Mental and Emotional Injuries in Employment Litigation

Second Edition

Mental and Emotional Injuries in Employment Litigation

Second Edition

James J. McDonald, Jr.
Fisher & Phillips LLP

Francine B. Kulick
Kulick Psychological Corporation

The Bureau of National Affairs, Inc., Washington, D.C.

Copyright © 2001
The Bureau of National Affairs, Inc.

Authorization to photocopy items for internal or personal use, or the internal or personal use of specific clients, is granted by BNA Books for libraries and other users registered with the Copyright Clearance Center (CCC) Transactional Reporting Service, provided that $1.00 per page is paid directly to CCC, 222 Rosewood Dr., Danvers, MA 01923. 1-57018-274-4/01/$0 + $1.00.

Published by BNA Books
1231 25th St., NW, Washington, DC 20037
http://www.bnabooks.com

International Standard Book Number: 1-57018-274-4
Printed in the United States of America

Dedicated to

James & Pat McDonald

and

Dorothy & Sidney Kulick

ACKNOWLEDGMENTS

The editors acknowledge the support and contributions of Sunny Dalton, Christine Silletto Ramirez, Deborah Chagal, and the law firm of Fisher & Phillips LLP. The editors also are extraordinarily grateful for the support and encouragement of Timothy J. Darby, Brian M. Malsberger, and the staff of BNA Books.

The editors are especially indebted to the late Sara P. Feldman-Schorrig, M.D., whose insightful work in forensic psychiatry served as a source of inspiration for the first edition of this treatise, and whose untimely death prevented her from participating in this edition.

ABOUT THE EDITORS

James J. McDonald, Jr., J.D., is a partner in and co-founder of the Irvine, California office of the national labor and employment law firm of Fisher & Phillips LLP. Mr. McDonald received his law degree *cum laude* from Georgetown University and he is a member of the California and Georgia Bars. He is the author of numerous publications on mental health and employment law and he is a frequent public speaker in this area as well. Mr. McDonald also teaches labor and employment law at the University of California—Irvine. He is a member of the Editorial Advisory Board of the *Employee Relations Law Journal*, a member of the Advisory Board of the American College of Forensic Psychiatry, and a member of the Labor and Employment Law Section of the American Bar Association, Division 41 (Psychology and the Law) of the American Psychological Association, the Society for Human Resources Management, and the Defense Research Institute.

Francine B. Kulick, Ph.D., is a clinical psychologist in private practice in Santa Monica, California. Her specialty is forensic psychology, with an emphasis on evaluation and litigation consulting. She received her doctorate in clinical psychology from the University of Miami in 1978, having completed her internship at Patton State Hospital in San Bernardino, California. She served as a clinical psychologist at Jackson Memorial Hospital and was an adjunct faculty member at the University of Miami Medical School. She was a senior psychologist, and later Assistant Clinic Director of Family Court Mental Health Services in Brooklyn, New York. She has practiced in the area of forensic psychology for more than 20 years. She is a member of Division 41 (Psychology and the Law) of the American Psychological Association, and a Diplomate and Fellow of the American College of Forensic Examiners. She is licensed to practice psychology in California, New York, and Florida.

ABOUT THE AUTHORS

Elissa P. Benedek, M.D. is a Consultant at the Center for Forensic Psychiatry in Ann Arbor, Michigan, and she also maintains a private practice in child, adolescent, and forensic psychiatry. She obtained her medical degree from the University of Michigan Medical School and completed her residency at the Neuropsychiatric Institute at the University of Michigan Medical Center. She is a Diplomate of the American Board of Psychiatry and Neurology with Added Qualifications in Forensic Psychiatry and a Diplomate of the American Board of Forensic Psychiatry. Dr. Benedek is a Life Fellow and former President of the American Psychiatric Association. She is also a Clinical Professor of Psychiatry at the University of Michigan, Michigan State University, and Wayne State University. She is the author of nine books and more than 100 articles and book chapters on clinical and forensic psychiatry.

Archie Brodsky, B.A. is a research associate in the Program in Psychiatry and the Law, Harvard Medical School at Massachusetts Mental Health Center, and at the Heller Graduate School of Brandeis University. He is co-author of *Decision Making in Psychiatry and the Law, The Truth About Addiction and Recovery, Resisting 12-Step Coercion,* and a dozen other trade and professional books as well as numerous journal articles on medical decision making, clinical ethics, risk management, substance abuse, and health policy. He was co-recipient of the 1998 Manfred S. Guttmacher Award, given by the American Psychiatric Association and the American Academy of Psychiatry and the Law for outstanding contribution to the literature in forensic psychiatry. A former chair of the Human Rights Committee at Massachusetts Mental Health Center, he is currently involved in a Brandeis University study to evaluate community-based substance-abuse prevention efforts in the Robert Wood Johnson Foundation's "Fighting Back" program.

Peter Brown, M.D., FRCP(C) is Medical Director of the Psychiatric Unit for UnumProvident Corporation of Chattanooga Tennessee, the nation's largest disability insurance provider. He obtained his medical degree at the University of Western Ontario, London, Ontario in 1975. He completed his psychiatric training at the University of Toronto in 1979. Dr. Brown is a former Associate Professor of Psychiatry at the University of Toronto and he is the author of *The Hypnotic Brain: Hypnotherapy and Social Communication*, published by Yale University Press in 1991.

Harold J. Bursztajn, M.D. is Associate Clinical Professor of Psychiatry and Co-Director of the Program in Psychiatry and the Law at Harvard Medical School. He also maintains a psychiatry practice with clinical appointments at Beth Israel Hospital and the Massachusetts Mental Health Center. He is a *magna cum laude* graduate of Princeton University, he received his medical degree from Harvard Medical School, and he completed his psychiatric residency at the Massachusetts Mental Health Center. He is a Diplomate of the American Board of Psychiatry and Neurology, with Added Qualifications in Forensic Psychiatry. Dr. Bursztajn is co-author of the book, *Decision Making in Psychiatry and the Law,* and his publications reflect over twenty years of research in evaluating employment-related claims including ADA, sexual harassment, worker's compensation, wrongful termination, and workplace violence issues.

Myra C. Creighton, J.D. is a partner in the Atlanta, Georgia office of Fisher & Phillips LLP, a national labor and employment law firm. She received her law degree *cum laude* from the University of Georgia in 1991 where she was a member of the 1990 Phillip C. Jessup Moot Court Team that won the national and world championships in international law. Ms. Creighton also served as a law clerk to Judge Duross Fitzpatrick of the United States District Court for the Middle District of Georgia following graduation from law school. Ms. Creighton's practice focuses on litigation and advice to clients involving the Americans with Disabilities Act, the Family and Medical Leave Act, and sexual harassment.

Rodney J. S. Deaton, M.D., J.D. is a psychiatrist in private practice in Indianapolis, Indiana and an Assistant Professor of Psychiatry at the Indiana University School of Medicine. He is a graduate of the Indiana University School of Medicine and a *magna cum laude* graduate of the Harvard Law School. He did his residency training in adult psychiatry at Duke University and in child/adolescent psychiatry at the Boston Children's Hospital/Judge Baker's Children's Center, Harvard Medical School.

David D. Fox, Ph.D. is a clinical psychologist in private practice in Glendale, California, where his specialties include psychological and neuropsychological assessment of adolescents, adults, and seniors, as well as psychological assessments in the workplace. He is also Director of Consultants in Clinical Assessment, which provides interpretation of psychological testing and consultation in psychological assessment. He is also an adjunct faculty member at the Pepperdine University Graduate School of Education and Psychology. Dr. Fox received his Ph.D. in clinical psychology in 1979 from Wayne State University.

Liza H. Gold, M.D. is a psychiatrist in private practice in McLean, Virginia. She is a Diplomate of the American Board of Psychiatry and Neurology with a subspeciality certification in Forensic Psychiatry. She is a *magna cum laude* graduate of Harvard/Radcliffe College, she received her medical training at the New York University School of Medicine, and she completed her psychiatric residency at Boston University. Dr. Gold is a Clinical Assistant Professor of

Psychiatry in the Program in Psychiatry and Law of the Department of Psychiatry at Georgetown University Medical Center. She is the author of the forthcoming book, *Sexual Harassment, Psychiatry and the Law: Forensic Assessment in Litigation*, to be published in 2002 by the American Psychiatric Press. Dr. Gold has extensive experience in the diagnostic evaluation and treatment of posttraumatic, mood, anxiety, and personality disorders.

Daniel P. Greenfield, M.D., M.P.H., M.S. is a psychiatrist and addiction medicine specialist in private practice in Millburn/Short Hills, New Jersey. A graduate of the University of North Carolina School of Medicine, Dr. Greenfield's postgraduate residency training was in general preventive medicine at Harvard Medical School and in psychiatry at Cornell Medical Center and Rutgers Medical School. Dr. Greenfield has also been educated at the University of London and he received both the M.P.H. degree and the M.S. degree in Health Services Administration from the Harvard University School of Public Health. Dr. Greenfield is board-certified in General Preventive Medicine and in Psychiatry. Dr. Greenfield holds clinical faculty teaching appointments at the Albert Einstein College of Medicine at Montefiore Medical Center in Bronx, New York, and at the Seton Hall University's School of Graduate Medical Education/New Jersey Neuroscience Institute at JFK Medical Center in South Orange and Edison, New Jersey. Dr. Greenfield is also author of the book, *Prescription Drug Abuse and Dependence*, published in 1995.

Mae F. Keller, Ph.D. is a clinical and forensic psychologist in private practice in Ann Arbor, Michigan, where her practice includes forensic evaluation, psychological testing, and psychotherapy. She received her doctorate in clinical psychology from the University of Michigan in 1986. Dr. Keller is on the staff of the Center for Forensic Psychiatry, which conducts psychological assessment in criminal cases and is involved in the development of hospital-based treatment services for the forensic population. Dr. Keller is a past president of the Michigan Society of Forensic Psychology, and she is a member of Division 41 (Psychology and Law) of the American Psychological Association and of the Society for Personality Assessment.

Francine B. Kulick, Ph.D. is a clinical psychologist in private practice in Santa Monica, California. Her specialty is forensic psychology, with an emphasis on evaluation and litigation consulting. She received her doctorate in clinical psychology from the University of Miami in 1978, having completed her internship at Patton State Hospital in San Bernardino, California. She served as a clinical psychologist at Jackson Memorial Hospital and was an adjunct faculty member at the University of Miami Medical School. She was a senior psychologist and, later, Assistant Clinic Director of Family Court Mental Health Services in Brooklyn, New York. She has practiced in the area of forensic psychology for more than 20 years. She is a member of Division 41 (Psychology and the Law) of the American Psychological Association, and a Diplomate and Fellow of the American College of Forensic Examiners. She is licensed to practice psychology in California, New York, and Florida.

Paul R. Lees-Haley, Ph.D., ABPP is a clinical and forensic psychologist and neuropsychologist in private practice in Huntsville, Alabama. He received his doctorate in clinical psychology from the University of Tennessee in 1978 where he was a Woodrow Wilson Fellow, and he is a Diplomate of the American Board of Professional Psychology. He is a nationally-renowned speaker and author of nearly 200 articles on psychological testing and the evaluation and treatment of trauma, and he won the Nelson Butters National Academy of Neuropsychology Award for Research Contributions to Clinical Neuropsychology in 1994.

Mark S. Lipian, M.D., Ph.D. is a clinical and forensic psychiatrist in private practice in San Francisco and Newport Beach, California. A graduate of the University of California at Berkeley where he was Phi Beta Kappa, Dr. Lipian went on to receive his medical degree and doctorate in psychology from Yale and Oxford Universities. He then completed his residency in psychiatry and a fellowship in forensic psychiatry at UCLA's Neuropsychiatric Institute. He is an Assistant Clinical Professor of Psychiatry at both UCLA and University of California - Irvine. He has published and lectured nationally on such subjects as the prevention of workplace violence, workplace harassment and discrimination issues, Posttraumatic Stress Disorder and malingering. His practice includes clinical work with private patients and forensic consultation with attorneys, businesses, and government and law enforcement agencies. He is also Medical Director of the Orange County Conditional Release Program, a clinic for court-mandated treatment of mentally ill offenders. He is a member of the American Psychiatric Association, the American Academy of Psychiatry and the Law, and the American Academy of Forensic Sciences.

James J. McDonald, Jr., J.D. is a partner in and co-founder of the Irvine, California office of the national labor and employment law firm of Fisher & Phillips LLP. Mr. McDonald received his law degree *cum laude* from Georgetown University and he is a member of the California and Georgia Bars. He is the author of numerous publications on mental health and employment law and he is a frequent public speaker in this area as well. Mr. McDonald also teaches labor and employment law at the University of California - Irvine. He is a member of the Editorial Advisory Board of the *Employee Relations Law Journal,* a member of the Advisory Board of the American College of Forensic Psychiatry, and a member of the Labor and Employment Law Section of the American Bar Association, Division 41 (Psychology and the Law) of the American Psychological Association, the Society for Human Resources Management, and the Defense Research Institute.

Jane M. McFetridge, J.D. is a partner in the Chicago, Illinois office of Fisher & Phillips LLP, a national labor and employment law firm, where she represents employers in employment litigation. She obtained her B.S. in accounting with honors from the University of Illinois at Champaign and her J.D. from Northwestern University Law School. Her practice covers the spectrum of employment litigation, including both state and federal claims, and individual and class action suits. She also has an extensive appellate practice, including oral arguments before the Seventh Circuit Court of Appeals, the Illinois Supreme Court, the Illinois Appellate Courts, and the Michigan Court of Appeals. Ms. McFetridge has served as a faculty member for the American Bar Association's

National Institute on Sexual Harassment, and she is active in the Defense Research Institute's Employment Law Committee and the Labor and Employment Law Committee of the Chicago Bar Association. She is also a Certified Public Accountant.

David R. Price, Ph.D. is the Director of the Forensic Psychiatry Program for The Institute of Psychiatry, Department of Psychiatry and Behavioral Sciences, of the Medical University of South Carolina in Charleston, South Carolina. He is also Administrative Director of the Forensic Psychiatry Research Foundation for the Medical University of South Carolina and President of The Forensic Network located in Greenville, South Carolina. Dr. Price received his Ph.D. in clinical psychology from Auburn University in 1982. He is a Fellow of the Academy of Learning and Developmental Disorders, a Diplomate of the American Board of Psychological Specialities in Forensic Clinical Psychology; a Diplomate of the American Board of Psychological Specialities in Forensic Neuropsychology; and a Diplomate of the American Board of Professional Disability Consultants. He is the senior editor of the book, *The Insurer's Handbook of Psychological Injury Claims*. Dr. Price also lectures nationally on the evaluation of psychological injury claims and brain injury claims.

Jonathan P. Rosman, M.D. is a psychiatrist in private practice in clinical and forensic psychiatry in Pasadena, California. He obtained his medical degree from the University of Pretoria in South Africa in 1980. He then completed his psychiatric residency training at McMaster University in Ontario, Canada, and Case Western Reserve University in Cleveland, Ohio. He subsequently completed fellowship training in forensic psychiatry at Case Western Reserve University. He obtained his specialist certification in psychiatry from the Royal College of Physicians and Surgeons of Canada, and he is a Diplomate of the American Board of Psychiatry and Neurology. He is also Board Certified in the subspecialties of Forensic Psychiatry and Addiction Psychiatry. Dr. Rosman has lectured and published in the areas of necrophilia, the psychiatric rehabilitation of the elderly, and sexual harassment.

Robert I. Simon, M.D. is Clinical Professor of Psychiatry and Director of the Program in Psychiatry and Law at Georgetown University School of Medicine in Washington, D.C., and Adjunct Professor of Psychiatry at the Uniformed Services University of the Health Sciences, F. Edward Hebert School of Medicine in Bethesda, Maryland. He also maintains a private psychiatry practice in Bethesda, Maryland. Dr. Simon received his medical training at Tufts University School of Medicine and completed his residency in psychiatry at the University of Miami School of Medicine/Jackson Memorial Hospital. He is a Diplomate of the American Board of Psychology and Neurology, with Added Qualifications in Forensic Psychiatry, and a Diplomate of the American Board of Forensic Psychiatry. Dr. Simon has authored more than 60 articles and 33 book chapters, and he has authored or edited 21 books, including *A Concise Guide to Psychiatry and Law for Clinicians* (3d ed. 2001), *The Mental Health Professional and the Law: A Comprehensive Handbook* (1998), and *Bad Men Do What Good Men Dream: A Forensic Psychiatrist Illuminates the Darker Side of Human Behavior* (1996).

SUMMARY TABLE OF CONTENTS

	Page
ABOUT THE EDITORS	vii
ABOUT THE AUTHORS	viii
DETAILED TABLE OF CONTENTS	xv
LIST OF TABLES, FIGURES, AND EXHIBITS	xxxii
PREFACE	xxxvi
CHAPTER 1 — THE LEGAL CONTEXT	1
CHAPTER 2 — THE ROLE OF THE MENTAL HEALTH PROFESSIONAL IN EMPLOYMENT LITIGATION	50
CHAPTER 3 — CLINICAL EVALUATION AND CASE FORMULATION OF MENTAL AND EMOTIONAL INJURY CLAIMS	72
CHAPTER 4 — THE DIAGNOSTIC AND STATISTICAL MANUAL OF MENTAL DISORDERS	117
CHAPTER 5 — MENTAL DISORDERS COMMONLY ENCOUNTERED IN EMPLOYMENT LITIGATION	158
CHAPTER 6 — PERSONALITY DISORDERS IN EMPLOYMENT LITIGATION	212
CHAPTER 7 — PREPARING THE CASE FOR THE EXPERT	262
CHAPTER 8 — THE RIGHT TO PRIVACY VERSUS THE NEED FOR DISCOVERY	284
CHAPTER 9 — THE MENTAL EXAMINATION	328
CHAPTER 10 — THE USE AND MISUSE OF PSYCHOLOGICAL TESTING	364
CHAPTER 11 — MALINGERING: DISTORTION AND DECEPTION IN EMPLOYMENT LITIGATION	409
CHAPTER 12 — PHARMACOLOGY AND PSYCHOPHARMACOLOGY	454
CHAPTER 13 — POSTTRAUMATIC STRESS DISORDER IN EMPLOYMENT CASES	502
CHAPTER 14 — SPECIAL ISSUES IN SEXUAL HARASSMENT CASES	574
CHAPTER 15 — AVOIDING AND ATTACKING "JUNK SCIENCE" IN EMPLOYMENT LITIGATION	631

CHAPTER 16	MENTAL DISABILITIES UNDER THE AMERICANS WITH DISABILITIES ACT	659

APPENDIXES

APPENDIX 1:	EEOC POLICY GUIDE ON COMPENSATORY AND PUNITIVE DAMAGES UNDER 1991 CIVIL RIGHTS ACT	777
APPENDIX 2:	AMERICAN ACADEMY OF PSYCHIATRY AND THE LAW: ETHICAL GUIDELINES FOR THE PRACTICE OF FORENSIC PSYCHIATRY	783
APPENDIX 3:	SPECIALTY GUIDELINES FOR FORENSIC PSYCHOLOGISTS	789
APPENDIX 4:	MODEL ENGAGEMENT LETTERS FOR MENTAL HEALTH EXPERTS	799
APPENDIX 5:	RULE 412, FEDERAL RULES OF EVIDENCE	805
APPENDIX 6:	RULE 702, FEDERAL RULES OF EVIDENCE	813
APPENDIX 7:	SAMPLE CROSS-EXAMINATION OF PLAINTIFF'S EXPERT	821
TABLE OF CASES		833
INDEX		859

DETAILED TABLE OF CONTENTS

	Page
ABOUT THE EDITORS	vii
ABOUT THE AUTHORS	viii
SUMMARY TABLE OF CONTENTS	xiii
LIST OF TABLES, FIGURES, AND EXHIBITS	xxxii
PREFACE	xxxvi

		Page
CHAPTER 1	THE LEGAL CONTEXT	1
I.	Actions in Which Emotional Distress Damages Are Available	2
	A. Statutory Bases for Recovery of Emotional Distress Damages	3
	1. The Civil Rights Act of 1991	3
	2. Sections 1981 and 1983	4
	3. Age Discrimination in Employment Act	4
	4. State Employment Discrimination Statutes	4
	B. Common Law Bases for Recovery of Emotional Distress Damages	5
	1. Intentional Infliction of Emotional Distress	5
	a. Extreme or Outrageous Conduct	6
	b. Severe Emotional Distress	9
	2. Negligent Infliction of Emotional Distress	9
	3. Wrongful Discharge in Violation of Public Policy	10
	4. Assault and Battery	12
	5. False Imprisonment	13
	6. Invasion of Privacy	13
	a. Intrusion on Seclusion	14
	b. False-Light Publicity	14
	c. Public Disclosure of Private Facts	14
	7. Defamation	15
	8. Fraud and Misrepresentation	15
	9. Tortious Interference With Contract	16

10. Loss of Consortium	16
11. Negligence	17
II. Proof and Calculation of Emotional Distress Damages	19
A. Proof of Damages	20
B. Measure of Damages	23
C. Hedonic Damages	27
1. Hedonic Damages After *Daubert*	28
2. Hedonic Damages in Employment Cases	29
D. Preexisting Conditions and the "Eggshell Plaintiff" Rule	32
III. Psychological Issues in the Liability Phase	34
IV. Other Legal Issues	41
A. Availability of Damages for Stress of Litigation	41
B. Emotional Distress Claims in Class Actions	41
1. Class Actions: The Basics	42
2. The Response of the Courts	42
3. Class Treatment of Emotional Distress Claims	46
4. Liability Issues	47
C. Statutes of Limitations	48

CHAPTER 2   THE ROLE OF THE MENTAL HEALTH PROFESSIONAL IN EMPLOYMENT LITIGATION 50

I. Qualifications of Mental Health Expert Witnesses	52
A. Types of Mental Health Professionals	52
1. Psychiatrists	52
2. Clinical Psychologists	53
3. Psychiatric Social Workers	53
4. Marriage and Family Therapists	54
5. Other Specialties	54
B. Additional Professional Qualifications	54
II. Factors to Guide the Selection of an Expert	55
A. Clinical Expertise	55
B. Forensic Expertise	56
C. Problems with Interpersonal Issues	57
III. Retaining the Expert	58
A. Whether to Use the Plaintiff's Treating Therapist	58
B. When to Retain the Expert	61
C. Practical Aspects of Retaining an Expert	61
1. Scheduling Issues	62
2. Budgetary Issues	62
3. Billing Issues	62
4. Payment Issues	62
IV. The Expert's Approach to the Conduct of the Evaluation	63
A. Record Review	63
B. The Forensic Interview	63
C. Psychological Testing	65
V. The Nature and Scope of the Expert's Testimony	65
A. Qualification of the Expert	65

	B. Admissibility Issues	66
	C. The Expert's Opinion	67
VI.	Expert's Vulnerabilities in Court	68
	A. Problems with Limited Evaluations	69
	B. Financial Bias	70
	C. Ethical Issues	71
VII.	The Mental Health Expert as Litigation Consultant	71

CHAPTER 3 CLINICAL EVALUATION AND CASE FORMULATION OF MENTAL AND EMOTIONAL INJURY CLAIMS ... 72

I.	Overview of Mental and Emotional Injury Claims and Issues	72
II.	Evaluating the Context of the Injury Claim	75
	A. Severity of the Injury Alleged	75
	B. Treatment Provided	76
	C. Qualifications of Treaters and Experts	77
III.	Evaluating the Diagnosis	78
	A. Multiaxial Diagnoses	79
	B. Reliability of Diagnoses	80
	C. Assessment of Premorbid Functioning	82
	D. Assessment of the Effects of Litigation	83
	E. Assessment of Potential for Malingering and Symptom Exaggeration	83
	F. Assessment of Iatrogenic Effects	84
IV.	Examples of Preexisting and Comorbid Psychiatric Disorders	85
	A. Developmental Disorders	85
	1. Attention Deficit/Hyperactivity Disorder	85
	2. Intellectual Disorders	86
	3. Learning Disorders	87
	B. Substance Abuse	88
	C. Anxiety Disorders	89
	D. Mood Disorders	90
	E. Organic Disorders	93
	F. Personality Disorders	94
	G. Thought Disorders	98
V.	Physical Disorders That Produce Psychological Symptoms	99
VI.	Psychosocial Stressors	108
VII.	The Role of Psychological Testing	110
VIII.	Discovery Issues	111
IX.	Case Conceptualization	114

CHAPTER 4 THE DIAGNOSTIC AND STATISTICAL MANUAL OF MENTAL DISORDERS ... 117

I.	Introduction	117
II.	Historical Background	118
	A. Classification Prior to *DSM-III*	118

B. *DSM-III* and *DSM-III-R* 120
C. *DSM-IV* 122
D. *DSM-IV-TR* 125
E. *DSM-V* 126
III. Categories, Dimensions, and Prototypes 126
IV. The Multiaxial Evaluation 128
    A. Axis I: The Clinical Disorders 130
        1. Disorders Usually First Diagnosed in Infancy,
           Childhood, or Adolescence 131
        2. Delirium, Dementia, Amnestic, and Other Cognitive
           Disorders 132
        3. Mental Disorders Due to a General Medical Condition 132
        4. Substance-Related Disorders 133
        5. Schizophrenia and Other Psychotic Disorders 133
        6. Mood Disorders 133
        7. Anxiety Disorders 134
        8. Somatoform Disorders 134
        9. Factitious Disorders 134
        10. Dissociative Disorders 135
        11. Sexual and Gender Identity Disorders 135
        12. Eating Disorders 136
        13. Sleep Disorders 136
        14. Impulse-Control Disorders 136
        15. Adjustment Disorders 136
        16. Other Conditions That May Be the Focus of Clinical
            Attention 137
    B. Axis II: Personality Disorders and Mental Retardation 137
    C. Axis III: General Medical Conditions 139
    D. Axis IV: Psychosocial and Environmental Problems 139
    E. Axis V: Global Assessment of Functioning 140
    F. The Appendixes 143
V. Commonly Used Terms in *DSM-IV-TR* 143
    A. Mental Disorder 143
    B. Clinically Significant Impairment or Distress 144
    C. Numerical Codes 144
    D. Subtypes and Specifiers 144
    E. Principal Diagnosis (Reason for Visit) 145
    F. Differential Diagnosis 145
    G. Inclusion and Exclusion Criteria 146
    H. Indicating Diagnostic Uncertainty (Deferred, Unspecified,
       Provisional, and Not Otherwise Specified Diagnoses) 147
VI. The Importance of Clinical Judgment 149
VII. Using *DSM-IV-TR* in Employment Litigation 150
VIII. *DSM-IV-TR*: Present Status and Future Directions 152
    A. The Medical Model 153
    B. The Proliferation of Diagnoses 153
    C. "Psychiatrization" of the Normal 153
    D. Comorbidity 154

E. Absence of a Gold Standard (External Validating Criteria)	155
F. Theory and Empiricism	156

CHAPTER 5 MENTAL DISORDERS COMMONLY ENCOUNTERED IN EMPLOYMENT LITIGATION ... 158

I. Introduction	158
A. Origins, History, and Definitions	158
1. Psychiatry and Psychology	158
2. Physical Illnesses and Mental Disorders	159
3. *DSM-IV-TR*	159
4. Psychiatric Symptoms	159
a. Psychotic Symptoms	160
b. Affective Symptoms	160
c. Anxiety Symptoms	161
d. Conversion Symptoms	161
e. Cognitive Symptoms	161
f. Unreasonable Attitudes and Expectations	161
B. Factors Affecting Mental Health	162
1. Organic Versus Functional Pathology	162
2. Nature Versus Nurture	162
C. Formal Diagnosis	163
II. Overview of Axis I Disorders Commonly Encountered in Employment Litigation	164
A. Thought Disorders	164
1. Schizophrenia	165
2. Delusional Disorder	170
B. Mood Disorders	173
1. Major Depressive Disorder	173
2. Dysthymic Disorder	178
3. "Double Depression"	180
4. Bipolar Affective Disorder	181
5. Bipolar I Disorder Versus Bipolar II Disorder	184
C. Anxiety Disorders and Dual Diagnosis	187
1. Panic Disorder and Agoraphobia	188
2. Obsessive-Compulsive Disorder	192
3. Generalized Anxiety Disorder	195
4. Posttraumatic Stress Disorder	197
D. Somatoform Disorders	200
1. Somatization Disorder	200
2. Conversion Disorder	203
3. Pain Disorder	205
E. Adjustment Disorders	206
III. Effective Forensic Mental Health Workup of Axis I Claims in Employment Litigation	210

CHAPTER 6 PERSONALITY DISORDERS IN EMPLOYMENT LITIGATION .. 212

I. Introduction	212

A. Qualities of Personality 213
   1. Traits Versus States 213
   2. Personality Traits Versus Personality Disorders 214
B. Factors Affecting Personality Development 215
   1. Nature Versus Nurture 215
      a. Bonding Theories 216
      b. Efficacy and Interaction Theories 216
      c. Trauma Theories 217
      d. Genetic Theories 217
      e. Temperament Theories 218
      f. Arousal Theories 218
   2. Etiologic Conclusions 219
II. The Role of Personality Disorders in Employment Litigation 219
III. Personality Disorders That May Be Found in the Workplace 220
   A. Cluster A Disorders 221
      1. Paranoid Personality Disorder 221
      2. Schizoid and Schizotypal Personality Disorders 223
   B. Cluster B Disorders 226
      1. Antisocial Personality Disorder 227
      2. Borderline Personality Disorder 231
      3. Histrionic Personality Disorder 235
      4. Narcissistic Personality Disorder 237
   C. Cluster C Disorders 239
      1. Avoidant Personality Disorder 240
      2. Dependent Personality Disorder 242
      3. Obsessive-Compulsive Personality Disorder 245
      4. Personality Disorder Not Otherwise Specified 247
IV. Personality Disorders in the Workplace and Courtroom:
    Dangerousness and "Righteous Rage" 248
   A. Personality Disorders and Workplace Violence 248
   B. Personality Disorders and "Righteous Rage" 251
V. Treatment of Personality Disorders 253
   A. Acute Intervention and Crisis Management 253
   B. Long-Term Treatment and Restructuring 254
VI. Effective Forensic Mental Health Workup of Personality
    Disorders in Employment Litigation 254

CHAPTER 7   PREPARING THE CASE FOR THE EXPERT 262

I. The Expert's Role 262
   A. Formulating a Forensic Opinion 262
   B. Formulating the Theory of a Case 264
II. The Responsibility of the Attorney 268
   A. Orientation of Less Experienced Counsel 268
   B. Timing of Expert Selection 269
   C. Preliminary Matters 269
      1. The Expert's Background 269
      2. Orientation of the Expert to the Litigation Process 269

3. Experts from Outside the Jurisdiction 269
4. Areas Outside the Expert's Expertise 270
5. Financial Arrangements 270
D. Obtaining Discovery of the Information That the Expert Will Need 271
1. Legal Documents to Provide to the Expert 271
2. Records to Obtain and Provide to the Expert 271
   a. Psychotherapy and Other Treatment Records 271
   b. Prior Medical Records 272
   c. Personnel Records 276
   d. Educational Records 276
   e. Records of Divorce and Child Custody Proceedings 277
   f. Prior Court Cases 278
   g. Workers' Compensation Files 278
3. Information to Obtain During the Plaintiff's Deposition 279
E. Setting the Stage for the Mental Examination of the Plaintiff 282

CHAPTER 8 THE RIGHT TO PRIVACY VERSUS THE NEED FOR DISCOVERY 284

I. Scope and Waiver of Privileges 285
   A. Medical and Psychotherapy Records 285
      1. Cases Viewing Waiver Broadly 286
      2. Cases Viewing Waiver Narrowly 292
      3. Cases Taking a Balanced View 295
      4. Cases Applying a Rule 35 Analysis 295
   B. Discovery of Other Records 297
   C. Depositions 298
   D. Interrogatories 299
II. Discovery of Plaintiff's Sexual History 300
   A. Amendments to Rule 412 of the Federal Rules of Evidence 301
   B. Application of Rule 412 to Volitional Conduct 303
      1. Types of Sexual Behavior Covered 304
      2. Application of Rule 412 to the Welcomeness Issue 305
   C. Application of Rule 412 to Emotional Damages Issues 310
   D. Application of Rule 412 to Summary Judgment Motions 313
   E. Application of Rule 412 in Discovery 313
   F. Application of Rule 412 to Nonparty Witnesses 317
   G. Application of Rule 412 to Prior Sexual Abuse 318
      1. Alternative Causation of Damages 320
      2. Impact on Plaintiff's Credibility 321
         a. Borderline Rage 322
         b. Dissociation 322
      3. The Reasonable Woman/Reasonable Person Standard 323
      4. Repetition Compulsion and the Welcomeness Defense ... 325

Chapter 9 The Mental Examination 328

- I. Introduction 328
- II. When Is a Mental Examination Available? 330
  - A. The "In Controversy" Requirement 331
    1. "Garden Variety" Emotional Damages Claims 333
    2. Factors Likely to Lead to a Finding of "In Controversy" 335
       - a. Separate Claim for Intentional Infliction of Emotional Distress 335
       - b. Alleged Presence of a Specific Psychiatric Disorder 336
       - c. Plaintiff's Use of a Mental Health Expert 337
       - d. Allegation of Continuing Emotional Injury 338
       - e. Allegation of Severe Emotional Injury 340
       - f. Plaintiff Concedes That Mental Condition Is in Controversy 341
  - B. The Good Cause Requirement 341
- III. Terms Under Which a Mental Examination Shall Proceed 344
  - A. Timing of the Examination 344
  - B. Presence of Observers 345
  - C. Recording the Examination 348
  - D. Limitations on the Duration of the Examination 349
  - E. Restrictions on the Scope of the Examination 349
  - F. Conduct of Psychological Testing As Part of the Examination 353
    1. Limitations on Tests That May Be Used 354
    2. Obligation to Identify Tests in Advance 356
- IV. Conducting the Clinical Interview 356
  - A. The Examiner's Approach 357
  - B. The Components of the Mental Examination 358
    1. Mental Status Examination 358
    2. Past History 359
    3. Account of Events in the Workplace 360
    4. Assessment of Current Functioning 361
    5. Psychological Testing 362
  - C. Forming a Clinical Opinion 362

Chapter 10 The Use and Misuse of Psychological Testing 364

- I. Introduction 364
- II. Testing Terminology 366
- III. Psychological Tests Most Frequently Found in Employment Lawsuits 368
  - A. Minnesota Multiphasic Personality Inventory-2 368
    1. MMPI-2 Validity Scales 369
       - a. L Scale 369
       - b. F Scale 369
       - c. K Scale 370

   d. F Minus K Index 370
   e. Weiner-Harmon Subtle-Obvious Subscales 371
   f. Dissimulation Scale-Revised 372
   g. Fake Bad Scale 372
   h. F Back Scale 373
   i. Variable Response Inconsistency Scale 374
   j. True Response Inconsistency Scale 374
  2. MMPI-2 Clinical Scales 374
   a. Hypochondriasis (*Hs*) Scale 375
   b. Depression (*D*) Scale 375
   c. Hysteria (*Hy*) Scale 375
   d. Psychopathic Deviate (*Pd*) Scale 376
   e. Masculinity-Femininity (*MF*) Scale 376
   f. Paranoia (*Pa*) Scale 376
   g. Psychasthenia (*Pt*) Scale 377
   h. Schizophrenia (*Sc*) Scale 377
   i. Hypomania (*Ma*) Scale 377
   j. Social Introversion (*Si*) Scale 377
  3. MMPI-2 Content Scales 378
  4. MMPI-2 Supplementary Scales 378
  5. Interpretation of the MMPI-2 379
  6. MMPI-2 Code Types 380
 B. Millon Clinical Multiaxial Inventory-III 381
 C. Wechsler Adult Intelligence Scale-III 384
  1. WAIS-III Verbal Tests 384
  2. WAIS-III Performance Tests 385
  3. Scoring 385
IV. Other Testing Instruments That May Appear in Employment
 Lawsuits 387
 A. Beck Anxiety Inventory 387
 B. Beck Depression Inventory 387
 C. Beck Hopelessness Survey 388
 D. Hamilton Anxiety Rating Scale 389
 E. Hamilton Depression Rating Scale 390
 F. Hamilton Depression Inventory 391
 G. Human Figure Drawing 391
 H. Impact of Event Scale 392
 I. Posttraumatic Stress Diagnostic Scale 394
 J. Profile of Mood States 395
 K. Rorschach Ink Blot Test 396
 L. Sentence Completion Test 398
 M. Shipley Institute of Living Scale 398
 N. State-Trait Anxiety Inventory 399
 O. Symptom Checklist 90-R 399
 P. Thematic Apperception Test 401
 Q. Other Instruments 402
V. Misuse of Psychological Testing 402
 A. Lack of Examiner Qualifications 403

B. Test Administration 404
C. Scoring 404
D. Interpretation 405
E. Validity Issues 406
F. Coaching 407
VI. Conclusion 408

CHAPTER 11 MALINGERING: DISTORTION AND DECEPTION
IN EMPLOYMENT LITIGATION 409

I. Introduction 409
II. Definition of Terms: Classification of Distortion 410
  A. Conscious Distortion 410
    1. Evasion 410
    2. Deception 411
  B. Subconscious Distortion 413
    1. Subconscious Distortion Due to Axis I Conditions 413
    2. Subconscious Distortion Due to Axis II Conditions 414
    3. Subconscious Distortion Due to Emotionally Charged
       Life Events 414
III. Opportunities for Distortion and Deception in Employment
   Litigation 415
  A. Distortion by a Plaintiff 415
    1. Downplaying Alternative Causes of Symptoms 415
    2. Distortion of the Nature of the Work Environment 416
    3. The Plaintiff's Misconstruing Normal Behaviors As
       Sexual and/or Harassing 417
    4. Avoidance of Responsibility 420
  B. Distortion by an Expert 421
    1. Distortion by Plaintiff's Expert 421
      a. Exaggeration of the Diagnosis 421
        i. Overdiagnosed PTSD 421
        ii. The Existence of a "Mental Disability" Under
            the ADA 422
      b. Downplaying the Importance of Alternative Causes
         of Symptoms 423
      c. Exaggerating the Severity of the Prognosis and the
         Expected Duration of Further Treatment 424
      d. Distorting the Expert's Own Role 424
    2. Distortion by a Defense Expert 425
IV. Malingering in the Workplace 425
  A. Malingering of a Psychiatric Disability to Avoid Work 426
  B. Fabrication of Harassment or Discrimination Claims 427
  C. Exaggerated Effect of Medical or Psychological Condition
     on "Major Life Activities" 430
  D. Exaggeration of Symptoms 431
    1. The Nature and Severity of the Impairment 431
    2. The Duration of the Impairment 432

    3. The Permanent or Long-Term Impact of
     an Impairment 433
  E. Misattribution of the Cause of Symptoms to the
   Workplace 434
    1. The Use of the Logical Fallacy of *Post Hoc Ergo
     Propter Hoc* 435
    2. Reversal of Cause and Effect 435
 V. Dissimulation in the Workplace 436
 VI. The Detection of Distortion and Deception in Employment
  Litigation 437
  A. The Use of Collateral Sources of Information 438
  B. The Use of Psychological Testing 439
  C. Understanding Normal Responses to Traumatic Events 440
  D. The Forensic Interview of the Plaintiff 441
    1. Know the Collateral Data 441
    2. Obtain a Thorough Background History to Establish a
     Pattern of Behavior and Reaction to Various Kinds of
     Stresses 442
    3. Ask Open-Ended Questions 442
    4. Ask Leading Questions in the Wrong Direction 442
    5. Ask Detailed Questions, Particularly When Responses
     Are Vague and Generalized 442
    6. Evaluate Every Symptom in Detail 443
    7. Look for Verbal Cues of Vagueness and Evasiveness 444
    8. Look for Nonverbal Cues 444
    9. Look for Inconsistencies in the Interview 445
    10. Evaluate the Impact of the Legal Process 445
    11. Evaluate Plaintiffs' Attitudes Toward Their Alleged
     Emotional Distress 446
    12. Look for Alternative Motives for the Lawsuit 446
 VII. Problems and Pitfalls in the Detection of Distortion and
  Deception 447
  A. Inadequate or Blocked Discovery 447
  B. Failure to Recognize Therapeutic Bias 448
  C. Failure to Evaluate a Plaintiff Adequately 448
    1. Failure to Establish the Appropriate Parameters for an
     Evaluation 448
    2. Failure to Evaluate the Effects of Major Life Events 449
    3. Failure to Evaluate for Personality Defects, Poor
     Judgment, or Short Temper 449
  D. Over- or Underdiagnosing Malingering 450
  E. Failing to Evaluate the Ability to Work in Other, Similar
   Job Environments 451
  F. Working with Outdated Knowledge 452
 VIII. Conclusion 453

CHAPTER 12 PHARMACOLOGY AND PSYCHOPHARMACOLOGY 454

 I. Basic Principles of Psychopharmacology 456

A. Fundamentals of Psychiatric Diagnosis 457
B. Fundamentals of Pharmacology and
   Psychopharmacology 458
   1. Dose-Response Relationship 458
   2. Desired Versus Undesired Effects 459
   3. Pharmacologic Interactions 460
C. Classes of Pharmacologic Agents 461
   1. Classification According to Lawfulness of Use 464
   2. Classification According to Effect 465
   3. Classification According to Clinical Purpose 465
   4. Four Additional Classes 466
II. Classes and Properties of Psychotropic Medications 468
   A. Stimulants 468
   B. Depressants 469
   C. Hallucinogens 469
   D. The Fourteen "Antis" 470
      1. Anti-Addiction Agents 470
      2. Anti-Anxiety Agents 472
      3. Anti-Appetite Agents 473
      4. Anti-Convulsant Agents 474
      5. Anti-Dementia Agents 475
      6. Anti-Depressant Agents 475
      7. Anti-ADHD Agents 477
      8. Anti-Insomnia Agents 478
      9. Anti-Manic Agents 479
     10. Anti-Obsessive Agents 480
     11. Anti-Pain Agents 480
     12. Anti-Panic Agents 482
     13. Anti-Psychotic Agents 483
     14. Anti-Sex Agents 485
III. Psychiatric Aspects of Nonpsychotropic Agents 486
IV. Synthesis and Summary 488
V. Suggestions for Further Reading and Research 500

CHAPTER 13 POSTTRAUMATIC STRESS DISORDER IN EMPLOYMENT
           CASES 502

I. Introduction 502
II. PTSD in the Clinical Context 504
   A. Diagnostic Criteria 504
      1. Criterion A: The Traumatic Stressor 505
      2. Criteria B, C, and D: The Symptoms of PTSD 509
      3. Criteria E and F: Duration of Symptoms and Functional
         Impairment 511
   B. Epidemiology 514
      1. Factors Predictive of the Development of PTSD 514
         a. Pretrauma Vulnerabilities 515
         b. Magnitude of the Stresssor 515
         c. Preparedness for the Event 516

d. Immediate and Short-Term Responses 516
e. Postevent "Recovery" Factors 517
2. Subthreshold PTSD 518
C. PTSD and Comorbidity 520
D. Course and Prognosis 522
1. Acute Stress Disorder 522
2. Chronic PTSD 522
3. Prognosis 525
E. Treatment and Treatment Outcomes 527
III. The Forensic Evaluation of PTSD 531
A. Guidelines for the Forensic Assessment of PTSD 532
B. Importance of Review of Records 533
C. Testing in the Diagnosis of PTSD 535
1. Physiological Testing 535
2. Psychological Testing 536
D. Bias and the Misdiagnosis of PTSD 539
IV. Special Issues in the Forensic Assessment of PTSD 543
A. Trauma History, Comorbid Disorders, and Proximate
Cause 543
B. Personality Disorders and PTSD 547
1. Borderline Personality Disorder: Clinical
Presentation 551
a. BPD and Trauma 553
b. The "Sitting Duck" Syndrome 553
c. Repetition Compulsion 555
2. Forensic Assessment of Personality Disorders 556
3. The Interplay of Personality Disorders and PTSD 558
C. Functional Impairment and the Assessment
of Damages 561
D. PTSD Used as Syndrome Evidence 565
E. Malingering 567
V. Conclusion 573

CHAPTER 14   SPECIAL ISSUES IN SEXUAL HARASSMENT CASES 574

I. History and Legal Context 574
A. Legal Definitions and Milestones 575
B. Developments in Sexual Harassment 579
1. Sexual Harassment in School Settings 579
2. Same-Sex Harassment 580
3. Employer Precautions and Employee
Responsibility 581
C. Alternatives to Litigation: Complaint Procedures,
Mediation, and Arbitration 581
D. Intellectual History and Controversies in Sexual
Harassment 583
II. Social Science Perspectives and Selected Empirical Studies:
Uses and Limitations 584
A. Types of Sexual Harassment 585
B. Prevalence of Sexual Harassment 586

C. Gender Differences in Perceptions Related to Sexual
Harassment 588
D. Victim Characteristics and Patterns of Sexual
Harassment 589
E. Offender and Organizational Characteristics 589
F. Individual Responses and the Effects of
Harassment 590
G. The Effects of Harassment Upon Organizations 592
H. Legal Standards: Reasonable Victim/Woman/Person 592
I. Integrating Social Science Perspectives and Legal
Issues 593
III. Special Issues in Sexual Harassment Cases:
Selected Literature 594
A. Background and Overview 594
B. The Extent of the Expert's Role in Sexual
Harassment Cases 594
C. Issues of Scope, Focus, and Assessment Practices in
Sexual Harassment Cases 599
IV. Forensic Assessment in Sexual Harassment Cases 601
A. The Role of the Forensic Expert 601
B. Ground Rules 601
C. Relevant Areas of Expertise 602
D. Examiner Objectivity and Possible Bias 603
1. The Distinction Between Therapist and Evaluator 603
2. The Importance of Avoiding Ideology 604
3. The Examiner's History 604
V. The Evaluation Process 605
A. The Forensic Interview in Sexual Harassment Cases:
Content and Process 605
B. Psychological Testing: Uses and Limitations 609
1. Issues of Test Validity and Claimant Credibility 609
2. Psychological Tests and Assessment of Personality
and Symptoms 612
C. The Forensic Examiner's Testimony in Sexual Harassment
Cases 613
1. The Obligation to Provide Complete and Balanced
Information 613
2. Avoiding Excessive Inference 614
3. Assessing Credibility Versus Usurping the Role of the
Trier of Fact 614
VI. Special Assessment Issues in Sexual Harassment Cases 615
A. Overview 615
B. Childhood Sexual Abuse 616
C. Personality Disorders 618
D. Reasonable Person/Woman Exceptions: The
"Hypersensitivity" Issue 619
E. Welcomeness and Plaintiff Response 620
F. Assessment of Severity of Emotional Damages 623

VII. Psychological Treatment in Sexual Harassment Cases	625
A. The Decision to Litigate	625
B. Confidentiality Issues	626
C. The Therapist/Evaluator Distinction Revisited	627
D. Treatment Approaches with Sexual Harassment Claimants	628

CHAPTER 15 AVOIDING AND ATTACKING "JUNK SCIENCE" IN EMPLOYMENT LITIGATION 631

I. The Development of the Law Against Junk Science	632
A. *Daubert*	632
B. *Kumho Tire*	637
C. Revised Federal Rule of Evidence 702	639
II. Junk Science in Employment Cases	641
A. The Expert's Training and Experience	642
1. Education and Training	642
2. Clinical Experience	645
B. The Expert's Diagnostic Technique	647
1. Failure to Use *DSM-IV-TR*	648
2. Failure to Conduct Differential Diagnosis	652
C. Misuse of Psychological Testing	654
1. Lack of Expert's Qualifications in Testing	654
2. Lack of Scientific Basis in the Test	655
3. Improper Test Administration	656
4. Improper Scoring of Tests	657
5. Improper Interpretation of Tests	657

CHAPTER 16 MENTAL DISABILITIES UNDER THE AMERICANS WITH DISABILITIES ACT 659

I. Introduction	659
II. The Definition of "Mental Disability" Under the ADA	660
A. Mental Impairment That Substantially Limits a Major Life Activity	661
1. What Constitutes an Impairment	661
a. Mental Disorders Listed in the *DSM*	661
b. Other Conditions Described in the *DSM*	663
c. Conditions Not Contained in the *DSM*	663
d. Personality Disorders and Pathological Personality Traits	665
2. Substantial Limitation	667
a. Temporary Nonchronic Impairments	669
b. Mitigating Measures	672
3. Major Life Activities	675
a. Interacting With Others	676
b. Engaging in Sexual Relations	679
c. Reproduction	681
d. Sleeping	682

	e. Cognitive Functions	684
	f. Caring for Oneself	685
	g. Traveling	687
	h. Working	687
	i. Inability to Tolerate Stress	690
	ii. Personality Conflicts with Supervisors	691
	iii. Shift Work and Overtime	692
B.	Conditions Excluded From Coverage	693
C.	Record of Disability	693
D.	Being Regarded as Disabled	695
	1. Referrals to Counseling or to an Employee Assistance Program	698
	2. Expressions of Concern	699
	3. Perception of Personality Traits	699
	4. Knowledge of Symptoms	700
	5. Offer of Accommodation	701
	6. Safety Concerns	702
	7. Request for Medical Evaluation	702

III. Qualified Individual with a Disability 703
  A. Attendance 707
  B. Punctuality 710
  C. Shifts/Hours Worked 712
  D. Ability to Get Along with Coworkers and Supervisors 713
  E. Interacting with Customers or General Public 714
  F. Security Clearance 715
  G. Other Essential Functions 715

IV. Reasonable Accommodation 716
  A. Defining "Reasonable" Accommodations 717
  B. Burden of Proof in Establishing That Accommodation Is Reasonable 717
  C. What Triggers the Accommodation Obligation 718
  D. The Interactive Process 723
    1. Steps in the Process 724
    2. Liability for Failure to Engage in the Process 724
  E. Common Forms of Accommodation Requested by Mentally Disabled Individuals 727
    1. Unpaid Leave 727
    2. Modified Work Schedule 730
    3. Part-Time Work 733
    4. Shift Changes 734
    5. Working at Home 734
    6. Transfer 735
    7. Accommodation of Employee Misconduct 737
    8. Requirement That Employee Obtain Treatment 741
  F. Accommodations Not Required 743
  G. Undue Hardship 745

V. Drug and Alcohol Abuse 746
  A. Drug Use 746

	B. Alcoholism	749
VI.	Benefit Plans	750
VII.	Medical Examinations and Inquiries	751
	A. Preemployment Inquiries	752
	1. General	752
	2. Preemployment Psychological Testing	754
	3. Preemployment Drug Testing	755
	B. Post-Offer Preemployment Examinations and Inquiries	756
	C. Postemployment Medical Inquiries	758
	D. Performance-Related Concerns	760
	1. Direct Threat	762
	2. Disclosures of Prescription Medication Use	763
	3. Monitoring and/or Requiring Medication or Treatment	764
	4. Employee Refusal to Respond to Medical Inquiry or Submit to Medical Examination	766
VIII.	Violence and Threats	767
	A. Introduction	767
	B. Burden of Proof	768
	C. Magnitude of Threat	770
	D. Suicide Threats	773
	E. Conflicting Medical Information	774

APPENDIXES

APPENDIX 1:	EEOC POLICY GUIDE ON COMPENSATORY AND PUNITIVE DAMAGES UNDER THE 1991 CIVIL RIGHTS ACT	777
APPENDIX 2:	AMERICAN ACADEMY OF PSYCHIATRY AND THE LAW: ETHICAL GUIDELINES FOR THE PRACTICE OF FORENSIC PSYCHIATRY	783
APPENDIX 3:	SPECIALTY GUIDELINES FOR FORENSIC PSYCHOLOGISTS	789
APPENDIX 4:	MODEL ENGAGEMENT LETTERS FOR MENTAL HEALTH EXPERTS	799
APPENDIX 5:	RULE 412, FEDERAL RULES OF EVIDENCE	805
APPENDIX 6:	RULE 702, FEDERAL RULES OF EVIDENCE	813
APPENDIX 7:	SAMPLE CROSS-EXAMINATION OF PLAINTIFF'S EXPERT	821

TABLE OF CASES 833

INDEX 859

LIST OF TABLES, FIGURES, AND EXHIBITS

Tables

		Page
3-1	Conceptualization of the Mental Disorder	115
4-1	The Multiaxial System	128
4-2	Axis I Disorders	131
4-3	Other Conditions That May Be a Focus of Clinical Attention	131
4-4	Axis II Personality Disorders	138
4-5	Axis V Global Assessment of Functioning (Rating of Severity of Symptoms or Impairment)	140
5-1	Axis I Disorders Commonly Encountered in Employment Litigation	164
5-2	*DSM-IV-TR* Diagnostic Criteria for Schizophrenia	166
5-3	*DSM-IV-TR* Subtypes of Schizophrenia	167
5-4	*DSM-IV-TR* Diagnostic Criteria for Delusional Disorder	171
5-5	Subtypes of Delusional Disorder	172
5-6	*DSM-IV-TR* Diagnostic Criteria for Major Depressive Episode	175
5-7	*DSM-IV-TR* Diagnostic Criteria for Major Depressive Disorder, Single Episode	176
5-8	*DSM-IV-TR* Diagnostic Criteria for Major Depressive Disorder, Recurrent	177
5-9	*DSM-IV-TR* Diagnostic Criteria for Dysthmic Disorder	179
5-10	*DSM-IV-TR* Diagnostic Criteria for Manic Episode	182
5-11	*DSM-IV-TR* Diagnostic Criteria for Mixed Episode	183
5-12	*DSM-IV-TR* Diagnostic Criteria for Hypomanic Episode	185
5-13	*DSM-IV-TR* Diagnostic Criteria for Bipolar I Disorder	185

5-14	*DSM-IV-TR* DIAGNOSTIC CRITERIA FOR BIPOLAR II DISORDER	186
5-15	*DSM-IV-TR* DIAGNOSTIC CRITERIA FOR A PANIC ATTACK	189
5-16	*DSM-IV-TR* DIAGNOSTIC CRITERIA FOR PANIC DISORDER WITH AGORAPHOBIA	190
5-17	*DSM-IV-TR* DIAGNOSTIC CRITERIA FOR PANIC DISORDER WITHOUT AGORAPHOBIA	191
5-18	*DSM-IV-TR* DIAGNOSTIC CRITERIA FOR OBSESSIVE-COMPULSIVE DISORDER	193
5-19	*DSM-IV-TR* DIAGNOSTIC CRITERIA FOR GENERALIZED ANXIETY DISORDER	195
5-20	*DSM-IV-TR* DIAGNOSTIC CRITERIA FOR POSTTRAUMATIC STRESS DISORDER	198
5-21	*DSM-IV-TR* DIAGNOSTIC CRITERIA FOR SOMATIZATION DISORDER	201
5-22	*DSM-IV-TR* DIAGNOSTIC CRITERIA FOR CONVERSION DISORDER	204
5-23	*DSM-IV-TR* DIAGNOSTIC CRITERIA FOR PAIN DISORDER	205
5-24	*DSM-IV-TR* DIAGNOSTIC CRITERIA FOR ADJUSTMENT DISORDER	209
5-25	SUBTYPES OF ADJUSTMENT DISORDERS	209
6-1	*DSM-IV-TR* DIAGNOSTIC CRITERIA FOR A PERSONALITY DISORDER	214
6-2	*DSM-IV-TR* PERSONALITY DISORDERS, GROUPED BY CLUSTER	221
6-3	*DSM-IV-TR* DIAGNOSTIC CRITERIA FOR PARANOID PERSONALITY DISORDER	223
6-4	*DSM-IV-TR* DIAGNOSTIC CRITERIA FOR SCHIZOID PERSONALITY DISORDER	224
6-5	*DSM-IV-TR* DIAGNOSTIC CRITERIA FOR SCHIZOTYPAL PERSONALITY DISORDER	225
6-6	*DSM-IV-TR* DIAGNOSTIC CRITERIA FOR ANTISOCIAL PERSONALITY DISORDER	230
6-7	*DSM-IV-TR* DIAGNOSTIC CRITERIA FOR CONDUCT DISORDER	230
6-8	*DSM-IV-TR* DIAGNOSTIC CRITERIA FOR BORDERLINE PERSONALITY DISORDER	234
6-9	*DSM-IV-TR* DIAGNOSTIC CRITERIA FOR HISTRIONIC PERSONALITY DISORDER	237
6-10	*DSM-IV-TR* DIAGNOSTIC CRITERIA FOR NARCISSISTIC PERSONALITY DISORDER	239
6-11	*DSM-IV-TR* DIAGNOSTIC CRITERIA FOR AVOIDANT PERSONALITY DISORDER	241
6-12	*DSM-IV-TR* DIAGNOSTIC CRITERIA FOR DEPENDENT PERSONALITY DISORDER	244
6-13	*DSM-IV-TR* DIAGNOSTIC CRITERIA FOR OBSESSIVE-COMPULSIVE PERSONALITY DISORDER	247

6-14	DSM-IV-TR DIAGNOSTIC CRITERIA FOR PERSONALITY DISORDER NOT OTHERWISE SPECIFIED	248
6-15	THE AXIS II DISORDERS, CHARACTERISTIC BASELINE BEHAVIORS, AND POTENTIALLY DANGEROUS RESPONSES TO CHARACTEROLOGICALLY PERCEIVED THREAT OF ATTACK	249
6-16	FORENSIC PSYCHIATRIC DATA RELEVANT TO ASSESSING PLAUSIBILITY OF EMPLOYMENT LITIGATION CLAIMS	256
6-17	CHECKLIST OF SUGGESTED DOCUMENTS TO PROCURE IN DISCOVERY FOR PSYCHIATRIC EVALUATION OF EMPLOYMENT LITIGATION CLAIMS INVOLVING POSSIBLE CONTRIBUTORY AXIS II PATHOLOGY	257
7-1	COMMON ANTIDEPRESSANT MEDICATIONS	273
7-2	COMMON ANTIANXIETY MEDICATIONS	274
7-3	CHECKLIST FOR PREPARATION OF CASE FOR THE EXPERT	283
10-1	MMPI-2 CLINICAL SCALES	375
10-2	MMPI-2 CONTENT SCALES	378
10-3	MMPI-2 SUPPLEMENTARY SCALES	378
10-4	MCMI-III SCALES	382
12-1	EXAMPLES OF NONPSYCHOTROPIC MEDICATIONS CLASSIFIED BY ORGAN SYSTEM AFFECTED	461
12-2	EXAMPLES OF NONPSYCHOTROPIC MEDICATIONS CLASSIFIED BY DISEASE TREATED	462
12-3	LICIT AND ILLICIT PSYCHOTROPIC AGENTS	464
12-4	EXAMPLES OF ILLICIT PSYCHOTROPIC AGENTS	464
12-5	LICIT PSYCHOTROPIC AGENTS: THE FOURTEEN "ANTIS"	465
12-6	ANTI-PARKINSONIAN MEDICATIONS	466
12-7	ANTI-ADDICTION AGENTS	471
12-8	ANTI-ANXIETY AGENTS	473
12-9	ANTI-APPETITE AGENTS	474
12-10	ANTI-CONVULSANT AGENTS	475
12-11	ANTI-DEPRESSANT AGENTS	476
12-12	ANTI-ATTENTION DEFICIT HYPERACTIVITY DISORDER [ADHD] AGENTS (STIMULANT CLASS)	478
12-13	ANTI-INSOMNIA AGENTS	478
12-14	ANTI-MANIC AGENTS	480
12-15	ANTI-OBSESSIVE AGENTS	480
12-16	ANTI-PAIN ("ANALGESIC") AGENTS	481
12-17	ANTI-PANIC AGENTS	483
12-18	ANTI-PSYCHOTIC AGENTS I: TRADITIONAL MEDICATIONS	484
12-19	ANTI-PSYCHOTIC AGENTS II: "ATYPICAL" ANTI-PSYCHOTIC MEDICATIONS	485
12-20	NONPSYCHOTROPIC AGENTS USED TO TREAT SIDE EFFECTS OF PSYCHOTROPIC AGENTS	486
12-21	NONPSYCHOTROPIC MEDICATIONS USED TO TREAT PSYCHIATRIC CONDITIONS AND SIGNS/SYMPTOMS OF PSYCHIATRIC DISORDERS	487
12-22	SUMMARY OF MEDICATION SIDE EFFECTS	488
12-23	ALPHABETICAL LISTING OF MEDICATIONS BY GENERIC NAME	491

12-24	ALPHABETICAL LISTING OF MEDICATIONS BY BRAND NAME	494
12-25	DEPOSITION QUESTIONS CONCERNING PAST MEDICAL HISTORY	498
13-1	*DSM-IV-TR* DIAGNOSTIC CRITERIA FOR POSTTRAUMATIC STRESS DISORDER	504
13-2	EXAMPLES OF TRAUMATIC EVENTS THAT QUALIFY AS A CRITERION A STRESSOR	506
13-3	THE CLINICAL SYMPTOMS OF PTSD	509
13-4	FACTORS PREDICTIVE OF THE DEVELOPMENT OF PTSD	515
13-5	*DSM-IV-TR* DIAGNOSES ASSOCIATED WITH TRAUMA RESPONSES	521
13-6	FACTORS ASSOCIATED WITH CHRONIC PTSD	523
13-7	SYMPTOM CLUSTERS IN PTSD	529
13-8	MEDICATIONS USED IN THE TREATMENT OF PTSD	529
13-9	DOCUMENTATION REQUIREMENTS FOR THE FORENSIC EVALUATION	534
13-10	*DSM-IV-TR* DIAGNOSTIC CRITERIA FOR BORDERLINE PERSONALITY DISORDER	551

Figures

6-1	A TWO-STEP APPROACH TO THE FORENSIC MENTAL HEALTH EVALUATION OF EMPLOYMENT LITIGATION CLAIMS POTENTIALLY INVOLVING PERSONALITY PATHOLOGY	256
6-2	SCENARIOS UNDERLYING IMPLAUSIBLE CLAIMS	259
6-3	SCENARIOS UNDERLYING IMPLAUSIBLE CLAIMS: PLAINTIFF KNOWS CLAIM IS FALSE	259
6-4	SCENARIOS UNDERLYING IMPLAUSIBLE CLAIMS: PLAINTIFF BELIEVES CLAIM IS TRUE	260
6-5	SCENARIOS UNDERLYING IMPLAUSIBLE CLAIMS: PLAINTIFF KNOWS CLAIM IS FALSE	260
6-6	SUMMARY: FORENSIC PSYCHIATRIC APPROACH TO THE EVALUATION OF EMPLOYMENT LITIGATION CLAIMS	261
10-1	MMPI-2 PROFILE	380
12-1	THEORETICAL DOSE-RESPONSE CURVE	459

Exhibits

7-1	SAMPLE LANGUAGE FOR SUBPOENA FOR PSYCHIATRIC OR PSYCHOLOGICAL TREATMENT RECORDS	272
7-2	SAMPLE LANGUAGE FOR SUBPOENA FOR MEDICAL RECORDS	272
7-3	SAMPLE LANGUAGE FOR SUBPOENA FOR PERSONNEL RECORDS	276
7-4	SAMPLE LANGUAGE FOR SUBPOENA FOR SCHOOL RECORDS	277

PREFACE

The Growing Importance of Mental Health Issues in Employment Law

In the last decade, mental health issues have grown to become a significant issue for many employment attorneys, and the workplace has become a focus of considerable attention for many psychiatrists and clinical psychologists. Two leading factors have contributed to this result.

First and most significant was the enactment of two groundbreaking pieces of federal legislation. One statute, the Civil Rights Act of 1991,[1] provides plaintiffs in federal employment discrimination cases the right to recover damages for emotional distress (as well as punitive damages) of up to $300,000, in addition to the traditional remedies of lost wages and benefits and attorneys fees. As a result, virtually every federal employment discrimination lawsuit[2] now contains an allegation that the plaintiff suffered mental and emotional distress at the hands of the defendant employer. Most such lawsuits also include allegations under state fair employment statutes, or tort theories such as violation of public policy or intentional infliction of emotional distress, which often carry the potential for recovery of unlimited emotional distress damages. As a result, "dueling mental health experts" have become a common feature in the trial of many employment lawsuits, opining about whether and to what extent the plaintiff suffered emotional injury and who is to blame.

The other statute, the Americans with Disabilities Act of 1990 (which became effective in 1992), prohibits discrimination against—and requires accommodation of—employees with disabilities. Although in many respects the ADA was written with physical disabilities in mind, mental disabilities now account for the largest category of charges filed with the Equal Employment Opportunity Commission.[3] Under the ADA, mental health professionals play increasingly important roles in determining whether employees are psychologi-

---

[1] 42 U.S.C. § 1981A.

[2] Except for federal age discrimination lawsuits, as the Age Discrimination in Employment Act was not amended by the Civil Rights Act of 1991.

[3] In the last fiscal year for which statistics are available, the EEOC reported that charges relating to mental disabilities accounted for 16.9% of all ADA charges filed. The next-highest category, back problems, accounted for 15.6 % of charges filed. *Source:* www.eeoc.gov/stats/ada.

cally fit for duty, what types of accommodations of mental disabilities might be appropriate, and even whether an employee allegedly discriminated against because of his or her mental disability suffered compensable emotional distress as a result.

The second contributing factor is what we referred to in the Preface of the first edition of this volume as the "psychologization" of the workplace. What once might have been viewed as merely a difficult place to work is now viewed as the breeding ground for a variety of psychological disorders. As Charles J. Sykes pointed out in his book, *A Nation of Victims:*

> It was once taken for granted that many jobs were merely compensated drudgery. That the boss was a jerk, the work tedious, the social milieu isolated, and appreciation and affection in short supply was simply regarded as a fact of life—not as the seed of mental breakdown.[4]

An increasing number of employees have come to expect their jobs to provide them with more than just a paycheck. Many workers expect parenting, nurturing, rapid career advancement, interesting work and polite and accommodating supervisors who will look out for their emotional well-being. The rise in popularity of employee assistance programs (EAPs) is one aspect of this trend. The ever-broadening layperson's definition of "harassment" is another; it has produced a growing number of harassment lawsuits alleging rudeness and insensitivity on the part of the boss rather than sexual advances or vulgar conduct,[5] and virtually all of them include substantial damage claims for the emotional stress experienced as a result of working for a difficult supervisor. An example of this is found in *Freeman v. Chicago Park District*,[6] a racial harassment case in which the jury found no racial basis for the alleged harassment but awarded the plaintiff $45,000 anyway.

As a result of these factors, mental health issues are now an integral part of many employment lawsuits, and claims for emotional injuries represent a substantial portion of a defendant's monetary exposure. The magnitude of this exposure can be calculated in any given case by subtracting the value of the plaintiff's claim for lost pay and benefits from the plaintiff's total claim for compensatory damages. For example, if a plaintiff in a wrongful discharge case sues for $1 million, and that individual was paid $60,000 annually plus $15,000 in benefits at the time of discharge and was out of work for a year, $925,000 of the plaintiff's compensatory damage claim would be attributable to emotional distress damages. If such a plaintiff demands $300,000 to settle his or her claim, $225,000 of the settlement demand would be attributable to emotional distress damages. When viewed in this light, it quickly becomes apparent how important is the ability to objectively gauge whether, and to what extent, the plaintiff actually suffered psychological damages.

---

[4]CHARLES J. SYKES, A NATION OF VICTIMS: THE DECAY OF THE AMERICAN CHARACTER 156 (1992).

[5]*See* James J. McDonald, Jr., *The Equal Opportunity Jerk*, 26 EMPL. REL. L.J. 89 (1999).

[6]189 F.3d 613, 80 FEP Cases 1678 (7th Cir. 1999).

The Challenge of Evaluating Psychological Injury Claims

Unfortunately, it is often difficult to detect and measure a purely psychological injury that is claimed to have arisen in the workplace. When considered in the context of a *physical* injury, the concept of "pain and suffering" has a more tangible quality. First, of course, there is usually little doubt that the injury actually occurred. There may be considerable argument over who is responsible for the injury, but there ordinarily is some objective physical manifestation of the injury (such as a scar or x-rays) to establish conclusively that the injury occurred. Second, while such a concept can never be measured exactly, the suffering that accompanies a physical injury such as a broken leg or a burned hand is within the realm of experience of most courts and juries. In addition, ranges of jury verdicts for various types of physical injuries are routinely published and can assist counsel on both sides of a case to reach a fair settlement value for a case involving a physical injury.

By contrast, the injuries alleged in employment litigation (outside of workers' compensation cases involving physical injuries) are almost exclusively psychological. There is no physical manifestation of the alleged injury available to prove that it occurred. Typically, the claim is based solely on the plaintiff's own report of symptoms experienced—symptoms often described in such ambiguous terms as "anxiety," "depression," "panic," or "flashbacks." While a plaintiff may exhibit various symptoms that are relatively objective such as insomnia, headaches or gastrointestinal distress, there is ordinarily no way to verify conclusively whether those symptoms are the result of events in the workplace. It is even more difficult to gauge precisely the magnitude of a purely psychological injury.

The difficulty in determining the existence and severity of a purely psychological injury is the result of several factors. First, incidents such as loss of a job or unwanted sexual overtures affect different people in vastly different ways, depending on a host of factors including the individual's background and coping mechanisms. An incident that one employee might shrug off without a second thought might cause another employee to suffer extreme and disabling emotional distress.

Second, the sciences of psychiatry and psychology are relatively inexact ones. Two mental health professionals can—and do—arrive at different diagnoses of the same patient. This may be the result of different training and experience, different clinical approaches, or different interpretation of psychological test results (most of which provide a large field for interpretation). In addition, the various diagnostic categories can be somewhat slippery. The American Psychiatric Association's *Diagnostic and Statistical Manual of Mental Disorders,* the diagnostic bible of the mental health professions, is revised every seven years or so.[7] In the course of these revisions, new mental disorders are

---

[7]The third edition of the *Diagnostic and Statistical Manual of Mental Disorders,* known as "DSM-III," was published in 1980. It was revised in 1987 with such revision becoming known as "DSM-III-R." It was revised again in 1994, with the fourth edition

added and others are deleted, and the diagnostic criteria for still others are modified. While the revision process is intended to account for new developments in science, politics can play a part as well since the manual is written by various committees of psychiatrists and psychologists and disputes over diagnostic criteria are resolved by majority vote.[8]

Third, the diagnosis of a mental disorder depends in large part on the patient's self-report of various symptoms. While psychological testing and the clinician's[9] own observation of the patient certainly play a role in formulating a diagnosis, they really are adjuncts to the patient's own description of the symptoms experienced. The obvious problem with this is that the patient's account may not be wholly reliable. This may or may not involve intentional deception on the patient's part; it may simply be the result of poor memory, for example. But in the context of litigation in which a substantial amount of money is at stake and the primary vehicle for obtaining that money is a claim for mental and emotional injuries, the possibility of conscious deception on the part of the patient is quite real.

Fourth, it is sometimes difficult for the clinician to move from the therapeutic role to the forensic role. The term "forensic" refers to the application of scientific or medical knowledge in a legal context. In the forensic realm, the clinician ideally takes on the role of objective observer; albeit as an expert witness retained by the plaintiff or the defendant. Mental health professionals are trained primarily to help people, however. They are not typically trained to be skeptical of a patient's report of symptoms, as a purely objective observer might be. In fact, to betray any such skepticism would jeopardize severely the therapeutic alliance between clinician and patient. In the forensic context, by contrast, the clinician must be more of a detective than a therapist. A skeptical approach is essential (regardless of which side has retained the clinician) if an objective appraisal of the litigant's condition is to be obtained. The litigant's account cannot simply be accepted as true; rather, it must be thoroughly scrutinized for any evidence of fabrication, exaggeration, or misattribution of symptoms. Many clinicians are uncomfortable in this role, however, and the accuracy of their conclusion about a plaintiff's mental condition may suffer as a result.

Fifth, even where there is some certainty that a plaintiff is suffering from a form of psychopathology, it is sometimes difficult to establish a causative link between the workplace incident at issue and the psychopathology. Just because a plaintiff (1) was fired and (2) is depressed does not necessarily mean that the firing caused the depression, although such *post hoc, ergo propter hoc* reasoning is unfortunately quite common in litigation over emotional damage claims. Perhaps the plaintiff was treated for clinical depression prior to ever

---

known as "DSM-IV." A "text revision" of DSM-IV was issued in 2000, known as "DSM-IV-TR."

[8]*See* JAY ZISKIN, COPING WITH PSYCHIATRIC AND PSYCHOLOGICAL TESTIMONY 157–58 (5th ed. 1995).

[9]The term "clinician" will be used throughout this book to refer interchangeably to psychiatrists and clinical psychologists.

having come to work for the defendant. Perhaps the plaintiff suffered a significant loss outside of the workplace around the time of the termination. Many employees bring a whole range of mental and emotional problems and concurrent stressors with them into the workplace. Certain of these conditions—such as personality disorders and bipolar (manic-depressive) disorders—can produce the same symptoms of anxiety and depression that often are claimed to follow workplace incidents such as termination of employment, discrimination, or harassment. Establishing blame—or lack thereof—for a plaintiff's current mental condition is often the core issue addressed by opposing mental health experts in an employment lawsuit.

A Rapidly Developing Area of Law and Clinical Practice

When the first edition of this treatise was published in 1994, *Daubert v. Merrill Dow Pharmaceuticals, Inc.*[10] had just been decided. Rule 412 of the Federal Rules of Evidence was about to be amended to apply to sexual harassment lawsuits. The Fourth Edition of the American Psychiatric Association's *Diagnostic and Statistical Manual of Mental Disorders*[11] had just been published. There was little understanding among many attorneys of even the basic tenets of forensic psychiatry and psychology, and there was a lack of familiarity among many mental health professionals as well as attorneys of how an employee's psychopathology can cause workplace incidents alleged to be harassment or discrimination, instead of vice-versa. Much has happened in the development of the law and clinical practice since 1994 to make mental health issues an integral part of most employment litigation. Three trends in particular have been highlighted in the development of the law and clinical practice concerning emotional injuries in the workplace.

The first trend involves the increasing scrutiny by the courts of expert testimony, designed to ferret out "junk science" that may seem impressive to a jury but that is scientifically dubious. This trend began with the Supreme Court's decision in *Daubert*,[12] which established the trial court as a "gatekeeper" to ensure that only scientifically sound evidence reaches the jury, and it continued with the Court's most recent decision in *Kumho Tire Co. v. Carmichael*,[13] which extended the *Daubert* rule to expert testimony that does not involve pure science. Such scrutiny is being applied with greater frequency to the testimony of mental health experts, particularly where such "experts" lack the requisite qualifications or experience, or they fail to employ commonly accepted diagnostic procedures, or they administer psychological "tests" that are really little more than subjective symptom inventories. Some courts have struggled

---

[10] 509 U.S. 579 (1993).
[11] American Psychiatric Association, Diagnostic and Statistical Manual of Mental Disorders (4th ed. 1994).
[12] *Supra* note 10.
[13] 526 U.S. 137 (1999).

with the application of *Daubert* principles in employment cases, however. For example, one judge derisively characterized the Minnesota Multiphasic Personality Inventory (MMPI)—the first edition of the most widely used and extensively validated personality inventory in existence—as a "mind control device."[14] Another court affirmed a jury award for emotional distress damages, noting that the plaintiff's psychological expert had diagnosed posttraumatic stress disorder (PTSD) as a result of her being terminated and having to listen to foul language in the workplace[15]—a plainly invalid basis for a PTSD diagnosis. Nonetheless, although psychiatry and psychology differ from "hard" sciences such as chemistry or physics, they are still sciences, the basic principles of which are derived through the scientific method, and the courts are well-justified in requiring that expert testimony on mental health issues meet at least minimum scientific standards.

A corollary to this trend in the courts toward good science can be found in movements among forensic psychiatrists and psychologists to avoid practices that lack scientific rigor. Examples include the *Ethical Guidelines for the Practice of Forensic Psychiatry* republished by the American Academy of Psychiatry and the Law in 1995,[16] which discourage the "therapeutic bias" that results when a plaintiff's treating therapist attempts to serve also as expert witness, and the "Georgetown Guidelines" for the assessment of PTSD,[17] which decry the use of idiosyncratic diagnostic criteria.

The second trend, which is sometimes in tension with the first, involves the ongoing and intensifying conflict between a plaintiff's right to privacy and a defendant's right to a fair trial. Where a plaintiff asserts a claim for emotional damage allegedly arising out of a workplace incident, the defendant may attempt to defend itself by searching, via the discovery process, for alternative causes of the plaintiff's condition. These might include previously-diagnosed depression, a prior rape or other trauma, a personality disorder, or a concurrent stressor such as marital problems or financial distress. Such an approach is grounded in good science, as the scientific method requires that all potential causes of a condition be considered and ruled out before the actual cause is settled upon. Such an approach is also perceived to constitute an affront to a plaintiff's privacy rights in many instances, however.

As a result, a considerable amount of law has developed since the publication of the first edition of this treatise on issues such as whether (and under what conditions) the plaintiff should be compelled to submit to a Rule 35[18]

---

[14]Usher v. Lakewood Usher Eng'g & Mfg. Co., 158 F.R.D. 411, 66 FEP Cases 558 (N.D. Ill. 1994).

[15]Baty v. Willamette Indus., Inc., 985 F. Supp. 987 (D. Kan. 1997), *aff'd*, 172 F.3d 1232, 79 FEP Cases 1451 (10th Cir. 1999).

[16]These Guidelines are reproduced in Appendix 2.

[17]*See* Robert I. Simon, *Toward the Development of Guidelines in the Forensic Psychiatric Examination of Posttraumatic Stress Disorder Claimants*, in POSTTRAUMATIC STRESS DISORDER IN LITIGATION: GUIDELINES FOR FORENSIC ASSESSMENT 31 (Robert I. Simon ed., 1995).

[18]Fed. R. Civ. P. 35.

mental examination, whether the defendant should have access to the plaintiff's medical and psychotherapy records, and whether the defendant may conduct discovery into various aspects of the plaintiff's sexual history. Thus far, the law has not developed uniformly. Congress, for its part, and over the objection of the Supreme Court, amended Rule 412 of the Federal Rules of Evidence[19] in 1994 to limit the discovery of the sexual history of a sexual harassment plaintiff. The line drawn by Congress is a fuzzy one, however, and it fails to distinguish adequately between prior *consensual sexual activity* with persons other than co-workers (which ordinarily is of little relevance to the issues in the case) and prior *sexual trauma* (which may be of extreme relevance in a given case).

The amended Rule 412 and similar judicial efforts to safeguard the privacy of plaintiffs do protect some plaintiffs from abusive discovery tactics designed to achieve little more than embarrassment and intimidation. They also, however, can constitute significant impediments to finding the truth.[20] Justice Antonin Scalia lamented the trend in the law toward creating ever more privileges and restrictions on discovery in his dissenting opinion in *Jaffee v. Redmond*,[21] which recognized a psychotherapist–patient privilege under federal common law. Scalia wrote:

> The Court has discussed at some length the benefit that will be purchased by creation of the evidentiary privilege in this case: the encouragement of psychoanalytic counseling. It has not mentioned the purchase price: occasional injustice. That is the cost of every rule which excludes reliable and probative evidence—or at least every one categorical enough to achieve its announced policy objective. In the case of some of these rules, such as the one excluding confessions that have not been properly "Mirandized," . . . the victim of the injustice is always the impersonal State or the faceless "public at large." For the rule proposed here, the victim is more likely to be some individual who is prevented from proving a valid claim—or (worse still) prevented from establishing a valid defense. The latter is particularly unpalatable for those who love justice, because it causes the courts of law not merely to let stand a wrong, but to become themselves the instruments of wrong.[22]

If the goal of the judicial process is to provide an objective and accurate assessment of causation and damages, concern for the plaintiff's privacy rights cannot be permitted to override the defendant's need to obtain sufficient background information on the plaintiff to permit such an assessment to occur. Many plaintiffs, unfortunately, enter the litigation process unaware that if they place their mental condition in issue by seeking an award for emotional damages, they most likely will open up their background to searching scrutiny by the

---

[19]The text of the amended Rule 412 is set forth in Appendix 5.
[20]*See* John Gibeaut, *Shield a Prosecution Sword*, A.B.A. J. 36 (Dec. 1997) (describing how "rape shield" laws may deprive defendants of their right to due process).
[21]518 U.S. 1 (1996).
[22]*Id.* at 18–19.

opposing attorney. It is incumbent upon plaintiffs' attorneys to disclose this potential to a client who is considering asserting such a claim. In any event, the courts are likely to continue to struggle with this issue for some time to come.

The third trend is the increasing willingness of the courts to examine the role of a plaintiff's own prior psychological problems in the genesis of the workplace dispute at issue in litigation. For example, in an early case, *Lowe v. Philadelphia Newspapers, Inc.*,[23] the court admitted a psychiatrist's testimony that the plaintiff was oversensitive and may have overreacted to events on the job. As the court observed:

> Testimony concerning a . . . plaintiff's mental disorder which causes him or her to perceive criticism as harassment, and to perceive racial slurs where no racial motivation is present, is highly relevant to the question whether plaintiff's perception of racial harassment is correct.[24]

Often, a plaintiff's prior psychopathology takes the form of a personality disorder,[25] which is a chronic and pathological means of perceiving and interpreting one's environment and relating to others. An employee with a Borderline Personality Disorder, for example, may initiate sexual-related conversations with co-workers and then suddenly accuse the same co-workers of sexual harassment when they respond. A manager with a Narcissistic Personality Disorder may be insensitive to the needs of his subordinates and unable to comprehend why his abusive manner produces a high rate of turnover.

The most recent and comprehensive recognition to date by a court of the role of personality disorders in the genesis of harassment and discrimination claims occurred in *Pascouau v. Martin Marietta Corporation.*[26] In that harassment lawsuit, the court concluded that "the conduct that could be described as harassment was not based on gender, but rather on Plaintiff's demonstrated lack of interpersonal skills." In its discussion of the facts of the case, the court described at some length the plaintiff's pre-existing psychological problems, many of which arose from the plaintiff's dysfunctional childhood. The *Pascouou* court explained the relevance of the plaintiff's personality disorder:

> The personality disorder is a condition, largely the product of being raised in a dysfunctional home with dysfunctional parents, in which Plaintiff did not learn how to solve problems effectively or to communicate effectively with other people. The disorder leads to the formulation of implausible perceptions and thus different kinds of conclusions about what other people's actions and behavior

---

[23]594 F. Supp. 123, 54 FEP Cases 167 (E.D. Pa. 1984).

[24]*Id.* at 126, 54 FEP Cases at 169. *See also* Davis v. United States Steel Corp., 539 F. Supp. 839, 54 FEP Cases 203 (E.D. Pa. 1982) (incidents alleged by plaintiff to be racial harassment held to be legitimate criticism and discipline inaccurately perceived by plaintiff because of emotional disorder).

[25]For a full discussion of the role of personality disorders in employment disputes, see Chapter 6, Personality Disorders in Employment Litigation.

[26]994 F. Supp. 1276, 76 FEP Cases 651 (D. Colo. 1998), *aff'd in relevant part,* 185 F.3d 874 (10th Cir. 1999) (table).

mean as distinguished from what a reasonable person not subject to such a disorder would perceive them to mean.[27]

The *Pascouau* court then remarked, concerning the testimony of the defense psychiatrist:

> When asked if Plaintiff's allegations had any role in the causes of Plaintiff's disorders, Dr. Plezak replied that the situation is reversed in that the disorders are causes of the allegations. The incidents Plaintiff related were characterized by misinterpretations of events and interactions with fellow employees that were far more intense than would be interpreted by a reasonable person.[28]

This is a dramatic acknowledgment of the important role that many plaintiffs' own prior psychopathology may play in the genesis of harassment and discrimination cases. This case is particularly significant because it indicates that testimony of psychiatric or psychological experts may be directed to issues of liability as well as damages. In circumstances where the courts allow experts to focus on possible personality pathology ("Axis II disorders" in the parlance of the mental health professions) in addition to emotional distress damages, the need for adequate discovery into the plaintiff's prior life history is even more acute, increasing the likelihood of legal skirmishes over the scope of permissible discovery. The diagnosis of a personality disorder can often supply the key to an understanding of the events that led up to the lawsuit—particularly in difficult "he said/she said" cases where there are no third-party witnesses to break the impasse.

The Challenge for Attorneys and Mental Health Professionals

Employment lawyers thus are faced with a significant challenge. Mental and emotional injury claims now constitute a substantial bulk of exposure in most contemporary employment litigation, yet many attorneys are still unfamiliar with the techniques used to assess such injuries in the employment litigation context—and even less familiar with how to determine whether the plaintiff's psychopathology might have caused or contributed to the events at issue in the litigation. An attorney encountering a case involving a claim of mental or emotional injury typically is confronted by a bewildering array of esoteric jargon, expert witnesses with diametrically opposite positions, and alleged symptoms on the part of the plaintiff that may be difficult to distinguish from the ordinary emotional tribulations of everyday life. It is the goal of this book to provide attorneys with a basic understanding of the content and process of forensic psychiatry and psychology, and to demystify matters such as personality disorders, diagnostic criteria, differential diagnosis, pharmacology, and psychological testing. The desired result is that attorneys will be less intimidated by

---

[27]*Id.* at 1279, 76 FEP Cases at 653–54.
[28]*Id.*, 76 FEP Cases at 654.

mental and emotional injury claims and better equipped to evaluate them objectively.

This book should be of interest to mental health professionals as well, both experienced forensic clinicians and those without significant prior exposure in the forensic area. Not only do the authors tailor various forensic concepts and techniques to fit in the context of employment litigation, but several of the chapters that follow represent the state of the art of forensic practice. Forensic psychiatry and psychology historically have focused on whether and how badly a plaintiff was injured, and whether and to what extent alternative stressors may have played a role. Several of the chapters in this book also consider the possibility that a plaintiff in an employment lawsuit may not have been merely the passive victim of workplace events. Mental health professionals may find helpful the discussion regarding the role of personality disorders and other serious chronic conditions in bringing about incidents in the workplace that ultimately lead to litigation.

The goal of the editors has been to provide an objective treatment of the various legal and clinical issues discussed in this work. The focus here will not just be upon techniques designed to assist a plaintiff or a defendant to win a case. Rather, the intent of this book is to stimulate dialogue and debate among attorneys, clinicians, and the courts, in the hope that future developments in the law and in forensic practice in this important area will be sound and well reasoned.

A Word of Caution

A work as broad in scope as this one could not be written by one person; it requires collaboration by authors representing a wide variety of expertise. The editors have endeavored to select authors who are among the leading authorities in the areas covered by their chapters. With such a diverse collection of prominent professionals comes a diversity of perspective, however. The editors have encouraged the authors to present their unique perspectives. The viewpoint of any one author or authors should not be attributed, therefore, to the other authors or to the editors.

JAMES J. MCDONALD, JR.
FRANCINE B. KULICK
(November 2001)

CHAPTER 1

THE LEGAL CONTEXT

James J. McDonald, Jr., J.D.[*]

Mental and emotional injuries are relevant in employment litigation because of the growing collection of statutes and common law causes of action that permit recovery of damages in employment lawsuits for mental anguish, emotional distress, pain and suffering, and the like. Variously referred to as *compensatory damages, extracontractual damages,* and *emotional distress damages,* these damage claims account for the bulk of the employer's exposure in most employment lawsuits.

Emotional distress may manifest itself as fright or a traumatic reaction at the time of the injury, anxiety or depression as a result of the injury, or humiliation and embarrassment in connection with the injury. One standard jury instruction defines *emotional distress* as "mental distress, mental suffering or mental anguish. It includes all highly unpleasant mental reactions, such as fright, nervousness, grief, anxiety, worry, mortification, shock, humiliation and indignity, as well as physical pain."[1]

There is no legal requirement that emotional distress be diagnosable as a mental disorder to be compensable; the testimony of lay witnesses—even the plaintiff's own uncorroborated testimony—may suffice to support an award of emotional distress damages.[2] Nonetheless, emotional distress often is manifested

---

[*]The author gratefully acknowledges the contribution of David D. Kadue, Esq. of the Los Angeles office of Seyfarth Shaw. Mr. Kadue authored a chapter in the first edition of this volume, which provides the foundation for part of this chapter.

[1]CALIFORNIA BOOK OF APPROVED JURY INSTRUCTIONS (BAJI) (8th ed. 2001), BAJI 12.72. This definition closely resembles that in the RESTATEMENT (SECOND) OF TORTS §46 cmt. j (1965), which defines *emotional distress* to include "mental suffering, mental anguish, mental or nervous shock" and "all highly unpleasant mental reactions, such as fright, horror, grief, shame, humiliation, embarrassment, anger, chagrin, disappointment, worry, and nausea."

[2]*See, e.g.,* Williams v. Trans World Airlines, 660 F.2d 1267, 1273, 27 FEP Cases 487 (8th Cir. 1981).

by one or more mental disorders diagnosable by a psychiatrist or psychologist in accordance with the American Psychiatric Association's *Diagnostic and Statistical Manual of Mental Disorders*.[3] A plaintiff's case may become more valuable if supported by testimony from the plaintiff's psychotherapist and/or an expert witness' analysis of the plaintiff's clinically diagnosed mental disorder. This analysis can help the plaintiff establish both the existence and the severity of emotional distress, as well as the connection between that distress and the defendant's conduct. In most instances, however, a plaintiff who seeks to introduce testimony of a mental health expert or treating therapist opens the door to intrusive discovery by the defendant into the plaintiff's medical, psychological, and social history as well as a mental examination by an expert retained by the defense.[4] Particularly if the plaintiff's mental anguish was more in the nature of embarrassment and humiliation as opposed to a psychiatric disorder, such a plaintiff may find it preferable to describe his or suffering to the jury in lay terms rather than introduce expert testimony.

The defendant must also make a tactical decision whether to introduce expert testimony. On one hand, the defendant's argument that the plaintiff has suffered very little or no emotional distress may be more convincing if supported by an expert opinion that minimizes the severity and significance of the plaintiff's alleged condition. An expert might opine, for example, that the plaintiff is suffering from no mental disorder, is suffering from only a minor and easily treatable disorder, or is suffering from a mental disorder that preexisted the events at issue in the litigation. On the other hand, the defendant's putting too much emphasis on the emotional damage issue can backfire, particular where the plaintiff's emotional damage claim is relatively weak, or where it is presented in lay terms by the plaintiff. An extensive defense presentation can actually tend to bolster a weak claim in the eyes of a jury. It can also detract attention from a strong defense case on the merits.

Both sides in an employment lawsuit, therefore, must make several tactical decisions regarding whether and how extensively to prosecute or defend a claim for emotional distress damages. A variety of legal and clinical issues must be taken into account.

I. Actions in Which Emotional Distress Damages Are Available

Legal actions for recovery of damages fall into two broad categories—statutory and common law. Statutes either expressly provide for recovery of emotional distress damages or are construed in that manner by the courts. Common law

---

[3] *See* AMERICAN PSYCHIATRIC ASSOCIATION, DIAGNOSTIC AND STATISTICAL MANUAL OF MENTAL DISORDERS (4th ed. text rev. 2000).

[4] See discussion of the plaintiff's right to privacy versus the defendant's right to discovery in Chapter 8, The Right to Privacy vs. the Need for Discovery, and of the availability of a mental examination of the plaintiff in Chapter 9, The Mental Examination of the Plaintiff.

theories that permit recovery of emotional distress damages have developed in an incremental fashion over many years of appellate court decisions.

A. Statutory Bases for Recovery of Emotional Distress Damages

Several statutes involving employment law provide for recovery of emotional distress damages.

1. Civil Rights Act of 1991

Title VII of the Civil Rights Act of 1964, which prohibits discrimination by employers of 15 or more employees on the basis of race, color, religion, sex, and national origin,[5] originally did not provide for recovery of emotional distress or other forms of compensatory damages. Nor did the Americans With Disabilities Act (ADA), which prohibits discrimination against persons with physical or mental disabilities.[6] With the enactment of the Civil Rights Act of 1991, however, plaintiffs in federal employment discrimination lawsuits brought under Title VII or the ADA were permitted to recover compensatory and punitive damages for intentional discrimination in addition to the back wages and other equitable relief previously available. Compensatory damages include "emotional pain, suffering, inconvenience, mental anguish, loss of enjoyment of life, and other nonpecuniary losses."[7] The amount of combined compensatory and punitive damages that may be recovered is limited under the Civil Rights Act of 1991, however, depending on the size of the employer. The damage limitations are as follows:

15 to 100 employees	$ 50,000
101 to 200 employees	$100,000
201 to 500 employees	$200,000
More than 500 employees	$300,000

These limitations are on compensatory and punitive damages combined that may be awarded in a single action.[8] The maximum damage amounts do not include awards for "front pay."[9] Nor do the federal damages caps prohibit larger damage awards under applicable state laws for the same conduct.[10] Moreover, where a plaintiff succeeds on state law claims as well as federal

---

[5]42 U.S.C. §2000e et seq. Sexual harassment, which is considered a form of discrimination based on sex, is also actionable under Title VII. *See, e.g.,* Harris v. Forklift Sys., Inc., 510 U.S. 17, 63 FEP Cases 225 (1993); Meritor Sav. Bank v. Vinson, 477 U.S. 57, 40 FEP Cases 1822 (1986).

[6]42 U.S.C. §12101 et seq.

[7]42 U.S.C. §1891A(b)(3).

[8]Hogan v. Bangor & Aroostook R.Co., 61 F.3d 1034, 4 AD Cases 1251 (1st Cir. 1995).

[9]Pollard v. E.I. duPont de Nemours & Co., ___ U.S. ___, 121 S. Ct. 1946, 85 FEP Cases 1217 (2001).

[10]Kimzey v. Wal-Mart Stores, Inc., 107 F.3d 568, 73 FEP Cases 87 (8th Cir. 1997).

claims, damages in excess of the federal cap may be allocated by the court to the state law claims.[11]

The Equal Employment Opportunity Commission (EEOC), which enforces Title VII, has issued a policy guide on the recovery of damages now permitted by the Civil Rights Act of 1991.[12] That part of the policy guide that discusses emotional distress damages appears as Appendix 1.

2. Sections 1981 and 1983

The Civil Rights Act of 1866[13] forbids race discrimination in employment by private and nonfederal public employers. The Civil Rights Act of 1871[14] forbids state government employers from discriminating on the basis of race, sex, religion, and national origin. Under both sections 1981[15] and 1983,[16] compensatory damages may be awarded for emotional distress.

3. Age Discrimination in Employment Act

The Age Discrimination in Employment Act of 1967 (ADEA)[17] forbids discrimination against employees or applicants who are 40 years of age or older. In an ADEA action, unlike in a Title VII action, damages for pain and suffering and mental distress are not compensable.[18] This is because the ADEA is modeled after the Fair Labor Standards Act, which authorizes awards of only back wages and liquidated damages.[19] Also, the Civil Rights Act of 1991 does not apply to claims brought under the ADEA.

4. State Employment Discrimination Statutes

Most states have fair employment practice statutes (modeled after Title VII) that forbid employment discrimination, generally on the same grounds covered

---

[11] Passantino v. Johnson & Johnson Consumer Prods., Inc., 212 F.3d 493 (9th Cir. 2000).

[12] POLICY GUIDE ON COMPENSATORY AND PUNITIVE DAMAGES UNDER 1991 CIVIL RIGHTS ACT (July 7, 1992), *reprinted in* 8 Fair Empl. Prac. Man. (BNA) 405:7091–7102.

[13] Codified in part at 42 U.S.C. §1981.

[14] Codified in part at 42 U.S.C. §1983.

[15] Johnson v. Railway Express Agency, Inc., 421 U.S. 454, 10 FEP Cases 817 (1975).

[16] *See, e.g.,* Carey v. Piphus, 435 U.S. 247, 262 (1978) (student who can prove denial of due process can recover for emotional distress caused directly thereby); King v. Board of Regents, 898 F.2d 533, 537, 52 FEP Cases 809 (7th Cir. 1990) (plaintiff may recover compensatory damages under §1983 claim for environmental sexual harassment).

[17] 29 U.S.C. §621 et seq.

[18] *E.g.,* Perrell v. FinanceAmerica Corp., 726 F.2d 654, 33 FEP Cases 1728 (10th Cir. 1984); Hill v. Spiegel, Inc., 708 F.2d 233, 31 FEP Cases 1532 (6th Cir. 1983); Naton v. Bank of California, 649 F.2d 691, 27 FEP Cases 510 (9th Cir. 1981).

[19] 29 U.S.C. §216.

by Title VII and ADEA. Several of these states permit plaintiffs to recover compensatory damages.[20] Some state statutory schemes, however, expressly limit the amount of compensatory damages that can be awarded in a state administrative proceeding.[21]

B. Common Law Bases for Recovery of Emotional Distress Damages

There are a variety of causes of action based on the common law that permit the recovery of emotional distress damages. These damages generally are not available in suits for breach of contract because in contract actions the damages are measured by the benefit of the party's bargain, the nature of which rarely involves emotional tranquility. In contrast, emotional distress damages generally are available in tort actions because tort actions usually entitle the plaintiff to compensatory damages—relief designed to make the plaintiff whole. In fact, emotional distress is the principal element of damages in many torts.[22]

As discussed in the following sections, many—but not all—tort theories entitle a plaintiff to recovery for emotional distress. The principal tort theories available in employment litigation that may allow recovery for emotional distress damages are intentional and negligent infliction of emotional distress, violation of public policy, assault and battery, false imprisonment, invasion of privacy, defamation, misrepresentation, loss of consortium, and negligent hiring or retention.

1. Intentional Infliction of Emotional Distress

The tort of intentional infliction of emotional distress has four essential elements: (1) extreme and outrageous conduct; (2) an intent to cause, or reckless disregard of the probability of causing, emotional distress; (3) severe emotional distress suffered by the plaintiff; and (4) a causal connection between the conduct complained of and the plaintiff's emotional distress.[23]

---

[20]*See, e.g.,* State Personnel Bd. v. Fair Employment & Hous. Comm'n, 39 Cal. 3d 422, 429 (1985) (in private actions under California's fair employment practices statute, courts may award compensatory and punitive damages).

[21]*See, e.g.,* CAL. GOV'T CODE §12970(a)(3) (agency may not award more than $50,000 for "emotional pain, suffering, inconvenience, mental anguish, loss of enjoyment of life, and other nonpecuniary losses"); KAN. STAT. ANN. §44-1005(k) (agency may award no more than $2,000 for "pain, suffering, and humiliation"); MINN. STAT. ANN. §363.071(2) (administrative law judge may award "compensatory damages" in amount up to three times actual damages sustained); WASH. REV. CODE §49.60.250(5) (administrative law judge may award no more than $10,000 for "humiliation and mental suffering").

[22]RESTATEMENT (SECOND) OF TORTS §905 cmt. c (1979).

[23]3 E. DEVITT ET AL., FEDERAL JURY PRACTICE AND INSTRUCTIONS §81.05 (1987) (4th ed. 1987); W. PROSSER & P. KEETON, HANDBOOK ON THE LAW OF TORTS 60 (5th ed. 1984) ("liability for conduct exceeding all bounds usually tolerated by decent

A. Extreme or Outrageous Conduct The element of proof on which liability most often hinges is whether the conduct complained of is sufficiently outrageous.[24] Findings of outrageous conduct typically have occurred where the defendant has engaged in violent conduct,[25] sexual exposure,[26] or offensive touching.[27]

Plaintiffs in harassment and discrimination cases also often plead state law claims for intentional infliction of emotional distress in an attempt to collect damages exceeding the $300,000 limit on federal compensatory and punitive

---

society, of a nature which is especially calculated to cause, and does cause, mental distress of a very serious kind").

[24]The RESTATEMENT (SECOND) OF TORTS defines *outrageous conduct* as follows: Liability has been found only where the conduct has been so outrageous in character, and so extreme in degree, as to go beyond all possible bounds of decency, and to be regarded as atrocious, and utterly intolerable in a civilized community. Generally, the case is one in which the recitation of the facts to an average member of the community would arouse his resentment against the actor, and lead him to exclaim, "Outrageous!"

Id. at §46 cmt. d. An emotional distress claim failed in *Miller v. Aluminum Co. of America*, 679 F. Supp. 495, 45 FEP Cases 1775 (W.D. Pa. 1988), *aff'd*, 856 F.2d 184, 52 FEP Cases 1472 (3d Cir. 1988), where the complainant alleged that she had been assigned to menial, routine work, disadvantaged by sexual favoritism, and subjected to an embarrassing remark by a male plant manager about her breasts. Summary judgment was granted against her because the conduct was not "actionable outrageous behavior." *Id.*, 52 FEP Cases, at 1779, 1784.

[25]*E.g.,* Arnold v. City of Seminole, 614 F. Supp. 853, 857, 861, 40 FEP Cases 1539, 1541, 1544 (E.D. Okla. 1985) ($150,000 compensatory damage award for intentional infliction of emotional distress; touching consisted of pushing plaintiff across room and into file cabinet).

[26]*E.g.,* Priest v. Rotary, 634 F. Supp. 571, 575, 40 FEP Cases 208, 209 (N.D. Cal. 1986) (defendant "exposed his genitals to plaintiff . . . as [she] was having a cup of coffee following the end of [her] shift").

[27]*E.g.,* Shrout v. Black Clawson Co., 689 F. Supp. 774, 779–82, 46 FEP Cases 1339, 1343–46 (S.D. Ohio 1988) ($75,000 in compensatory damages awarded for intentional infliction of emotional distress where defendant's conduct included "touch[ing] her intimately"); Gilardi v. Schroeder, 672 F. Supp. 1043, 1047, 45 FEP Cases 283 (N.D. Ill. 1986) (male employer drugged plaintiff, sexually assaulted her while she was unconscious, then put her in bed with his wife; court awarded plaintiff $100,000), *aff'd*, 833 F.2d 1226, 45 FEP Cases 346 (7th Cir. 1987); Pease v. Alford Photo Indus., 667 F. Supp. 1188, 1190, 1203, 49 FEP Cases 497, 498, 507–09 (W.D. Tenn. 1987) ($2,500 in compensatory damages awarded for "serious mental injury" based on tort of "outrageous conduct" where defendant's conduct included "unwelcomed, unwanted, unconsented to, sexually harassing and humiliating touching"); *Priest*, 634 F. Supp. at 578, 584, 40 FEP Cases at 212, 217 ($95,000 in compensatory damages awarded where pattern of conduct included unwelcome touching of plaintiff's breasts and unzipping the front of plaintiff's uniform, constituting emotional distress consisting of "highly unpleasant mental reactions, including fright, humiliation, shock, surprise, sickness, nervousness, apprehension, disgust, emotional pain, intimidation, embarrassment, anger, sleeplessness, nausea, and anxiety").

damages imposed by the Civil Rights Act of 1991. The workplace context makes the outrageous conduct element easier to prove than it is in some other claims for emotional distress in that the plaintiff can emphasize the nature of the employment relationship that gave the defendant extraordinary power to damage the plaintiff's interests.[28] As one court has observed: "The standards for intent and for socially tolerable conduct depend on the type of relationship which exists between plaintiff and defendant. An employer-employee relationship . . . imposes a greater obligation to refrain from inflicting mental distress than the obligation which exists between strangers."[29] Similarly, in *Fisher v. San Pedro Peninsula Hospital*,[30] the California Court of Appeal held that "[g]iven an employee's fundamental, civil right to a discrimination free work environment" under statutory law, sexual harassment at work is inherently outrageous, "as it exceeds all bounds of decency usually tolerated by a decent society."[31]

Not all courts hold that a federal Title VII violation necessarily equates with a state law cause of action for intentional infliction of emotional distress, however. In *Hadley v. VAMPTS*,[32] the court applied a different standard of proof for recovery of emotional distress damages under Title VII and for the common law cause of action for intentional infliction of emotional distress. The plaintiff in *Hadley* was awarded emotional distress damages on his Title VII claim but not on his claim for intentional infliction of emotional distress. He argued that there was no difference between the two claims, but the court disagreed. It explained:

---

[28]*E.g.*, Dias v. Sky Chefs, 919 F.2d 1370, 54 FEP Cases 852 (9th Cir. 1990) (affirming jury verdict of liability where manager created hostile work environment and recommended discharge of plaintiff in retaliation for her complaints; duty under Oregon law to refrain from abusive employment behavior is closer to that of physician toward patient than that of police officer toward citizen not in custody); Lucas v. Brown & Root, Inc., 736 F.2d 1202, 1206, 35 FEP Cases 1855 (8th Cir. 1984) (alleged sexual advances that threatened plaintiff's job security, coupled with misrepresentations respecting plaintiff's unemployment compensation, stated claim); Stewart v. Thomas, 538 F. Supp. 891, 894, 30 FEP Cases 1609 (D.D.C. 1982) (supervisor made advances, used abusive language, engaged in offensive touching, and threatened plaintiff with adverse job consequences if she rejected his advances); Rice v. United Ins. Co., 465 So. 2d 1100, 36 FEP Cases 1641 (Ala. 1984) (sustaining claim based on plaintiff's allegations that supervisor tried to force her to take disability leave following her pregnancy and misrepresented vital business information); Howard Univ. v. Best, 484 A.2d 958, 36 FEP Cases 482 (D.C. App. 1984) (sustaining claim brought by discharged employee, stressing history of female subordination in workplace).

[29]*Dias*, 919 F.2d at 1373, 54 FEP Cases at 854.

[30]214 Cal. App. 3d 590, 262 Cal. Rptr. 842, 54 FEP Cases 584 (1989).

[31]*Id.* at 618, 262 Cal. Rptr. at 858, 54 FEP Cases at 596. *But see* Andrews v. City of Philadelphia, 895 F.2d 1469 (3d Cir. 1990) (sexual harassment alone does not usually rise to the level of outrageousness necessary to make out cause of action for intentional infliction of emotional distress).

[32]44 F.3d 372, 67 FEP Cases 186 (5th Cir. 1995).

> While it is true that compensatory damages under Title VII can overlap with actual damages suffered as a result of intentional infliction of emotional distress, the severity of injury necessary for each is markedly different. In order to be compensable, emotional distress under the state law of intentional infliction of emotional distress must be severe. There is no such requirement for compensable emotional harm under Title VII.[33]

This difference in standards of proof has become relevant to claims for intentional infliction of emotional distress based upon an organization's failure to promptly remedy sexual harassment. In *Codrington v. Virgin Islands Port Authority*,[34] the court held that the employer's failure to take prompt remedial action following a claim of sexual harassment constituted a violation of Title VII but was not conduct "so outrageous and so beyond all bounds of decency to be considered atrocious and utterly intolerable in a civilized society so as to support a cause of action for intentional infliction of emotional distress."[35] In *Prunty v. Arkansas Freightways, Inc.*,[36] by contrast, the corporate employer was held liable for intentional infliction of emotional distress based upon a vice president's knowledge of a manager's sexual harassment of a subordinate and the vice president's failure to take corrective action. The court reasoned that the vice president, on behalf of the corporation, had ratified the manager's harassment. The court noted, however, that liability for intentional infliction of emotional distress will not arise out of an "ordinary employment dispute." Only in "extreme and outrageous" situations will liability attach.[37]

In *Walker v. Thompson*,[38] the Fifth Circuit affirmed summary judgment for the employer on an intentional infliction of emotional distress claim based on a series of racist remarks in the workplace. It noted that "insults, indignities, threats, annoyances, or petty oppressions, without more, do not rise to the level of intentional infliction of emotional distress."[39] In *Gray v. Sears, Roebuck & Co.*[40] a district court, citing a Texas Supreme Court case, maintained that "[a] claim for intentional infliction of emotional distress does not lie for ordinary employment disputes." Quoting another Texas Supreme Court case, the court observed: "Even the wrongful transfer, failure to promote, or termination of an employee does not, standing alone, constitute intentional infliction of emotional distress."[41] That court held that an employer's failure to reinstate an employee

---

[33]*Id.* at 372, 67 FEP Cases at 187.

[34]911 F. Supp. 907, 70 FEP Cases 213 (D.V.I. 1995).

[35]*Id.* at 915, 70 FEP Cases at 219.

[36]16 F.3d 649, 9 IER Cases 911 (5th Cir. 1994).

[37]*Id.* at 654, 9 IER Cases at 915.

[38]214 F.3d 615, 83 FEP Cases 243 (5th Cir. 2000).

[39]*Id.* at 628, 83 FEP Cases at 252. *See also* Durley v. APAC, Inc., 236 F.3d 651, 658, 84 FEP Cases 1177, 1181 (11th Cir. 2000) ("Rudeness and insensitivity that result in hurt feelings will not, in and of themselves, establish liability.").

[40]131 F. Supp. 2d 895, 904 (N.D. Tex. 2001) (citing GTE Southwest v. Bruce, 998 S.W.2d 605, 611 (Tex. 1999)).

[41]*Id.* (quoting City of Midland v. O'Bryant, 18 S.W.3d 209, 217 (Tex. 2000)).

in his old job upon his return from medical leave and transfer of the employee to a location 20 miles away was not conduct that was sufficiently outrageous to qualify.

B. SEVERE EMOTIONAL DISTRESS As noted previously, one limitation on liability is the requirement that the emotional distress inflicted be "severe." As the *Restatement (Second) of Torts* explains: "Complete emotional tranquility is seldom attainable in the world, and some degree of transient and trivial emotional distress is a part of the price of living among people. The law intervenes only where the distress inflicted is so severe that no reasonable man could be expected to endure it."[42] Further, for purposes of establishing this tort, the distress must be "reasonable and justified under the circumstances," although liability will result if the distress has resulted from a peculiar susceptibility to emotional distress of which the defendant was aware.[43]

In *Barrett v. Applied Radiant Energy Corp.*,[44] the Fourth Circuit affirmed the district court's dismissal of the plaintiff's claim for intentional infliction of emotional distress, noting that she failed to allege any interference with work or outside activities or allege that she suffered any physical symptoms of stress. The court observed that a showing of

> severe emotional distress, as opposed to generalized emotional distress, is required because "the injuries in such cases are too hard to determine with any reasonable certainty—are more often assumed than real—and the suit too liable to be wholly speculative. If everyone was allowed damages for injuries to his feelings caused by someone else, the chief business of mankind might be fighting each other in the courts."[45]

One court recently denied the claim for intentional infliction of emotional distress of a plaintiff who was terminated without warning after eight years of employment where the plaintiff had not seen a doctor for treatment, did not suffer any significant physical symptoms, and had experienced other emotional stressors unrelated to the workplace.[46]

2. Negligent Infliction of Emotional Distress

Although many jurisdictions authorize recovery for emotional distress caused by negligent conduct, courts vary in the degree of objective symptomatology they require.[47] Some courts hold that one cannot recover for negligent infliction

---

[42] RESTATEMENT (SECOND) OF TORTS §46 cmt. j (1965).
[43] *Id.*
[44] 240 F.3d 262, 85 FEP Cases 252 (4th Cir. 2001).
[45] *Id.* at 269, 85 FEP Cases at 258–59 (quoting Ruth v. Fletcher, 377 S.E.2d 412, 415 (Va. 1989)).
[46] Yelverton v. Graebel/Houston Movers, Inc., 121 F. Supp. 2d 604 (E.D. Tex. 2000).
[47] *See generally* Atchison, Topeka & Santa Fe Ry. v. Buell, 480 U.S. 557, 570–71 (1987).

of emotional distress without also suffering a physical injury.[48] Other courts are more generous. For example, in *Olson v. Connerly*,[49] the plaintiff's "panic attacks" resulting from outrageous conduct by her former physician were held to be a sufficient physical manifestation to allow recovery for mental distress arising from the physician's negligent conduct.

In some jurisdictions, negligence claims (including claims for negligent infliction of emotional distress) are preempted by workers' compensation exclusivity. California is a leading example. In *Livitsanos v. Superior Court*,[50] the California Supreme Court held that claims for negligent infliction of emotional distress are preempted by workers' compensation regardless of whether they are compensable under the workers' compensation system.

Finally, in *Malik v. Carrier Corp.*,[51] the Second Circuit held that an employee may not bring a claim for negligent infliction of emotional distress based upon his employer's investigation of sexual harassment allegations against him. The court recognized that such an investigation might well cause an employee to suffer emotional distress:

> Such investigations forseeably produce emotional distress—often in copious amounts—in alleged harrassers, whether guilty or innocent. As with any investigation into potentially embarrassing personal interactions, confidentiality is difficult or impossible to maintain if all pertinent information is to be acquired from all possible sources. Denials of an accused cannot by themselves bring the matter to an end. Even if the charge proves demonstrably baseless, the very existence of the charge may give the charge temporary or even permanent credibility among some persons.[52]

Nonetheless, the court maintained that because such an investigation is mandated by federal law, any emotional distress claims arising out of such an investigation must fail as a matter of law.[53]

3. Wrongful Discharge in Violation of Public Policy

Courts in most states recognize that public policy may limit an employer's right to discharge even an at-will employee.[54] Courts typically have recognized

---

[48]*See, e.g.,* Rogers v. Loew's L'Enfant Plaza Hotel, 526 F. Supp. 523, 529–30, 29 FEP Cases 828 (D.D.C. 1981) (citing rule); Miller v. Aluminum Co. of Am., 679 F. Supp. 495, 45 FEP Cases 1775 (W.D. Pa. 1988) (negligent infliction actionable only with physical impact or threat thereof or contemporary observance of injury by family member).

[49]151 Wis. 2d 663, 445 N.W.2d 706 (1988), *aff'd,* 156 Wis. 2d 488, 457 N.W.2d 479 (1990).

[50]2 Cal. 4th 744, 7 Cal. Rptr. 2d 808, 7 IER Cases 745 (1992).

[51]202 F.3d 97, 81 FEP Cases 1275 (2d Cir. 2000).

[52]*Id.* at 106, 81 FEP Cases at 1281–82.

[53]*Id.* at 109, 81 FEP Cases at 1283.

[54]*E.g.,* Petermann v. Teamsters Local 396, 174 Cal. App. 2d 184, 344 P.2d 25 (1959) (termination of employee for refusing to commit perjury violated public policy of state as reflected in the penal code). For a listing of those states that recognize the tort of wrongful discharge in violation of public policy, see IER Manual (BNA) 505:51–52.

a public policy cause of action where an employee has been discharged for refusing to commit an unlawful act.[55] The bases cited for public policy claims have been state statutes,[56] state constitutions,[57] and policies forbidding discharges in retaliation for performing an act that the public would encourage or for refusing to do something that the public would condemn.[58] These grounds support a tort action that entitles the plaintiff to compensatory damages, including emotional distress damages.

When an employee brings a public policy claim alleging that he or she was discharged in violation of the public policy against employment discrimination (as articulated in Title VII, a state employment discrimination statute, or elsewhere), courts have raised two basic questions as to whether such a claim will be recognized. First, some courts have questioned the need to recognize a public policy tort action for employment discrimination, as a common law action should be available only where there otherwise would be no remedy. Under this doctrine, the existence of remedies under Title VII or any state employment discrimination statute undermines the justification for a public policy tort.[59]

---

[55]*E.g.*, Tameny v. Atlantic Richfield Co., 27 Cal. 3d 167, 610 P.2d 1330, 164 Cal. Rptr. 839 (1980) (unlawful to discharge employee who refused to participate in illegal price fixing); Sabine Pilot Serv. v. Hauck, 687 S.W.2d 733, 735, 119 LRRM 2187 (Tex. 1985) (unlawful to fire employee for refusing to illegally dump bilge into bay waters); Trombetta v. Detroit, Toledo & Ironton R.R., 81 Mich. App. 489, 265 N.W.2d 385 (1978) (unlawful to discharge employee who refused to falsify pollution records).

[56]Dias v. Sky Chefs, 919 F.2d 1370, 54 FEP Cases 852 (9th Cir. 1990) (under Oregon law, unlawful to discharge employee for complaining about sexual harassment on the job, given that sexual harassment is prohibited under state and federal law); Chamberlin v. 101 Realty, 915 F.2d 777, 54 FEP Cases 101 (1st Cir. 1990) (female employee discharged for rebuffing employer's sexual advances had claim under New Hampshire law for wrongful termination based on public policy); Handley v. Phillips, 715 F. Supp. 657, 662, 52 FEP Cases 195 (M.D. Pa. 1989) (allegations that female employee's dismissal constituted a breach of public policy); Holien v. Sears, Roebuck & Co., 298 Or. 76, 689 P.2d 1292, 36 FEP Cases 137 (1984) (sexual harassment supports wrongful discharge claim based on public policy under both state and federal law prohibiting harassment).

[57]Rojo v. Kliger, 52 Cal. 3d 65, 276 Cal. Rptr. 130, 54 FEP Cases 1146 (1990) (citing California constitution in deciding that plaintiff may pursue public policy claim without regard to state statutory remedies); Drinkwalter v. Shipton, 225 Mont. 380, 732 P.2d 1335, 1336, 50 FEP Cases 616, 617 (1987) (sexual harassment violates public policy embodied in Montana constitution).

[58]Lucas v. Brown & Root, Inc., 736 F.2d 1202, 1205, 35 FEP Cases 1855 (8th Cir. 1984) (discharge of female employee for denying sex to her boss breached Arkansas public policy against prostitution); Clemens v. Gerber Scientific, 1989 U.S. Dist. LEXIS 376 (E.D. Pa. 1989) (public policy claim stated under Pennsylvania law for retaliation against woman for resisting sexual advances, with specific intent to harm her).

[59]*E.g.*, Haw-Len v. F.W. Woolworth Co., 737 F. Supp. 1104, 1106-08 (D. Haw. 1990) (where plaintiff sues for breach of public policy that inheres in employment discrimination statute, statutory remedy is exclusive); Harrison v. Edison Bros. Apparel

Second, because Title VII by its terms does not preempt any state law action, courts in several states have held that the state employment discrimination statute was intended to provide the exclusive state law remedy for acts of employment discrimination.[60] Other courts have permitted plaintiffs to pursue public policy claims despite the existence of a statutory remedy.[61]

4. Assault and Battery

The traditional torts of assault and battery provide a common law remedy for persons threatened with and subjected to offensive physical contact. Although battery and assault constitute separate torts, usually they are asserted as companion causes of action.[62]

Liability for battery requires a harmful or offensive contact with a person, resulting from an act intended to cause the plaintiff or a third person to suffer the contact.[63] A battery results whenever the offensive contact extends to any

---

Stores, 724 F. Supp. 1185, 1191–93 (M.D.N.C. 1989) (no "public policy" exception to employment at will where statutory remedy exists).

[60]*E.g.*, Wolk v. Saks Fifth Ave., 728 F.2d 221, 34 FEP Cases 193 (3d Cir. 1984).

[61]*Rojo*, 52 Cal. 3d 65, 276 Cal. Rptr. 130, 54 FEP Cases 1146 (California fair employment practices statute does not bar "public policy" claim; sexual harassment victims may pursue administrative or common law remedies, or both); Hallquist v. Mak Fish Plumbing & Heating Co., 46 FEP Cases 1855, 1860 (D. Mass. 1987), *aff'd*, 843 F.2d 18, 47 FEP Cases 323 (1st Cir. 1988) (sexual harassment complainant who was laid off entitled to both back pay under Title VII and compensatory damages for termination in violation of public policy under Massachusetts law).

[62]*E.g.*, Fields v. Cummings Credit Union, 540 N.E.2d 631, 53 FEP Cases 1613, 1618 (Ind. App. 1989) (claim for assault and battery stated on basis of touching face, shoulders, and buttocks and attempted kiss, all without complainant's consent); Waltman v. International Paper Co., 47 FEP Cases 671 (W.D. La. 1988) (allegations of unwelcome touching and pinching of breasts and thighs and the placing of an air hose between plaintiff's legs by male coworkers supported claim for assault and battery), *rev'd on other grounds*, 875 F.2d 468, 50 FEP Cases 179 (5th Cir. 1989); Dockter v. Rudolf Wolff Futures, 684 F. Supp. 532, 46 FEP Cases 1129 (N.D. Ill. 1988) (unwelcome petting and breast fondling by supervisory employee constituted assault and battery under Illinois law), *aff'd*, 913 F.2d 456, 53 FEP Cases 1642 (7th Cir. 1990); Valdez v. Church's Fried Chicken, 683 F. Supp. 596, 47 FEP Cases 1155 (W.D. Tex. 1988) (plaintiff awarded $46,525 in damages for sexual assault by male coworker); Pease v. Alford Photo Indus., 667 F. Supp. 1188, 49 FEP Cases 497 (W.D. Tenn. 1987) (plaintiff recovered compensatory and punitive damages for assault and battery resulting from employer's physical sexual harassment); O'Reilly v. Executone of Albany, 121 A.D.2d 772, 503 N.Y.S.2d 185 (1986) (assault and battery claim arising from allegations of intentional, repeated, and malicious sexual touching by male coworkers); Skousen v. Nidy, 90 Ariz. 215, 367 P.2d 248, 250 (1961) (employer liable for assault and battery for touching private parts of 65-year-old female employee as he tried to seduce her).

[63]RESTATEMENT (SECOND) OF TORTS §§13, 18 (1965).

part of the plaintiff's body or to practically anything attached to it,[64] although there need be no mental or physical harm to justify an award of damages.[65]

Liability for assault requires a showing that (1) the actor intended to cause harmful or offensive physical contact and (2) the victim was put in apprehension of such conduct.[66] Verbal conduct alone does not constitute an assault unless the circumstances somehow warrant an expectation of imminent physical contact.[67] Consequently, one who is the target only of insults and innuendo must pursue an alternative theory of relief.

Any claim of offensive or harmful touching, regardless of its nature, is sufficient to satisfy the element of an offensive contact.[68] Greater emotional distress is likely, however, whenever the touching is sexual in nature.[69]

5. False Imprisonment

The tort of false imprisonment involves an act intended to confine another person "within boundaries fixed by the actor," which results in a confinement of which the other person is conscious.[70] For example, an employee was held to have stated a claim for false imprisonment where he was "physically and forcibly restrained" by his supervisor and other employees when he tried to leave his office cubicle.[71] Some form of physical restraint is typically required, however. A cause of action for false imprisonment will not lie where an employer merely threatens an employee with discharge if the latter leaves the room.[72]

6. Invasion of Privacy

Several different torts fall under the general heading of *invasion of privacy*. The claims commonly asserted in support of emotional distress damages are

---

[64]*Id.*

[65]Boyd v. James S. Hayes Living Health Care Agency, 671 F. Supp. 1155, 44 FEP Cases 332 (W.D. Tenn. 1987) (where plaintiff sustained no compensable damage from offensive touching, judgment entered for defendant on battery claim).

[66]RESTATEMENT (SECOND) OF TORTS §21 (1965).

[67]*Id.* at §31.

[68]*See* Newsome v. Cooper-Wiss, Inc., 179 Ga. App. 670, 347 S.E.2d 619, 621–22 (1986) (plaintiff stated claim for assault and battery even though defendant never touched the private areas of her body).

[69]*See, e.g.,* Valdez v. Church's Fried Chicken, 683 F. Supp. 596, 47 FEP Cases 1155 (W.D. Tex. 1988) (plaintiff awarded damages against coworker in assault and battery action arising from sexual assault in the workplace); Gilardi v. Schroeder, 672 F. Supp. 1043, 45 FEP Cases 283 (N.D. Ill. 1986) (female employee entitled to punitive damages for civil battery after her employer intentionally drugged her and engaged in sexual intercourse with her while she was unconscious).

[70]RESTATEMENT (SECOND) OF TORTS §35 (1965).

[71]Ubelacker v. Cincom Sys., Inc., 48 Ohio App. 3d 268, 3 IER Cases 1853 (1988).

[72]Foley v. Polaroid Corp., 508 N.E.2d 72, 2 IER Cases 328 (Mass. 1987).

(1) intrusion on seclusion, (2) false-light publicity, and (3) public disclosure of private facts.

A. INTRUSION ON SECLUSION The tort of intrusion involves an intentional interference with the solitude or seclusion of one's person or private affairs and concerns.[73] The intrusion must be offensive or objectionable to a reasonable person, and it must encompass a truly private matter.[74]

Invasion of privacy sometimes involves persistent, unwelcome intrusions into the home, by telephone calls or otherwise, and on that basis, such actions have been held to give rise to a cause of action.[75] Some courts have held that even absent an intrusion into the home, invasion of privacy may lie with respect to a series of personal inquiries made by a supervisor in the workplace.[76]

B. FALSE-LIGHT PUBLICITY A second form of invasion of privacy consists of publicity that places the complainant in a false light before the public.[77] The false light, although it need not be defamatory, must be objectionable to the ordinary, reasonable person under the circumstances.[78]

C. PUBLIC DISCLOSURE OF PRIVATE FACTS Public disclosure of private facts is a third tort falling under the rubric of invasion of privacy. The elements of this tort are (1) the public disclosure of a private fact, (2) publicity that would be highly offensive and objectionable to a person of ordinary sensibilities, (3) the lack of a legitimate public interest in having the information made available, and (4) injury to the complainant as a result of the publicity.[79]

---

[73]PROSSER & KEETON, *supra* note 23, at 854.

[74]RESTATEMENT (SECOND) OF TORTS §652B (1965).

[75]Rogers v. Loew's L'Enfant Plaza Hotel, 526 F. Supp. 523, 29 FEP Cases 828 (D.D.C. 1981) (sustaining intrusion claim based on plaintiff's allegations that her immediate supervisor repeatedly called her at home and at work—when he was off duty—and made "leering comments" to her about her personal and sexual life, despite her requests that he stop).

[76]*E.g.*, Phillips v. Smalley Maint. Serv., 435 So. 2d 705 (Ala. 1983), *reprinted in relevant part at* 711 F.2d 1533–37, 32 FEP Cases 982–86 (plaintiff's employer subjected her to intrusive demands and threats, including inquiry into her sexual relationship with her husband; on one occasion, he slapped her buttocks; on another occasion, he covered his office window with paper, thereby obscuring the view of others, after telling her that sexual services were part of her job). *See also* Priest v. Rotary, 634 F. Supp. 571, 582, 40 FEP Cases 208, 215 (N.D. Cal. 1986) (defendant "made sexually suggestive comments to and about [plaintiff] in the presence of others which violated her right to privacy").

[77]PROSSER & KEETON, *supra* note 23, §117, at 863.

[78]RESTATEMENT (SECOND) OF TORTS §652E (1965).

[79]*Id.* §652D; PROSSER & KEETON, *supra* note 23, §117, at 856–57. Under Florida law, the publication must be to the public in general or to a large number of persons. *See* Steele v. Offshore Shipbuilding, 867 F.2d 1311, 1315, 49 FEP Cases 522 (11th Cir. 1989).

In *Cummings v. Walsh Construction Co.*,[80] an employee alleged that her supervisor's public disclosure of their sexual relationship amounted to an actionable invasion of privacy. The court dismissed her claim, holding that her discussion of the relationship with third persons effectually robbed her of the "veil of privacy."[81]

7. Defamation

A defamation action requires proof that (1) the defendant made a false or defamatory statement, (2) the statement constituted an unprivileged communication to a third party, (3) the defendant was at least negligent in communicating the statement, and (4) the communication was the proximate cause of harm to the plaintiff or the communication was actionable regardless of special harm.[82] Defamatory matter that is written historically has been regarded as *libel,* whereas orally communicated defamation constitutes *slander.*[83] Libel is actionable without any proof of special harm.[84] Slander, in contrast, generally is not actionable unless actual damage is proved.[85] However, proof of damage is not required where the slander involves the plaintiff's business, trade, or profession; the commission of a crime by the plaintiff; the "unchastity" of a female plaintiff; or the contraction of a "loathsome" disease.[86]

8. Fraud and Misrepresentation

The torts of fraudulent and negligent misrepresentation can occur when one misrepresents facts or intentions for the purpose of inducing another to act or to refrain from action when justifiable reliance on the misrepresentation causes pecuniary loss.[87]

With respect to property transactions, the general rule is that damages for emotional distress cannot be recovered in actions for fraud.[88] A typical statement of the rule is that mental distress is not an element of damages for fraud.[89]

---

[80]561 F. Supp. 872, 884, 31 FEP Cases 930 (S.D. Ga. 1983).

[81]*Id.* at 885.

[82]RESTATEMENT (SECOND) OF TORTS §558 (1965); PROSSER & KEETON, *supra* note 23, §111, at 774.

[83]PROSSER & KEETON, *supra* note 23, §112, at 786–87 (libel includes pictures, signs, statues, and motion pictures, although debate continues regarding the characterization of radio and television broadcasts).

[84]*Id.*

[85]*Id.* at 788; Kersul v. Skulls Angels, 130 Misc. 2d 345, 495 N.Y.S.2d 886, 42 FEP Cases 987 (Sup. Ct. 1985) (action for slander, which arose from employer's broadcast to others that plaintiff was crazy, was deficient for failure to plead special damages).

[86]PROSSER & KEETON, *supra* note 23, §112, at 788–93.

[87]*See, e.g.,* RESTATEMENT (SECOND) OF TORTS §525 (1965) (fraudulent misrepresentation); PROSSER & KEETON, *supra* note 23, §105, at 728 (same).

[88]Branch v. Homefed Bank, 6 Cal. App. 4th 793, 8 Cal. Rptr. 2d 182 (1992).

[89]Sierra Nat'l Bank v. Brown, 18 Cal. App. 3d 98, 103, 95 Cal. Rptr. 742 (1971). *See also* O'Neal v. Spillane, 45 Cal. App. 3d 147, 119 Cal. Rptr. 245 (1975); *In re*

Emotional distress damages have been awarded, however, in cases of fraud or misrepresentation in connection with the provision of personal services. In *Sprague v. Frank J. Sanders Lincoln Mercury, Inc.*,[90] the fraud consisted of misrepresentations concerning the repair of an automobile. The trial court had excluded evidence of damages for mental distress and suffering. Distinguishing cases of generalized deceit from cases involving fraud in the sale of property, the appellate court reversed, holding that "general damages for mental pain and suffering are recoverable in a tort action of deceit."[91]

The rule is different regarding negligent misrepresentation. Where the loss (other than emotional distress) is solely economic, there generally is no recovery for emotional distress.[92]

9. Tortious Interference With Contract

To prevail under a contractual interference theory, the plaintiff must show that the defendant intentionally and improperly interfered with the performance of a contract, either by inducing the termination of the contract or in some other way.[93] Proof of an unlawful motive is necessary.

The plaintiff generally must have an enforceable contract.[94] Because liability for tortious interference is founded only on the acts of an interfering third party,[95] agents of the other party to the contract cannot be liable for contractual interference unless they are shown to have acted outside their legitimate scope of authority.[96] Because the tort is designed to compensate only for economic harm resulting from the interference, this is an example of a tort for which emotional distress damages are not available.

10. Loss of Consortium

A claim for loss of consortium is a derivative action for the loss of sexual attentions, society, and affection resulting from an injury to one's marital

---

Marriage of McNeil, 160 Cal. App. 3d 548, 206 Cal. Rptr. 641 (1984); Adriana Int'l Corp. v. Thoeren, 913 F.2d 1406 (9th Cir. 1990).

[90] 120 Cal. App. 3d 412, 174 Cal. Rptr. 608 (1981).

[91] *Id.* at 417, 174 Cal. Rptr. 608. *See also* Murphy v. Allstate Ins. Co., 83 Cal. App. 3d 38, 51, 147 Cal. Rptr. 565 (1978) (intentional fraud and bad faith in the repair and restoration of plaintiffs' furniture); Schroeder v. Auto Driveaway Co., 11 Cal. 3d 908, 921, 114 Cal. Rptr. 622, 528 P.2d 662 (1974) (intentional tort—"malice, fraud and oppression"—in the loss and destruction of personal property by a moving company).

[92] Branch v. Homefed Bank, 6 Cal. App. 4th 793, 8 Cal. Rptr. 2d 182 (1992).

[93] Romero v. Mason & Hanger-Silas Mason Co., 739 F. Supp. 1472, 1477 (D.N.M. 1990) (citing RESTATEMENT (SECOND) OF TORTS §766 (1977)).

[94] *See* Cummings v. Walsh Constr. Co., 561 F. Supp. 872, 31 FEP Cases 930 (S.D. Ga. 1983) (no interference claim viable if plaintiff is an at-will employee).

[95] RESTATEMENT (SECOND) OF TORTS §766 (1977).

[96] Favors v. Alco Mfg. Co., 186 Ga. App. 480, 367 S.E.2d 328 (1988) (supervisory employee liable only when acting outside scope and course of employment).

partner.[97] Loss-of-consortium claims have been asserted by men whose wives have suffered physical and emotional injuries arising from sexual harassment in the workplace.[98]

In *Brown v. Youth Services International of Baltimore*,[99] the court noted that "federal courts almost unanimously have dismissed loss of consortium claims based upon federal civil rights violations."[100] The *Brown* court went on to point out that although Congress amended Title VII of the Civil Rights Act of 1991 to provide for compensatory damages for various forms of loss, it did not specifically provide for loss of consortium. The *Brown* court concluded that it was inappropriate for a court to add a remedy that Congress had failed to provide.

Loss-of-consortium claims may accompany the other spouse's actions for assault and battery, intentional infliction of emotional distress, or similar common law tort actions, however. In *Eide v. Kelsey-Hayes Co.*,[101] the court concluded that a derivative claim for loss of consortium was cognizable under a state employment discrimination statute. A loss-of-consortium claim does not require that the primary injured spouse has suffered a physically disabling injury. In *Bowersox v. P.H. Glatfelter*,[102] the court held that such symptoms as depression, headaches, nausea, and severe emotional distress can result in the deprivation of society and companionship, thereby warranting a remedy for loss of consortium.

11. Negligence

The general rule is that emotional distress damages are not available in negligence cases. Exceptions to this rule apply in cases of physical impact or injury,

---

[97]PROSSER & KEETON, *supra* note 23, §125, at 931–32.

[98]*E.g.,* Handley v. Phillips, 715 F. Supp. 657, 662, 52 FEP Cases 195 (M.D. Pa. 1989) (granting summary judgment on husband's consortium claim); Bowersox v. P.H. Glatfelter Co., 677 F. Supp. 307, 312, 45 FEP Cases 1443 (M.D. Pa. 1988) (husband stated claim against wife's former supervisor for loss of consortium); Eide v. Kelsey-Hayes Co., 427 N.W.2d 488, 489, 47 FEP Cases 1050 (Mich. 1988) (sexual harassment victim's husband awarded $28,000 in damages for loss of consortium); Spoon v. American Agriculturalists, 120 A.D.2d 857, 502 N.Y.S.2d 296 (1986) (husband of complainant stated derivative claim for loss of consortium arising from employer's alleged intentional torts against wife).

[99]904 F. Supp. 469, 69 FEP Cases 991 (D. Md. 1995).

[100]*Id.* at 470, 69 FEP Cases at 992, (citing Godby v. Electrolux Corp., 65 FEP Cases 211 (N.D. Ga. 1994)); Quitmeyer v. Southeastern Pa. Trans. Auth., 740 F. Supp. 363 (E.D. Pa. 1990); Tauriac v. Polaroid Corp., 716 F. Supp. 672, 48 FEP Cases 1256 (D. Mass. 1989).

[101]427 N.W.2d 488, 489, 47 FEP Cases 1050 (Mich. 1988) (husband stated viable derivative claim for loss of consortium where wife stated sexual harassment claim under Michigan's statute). In contrast, a loss-of-consortium claim cannot be sustained to the extent it is predicated on a Title VII sexual harassment claim. Pryor v. U.S. Gypsum, 585 F. Supp. 311, 317, 47 FEP Cases 159 (W.D. Mo. 1985).

[102]677 F. Supp. 307, 45 FEP Cases 1443 (M.D. Pa. 1988).

malice, breach of fiduciary duty, or other unusually extreme or outrageous circumstances where the negligence by its nature will predictably cause highly unusual emotional distress.[103] Emotional distress recovery has also been allowed when the negligence arises in a situation involving breach of fiduciary or quasi-fiduciary duties, such as bad-faith refusals to pay insurance proceeds.[104] Emotional distress injuries arising from negligence may also be recovered in some states in the special case of witnessing physical injury to a close relative.[105]

In *Branch v. Homefed Bank*,[106] an employee was hired with negligent misrepresentations about his salary. He suffered distress when, after joining the organization, he found that his salary would be much lower than was promised and that his employer would not make good on its word. The jury awarded $45,000 in economic damages and $60,000 in emotional distress damages. The court overturned the emotional distress award, reasoning that this was a case subject to the general rule against recovery of emotional distress damages in negligence cases: "Injury resulting from the economic loss in terms of emotional distress is not compensable. Recovery for worry, distress and unhappiness as the result of damage to property, loss of job or loss of money is not permitted when the defendant's conduct is merely negligent."[107]

Negligent retention and supervision claims are sometimes asserted against employers in an attempt to hold them liable for the torts of their employees.[108] Liability for negligent retention is predicated on an employer's knowledge of an employee's propensity to engage in tortious conduct and the subsequent

---

[103]Allen v. Jones, 104 Cal. App. 3d 207, 215, 163 Cal. Rptr. 445 (1980) (mishandling of the cremated remains of plaintiff's brother); Molien v. Kaiser Found. Hosps., 27 Cal. 3d 916, 930, 167 Cal. Rptr. 831, 616 P.2d 813 (1980) (negligent advice to patient that she suffered from syphilis, resulting in severe distress to her husband).

[104]Crisci v. Security Ins. Co., 66 Cal. 2d 425, 58 Cal. Rptr. 13, 426 P.2d 173 (1967); Gruenberg v. Aetna Ins. Co., 9 Cal. 3d 566, 108 Cal. Rptr. 480, 510 P.2d 1032 (1973); Jarchow v. Transamerica Title Ins. Co., 48 Cal. App. 3d 917, 122 Cal. Rptr. 470 (1975).

[105]Dillon v. Legg, 68 Cal. 2d 728, 69 Cal. Rptr. 72, 441 P.2d 912 (1968); Thing v. La Chusa, 48 Cal. 3d 644, 257 Cal. Rptr. 865, 771 P.2d 814 (1989).

[106]6 Cal. App. 4th 793, 8 Cal. Rptr. 2d 182 (1992).

[107]*Id.*, 8 Cal. Rptr. 2d at 187.

[108]Harrison v. Edison Bros. Apparel Stores, 724 F. Supp. 1185, 1190 (M.D.N.C. 1989) (negligent retention claim asserted against employer arising from tortious acts of coworker); Byrd v. Richardson-Greenshields Sec., 552 So. 2d 1099 (Fla. 1989) (negligent hiring and retention action brought by female plaintiff who alleged repeated touching and verbal sexual advances by her supervisor); Carr v. U.S. W. Direct Co., 98 Or. App. 30, 779 P.2d 154 (1989) (negligent supervision claim against employer arising from supervisor's sexual harassment and rape of female sales representative); Kresko v. Rulli, 432 N.W.2d 764, 769 (Minn. Ct. App. 1988) (plaintiff asserted negligent retention claim against her employer for alleged sexual harassment by her supervisor); Hart v. National Mortgage & Land Co., 189 Cal. App. 3d 1420, 235 Cal. Rptr. 68 (1987) (male plaintiff asserted negligent retention claim against his employer based on sexual harassment by his male supervisor).

failure to address this inappropriate conduct.[109] An employer charged with negligent retention may not assert an assumption-of-risk defense against the complainant.[110]

Claims of negligence regarding the employment relationship generally are vulnerable to the argument that they are torts barred by the exclusivity provisions of state workers' compensation statutes.[111] Exceptions have been made, however, in cases involving allegations of employment discrimination. In *Byrd v. Richardson-Greenshields Securities*,[112] the Florida Supreme Court declined to apply the exclusivity provision of the workers' compensation law to negligent hiring and retention claims based on sexual harassment in the workplace. The court reasoned that workers' compensation laws were never intended to encompass acts of sexual harassment, particularly because state and federal policies are strongly committed to outlawing and eliminating sexual discrimination in the workplace.[113]

II. Proof and Calculation of Emotional Distress Damages

Plaintiffs who are victims of unlawful discrimination or harassment are not automatically entitled to recover emotional distress damages. They must prove in addition that the unlawful discrimination caused them to suffer mental or emotional injury. This point grows out of the decision of the U.S. Supreme Court in *Carey v. Piphus*.[114] In that case, arising under 42 U.S.C. §1983, the Court held that compensable emotional distress damages must be proven; they will not be presumed to have been suffered even if liability is established.

---

[109] Perkins v. Spivey, 911 F.2d 22, 53 FEP Cases 973 (8th Cir. 1990) (although employer has no duty under Kansas common law to maintain workplace free from the psychological harm of sexual harassment, it does have a duty not to retain an employee it knows or should know is emotionally harming coworkers to the extent they suffer physical injuries).

[110] *Id.* (rejecting defense as inconsistent with modern views toward women and abuse).

[111] *E.g.*, Fields v. Cummings Employees Fed. Credit Union, 540 N.E.2d 631, 53 FEP Cases 1613 (Ind. Ct. App. 1989) (negligent retention claims barred by the exclusivity of Indiana's Workers' Compensation Act); Brooms v. Regal Tube Co., 881 F.2d 412, 421, 50 FEP Cases 1499, 1509 (7th Cir. 1989) (Illinois Workers' Compensation Act precluded plaintiff's negligence action against employer arising from sexual harassment in the workplace).

[112] 552 So. 2d 1099 (Fla. 1989).

[113] *Id.* at 1103–04; *see also* Hogan v. Forsyth Country Club Co., 79 N.C. App. 483, 340 S.E.2d 116, 124 (plaintiff's negligent retention claim not barred by workers' compensation statute), *review denied*, 317 N.C. 334, 346 S.E.2d 141 (1986).

[114] 435 U.S. 247 (1978).

A. Proof of Damages

Proof of emotional distress does not require any particular kind of physical evidence or testimony. A plaintiff may recover emotional distress damages, for example, without any expert testimony.[115] Because of the inherent difficulties involved, however, proof of emotional distress damages will often involve the assistance of psychiatric or psychological experts.

As noted earlier, the EEOC has issued a policy guide on the recovery of damages now permitted by the Civil Rights Act of 1991.[116] Part of that policy guide, which appears as Appendix 1, discusses the means of proving a claim for emotional distress damages. Although the EEOC policy guide is not binding on the courts, it is likely to be given persuasive weight by courts in employment discrimination lawsuits where emotional distress damages are at issue.

In the policy guide, the EEOC recognizes that a "claim of emotional harm will be seriously undermined if the onset of symptoms of emotional harm preceded the discrimination." Nonetheless, a plaintiff who is unusually emotionally sensitive is entitled to recovery for the entirety of any emotional distress caused by the discrimination at issue, according to the EEOC, even if someone who is normally sensitive would suffer less; the wrongdoer is considered to take its victims as it finds them.[117]

The EEOC will consider, however, to what extent the employer caused the emotional harm. Relevant here would be such factors as (1) whether the discrimination was overt or merely covert, (2) whether upper management was aware of the discrimination, (3) whether the plaintiff sought counseling, and (4) "other factors which probably contributed to the plaintiff's mental distress."[118] Thus, according to the EEOC, "where a complaining party's emotional harm is due in part to personal difficulties, which were not caused or exacerbated by the discriminatory conduct, the employer is liable only for the harm resulting from the discriminatory conduct."[119]

In the conciliation negotiations that it conducts when it finds that discrimination has occurred, the EEOC typically will require medical evidence of emotional harm to seek damages for such harm. Although testimonial evidence alone sometimes will suffice, "for conciliation or settlement purposes" the EEOC states that "testimony solely by the complaining party may not be sufficient to establish emotional harm," and it looks for "corroborating testimony by the complaining party's co-workers, supervisors, family, friends, or anyone else with knowledge of the emotional harm."[120]

---

[115]*E.g.*, Williams v. Trader Pub'lg Co., 218 F.3d 481, 486, 83 FEP Cases 668 (5th Cir. 2000) (affirming award of damages based only on plaintiff's testimony of sleep loss, weight loss and increased smoking as a result of loss of job).

[116]POLICY GUIDE ON COMPENSATORY AND PUNITIVE DAMAGES UNDER 1991 CIVIL RIGHTS ACT (July 7, 1992), *reprinted in* 8 Fair Empl. Prac. Man. (BNA) 405:7091–7102.

[117]*Id.* at 7096–97.

[118]*Id.* at 7097.

[119]*Id.*

[120]*Id.* at 7098.

The EEOC has indicated that it expects that damage awards for emotional harm under Title VII will vary significantly because there are no definitive rules governing the amounts to be awarded. The EEOC maintains that the computation of these awards should consider the severity of harm and how long the complaining party has suffered from the harm. To determine severity the EEOC considers, for example, whether the harm consisted of occasional sleeplessness as opposed to a "nervous breakdown resulting in years of psychotherapy." As to the length of time that the complaining party has suffered, the EEOC would consider, for example, whether the complaining party has suffered from severe depression for two months or a year.[121]

In *Jenson v. Eveleth Taconite Co.*,[122] the Eighth Circuit required the plaintiffs to show that sex discrimination and sexual harassment were "substantial factors" in causing their emotional harm.[123] Although the Eighth Circuit differed in a number of respects with the lower court's handling of the plaintiffs' damage claims, it found no error of law or abuse of discretion in that court's rejection of the plaintiffs' attempt to divide their mental anguish claims into separate impairments (for example, anger, shame, wounded pride) and seek a separate monetary award for each type of impairment.[124]

Other courts have varied in the standards that they have required plaintiffs to meet to qualify for emotional distress damages in employment cases; no single, clear standard has crystallized to date. Most courts have held that a plaintiff's own testimony is enough to sustain an award for emotional distress damages, although many courts subject awards based solely upon the plaintiff's own testimony to greater scrutiny than where other objective evidence of such injury also exists.[125]

In *Patterson v. P.H.P. Healthcare Corp.*,[126] the Fifth Circuit, relying on *Carey*[127] and the EEOC's policy guide, expressed some doubt that mere "hurt feelings" on the part of a plaintiff can justify an award of emotional distress damages. Rather, maintained the *Patterson* court, the proof necessary for an award of emotional distress damages

> requires a degree of specificity which may include corroborating testimony or medical or psychological evidence in support of the damage award. Hurt feelings,

---

[121]*Id.* at 7099.

[122]130 F.3d 1287 (8th Cir. 1997).

[123]*Id.* at 1294.

[124]*Id.* at 1290 n.5. *See also* Reynolds v. Octel Communications Corp., 924 F. Supp. 743, 69 FEP Cases 1178 (N.D. Tex. 1995) (although plaintiff was discriminated against based upon both her sex and her age, she suffered but one injury and cannot recover the same damages twice).

[125]*See* Price v. City of Charlotte, 93 F.3d 1241, 1251, 71 FEP Cases 1289 (4th Cir. 1996) ("A survey of the case law reveals that a plaintiff's own testimony, standing alone, may support a claim of emotional distress precipitated by a constitutional violation. . . . Equally, however, the case law reveals that courts scrupulously analyze an award of compensatory damages for a claim of emotional distress predicated exclusively on the plaintiff's testimony.").

[126]90 F.3d 927, 72 FEP Cases 613 (5th Cir. 1996).

[127]435 U.S. 247 (1978).

anger and frustration are part of life. Unless the cause of action manifests some specific discernable injury to the claimant's emotional state, we cannot say that the specificity requirement has been satisfied.[128]

The court noted that "a number of our sister circuits have recognized that a claimant's testimony alone may not be sufficient to support anything more than a nominal damage award."[129] It went on to vacate the lower court's emotional distress damage award of $40,000 and to hold that no more than nominal damages may be recovered where the plaintiff presents no corroborating testimony in support of his damage claim and offers no medical or psychological evidence. It vacated an award of $150,000 in favor of a coplaintiff on similar grounds. The court noted that although a retaliatory discharge "caused a substantial disruption" in the plaintiff's daily routine, no proof of actual injury existed, and an award of more than nominal damages was unwarranted.

In *Forshee v. Waterloo Industries, Inc.*,[130] the Eighth Circuit overturned an award of emotional damages in the amount of $9,631 in a sexual harassment case, holding that the district court erred in submitting the issue of emotional distress damages to the jury. The plaintiff had alleged that her supervisor had made a sexual advance, which she rejected, and that she was subsequently terminated as a result. The court noted that the plaintiff's evidence of emotional distress was based entirely upon her own testimony. The plaintiff had testified that after being terminated she went home and cried about it for the rest of the day and that she was thereafter forced to work at two lower-paying jobs. The court observed that "[w]hile a compensatory damage award may be based solely on plaintiff's own testimony," the plaintiff "did not identify and describe the kind of severe emotional distress" that warrants a damage award. The court further pointed out that the plaintiff suffered no physical injury and was not medically treated for any psychological or emotional injury, and no other witnesses corroborated any outward manifestation of emotional distress. It noted that the plaintiff found a new job almost immediately, and although it was lower-paying, her award for lost wages would make up for the difference. Finally, the court recognized that although the supervisor's sexual advance was "disgusting," it did not humiliate the plaintiff in front of her coworkers and, by the plaintiff's own admission, was not the cause of her emotional distress.[131] The *Forshee* court curiously refused to disturb the jury's finding that the

---

[128]90 F.3d at 940, 72 FEP Cases at 623–24.

[129]*Id.* at 938, 72 FEP Cases at 622 (citing Fitzgerald v. Mountain States Tel. & Tel. Co., 68 F.3d 1257, 69 FEP Cases 163 (10th Cir. 1995); Gunby v. Pennsylvania Elec. Co., 840 F.2d 1108, 45 FEP Cases 1818 (3d Cir. 1995); Erebia v. Chrysler Plastic Prods. Corp., 772 F.2d 1250, 37 FEP Cases 1820 (6th Cir. 1985); Vance v. Southern Bell Tel. & Tel. Co., 863 F.2d 1503, 50 FEP Cases 742 (11th Cir. 1989)). In *Bailey v. Runyon*, 220 F.3d 879, 82 FEP Cases 892 (8th Cir. 2000), the Eighth Circuit affirmed an award of nominal damages where the plaintiff's emotional distress claim was supported only by his own testimony.

[130]178 F.3d 527 (8th Cir. 1999).

[131]*Id.* at 531.

plaintiff's refusal of the supervisor's sexual advance resulted in her termination, yet held that no emotional distress damages were recoverable because the plaintiff attributed her emotional distress to the loss of her job as opposed to the sexual advance. *Forshee* may therefore be of questionable precedential value.

In contrast to purely emotional injuries (which in the view of most courts may be established without expert testimony), a *physical* disorder alleged to have been caused or exacerbated by workplace events (or the stress produced thereby) requires expert medical testimony. For example, in *Hrabak v. Marquip, Inc.*,[132] the court granted the defendant's motion in limine to exclude evidence of the plaintiff's miscarriage. The court held that, without presenting the testimony of a physician, the plaintiff could not attempt to show that emotional distress resulting from sexual harassment caused her to miscarry. In *Shea v. Icelandair*,[133] by contrast, the plaintiff put on the testimony of medical witnesses to the effect that his unlawful demotion caused his Parkinson's disease to worsen and caused him to suffer cardiac problems and suffer emotional distress. Although the courts reduced the plaintiff's compensatory damages award by $75,000, it held that the plaintiff could still recover $175,000.

In *Karcher v. Emerson Electric Co.*,[134] the court cited the testimony of the plaintiff's treating psychiatrist and treating psychologist in rejecting the defendant's argument that a jury award of $150,000 for emotional distress in a sex discrimination case was invalid. The court noted that the two doctors had linked the plaintiff's depression and emotional stress to her job-related problems.

B. Measure of Damages

Emotional distress damages, unlike economic damages, are not subject to any form of numerical certainty. Rather, the amount of emotional distress damages is left to the best judgment of the jury. The *Restatement (Second) of Torts* explains: "There is no rule of certainty with reference to the amount of recovery permitted for any particular type of emotional distress; the only limit is such an amount as a reasonable person could possibly estimate as fair compensation."[135]

The California Supreme Court has commented at length on the inherent difficulties a jury faces in assessing the measure of emotional distress damages:

> No method is available to the jury by which it can objectively evaluate such damages, and no witness may express his subjective opinion on the matter. . . . In a very real sense, the jury is asked to evaluate in terms of money a detriment for which monetary compensation cannot be ascertained with any demonstrable accuracy. As one writer on the subject has said, "Translating pain and anguish into dollars can, at best, be only an arbitrary allowance, and not a process of

---

[132] 58 FEP Cases 908 (W.D. Wis. 1992).
[133] 925 F. Supp. 1014, 70 FEP Cases 1544 (S.D.N.Y. 1996).
[134] 94 F.3d 502, 71 FEP Cases 1651 (8th Cir. 1996).
[135] RESTATEMENT (SECOND) OF TORTS §905, at 460 (1979).

measurement, and consequently the judge can, in his instructions, give the jury no standard to go by; he can only tell them to allow such amount as in their discretion they may consider reasonable. . . . The chief reliance for reaching reasonable results in attempting to value suffering in terms of money must be the restraint and common sense of the jury."[136]

Among the factors a jury will assess in determining the amount of emotional distress damages are

- the length of time during which the pain or other harm to the feelings has occurred;
- the length of time during which the pain or harm to feelings will continue;
- the plaintiff's reasonable susceptibility to this kind of harm, taking into account the plaintiff's age, sex, and condition in life; and
- any provocation by the plaintiff (as a factor in mitigation of damages).[137]

Weighing such factors, juries have an enormous amount of discretion in determining the amount of emotional distress damages that are recoverable. Nevertheless, a trial court may reduce a damages award as excessive,[138] and an appellate court may reduce a verdict that is so large it shocks the court's sense of justice.[139]

The inherently arbitrary nature of determining the amount of emotional distress damages has led some courts to limit the methods by which the amount may be argued. Although a plaintiff can always specify the amount he or she desires the jury to award as compensation for emotional distress, some courts have held that the plaintiff's counsel may not suggest a mathematical formula for the jury to use by suggesting the award of given amounts over specific periods of time. This has been labeled the *per diem argument* (e.g., "It would be appropriate to award my client $1,000 per day for the mental suffering she endured during the month that she was recovering from the injuries caused by the defendant"). The primary argument against permitting use of the per diem argument is that any kind of mathematical formula inherently misleads the jury for purposes of computing an emotional distress damage award.[140]

Although there is a split in authority, most courts, however, permit use of the per diem argument.[141] They generally reason that since the plaintiff is

---

[136]Beagle v. Vasold, 65 Cal. 2d 166, 53 Cal. Rptr. 129, 131 (1966) (citations omitted).

[137]RESTATEMENT (SECOND) OF TORTS §905, at 460 (1979).

[138]*See, e.g.,* Seffert v. Los Angeles Transit Lines, 56 Cal. 2d 498, 507, 15 Cal. Rptr. 161, 166 (1961).

[139]*See, e.g.,* Johnston v. Long, 30 Cal. 2d 54, 57, 76, 181 P.2d 645 (1947).

[140]*See, e.g., Beagle,* 53 Cal. Rptr. at 132–34 (Traynor, C.J., dissenting) (it is "unrealistic to seek an appropriate award for pain and suffering by the use of any so-called per diem formula").

[141]*See generally Beagle,* 65 Cal. 2d 166, 53 Cal. Rptr. 129 (citing the cases and law review commentary on either side of the issue). *See also* 2 DOBBS, LAW OF REMEDIES, §8.1(4), at 395 (2d ed. 1993) ("most courts are willing to allow at least

free to ask for a total amount of emotional distress damages, it is logical to permit the plaintiff to ask for certain damages attributable to certain periods of time.

Whereas courts generally have permitted per diem arguments, they have limited other arguments that create an unacceptable risk of appealing to a jury's personal prejudice and passion. Courts thus have frowned on use of the so-called golden rule argument, by which juries are asked to put themselves in the plaintiff's place and to consider whether they would want to undergo what the plaintiff has undergone. This argument is considered impermissible because it appeals to the jurors' self-interest.[142]

In numerous cases, district courts or courts of appeals have ordered substantial reductions in large jury verdicts for emotional distress. For example, in *Hetzel v. County of Prince William*,[143] the Fourth Circuit reversed and remanded an award of $500,000 in emotional distress damages to a police officer found to have been terminated in retaliation for her complaints about sex and national origin discrimination. The plaintiff had offered only her own testimony that she had suffered headaches, stress, trouble reading to her daughter, and problems with her family life. She reported no physical illnesses or injuries, she sought no medical attention, and she continued to perform her job and receive favorable performance evaluations. She also failed to put on corroborating testimony regarding her damages. Moreover, the court noted that much of the plaintiff's claimed distress was actually caused by her erroneous belief that she was herself the victim of discrimination. The court distinguished high awards for emotional distress in other cases on the grounds that the plaintiffs in those cases were in fact the victims of discrimination, or they lost their jobs and had difficulty finding new employment, or they suffered serious and often permanent physical injuries.

In *Fitzgerald v. Mountain States Telephone & Telegraph Co.*,[144] the court reversed emotional distress damage awards in the amount of $250,000 apiece for two plaintiffs in a Section 1981 case, reasoning that such high awards were the product of "passion or prejudice." Neither plaintiff put on testimony from a treating psychologist or physician, and both continued working in their fields. One plaintiff testified merely that discriminatory remarks made during a diversity training session "left her devastated" and "stripped her dignity away," and caused her to have more frequent herpes outbreaks. The other plaintiff testified that he felt angry and insulted, had headaches, and missed more than three weeks of work. The court ordered a new trial on compensatory damages.

In *Rush v. Scott Specialty Gases, Inc.*,[145] the court reduced a $1 million compensatory damages award to $100,000 in a sexual harassment case, finding that although the plaintiff presented adequate evidence that she suffered

---

some form of mathematical argument"); Annotation, *Per Diem or Similar Mathematical Basis for Fixing Damages for Pain and Suffering*, 3 A.L.R.4th 940 (1981).

[142]2 DOBBS, *supra* note 141, §8.1(4), at 383.

[143]89 F.3d 169, 71 FEP Cases 520 (4th Cir. 1996).

[144]68 F.3d 1257, 69 FEP Cases 163 (10th Cir. 1995).

[145]930 F. Supp. 194, 73 FEP Cases 1429 (E.D. Pa. 1996), *rev'd on other grounds*, 113 F.3d 476, 74 FEP Cases 1745 (3d Cir. 1997).

emotional injury, the damage award was excessive. Other courts have ordered similar reductions.[146]

In *Blakey v. Continental Airlines*,[147] the court reduced an emotional damage award of $500,000 to a plaintiff in a sexual harassment case to $250,000. The court observed that it may consider awards in other cases—including cases from other circuits—involving similar injuries as a "helpful guide" to whether a particular damage award is excessive.[148] It then noted that the only evidence of emotional damage presented at trial was the plaintiff's own testimony and that of her psychiatric expert, who had met with her for two hours and reviewed her records for 90 minutes. Her expert testified that the plaintiff suffered some emotional distress as a result of events at work but that other events outside work—including her volatile relationship with her boyfriend's ex-wife, who had her arrested and threatened her with physical violence—contributed to her emotional distress. Her expert also testified that most of the plaintiff's emotional problems had resolved more than three years prior to trial. The court also noted that the plaintiff was never hospitalized and she was not disabled from future employment. In fact, the court noted the plaintiff's testimony that her job as an airline pilot was inherently stressful, and that she was medically able to perform it during the entire period she was also suffering from emotional distress. The court then remarked: "This is not the kind of evidence that $500,000 awards are made of."[149] It then remitted the award to $250,000, which it noted was "high, but within the realm of reason."[150] In support of such an award, the court cited that fact that the plaintiff had been subjected to pornography in the workplace for at least three years, and that she received psychological counseling and psychotropic medication as a result.

In other cases, courts have affirmed emotional distress damage awards in widely varying amounts, where the damages were said to be caused by sexual

---

[146]*E.g.*, Ramirez v. New York City Off-Track Betting Corp., 112 F.3d 38, 73 FEP Cases 573 (2d Cir. 1997) ("pain and suffering" award of $1,145,625 reduced to $500,000 where defendant's actions left mentally ill plaintiff permanently disabled); Delli Santi v. CNA Ins. Co., 88 F.3d 192, 71 FEP Cases 143 (3d Cir. 1996) (affirming district court's reduction of $300,000 emotional damage award to $5,000 in retaliation case); Williams v. Pharmacia, Inc., 956 F. Supp. 1457, 73 FEP Cases 294 (N.D. Ind. 1996) (reduction of $250,000 emotional damage award to $40,000 in lost promotion case); McIntosh v. Irving Trust Co., 887 F. Supp. 662, 74 FEP Cases 99 (S.D.N.Y. 1995) (reduction of $219,428 emotional damage award to $20,000 in failure to promote and wrongful termination case); Lightfoot v. Union Carbide Corp., 901 F. Supp. 166, 71 FEP Cases 269 (S.D.N.Y. 1995) (reduction of $750,000 emotional damage award to $75,000 in age discrimination case; verdict was a "material deviation from the norm"); Abrams v. Lightolier, 841 F. Supp. 584, 65 FEP Cases 1149 (D.N.J. 1994) ($100,000 "pain and suffering" award in age discrimination case reduced to $2,500; plaintiff testified only that he was "very, very upset" about having been accused of bribery by employer).

[147]992 F. Supp. 731, 76 FEP Cases 280 (D.N.J. 1998).
[148]*Id.* at 736, 76 FEP Cases at 285.
[149]*Id.*
[150]*Id.* at 740, 76 FEP Cases at 288.

harassment,[151] wrongful or discriminatory termination,[152] or wrongfully denied promotions.[153]

C. Hedonic Damages

The theory of "hedonic" damages (derived from the Greek word for "pleasure"), attempts to compensate plaintiffs for the lost value of the enjoyment of life separate from any economic or physical loss. Hedonic damages valuation is based on the theory that the value of human life above and beyond a person's earning capacity may be derived by examining societal decisions that involve the expenditure of money to avoid risks to life or health.[154] The primary method used to establish such a value is called the willingness-to-pay model. This model is based upon the assumption that people are willing to pay more for products that will prolong or protect their lives and that people often will demand higher pay to do jobs that involve life-threatening activities. The factors used in these studies vary, but they focus on consumer behavior and purchases of safety devices, wage risk premiums, and regulatory cost-benefit analysis. A survey model is also sometimes used in which individuals are asked to state what they would be willing to pay to reduce their chance of dying by a specified percentage. From these statistics, some economists claim they can determine the value of the enjoyment of life. For example, if it is supposed that consumers are willing to spend $30 for a smoke detector, and if one life is saved for every 100,000 smoke detectors purchased, then it costs $3,000,000 to reduce the death rate from fire by one life. Thus, the starting point for valuing a life according to this theory is $3,000,000.

The theory of hedonic damages was originally designed to apply to wrongful death cases. It was first accepted by a court in *Sherrod v. Berry*,[155] a Section 1983 case involving the killing of a suspect during a police stop. The district

---

[151]*E.g.*, Kelly-Zurian v. Wohl Shoe Co., Inc., 22 Cal. App. 4th 397, 27 Cal. Rptr. 2d 457, 64 FEP Cases 603 (1994) ($125,000); Farpella-Crosby v. Horizon Health Care, 97 F.3d 803, 72 FEP Cases 254 (5th Cir. 1996) ($7,500); McKinnon v. Kwong Wah Rest., 83 F.3d 498, 70 FEP Cases 1037 (1st Cir. 1996) ($2,500).

[152]*E.g.*, Ross v. Douglas County, 234 F.3d 391, 84 FEP Cases 791 (8th Cir. 2000)($100,000); Lussier v. Runyon, 1994 WL 129776, 3 AD Cases 223 (D. Me. 1994) ($75,000); U.S. EEOC v. AIC Sec. Investigations, Ltd., 55 F.3d 1276, 4 AD Cases 693 (7th Cir. 1995) ($50,000); Hearn v. General Elec. Co., 927 F. Supp. 1486, 71 FEP Cases 435 (M.D. Ala. 1996) ($50,000); Luciano v. Olsten Corp., 912 F. Supp. 663, 73 FEP Cases 221 (E.D.N.Y. 1996) ($11,400); Keys v. U.S. Welding, Fabrication & Mfg., Inc., 59 FEP Cases 1537 (N.D. Ohio 1992) ($2,500).

[153]*E.g.*, McClam v. City of Norfolk Police Dep't, 877 F. Supp. 277, 71 FEP Cases 757 (E.D. Va. 1995) ($15,000); Odima v. Westin Tucson Hotel, 53 F.3d 1484, 67 FEP Cases 1222 (9th Cir. 1995) ($10,000); McNight v. Circuit City Stores, Inc., 73 FEP Cases 841 (E.D. Va. 1997) ($2,700).

[154]*See* Kurncz v. Honda N. Am., Inc., 166 F.R.D. 386, 388 (W.D. Mich. 1996).

[155]827 F.2d 195 (7th Cir. 1987).

court denied the defendant's motion in limine to exclude an expert's testimony on hedonic damages as speculative, and the Seventh Circuit affirmed. Soon the theory of hedonic damages was being applied in cases involving nonfatal injuries. In these cases, both an economist and a psychologist would testify. The economist would estimate the value of a human life, and the psychologist would then opine that the plaintiff had lost a certain percentage of his or her capacity to enjoy life by reason of the events at issue in the litigation.[156]

1. Hedonic Damages After Daubert

The Supreme Court's decision in *Daubert v. Merrill Dow Pharmaceuticals, Inc.,*[157] dampened the courts' early enthusiasm for hedonic damages. Hedonic damages became a frequent casualty of the courts' new rigorous requirements for expert scientific testimony. *Daubert* established two primary tests to be used in determining whether such testimony should be admissible. First, the testimony must be reliable, by which the Court means it must be scientifically valid. This can be determined through the following inquiries: (1) whether the theory can be tested, (2) whether it has been subject to peer review, (3) whether it has a measurable error rate, and (4) whether the theory has been generally accepted in the relevant scientific community. If the test for reliability is met, a court must then inquire whether the testimony is relevant under Rule 403 of the Federal Rules of Evidence, requiring that the evidence must assist a jury in determining the existence of any fact of consequence without resulting in a waste of time or confusion of the issues.

Hedonic damage theory can never be tested, so the first prong of *Daubert*'s test for reliability cannot be met. Unlike other controversial topics that can be validated in retrospect, such as predicted rates of inflation and average life expectancies, the value of the enjoyment of life will always, by nature, be speculative. The creator of this theory has himself acknowledged that the theory cannot be tested.[158] As a result, there is no reliable method for determining whether hedonic damages theories are correct or not. It necessarily follows that the second prong of the reliability test cannot be met, as there can be no known error rate to inform a jury of the theory's reliability. The third prong of the test involving peer review arguably can be met, but not satisfactorily. As one court has observed, "[t]here is no basic agreement among economists as to what elements ought to go into the life evaluation."[159]

Hedonic damages valuation theories also fail to satisfy Rule 403. Where the law allows recovery for hedonic damages, juries may be best equipped to determine the measure of damages. Hedonic damages calculations used by forensic economists are often so complex and questionable that courts find that

---

[156]In some cases, the jury is left to determine for itself the percentage by which the plaintiff has lost his or her capacity to enjoy life. *See* Saia v. Sears Roebuck & Co., 47 F. Supp. 2d 141 (D. Mass. 1999).
[157]509 U.S. 579 (1993). *Daubert* is discussed in more detail in Chapter 15, Avoiding and Attacking Junk Science.
[158]*Saia*, 47 F. Supp. 2d *at* 149.
[159]*Kurncz,* 166 F.R.D. at 389.

they will not assist the jury in understanding the evidence or determining any fact in issue.[160] Many courts take the view that jurors are just as able as so-called experts to quantify the value of the enjoyment of life. As the Seventh Circuit observed in confirming the exclusion of expert testimony on hedonic damages: "A witness who knows no more than the average person is not an expert."[161] Another court similarly excluded expert testimony on hedonic damages, finding that it was not sufficiently reliable for the jury to obtain any value from it. That court maintained that if the jury is to decide the question of hedonic damages, it should decide it from the beginning.[162]

Although the theory of hedonic damages has not fared well under *Daubert* and its progeny, two appellate courts recently affirmed the admission of hedonic damages testimony in cases involving non-fatal injuries.

In *Smith v. Ingersoll-Rand Co.*,[163] the plaintiff was injured by a piece of road grading equipment, which injury required the amputation of his leg above the knee. The jury awarded more than $27,000,000 in damages after hearing expert testimony on hedonic damages, and the Tenth Circuit affirmed. Although the district court did not permit the expert to quantify the plaintiff's loss of enjoyment of life as the result of his injury (which the expert had estimated to fall between $1,742,514 and $2,323,411), the court did allow the expert to testify about the meaning of hedonic damages. The Tenth Circuit, noting that all federal courts which have considered allowing testimony on the quantification of hedonic damages since *Daubert* have excluded such testimony, approved of the district court's allowing the expert to testify about the nature of such damages.

In *Lewis v. Alfa Laval Separation, Inc.*,[164] the plaintiff was injured at work when a centrifuge exploded and hot corn mash was blown into his ear. Expert testimony was allowed to the effect that our country presently values a life at $3,500,000. Subtracting $900,000 in wages that an average American would earn leaves $2,600,000 in noneconomic value, or $77,000 per year spread over the life of the plaintiff in that case. Noting a psychologist's testimony that the plaintiff lost between six and nine percent of his functioning as a result of the accident, the expert estimated that the plaintiff had lost between $4,000 and $5,000 per year's worth of life's pleasures as a result of the accident. The jury awarded a total of $650,000 and the court of appeals affirmed. It classified the hedonic damages testimony as "shaky but admissible" under *Daubert* and noted that while there were "cogent reasons for excluding" the testimony, it was not an abuse of discretion for the trial court to admit it.

2. Hedonic Damages in Employment Cases

Although the Civil Rights Act of 1991 provides for recovery of damages for "loss of value of life" as a type of compensatory damages recoverable in federal

---

[160]*Saia*, 47 F. Supp. 2d at 149–50; Hein v. Merck & Co., 868 F. Supp. 230, 233 (M.D. Tenn. 1994).
[161]Mercado v. Ahmed, 974 F.2d 863, 870 (7th Cir. 1992).
[162]*Saia*, 47 F. Supp. 2d at 150.
[163]214 F.3d 1235 (10th Cir. 2000).
[164]714 N.E.2d 426 (Ohio App. 1999).

employment discrimination cases,[165] in the only two published cases thus far on the subject courts have refused to apply hedonic damages in the employment context.

In *Mister v. Illinois Central Gulf Railroad*,[166] a pre-*Daubert* case, the plaintiff in a discriminatory failure-to-hire class action sought to recover hedonic damages as part of his claim for emotional distress. The court denied the claim. It observed:

> In this case . . . the only hedonic loss is caused by a lack of a job. The back pay award fully compensates the class for any hedonic damage. Once the class is awarded back pay, the past lost ability to enjoy life is fully restored, since the class has received the object which caused the deprivation. For example, in the personal injury context, a plaintiff who has lost an arm may have a claim for hedonic damages. However, if the arm was restored to him, his claim for hedonic damages would disappear, since he could no longer claim that he cannot enjoy the more subjective pleasures of life to the fullest. Similarly here, the plaintiff class has been made whole by an award of back pay. To allow hedonic damages on top of the back pay would be equivalent to a double recovery.[167]

In *McGuire v. City of Santa Fe*,[168] a wrongful termination case, the court relied upon *Daubert* to exclude testimony regarding hedonic damages. The plaintiff had proffered the testimony of an economist and a psychologist on hedonic damages. The economist used wage studies to conclude that the economic value of a human life generally ranges from $928,000 to $18,464,000. The psychologist then determined that the plaintiff had lost a specified percentage of the enjoyment of his life as a result of being fired. The economist multiplied that percentage by his estimate of the value of the plaintiff's life to produce the conclusion that the plaintiff's lost enjoyment of life was worth between $1,430,000 and $2,300,000. The court refused to admit this testimony. It first noted that, prior to *Daubert,* a trend had developed allowing testimony on hedonic damages but after *Daubert* courts have rejected hedonic damages as a proper subject for expert testimony. Then it pointed out that the first question under *Daubert* is whether the theory at issue can be tested. The court observed that there were no widely accepted standards for uniformly measuring life's pleasures, and the fact that the economist's estimated life value, ranging from $928,000 to $18,464,000, and his calculations that Defendants' actions deprived Plaintiff of between $1,430,000 and $2,300,000 in lost pleasure, "suggests any such test would have very broad and flexible parameters."[169]

The *McGuire* court then addressed the *Daubert* issue of peer review. It noted that "the economic foundations of hedonic damages have, however . . . been assailed as lacking any verifiable basis by respected economists."[170] The

---

[165]42 U.S.C. §1981a(b)(3).
[166]790 F. Supp. 1411, 61 FEP Cases 1391 (S.D. Ill. 1992).
[167]*Id.* at 1421, 61 FEP Cases at 1398.
[168]954 F. Supp. 230 (D.N.M. 1996).
[169]*Id.* at 232.
[170]*Id.*

court also cited an article in an economic journal indicating that "pain and suffering awards will consume up to fifteen percent of the country's annual gross national product if hedonic damages become the standard for nonpecuniary awards."[171] Next, the court addressed the existence of a known error rate. It noted that the "Lost Pleasure of Life Scale" utilized by the psychologist in *McGuire* has been determined to be only "moderately reliable," which means that it produces results that are greater than chance. The court remarked: "This is hardly a quantifiable error rate and it hardly seems useful to provide the fact finder with 'expert' testimony on figures that are only touted as more reliable than those which might be drawn out of a hat."[172] The *McGuire* court concluded that hedonic damages are not a proper element of damages in an employment discrimination case.

The weaknesses of the theory of hedonic damages are perhaps most apparent in the employment context, where the injuries involved are almost exclusively psychological. In such instances, the use of a putative "average person" as the standard for calculating damages seems particularly inappropriate. For, as one court has observed, "[i]t seems obvious . . . that some people enjoy life more than others."[173] In a similar vein, forensic psychologist Paul R. Lees-Haley responds to the proponents of hedonic damages theory:

> If the case is about the loss of life of a severely depressed patient who denies having any pleasure in existence, and reports mostly pain and suffering pre-injury, what is the resulting quotient by your method? It is difficult to imagine that you would follow your own logic and report a negative balance, as if the plaintiff owes the defendant money....
>
> Do you give drug addicts or alcoholics more money because they get high a lot and enjoy themselves more frequently than puritans who lead a rather austere existence? Are the lives of Hedonists worth more in your scheme than the lives of Stoics and persons who sacrifice their personal interests for their community? Do you give lower damages awards to minorities who lead unhappy lives because they are downtrodden by abusive majorities in their cultures? . . .
>
> How do you correct for the presence of numerous other stressors in the individual's life? Do you have norms to adjust for the individuals who are in the middle of a divorce, or who have experienced an unrelated death of a loved one, or have various uncomfortable diseases? How many Hedons are subtracted for people with pre-existing stressors, and by what reliable and valid methodology is this correction made?[174]

These critiques make it apparent that hedonic damages are unlikely ever to satisfy the *Daubert* standards for admissibility in employment cases. When the theory of hedonic damages is imported into the realm of employment

---

[171]*Id.* at 232–33.
[172]*Id.* at 233.
[173]Hein v. Merck & Co., 868 F. Supp. 230, 233 (M.D. Tenn. 1994).
[174]Paul R. Lees-Haley, *Hedonic Damages Testimony: Is It Science or Snake Oil?* AM. PSYCHOL.-L. SOC'Y NEWS, Winter 2000, at 6.

litigation, absurd results can occur. The wrongfully terminated plaintiff might collect hedonic damages yet go on to a become a much greater success at her next job than she ever could have been at the job she lost. An award of hedonic damages to a plaintiff who was harassed or discriminated against necessarily presupposes that the plaintiff will forever wallow in despair over his poor treatment by the defendant, rather than pick himself up and move forward toward a better life. While it is tempting for both plaintiff and defense counsel to seek a measure of emotional distress damages that might add an element of predictability to the uncertain process of assessing emotional harm resulting from intangible events such as the loss of a job or experiencing on-the-job harassment, the theory of hedonic damages does not seem sufficient.

D. Preexisting Conditions and the "Eggshell Plaintiff" Rule

Much controversy has arisen over application of the "eggshell plaintiff" rule in employment cases. Evidence of preexisting mental disorders significantly clouds the issue of causation where workplace events are alleged to have produced a mental condition similar to that which was preexisting. The recent trend in the case law indicates that the eggshell plaintiff rule will not be applied to liability issues in employment lawsuits, but it will be applied to damage issues.

For example, in *Sudtelgte v. Reno*,[175] the court declined to apply the eggshell plaintiff rule with respect to liability in a sexual harassment case. Reasoning that to apply a different liability threshold to abnormally sensitive plaintiffs than is applied to plaintiffs in general would be inconsistent with the "reasonable woman" standard used to determine liability for harassment,[176] the *Sudtelgte* court maintained that harassment claims "based on abnormal sensitivity, whether or not the sensitivity was simply unusual or produced by mental illness," are not viable.[177]

A similar approach was taken in *Poole v. Copland, Inc.*,[178] involving a claim for intentional infliction of emotional distress allegedly resulting from various acts of sexual harassment in the workplace. The plaintiff in that case had an extensive history of prior trauma, including having been sexually molested by a neighbor at age 9, a marriage to an abusive drug addict at age 16, molestation by an uncle at age 18, a two-week kidnap and rape experience also at age 18, and having been beaten by her father when she was 19. Psychiatrists testified that the plaintiff suffered from a dissociative disorder as a result. The state court of appeals in *Poole* held that although the eggshell plaintiff rule applies to mental as well as physical injuries, where an eggshell plaintiff is involved, special jury instruction must be given on the issue of liability, "requiring the

---

[175] 63 FEP Cases 1257 (W.D. Mo. 1994).
[176] *See* Ellison v. Brady, 924 F.2d 872, 879, 54 FEP Cases 1346, 1353 (9th Cir. 1991).
[177] 63 FEP Cases at 1267.
[178] 481 S.E.2d 88, 12 IER Cases 833 (N.C. App. 1997).

jury to find that the alleged conduct could reasonably be expected to injure a person of ordinary mental condition."[179] Thus, only if the harassment would injure a person of "ordinary susceptibility," maintained the *Poole* court, will it be actionable.

Where damage awards are concerned, however, the EEOC and most federal courts will apply the eggshell plaintiff rule. In its Policy Guide, the EEOC states:

> The claim of emotional harm will be seriously undermined if the onset of symptoms of emotional harm preceded the discrimination. However, if a complaining party had preexisting emotional difficulties and his mental health deteriorates as a result of the discriminatory conduct, the additional harm may be attributed to the respondent. The fact that the complaining party may be unusually emotionally sensitive and incur great emotional harm from discriminatory conduct will not absolve the respondent from responsibility for the greater emotional harm. For example, suppose the Commission finds that the respondent is liable for sexual harassment against three female employees, one of whom is an incest victim. The incest victim incurred much greater emotional harm from the sexual harassment than did her two co-workers. The respondent is liable for the greater emotional harm that the incest victim suffered.[180]

The court in *Shea v. Icelandair*[181] followed a similar approach. In that case, the plaintiff claimed that his being demoted caused his Parkinson's disease to worsen. Noting that "[i]t is well settled that aggravation of a pre-existing condition gives rise to liability,"[182] the court permitted the plaintiff to recover damages for the worsening of the symptoms of his preexisting disease.

A more difficult situation is presented, however, where a plaintiff does not claim that the defendant's conduct exacerbated a preexisting physical or mental disorder, but rather where the existence of such a disorder is discovered by the defendant and used to challenge the plaintiff's claim that *all* of the emotional distress that he or she is suffering must be attributed to the defendant. This actually tends to be the more common circumstance, as relatively few plaintiffs will readily acknowledge that they had psychological difficulties prior to entering the defendant's workplace. Most courts in this situation will take a plaintiff's prior traumatic experiences and mental health history into account as mitigating factors in awarding emotional distress damages.

In *Jenson v. Eveleth Taconite Co.*,[183] for example, the Eighth Circuit rejected the trial court's assertion that there is "no scientifically developed psychiatric model or procedure for determining whether a particular stress caused a particular symptom or mental state,"[184] and maintained that "[t]o limit its liability through apportionment, a defendant must prove that a plaintiff's

---

[179] *Id.* at 94.

[180] POLICY GUIDE, *supra* note 11, at 7097 (citing Williamson v. Handy Button Mach. Co., 817 F.2d 1290, 43 FEP Cases 1465 (7th Cir. 1987)).

[181] 925 F. Supp. 1014, 70 FEP Cases 1544 (S.D.N.Y. 1996).

[182] *Id.* at 1025.

[183] 130 F.3d 1287 (8th Cir. 1997).

[184] *Id.* at 1297.

damages are divisible, and other outside factors contributed to the plaintiff's harm."[185]

In *McKinnon v. Kwong Wah Restaurant*,[186] the First Circuit, rejecting plaintiffs' argument on appeal, affirmed the district court's award of $2,500 apiece to two plaintiffs for emotional distress in a sexual harassment case. The court of appeals noted that "both plaintiffs were suffering from emotional distress caused by sources independent from their employment."[187] The court noted that one plaintiff had separated from her boyfriend after the discovery of an unplanned pregnancy and that the other had been sexually abused by her stepfather from age 5 to age 17. The court of appeals concluded that in spite of the difficulty in "distinguishing between plaintiffs' trauma caused by the defendants' harassment and that arising from other causes," the district court's damage awards were proper.[188]

In *Hurley v. Atlantic City Police Department*,[189] the court reduced the jury's award of $575,000 for emotional distress damages in a sexual harassment case to $175,000. Although the court found that the sexual harassment had caused the plaintiff to suffer "serious harm," the court also noted that the testimony of the defendant's psychological expert

> strongly suggests that the difficulties plaintiff has faced and continues to face are rooted in sources other than workplace harassment, such as a troubled childhood marked by sexual molestation, abandonment, and foster homes; physical abuse by both her husbands; and other severe personal, marital and family problems unrelated to her work environment.[190]

The fact that a plaintiff may have experienced prior traumas therefore may significantly affect the value of the plaintiff's emotional damage claim, even where liability is established. The trend among courts appears to be toward taking evidence of prior significant emotional traumas into account in determining the value of an emotional damage claim.

III. Psychological Issues in the Liability Phase

While traditionally the psychological issues in most employment lawsuits have involved damages, the plaintiff's psychological condition may also be quite relevant to liability issues in the case. This is because it is possible that the plaintiff's psychological problems caused the workplace dispute in question,

---

[185]*Id.* at 1294. The *Jenson* court also noted that plaintiffs do not bear the burden of proving that other factors did not contribute to their emotional harm. *Id.*

[186]83 F.3d 498, 70 FEP Cases 1037 (1st Cir. 1996).

[187]*Id.*, 70 FEP Cases at 1043.

[188]*Id.*

[189]933 F. Supp. 396, 72 FEP Cases 1828 (D.N.J. 1996).

[190]*Id.* at 424, 72 FEP Cases at 1850.

instead of vice versa.[191] The courts have become increasingly willing to consider the role of a plaintiff's own prior psychopathology in the genesis of the workplace dispute at issue in litigation. Most often these prior problems take the form of a personality disorder, which is a chronic and pathological means of perceiving and interpreting one's environment and relating to others.[192] Personality disorders are relevant to the issue of employer liability in employment lawsuits in at least two respects.

First, personality disorders often cause conflicts between a plaintiff and his or her coworkers that lead to claims by the plaintiff of victimization. In this sense, a plaintiff suffering from a personality disorder may not merely be the innocent victim of another's unprovoked wrongdoing. Such a plaintiff's own irritability, perfectionism, manipulation of others, or sexually suggestive behavior is often the beginning of a chain of events that ultimately leads to a claim of wrongful termination, harassment, or discrimination. For example, an employee with a Borderline Personality Disorder may direct sexually suggestive comments or even blatantly seductive conduct toward a supervisor and then angrily accuse the supervisor of sexual harassment should he respond. Borderline personalities tend to view others (particularly those in positions of authority) in extreme terms as either "all good" or "all bad." In the eyes of the Borderline, a boss can go from hero to defendant almost instantly. Such an employee may idolize her supervisor until he criticizes her work performance and then react with rage and accuse him of misconduct.[193]

Another example is a manager with a Narcissistic Personality Disorder, whose insensitivity toward others may cause subordinates to seek to avoid him or complain of mistreatment, which may ultimately lead to his failure as a manager. He will likely react with rage when demoted or terminated, blaming everyone but himself for his troubles in the ensuing litigation. Still another example is an employee with Obsessive-Compulsive Personality Disorder, whose rigid perfectionism and lack of interpersonal skills may not be problematic while he is a nonsupervisory employee, but which may cause him to fail when he is promoted into management. Most people with personality disorders are wholly lacking in insight into their situation. In their view, they are fine; it is everyone else who has problems. Accordingly, when they typically fail in the workplace, they begin the hunt for a culprit that often ends in a lawsuit.

---

[191]*See* James J. McDonald, Jr. & Paul R. Lees-Haley, *Personality Disorders in the Workplace: How They May Contribute to Claims of Employment Law Violations*, 22 EMPL. REL. L.J. 57 (1996).

[192]Personality disorders are discussed in detail in Chapter 6, Personality Disorders in Employment Litigation.

[193]In *Ramirez v. Kelly,* 1997 WL 223053 (N.D. Ill. May 1, 1997), the plaintiff and the defendant, who was above the plaintiff in the chain of command, had a sexual relationship. After the plaintiff found out that the defendant was married, the plaintiff sued for sexual harassment, claiming that she had been raped and coerced to carry on the relationship. The plaintiff was diagnosed by the defense psychiatric expert as having Borderline Personality Disorder, although the court expressed some skepticism about the psychiatrist's diagnostic methods.

Second, personality disorders often are relevant to a plaintiff's perception of the events that precede litigation. Individuals with personality disorders often interpret events in a distorted fashion. This frequently accounts for the diametrically opposite characterization of the very same event by plaintiff and defendant in so many employment lawsuits, particularly in "he said/she said" cases where there are no third-party witnesses to help break the credibility impasse. Unlike psychotic individuals with patently bizarre perceptions, employees with personality disorders have relatively good contact with reality. Thus, their accusations of coworker misconduct, although false, are not obviously bizarre and on the contrary may sound quite plausible. Often, to the personality-disordered individual, "believing is seeing." For example, if on account of a personality disorder one presumes that another person is thinking in sexual terms, a variety of behaviors can be construed as sexual in nature—choice of clothing, a smile, an inadvertent touch, a compliment, any sort of effort to engage in joint activities, how close one stands, an invitation to lunch, humorous remarks, gestures, the amount of eye contact, glances, references to other relationships—the list is endless. Similarly, if one assumes that others are discriminating, this assumption becomes a self-fulfilling prophecy—one perceives discrimination to be lurking around every corner. Inattention, inadvertent slights, nonspecific discourtesy, lack of personal concern, random acts of preference, and numerous other ordinary events are consistent with such an assumption and may be construed by the personality disordered individual as evidence of discrimination.

Courts have begun to recognize the role that personality disorders play in the genesis of disputes involving alleged workplace harassment and discrimination. In *Lowe v. Philadelphia Newspapers, Inc.*,[194] a racial harassment case, the court admitted the testimony of a psychiatrist to show that, because of a personality disorder, the plaintiff was oversensitive to ordinary criticism and perceived it as harassment. The plaintiff had attempted to have the court bifurcate the liability and damages issues of the case and exclude testimony of defense psychiatrists concerning her personality disorder from the liability phase. In denying the plaintiff's motion, the court observed that the psychiatrists' testimony was relevant to "whether the alleged harassment claimed by plaintiff is racial and is harassment at all." The court noted that one defense psychiatrist had testified on deposition that, because of her personality disorder, the plaintiff was overly sensitive and may have overreacted to events on the job. As the *Lowe* court explained:

> Testimony concerning a ... plaintiff's mental disorder which causes him or her to perceive criticism as harassment, and to perceive racial slurs where no racial motivation is present, is highly relevant to the question whether plaintiff's perception of racial harassment is correct.[195]

---

[194] 594 F. Supp. 123, 54 FEP Cases 167 (E.D. Pa. 1984).

[195] *Id.* at 125–26, 54 FEP Cases at 169. The *Lowe* court cited *Davis v. U.S. Steel Corp.*, 539 F. Supp. 839, 54 FEP Cases 203 (E.D. Pa. 1982), in which incidents alleged by the plaintiff to be racial harassment were held to be legitimate criticism inaccurately perceived by the plaintiff because of an emotional disorder.

A personality disorder was found to be at the root of a sexual harassment claim in *Spencer v. General Electric Co.*[196] Although the court in that case found a hostile working environment to exist based upon sexual joking and horseplay on the part of the plaintiff's supervisor and coworkers, it rejected the plaintiff's allegations of more serious misconduct, including "more than 100 sexual assaults" by her supervisor in the workplace during the workday, none of which were corroborated by third-party witnesses. The plaintiff attempted to explain the numerous inconsistencies in her story by presenting testimony from her psychiatrist that the harassing events caused her to develop a posttraumatic stress disorder that impaired her ability to recall details. The court rejected this notion and instead credited the testimony of the defense psychiatrist, which was that the plaintiff's "memory problems" resulted from "convenient selectivity rather than emotional trauma," and that the plaintiff suffered from Histrionic Personality Disorder. The court cited the characteristics of such a disorder, including "immaturity, shallowness, self-centeredness, obsession with one's personal appearance and exaggerated emotionality," and then observed that having heard hours of testimony from and about the plaintiff, the defense psychiatrist's conclusions "ring true."

In *Sudtelgte v. Reno*,[197] the court admitted extensive psychiatric testimony in a sexual harassment lawsuit concerning the fact that the plaintiff suffered from a Paranoid Personality Disorder that adversely affected her ability to get along with supervisors and coworkers and that caused her to feel persistently "picked on." The plaintiff alleged a variety of "harassing" conduct, such as coworkers asking to borrow her car, urging her to drink beer with them, and once photographing her with her finger in her nose. Several psychiatrists and psychologists testified at the trial—all to the same general effect—that the plaintiff had numerous preexisting chronic mental problems, including a personality disorder, that interfered with her ability to get along with others and that caused her to misperceive events and the motivations of others. The *Sudtelgte* court held that although the plaintiff may have felt subjectively harassed, this was the result of the abnormal sensitivity caused by her personality disorder, and she could not show that a "reasonable woman" would have been similarly offended. The *Sudtelgte* court also noted the impact of the plaintiff's personality disorder on her credibility, observing that the plaintiff's "current perceptions of present and past events are grossly unreliable, probably because of her mental illness."[198]

The most recent and dramatic recognition by a court of the role of personality disorders in the genesis of harassment and discrimination claims occurred in *Pascouau v. Martin Marietta Corp.*[199] In that case, in which the plaintiff claimed coworkers called her names and passed gas in her presence, the court

---

[196]697 F. Supp. 204, 51 FEP Cases 1696 (E.D. Va. 1988), *aff'd*, 894 F.2d 651, 51 FEP Cases 1725 (4th Cir. 1990).

[197]63 FEP Cases 1257 (W.D. Mo. 1994).

[198]*Id.* at 1257.

[199]994 F. Supp. 1276 (D. Colo. 1998), *aff'd in relevant part*, 185 F.3d 874 (10th Cir. 1999) (table).

concluded that "the conduct that could be described as harassment was not based on gender, but rather on Plaintiff's demonstrated lack of interpersonal skills." In its discussion of the facts of the case, the court described at some length the plaintiff's preexisting psychological problems, many of which arose from the plaintiff's dysfunctional childhood. The court noted that the plaintiff still suffered symptoms of Posttraumatic Stress Disorder as a result of an incident when she was eight years old in which her mother forced her and her sister into a car at knifepoint and then drove the car off a bridge in a suicide attempt.

One of the *Pascouau* plaintiff's preexisting conditions was a mixed personality disorder with borderline and narcissistic characteristics—a condition that occurs somewhat frequently among sexual harassment plaintiffs. The *Pascouou* court explained the relevance of the plaintiff's personality disorder:

> The personality disorder is a condition, largely the product of being raised in a dysfunctional home with dysfunctional parents, in which Plaintiff did not learn how to solve problems effectively or to communicate effectively with other people. The disorder leads to the formulation of implausible perceptions and thus different kinds of conclusions about what other people's actions and behavior mean as distinguished from what a reasonable person not subject to such a disorder would perceive them to mean.
>
> Consistent with this disorder, Plaintiff makes judgments that are highly personalized and overly emotional. She sees things in black and white terms rather than shades of gray that permit allowances and generally feels whatever goes wrong is someone else's fault and she had no role in the misadventure. Persons with this disorder take no responsibility for what goes wrong in their lives.[200]

The court then went on to discuss the role in the case of the symptoms of Borderline Personality Disorder exhibited by the plaintiff:

> The essence of the Plaintiff's complaints in this case is the product of Plaintiff's "splitting," a psychiatric term meaning the patient initially over-evaluates and over-values other people, and then, when the slightest thing goes wrong, demeans those people and becomes angry and upset with them. The major affective characteristic is anger or rage. Secondarily, such a person is fearful of being abandoned or not being liked and does not want to be alone. As a result, the borderline personality very often gets involved in unsuccessful intimate relationships. Depression frequently accompanies this personality disorder because the unsuccessful outcomes of interactions with other people lead to prolonged disappointment.[201]

The court credited the testimony of the defense psychiatrist, a Dr. Plezak, noting:

> When asked if Plaintiff's allegations had any role in the causes of Plaintiff's disorders, Dr. Plezak replied that the situation is reversed in that the disorders

---

[200]*Id.* at 1279, 76 FEP Cases at 653–54.
[201]*Id.,* 76 FEP Cases at 654.

are causes of the allegations. The incidents Plaintiff related were characterized by misinterpretations of events and interactions with fellow employees that were far more intense than would be interpreted by a reasonable person.[202]

Conversely, the court rejected the view of the plaintiff's psychiatrist that all of the plaintiff's emotional difficulties were the result of her experiences in the workplace, noting that "his conclusion dismisses the profuse psychiatric history of the Plaintiff which accounts for the symptoms she had displayed all her life and continued to display even at the time of trial."[203]

In *Lanni v. New Jersey*,[204] the plaintiff filed a motion in limine to exclude the testimony of the defendant's psychiatrist, who had diagnosed the plaintiff as having Narcissistic Personality Disorder, among other conditions. In denying the motion, the court stated that it had reviewed the psychiatrist's report, which detailed how the plaintiff's psychiatric condition might explain the plaintiff's perception that he was being mistreated at work. The court found that the psychiatrist's testimony would "not only assist the trier of fact in understanding various mental and cognitive conditions, but will also assist in sorting out issues of causation."[205]

In *Newberry v. East Texas State University*,[206] an Americans With Disabilities Act case, the plaintiff's psychiatrist testified that the plaintiff suffered from an Obsessive-Compulsive Personality Disorder. The plaintiff himself had testified that this disorder interfered with his relations with others by instilling in him a rigid perfectionism, rigidly ethical behavior, and an insistence on addressing all details of his interpersonal relationships.[207]

In *Stafford v. Noramco of Delaware, Inc.*,[208] the plaintiff claimed that he was not hired for a job for which he applied on account of his race and age. In granting the employer's motion for summary judgment, the court noted that the defendant had cited a determination by a Social Security Administrative Law Judge that the plaintiff was disabled on account of a "severe personality disorder" and that he was "suspicious, hostile, and continually feels victimized." The court explained: "While this finding, in and of itself, does not suggest [the plaintiff] is unqualified for the position, it suggests why, despite overwhelming evidence, he continues to believe Noramco discriminated against him.[209]

In *Frazier v. Topeka Metal Specialties, Inc.*,[210] the plaintiff alleged race discrimination in the form of unequal pay, unequal discipline, discriminatory discharge, and harassment. His psychiatrist diagnosed Paranoid Schizophrenia

---

[202]*Id.*
[203]*Id.*
[204]177 F.R.D. 295 (D.N.J. 1998).
[205]*Id.* at 302.
[206]161 F.3d 276, 8 AD Cases 1595 (5th Cir. 1998).
[207]*Id.* at 278, 8 AD Cases at 1597.
[208]2000 WL 1868179 (D. Del. Dec. 15, 2000).
[209]*Id.*, at *3 n. 13.
[210]2001 WL 138893 (D. Kan. Feb. 15, 2001).

and Antisocial Personality Disorder and stated that he believed the plaintiff's problems at work were the result of his "inability to perceive or process what was going on around him." In denying the employer's motion for summary judgment as to the plaintiff's harassment claim, the court observed as to the harassment allegations: "Whether these complaints were valid or the product of [the plaintiff's] mental condition and his inability to perceive events around him is a credibility issue to be determined by the jury, not an issue for summary judgment."[211]

In other recent cases, even though no personality disorder was diagnosed, the court attributed the plaintiffs' difficulties in the workplace to their own manner of relating to others as opposed to harassment or discrimination. For example, in *Munday v. Waste Management of North America*,[212] the plaintiff complained that she was harassed because of her gender and treated differently than male employees. Although finding that coworkers had made some inappropriate comments, the court rejected the plaintiff's hostile environment claim, and then explained:

> Munday herself greatly contributed to the difficulties of which she complains by her own abrasive conduct and by her tendency to blame her problems on others and to assume little responsibility for her own errors, as well as by her general dissatisfaction with her own life.[213]

The *Munday* court went on to observe of the plaintiff: "As a result of her workplace demeanor, she appears to have herself initiated many of the perceived—and sometimes real—problems which she claims she suffered."[214]

Similarly, in *Jensvold v. Shalala*,[215] the court rejected the plaintiff's claims of gender discrimination in terms and conditions of employment. In doing so, the court remarked:

> Plaintiff's version of events remains an illusion. Her skewed perception of events, whether after-the-fact rationalizations borne of a personal sense of failure, or a contemporaneous self-fulfilling prophesy, is entirely of her own creation. Dr. Jensvold was ready to see sinister motive in any action she perceived as remotely critical of her. This is unfortunate, for she obviously had promise as a medical researcher. Instead of trying harder, she sought to lay blame on others.[216]

The courts therefore are increasingly willing to examine the plaintiff's role in the events that the plaintiff alleges give rise to the defendant's liability.

---

[211]*Id.* at *10.
[212]858 F. Supp. 1364, 72 FEP Cases 471 (D. Md. 1994), *rev'd in part on other grounds,* 126 F.3d 239, 74 FEP Cases 1478 (4th Cir. 1997).
[213]*Id.* at 1372, 72 FEP Cases at 477.
[214]*Id.* at 1374, 72 FEP Cases at 478.
[215]925 F. Supp. 1109, 70 FEP Cases 788 (D. Md. 1996).
[216]*Id.* at 1114, 70 FEP Cases at 792.

IV. Other Legal Issues

A. Availability of Damages for Stress of Litigation

With increasing frequency, plaintiffs in employment cases attribute some portion of their emotional distress to the stress of litigation, such as testifying at depositions and in court, undergoing a mental examination conducted by a defense examiner, and encountering an ex-boss, harasser, or coworkers at depositions or court proceedings. In *Blakey v. Continental Airlines*,[217] the court noted that some of the plaintiff's stress "may be due to the contentiousness of this litigation." It then observed, however, that "[s]he cannot recover for emotional distress caused by litigation.[218]

B. Emotional Distress Claims in Class Actions

Class actions, which were the vehicle of choice for eliminating systemic discrimination following the enactment of Title VII of the Civil Rights Act of 1964, have seen a recent resurgence in popularity in employment litigation. It is the rare large corporation today that has not been targeted by such an action alleging discrimination or harassment against a substantial number of employees. The Civil Rights Act of 1991 added considerable complication to class treatment of employment discrimination and harassment cases, however. That legislation increased the stakes of a discrimination or harassment class action by permitting plaintiffs to recover compensatory and punitive damages. Where compensatory damages for emotional distress are sought, however, treatment of the action as a class action may well be inappropriate due to the necessarily individualized nature of the claims at issue. Courts and commentators[219] have struggled with this concept without any clear resolution, although to date there has yet to be any extensive examination of the peculiar ironies of handling claims for emotional injury via class action. While it may be superficially appealing to argue that there is nothing wrong with assuming that if a class of employees suffered discrimination or harassment each individual employee must also have suffered compensable emotional distress, the argument for classwide treatment collapses

---

[217]992 F. Supp. 731, 76 FEP Cases 280 (D.N.J. 1998).

[218]*Id.* at 736 n.3, 76 FEP Cases at 384 n.3.

[219]For discussions of the problems that discrimination and harassment class actions present following the Civil Rights Act of 1991, see Gary M. Kramer, *No Class: Post-1991 Barriers to Rule 23 Certification of Across-the-Board Employment Discrimination Cases*, 15 LAB. LAW. 415 (2000), and Ashley W. Jordaan & John R. Webb, *The Growing Tension Between Rule 23 Class Actions and Hostile Environment Sexual Harassment Claims*, 26 EMPL. REL. L.J. 63 (2000). For an argument in favor of continued class treatment of discrimination and harassment claims, see Lesley Frieder Wolf, *Evading Friendly Fire: Achieving Class Certification After the Civil Rights Act of 1991*, 100 COLUM. L. REV. 1847 (2000).

when it comes to determining just how much to award each plaintiff in emotional damages. This argument does not account for the possibility, moreover, that the liability question for some plaintiffs might hinge on their own preexisting psychological conditions, and it also fails entirely to address the absurdity of awarding emotional distress damages to some plaintiffs who were not even aware that they suffered discrimination, let alone that they suffered emotional distress as a result.

1. Class Actions: The Basics

Federal class actions are governed by Rule 23 of the Federal Rules of Civil Procedure. There are essentially two sets of requirements that a class action must meet in order to be maintainable—all of those set forth in Rule 23(a), and at least one of those set forth in Rule 23(b).

Rule 23(a) provides that a class action may be brought only if:

> (1) the class is so numerous that joinder of all members is impracticable, (2) there are questions of law or fact common to the class, (3) the claims or defenses of the representative parties are typical of the claims or defenses of the class, and (4) the representative parties will fairly and adequately protect the interests of the class.

In addition, one of the subsections of Rule 23(b) must also be met, with subsections (2) and (3) being the two most relevant to employment cases:

> (2) the party opposing the class has acted or refused to act on grounds generally applicable to the class, thereby making appropriate final injunctive relief or corresponding declaratory relief with respect to the class as a whole; or
> (3) the court finds that the questions of law or fact common to the members of the class predominate over any questions affecting only individual members, and that a class action is superior to other available methods for the fair and efficient adjudication of the controversy. The matters pertinent to the findings include: (A) the interest of members of the class in individually controlling the prosecution or defense of separate actions; (B) the extent and nature of any litigation concerning the controversy already commenced by or against members of the class; (C) the desirability or undesirability of concentrating the litigation of the claims in the particular forum; (D) the difficulties likely to be encountered in the management of the class action.

In most putative class actions for harassment or discrimination to date, courts have assumed that the Rule 23(a) criteria were met, and the controversy has focused on the Rule 23(b) criteria. Most plaintiffs have attempted to have their class actions certified under Rule 23(b)(2). The problem with this is that although Rule 23(b)(2) is silent as to whether monetary remedies may be sought in conjunction with injunctive or declaratory relief, the Advisory Committee Notes on Rule 23 state that class certification under (b)(2) "does not extend to cases in which the appropriate final relief relates exclusively or predominantly to money damages." Though back pay awards in class action cases were common prior to the Civil Rights Act of 1991, they were not as problematic under this provision because they were considered a form of equitable relief[220] and both liability and damages were determined by judges as opposed to juries.

With compensatory and punitive damages and jury trials becoming available under the Civil Rights Act of 1991, the continued appropriateness of (b)(2) class certifications has been brought into question because no longer is equitable relief the "predominant" form of relief sought; rather, money damages for emotional distress and punitive damages have become predominant.

2. The Response of the Courts

Courts have taken varying approaches to certifications of class actions in discrimination and harassment cases since the enactment of the Civil Rights Act of 1991. The leading case in the area and the first court of appeals decision on the subject is the Fifth Circuit's decision in *Allison v. Citgo Petroleum Corp.*[221] The Fifth Circuit in *Allison* rejected class certification in a case alleging race discrimination in hiring, promotion, compensation, and training, where the plaintiffs sought injunctive, declaratory, and monetary relief, including "compensatory and punitive damages to the maximum amount permissible under the law." The district court denied class certification under Rule 23(b)(2) and (b)(3), and the Fifth Circuit affirmed. The *Allison* court maintained that (b)(2) certification is appropriate where "uniform group remedies" are sought, which may be awarded "without requiring a specific or time-consuming inquiry into the varying circumstances and merits of each class member's individual case."[222] The *Allison* court determined that monetary relief "predominates" in a case unless it is "incidental" to injunctive or declaratory relief. The court went on to state that liability for "incidental" damages should not require additional hearings "to resolve the disparate merits of each individual's case; it should neither introduce new and substantial legal or factual issues, nor entail complex individualized determinations."[223]

The *Allison* court went on to note that recovery of compensatory and punitive damages requires "particularly individualized proof of injury, including how each class member was personally affected by the discriminatory conduct."[224] As a result, held the court, such claims are not merely incidental to the injunctive and declaratory relief also being sought. The court started from the premise that "compensatory damages for emotional distress and other forms of intangible injury will not be presumed from a mere violation of constitutional or statutory rights."[225] It noted that specific, individualized proof is necessary,

---

[220]*See* Johnson v. Georgia Highway Express, Inc., 417 F.2d 1122, 1125 (5th Cir. 1969) (a claim for back pay "is not in the nature of damages, but rather is an integral part of the statutory equitable remedy").

[221]151 F.3d 402, 81 FEP Cases 501 (5th Cir. 1998).

[222]*Id.* at 413, 81 FEP Cases at 509.

[223]*Id.* at 415, 81 FEP Cases at 510–11.

[224]*Id.* at 416, 81 FEP Cases at 512.

[225]The *Allison* court cited *Patterson v. P.H.P. Healthcare Corp.*, 90 F.3d 927, 938–40, 72 FEP Cases 613 (5th Cir. 1996), for the point that the proof necessary for

and testimony from the plaintiff alone is not ordinarily sufficient. The *Allison* court continued:

> Compensatory damages may be awarded only if the plaintiff submits proof of actual injury, often in the form of psychological or medical evidence, or other corroborating testimony from a third party. The very nature of these damages, compensating plaintiffs for emotional and other intangible injuries, necessarily implicates the subjective differences of each plaintiff's circumstances; they are an individual, not class-wide, remedy. The amount of compensatory damages to which any individual class member might be entitled cannot be calculated by objective standards. Furthermore, by requiring individualized proof of discrimination and actual injury to each class member, compensatory damages introduce new and substantial legal and factual issues. Clearly . . . compensatory damages under Title VII and 42 U.S.C. § 1981 are not incidental to class-wide injunctive or declaratory relief for discrimination.[226]

The court went on to explain that punitive damages are not incidental either, because they must necessarily turn on the recovery of compensatory damages.

The *Allison* court then went on to address the plaintiffs' argument that the district court should have certified a "hybrid" class action, in which the claims for compensatory and punitive damages would be certified under Rule 23(b)(3) and the rest of the class action would be certified under Rule 23(b)(2). The Fifth Circuit affirmed the district court's finding that (b)(3) certification was inappropriate because compensatory and punitive damages could be established only through examination of each plaintiff's individual circumstances. As the court explained:

> The plaintiffs' claims for compensatory and punitive damages must therefore focus almost entirely on facts and issues specific to individuals rather than the class as a whole: what kind of discrimination was each plaintiff subjected to; how did it affect each plaintiff emotionally and physically, at work and at home; what medical treatment did each plaintiff receive and at what expense; and so on and so on. Under such circumstances, an action conducted nominally as a class action would degenerate in practice into multiple lawsuits separately tried.[227]

Thus, concluded the court, as issues of law and fact common to the class would not predominate over issues specific to individuals, (b)(3) class certification was not appropriate.

Several district court cases decided after *Allison* have reached the same result.[228] Class certification was denied in a sexual harassment case, in *Cox v.*

---

an award of emotional distress damages "requires a degree of specificity which may include corroborating testimony or medical or psychological evidence in support of the damage award. Hurt feelings, anger and frustration are part of life. Unless the cause of action manifests some specific discernable injury to the claimant's emotional state, we cannot say that the specificity requirement has been satisfied."

[226] 51 F.3d at 417, 81 FEP Cases at 512.

[227] *Id.* at 419, 81 FEP Cases at 514.

[228] A similar result was reached in *Abrams v. Kelsey-Seybold Medical Group, Inc.*, 178 F.R.D. 116 (S.D. Tex. 1997), which was decided prior to *Allison*.

Indian Head Industries, Inc.,[229] and in *Legrand v. New York City Transit Authority*,[230] a pregnancy discrimination case. In the latter, the court noted that the fact that each plaintiff sought $1 million in compensatory damages and $1 million in punitive damages "makes clear that the final relief here relates predominantly to money damages."[231] Class certification in a race and sex discrimination action similarly was denied in *Burrell v. Crown Central Petroleum, Inc.*,[232] and in race discrimination cases in *Robinson v. Metro-North Commuter Railroad*[233] and *Reid v. Lockheed Martin Aeronautics Co.*[234]

Other courts have reached contrary results, however. In *Bremiller v. Cleveland Psychiatric Institute*,[235] the court certified a class of plaintiffs in a sexual harassment lawsuit, rejecting the defendant's argument that compensatory damages were not incidental to injunctive relief. It relied upon a number of cases that preceded the Civil Rights Act of 1991, however. That court did require that notice be provided to each class member advising of the right to opt out of the class. In *Jefferson v. Ingersoll International Inc.*,[236] the Seventh Circuit held that (b)(2) class certification in a race discrimination lawsuit was inappropriate, but it remanded the case to the district court for a determination of whether a (b)(3) certification or a "hybrid" (b)(2) certification for liability issues and (b)(3) certification for damages issues would be appropriate.

Finally, two appellate cases have examined the award of compensatory damages in class action cases following a class finding on liability. In *Jenson v. Eveleth Taconite Co.*,[237] a sexual harassment and discrimination case, the district court found liability classwide based on the pervasive nature of the sexual harassment involved, but it addressed the damage claim of each plaintiff separately, via a special master. The Eighth Circuit reversed and remanded the special master's award of compensatory damages under state law for emotional distress, finding that the special master applied the wrong standards, improperly excluded the testimony of the plaintiffs' experts, and awarded too little in monetary damages. In *Berger v. Iron Workers Reinforced Rodmen Local 201*,[238] the court affirmed a special master's award of compensatory damages for emotional distress to certain class members following a class finding of race discrimination and individual trials concerning damages. The use of special masters to determine specific compensatory damage awards following a class finding on liability in these two cases is a deceptively simple solution, however. First, the use of a special master will not be viable for claims arising after enactment of the Civil Rights Act of 1991, in light of that law's granting the

---

[229] 187 F.R.D. 531 (W.D.N.C. 1999).
[230] 83 FEP Cases 1817 (E.D.N.Y. 1999).
[231] *Id.* at 1823.
[232] 197 F.R.D. 284 (E.D. Tex. 2000).
[233] 197 F.R.D. 85, 84 FEP Cases 151 (S.D.N.Y. 2000).
[234] 199 F.R.D. 379 (N.D. Ga. 2001).
[235] 898 F. Supp. 572, 66 FEP Cases 1738 (N.D. Ohio 1995).
[236] 195 F.3d 894, 81 FEP Cases 170 (7th Cir. 1999).
[237] 130 F.3d 1287, 75 FEP Cases 852 (8th Cir. 1997).
[238] 170 F.3d 1111, 79 FEP Cases 1018 (D.C. Cir. 1999).

right to a jury trial of all issues to both sides in a case. Second, relatively few class members were affected—16 in *Jenson* and 18 in *Berger*. Third, in spite of the relatively few claimants involved, the separate hearings on damages (not counting appeals) in those two cases took more than three years to conclude in *Jensen* and more than five years in *Berger*, which makes it questionable whether any judicial economies were achieved.

3. Class Treatment of Emotional Distress Claims

The notion that it can be inferred that a class of people have suffered emotional distress without specific proof of it seems peculiar, but some courts have not been so troubled by the concept. In *Berger v. Iron Workers*, the District of Columbia Circuit approved an award of emotional distress damages to 18 class members who completed an apprenticeship training program that the court deemed unnecessary. The court remarked that "courts may properly infer emotional distress from factual circumstances—and award damages to compensate for that distress,"[239] and then explained:

> There can be little doubt that claimants, who were experienced rodmen, suffered emotional distress by having to subject themselves to an unnecessary training program for up to two years before being permitted to take the union entrance exam. Those circumstances more than adequately support the extremely modest awards granted here, which range from $2,500 to $25,000.[240]

As the Fifth Circuit in *Allison* recognized, an award of emotional distress damages requires an examination, *with respect to each plaintiff*, of the nature of the stressful event(s), and the impact of the event or events on the plaintiff. Specifically, such an analysis requires consideration of numerous factors unique to each plaintiff, such as:

- How serious was the stressor?
- Was there a single stressor or multiple stressors?
- What symptoms did the stressor produce?
- How long did each symptom last?
- What impact, if any, did each symptom have on the plaintiff's life?
- Was medical treatment or psychotherapy required?
- Could the symptoms have been produced by a preexisting or concurrent stressor?
- Could the symptoms have been related to a preexisting mental or personality disorder?
- Could the symptoms have been fabricated or exaggerated?
- Did the plaintiff have an "eggshell skull" that caused the stressor to produce more severe symptoms than otherwise might have been expected?

This analysis cannot be avoided if an award of emotional distress damages is to be fixed accurately.

---

[239]*Id.* at 1138, 79 FEP Cases at 1040.
[240]*Id.*, 79 FEP Cases at 1040–41.

Estimation by a court of the value of emotional damages that "probably were" suffered, without submission of actual proof, is a difficult and dangerous undertaking. As noted above, the Equal Employment Opportunity Commission, in its *Policy Guide on Compensatory and Punitive Damages Under the 1991 Civil Rights Act,* maintains that "[e]motional harm will not be presumed merely because the complaining party is a victim of discrimination. The existence, nature and severity of emotional harm must be proved."[241]

There thus does not seem to be any viable way around the requirement that if emotional damages are to be awarded in a class action, they must be based upon an examination of each plaintiff's specific situation. That examination, in turn, makes class treatment of the claims inappropriate, as a separate trial essentially must occur as to damages for each plaintiff.

4. Liability Issues

An individualized inquiry sometimes may also be necessary with respect to liability, at least in harassment cases, that would make class treatment of liability issues as well as damages issues inappropriate. *Harris v. Forklift Systems, Inc.,*[242] established that there are both a subjective and an objective component to determining liability for harassment; the Supreme Court maintained that "if the victim does not subjectively perceive the environment to be abusive, the conduct has not actually altered the conditions of the victim's employment."[243] Such a subjective perception cannot typically be determined on a classwide basis, as each class member's experience of the allegedly harassing events will likely differ. The court in *Cox v. Indian Head Industries, Inc.,*[244] in refusing to certify a class in a sexual harassment case, recognized this and maintained in addition that a plaintiff's own role in the genesis of the events at issue is also an element that must be considered. That court explained:

> While many of the allegations involve egregious conduct, most of those incidents relate solely to the named Plaintiffs. Those involving putative class members are not solely sexual in nature. Some incidents include "horseplay" while others are questionably consensual in nature. And, although not clear, some individuals seem to have been dating others. One incident involved viewing obscene drawings in the men's restroom, raising the issue of why the female employee was present there. Another incident involved male employees' sexual remarks to a female employee whose husband had obtained a penile implant, again raising the issue of why such information became public knowledge. Some of the described incidents involved humor in which the female employees appear to have joined. It cannot be said that "as goes the claim of the named plaintiff, so go the claims of the class."[245]

---

[241]POLICY GUIDE, *supra* note 12, at 7096.
[242]510 U.S. 17, 63 FEP Cases 225 (1993).
[243]*Id.* at 21, 63 FEP Cases at 228.
[244]187 F.R.D. 531 (W.D.N.C. 1999).
[245]*Id.* at 534.

C. Statutes of Limitations

In *Stoll v. Runyon*,[246] the Ninth Circuit held that the limitations period for a plaintiff to file a sexual harassment charge under Title VII would be tolled on account of the psychological injuries suffered by the plaintiff as a result of the harassment. In *Stoll*, the plaintiff was raped by a supervisor, and she was repeatedly asked by supervisors and coworkers to perform oral sex on them. Her male coworkers rubbed up against her, pressing their erect penises on her back, and followed her into the women's restroom, and her supervisor refused to allow her to go to the restroom when she was menstruating. The plaintiff was diagnosed with severe major depression, severe generalized anxiety disorder, and somatic pain disorder. Her psychiatrist testified that she might never recover from the abuse and might never work again. She attempted suicide four times and was on psychiatric disability leave.

The plaintiff had pursued a Title VII claim, which was heard by an administrative law judge of the Equal Employment Opportunity Commission. The judge did not award her front pay, and she appealed the ruling to the Office of Federal Operations. That agency also denied her request for front pay. Almost a year later, the plaintiff filed a handwritten *pro se* complaint in federal court under Title VII. The defendant moved to dismiss on the ground that the complaint was not filed within the 90-day limitations period following the plaintiff's exhaustion of her administrative appeals, and the court granted the motion over the plaintiff's objection that the statute had been equitably tolled.

Noting that equitable tolling applies when the plaintiff is prevented from asserting a claim by wrongful conduct by the defendant, or when extraordinary circumstances beyond the plaintiff's control make it impossible to file a claim on time, the Ninth Circuit reversed. It held that both grounds for equitable tolling had been met. The court maintained that "the Post Office is not entitled to benefit from the fact that its own admittedly outrageous acts left Stoll so broken and damaged that she cannot protect her own rights."[247] It also held that the plaintiff was mentally incapacitated, which prevented her from relating effectively with her lawyer so as to have filed her lawsuit on time. Specifically, the court cited evidence that the plaintiff was unable to open her mail without suffering a panic attack and could not concentrate well enough to read. The plaintiff testified that she was unable to communicate directly with her own lawyer about matters involving the case. Instead, her lawyer would send all correspondence relating to the case to the plaintiff's psychiatrist's office, where a receptionist would open it and explain it to her. Her psychiatrist testified that the plaintiff was heavily medicated on Valium and Vicodin and was unable to understand her legal rights.

---

[246] 165 F.3d 1238, 78 FEP Cases 1312 (9th Cir. 1998).
[247] *Id.* at 1242, 78 FEP Cases at 1315.

Although the facts in *Stoll* are much more extreme than those encountered in most harassment and discrimination cases, the Ninth Circuit's result suggests that some courts may find the limitations period to be tolled where the plaintiff is mentally incapacitated[248]—particularly if the mental damage flowed from the workplace events at issue.[249] Courts will have to use care, however, to ensure that the element of extreme mental incapacity present in *Stoll* is not trivialized in future cases such that every plaintiff who suffers some emotional distress from discrimination or harassment might argue for tolling of the statute of limitations.

---

[248]*See* Tsai v. Rockefeller Univ., 137 F. Supp. 2d 276, 85 FEP Cases 358 (S.D. N.Y. 2001) (motion to dismiss lawsuit denied where plaintiff filed EEOC charge three years after termination; plaintiff claimed that "nervous break-down" resulting from wrongful termination prevented timely exercise of her rights).

[249]*But see* Elshirbiny v. Hewlett Packard Co., 2001 WL 590034 (N.D. Cal. May 24, 2001) (plaintiff's unsworn statement that Chronic Fatigue Syndrome and other unspecified conditions prevented timely filing of EEOC charge rejected; court noted that plaintiff was able to file workers' compensation claim during limitations period; Eber v. Harris County Hosp. Dist., 130 F. Supp. 2d 847 (S.D. Tex. 2001) (limitations period tolled while plaintiff in a coma but not during subsequent period of depression; noting that plaintiff filed unemployment compensation claim during limitations period, which required "skills and mental functions . . . similar to those necessary for filing a charge with the EEOC"); St. Andre v. Henderson, 2000 WL 1677967 (N.D. Cal. Nov. 6, 2000) (equitable tolling denied where plaintiff was not mentally incapacitated at time statute was running); David v. Trugreen Ltd. P'ship, 1999 WL 288686 (N.D. Tex. May 5, 1999) (rejecting tolling argument based on plaintiff's mental illness not alleged to be caused by the workplace, and noting that the plaintiff was competent to seek legal counsel and apply for an auto loan, and was released by his doctor to return to work, during the limitations period).

CHAPTER 2

THE ROLE OF THE MENTAL HEALTH PROFESSIONAL IN EMPLOYMENT LITIGATION

Rodney J. S. Deaton, M.D.
Harold J. Bursztajn, M.D.
Archie Brodsky, B.A.

Mental health professionals have long played a role in legal proceedings. Most laypeople think of psychiatrists, psychologists, and other clinicians as providing testimony in criminal proceedings. In such cases they help courts determine whether individuals are competent to stand trial or whether they were sane or insane at the time of the crime's commission. From the Daniel M'Naughten trial in late-nineteenth-century England to the trials of John Hinckley and the Unabomber in late-twentieth-century America, for good or for ill, mental health professionals have played a major role in the public debate about mental illness and responsibility.[1]

Yet in civil and administrative matters as well, mental health professionals have played an important role in a variety of legal contexts, from malpractice cases to will contests to disability determinations.[2] In the context of employment litigation, they have been important for determining the nature and extent of emotional damages and, since the advent of the Americans With Disabilities Act (ADA) of 1990,[3] psychological fitness for duty and the need for reasonable accommodation. It is thus quite important for an attorney to understand the strengths and weakness of mental health testimony so as to pursue or defend an employment claim as successfully as possible.

---

[1] *See generally* Marvin Prosono, *History of Forensic Psychiatry, in* PRINCIPLES AND PRACTICE OF FORENSIC PSYCHIATRY 13 (Richard Rosner ed., 1994) [hereinafter PRINCIPLES AND PRACTICE].

[2] Thomas G. Gutheil, *Legal Issues in Psychiatry, in* COMPREHENSIVE TEXTBOOK OF PSYCHIATRY/VI 2747 (Harold I. Kaplan & Benjamin J. Sadock eds., 1995).

[3] 42 U.S.C. §12101 et seq.

This chapter will describe the various professionals who might prove helpful to an attorney in an employment litigation claim involving some mental health issue. It will address practical concerns with respect to the hiring of the professional, as well as the preparation of the professional for the attorney's particular litigation needs, whether these involve consultation, evaluation, or testimony.

This chapter will address two ways in which mental health professionals can assist attorneys. The first is the more "standard" of the two, and it involves the diagnosis of mental disorders that might be relevant to the litigation at issue. This requires that an expert be well acquainted with standard descriptions of emotional problems and disorders, as well as with the various treatments available for them. Experts who possess a high degree of skill in diagnosis and treatment tend to provide more accurate assessments of the merits of a case, as well as provide more persuasive and useful evaluations and testimony.

In addition, however, an expert should be sought who possesses not only excellent diagnostic skills but also excellent skills in understanding the nuances of interpersonal relations and intrapsychic functioning. Although it is fashionable in some circles to downplay the importance of these skills, given that they are not as amenable to certain types of experimental protocols, attorneys should seek out experts who also have expertise in these more "subjective" areas, both in the diagnostic assessment and the psychotherapeutic treatment of these problems.[4] Such experts can aid attorneys in the more subtle aspects of a case, pointing out potential problems and strengths as attorneys deal with clients, opposing parties, and even opposing counsel.

Finally, this chapter will stress the importance of finding experts who are comfortable assessing and communicating the relative certainties and uncertainties of their opinions. Unfortunately, too often mental health professionals promise more than they can deliver—a definite diagnosis or assessment, with clear ramifications for damages or needs. Given that the "experts" are making these "definite" statements, even seasoned attorneys can sometimes forget the common sense that they carry with them in their daily lives. They forget how uncertain life is, let alone how uncertain litigation typically is.

The best expert is not afraid to be certain when (albeit relative) certainty is warranted—for example, when symptom pictures are clear, when causal relationships are straightforward, and when treatment courses are easily definable. But opportunities for such absolute certainty are quite rare. The attorney will be best served by finding experts who are willing to consider various explanations for the data given them and who can then argue cogently and persuasively for one course of action over another, recognizing the pros and cons of all possible antecedents and outcomes. In other words, sometimes the best experts are more uncertain than certain.[5]

---

[4]Drew Westen, *The Scientific Status of Unconscious Processes: Is Freud Really Dead?* 47 J. AM. PSYCHOANALYTIC ASS'N 1061 (2000).

[5]Harold J. Bursztajn & Archie Brodsky, *Ethical and Effective Testimony After Daubert*, in THE MENTAL HEALTH PRACTITIONER AND THE LAW 262 (Lawrence E. Lifson & Robert I. Simon eds., 1998).

I. Qualifications of Mental Health Expert Witnesses

The rules of evidence typically do not require that mental health expert witnesses have any particular qualifications. Indeed, Federal Rule of Evidence 702, which provides for expert witness testimony, is broadly written:

> If scientific, technical, or other specialized knowledge will assist the trier of fact to understand the evidence or to determine a fact in issue, a witness qualified as an expert by knowledge, skill, experience, training or education, may testify thereto in the form of an opinion or otherwise, if (1) the testimony is based upon sufficient facts or data, (2) the testimony is the product of reliable principles and methods, and (3) the witness has applied the principles and methods reliably to the facts of the case.[6]

The requirements to be qualified to testify as an expert witness therefore are not particularly stringent, although courts are subjecting the substance of an expert's testimony to greater scrutiny. Although with a few exceptions, most mental health professionals will qualify to give expert testimony,[7] the specific qualifications and credentials of expert witnesses are very important in that they generally lend considerable weight in the eyes of the trier of fact to the credibility of the expert's conclusions.

A. Types of Mental Health Professionals

1. Psychiatrists

Psychiatrists are physicians who complete the same four-year medical school curriculum as other medical specialists. Upon receiving their medical degrees, future psychiatrists then enroll in a residency program devoted to psychiatric training. During this residency the psychiatrists-in-training care for patients in inpatient and outpatient settings under the supervision of more experienced psychiatrists. The residency lasts at least four years, during which time residents are continuously treating patients suffering from a variety of psychiatric disorders, using both psychotherapeutic and medical (e.g., medication, electroshock treatments) modalities.

In the United States, upon completion of psychiatric training, psychiatrists become *board-eligible*, which means they are eligible to take a national certifi-

---

[6]FED. R. EVID. 702. Some states do have minimum experience requirements for providing expert witness testimony. For example, Section 2032(b) of the California Code of Civil Procedure provides:
> A mental examination conducted under this section shall be performed only by a licensed physician, or by a licensed clinical psychologist who holds a doctoral degree in psychology and has had at least five years of postgraduate experience in the diagnosis of emotional and mental disorders.

[7]See Chapter 15, Avoiding and Attacking "Junk Science," for a discussion of minimum qualifications established by some courts for experts who seek to testify.

cation test, commonly called "the boards." Upon passing the examination, psychiatrists become *board-certified* by the American Board of Psychiatry and Neurology. To assure that they are retaining experts who have demonstrated a certain level of competence and experience, attorneys should use only board-certified psychiatrists.

Because of their medical training, psychiatrists can address the medical aspect of the litigant's claim as well as the psychological aspect. For example, they can evaluate the use and efficacy of psychopharmacologic treatments. Sometimes the psychological symptoms reported by a litigant (e.g., sleep disturbance or sexual dysfunction) are a side effect of psychotropic medication rather than the product of adverse workplace events. Psychiatrists can also evaluate the role that underlying, nonneuropsychiatric illness might play in the development of psychological symptoms. Hypo- and hyperthyroidism are examples of medical conditions that can produce direct psychological symptoms.

2. Clinical Psychologists

Clinical psychologists are doctoral-level professionals who have received extensive training in the psychological aspects of mental health or illness. They complete an extended curriculum of study leading to a doctorate of philosophy (Ph.D.) in psychology or a doctorate in psychology (Psy.D.). Because of the traditional focus on social science and empirical validation found in most psychology programs, clinical psychologists also receive extensive training in psychological testing. Clinical psychologists typically have expertise in the diagnosis of the signs and symptoms of mental illness. They may also have had training in various psychotherapeutic treatments for mental illness.

After earning their degree, clinical psychologists then work for at least one year in a clinical internship. The training program and the internship should be accredited by the American Psychological Association. Ideally, the internship should be done in a clinical setting where there is access to the treatment of mentally ill inpatients so that the psychologist can gain an understanding of the full range of psychopathology. After completing degree requirements, a clinical psychologist must still be licensed to practice independently. Each state has different requirements, but most require one year of predoctoral and one year of postdoctoral clinical experience to sit for the examination. Educational credentials are reviewed as well. All candidates for licensure must pass a national examination, and many states require an additional written or oral examination. There are also various credentialing boards of professional psychology. The American Board of Professional Psychology and the American Board of Forensic Psychology are leading examples. Credentialing by these organizations is comparable to more specific credentialing in psychiatry beyond that profession's board certification.

3. Psychiatric Social Workers

Psychiatric social workers have earned a master's degree in social work from an accredited school of social work. The degree requires two years of classroom work accompanied by practicum training in a mental health setting, such as a mental health clinic or a psychiatric inpatient unit. After completing their degree, they become eligible to take either a state or a national certification examination that tests knowledge of both the diagnosis of the signs and symptoms of mental illness and the psychotherapeutic treatment of mental illness. Social workers also receive special training in the evaluation and integration of family and social services within a community.

Since the focus of social work training is on social systems, psychiatric social workers may have special training in marital and family evaluation and treatment.

4. Marriage and Family Therapists

Marriage and family counselors or therapists (sometimes known as MFCCs, or MFTs) typically complete a master's degree program in counseling. These professionals are trained to assist clients with marital and family problems; they rarely receive training in the diagnosis and treatment of mental illness. Some states have licensing or certification procedures for master's-level counselors; some do not. Even states that license these counselors do not license them to diagnose mental illness.[8] For this reason, these individuals are an extremely poor choice as expert witnesses in employment lawsuits.

5. Other Specialties

Mental health professionals may have a variety of other degrees and professional backgrounds. Some clinicians may have a master's degree in counseling or psychology. Like clinical psychologists, most of these individuals have had at least some practical experience working with clients, usually under the supervision of a licensed counselor.

Attorneys should be advised, however, that clinicians who have not had doctoral-level training are much more open to problems on cross-examination, especially if the retaining attorney has attempted to have the master's-level clinician testify about matters that could involve making assessments of medical or testing issues.

B. Additional Professional Qualifications

Many mental health subspecialties have specialized training programs to teach interested clinicians about the legal profession and forensic practice. Both psychiatrists and psychologists, for example, have specialized examinations leading to special certification in forensic psychiatry or psychology.

Given the complexity of most employment litigation cases, an attorney should try first to find an expert who has such specialized qualifications. This will ensure that the expert not only has solid, basic qualifications in psychiatry

---

[8] *See, e.g.*, CAL. BUS. & PROF. CODE §4980.02.

or psychology, but also has specialized knowledge in basic legal procedure and the clinical issues that often arise in legal contexts.

Once again, however, the attorney should not assume that such credentials are the only ones the expert needs. Ideally, the forensically trained evaluator practices more than legal medicine or psychology. In the best case, such a clinician also sees patients in a clinical practice, thus keeping up with the many changes in routine clinical care. Also, the attorney should still make certain that the forensically trained expert has relevant clinical experience in the area at issue in the case. The attorney should never be reticent to ask the expert about his or her specific experience in a relevant area.

Most mental health professions also have organizations that cater to the professional and educational needs of forensic specialists. Psychiatrists in the United States, for example, have the American Academy of Psychiatry and the Law, an affiliate of the major psychiatric organization in America, the American Psychiatric Association. Psychologists have the American Psychology-Law Society, also known as Division 41 of the American Psychological Association. Though membership in such an organization does not per se guarantee any expertise in forensic mental health, it does indicate that the expert is associated with like-minded clinicians who are involved in research and the development of more uniform, ethical forensic evaluations.

Finally, attorneys should acquaint themselves with any specific legal requirements that their particular jurisdiction requires in the licensing or use of mental health professionals in legal proceedings. Some states consider the giving of forensic testimony to constitute the practice of medicine or psychology, which requires licensure in that state or at least a grant of special permission by the state medical board.

II. Factors to Guide the Selection of an Expert

A. Clinical Expertise

When hiring an expert, an attorney should look for various areas of expertise. Generally, the expert should have the skills to do standard descriptive diagnosis and should know about the natural course of the particular illness that the litigant suffers from. The expert should know the range of treatment modalities available to treat the litigant's particular problem, using both medical and psychological treatment. As more is learned about the complex interaction between the brain and other parts of the body, it will become increasingly important to find an expert who has the training and experience to discuss how to integrate these treatment approaches.

Specifically, the clinician who is selected should have expertise in the condition or conditions at issue in the litigation. For example, if a plaintiff claims to have suffered depression as a result of being fired but a cursory review of medical records indicates that the plaintiff has a long history of treatment with antidepressant medications prior to having been fired, a clinician throughly familiar with depression and its treatment should be selected. If a personality disorder may have played a role in the workplace events at issue or the symptoms alleged to have occurred as a result,[9] a clinician with expertise and experience in personality disorders should be chosen.

Some evaluators may seek to avoid giving standard diagnoses because they believe that diagnoses "medicalize" a patient or do not capture the essence of a client's problems. Such an approach may at times be laudable in the clinical setting. Yet in the forensic setting, an attorney should not select an expert who does not feel comfortable making standardized diagnoses.[10] Such an expert might miss important neuropsychiatric syndromes or be unable to articulate clinical findings in terms that are commonly understood. For example, is a clinician who diagnoses "Traumatic Stress Reaction Syndrome" talking about Posttraumatic Stress Disorder or something else?

In addition, the attorney should attempt to find and retain an expert who has expertise in formulating and explaining the client's interpersonal and intrapsychic processes. Although many in the mental health community doubt the utility or even validity of such "psychodynamic" concepts, attorneys should be wary of experts who completely ignore such concepts and formulations. An expert who understands how psychological experience can influence behavior, thoughts, and feelings can more thoroughly place a particular clinical diagnosis in its appropriate interpersonal and intrapersonal context.

B. Forensic Expertise

Today many clinicians who testify have had some type of specialized training in mental health and law. For example, psychiatrists can obtain a post-residency fellowship in forensic psychiatry. In this training the psychiatrist works under the supervision of senior clinicians who teach the psychiatrist how to perform examinations that can be used in various legal contexts. Many programs offer access to law school courses in subjects such as criminal law and evidence. Some specialists even go so far as to obtain a law degree.

In addition to asking about specialized training, attorneys should also inquire about the types of cases the expert has evaluated. Some experts specialize in evaluating certain types of cases. They bring the advantage of much expertise in one particular area. They have the disadvantage, however, of not having evaluated clients in other contexts that might have given them a broader view of the legal system. For example, an expert whose primary experience has been in evaluating criminal defendants would be a poor choice for a sexual harassment case involving complex Axis II issues and a claim of traumatic injury.

Because treatment issues often come into play in these cases, one should find an expert who has broad experience in a variety of treatment modalities, or

---

[9]*See* Chapter 6, Personality Disorders in Employment Litigation.

[10]In the United States and Canada, the authoritative text outlining the major psychiatric diagnoses is AMERICAN PSYCHIATRIC ASSOCIATION, DIAGNOSTIC AND STATISTICAL MANUAL OF MENTAL DISORDERS (4th ed. text rev. 2000) [hereinafter DSM-IV-TR].

who is at least familiar with the basics of a variety of treatments. Psychodynamic treatments, for example, may or may not be the treatments of choice for most litigants. Yet it will be helpful to the attorney if the expert is familiar with basic psychodynamic concepts. Often these concepts can help make sense out of seemingly irrational behavior.

Prior courtroom experience is important. The more courtroom experience an expert has, the more at ease he or she will be in both evaluating the case and presenting it to the court or jury. Basic communication skills are very important but sometimes overlooked in selecting an expert. Be wary of the expert who cannot translate diagnostic opinions into lay language. Even though some attorneys think that an expert with outstanding credentials can impress juries with erudition, such is rarely the case. Jurors find experts who are easily understood to be more credible. Even the most complicated psychodynamic material, for example, can be easily translated into such basic concepts as dependence/independence, or closeness/competition. How well the expert can explain psychological issues to the attorney is usually a good predictor of how well he or she will be able to communicate with the jury.

Finally, the attorney should probe the expert for any ideological biases that may affect the expert's objectivity. Has the expert been retained almost exclusively by plaintiffs or by defendants? Has the expert gone on record in symposia or publications to say, for example, that it is wrong to "blame the victim" in a sexual harassment case by investigating her prior mental health history, or that most emotional injury claims are grossly exaggerated? Does the expert have a personal history with mental illness, sexual harassment or abuse, or unfair treatment in the workplace that may bring about a potential bias? As one commentator has observed, "the issue of sexual harassment arouses strong feelings in individuals with differing opinions regarding aspects of civil rights and feminism."[11] As this authority notes, extreme positions with respect to the issue of sexual harassment rooted in ideological positions will render an expert's opinion suspect:

> The position that any personal comment made by a male coworker toward a woman in the workplace is sexual harassment demonstrates unfamiliarity with the definition of sexual harassment. However, the position that sexual harassment is not a legitimate problem in the workplace and does not result in significant consequences is also an uninformed opinion, which equally reflects bias.[12]

Not only can these types of biases (sometimes unwittingly) affect an expert's ability to be objective, but they can also be exploited by opposing counsel on cross-examination if they are discovered.

C. Problems with Interpersonal Issues

Certainly an attorney should not retain an expert who appears to have his or her own interpersonal difficulties—one who, for example, is cold or aloof in

---

[11]Liza M. Gold, *Addressing Bias in the Forensic Assessment of Sexual Harassment Claims*, 26 J. AM. ACAD. PSYCHIATRY & L. 563, 565 (1998).

[12]*Id.* at 566.

interactions with the attorney, or who is often prickly and difficult. Other interpersonal issues are less obvious yet equally important to consider as one works with an expert in a case.

Every interaction between evaluator and plaintiff is a human interaction. An evaluator often can get information from a plaintiff only by forming some type of helpful alliance with the plaintiff. When the plaintiff is hostile toward the expert, it is often difficult to form such an alliance. Timid plaintiffs may be frightened by more confident evaluators, and timid evaluators may be intimidated by confident, confrontative plaintiffs. Class differences also can make a great difference in the amount of information shared between an evaluator and a plaintiff. Men and women may bring different expectations of gender roles. Often these types of interpersonal issues cannot be changed and instead must simply be taken into account. Yet the attorney should ask the evaluator to consider what cultural and interpersonal factors may be at stake in an evaluation, to make sure that the evaluator is both considering the issues and addressing them in a logical way.

III. Retaining the Expert

A. Whether to Use the Plaintiff's Treating Therapist

One of the most important questions that a plaintiff's attorney must address when retaining an expert is whether to use the plaintiff's treating clinician as an expert or whether to hire another evaluator to do a separate evaluation.

Many attorneys prefer to use treating clinicians. First, it is easiest. One does not have to find an evaluator who specializes in forensic examinations, which is sometimes a problem in certain areas, where there are not many mental health professionals or where none of them wish to go to court to testify. Second, the treating clinician already knows the client's history in depth. Attorneys can save a great deal of money in evaluation expenses.

If at all possible, however, attorneys should avoid using the treating clinician as a forensic expert. Instead, they should hire another evaluator, ideally one who has forensic training and experience, to perform the forensic examination. The problems faced by the treating clinician who also attempts to serve as expert are of a practical and ethical nature.[13]

From a practical standpoint, some treating clinicians are so immersed in the worldview of their patients that they have difficulty even considering hypotheses other than those put forth by their patients. Mental health professionals are trained to help people and are not typically trained to be skeptical of a patient's report of symptoms. Accordingly, the clinician typically accepts the patient's account of symptoms. What is important in the therapeutic context

---

[13]Larry H. Strasburger, Thomas G. Gutheil & Archie Brodsky, *On Wearing Two Hats: Role Conflict in Serving As Both Psychotherapist and Expert Witness*, 154 AM. J. PSYCHIATRY 448 (1997).

is not so much rendering a precise diagnosis or assessing causation as helping the patient improve his or her functioning. Thus, a treating clinician may overlook crucial data or diagnoses that may not, for example, have much relevance to the course of a particular therapy but that may shed important light on a litigant's legal claim.

Yet even if the treating clinician is able to entertain alternative hypotheses for the patient's problems, these hypotheses can often impede treatment as much as help it. For psychotherapy to be successful, the clinician must usually pay attention to the meaning that a patient assigns to a particular event. Whether a particular event happened in a certain way is not as important as the feeling that the patient still carries from the event. If a clinician is always considering alternative hypotheses or constructions of an event, he or she may fail to empathize enough with the patient's current beliefs to allow the patient to find new, more positive meaning from the event.

Finally, if a treating clinician testifies, the effect of the testimony itself can often be quite detrimental to the therapeutic relationship. It is not that treating clinicians need to protect patients from alternative versions of an event. But they may choose putting off discussion of a particular version of events until a more propitious time, or they may choose to avoid certain subjects altogether, for the subjects may not be necessary for a patient's current progress. Once the treating clinician is on the stand, however, he or she may be forced to consider and discuss hypotheses or versions of fact that may be radically at odds with the patient's formulation. When the patient hears the therapist talk of these alternatives, especially if the discussion is clinically premature or if the treating clinician has not had adequate time to explore all the alternatives with the patient, the patient might become hurt or angered at the treating clinician's formulations. This may result in having to reestablish an alliance that was damaged by inopportune testimony.[14]

From an ethical standpoint, the treating clinician always enters more tenuous ground by also assuming a forensic role in the same case. Immediately, the clinician becomes an agent of two parties—the agent of the patient as therapist, but also the agent of the court as objective evaluator. In the role of expert, the clinician must play the role of detective. A skeptical approach is essential (regardless of which side has retained the clinician) if an objective appraisal of the litigant's condition is to be obtained. The litigant's account cannot simply be accepted as true. Rather, it must be thoroughly scrutinized for any evidence of fabrication or exaggeration of symptoms. This is a very difficult approach for most treating therapists to take, however, and the accuracy of their conclusions about a patient's condition may suffer as a result. Conversely, to the extent a plaintiff's treating therapist perceives his or her role as assisting the plaintiff in obtaining relief through litigation as a means of resolving an underlying mental disorder, that clinician's role as expert witness is obviously compromised. As one leading commentator recently observed:

---

[14]Larry H. Strasburger, *"Crudely, Without Any Finesse": The Defendant Hears His Psychiatric Evaluation*, 15 BULL. AM. ACAD. PSYCHIATRY & L. 229 (1987).

In general, these two roles—treater and expert—are considered incompatible because the clinical, legal and ethical mandates are markedly different for them. . . . [T]he treater's job is to place the patient's welfare first—to help and to heal—whereas the expert's job is, by testimony, to inform and teach the judge or jury, regardless of whether the expert's testimony helps or harms the patient. The treater's "client" is the patient; the expert's client is the court. *The very need of the treater to help the patient constitutes, from a forensic perspective, a form of bias through lack of the requisite objectivity and investment in the outcome.*[15]

As another leading forensic psychiatrist has similarly observed:

The treater-examiner dichotomy is [a] source of bias. The treater is the natural ally of the plaintiff. The key therapeutic tasks involve the provisions of empathy, validation, and empowerment. In order to avoid re-victimization in therapy, some have recommended that therapists should assume the harassment occurred, that the patient has an adequate work record and that if a complaint was filed, some type of retaliation took place.[16]

Obviously, a clinician who commences an examination with those kinds of assumptions cannot perform an objective scientific evaluation of a plaintiff. Yet often a plaintiff's mental health expert, who happens to double as the plaintiff's treater, when questioned about his or her conclusion that workplace events caused the plaintiff to suffer one or more mental disorders, responds with: "Well, this is what my patient believes to be the case and I have no reason to think that my patient would lie to me." Such an approach is decidedly unscientific.

For this reason, many forensic specialty organizations strongly discourage members from serving as both treating clinician and forensic evaluator.[17] For example, the *Ethical Guidelines for the Practice of Forensic Psychiatry* of the American Academy of Psychiatry and the Law provide: "Treating psychiatrists should generally avoid agreeing to be an expert witness or to perform evaluations of their patients for legal purposes because a forensic evaluation usually requires that other people be interviewed and testimony may adversely affect the therapeutic relationship."[18]

Thus, even though there are some advantages of ease in using the treating clinician, overall the disadvantages far outweigh them. Attorneys will do far better for their clients and for their case if they hire a specialized forensic expert to evaluate the case and, if necessary, testify. That forensic evaluator can thoroughly interview the treating clinician to get that person's perspective and incorporate it into the overall evaluation.

---

[15]THOMAS G. GUTHEIL, THE PSYCHIATRIST IN COURT 27 (1998) (emphasis added).

[16]Robert I. Simon, *The Credible Forensic Psychiatric Evaluation in Sexual Harassment Litigation,* 26 PSYCHIATRIC ANNALS 139, 141 (1996).

[17]*See, e.g.,* AMERICAN ACADEMY OF PSYCHIATRY AND THE LAW, ETHICAL GUIDELINES FOR THE PRACTICE OF FORENSIC PSYCHIATRY (1991). These Ethical Guidelines appear in Appendix 2.

[18]*Id.* at §IV commentary.

B. When to Retain the Expert

The relationship between the attorney and the expert should be collaborative, not sterile. Too often, attorneys and mental health experts view one another as remote and unapproachable. This is a mistake. In spite of the necessity for objectivity on the part of the psychiatric expert, the expert is an important member of the legal team.

The mental health expert should be retained early in the case. This will permit the expert to help educate the attorney concerning the mental health issues involved in the case, and if the expert arrives at an adverse conclusion about the case, another expert may be chosen before the designation deadline. The first expert can then be treated as a consultant, and all communications between that expert and the attorney can be protected by the work product privilege.

If possible, the expert should be involved in the development of the theory of the case. For example, in a sexual harassment case, the defendant might seek to defend the case by steadfastly denying that any of the alleged conduct occurred (even though this might not be entirely true). The expert's evaluation of the plaintiff, however, might reveal a hypersensitivity to sexual cues on the part of the plaintiff suggesting that the plaintiff did not react to the alleged harasser's compliments and requests for dates as a "reasonable woman" would have done. The time to reconcile these inconsistent defenses is early in the case, not on the eve of trial after depositions of the accused harasser and the expert have been taken.

In addition, since experts do not themselves have subpoena power, and since the actual mental examination of the plaintiff is relatively short and the plaintiff may not be completely forthcoming about all aspects of his or her life, it is essential that the expert work with the attorney to ensure that a variety of records are obtained to permit the expert to render a fully informed opinion, and particularly one that may assist the expert in determining whether the cause of the plaintiff's condition is the workplace incident at issue or something else.[19]

C. Practical Aspects of Retaining an Expert

After an appropriate expert has been selected, it is important to structure the relationship between the attorney and the expert in a manner designed to avoid conflicts and problems and to maximize the expert's effectiveness. The expert and attorney may wish to formalize the terms of their relationship in an engagement letter agreement, so that no misunderstandings develop later.[20] Regardless of whether a formal letter agreement is used, the following items should be considered.

---

[19]*See* Chapter 7, Preparing the Case for the Expert.
[20]Sample engagement letters appear in Appendix 4.

1. Scheduling Issues

The reality of forensic practice is that the expert (like the attorneys and the parties) is largely at the mercy of the court with respect to scheduling. Trials may be continued without notice, or delays may occur that would require changing an expert's anticipated time to testify. This requires that the expert remain somewhat flexible in scheduling. The attorney should explain all scheduling issues to the expert, and the expert should advise the attorney as soon as possible of any scheduling limitations that may be salient.

2. Budgetary Issues

The attorney and the expert should establish a budget at the outset of their relationship. Whether the expert will be paid by a plaintiff's attorney advancing expenses, a party, or an insurance company, resources typically are not unlimited, and it is essential that both the attorney and the expert have a clear understanding of how much the expert's services will cost. The expert must stay reasonably within the budget or obtain approval from the attorney in the event of unforeseen complications that will increase costs. In addition, if the expert intends to incur significant costs, such as travel, rental of an examination facility, or psychological testing, this should be cleared with the attorney in advance.

3. Billing Issues

The attorney should become familiar with the expert's billing policies and practices. Some of these issues include the following:

- Will different billing rates be used for record review as opposed to testimony?
- Will the expert charge for travel, and if so, at what rate?
- Does the expert have a minimum charge (for example, two or four hours) for depositions or other testimony?
- How often will bills be submitted?
- Will a cancellation charge apply if a deposition is canceled or a trial is postponed?

4. Payment Issues

Although in most cases the expert will submit billing statements to the attorney, the attorney and the expert should have a clear understanding of who is responsible for paying the bills. On the plaintiff's side, will the plaintiff's attorney be advancing costs or will the bills be paid directly by the plaintiff? On the defense side, will the attorney pay the bills and seek reimbursement from the client, or will the bills be forwarded to the client or to an insurance carrier for payment? If the bills are to be paid by someone other than the attorney (i.e., plaintiff, defendant employer, or insurance carrier), that person or entity should also execute the engagement agreement if one is used. This provides the expert with the option of suing the responsible party directly in the event of nonpayment, instead of having to sue an attorney from whom the expert might wish to obtain future engagements.

IV. The Expert's Approach to the Conduct of the Evaluation

The attorney should become familiar with the expert's approach to conducting the forensic evaluation of the plaintiff. These matters are treated substantively elsewhere in this volume,[21] and the attorney should be aware of the expert's approach to them in order to ensure that a comprehensive evaluation of the plaintiff will occur and that issues relevant to the litigation will be fully developed.

A. Record Review

The attorney should inquire of the expert which records are needed for the expert's review so that they may be obtained and furnished to the expert. Records commonly required include the plaintiff's medical records, psychotherapy records, employment records, school records, and court records from any criminal, divorce, bankruptcy, or other civil cases. Other records may be needed as well. The attorney should be wary of an expert who professes to have little or no need to review records, as these records provide an essential component of the plaintiff's clinical picture.

B. The Forensic Interview

Each evaluator will have his or her particular style of examination. Several elements, however, should be uniform across most examinations.[22] At the beginning of the evaluation, the evaluator should explain the context and purposes of the examination to the plaintiff and inform him or her that the information provided will become part of the litigation process and will not be confidential. The evaluator should then obtain as thorough a history as possible from the plaintiff about the events leading up to the particular issue at dispute in the employment litigation. The evaluator also should elicit from the plaintiff as much history as possible about his or her life outside work. The evaluator should inquire about past medical and psychiatric history, focusing on particular

---

[21]*See* Chapter 7, Preparing the Case for the Expert; Chapter 9, The Mental Examination of the Plaintiff, and Chapter 10, Psychological Testing.

[22]Gordon D. Strauss, *The Psychiatric Interview, History, and Mental Status Examination, in* COMPREHENSIVE TEXTBOOK OF PSYCHIATRY/VI, *supra* note 2, at 521.

symptom patterns that have occurred through the years, and about current and prior substance abuse.

The evaluator should also explore whether the plaintiff suffered physical, sexual, or emotional abuse as a child. Other relevant inquiries include whether the plaintiff has any history of self-inflicted violence or violence toward others. Has the plaintiff contemplated either? How does the plaintiff manage conflict and feelings of anger—does he or she use threats or intimidation as a means to control interpersonal relationships? Such assessments can be crucial in assessing not only the plaintiff's legal claim (e.g., how the plaintiff interprets events and how he or she may have contributed to an escalating dynamic of hostility), but also the plaintiff's current emotional status as the litigation is proceeding.

The evaluator should also inquire about the plaintiff's family—the plaintiff's own marital family and children, if applicable, as well as the plaintiff's family of origin. The evaluator should examine whether other members of the plaintiff's family have suffered from medical or mental illnesses. The evaluator should also ask about interpersonal relations within the family. How does the plaintiff relate to his or her relatives? One should certainly not assume that such information is irrelevant to an examination about employment. Almost uniformly people will relate to adults in their current situation (including employers and fellow employees) quite similarly to the ways in which they relate to family members. Similar inquiries should be made about the plaintiff's interpersonal relations with peers and teachers in school, as well as the nature and quality of the plaintiff's current friendships.

The evaluator should additionally inquire extensively about the plaintiff's work history, including, if relevant, any military history. The evaluator should explore whether patterns of relationships in other areas of the plaintiff's life (e.g., patterns relating to family, friends, and teachers) recur within the work environment as well.

The evaluator should also explore the relationship the plaintiff has had with litigation and the legal system. Has there been a history of grievances or litigation associated not only with the work setting, but with events outside it as well? Does the plaintiff have a criminal history? Is there a history of using litigation to resolve or avoid certain interpersonal conflicts?

Throughout the examination, the evaluator assesses two other important areas of the plaintiff's functioning. First is the plaintiff's overall judgment. Does the plaintiff act appropriately in given situations? Does the plaintiff repeatedly place himself or herself in difficult, or even dangerous, situations? Second is the plaintiff's level of insight. The more insight the plaintiff has, the more likely he or she will benefit from treatment, and possibly the more likely he or she will act reasonably during the course of litigation. The less insight the plaintiff has, the more he or she will blame problems on external factors. Persons with poor insight often will blame others, including employers and fellow employees, for problems that clearly are rooted in other areas of the litigant's life.

In a comprehensive evaluation, the evaluator will gather crucial information from each of these lines of inquiry. It is therefore important for the evaluator to spend as much time as possible with the plaintiff. A potential expert who can spend only a limited amount of time with the plaintiff, or who insists that an evaluation lasting only an hour or two is sufficient, should be avoided.

C. Psychological Testing

Often evaluators use personality tests or inventories.[23] In general, these psychological tests are sets of questions or other stimuli, such as pictures, that require an individual to respond in a certain way. In some tests, the examinee chooses a particular alternative, or fills in a blank, or describes a statement as true or false. In other tests, the examinee describes a picture or tells a story, while the examiner focuses the examinee's responses on certain topics or questions.

Psychological testing can greatly aid an evaluator in a case. Yet while these tests may be an important component of the psychological evaluation of a plaintiff, none of them—no matter how standardized or validated—can provide certainty. Many attorneys falsely assume that psychological testing gives "real" answers that are somehow more reliable than data obtained in clinical interviews. Some forensic evaluators even make claims about litigants based solely on the results of psychological testing, without benefit of a personal interview of the litigant. Such "blind" evaluations should be viewed with much caution. Attorneys are well advised not to proceed with expert testimony about psychological testing without having first given the evaluator an opportunity to do a thorough interview of the plaintiff as well as review records, unless the testimony is intended solely to rebut an opposing expert's opinions concerning testing.

The attorney should also ensure that the expert has sufficient expertise in administering and interpreting psychological tests. Psychiatrists—unlike psychologists—ordinarily do not receive substantial training in psychological testing, although many psychiatrists have sufficient familiarity with the Minnesota Multiphasic Personality Inventory-2 (MMPI-2) to use it as a supporting component of their evaluation. If psychological testing is to be a salient issue in an employment lawsuit and a party's desired expert is a psychiatrist, consideration should be given to having the expert associate with a psychologist who will administer and interpret psychological testing.

V. The Nature and Scope of the Expert's Testimony

A. Qualification of the Expert

Attorneys should qualify a mental health expert using the same litigation techniques they use to qualify any other type of expert. By use of an affidavit or direct testimony, they should establish a foundation for the expert's qualifications and experience. They should highlight any special training or expertise the expert has in the area of forensic mental health, as well as prior experience in evaluating plaintiffs in employment lawsuits. Similarly, attorneys should elicit the expert's opinion, either via a report or by testimony, using standard report formats or standard questions.

---

[23] *See generally* Robert W. Butler & Paul Satz, *Personality Assessment of Adults and Children, in* COMPREHENSIVE TEXTBOOK OF PSYCHIATRY/VI, *supra* note 2, at 544.

The more familiar the expert is with legal procedure, through either training or experience, the less the attorney will have to acquaint the expert with such concepts as relevance, prejudice, or the permissible scope of expert testimony. If the expert does not have extensive experience in forensic evaluation and testimony, though, the attorney will have to educate the expert exhaustively in the pragmatic aspects of legal procedure and etiquette. Most standard training programs in mental health provide little, if any, exposure to forensic practice. The average mental health professional is almost as ignorant as the layperson of even the most common aspects of litigation and may need extended coaching in such basic areas as cogency and style of presentation.

Yet whether the attorney is dealing with seasoned experts or neophytes, all expertise in mental health is filled with clinical uncertainty.[24] It is true that many, if not most, mental health treatments now have solid scientific studies behind them demonstrating efficacy and accuracy. Modern mental health practice is much more about science than it was even 25 years ago. Nevertheless, human behavior is exceedingly difficult to quantify or predict.

The attorney should allow, and if necessary encourage, the expert to be definitive when appropriate and yet tentative when appropriate. Even seasoned experts can fall into the trap of believing that litigation requires them to be "certain" about the evaluations. Unfortunately, many attorneys give the expert this impression or even demand it of them. This will only lead to trouble for the expert and for the attorney. An evaluation will be much more credible— and will be much more likely to survive cross-examination and opposing testimony—if it is couched in words that show thoroughness of opinion and evaluation, yet also humility in the reporting and prediction of results.

B. Admissibility Issues

Ever since the United States Supreme Court set federal standards for the admissibility of expert testimony in the case of *Daubert v. Merrill Dow Pharmaceuticals, Inc.*[25] (after which most states adopted similar standards for admissibility under their particular state rules), attorneys have been focusing more on the strength and substance of experts' opinions. Although the requirements of *Daubert* and its progeny are more fully outlined elsewhere in this volume,[26] a few points are worth noting.

In general, if an expert has done a thorough evaluation similar to the one described herein and has then formulated that evaluation at least partially in the language of *DSM-IV-TR*, the attorney calling the expert should not have any *Daubert* problems. The diagnostic categories of *DSM-IV-TR* have been

---

[24]Harold J. Bursztajn, Albert E. Scherr, & Archie Brodsky, *The Rebirth of Forensic Psychiatry in Light of Recent Historical Trends in Criminal Responsibility,* 17 PSYCHIATRIC CLINICS N. AM. 611 (1994).

[25]509 U.S. 579 (1993).

[26]See Chapter 15, Avoiding and Attacking "Junk Science."

and continue to be exhaustively tested in rigorous scientific trials. Furthermore, the interview and examination techniques discussed earlier are standard and are taught in all reputable programs of mental health training.

If the expert is providing information based on psychological testing, the expert should know about the reliability and validity data of the test being discussed. If the expert uses a well-established test such as the MMPI-2, such data are extensive and well recognized. Some tests or questionnaires, however, may be quite idiosyncratic. Without adequate data to support them, such tests could face admissibility problems as well as vigorous attack on cross-examination.

In addition, testimony about interpersonal or intrapsychic processes will likely be admissible if presented properly. Even though it is fashionable in some circles to downplay unconscious processes as "psychobabble,"[27] the scientific evidence for such processes is very strong.[28] Moreover, in spite of a flurry of recent theories questioning the importance of early family interactions in the development of adult behavior patterns, the evidence is also quite strong that there remains a significant correlation between childhood attachment patterns with caregivers and adult patterns of interpersonal relationships.[29]

The attorney should be concerned, however, about experts who eschew standardized diagnostic patterns in favor of "syndromes" that are not described in *DSM-IV-TR*. Such syndromes may not be well established and, even worse, may be a product of the expert's own particular ideology. For example, an expert may speak of a "patient-therapist (or in this context, employee-employer) sex syndrome," in which a patient or employee shows particular symptoms and signs of trauma following sexual relations with a therapist or supervisor. Such symptoms and signs may indeed be present in the plaintiff, but they could well be the same symptoms or signs of distress that follow any significant, painful event. There may be nothing special about this syndrome except its label, which merely restates the conditions of the event without adding any new information to the diagnosis.

C. The Expert's Opinion

Different causes of action in employment litigation—wrongful termination, discrimination or harassment claims, ADA claims, for example—focus on

---

[27] Linda Stout Saunders, Harold J. Bursztajn & Archie Brodsky, *Recovered Memory and Managed Care: HB 236's Post-Daubert "Science" Junket,* 17 N.H. TRIAL BAR NEWS 27 (1995) (describing attempts to forbid, via legislation, testimony based on certain types of psychotherapy because they allegedly are not "scientific").

[28] *See, e.g.,* COGNITIVE SCIENCE AND THE UNCONSCIOUS (Dan J. Stein ed., 1997); EMPIRICAL PERSPECTIVES ON THE PSYCHOANALYTIC UNCONSCIOUS (Robert F. Bornstein & Joseph M. Masling eds., 1998).

[29] *See, e.g.,* DANIEL J. SIEGEL, THE DEVELOPING MIND: TOWARD A NEUROBIOLOGY OF INTERPERSONAL EXPERIENCE (1999); JIM GRIGSBY & DAVID STEVENS, NEURODYNAMICS OF PERSONALITY (2000).

different elements of mental health functioning. In general, though, an expert's opinion can cover as many as four main areas.

First, the expert can give an opinion concerning the presence or absence of one or more mental disorders, as well as the severity of each such illness. A diagnosis of no mental disorder does not necessarily mean that the employee did not suffer emotional distress, just that the distress, if it existed, was not so serious as to constitute or result in a mental disorder.

Second, the expert can describe the prognosis and possible treatment for the disorder(s) diagnosed. This information usually helps determine the scope of the damages claimed. Some disorders have clear prognoses and treatments. Others are far more ill defined, requiring more speculation as to the course and efficacy of treatment.

Third, the expert may opine concerning whether the mental disorder diagnosed as caused by events in the workplace or instead brought about by other causes. Some cases are quite clear. If a person sustains a head injury at work, for example, leading to serious psychological changes in behavior that had never before been noted, one can easily link the cause (the work accident) to the effect (brain damage). For most cases not involving a physical trauma, however, the issue of causation is far from easy. Multiple factors lead to and exacerbate emotional illness. A good forensic evaluator should consider credible alternative explanations for a plaintiff's condition, even if the plaintiff and his or her attorney are reluctant to do so. An evaluator should be able to articulate such possibilities while still coming to a reasonably certain opinion as to the most likely causes of the plaintiff's condition.

Fourth, an expert can offer an opinion as to what role, if any, the plaintiff's psychopathology played in the workplace incidents at issue in the litigation. This is particularly true in harassment and discrimination cases where the plaintiff has a personality disorder or disorders that predated the incident being litigated.[30] An evaluator who has conducted a thorough evaluation will have gleaned much information about the plaintiff's intrapsychic and interpersonal issues. For example, how does the plaintiff balance issues of independence and dependence? How does he cope with strong emotion? What patterns of interpersonal relationships are there in her life? How do these patterns play out in the work setting? Often a plaintiff with a personality disorder will instigate or exacerbate dysfunction in the workplace that ultimately leads to the filing of a lawsuit for harassment or discrimination.

VI. Expert's Vulnerabilities in Court

When using mental health experts in employment litigation, the attorney should consider several vulnerabilities that all mental health experts face when preparing legal reports and testimony. Even though no particular expert will have all

---

[30]For a detailed discussion of personality disorders, see Chapter 6.

of these vulnerabilities, every expert will have at least some of them. The attorney should discuss these potential issues with the expert throughout the course of the litigation, so that neither party overlooks them and thus remains unprepared for adverse consequences from them.

A. Problems with Limited Evaluations

Every forensic evaluation is a limited evaluation. Even if an evaluator spends eight or nine hours with a litigant—a substantial amount of time for most routine mental health evaluations—the evaluator has still only seen the litigant in a limited setting, without the benefit of observing him or her over an extended period of time. Most mental illnesses wax and wane over time. Even though one can strengthen the findings of an examination with information from adequate record review and other collateral sources, such information is still secondhand. The adequately prepared expert acknowledges these limitations and accordingly does not overargue the case—while also not downplaying the wealth of very useful information that can be gleaned even from examinations as short as a few hours.

A corollary problem is the problem of accidental or, even worse, willful misinformation. When an evaluator meets a litigant for only a few hours, the evaluator must always keep the diagnosis of malingering (including the exaggeration of symptoms that do exist) in mind. In a routine clinical evaluation, the treating clinician rarely considers that a patient is faking problems. Even if it appears that the patient is faking some problems, the clinician may still not choose to address that situation immediately, preferring to wait until an opportune time to explore why the patient feels the need to dissimulate with the therapist.

In contrast, every forensic evaluator must bear in mind the potential that the litigant is malingering. Several excellent resources are available to help clinicians and lawyers spot malingering.[31] As discussed above, results of the MMPI-2 may also be helpful in spotting the problem. An attorney should make sure that the expert she has retained is at least aware of the problem of malingering and can explain how she will examine for it to try to confirm or disconfirm it.

For example, evaluators should always at least consider the possibility of malingering when they are examining a litigant who is claiming to suffer from Posttraumatic Stress Disorder (PTSD). The symptoms of PTSD are, for the most part, self-reported, so they are easy to fake. The diagnosis is also well known to the general public, so litigants may have easy access to a list of the symptoms of the disorder. In contrast to those who malinger PTSD, plaintiffs who suffer from true PTSD (1) attempt to minimize the association between

---

[31] *See, e.g.,* Chapter 11, Malingering: Distortion and Deception in Employment Litigation; Phillip J. Resnick, *Malingering, in* PRINCIPLES AND PRACTICE, *supra* note 1, at 417; Mark J. Mills & Mark S. Lipian, *Malingering, in* COMPREHENSIVE TEXTBOOK OF PSYCHIATRY/VI, *supra* note 2, at 1614.

the symptoms and the traumatic event, (2) blame themselves for the event's occurrence, (3) initially deny the emotional impact of the event, (4) are reluctant to recount any details of the stressor, and (5) feel angry at themselves for being unable to overcome the symptoms.[32] An evaluator should look carefully for the presence—or more important, the absence—of these factors during the examination of a litigant who is claiming to suffer from PTSD.

Finally, no evaluator ever has "complete enough" access to outside information. The expert who has only limited access to outside information should be quite tentative in his or her conclusions. Yet even with access to large amounts of outside information, the expert should always hold open the possibility that new information could disconfirm hypotheses based on information that is already known.

B. Financial Bias

The *Ethical Guidelines for the Practice of Forensic Psychiatry* of the American Academy of Psychiatry and Law state that "[c]ontingency fees, because of the problems that these create in regard to honesty and efforts to obtain objectivity, should not be accepted."[33] The bias of an expert who will be paid only if the side retaining him or her wins is obvious. Yet many plaintiff's experts who also serve as the treating clinician essentially work on a contingency fee basis when they perform therapy or other treatment for the plaintiff on a lien basis. Such liens are common in the workers' compensation context, but they occur as well in civil lawsuits, particularly where the plaintiff's attorney refers the plaintiff to the clinician for treatment. An expert whose lien will likely go unsatisfied if the plaintiff fails to win a monetary award is vulnerable to being attacked as biased.

Whether or not the treating clinician formally asserts a lien for services rendered against the litigation proceeds is immaterial. The net result is that the plaintiff will owe the clinician a substantial amount of money that likely will be uncollectible if the plaintiff fails to recover damages, and the clinician's opinion is instrumental toward such a recovery. The clinician therefore will be vulnerable to attack on cross-examination as essentially working on a "contingent fee"; that is, if the expert's opinion does not produce a victory for the plaintiff, the expert is not likely to get paid.

This problem can arise on the defense side as well, if the expert has a large receivable balance going into trial. Opposing counsel might suggest that the expert will not get paid if the defense loses, thereby tainting the objectivity of the expert. The obvious solution is for the expert—whether retained by plaintiff or defense—to get paid up to date just before trial.

---

[32]Harold J. Bursztajn, P.T. Joshi, S.M. Sutherland & D.A. Tomb, *Recognizing Posttraumatic Stress*, PATIENT CARE, Mar. 30, 1995, at 40.

[33]*Id. See also* Report 18 of the Board of Trustees of the American Medical Association (1998) ("the physician as a witness . . . should not accept compensation that is contingent upon the outcome of the litigation").

C. Ethical Issues

Both the psychiatric and psychological professions have established ethical guidelines to govern forensic practice in their respective fields. The American Academy of Psychiatry and the Law has adopted *Ethical Guidelines for the Practice of Forensic Psychiatry*.[34] The Committee on Ethical Guidelines for Forensic Psychologists of Division 41 of the American Psychological Association and the American Board of Forensic Psychology have promulgated *Specialty Guidelines for Forensic Psychologists*.[35] These guidelines address numerous ethical issues of forensic practice, including confidentiality and disclosures, competence, maintaining objectivity, and conflicts of interest. While violation of these standards may carry consequences for a clinician within his or her profession, such violations might also be highlighted on cross-examination of the expert. Attorneys therefore should familiarize themselves with these ethical standards.

VII. The Mental Health Expert as Litigation Consultant

A mental health professional can be very valuable as a consultant throughout the litigation process, even though not eventually retained to provide evaluation and testimony. Before the attorney even takes on a case, the consultant can review materials to see the strengths and weaknesses of the case. Although many attorneys use medically trained personnel such as nurses to review cases in which nonpsychiatric issues are raised, attorneys would be well advised to use a mental health professional to evaluate cases in which psychological and psychiatric issues are at stake. Most standard training for nurses and other allied health personnel does not include enough specialized training in mental health issues to provide such screeners adequate understanding of all the complexities of a mental health case.

Once litigation begins, the consultant then can help the attorney in all phases of the case. In the discovery phase of litigation, the consultant can help the attorney determine which material is relevant to the mental health issues, aiding in the preparation of focused interrogatories, document requests, and deposition questions. The consultant can also help the attorney understand the strengths and weaknesses of reports prepared by opposing experts, aiding the attorney in the preparation of appropriate rebuttal materials and cross-examination questions. If the consultant is not to be called to testify during the litigation, most state procedural rules allow the attorney to claim that the expert's opinions fall under the attorney's work product. Thus opposing counsel cannot force discovery of the consultant's impressions and opinions.

---

[34] These are set forth in Appendix 2.
[35] These are set forth in Appendix 3.

CHAPTER 3

CLINICAL EVALUATION AND CASE FORMULATION OF MENTAL AND EMOTIONAL INJURY CLAIMS

David R. Price, Ph.D.

I. Overview of Mental and Emotional Injury Claims and Issues

Claims of psychological injury for compensation have increased significantly in recent times. In fact, they have become increasingly common since their introduction in the late 1800s with the concept of "railway spine,"[1] the ancestor of present day Posttraumatic Stress Disorder (PTSD). Psychiatric disability claims have risen approximately 200 percent in the 1990s alone.[2] It is often difficult to evaluate claims of psychological injury that are attributed to a specific cause (such as an adverse employment event) since at any one time more than 28 percent of the adult population in the United States has a diagnosable psychiatric or substance abuse disorder[3] and over 25 percent of the population reports being on the verge of a nervous breakdown yearly.[4] This estimate does not include the percentage of the population who have normally occurring psychological symptoms that do not rise to the threshold of a diagnosable mental disorder. For example, it is extremely important to differentiate between whether someone is experiencing a true clinical depression or just the "blues" that all of us normally experience.

---

[1] SHOBAL V. CLEVENGER, SPINAL CONCUSSION (1889).
[2] Deborah Griffin, *Managing the Early Resolution of Psychiatric Claims*, presentation at International Claims Association's 89th Annual Meeting (1998).
[3] Darrel Regier et al., *The De Facto U.S. Mental and Addictive Disorders Service System*, 50 ARCHIVES GEN. PSYCHIATRY 85 (1993).
[4] Ralph Swindle et al., *Responses to Nervous Breakdowns in America Over a 40-Year Period: Mental Policy Implications*, 55 AM. PSYCHOLOGIST 740 (2000).

Mental disorders commonly occur in the adult population, but this does not mean that they necessarily result in a psychiatric impairment that affects one's ability to be employed. With more than 28 percent of our adult population having a psychiatric or addictive disorder (which means that in excess of 50 million adults have a diagnosable mental disorder), a substantial portion of these persons are employed. It may well be, therefore, that a psychiatric or psychological disorder that is claimed to be the result of some specific cause of action in the employment setting may actually have been a preexisting disorder, a substance abuse disorder, or a personality disorder unrelated to one's employment.

Unfortunately, most symptoms common to psychiatric disorders are homogenous rather than heterogenous. That is to say, one symptom, such as a loss of concentration or depressed mood, may be prevalent in a number of disorders. Depressed mood is often the easiest to confuse. Twenty different diagnosable depressive disorders are listed in the American Psychiatric Association's *Diagnostic and Statistical Manual of Mental Disorders (DSM-IV-TR)*,[5] and depressed mood is found as a symptom or associated feature in over 200 other mental and physical disorders. Depressed mood also routinely occurs in normal, everyday life and does not reach a diagnostic threshold for depression. Ideally for purposes of diagnostic certainty, a symptom would not occur in normal everyday functioning but would occur only with a pathological state, such as in the case of a fractured bone. This situation does not exist with mental disorders, which may be characterized by many overlapping symptoms and few unique and specific symptoms. It takes a well-trained mental health professional with considerable diagnostic skill to look at the overall constellation of symptoms, the etiology, the course, and the duration of a disorder in order to render an acceptable diagnosis. This is often best accomplished by a careful analysis of the individual's medical and psychiatric history in addition to a face-to-face interview, which can produce only a self-report of subjective symptoms.

Face-to-face interviews in and of themselves are not necessarily adequate for a valid mental diagnosis. Many diagnoses of psychiatric or psychological disorders in mental and emotional injury claims are accomplished solely via interview of the litigant and based upon the litigant's own self-reported symptoms, which can often result in error. The Social Security Administration routinely employs psychologists and psychiatrists to review medical and psychiatric records to determine if a person has an acceptable psychiatric impairment. So as to avoid bias, the SSA specifically directs the psychologists and psychiatrists not to base their decisions on face-to-face evaluations. Research has indicated that psychologically naive individuals can report the symptoms necessary in a face-to-face interview to receive diagnoses of Posttraumatic Stress Disorder, Major Depression, Anxiety Disorder, or brain

---

[5] AMERICAN PSYCHIATRIC ASSOCIATION, DIAGNOSTIC AND STATISTICAL MANUAL OF MENTAL DISORDERS (4th ed. text rev. 2000) [hereinafter DSM-IV-TR].

injury.⁶ There is also evidence indicating that litigants respond differently than nonlitigants regarding their symptoms and report a higher percentage of symptoms than do nonlitigants.⁷ Recent research reveals that people in litigation versus people with similar injuries who are not in litigation report superior preinjury functioning and lower postinjury functioning.⁸ This suggests that the litigation process may affect the reporting of symptoms. There is also research indicating that the presence of financial incentives causes an exaggeration of symptoms of pain⁹ and brain injury¹⁰ and that individuals' reports of their symptoms, such as their memory functioning, are unreliable when compared with their performance on diagnostic tests, even when malingering is ruled out.¹¹ In summary, research suggests that one should be cautious about overly relying on the self-report of an individual who is involved in the litigation process or who has the potential for compensation.

Indeed, *DSM-IV-TR* advises clinicians to carefully evaluate the potential for malingering if the case is in a medicolegal context (i.e., attorney referral), because litigation may distort a patient's self-reports.¹² Because of the complexity of mental disorders and the likelihood of having comorbid and premorbid disorders, it is often advisable to have a careful evaluation and formulation of the mental and emotional injury claim by a skilled forensic mental health professional. *DSM-IV-TR* recognizes that emotional symptoms arise from a variety of sources and recommends that a multiaxial diagnostic system be utilized in evaluating and diagnosing mental disorders, stating that "the use of the multiaxial system facilitates comprehensive and systematic evaluation with attention to the various mental disorders and general medical conditions, psychosocial and environmental problems, and level of functioning that might be overlooked if the focus was on assessing a single presenting problem."¹³ This is exactly what one's case formulation and case analysis should accomplish—a thorough and systematic evaluation of a claim and its merits. Should one complete such a case formulation and analysis, one may well discover that the

---

⁶Paul R. Lees-Haley & John T. Dunn, *The Ability of Naive Subjects to Report Symptoms of Mild Brain Injury, Posttraumatic Stress Disorder, Major Depression, and Generalized Anxiety Disorder*, 50 J. CLINICAL PSYCHOL. 252 (1994).

⁷Paul R. Lees-Haley & Richard S. Brown, *Neuropsychological Complaint Base Rates of 170 Personal Injury Claimants*, 8 ARCHIVES CLINICAL NEUROPSYCHOLOGY 8 (1993).

⁸Paul R. Lees-Haley, et al., *Response Bias in Plaintiffs' Histories*, 11 BRAIN INJURY 791 (1998).

⁹Martin L. Rohling, Laurence M. Binder, & Jennifer Langhinrichsen-Rohling, *A Meta-Analytic Review of the Association Between Financial Compensation and the Experience and Treatment of Chronic Pain*, 14 HEALTH PSYCHOL. 537 (1995).

¹⁰Laurence M. Binder & Martin L. Rohling, *Money Matters: A Meta-Analytic Review of the Effects of Financial Incentives on Recovery after Closed-head Injury*, 153 AM. J. PSYCHIATRY 7 (1996).

¹¹Carl B. Dodrill, *Myths of Neuropsychology*, 11 CLINICAL NEUROPSYCHOLOGIST 1 (1997).

¹²DSM-IV-TR, *supra* note 5, at 739.

¹³*Id.* at 27.

person's symptoms do not deviate from normalcy sufficiently to merit a diagnosis. The clinician may have alternative explanations for the symptoms, or the symptoms may indeed be incident-specific and related to the cause of action. Additionally, the clinical disorder may occur along with the existence of other mental disorders (known as comorbid disorders; personality disorders are common examples) that have been exacerbated by the litigation process or may actually be the driving force behind the litigation claim. It therefore is well advisable for legal counsel handling an employment law claim to have such a claim reviewed by competent mental health professionals skilled in case analysis so as to determine both the value and veracity of the claim.

A thorough case formulation and analysis should be of benefit to both the defense and the plaintiff's attorney. For the defense attorney it will reveal the inherent flaws of the plaintiff's claims and may suggest alternative causes for the plaintiff's symptoms, indicate symptom exaggeration, or even document malingering. It may also indicate that the plaintiff indeed had an incident-specific disorder that is in remission but for which the claimed symptoms remain as litigation artifacts. A case analysis will also benefit the plaintiff's attorney as it may well be that the plaintiff has a preexisting mental disorder that made him or her more vulnerable to adverse workplace events; for example, a person with Dependent Personality Disorder may be especially susceptible to sexual harassment. Alternatively, the plaintiff may have had a preexisting mood disorder that had been exacerbated by workplace difficulties. The case formulation is beneficial to help all participants in litigation determine whether:

- Workplace events caused the mental disorder;
- The mental disorder occurred first and contributed to the cause of action;
- The mental disorder came first and was exacerbated by the cause of action; or
- There is a mental disorder present but completely unrelated to the cause of action.

This chapter will recommend a procedure for case formulation and analysis, including the analysis of the claim and the cause of action, make recommendations for the evaluation of allegations of mental disorders, and suggest types of discovery necessary for the claim evaluation and analysis.

II. Evaluating the Context of the Injury Claim

In evaluating a mental or emotional injury claim, it is necessary to look at the climate and the context in which the claim occurred. For example, did the claimed psychological injury arise before the onset of litigation or after an attorney referral for evaluation and even months after the initiation of the litigation? One should remember that if the claim of mental injury arose after the attorney referral, that puts the burden upon the evaluating clinician to evaluate for malingering.

A. Severity of the Injury Alleged

The first step in analyzing a mental and emotional injury is to evaluate the severity of the alleged workplace events at issue. For example, Posttraumatic

Stress Disorders are known to occur following life-threatening stressors such as violent assault or being threatened with a life-threatening illness. PTSD does not routinely follow verbal sexual harassment absent a sexual assault. One should evaluate whether the cause of action was an acute event such as a job termination or a chronic event such as a long and extensive experience of discrimination or harassment. Occupational difficulties or termination from work are usually associated with the occurrence of brief disorders called Adjustment Disorders as opposed to chronic disorders, such as a Major Depressive Episode. In evaluating the context of the cause of action, counsel should always evaluate carefully the claimed cause of the injury and determine the following:

- Was there any real physical injury?
- Was the cause of action an acute event occurring once or was it a series of events occurring across time?
- What did the individual observation of the alleged workplace event(s) indicate? For example, what do the reports of coworkers, company medical personnel, or other employees suggest?
- Did the claimed mental disorder arise immediately after the event or events at issue or did it occur afterwards upon the initiation of litigation or attorney referral?

B. Treatment Provided

Similarly, it is advisable to evaluate the context of treatment, to determine who rendered the treatment and if the treatment protocol seemed reasonable. For example, if a plaintiff is alleging total disability due to depression secondary to a work-related event, it must be determined if the plaintiff is in fact being treated aggressively for that alleged depression and whether inpatient treatment or antidepressant medication was required, or whether the plaintiff simply underwent outpatient psychotherapy. It is also important to determine if the initial referral was from the plaintiff's primary care physician or some other individual, such as an attorney or a coworker involved in similar litigation. In evaluating the context of referral for psychological or psychiatric treatment one should carefully evaluate the following issues:

- Who made the referral? Note that it is a red flag for malingering if the plaintiff's attorney made the referral. This has been recognized by the plaintiffs' bar, which now often recommends a "clean medical handoff" in referring a patient for treatment by asking him or her to go see the family doctor and request a referral to a certain expert so as to "not cast any suspicion."[14] The issue of proper referral needs to be carefully explored.

---

[14]*See* C. Michael Bee, *How to Identify and Win the Mild Closed Head Injury Case*, paper presented at the Arkansas Trial Lawyers Association 1995 Annual Meeting (1995).

- How is the treatment provider paid? If treatment is provided on a lien basis, it should be scrutinized to ensure that it was all in fact necessary. Without the review of a health plan claims administrator and no limit on how many treatment sessions will be reimbursed, the number of treatment sessions performed on a lien basis is sometimes excessive and can make the plaintiff's condition appear more serious than it really is. In addition, where the plaintiff's expert is providing services on a lien basis, his or her testimony should be regarded with suspicion since the expert will have a financial investment in the outcome of the case.
- If the individual has had treatments by multiple providers, all of short duration, this may suggest litigation file building, a Somatoform Disorder (in which doctor shopping commonly occurs), or a characterological disorder such as a personality disorder. Personality disorders would be unrelated to the cause of action and would clearly preexist the employment issues. The presence of personality disorders should be carefully evaluated as they may have actually caused the employment difficulties at issue.
- Does the treatment meet a standard of common sense in relation to the severity of the alleged injury? Determine whether the treatment is of an intense, frequent nature, such as weekly psychotherapy, or intermittent, such as random or yearly contacts with one's treatment provider. Evaluate the specific nature of the treatment. A professional claiming to have been treating a litigant for a year may actually have done one evaluation and three follow-up medication checks at 90-day intervals.
- Always evaluate whether the treatment was comprehensive in nature. Did it include medication and psychotherapy? Evaluate the type of psychotherapy— was it individual psychotherapy, group psychotherapy or marital therapy? The individual may be receiving treatment for issues unrelated to the cause of action, such as marital therapy, which would cloud the claims related to the cause of action.
- Always examine the insurance codes that have been offered on billing or insurance statements for the treatment to see what type of treatment was rendered. These are codes that identify what treatment was rendered (e.g., 90844 would reflect 45–50 minutes of psychotherapy). Also verify any diagnostic codes related to the *DSM-IV-TR* that may have been turned over to a health insurer for reimbursement under third-party treatment coverage in case they are inconsistent with the alleged compensable disorder. For example, a plaintiff's therapist may report that the plaintiff has a Major Depressive Disorder, Single Episode (*DSM-IV-TR* 296.20) as a compensable injury when the therapist's billing or insurance records report a *DSM-IV-TR* code of 296.30, which is Major Depressive Disorder, Recurrent. This identifies the depression as a preexisting condition.

C. Qualifications of Treaters and Experts

One should always carefully evaluate the opposing treater and expert. Was the treater competent to render the treatment given for the diagnostic condition that was diagnosed? Is the expert qualified to diagnose the condition? For example, sometimes a case will be encountered where a marital or family therapist will have rendered a diagnosis of Posttraumatic Stress Disorder for a plaintiff and then set out upon a course of treatment. Such diagnosis and treatment may be beyond the scope of the therapist's qualifications and license, however. Thus the credentials of the opposing treater and expert, including education and training, licensure, and experience, should be carefully evaluated. It is always advisable to make the following evaluations when looking at treaters and experts:

- Is the person's degree in a relevant specialty for which the diagnosis and treatment are being rendered? For example, does the person hold an M.D. degree with board certification in psychiatry, or instead a doctorate of education degree in educational counseling? The latter credential may not be sufficient qualification to diagnose mental illness in a litigation context.
- Does the treater or expert have sufficient expertise in the area in which he or she is rendering an opinion, such as Posttraumatic Stress Disorder?
- Has the treater or expert published books or articles or made relevant presentations in the area in which expertise is asserted?
- Did the treater or expert actually perform the treatment or evaluation as claimed or did someone else within his or her office, such as an unlicensed assistant, render such treatment?
- Did the treater or expert have a preexisting relationship with the litigant or attorneys involved?
- Did the treater or expert bill the attorney directly for his or her services, rather than billing the plaintiff or a health insurer?

III. Evaluating the Diagnosis

Oftentimes diagnoses in cases where mental and emotional injury claims are alleged are inadequate or incomplete. The naive mental health professional, particularly one who does not possess a doctorate, may offer overly simple descriptions of symptoms or syndromes that he or she then relates to some allegedly traumatic event solely on the basis of the litigant's self-report. These descriptions are often posed such as "Depression secondary to . . ." or "Posttraumatic . . . as a result of. . . ." They are not *DSM-IV-TR* criterion-related diagnoses and may not survive a Rule 702 challenge.[15] These diagnoses are typically not reimbursable by third-party health insurers and do not come accompanied with diagnostic codes. They are not published, are not testable, and are not accepted by the relevant scientific peer community.

A diagnosis therefore should be evaluated according to the following criteria:

---

[15]See Chapter 15, Avoiding and Attacking "Junk Science" in Employment Litigation.

- Is it a diagnosis contained in *DSM-IV-TR* or *ICD-10*[16]
- Is it a comprehensive multiaxial diagnosis recommended by *DSM-IV-TR*?
- Is treatment being provided for the condition diagnosed?
- Has the disorder been previously diagnosed in the litigant?
- Are there multiple diagnoses rendered?

A. Multiaxial Diagnoses

Diagnoses are often made on the basis of subjectively reported symptoms, self-reported descriptions, and/or observable behavior at any given point in time. The mental health professional can determine that a person may be depressed now but cannot say with 100 percent certainty, judging solely from the claimant's subjective self-report, that the depression was caused by any given event in the past. From the *Diagnostic and Statistical Manual of Mental Disorders—Third Edition*[17] in 1980 to the current text, *DSM-IV-TR*, this manual has recommended that clinicians diagnose mental and emotional disorders on a multiaxial system. It advises a "systematic evaluation with attention to the various disorders and general medical conditions, psychosocial and environmental problems, and level of functioning, that might be overlooked if the focus was on assessing a single presenting problem."[18] Without the use of this system, the typical clinician may look at a self-reported problem or focus on just a narrow range of symptoms and miss the pre-existing or concurrent disorders that may provide alternative explanations of the individual's symptoms. Just as an emergency room physician would not diagnose and treat a fractured femur while ignoring a gaping laceration, the mental health professional should not diagnose a self-reported depression and ignore an Alcohol Dependence or Partner Relational Problem.

One may find clinicians using the *International Classification of Diseases, Ninth Revision, Clinical Modification*[19] or the *ICD-10* in diagnosing mental disorders. *ICD-10's* Chapter V on "Mental and Behavioral Disorders" has codes and terms fully compatible with those of *DSM-IV-TR*. Mental health treatment providers typically will use a *DSM-IV-TR* code type primarily for reimbursement by third-party insurers or the federal government since its use has been mandated by the Health Care Finance Administration for purposes of reimbursement

---

[16] The official international coding system is set forth in WORLD HEALTH ORGANIZATION, INTERNATIONAL STATISTICAL CLASSIFICATION OF DISEASES AND RELATED HEALTH PROBLEMS (10th rev. 1992)(*ICD-10*). Cooperation between the American Psychiatric Association and the World Health Association has resulted in compatibility between *DSM-IV-TR* and *ICD-10*.

[17] AMERICAN PSYCHIATRIC ASSOCIATION, DIAGNOSTIC AND STATISTICAL MANUAL OF MENTAL DISORDERS (3rd ed. 1980).

[18] DSM-IV-TR, *supra* note 5, at 27.

[19] WORLD HEALTH ORGANIZATION, INTERNATIONAL CLASSIFICATION OF DISEASES (9th rev.1979).

under the Medicare system.[20] Additionally, the use of the multiaxial system is required by the American Medical Association's *Guide to the Evaluation of Permanent Impairment*.[21] Hence, the treater's records should be examined, along with billing records, to determine whether the diagnostic code numbers used across the board are consistent, not only within the litigation context but also for the health care treatment provider's reimbursement. Significant inconsistencies often occur between treatment notes, billing invoices, and insurance invoices. For example, the billing invoice to the health insurer may reflect that a doctor rendered psychiatric care while treatment records document that a social worker, in the doctor's employment, actually was the treatment provider. The treatment records may also reflect that the claimant was receiving marital counseling, while the invoices reflected a CPT code for individual counseling, since health insurers do not typically reimburse for marital therapy. Finally the claimant receiving marital therapy may have a listed diagnosis for the insurer of 309.0, an Adjustment Disorder with Depressed Mood, while in office records reflect a diagnosis of V61.10, Partner Relational Problem. Again, since health insurers do not usually reimburse for marital counseling, an inaccurate diagnosis of a form of depression may be listed in order to obtain reimbursement.

B. Reliability of Diagnoses

It has been noted that psychiatric diagnoses are not very reliable. In fact, research has found that agreement in diagnosis between two psychiatrists does not exceed 60 percent, with a reliability of about 40 percent.[22] In fact, one observer has commented about psychiatric diagnosis: "Doctors are loath to find nothing and say that nothing is wrong because they are afraid they might miss something. Doctors will typically rely on their patients' subjective complaints and offer a large number of diagnoses based on minimal objective findings."[23] Symptoms of a subjective self-reported nature of alleged distress are subject to interpretation not only by the examiner but by the reporter as well and this may serve to contaminate the diagnosis. In fact, research has documented that attorneys contaminate self-reports,[24] as does the litigation process.[25] As the individual claimants continue to report their history, they often inflate their

---

[20]DSM-IV-TR, *supra* note 5, at 1.
[21]AMERICAN MEDICAL ASSOCIATION, GUIDES TO THE EVALUATION OF PERMANENT IMPAIRMENT (5th ed. 2000).
[22]Bruce J. Ennis & Thomas R. Litwack, *Psychiatry and the Presumption of Expertise: Flipping Coins in the Courtroom*, 62 CAL. L.R. 701, 702 (1974).
[23]Eric H. Marcus, *The Psychiatric Diagnosis: Validity and Credibility Issues*, in THE INSURER'S HANDBOOK OF PSYCHOLOGICAL INJURY CLAIMS 1, 2 (David R. Price & Paul R. Lees-Haley eds., 1995).
[24]Paul R. Lees-Haley, *Attorneys Influence Expert Evidence in Forensic Psychological and Neuropsychological Cases*, 4 ASSESSMENT 321, 324 (1997).
[25]Lees-Haley et al., supra note 8; Lees-Haley & Brown, *supra* note 7.

preinjury functioning and magnify their postinjury symptoms and losses. It is unreasonable to assume that only those individuals of superoptimal functioning ever experience a traumatically induced mental injury. Claimants also tend to report symptoms that are not usually associated with psychiatric disorders but that are more often associated with central nervous system disorders, such as attention, concentration, and memory complaints.

In order for a psychiatric diagnosis ever to be reliable, it must reflect the same operational definition of diagnostic criteria that uniformly defines the diagnosis. The use of systematic and regular criteria to diagnose mental and emotional injuries facilitates consensus, allows the uniform collection and retrieval of information, and will facilitate effective and reliable communication between experts regarding the condition and associated features of that disorder. In *Daubert v. Merrill Dow Pharmaceuticals Inc.*,[26] the U.S. Supreme Court identified guidelines regarding the reliability of an expert's opinion and established four standards for ascertaining such reliability:

1. Whether the theory is capable of being or has been tested;
2. Whether it has been subject to peer review and publication;
3. The known rate of errors; and
4. Whether the theory or methodology meets with the general acceptance in the relevant scientific community.

Any diagnosis or diagnostic criteria not found in *DSM-IV-TR* or its companion work, the *ICD-10,* may well be inadmissible. The diagnoses found in *DSM-IV-TR* do meet universal acceptance, and more than 60 health organizations have endorsed or contributed to the compilation of the diagnoses contained therein.[27] In evaluating the reliability of a diagnosis, therefore, the following should be considered:

- Is the diagnosis based on criteria set forth in *DSM-IV-TR, ICD-9,* or *ICD-10?*
- Is the diagnosis a complete multiaxial diagnosis that includes a diagnosis of clinical disorders, developmental disorders, personality disorders, physical conditions, general medical disorders, and psychosocial stressors and that also assesses the subject's general level of functioning?
- Does the diagnosis support the treatment protocol rendered? If a plaintiff is alleging a permanent disabling condition, is appropriate treatment being rendered? For example, if plaintiff is claiming a permanent disabling depression but is receiving only sporadic treatment from a psychologist and not psychiatric care with antidepressant medication, the diagnosis should be viewed with suspicion and investigated further.
- Do the diagnoses rendered in the litigation or forensic evaluation match those rendered to a third-party payor such as a health insurer? These diagnostic codes can be located on "superbills," invoices, or receipts.

---

[26]509 U.S. 579 (1993).
[27]*DSM-IV-TR, supra* note 5, at 927.

- Has the examiner appropriately evaluated psychosocial stressors the individual may be having unrelated to the cause of action or as a consequence of it, and included a reporting of those stressors on Axis IV of the multiaxial diagnosis?

C. Assessment of Premorbid Functioning

Recent research has indicated that the self-reported premorbid functioning of persons in litigation is unreliable and likely exaggerated.[28] Other research has shown that the reports of self-reported memory are unreliable[29] and that litigants may overreport symptoms.[30] Premorbid functioning must therefore be evaluated objectively and carefully. It is best determined not by the self-report of the litigant but by review of academic, medical, and employment records. In evaluating preexisting intellectual condition and academic functioning, the following should be reviewed:

- Academic performance,
- Whether all course work was actually completed,
- Whether discipline was imposed for academic or misconduct reasons,
- Attendance records, and
- Participation in extracurricular activities.

The plaintiff's premorbid occupational history should also be evaluated, especially the following aspects:

- Evaluations and performance reviews,
- Disciplinary notices,
- Longevity and stability versus transient job behavior,
- Whether there was steady upward progression throughout a job or career, versus a drift downward that may be attributable to a premorbid condition, and
- Litigiousness, as reflected in lawsuits, grievances, and workers' compensation claims.

Similarly, the plaintiff's preexisting medical records must be reviewed carefully:

- Look for any record of a preexisting mental disorder such as depression, anxiety, PTSD, or bipolar disorder, including references to "nerves," or "nervousness," or "stress," as these may indicate a preexisting mental disorder.
- Search for any record of preexisting physical disorder that also presents psychiatric symptoms of agitation, anxiety, sleep disturbance, lethargy, or fatigue.
- Research pharmaceutical records. These should reveal the plaintiff's treating doctors and medications prescribed. Compare the records of the medications prescribed with the records of the medications actually purchased, to determine if the plaintiff was following the prescribed course of treatment. Look also

---

[28]Lees-Haley et al., *supra* note 8.
[29]Dodrill, *supra* note 11, at 7–9.
[30]Lees-Haley & Brown, *supra* note 7.

for multiple physicians prescribing controlled substances, which may indicate substance dependence.

Other premorbid stressors such as divorces, arrests, or financial distress must also be evaluated. These stressors may cause or exacerbate mental disorders that are being alleged to be the result of workplace events.

D. Assessment of the Effects of Litigation

Research indicates that litigation, with its possibility of compensation, has an effect on self-reported symptoms.[31] When groups of individuals with injuries for which there is the possibility of compensation are compared with persons with comparable injuries but no possibility of compensation, we see that those with the likelihood of compensation are less likely to profit from treatment and more likely to see themselves as disabled.[32] There is also research indicating that individuals in litigation may report symptoms that are not related to the litigation.[33] Litigation effects therefore must be considered in evaluating a case. A mental injury might be exacerbated by the claimant's obsessing over depositions, trial, or the costs of litigation. On the other hand, plaintiffs might be "educated" by their attorneys about various symptoms that might exist, which may lead naive and unsophisticated litigants to believe they have a disorder when, in fact they do not, even when malingering has been ruled out. To evaluate the effects of litigation on a claim, the following should be examined:

- Whether the claimed symptoms arose some time after the workplace events at issue;
- Whether symptoms were reported or treatment rendered before or after legal representation was obtained;
- Whether the plaintiff was sent by an attorney for treatment;
- Whether the plaintiff's attorney is the responsible party for payment for treatment (attorneys commonly are billed for evaluations of a plaintiff);
- Whether the plaintiff's medical records contain mention of litigation-induced stress or anxiety.

E. Assessment of Potential for Malingering and Symptom Exaggeration

In the evaluation of any mental and emotional injury claim, the possibility of malingering or symptom exaggeration must be considered. Certainly in any

---

[31] Lees-Haley et al., *supra* note 8.
[32] Binder & Rohling, *supra* note 10; Rohling, Binder & Langhinrichsen-Rohling, *supra* note 9.
[33] Lees-Haley & Brown, *supra* note 7.

cases involving financial compensation, symptom exaggeration is a concern. One authority has identified five types of malingering[34] that should be considered in claims involving compensation. They include the following, to which this author would add a sixth:

1. *Simulation*: The citing of symptoms that do not exist;
2. *Dissimulation*: The concealment or minimization of existing symptoms;
3. *Pure Malingering*: The citing of a disease does not exist at all;
4. *Partial Malingering*: The conscious exaggeration of existing symptoms or the assertion that prior genuine symptoms are still present;
5. *False Imputation*: Attribution to the injury of authentic symptoms consciously recognized to have no relationship to it;
6. *Iatrogenic Imputation*: Attribution by an examiner or treatment provider of genuine symptoms unrelated to an injury to that injury.

All of these need to be carefully evaluated within the litigation context. Malingering and symptom exaggeration are examined in substantial detail in Chapter 11, Malingering: Distortion and Deception in Employment Litigation.

F. Assessment of Iatrogenic Effects

An iatrogenic effect is a medical phenomenon that occurs when an examiner forms an opinion that an alleged condition produced symptoms but when no disease is actually present. That opinion is then communicated to the patient, who begins to believe he is suffering from a real disorder. This belief can be engendered not only by an examiner but by a litigant's attorney through various educational material that may be provided.

One observer has noted: "Psychiatric evaluation reports typically begin by referring to the individual being examined as a 'patient.' This can generate the automatic assumption that the individual has an illness. This automatic assumption then sets up for bias in which most every occurrence is taken as a 'symptom.' "[35] Iatrogenically triggered symptoms can also occur as a result of a litigant's own self-education, as information on the symptoms of various mental disorders are readily available at libraries, in bookstores, or on the Internet. Iatrogenic effects may be detected by the following:

- There is no evidence that the disorder actually occurred.
- The self-reported symptoms and claimed stress are inconsistent with a known diagnostic pattern.
- The perception of having a disorder begins after the initial relationship with a specific medical or mental health professional even when the report from that

---

[34]J. Randall Price, *Malingering and Symptom Exaggeration*, in THE INSURER'S HANDBOOK OF PSYCHOLOGICAL INJURY CLAIMS 21, 22 (David R. Price & Paul R. Lees-Haley eds., 1995).
[35]Marcus, *supra* note 23, at 2.

mental health professional is contradicted by other professionals involved in the case.
- There is evidence that one's legal representative has provided education to the litigant.
- There are indications that the medical/psychological examiner has provided information about the disorder to "educate" the litigant.

IV. Examples of Preexisting and Comorbid Psychiatric Disorders

There are a number of psychiatric disorders that may preexist or exist concomitantly with a disorder or disorders claimed to be the result of adverse workplace events. Counsel and the forensic examiner should be familiar with these disorders and their potential effect on the clinical presentation of the plaintiff.

A. Developmental Disorders

Developmental Disorders are essentially disorders that were in existence by childhood and would clearly predate any adverse employment action or interaction. The relevance of Developmental Disorders is that they predispose the individual to have other comorbid disorders, affect his or her ability to learn, think, and concentrate, and present an issue regarding reasonable accommodation. Developmental disorders generally encompass three groups: Attention Deficit Disorders, Intellectual Disorders, and Learning Disorders.

1. Attention Deficit/Hyperactivity Disorder

This is a disorder that arises in childhood and involves inattention, hyperactivity, impulsivity, or difficulties in accommodation. The Attention Deficit/Hyperactivity Disorder (ADHD) is characterized by the inability to sustain attention and concentration along with poor frustration tolerance. It is known to coexist with learning disabilities, especially dyslexia, and may lead to the development of conduct disorders. Individuals with this disorder often have poor academic records, a fact that may lead to a poor occupational history as well. Individuals with ADHD can also show abnormalities on a neuropsychological exam.

Theoretically these disorders are diagnosable in childhood prior to age six. The presence of these disorders is very rarely scrutinized in adults. Historically, it was commonly believed that people with ADHD grew out of it in their teens. Now it is recognized that ADHD continues into adult life and many individuals are often medicated to treat this condition through their adult life. Psychostimulants such as Ritalin or Adderall are the medications of choice in the treatment of ADHD.

Concurrent disorders often seen with Attention Deficit/Hyperactivity Disorder include the following:

Communication Disorders   Conduct Disorder
Functional Encopresis   Functional Enuresis
Generalized Anxiety Disorder   Learning Disorders
Major Depression   Oppositional Defiant Disorder
Specific Developmental Disorders   Tourette's Syndrome

In evaluating whether an Attention Deficit/Hyperactivity Disorder may be present, the following should be considered:

- Any notation in medical records, particularly pediatric records, that documents the prescription of stimulant medication such as Ritalin, Cylert, or Dexedrine is an indication that ADHD may be present.
- A previous diagnosis of Dyslexia or another learning disability may indicate the presence of ADHD.
- Academic records that reflect that a person has been in a self-contained class for the emotionally or educationally handicapped is a red flag for this condition.
- Key words such as "hyperactivity" or "Attention Deficit Disorder" located in pediatric or academic records are be an indication that this disorder may be present.

2. Intellectual Disorders

Traditionally, disorders of intellect were not presented as an issue in the workplace. However, more and more frequently these disorders are becoming a problem in the workplace, whether they are the result of Dementia (the loss of acquired intelligence as a result of a traumatic brain injury) or whether they are seen in individuals in the Borderline Range of Intelligence or in the Mild Range of Mental Retardation. Individuals in these areas can be found in the workforce, particularly in light of efforts to employ the disabled as a result of the Americans with Disabilities Act or voluntary employer initiatives. Persons with Borderline Intelligence (the range between retardation and average intellect, involving IQs of between 70 and 80) can actually acquire the skills necessary to be employed in semiskilled or skilled trade occupations. Individuals with Mild Mental Retardation (IQs from 55 to 69) may actually also be employed in unskilled, structured settings. Individuals with intellectual disorders are four times as likely as the general population to have comorbid psychiatric disorders.[36] Individuals functioning within this range can acquire academic skills up to the sixth to eighth grade level. Individuals with intellectual disorders can often show deficits on neuropsychological testing that would be secondary to the intellectual disorder and not an acquired cerebral insult. The typical individuals with intellectual disorders encountered in the workplace would likely be those with IQs between 60 and 79. Persons in this range can be frustrating to manage because they will sometimes attempt to mask their deficiency by stating that they understand something when in fact they do not. In evaluating the presence of any disorder of intellect, the following should be reviewed:

---

[36]*DSM-IV-TR, supra* note 5, at 45.

- Academic records, which are likely to document preexisting intellectual deficits and often will indicate specialized education or the interruption of education;
- Previous evaluations, in particular intellectual evaluations, that should document IQ;
- Evidence that the person has ever participated in any sheltered workshops for the vocational training of those with intellectual deficits.

3. Learning Disorders

Learning disorders have as their predominant characteristic impairment in the acquisition of social, cognitive, language, and intellectual academic skills. Specifically, such skills as reading, writing, arithmetic, and auditory comprehension may be impaired. This class of disorders includes the following:

Reading Disorder	Mathematics Disorder
Disorder of Written Expression	Development Coordination Disorder
Expressive Language Disorder	Mixed Receptive-Expressive Language Disorder
Phonological Disorder	Stuttering

Associated features of learning disorders can include the following:

40 percent school dropout rate	Deficits in attention and memory
Deficits in visual perception	Deficits in linguistic processes
Deficits in social skills	Language delays
Low self-esteem problems in cognitive processing[37]	Occupational difficulties

Individuals with pronounced learning disorders often have a corresponding impairment in their personal relationships. They typically have some difficulty in the development of perception and interpretation of social cues resulting in impaired social skills. Individuals with learning disorders are likely to have impairment in their frustration tolerance and in their ability to learn new concepts.

In evaluating whether a learning disorder is present, the following should be considered:

- Review all academic transcripts and pay particular attention to achievement testing such as the Otis-Lenin, Stanford Achievement Test, or the Comprehensive Test of Basic Skills. Compare test performances across nonverbal and verbal skills from the various cognitive skills assessed. These performances are often given in terms of standard scores, stanines, scaled scores, and percentile scores. Look for a pronounced variation in these abilities.
- In reviewing academic records, look for enrollment in special education classes.
- Determine whether the person was enrolled in an individualized educational program (i.e., designed for students with learning disabilities).

---

[37]*Id.* at 50.

- Look for key words such as "dyslexia," "learning disability," or "developmental disorder."

B. Substance Abuse

The evaluation of substance abuse and dependence in litigants is often neglected. Individuals in our society routinely abuse substances ranging from alcohol to prescribed medications to illegal drugs, which all can produce significant psychological and psychiatric symptoms. Substance addiction also impairs recovery from psychological and psychiatric disorders, and in fact, the medical standard remains that for one to profit from psychological or psychiatric intervention one must maintain sobriety. The authoritative text for the diagnosing of mental disorders (*DSM-IV-TR*) currently recognizes 124 individual abuse/dependence-related disorders,[38] including disorders related to alcohol, amphetamine, caffeine, cannabis, cocaine, hallucinogens, inhalants, nicotine, opioids, phencyclidine, sedatives, hypnotic or anxiolytic drugs, and polysubstance abuse. Research indicates that lifetime rates for alcohol abuse disorders include almost 25 percent of men and 5 percent of women.[39] Other studies report that as high as 50 percent of the male general population and 20 percent of the female general medical patients meet the rigorous criteria for alcoholism.[40]

Symptoms related to substance abuse can include:

Academic problems
Antisocial behavior
Inability to sustain consistent work behavior
Irritable mood
Symptom exaggeration
Failure to fulfill major role obligations
Interpersonal problems
Marital difficulties
Multiple legal problems
Occupational problems
Poor work performance
Recurrent social problems
Repeated use in hazardous situations

In the evaluation of whether substance abuse may be an issue in litigants one should look for the following:

---

[38] *Id.* at 191–295.

[39] Rosa M. Crum, *Epidemiology of Alcohol and Drug Addiction*, in PRINCIPLES OF ADDICTION MEDICINE 1, 2 (Norman S. Miller ed., 1994).

[40] Marc A. Schuckitt & Michael Irwin, *Diagnosis of Alcoholism*, 72 MED. CLIN. OF N. AM. 1133, 1134 (1988).

- A record of a DUI or DWI
- Arrest for any alcohol-related event such as drunkenness and disorderly conduct
- Past participation in Alcoholics Anonymous or Narcotics Anonymous
- Multiple divorces
- Termination from work related to substance abuse
- Documentation of substance abuse such as through drug screens
- Medical evidence of substance abuse such as abnormal liver functions or blood work
- Documentation of medical concern for drug, alcohol, or prescribed medication abuse
- Prior experience with or referrals to twelve-step programs.

C. Anxiety Disorders

Anxiety is a disorder as well as a symptom. It is commonly related to other symptoms such as insomnia, inability to sustain attention and concentration, and gastrointestinal problems. Anxiety is a common symptom of both physical and mental disorders. In fact, *DSM-IV-TR* even documents a disorder entitled "Anxiety Disorder Due to a General Medical Condition."[41] Medical causes of anxiety include the following:

cerebral vascular disorder	sequelae to head injury
multiple sclerosis	brain tumor
tumors of the third ventricle	diencephalic autonomic epilepsy
posterior lateral sclerosis	Wilson's disease
Huntington's Chorea	combined systemic disease
mysthenias gravis	polyneuritis
hyperthyroidism	hypothyroidism
hypopituitarism	hyperpituitarism
hypoparathyroidism	hyperparathyroidism
ovarian dysfunction	testicular deficiencies
hyperglycemia	diabetes mellitus
pancreatic carcinoma	adrenal cortical insufficiency
adrenal cortical hyperplasia (Cushing's disease)	(Addison's disease)
adrenal tumors	atypical viral pneumonia
viral hepatitis	mononucleosis
rheumatoid arthritis	Lupus
polyarteritis nodosa	temporal arteritis
anemia	cerebral anoxia
renal insufficiency	paroxysmal atrial tachycardia
coronary insufficiency	Meniere's disease[42]

---

[41] *DSM-IV-TR*, *supra* note 5, at 476.

[42] Richard C. W. Hall, *Anxiety*, in PSYCHIATRIC PRESENTATIONS OF MEDICAL ILLNESS: SOMATOPSYCHIC DISORDERS 17 (Richard C. W. Hall ed., 1980).

Note that a variety of substances such as over-the-counter antihistamines, caffeine, and even food additives such as monosodium glutamate can cause anxiety symptoms and would need to be carefully considered.

Anxiety disorders reflect a broad range of mental disorders including the following:

Adjustment Disorder with Anxious Mood
Adjustment Disorder with Mixed Anxiety and Depressed Mood
Agoraphobia without History of Panic Disorder
Specific Phobia
Obsessive-Compulsive Disorder
Acute Stress Disorder
Anxiety Disorder Due to a General Medical Condition
Adjustment Disorder with Anxiety
Panic Disorder without Agoraphobia
Panic Disorder with Agoraphobia
Social Phobia
Separation Anxiety Disorder
Posttraumatic Stress Disorder
Generalized Anxiety Disorder
Substance Induced Anxiety Disorder
Anxiety Disorder Not Otherwise Specified

Anxiety can appear in mental disorders that last from less than 28 days (Acute Stress Disorder)[43] to less than six months (Adjustment Disorder),[44] as well as in more serious, chronic disorders. One must carefully evaluate claims of anxiety to differentiate among these related disorders. To appropriately evaluate any claims of anxiety, the following steps should be taken:

- Review medical records for references to anxiety, nervousness, stress-related symptoms, stress disorder, or insomnia.
- Evaluate medical records for any medical condition and its symptoms.
- Review pharmaceutical records to identify all medications consumed, whether by prescription or over the counter and refer to the *Physicians' Desk Reference* for possible side effects. Evaluate for substance abuse. Review pharmaceutical records for specific antianxiety medications such as muscle relaxants, hypnotic medications, and antidepressants as well as sleep medications.
- Inquire as to anxiety disorders in first-degree biological relatives.

D. Mood Disorders

Mood disorders most commonly involve depression but can also involve mania. *DSM-IV-TR* recognizes 29 specific mood disorders.[45] These include the following:

Vascular Dementia with Depressed Mood
Alcohol Induced Mood Disorder

---

[43]*DSM-IV-TR, supra* note 5, at 469.
[44]*Id.* at 680.
[45]*Id.* at 159, 369–410, 679–80, 740.

- Amphetamine Induced Mood Disorder
- Cocaine Induced Mood Disorder
- Hallucinogen Induced Mood Disorder
- Inhalant Induced Mood Disorder
- Opioid Induced Mood Disorder
- Phencyclidine Induced Mood Disorder
- Sedative, Hypnotic, Anxiolytic Induced Mood Disorder
- Other (or Unknown) Induced Mood Disorder
- Schizoaffective Disorder
- Major Depressive Disorder, Single Episode
- Major Depressive Episode, Recurrent
- Dysthymic Disorder
- Depressive Disorder, NOS
- Bipolar I Disorder, Single Episode Manic
- Bipolar I Disorder, Most Recent Episode Hypomanic
- Bipolar I Disorder, Most Recent Episode Manic
- Bipolar I Disorder, Most Recent Episode Mixed
- Bipolar I Disorder, Most Recent Episode Depressed
- Bipolar I Disorder, Most Recent Episode Unspecified
- Bipolar II Disorder
- Cyclothymic Disorder
- Bipolar Disorder, NOS
- Mood Disorder Due to a General Medical Condition
- Mood Disorder, NOS
- Adjustment Disorder With Depressed Mood
- Adjustment Disorder With Mixed Anxiety and Depressed Mood
- Bereavement

Depression is perhaps the most common type of emotional distress alleged as a result of job loss or other adverse workplace events. It is not only a disorder but a common symptom of other conditions as well, however, so it is important to determine whether the origin of the depressed mood is in fact the workplace or some other condition. Additionally, depressed mood appears as a symptom or associated feature in over 200 mental disorders, and a variety of medical illnesses may also induce depression.[46] The following medical disorders may produce symptoms of depression:

pernicious anemia	folic acid deficiency
multiple sclerosis	influenza
viral hepatitis	cirrhosis
uremia	carcinoma of the lung
lymphoma	chronic myelogenous leukemia
carcinoma of the pancreas	Cushing's disease
hyperaldosteronism	Addison's disease

---

[46] Richard C. W. Hall, *Depression*, in PSYCHIATRIC PRESENTATIONS OF MEDICAL ILLNESS: SOMATOPSYCHIC DISORDERS 40 (Richard C. W. Hall ed., 1980).

hyperparathyroidism	hypoparathyroidism
hyperthyroidism	hypothyroidism
acromegaly	systemic lupus erythematosus
ulcerative colitis	regional enteritis
Whipple's disease	amyloidosis
HIV (AIDS)	hypoglycemia
infectious mononucleosis	irritable bowel syndrome

Depression may also be a symptom related to life circumstance such as divorce, financial reversal, or failure to reach a goal. Millions of Americans are being treated for depression not only by mental health professionals but by their family practitioners, gynecologists, internists, and pastoral counselors. The World Health Organization rates depression as the world's fourth greatest health problem.[47] Depressed mood is also a common side effect of substance abuse, prescribed medications, or physical disorders, and it directly affects such issues as occupation performance and personal relationships and even performance on psychological testing.

Depression can be a chronic disorder. If one has had one major depressive episode, there is a 50 percent chance of having a second; after having two major depressive episodes, there is a 75 percent chance of having a third; after three major depressive episodes, there is a 90 percent chance of future depression.[48] Investigation of possible depressive episodes therefore should occur when a plaintiff complains of having suffered depression as a result of a workplace incident.

Depression is differentiated from other mood disorders such as Mania. Mania is the result of an elevated mood and is typically seen in Bipolar Disorder, but it may also be secondary to substance intoxication or abuse. Mania is essentially a persistently elevated, expansive, or irritable mood that often includes a decreased need for sleep, grandiosity, pressured speech, racing thoughts, distractibility, increase in goal-directed activities and an excessive involvement in pleasurable activities. Mania is conceptually divided into Hyermania and Hypomania. The difference between them is that the mood changes in Hypomania do not cause marked impairment in social or occupational functioning. Hypermanic individuals, on the other hand, are often institutionalized for their own safety. Hypomanic individuals may often be found in the workplace and cause difficulty with their gross disorganization, their flightiness, and their hypersexuality. Where depression is alleged, the following should be considered:

- Is there the presence of a mood disorder in first-degree biological families? This may suggest a genetically related illness.
- All physical disorders documented should be reviewed to determine whether depression may be a side effect of those conditions or even produce symptoms commonly related to depression such as fatigue, malaise, or weakness.

---

[47]Christopher J. L. Murray & Alan D. Lopez, *Evidence-Based Health Policy: Lessons from the Global Burden of Disease Study*, 274 SCIENCE 740 (1996).

[48]*DSM-IV-TR, supra* note 5, at 372.

- Determine if there was any preexisting treatment for substance abuse or continued substance abuse. This may indicate that the mood disorder is secondary to the substance abuse or that the substance abuse is a comorbid disorder.
- Look for a prior history of treatment for a mood disorder such as through the use of an antidepressant or a mood stabilizer such as Lithium, Depakote, or Tegretol. Note that oftentimes family practitioners initially treat the agitation secondary to a mood disorder with a sedative or hypnotic such as Valium or Librium.

E. Organic Disorders

Organic disorders comprise a group of mental or emotional disorders whose etiology is presumed to be caused by physical insult such as toxic exposure, central nervous system insult such as a brain injury, substance abuse, physical injury, or even a physical condition such as vascular disease or stroke. Many of the symptoms related to an organic disorder are much like those of other mental disorders, including mentation difficulties such as loss of concentration, attention, and memory, as well as associated depression and fatigue. Organic disorders can be progressive, such as in a vascular disease resulting in Vascular Dementia, Dementia Due to Alzheimer's Disorder, and Dementia Due to HIV Disease, or they can result from an acute event, such as in Dementia Due to Head Trauma. Symptoms seen in organic disease can include depression, mania, psychotic disturbance, agitation, and cognitive difficulty. In evaluating whether an organic condition is present, the following steps should be taken:

- Determine whether there is a history of toxic exposure, in particular to heavy metals.
- Document any previous physical disorder diagnosed in past treatment to see if it may be related to the mental disorder. Such conditions as HIV disease, cerebral vascular disease, Parkinson's disease, Huntington's disease, and Pick's disease can all produce symptoms associated with Dementia.
- Look for medical conditions that can cause organic illness, such as brain tumors, subdural hematomas, hydrocephalus, hyperthyroidism, hypercalcemia, and hyperglycemia as well as deficiencies of thiamine, niacin, and Vitamin B_{12}, and infectious conditions such as neurosyphilis and cryptococcosis.[49]
- As the presence of an organic disorder is likely to be documented in medical records, such records should be scrutinized as far back as pediatric records. Review any prior psychological or neuropsychological testing results.
- Evaluate all medications that may be utilized and their side effects, as well as recreational drug abuse, including illegal drugs.
- Look for any history of cerebral insults, central nervous system insults, or seizure disorders.

---

[49] *DSM-IV-TR*, *supra* note 5, at 151.

F. Personality Disorders

Personality disorders are one of the most underdiagnosed areas of mental disorders. They are often misunderstood even by mental health professionals who have adequate training. Personality disorders are in existence by late adolescence or early adulthood and usually present with comorbid disorders that predispose the individual to develop other psychiatric disorders. Personality disorders are difficult to diagnose because in order to detect them one must not only do a thorough clinical evaluation and psychological testing but also review medical records over time. Personality disorders are frequently not diagnosed by the mental health professional because most insurers will not pay for their treatment. These disorders will not be discussed in depth in this chapter as they are more fully discussed in Chapter 6, Personality Disorders in Employment Litigation.

There are eleven specific types of personality disorders found in *DSM-IV-TR*. A person may also have a combination of personality disorders and Personality Disorder Not Otherwise Specified. The following table summarizes frequent coexisting conditions often found with personality disorders:

Paranoid Personality Disorder

Frequent co-existing conditions: Brief Reactive Psychosis
Delusional Disorder
Noncompliance With Treatment
Occupational Problem
Parent-Child Relational Problem
Partner Relational Problem
Schizophrenia
Major Depressive Disorder

Schizoid Personality Disorder

Frequent co-existing conditions: Avoidant Personality Disorder
Borderline Personality Disorder
Brief Reactive Psychosis
Major Depressive Disorder
Paranoid Personality Disorder
Schizophrenia
Schizotypal Personality
    Disorder

Schizotypal Personality Disorder

Frequent co-existing conditions: Avoidant Personality Disorder
Borderline Personality Disorder
Brief Reactive Psychosis
Delusional Disorder
Major Depressive Disorder
Paranoid Personality Disorder
Schizoid Personality Disorder

Schizotypal Personality Disorder
    Frequent co-existing conditions: Schizophreniform Disorder
    continued   Schizophrenia

Antisocial Personality Disorder
    Predisposing conditions: Attention Deficit/Hyperactivity Disorder
    Conduct Disorder
    Oppositional Defiant Disorder

    Frequent co-existing conditions: Substance Abuse Dependence Disorders
    Anxiety Disorders
    Borderline Personality Disorder
    Depressive Disorder
    Histrionic Personality Disorder
    Malingering
    Narcissistic Personality Disorder
    Noncompliance with Treatment
    Occupational Problem
    Parent-Child Relational Problem
    Partner Relational Problem
    Pathological Gambling
    Somatization Disorder

Borderline Personality Disorder
    Predisposing conditions: Bulimia Nervosa
    Identity Disorder

    Frequent co-existing conditions: Antisocial Personality Disorder
    Attention Deficit/Hyperactivity Disorder
    Bipolar Disorder
    Brief Reactive Psychosis
    Dependent Personality Disorder
    Dysthymic Disorder
    Histrionic Personality Disorder
    Major Depression
    Dissociative Identity Disorder
    Narcissistic Personality Disorder
    Paranoid Personality Disorder
    Substance Abuse/Dependence Disorder
    Schizophrenia
    Schizotypal Personality Disorder
    Trichotillomania

Histrionic Personality Disorder

Frequent co-existing conditions: Brief Reactive Psychosis
Dysthymic Disorder
Conversion Disorder
Somatization Disorder
Substance Abuse/Dependence Disorder
Anorexia Nervosa
Bulimia Nervosa
Attention Deficit/Hyperactivity Disorder
Borderline Personality Disorder
Antisocial Personality Disorder

Narcissistic Personality Disorder

Frequent co-existing conditions: Academic Problems
Anorexia Nervosa
Antisocial Personality Disorder
Borderline Personality Disorder
Brief Reactive Psychosis
Dysthymic Disorder
Histrionic Personality Disorder
Major Depressive Disorder
Occupational Problem
Paranoid Personality Disorder
Partner Relational Problem
Substance Abuse/Dependence Disorder

Avoidant Personality Disorder

Frequent co-existing conditions: Agoraphobia without History of Panic Attacks
Anxiety Disorder
Borderline Personality Disorder
Delusional Disorder
Dependent Personality Disorder
Dysthymia
Paranoid Personality Disorder
Schizoid Personality Disorder
Schizotypal Personality Disorder
Social Phobia

Dependent Personality Disorder

    Predisposing conditions: Chronic Physical Illness in Childhood or Adolescence
Separation Anxiety Disorder in Childhood or Adolescence

    Frequent co-existing conditions: Anxiety Disorders
Adjustment Disorders
Avoidant Personality Disorder
Borderline Personality Disorder
Conversion Disorder
Dysthymia
Histrionic Personality Disorder
Major Depressive Disorder

Obsessive-Compulsive Personality Disorder

    Frequent co-existing conditions: Dysthymic Disorder
Hypochondriasis
Major Depressive Disorder
Obsessive-Compulsive Disorder

Passive-Dependent Personality Disorder

    Frequent co-existing conditions: Depressive Personality Disorder
Dysthymic Disorder
Major Depressive Disorder
Substance Abuse/Dependence Disorder

Beginning with the *Diagnostic and Statistical Manual of Mental Disorders, Fourth Edition*,[50] personality traits that are short of full-blown personality disorders yet still clinically significant may also be diagnosed. The documentation of these personality traits in medical and psychological or psychiatric records may be indicative of the presence of a personality disorder. When reviewing medical or psychiatric records, one should pay attention to descriptions such as:

Antisocial	Avoidant	Borderline
Compulsive	Dependent	Depressive
Grandiose	Histrionic	Hysterical
Narcissistic	Obsessive-Compulsive	Paranoid
Passive-aggressive	Sadistic	Passive-dependent
Self-defeating	Schizoid	Schizotypal
Sociopathic		

---

[50] AMERICAN PSYCHIATRIC ASSOCIATION, DIAGNOSTIC AND STATISTICAL MANUAL OF MENTAL DISORDERS 631 (4th ed. 1994).

The following measures should also be considered when evaluating for a personality disorder:

- Scrutinize psychological evaluations of the plaintiff for personality descriptions that imply chronic personality traits or behaviors—for example, the use of phrases such as "characterological" or "disturbed interpersonal relationships."
- Obtain all psychological testing previously administered. Tests such as the Minnesota Multiphasic Personality Inventory-2 and the Millon Clinical Multiaxial Inventory-III will often recommend diagnoses of personality disorders when appropriate. These findings may be minimized or ignored by previous examiners. It is always advisable to get the raw test data and have it independently scored and interpreted.
- Review occupational history. Frequent job changes may suggest a personality disorder.
- Check financial records and other financial obligations that can be suggestive of personality disorders. Excessive debt, loan defaults, bankruptcies, and foreclosures can all be signs of an underlying personality disorder.
- Review marital and relational history. Two or more divorces and/or stormy and chaotic personal relationships can indicate characterological problems.
- The presence of documented substance abuse may also indicate characterological problems, but if the abnormal personality traits followed a history of drug dependence, then they may be substance-related and not a personality disorder.

G. Thought Disorders

Formal thought disorders are very severe psychiatric conditions that typically have an insidious onset and become chronic following their acute manifestation. Often the presence of these disorders has a profound impact on one's employability. They are often unrelated to any type of event in the individual's life and may be the result of a genetic process. Disorders that disrupt thought processes are termed psychoses and can range from Schizophrenia to Schizoaffective Disorder (which is a combination of Schizophrenia and Depression) to a full-blown Delusional Disorder. Individuals with these disorders may experience auditory and visual hallucinations as well as have delusions. Delusions are mistaken beliefs that may have a bizarre theme, as found in Schizophrenia, or be nonbizarre, as found in Delusional Disorders.

The median age of the onset of the first episode of Schizophrenia is in the mid-20s, and the onset may be insidious or very abrupt. Conversely, the onset of a Delusional Disorder is generally in middle or late adult life, but it can occur earlier. Common types of Delusional Disorder can include Erotomanic, Grandiose, Jealous, Persecutory, Somatic, and Mixed Type. Usually social, marital, or work problems result from delusional beliefs, psychotic symptoms, and Schizophrenia.

In evaluating for thought disorders, the following should be considered:

- Check medical and psychiatric records specifically for mentions of delusions, auditory hallucinations, or visual hallucinations.

- Look in medical and psychiatric records for mention of grossly disorganized behavior.
- Review all psychiatric admissions. Often thought disorders will result in inpatient treatment and even involuntary commitment proceedings that force the person to seek treatment. Specifically review the records for mention of Schizophreniform Disorder, Schizophrenia, Schizoaffective Disorder, or Delusional Disorder.
- Review medications prescribed to see if they include antipsychotic drugs such as Risperdal, Haldol, or Thorazine.
- Review emergency room records to determine if admission or treatment was for acute psychiatric symptoms.

V. Physical Disorders That Produce Psychological Symptoms

Persons who claim mental or emotional injury may also present with one or more physical disorders. It is very important to have those disorders evaluated. Physical disorders may produce psychological symptoms such as loss of sleep, loss of libido, poor concentration, depressed mood or fatigue, as can their prescribed medications' side effects. For example, mitral valve prolapse can cause anxiety problems. Diabetes can produce neuropathies that may be mistaken for toxic exposure. High blood pressure and its medication can cause loss of libido. High blood pressure has also been implicated in producing deficits on neuropsychological testing that may mimic brain injury. Physical disorders should be carefully reviewed for their potential psychiatric symptoms and side effects that may mimic these symptoms.

The following list contains common physical disorders and their associated psychiatric symptom manifestations. Psychiatric symptoms have been grouped under three general areas, Anxiety, Depression and Cognitive Impairment. Cognitive Impairment would include symptoms related to intellect, memory, and neuropsychological symptoms such as attention or concentration deficits.

Acute Intermittent Porphyria
Symptoms:
Depression

Addison's Disease
Symptoms:
Anxiety
Cognitive impairment
Depression

Alzheimer's-Type Dementia
Symptoms:
Anxiety
Cognitive impairment
Depression

Amyloidosis
Symptoms:
Depression

Amyotrophic Lateral Sclerosis
Symptoms:
Cognitive Impairment
Depression

Anemia
Symptoms:
Anxiety
Depression

Brain Tumors
Symptoms:
Anxiety
Cognitive impairment
Depression

Brucellosis
Symptoms:
Anxiety
Depression

Cerebrovascular Disease
Symptoms:
Anxiety
Cognitive impairment
Depression

Chronic Obstructive Pulmonary Disease
Symptoms:
Anxiety
Cognitive impairment
Depression

Cirrhosis
Symptoms:
Depression

Combined Systems Disease
Symptoms:
Anxiety
Cognitive impairment
Depression

Congestive Heart Failure
Symptoms:
Anxiety
Depression

Coronary Artery Disease
Symptoms:
Anxiety
Cognitive impairment
Depression

Coronary Insufficiency
Symptoms:
Anxiety

Creutzfeldt-Jakob Disease
Symptoms:
Cognitive impairment
Depression

Cushing's Syndrome
Symptoms:
Anxiety
Cognitive impairment
Depression

Diabetes
Symptoms:
Anxiety
Cognitive impairment
Depression

Electrolyte Imbalance (*Hyponatremia:* a decrease in serum sodium below normal due to excess H_2O relative to solute. *Hypernatremia:* elevation of serum sodium above normal range due to a deficit in body water relative to sodium.)
Symptoms:
Cognitive impairment
Depression

Electrolyte Imbalance: Calcium (hypocalcemia)
Symptoms:
Cognitive impairment
Depression

Electrolyte Imbalance: HCO_3 (metabolic acidosis and respiratory acidosis)
Symptoms:
Anxiety
Depression

Electrolyte Imbalance: Potassium (hypokalemia and hyperkalemia)
Symptoms:
Anxiety
Cognitive impairment
Depression

Electrolyte Imbalance: Magnesium (hypo- and hypermagnesemia)
Symptoms:
Depression

Encephalitis
Symptoms:
    Anxiety
    Cognitive impairment
    Depression

Endocrinopathies: Pancreas (hyperinsulinism caused by hyperglycemia)
Symptoms:
    Anxiety
    Depression

Epilepsy
Symptoms
    Anxiety
    Cognitive impairment
    Depression

Gout
Symptoms:
    Depression

Guillain-Barre Syndrome
Symptoms:
    Anxiety
    Depression

Hepatic Encephalopathy
Symptoms:
    Anxiety
    Cognitive impairment
    Depression

Hepatitis B
Symptoms:
    Anxiety
    Depression

Herpes Simplex
Symptoms:
    Depression

Herpes Simplex Encephalitis
Symptoms:
    Anxiety
    Cognitive impairment

HIV (AIDS)
Symptoms:
    Anxiety
    Cognitive impairment
    Depression

Homocystinuria
Symptoms:
Anxiety
Cognitive impairment
Depression

Huntington's Disease
Symptoms:
Anxiety
Cognitive impairment
Depression

Hypercortisolism
Symptoms:
Anxiety
Depression

Hyperglycemia
Symptoms:
Cognitive impairment
Depression

Hyperparathyroidism
Symptoms:
Anxiety
Cognitive impairment
Depression

Hypertension
Symptoms:
Anxiety
Cognitive impairment

Hypertensive Encephalitis
Symptoms:
Anxiety
Cognitive impairment
Depression

Hyperthyroidism
Symptoms:
Anxiety
Depression

Hyperprolactinemia
Symptoms:
Anxiety
Depression

Hypocortisolism
Symptoms:
Cognitive impairment
Depression

Hypoglycemia
Symptoms:
Anxiety
Cognitive impairment
Depression

Hypoparathyroidism
Symptoms:
Anxiety
Cognitive impairment
Depression

Hypotension
Symptoms:
Cognitive impairment

Hypothyroidism
Symptoms:
Anxiety
Cognitive impairment
Depression

Infectious Mononucleosis
Symptoms:
Anxiety
Depression

Irritable Bowel Syndrome
Symptoms:
Anxiety
Depression

Leukemia
Symptoms:
Anxiety
Cognitive impairment
Depression

Lupus Erythematosus, Systemic
Symptoms:
Anxiety
Cognitive impairment
Depression

Lymphoma
Symptoms:
Anxiety
Depression

Malaria
Symptoms:
Anxiety
Depresssion

Marchiafava-Bignami
Symptoms:
Anxiety
Cognitive impairment
Depression

Ménière's Disease
Symptoms:
Anxiety
Cognitive impairment

Meningitis
Symptoms:
Cognitive impairment

Menopause
Symptoms:
Depression

Mitral Valve Prolapse
Symptoms:
Anxiety

Multiple Sclerosis
Symptoms:
Anxiety
Cognitive impairment
Depression

Myasthenia Gravis
Symptoms:
Depression

Myocardial Infarction
Symptoms:
Anxiety
Depression

Nephritis
Symptoms:
Anxiety

Nieman Pick Disease
Symptoms:
Cognitive impairment
Depression

Normal Pressure Hydrocephalus
Symptoms:
Cognitive impairment

Ovarian Dysfunction
Symptoms:
Depression

Pancreatic Carcinoma
Symptoms:
Anxiety
Depression

Pancreatitis
Symptoms:
Anxiety
Depression

Parkinson's Disease
Symptoms:
Anxiety
Cognitive impairment
Depression

Paroxysmal Atrial Tachycardia
Symptoms:
Anxiety

Pernicious Anemia
Symptoms:
Anxiety
Cognitive impairment
Depression

Pheochromocytoma (endocrinopathies)
Symptoms:
Anxiety

Pneumonia
Symptoms:
Anxiety
Depression

Polyneuritis
Symptoms:
Anxiety

Porphyria
Symptoms:
Cognitive impairment
Depression

Postconcussive Syndrome
Symptoms:
Anxiety
Cognitive impairment
Depression

Premenstrual Syndrome
Symptoms:
Anxiety
Depression

Progressive Supranuclear Palsy
Symptoms:
Cognitive impairment
Depression

Psoriasis
Symptoms:
Depression

Regional Enteritis
Symptoms:
Depression

Rheumatoid Arthritis
Symptoms:
Anxiety
Depression

Shy-Dager Syndrome
Symptoms:
Cognitive impairment
Depression

Sleep Apnea
Symptoms:
Depression

Syphilis
Symptoms:
Anxiety
Cognitive impairment
Depression

Toxoplasmosis
Symptoms:
Depression

Transient Cerebral Ischemia
Symptoms:
Anxiety
Depression

Tuberculosis
Symptoms:
Anxiety
Depression

Ulcerative Colitis
Symptoms:
Anxiety
Depression

Uremia
Symptoms:
Cognitive impairment
Depression

Vitamin Deficiency: B1
Symptoms:
Anxiety

Vitamin Deficiency: Niacin (causes pellagra)
Symptoms:
Anxiety
Cognitive impairment

Wilson's Disease
Symptoms:
Anxiety
Cognitive impairment
Depression

The following should be considered in determining whether physical disorders play a role in a person's psychological condition:

- Note any physical disorders that have been diagnosed or referenced in medical records. Consider retaining an expert medical consultant to evaluate their significance or refer to published treatises that can be found in libraries or online[51] so that the physical disorder and its common symptoms can be researched.
- Evaluate the side effects of all prescribed medications. This can easily be done by referring to the current *Physicians' Desk Reference.*[52]

VI. Psychosocial Stressors

Psychosocial stressors are events whose presence can affect one's psychiatric diagnosis, prognosis, and treatment. They can be biologically based, environmentally based, occupationally related, or induced by social or traumatic events. Psychiatric diagnosis typically addresses only negative psychosocial stressors such as physical illness, financial problems, demotions at work, death, or assault, but positive stressors, such as job promotions, marriage, and birth of a child, can have negative effects as well. Psychosocial stressors can produce emotional symptoms such as depressed mood, anxiety, sleeplessness, loss of libido, and concentration difficulties, as well as mental disorders. Stressors such as long work hours are known to produce disorders such as an Adjustment Disorder,

---

[51]Such texts include THE MERCK MANUAL OF DIAGNOSIS AND THERAPY (Mark Beers & Robert Berkow eds., 1999); PSYCHIATRIC PRESENTATIONS OF MEDICAL ILLNESS: SOMATOPSYCHIC DISORDERS (Richard C. W. Hall ed., 1980).
[52]PHYSICIANS' DESK REFERENCE (2000).

which can also be caused by seasonal business difficulties.[53] Even pleasurable stressors such as taking out a mortgage to buy a new home, the addition of a new family member, or a job promotion can produce significant stress.[54] Psychosocial stressors need to be carefully evaluated and integrated into a diagnostic picture. *DSM-IV-TR* recognizes the impact that these stressors have on a person's emotional functioning and provides an axis (Axis IV) for them to be identified as part of the clinical assessment. *DSM-IV-TR* also recognizes that psychosocial stressors can produce conditions that may be a focus of mental health treatment or evaluation but are not in and of themselves a mental disorder. These conditions are called "V-code conditions,"[55] and they address such issues as Occupational Problems, Partner Relational Problems, Parent-Child Problems, and Phase of Life Problems. The following is a list of such conditions.

Relational Problems
  Relational Problem Related to a Mental Disorder
  or General Medical Condition
  Parent-Child Relational Problem
  Partner Relational Problem
  Sibling Relational Problem
  Relational Problem Not Otherwise Specified

Problems Related to Abuse or Neglect
  Physical Abuse of Adult by Partner
  Physical Abuse of Adult by Person Other Than Partner
  Sexual Abuse of Adult by Partner
  Sexual Abuse of Adult by Person Other Than Partner

Additional Conditions That May Be a Focus of Clinical Attention
  Noncompliance With Treatment
  Adult Antisocial Behavior
  Child or Adolescent Antisocial Behavior
  Bereavement
  Academic Problem
  Occupational Problem
  Identity Problem
  Religious or Spiritual Problem
  Acculturation Problem
  Phase of Life Problem

Many individuals, if properly evaluated by the mental health professional, will have corresponding V-code conditions along with a diagnosis of a primary

---

[53] *DSM-IV-TR*, *supra* note 5, at 679.
[54] Debra C. Price & Craig A. Horn, *Psychosocial Stressors*, in THE INSURER'S HANDBOOK OF PSYCHOLOGICAL INJURY CLAIMS 104 (David R. Price & Paul R. Lees-Haley eds., 1995); Thomas H. Holmes, *The Social Readjustment Scale*, 11 J. PSYCHOSOMATIC RES. 213 (1967).
[55] *DSM-IV-TR*, *supra* note 5, at 736–42.

clinical disorder. In evaluating a psychological injury for the presence of psychosocial stressors, it is advisable to do the following:

- Review depositions and other discovery materials to determine the existence of any substantial life events such as change of income, recent move, job change, the addition or loss of a loved one, marriage, divorce, or separation.
- Identify all occupational stressors that may have been present during the course of employment, including promotions, demotions, significant overtime, performance problems, or difficulties in getting along with supervisors or coworkers.
- Review medical and psychological records for mention of marital discord or chronic illness.
- Remember that litigation can be a significant psychosocial stressor.

VII. The Role of Psychological Testing

Psychological test results should be scrutinized very carefully. They can carry an aura of scientific credibility and usefulness, but in fact the conclusions can be completely invalid and speculative.[56] In evaluating psychological tests one may wish to refer to the research literature, the test manuals, or published reviews of the test. Instruments that are labeled psychological tests can vary widely from objective empirically validated instruments such as the Minnesota Multiphasic Personality Inventory (MMPI), to checklists that simply quantify subjective self-reports, to projective tests that have no scoring system at all, such as the Thematic Apperception Test. Tests can be objective, in which claimants respond to an instrument with a behavior or with a four-choice method that can be statistically translated and compared with normative data, or subjective, such as projective tests.

Projective tests are tests in which an individual responds to ambiguous stimuli and the clinician then interprets those responses. Such tests have been criticized as being unreliable.[57] Many of these tests, such as the Incomplete Sentence Blank and Thematic Apperception Test, actually have no scoring system, leaving the interpretations regarding the individual's functioning as pure speculation. Tests can also include surveys and rating scales, which are not themselves tests but provide a way of organizing an individual's self-report. They are also often unreliable and invalid. Major concerns in the administration of psychological tests include that the administration is often not supervised, the scoring is not objective, and the test-taking individuals were coached by their legal counsel prior to taking tests.[58]

---

[56]Paul E. Meehl, *What Social Scientists Don't Understand*, in METATHEORY IN SOCIAL SCIENCE 325 (Donald W. Fiske & Richard Shweder eds., 1986).

[57]Paul R. Lees-Haley & James J. McDonald, Jr., *The Use (and Misuse) of Psychological Testing in Employment Litigation*, 23 EMPL. REL. L.J. 37 (1995); Paul R. Lees-Haley, *Attorneys Influence Expert Evidence in Forensic Psychological and Neuropsychological Cases*, 4 ASSESSMENT 321 (1997).

[58]Lees-Haley, *supra* note 57, at 324.

In reviewing psychological and neuropsychological test results, the following should be considered:

- Who actually administered the test? Was it the expert clinician or some subordinate with less training and expertise?
- Was the individual who administered the tests and interpreted them qualified to do so by research, training, and professional licensure?
- Was the test administered in a controlled supervised structure, such as an office, or was the individual allowed to take the test home to complete and return?
- Was the test an objective test (i.e., MMPI-2, MCMI-III, WAIS-III) or projective (i.e., Rorschach, Incomplete Sentence Blank, Thematic Apperception Test)? The latter tests have poor reliability and validity.
- Were standardized scoring methods used, and were those scores then compared to those of a normative population, or was the instrument scored idiosyncratically and the interpretation of the individual's performance solely up to the clinician?
- Instruments identified as checklists, rating scales, or surveys are not psychological tests and should not be treated as such.
- Was the test administered in its entirety or in an abbreviated form? If administered in an abbreviated form, it is likely to be an invalid estimate of the person's functioning.
- Was the most recent version of the test administered or was an outdated version utilized? Using an older version commonly occurs and should call the expert's performance credibility into question.

VIII. Discovery Issues

The appropriate evaluation of the psychological injury claim begins with a thorough discovery of all relevant documents and history rather than through an immediate independent mental examination. A qualified forensic expert will request all the medical and psychological records for review so as to obtain the complete picture of the plaintiff through as many objective external sources as possible. It is often useful for the litigator to retain a qualified psychiatric or psychological consultant to assist in identifying what records should be obtained in discovery and what the information contained in those records reflects. Also, information contained in those records might help indicate what type of mental health professional should be retained as an expert to evaluate and possibly provide an expert opinion at trial.

The following information is often useful and necessary in evaluating a psychological injury claim and can be obtained by counsel in depositions, from third parties via subpoena, or by the clinician in the course of the mental examination of the plaintiff.

Developmental History

- Does the plaintiff have a history of meeting developmental milestones normally?
- Did the plaintiff have any significant physical disease, trauma, or illness as a child?

- Were any psychological disorders present in childhood, such as a Separation Anxiety Disorder or Learning Disability?
- Was the plaintiff the product of a divorced home, custody battle, or dysfunctional relationships with stepparents?
- Did the plaintiff experience multiple moves as a child?
- Did the plaintiff experience sexual or physical abuse as a child?

Social History

- As a child, did the plaintiff come into contact with governmental agencies such as Social Services or Youth Services?
- Was the plaintiff either the victim or perpetrator of any crimes?
- Was the plaintiff involved in multiple marriages or a succession of chaotic, stormy relationships?

Educational History

- Did the plaintiff have any learning disabilities or behavioral disorders?
- Did the plaintiff start and graduate from school on time?
- What was the plaintiff's social progress through high school?
- Was the plaintiff involved in extracurricular activities or the recipient of academic honors?
- Was the plaintiff the subject of academic discipline or discipline for misconduct?
- Did the plaintiff start and stop attending college on numerous occasions?

Employment History

- Examine work history for terminations or chronic "job-hopping."
- Review job applications from various employers to locate inconsistencies in work history.
- Look for reprimands, counseling reports, or discipline for misconduct or poor work performance.
- Assess income history to determine whether it shows a consistent upward trajectory or a flat or downward trajectory that may indicate career reversals.

Military Records

- Look for type of discharge and any record of discipline or misconduct.
- Look for any relevant medical information.

Medical History

- Identify all treatment providers, physical disorders diagnosed, treatment, medications used, indications of addictive habits, and number of treatment providers. Short-term doctor/patient relationships may be indicative of a Somatoform Disorder, symptom exaggeration, or treatment noncompliance.
- Obtain medical records as far back as possible. Generally it is advisable to request pediatric, family practice, ob/gyn, and internists' records in addition to any other specialties involved.
- When reviewing medical records, always look for reports, intake forms, progress notes, test results, other treating or examining doctors' names, correspondence, insurance forms filed, billing information, and diagnoses.

- Always compare the diagnoses found in the chart to those located in correspondence, insurance forms, and billing information for any inconsistencies.
- Determine whether the course of treatment provided was appropriate to the diagnosis and was effective.
- Evaluate possible side effects of treatment.

Hospitalization Records

- Obtain all hospital files; even if the primary purpose of the hospitalization was not psychiatric in nature, the condition involved might nonetheless have produced psychiatric symptoms.
- Review every record, including the emergency room records, social work reports, and nursing observations.
- Carefully review patient questionnaire and history forms for medical and psychiatric history information.

Psychiatric and Psychological History

- Obtain complete and unredacted records, including handwritten progress notes, raw test data, and correspondence.
- Examine diagnoses, diagnostic codes, intake forms, billing information, reports, and insurance forms for consistency.
- Document all prior diagnoses of mental disorders and the nature of treatment received.
- Obtain records of marital and pastoral counselors; while these individuals do not typically diagnose and treat mental disorders, their notes may contain important information about a plaintiff's history and condition.
- Look for prior diagnoses of the condition (e.g., depression) at issue in the present litigation, suggesting a chronic or recurring condition.

Current Diagnoses and Treatment

- Identify the individual's diagnosis and specifically what he or she is being treated for. The diagnosis and treatment may not be consistent; e.g., the plaintiff may be diagnosed as suffering Posttraumatic Stress Disorder from a workplace incident but actually be receiving counseling for a marital problem.
- Look to see if a plaintiff who is alleged to be disabled is receiving any treatment for the allegedly disabling condition.
- Determine if the diagnosis is a criterion-referenced diagnosis such as set forth in *DSM-IV-TR* or instead an idiosyncratic description.
- Evaluate medication and pharmacy records to determine use of prescribed and over-the-counter medications and compare those to the medications actually prescribed.
- Pay particular attention to early prescription refills as they may be an indication of substance abuse.

Substance Abuse History

- Note any reference to concern for alcohol usage, abnormal blood or liver screens, or medical notations expressing concern over prescribed medication abuse or alcohol abuse.
- Any physician notation indicating the refusal to prescribe additional medications can be a red flag for substance abuse.

- History of DUIs or DWIs should be evaluated.
- Multiple marriages and divorces may also be indicative of substance dependence.

Criminal History

- Contact with the criminal justice system, particularly such events as arrests, trials or guilty pleas, and incarcerations, may be a significant alternative stressor.
- Criminal records should be evaluated for any issues related to substance abuse, fraud, or domestic violence inflicted or received.

Marital History

- Look for age at first marriage, number of marriages, or grounds for divorce.
- Look for any history of being involved in custody disputes, failure to pay child support, visitation or custody disputes, or hints of abuse.

Financial Records

- Changes in income, failure to honor financial obligations, foreclosures, repossessions, mortgages, or heavy debt ratios indicate significant psychosocial stressors.
- Chronic financial problems can also suggest a predisposition for malingering for financial gain or the presence of a personality disorder.

IX. Case Conceptualization

The final step in evaluating a case is the case conceptualization. Essentially, this involves evaluating whether the plaintiff in fact suffered a mental injury or disorder that was proximately caused by a workplace event and whether such a disorder has occurred in isolation or along with other disorders. If, for example, a plaintiff has suffered a pure psychological disorder induced by trauma, such as Posttraumatic Stress Disorder, and the plaintiff has no history of prior mental disorders or traumas, then such a claim would have more veracity and value than a claim in which a plaintiff with a well-documented history of recurrent depression now claims to be depressed as a result of some adverse workplace event.

Table 3-1 may be useful to the litigator attempting to evaluate a psychological injury claim. If a plaintiff has a mental disorder, such as depression, that did not exist prior to the workplace event and is currently in existence or has been in existence and is now in remission, this would suggest that the depression was related to the workplace event. If, by contrast, a plaintiff has one or more physical disorders, a personality disorder, substance abuse that can produce depressive symptoms, or a prior chronic or recurrent depression, then the causation of the plaintiff's present condition is less certain. V-code psychosocial stressors also may be present, such as an Occupational Problem or a Partner Relational Problem, and they may be producing stress and symptoms in the plaintiff that would provide an alternative explanation of the depressed mood.

It is also important to determine whether symptom exaggeration is present. Symptom exaggeration may occur either in the exaggeration of genuine symptoms or in the false production of symptoms (malingering). Alternatively, a plaintiff could consciously produce symptoms in order to assume the role of a patient, which is a Factitious Disorder with different clinical significance. In Factitious Disorders the patient is driven to assume the sick role without any external incentives such as compensation. This disorder usually occurs in intermittent episodes and not as a chronic illness.

Individuals can also produce symptoms unconsciously, creating a disorder that has a temporal but not a proximate relationship to the adverse work situation. This is called Conversion Disorder. Conversion Disorders consist of symptoms that affect voluntary motor or sensory functions and are related to psychological factors. The psychological factors are assumed to be related to this disorder since it is preceded by conflicts, stressors, or interpersonal difficulty. This disorder may be associated with the presence of secondary gain. Examples of secondary gain include maintaining or enhancing ones status in one's family, avoiding sex, or converting a socially unacceptable disability (such as a psychiatric disorder) into a socially acceptable disability (a personal injury).

Finally, if other mental disorders are present, they may impact upon the symptom presentation and confound an effort to determine precise causation of the symptoms at issue. For example a preexisting personality disorder may have predisposed an individual to having a substance abuse problem, a recurrent depression, and Somatoform Disorder.

Table 3-1   Conceptualization of the Mental Disorder

Factors to Consider

Other mental disorders
Unconscious symptom production (Conversion Disorder)
Conscious symptom production (Malingering)
Symptom exaggeration
Psychosocial stressors
V Code Conditions
Personality disorder
Substance abuse/dependence
Physical disorders
Mental disorder was exacerbated by employment
Mental disorder is not currently in existence (in remission)
Mental disorder is currently in existence
No mental disorder is present
Psychiatric treatment for alleged disorder

It is necessary to consider whether there was a mental disorder in existence preinjury and whether that disorder currently still exists or is in remission. It is possible that the preexisting condition was exacerbated by the adverse work event or may be the basis for a claim of accommodation. For example, again, if the disorder is exacerbated, this may be supported by the adverse work situation if there seems to be a temporal or proximate relationship. However, if it is exacerbated by substance abuse or a personality disorder or other mental disorders, then it is likely not related to the adverse work situation. False imputation[59] and iatrogenic imputation,[60] in which symptoms that genuinely occur are wrongfully attributed to a specific event, must also be considered and ruled out. This can often happen in litigation.

Additionally, it is important to evaluate whether a mental disorder may be present but could be completely unrelated to employment. Conditions such as a Mood Disorder Secondary to Alcohol Dependence would obviously be unrelated to employment, as would a Personality Disorder or even psychosocial stressors. They should all be carefully evaluated.

Finally, if no mental disorder is present but one is being alleged, then Malingering, a Factitious Disorder, or Conversion Disorder would have to be considered, all of which have implications for the value and veracity of the claim.

---

[59]See Chapter 11, Malingering: Distortion and Deception in Employment Litigation.

[60]David R. Price, *The Role of Financial Incentives in the Production of Mental and Emotional Symptoms*, Defense Research Institute Seminar on Defense of Damages (1997).

CHAPTER 4

THE DIAGNOSTIC AND STATISTICAL MANUAL OF MENTAL DISORDERS

Peter Brown, M.D., FRCP(C)

I. Introduction

Published in 2000 by the American Psychiatric Association, the "text revision" of the fourth edition of the *Diagnostic and Statistical Manual of Mental Disorders (DSM-IV-TR)* is currently the single most influential text in clinical psychology and psychiatry. Like its immediate predecessors, *DSM-III* and *DSM-III-R*,[1] its influence belies the dry title.

DSM-IV-TR provides a common language and overarching conception of mental disorder. Its effects extend beyond the narrowly clinical and can be seen in research, education, health care planning, the courts, and even in the perception of mental disorder in the media and among the general public. Moreover, since it has been translated into more than one dozen languages, its influence is now global.

Despite these far-reaching effects, the goals of *DSM-IV-TR* are both modest and narrow. According to the introduction, the

> highest priority has been to provide a helpful guide to clinical practice. We hoped to make DSM-IV-TR practical and useful for clinicians by striving for brevity of criteria sets, clarity of language, and explicit statements of the constructs embodied in the diagnostic criteria. An additional goal was to facilitate research and improve communication among clinicians and researchers. We were also mindful of the use of DSM-IV-TR for improving the collection of clinical information and as an educational tool for teaching psychopathology.[2]

---

[1] AMERICAN PSYCHIATRIC ASSOCIATION, DIAGNOSTIC AND STATISTICAL MANUAL OF MENTAL DISORDERS (3d ed. 1980, 3d ed. rev. 1987).

[2] AMERICAN PSYCHIATRIC ASSOCIATION, DIAGNOSTIC AND STATISTICAL MANUAL OF MENTAL DISORDERS xxiii (4th ed. text rev. 2000) (hereinafter DSM-IV-TR).

The result is a useful, even essential, tool for patient care. The goal of the *DSM* is to provide a single standardized system and language for the diagnosis and classification of psychiatric disorders. It allows for communication among clinicians of different disciplines and orientations. The *DSM* is also used routinely in research, in education, and in collecting statistical information that can be used for health care, public policy, and/or economic analyses and planning. It has also found its way into the courtroom (often with distinctly mixed results). A clear understanding of what the *DSM* can and cannot do substantially increases its utility in medicolegal settings.

II. Historical Background

A. Classification Prior to *DSM-III*

"The need for classification of mental disorders has been clear throughout the history of medicine, but there has been little agreement on which disorder should be included, and the optimal method for their organization."[3] Every literate culture has had some system of disease classification. These systems were typically based on a combination of causal theories and random observations of patients. Modern medical classification began in the seventeenth century with the writings of Thomas Sydenham and others, who emphasized the need for careful observation and description leading to diagnostic categories (syndromes or disorders), formed by describing common features (signs and symptoms) that occurred together, suggesting an underlying pathophysiology (disease).[4] Medical nosologists of the next two centuries modeled themselves on the taxonomists in chemistry, geology, zoology, and the botanical sciences who were busy charting the material world. They emphasized painstaking observation, independent of speculation about possible causation. By the late nineteenth century, the work of a generation of (primarily) German-speaking investigators had identified most of the major psychiatric syndromes. While most of these observations were based on studies of the populations of huge mental hospitals, other clinicians, such as Sigmund Freud, made important contributions in the description of an increasingly varied group of patients in office practice.

The syndromal approach remains the cornerstone of modern medicine:

> A syndrome is a group or pattern of symptoms, affects, thoughts, and behaviors that tend to appear together in clinical presentations. The assumption is that the symptoms cluster together because they are associated in some clinically meaningful way, which perhaps may reflect a common etiological process, course, treatment or response. The most important advantage of the syndromal approach is in facilitating the understanding and treatment of mental disorders. The very

---

[3]DSM-IV-TR, supra note 2, at xxiv.
[4]AMERICAN PSYCHIATRIC ASSOCIATION, DSM-IV GUIDEBOOK 3 (1995):

process of delimiting groups of patients based on patterns of core symptoms aims to define some populations that share intrinsic features like response to treatment, degree of impairment, course, family history, biological markers, and co-morbid disorders. . . .[5]

Apart from clinical and scientific needs, public health and economic pressures have also contributed to the need to classify. Formal psychiatric classification in the United States dates back a little over 100 years and originally arose out of the need to have a single system for collecting statistical information about the inmates of the large public mental hospitals of that era. The focus was thus heavily weighted toward the most severe and disabling disorders. The Committee on Statistics of the American Medico-Psychological Association (which became the American Psychiatric Association in 1921) published classifications in 1917 and 1935.[6]

After the Second World War, further impetus was provided by the need of the Veterans Administration to coordinate inpatient and outpatient services for the substantial number of veterans with mental disorders. The goal was to expand the existing system to cope with the dramatically different population of patients requiring psychiatric and psychological treatment during and after World War II (i.e., relatively more acute and reactive disorders often with obvious relationships to clear psychosocial stressors). This widening of the focus of psychiatry also reflected the growing influence of academic, psychoanalytically oriented psychiatrists who treated a far more heterogeneous population than were found in the traditional mental hospitals.

At the same time, the World Health Organization published the sixth edition of the *International Classification of Diseases, Injuries and Causes of Death (ICD-6)* including for the first time a section on the classification of mental disorders.[7] The differences between the ICD and the classification systems used in the United States highlighted the need for a further update.

The immediate result was the publication of the first edition of the *Diagnostic and Statistical Manual of Mental Disorders (DSM-I)* in 1952 by the American Psychiatric Association. Heavily influenced by the prevailing psychobiological model of the time, as expounded by Adolph Meyer, *DSM-I* contained a list of disorders and clinical features together with a small glossary. The manual did not meet with widespread acceptance. Clinicians from competing theoretical schools found many of the concepts incompatible with, and irrelevant to, their daily clinical practice. Its brevity also limited day-to-day utility. Awareness of these shortcomings, and of the gradual changes in the knowledge base of psychiatry, led to work on the second edition of the *DSM*, known as *DSM-II*, which was published in 1968. The result was largely underwhelming, with all of the original problems in *DSM-I* still largely unresolved. Furthermore, the pace

---

[5]*Id.* at 17.

[6]American Psychiatric Association, *Notes and Comment: Revised Classified Nomenclature of Mental Disorders*, 90 AM. J. PSYCHIATRY 1369 (1933).

[7]WORLD HEALTH ORGANIZATION, INTERNATIONAL CLASSIFICATION OF DISEASES, INJURIES AND CAUSES OF DEATH (1948).

of psychiatric research had increased dramatically, leaving *DSM-II* obsolete by the time it was completed.

B. *DSM-III* and *DSM-III-R*

DSM-I and its successor, *DSM-II*, were terse, brief, vague, and arbitrary. Their content reflected the opinions and clinical experience of a relatively small group of academic psychiatrists rather than the (admittedly exiguous) existing scientific evidence. The results were documents of minimal value and negligible impact. Studies of reliability (in terms of either consistency over time or agreement between clinicians) were uniformly poor.[8]

The decision to produce a new edition, taking a radically different approach, was strongly influenced by the writings of Erwin Stengel, an English psychiatrist who was a consultant to the World Health Organization.[9] Stengel reviewed the existing classifications, noted their shortcomings, and recommended a methodology to enhance the scientific and clinical value of future classifications. He promoted the notion that explicit lists of diagnostic criteria based on careful definitions of terms were essential elements in standardization. He also emphasized the need for an atheoretic approach, so that clinical observations could be separated from speculations about causes. While this might appear to be a simple, commonsense approach, at the time this was by no means a universally accepted viewpoint. It conflicted with most of the prevalent schools of psychiatry, each of whom had an explanatory theory, a self-contained vocabulary, and little interest in challenging its own assumptions. However, a number of developments were beginning to challenge this complacency.

The foremost development was a growing awareness of the weaknesses in contemporary psychiatric diagnosis. Studies in the 1960s and early 1970s had demonstrated poor diagnostic agreement among psychiatrists.[10] Surveys showed marked national or even regional differences in diagnoses, arising from a variety of social and cultural factors, including individual practitioner idiosyncrasies and differences in theoretical orientation. Psychiatrists came to different diagnoses largely because they used different criteria for making them.

With a growing consensus as to the nature of the problems, remedies could be instituted. In the United States, work to address these problems was led by Robert Spitzer and his colleagues at the New York State Psychiatric Institute and Eli Robins, Samuel Guze, and colleagues from the Washington University Department of Psychiatry. There was a gradual but steady shift away from anecdotal and theoretically based descriptions of individuals or small numbers of patients toward larger, methodologically well-designed studies with results that could be generalized to similar patients in different settings.

---

[8] Andrew E. Skodol & Robert L. Spitzer, AN ANNOTATED BIBLIOGRAPHY OF DSM-III (1987).
[9] ERWIN STENGEL, CLASSIFICATION OF MENTAL DISORDERS (1960).
[10] Skodol & Spitzer, *supra* note 8.

The goal was to standardize, as much as possible, the way in which data were gathered, which elements were considered important, and the way in which diagnostic decisions were made. By establishing consensus on these elements, a great deal of the unreliability of psychiatric diagnosis could be eliminated. Field studies designed to test these new instruments revealed a dramatic improvement in diagnostic agreement, or "interrater reliability."

The Washington University Department of Psychiatry published an initial set of psychiatric disorders, each with a list of explicit diagnostic criteria.[11] The National Institute of Mental Health's collaborative project on depression refined the Washington University criteria into the Research Diagnostic Criteria (RDC) and then developed a structured interview known as the Schedule for Affective Disorders in Schizophrenia (SADS) to increase the use of the RDC in clinical research. These developments heavily influenced the shape of *DSM-III*.

The onset of the modern era of psychopharmocology also heralded a new interest in accuracy of diagnosis. In the era before effective drug treatment of many psychiatric disorders, diagnostic precision was largely of purely theoretical interest. If patients with severe mental disorders were simply going to be institutionalized and patients with less severe disorders were automatically going to receive psychotherapy or psychoanalysis, then more precise diagnosis was of limited value. Once there were more specific and effective treatments for a growing number of psychiatric syndromes, accuracy in diagnosis became progressively more important.

The six years of development of *DSM-III*, prior to its publication in 1980, was an effort unique in the history of American psychiatry. Coordinated by Robert Spitzer, a central committee with fourteen advisory committees worked on the project. The inclusive nature of the decision-making process was unprecedented. The goal was to provide a document that would be useful for clinicians of various theoretical schools and enhance communication among disciplines by providing clear, operational definitions of the core features of the disorders while maintaining a biopsychosocial model and an atheoretical orientation. The two principal methodologic innovations of *DSM-III* were (1) specified diagnostic criteria (both inclusion and exclusion) for each of a specified number of disorders with explicit decision rules for making diagnostic judgments, and (2) a multiaxial system instituted to ensure that important information in a variety of domains was not neglected. *DSM-III* field trials, using the combination of explicit criteria sets and standardized interviews, found a marked improvement in reliability for most diagnoses while problem areas, particularly in the diagnosis of children's psychiatric disorders, were clearly identified.

Though the manual quickly became widely used, there were also a number of criticisms as well as concerns about potential misuse. The most telling concern was that, without appropriate clinical judgment, the criteria could be used in an unnaturally mechanical or rigid manner that would obscure genuine clinical differences and by "rounding off" and failing to recognize individuality

---

[11]J.P. Feighner et al., *Diagnostic Criteria for Use in Psychiatric Research*, 26 ARCHIVES GEN. PSYCHIATRY 57 (1972).

of each patient, lump them into procrustean diagnostic categories. There were also concerns and controversies about the inclusion or exclusion of particular diagnoses, protests about the elimination of popular but confusing terms (such as "neurosis") and other, more general, criticisms on professional, forensic, economic, social, or philosophical grounds. In addition, once the manual was in widespread use, imperfections and inconsistencies were discovered, which led to a considerable number of post hoc suggestions for improvements. The combination of inevitable complaints and problems in implementation of *DSM-III* led to the decision to make some, hopefully simple, revisions without having to wait for a full new edition. The result was *DSM-III-R*, which was published in 1987.

The reaction to *DSM-III-R* was mixed. The revised edition retained the key strengths of *DSM-III*, but the specific changes were not unalloyed or obvious improvements in all cases. For many users, there appeared to be rather more changes than were warranted, suggesting that the revision had come too rapidly on the heels of *DSM-III* for easy assimilation. On the other hand, some specific interest groups of clinicians and researchers were disappointed that the changes were not dramatic enough. There was also widespread concern that the decision-making process had still been too restricted, with the opinions of a few highly influential clinicians and researchers carrying disproportionate weight. "Participants in the DSM-III and the DSM-IIIR process often thought that it was unclear how and why particular decisions were made, and there was little or no documentation of the supporting evidence and rationale."[12] To its credit, the American Psychiatric Association rightly recognized that, whatever the absolute merits of any or all of these criticisms, the perception that the process had been arbitrary could seriously undermine confidence in *DSM* use. Consequently, a decision was made to provide a new revision (to be released to coincide with ICD-10) that would address these concerns.

C. *DSM-IV*

DSM-IV represents an *evolution* of *DSM-III-R* rather than a *revolution.* The greatest single innovation was in expanding and opening to greater scrutiny the way that changes were made. In addition to careful documentation of the underlying scientific rationale for or against any proposed changes, the *DSM-IV* Task Force took two additional steps to minimize avoidable bias: (1) the inclusion of as large as possible number of experts in the process and (2) an extensive effort to publicize every step of the decision-making process.[13] The basic goals of *DSM-III* and *DSM-III-R* remained unchanged. *DSM-IV*'s editors explained: "It is our belief that the major innovation of DSM-IV lies not in any of its specific content changes, but rather in the systematic and explicit process by which it was constructed and documented. More than

---

[12]DSM-IV GUIDEBOOK, *supra* note 4, at 28.
[13]*Id.* at 34.

any other nomenclature of mental disorders, DSM-IV is grounded in empirical evidence."[14]

The decision was also made, early in the inception of *DSM-IV*, to take a consistently minimalist approach to revisions. This involved allowing changes in the system only when they were driven by empirical data and not simply as a convenience to researchers or other special interest groups. In addition, because of the continued concern with a real or perceived potential proliferation of the number of disorders, the Task Force also took care to limit the number of new categories. The Task Force received suggestions for over 100 additional diagnoses. Very few came close to the standards required for serious consideration, however, and most were easily excluded. In the end, there was no increase in the number of diagnostic categories. The minimalist approach ensured that the revision focus would be limited to a few specific identified problems largely involving refinements of the criteria sets.

A final significant difference was, quite simply, that *DSM-IV* had the advantage of being preceded by *DSM-III*. Prior to *DSM-III*, the scientific literature on psychopathology was relatively meager. *DSM-III* began a bootstrap operation providing a common language which stimulated research and thereby vastly strengthened the scientific basis for all of psychiatry and psychology.

By the spring of 1989, the methodology and organizational structure for preparing *DSM-IV* was set up. It is worthwhile to consider the sheer size and extent of the effort by the thousands of clinicians involved in the creation of *DSM-IV*. A task force of 27 members divided the system into 13 areas and recruited a work group for each one. The 13 groups, each composed of a minimum of five members, were charged with reviewing the existing scientific literature for their particular topic. The goals were to identify specific questions, provide the widest and most detailed pool of information possible, include representations from all interested points of view, design studies to provide any relevant empirical data to help select the recommended options that best answered the original questions, and develop a transparent decision-making process that would allow close scrutiny of each decision. The progress of the work groups was reviewed, assisted, and critiqued by over 1,500 advisers. An extensive effort was made to include clinicians of varying viewpoints, and to encourage extensive contributions from other disciplines, as well as other countries. In the end, more than 60 organizations and associations were consulted. The process was facilitated by the close consultation that developed between the *DSM-IV* Task Force and their counterparts in the development of *ICD-10*. There were regular conferences, semiannual newsletters, and a regular column on the ongoing revisions in a widely read psychiatric journal. In addition, two years before the publication of *DSM-IV* the list of likely revisions were published as the "*DSM-IV* Options Book."

The revision process involved three steps:

- *Literature Reviews*. After intensive method conferences which provided training in a systematic procedure for finding, extracting, aggregating, and interpreting

---

[14]DSM-IV-TR, *supra* note 2, at xxiv.

data in a comprehensive and objective fashion, the members of the work groups identified 150 topics for consideration and did multiple computerized searches to identify and review all the relevant scientific literature. These literature reviews were required to specify (1) the nature and significance of the issues, (2) the methodology used in assigning weight to the existing literature, (3) the results (including a methodological review of the studies involved), and (4) the advantages and disadvantages of the various options under consideration. In order to further reduce the bias created by any advocacy of a personal opinion, the reviewers were required to take the perspective of "consensus scholars" who would begin the process of data aggregation and interpretation without a preconceived conclusion. The goal of this elaborate process was to provide a database that included all of the best available clinical and research literature, emphasizing both its strengths and limitations.

- *Data Reanalyses.* When significant conflicts in the literature or an inadequate data base were identified, the work groups requested further published and unpublished data sets from researchers in that particular field. Supported financially by the John D. and Catherine T. MacArthur Foundation, more than forty reanalyses of data sets were done to examine the comparative merits of competing criteria sets. These reanalyses were mostly of data sets from large clinical studies or epidemiologic surveys. Because of the formalized rules, the process of compiling *DSM-IV* was notably less acrimonious and politicized than that for *DSM-III* or *DSM-III-R*.[15] In cases when the literature clearly favored one perspective, the conclusions were relatively straightforward. When the review of the literature revealed either a lack of consensus or a lack of basic evidence, it was clear that further data would be needed. This process helped to refine and clarify the options so that prospective studies or field trials could be set in motion.

- *Field Trials.* Once the options were structured in a testable manner, 12 field trials to compare the alternatives and to measure the impact of proposed changes were performed under the sponsorship of the National Institute of Mental Health in collaboration with the National Institute on Drug Abuse and the National Institute on Alcohol Abuse and Alcoholism. This final step illustrates the fundamental notion of *DSM-IV* as a scientific document: in the end, the types of disorders and their features should be determined by the best evidence available in carefully designed studies. While the preparation of both *DSM-III* and *DSM-III-R* had also involved field trials, these had been on a comparatively restricted budget. The availability of a substantially larger funding base gave researchers access to a much more elaborate and more representative database. In order to ensure that the conditions reflected clinical realities, multiple sites were selected to obtain the widest range of subjects from a variety of sociocultural and ethnic backgrounds. For the 12 field trials, more than 70 sites were included and a total of more than 6,000 subjects participated. Each field trial collected information on the reliability and performance characteristics of each criteria set as a whole, as well as specific items within the criteria set. The field trials served several

---

[15]DSM-IV GUIDEBOOK, *supra* note 4, at 28.

purposes. They helped to select the optimum definition of the various disorders and reduced the risk that changes would result in unanticipated shifts in the definition and prevalence of the various disorders. Field trials are an important link between clinical research and clinical practice. For the most part, the empirical data derived from the literature review and data reanalyses had been collected under tightly controlled protocols and university settings under conditions emphasizing the protection of the internal validity of the study. As a result, most of the existing literature might or might not generalize to the very different clinical settings in which *DSM-IV* is also used.[16]

In keeping with the more open approach, the decision was made to insist on an explicit threshold for revisions that minimized the possibility of the work groups' being influenced by subjective biases. Any changes that were made had to be substantiated by explicit rationales and backed up by the empirical data.

The results of the field trials and their recommendations were then submitted by the work groups to the overall task force. This ensured that changes, which might make sense at the work group level when looking at one specific disorder, would not have unforeseen, wider consequences and complications for the system as a whole. Once the task force had completed its reviews, the recommendations were sent for approval to the Committee on Diagnosis and Assessment, the Council on Research, the Assembly, and finally, the Board of Trustees of the American Psychiatric Association. Though intensely scrutinized by each of these bodies, the recommendations were accepted without change. As a final, post-publication step to allow scholarly documentation and review of the entire process, the 150 literature reviews, the reports of the 40 data reanalyses, the results of the 12 field trials, and the final executive summary of the rationale for the decisions made by each work group have been published in a massive four-volume work, the *DSM Sourcebook*.[17]

D. *DSM-IV-TR*

The latest development, a "text revision" of *DSM-IV*, was begun in 1997 and published in 2000. *DSM-IV-TR* was the product of the same careful, systematic, and open work group approach used for *DSM-IV*. The goals of the revision were deliberately modest. The diagnostic criteria themselves were left unchanged. The changes were limited to (1) an update and correction of supporting material (from any relevant research reported since the original reviews in 1992), and (2) more detail on differential diagnosis (i.e., how one diagnosis is arrived at by systematically excluding the alternatives) and the use of Axis V. A new Appendix in *DSM-IV-TR* explicitly identifies and describes all of the changes.[18]

---

[16]*Id.* at 34.
[17]AMERICAN PSYCHIATRIC ASSOCIATION, DSM-IV SOURCEBOOK (vol. 1, 1994; vol. 2, 1996; vol. 3, 1997; vol. 4, 1998).
[18]DSM-IV-TR, *supra* note 2, at 829–43.

E. *DSM-V*

Work has begun on a fifth edition of the *DSM*, which is expected to be available sometime after 2010. The work in preparation involves studies on the validity of psychiatric diagnoses. Work groups have been organized to identify problems and possible solutions in six areas: (1) developmental diagnoses, (2) gaps in the current diagnostic system, (3) disability and impairment, (4) neuroscience, (5) nomenclature, and (6) cross-cultural issues.

III. Categories, Dimensions, and Prototypes

The *DSM Guidebook* cautions:

> The main disadvantage of syndromal classifications is the tendency for the descriptively defined syndromes to become reified and treated as if they truly represent independent disease entities. Therefore, it is important for the user of syndromal classification to realize that the syndromal groupings reflect only the state of understanding that was obtained during the drafting of that version of the classification. Regular revisions in the classification system are needed to allow the syndromes to be redefined in order to reflect the evolving understanding of the pathophysiology of mental disorders, with the ultimate goal of arriving at definitions that correspond more fully to underlying pathogenic entities and targets of treatment.[19]

One of the most important contributions of the *DSM* has been to demystify the diagnostic process in psychiatry and psychology. Making diagnoses means assigning individual cases to preexisting categories. Placing items into categories is a universal and fundamental cognitive skill essential in daily life but one that we rarely have a need to study. In everyday life we use different ways of categorizing information that usually vary according to our needs. For some items we use a categorical approach, which divides things among discrete entities (e.g., guilty or not guilty). For others that involve quantitative measurements along a scale (e.g., height, weight, or temperature), if we have an appropriate instrument, we can apply a dimensional system.

This distinction extends to categorizing human behavior. The syndromal approach, generally used in medicine and psychiatry, is a categorical system. Any diagnostic system has to be able to effectively distinguish between (1) people who have a mental disorder and those who do not, and (2) people who have different disorders. The strengths of the categorical approach include its relative simplicity and the ability that it gives to collect items in homogeneous groups. It works best when there are clear boundaries between various categories (such as when they are mutually exclusive). It works less well when there is significant overlap between the categories or when there is marked within-

---

[19] DSM-IV GUIDEBOOK, *supra* note 4, at 17.

category variation. When the boundaries are arbitrary or when there is a great deal of variation within the population, dimensional approaches (e.g., thermometers to measure temperature or yardsticks to measure length) should be more useful.

The decision to use one approach or another is a complex, real-world process based on an examination of the existing options, usually in the absence of a preexisting ideal system. The *DSM* has opted for a categorical approach to classifying mental disorders for a variety of heuristic reasons—comparative simplicity (when compared with the alternatives), synchronization with the universally accepted biomedical model (and with *ICD-10*), and the general success the categorical/syndromal approach has had in characterizing both the general medical conditions and the major psychiatric disorders.[20] This is not to say that the *DSM* implies that reality conforms to the system. Rather, the system is an attempt to model reality.

As *DSM-IV-TR* explains:

> In DSM-IV-TR, there is no assumption that each category of mental disorder is a completely discrete entity with absolute boundaries dividing it from other mental disorders or from no mental disorder. There is also no assumption that all individuals described as having the same mental disorder are alike in all important ways. The clinician using DSM-IV-TR should therefore consider that individuals sharing diagnosis are likely to be heterogeneous, even in regard to the defining features of the diagnosis and that boundary cases will be difficult to diagnoses in anything but a probabilistic fashion.[21]

Prototypes of disorders and "polythetic" criteria sets are important conceptual tools in using categories effectively and in understanding the limitations of this process. A prototype is a member of a category that possesses all the distinguishing features of the category. If typical cases are considered central and less typical cases are on the periphery, or nearer the boundary of the category, then a prototypical case is a "bull's-eye." Such a case would have all of the symptoms listed for that disorder. The closer a case is to the prototype, the greater the degree of diagnostic confidence. Unfortunately, prototypical cases, with all the features of a particular disorder and clear boundaries from other disorders, are more common in textbooks than in real life. They serve principally to enhance recognition by highlighting the key features that create a "family resemblance." *DSM-IV-TR* sees prototypes as a potential bridge between categorical and dimensional approaches that allows aspects of both to be applied.[22]

Polythetic criteria sets require that a certain, predetermined minimum number, but not all, of the possible symptoms be present in order to make a diagnosis. In contrast, in a monothetic (all or nothing) criteria set all the items must be present in order to make a diagnosis. Polythetic sets reflect

---

[20] DSM-IV-TR, *supra* note 2, at xxxi.
[21] *Id.* at xxxi–xxxii.
[22] DSM-IV GUIDEBOOK, *supra* note 4, at 19.

the heterogeneity of clinical presentations and the wide variety of individual differences in patients. Ideally, the range of a particular disorder will be determined by the degree of variation between the prototype and the minimum number of symptoms or cutoff point of the diagnostic criteria.

As the *DSM-IV Guidebook* notes:

> The prototypal approach recognizes the fuzzy boundaries and heterogeneity within the DSM-IV-TR criteria sets. Definitions are seen as the prototypal forms of the disorder, and individual class members are expected to vary greatly in the degree to which they resemble one or another. ... If one regards the DSM-IV-TR categories as prototypes, one is less likely to reify categories and more likely to respect boundary cases rather than trying to force them into one or another category.[23]

IV. The Multiaxial Evaluation

The evolution of the *DSM* has brought changes both in content and in process. One of the most significant changes in process was the addition, in *DSM-III*, of a multiaxial evaluation. This involves assessment on five different axes or domains of information, each of which may be important in diagnosis, treatment planning, or prognosis. The five axes of *DSM-IV-TR* are by no means exhaustive of every potential dimension of human behavior. Proposals for as many as twenty-three different axes were considered for *DSM-IV*. However, the decision was made to produce a system that was reasonably comprehensive without being excessively cumbersome. The domains of information that were included were those that had the best empirical support and the greatest utility. The overall goal was to develop a system that could be used to form a composite clinical picture to communicate a body of clinically relevant information—as well as to indicate what information is yet needed and thus structure further data gathering. The five axes of the current multiaxial system are illustrated in Table 4-1.

Table 4-1 The Multiaxial System

Axis I: Clinical Disorders (and other conditions that may be a focus of clinical attention)
Axis II: Personality Disorders and Mental Retardation
Axis III: General Medical Conditions
Axis IV: Psychosocial and Environmental Problems
Axis V: Global Assessment of Functioning Scale

---

[23]*Id.* at 18–19.

Taking a biopsychosocial orientation (i.e., the assumption that biological, psychological, and social factors are relevant in all psychiatric disorders), the goal of the multiaxial system is to encourage and facilitate comprehensive and systematic evaluation and to encourage clinicians of various orientations to at least consider each of the various categories and to provide a "convenient format for organizing and communicating clinical information, for capturing the complexity of clinical situations, and for describing the heterogeneity of individuals presenting with the same diagnosis."[24] The multiaxial system was designed to address several specific problems. These included:

- *Overlooking diagnoses.* There is a tendency for acute distress or symptoms to obscure important underlying chronic conditions and patterns. Mental retardation, personality disorders, and general medical conditions are all easily overlooked when the field of inquiry is too narrowly, or rapidly, restricted. The addition of Axes II and III in particular address this issue. The insistence that each clinician consider each patient along the first three axes made it much more difficult to avoid at least considering these possibilities.
- *The role of specific stressors and circumstances.* There is also a tendency of single categories to obscure what is unique about individuals. Rather than having a patient conform to a single, procrustean bed, defined by a preexisting theoretical orientation, or based on the availability or preference for particular treatments, the range of axes insists on at least the consideration of all relevant biopsychosocial factors. The fourth axis of the *DSM* allows for the consideration of the current life predicament and the complex relationship of stressors and reactions that may influence clinical status.
- *Quantifying impairment.* There is a need to quantify impairment for comparative purposes. Given the heterogeneity of patient populations, there was no way of providing useful comparative measures by diagnosis alone. The fifth axis, rating the level of function of each individual in relationship to the overall population, allows for a quick shorthand indicating issues such as the need for treatment.

Apart from the limiting conditions of adequate scientific evidence, there is no inherent reason why the axes of the *DSM* should always be limited to the current five. The divisions are arbitrary and the number selected was based on balancing the possible advantage of adding useful information (particularly when they were based on well-validated instruments) with the disadvantage of making the system progressively more cumbersome and complex and increasing the number of determinations that a clinician is expected to make.

The multiaxial system is an attempt to strike a balance between utility and detail. The goal is to convey the maximum amount of clinical relevant information in order to encourage systematic assessment and a more detailed view of the individual patient than can be conveyed by a simple diagnosis. It is quite likely with ongoing research that axes may be added, deleted, or

---

[24]DSM-IV-TR, *supra* note 2, at 27.

modified in subsequent *DSM* editions. However, the general approach of a multiaxial evaluation appears likely to be a permanent fixture in future editions.

A. Axis I: The Clinical Disorders

The body of *DSM-IV-TR* consists of criteria sets and descriptive text for the major diagnostic classes of disorders (these are set forth in Table 4-2) and "other conditions that may be a focus of clinical attention" (which are set forth in Table 4-3) and are coded on Axis I or Axis II. The disorders are grouped together either by similarities in cause or by common clinical features. The text for each disorder includes nine subsections:

- The criteria sets of specific diagnostic features
- Subtypes and their specifiers
- Specific instructions for recording procedures
- Associated features and disorders, including (1) clinical features that are common and may be helpful, but are not essential, for making the diagnosis; (2) laboratory findings that are diagnostic, simply associated, or common complications of the disorder; and (3) findings in the physical examination that may be helpful in the differential diagnosis
- Specific cultural, age, or gender features (what is known about the effect of these factors on the prevalence rates or presentations of the specific disorder)
- Available data on both lifetime and point prevalence, incidence, and lifetime risk in different clinical settings.
- Course (the progression over time of typical patterns of symptoms)
- Familial pattern (the relative frequency of the disorder among first-degree relatives of those with the disorder compared with the frequency in the general population)
- Differential diagnosis (i.e., the decision sequence that is to be used to differentiate the disorder from others that have similar characteristics and presenting features).

In order to increase the sensitivity of clinicians to the role that cultural or ethnic factors may play, *DSM-IV-TR* includes a discussion of common cultural variations in clinical presentations and two related appendixes. One involves a description of culture-bound syndromes, or "the ways in which varied cultural backgrounds affect the content and form of the symptom presentation . . . preferred idioms for describing distress, and information on prevalence." The second provides an outline for cultural formulation to "increase sensitivity to variations in how mental disorders may be expressed in different cultures" to "reduce the possible effect of unintended bias stemming from the clinician's own cultural background."[25]

---

[25]*Id.* at xxxiv. For a more detailed discussion, see also 3 DSM-IV SOURCEBOOK, *supra* note 17, at 861–1016.

Table 4-2 Axis I Disorders

Disorders usually first diagnosed in infancy, childhood, or adolesence
Delirium, dementia, amnestic, and other cognitive disorders
Mental disorders due to a general medical condition
Substance-related disorders
Schizophrenia and other psychotic disorders
Mood disorders
Anxiety disorders
Somatoform disorders
Factitious disorders
Dissociative disorders
Sexual and gender identity disorders
Eating disorders
Sleep disorders
Impulse-control disorders
Adjustment disorders

Table 4-3 Other Conditions That May Be a Focus of Clinical Attention

Psychological factors affecting general medical conditions
Medication-induced disorders
Relational problems
Problems associated with abuse or neglect
Additional conditions (noncompliance with treatment, malingering, antisocial behavior, borderline intellectual function, age-related cognitive decline, bereavement, and educational, occupational, identity, religious, acculturation, or phase-of-life problems)

Diagnoses on Axis I should be listed in order of their immediate clinical importance. In each section the category "not otherwise specified" is included to assist clinicians doing preliminary evaluations or when they are confronted with patients who do not fit the existing categories. The list of Axis I disorders includes the following categories.

1. Disorders Usually First Diagnosed in Infancy, Childhood, or Adolescence

These diagnoses are most often identified in childhood and usually have a lifelong pattern. Particularly in the case of some of the milder disorders, or in circumstances where access to psychiatric care has not been readily available, however, these diagnoses may not actually be made until adulthood. The reliability of diagnoses in children has lagged behind those for most other Axis I disorders. The inherent difficulties of evaluating children (e.g., multiple biases, fears of stigma, the role of developmental factors, environmental influences, and the relative difficulty of most children in describing their experiences in adult terms) all continue to make this section a priority for ongoing improvement.

2. Delirium, Dementia, Amnestic, and Other Cognitive Disorders

This group of disorders includes three general patterns of cognitive deficits:

- Disturbances in consciousness with associated changes in cognition (delirium)
- Multiple cognitive deficits of a chronic and generally progressive type (dementia)
- Problems of memory in the absence of other significant cognitive deficits (amnestic disorder)

The grouping of disorders in *DSM-III-R,* under the single heading of Organic Mental Syndromes, has been subdivided in *DSM-IV-TR* into three sections: Delirium, Dementia, Amnestic, and Other Cognitive Disorders; Mental Disorders Due to a General Medical Condition; and Substance-Related Disorders. The term "organic" has been eliminated from *DSM-IV-TR* because of the possible misleading inference that other diagnoses were not organic (i.e., did not have a biological basis). However, the sections remain clustered together because of their priority in differential diagnosis (i.e., they must be excluded prior to making other *DSM-IV-TR* diagnoses).

3. Mental Disorders Due to a General Medical Condition

These are disorders of brain function directly related to the physiologic effects of a general medical condition (as opposed to being a psychological reaction to having the condition or its consequences). Clinicians should always consider general medical conditions as a possible cause of psychiatric symptoms for three important reasons:

- Identification and treatment of the underlying condition are critical.
- There are no specific, pathognomonic features of a mental disorder caused by general medical condition. Any psychiatric disorder can, at least potentially, be the result of a general medical condition.
- There is a particular contemporary concern related to the way health care is provided, such that when general medical and psychiatric treatment systems are separated, clinicians in one or the other system are more likely to overlook possible alternatives. There is good evidence that psychiatric clinicians may not recognize general medical conditions, while focusing primarily on psychiatric conditions, and there is substantial evidence that florid psychiatric disorders can go unrecognized or untreated in medical or surgical settings.[26] *DSM-IV-TR* makes a determined effort to alert clinicians to the ongoing need for careful medical screening by thorough history, physical examination, and appropriate laboratory investigations.

---

[26]*Id.* at 401–07; *DSM-IV-TR, supra* note 2, at 765–70.

4. Substance-Related Disorders

The two major types of substance-related disorders are (1) *substance-use* disorders (dependence and abuse), and (2) *substance-induced* disorders (intoxication, withdrawal, or other clinical syndromes). As with the disorders secondary to a general medical condition, substance-related disorders must be given a high diagnostic priority by virtue of their frequency and their specific treatment implications. At the same time, their identification can be particularly difficult. For a variety of reasons, patients may deny or minimize substance use. The substance-induced disorders (as with the disorders that are due to a general medical condition) can mimic virtually any psychiatric presentation. Effective identification of this group involves a high index of clinical suspicion with alertness to any of the subtle warning cues, information gathering from other sources, sensitivity to cultural or other contexts, physical examinations, and the appropriate use of laboratory testing.

5. Schizophrenia and Other Psychotic Disorders

This group includes the typically severe and pervasive group of clinical syndromes that are referred to under the heading of schizophrenia and other presentations that are diagnostically similar (Schizophreniform Disorder, Schizoaffective Disorder, Delusional Disorder, Brief Psychotic Disorder, and Shared Psychotic Disorder). The traditional subtypes of schizophrenia (Paranoid, Disorganized, Catatonic, Undifferentiated, and Residual) were retained, despite continued concerns about their utility. Research in this area strongly predicts the likely eventual adoption of the three-factor dimensional system (psychotic, disorganized, and negative) that is included in Appendix B of *DSM-IV-TR*.[27]

6. Mood Disorders

This group encompasses disorders including depressed mood or forms of elation. The basic list of disorders is supplemented by description of four types of mood episode that can be used as diagnostic building blocks. The presence or absence of depressed, manic, mixed, or hypomanic episodes is used to subclassify the presentation of a mood disorder into *unipolar* (depression alone) or *bipolar* (periods of depression alternating with periods of elation) disorders. Unipolar disorders are further subdivided into major depression or dysthymia. Bipolar disorder is subdivided into types I or II on the basis of the presence (I) or absence (II) of full-blown manic episodes. The rules for making these diagnoses may initially appear quite complicated because mood disorders have a wide variety of presentations, levels of severity, clinical course, and response to treatment. In addition to accurate descriptions of current symptoms, correct diagnosis requires a careful history, which includes a consideration of the natural history or progression of the disorder and its response to treatment.

---

[27]DSM-IV-TR, *supra* note 2, at 765–70.

Careful documentation of the symptoms and the way they change over time can resolve many diagnostic dilemmas. Review of old records and collateral sources can be extremely helpful.

7. Anxiety Disorders

This group of disorders is subdivided into:

- Episodes of severe anxiety (panic attacks)
- Anxiety related to particular situations (phobias, acute stress, or Posttraumatic Stress Disorder)
- Anxiety that is associated with the presence of obsessions or compulsions
- More generalized anxiety.

The inclusion of Posttraumatic Stress Disorder and Acute Stress Disorder with the other anxiety disorders was a controversial measure but one which, on the basis of existing information, was believed to make the most nosologic sense.[28]

8. Somatoform Disorders

These disorders are characterized by the presence of physical symptoms that are:

- Not fully accounted for by a general medical condition (somatization, conversion, pain disorder)
- A preoccupation with illness (hypochondriasis) or
- Associated with an imagined physical defect (body dysmorphic disorder)

These diagnoses must be carefully considered in patients with diagnoses of controversial syndromes such as chronic fatigue syndrome, fibromyalgia, and multiple chemical sensitivity.

9. Factitious Disorders

This heading includes an intentional feigning of physical or psychological symptoms to assume the sick role. It should be distinguished from malingering, which is intentional feigning of physical or psychological symptoms for an external motivation. Factitious Disorder (historically referred to as "Munchausen's Syndrome") is considered a mental disorder, while malingering is not (see below under "other conditions that may be a focus of clinical attention"). However, both Factitious Disorder and malingering are among the most difficult determinations for clinicians to make as clinicians typically depend heavily on the accuracy of what patients tell them. Balancing between excessive skepticism and gullibility is an ongoing challenge to clinical judgment that requires consideration of the context in which the symptoms occur, with special attention paid to atypical or unusual presentations (especially regarding the nature, severity, or duration of symptoms), frequent hospitalizations without

---

[28] DSM-IV GUIDEBOOK, *supra* note 4, at 264.

follow-up, and noncompliance with treatment. Evidence from collateral sources is always important.

10. Dissociative Disorders

These disorders involve a disturbance in integrative functions of memory (dissociative amnesia), consciousness (dissociative fugue), perception (depersonalization), or identity (Dissociative Identity Disorder). The dissociative disorders are related in a hierarchic manner, with the more inclusive identity disorder taking precedence over the others. Dissociative Identity Disorder was previously included in *DSM-III* as Multiple Personality Disorder. Three reasons were provided for the change: (1) to underline the common role of dissociation and underlying continuity of these disorders, (2) to eliminate the notion that Multiple Personality Disorder is a personality disorder,[29] and (3) the empirical evidence suggests that the distinct identities or personality states experienced or manifested by these patients are better considered as dissociated or inadequately integrated aspects of a single personality rather than reified as discrete and separate personalities within a single individual.[30] The changes reflect a sharp disagreement about the actual prevalence of the disorder. Noting this controversy, the *Guidebook* opines that, circa 1995, "Dissociative Disorders are probably overdiagnosed because of wide media coverage, iatrogenic suggestions, and the assumption that all cases of childhood sexual abuse result in these disorders."[31] In light of this tendency toward overdiagnosis, the *Guidebook*'s editors conclude with a caution that symptoms of these disorders can be found as associated features of many other disorders, and these alternatives "should be carefully considered and ruled out before a diagnosis of Dissociative Disorder is made."[32] In the section on differential diagnosis of Dissociative Identity Disorder, *DSM-IV-TR* takes the additional step of reminding clinicians of the need to note the context and be particularly aware of the possibility of malingering or factitious disorder.[33]

11. Sexual and Gender Identity Disorders

This section includes (1) disturbances of sexual function (including diminished desire or arousal, some types of pain during intercourse, and failure to reach orgasm); (2) the paraphilias (disorders characterized by "recurrent, intense sexually arousing fantasies, sexual urges or behaviors"[34] involving children or other nonconsenting persons (e.g., pedophilia and exhibitionism), nonliving objects (e.g., fetishism), and humiliation or suffering of oneself or one's partner

---

[29]For a discussion of personality disorders, see Chapter 6, Personality Disorders.
[30]2 DSM-IV SOURCEBOOK, *supra* note 17, at 973–1005.
[31]DSM-IV GUIDEBOOK, *supra* note 4, at 307.
[32]*Id.* at 307.
[33]DSM-IV-TR, *supra* note 2, at 529.
[34]*Id.* at 566.

(e.g., sexual masochism or sadism)); and (3) gender identity disorders characterized by "severe and persisting problems in one's sense of gender identification as a male or female."[35]

12. Eating Disorders

This includes Anorexia Nervosa, Bulimia, and their variants, including Binge Eating Disorder.

13. Sleep Disorders

This group includes primary sleep disorders and those that are secondary to a mental disorder, a general medical condition, or substance use. The frequency and heterogeneity of sleep complaints make the diagnosis of many primary sleep problems especially difficult. While some sleep disorders are easily characterized, others (such as Circadian Rhythm Sleep Disorder) can be difficult to distinguish quantitatively or qualitatively from the vicissitudes of daily life.

14. Impulse-Control Disorders

This grouping of relatively rare, and poorly studied, disorders includes failure to control an impulse to harm self or others that is not better accounted for by other psychiatric diagnoses. Further studies are needed to establish better diagnostic reliability for all the disorders in this grouping.

15. Adjustment Disorders

Changes in thinking, emotions, or behavior are common in response to stressful life events. Adjustment disorders form a residual diagnostic category that includes a variety of responses to acute or chronic stressors that are clinically significant yet do not meet the diagnostic thresholds for the other specific *DSM-IV-TR* disorders. In the differential diagnostic process, consideration of whether or not the person has an adjustment disorder is the final step before concluding that no psychiatric disorder is present. As a residual category it presents methodological problems for researchers, and thus the scientific literature is far less extensive than the literature on most other psychiatric disorders, particularly with regard to prognosis and appropriate treatment.

As a category, adjustment disorders can have particular significance in employment cases in a number of ways. First, as one of the few *DSM-IV-TR* categories with a presumed etiology (i.e., by definition the presenting symptoms are the consequence a specific stressor or stressors), the diagnosis may have significant legal implications. Care must be taken to use clinical judgment to establish if this is indeed the most parsimonious explanation (i.e., whether the presentation is best conceptualized as an adjustment disorder or as part of a

---

[35]*Id.* at 576.

preexisting disorder). One common problem can be distinguishing between adjustment disorder and a personality disorder. In the section on differential diagnosis, *DSM-IV-TR* notes, "Because Personality Disorders are frequently exacerbated by stress, the additional diagnosis of Adjustment Disorder is usually not made."[36] Similarly, it is important to determine if the ostensible stressor is indeed responsible for the symptoms or whether it can better be understood as a consequence of other stressors. When litigation and possible compensation are at issue, other possible and common stressors such as marital or family conflict may be overlooked or downplayed. Similarly the very state of not working, or "worklessness," can by itself be a potent cause of psychological distress because of the important role that work plays in our culture in defining personal identity and helping one maintain self-esteem.[37] Consequently, symptoms that are attributed to an event in the workplace that lead to stopping work may actually be more accurately seen as a result of the decision to stop working and the resulting role change. Finally, as the last step before diagnosing no mental disorder, financial pressures on both the patient and clinician (e.g., mental health benefits typically only cover *DSM-IV-TR* diagnoses) may encourage a form of diagnostic "grade inflation" and discourage the use of the a more appropriate designation of "Other Conditions That May Be a Focus of Clinical Attention."

16. Other Conditions That May Be the Focus of Clinical Attention

This grouping includes a number of common life predicaments (Table 4-3). People who receive a "V code" diagnosis present with a problem that is the focus of clinical attention and may require evaluation and an intervention (e.g., education, support, reassurance, or advice) of a common life problem without receiving a formal psychiatric diagnosis. Appropriate use of this category serves to remind clinicians that people can find themselves in circumstances that cause emotional distress without necessarily having a psychiatric disorder. Clearly, such work has been an important part of what physicians do, and inclusion of this category clearly undermines the occasionally heard argument that the *DSM* excessively "psychiatrizes" human behavior. Unfortunately, the usefulness of this category has been vitiated in the United States by a number of influences that stem indirectly or directly from a managed mental health care system that often arbitrarily restricts payment for services to a number of predetermined diagnoses.

B. Axis II: Personality Disorders and Mental Retardation

Personality disorders are manifested by enduring pervasive and inflexible patterns of inner experience and behavior as manifested in thinking, impulse

---

[36] *Id.* at 682.

[37] B. Schulman, *Worklessness and Disability: Expansion of the Biopsychosocial Perspective,* 4 J. OCCUP. REHAB. 113 (1994).

control, and emotional expression or interpersonal functioning which are not accounted for by cultural differences, and which result in significant impairment or distress.[38] Diagnosis involves a two-step process: (1) establishing whether or not the generic personality disorder criteria are met (i.e., does the person have a personality disorder or not?); and (2) establishing whether the disorder meets criteria for any of the specific subtypes. In addition, clinicians are encouraged to list maladaptive personality traits that do not meet the diagnostic threshold, especially if they believe the traits will prove to be clinically relevant.

For convenience, the subtypes of personality disorders (Table 4-4) can be grouped into three clusters: (1) odd–eccentric, (2) dramatic–emotional, and (3) anxious–fearful. It is the nature of the subtypes and differentiating among them that cause most of the difficulties in this controversial, but essential, category. Studies suggest a high degree of overlap between the subtypes categories. In the best studies done to date, multiple diagnoses of different personality subtypes are the rule rather than the exception, with patients receiving an average of between 2.8 and 4.6 different subtype diagnoses.[39] According to the current system, clinicians should adopt a strictly empirical approach and diagnose as many of the patterns as are present but without assuming that each personality subtype diagnosis implies a separate diagnostic entity,[40] with the result that multiple diagnoses should be common.

Table 4-4 Axis II Personality Disorders

CLUSTER A: "odd/eccentric" (Paranoid, Schizoid, Schizotypal)
CLUSTER B: "emotional/dramatic" (Histrionic, Antisocial, Narcissistic, Borderline)
CLUSTER C: "anxious/fearful" (Avoidant, Dependent, Obsessive-Compulsive)

Axis II also includes a not otherwise specified (NOS) subgroup for people who meet the general criteria without meeting the criteria for a specific subcategory.

Significant concern has been expressed about the limitations of the current system of Axis II diagnostic categories. Although careful use of the system is reasonably effective at identifying patients who have personality disorders, the utility of the subtypes has not been clearly established.[41] However, the greater focus of attention on this group of disorders is, by itself, worth the controversy. Prior to *DSM-III,* studies had demonstrated that Axis II diagnoses were frequently overlooked by clinicians while dealing with Axis I disorders.[42] This

---

[38] DSM-IV Guidebook, *supra* note 4, at 358–59.
[39] 4 DSM-IV Sourcebook, *supra* note 17, at 1123.
[40] DSM-IV Guidebook, *supra* note 4, at 365.
[41] 4 DSM-IV Sourcebook, *supra* note 17, at 1123–37.
[42] C. Robert Cloninger, Personality and Psychopathology 377–506 (1999).

oversight frequently had far-reaching repercussions, as people with personality disorders or mental retardation are much more likely to have complicated psychiatric or medical presentations and to require lengthier, or modified, treatment.[43] Most clinicians and researchers agree, however, that the shortcomings of the current system, both perceived and real, have stimulated innovative approaches that will eventually have an impact on clinical practice.

C. Axis III: General Medical Conditions

Axis III requires the clinician to identify possible general medical conditions and to consider their possible roles in the current presentation. A general medical condition can be related to Axis I or II diagnoses in a number of ways:

- It may be a direct cause of psychological disturbances (such as when hypothyroidism causes symptoms of depression).
- It may provoke a psychological reaction (e.g., an Adjustment Disorder with Depressed Mood in an adolescent with diabetes).
- It may be a complicating factor that may have important treatment or prognostic implications (e.g., when a diagnosis of Parkinson's Disease has to be considered because of the potential side effects of psychotropic medication, which may exacerbate the neurologic condition).
- It may be present but currently unimportant with respect to the psychological status of the person.

A list of the most commonly used general medical diagnoses from the *ICD-9* is included in an appendix of the *DSM-IV-TR*.[44]

On Axis III, *DSM-IV* replaced the *DSM-III-R* term "Physical Disorder" with "General Medical Condition" to underscore the belief that the distinction between "mental" and "physical" disorders is a misleading bias that does not recognize the interplay of biological, psychological, and sociological factors in every illness. It is to the credit of *DSM-IV-TR* that it does not create hard-and-fast distinctions where none exist.

D. Axis IV: Psychosocial and Environmental Problems

Adverse life events can trigger, worsen, or perpetuate mental disorders. Axis IV is used to identify psychosocial and environmental problems that may influence the clinical presentation, the course of treatment, or the prognosis for Axis I and Axis II disorders. Axis IV encourages clinicians to consider factors that may be critical in the overall management of the patient.

DSM-IV-TR groups psychosocial problems under the following specific categories:

---

[43]DSM-IV GUIDEBOOK, *supra* note 4, at 380.
[44]DSM-IV-TR *supra* note 2, at 867.

- Problems with the primary support group
- Problems related to the social environment
- Educational problems
- Occupational problems
- Housing problems
- Economic problems
- Problems with access to health care services
- Problems related to integration with the legal system/crime
- Other psychosocial and environmental problems

Clinicians have the option of using the checklist of problems listed and/or then specifying the exact nature of the problem or problems. Typically, the stressors are restricted to those that have occurred in the past year. However, long-standing, chronic, or severe problems that occurred many years in the past that still have an enduring influence are also recorded. Psychosocial and environmental problems that become the primary focus of clinical attention (usually in the absence of another psychiatric diagnosis) are recorded on Axis I.

Researchers noted that for *DSM-III* and *DSM-III-R*, a substantial number of clinicians were either misusing Axis IV or ignoring it completely. In addition, the limited research found only modest levels of reliability and uncertain levels of validity.[45] There are detailed methodologies for evaluating and measuring psychosocial stressors that demonstrate high levels of reliability, but they are currently too complex for routine clinical use. The *DSM-IV* work group for Axis IV reviewed a number of proposed alternatives, for both their scientific credentials and their convenience, without being able to identify a solution.[46] The actual changes accepted were very minor and were made in the hope that greater user-friendliness might improve utilization.

E. Axis V: Global Assessment of Functioning

Axis V, the Global Assessment of Functioning (GAF) Scale, is an overall clinical impression of the degree of impairment and its changes over time. The scale, which is set forth in Table 4-5, provides a single numeric value that can be used to compare the social, psychological, and occupational functioning of the individual patient with the full range of human function.

Table 4-5 Axis V: Global Assessment of Functioning (Rating of Severity of Symptoms or Impairment)

100–91 Superior function
90–81 Good function
80–71 Transient symptoms or slight impairment

---

[45] 4 DSM-IV SOURCEBOOK, *supra* note 17, at 941.
[46] 3 *Id.* at 409–22; 4 *id.*, at 942.

70–61 Mild symptoms or impairment
60–51 Moderate symptoms or impairment
50–41 Serious symptoms or impairment
40–31 Major impairment in several areas or impaired communication and/or reality testing
30–21 Serious impairments in behavior, communication, or judgment or inability to function in almost all areas
20–11 Gross impairment in personal hygiene or communication or some danger to self or others
10–1 Persistent, imminent danger to self or others, incoherent, mute, or inability to maintain minimal personal hygiene
0 Inadequate information

Axis V requires the clinician to record a single score for overall psychological, social, and occupational functioning along a hypothetical continuum from superior functioning (100) in a wide range of activities to extreme and persistent dysfunction (1).[47] "In making the single GAF rating, two separate assessments are required: (1) how serious the symptoms are, and (2) how serious the impairment in school, work, or social function is. The final rating is based on whichever of the two assessments is the worst. As the GAF scale is usually used, the symptom rating tends to overshadow the ratings of functional impairment."[48]

In order to facilitate its use, the GAF scale is provided with particular verbal descriptions as anchor points for each ten-point increment. *DSM-IV-TR* recommends a four step method to determine the GAF. Clinicians are instructed to (1) start at the top of the scale and (2) move down to find the description of the symptom severity or level of impairment (whichever is worse) that best fits. On finding the appropriate decile (ten-point range), the clinician should then (3) double check, by examining the next range below, and then (4) determine which score within that ten-point range fits most closely by comparing the upper and lower ends of the range.[49]

Axis V has a number of limitations in actual practice that must remain in the forefront of clinical awareness. It specifically excludes impairments that are related to physical or environmental limitations. In practice, such impairments can be very significant for patients in extreme environments (e.g., prison) or who have significant medical impairments. Identifying which issues are psychological or social and which ones are physical or environmental can be highly arbitrary.

Numeric values are beloved of data collectors everywhere, and managed care companies and various other insurers have insisted on having a score provided, sometimes to the neglect of other, more pertinent information, simply because a number (even if it is not accurate) is more manageable than verbal descriptions. This has resulted in an increased reliance on the scale without

---

[47] DSM-IV-TR, *supra* note 2, at 32.
[48] DSM-IV GUIDEBOOK, *supra* note 4, at 77.
[49] DSM-IV-TR, *supra* note 2, at 33.

necessarily assessing its clinical relevance. Certainly, a single numeric score appears to allow a quick and simple representation of current function as well as measuring change in level of function over time. This means that it can be a general indicator of response to treatment or a potential worsening of the clinical state. The very simplicity of a single numeric value that makes it so appealing to various organizations who have a need to quantify the level of psychological impairment means that it is potentially vulnerable to misuse, however.

As with Axis IV, surveys of practicing clinicians indicated that Axis V was not being widely used and was frequently misused. The *DSM-IV* Committee determined that this was the result of an interplay of lack of clinical utility and scientific validity, a lack of training and experience for most clinicians for making such ratings, and a lack of user-friendliness.[50] The principal problem with the scale has been that the need to make it flexible and general enough for many clinical settings has resulted in a system that can be interpreted in too many different ways by clinicians. As with Axis IV, all the proposed amendments in the scale had disqualifying disadvantages, and the final changes contained in *DSM-IV* were relatively minor and designed for greater user-friendliness.

Studies of how the GAF performs have reported that the correlation with more detailed symptom ratings was good but the correlation with degree of impairment of function as rated by better-established measures was poor.[51] Also, the levels of agreement among clinician ratings can be very high in a relatively homogeneous patient population.[52]

The principal potential limitation of the GAF scale is that it is more reliably used in rating symptom severity than in rating the level of associated impairment. This appears to be related to the reality that most clinicians are more meticulous about reviewing current symptoms and their severity than they are about establishing levels of psychosocial function. With all of the reservations in mind, there are obvious advantages nonetheless to persisting in the development of a scale, or scales, that can reliably rate the overall severity of symptoms or impairment and can be used to indicate changes over time. As *DSM-IV-TR* points out, there is no necessary connection between level of function and any particular diagnosis.[53] Individuals within the same diagnostic category can vary widely with respect to their psychological health and their level of social functioning. A reliable shorthand for indicating what level of treatment (e.g., inpatient vs. outpatient or type, frequency, or duration of treatment) and measuring improvement or response to treatment would be highly desirable. Finally, while developments in specialized rating scales can be helpful in specific

---

[50]3 DSM-IV SOURCE BOOK, *supra* note 17, at 439.

[51]Peter P. Roy-Byrne et al., *Evidence for Limited Validity of the Revised Global Assessment of Functioning Scale*, 47 PSYCHIATRIC SERVICES 864 (1996).

[52]Mark J. Hilsenroth, et al., *Reliability and Validity of DSM-IV Axis V*, 157 AM. J. PSYCHIATRY 1858 (2000).

[53]DSM-IV-TR, *supra* note 2, at xxxiii.

settings, unless there is an overall system such as the GAF, it will be impossible to translate these findings to different settings.

F. The Appendixes

The final section of *DSM-IV-TR* is a group of appendixes including:

- Decision trees for differential diagnosis that outline the important features of the decision-making process given a particular presenting symptom
- A set of twenty-six research criteria sets for disorders, and three optional axes described below.
- Glossary of technical terms
- A description of changes in *DSM-IV-TR*
- Alphabetical and numerical lists of the *DSM-IV-TR* diagnoses
- A list of *ICD-9CM* codes (see Section V.C) for the most common associated general medical conditions
- A *DSM-IV-TR* classification with the *ICD-10* codes that will eventually supersede the ICD-9CM coding
- An outline for cultural formulation and a glossary of culture-specific syndromes

The three optional axes contained in the appendixes to *DSM-IV-TR* are as follows:

- *The Defensive Functioning Scale* is a measure, based on psychoanalytic models, that identifies the particular defense mechanisms used by an individual.
- *The Global Assessment of Relational Functioning Scale (GARF)* is analogous to the GAF used for individuals and can be used to rate the level of function of a family or other ongoing relationship.
- *The Social and Occupational Functioning Assessment Scale (SOFAS)* is a scale similar to the GAF, but which focuses solely on social and occupational functioning.

These additional axes were considered to have insufficient current empirical evidence to be included with the official diagnostic categories but were felt to warrant further study.

V. Commonly Used Terms in *DSM-IV-TR*

A. Mental Disorder

DSM-IV-TR attempts to categorize the nature and extent of what is known about the range of mental disorders. According to *DSM-IV-TR*,

> each of the mental disorders is conceptualized as a clinically significant behavioral or psychological pattern that occurs in an individual that is associated with present distress (*e.g.*, a painful symptom) or disability (*i.e.*, impairment in one or more important areas of functioning) or with a significantly increased risk of suffering,

death, pain, disability, or an important loss of freedom. In addition, this syndrome or pattern must not merely be an expectable or culturally sanctioned response to a particular event, for example, the death of a loved one. Whatever its original cause, it must currently be considered a manifestation of a behavioral, psychological, or biological dysfunction in the individual. Neither deviant behavior (*e.g.*, political, religious, or sexual) nor conflicts that are primarily between the individual and society are mental disorders unless the deviance or conflict is a symptom of a dysfunction in the individual, as described above.[54]

B. Clinically Significant Impairment or Distress

In addition to meeting the specific diagnostic criteria for a mental disorder, *DSM-IV-TR* requires for most disorders that the features have "clinical significance," or be sufficiently serious so as to warrant clinical attention. This is usually worded as "[c]auses clinically significant distress or impairment in social, occupational, or other important areas of functioning."[55]

C. Numerical Codes

All illnesses and disorders in every branch of medicine in the United States are assigned a numerical code from the *International Classification of Diseases, 9th Revision, Clinical Modification (ICD-9CM)*. The numerical codes with each diagnosis have a variety of administrative uses, including reimbursement of clinicians collecting statistics on the various disorders, and utilization review for managed care. The three- to-five digit codes that accompany each *DSM* diagnosis are those of *ICD-9CM*.

D. Subtypes and Specifiers

The *DSM-IV Guidebook* explains: "One of the weaknesses of the DSM system has been its excessive emphasis on the cross sectional symptom presentation at the expense of providing information concerning the longer term course features of the disorder. Often, the past history of the disorder is the best predictor of the future course and response to treatment."[56] In an attempt to address this problem, certain *DSM-IV-TR* diagnostic codes contain an "x," indicating that specifiers describing a level of severity or subtype of the disorder should be included.

Specifiers come in two forms—(1) severity (mild, moderate, or severe) and (2) course (in partial remission, in full remission, or prior history). The

---

[54]*Id.* at xxxi.
[55]*Id.* at xxxi–xxxii.
[56]DSM-IV GUIDEBOOK, *supra* note 4, at 56.

severity specifiers are based on consideration of the number of symptoms and the degree of associated social or occupational functional impairment. The course specifier helps to compare the current presentation (generally, the peak severity over the past month) with previous levels of severity. For example, if the current symptom picture does not meet the full criteria, but did so in the past, the specifier "in partial remission" is used. For patients who have improved to the point that no criteria are present any longer, clinicians may elect to use the specifiers "full remission" or "prior history," or no longer record the diagnosis. The distinction between the "full remission" and "prior history" is made to raise the question as to whether continued treatment is required to prevent relapse.

In order to make use of the specifiers easier, the text sections describing the characteristic course of each disorder were expanded in *DSM-IV* to cover the following:

- Age at onset
- Mode of onset (e.g., sudden, insidious)
- Whether the disorder is typified by single episode, recurrent episode with symptom-free periods, or a continuous course
- The number of episodes and their typical duration
- Overall progression of the condition (e.g., worsening or improving with age)
- If there is more than one condition, the temporal sequencing of those conditions.[57]

E. Principal Diagnosis (Reason for Visit)

The term *principal diagnosis* is used in inpatient settings for the condition that is the principal cause for the admission. In an outpatient setting, the term *reason for visit* is the diagnosis that is the main focus of attention or treatment. Other diagnoses should be listed in order of priority of clinical need.

F. Differential Diagnosis

In making a diagnosis, clinicians explicitly or implicitly use a decision tree, or algorithm, moving from a description of current symptoms toward a specific diagnosis by progressively eliminating the plausible alternatives. Without explicit criteria, this differential diagnosis process is often haphazard and idiosyncratic. The appendix of differential diagnosis decision trees displays an explicit systematic and consistent application of the rules.[58]

The differential diagnosis process involves a sequence of six basic steps:

1. *Rule out Malingering/Factitious Disorder. DSM-IV-TR* directs the clinician to first answer the question, "Is the presenting symptom for real?" The *DSM-IV-TR*

---

[57]*Id.* at 58.
[58]DSM-IV-TR, *supra* note 2, at 745–58.

editors comment: "We include this as our first step because it is so often missed in clinical practice."[59] They point out that it is naïve to believe that the clinician-patient relationship is always based on mutual trust and total honesty and they suggest that an appropriate stance involves sensitivity to the context in which symptoms are presented.
2. *Rule out substance abuse etiology.*
3. *Rule out a disorder due to a General Medical Condition.*
4. *Determine the specific primary disorder, if any.* If Malingering/Factitious Disorder, substance abuse etiology, and a disorder due to a general medical condition are all ruled out, the next step is to make the clinical judgment as to whether the presentation meets the diagnostic threshold for any of the other specific *DSM-IV-TR* diagnoses.
5. *Differentiate between "Not Otherwise Specified" (NOS) and an "Adjustment Disorder."* If the presentation does not meet the diagnostic threshold for any specific diagnosis apart from an Adjustment Disorder, the next step is to make a clinical judgment of whether or not the reported symptoms have developed as a maladaptive response to a psychosocial stressor. If they have, the diagnosis of adjustment disorder is made. If the symptoms are judged not to be a response to such a stressor, then the relevant NOS diagnosis should be made.
6. *Consider a diagnosis of "No Mental Disorder."* The editors note, "This is generally the last step in each of the decision trees but it is by no means the least important or easiest to make. Taken individually, many of the symptoms included in DSM-IV-TR are fairly ubiquitous and are not by themselves indicative of the presence of a mental disorder. During their lives, most people may experience periods of anxiety, depression, sleeplessness, or sexual dysfunction that may be considered as no more than an expected part of the human condition."[60] It is also at this point that the category "other conditions that may be the focus of clinical attention" should be considered.

G. Inclusion and Exclusion Criteria

Inclusion criteria are the items that must be present for a diagnosis to be made. Exclusion criteria are the states or conditions that would preclude the diagnosis. The combination is used to establish useful boundaries between the diagnoses and to assist in the process of differential diagnoses.

The following types of exclusion criteria are found in the *DSM-IV-TR*:

- "Not due to the direct physiologic effects of a substance (*e.g.*, a drug of abuse, or a medication) or general medical condition."

---

[59]Michael B. First, Allen Frances & Harold Alan Pincus, *DSM-IV Handbook of Differential Diagnosis* 1 (1995).
[60]*Id.* at 11.

- "Criteria are not met for . . ."
- "Criteria have never been met for . . ."
- "Does not occur exclusively during the course of . . ."
- "Not better accounted for by . . ."[61]

DSM-IV-TR provides some guidance as to the use of exclusion criteria that are important in preventing unnecessary multiple diagnoses:

- The most important exclusion criteria are that the disturbance is not due to the direct physiological effects of a substance (*e.g.*, drug of abuse, or medication) or of a general medical condition.
- More severe and pervasive disorders should take precedence over less pervasive disorders in accounting for symptomatology. In these cases the diagnoses are arranged in a hierarchy. This means that the clinical presentation of the less pervasive disorder is considered a subset of a pattern of the more extensive disorder (e.g., a diagnosis of Bipolar Disorder excludes the diagnosis of Major Depressive Disorder and the diagnosis of Substance Dependence excludes the diagnosis of Substance Abuse).
- Clinical judgment is necessary and extra attention should be paid to differential diagnosis when the presenting symptoms appear to overlap a boundary condition between two similar disorders. The goal is to minimize needless diagnostic proliferation while not neglecting true comorbidity that would have significant treatment or prognostic implications (such as when a patient with a primary psychiatric disorder also has problems with substance use).

H. Indicating Diagnostic Uncertainty (Deferred, Unspecified, Provisional, and Not Otherwise Specified Diagnoses)

In the clinical setting, information gathering is an ongoing process. Diagnostic confidence can reasonably be expected to vary according to both the amount of information available and the circumstances in which it is presented. An overly rigid adherence to a preliminary diagnosis at the expense of developing a more complete and comprehensive assessment is a fundamental error. Clinicians are expected to keep an open mind and entertain an adequate number of possibilities especially when operating under conditions when significant information may not be available. Over time, the clinician uses subsequent information to refine the diagnosis (i.e., always keeping an open mind in order to ensure that new information can be given a fair and reasonable evaluation). Response, or lack of response, to treatment also should be included in the developing data base. Without this open-minded stance, prolonged contact with the patient may simply serve to compound initial error.

DSM-IV-TR encourages flexibility, particularly when clinicians must make decisions while working under conditions of limited information and clinical urgency. It is an unavoidable irony that the most acutely ill patients, who

---

[61]DSM-IV-TR, *supra* note 2, at 5–6.

may require the most dramatic interventions (e.g., emergency treatment), often present with the least available information (the patient may be uncommunicative or incoherent, family members or previous treating physicians may not be available, and medical records may be inaccessible).

In such circumstances, specifically indicating a lesser degree of clinical certainty and underlining the need for further data collection is the wisest course. A diagnosis may be qualified as deferred, unspecified, provisional, or not otherwise specified (NOS), depending on the relative lack of diagnostic certainty. A deferred diagnosis indicates that the available information is inadequate for any diagnostic judgment. "Unspecified Mental Disorder (nonpsychotic)" can be diagnosed when psychotic disorders can be ruled out but information is not adequate to proceed any further diagnostically. Specifying that a diagnosis is "provisional" allows the clinician to have a working hypothesis but to indicate the importance of a greater continued degree of diagnostic scrutiny than usual. As further observations are made over time and other sources of information can be contacted, the diagnostic certainty can grow until a more specific diagnosis is reached.

Finally, an NOS diagnosis is may be appropriate when:

- the diagnostic process is incomplete, as when there is insufficient information to make a more specific diagnosis or there is uncertainty as to whether the diagnosis is primary, substance-induced, or due to a general medical condition; or
- the diagnosis is used as a residual category, as when the presentation is "subthreshold" (i.e., the number of symptoms does not quite meet the symptom or duration thresholds for the specific disorders, but does involve a clinically significant condition) or the presentation "conforms to a symptom pattern that has not been included in the DSM-IV Classification but that causes clinically significant distress or impairment."[62]

Examples of such symptom patterns (i.e., proposed categories for which the empirical evidence is not sufficient for inclusion in the classification but for which explicit criteria will allow further research) are included in a *DSM-IV-TR*'s Appendix B. Concern has been expressed that this use of the NOS category may lead to diagnostic imprecision or even open the floodgates of clinical imagination and allow an unlimited assortment of new diagnoses to be made. However, careful attention to how it is used can preserve the benefits and minimize the disadvantages.

To this end, there are two important points to be kept in mind. First, the *DSM* classification does not, and cannot, correctly and exhaustively describe every possible clinical presentation. The range of human behavior and experience is protean and all too often irritatingly oblivious to preconceived categories. Rather than arbitrarily assigning these patients to a procrustean bed of a limited number of hard-and-fast groups, the *DSM* takes a position of encouraging flexibility. Second, the very use of the NOS diagnosis is a signal of the clinician's

---

[62]*Id.* at 4.

acknowledging (1) more than ordinary diagnostic uncertainty and (2) less than ordinary empirical data to support the proposed diagnosis and the way in which it was reached. A diagnosis that may be a useful tool for clinical work or research may not be adequate in the legal arena (can a diagnosis be reached "to a reasonable degree of medical certainty" if the clinician must acknowledge that it is uncertain whether there is sufficient evidence to support it?). Clinicians who use the diagnosis within the medicolegal context must reasonably expect greater than ordinary skepticism and be prepared to provide greater than ordinary exposition of the diagnostic process.

In summary, by providing various terms to indicate diagnostic uncertainty, *DSM-IV-TR* encourages clinicians to recognize and communicate relative degrees of diagnostic uncertainty, remembering that the information base is always subject to change, and to continue to question the reliability of that data for as long as is clinically necessary.[63]

VI. The Importance of Clinical Judgment

Making diagnostic sense of the things that people do or say always requires the use of clinical judgment. This can be defined as a level of skill in assessing patients, developed by a combination of training and experience, that is the professional version of common sense. The *DSM-IV Guidebook* makes the point that the *DSM* is a "tool to help inform clinical judgment; it is not a substitute for it."[64] *DSM-IV-TR* emphasizes that it is not designed to be a "cookbook" that can be used with equal facility by trained or untrained individuals.[65] Clinical judgment is essential in determining how the criteria should be applied. Clinical judgment will also include familiarity with the salient scientific and clinical literature, the ability to appraise its relative strengths and weaknesses, and the capacity to apply it to the clinical situation. This implies that pertinent factors will be identified and given the appropriate weight within a particular context.

Clinical judgment will also include ways of recognizing and minimizing avoidable error. Diagnosis is never simply a listing of symptoms. Inexperienced interviewers usually make errors by too rapidly restricting their initial list of possibilities. Generally, this is the result of placing too much emphasis on inclusion criteria and not giving sufficient weight to exclusion criteria. By ignoring or distorting the decision rules in this way, it is impossible to use systematic decision trees or prevent avoidable error. In order to use the system effectively and consistently, clinicians must be aware of the general principles and decision rules of the overall system as well as the criteria for any particular disorder.

---

[63] *Id.* at 4–5.
[64] DSM-IV GUIDEBOOK, *supra* note 4, at x.
[65] DSM-IV-TR, *supra* note 2, at xxxii.

Clinical judgment will also be required to recognize the source and significance of clinical disagreement. If they use the same explicit system, reasonable clinicians can still have disagreements. While error is inevitable in every human enterprise, it is helpful to distinguish between avoidable and unavoidable error and to try to identify the source of that error. There are five types of variation that affect the reliability of psychiatric diagnoses. They include:

- Subject variance (the patient's symptoms change over time)
- Occasion variance (certain symptoms may be more prominent, or troublesome, or otherwise a greater focus for attention at any one time)
- Information variance (two clinicians ask different questions and thereby collect a different information base)
- Observer variance (clinicians rate the same information in different ways)
- Criterion variance (there are differences in how the criteria are applied).

Low interrater agreement (high rates of diagnostic disagreement between two clinicians) can be the result of any of these. Awareness of these potential variations, careful attention to the data, and a longitudinal perspective can all contribute to greater reliability. More particularly, while subject or occasion variance usually pertain to patient reports, information, observer, or criterion variance normally derive from the behavior of clinicians.

VII. Using *DSM-IV-TR* in Employment Litigation

In its foreword, *DSM-IV-TR* pointedly warns against assuming any necessary correlation between a diagnosis and a specific level of impairment or any particular legal standard or legal definitions of human behavior.[66] It goes on to state:

> It is to be understood that inclusion here for clinical and research purposes, of a diagnostic category does not imply that the condition meets legal or other nonmedical criteria for what constitutes mental disease, mental disorder, or mental disability. The clinical and scientific considerations involved in categorization of these conditions as mental disorders may not be wholly relevant to legal judgments, for example, that take into account such issues as individual responsibility, disability and determination, and competency.[67]

Legal definitions have developed for the purposes of the courts, and both clinicians and members of the bar must constantly be aware of the differences between legal and clinical concepts. They must resist the temptation to conflate the two types of concepts and blur necessary and important distinctions.

Apart from providing a framework to ensure that the most accurate and pertinent clinical data can be made available, *DSM-IV-TR* does not resolve the

---

[66] *Id.* at xxxi–xxxii.
[67] *Id.* at xxviii.

traditional problem that medical and legal terminology, goals, and assumptions are often quite different. Clinicians in medicolegal contexts must be vigilant to ensure that clinical tools are not misused or their purposes distorted. The *DSM-IV Guidebook* warns:

> It is actually quite remarkable (and somewhat unsettling) how often DSM-IV-TR makes an appearance in the courtroom. No doubt these frequent appearances partly reflect the usefulness of the diagnostic system in helping to inform discussions on issues. . . . Unfortunately, however, the diagnostic system is often incorrectly applied in forensic context. It must be noted that there is something of a mismatch between the goals and limitations of DSM-IV-TR and the requirements of the legal system. DSM-IV-TR is a clinical document that is intended for collegial use in an atmosphere that is very different from the adversarial nature of the typical forensic proceeding. Statements in DSM-IV-TR can be read out of context to make points that may be much at odds with the thrust of its use in clinical practice. Most legal questions require a black and white dichotomization that is very much at odds with the shades of gray that characterize most clinical situations. Moreover, there is a tendency in legal settings to assume that the assigning of a diagnostic label applies and that all of the prototypical features of the disorder apply to the particular individual who is the focus of the legal question. In fact, clinical presentations of any given diagnosis are quite heterogeneous so that two individuals with the same DSM-IV-TR diagnosis can, and do, differ in many ways that are likely to be important in answering forensic questions (*e.g.*, legal responsibility). Perhaps, most fundamentally, the clinical definition of mental disorder in DSM-IV-TR is not at all equal to legal definitions of mental disorder, mental disability, mental disease, and mental defect.[68]

In forensic settings, *DSM-IV-TR* must always be used with caution, common sense, and the awareness that the adversarial system may result in distortions. Particularly egregious examples of the misuse of the diagnostic system in recent years include the use of relatively rare diagnostic labels as common explanations for criminal behavior, the recovered memory syndrome, and the overuse of posttraumatic stress disorder to increase damage awards and disability entitlement and to diminish criminal responsibility.[69] With constant awareness of these risks and limitations, the *DSM* may still serve as a valuable tool for clinicians who interact with the courts. The use of the system will help to enhance the validity, value, and reliability of medicolegal determinations and also serve as a "check on ungrounded speculation about mental disorders and the functioning of a particular individual."[70]

With these caveats in mind, it is possible to address two important ways that *DSM IV-TR* can be used in the courtroom. The first is when it is employed by the mental health expert to:

---

[68]DSM-IV GUIDEBOOK, *supra* note 4, at 65.
[69]*Id.*
[70]DSM-IV-TR, *supra* note 2, at xxxiii.

- Structure data gathering
- Establish the presence or absence of a psychiatric disorder
- Describe the signs and symptoms with their respective frequency and severity
- Relate reported symptoms to any reported associated impairment in psychological, social, or occupational function
- Describe what is known about the possible relationship of these features (including prognosis) and the ways in which they would be related to the relevant legal criteria

The reciprocal use of *DSM-IV-TR* is as a tool for quality control of expert information gathering, reasoning, and conclusions by comparing individual performance with accepted standards. The value of an expert opinion always depends in large measure upon the care and thoroughness with which the data have been gathered and the diagnostic rules have been applied. The explicit nature of *DSM-IV-TR* serves to demystify the process of rendering an expert opinion as well as to make such an opinion more susceptible to confirmation or refutation. It is one reasonable measure for assessing the way in which information was evaluated and organized and the degree to which the data are consistent with the reasoning and conclusions provided. The criteria, terminology, and decision rules form a foundation on which the remainder of the opinion is based. The firmness of that foundation is critical to the credibility of the subsequent structure of the opinion, irrespective of its creativity, rhetorical force, or subjective attractiveness.

DSM-IV-TR therefore is a useful tool in medicolegal settings if its limitations are respected and if it is properly applied. It is a useful tool for the expert doing an evaluation, inasmuch as it helps to organize information and to align clinical and legal concepts so that a determination may be made as to how relevant clinical information is to the legal decision making. It can also be an effective tool for scrutinizing psychiatric testimony to ensure its scientific and ethical reliability. *DSM-IV-TR* can help constrain unchallenged expert testimony in general and force the expert to acknowledge the consensus of scientific and clinical standards. When the mental health expert is seen to deviate from this system, the onus is then placed upon the expert to make explicit the reasoning and justification for that deviation. Explicit rules have the further advantage of minimizing the ways in which the adversarial system can distort expert testimony. By insisting on an explicit process of data collection, reasoning and diagnosis, the trier of fact may be more clearly able to evaluate the extent, source and significance of both expert conclusions and expert disagreement.

VIII. *DSM-IV-TR*: Present Status and Future Directions

Thoughtful criticism is an important way of improving the utility of any human construct. The most frequent criticisms of *DSM-IV-TR* have included its overadherence to the medical model, its proliferation of diagnoses, its psychiatrization of behavior (viewing normal variations as pathological), its high reported levels of comorbidity, its ignoring of dimensional measures, the absence of a diagnostic gold standard, and the obscuring of the value of theory by a descriptive atheoretical approach.[71]

A. The Medical Model

It may seem strange to criticize a branch of medicine for adhering to a medical model, but this objection reflects the ambivalence with which psychiatry is often regarded, as well as the complexity and variety of human behavior and the way they often defy simple categorization. Neither *DSM-IV-TR* in particular nor the medical model in general completely covers the range of that complexity. Nor do they preclude other systems of explanation. However, it is also important to remember that the *DSM* is explicitly based on a biopsychosocial model that insists that each of these domains is and always will be critical in understanding human behavior and that none of them can be neglected without seriously limiting the value of the system. Properly understood, the model is a defense against the recurrent temptation to reductionism in clinical practice.

B. The Proliferation of Diagnoses

Contrary to popular belief, there has been no increase in the number of psychiatric diagnoses since *DSM-III-R*. The only changes in the criteria sets have been attempts to clarify ambiguities, modifications supported by empirical evidence, or attempts to make the various aspects of the system (particularly Axis IV and Axis V) more user-friendly. These limited changes have been the product of an inherently conservative approach. The actual concern that underlies this criticism appears to be about how a boundary is established between the extremes of normal behavior and what can be defined as psychiatric disorder. This concern is that a wide range of ordinary thoughts, feelings, or actions may be "psychiatrized" (i.e., labeled as manifestations of psychiatric disorders).

C. "Psychiatrization" of the Normal

The "anti-psychiatry" movement of the 1960s, as exemplified by the writings of Thomas Szasz or R.D. Laing, was critical of the very idea of the diagnosis in psychiatry.[72] Quite apart from the very real problems with standards of clinical diagnostic reliability at the time, there were also a number of wider philosophical concerns that may still be relevant. At the heart of the argument is a concern about the effects of the diagnostic process on the perceptions and beliefs of both doctor and patient. These include (1) social stigma, (2) labeling effects (categorizing an individual in a particular way may cause the person

---

[71] JAMES W. BARRON, MAKING DIAGNOSIS MEANINGFUL 3 (1998).
[72] *Id.* at 230.

to behave according to the expectations of that label), (3) a reductionism that will narrow our view of humanity and limit our ways of expressing individual differences, and (4) an expansion of psychiatric concepts into a wide variety of human realms that are better dealt with in other ways.[73]

All of these concerns express important values. The diagnostic system works best when potential problems are kept in mind. If the purpose of the system is to improve clinical knowledge and communication, then whether or not the advantages of a diagnostic system outweigh the disadvantages must frequently be examined. The *DSM* diagnostic system has shown widely accepted advantages for communication, education, and research. That should not mean that its limitations or potential disadvantages must be ignored.

D. Comordibity

DSM-IV-TR is sometimes criticized because of the level of reported comorbidity (i.e., the frequency of patients receiving multiple diagnoses). This is often taken to indicate that the system is arbitrary and fits poorly with human complexity.[74] This viewpoint ignores the fact that reality is seldom as tidy as we would like. True comorbidity is a well-known and common phenomenon in all of clinical medicine, with a number of important implications. For example, certain risk factors make it likely that some individuals will develop more than one disorder (e.g., obesity increases the risk that a patient may have both diabetes and coronary artery disease). The illnesses associated with that risk factor may be completely unrelated or causally connected, or may represent different manifestations of the same underlying pathophysiologic mechanism.

Awareness of these patterns has been critical in the attempt to understand these relationships. In psychiatry, one common and important type of comorbidity occurs when diagnoses are given on the two clinical axes. The division of disorders into Axis I and Axis II is meant to be a heuristic device to facilitate comprehensive evaluation and not a statement of a fundamental dichotomy. It is clinically useful to distinguish between relatively time-limited events and more enduring patterns of behavior. Axis I and Axis II disorders may represent a single underlying pattern or types of behavior that have a causal relationship. There is evidence that understanding patterns of comorbidity may help us to understand those underlying mechanisms. For example, a variety of personality patterns are associated with increased rates of unipolar depression, but bipolar disorder is most strongly associated with the Cluster B Personality Disorders. Similarly, strong associations between one personality disorder and a specific Axis I disorder (e.g., avoidant personality and social phobia, schizotypal personality and schizophrenia) support the predicted continuum in these disorders while the absence of such an association for others (e.g., the lack of an association between obsessive compulsive personality and obsessive compulsive disor-

---

[73]DSM-IV GUIDEBOOK, *supra* note 4, at 23.
[74]BARRON, *supra* note 71, at 111.

der) can help us to identify underlying connections. Differential patterns of comorbidity for some particular types of personality disorders and certain Axis I disorders (e.g., anorexia nervosa and avoidant personality, bulimia nervosa with borderline personality) but not for others argue strongly for the value of these distinctions. The ability of these studies to identify these particular correlations indicates the value of *DSM-IV-TR* as a research tool and the need to accept true comorbidity as a necessary, if frustrating, fact of clinical life.

Finally, comorbidity may also be more apparent than real, the consequence of where diagnostic thresholds are set or how specific criteria are worded. Diagnosis must balance sensitivity with specificity in an attempt to reach the most clinically useful balance. Any attempt to make an instrument more sensitive decreases its specificity and vice versa. Requiring that a specific presentation meet the minimum number of symptoms and duration requirements attempts to minimize the number of false positives (i.e., making a diagnosis when one is not truly present). This is always done at the expense of producing relatively more false negatives (i.e., of potentially excluding individuals who actually have the diagnosis). A decision as to where a particular threshold needs to be placed always involves a balance between these two pressures and is typically resolved by the best available data on the natural history of the particular disorder(s). As the *DSM-IV Guidebook* explains:

> The allowance for multiple diagnoses means that information is saved, reliability is improved, and one avoids assumptions about priority and causality that are difficult to make in clinical practice and are unsupported by empirical evidence.... Use of multiple diagnoses is, in itself, neither good nor bad, so long as the implications are understood. The major point to keep in mind is that having more than one DSM-IV-TR diagnosis does not mean that an individual has more than one underlying pathophysiological process. Instead, DSM-IV-TR diagnoses should be considered descriptive building blocks useful for communicating diagnostic information.[75]

E. Absence of a Gold Standard (External Validating Criteria)

One important adjunct to the syndromal approach is the potential use of external validating criteria, such as laboratory tests, to confirm diagnoses. The test results may give a more direct assessment of the underlying process and provide a measure of convergent validity for a clinical diagnosis. A well-standardized test can be used as a "gold standard" against which diagnostic validity can be measured. While such tests are available in many areas of modern medicine, in psychiatry a wide variety of biological markers have been studied but all remain primarily of research interest and have yet to provide a contribution in improving diagnosis.[76] For the present, beyond its usefulness in screening out

---

[75]DSM-IV GUIDEBOOK, *supra* note 4, at 20.
[76]Stephen V. Faraone & Ming T. Tsuang, *Measuring Diagnostic Accuracy in the Absence of a "Gold Standard,"* 151 AM. J. PSYCHIATRY 650 (1994).

and identifying Axis III disorders, laboratory medicine has only a promissory role in psychiatric diagnosis.

There is hope that this may change. In particular, neuroimaging techniques (such as positron emission tomography or magnetic resonance imaging) offer a tantalizing glimpse into brain functioning. At present, these techniques remain in their (perhaps late) infancy, and our capacity to interpret their significance is limited. It can reasonably be expected that these techniques, in combination with genetic studies, treatment outcome measures, and other research techniques, will one day contribute to diagnosis and treatment for at least some psychiatric disorders. It is also reasonably certain that (as in the rest of medicine) these measures will augment and not replace careful clinical evaluation.

F. Theory and Empiricism

DSM-IV-TR is not universally beloved, but it is generally accepted. It also represents the best available system, not an ideal one. Criticism of *DSM-IV-TR* remains, but the intensity has been dramatically reduced as the goals of the system are more clearly understood. Clinicians also have to remember that the diagnostic process is only one step in assessment and treatment. A variety of other factors unique to the individual, such as self-perceptions, coping styles, family history, relationships with others, and a variety of other psychosocial factors, must be recognized and included. The *DSM-IV Guidebook* deplores, equally, extremes of *DSM* idolatry and *DSM* dismissal: "Being mindful of the many epistemological limitations of DSM-IV will result in a more flexible and clinically practical perspective that does not put more weight on the system than it can bear. Perhaps the most important rule applying to DSM-IV is not to take the rules so seriously that one's clinical judgment is blinded."[77]

In a sense, the *DSM* has been criticized for not achieving goals that it never set out to accomplish.[78] Put together for universal use, consensus documents will rarely satisfy all, or even most, minority concerns or special interests. Indeed, one hallmark of a balanced viewpoint is that it is attacked equally from various extremes.

In reviewing the range of criticisms, it also seems clear that the *DSM* as an "official" document has come to serve as a lightning rod for much of the current, pervasive dissatisfaction with the direction that the health care system in general and mental health care in particular have taken in recent years. The tone of these criticisms is often one of nostalgia for a past (if imaginary) golden age before the advent of managed care. In one viewpoint, the *DSM* classification is a tool being used by an unfeeling bureaucracy to restrict care, particularly talk therapies. Another criticism takes the opposite tack, saying that *DSM* pathologizes normal behavior to create more business for mental health practitioners. Yet even some of the most astute critics have generally noted the

---

[77]DSM-IV GUIDEBOOK, *supra* note 4, at 24.
[78]BARRON, *supra* note 71, at 29.

accumulation of the literature in support of the *DSM* system. They have also noted that whatever the merits of the various criticisms, the empirical evidence to support viable alternatives has not yet arrived.[79] *DSM-IV-TR* remains, quite simply, not a perfect system but the best available instrument.

The principal concern of many of the criticisms is not about the use of *DSM-IV-TR* but about potential misuse. There are concerns that it may promote a false dichotomy between "biologic" and "psychologic" disorders, may be a source of reification of a variety of nonpathological behaviors into syndromes, or, because of its atheoretical stance may somehow deemphasize the need for theories to understand human behavior. Criticism of the *DSM* is often accompanied by the further complaint that it has unreasonably neglected a particular viewpoint, usually that of the particular critic in question.[80]

DSM-IV-TR was not constructed with a view to making it infallible or permanent. As with any scientific tool, *DSM-IV-TR* has the ultimate aim of making itself obsolete by stimulating research that will produce far-reaching changes as our knowledge base expands.

DSM-IV-TR's editors have repeatedly warned that it is neither cookbook nor bible. At the heart of the matter, this is yet another attempt to emphasize that clinical judgment and common sense are critically important in using the system to diagnose and treat patients. It is not a cookbook if a cookbook means that it can be applied by anyone who can read in equal fashion regardless of level of training. Nor is it a bible inasmuch as it is not unchanging, inerrant, or applicable to every person in every situation. It is the product of the best available information and as such is subject to change. Neither is it a bible that all psychiatrists must believe verbatim and accept as holy writ. Psychiatrists still can, and do, legitimately disagree with one another, as well as with particular elements of *DSM-IV-TR*. If there is a biblical analogy (and several do come to mind), the most apt is that it is a way of escaping Babel. Prior to the *DSM-III* process, psychiatrists, psychologists, and other mental health professionals were extremely restricted in their ability to communicate with one another. By providing a common language, DSM provides a means for clinicians to communicate and develop the foundation for a more comprehensive, empirically based understanding of mental disorders.

---

[79]*Id.*
[80]*Id.* at 73.

CHAPTER 5

MENTAL DISORDERS COMMONLY ENCOUNTERED IN EMPLOYMENT LITIGATION

Mark S. Lipian, M.D., Ph.D.

I. Introduction

Undetected and unaddressed, mental disorders in the workplace can escalate to become an employer's worst nightmare. They can fuel employee discomfort and discontent. They can underlie seemingly groundless interpersonal attacks, both verbal and legal. They can, in the most extreme instances, motivate workplace violence and tragedy.

Yet, despite their growing importance in the workplace, mental health issues remain scary, shadowy topics, cloaked in mystery, mythologized, banished to the similarly destructive realms of uninformed prejudicial distortion and misinformed, mass media popularization. General cultural confusion surrounding mental disorders and psychiatry often is compounded when mental health becomes a central issue in employment litigation. Intentionally or not, common myths are turned all the more mythological; popular fantasies are spun all the more fantastically. This chapter and the next are proposed as initial antidotes to that process.

A. Origins, History, and Definitions

1. Psychiatry and Psychology

Psychiatry is a medical subspecialty, and as such has its origins in the orientations and beliefs of medical science. Psychiatrists are medical doctors (M.D.s) who, after completing training in general medicine, go on to specialty training in the treatment of mental disorders through medications and psychotherapy.

Psychology is a social science, and like other social sciences, has its roots in an attempt to bring experimental method into the realm of philosophical debate. While many subfields of psychology remain academic and research-based (e.g., social psychology, developmental psychology), clinical psychology has evolved as a more pragmatic application, attempting to marshal psychological principles of behavior in the service of behavioral change. Clinical psychologists are doctors of philosophy (Ph.D.s) who, after completing training in general psychology, go on to specialty training in abnormal behavior and its modification through psychotherapy.

2. Physical Illnesses and Mental Disorders

To understand the concept of mental disorders, it is helpful to reflect upon psychiatry's medical heritage. In general medicine, illnesses are first identified as symptom clusters—patterns of phenomena (e.g., deep, hacking cough; yellow productive sputum; high temperature; chest pain; night sweats) that have been noted to occur together repeatedly, across cultures, across epochs, across socioeconomic classes, and across ethnicities. Such clusters, once identified, are labeled "syndromes"; when the etiologic agent responsible for their appearance has been isolated, they are called "illnesses" (e.g., pneumonia).

Mental disorders are the psychiatric equivalents of physical illnesses. Clusters of symptoms (e.g., hallucinations, delusions, emotional flattening, decreasing social comfort over time) are recognized as co-occurring in reliable patterns, across cultures, across epochs, across socioeconomic classes, and across ethnicities. Because the etiologic agents causing various forms of psychiatric dysfunctions have yet to be definitively identified, such clusters are termed "disorders" (e.g., schizophrenia), rather than "illnesses" or "diseases."

3. DSM-IV-TR

The American Psychiatric Association's *Diagnostic and Statistical Manual of Mental Disorders, Fourth Edition - Text Revision (DSM-IV-TR)*[1] is essentially a compendium of replicable, identifiable psychiatric symptom clusters—psychiatric disorders—as they are most accurately characterized today. Diagnostic labels are identified and defined by those co-occurring symptoms that must minimally be present to correctly assign a patient the selected diagnosis. In addition to the particular pattern of symptoms required for a diagnosis, typically the symptoms must rise to a specified level of "clinical significance" (interfere in some meaningful way with the individual's social and/or vocational functioning) for the diagnosis to be made correctly, and they must be present continuously for some specified period of time.

4. Psychiatric Symptoms

Simply experiencing psychiatric dysfunction, even if that dysfunction takes the form of specific symptom manifestation, does not necessarily equate to qualify-

---

[1]AMERICAN PSYCHIATRIC ASSOCIATION, DIAGNOSTIC AND STATISTICAL MANUAL OF MENTAL DISORDERS (4th ed. text rev. 2000) [hereinafter *DSM-IV-TR*].

ing for a diagnosable psychiatric disorder. In fact, just as in the case of physical medicine, particular symptoms (a cough, an auditory hallucination) may arise out of any one of numerous pathological processes (an allergy vs. a flu vs. lung cancer; a medication side effect vs. a psychotic Major Depressive Episode vs. Schizophrenia).

Broadly, psychiatric symptoms can be conceptualized as falling into one of six types—psychotic, affective, anxiety, conversion, cognitive, or unreasonable attitudes and expectations. Each of the six symptom types may manifest itself in any one of numerous psychiatric disorders.

A. PSYCHOTIC SYMPTOMS Psychotic symptoms involve experience not based in consensual reality. Such non-reality-based phenomena may be perceptual, conceptual, or affect the form and content of thought.

- *Hallucinations* are false perceptions. They arise in any of the five senses, but are most typically auditory (hearing voices), visual (seeing things that are not there), or tactile (feeling things crawling on the skin).
- *Delusions* are false conceptions or false belief systems. They may take any form but are most typically persecutory ("others are trying to harm me"), grandiose ("I am capable of objectively impossible accomplishments"), or referential ("my mind is permeable and can be read;" "my thoughts are broadcast for all to hear;" "special messages are being conveyed to me by newspaper or television").
- *Formal Thought Disorder* involves the ungluing of the logic that typically binds ideas or communications together. Verbal and/or written utterances cease to convey meaning to others; ideas cease to coalesce into intelligible wholes. Coherence is lost.

CASE EXAMPLE

Ms. A, an ebullient sales representative working for a large publishing company, made no secret of her diagnosis as a "Manic Depressive" (Bipolar Affective Disorder). Properly medicated, Ms. A was stable and highly effective interpersonally—charming, charismatic, and verbally adept.

However, colleagues knew instantly on the several occasions when Ms. A elected to discontinue the medications that held her Bipolar Disorder in check. There was an almost complete collapse of logic in her utterance: "I came to work today to play hooray; the play's the thing and I can sing; sing song, sing song; Gary, got any coffee? Can you believe the shining light in here at the end of the tunnel; it's so bright and I'm so bright and it's just a tunnel of love, my friend. Where is my sales book—I'm booked for love and times are changing, you know; you've got to do unto others or they will do unto you, so you might as well sell it through and through!" These types of verbalizations are characteristic manifestations of psychosis clad as formal thought disorder.

B. AFFECTIVE SYMPTOMS Affective symptoms are disturbances of mood or emotion. They may take the form of abnormally extended episodes of a single pathological mood state (e.g., despair, euphoria), or of abnormal cycling between extremes of mood state (e.g., repeated, dysregulated swings between despair and euphoria).

Affective symptoms may involve degree, duration, or situational appropriateness of emotional experience. An otherwise normal mood state may occur at abnormal or inappropriate times (e.g., giggly euphoria upon learning of a colleague's hardship). It may occur to abnormal intensity (e.g., tearful misery upon hearing of a fifteen-minute delay of a business flight). Or it may appear and disappear with abnormal lability (e.g., rapid fluctuation among happiness, sadness, rage, and meekness, all within moments and without apparent environmental provocation).

C. ANXIETY SYMPTOMS Anxiety symptoms surround dysregulation of levels of arousal, such that one is inappropriately anxious at inappropriate times. Such dysregulation may be chronic (generalized anxiety) or it may be acute and episodic (panic attacks). It may be triggered by specific inappropriate environmental stimuli, or it may be free-floating, seemingly devoid of contextual connection.

D. CONVERSION SYMPTOMS Conversion symptoms comprise physical experiences that have no physiological underpinning. Purely psychological forces manifest themselves in the form of physical pathology, for which there is no identifiable biochemical or anatomic cause. Conversion symptoms may be circumscribed (e.g., paralysis of a given extremity without neurologic or orthopedic basis) or more generalized (an overall fatigue without metabolic explanation). Universal, however, is the experiential reality; the individual manifesting a conversion symptom is not faking or malingering. For that individual, the subjective pathological experience is very real; for the outside medical evaluator, no objective, medically measurable explanation for the reported and demonstrated pathology can be found.

E. COGNITIVE SYMPTOMS Cognitive symptoms describe abnormalities in the functions of orderly thinking—memory, attention, concentration, task sequencing, problem solving. Although typically attributed to acute brain injury (direct tissue damage due to traumatic insult), such symptoms may arise as a function of many psychiatric disorders not involving sudden brain damage. They may be circumscribed or pervasive within any given domain (e.g., memory, problem solving), and they vary in degree, in longevity, and in breadth of domains affected.

F. UNREASONABLE ATTITUDES AND EXPECTATIONS The final class of psychiatric symptoms is the hallmark of the personality disorders, pathology that is the subject of Chapter 6. Personality disorders consist of patterns of unreasonable expectations, interpretations, attitudes, and demands of one's interpersonal environment that are lifelong, and that consistently interfere with one's ability to interact successfully and fulfillingly with others. Affecting both work and play, the particular pathological beliefs and social distortions overlap somewhat among the different disorders but tend to cluster into patterns that define the various personality diagnoses. While such "traits" are present to some extent in virtually every human being, their extremity, their pervasiveness, and their consistently adverse effects upon social and/or occupational functioning differentiate those with diagnosable personality disorders from the population at large.

B. Factors Affecting Mental Health

1. Organic Versus Functional Pathology

A distinction is often drawn between symptomatology caused by an acute, physical insult to the brain (e.g., a blow to the head, exposure to a toxin, a hypoxic episode) and that resulting from psychiatric disorders that do not involve acute, identifiable tissue damage (e.g., Schizophrenia; Bipolar Affective Disorder; Panic Disorder). Symptoms arising in the context of novel, measurable brain injury and tissue damage are referred to as *organic*. Those that are the products of non-brain-injury related mental disorders are termed *functional*.

As noted earlier, etiology cannot be inferred through specific symptom identification alone in psychiatry any more than it can in other medical specialties. Both organic and functional psychiatric disorders can give rise to identical psychotic symptoms, for example. Both can produce indistinguishable disturbances of mood and arousal. Diagnosis must be the product of analysis of symptom patterns, in the context of a thorough and detailed genetic, environmental, medical, and social history.

2. Nature Versus Nurture

Apart from the personality disorders (which are reviewed in Chapter 6), it is increasingly clear that most major psychiatric disorders involve at least a significant biological component.[2] They tend to recur in families through hereditary bloodlines; they respond to medications; they reappear episodically throughout the individual's lifetime. They seem to surround genetically dictated imbalances and dysregulations of relative concentrations of the myriad neurotransmitters of the brain, chemicals and chemical combinations underlying all emotional and intellectual experience, common to all human beings to greater or lesser degree and in greater or lesser relative proportion.

---

[2]The single, outstanding exception to this generalization is Posttraumatic Stress Disorder (PTSD), by definition a significant symptomatic reaction to an acute, overwhelming environmental stressor (see Chapter 13, Posttraumatic Stress Disorder in Employment Litigation). Contemporary research increasingly suggests that even PTSD involves significant biological loading; those with family history of mood or anxiety disorder appear substantially more "vulnerable" to the development of PTSD than those exposed to the same or equivalent stressor, but without such genetic predisposition. *See* W.R. True, et al., *A Twin Study of Genetic and Environmental Contributions to Liability for Posttraumatic Stress Symptoms,* 50 ARCHIVES GEN. PSYCHIATRY 257 (1993).

Consistent with this nature-driven model of major psychiatric pathology is the fact that many psychiatric disorders follow a biologically driven, recurrent, episodic course. Thus, one who has suffered a circumscribed, time-limited episode of Major Depressive Disorder is likely to suffer further such episodes later in his or her life, and those subsequent episodes may well occur spontaneously without an identifiable environmental trigger. The same is true of the periodic, episodic decompensations of Schizophrenia and of the acute swings of the Bipolar (Manic Depressive) pendulum.

Equally clear, however, is that environmental circumstances (nurture) can have profound interactive impact upon the course of psychiatric illness in those who are biologically predisposed. The onset of a first psychotic "break" (or episode) tends to occur during the mid-teens for those genetically coded to suffer Schizophrenia; but specific timing often correlates to immediate stress in the environment at that juncture (leaving home for college or a stressful romantic breakup, for example). Similarly, while individual episodes of Major Depressive Disorder or of Bipolar Affective Disorder may occur spontaneously, they may also be triggered by environmental stressors occurring at the time.

Particularly important to tease apart in the context of litigation, then, are concepts of *causation*, *triggering*, and *exacerbation*. A biological condition like Major Depressive Disorder or Bipolar Affective Disorder cannot be *caused* by environmental events (such as those often at issue in employment litigation). One is born with these disorders; very often one has experienced episodes related to them well before setting foot into the workplace currently under scrutiny. A given episode of a preexisting disorder may or may not have been triggered by events at issue; or, if its onset predates those events, symptoms may or may not have been exacerbated by litigation-related experience. Careful, meticulous discovery, document review, and if available, psychiatric examination, are critical to the isolation and evaluation of these entangled possibilities.

C. Formal Diagnosis

Formal diagnosis in psychiatry is typically reported employing five diagnostic "axes," each presenting a somewhat different facet of the complete diagnostic construction.

- *Axis I* defines the acute, "major" psychiatric disorders. With the exception of Posttraumatic Stress Disorder and most Adjustment Disorders, these are primarily biological conditions. They have a hereditary component, they respond to medications, and they seem to involve imbalances in the chemicals (neurotransmitters) of the brain. Frequently, they are recurrent and episodic throughout a lifetime. Episodes often remit completely with proper treatment. Even without such treatment, many Axis I disorder episodes disappear on their own over time.
- *Axis II* defines the *personality disorders*. These are patterns of action upon and interaction with the environment that are primarily learned rather than biologically determined. They are lifelong "styles" of social expectation, interpretation, and demand that are maladaptive, causing recurrent difficulties in interpersonal interactions in the social and/or vocational spheres.

- *Axis III* defines any nonpsychiatric medical conditions that may be interacting with Axis I or Axis II disorders so as to influence behavior or experience through the "lens" of the ongoing psychiatric pathology.
- *Axis IV* identifies and quantitates any psychosocial stressors in the individual's life that may be interacting with the Axis I or Axis II disorders so as to influence behavior or experience. External events affect pathology again through the lens of the ongoing psychiatric condition.
- *Axis V* reports the *Global Assessment of Functioning* (G.A.F.) Scale, a 1–100 summarization of how well the individual is functioning currently, relative to his or her highest function within the past year.

II. Overview of Axis I Disorders Commonly Encountered in Employment Litigation

Axis I psychiatric disorders most frequently encountered in employment litigation can be conceptualized as falling into one of five types: Thought Disorders, Mood Disorders, Anxiety Disorders, Somatoform Disorders, and Adjustment Disorders. Table 5-1 organizes some diagnoses commonly alleged in litigation contexts within these categories.

Table 5-1   Axis I Disorders Commonly Encountered in Employment Litigation

Thought Disorders	*Mood Disorders*	*Anxiety Disorders*	*Somatoform Disorders*	*Adjustment Disorders*
1. Schizophrenia	1. Major Depressive Disorder	1. Panic Disorder	1. Somatization Disorder	1. With Depressed Mood
2. Delusional Disorder	2. Dysthymic Disorder	2. Obsessive-Compulsive Disorder	2. Conversion Disorder	2. With Anxious Mood
	3. Bipolar Affective Disorder a. Type I b. Type II	3. Generalized Anxiety Disorder	3. Pain Disorder	3. Mixed
		4. Posttraumatic Stress Disorder		

A. Thought Disorders

Thought disorders are centrally characterized by disturbances of thinking, most commonly by non-reality-based (psychotic) ideation. Those with a thought disorder may additionally develop a pathological mood (e.g., a schizophrenic may experience a Major Depressive Episode). Furthermore, although psychosis is the hallmark of the thought disorders, it is not a phenomenon exclusive to them (e.g., a person with a Major Depressive Disorder may become actively delusional).

1. Schizophrenia

CASE EXAMPLE

Ms. B was an atomic engineer who, in her mid-30s, filed a sexual harassment suit against her employer, alleging that her immediate supervisor had acted in various inappropriately intimate ways over the two-year course of her employment. The suit came as a surprise to the employer and supervisor alike, who viewed Ms. B as a loner and somewhat eccentric in her speech and dress, but certainly as an honest and hardworking employee.

Thorough investigation produced no evidence that harassment had occurred. However, meticulous discovery revealed a recurrent pattern of early employment success followed by work deterioration as job responsibility increased. When performance was correspondingly criticized at two previous jobs as well as at the current one, Ms. B became convinced she was being hounded and persecuted by the criticizing superior, because he (or in one case, she) "is sexually attracted to me, and can't let go."

Forensic psychiatric examination confirmed not only the tenacious nature of these persecutory delusional beliefs, but further psychotic thought process in the form of a conviction that newspaper articles pertaining to sexual harassment had "special, hidden messages encoded" just for Ms. B, and that "evil men, perhaps former university teachers" were somehow in cahoots with her sexually frustrated supervisors/suitors and were periodically following her on the freeway driving "dark, creepy vans" just to add to her sense of discomfort and personal invasion. Further, personal history included the belief that university professors in China, Germany, and the United States had attempted to seduce—once even rape—Ms. B, and that apartment managers in Germany had done the same.

Generally, Ms. B's life had been one of increasing social isolation, fear, and confused frustration as her teens gave way to her 20s. Her 30s, and her sexual harassment suit, reflected no more than the continuation of this ongoing, deteriorating course.

Schizophrenia is arguably the most potentially devastating of the Axis I disorders. As such, it appears in the context of employment litigation relatively infrequently, typically having ravaged its victims beyond employability long before an employment lawsuit will have had occasion to arise. Certain of its subtypes do not so completely impair performance as to totally disable those they strike, however, and as in the vignette above, manifest themselves cloaked in intuitively implausible and apparently bizarre workplace behaviors and claims.

Often first becoming symptomatic during the adolescent to late teen years, Schizophrenia is estimated to afflict about 1 percent of the nation's general population. It is classically characterized by a combination of so-called *positive* and *negative* symptoms. Positive symptoms of Schizophrenia tend to occur intermittently during acute, circumscribed episodes, or "schizophrenic breaks." Negative symptoms, meanwhile, follow a chronic, continuing, deteriorating course over the second, third, and fourth decades of life, finally tending to level off in the late 40s to early 50s as the disorder naturally diminishes.

Positive symptoms of Schizophrenia consist of an aberrant excess of mental activity: psychotic experiences such as hallucinations, delusions, or disorganized, chaotic thinking and speech—the stereotypic displays of the "crazy." Such symptoms generally occur as periodic, episodic decompensations that may or may not be triggered by environmental stressors (interpersonal pressures, natural phenomena such as earthquakes or fires, or even illicit drug use).

Negative symptoms of Schizophrenia refer to deficiencies of mental content or function that is normally present in the nonschizophrenic population—affective flattening or "blankness," lack of interest in social stimulation or contact ("asociality"), and marked poverty of richness or color of speech ("alogia"). Generally, negative symptoms are present as a backdrop, a baseline upon which episodes of positive symptoms are superimposed. That baseline follows a classically deteriorating course (increasing dissociation of feeling from thought, decreasing social proclivity) as the illness runs its natural course.

DSM-IV-TR captures the various psychopathological facets of Schizophrenia in its formal diagnostic criteria, outlined in Table 5-2.

Table 5-2 *DSM-IV-TR* Diagnostic Criteria for Schizophrenia

A. *Characteristic symptoms*: Two (or more) of the following, each present for a significant portion of time during a 1-month period (or less if successfully treated):
   (1) delusions
   (2) hallucinations
   (3) disorganized speech (e.g., frequent derailment or incoherence)
   (4) grossly disorganized or catatonic behavior
   (5) negative symptoms, i.e., affective flattening, alogia, or avolition
   Note: Only one Criterion A symptom is required if delusions are bizarre or hallucinations consist of a voice keeping up a running commentary on the person's behavior or thoughts, or two or more voices conversing with each other.

B. *Social/occupational dysfunction*: For a significant portion of the time since the onset of the disturbance, one or more major areas of functioning such as work, interpersonal relations, or self-care are markedly below the level achieved prior to the onset (or when the onset is in childhood or adolescence, failure to achieve expected level of interpersonal, academic, or occupational achievement).

C. *Duration*: Continuous signs of the disturbance persist for at least 6 months. This 6-month period must include at least 1 month of symptoms (or less if successfully treated) that meet Criterion A (i.e., active-phase symptoms) and may include periods of prodromal or residual symptoms. During these prodromal or residual periods, the signs of the disturbance may be manifested

by only negative symptoms or two or more symptoms listed in Criterion A present in an attenuated form (e.g., odd beliefs, unusual perceptual experiences).
D. *Schizoaffective and Mood Disorder exclusion*: Schizoaffective Disorder and Mood Disorder With Psychotic Features have been ruled out because either (1) no Major Depressive, Manic, or Mixed Episodes have occurred concurrently with the active-phase symptoms; or (2) if mood episodes have occurred during active-phase symptoms, their total duration has been brief relative to the duration of the active and residual periods.
E. *Substance/general medical condition exclusion*: The disturbance is not due to the direct physiological effects of a substance (e.g., a drug of abuse, a medication) or a general medical condition.
F. *Relationship to a Pervasive Developmental Disorder*: If there is a history of Autistic Disorder or another Pervasive Developmental Disorder, the additional diagnosis of Schizophrenia is made only if prominent delusions or hallucinations are also present for at least a month (or less if successfully treated).

Source: Reprinted with permission from the *Diagnostic and Statistical Manual of Mental Disorders, Fourth Edition, Text Revision*, 312–13. Copyright 2000 American Psychiatric Association.

Five subtypes of Schizophrenia have been identified, and they are outlined in Table 5-3. Of these, the most likely to arise in an employment setting is the Paranoid Type (that presented in the case example above). Schizophrenia, Paranoid Type tends to have a more circumscribed character than other forms, its manifestation primarily in persecutory delusions and possibly minor hallucinatory experiences, but with intellectual and interpersonal functioning preserved to greater extent than in other subtypes. Thus, paranoid schizophrenics, particularly if intelligent, will often manage to mask their inner experience and achieve relatively high function vocationally. Unfortunately, as in the vignette, environmental stress (including work-related demands) can cause symptoms to become more prominent and obvious, resulting in seemingly inexplicable workplace behaviors, beliefs, and accusations.

Table 5-3 *DSM-IV-TR* Subtypes of Schizophrenia

Subtype	DSM-IV-TR *Criteria*	Typical Features and Manifestations
Paranoid	A. Preoccupation with one or more delusions or frequent auditory hallucinations. B. None of the following is prominent: disorganized speech, disorganized or catatonic behavior, or flat or inappropriate affect.	Generalized irritability and anger, thematic but fluctuating delusional belief systems, anxiety, suspiciousness. A stilted, guarded, emotionally flat style of interpersonal interaction that may become surprisingly intense if challenged.

continued

Table 5-3 Continued.
***DSM-IV-TR* Subtypes of Schizophrenia**

Subtype	*DSM-IV-TR* Criteria	*Typical Features and Manifestations*
Disorganized	A. All of the following are prominent: (1) disorganized speech (2) disorganized behavior (3) flat or inappropriate affect B. The criteria are not met for Catatonic Type.	Silly, effervescent, childlike, giddy. Typically results in extreme social impairment, poor long-term functioning, and serious vocational interference.
Catatonic	A. Motoric immobility as evidenced by catalepsy (including waxy flexibility) or stupor. B. Excessive motor activity (that is apparently purposeless and not influenced by external stimuli). C. Extreme negativism (an apparently motiveless resistance to all instructions or maintenance of a rigid posture against attempts to be moved) or mutism. D. Peculiarities of voluntary movement as evidenced by posturing (voluntary assumption of inappropriate or bizarre postures), stereotyped movements, prominent mannerisms, or prominent grimacing. E. Echolalia or echopraxia.	Unusual motor behavior classic: rigid stiffness, "plastic elasticity," other unusual psychomotor disturbances. Can become a medical emergency if muscular rigidity is prolonged, with a possibility of resultant hyperpyrexia, malnutrition, or related self-injury.
Undifferentiated	A type of Schizophrenia in which symptoms that meet Criterion A are present, but the criteria are not met for the Paranoid, Disorganized, or Catatonic Type.	Most pervasive and probably most common clinical presentation. Broad spectrum of positive symptoms during episodic decompensations or schizophrenic breaks, against a background of chronically deteriorating negative symptomatology: social deficits, emotional flattening and distancing between thought and affect, apathy, and poverty of speech.

Residual	A. Absence of prominent delusions, hallucinations, disorganized speech, and grossly disorganized or catatonic behavior. B. There is continuing evidence of the disturbance, as indicated by the presence of negative symptoms or two or more symptoms listed in Criterion A for Schizophrenia, present in an attenuated form (e.g., odd beliefs, unusual perceptual experiences).	Absence of episodes of "positive symptoms" (i.e., psychosis), but "negative" symptoms remain prominent: emotional blunting, social distancing. There may also remain moderate (subpsychotic) "eccentric" behavior, "illogical" thinking, loosening of associations.

There is no cure for Schizophrenia. No medication can reverse or permanently correct the neurotransmitter abnormalities that cause the disorder. No psychotherapy exists through which an individual can completely undo its behavioral effects and its psychotic inner experiences.

Medications are, however, available that assist greatly in the management of Schizophrenia. Antipsychotic (neuroleptic) agents tend to reduce psychosis, often completely eliminating positive symptoms such as hallucinations, delusions, and grossly disorganized thought. Newer medicines like olanzapine and risperidone are even somewhat effective at reducing negative symptoms, an area of schizophrenic experience that has traditionally proven frustratingly resistant to psychopharmacologic intervention.

A critical feature of serious psychiatric disorders like Schizophrenia and their care is recognition by the afflicted individual. He or she must come to understand and accept that he or she has a chronic psychiatric disorder, understand the signs and symptoms of that disorder and the warnings of an imminent episode or decompensation into acute symptomatic experience, and know how best to intervene early so as to prevent such episodes, as well as to cope with ongoing baseline symptoms.

Psychotherapy in a disorder as serious as Schizophrenia centrally involves assisting the individual to develop insight into and familiarity with his or her own pathological process. Once this is accomplished, therapy switches to a development of symptom-specific coping strategies, an exploration of realistic possibilities in the worlds of work and societal participation, and basic support and assistance coping with the frustrations and difficulties that inevitably result from limitations and experiences inherent to the disorder.

Prognosis is largely a function of schizophrenic subtype. Disorganized and catatonic schizophrenics tend to face a relatively dismal future of limited function and participatory capacity, even if optimally treated. Paranoid schizophrenics, with proper management, may do much better, with the potential for productive and satisfying lives, albeit typically lives more isolated and stress-intolerant than that of the average individual.

As proves to be the case in all of the Axis I psychiatric disorders to an enormous extent, ultimate life outcome and quality are products of the interactive impact of related but independent forces—biological underpinning, individual motivation and attitude, quality of medical care, and nature of coincidental social and environmental experiences.

2. Delusional Disorder

CASE EXAMPLE

Ms. C was a high-level claims manager at a large insurance company. She was well liked, socially active, intelligent, and highly competent.

The company was surprised and concerned when Ms. C unexpectedly complained of sexual harassment by "most of the men" who worked around her. She alleged hostile, sexualized, and demeaning remarks on a daily basis emanating from her male colleagues. Further, she insisted that these comments had persisted since the earliest days of her one-and-a-half year employment with the company, but that she was only now "fed up" enough with them to report.

Investigating managers elicited no confirmation of Ms. C's claim by either male or female colleagues, and uncovered no tangible evidence to support it. Yet, Ms. C appeared genuinely upset and shaken by her reported experience, asking only that "it stop, so I can do my work."

On voluntary psychiatric examination (suggested by management in response to Ms. C's upset and concern about her workplace situation), Ms. C revealed that she knew her male floor-mates were harassing her because she was able to read their minds, and they were perpetually thinking "thoughts unsavory." Furthermore, Ms. C could read the examiner's mind and thereby determined that his thoughts were "righteous;" therefore, she was safe in revealing her supernatural secret for the first time.

Apart from this specific belief system, examination revealed absolutely nothing abnormal about Ms. C: her affect was full and appropriate; she was troubled by the "harassment" but certainly not clinically depressed (or manic); she was an intelligent, charming, vivacious young woman with a fine sense of humor.

Subsequent medical workup (biochemical evaluation, structural and electrical brain testing, neurological consultation) was entirely benign. Yet Ms. C's tightly circumscribed but apparently bizarre belief system remained firm and imperturbable.

Delusional Disorder often proves the most peculiar of the psychiatric disorders because outwardly the affected individual seems so "normal." Indeed, the disorder is centrally characterized by one (or occasionally more) nonbizarre delusions that are circumscribed and isolated and occur against a backdrop of otherwise fully conventional belief and behavior.

Delusional Disorder does not condemn an individual to the generally deteriorating course of Schizophrenia, nor does it produce Schizophrenia's multiple episodes of acute positive symptoms or its chronic oddness and isolation (negative symptoms). Thus, individuals suffering from Delusional Disorder are more likely than schizophrenics to seek, attain, and successfully maintain employment, and psychotic beliefs resulting from Delusional Disorder are more likely than those rooted in Schizophrenia to underlie complaints about workplace events that may seem peculiar.

Table 5-4 outlines the *DSM-IV-TR* diagnostic criteria for Delusional Disorder.

Table 5-4   *DSM-IV-TR* Diagnostic Criteria for Delusional Disorder

A. Nonbizarre delusions (i.e., involving situations that occur in real life, such as being followed, poisoned, infected, loved at a distance, or deceived by spouse or lover, or having a disease) of at least 1 month's duration.
B. Criterion A for Schizophrenia has never been met. *Note:* Tactile and olfactory hallucinations may be present in Delusional Disorder if they are related to the delusional theme.
C. Apart from the impact of the delusion(s) or its ramifications, functioning is not markedly impaired and behavior is not obviously odd or bizarre.
D. If mood episodes have occurred concurrently with delusions, their total duration has been brief relative to the duration of the delusional periods.
E. The disturbance is not due to the direct physiological effects of a substance (e.g., a drug of abuse, a medication) or a general medical condition.

Source: Reprinted with permission from the *Diagnostic and Statistical Manual of Mental Disorders, Fourth Edition, Text Revision,* 329. Copyright 2000 American Psychiatric Association.

By far the most frequently encountered variant of Delusional Disorder both in and out of employment settings is the Persecutory Type. Here, the central theme is a delusional belief that the individual is being conspired against, maligned, cheated, harassed, or otherwise maliciously harmed in some way.[3] In situations of unwelcomed pursuit (stalking), the Erotomanic Type may be present. This involves a delusional belief that the target is in love with the pursuer (the delusional individual). Typically, an idealized, romantic love predominates; but that love is at risk for being transformed into an equally extreme devaluation ("the 'chaste goddess' turned out to be a 'demonic temptress,' and must be punished!") if the unsuspecting target is perceived as somehow having defiled the (psychotically conceived) ideal.

Table 5-5 lists the various subtypes of Delusional Disorder, describing the defining characteristics of each.

---

[3]Delusional Disorder Persecutory Type may result in numerous lawsuits or complaints to regulatory or governmental agencies filed by an individual who believes himself or herself to be the victim of multiple injustices. This condition is sometimes referred to as "querulous paranoia."

Table 5-5 Subtypes of Delusional Disorder

Subtype	Typical Features and Manifestations
Persecutory Type	Central theme is belief in malicious treatment of some kind; conspiracy, harassment, cheating, spying, following, poisoning or drugging, discriminating. May result in frequent reporting to regulatory agencies or filing of lawsuits (querulous paranoia). In extreme cases, may give rise to resentment, anger, and even violence toward those believed to be acting malignantly toward the individual.
Erotomanic Type	Central false belief that a specific individual (often a celebrity or public figure, or someone in authority) is in love with the individual. Usually idealized, romantic love is more involved than sexual attraction. Can result in uninvited pursuit (stalking), misguided efforts to rescue the target from imagined dangers, or extremely, in vilification and possible retaliatory attack if the idealized target has somehow acted to defile his or her romanticized status.
Somatic Type	Central theme is delusional belief in noxious bodily functions or sensations: foul odors, invading parasites, misshapen or ugly body parts, nonfunctioning body parts (e.g., the kidneys).
Grandiose Type	Central false belief of having some extraordinary but unrecognized talent, insight, or knowledge. May take the form of having a "special" (but non-love) relationship with a public figure or deity.
Jealous Type	Central delusion that a spouse or lover is or has been unfaithful.
Mixed Type	No central delusional theme predominates.
Unspecified Type	Central delusional belief cannot be identified, or does not fall clearly into any of the above categories.

By definition, those with Delusional Disorder (particularly Persecutory Type) are suspicious. Convincing such individuals even to consider treatment can be highly problematic. Often, the option of medical intervention can best be couched in terms of possibly reducing anxiety, dysphoria and upset caused by the (delusionally perceived) insults to which the potential patient feels he or she is being subjected.

Once rapport has been established, medication may be introduced, often similarly cloaked in the prospect of reducing anxiety or turmoil. Only after the delusion has been somewhat cracked or penetrated—i.e., the individual has begun to at least question its logical consistency, if not its veracity—can direct confrontation of the fantastic belief system be constructively initiated.

Typically, the same neuroleptic biochemical approach is employed in the treatment of Delusional Disorder as is effected in the treatment of Schizophrenia. Unfortunately, paranoid delusions tend to be the psychiatric symptoms most stubbornly resistant to psychopharmacologic intervention, and often they can be at best only partially eradicated. Then psychotherapy must be invoked, to assist the individual in understanding and accepting the paradox that even though he or she may have an idea or belief that seems very real (and persists in seeming so in the face of logical contradiction), it is not. It is just a byproduct of psychiatric disorder, and best kept to oneself except within very specific, clearly delineated venues (the therapist's office or with a select friend or two). If such a state of psychiatric equilibrium can be achieved and maintained, prognosis for the otherwise intact, high-functioning individual is likely very good.

B. Mood Disorders

Mood Disorders, also known as Affective Disorders, are characterized by some dysregulation of or inability to modulate mood state.[4] While abnormal mood is this group's central and organizing quality, such affective pathology may be accompanied by abnormal thinking and perception (including frank psychosis), as well as by profound anxiety.

Mood abnormality may be characterized by degree of intensity and duration of a single state (single mood too extreme for too long); degree of intensity and duration of fluctuating states (fluctuating moods too extreme, and for inappropriate spans of time); or degree of fluctuation between states of normal intensity (appropriate moods, but inappropriately fleeting or resistant to change). A mood disorder may be *unipolar* (involving only one mood extreme—depression—experienced with abnormal intensity and longevity), or *bipolar* (involving two or more mood extremes—mania and depression—both experienced with abnormal intensity and fluctuating at variable frequencies).

1. Major Depressive Disorder

CASE EXAMPLE

Mr. D was a customer service representative for a computer software company that prides itself on its progressive workplace environment—hours are flexible, management is employee-focused, and restrooms are unisex.

Mr. D thrived in this atmosphere for several years. Then a number of personal calamities seemed to cascade upon Mr. D in rapid, coincidental succession. His 59-year-old father suffered a sudden stroke and shortly thereafter committed suicide. His

---

[4]The terms *mood* and *affect* are often confused and frequently used interchangeably. Technically, *mood* refers to emotional state at one particular point: a cross-sectional "snapshot" frozen in time. *Affect* denotes the ongoing flux of emotional tone, the general flow of feelings from which mood is cross-sectionally extracted.

wife unexpectedly miscarried the couple's first child at five months. A large investment went sour. Seven months after Mr. D's father's death, Mr. D's mother succumbed to an (apparently intentional) overdose of her antidepressant medication. Not long after his father's death, Mr. D's work product began to deteriorate. Assignments were not completed or were completed sloppily. Usually social and outgoing, Mr. D was noted to be uncharacteristically irritable around peers, and snappy and aggressive with colleagues and clients alike. His personal hygiene deteriorated, as did his judgment. One customer reported Mr. D for spontaneously sharing with her how "it was I who had to identify my father's maggot-ridden body when he blew his brains away."

Finally, things reached a head when Mr. D complained that a cherub painted in the unisex restroom admonishing the user to "please put the toilet seat down after use" was actually meant to be a mean-spirited personal attack upon Mr. D's masculinity. Mr. D complained to management, demanding that a "reasonable accommodation" be made to his needs by converting all twenty-two of the company's unisex restrooms into male-only or female-only versions.

When the company refused, Mr. D resigned and initiated a lawsuit claiming constructive termination. Later, violation of the Americans with Disabilities Act was added to the lawsuit, based upon Mr. D's subsequent diagnosis of Major Depressive Disorder.

Major Depressive Disorder is the "Great Imitator" of psychiatry, in that the psychopathology may present itself in so many variable ways. Certainly, Major Depressive Disorder's hallmark symptom is a marked alteration of mood that does not vary over time, but that altered mood may be sadness, anger, irritability, apathy, guilt, or despair. The depressed person may first note physiological changes such as inability to sleep beyond a specific predawn hour (early morning awakening) or decrease in appetite, or their exact opposites (hypersomnolence and/or appetite increase). There may be changes in cognition—difficulty with concentration, memory, or attention. There may also be diffuse, nonspecific physical discontent—aches and pains or chronic fatigue. Psychotic symptoms may even develop.

As suggested by the name, however, the classic, core abnormality in Major Depressive Disorder is an alteration of mood—a marked period of sadness, despondency, or despair, or of tenseness, irritability, or anger. Such uncharacteristic, uncomfortable, pervasive mood state is typically accompanied by "neurovegetative" symptoms of depression: changes in physiologic regulation such as altered sleep, altered appetite, altered motor activity ("psychomotor retardation"—a literal slowing down of ambulation and body movements). Superimposed upon all these symptoms may be cognitive changes, psychotic changes, and a morbid preoccupation with death that can lead, most extremely, to violence in the form of suicide, homicide, or both.

Major Depressive Disorder is one of the most commonly encountered of the Axis I diagnoses. It is believed to occur with a prevalence of 5 to 10 percent in the population at large. Lifetime risk appears to be between 10 and 25 percent, with a slightly higher likelihood of occurrence in females than in males. Episodes may begin at any age, with average age of onset in the mid-20s.

Major Depressive Disorder is episodic, with circumscribed, acute major depressive episodes reoccurring throughout the lifetime. Individual episodes are typically time-limited, with symptoms receding naturally and even without treatment after one to two years. Between individual episodes, the disorder is said to be in remission. The affected individual is often returned to his or her psychological baseline entirely symptom-free.

Major Depressive Disorder is a biological phenomenon, passed through the generations genetically. It involves imbalances in the relative concentrations of neurotransmitters of the brain, and it is responsive to biochemical (medical) interventions. Individual episodes may be triggered by stressful environmental events, or they may occur spontaneously, without noticeable external provocation. Approximately 50 to 60 percent of individuals with Major Depressive Disorder, Single Episode can be expected to have a recurrent episode at some later point in their lives. The probability of further episodes increases with each successive bout endured.

In the context of employment litigation and other nonmedical circumstances, it becomes particularly critical to differentiate emotional upset—reactive feelings of sadness, despondency, anger, or irritability that arise in response to environmental provocation but that fade shortly following the removal of the environmental stressor—from the biological psychopathology of Major Depressive Disorder. Overlap of vocabulary and experience lends itself to misunderstanding and even frank exploitation and abuse in a contentious legal arena. Simple feelings of sadness or indignation—even though described in the vernacular as "depression"—are normal human responses to stress and should not be misconstrued as rising to the level of diagnosable psychiatric disorder.

DSM-IV-TR diagnostic criteria are designed to establish the minimal constellation of symptoms necessary to warrant the hypothesis that an episode of Major Depressive Disorder underlies presenting complaints of altered mood. Symptom criteria required for diagnosis of a Major Depressive Episode are set forth in Table 5-6. Those necessary to diagnose Major Depressive Disorder, Single Episode are outlined in Table 5-7, and those involved in a diagnosis of Major Depressive Disorder, Recurrent are listed in Table 5-8.

Table 5-6 *DSM-IV-TR* Diagnostic Criteria for Major Depressive Episode

A. Five (or more) of the following symptoms have been present during the same 2-week period and represent a change from previous functioning; at least one of the symptoms is either (1) depressed mood or (2) loss of interest or pleasure.

Note: Do not include symptoms that are clearly due to a general medical condition, or mood-incongruent delusions or hallucinations.

   (1) depressed mood most of the day, nearly every day, as indicated by either subjective report (e.g., feels sad or empty) or observation made by others (e.g., appears tearful). *Note:* In children and adolescents, can be irritable mood.

   (2) markedly diminished interest or pleasure in all, or almost all, activities most of the day, nearly every day (as indicated by either subjective account or observation made by others)

continued

Table 5-6 *Continued.*
***DSM-IV-TR* Diagnostic Criteria for Major Depressive Episode**

   (3) significant weight loss when not dieting or weight gain (e.g., a change of more than 5% of body weight in a month), or decrease or increase in appetite nearly every day. *Note:* In children, consider failure to make expected weight gains.
   (4) insomnia or hypersomnia nearly every day
   (5) psychomotor agitation or retardation nearly every day (observable by others, not merely subjective feelings of restlessness or being slowed down)
   (6) fatigue or loss of energy nearly every day
   (7) feelings of worthlessness or excessive or inappropriate guilt (which may be delusional) nearly every day (not merely self-reproach or guilt about being sick)
   (8) diminished ability to think or concentrate, or indecisiveness, nearly every day (either by subjective account or as observed by others)
   (9) recurrent thoughts of death (not just fear of dying), recurrent suicidal ideation without a specific plan, or a suicide attempt or a specific plan for committing suicide
B. The symptoms do not meet criteria for a Mixed Episode.
C. The symptoms cause clinically significant distress or impairment in social, occupational, or other important areas of functioning.
D. The symptoms are not due to the direct physiological effects of a substance (e.g., a drug of abuse, a medication) or a general medical condition (e.g., hypothyroidism).
E. The symptoms are not better accounted for by Bereavement, i.e., after the loss of a loved one, the symptoms persist for longer than 2 months or are characterized by marked functional impairment, morbid preoccupation with worthlessness, suicidal ideation, psychotic symptoms, or psychomotor retardation.

Source: Reprinted with permission from the *Diagnostic and Statistical Manual of Mental Disorders, Fourth Edition, Text Revision,* 356. Copyright 2000 American Psychiatric Association.

Table 5-7 *DSM-IV-TR* Diagnostic Criteria for Major Depressive Disorder, Single Episode

A. Presence of a single Major Depressive Episode.
B. The Major Depressive Episode is not better accounted for by Schizoaffective Disorder and is not superimposed on Schizophrenia, Schizophreniform Disorder, Delusional Disorder, or Psychotic Disorder Not Otherwise Specified.
C. There has never been a Manic Episode, a Mixed Episode, or a Hypomanic Episode.

Note: This exclusion does not apply if all of the manic-like, mixed-like, or hypomanic-like episodes are substance or treatment induced or are due to the direct physiological effects of a general medical condition.

Source: Reprinted with permission from the *Diagnostic and Statistical Manual of Mental Disorders, Fourth Edition, Text Revision,* 375. Copyright 2000 American Psychiatric Association.

Table 5-8 *DSM-IV-TR* Diagnostic Criteria for Major Depressive Disorder, Recurrent

A. Presence of two or more Major Depressive Episodes. *Note:* To be considered separate episodes, there must be an interval of at least 2 consecutive months in which criteria are not met for a Major Depressive Episode.
B. The Major Depressive Episodes are not better accounted for by Schizoaffective Disorder and are not superimposed on Schizophrenia, Schizophreniform Disorder, Delusional Disorder, or Psychotic Disorder Not Otherwise Specified.
C. There has never been a Manic Episode, a Mixed Episode, or a Hypomanic Episode. *Note:* This exclusion does not apply if all of the manic-like, mixed-like, or hypomanic-like episodes are substance or treatment induced or are due to the direct physiological effects of a general medical condition.

Source: Reprinted with permission from the *Diagnostic and Statistical Manual of Mental Disorders, Fourth Edition, Text Revision,* 376. Copyright 2000 American Psychiatric Association.

Notable in the *DSM-IV-TR* diagnostic system is the attempt to differentiate Major Depressive Disorder from phenomenological "masqueraders"—i.e., transient and minimally pathologically significant changes in affective status. Symptoms of Criterion A define the biologic character of Major Depression, and they must be present for at least two continuous weeks to rule out reactive, fleeting mood fluctuation. Criteria B, C, and D attempt to distinguish other conditions whose symptoms overlap those of Major Depressive Disorder, such as Bipolar Affective Disorder (Manic Depressive Illness); mood dysregulation induced artificially through toxin administration (e.g., barbiturates, alcohol); mood disorder produced as a side effect of a general medical (nonpsychiatric) condition (e.g., hypothyroidism, cancer); or disturbance in mood resulting from the universal, nonpathological circumstance of bereavement. Criterion C operationalizes the concept of clinical significance—symptoms present must provoke notable, meaningful impairment in social, occupational, or other important areas of functioning.

Treatment success rates are extremely high for Major Depressive Disorder. Antidepressant medications are abundant and exist in several chemical classes, such that a patient who reacts badly to one is more than likely to respond to another, or to some combination. Specific forms of psychotherapy (e.g., cognitive or behavioral therapy) have been developed that are highly effective, in and of themselves. Ideally, treatment of an episode should include both appropriate medication management and psychotherapy of the appropriate type, administered by a practitioner trained and experienced in the use of these techniques.

Correctly managed, most Major Depressive Episodes will resolve in less than six months. Occasionally, residual symptoms will remain longer, fading more slowly over time. Rarely will such residual symptoms be of sufficient magnitude to significantly impede effective day-to-day social or vocational functioning, however.

Rare individuals will prove resistant even to skillful psychopharmacologic and psychotherapeutic management. For these patients, Electroconvulsive Therapy (E.C.T.) becomes the treatment of choice. Contemporary E.C.T. is actually the safest, most effective treatment there is for the treatment of serious bouts of Major Depression, a far cry from stereotypic images of "shock treatment" popularized in movies and in television tabloids. Typically, with a short (two- to three-week) course of E.C.T., a patient can safely and painlessly be relieved of symptoms of Major Depression, entering a period of remission at least as resistant to relapse as that induced through medication or psychotherapeutic management, with fewer concurrent side effects and with virtually no clinically meaningful side effects.

2. Dysthymic Disorder

CASE EXAMPLE

Dr. E was an anesthesiologist working as an employee in a large HMO. For years, Dr. E complained to friends and associates about chronic feelings of fatigue, low self-esteem, and being "down in the dumps."

Financial circumstances forced the HMO to downsize, and remaining staff physicians including Dr. E were required to assume extra duties and extra on-call hours, and also to accept a 20 percent pay cut. Dr. E loudly and publicly protested these changes and led an unsuccessful campaign to have them reversed. Nonetheless, Dr. E continued working; he neither complained of, nor was he noted by anyone to display, any increase in or exacerbation of his perpetual low-level symptoms of disgruntlement.

Three months after the downsizing and Dr. E's failed attempt at insurrection, Dr. E presented to the HMO administration a note from his psychiatrist diagnosing Dr. E with "Severe Major Depression" and requesting, on this basis, an Americans with Disabilities Act "reasonable accommodation."

The accommodation proposed to the HMO (no on-call time, only daytime work hours, no more operating room time than had been required prior to downsizing) was deemed administratively unacceptable (and impossible), and Dr. E was terminated when he refused to honor the HMO's performance requirements. A lawsuit soon was filed on Dr. E's behalf, alleging violation of the ADA as well as wrongful termination.

Dysthymic Disorder is best thought of as a chronic, low-level depression. It may be biologically determined like Major Depressive Disorder (with a clear family history and responsive to medication), or it may be characterologic, with its origins in chronic discontent engendered by the perpetual dissatisfactions, failed expectations, and unreasonable interpersonal demands of a personality disorder. (The latter phenomenon is reflected in older nomenclatures for Dysthymic Disorder—terms such as "depressive neurosis" or "characterologic depression.")

Fundamental to Dysthymic Disorder is the chronic, unwavering nature of the depressive experience; while there may be mild ups and downs, depressed mood is prominent for most of the day, more days than not, for most of the individual's life (technically, for two or more years continuously). Equally fundamental is the relatively moderate to mild degree of the disturbance. Those with Dysthymic Disorder may not be fun or luminous, but they are seldom totally disabled from their occupation or unable to engage in ordinary social interaction.

Table 5-9 sets forth the *DSM-IV-TR* diagnostic criteria for Dysthymic Disorder. Most evident in these criteria is the chronicity component. While symptoms must, as always, cause clinically significant distress or impairment in social, occupational, or other functioning to rise to diagnosable significance, they must do so continuously for a minimum of two years. Dysthymic Disorder is not a reactive condition, as is sometimes erroneously alleged in litigation; it cannot be caused or triggered by isolated, commonly litigated workplace events such as harassment, discrimination, or termination (wrongful or legitimate); and it is, in fact, one of the preexisting conditions most likely misattributed to alleged adverse workplace events by hasty and superficial forensic evaluators.

Table 5-9 *DSM-IV-TR* Diagnostic Criteria for Dysthymic Disorder

A. Depressed mood for most of the day, for more days than not, as indicated either by subjective account or observation by others, for at least 2 years. *Note:* In children and adolescents, mood can be irritable and duration must be at least 1 year.
B. Presence, while depressed, of two (or more) of the following:
   1) poor appetite or overeating
   2) insomnia or hypersomnia
   3) low energy or fatigue
   4) low self-esteem
   5) poor concentration or difficulty making decisions
   6) feelings of hopelessness
C. During the 2-year period (1 year for children or adolescents) of the disturbance, the person has never been without the symptoms in Criteria A and B for more than 2 months at a time.
D. No Major Depressive Episode has been present during the first 2 years of the disturbance (1 year for children and adolescents); i.e., the disturbance is not better accounted for by chronic Major Depressive Disorder, or Major Depressive Disorder, In Partial Remission.

continued

> **Table 5-9 Continued.**
> **DSM-IV-TR Diagnostic Criteria**
> **for Dysthymic Disorder**
>
> *Note:* There may have been a previous Major Depressive Episode provided there was a full remission (no significant signs or symptoms for 2 months) before development of the Dysthymic Disorder. In addition, after the initial 2 years (1 year in children or adolescents) of Dysthymic Disorder, there may be superimposed episodes of Major Depressive Disorder, in which case both diagnoses may be given when the criteria are met for a Major Depressive Episode.
>
> E. There has never been a Manic Episode, a Mixed Episode, or a Hypomanic Episode, and criteria have never been met for Cyclothymic Disorder.
> F. The disturbance does not occur exclusively during the course of a chronic Psychotic Disorder, such as Schizophrenia or Delusional Disorder.
> G. The symptoms are not due to the direct physiological effects of a substance (e.g., a drug of abuse, a medication) or a general medical condition (e.g., hypothyroidism).
> H. The symptoms cause clinically significant distress or impairment in social, occupational, or other important areas of functioning.
>
> *Specify if:*
> Early Onset: if onset is before age 21 years
> Late Onset: if onset is age 21 years or older
>
> *Source:* Reprinted with permission from the *Diagnostic and Statistical Manual of Mental Disorders, Fourth Edition, Text Revision,* 380–81. Copyright 2000 American Psychiatric Association.

Clinical management of Dysthymic Disorder is similar to that of Major Depressive Disorder, particularly when a biological component is prominent. The same antidepressant medications with the same approaches to psychopharmacology (single agents or rationally derived combinations) are employed. The same (Cognitive-Behavioral) psychotherapy is also effective.

Where characterological etiology looms large, treatment may prove more difficult and is definitely a longer-term undertaking. Medications may still be helpful, but their efficacy is less predictable. Significantly, psychotherapy must switch from the didactic, "here and now" orientation of Cognitive-Behavioral treatment to a longer-term, more exploratory psychodynamic focus. In order to alleviate misery born of the self-fulfilling prophecies, passive-aggressive self-sabotages, and irrational demands and expectations of personality pathology, that pathology itself must be uncovered, identified, confronted, and ultimately rejected by the patient. Such process, successfully undertaken, will invariably alleviate dysthymic byproduct along the way.

3. "Double Depression"

Individuals who are chronically discontent and unhappy as a function of Dysthymic Disorder will sometimes—perhaps in response to identifiable environmental stressors or perhaps not—develop an acute Major Depressive Episode superimposed upon chronic, baseline symptoms. Such an episode is circumscribed, time-limited, and governed by all the laws of Major Depressive Episodes not experienced in conjunction with Dysthymic Disorder. Though not a formal *DSM-IV-TR* diagnostic entity, this state of psychological affairs is often termed "Double Depression."

The superimposed Major Depressive Episode, treated in the same way as is any Major Depressive Episode, subsequently clears, and the individual returns to his or her chronic state of mild to moderate discontent. Typically, the post-episode symptom picture is, upon careful scrutiny, indistinguishable from the pre-episode picture.

In litigation-related evaluation, a bout of Double Depression obviously must be carefully distinguished from a case of a new Major Depressive Disorder with refractory, treatment-resistant post-episode symptoms. Meticulous discovery of pre-episode functioning—via review of medical and mental health records, as well as employment, school, and military records—generally provides the basis for such differentiation.

4. Bipolar Affective Disorder

CASE EXAMPLE

A lawsuit was filed against the U.S. government when Ms. F, a custodian at a U.S. Air Force base, slipped on wet, slippery tundra at the base, allegedly because she had been "supremely upset" by an ethnically tainted joke she had just been told by one of the base's senior officers. Although there was no documented loss of consciousness or visible physical lesion, orientation and memory were intact in the emergency room, and brain scan, E.E.G. and neurologic workup were all within normal limits, Ms. F was noted by E.R. personnel to be excessively talkative and pressured of speech, giddy, and "hyper." A mild closed head injury was diagnosed, and Ms. F went on within the week to file a lawsuit claiming severe cognitive deficits as damages.

A few months after the alleged head injury, Ms. F was psychiatrically hospitalized when police found her naked in a park, on her knees, praying to an unspecified deity. At the hospital Ms. F was noted to be giddy, hypersexual, uninhibited, speaking unintelligibly, and somewhat delusional, claiming to be "the Earth Mother" and "the Mother of Us All." Ms. F was treated with antipsychotic medications as well as the mood stabilizer lithium and released as stable. Within the month, Ms. F stopped taking her medications and was similarly rehospitalized. She expanded her legal claim against the United States, adding damages described as "Traumatically Induced Manic Depression" to her earlier alleged "severe cognitive deficits." Forensic psychiatric evaluation revealed a recurrent religious delusional theme permeating Ms. F's post-incident psychotic episodes, as well as a propensity to flop down on the ground in religious ecstasy at such times. This led to discovery of documentation showing that pre-event, Ms. F was divorced by her first husband as a result of episodes of disinhibition, indiscreet hypersexuality and spending, and hyperreligiosity that included "physically inappropriate behavioral displays of public praying."

In light of the objectively minimal nature of any head injury sustained at the U.S. Air Force Base, embedded as it was in this striking psychiatric history, the court adopted the evaluating psychiatrist's opinion that no fall had occurred at all on government tundra. Instead, Ms. F, entering yet another of her manic episodes, simply lay down on the ground that evening to pray. No head injury. No damages. No hostile working environment was found to have existed; in fact, the court observed that such an environment was "more likely than not delusional."

Bipolar Affective Disorder (formerly known as Manic-Depressive Disorder) is a cyclic condition in which an individual alternates between three general mood states: Mania, Euthymia, and Major Depression. Cycling may vary in frequency just as states may vary in duration. States may be relatively pure, or mixed, including features of both Mania and Depression at the same time.

Broadly, just as a Major Depressive Episode can be thought of as a period of slowdown, where the individual is more gloomy and more lethargic than usual, a Manic Episode can be conceived of as a period of speedup. The individual is uncharacteristically high, with elevated, expansive mood and enthusiastic, infectious energy. Little sleep is needed, and projects typically requiring days are completed (albeit not very well) in hours. The individual may be disinhibited, inappropriately violating sexual taboos or rationally imposed spending limits. Where psychosis is present, it classically takes the form of grandiose delusion—omnipotence and omniscience, supernatural ability (to fly, to dodge bullets), self-definition as a powerful historical figure (Napoleon, Cleopatra, the Messiah).

Just as Major Depression may occasionally paradoxically present without depressed mood (with irritability or anger in its place), so may mania present from time to time without giddy euphoria or enthusiasm. Instead, a "dark" Manic Episode may be dominated by extraordinary but negative energy—free-floating rage, extreme irritability and demandingness, even physical restlessness leading to disinhibited assault. Obviously, manics of this latter type can be highly dangerous and difficult to manage.

DSM-IV-TR criteria for a Manic Episode are outlined in Table 5-10.

Table 5-10 *DSM-IV-TR* Diagnostic Criteria for Manic Episode

A. A distinct period of abnormally and persistently elevated, expansive, or irritable mood, lasting at least 1 week (or any duration if hospitalization is necessary).
B. During the period of mood disturbance, three (or more) of the following symptoms have persisted (four if the mood is only irritable) and have been present to a significant degree:
   (1) inflated self-esteem or grandiosity
   (2) decreased need for sleep (e.g., feels rested after only 3 hours of sleep)
   (3) more talkative than usual or pressure to keep talking
   (4) flight of ideas or subjective experience that thoughts are racing
   (5) distractibility (i.e., attention too easily drawn to unimportant or irrelevant external stimuli)
   (6) increase in goal-directed activity (either socially, at work or school, or sexually) or psychomotor agitation

(7) excessive involvement in pleasurable activities that have a high potential for painful consequences (e.g., engaging in unrestrained buying sprees, sexual indiscretions, or foolish business investments)
C. The symptoms do not meet criteria for a Mixed Episode.
D. The mood disturbance is sufficiently severe to cause marked impairment in occupational functioning or in usual social activities or relationships with others, or to necessitate hospitalization to prevent harm to self or others, or there are psychotic features.
E. The symptoms are not due to the direct physiological effects of a substance (e.g., a drug of abuse, a medication, or other treatment) or a general medical condition (e.g., hyperthyroidism).
Note: Manic-like episodes that are clearly caused by somatic antidepressant treatment (e.g., medication, electroconvulsive therapy, light therapy) should not count toward a diagnosis of Bipolar I Disorder.

Source: Reprinted with permission from the *Diagnostic and Statistical Manual of Mental Disorders, Fourth Edition, Text Revision,* 362. Copyright 2000 American Psychiatric Association.

Euthymia refers to a period of baseline, normal mood, characterized by neither manic nor depressive feelings or behavior. The life experience of one suffering from Bipolar Affective Disorder alternates between experiencing a Manic Episode (one pole); experiencing a Major Depressive Episode (the other pole); and being Euthymic (of normal mood).[5]

Not all Manic Episodes are pure ones. A person may alternate between Major Depressive Episodes, euthymia, and so-called mixed states, periods during which symptoms of both mania and depression coexist. Such an individual is still considered to suffer from Bipolar Affective Disorder. The criteria for a Mixed Episode are outlined in Table 11.

Table 5-11 *DSM-IV-TR* Diagnostic Criteria for Mixed Episode

A. The criteria are met both for a Manic Episode and for a Major Depressive Episode (except for duration) nearly every day during at least a 1-week period.
B. The mood disturbance is sufficiently severe to cause marked impairment in occupational functioning or in usual social activities or relationships with others, or to necessitate hospitalization to prevent harm to self or others, or there are psychotic features.
C. The symptoms are not due to the direct physiological effects of a substance (e.g., a drug of abuse, a medication, or other treatment) or a general medical condition (e.g., hyperthyroidism).

continued

---

[5]Technically, the Bipolar Affective Disorder diagnosis is assigned after a single Manic Episode has occurred, even if no Major Depressive Episode has yet descended upon the individual. This is based upon predictive power. In contrast, Major Depressive Disorder is diagnosed when one or more Major Depressive Episodes—but no Manic Episodes—have been experienced.

Table 5-11 Continued.
DSM-IV-TR Diagnostic Criteria for Mixed Episode

Note: Mixed-like episodes that are clearly caused by somatic antidepressant treatment (e.g., medication, electroconvulsive therapy, light therapy) should not count toward a diagnosis of Bipolar I Disorder.

Source: Reprinted with permission from the *Diagnostic and Statistical Manual of Mental Disorders, Fourth Edition, Text Revision,* 365. Copyright 2000 American Psychiatric Association.

5. Bipolar I Disorder Versus Bipolar II Disorder

For many years, clinicians have been aware of certain individuals whose baseline, lifelong functioning appears somewhat sped up relative to the average. These people were natural leaders; often highly charismatic, verbal and intelligent, with ready wit and powerful persuasive skills, they usually excelled in most areas of endeavor.

A price appeared to be extracted, however, for the ease with which such individuals seemed to glide through life. Periodically, they would experience a brief phase (days to a week or two) of being too "on"—almost hyper, lacking judgment, inhibition, and tactful restraint usually seen as their defining characteristics. And, from time to time, such individuals appeared to plunge into bouts of overwhelming, intractable hopelessness and despair.

In 1994 (with the publication of *DSM-IV*[6]) this phenomenology was crystallized into a formal diagnostic category. A state of Hypomania ("just below mania") was defined to capture periods of relative disinhibition, excess energy, and poor judgment, surpassing the individual's charismatic baseline, but certainly not of sufficient magnitude to be considered a full-blown Manic Episode. Where fluctuation between classic mania, euthymia, and Major Depression became known as Bipolar I disorder, those who fluctuated between Hypomania and the depressive pole were designated Bipolar II.

Formal diagnostic criteria for a Hypomanic Episode are outlined in Table 5-12. Those for Bipolar I Disorder are set forth in Table 5-13, and those for Bipolar II Disorder are contained in Table 5-14. Note that either Bipolar I or Bipolar II Disorder may be "rapid cycling" (technically, at least four episodes of mood disturbance—Major Depressive, Manic, Mixed, Hypomanic—within a 12-month period; often many more). Either may have a "seasonal pattern" (with particular mood episodes routinely occurring at particular times of year). Episodes of either may, but need not, be triggered by external, environmental, or naturally occurring internal events (e.g., the menstrual cycle), or by medically pathological internal events (serious illness). Both are biological entities at core and cannot in and of themselves be "caused" by psychosocial stressors of any magnitude. Specific, circumscribed episodes of each, however, can be triggered by such stressors.

---

[6]AMERICAN PSYCHIATRIC ASSOCIATION, DIAGNOSTIC AND STATISTICAL MANUAL OF MENTAL DISORDERS (4th ed. 1994).

Table 5-12 *DSM-IV-TR* Diagnostic Criteria for Hypomanic Episode

A. A distinct period of persistently elevated, expansive, or irritable mood, lasting throughout at least 4 days, that is clearly different from the usual nondepressed mood.
B. During the period of mood disturbance, three (or more) of the following symptoms have persisted (four if the mood is only irritable) and have been present to a significant degree:
   (1) inflated self-esteem or grandiosity
   (2) decreased need for sleep (e.g., feels rested after only 3 hours of sleep)
   (3) more talkative than usual or pressure to keep talking
   (4) flight of ideas or subjective experience that thoughts are racing
   (5) distractibility (i.e., attention too easily drawn to unimportant or irrelevant external stimuli)
   (6) increase in goal-directed activity (either socially, at work or school, or sexually) or psychomotor agitation
   (7) excessive involvement in pleasurable activities that have a high potential for painful consequences (e.g., the person engages in unrestrained buying sprees, sexual indiscretions, or foolish business investments)
C. The episode is associated with an unequivocal change in functioning that is uncharacteristic of the person when not symptomatic.
D. The disturbance in mood and the change in functioning are observable by others.
E. The episode is not severe enough to cause marked impairment in social or occupational functioning, or to necessitate hospitalization, and there are no psychotic features.
F. The symptoms are not due to the direct physiological effects of a substance (e.g., a drug of abuse, a medication, or other treatment) or a general medical condition (e.g., hyperthyroidism).
Note: Hypomanic-like episodes that are clearly caused by somatic antidepressant treatment (e.g., medication, electroconvulsive therapy, light therapy) should not count toward a diagnosis of Bipolar II Disorder.

Source: Reprinted with permission from the *Diagnostic and Statistical Manual of Mental Disorders, Fourth Edition, Text Revision,* 368. Copyright 2000 American Psychiatric Association.

Table 5-13 *DSM-IV-TR* Diagnostic Criteria for Bipolar I Disorder

A. Criteria, except for duration, are currently (or most recently) met for a Manic, a Hypomanic, a Mixed, or a Major Depressive Episode.
B. There has previously been at least one Manic Episode or Mixed Episode.
C. The mood symptoms cause clinically significant distress or impairment in social, occupational, or other important areas of functioning.
D. The mood symptoms in Criteria A and B are not better accounted for by Schizoaffective Disorder and are not superimposed on Schizophrenia, Schizophreniform Disorder, Delusional Disorder, or Psychotic Disorder Not Otherwise Specified.

continued

Table 5-13 *Continued.* DSM-IV-TR Diagnostic Criteria for Bipolar I Disorder

E. The mood symptoms in Criteria A and B are not due to the direct physiological effects of a substance (e.g., a drug of abuse, a medication, or other treatment) or a general medical condition (e.g., hyperthyroidism).

Source: Reprinted with permission from the *Diagnostic and Statistical Manual of Mental Disorders, Fourth Edition, Text Revision,* 392. Copyright 2000 American Psychiatric Association.

Table 5-14 DSM-IV-TR Diagnostic Criteria for Bipolar II Disorder

A. Presence (or history) of one or more Major Depressive Episodes.
B. Presence (or history) of at least one Hypomanic Episode.
C. There has never been a Manic Episode or a Mixed Episode.
D. The mood symptoms in Criteria A and B are not better accounted for by Schizoaffective Disorder and are not superimposed on Schizophrenia, Schizophreniform Disorder, Delusional Disorder, or Psychotic Disorder Not Otherwise Specified.
E. The symptoms cause clinically significant distress or impairment in social, occupational, or other important areas of functioning.

Source: Reprinted with permission from the *Diagnostic and Statistical Manual of Mental Disorders, Fourth Edition, Text Revision,* 397. Copyright 2000 American Psychiatric Association.

The lifetime prevalence (percentage of the population suffering the disorder during an "average" lifetime) of Bipolar I Disorder is estimated at between 0.4 percent and 1.6 percent. That of Bipolar II Disorder is thought to be approximately 0.5 percent[7] (probably an underestimate due to underreporting). Both subtypes may first appear during virtually any decade of life, from the prepubertal through the geriatric years.

The hallmark treatment of Bipolar Affective Disorder (Type I or II) is psychopharmacologic, in the form of one or a combination of "mood stabilizers." These medications reduce the frequency of occurrence of abnormal mood episodes at either pole, and reduce the intensity of such episodes if and when they do occur.

Occasionally, additional pharmacologic intervention is indicated—a neuroleptic (antipsychotic) for psychotic symptoms, a tranquilizer for extreme agitation, an antidepressant for profound dysphoria, or some combination. Like Major Depressive Disorder, Bipolar Affective Disorder will, in the vast majority of cases, be fully and effectively managed with appropriate psychopharmacology. So managed, residual symptoms, if present at all, are characteristically minimal and insignificant relative to overall social and vocational function.

---

[7]*DSM-IV-TR, supra* note 1, at 385.

From time to time, a patient presents with obvious symptoms of a Major Depressive Episode, no symptoms or history of Mania, and no known family history. Treated with an appropriate antidepressant medication, such a patient then goes on to develop classic symptoms of a Manic Episode. Subsequent addition of a mood stabilizer restores normal function. Such patients are believed to suffer from an underlying biological Bipolar I Disorder, the first manifestation of which happened to be a Major Depressive Episode. Without a "ceiling" of mood stabilizer present, the antidepressant pushes the biologically predisposed patient into the opposite, manic pole. Often, post hoc scrutiny uncovers a subtle family history of Bipolar Disorder, or even of (unrecognized, unsuspected) prior Manic or Hypomanic behavior in the individual himself or herself. This phenomenon is sometimes referred to in psychiatric literature as Bipolar III. It has yet to be recognized as a formal diagnostic entity, and indeed probably should not be, since it really constitutes no more than a pharmacologically induced manifestation of Bipolar I or II.

Unfortunately for those suffering from Bipolar Affective Disorder and for those close to them, the Manic state can actually prove quite enjoyable, a "natural high" not unlike that produced by certain psychostimulants and inhalants. Consequently, these individuals may be loath to give up the energy, "hyperacuteness," and euphoric attitude that are the benchmarks of their Mania.

Thus, in addition to the general need to overcome resistance to acknowledgment of a chronic mental illness and to develop insight (a thorough understanding of one's own warning signs for impending psychological deterioration, and development of strategies of response), psychotherapy in Bipolar Affective Disorder must confront volitional issues. For example, the costs versus the benefits of taking, or not taking, one's medication; of neutralizing, or not neutralizing, one's natural patterns of pathology must be confronted and resolved. Sadly, in many cases it is only after a young manic has repeatedly suffered adverse consequences of his or her untempered illness (such as recurrent police confrontations, physical altercations, financial and vocational debacles, sexual fiascos) that he or she becomes willing to give up the "pleasures" the disorder can intermittently produce.

C. Anxiety Disorders and Dual Diagnosis

Anxiety Disorders are characterized by an impairment of the ability of a person to modulate arousal. Anxiety is a universal phenomenon, adaptive as a warning signal in circumstances of impending danger, and energizing as a source of stimulation in situations where heightened attention or effort is required. Only when levels of anxiety become excessive, or when they are experienced at inappropriate times, do they interfere with performance and become pathological.

In the context of employment litigation, complaints involving anxiety symptoms almost invariably are accompanied by complaints surrounding dysfunctional mood (e.g., panic attacks accompanying depression). When comorbid symptoms of two disorders are of sufficient magnitude to warrant the assignment of both diagnoses, this is termed a situation of "dual diagnosis."

While traditionally dual diagnosis has connoted the coexistence of a substance abuse disorder (e.g., Alcohol Dependence) along with a functional psychiatric disorder (e.g., Major Depressive Disorder), in fact the phrase correctly refers to any two, distinct, co-occurring Axis I conditions.

It has historically been assumed that the Mood Disorders are a group entirely distinct from the Anxiety Disorders, differing not only in expression but also in course, biological underpinning, etiology, prognosis, and treatment. However, as research begins to illuminate the still murky waters of the actual biophysiological pathology expressing itself as functional psychiatric symptoms, it becomes increasingly certain that Mood Disorders and Anxiety Disorders are in truth close cousins, probably just different ends of a common biopathological spectrum. Hereditary patterns overlap. Neurotransmitter abnormalities are strikingly similar. Identical medications treat both classes of psychopathology.

Of most practical import, the one category of disorder will frequently give way to the other over time. An individual may first experience illness in the form of panic attacks but soon develop symptoms of a Major Depressive Episode. Another may be in the throes of Major Depression and inexplicably suffer his or her first panic attack. Thus, unlike other areas of pathology where, in a medicolegal context, progressive reporting of ever-increasingly elaborated symptoms over time is a sign of possible malingering (sometimes known as "chart creep"), such a progression from Mood Disorder to Anxiety Disorder, or vice versa, may be entirely natural and legitimate.

1. Panic Disorder and Agoraphobia

CASE EXAMPLE

Mr. G, a promising young advertising executive, was admired for his wildly creative ideas and campaigns for television commercial clients. He was equally known for his shyness and refusal to participate in the public presentations central to pitching his product. Such marketing was left to his partner, a more gregarious and outgoing (if less imaginative) character.

The company founder was concerned that Mr. G's reticence might handicap an otherwise promising career, and he became determined to coax Mr. G out of his false modesty. On a Monday morning, unannounced and in the middle of an important meeting with key, lucrative clients, the founder announced that Mr. G, not his partner, would be pitching the proposed new multimillion-dollar campaign that day.

Mr. G had already finished two cups of coffee, and as he stood up to speak, his heart began to race and he felt hot and sweaty. His hands began to shake. Soon, he was gasping for air. He ran out of the room terrified, thinking his body might literally explode.

For the next several months, Mr. G experienced unpredictable, apparently trigger-free episodes—each similar to the first, building in intensity for about ten minutes before beginning to recede—as many as four a day. His mood began to change, and he became increasingly morose. His sleep was fitful and interrupted. He lost his appetite, and he lost weight.

About two months after his initial episode, Mr. G was noted by colleagues to be confused and rambling. He came to work unshaven, wearing inappropriate, rumpled clothing. He seemed hostile and irritable.

On the eleventh week after his first panic attack, Mr. G filed a complaint of discrimination with the Equal Employment Opportunity Commission (EEOC), copied to his company's Director of Human Resources. In a loose, convoluted, illogical logic, Mr. G explained that he was the victim of religious harassment and discrimination at the hands of the company founder. Being of Jewish descent, Mr. G reasoned that this stemmed from his parents' survival through a terrifying internment in one of the Nazi concentration camps during World War II. He complained that the company founder, a German American, "has taken it upon himself to avenge my parents' fortitude, and redeem the honor of his forefathers by maligning, persecuting, and torturing me."

Panic Disorder, with or without comorbid Agoraphobia or Major Depression, is a frequently encountered complaint in employment litigation settings, particularly where an alleged inability to work is asserted. For example, a lawyer may become unable to litigate, for fear of experiencing a panic attack upon entering the courtroom. A surgeon may become unable to operate, for fear of jerking the scalpel, or a gynecologist may become unable to deliver for fear of dropping the baby. With Agoraphobia, the employee is too afraid of potential panic attack even to venture forth from his or her home.

Panic attacks are appropriate physiologic arousal functions occurring at inappropriate times. The organism's normal, biologically adaptive adrenergic nervous system response—the "fight or flight" set of physiologic adaptations that energizes animals to deal instantaneously with threat by either fighting it off or fleeing—is being activated spontaneously and inappropriately, when in fact there is no environmental menace present. The individual suffering a panic attack is, in essence, being prepared for an attack by a wild animal when in fact no such animal is in sight.

Panic attacks may be spontaneous—occurring with no identifiable stimulus—or they may be predictably triggered by specific situations or stimuli such as driving in rain or being in a large, crowded mall. The attacks are classically characterized by an abrupt onset of characteristic symptoms such as heart palpitations, shortness of breath and hyperventilation, dizziness, or tremor. Onset to peak episode intensity is usually within 10 to 15 minutes, followed by gradual waning of symptoms. Table 5-15 exhibits the specific *DSM-IV-TR* definition of a Panic Attack.

Table 5-15 *DSM-IV-TR* Diagnostic Criteria for a Panic Attack

A discrete period of intense fear or discomfort, in which four (or more) of the following symptoms developed abruptly and reached a peak within 10 minutes:
    (1) palpitations, pounding heart, or accelerated heart rate
    (2) sweating
    (3) trembling and shaking

continued

Table 5-15 Continued.
DSM-IV-TR Diagnostic Criteria for a Panic Attack

(4) sensations of shortness of breath or smothering
(5) feeling of choking
(6) chest pain or discomfort
(7) nausea or abdominal distress
(8) feeling dizzy, unsteady, lightheaded, or faint
(9) derealization (feelings of unreality) or depersonalization
(10) fear of losing control or going crazy
(11) fear of dying
(12) paresthesias (numbness or tingling sensations)
(13) chills or hot flashes

Source: Reprinted with permission from the *Diagnostic and Statistical Manual of Mental Disorders, Fourth Edition, Text Revision,* 432. Copyright 2000 American Psychiatric Association.

"Agoraphobia" is a term often used inappropriately in lay contexts, including those surrounding employment litigation. Common misinterpretations include "fear of leaving the home," "fear of social situations," "fear of crowds," and "fear of public places."

Correctly, Agoraphobia denotes a single, very specific condition. It is a state of profound anxiety that arises when one finds oneself in places or situations from which escape might be difficult or humiliating (or in which help might not be readily available) in the event of having a panic attack or significant panic-like symptoms (e.g., chest pain, sudden diarrhea). Such anxiety typically gives rise to avoidance of a variety of situations. At its most extreme, it may result in a refusal to leave one's home or to be alone in one's house. Less crippling are situation-specific agoraphobic avoidances, such as being in a crowded movie theater or in a car, traveling by plane or train, being in an elevator, going through a tunnel. Sometimes, the avoidance is total. Other times, the individual is willing to confront feared stimuli, but only in the presence of a trusted friend or relative who can effect a rescue if necessary.

Panic Disorder is diagnosed when the presence of recurrent, unexpected panic attacks is followed by at least one month of worrying about or acting in response to worry about further attacks. As Tables 5-16 and 5-17 display, Panic Disorder may be diagnosed with or without Agoraphobia.

Table 5-16 DSM-IV-TR Diagnostic Criteria for Panic Disorder With Agoraphobia

A. Both (1) and (2):
  (1) recurrent unexpected Panic Attacks
  (2) at least one of the attacks has been followed by 1 month (or more) of one (or more) of the following:
    (a) persistent concern about having additional attacks
    (b) worry about the implications of the attack or its consequences (e.g., losing control, having a heart attack, "going crazy")
    (c) a significant change in behavior related to the attacks

B. The presence of Agoraphobia.
C. The Panic Attacks are not due to the direct physiological effects of a substance (e.g., a drug of abuse, a medication) or a general medical condition (e.g., hyperthyroidism).
D. The Panic Attacks are not better accounted for by another mental disorder, such as Social Phobia (e.g., occurring on exposure to feared social situations), Specific Phobia (e.g., on exposure to a specific phobic situation), Obsessive-Compulsive Disorder (e.g., on exposure to dirt in someone with an obsession about contamination), Posttraumatic Stress Disorder (e.g., in response to stimuli associated with a severe stressor), or Separation Anxiety Disorder (e.g., in response to being away from home or close relatives).

Source: Reprinted with permission from the *Diagnostic and Statistical Manual of Mental Disorders, Fourth Edition, Text Revision,* 441. Copyright 2000 American Psychiatric Association.

Table 5-17 *DSM-IV-TR* Diagnostic Criteria for Panic Disorder Without Agoraphobia

A. Both (1) and (2):
  (1) Recurrent unexpected Panic Attacks
  (2) At least one of the attacks has been followed by 1 month (or more) of one (or more) of the following:
    (a) persistent concern about having additional attacks
    (b) worry about the implications of the attack or its consequences (e.g., losing control, having a heart attack, "going crazy")
    (c) a significant change in behavior related to the attacks
B. Absence of Agoraphobia.
C. The Panic Attacks are not due to the direct physiological effects of a substance (e.g., a drug of abuse, a medication) or a general medical condition (e.g., hyperthyroidism).
D. The Panic Attacks are not better accounted for by another mental disorder, such as Social Phobia (e.g., occurring on exposure to feared social situations), Specific Phobia (e.g., on exposure to a specific phobic situation), Obsessive-Compulsive Disorder (e.g., on exposure to dirt in someone with an obsession about contamination), Posttraumatic Stress Disorder (e.g., in response to stimuli associated with a severe stressor), or Separation Anxiety Disorder (e.g., in response to being away from home or close relatives).

Source: Reprinted with permission from the *Diagnostic and Statistical Manual of Mental Disorders, Fourth Edition, Text Revision,* 440. Copyright 2000 American Psychiatric Association.

Prevalence of Panic Disorder is estimated at between 1 percent and 3 percent of the general population. About one-third to one-half of those in the community with Panic Disorder also suffer from Agoraphobia. As mentioned earlier, comorbidity of symptoms of Panic Disorder and symptoms of Major Depressive Disorder is notably high.

The same medications most often employed in the treatment of Major Depressive Disorder—so-called Selective Serotonin Reuptake Inhibitors (SSRIs) and Tricyclic Antidepressant Agents (TCAs)—prove to be remarkably effective in the treatment of Panic Disorder. These medications often require several weeks of gradual dosage increase before beginning to take effect. If symptoms are profound, many practitioners will initially administer a short-term tranquilizer (benzodiazepine) to help "turn down the volume." For reasons that remain pharmacologically mysterious, average antidepressant dosages required to diminish panic and anxiety tend to be higher than those successful in treating Major Depression.

In addition to highly effective psychopharmacological options, effective psychotherapeutic approaches to the treatment of Panic Disorder have been developed. Cognitive-behavioral in nature, such therapies employ didactics, behavioral methods, and exercises specifically tailored to individual patients. In skillful hands, they achieve significant and lasting results. As is true for most other forms of psychopathology, the most effective treatment for Panic Disorder (with or without Agoraphobia) has been shown to be a combination of appropriate medications and appropriate verbal interventions.

2. Obsessive-Compulsive Disorder

CASE EXAMPLE

Ms. H was one of numerous legal secretaries at a large firm. Valued for her intelligence and detail orientation, Ms. H was also resented by other secretaries for her tendency to monopolize community facilities (copy machine, microwave), literally locking herself in the machine room or kitchen and remaining there for hours accomplishing tasks typically completed in minutes by others. When Ms H's "special techniques" (as she cryptically explained her hidden behaviors) finally resulted in several missed court filing deadlines and she continued to resist intelligible explanation, Ms. H was referred for a fitness-for-duty psychiatric evaluation.

Examination revealed that in the copy room, Ms H went through an elaborate, ritualistic sequence of loading and unloading, toner checking, reloading, paper checking, and miscellaneous button pushing before a single copy could be produced, and she repeated it every few pages thereafter. Similar special techniques were employed in community kitchen and restroom. Failure to perform a given special technique would, Ms. H feared, result in something violent and painful happening to her boyfriend, who currently lived thirteen states distant. Ms. H reported that she was fully aware of the illogic and the utter bizarreness of this belief, but she was equally fully unable to shake herself of it or dare to behave so as to challenge its nonsensical prediction.

Obsessive-Compulsive Disorder (OCD) is most likely to present itself in workplace litigation in the context of compulsion interfering with work efficiency, with resultant raising of fitness-for-duty concerns or requests for accommodation under the Americans with Disabilities Act.[8] Typically first manifesting as early as the teens and seldom beyond the late thirties, and with a prevalence

---

[8] *See* Humphrey v. Memorial Hosp. Ass'n, 239 F.3d 1128 (9th Cir. 2001).

in the general population of around 1 percent, OCD is profoundly painful for those it afflicts, not only because of the eccentric (and inconvenient) nature of the thoughts and behaviors that define it, but because of the fully rational awareness of the sufferer that his or her unavoidable ideas and rituals are utterly bizarre.

Obsessions are recurrent ideas, thoughts, or images that persist and are experienced as intrusive, inappropriate, and anxiety-producing. Where the psychotic individual with a delusional belief system thinks that the tenets of that system are completely reasonable and rational ("You'd be paranoid too, if everyone were out to get you!"), the obsessive thinker is fully aware and will readily agree that his or her idea is unreasonable and unrealistic. Yet the idea persists, and it produces great anxiety.

Compulsions are ritualized, repetitive, intentional physical behaviors or mental acts performed in response to obsessions, usually according to "rules" that, if broken, negate the effectiveness of the entire behavioral sequence. Compulsions may be believed necessary in order to prevent irrationally dreaded events (a handwashing ritual must be performed to prevent one's child from having a terrible school accident, for example), or at least to relieve the anxiety produced by obsessional ideas. As with obsessions, the individual is aware of—and often repelled by—the illogic and "weirdness" of his or her belief system, yet feels compelled to adhere to it. Because of such awareness, obsessive beliefs and compulsive rituals frequently remain dark, closely guarded, and profoundly embarrassing secrets.

DSM-IV-TR diagnostic criteria for OCD are set forth in Table 5-18. Note that formal *DSM-IV-TR* definitions for obsessions and compulsions are encompassed in the criteria.

Table 5-18 *DSM-IV-TR* Diagnostic Criteria for Obsessive-Compulsive Disorder

A. Either obsessions or compulsions:
Obsessions as defined by (1), (2), (3), and (4):
 (1) recurrent and persistent thoughts, impulses, or images that are experienced, at some time during the disturbance, as intrusive and inappropriate and that cause marked anxiety or distress
 (2) the thoughts, impulses, or images are not simply excessive worries about real-life problems
 (3) the person attempts to ignore or suppress such thoughts, impulses, or images, or to neutralize them with some other thought or action
 (4) the person recognizes that the obsessional thoughts, impulses, or images are a product of his or her own mind (not imposed from without as in thought insertion)
Compulsions as defined by (1) and (2):
 (1) repetitive behaviors (e.g., hand washing, ordering, checking) or mental acts (e.g., praying, counting, repeating words silently) that the person feels driven to perform in response to an obsession, or according to rules that must be applied rigidly

continued

Table 5-18 Continued.
***DSM-IV-TR* Diagnostic Criteria for Obsessive-Compulsive Disorder**

  (2) the behaviors or mental acts are aimed at preventing or reducing distress or preventing some dreaded event or situation; however, these behaviors or mental acts either are not connected in a realistic way with what they are designed to neutralize or prevent or are clearly excessive
B. At some point during the course of the disorder, the person has recognized that the obsessions or compulsions are excessive or unreasonable.
   Note: This does not apply to children.
C. The obsessions or compulsions cause marked distress, are time consuming (take more than 1 hour a day), or significantly interfere with the person's normal routine, occupational (or academic) functioning, or usual social activities or relationships.
D. If another Axis I disorder is present, the content of the obsessions or compulsions is not restricted to it (e.g., preoccupation with food in the presence of an Eating Disorder; hair pulling in the presence of Trichotillomania; concern with appearance in the presence of Body Dysmorphic Disorder; preoccupation with drugs in the presence of a Substance Use Disorder; preoccupation with having a serous illness in the presence of Hypochondriasis; preoccupation with sexual urges or fantasies in the presence of a Paraphilia; or guilty ruminations in the presence of Major Depressive Disorder).
E. The disturbance is not due to the direct physiological effects of a substance (e.g., a drug of abuse, a medication) or a general medical condition.

Source: Reprinted with permission from the *Diagnostic and Statistical Manual of Mental Disorders, Fourth Edition, Text Revision,* 462–63. Copyright 2000 American Psychiatric Association.

For many years, OCD was pessimistically viewed as one of the psychiatric disorders most resistant to treatment. However, recognition of the biochemical kinship between Mood Disorders and Anxiety Disorders has drastically revised such assessment, and OCD is today as susceptible to psychopharmacologic and psychotherapeutic intervention as are the more traditionally "treatable" conditions.

The mainstay of pharmacotherapy for OCD is, not surprisingly, the same SSRI and Tricyclic Antidepressant array as is employed in treating Mood and Anxiety Disorders already discussed. Like Panic Disorder, OCD will sometimes require higher dosages of antidepressants than will Major Depression for full effect; since such dosages must be achieved through gradual titration and/or systematic combination therapy, the lag time between treatment onset and clinical effect can be weeks (even months), a fact of which patients must be apprised from the outset so as to avoid frustration and still further anxiety. As in the case of Panic Disorder, initial anxiety reduction with a benzodiazepine is often helpful, to be weaned as antidepressant dosage becomes therapeutic and effective.

Following the mold for Panic Disorder, specific and innovative cognitive-behavioral protocols for the treatment of Obsessive-Compulsive Disorder have been developed and continue to be refined. Advocates report marked improvement of symptoms in 60 to 70 percent of patients who regularly employ such techniques. Combination of psychopharmacology and psychotherapy proves multiplicatively more effective than treatment via either approach alone.

3. Generalized Anxiety Disorder

Generalized Anxiety Disorder is something of a catchall diagnosis, encompassing people who are excessively worried and emotionally aroused most of the time, but whose symptoms do not fit the patterns of any of the more specifically delineated psychiatric entities. There are some who question the existence of a unique, "Generalized Anxiety Disorder" condition altogether, hypothesizing that those so diagnosed are actually more correctly manifesting symptoms of Mood Disorder, another Anxiety Disorder, Personality Disorder, or most likely, some combination of character pathology and Axis I symptomatology.

Phenomenologically, individuals said to have Generalized Anxiety Disorder spend most of their time worrying about things. They worry about health. They worry about finances. They worry about acceptance. And their worry exceeds pathological threshold in its pervasiveness, its intensity, and its invasion into other domains including cognitive efficiency, physical sense of well-being, and ability to sleep or interact socially.

Population prevalence rate for Generalized Anxiety Disorder is estimated at between 2 percent and 3 percent. Table 5-19 outlines formal *DSM-IV-TR* criteria for the diagnosis.

Table 5-19 *DSM-IV-TR* Diagnostic Criteria for Generalized Anxiety Disorder

A. Excessive anxiety and worry (apprehensive expectation), occurring more days than not for at least 6 months, about a number of events or activities (such as work or school performance).
B. The person finds it difficult to control the worry.
C. The anxiety and worry are associated with three (or more) of the following six symptoms (with at least some symptoms present for more days than not for the past 6 months). *Note:* Only one item is required in children.
   (1) restlessness or feeling keyed up or on edge
   (2) being easily fatigued
   (3) difficulty concentrating or mind going blank
   (4) irritability
   (5) muscle tension
   (6) sleep disturbance (difficulty falling or staying asleep, or restless unsatisfying sleep)

continued

Table 5-19   *Continued.*
***DSM-IV-TR* Diagnostic Criteria for Generalized Anxiety Disorder**

D. The focus of the anxiety and worry is not confined to features of an Axis I disorder, e.g., the anxiety or worry is not about having a Panic Attack (as in Panic Disorder), being embarrassed in public (as in Social Phobia), being contaminated (as in Obsessive-Compulsive Disorder), being away from home or close relatives (as in Separation Anxiety Disorder), gaining weight (as in Anorexia Nervosa), having multiple physical complaints (as in Somatization Disorder), or having a serious illness (as in Hypochondriasis), and the anxiety and worry do not occur exclusively during Posttraumatic Stress Disorder.
E. The anxiety, worry, or physical symptoms cause clinically significant distress or impairment in social, occupational, or other important areas of functioning.
F. The disturbance is not due to the direct physiological effects of a substance (e.g., a drug of abuse, a medication) or a general medical condition (e.g., hyperthyroidism) and does not occur exclusively during a Mood Disorder, a Psychotic Disorder, or a Pervasive Developmental Disorder.

Source: Reprinted with permission from the *Diagnostic and Statistical Manual of Mental Disorders, Fourth Edition, Text Revision,* 476. Copyright 2000 American Psychiatric Association.

Because it is so often a camouflage for underlying, more specific and fundamental psychopathology, suspicion of a Generalized Anxiety Disorder, particularly in a forensic psychiatric context, should trigger even more fastidious than average documentary and historical search for a Mood Disorder, Personality Disorder, other Anxiety Disorder, or even psychosis. Even more scrupulously than usual, an underlying general medical illness must be ruled out through examination and appropriate diagnostic testing. Even more painstakingly than per routine, drug, alcohol, or other toxin exposure must be considered. Only when such alternatives have been either completely treated or thoroughly ruled out should a clinician be content to diagnose, and proceed to treat, amorphous Generalized Anxiety Disorder.

Psychopharmacologic management of Generalized Anxiety Disorder tends to reflect the diffusion of the diagnosis itself. Tricyclic antidepressants have been tried and said to be effective, most probably due to their sedating side effects. Antipsychotics have been employed and reported helpful, most likely because they have even greater sedating side effects than tricyclics. Benzodiazepines have been useful, but must be strictly time- and dosage-limited because of patients' potential to build up physical tolerance to, and psychological dependence upon, these agents. The nonbenzodiazepine buspirone avoids such dangerous complications, but opinion is sharply divided between practitioners who insist buspirone has no positive effects and those who almost literally sing its praises.

Psychotherapy for Generalized Anxiety Disorder tends to be pragmatic. Relaxation techniques and strategies are taught, exercise and meditative regimens are prescribed, psychoeducation and stress avoidance and reduction counseling are offered. Often, involvement of the family is helpful in identifying entrenched habits and patterns of interpersonal/intrafamilial interaction that are as obviously certain to outside observers to nourish a chronic crisis climate in the home as they are undetectably second nature to the participants.

4. Posttraumatic Stress Disorder

CASE EXAMPLE

Ms. I, a computer programmer at the corporate headquarters of a large publishing concern, was dating a software engineer at the same company. Ms. I broke up with the coworker when she discovered she was pregnant with another man's baby. The coworker took the breakup hard, becoming increasingly irritable, depressed, and morbid over the next few months.

On the three-month anniversary of the breakup, the coworker followed Ms. I home and confronted her on her lawn. Verbal attacks escalated to pushing and shoving and the two tumbled to the ground. Ms. I managed to knee her coworker in the groin, which served to inflame him further.

The coworker grabbed a large stone from the property's landscaping and began beating Ms. I wildly. He broke her rib and crushed her hand. He thrashed her face, and then he finally regained control and fled the scene.

Two days later, the coworker turned himself into the police. Ms. I, who had remained conscious throughout the ordeal, survived her physical injuries. However, for months following the assault, she was terrified to leave her mother's home. She could not approach her own house. She became nauseous when she approached company buildings. The sight of a computer made her panicky. The ringing of a telephone made her jump. She wanted to see no one, do nothing, say nothing. Again and again, memories of the attack flooded her consciousness, unbidden, unwanted, and irrepressible.

Posttraumatic Stress Disorder (PTSD) is of sufficient importance in the arena of employment litigation to warrant expanded treatment in this volume; it is the subject of Chapter 13, and therefore will not be discussed extensively here. The latest diagnostic refinement of a phenomenon variously termed Shell Shock, Battle Fatigue, or Traumatic Neurosis, PTSD is the only major psychiatric diagnosis formulated in such a way as to embed a specific external attribution of causality within the diagnosis itself. As such, PTSD has become a phenomenon ripe for lay misunderstanding, popular misconception, and professional overuse and exploitation by both medical and the legal practitioners.

Posttraumatic Stress Disorder is the diagnostic embodiment of the intuitive belief that an external, traumatizing event can give rise to an identifiable, lasting set of symptoms. Fundamental to a realistic understanding of the disorder, however, are two psychiatric facts: (1) not all traumatic events will cause PTSD, and (2) relatively few individuals, even if exposed to an event of the magnitude necessary to provoke PTSD, will actually develop the disorder. *DSM-IV-TR* criteria for Posttraumatic Stress Disorder are outlined in Table 5-20.

Table 5-20   DSM-IV-TR **Diagnostic Criteria for Posttraumatic Stress Disorder**

A. The person has been exposed to a traumatic event in which both of the following were present:
   (1) the person experienced, witnessed, or was confronted with an event or events that involved actual or threatened death or serious injury, or a threat to the physical integrity of self or others
   (2) the person's response involved intense fear, helplessness, or horror. *Note:* In children, this may be expressed instead by disorganized or agitated behavior.
B. The traumatic event is persistently reexperienced in one (or more) of the following ways:
   (1) recurrent and intrusive distressing recollections of the event, including images, thoughts, or perceptions
   Note: In young children, repetitive play may occur in which themes or aspects of the trauma are expressed.
   (2) recurrent distressing dreams of the event
   Note: In children, there may be frightening dreams without recognizable content.
   (3) acting or feeling as if the traumatic event were recurring (includes a sense of reliving the experience, illusions, hallucinations, and dissociative flashback episodes, including those that occur on awakening or when intoxicated)
   Note: In young children, trauma-specific reenactment may occur.
   (4) intense psychological distress at exposure to internal or external cues that symbolize or resemble an aspect of the traumatic event
   (5) physiological reactivity on exposure to internal or external cues that symbolize or resemble an aspect of the traumatic event
C. Persistent avoidance of stimuli associated with the trauma and numbing of general responsiveness (not present before the trauma), as indicated by three (or more) of the following:
   (1) efforts to avoid thoughts, feelings, or conversations associated with the trauma
   (2) efforts to avoid activities, places, or people that arouse recollections of the trauma
   (3) inability to recall an important aspect of the trauma
   (4) markedly diminished interest or participation in significant activities
   (5) feeling of detachment or estrangement from others
   (6) restricted range of affect (e.g., unable to have loving feelings)
   (7) sense of a foreshortened future (e.g., does not expect to have a career, marriage, children, or a normal life span)
D. Persistent symptoms of increased arousal (not present before the trauma), as indicated by two (or more) of the following:
   (1) difficulty falling or staying asleep
   (2) irritability or outbursts of anger
   (3) difficulty concentrating
   (4) hypervigilance
   (5) exaggerated startle response
E. Duration of the disturbance (symptoms in Criteria B, C, and D) is more than 1 month.
F. The disturbance causes clinically significant distress or impairment in social, occupational, or other important areas of functioning.

Source: Reprinted with permission from the *Diagnostic and Statistical Manual of Mental Disorders, Fourth Edition, Text Revision*, 467–68. Copyright 2000 American Psychiatric Association.

Several points bear brief emphasis here. First is that the threshold stressor criterion, Criterion A, is an extreme one. In order to be capable of shocking the human organism's naturally buffering adrenergic nervous system sufficiently to cause lasting symptoms, the stressful event must be sudden, of enormous intensity, startling, and overwhelming. It must be like a lightning bolt from the sky; a threat to life or limb shattering normal equilibrium and displacing it with fear, helplessness, or horror. Accordingly:

- Lesser, repetitive stressors of minor to moderate intensity, such as sexual harassment with no threat of violence, or interpersonal or physical irritations in the workplace, cannot add up to produce PTSD.
- Events experienced as pleasurable at the time of occurrence but later regretted, such as an inappropriate but voluntary sexual liaison, cannot retrospectively cause PTSD.
- Objectively minor stressors which because of distorted perceptions are experienced as severe, such as a verbal slight or performance admonishment from a supervisor perceived as a narcissistic wound by a personality prone to entitlement and intolerance of criticism, cannot be magnified so as to give rise to PTSD.

In addition, fundamental to the production of PTSD is a conscious, cognizant awareness of the traumatic event as it transpires. Without this, the requisite overwhelming emotional reaction cannot occur. Thus, certain common events claimed to cause PTSD in the context of litigation obviously cannot do so:

- Being blindsided by a blow to the head, such that consciousness is lost.
- Being rear-ended or otherwise struck by a motor vehicle in such a manner as to preclude knowledge of the event's imminence (with no frightening sequelae immediately following impact).
- Suffering a sudden fall or other accident with immediate loss of consciousness.

As is seen in *DSM-IV-TR* Criteria B, C and D, PTSD symptoms overlap with many of the symptoms of other psychiatric disorders, directly mimicking symptoms of Major Depressive Disorder (and other mood disorders), as well as those of Panic Disorder (and other anxiety disorders). Such overlap results in the erroneous diagnosis of PTSD in many persons who coincidentally undergo an unpleasant event during the course of a preexisting depressive or anxiety disorder. Thorough investigation usually permits a clear and orderly differentiation among cases in which a novel stressor caused PTSD, aggravated (or triggered an episode of) a preexisting depressive or anxiety disorder, caused PTSD symptoms to be superimposed upon a preexisting depressive or anxiety disorder, or had no significant effect upon the natural history of a preexisting depressive or anxiety disorder.

Specifically excluded from the diagnosis of PTSD are cases in which symptoms occur only during the one-month period following the stressor. Such cases receive the *DSM-IV-TR* diagnosis of Acute Stress Disorder, reflecting growing evidence that brief periods of PTSD-like symptoms commonly occur in the immediate aftermath of severe stressors. These symptoms typically remit within a few weeks of the event.

Impairment among those suffering PTSD is highly variable, apparently contingent more on psychosocial history, personality factors, and current social situation than on anything intrinsic to the disorder itself. Some individuals are limited only with respect to specific circumscribed activities; others are more globally impaired because symptoms interfere with important relationships or capacity to work. Some are affected for little more than the one month required to make the diagnosis; others may still suffer symptoms years after actual occurrence of the traumatic event.

Both spontaneous remission and successful treatment frequently occur. Treatment efficacy has been reported with brief cognitive-behavioral therapy, with medications, and with other methods. Exposure-based psychotherapies have proven especially effective. Research on medication effects is helping to identify which agents are most helpful for which symptoms. Pharmacotherapy, as well as a rational course of psychotherapy, must be tailored to each individual case of PTSD.

D. Somatoform Disorders

Somatoform Disorders are defined by the paradoxical existence of physical symptoms lacking identifiable physiologic etiology or anatomic pathology. Thus, although there can be found no underlying organic lesion to explain the physical complaint being reported, the subjective experience of physical dysfunction driving that complaint remains very real. A limb cannot be mobilized despite intact neuromusculature, or pain is present despite lack of physical injury or tissue damage.

The Somatoform Disorders must be clearly distinguished from Malingering, in which an individual consciously fakes the existence of symptoms to gain an external reward of some tangible kind, and from Factitious Disorder, in which the individual also consciously fakes symptoms, in this case so as to secure the nurturance and sympathy inherent to playing the "sick" role. In the Somatoform Disorders, the conversion of mental need into physical manifestation is unconscious, and it is complete. Symptoms are unambiguously present and nonvolitional, but they cannot be mapped to any corresponding organic pathology.

1. Somatization Disorder

CASE EXAMPLE

Ms. J, a receptionist nearing her three-year employment anniversary, was charming and cordial with visitors, but also notably fragile. In each of her three years she had used up all of her sick days and vacation and personal days treating, and recovering from, multiple diffuse, vague bodily aches, pains, and sundry dysfunctions. At one point, Ms. J went out on a two-week "stress leave." At another, she returned from a doctor declaring she had been diagnosed with Multiple Sclerosis. That diagnosis was one month later withdrawn, and rumors swirled among peers that she had AIDS, syphilis, and even a "rare African liver disease."

Finally, having exhausted all conventional forms of paid time off, toward the end of her third year Ms. J was removed from the workplace on a medical disability leave. Initial diagnosis was Chronic Fatigue Syndrome. Later this was replaced (by a different physician) with Fibromyalgia.

When her short-term disability expired, Ms. J returned to work requesting a doctor-approved ADA "reasonable accommodation," based upon her new working diagnosis of "Chronic Epstein-Barr Virus Syndrome definitively confirmed through objective laboratory testing." Ms. J claimed she could continue working in her occupation as a receptionist, but only under the following conditions:

(1) No telephones (they "exacerbate headaches").

(2) No bright lights (she was "photosensitive;" this was to include desk lamps and, specifically, neon or halogen bulbs).

(3) No more than "two simultaneous conversations at a time" ("too stressful").

(4) Twenty-minute break every 2.5 hours (for "recovery and muscle stretching").

(5) A backup employee to cover for her at the receptionist desk and telephones as "multiple bathroom breaks will be needed." This was explained on the basis of I.B.S. (Irritable Bowel Syndrome) symptoms "growing out of Chronic E-B Infection," and resultant "Ravaged Colon Syndrome."

Somatization Disorder is in some ways the quintessential Somatoform Disorder, in that it involves the most widespread, diffuse, vague, nondescript symptomatology of this family of disorders. In fact, as outlined in Table 5-21, the *DSM-IV-TR* diagnostic criteria for Somatization Disorder specifically demand its manifestation in multiple organ systems affecting multiple body functions. All such symptoms, of course, must lack discernable physiologic underpinning.

Table 5-21 *DSM-IV-TR* Diagnostic Criteria for Somatization Disorder

A. A history of many physical complaints beginning before age 30 years that occur over a period of several years and result in treatment being sought or significant impairment in social, occupational, or other important areas of functioning.

B. Each of the following criteria must have been met, with individual symptoms occurring at any time during the course of the disturbance:

    (1) *four pain symptoms:* a history of pain related to at least four different sites or functions (e.g., head, abdomen, back, joints, extremities, chest, rectum, during menstruation, during sexual intercourse, or during urination)

    (2) *two gastrointestinal symptoms:* a history of at least two gastrointestinal symptoms other than pain (e.g., nausea, bloating, vomiting other than during pregnancy, diarrhea, or intolerance of several different foods)

continued

Table 5-21 Continued.
***DSM-IV-TR* Diagnostic Criteria for Somatization Disorder**

(3) *one sexual symptom:* a history of at least one sexual or reproductive symptom other than pain (e.g., sexual indifference, erectile or ejaculatory dysfunction, irregular menses, excessive menstrual bleeding, vomiting throughout pregnancy)

(4) *one pseudoneurological symptom:* a history of at least one symptom or deficit suggesting a neurological condition not limited to pain (conversion symptoms such as impaired coordination or balance, paralysis or localized weakness, difficulty swallowing or lump in throat, aphonia, urinary retention, hallucinations, loss of touch or pain sensation, double vision, blindness, deafness, seizures; dissociative symptoms such as amnesia; or loss of consciousness other than fainting)

C. Either (1) or (2):
  (1) after appropriate investigation, each of the symptoms in Criterion B cannot be fully explained by a known general medical condition or the direct effects of a substance (e.g., a drug of abuse, a medication)
  (2) when there is a related general medical condition, the physical complaints or resulting social or occupational impairment are in excess of what would be expected from the history, physical examination, or laboratory findings

D. The symptoms are not intentionally produced or feigned (as in Factitious Disorder or Malingering).

Source: Reprinted with permission from the *Diagnostic and Statistical Manual of Mental Disorders, Fourth Edition, Text Revision,* 490. Copyright 2000 American Psychiatric Association.

Notable in Somatization Disorder is the tendency of symptom foci to "wander"—a patient's myriad diffuse, multisystemic physical complaints typically metamorphose into new, different, diffuse multisystemic complaints. Mismanaged, such complaints can become chronic and ingrained, and the lives of individuals suffering from Somatization Disorder often revolve around their countless medical problems and the care and management of those problems. Further complicating the medical picture is the tendency of well-meaning but misguided health care providers to inadvertently make matters worse by failing to recognize and address an underlying Somatization Disorder. Thus, they not only reinforce the physical illness focus of the individual, but they also subject their patient to unnecessary, dangerous, painful and costly diagnostic and therapeutic procedures for each new symptom manifested. Contraindicated analgesic and anxiolytic medications also often enter the clinical fray, with oversedation, confusion, and addiction the inevitable outcomes.

Once a diagnosis of Somatization Disorder has been made (after physical, nonpsychiatric pathology has been ruled out and other psychiatric diagnoses and Malingering have been eliminated), treatment focuses on support, reassurance, and education and the avoidance of unnecessary and dangerous medical interventions. Ideally, a single physician can establish a long-term, trusting relationship with the patient, thus minimizing disgruntled "doctor shopping" and centralizing treatment plan and progress monitoring. Regularly scheduled visits at frequent intervals replace "as needed" consultations, relaying to the patient a message that he or she is of interest and concern, whether or not actively symptomatic. As trust and relationship build, attention and focus are gently shifted away from somatic complaints and preoccupations and toward psychosocial conflicts, concerns, and deficits. Potentially addictive medications must be avoided at all costs, but non-habit-forming psychotropic agents can be useful in addressing depressive or anxiety symptoms as they become more directly apparent.

2. Conversion Disorder

CASE EXAMPLE

Ms. K, an associate at a prominent law firm, had been a promising classical pianist growing up and always dreamed of a professional concert career. However, a combination of Depression-era cautiousness and middle-class sensibility led her parents to oppose such a career and to focus her instead on a more practical career in medicine or law.

Ms. K thrived academically and sailed through law school, but resentment, cynicism, and bitterness ran deeply beneath a seemingly efficient and positive surface attitude.

After two successful years in training as an associate attorney, Ms. K was given the opportunity to try her first case. She prepared tirelessly and enthusiastically. When the time for opening arguments came, she felt ready.

But when the young attorney stood to address the jury, her mouth opened yet no words came out. Ms. K could neither vocalize nor move her jaw. She was rushed to the hospital and accorded the finest of neurological evaluation and care. No physical, physiological, or anatomical lesion could be identified; no neurological explanation could be offered for her aphonia. Yet Ms. K was not malingering. Her predicament was genuine and terrifying. She could not speak, and if she could not speak, dreams of life as a brilliant trial lawyer were about to become no more pragmatically possible than childhood fantasies of a dazzling concert career.

While Somatization Disorder is heralded by the vagueness of its diffuse, nonspecific symptom picture, Conversion Disorder presents in just the opposite way—as a circumscribed symptomatic complaint, specifically but symbolically related to some psychological conflict the individual is consciously or unconsciously grappling with. Thus, the diagnosis requires the presence of one or more nonfeigned symptoms or deficits affecting voluntary motor or sensory function, suggesting but not demonstrably based in neurological or general medical pathology. Psychological factors must be found that are associated with the symptom, such that a conflict-laden situation somehow and to some extent is resolved by the symptom's presence and/or consequences.

Conversion Disorder is the contemporary formulation of Freud's original concept of "conversion neurosis," or what has often been referred to in popular culture as a "hysterical" reaction or phenomenon.[9] The current *DSM-IV-TR* diagnostic criteria for Conversion Disorder are delineated in Table 5-22.

Table 5-22 *DSM-IV-TR* Diagnostic Criteria for Conversion Disorder

A. One or more symptoms or deficits affecting voluntary motor or sensory function that suggest a neurological or other general medical condition.
B. Psychological factors are judged to be associated with the symptom or deficit because the initiation or exacerbation of the symptoms or deficit is preceded by conflicts or other stressors.
C. The symptom or deficit is not intentionally produced or feigned (as in Factitious Disorder or Malingering).
D. The symptom or deficit cannot, after appropriate investigation, be fully explained by a general medical condition, or by the direct effects of a substance, or as a culturally sanctioned behavior or experience.
E. The symptom or deficit causes clinically significant distress or impairment in social, occupational, or other important areas of functioning or warrants medical evaluation.
F. The symptom or deficit is not limited to pain or sexual dysfunction, does not occur exclusively during the course of Somatization Disorder, and is not better accounted for by another mental disorder.

Specify type of symptom or deficit:
 With Motor Symptom or Deficit
 With Sensory Symptom or Deficit
 With Seizures or Convulsions
 With Mixed Presentation

Source: Reprinted with permission from the *Diagnostic and Statistical Manual of Mental Disorders, Fourth Edition, Text Revision*, 498. Copyright 2000 American Psychiatric Association.

Conversion Disorder is thought to be fairly common. It has sometimes been estimated that between 5 percent and 14 percent of general hospital patients have a history of conversion symptoms, that 1 percent of all neurological hospital admissions have such symptoms, and that 25 percent of "normal" postpartum and medically ill women have experienced conversion symptoms sometime during their lives.

Specific, individual symptoms may quickly and spontaneously abate, but as many as 20 to 25 percent of patients will relapse within one year, manifesting

---

[9] The original scientific conceptualization of hysteria probably dates back to Egyptian thinking of around 3,000 B.C. Egyptian physicians hypothesized that a displacement of the uterus to a wayward anatomic site underlay otherwise inexplicable symptoms, and treatment consisted of attempting to lure the "wandering womb" back to its proper physical location. *See* FRANZ G. ALEXANDER & SHELDON T. SELESNICK, THE HISTORY OF PSYCHIATRY: AN EVALUATION OF PSYCHIATRIC THOUGHT AND PRACTICE FROM PREHISTORIC TIMES TO THE PRESENT (1995).

the same or new conversion symptoms. Careful history gathering and document review will often reveal a historical template for particular conversion symptoms; they will prove to be unconsciously modeled upon symptoms encountered during prior (physiologically based) illness, or witnessed in an important figure in the Conversion Disorder patient's life (such as a family member or mentor).

Conversion Disorder patients are typically highly suggestible people, and suggestion (in such therapeutic forms as hypnosis, narcoanalysis, or relaxation and visualization techniques) remains the mainstay of treatment for the disorder. In some cases of mass hysteria—where, for example, workplace exposure to an objectively benign toxin seemingly gives rise to similar symptoms, all similarly lacking in organic basis, among large numbers of "victims"—a group process of suggestion and panic appears to create a Conversion Disorder epidemic. Segregation of afflicted parties from one another, and individual reassurance and education by respected, informed authority figures, often go far in stemming such an "epidemic" early in its course.

3. Pain Disorder

The contemporary formulation of Pain Disorder is of importance primarily in its acknowledgment that psychiatric factors often play a significant role in exacerbating the intensity, longevity, or behavioral and social consequences of an individual's subjective pain experience, even if that experience does originate in tangible injury and identifiable tissue damage of some kind. Psychoemotional factors contribute to produce a pain experience that, although originating in measurable injury, reaches an incongruent intensity and produces a disproportionate effect. Thus, the label Pain Disorder is in practice applied to a spectrum of maladies, some purely psychiatric, some purely physiologic, but most typically a combination of the two.

In employment litigation, Pain Disorder is most likely to arise as an issue under the cloak of a workers' compensation claim or of an ADA request for reasonable accommodation. As in the case of Somatization Disorder, once Malingering and Factitious Disorder have been addressed, the focus of forensic analysis and evaluation is generally upon management. Has treatment been appropriately sensitive to, and sensitively but aggressively addressed, psychiatric issues that are complicating and prolonging recovery? Or is illness and pain behavior being reinforced, leading to further entrenchment of complaints, further injury through unnecessary and dangerous medical procedures, and possibly to drug addiction and unwarranted, chronic disability?

DSM-IV-TR clinical criteria required for a diagnosis of Pain Disorder are shown in Table 5-23.

Table 5-23 *DSM-IV-TR* Diagnostic Criteria for Pain Disorder

A. Pain in one or more anatomical sites is the predominant focus of the clinical presentation and is of sufficient severity to warrant clinical attention.
B. The pain causes clinically significant distress or impairment in social, occupational, or other important areas of functioning.

continued

Table 5-23 *Continued.*
***DSM-IV-TR* Diagnostic Criteria for Pain Disorder**

C. Psychological factors are judged to have an important role in the onset, severity, exacerbation, or maintenance of the pain.
D. The symptom or deficit is not intentionally produced or feigned (as in Factitious Disorder or Malingering).
E. The pain is not better accounted for by a Mood, Anxiety, or Psychotic Disorder and does not meet criteria for Dyspareunia.

Pain Disorder Associated With Psychological Factors: psychological factors are judged to have the major role in the onset, severity, exacerbation, or maintenance of the pain. (If a general medical condition is present, it does not have a major role in the onset, severity, exacerbation, or maintenance of the pain.) This type of Pain Disorder is not diagnosed if criteria are also met for Somatization Disorder.
Specify if:
  Acute: duration of less than 6 months
  Chronic: duration of 6 months or longer

Pain Disorder Associated With Both Psychological Factors and a General Medical Condition: both psychological factors and a general medical condition are judged to have important roles in the onset, severity, exacerbation, or maintenance of the pain. The associated general medical condition or anatomical site of the pain is coded on Axis III.
Specify if:
  Acute: duration of less than 6 months
  Chronic: duration of 6 months or longer

Source: Reprinted with permission from the *Diagnostic and Statistical Manual of Mental Disorders, Fourth Edition, Text Revision*, 503. Copyright 2000 American Psychiatric Association.

E. Adjustment Disorders

CASE EXAMPLE

Mr. L had always been a proud man. The eldest of four children, he early took on a "parenting" role in his native Latin American country. He was the only son in his family to earn any sort of degree, graduating from trade school as an automobile mechanic. He took great pride in helping his parents to pay rent for the family home. And when he came to the United States at the age of 22, it was with the dream of doing well enough to bring his brothers, sisters, and aging parents to live with him in the beautiful new house he would buy someday.

  Mr. L seemed on the road to fulfilling his self-imposed destiny when he secured a job in the auto shop of a suburban branch of a large retail chain. A diligent, hard worker, he rapidly stood out from other mechanics, earning praise and kudos from customers and management alike. Within a year, Mr. L was lead mechanic, and six months after that he was appointed auto shop assistant manager.

As he approached his second year with the company, Mr. L was offered a transfer to the chain's more troubled downtown store, where he was to become manager of the auto shop. He accepted the challenge enthusiastically: Within another year at his new manager's wage, he would be able to afford to bring his family to the U.S. He could possibly even put a down payment on a home. Mr. L swelled with pride.

But things did not go well in the new position. Mr. L found himself managing a crew of 12 young men, none of them enthusiastic about conforming to the standards of the new manager who was rocking their formerly comfortable boat. The crew showed Mr. L little respect and less willingness to comply. Early jokes about being a "goody-goody" and a "brainless work horse" gave way to increasingly vicious ethnic slurs and blatant insubordination. Production and work quality declined sharply, as initial passive resistance turned to active sabotage of Mr. L's command.

Unaccustomed to such personal disdain and new to professional failure, Mr. L became increasingly anxious and despondent. His sleep deteriorated—he awakened frequently throughout the night sweating and shaking—and he suffered from nausea and diarrhea in the mornings before work. Matters became worse when he was confronted by the store manager with multiple customer complaints about poor workmanship on cars and was advised of plummeting departmental revenue. When Mr. L explained that he felt he was being victimized by his crew because of his ethnicity, he was told, "Stop whimpering with that kind of malarkey. Either you have it as a manager or you don't. Don't give me that discrimination garbage. Show me something in the next few months, or you're out of here."

The more Mr. L tried to control the situation in his department, however, the more his crew sensed victory and the more defiant they became. Ethnic slurs were progressively more blatant and unabashed, occurring nearly every day. Refusal to follow directives was increasingly belligerent and absolute. Workers frequently yelled at him, laughed at him, walked away from him even as he spoke to them.

The situation finally boiled over when one particularly disgruntled subordinate actually shoved Mr. L into a wall. Though the two were split up before blows were exchanged and Mr. L was not seriously threatened or physically hurt, he found himself humiliatingly reduced to tears.

Several days later, Mr. L was called into the store manager's office and blamed for the shoving incident. When he again explained about the discriminatory hostility he perceived to be surrounding him, the store manager expressed only contempt. "You can't even fail like a man. You couldn't make it; face it, and don't try to blame it on some girl's excuse about being from Latin America!" Mr. L was advised that he could resign or be terminated for inadequate performance.

Mr. L visited an attorney three days after resigning. At that meeting, he shook openly as he related his story; more than once his eyes welled with tears. His appetite was shot and he had lost eleven pounds in the prior four weeks. He could not sleep.

Eight months after that meeting, however, when he was examined by independent evaluating psychiatrists concerning his ethnic discrimination and wrongful termination lawsuit, Mr. L's symptoms had fully resolved. In fact, within seven weeks of leaving his toxic workplace, he returned to normal function, sleeping and eating regularly. He was in reasonably good cheer upon commencement of his new job as lead mechanic at an independent repair shop, a position he secured two months after his upsetting termination and all the events that preceded it.

Symptom resolution notwithstanding, on the basis of history, prior symptoms, and ongoing anger about the experience, the plaintiff's expert psychiatrist diagnosed

Mr. L with Posttraumatic Stress Disorder: "PTSD is, in this case, the product of the cumulative impact of the many traumatic experiences this man encountered at his former workplace, all this against the backdrop of a fear of failing his family that rendered him particularly vulnerable to those very traumata."

The defense expert disagreed, diagnosing an Adjustment Disorder with Mixed Anxiety and Depressed Mood. He opined, "While Mr. L was certainly hurt by workplace events, and his symptoms were certainly real, neither the stressor involved in giving rise to the symptoms, nor the quality and duration of the symptoms themselves, approach a magnitude consistent with a diagnosis of PTSD. Mr. L's was a transient, reactive phenomenon; once the troublesome circumstances passed, the symptoms passed as well. There are no clinically significant residual effects evident or to be anticipated."

Adjustment Disorders are the psychiatric conditions most likely to be diagnosed to describe symptoms that follow some stressful event. In fact, Adjustment Disorders are the more correct diagnoses for the vast majority of individuals erroneously diagnosed with Posttraumatic Stress Disorder in the context of employment litigation. Adjustment Disorders can be thought of as a formalization of the critical boundary differentiating the "normal" upset reactions human beings experience when they are faced with stressful life events from the experience that must minimally be present to consider an individual's reaction "pathological."

Three elements must exist for one to be diagnosed with an Adjustment Disorder:

- There must be some identifiable environmental event or events to which the individual develops a response, the response manifesting itself within three months of stressor(s)' onset.
- The individual must react to the stressor(s) with marked distress, exceeding that which would be expected in the "average person" exposed to the event; or behaviors or symptoms in response to the stressor(s) must result in significant impairment in social or occupational functioning.
- Symptoms must last no more than six months after termination of the stressful event or of its direct consequences.

In marked contrast to the strictly delineated threshold event of Posttraumatic Stress Disorder, the nature and magnitude of the original Adjustment Disorder stressor are not specified. It may be a single experience (loss of a job), or there may be multiple upsets (repeated incidences of sexual harassment, plus difficulties during a divorce and custody battle). Stressors may be recurrent but periodic (encounters when a traveling manager intermittently comes to town) or continuous (working as a visiting nurse in a dangerous, hostile neighborhood).

Predominant symptoms affecting an individual with Adjustment Disorder may be those of mood (sadness, tearfulness, hopelessness), those of anxiety (nervousness, worry, jitteriness), or both. Disturbance may also take the form of unaccustomed "acting out" (violation of age-appropriate social rules, reckless driving, fighting, truancy).

Table 5-24 contains the *DSM-IV-TR* criteria for Adjustment Disorder. The various subtypes are identified in Table 5-25.

Table 5-24 *DSM-IV-TR* Diagnostic Criteria for Adjustment Disorder

A. The development of emotional or behavioral symptoms in response to an identifiable stressor(s) occurring within 3 months of the onset of the stressor(s).
B. These symptoms or behaviors are clinically significant as evidenced by either of the following:
   (1) marked distress that is in excess of what would be expected from exposure to the stressor
   (2) significant impairment in social or occupational (academic) functioning
C. The stress-related disturbance does not meet the criteria for another specific Axis I disorder and is not merely an exacerbation of a preexisting Axis I or Axis II disorder.
D. The symptoms do not represent Bereavement.
E. Once the stressor (or its consequences) has terminated, the symptoms do not persist for more than an additional 6 months.

Specify if:
   Acute: if the disturbance lasts less than 6 months
   Chronic: if the disturbance lasts for 6 months or longer

Source: Reprinted with permission from the *Diagnostic and Statistical Manual of Mental Disorders, Fourth Edition, Text Revision,* 683. Copyright 2000 American Psychiatric Association.

Table 5-25 Subtypes of Adjustment Disorders

Subtype	Typical Symptoms
With Depressed Mood	Sadness, dysphoria, tearfulness, hopelessness
With Anxiety	Nervousness, worry, jitteriness, irritability
With Mixed Anxiety and Depressed Mood	Symptoms of both depression and anxiety are prominent.
With Disturbance of Conduct	Violations of others' rights or of major age-appropriate societal norms and rules, vandalism, reckless driving, fighting, truancy
With Mixed Disturbance of Emotions and Conduct	Both emotional dysregulation (depression, anxiety) and behavioral dyscontrol (disturbance of conduct) are prominent.
Unspecified	Other types of maladaptive reactions (social withdrawal, anorexia without mood change) are predominant.

Adjustment Disorders are by definition self-limited, but even their mandated six-month maximal course can usually be reduced through supportive psychotherapy, teaching of coping or relaxation techniques, or sometimes simply via some "ventilation port" such as a sympathetic manager, an Employee Assistance Program, or a diary. If elements (or consequences) of the original stressor(s) continue to affect the individual's environment and to exacerbate symptoms, assistance in removal of the irritants, or in removal of the individual from the irritants, will often prove the most efficacious treatment available.

Generally, psychotropic medications are not indicated in the treatment of Adjustment Disorders. However, if particular symptoms (anxiety, tension headache) are especially acute or bothersome, targeted short-term use of symptom-specific psychopharmocologic agents (anxiolytics, analgesics) may be appropriate for immediate relief.

III. Effective Forensic Mental Health Workup of Axis I Claims in Employment Litigation

Like most medicolegal evaluations involving psychiatric claims, the analysis of those emerging in employment litigation can be organized around three core issues:

- Does there exist a diagnosable psychiatric disorder, and if so, what is the appropriate diagnosis?
- If there does exist a diagnosable psychiatric disorder, how, if at all, does that disorder interact with events at issue in the litigation?
- Has treatment to date been appropriate, what is the prognosis, and are there any suggestions for future case management?

The first of these issues surrounds the medical notion of diagnosis and is critical to the legal concept of damages. The second involves the medical question of differential diagnosis and it relates to the legal concept of causation. The third focuses upon the medical area of treatment and prognosis and addresses legal concerns of extent of injury and possibly of mitigation.

As has been evident in the foregoing review of commonly encountered Axis I disorders, not only is there frequent symptom overlap among these disorders, but many of the disorders are episodic and recurrent. Thus, diagnosis in legal contexts must be exquisitely sensitive not only to symptom pattern but also to symptom history and the correlation of symptoms to timing of events alleged in litigation. Since potential motivational factors (such as financial gain and revenge) are fueled by potential interpersonal factors (such as rage, insult, and envy), those engaging in forensic psychiatric evaluation must include the entire psychosocial, motivational matrix of the employment setting in their analysis. Simply listening to a plaintiff list his or her complaints and describe his or her experiences (as one would do in basic clinical work) is a road certain to lead the forensic examiner to distortion and distorted conclusions, intentionally instilled or not. Extensive data gleaned through review of written materials must be incorporated into any conclusions suggested via psychiatric examination alone.

Review of written documents, most helpfully concluded prior to ever beginning the actual psychiatric examination, provides a behavioral, psychosocial, vocational, and factual background through which hypotheses are generated, to be transformed into specific questions and tested at examination or through further document procurement. When the scope of documents obtained is broad, a more factually based psychiatric analysis can be performed, a more comprehensive set of hypotheses can be generated, and those hypotheses can be tested more effectively.

The threshold step in the evaluation of psychiatric disorder is to rule out the existence of any underlying physical, anatomical, pathophysiological lesion or illness process, externally introduced toxin, or medication side effect that could account for presenting symptoms. Medical problems such as thyroid dysregulation, autoimmune disorders, or neoplastic processes can produce symptoms indistinguishable from those of the Axis I psychiatric disorders. Drugs of abuse can do the same, whether originally procured by prescription or illegally. Even side effects of appropriately administered medications can precisely mimic symptoms of depression, anxiety, and even psychosis.

Once it is fairly certain that medical or pharmacological factors cannot account for symptoms, the possible existence of a non-litigation-related psychiatric disorder or of incorrect diagnosis must be entertained. The exact character of symptoms, their exact patterns, and the details of their onset, course, development, and response to environmental events and interventions must be elucidated. Documents must be scoured for evidence of prior bouts of illness or of pre- or post-event emergence of symptoms.

The third diagnostic step is to rule out Malingering or Factitious Disorder. This exercise can be extremely difficult; especially if one is confronted with a talented liar, it is foolhardy and fallacious to imagine that it can be accurately accomplished through examination alone. Typically, a determination of Malingering (or Factitious Disorder) in a medicolegal context must be the product of a convergence of multiple data indexes of multiple types, extracted from multiple sources, that render the opinion of Malingering an all but inevitable one. This complicated area is addressed in more detail in Chapter 11.

Finally, the interplay of Axis I claims and Axis II pathology must be explored. Personality Disorders present themselves as critical components of employment litigation claims under many guises. They may, under certain circumstances, literally decompensate into "mini-episodes" of Axis I pathology of different types. They may give rise to distorted perceptions and beliefs underlying otherwise inexplicable workplace allegations or events. They may fuel a "righteous rage" driving those whose behavior and judgment they govern to feel justified in lying, conniving, and blatantly falsely accusing in order to exact revenge upon an individual or employer they (erroneously) believe has wronged them so profoundly as to deserve such treatment. These sorts of interactions and distortions, as well as the personality disorders that create and fuel them, are the subject of Chapter 6.

CHAPTER 6

PERSONALITY DISORDERS IN EMPLOYMENT LITIGATION

Mark S. Lipian, M.D., Ph.D.

I. Introduction

Personality disorders are long-standing patterns of maladaptive behavior; deeply ingrained coping styles, traits of which are often evident in childhood but emerge full-blown by the later teenage years. Personality disorders surround habitually distorted expectations, perceptions, interpretations, and demands of the interpersonal, social world, and they result in chronically, recurrently, and predictably impaired ability to relate to and interact with others. The outcome for the afflicted individual is a lifetime pattern of frustration and of unsatisfying, unsuccessful relationships in social, vocational, and associated interpersonal settings.

That people have distinct "personalities"—characteristic, recurring ways of perceiving, acting upon, and interacting with situations that are predictive of the individual rather than the setting—is a notion that can be traced back to the dawn of civilization. Ancient Greeks elaborated a system of four "temperaments" (sanguine, choleric, melancholic, phlegmatic) to describe variations of personality type. These temperaments were believed to be embodiments of the four physical elements (earth, air, fire, water). While the mythology has varied through the ages, the descriptions have not changed much. Terms such as "melancholic," "sanguine," and "choleric" remain part of our descriptive arsenal today.

The concept that certain individuals develop *abnormal* personalities—pervasive, predictable patterns of expectation, interpretation, demand, and reaction that lie outside the community norm and are maladaptive for the individual—also is historically well grounded. In the 1800s, the French psychiatrist Pinel coined the term *manie sans délire* to describe individuals prone to unexplained outbursts of rage and violence, but who were not "insane."[1] The Scottish

---

[1] PHILLIPPE PINEL, A TREATISE ON INSANITY (1806).

physician Prichard referred to "moral insanity"—in persons who wantonly and repeatedly violated social norms, but who were neither intellectually impaired nor psychotic.[2]

Finally, the idea that personality—both normal and abnormal—has its origins (genetic or environmental or both) early in human development can also be traced historically. Freud's was the first grand theory of character formulation. Fixation (caused by pivotal environmental events and experiences) at various stages of psychosexual development (a universal, biologically driven developmental progression of childhood) leads to particularly prominent character traits.[3] Like the "elemental" theory of the Greeks, this particular Freudian etiologic hypothesis has been largely scientifically rejected. But the concept—personality as an enduring, deeply ingrained set of qualities (traits) emergent early in development; crystallized by adolescence; guiding expectation, belief, demand, interpretation, and interaction in predictable ways (pathologic or not) throughout the lifetime—has endured, and it shapes medical, psychiatric, and psychological thinking today.

A. Qualities of Personality

Contemporary concepts of personality are both categorical and dimensional. Individual personalities are defined in terms of traits (categories such as obsessiveness, impulsiveness, affective lability). Each such category, however, is conceived of as a continuum of behaviors within the category (degree of obsessiveness, degree of impulsiveness) rather than as an all-or-nothing, on-or-off phenomenon (is or is not obsessive; is or is not impulsive).

One's personality can be conceived of as a behavioral "batting average." With a certain probability, a given individual is likely to behave in ways defined by his or her personality, across interpersonal circumstances and across environmental situations. He or she may not always do so, but he or she will do so more likely, and more often, than not.

1. Traits Versus States

Personality traits are the enduring, deeply ingrained patterns that guide an individual in his or her interactions with the environment. They are habitual

---

[2] JAMES C. PRICHARD, A TREATISE ON INSANITY (1835).

[3] Freud suggested that fixation at the earliest ("oral") developmental stage would result in demanding, dependent traits (Dependent Personality Disorder). Fixation at the next ("anal") stage would give rise to obsessiveness, rigidity, and emotional detachment (Obsessive-Compulsive Personality Disorder). Fixation at the third ("phallic") stage would produce emotional and intellectual shallowness and difficulties with meaningful intimacy (Histrionic Personality Disorder). To date little evidence has been gathered to support Freud's linkage of traumatic experience, particular to psychosexual developmental stage, as the universal etiology underlying the specific symptom clusters hypothesized.

ways of perceiving, relating to, thinking about, understanding, and predicting the responses of one's world and oneself. As such, they dictate recurrent patterns of an individual's behavior across a broad range of experiential and interpersonal contexts.

Personality traits interact with environmental circumstance to dictate one's dispositional "state" at any immediate point in time. For example, one who is high in the trait of "suspiciousness," presented with an ambiguous environmental circumstance, is likely to become more agitated and uncomfortable than he or she is at baseline state. The enduring trait ("high suspiciousness") predicts response to the situation (contextual ambiguity) giving rise to the immediate state (agitation). The prediction is not an absolute one, but rather probabilistic. Most such situations will give rise to this state in this individual, but humans being humans, the prediction can never be made with 100 percent certainty.

2. Personality Traits Versus Personality Disorders

Personality is defined as the overall pattern of personality traits present in an individual. When those traits are maladaptive, causing predictable patterns of functional impairment that recur across contexts, environments, and circumstances, the individual is considered to be exhibiting character psychopathology.

A *personality disorder* is an enduring pattern of inner experience and behavior—of personality traits—that deviates markedly from the individual's cultural norms and significantly affects such fundamental social functions as interpretation, expectation, emotional reaction, interpersonal interaction, and impulse control. The identified pattern must be inflexible and recurrent, manifesting itself across a broad range of social, occupational, or other areas of interpersonal functioning. Manifestations of the pattern may be identified as early as childhood, with full-fledged onset of personality disorder in late adolescence or early adulthood.

The American Psychiatric Association's *Diagnostic and Statistical Manual of Mental Disorders* (*DSM-IV-TR*) identifies a number of specific patterns of pathological traits, defining reliably replicable clusters as Axis II diagnostic entities (personality disorders), much as reliably clustered psychopathological symptoms and signs are concretized as Axis I diagnoses. As is the case with symptom identification in diagnosing Axis I disorders, Axis II diagnostic categories define a minimal number of pathological traits that must be present for a diagnosis of personality disorder to be made. General *DSM-IV-TR* criteria for the diagnosis of a Personality Disorder are outlined in Table 6-1.

Table 6-1 *DSM-IV-TR* Diagnostic Criteria for a Personality Disorder

A. An enduring pattern of inner experience and behavior that deviates markedly from the expectations of the individual's culture. This pattern is manifested in two (or more) of the following areas:
   (1) cognition (i.e., ways of perceiving and interpreting self, other people, and events)

    (2) affectivity (i.e., the range, intensity, lability, and appropriateness of emotional response)
    (3) interpersonal functioning
    (4) impulse control
B. The enduring pattern is inflexible and pervasive across a broad range of personal and social situations.
C. The enduring pattern leads to clinically significant distress or impairment in social, occupational, or other important areas of functioning.
D. The pattern is stable and of long duration, and its onset can be traced back at least to adolescence or early adulthood.
E. The enduring pattern is not better accounted for as a manifestation or consequence of another mental disorder.
F. The enduring pattern is not due to the direct physiological effects of a substance (e.g., a drug of abuse, a medication) or a general medical condition (e.g., head trauma).

Source: Reprinted with permission from the *Diagnostic and Statistical Manual of Mental Disorders, Fourth Edition, Text Revision,* 689. Copyright 2000 American Psychiatric Association.

Captured in the *DSM-IV-TR* criteria are the fundamental characteristics and manifestations of personality disorder:

- The pattern of inner experience and behavior deviates remarkably from the cultural norm, manifesting itself in critical interpersonal domains of cognition (perception, expectation, interpretation and demand); of affect (emotional responsiveness, tone, and lability); of social functioning; and of impulse control (Criterion A).
- The pattern is enduring, inflexible, and maladaptive, and extends across situations, circumstances, and age domains (Criterion B).
- The pattern recurrently and chronically gives rise to frustration and subjective distress, resulting in predictably repetitive dysfunction in social, occupational, or other interpersonal endeavors (Criterion C).
- The emergence of the enduring pattern can be traced back to adolescence; untreated, it is lifelong and pervasive (Criterion D).
- Neither another physical or mental disorder nor the direct physiological effects of a substance (medication or toxin) can account for the behavioral pattern identified (Criteria E and F).

B. Factors Affecting Personality Development

1. Nature Versus Nurture

The exact mechanism by which personality develops, and how the program goes awry to give rise to the various personality disorders, remains uncertain and highly controversial. Clearly, an enormous contributor to the process is experience ("nurture"), perhaps as early as the first days of life ("bonding" theories), perhaps confined to the first two or three years ("efficacy" and "interaction" theories), perhaps extending throughout the preschool years and even beyond ("trauma" theories).

Equally certain, however, are the contributions of biology ("nature")—hereditary predispositions ("genetic" theories), inborn behavioral proclivities ("temperament" theories), and biologically determined needs for stimulation and patterns of autonomic response ("arousal" theories). In truth, as is so frequently the case in psychiatry, some combination of aberrant nature and nurture is the most realistically hypothesized etiology for personality disorders.

A. BONDING THEORIES Largely deriving their concepts from the imprinting studies of ethologist Konrad Lorenz, bonding theorists have suggested that there is a critical period during which human infants must bond to principal caretakers if a secure attachment is to be forged.[4] This secure attachment, in turn, is prerequisite to healthy personality development. The critical period may be as early as the first days or even the first hours of the infant's life.

According to this theory, any forces that might interfere with the natural, biologically programmed early interactive patterns of infant and caretaker can lead to aberrant personality development. Thus, placement in a newborn I.C.U. because of premature delivery or other complication, caretaker illness or isolation from the child, or severe emotional or psychiatric impairment on the part of the caretaker could prove disastrous to caretaker-infant bonding during this critical period and hence to later personality integration.

B. EFFICACY AND INTERACTION THEORIES Efficacy and interaction theories are probably the most scientifically grounded of the current environmental explanations for the development of personality disorder, but they account best for only one subset, the Cluster B or *identity* disorders (Antisocial, Borderline, Histrionic, Narcissistic). The common theme among individuals with these conditions is an incompletely developed sense of "self" as a stable entity constant through space and time. For such self-concept to exist, there must be clear, unambiguous differentiation between *self* and *other*. The boundary between the individual and his or her environment must be fully resolved and impermeable.

Working with newborns, young infants, and young toddlers, developmental psychologist Jerome Bruner and his followers have impressively demonstrated that from the very first moments of life onward, there exist predictable, universal "turn-taking games" played between caretaker and infant. Early on, these are nonverbal—such behaviors as referencing (infant looks, caretaker follows; caretaker looks, infant follows); touching (caretaker touches, infant reacts; infant touches, caretaker reacts); and smiling (caretaker smiles, infant responds; infant smiles, caretaker responds). Over time, these games expand to include verbalization (taking turns "cooing" or "clucking") and increasingly complex behavioral sequences.[5]

It is hypothesized that under normal developmental circumstances, where caretaker response to infant behavior in turn-taking games is reliable and

---

[4]JOHN BOWLBY, ATTACHMENT (1969).

[5]MARK H. BORNSTEIN & JEROME S. BRUNER, INTERACTION IN HUMAN DEVELOPMENT (1989).

predictable, these interactions are fundamental to the infant's developing ability to differentiate self from other. There is an "I" who can act upon my environment ("you") and cause response. When response is routine, calm, and orderly, efficacy develops. The infant acquires a sense of control, purpose, and power. Such primitive differentiation, boundary formation, and behavioral efficacy go on to become the template for development of a sense of integrated self, as well as for development of language, empathy, conscience, and related fundamental characterologic phenomena.

Where something goes awry in early turn-taking games—if a caretaker is psychiatrically impaired and unable to respond in predictable and orderly ways, or presents chaotic or hostile mixed messages in response to bouts of substance abuse, or is absent altogether due to illness or lack of interest—differentiation of "self" from "non-self" does not effectively occur for the child, and efficacy is not fully experienced. A stable sense of boundaried self is not constructed, and maladaptive behaviors, expectations, and interpretations, which give rise to a personality disorder, are learned instead. While full-blown, diagnosable personality disorder does not emerge until mid- to late teens, it is during the first two or three years that the critical foundations for healthy versus impaired interpersonal functioning are formidably cast.

C. Trauma Theories The most prominent current trauma theories report correlation between childhood abuse (particularly sexual abuse) and the ultimate development of personality disorder (particularly Borderline Personality Disorder). While such correlation is certainly suggestive, it is far from perfect. It is probably more accurate to ascribe Borderline Disorder (as well as other implicated "Cluster B" disorders, e.g., Narcissistic Personality Disorder; Histrionic Personality Disorder) to generalized chaotic home life, of which sexual abuse may be one manifestation among many others, all potent in giving rise, ultimately, to pathological psychiatric outcomes. The body of literature that has exposed sexual and physical abuse in childhood as significant predictors of adult Borderline Personality Disorder has failed to control for more generalized patterns of caretaker impulse control dysregulation, passive-aggressive manipulative power struggle, and otherwise pathologic ambivalence in the homes of children studied. Such broader maladaptive experience tends to pervade the early lives of these youngsters, and is a more psychologically parsimonious and theoretically coherent explanation for development of identity disorder and, ultimately, character pathology than is childhood abuse conceived as an isolated phenomenon.

D. Genetic Theories To some limited extent, nature in the form of hereditary biological predisposition (genetic theories) appears to explain certain of the personality disorders, particularly those of Cluster A (Paranoid, Schizoid, Schizotypal), all of which may be linked, to greater or lesser degree, to Schizophrenia. Family, twin, and adoption studies imply a particular linkage of Schizotypal Personality Disorder to familial history of Schizophrenia.[6] There is even

---

[6]Larry J. Siever, *Schizophrenia Spectrum Disorders*, in 11 Review of Psychiatry 25–42 (Allan Tasman & Michelle B. Riba eds., 1992).

fairly strong evidence from family and adoption studies of a genetic component to the development of Antisocial and Borderline Personality Disorders.[7]

To date, genetic theories remain tenuous in the realm of personality disorders. Many potential pitfalls and intervening, complicating variables prevent ascribing too much validity to them. For example, researchers have suggested that it is actually certain basic dimensions of personality (e.g., intimacy craving, callousness) that are inherited along a continuum of normality, and that caretaker response to infant behavior along these dimensions is what ultimately gives rise to one personality or another, disordered or not. Thus, continuum behavior is inherited; personality or personality disorder is not.

E. TEMPERAMENT THEORIES One particularly extensively studied behavioral dimension—temperament—certainly does seem to be present from the moment of birth, to be transmitted genetically, and to be somewhat predictive of behavior throughout the lifetime. However, as is true for all "genetic" theories, research on temperament has primarily served to highlight how a child's inborn, biological proclivities can actively provoke his or her environment into interacting with that child in certain ways. The overall developmental outcome (healthy personality or personality disorder) is drawn out, shaped, and modified by the child's active interaction with his or her environment. Thus, such theories allow for a great deal of plasticity in development. Continuum traits born into the infant (fearful, shy, and timid versus bold, outgoing, and aggressive) are modified and shaped by a specific environment providing unique experience, teaching, and behavioral control. The optimistic vision of such theories is that individual parental errors, or even specific traumatic events in a given child's early life, need not dictate fixed, inevitable pathologic consequences. Corrective response is possible.

F. AROUSAL THEORIES A final nature theory with significant empirical validation addresses specifically Antisocial Personality Disorder (formerly known as "psychopathy" or "sociopathy"). "Arousal" theory notes that human beings are born with genetically determined variations in arousability, which is the tendency of the autonomic nervous system to respond to environmental stimuli. Certain people have especially low arousability; such individuals require far higher levels of stimulation in order for their adrenergic response system to kick in. Arousal theorists propose that infants endowed with low arousability predictably develop into risk takers. Requiring higher baseline stimulation than average youngsters, they tend to run harder and play riskier than their peers.

How caretakers respond to this endowment of arousability will, according to theory, produce personality. In a responsive, healthy, nurturing home, "high stimulation" children will develop into society's heroes—firefighters, police

---

[7] John G. Gunderson & Mary C. Zanarihi, *Pathogenesis of Borderline Personality*, in 8 REVIEW OF PSYCHIATRY 25–48 (Allan Tasman, Robert E. Hales & Allan J. Francis eds., 1989).

officers, military pilots. In a troubled, chaotic, uncaring, or disconnected home, however, these youngsters may mature into society's villains—criminals and even killers without conscience or remorse. They will come to manifest Antisocial Personality Disorder.[8]

2. Etiologic Conclusions

Obviously, much remains to be learned about the exact etiology of the various personality disorders. Certain specific theories (efficacy theory, arousal theory) appear particularly adept at explaining development of subsets of pathology (Cluster B Disorders, Antisocial Personality Disorder). But more generally, personality is surely the interactive dynamic outcome of some interplay of genetic predisposition, extremely early biological and interpersonal experiences, later psychological predispositions and behavioral encounters, parental psychology and health, cultural and societal child-rearing methods and attitudes, reality factors in the immediate and potential environment, and coincidence and luck. The specific mechanism by which peculiar traits develop and cluster to formulate particular personalities and personality disorders remains unproven, endlessly theorized, and fiercely debated by philosophers, behavioral scientists, and clinicians alike.

II. The Role of Personality Disorders in Employment Litigation

Certain qualities inherent in the personality disorders mean that these disorders frequently have a pivotal role in the health (or ill health) of a workplace environment, and consequently in employment litigation. Personality disorders produce cognitive distortions and unreasonable expectations and demands that may impact liability issues in an employment lawsuit. They lead to social dysfunction, boundary violation and permeability, and a tendency toward passive-aggressive control that may undermine employee morale and create factions and alienation in a workforce. Certain personality disorders can give rise to intense rage, acute exacerbation of baseline characterologic tendencies, and heightened impairment of impulse control, leading to retaliatory behavior and even potential violence. Under more prolonged disorder-related stress, an employee with a personality disorder can "decompensate," so as to develop a full-fledged Axis I thought, affective, or anxiety disorder.

Issues of causation as well as damages can become highly clouded in a lawsuit where a personality disorder is involved. What is claimed to be sexual harassment, for example, may turn out to have been provoked. What is reported

---

[8] Don C. Fowles, *Electrodermal Hyporeactivity, Motivation, and Psychopathy: Theoretical Issues*, in PROGRESS IN EXPERIMENTAL PERSONALITY AND PSYCHOPATHOLOGY RESEARCH 263 (Don C. Fowles, Patricia B. Sutker & Sherryl Goodman eds., 1994).

(and believed) to be ethnic discrimination may be the product of a never-ending and hypervigilant search for "subtle clues" of mistreatment or bias that do not, to the objective observer, really exist. A Major Depressive Episode, genuine and genuinely new, may not be the result of unreasonable employer demands, as claimed, but rather the consequence of severe Narcissistic Personality Disorder facing the insult of an adverse performance evaluation. Because deeply ingrained lifelong patterns of behavior are involved (rather than the acute symptoms of Axis I pathology), potential problems may go undetected for quite some time until they become manifest in an unexpected, seemingly unprovoked allegation of harassment, discrimination, or other alleged mistreatment in the workplace.

III. Personality Disorders That May Be Found in the Workplace

DSM-IV-TR recognizes ten personality disorders, as well as Personality Disorder Not Otherwise Specified, a diagnosis reserved for individuals exhibiting a mixed picture of traits of several disorders, none clustering sufficiently to justify any specific diagnosis but all of which taken together cause clinically significant impairment for the individual. Diagnoses are grouped into three clusters (A, B, and C). The clusters are comprised of disorders that are phenomenologically and etiologically similar, or the traits of which tend to overlap. Interestingly, the clusters also roughly correspond to the broad Axis I division of psychopathology into the categories of thought disorders, mood disorders, and anxiety disorders.

Cluster A contains the "odd" or eccentric disorders: Paranoid, Schizoid, and Schizotypal Personality Disorders. Common to these (and reminiscent of Axis I thought disorders) is a pervasive, chronic pattern of abnormal cognitive style (e.g., suspiciousness and hypervigilance), expressive style (e.g., odd, idiosyncratic speech), and relating style (e.g., seclusiveness and interpersonal detachment).

Cluster B disorders are dramatic and emotional in nature; they thus hold some kinship to Axis I mood disorders. They consist of Antisocial, Borderline, Histrionic, and Narcissistic Personality Disorders. Cluster B disorders share a pervasive willingness to violate social norms (e.g., lying, stealing), impulse control dysregulation (e.g., substance abuse, ill-advised sexuality), excessive emotionality, grandiosity and reflexive projection of responsibility outward, and a great deal of underlying rage.

Cluster C contains the "anxious" disorders (thus, the similarity to Axis I anxiety disorders): Avoidant, Dependent, and Obsessive-Compulsive Personality Disorders. Common to Cluster C pathology is a chronic pattern of excessive fear surrounding social interaction, separation, rejection, and environmental control.

Table 6-2 displays the various *DSM-IV-TR* Personality Disorders, grouped by cluster.

Table 6-2 *DSM-IV-TR* **Personality Disorders, Grouped by Cluster**

Cluster A	Cluster B	Cluster C	Other
Paranoid	Antisocial	Avoidant	Personality Disorder N.O.S. ("Mixed Personality Disorder")
Schizoid	Borderline	Dependent	
Schizotypal	Histrionic	Obsessive-Compulsive	
	Narcissistic		

A. Cluster A Disorders

Cluster A personality disorders share oddities or eccentricities of thinking, speech, and manner. While individuals with such disorders are often fairly readily identifiable, their belief systems and behaviors do not deviate sufficiently from the societal norm to be considered psychotic. Still, these are probably the most biologically oriented of the personality disorders in terms of etiology, and indeed individuals diagnosed with Cluster A pathology are much more likely than those not so diagnosed to go on to manifest frank Delusional Disorder or Schizophrenia later in life.

1. Paranoid Personality Disorder

CASE EXAMPLE

Ms. A was a salesperson for a cellular telephone company. Shortly after commencing employment, Ms. A felt that her male supervisor was attracted to her sexually, although she "knew" it was only because of her ethnic background and therefore not to be taken seriously.

Ms. A was not particularly successful in her sales endeavors and received feedback that, although encouraging and supportive, suggested potential ways to improve performance. This she interpreted as hostile and aggressive, and when her supervisor proposed a weekly meeting with Ms. A to "coach" her and "teach her the ropes," Ms. A became extremely upset. She literally ran to her district manager in tears to report this latest in the series of "threats" levied by her supervisor. The malevolent treatment was based, Ms. A was certain, upon her supervisor's anger at having been stymied in his sexual pursuits. She explained, "I let him know, by being very nice, but making clear I was not the type he was hoping for. This made him very angry, I am sure of it."

Over the next year of her employment, Ms. A became increasingly isolative, disclosing her problems to no one for fear peers were close with her supervisor. She determined that her sales territory was somehow inferior to those of her colleagues (though in years past, it had proven the company's most lucrative), and she demanded a larger area. When the company failed to meet a deadline Ms. A set for granting her a larger territory, Ms. A announced the situation was intolerable. She resigned and filed a lawsuit alleging sexual and ethnic discrimination and constructive termination.

Ms. A received a large settlement from her erstwhile employers but became deeply distressed to discover she would be taxed not only on her portion of the recovery, but on her attorney's percentage as well. She filed a legal malpractice action against the attorney, claiming he had forced her to settle the case and lied to her about the tax ramifications.

During forensic psychiatric evaluation of Ms. A's emotional distress claim in the legal malpractice action, it came to light that at previous and subsequent jobs, Ms. A had "sensed" problems with her respective male supervisors. Both supervisors, she reasoned, were jealous of and intimidated by her and had therefore attempted to "sabotage" her, leading her to premature departure from the respective positions. In addition, Ms. A disclosed, her ex-husband had "betrayed" her through multiple extramarital liaisons (a state of affairs she sensed, he denied, and she could never prove). At the time of her psychiatric examination, six years after the divorce, Ms. A continued a campaign to undermine her ex-husband's credibility within the community. She announced: "He deserves every bit of Hell I can give him and he always will. He, my supervisor, my attorney—they are all monsters!"

Those with Paranoid Personality Disorder often present themselves impressively at first, with excellent academic records (they are competitive and highly controlled), potent resumes, and an appearance of confidence and power. However, over time, problems arise in the form of unfounded suspicions, undue defensiveness at "injustices" or "insults" perceived by no one else, excessive rigidity, an absolute unwillingness to consider compromise, and a demand for control coupled with a suspicious aloofness and reluctance to confide.

Once crossed, such individuals frequently bear grudges for years and are unwilling to forgive. Driven by a moralistic sense of virtue, they may carry on the battle via methods perceived by others as crafty, devious, sly, or outright dishonest. Very much attuned to and focused upon relative power relationships and perceived interpersonal rivalries and jealousies, individuals with Paranoid Personality Disorder will often treat subordinates or even peers with disdain, while scheming and manipulating to secure power over superiors they construe as jealous, treacherous, and otherwise hostile.

When one with Paranoid Personality Disorder perceives himself or herself to have been threatened, demeaned, or criticized, the response is likely to be rapid, angry, and absolute. A counterattack is likely to occur accompanied by fear, with immediate devaluation of the perceived attacker and an increase in isolative suspiciousness. Frank decompensation into a brief psychotic episode, into overt obsessive-compulsive behavior, or into a Major Depressive Episode may also occur. Paranoid Personality Disorder is sometimes a premorbid marker for later development of Delusional Disorder or Schizophrenia; like the other Cluster A diagnoses, it appears to have a biological etiologic component.

Generally, an individual with Paranoid Personality Disorder will function most effectively in solo workplace settings, interacting best with machines or paperwork rather than with people. Supervision and instruction should be as explicit and structured as possible; these are not employees who deal well with subtle or inferential management styles.

DSM-IV-TR criteria for Paranoid Personality Disorder are displayed in Table 6-3.

Table 6-3 *DSM-IV-TR* Diagnostic Criteria for Paranoid Personality Disorder

A. A pervasive distrust and suspiciousness of others such that their motives are interpreted as malevolent, beginning by early adulthood and present in a variety of contexts, as indicated by four (or more) of the following:
  (1) suspects, without sufficient basis, that others are exploiting, harming, or deceiving him or her
  (2) is preoccupied with unjustified doubts about the loyalty or trustworthiness of friends or associates
  (3) is reluctant to confide in others because of unwarranted fear that the information will be used maliciously against him or her
  (4) reads hidden demeaning or threatening meanings into benign remarks or events
  (5) persistently bears grudges, i.e., is unforgiving of insults, injuries, or slights
  (6) perceives attacks on his or her character or reputation that are not apparent to others and is quick to react angrily or to counterattack
  (7) has recurrent suspicions, without justification, regarding fidelity of spouse or sexual partner
B. Does not occur exclusively during the course of Schizophrenia, a Mood Disorder With Psychotic Features, or another Psychotic Disorder and is not due to the direct physiological effects of a general medical condition.

Source: Reprinted with permission from the *Diagnostic and Statistical Manual of Mental Disorders, Fourth Edition, Text Revision,* 694. Copyright 2000 American Psychiatric Association.

2. Schizoid and Schizotypal Personality Disorders

CASE EXAMPLE

Mr. B worked as a payroll clerk in a small bank devoted to supporting investment within the Asian-American community. Mr. B labored diligently and conscientiously, alone in an office on the top floor of the three-story structure. He often told his supervisor how much he liked his job and his office: "They leave me alone to do my work, and proximity-wise, it's A-O.K. to connect so well to the waves!" Mr. B wore a baseball cap with aluminum foil encasing its visor; he explained the foil enhanced his ability to "tune in positive waves" he believed were directed toward him from a metal structure on the roof of the building.

A slight, Asian-American male with what his supervisor warmly called a "screwball smile," Mr. B still lived with his parents at the age of 32. He did not date; he did not socialize; he bothered no one and no one bothered him. He quietly, efficiently did his job for over ten years, the foil cap never leaving his head.

The bank where Mr. B worked was later merged into a much larger bank, and Mr. B's office was to be moved to a cubicle on the first floor of a nearby skyscraper. As the move date approached, Mr. B's work product deteriorated and he became visibly agitated and upset. He came to work wearing a new T-shirt with a fluorescent orange skeleton painted on its chest. He explained to his supervisor that the skeleton was to protect him from "demon waves, yellow demon waves." The foil cap became inverted, worn upside down to "catch any good waves that still might fall."

On psychiatric fitness for duty evaluation, Mr. B disclosed that "demon waves, yellow demon waves" come from beneath; "good" waves descend from above. By moving to the first floor, Mr. B was being put in "great metaphysical and philosophical danger, possibly terrifying to lay people." Aside from his supervisor, he had no friends or confidants within or outside the bank with whom he could share this urgent information, and he feared for his parents' health if they were to become aware. Yet in spite of his obvious concern about these matters, Mr. B appeared oddly detached throughout his examination, unemotional and removed.

Upon the evaluating psychiatrist's recommendation, Mr. B's concerns were accommodated by moving him to a small office on the top floor of the new building. The skeleton shirt disappeared one day after the move. The cap returned to its normal position right side up on Mr. B's head a week thereafter. Within that same week, the screwball smile once again stretched across Mr. B's face. The world's waves had been restored to harmony.

Schizoid and Schizotypal Personality Disorders are centrally characterized by the peculiar, idiosyncratic belief systems and behaviors they engender. Thought by many to actually represent minor manifestations of the Schizophrenia gene, they in fact do seem close cousins to that disorder, with Schizoid Personality Disorder reminiscent of the "negative" symptoms of Schizophrenia and Schizotypal Personality Disorder evocative of its "positive" manifestations. Often, traits of the two personality disorders overlap in a single individual.

Those manifesting Schizoid Personality Disorder tend toward social isolation. Devoid of any tangible desire or apparent need for intimacy, Schizoid individuals have little or no interest in romance or sexual experience, and they take pleasure in few activities. They tend to lack close friends, yet they remain extremely attached to the family of origin. Often, they come across as bland, removed, almost devoid of affect, and seem to be little touched by either praise or criticism from others.

Formal *DSM-IV-TR* criteria for Schizoid Personality Disorder are set forth in Table 6-4.

Table 6-4 *DSM-IV-TR* Diagnostic Criteria for Schizoid Personality Disorder

A. A pervasive pattern of detachment from social relationships and a restricted range of expression of emotions in interpersonal settings, beginning by early adulthood and present in a variety of contexts, as indicated by four (or more) of the following:

(1) neither desires nor enjoys close relationships, including being part of a family
(2) almost always chooses solitary activities
(3) has little, if any, interest in having sexual experiences with another person
(4) takes pleasure in few, if any, activities
(5) lacks close friends or confidants other than first-degree relatives
(6) appears indifferent to the praise or criticism of others
(7) shows emotional coldness, detachment, or flattened affectivity

B. Does not occur exclusively during the course of Schizophrenia, a Mood Disorder With Psychotic Features, another Psychotic Disorder, or a Pervasive Developmental Disorder, and is not due to the direct physiological effects of a general medical condition.

Source: Reprinted with permission from the *Diagnostic and Statistical Manual of Mental Disorders, Fourth Edition, Text Revision,* 697. Copyright 2000 American Psychiatric Association.

Like the active symptoms of Schizophrenia, symptoms of Schizotypal Personality Disorder tend to be more flamboyant and extrovertly odd than those of Schizoid Personality Disorder. Persons with this disorder may speak using unusual, idiosyncratic syntactic constructions, and they display "ideas of reference" (the belief that others can "tap into" their thoughts or that they can spy on the thoughts of others, or the conviction that hidden meanings can be detected in particular mystical numbers or dates, or be deciphered in newspaper or television snippets). Schizotypal individuals may be somewhat superstitious and even suspicious of others' not adhering to the same quasi-magical beliefs.

Like those who are Schizoid, Schizotypal people tend toward social isolation and social anxiety. Like Schizoid Disorder, Schizotypal Disorder is frequently characterized by affective flattening and emotional blankness.

DSM-IV-TR requirements for a diagnosis of Schizotypal Personality Disorder are set forth in Table 6-5.

Table 6-5 *DSM-IV-TR* Diagnostic Criteria for Schizotypal Personality Disorder

A. A pervasive pattern of social and interpersonal deficits marked by acute discomfort with, and reduced capacity for, close relationships as well as by cognitive or perceptual distortions and eccentricities of behavior, beginning by early adulthood and present in a variety of contexts, as indicated by five (or more) of the following:
(1) ideas of reference (excluding delusions of reference)
(2) odd beliefs or magical thinking that influences behavior and is inconsistent with subcultural norms (e.g., superstitiousness, belief in clairvoyance, telepathy, or "sixth sense"; in children and adolescents, bizarre fantasies or preoccupations)
(3) unusual perceptual experiences, including bodily illusions
(4) odd thinking and speech (e.g., vague, circumstantial, metaphorical, over-elaborate, or stereotyped)

continued

Table 6-5 Continued.
DSM-IV-TR Diagnostic Criteria for Schizotypal Personality Disorder

(5) suspiciousness or paranoid ideation
(6) inappropriate or constricted affect
(7) behavior or appearance that is odd, eccentric, or peculiar
(8) lack of close friends or confidants other than first-degree relatives
(9) excessive social anxiety that does not diminish with familiarity and tends to be associated with paranoid fears rather than negative judgments about self

B. Does not occur exclusively during the course of Schizophrenia, a Mood Disorder With Psychotic Features, another Psychotic Disorder, or a Pervasive Developmental Disorder.

Source: Reprinted with permission from the *Diagnostic and Statistical Manual of Mental Disorders, Fourth Edition, Text Revision,* 701. Copyright 2000 American Psychiatric Association.

In contrast to the petulance typically displayed by individuals suffering Paranoid Personality Disorder who perceive threat, those with Schizoid or Schizotypal Personality are more likely to withdraw into an inner world of tumult and fear when they experience criticism or attack. Over 50 percent of such individuals have a history of decompensation into at least one Major Depressive Episode at some time in their lives. They may become frankly psychotic under perceived siege, with odd beliefs briefly degenerating into outright delusional systems and idiosyncratic superstitions transiently giving way to blatant hallucinations. As is the case with Paranoid Personality Disorder, for some, Schizoid or Schizotypal Personality Disorder may actually constitute a precursor for a later emerging Delusional Disorder, Schizophreniform Disorder, or outright Schizophrenia.

If they make it into the workforce at all, Schizoid and Schizotypal employees are likely to present difficulties primarily by passively causing discomfort in those around them. Oddities in dress, in speech, in behavior, and occasionally in hygiene may all generate upset among colleagues or customers. Essentially submissive and cooperative, the Schizoid or Schizotypal employee is apt to promptly follow corrective management directives presented in a frank, nonjudgmental manner. As with Paranoid Personality Disorder, ideal jobs for Schizoid and Schizotypal employees involve isolated, self-motivated working assignments in relatively quiet, nonthreatening surroundings, with minimal need for interaction with supervisors, customers, or peers.

B. Cluster B Disorders

Cluster B Personality Disorders are in many ways the most difficult of the Axis II conditions to deal with in the context of employment law, because those so diagnosed are often the most publicly demonstrative of their pathology, while at the same time remaining personally oblivious to the possibility that there exists any pathology at all. Cluster B individuals are angry, dramatic people who frequently act out by expressing their pathological traits in overt behavioral displays. This results in tantrum-like outbursts of abusive behavior (directed toward self, others, or both), or in passive-aggressive, sadomasochistic manipulations designed to "get back" at others by showing how much anguish they have caused. There is a pervasive tendency in Cluster B individuals to project responsibility outward, and to react with angry indignation and dismissal to any suggestion that the Cluster B individual may have contributed to, provoked, or even made inevitable the unhappy, "victimized" outcomes he or she recurrently decries. In workplace settings, Cluster B individuals are often experienced as annoying, manipulative, demanding, seductive, unstable, or unreasonable.

The common experiential theme of the Cluster B Disorders is erratic emotionality; an affective lability born of a profound failure to have developed a stable sense of self and to have established adequately circumscribed boundaries between self and others. As described earlier, these so-called identity disorders appear to result mainly from faulty, ambivalent, confusing, or abusive interactions with caretakers during the first few years of life. Lacking a defined, insulated self or an integrated sense of efficacy, environmental mastery, and control, these individuals develop characteristic patterns of interaction with others that are predictable and repetitious. Such trait-dictated patterns cause them to be perceived as difficult, needy, manipulative, or obnoxious to those whose lives they touch.

A defining characteristic of personality disorders as a class and those falling into Cluster B in particular is that they tend to be *ego-syntonic*. This means that the person with the disorder generally is unaware of the fact that his or her behavior departs from the norm and adversely affects others. Many personality-disordered individuals—especially those with Cluster B pathology—experience chronic psychological distress as well as somewhat chaotic, dysfunctional lives. Rarely, however, do they attribute their distress or misfortune to a personality disorder, or to any behavioral provocation or contribution of their own. Instead, a hunt for some external culprit is usually undertaken. The Cluster B employee may conclude that his or her anxiety, depression, broken relationships, stunted career growth, and repeated feeling of victimization are the fault of discriminating bosses or harassing coworkers. The suggestion that the employee's own interpersonal style and manner of coping may have played a role in the genesis of any employment dispute at issue is met with surprise, outrage, and denial.

As is true generally of the personality disorders, while a given individual will often exhibit traits sufficient to warrant one or more specific Axis II, Cluster B diagnoses, those traits will nearly always be accompanied by several others more typical of alternate designations. A "pure" personality disorder, within or even between clusters, is rare.

1. Antisocial Personality Disorder

CASE EXAMPLE

Mr. C, the manager of a large commercial real estate project in the heart of a large American city, did not like his new boss. The suave superior seemed to advocate a very different vision for the project than that favored by Mr. C, and Mr. C's days in his lucrative, high-profile position seemed numbered.

Bothered, Mr. C considered his alternatives. He could fight the new boss politically; he would surely lose. He could resign; this would be a dignified approach, but then his pleasant lifestyle would be jeopardized. He decided instead to eliminate the irritant altogether, much as he had coolly and efficiently "wiped out" competition in his younger days in business.

Mr. C meticulously went about preparing a suitable means for the elimination of his nemesis. He quietly obtained explosive, primer, and fuse, careful to camouflage and code at each purchase step so as to cover his tracks. He then sent a live letter bomb to his supervisor's front door.

The bomb did not detonate as planned, and police investigation ultimately led to Mr. C's arrest. He coolly went about preparing a defense for his attorney to use, focusing upon police ineptitude and "reasonable doubt." When the elaborate plan was rejected by counsel, he arranged (through creative storytelling and re-creating history) to convince a prominent psychiatrist that he was insane.

The jury rejected the insanity defense, but the waiting period before trial was sufficient for Mr. C to convince the evaluating psychiatrist to certify that he was "treating" Mr. C (he saw Mr. C twice in eight months), and that Mr. C was "totally psychiatrically disabled" by the Bipolar I Disorder allegedly accounting for his crime (but that had never interfered with his work as a property manager of a massive commercial development nor with his elaborate postarrest legal machinations). When Mr. C finally went to prison convicted of attempted murder, he went there receiving over half a million dollars per annum in tax-free psychiatric disability benefits.

For six years, Mr. C's "treating" psychiatrist sent the disability carrier monthly re-certification updates, never once examining Mr. C in prison throughout this period. For his part, Mr. C mailed typed, detailed memoranda to his attorney instructing him on appeal strategy; to his wife instructing her on real estate investments; to investment partners discussing the merits of new enterprises. Simultaneously, Mr. C sent scanty, handwritten, pathetically confused notes to his disability carrier describing his supposedly deteriorating mental status.

When the carrier ultimately challenged Mr. C's ongoing psychiatric disability, he sued for bad faith and intentional infliction of emotional distress. The case was dismissed on a defense motion for summary judgment supported by forensic psychiatric testimony regarding Antisocial Personality Disorder.

Antisocial Personality Disorder was first formally noted in writings of the nineteenth century, when terms such as *manie sans délire* and *moral insanity* were used to describe unabashedly manipulative, amoral behavior unaccompanied by discernible impairment in reasoning. Also formerly termed *psychopathy* or *sociopathy*, Antisocial Personality Disorder is centrally characterized by lack of development of conscience and remorse as core regulatory components of the personality. Stemming from this developmental failure is a lifelong pattern of socially irresponsible, guiltless, manipulative, and exploitative behavior and of chronic disregard for the rights, feelings, and values of others.

Those with Antisocial Personality Disorder are often perceived as reckless, sensation-seeking, and contemptuous of the rules and restrictions subscribed to by the society around them. Common workplace behaviors include repeated lying, cynical manipulativeness, and possibly an undisclosed criminal record. Such individuals have a remarkable disregard for the feelings, wishes, and rights of others (often in the face of suave, charismatic likability). Their records often disclose a tendency toward sadistic, aggressive "retribution" for perceived slights; a history of impulsive behavior without regard for consequences; of cheating, conning, lying to, manipulating, or undermining fellow employees; or of consequence-defiant substance abuse. In general, theirs is a "cost versus benefit" rather than a morally driven view of the interpersonal world. If one with Antisocial Personality Disorder perceives likely outcome to outweigh potential consequence, he or she will act, regardless of societal norms of conduct.

When Antisocial individuals understand themselves to be demeaned or criticized, they are likely to refuse to accept responsibility. Instead, they typically will distort or lie to attempt to prove their innocence. They may attempt to gain the upper hand through slick double-talk or through aggressive intimidation, or they may actively retaliate against the threat. Such retaliation in an employment setting may take the form of mean practical jokes, of propagation of blatantly false accusations or rumors, or of arranging "setups" to bring down the target antagonist.

When seriously stressed (usually by having been caught in some serious act of rule violation), individuals with Antisocial Personality Disorder may decompensate into brief periods of anxiety or depression, sometimes taking such forms as Panic Attacks or a Major Depressive Episode. Recourse to substance abuse is also common under threat, and individuals with Antisocial Personality Disorder have more than the average tendency to develop somatization phenomena such as Conversion Disorder or Somatoform Disorder.

In any litigation context, malingering of Axis I symptoms or disorders must be carefully considered in litigants manifesting Antisocial Personality Disorder. The presence of Antisocial Personality Disorder diagnosed in a subject presenting symptoms in a medicolegal setting is, in fact, one of the four indicia cited by *DSM-IV-TR* as a situation warranting particularly scrupulous inquiry into possible feigning or exaggerating of claimed symptomatic distress.[9]

Antisocial Personality Disorder is unique among the Axis II diagnoses in requiring that symptoms of a prior childhood condition (Conduct Disorder) be positively identified before the diagnosis can be made (Criterion C). Conduct Disorder describes a pattern of recurrent violations of the rights of others (or of major age-appropriate social norms) before the age of fifteen years. Conduct Disorder infractions fall into four groups—aggression directed toward people or animals, destruction of property, deceitfulness and/or theft, or other major rule violation. *DSM-IV-TR* criteria for the diagnosis of Antisocial Personality Disorder are laid out in Table 6-6; those for Conduct Disorder are listed in Table 6-7.

---

[9]AMERICAN PSYCHIATRIC ASSOCIATION, DIAGNOSTIC AND STATISTICAL MANUAL OF MENTAL DISORDERS 739–40 (4th ed. text rev. 2000) [hereinafter *DSM-IV-TR*].

Table 6-6 *DSM-IV-TR* Diagnostic Criteria for Antisocial Personality Disorder

A. There is a pervasive pattern of disregard for and violation of the rights of others occurring since age 15 years, as indicated by three (or more) of the following:
   (1) failure to conform to social norms with respect to lawful behaviors as indicated by repeatedly performing acts that are grounds for arrest
   (2) deceitfulness, as indicated by repeated lying, use of aliases, or conning others for personal profit or pleasure
   (3) impulsivity or failure to plan ahead
   (4) irritability and aggressiveness, as indicated by repeated physical fights or assaults
   (5) reckless disregard for safety of self or others
   (6) consistent irresponsibility, as indicated by repeated failure to sustain consistent work behavior or honor financial obligations
   (7) lack of remorse, as indicated by being indifferent to or rationalizing having hurt, mistreated, or stolen from another
B. The individual is at least age 18 years.
C. There is evidence of Conduct Disorder with onset before age 15 years.
D. The occurrence of antisocial behavior is not exclusively during the course of Schizophrenia or a Manic Episode.

Source: Reprinted with permission from the *Diagnostic and Statistical Manual of Mental Disorders, Fourth Edition, Text Revision,* 706. Copyright 2000 American Psychiatric Association.

Table 6-7 *DSM-IV-TR* Diagnostic Criteria for Conduct Disorder

A. A repetitive and persistent pattern of behavior in which the basic rights of others or major age-appropriate societal norms or rules are violated, as manifested by the presence of three (or more) of the following criteria in the past 12 months, with at least one criterion present in the past 6 months.

Aggression to people and animals
   (1) often bullies, threatens, or intimidates others
   (2) often initiates physical fights
   (3) has used a weapon that can cause serious physical harm to others (e.g., a bat, brick, broken bottle, knife, gun)
   (4) has been physically cruel to people
   (5) has been physically cruel to animals
   (6) has stolen while confronting a victim (e.g., mugging, purse snatching, extortion, armed robbery)
   (7) has forced someone into sexual activity

Destruction of property
   (8) has deliberately engaged in fire setting with the intention of causing serious damage
   (9) has deliberately destroyed others' property (other than by fire setting)

Deceitfulness or theft
   (10) has broken into someone else's house, building, or car

(11) often lies to obtain goods or favors or to avoid obligations (i.e., "cons" others)
(12) has stolen items of nontrivial value without confronting a victim (e.g., shoplifting, but without breaking and entering; forgery)

Serious violations of rules
(13) often stays out at night despite parental prohibitions, beginning before age 13 years
(14) has run away from home overnight at least twice while living in parental or parental surrogate home (or once without returning for a lengthy period)
(15) is often truant from school, beginning before age 13 years
B. The disturbance in behavior causes clinically significant impairment in social, academic, or occupational functioning.

Source: Reprinted with permission from the *Diagnostic and Statistical Manual of Mental Disorders, Fourth Edition, Text Revision,* 98–99. Copyright 2000 American Psychiatric Association.

In the workforce, individuals with Antisocial Personality Disorder may be involved in illegal activities (embezzlement, fraud, forgery, theft) or in other problematic situations (malingering of on-the-job injuries for employment-related compensation, sexually harassing subordinates, substance abuse). Generally, they are best managed through rigid structure with unambiguous consequence: If costs of infraction outweigh benefits of misbehavior, infraction will not occur.

A common myth suggests that Antisocial Personality Disorder "burns out" around the age of 40 years. This notion is fueled by epidemiologic data confirming that people with Antisocial Personality Disorder have fewer legal and community difficulties in their senior years. However, other aspects of the disorder at least as relevant to employment litigation persist—substance abuse, impulsiveness, poor anger management, amorality, marital instability. If anything, these features can become more insidious and problematic to employers as the disordered individual hones his or her deceptive, manipulative skills with age and experience.

2. Borderline Personality Disorder

CASE EXAMPLE

Ms. D was a young female associate in a law firm. She boasted a sterling academic record, a delightful interpersonal style, and a crisp, analytic mind. Her only known blemish surrounded a law school summer clerkship at the same firm, during which a high-visibility romance with an associate went awry under mysterious circumstances, leading to some tension during the latter weeks of her clerkship tenure. However, the associate attorney had since resigned from the firm, and impressions of Ms. D otherwise remained so favorable that her summer indiscretion was deemed insignificant in the partners' greater vision for the future.

But then within months of Ms. D's hire, she became involved in a torrid affair with a married senior partner. When they were caught together unclothed in a conference room one evening, their intimate relationship ended noisily and publicly. Ms. D cut her wrists and overdosed on four capsules of the antidepressant medication she had been given by her secretary.

After brief psychiatric hospitalization and a month's medical leave, Ms. D returned to her office at the firm. She soon became romantically involved with two male colleagues—her paralegal and a third-year associate. Much tension and drama ensued, as Ms. D flipped seemingly month to month from one gentleman to the other, with increasing entanglement. She recruited allies from the firm (and designated antagonists) to support her reasoning for each realignment.

One night four months into their relationship, the paralegal found it possible to contain his rage no longer and slapped Ms. D during an altercation, opening a small cut over her upper lip. When the associate learned what had happened, he followed the paralegal home the following day, confronted him at his doorstep, and the two of them engaged in a fistfight.

The firm faced several lawsuits consequent to these events. They included a harassment, discrimination, and constructive termination suit levied by Ms. D (who resigned three days after the fight between her gentlemen admirers). Holding court from the hospital where she nursed wrists freshly sliced, Ms. D graced the press with accounts of how both paralegal and associate (with the tacit approval of senior management) had repeatedly accosted and sexually badgered her against her will; how this was only the latest manifestation of a pattern of promiscuous and exploitative behavior within the firm obvious to her from the days of her clerkship onward. She alleged that she had been "raped" by a senior partner on a conference room table "with full knowledge and consent of all the male partners in the firm," and that she was forced finally to sacrifice her career by leaving when the "overt hostility and threats from so many males just became totally intolerable."

The term Borderline Personality Disorder has its roots in the historical concept of "Borderline Schizophrenia"—the condition was thought to represent a gray zone between the *psychoses* (now encompassed in Axis I diagnoses) and the *neuroses* (now elements of Axis II conditions). Individuals so diagnosed were sometimes odd or eccentric at baseline, but they experienced transient psychotic episodes during regressive periods or while engaged in psychotherapy.

Today, what was once conceived of as a single diagnostic entity—Borderline Schizophrenia—is recognized to have erroneously encompassed an amorphous group of individuals suffering from very different disorders (Bipolar I or II Disorder; Schizophrenia or Schizophreniform Disorder; Schizotypal or Schizoid Personality Disorder; Cluster B Personality Disorders). Continued use of the term "borderline" to describe the diagnostic entity as it is currently conceived has become a somewhat confusing historical relic.

There are, in fact, no particular states between which Borderline Personality Disorder constitutes any sort of "border" or "line." Rather, Borderline Personality Disorder designates a Cluster B identity disorder in which lack of a fully developed and integrated self manifests as marked instability in a number of areas—of mood, of interpersonal valuation, of impulse control, of overt expression of rage. The subjective experience of the Borderline is one of emptiness, meaninglessness, boredom, and uncertain "anomie." Dull, chronic depression alternates with all-consuming passion and love, which in turn alternates with all-but-uncontrollable hatred and rage. The Borderline appears to those persons in his or her[10] immediate orbit as a person unpredictably varying between wildness, seductiveness, ragefulness, winsome withdrawal, passion, explosive self-destructiveness, and outwardly directed and potentially violent furor. The great English physician Thomas Sydenham captured the condition's essence when he wrote in 1682,

> All is caprice,
> they love without measure
> those whom they will soon hate without reason.[11]

Contemporary conceptualizations of Borderline Personality Disorder focus upon a pervasive pattern of volatile and intense interpersonal relationships destabilized by an overwhelming propensity toward "black or white," all-or-nothing thinking, such thinking resulting in extremes of overidealization and devaluation of individuals and institutions. Which extreme governs conscious awareness and guides behavior at any moment is determined by the Borderline individual's perception of the external entity's valuation of the Borderline at that moment. Lacking any stable sense of self, the Borderline perceives himself or herself to be all good if he or she is treated nicely or lovingly and all bad if treated meanly or rejected. In turn, others around the Borderline are either deemed all wonderful or all evil by the Borderline, the assignation subject to change with startling rapidity.

Such chaotically fluctuating thinking and feeling fundamentally govern the overall experience of one with Borderline Personality Disorder. Anger is inappropriate, sporadic, and intense. It may be directed inward (via depression or self-mutilating, self-destructive behavior), or outward (via rageful violence, or equally rageful but more subtle passive-aggressive undermining). There tend to be recurrent (but fleeting) suicidal thoughts, accompanied or not by suicidal gestures (such as self-mutilation, binges of substance abuse, and binges and purges typical of bulimic behavior). There is an overwhelming terror of aloneness (because alone there is nothing), and frantic efforts to avoid real (or imagined) abandonment prevail, again taking active or passive-aggressive form (pleading, stalking, threatening, and blackmailing; threats of suicide; sexual acting out; self-mutilation; and blatantly false allegations of victimization).

When a Borderline is provoked via a real or perceived interpersonal rejection or a serious devaluation of work product, the individual may decompensate into a transient psychotic episode (typically frank persecutory delusion or threatening auditory hallucination), or into depression sometimes assuming the form of Major Depressive Disorder. Brief episodes of Substance Abuse Disorder and/or Eating Disorder may also result.

---

[10]Borderlines tend to be predominantly (about 75%) female. *DSM-IV-TR, supra* note 10, at 708.

[11]THOMAS SYDENHAM, 2 THE WORKS OF THOMAS SYDENHAM, M.D. 88–89 (1850).

Many Borderline individuals are so deeply expectant of the recurrent tumult that is their lives that if they perceive themselves to be in a period of relative quiescence, they find themselves compelled to "stir things up," to provoke chaos in their surroundings so as to return to the familiar misery of their chaotic existence. Such often proves to be the case when a formerly benign workplace finds itself newly factionalized, alienated, and at war. Such is also frequently the dynamic when apparently manipulative seductive or impulsive behavior is followed by surprise, outrage, and often a legal claim or lawsuit.

Whether they have provoked the behavior or not, Borderlines who perceive themselves to be criticized, demeaned, or otherwise rejected may rapidly vilify the perceived persecutor and then move to pit others against him or her. A supervisor or peer may be "perfect" one day, and by the next have become the personification of evil and the cause of all things gone wrong in the Borderline's chronically chaotic existence.

Of particular note in the context of employment litigation is a baseline dysphoric mood that often accompanies Borderline Personality Disorder. Very frequently, such individuals are correctly diagnosed as suffering from long term Dysthymic Disorder reflective of their recurrently disappointing social and vocational lives. While unfortunate workplace events may indeed cause decompensation of such individuals into a full-blown, superimposed, Major Depressive Episode (also known as "double depression"),[12] it is incumbent upon forensic evaluators to establish that symptoms reported represent legitimate documentable exacerbation, and not just an unchanged, ongoing manifestation of an underlying Dysthymia, or even just the chronically fluctuating, generally dysphoric mood that characterizes Borderline Personality Disorder itself.

Table 6-8 sets forth the *DSM-IV-TR* diagnostic criteria for Borderline Personality Disorder.

Table 6-8 *DSM-IV-TR* Diagnostic Criteria for Borderline Personality Disorder

A pervasive pattern of instability of interpersonal relationships, self-image, and affects, and marked impulsivity beginning by early adulthood and present in a variety of contexts, as indicated by five (or more) of the following:
(1) frantic efforts to avoid real or imagined abandonment. *Note:* Do not include suicidal or self-mutilating behavior covered in Criterion 5.
(2) a pattern of unstable and intense interpersonal relationships characterized by alternating between extremes of idealization and devaluation
(3) identity disturbance: markedly and persistently unstable self-image or sense of self

---

[12]See Chapter 5, Mental Disorders Commonly Encountered in Employment Litigation.

(4) impulsivity in at least two areas that are potentially self-damaging (e.g., spending, sex, substance abuse, reckless driving, binge eating). *Note:* Do not include suicidal or self-mutilating behavior covered in Criterion 5.
(5) recurrent suicidal behavior, gestures, or threats, or self-mutilating behavior
(6) affective instability due to a marked reactivity of mood (e.g., intense episodic dysphoria, irritability, or anxiety usually lasting a few hours and only rarely more than a few days)
(7) chronic feelings of emptiness
(8) inappropriate, intense anger or difficulty controlling anger (e.g., frequent displays of temper, constant anger, recurrent physical fights)
(9) transient, stress-related paranoid ideation or severe dissociative symptoms

Source: Reprinted with permission from the *Diagnostic and Statistical Manual of Mental Disorders, Fourth Edition, Text Revision,* 710. Copyright 2000 American Psychiatric Association.

3. Histrionic Personality Disorder

CASE EXAMPLE

Ms. E was all the rage when she went to work as an executive secretary at a Hollywood studio. She was pretty and extroverted and bubbly and funny. Ms. E announced from the start that she was going to be an actress, and she often liked to show off her talent by reciting lines from favorite movies (usually, by assuming the character of a femme fatale); singing favorite torch songs; demonstrating risqué dance steps. Ms. E was particularly popular with male employees; she would wear very short skirts or very tight-fitting jeans and very low-cut neck lines.

Ms. E's aspirations to stardom were not kept secret from her boss, an upper-mid-level studio executive. Although he liked Ms. E (particularly because she flirted with him and joked about their having an affair), he was concerned about her basic work performance. Ms. E had an annoying vagueness to her communicative style and she had difficulty getting to the point.

Six months passed, and Ms. E's first performance evaluation came due. Her boss was not in good humor (his wife had recently admitted to her own ongoing extramarital affair), and he was more blunt in his evaluative comments than he might have been under better circumstances. The written evaluation noted Ms. E's inefficient way of communicating, her lack of focus, and her somewhat flighty attitude. "She seems more interested in pursuing an acting career than in doing the work immediately at hand," he wrote.

Ms. E was very upset by her boss's words and asked to meet with him for a drink so they could talk about the review "in a little more relaxed atmosphere." The boss distractedly agreed, and they went to a local lounge after work.

Ms. E expressed her profound disappointment at her evaluation: "I thought I meant more to you than this. Weren't we special?" Intrigued (and angry at his wife), the boss asked Ms. E if she thought they were "special." She looked incredulously at him, leaned forward, and cooed, "Yes, at least that's what I thought, anyway."

Now encouraged by both Ms. E and his extra dry martini, the boss looked into Ms. E's eyes and moved to kiss her. She reared back horrified, leaping off her chair and toward the door even as she hollered, "You pig! How can you do that? Pig!"

> *The next day, Ms. E resigned, at the same time formalizing a complaint of sexual harassment with the studio's personnel director, with the EEOC, and with an attorney. Her subsequent civil suit claimed chronic nightmares, fractured libido, and profound and pervasive distrust of men, all stemming from what she characterized as "the vicious rape attempt, including fellatio" that she "survived" that night when she was "cornered" by her boss.*

Individuals with Histrionic Personality Disorder are the "actors and actresses" of those diagnosed with Axis II pathology. Often deeply needy and craving of attention, Histrionic subjects tend to act in flirtatious, sexualized ways and to enjoy being the center of social focus. Yet, seemingly in direct contradiction to their provocative dress and overtly seductive behavior, those with Histrionic Personality Disorder often express unawareness, surprise, and disbelief at how others view their manipulations. They perceive themselves as exploited victims when they arouse a response that to most would be seen as predictable and appropriate given their provocation, and they are surprised and upset when others treat them as superficial or impressionistic. Yet, they typically interact in a vague, shallow, generalized manner.

Histrionic behavior in the workplace often manifests as a tendency toward high drama and attention seeking, inappropriately overt sexuality and seductiveness, vague, impressionistic speech, and a high degree of suggestibility. Employees with Histrionic Personality Disorder will exhibit discomfort if they are not the center of attention. They will engage freely in sexually provocative behavior and appearance, they will display rapidly shifting and shallow emotions, and they will relate through vague and highly dramatized verbal expression.

Such individuals often consider relationships more intimate than they really are, and are prone to alienate friends and acquaintances with their demand for constant admiration and attention. Highly suggestible, they are intrigued by current societal fads and are easily impressed with fringe groups and cults, parapsychological and New Age movements or beliefs, and mystical or natural approaches to spiritual and emotional well-being, and physical hygiene and healing.

If one with Histrionic Personality Disorder perceives himself or herself to have been threatened, attacked, or criticized, he or she is likely to react with behavior that is excessive and overemotional, and retaliation may take the form of vague, generalized allegations rather than specific complaints. Such individuals are highly prone to colorful exaggerations and flamboyant fabrications, and the histories of injustices they relate are seldom crisp, concise, or rich in specifics.

Under sustained or severe disorder-related stress, Histrionic Personality Disorder may decompensate into depressive disorders such as Dysthymic Disorder or Major Depressive Disorder, or into psychiatrically based physical symptoms constituting Conversion Disorder or Somatization Disorder. More frequently than with other Cluster B Disorders, those manifesting Histrionic Personality Disorder may experience objectively mild to moderate pain as excessively severe, developing diagnosable Pain Disorder and concomitant abusive dependence upon addictive prescription analgesic or anxiolytic medications.

DSM-IV-TR diagnostic criteria for Histrionic Personality Disorder are set forth in Table 6-9.

Table 6-9 *DSM-IV-TR* Diagnostic Criteria for Histrionic Personality Disorder

A pervasive pattern of excessive emotionality and attention seeking, beginning by early adulthood and present in a variety of contexts, as indicated by five (or more) of the following:
(1) is uncomfortable in situations in which he or she is not the center of attention
(2) interaction with others is often characterized by inappropriate sexually seductive or provocative behavior
(3) displays rapidly shifting and shallow expression of emotions
(4) consistently uses physical appearance to draw attention to self
(5) has a style of speech that is excessively impressionistic and lacking in detail
(6) shows self-dramatization, theatricality, and exaggerated expression of emotion
(7) is suggestible, i.e., easily influenced by others or circumstances
(8) considers relationships to be more intimate than they actually are

Source: Reprinted with permission from the *Diagnostic and Statistical Manual of Mental Disorders, Fourth Edition, Text Revision,* 714. Copyright 2000 American Psychiatric Association.

4. Narcissistic Personality Disorder

CASE EXAMPLE

Mr. F was a gardener. He never went to school for training in landscape architecture, yet he "knew" he was more than qualified in the field, and had no qualms advertising himself as a "qualified landscape architect" and printing this title (in dazzling fluorescent green) on the expensive business cards he designed to launch his new business. When, three years later, Mr. F was sued by a wealthy client for gross incompetence, he wrote the dissatisfaction off to the client's "inexorably constipated, bourgeois mindset" and vandalized her home and her car.

Despite this satisfying revenge, Mr. F needed a job—the suit (and a general paucity of patrons) had forced his business into bankruptcy. So he went to work as a groundskeeper for a local municipality.

Quickly, Mr. F concluded that his landscape architectural vision vastly eclipsed that of his team leader. Though he was put off by what he perceived as the supervisor's ineptitude, Mr. F tried hard not to be too critical—"I really wasn't bossy at all, just constructively suggestive," he remarked—because he found the team leader extremely attractive, and he was certain the supervisor found him so as well.

After several months, Mr. F grew restive: "The schmuck just wasn't learning anything I tried to teach him; and he won't make a move on me, either. He just kept teasing me with that flirting thing he did with his middle." Although he made it a policy never to be the aggressor, Mr. F finally could stand the situation no longer and bluntly propositioned the man, certain of positive response.

The response was curtly negative. The supervisor informed Mr. F that he was not gay; that even if he were gay, Mr. F's romantic approach was inappropriate on the job; and that Mr. F ought to focus a little more energy on cutting grass and a little less on "planting your own seeds all over creation." Mr. F professed to be "shocked, appalled, and genuinely, supremely crushed."

Surprise and pain gave way to festering, uncontrollable anger over the months that followed, as the team leader continued to instruct Mr. F on the proper methods of groundskeeping. When Mr. F's one-year review finally came up, the supervisor's feedback was almost uniformly negative. Mr. F's rage boiled over to the point that he could no longer handle it. He had to act.

He went to higher management to complain that his negative review was retaliatory and unfair. As the conversation progressed, Mr. F accused the team leader of exposing himself to Mr. F. When Mr. F indicated that he was offended by the act, he claimed the team leader turned hostile and vindictive. He had remained unreasonable and nasty since, according to Mr. F, the latest manifestation being the allegedly biased review.

Just as individuals with Antisocial Personality Disorder fundamentally fail to develop functional conscience, those with Narcissistic Personality Disorder do not develop genuine capacity to empathize. Preoccupied with their own self-importance, cleverness, and superiority, Narcissists are possessed of an overwhelming sense of entitlement and "specialness," so much so that they often consider it beneath them to have to put up with the mundane mediocrity of the population at large.

Grandiose and frequently preoccupied with fantasies of limitless power, success, brilliance, accomplishment, beauty, or ideal love, individuals with Narcissistic Personality Disorder tend to be shockingly insensitive to the wants or needs of others, while perpetually craving (and demanding) excessive praise, admiration, caring, and acknowledgment for feats real or imagined. Narcissists are frequently jealous of others and equally certain others are jealous of them.

As is the tendency with all the personality disorders and particularly those of Cluster B, Narcissistic individuals accept little responsibility for their behavioral outcomes, instead engaging in a perpetual search for outside agents responsible for their disappointments, distresses, and chronic social, vocational, and other interpersonal failures. Core to the disorder is extraordinary intolerance of criticism or perceived criticism. When individuals with Narcissistic Personality Disorder perceive themselves to be under threat or to have been demeaned in employment settings, they tend to become indignant, vindictive, and surprisingly given to rage, and to adopt a rigid and vengeful stance. They may act rapidly and sharply upon their rage, or they may plot revenge, allowing their anger to simmer at low boil and fuel elaborate plots to deliver perceived wrongdoers their due, sometimes months or even years after the occurrence of the Narcissistic insult.

It is thought that even more so than the traits of other personality disorders, Narcissistic traits tend to cluster not only with one another but with those of Cluster B Disorders as a whole. Thus, it is typical for one diagnosed with Narcissistic Personality Disorder to display profound Borderline, Antisocial, and Histrionic pathology as well. Such dovetailing of traits can create utter chaos in the workplace. Enraged by perceived criticism, an employee may devalue the criticism's source in a grossly exaggerated and distorted way, rapidly recruiting "allies" to share his or her point of view. In part, this may be accomplished by colorful re-creations of events bearing only the vaguest resemblance to reality. As factionalizing and backstabbing escalate, the disordered individual may work his or her way up the ranks of management, vilifying anyone not perceived as supportive en route. He or she may lie, ambush, or betray in what becomes an insatiable quest for vindication.

Under severe, prolonged, or recurrent disorder-specific stress, individuals with Narcissistic Personality Disorder may decompensate into bouts of intensified Dysthymia or Major Depressive Disorder. They may experience mini-psychotic episodes (usually in the form of persecutory delusion). While the lability of Borderline Personality Disorder more typically correlates with decompensation into the bingeing and purging of Bulimia Nervosa, Narcissistic grandiosity, imploded into feelings of persecution when the Narcissist is unsuccessful, more commonly gives way to the passive-aggressive self-mutilation of Anorexia Nervosa. As with the other Cluster B Disorders, substance abuse is frequently a part of the decompensated clinical picture.

Table 6-10 exhibits *DSM-IV-TR* criteria for the diagnosis of Narcissistic Personality Disorder.

Table 6-10   *DSM-IV-TR* Diagnostic Criteria for Narcissistic Personality Disorder

A pervasive pattern of grandiosity (in fantasy or behavior), need for admiration, and lack of empathy, beginning by early adulthood and present in a variety of contexts, as indicated by five (or more) of the following:
(1) has a grandiose sense of self-importance (e.g., exaggerates achievements and talents, expects to be recognized as superior without commensurate achievements)
(2) is preoccupied with fantasies of unlimited success, power, brilliance, beauty, or ideal love
(3) believes that he or she is "special" and unique and can only be understood by, or should associate with, other special or high-status people (or institutions)
(4) requires excessive admiration
(5) has a sense of entitlement, i.e., unreasonable expectations of especially favorable treatment or automatic compliance with his or her expectations
(6) is interpersonally exploitative, i.e., takes advantage of others to achieve his or her own ends
(7) lacks empathy: is unwilling to recognize or identify with the feelings and needs of others
(8) is often envious of others or believes that others are envious of him or her
(9) shows arrogant, haughty behaviors or attitudes

Source: Reprinted with permission from the *Diagnostic and Statistical Manual of Mental Disorders, Fourth Edition, Text Revision,* 717. Copyright 2000 American Psychiatric Association.

C. Cluster C Disorders

Cluster C—the "anxious" or "timid" personality disorders—resemble one another in that they share a chronic, pervasive pattern of excessive and distorted fears surrounding social interactions and judgments, potential for attachments and separations, and ability to modulate or control the behavior of self or others. Because of their pathologically low levels of assertiveness and high levels of submissiveness, individuals with Cluster C disorders may be vulnerable to harassment and discrimination in employment settings. What is actually terrified but painful stoicism in the face of inappropriate, demeaning treatment may be misinterpreted by perpetrators as consent or welcomeness, and sadistic colleagues may resort to ever-greater degrees of ugly conduct in an effort to get a rise out of their hapless victim.

Cluster C individuals are prone to present as claimants in employment litigation in workers' compensation or psychiatric disability cases, often when a new mental health treater has convinced them that what was never good for them is now disabling. They may also appear in cases with multiple plaintiffs all complaining of harassment or discrimination at the hands of an identified perpetrator, where the Cluster C individual in fact has experienced little or no bad behavior personally, but rather has been swept along with others toward the assertion of such a claim.

1. Avoidant Personality Disorder

CASE EXAMPLE

Dr. G always felt gloomy and alone. As a child, he was shunned for being unattractive and overweight. He had few friends and always felt as if he were on the outside, looking in. As a teenager and young adult, he never dated; certain of rejection, he did not ask a single girl out. In college, he felt inept and gawky, interpreting the social isolation to which he condemned himself as confirmation of his unattractiveness. What he lacked in social grace, however, he compensated for in academic prowess. He soothed himself by studying voraciously and succeeding spectacularly in the one area where he could. His grade point average never dipped below perfection; his standardized test results were routinely extraordinary.

He went to medical school, then on to residency in pediatrics and a fellowship in neonatology. In the high-tech, low-social-contact environment of the newborn intensive care unit, Dr. G finally found peace and relative fulfillment in his loneliness.

Ultimately, the neonatology group practice for which Dr. G worked was merged into a larger, full-service HMO, and Dr. G fell under the supervision of a new group of more critical physicians than those he had worked with early in his career. Dr. G sensed himself under increasing scrutiny. He was criticized for his "stodgy, methodical slowness," his "isolativeness," and his tendency to "leave the parent interaction to the nurses." Dr. G found himself progressively self-conscious in the hospital, anxious, and depressed.

Inner tension reached a pinnacle when Dr. G was called into his new chief's office one day and sharply criticized for his willingness to do what his colleagues considered "risky medical procedures." Dr. G's chief spoke dreaded words: "You can resign your position, or you can remain, but you will be under a closely supervised probationary period if you decide to stay. The choice is yours."

Upset and overwhelmed with anxiety, Dr. G left the group immediately to go on medical leave. He began treatment with a psychotherapist.

Within the month, Dr. G felt prepared to return to work. But his therapist encouraged otherwise: "Hasn't your whole life been a constant, bitter struggle? Hasn't it been miserable to get up every morning to face people you dread, confront judgments you hate? Why put yourself through that ever again?"

So encouraged by therapy, Dr. G did not return to work and instead filed a claim for permanent, total psychiatric disability on the basis of Major Depression. When Dr. G was examined by the psychiatrist hired by his insurance carrier to perform an evaluation, he was a truly miserable man. A lifetime of self-loathing and self-doubt rendered tolerable only by self-definition and success as a student and then as a neonatologist had come crashing down around him because his therapist had given him permission to succumb to his fears.

Avoidant Personality Disorder appears to reflect a very mild point along the Anxiety Disorder continuum that culminates in Social Phobia, much as Schizoid and Schizotypal Disorders seem to represent minor clinical manifestations along the Schizophrenia spectrum. Where Schizoid and Schizotypal individuals neither desire nor enjoy intimate relationships or social situations, those with Avoidant Personality Disorder dearly desire such experience but actively shun it because of perpetual fear of rejection, criticism, ridicule, and humiliation. Avoidant subjects desire to have relationships and be accepted but fear they never will, and they are hyperalert to potential signs of rejection. They tend to be extremely shy and unassertive, and to perceive themselves as unattractive or as social misfits. Thus, there is marked social impairment, and gravitation toward occupational and personal roles requiring minimal interpersonal interaction.

Individuals with Avoidant Personality Disorder are prone to avoid taking interpersonal chances or risks for fear of exposure under scrutiny. If the characterologic buttons of Avoidant Personality Disorder are pushed (e.g., by actual adverse judgments or personal rejections), defensive behaviors may include procrastination, absenteeism, abrupt resignation, or other forms of avoidance or self-destructive acting out. In situations of prolonged disorder-specific stress, Avoidant individuals may decompensate from typical baseline dysphoria (or Dysthymic Disorder) into a Major Depressive Episode or into a brief episode of psychosis, usually surrounding delusional beliefs of persecution, rejection, or disdainful loathing by others. Panic Attacks, Panic Disorder, Agoraphobia, and frank Social Phobia may develop out of Avoidant Personality Disorder.

Table 6-11 highlights *DSM-IV-TR* criteria for Avoidant Personality Disorder.

Table 6-11 *DSM-IV-TR* Diagnostic Criteria for Avoidant Personality Disorder

(1) avoids occupational activities that involve significant interpersonal contact, because of fears of criticism, disapproval, or rejection

continued

Table 6-11 Continued.
***DSM-IV-TR* Diagnostic Criteria for**
Avoidant Personality Disorder

(2) is unwilling to get involved with people unless certain of being liked
(3) shows restraint within intimate relationships because of the fear of being shamed or ridiculed
(4) is preoccupied with being criticized or rejected in social situations
(5) is inhibited in new interpersonal situations because of feelings of inadequacy
(6) views self as socially inept, personally unappealing, or inferior to others
(7) is unusually reluctant to take personal risks or to engage in any new activities because they may prove embarrassing

Source: Reprinted with permission from the *Diagnostic and Statistical Manual of Mental Disorders, Fourth Edition, Text Revision*, 721. Copyright 2000 American Psychiatric Association.

2. Dependent Personality Disorder

CASE EXAMPLE

Ms. H joined a mid-sized, family-owned plumbing firm in her early 20s, hired as a receptionist and bookkeeper. She was a notably loyal employee who never complained, readily took direction, and frequently volunteered for projects others considered tedious or unpleasant. If the company founder had any criticism of Ms. H at all, it was that she was too passive. She never took charge or made decisions, even after years of experience at the company. When the occasional new employee seemed to take advantage of Ms. H, asking her to do things outside her scope or treating her with less than the respect her seniority and devoted service dictated, Ms. H still seemed hesitant to complain. She preferred to be exploited than ever to "make a fuss."

After 23 years, the company founder retired and handed the plumbing business over to his two sons. Violently incompatible personalities, the two brothers began to clash almost immediately. Eight months of bitter feuding later, only the brasher, cruder, younger of the sons remained, his gentler, older rival preferring to retire from the family business altogether.

The younger brother began hiring fun-loving, rather uninhibited employees into the company. Soon, sexual innuendo and bawdy humor were commonplace. For Ms. H, the changes were particularly harsh and personally devastating. A quiet, stout, and somewhat matronly woman, Ms. H suddenly found herself the butt of endless "fat" jokes, "smell" jokes, "old" jokes, and "kinky sex" jokes. Particular delight was taken in commenting about her friendship with a disabled person who had worked with the firm for years. Jokes frequently circulated involving imagined sexual encounters between the two.

Ms. H became particularly hurt when people she had known and worked with for years leapt in to join the contagious fun. She began to wonder whether perhaps she really had become ugly, smelly, and vile. When she attempted to appease her coworkers by redoing her hair and updating her wardrobe, she became the target of only more vicious satire.

Still, Ms. H did not complain. Instead, she developed severe headaches and gastrointestinal problems. She began having nightmares in which she was grossly disfigured and burned at the stake as a witch. She developed spontaneous crying spells, which were worst on Sundays as she faced the start of still another workweek.

Ultimately, Ms. H awoke one Monday morning unable to move her legs. Having grown up caring for a sister stricken by polio, Ms. H instantly recognized paralysis. She dialed for emergency aid and was rushed to a local hospital.

Extensive medical testing uncovered no physiologic cause for Ms. H's inability to walk. Finally, she was evaluated by a psychiatrist, who diagnosed Conversion Disorder. When she subsequently admitted she was hearing unfamiliar voices in the room mocking and laughing at her, the psychiatrist's diagnosis was augmented to include atypical, psychotic depression.

Although Ms. H prevailed in the civil suit she later brought against her former employers, she was stifled in her ability to collect her jury award when the company strategically declared bankruptcy following the verdict. She remained devoted to the end. She commented: "I really feel better this way. I never would have wanted to do anything to seriously hurt that family; they were always so good to me. I hate to think I might have had anything to do with the hardships they're going to be living through now."

The proclivity toward passive-aggressive behavior—the art of punishing others by quietly failing to fulfill their desires or expectations, or even by behaving self-destructively so as to make others feel sorry for what they have done—is one encountered among many of the Axis II disorders, but it forms the centerpiece of Dependent Personality Disorder. Individuals with this disorder tend to rely excessively upon others for emotional support and for important decision making and goal determination. They also are prone to resist overt complaint or demand, relying instead upon indirect methods of communicating, protesting, or retaliating.

Dependent Personality Disorder is the contemporary formulation of Freud's "oral character," a needy, submissive disposition Freud believed to result from fixation (through significant environmental trauma) at the earliest, oral stage of psychosexual development. Such individuals, although overtly needy and reliant upon direction from others, in fact have a highly controlling, manipulative tinge to their character pathology. They essentially force others—intimates, colleagues, supervisors—to take charge of and assume responsibility for their lives. Individuals with Dependent Personality Disorder can never be held accountable, in their view, because they are simply doing what they are told.

Subjects with Dependent Personality Disorder seldom take initiative or make decisions, and they are loath to act independently on projects or generalized assignments unless specific instructions are outlined. These individuals deeply crave nurturance and praise, and they will go so far as to volunteer for duties others disdain in an effort to prove themselves to be dedicated employees. Dependent individuals are terrified of being alone (because they feel overwhelmed and inept if expected to care for themselves), and so they may remain in objectively exploitative, unsatisfying, or abusive relationships just to have some assurance they will be have their needs attended to.

In employment settings, employees with Dependent Personality Disorder are setups for exploitation, harassment, discrimination, and related forms of abuse. They tend to be meek and accepting of behavior others refuse to tolerate, suffering silently to the point of symptom development before standing up for themselves. However, once they are out of the toxic setting, powerful needs to avoid rejection and be liked are removed, and the person may come back to haunt his or her former tormentors with civil suits, or even passive-aggressive retaliatory acts such as industrial theft or sabotage, disclosure of trade secrets, or adverse publicity distributed anonymously to the media. When an employee with Dependent Personality Disorder perceives rejection, withdrawal of support, or excessive demand for initiative or independent thinking, he or she is likely to try all the harder to please, while developing increasing somatic symptoms (such as headaches or gastrointestinal distress), anxiety, and internal tension. The ultimate outcome may be passive-aggressive absenteeism or lateness, or work-product deterioration.

When severely stressed by demands from the environment that they act with autonomy and self-reliance, or as a result of overtly exploitative and demeaning management or peer behavior, subjects with Dependent Personality Disorder may decompensate into depressive syndromes (Dysthymic Disorder or Major Depressive Disorder); anxiety disorders (Panic Disorder with Agoraphobia is particularly common); and somatization disorders, in particular Conversion Disorder, with physiologic manifestation often bearing a fascinating symbolic kinship to perceived workplace stressors. An obedient soldier reluctantly promoted to drill sergeant develops an inability to speak. A female secretary encouraged to touch her male superior inappropriately develops paralysis of both arms. A young man relentlessly teased by coworkers about being "dirty" and "smelly" develops intolerable pain when shower water touches his skin.

Dependent traits are frequent partners to other full-blown Axis II Disorders. Table 6-12 sets forth the conditions necessary for a *DSM-IV-TR* diagnosis of Dependent Personality Disorder.

Table 6-12 *DSM-IV-TR* Diagnostic Criteria for Dependent Personality Disorder

A pervasive and excessive need to be taken care of that leads to submissive and clinging behavior and fears of separation, beginning by early adulthood and present in a variety of contexts, as indicated by five (or more) of the following:
(1) has difficulty making everyday decisions without an excessive amount of advice and reassurance from others
(2) needs others to assume responsibility for most major areas of his or her life
(3) has difficulty expressing disagreement with others because of fear of loss of support or approval. *Note:* Do not include realistic fears of retribution.
(4) has difficulty initiating projects or doing things on his or her own (because of lack of self-confidence in judgment or abilities rather than a lack of motivation or energy)

(5) goes to excessive lengths to obtain nurturance and support from others, to the point of volunteering to do things that are unpleasant
(6) feels uncomfortable or helpless when alone because of exaggerated fears of being unable to care for himself or herself
(7) urgently seeks another relationship as a source of care and support when a close relationship ends
(8) is unrealistically preoccupied with fears

Source: Reprinted with permission from the *Diagnostic and Statistical Manual of Mental Disorders, Fourth Edition, Text Revision,* 725. Copyright 2000 American Psychiatric Association.

3. Obsessive-Compulsive Personality Disorder

CASE EXAMPLE

Mr. I was mid-level manager at a nuclear power facility on the east coast. He was a diligent, hard worker, and known for his highly effective management style. Though Mr. I was perceived by a few workers as excessively rule-bound and perfectionistic, most of his subordinates appreciated his orderly logic, his attention to detail, and his oft-repeated ethical belief in "fairness for everyone, in every situation."

When Mr. I's company was purchased by a larger, international concern, he was transferred to a modernized plant in Southern California and given a promotion in acknowledgment of his years of impeccable service. The transfer was timed fortuitously; Mr. I had just been divorced by his second wife (who claimed "the only thing he can ever love is nuclear power"). He was ready for a change.

Within a few weeks of his arrival in Southern California, Mr. I realized his new position would be a challenge. He considered workers in California to be sloppy and lazy—they did not adhere to the quasi-militaristic schedule and command style customary back east—and they asked questions instead of following orders. Employees, in his view, were "way too prone to bend rules that are there for good reason."

Mr. I's dilemma was that despite its more laid-back culture and the greater individual decision-making authority allowed its rank and file, the California facility seemed to function superbly; if anything, it was producing better product for less cost than its East Coast counterpart. Any efforts Mr. I made to correct the laxity he perceived were met by stiff resistance, employee outrage, and a united union and management stance spotlighting the California facility's record of successes and workplace bonhomie.

Mr. I then began to notice things about his body, and he became increasingly concerned about their meaning. He was sure a mole was growing on his back and had irregular boundaries; no amount of reassurance from his dermatologist could convince him the intruder was not malignant. He thought his stools were becoming black and tarry; repeated blood-free laboratory analyses could not calm his concerns. He noticed a new asymmetry in his face, and related it to the series of strokes that felled his father when Mr. I was just 12 years old.

Within six months of his transfer to California, Mr. I left the workplace on a stress leave. The first medical leave he had taken in 12 years with the company, it also proved to be the last. Mr. I filed a whistleblower claim with the federal energy department while collecting workers' compensation benefits, alleging that the laxity at the Southern California facility made it unsafe, "a powder keg with a nuclear fuse." The allegation blossomed into civil litigation when Mr. I was deemed to be permanently psychiatrically disabled by the stress of having to do battle with what he considered an "intransigent and conspiratorial management" and an "abusive, corrupt union."

Unlike any other Axis II Disorder, Obsessive-Compulsive Personality Disorder can sometimes actually prove beneficial in the workplace, causing more of its innate problems in non-employment-related social settings. Central features include extreme attention to detail, perfectionism, orderliness, and control through strict moralistic adherence to rules, regulations, and procedures.

Those with Obsessive-Compulsive Personality Disorder are often unsettled, tormented souls, never satisfied that anything they have accomplished was done well enough. They tend to be extremely conscientious, and they are perceived by others as rigid and controlling, but only because of their strict adherence to whatever moralistic rule system they believe in. While they can be highly judgmental of those around them, individual decision making can be a painful ordeal for those with Obsessive-Compulsive Personality Disorder, since they feel compelled to carefully consider even seemingly trivial details to disproportionate excess in their drive to make the "perfect" decision.

In the workplace, while the perfectionism and detail orientation of Obsessive-Compulsive Personality Disorder can lead to great success in certain careers, it can result in a management (or interpersonal) style perceived by others as stifling, unreasonable, and preachy. Individuals with Obsessive-Compulsive Personality Disorder may clash with authority figures, and their difficulty making decisions may prove to be a profound impediment in certain environments.

Stressed by perceived criticism or questioning of ranks, rules, or beliefs, employees with Obsessive-Compulsive Personality Disorder are likely to retreat into ever-greater rigidity and obsessive, inflexible thinking. Then are often prone to bringing whistleblower claims should they perceive a violation of their own exceedingly high standards of ethics and morality.

Exposed to prolonged disorder-related stress, individuals with Obsessive-Compulsive Personality Disorder may develop symptoms of disturbed mood or anxiety. They also have a tendency to develop foci of personal or medical concern, sometimes of sufficient magnitude to warrant diagnosis of Hypochondriasis. Contrary to popular conceptions, Obsessive-Compulsive Personality Disorder does not inevitably predict later development of Axis I Obsessive-Compulsive Disorder. However, the two disorders may coexist, and the former does, in isolated cases, seem to serve as precursor to subsequent development of the latter, with its full-blown clinical array of intrusive, disturbing ideas or images recognized as inappropriate but irrepressible (obsessions); ritualized, repetitive behavior patterns deemed bizarre but necessary to prevent fantasized, dreaded events (compulsions); or both.

DSM-IV-TR Criteria for Obsessive-Compulsive Personality Disorder are set forth in Table 6-13.

Table 6-13 *DSM-IV-TR* Diagnostic Criteria for Obsessive-Compulsive Personality Disorder

A pervasive pattern of preoccupation with orderliness, perfectionism, and mental and interpersonal control, at the expense of flexibility, openness, and efficiency, beginning by early adulthood and present in a variety of contexts, as indicated by four (or more) of the following:
(1) is preoccupied with details, rules, lists, order, organization, or schedules to the extent that the major point of the activity is lost
(2) shows perfectionism that interferes with task completion (e.g., is unable to complete a project because his or her own overly strict standards are not met)
(3) is excessively devoted to work and productivity to the exclusion of leisure activities and friendships (not accounted for by obvious economic necessity)
(4) is over-conscientious, scrupulous, and inflexible about matters of morality, ethics, or values (not accounted for by cultural or religious identification)
(5) is unable to discard worn-out or worthless objects even when they have no sentimental value
(6) is reluctant to delegate tasks or to work with others unless they submit to exactly his or her way of doing things
(7) adopts a miserly spending style toward both self and others; money is viewed as something to be hoarded for future catastrophes
(8) hows rigidity and stubbornness

Source: Reprinted with permission from the *Diagnostic and Statistical Manual of Mental Disorders, Fourth Edition, Text Revision,* 729. Copyright 2000 American Psychiatric Association.

D. Personality Disorder Not Otherwise Specified

As noted previously, personality-disordered individuals usually display traits of several of the Axis II diagnoses; a "pure" personality disorder that fits neatly within one of the diagnostic categories is rare. While pathological traits are likely to cluster into the primary groups identified as individual disorders (and therefore meet the criteria for a given diagnosis), such clusters are often accompanied by additional traits formally assigned to alternate disorders.

Sometimes, an individual is encountered who manifests traits of several personality disorders, but those traits do not cluster sufficiently to warrant assignment of any one primary diagnosis. If such an individual clearly is significantly impaired in his or her social, occupational, or other interpersonal functioning by his or her assorted pathological character traits, the diagnosis Personality Disorder Not Otherwise Specified is assigned. This is also the appropriate diagnostic designation when multiple pathological traits have been identified and specific personality disorders are suspected, but their diagnoses cannot be supported by behavioral data amassed to date.

Table 6-14 lists *DSM-IV-TR* criteria for assignation of a diagnosis of Personality Disorder Not Otherwise Specified. Note that the criteria are identical to the diagnostic requirements for personality disorder in general.

Table 6-14 *DSM-IV-TR* Diagnostic Criteria for Personality Disorder Not Otherwise Specified

A. An enduring pattern of inner experience and behavior that deviates markedly from the expectations of the individual's culture. This pattern is manifested in two (or more) of the following areas:
   (1) cognition (i.e., ways of perceiving and interpreting self, other people, and events)
   (2) affectivity (i.e., the range, intensity, lability, and appropriateness of emotional response)
   (3) interpersonal functioning
   (4) impulse control
B. The enduring pattern is inflexible and pervasive across a broad range of personal and social situations.
C. The enduring pattern leads to clinically significant distress or impairment in social, occupational, or other important areas of functioning.
D. The pattern is stable and of long duration, and its onset can be traced back at least to adolescence or early adulthood.
E. The enduring pattern is not better accounted for as a manifestation or consequence of another mental disorder.
F. The enduring pattern is not due to the direct physiological effects of a substance (e.g., a drug of abuse, or a medication) or a general medical condition (e.g., head trauma).

Source: Reprinted with permission from the *Diagnostic and Statistical Manual of Mental Disorders, Fourth Edition, Text Revision,* 689. Copyright 2000 American Psychiatric Association.

IV. Personality Disorders in the Workplace and the Courtroom: Dangerousness and "Righteous Rage"

Two aspects of the interrelationship between personality disorders and employment litigation demand special attention. One is the potential for dangerousness and workplace violence such disorders engender. The other is the particular relevance of these disorders to allegations involving harassment, discrimination, or wrongful termination, and how they may give rise to the "righteous rage" sometimes underlying such allegations.

A. Personality Disorders and Workplace Violence

Many of the personality disorders, and particularly those comprising Cluster B, involve an enormous wellspring of rage held in abeyance to a greater or lesser extent, just below the surface of those whom they afflict.

The Borderline individual is a powder keg of anger, impulsively directed inwardly or outwardly under relevant environmental provocation. The Narcissistic subject responds to perceived devaluation with a rage that can literally reach homicidal proportion in the short term, or that may be nursed by the individual, smoldering over the longer term to drive retaliatory plot, preparation, and ultimate attack. The psychopath (Antisocial Personality Disorder), lacking conscience, feels unconstrained by any force other than probability of success in doing what it takes to achieve those outcomes he or she happens to desire.

Characterologically impaired employees are frequently aggravating, manipulative, or difficult to deal with at their baseline, but they are not dangerous in the sense that they might provoke or be parties to acts of workplace violence. However, when something in the environment causes the pathological features of such employees' long-term personality disorders to become especially salient—when some environmental situation or interpersonal phenomenon pushes the characterological buttons of the disordered employee—these individuals may indeed become vengeful, violent, and patently dangerous.

Forms of potentially violent, dangerous responses to adverse environmental stimulation are somewhat characteristic of the individual personality disorders and have been reviewed within discussions of those disorders themselves. Table 6-15 summarizes the ten *DSM-IV-TR* personality disorders, the classic baseline behaviors that characterize them, and potentially dangerous responses typical of particular disorders when the person perceives himself or herself to have been threatened, demeaned, or interpersonally attacked.

Table 6-15 The Axis II Disorders, Characteristic Baseline Behaviors, and Potentially Dangerous Responses to Characterologically Perceived Threat or Attack

Cluster	Disorder	Characteristic Baseline Behaviors	Potentially Dangerous Responses to Characterologically Perceived Threat or Attack
A	Paranoid	• Unfounded suspicions and defensiveness • Rigid unwillingness to compromise and demand for control • Overconcerns with "personal space," power relationships, perceived slights	• Angry, absolute counterattack through petulance and increased suspiciousness • Devaluation and "crafty, sly" retaliatory schemes • Unwillingness to forgive; festering anger
A	Schizoid	• Social isolation • Avoidance of intimacy • Bland, "removed" affect	• None; tend to withdraw into themselves or flee the scene
A	Schizotypal	• Magical, superstitious thinking and beliefs • Unusual, idiosyncratic dress, behavior, and speech • Social isolation and "affective flattening"	• None; tend to withdraw into themselves, decompensate into frank paranoia, and/or flee the scene • If become delusional, might respond to perceived threat with physically defensive behaviors, but highly unlikely to do so aggressively or proactively

continued

Table 6-15 Continued.
The Axis II Disorders, Characteristic Baseline Behaviors, and Potentially Dangerous Responses to Characterologically Perceived Threat or Attack

Cluster	Disorder	Characteristic Baseline Behaviors	Potentially Dangerous Responses to Characterologically Perceived Threat or Attack
B	Antisocial	• Lack of conscience or remorse • Recurrent rule violation and disregard for feelings of others • "Cost/benefit" analysis, rather than conventional morality, guides decision making and behavior	• Aggressive intimidation • Blatant lies and character assassination • Coldly conceived retaliatory acts, including planful violence
B	Borderline	• "Splitting": All-or-nothing, black-and-white thinking, overidealization alternating with devaluation • Impulsiveness and instability of mood, relationships, self-concept • Explosively passionate reactions, especially to perceived love or abandonment	• Vilification and factionalization in the workplace • Rage-filled outbursts resulting in violent acts directed inward or outward • Passive-aggressive attack through undermining
B	Histrionic	• "High drama" and theatricality • Seductiveness and overt sexuality in behavior and appearance • Impressionistic speech and vague, generalized reasoning	• Vague, generalized allegations often elaborated into colorful, fantastic false allegations • Excessive overemotionality and potential for impulsive violence
B	Narcissistic	• Lack of empathy, leading to self-absorption, insensitivity, feeling of entitlement • Unwillingness to accept responsibility for outcomes • Projection of blame outwards • Rage when perceive criticism, disrespect, or questioning of special privileges	• Immediate rage of potentially homicidal intensity • Rigid, vengeful stance often involving festering anger and planned, delayed violent retaliation
C	Avoidant	• Perpetual fear of ridicule and rejection, leading to avoidance of social or potentially judgmental situations • Hyperalertness to signs of rejection • Shy, unassertive	• None; tend toward passive-aggressive procrastination, absenteeism, abrupt resignation

C	Dependent	• Excessive dependence upon others for support, guidance, and direction • Resist complaint or demand, preferring indirect communication and response • Passive-aggressive resistance	• Little direct danger while within the setting • Once removed, passive-aggressive retaliation through industrial espionage or theft, disclosure of company secrets, adverse publicity, mail bombs or hit men in extreme cases
C	Obsessive-Compulsive	• Perfectionistic, moralistically rule-bound, conscientious, judgmental, detail-oriented • Difficult time making decisions • Overly rigid and monomaniacal	• None; tend to hypochondriasis and increased rigidity and stubbornness, but not violence

B. Personality Disorders and "Righteous Rage"

Personality disorders are relevant to the issue of employer liability in a harassment, discrimination, or wrongful termination lawsuit, in two broad respects.

First, personality disorders often provoke interactions between people which later are alleged to have been imposed upon the plaintiff by others. In this sense, the plaintiff is not merely an innocent victim of another's unprovoked wrongdoing. The plaintiff's own irritability, perfectionism, manipulation of others, or sexually suggestive behavior is often the beginning of a chain of events that ultimately leads to a claim of harassment, discrimination, violation of the Americans with Disabilities Act (ADA), or wrongful termination.

Second, personality disorders typically are relevant to the credibility of the plaintiff's account of the events in question. Individuals with a personality disorder often interpret events in a distorted fashion and rationalize their own unreasonable behavior. Unlike psychotic individuals with patently bizarre perceptions, employees with personality disorders maintain relatively good contact with reality on at least a superficial level. Thus, their accusations, although false, are not obviously bizarre, and on the contrary, may sound quite plausible.

Attorneys confronted with workplace harassment, discrimination, ADA, and wrongful termination claims, whether working for plaintiff or defense, usually are familiar with the use of a forensic psychiatrist or psychologist to assess the nature and extent of emotional distress or pain and suffering allegedly caused by wrongful workplace conduct. However, attorneys are often less familiar with the use of forensic psychiatry or psychology in addressing the validity of harassment, discrimination, ADA, or wrongful termination claims themselves. A forensic evaluation can be an integral component in the assessment of liability as well as of damages in many of these cases, and should be considered by attorneys early in their preparation.

Almost universally, allegations of harassment, discrimination, ADA violations, and wrongful termination arise in one of four broad contexts:

- *The allegation is true.* In this instance, psychiatric involvement is limited to an evaluation of damages. Document review and psychiatric examination focus upon descriptions of the emergence, quality, and degree of symptoms of psychiatric disorder. Questions of preexisting disorders, alternate causality, precipitation of new symptoms versus exacerbation of old ones, and effectiveness and appropriateness of treatment rendered are addressed. Malingering (symptom magnification, falsification, or misattribution) is evaluated with attention to consistency and psychiatric plausibility of symptom emergence, quality, and course, as described in documents reviewed and in various contexts of the examination. Personality traits or disorders resulting in particular vulnerabilities or sensitivities are explored and integrated into the analysis.

- *The allegation is false; the plaintiff knows it, but he or she is blatantly attempting to manipulate the legal system for financial reward.* Forensic psychiatric evaluation of possible malingering is critical in this instance; a detailed search through documents for systematic patterns of inconsistency, opportunistic distortion, and psychiatric implausibility is essential. Questions or situations are included in the psychiatric examination (if one is available), designed to uncover further psychiatric contradictions and implausibilities. Data are sought exemplifying a lifelong pattern of behavior evidencing minimal conscience and a willingness to cheat, steal, or hurt others for personal gain or advantage. Data supportive of a diagnosis of Antisocial Personality Disorder or traits are highly significant in this context.

- *The allegation is false, but the plaintiff sincerely believes it is true.* Forensic evaluation surrounds investigation of the origin of such false belief, usually stemming from either outright psychotic delusion or the distortion of severe personality disorder. In the case of delusion, magical thinking (mind reading, "vision," information from auditory hallucination) is detected in document review and then explored, if possible, at examination, with the goal an elucidation of the nature, quality, and extent of the false belief system. Personality disorders, as discussed earlier, manifest themselves in their characteristic patterns of maladaptive behavior, belief, and expectation (grandiosity or specialness, perpetual victimization and projection of responsibility outward, recurrent self-sabotage with labile fluctuation of mood), and document review and examination center upon a search for evidence of these and related patterns across age and situation. Once the pathological origin of the false allegation is understood, alleged damages become secondary as the forensic expert assists counsel, judge, and jury in understanding the psychiatrically driven misperceptions and distortions that have given rise to the claim.

- *The allegation is false; the plaintiff knows it but out of self-righteousness feels justified in seeking retribution against the employer.* As described earlier in this and Chapter 5, Mental Disorders Commonly Encountered in Employment Litigation, certain severe personality disorders (primarily from Cluster B) and some psychotic disorders give rise to a characteristic fury of extraordinary intensity—a righteous rage—when conditions exist that challenge the core pathological belief systems of the involved disorder. Examples include perceived criticism or humiliation in Narcissistic Personality Disorder, perceived abandonment in Borderline Personality Disorder, and perceived (delusional) threat in various paranoid psychotic disorders. The forensic examiner assists by detecting, in documentary descriptions or through examination questioning and observation, specific patterns of behavior and belief systems that identify the disorders at play. Having made the diagnosis, the examiner then reconstructs and explains how the workplace environment or individuals therein inadvertently inflamed the diagnosed disorders, giving rise to a righteous rage sufficiently intense to motivate a quest for vengeance. Alleged damages become a secondary issue.

To facilitate this level of input into the workup of workplace harassment, discrimination, ADA, and wrongful termination cases, it is most helpful to engage the forensic examiner as early as possible. Psychiatric or psychological input can assist in discovery strategy, including identification and production of documents, formulation of deposition questions, and specification of factual data. With this information, the forensic examiner can provide a focused, relevant independent mental examination of the plaintiff. A foundation of facts and observations is established from which the forensic examiner can provide medical or psychological insights, understandings, and diagnoses to plaintiff or defense legal team, and if necessary, to judge and jury.

V. Treatment of Personality Disorders

There is a widespread myth among some mental health practitioners that personality disorders, particularly those of Cluster B, cannot be treated. With the possible exception of Antisocial Personality Disorder, this information is untrue, and it is a lamentable disservice to those who suffer from these chronic conditions that it continues to be propagated.

It is true that individuals with a personality disorder can be successfully managed only when and if they are prepared to acknowledge that they actually do have a problem they need to address. Almost by definition, one of the central characteristics of Axis II pathology is the conviction on the affected individual's part that there is nothing wrong with him or her. It is the world that is foul; the Axis II subject is no more than an innocent, perpetual victim.

Over time, some of those persons afflicted with character pathology come to acknowledge that at least some proportion of their hitherto miserable life experience, and at least some contributory factor to their history of chronically unsatisfactory interpersonal relationships and volatile, disastrous workplace outcomes, must come from within them. When the Axis II patient is sufficiently fed up to accept that he or she may be playing an active part in his or her ongoing troubles, then and only then is that patient ready for treatment.

A. Acute Intervention and Crisis Management

In the short term, Axis II disorders tend to give rise to a series of acute crises, both in the personal lives of disordered individuals and in the workplace. Short-term management is supportive and goal-directed.

The Cluster B individual is given a venue in which to safely ventilate rage. The Cluster A patient is provided with a nurturant, reassuring therapeutic "container" in which to coalesce the personality, reestablish internal structure and reality testing, and explore what the conditions were that gave rise to the crisis in the first place and how to resolve their toxicity or avoid them in the future. Cluster B and Cluster C patients may be offered more adaptive, realistic strategies for coping with the transient stressors in their personal or vocational environments that are acutely pushing the buttons of their character pathology, and they may be provided with immediate avenues to immunize themselves against such adverse effects. Brief courses of antidepressant, anxiolytic, or antipsychotic medications may be helpful in this regard, and any reactive substance abuse or self-mutilating acting-out behavior (eating disorder, suicidal gesture, ill-advised sexuality) can be addressed through intensification of treatment frequency or even, if necessary, with brief hospitalization.

B. Long-Term Treatment and Restructuring

In the long term, the treatment of personality disorders involves the essential reconstruction by the disordered individual of his or her habitual patterns of interpersonal expectation, interpretation, understanding, demand, and response. The process is twofold. First, the habitually maladaptive patterns must be isolated, identified, and acknowledged by the patient. Second, they must be forsaken and exchanged for more reality-based, socially conventional, interpersonally sensitive expectations, responses, and beliefs. "Self" must gradually be reconstructed and accepted, and boundaries between "self" and "other" erected and fortified.

The therapeutic process is a long and often painful one of frequent psychodynamic encounter, gutsy self-examination and disclosure, and scary substitution of old, maladaptive but reassuringly familiar patterns of experience with new, unknown but ultimately more fulfilling relationships and interactions.

For years, old social reflexes and emotional response patterns will likely persist, although the patient may become more and more adept at recognizing them and stifling his or her propensity to act (with predictably catastrophic consequence) upon them. Over time, new patterns are explored, substituted, and generalized. Gradually, a more socially adaptive, interpersonally facile, reality-based individual emerges.

VI. Effective Forensic Mental Health Workup of Personality Disorders in Employment Litigation

The forensic psychiatric evaluation of mental health claims in employment litigation is complicated by the contributory role that Axis II pathology may play, both in the symptoms ultimately evidenced by the plaintiff at the time of examination and in the matrix of behaviors at the workplace that led to manifestation of the claim in the first place. If, as is recommended, forensic psychiatric consultation is secured early in case preparation, discovery can be oriented from the start to explore both liability and damages from a forensic psychiatric point of view.

A threshold step in the mental evaluation of the plaintiff is for the forensic examiner to establish a consensual frame of reference upon which to base hypotheses regarding Axis I and Axis II pathology. Such a frame of reference typically may include reliable testimony (in the form of affidavits, depositions, or evaluator interviews) from nonlitigant witnesses, describing their observations and experiences at the workplace and surrounding the behaviors and conditions at issue. Is the general consensus that the plaintiff is reality-based in his or her described experience? Or are his or her vision and reaction suggestive of interpretation and experience markedly different from that of others sharing the interpersonal environment under scrutiny? What is the average employee's experience of the plaintiff? Does the plaintiff seem demanding or entitled, volatile or impulsive, seductive yet oblivious to his or her manipulativeness? Does he or she harbor odd or magical beliefs, subscribe to supernatural abilities or mystical powers that have potentially colored workplace experience?

Certainly, determining the disposition of any "he said/she said" legal situation is the province of the finders of fact. However, if the forensic examiner can assist judge or jury by helping them, through psychiatric diagnosis and principle, to understand why there may be such discrepancy—how a psychotic individual might have come to believe discrimination is present through mind reading, or how a Borderline subject dousing fires of chronic rage with alcohol might have come to behave erratically and inappropriately on the job (with characterologically driven alcohol abuse, rather than racial prejudice, giving rise to negative reviews)—such input can prove highly useful to fact finders as they labor to render conclusions on the ultimate issue of liability.

A two-part model is proposed for forensic evaluation of employment litigation claims. The first and threshold step is an assessment of plausibility—does the consensual frame of reference suggest that events occurred as perceived and interpreted by the plaintiff, or does there appear to be significant discrepancy, suggesting fantasy, distortion, exaggeration, or outright historical re-creation?

If the claim appears reality-based and plausible, a standard forensic psychiatric evaluation of damages ensues, with the focus upon Axis I diagnoses and symptoms, preexisting diagnoses and symptoms, alternate stressors, symptom timing and intensity, treatment to date, and prognosis. If, however, the claim appears less plausible—or if contribution of character disorder to current symptom picture is suggested—then thorough assessment of Axis II pathology is indicated. Such analysis involves a detailed search through record review and (if possible) examination, for recurrent patterns of expectation, interpretation, demand, response, and distortion in the examinee's psychosocial interactions, that emerge in varying contexts and at varying times throughout the subject's life experience. Data might surface inferentially in employment records from different employers (including the military), or in legal papers from previous encounters with the courts. It might define itself in descriptions by fellow employees of behavioral patterns, and in interpretations by the plaintiff of his or her significant social relationships. It might be evident in behavior directly evidenced at examination, elicited and noted by a skillful examiner.

Figure 6-1 illustrates the two-stage model proposed for the psychiatric evaluation of employment litigation claims that potentially involve a personality disorder as contributory factor. Table 6-16 displays some of the data that must

Figure 6-1 A Two-Step Approach to the Forensic Mental Health Evaluation of Employment Litigation Claims Potentially Involving Personality Pathology

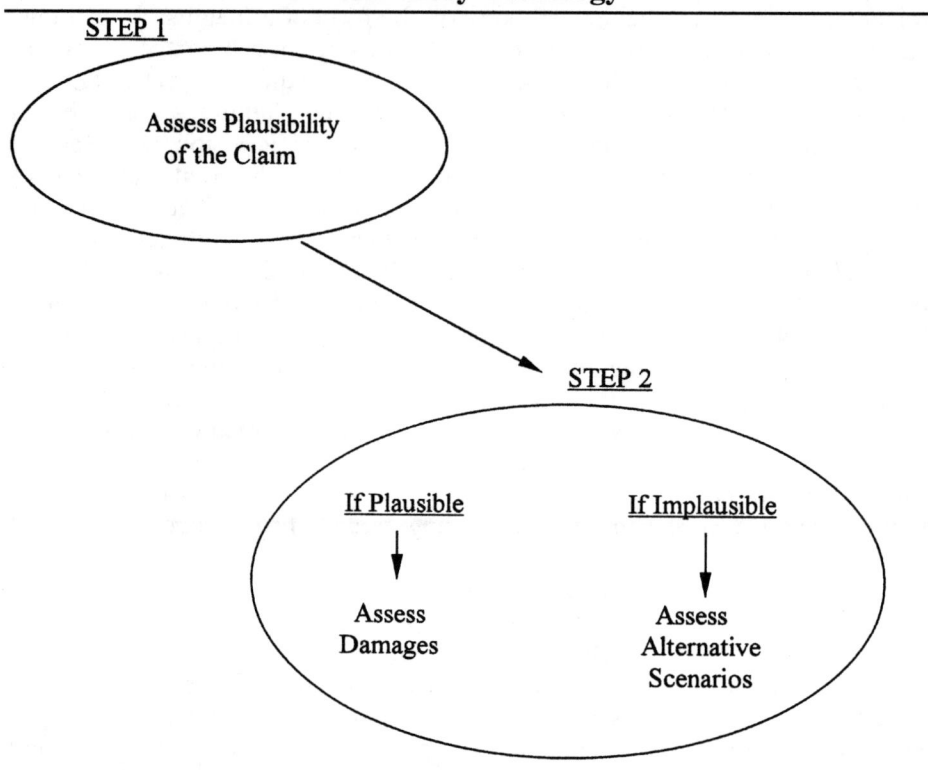

figure into a forensic psychiatric assessment of plausibility in these cases, and Table 6-17 presents a suggested checklist of documents to procure through discovery and to provide to the mental health evaluator involved in the assessment of an employment litigation claim potentially including contributory personality pathology.

Table 6-16 Forensic Psychiatric Data Relevant to Assessing Plausibility of Employment Litigation Claims

- Reliable Coworker Statements
- Timing of the Claims
- Timing of Medical Help Seeking
- Content of Performance Evaluations
- Prior Employment History and Experience
- "Victimization" History
- Psychiatric "Reasonableness" of Claim
- Prior Diagnosis of a Personality Disorder

Table 6-17 Checklist of Suggested Documents to Procure in Discovery for Psychiatric Evaluation of Employment Litigation Claims Involving Possible Contributory Axis II Pathology

- Personnel Records
- Coworker Depositions/Affidavits
- Performance Evaluations
- Prior Work Records
- School Records
- Military Records
- All Hospital Records

- All Medical Records
  - Pediatric
  - Family Practice
  - Internal Medicine
  - Ob-Gyn
  - Specialties

- All Mental Health Records
  - Psychiatry
  - Psychology
  - Counseling (Pastoral, School)
  - Social Work

- All "Alternate" Health Care Records
  - Chiropractor
  - Acupuncture
  - Massage Therapy
  - Hypnotherapy

- Legal Records
  - Workers' Compensation
  - Civil Litigation (Disability, Malpractice, Personal Injury)
  - Criminal Litigation
  - Family Law

- Case-Specific Documents
  - Complaint, Special Interrogatories
  - Depositions
  - Employer Internal Investigation Files

If the frame of reference that is developed suggests that the plaintiff's claims are less than plausible, three scenarios present themselves, and each must be systematically evaluated by the forensic psychiatrist or psychologist through document review and, if available, examination. The three scenarios were discussed earlier in this chapter, and they are outlined in Figure 6-2.

In the initial scenario, the plaintiff is well aware of his or her false claims and is making them simply to manipulate the system and amass undeserved reward. As illustrated in Figure 6-3, in this circumstance behavioral evidence is likely to support a conclusion of Malingering, perhaps driven by Antisocial Personality Disorder. Malingering is specifically addressed later in this text, in Chapter 11.

The second potential scenario is also straightforward. In this case, the allegations are false, but the plaintiff, driven by psychotic thinking (delusional belief and/or instruction delivered through hallucinatory experience) fully and unambiguously believes they are true. The psychosis may be the product of an Axis I disorder or emanate from a personality disorder in the throes of a decompensation (under disorder-specific stress) into a brief psychotic episode. The false belief can also be fueled by the chronically distorted perceptions of one of the severe Cluster A or B personality disorders. Such possibilities are illustrated in Figure 6-4.

The third and final scenario, like that initially described, surrounds a false set of claims knowingly concocted by the plaintiff. However, in this instance, the fabrication is driven by a conviction on the individual's part that he or she is justified in bending the truth in this circumstance, so as to exact revenge upon a person or an institution believed to have wronged the plaintiff so extremely as to deserve harsh punishment. If lying or cheating or conniving is required to realize that goal, the ends are seen as justifying the means. Such is the phenomenon of righteous rage described earlier, an alarmingly common product of the distorted perceptions and expectations, and the underlying chronic rage, of severe Axis II personality disorders. It is the same mechanism that may drive workplace violence when such individuals are "crossed," with their psychopathology ignited by environmental circumstance. Retaliation can be physical, or it can be litigious. In either case, the profound conviction of the actor is that retaliation is deserved and just.

Figure 6-5 depicts the righteous rage scenario and its most common diagnostic antecedents. In Figure 6-6, the forensic psychiatric approach to evaluation of an employment litigation claim is presented in overall summary display.

It is an unfortunate reality that employment settings, with their intrinsic propensity to engender close, intense interpersonal interaction; their fundamental need for supervision, correction, control, and discipline; their likelihood of generating periodic performance feedback and evaluation; and their tendency to foster the development of extracurricular social relationships, constitute as close to the ideal environment for irritation and eruption of character pathology as one might conceive. Acting out in the workplace by those with personality disorders is virtually certain to occur. Employment litigation—righteous, baseless, or founded in righteously believed but factually baseless delusion or lust for vengeance—is, and will remain, an inevitable outcome.

Figure 6-2 Scenarios Underlying Implausible Claims

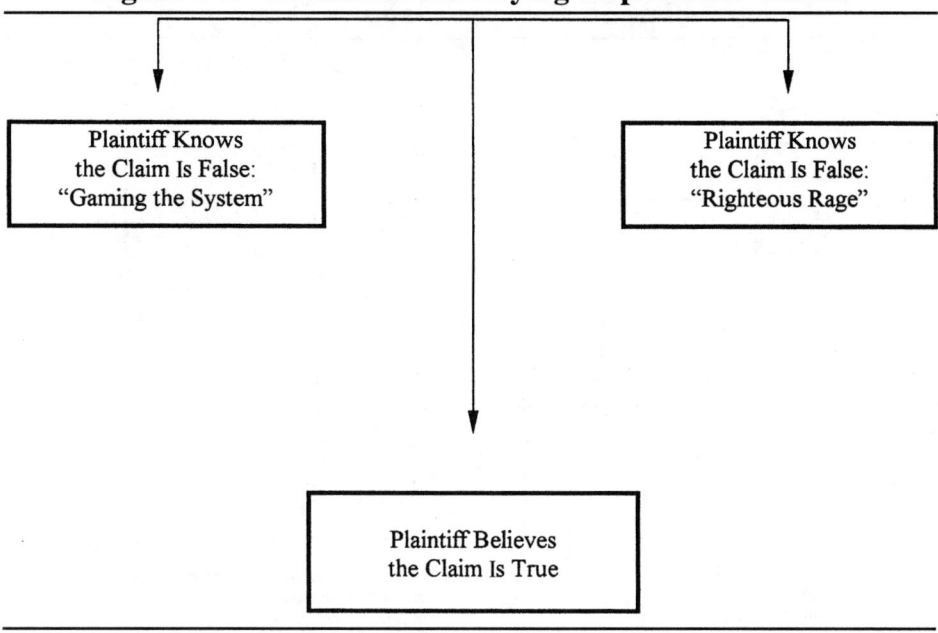

Figure 6-3 Scenarios Underlying Implausible Claims: Plaintiff Knows Claim Is False

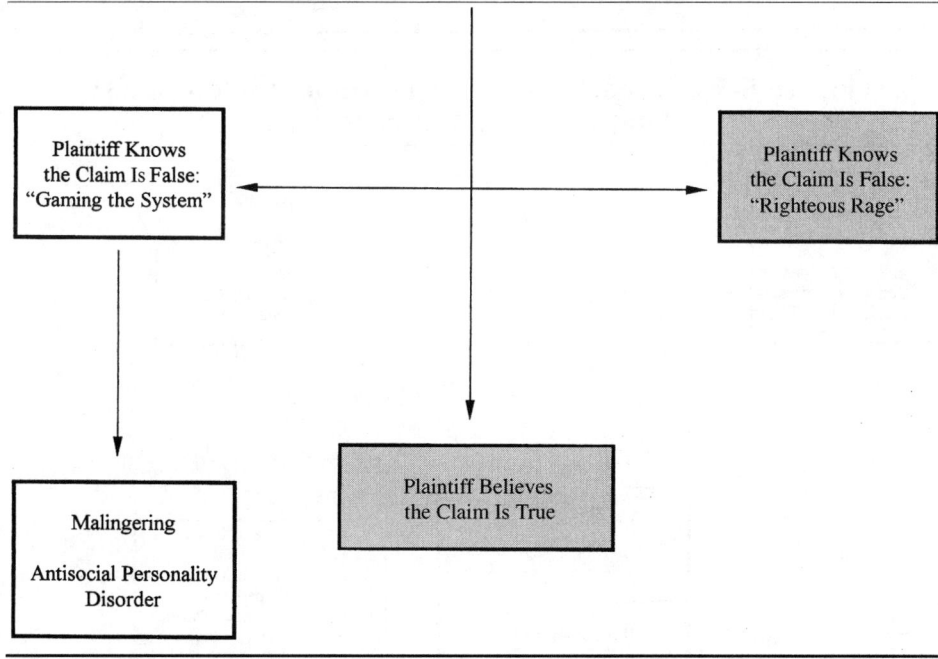

Figure 6-4 Scenarios Underlying Implausible Claims: Plaintiff Believes Claim Is True

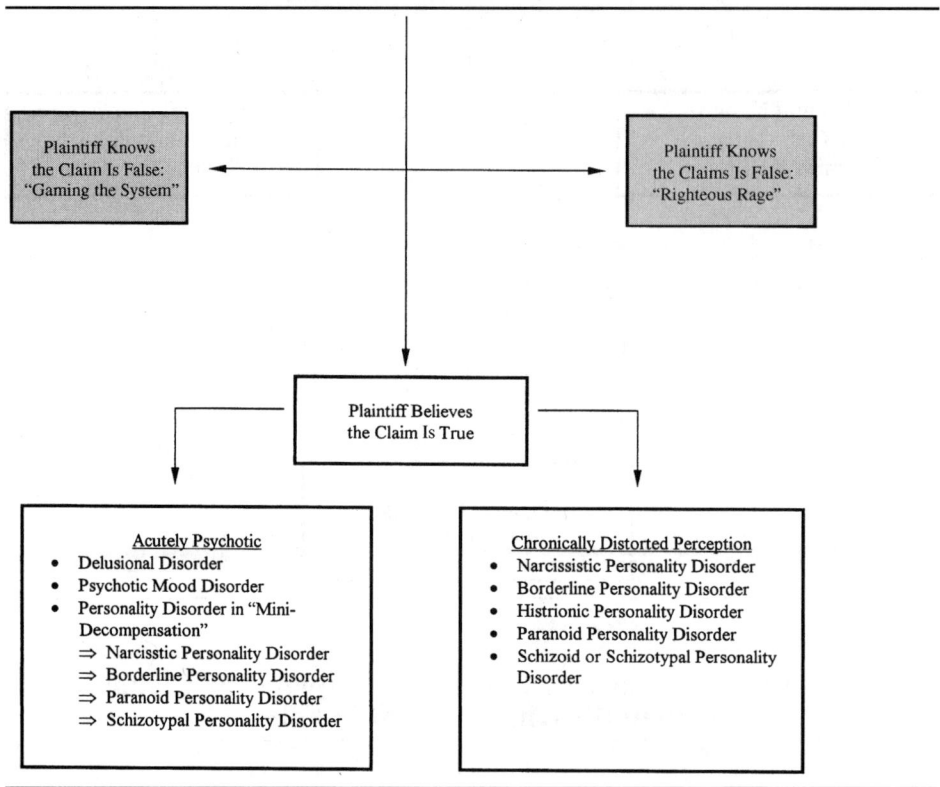

Figure 6-5 Scenarios Underlying Implausible Claims: Plaintiff Knows Claim Is False

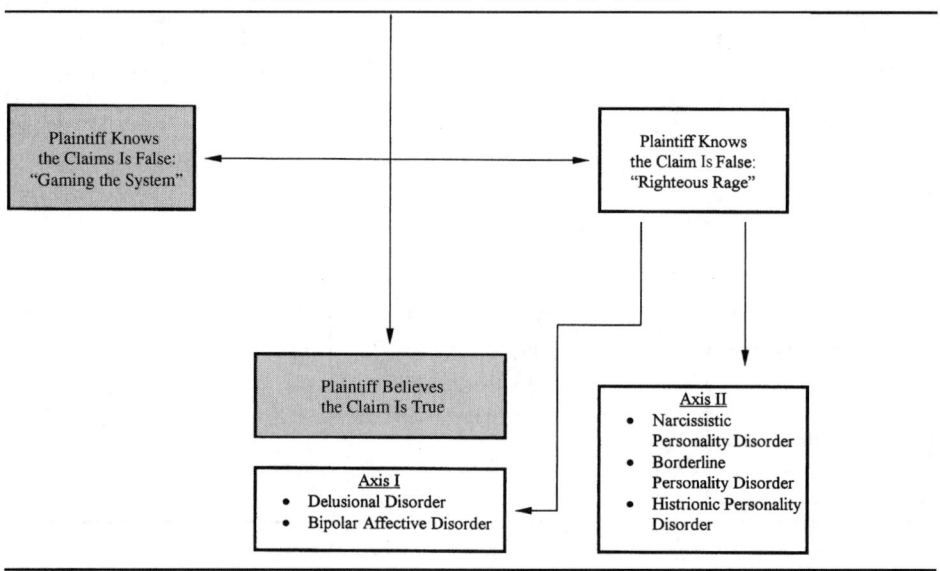

Figure 6-6 Summary:
Forensic Psychiatric Approach to the Evaluation of Employment Litigation Claims

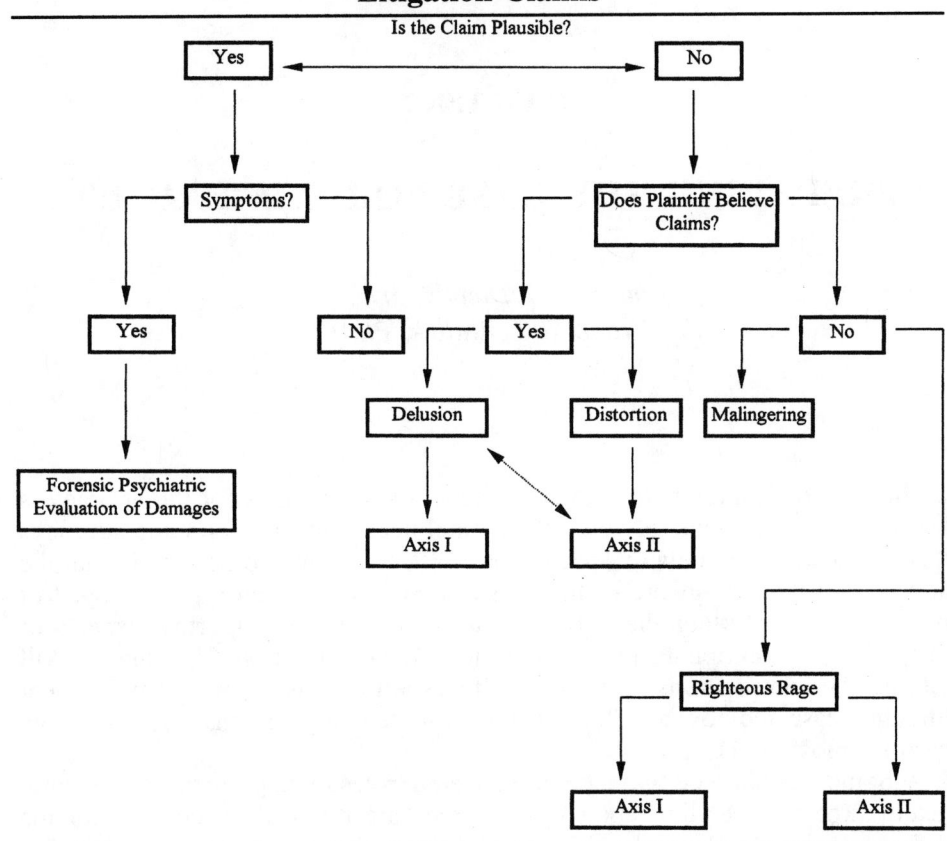

CHAPTER 7

PREPARING THE CASE FOR THE EXPERT

James J. McDonald, Jr., J.D.
Francine B. Kulick, Ph.D.

In the field of employment litigation one of the challenges for the attorney is learning to work effectively with the mental health expert. For some attorneys this will be a totally new experience. For others it will also be new in that the attorney may not be aware of the variety of ways in which a psychologist or psychiatrist can further the attorney's understanding of important aspects of the plaintiff's emotional functioning in this area of litigation. This chapter will discuss the contributions a mental health expert can make in an employment litigation case and how an attorney can facilitate matters so that the expert can perform most effectively.

Some would argue that there are different roles to be performed by mental health experts depending upon whether they are retained by counsel for the defense or for the plaintiff. Although the respective attorneys are performing different roles, the premise of this chapter will be that any expert should perform the same tasks in a forensic evaluation: review all essential records, conduct a clinical interview, and administer psychological testing. The aim should always be to formulate an educated and objective forensic opinion.

I. The Expert's Role

A. Formulating a Forensic Opinion

The expert's formulation of a forensic opinion is akin to using basic aspects of the scientific method. The mental health expert begins by formulating questions rather than presuming a specific sequence of events has occurred. In employment litigation the typical questions would be:

- Has the plaintiff suffered a diagnosable mental disorder at any time period relevant to the pending litigation?

- If so, what is its apparent cause—the workplace event(s) at issue in the litigation, some unrelated cause, or a combination of the two?
- If the workplace was at least partially the cause of the plaintiff's condition, how severe was the injury and what is the prognosis?
- What role, if any, did any preexisting mental or personality disorder of the plaintiff contribute to the workplace event(s) at issue in the litigation?

There is an analogy to be made to doing research. That is, various hypotheses are set forth regarding the plaintiff's emotional functioning. Data are collected from the review of medical records, the clinical interview, and administration of psychological testing which may or may not support these hypotheses. Obviously, one hypothesis is that the plaintiff is suffering a diagnosable mental disorder as defined in the text revision, fourth edition, of the *Diagnostic and Statistical Manual of Mental Disorders (DSM-IV-TR)*[1] and that the sole cause or causes are those alleged in the lawsuit. However, in order to reach an *objective* forensic opinion it is necessary to explore alternative hypotheses, determine whether any diagnosis should be made, and either accept or eliminate other possible causes. These causes might include preexisting and long-standing emotional problems, concurrent or preexisting stressors, or even malingering of a mental disorder. A thorough analysis of all pertinent information must be done in order to accept the explanation that best fits the available data.

A forensic expert is not functioning as a therapist. A therapist is meant to be a supportive figure in a patient's life, and an ally. A therapist takes statements made by a patient at face value. The assumption is made that the person is there only to get help and is entirely motivated to report feelings and events accurately. Unfortunately, an individual involved in litigation *may* also be motivated by secondary gain. That is, the potential for financial remuneration may lead to the fabrication or exaggeration of claimed symptoms or an emphasis on the allegations put forth in the lawsuit as the predominant or sole cause of any emotional difficulty the plaintiff has experienced.

Employment litigation differs somewhat from other civil actions such as personal injury because mental health experts can speak to diagnostic issues involving both liability and damages. Obviously the damages aspect is addressed through the determination of any acute diagnosis of the plaintiff and its apparent cause. Moreover, reports of alleged discriminatory events having occurred in the workplace are affected by an individual's perceptions of those events. The mental health expert may play a role here by determining whether the plaintiff had a lifelong personality disorder that preexisted the events that are the subject of the litigation.[2] For example, one feature of a personality disorder is that it can distort one's perceptions. Statements, actions, or events that may, when viewed objectively, seem innocent may be viewed as persecutory by a personality-disordered employee. The mental health expert can play an important role

---

[1] AMERICAN PSYCHIATRIC ASSOCIATION, DIAGNOSTIC AND STATISTICAL MANUAL OF MENTAL DISORDERS (4th ed. text rev. 2000) [hereinafter DSM-IV-TR].

[2] See Chapter 6, Personality Disorders in Employment Litigation, for a thorough discussion of personality disorders.

in helping the attorney to formulate a theory of the case that takes into account the plaintiff's past history as well as current functioning.

B. Formulating the Theory of a Case

The expert can be helpful in developing the theory of the case, with respect not only to emotional damage issues but often to liability issues as well. In fact, it is essential that counsel and the expert communicate early in the case to determine whether the anticipated role for the expert will be consistent with the overall theory of the case. For example, it would be inconsistent for the defense's fact witnesses to claim unequivocally in a sexual harassment case that the acts alleged by the plaintiff never occurred, while the defense's psychiatric expert simultaneously opines that the plaintiff has a personality disorder that causes her to be hypersensitive to sexual cues and to misperceive the actions and motivations of others. A better approach might be to determine whether there was in fact a kernel of truth to the plaintiff's allegations (i.e., that some relatively innocuous comments were in fact made, but that the plaintiff may have misperceived those comments or taken them out of context as a result of her personality disorder). Obviously, such a theory of the case needs to be fully developed before fact witnesses testify under oath at a deposition.

In most employment lawsuits, the plaintiff claims to have experienced some degree of emotional distress allegedly caused by some unlawful or tortious act in the workplace—typically wrongful termination, discrimination, or harassment. In formulating a theory of the case the expert must first be able to determine the plaintiff's baseline level of emotional functioning. This is a determination of how this person was doing psychologically prior to the claimed mistreatment at work. Determining this baseline is necessary because the expert must then form an opinion as to whether the plaintiff experienced any worsened mental functioning while at work. If this has occurred, a determination must be made as to whether it was related to work itself or to some other set of stressful events in the person's life, or is just another episode in the life of a person with a history of chronic mental problems.

The baseline of one's emotional functioning encompasses two broad areas—whether the individual has had prior episodes of *acute* mental conditions such as some level of anxiety, depression, or thought disturbance and whether he or she has had any lifelong *personality disorder*. Many individuals experience repeated episodes of anxiety or depression across their life spans. A predisposition to this type of mental problem must be distinguished from an emotional reaction to specific workplace events. Determining the presence or absence of such conditions typically requires access to the plaintiff's medical and psychiatric records. Although some background information about a plaintiff's prior psychological functioning is also gathered in the clinical interview, without access to medical and psychiatric records prior to the mental examination it is difficult to determine all potential relevant areas of inquiry into the plaintiff's history and past emotional functioning.

Unlike episodes of depression or anxiety, personality disorders and traits are relatively constant. They affect how people perceive the world and interact with others in their environment. Their presence is sometimes associated with repeated instances of maladjustment in jobs. These core features of an individual's personality are in place by late adolescence or early adulthood; they are not caused by events at work. A mental health expert's ability to form an opinion about an individual's functioning on this dimension is enhanced by access to other psychiatric records and personnel records as well as through the clinical interview and the administration of psychological testing.

Once the expert has been able to review documents and generate hypotheses about the individual's prior level of psychological functioning, it must be determined whether the plaintiff has experienced a diagnosable mental disorder at any point while at the job in question or subsequent to leaving it. This step is accomplished through clinical interview and psychological testing as well as review of pertinent records. Clinical interaction and record review enable the expert to determine all of the potentially stressful events in the plaintiff's life and where work fits into the picture.

When a comprehensive theory of a case has been formulated, the available data tell a story. In some instances, it will be the story of an individual with no prior emotional difficulties developing a well-established diagnosable mental disorder as a result of unlawful conduct in the workplace or adverse events at work. In other instances the story will be of someone who as a result of chronic mental problems, misperceives innocuous events in the workplace as deliberate mistreatment. Between these two extremes are a variety of other potential explanations. The unifying characteristic of any well-formulated theory of a case is that the information about an individual, gleaned from different sources, fits together to help explain what has happened.

Some case examples follow.

CASE EXAMPLE

Role of Concurrent and Preexisting Stressors
Ms. A claimed one primary event of sexually harassing behavior from a supervisor. In the clinical interview she denied having a prior psychiatric history or any other stressful events in her life. Her extensive medical file was obtained. Those records documented a history of outpatient psychotherapy and prescriptions for antianxiety and antidepressant medication prior to beginning her job. She carried diagnoses of chronic depression and anxiety. The records further showed that Ms. A had numerous medical problems. She had also given her physicians a history of several marriages and of having been treated abusively by former spouses. During the time period she was at her job she had marital problems, and her husband was unemployed and involved in his own employment-related lawsuit. She had told one physician that things were so bad she might have to file for bankruptcy.

The set of facts depicted above illustrates the importance of securing medical records (in addition to psychiatric records) for the expert to review. The resulting theory of the case was that the plaintiff had chronic emotional problems and numerous stressors in her life. Further, she had a financial motivation for filing a lawsuit because she had large debts and her spouse was unemployed.

CASE EXAMPLE

Role of Preexisting Personality Disorder

Ms. B was employed in the office area of a factory. She alleged that she had been propositioned and subjected to crude language by coworkers, leading to the development of emotional problems. Her history emerged through her medical records, which were voluminous for someone still in her early twenties. Her psychiatric history included bulimia, alcohol and drug abuse, and a hospitalization for depression. She had little contact with her extended family. In the past she had been both physically and sexually abused by several men. One abuser was a relative. She was in therapy while at the job in question. The treatment notes contained information about all of the stressful events in her life. However, there were no notes documenting complaints about the workplace. In fact, it was described as a safe haven in her otherwise chaotic existence. Following evaluation, testing, and review of records, the theory that received the most support was that she had taken out her anger at other men in her life on her coworkers, which was one consequence of numerous Borderline personality traits if not a full-fledged Borderline Personality Disorder.

In this case medical records helped to provide information about prior psychiatric history as well as prior and ongoing stressful events. The concurrent stressors involved men in her life, but those men were not her coworkers.

CASE EXAMPLE

Plaintiff's Misperception of the Workplace as a Result of a Personality Disorder

Mr. C was a civil servant who had been at the same job for many years. When faced with disciplinary action that held the threat of termination, he filed a lawsuit alleging race discrimination. A review of his voluminous personnel file coupled with extensive observation and clinical interview led to the conclusion that he had a Paranoid Personality Disorder and possibly a Delusional Disorder. He clearly misinterpreted events and easily read threatening meanings into harmless situations.

In this instance the most important element was the review of the personnel file. It was clear that this employee's problems with his superiors had been present for many years while he worked in several different departments. As things deteriorated, he insisted that the cause was discrimination and denied any problems with his functioning as an employee. Unfortunately, he had no insight into his long-standing psychological problems.

CASE EXAMPLE

Medical Explanation for Psychiatric Complaints

Ms. D had worked for many years in a clerical role in the same setting. After some changes in management she complained of sexual harassment by several of her *colleagues. Her medical records were quite complex and indicated a history of thyroid problems. The mental health expert's understanding of them was enhanced through consultation with an endocrinologist. According to the endocrinologist, the records revealed that her thyroid medication regimen was inappropriate. As a result, her hypothyroid condition (with symptoms that mimic depression) was overcorrected and had become a medication-induced hyperthyroid condition (with symptoms that mimic anxiety). The theory was formulated that she had become difficult to work with because her mood fluctuated in an unpredictable way as a result of these underlying medically caused symptoms, and these mood shifts led to conflicts with her coworkers that she perceived as harassment. Unfortunately, she had no insight into her medical problems and the subjective feeling of emotional discomfort that they could create. Her supervisors had no knowledge of her medical condition and simply thought she had developed a poor attitude toward work.*

In this instance medical records offered an alternative medical explanation for the symptoms of anxiety and depression the plaintiff experienced. Further, they provided support for the need for consultation with a medical expert in another area.

CASE EXAMPLE

Clear Major Depression Diagnosis but Uncertain Legal Import

Mr. E had been with the same employer for many years. He was accused of a violation of company rules and was demoted. He brought a claim for age discrimination and wrongful demotion. Medical records showed no prior history of depression. Further, there was no indication of other stressors in his life. Clinical interview and psychological testing both supported the diagnosis of an ongoing Major Depression. The only issue remaining was whether his demotion was lawful or not. In either case, the negative change in his job had clearly led to his becoming seriously depressed. What remained to be determined was a legal issue, outside the expertise of a mental health expert.

In this case the comprehensive review of records made it clear that the only explanation for this man's depression was that it was related to events in the workplace. The fact that an employee suffers a diagnosable mental disorder as a result of an adverse workplace event, however, does not establish a legal wrong. A determination that unlawful conduct occurred must be made before such a plaintiff will be entitled to compensation. The loss of a job can be a traumatic event, particularly for an older or long-term employee. The fact that the individual suffered significant emotional distress as a result of a disturbing workplace event does not automatically entitle the person to damages, however. Liability must still be established.

CASE EXAMPLE

Malingering

Ms. F made claims of sexual harassment and wrongful termination (which she alleged caused her to suffer severe emotional distress) when faced with a layoff at work. Her history indicated that she had filed numerous prior lawsuits and workers' compensation claims. In fact, because she had had several evaluations in the past, she had been administered the Minnesota Multiphasic Personality Inventory (MMPI) on five separate occasions. Examination of the test results showed a pattern. The testing always suggested the presence of malingering. Doctors who had evaluated her in the past also concluded that her psychological complaints were exaggerated. A similar conclusion was reached in this instance following records review, clinical interview, and psychological testing.

In this case the comparison of repeated administrations of the same psychological test was critical in determining a pattern of manipulative behavior coupled with an exaggeration of symptoms.

These case examples illustrate how the plaintiff's psychological condition can be made an integral part of the theory of the case, rather than just an adjunct issue. A mental health professional can provide valuable assistance in this regard, but counsel retaining the expert has an important role to play as well if the expert's contribution to the case is to be most effective.

II. The Responsibility of the Attorney

Even the most savvy and experienced forensic psychiatrist or psychologist will not be effective as an expert witness without substantial support and involvement on the part of the attorney who retains the expert. Counsel's thorough preparation of the case for the expert is essential to a successful resolution. Experts cannot be expected simply to show up with little preparation and give testimony that will win the case. Advance planning and the collection—usually via subpoena—of a considerable amount of background information on the plaintiff are both essential. Close communication with the expert and thorough preparation of the expert's testimony also are very important.

A. Orientation of Less Experienced Counsel

It is certainly common, particularly at large law firms, to have several lawyers working on one matter. The assignment of finding and retaining an expert is often given to the most junior person. This can be problematic if that attorney has no experience working with a mental health expert. To begin this process on the right note, it is important for a more senior attorney to ascertain the level of previous experience of the junior colleague in interacting with mental health experts. If the junior attorney has little or no such experience, a basic orientation should be provided or a more senior attorney should be assigned to the task. A basic orientation would include assisting the junior attorney to locate an expert,[3] establish the proper rapport, and make the necessary arrangements with that individual.

---

[3] Detailed information on the comparative qualifications of various mental health experts is set forth in Chapter 2, The Role of the Mental Health Professional.

B. Timing of Expert Selection

Various timing issues are relevant to engaging a mental health expert. These will of course be more obvious to the attorney seasoned in this area. If counsel hopes to have the expert involved in the development of the theory of the case, early selection and engagement of the expert are essential. The expert cannot be of much use in this regard if he or she is not engaged until just before trial, after all key depositions have been taken and discovery is almost closed. In any event, the attorney must communicate with the expert early enough to allow for the setting of a mental examination and obtaining the necessary records. If the critical time to obtain records and schedule the mental examination is allowed to elapse, the expert can be severely limited in his or her effectiveness.

C. Preliminary Matters

1. The Expert's Background

Counsel should inquire in advance of designating an expert whether the prospective expert has any blemishes in his or her background that might be exploited by the opposition on cross-examination. Examples include malpractice lawsuits, revocation of licenses or professional discipline, loss of hospital privileges, unpaid student loans, and similar matters. Such matters need not necessarily disqualify an expert, but counsel should be aware of them in advance and be prepared to explain them if they become an issue in the litigation.

2. Orientation of the Expert to the Litigation Process

If the expert is not experienced in forensic work, counsel should orient the expert in advance concerning the litigation process, including the unpredictability of court schedules and the nature of cross-examination. Mental health professionals who have not had some experience in the courtroom may be in for an unpleasant surprise if they do not know what to expect. The expert must also have and be willing to spend the time necessary to do a thorough job. The expert must take the time necessary to review all relevant documents prior to the mental examination of the plaintiff, to spend sufficient time conducting the examination, and to devote the time necessary to preparation of an adequate written report (if one is required) and deposition and trial testimony. If a potential expert's schedule will not accommodate these time commitments, counsel should consider whether another expert might be more suitable.

3. Experts from Outside the Jurisdiction

If the expert is coming in from out of town, counsel should ensure that arrangements are made to secure an adequate facility for conducting the mental examination of the plaintiff. Another mental health professional's office borrowed for the occasion, an executive suite facility, or a hotel conference room are the best options. Examinations should not be conducted in an attorney's office, as the atmosphere may be too adversarial. Hotel sleeping rooms similarly should be avoided—particularly where the plaintiff and the examiner are of opposite genders—for obvious reasons.

If the expert will be testifying in a jurisdiction in which he or she is not licensed, counsel must determine whether permission from or notification of the forum jurisdiction's licensing board is required. This is because the conduct of a forensic mental examination and the giving of expert testimony are considered the practice of medicine or psychology in most jurisdictions. Although it is not ordinarily difficult for an out-of-state expert to obtain permission to come into a jurisdiction for the limited purpose of performing a forensic evaluation, the failure to abide by local requirements in this regard could lead to disqualification of the expert or other adverse consequences.

4. Areas Outside the Expert's Expertise

In the course of evaluating a case, occasionally an expert will confront issues that are outside the scope of his or her expertise. For example, in the course of reviewing medical records a psychologist may find references to medications that carry relevant side effects or to a thyroid abnormality. While these items may rather easily be identified by a psychologist, their interpretation is normally outside a psychologist's training and expertise. Consultation between the expert and a psychiatrist, pharmacologist, internist, or endocrinologist may be appropriate. Conversely, a psychiatrist may encounter psychological testing data in the course of reviewing the records of the plaintiff's therapist or another evaluator. Consultation with a psychologist with training and experience in psychological testing would be appropriate.

In many such instances, the expert is already familiar with professional colleagues in related fields who can serve in such a consulting role. In other instances, counsel may need to assist the expert in locating a suitable consultant. Counsel should also expect that the consultant will charge a reasonable fee for his or her time and should ensure that the fee is paid.

5. Financial Arrangements

Counsel and the expert should develop a realistic budget for the cost of the expert's services, particularly if limited funds are available for expert fees. Failure to communicate in this regard can lead to an expert's bill that counsel's client may view as excessive, placing counsel in the difficult position of going into a trial with both an unhappy client and an unhappy expert. Any billing problems must be resolved in advance of trial. If a party owes its expert a substantial amount of money at the time of trial and this fact is exploited by the opposition, the expert's credibility can suffer in the eyes of the fact finder as it may appear that the expert's ability to collect outstanding fees may be contingent upon the outcome of the trial.

D. Obtaining Discovery of the Information That the Expert Will Need

The most effective way for an expert to prepare to conduct a clinical interview of the plaintiff is to review all pertinent documents in advance of the scheduled interview. As experts do not have subpoena power, it is the obligation of counsel to obtain and provide to the expert all the documents that the expert will need to conduct a thorough evaluation, such as records, pleadings, deposition transcripts, and the like. These should be provided to the expert *before* the mental examination of the plaintiff, if possible, so that the expert can develop a context in which to place the data obtained during the examination. On the other hand, counsel must be careful not to inundate the expert with unnecessary documents, as this will likely just confuse the issues and unnecessarily increase the cost of the expert's services.

1. Legal Documents to Provide to the Expert

Counsel should provide the expert with the following documents from counsel's own files or as they become available:

- Complaint or last amended version
- Transcripts of the deposition of the plaintiff
- Transcripts of the depositions of key defense witnesses, such as the decision maker in a termination case or the alleged harasser in a harassment case
- Any other discovery responses (for example, interrogatory responses, statement of damages) relating to alleged emotional injuries
- Transcripts of the depositions of opposing medical and psychological treatment providers and experts

The entire transcript of a particular deposition should be provided. If counsel provides only excerpts of the transcript, the expert could be vulnerable on cross-examination; for example: "Doctor, did you review all the material you considered important, or just that selected information that opposing counsel allowed you to see?"

2. Records to Obtain and Provide to the Expert

Counsel additionally should obtain and provide the following records to the expert.

A. PSYCHOTHERAPY AND OTHER TREATMENT RECORDS Records of all the plaintiff's treating physician(s) and psychotherapist(s) should be obtained, including patient questionnaires, treatment notes, billing records, and psychological testing materials and answer sheets (see Exhibit 7-1 for sample subpoena language).

Patient questionnaires should be obtained because these often contain a detailed account in the plaintiff's own handwriting of family history and even prior sexual abuse; prior major illnesses, hospitalizations, and mental health treatment; and a description of current symptoms.

Treatment notes may reveal a variety of useful information.[4] They often reflect discussions between patient and therapist concerning prior or concurrent alternative stressors, such as childhood sexual abuse or marital discord. They may additionally reflect treatment for medical conditions that produce psychological symptoms—for example, thyroid imbalances. They also may reveal that the patient is taking medications that may produce relevant side effects.

Billing records should be obtained for two purposes. First, they will ordinarily reveal whether the expert is owed any significant amount of money at the time of trial that may indicate a financial bias. Second, billing records should be matched with treatment notes to ensure that all such notes were produced. If there are billing entries but no therapy notes for particular therapy sessions, further inquiry of the treatment provider should be made.

Psychological testing materials and answer sheets should be obtained so that the tests may be rescored. Data-entry or hand-scoring errors are not uncommon, and sometimes an expert or treatment provider will take only selected portions of a test's results into account in rendering a diagnosis instead of the entire test profile. A rescoring of the test data and an interpretation of the entire test profile may reveal significant errors in the opposing expert's test interpretation. If the opposing expert or treatment provider refuses on ethical grounds to produce testing materials to counsel, arrangements should be made for the production of such materials directly to counsel's expert.

Exhibit 7-1 Sample Language for Subpoena for Psychiatric or Psychological Treatment Records

Any and all medical, psychiatric, and psychological records relating to the diagnosis and/or treatment of [NAME OF PLAINTIFF], SSN: _____, DOB: _____. This request includes, but is not limited to, any and all intake documents, patient questionnaires, patient history notes, patient diaries, clinical notes, MMPI/MMPI-2 and all other psychological testing materials (including answer sheets and scoring analyses), laboratory test results, therapy notes, treatment records, medications administered and/or prescriptions written, insurance records, billing records, medical-legal reports, correspondence with attorneys for the patient, records and correspondence relating to referrals of this patient to other health care providers, reports and records of other health care providers relied upon by you in diagnosing and treating this patient, and any other records or reports pertaining to the treatment and/or evaluation of this patient.

B. PRIOR MEDICAL RECORDS Records should be subpoenaed from the plaintiff's family or general practice physician, other physicians who treated

---

[4] *See* Magee v. Paul Revere Life Ins. Co., 178 F.R.D. 33 (E.D.N.Y. 1998) (where plaintiff's therapist refused to produce treatment notes covering therapy conducted during certain period, therapist was precluded from testifying at trial concerning any aspect of therapy conducted during that period).

the plaintiff in the past (including gynecologists for female plaintiffs), any providers of prior mental health treatment, and any hospitals in which the plaintiff was treated (see Exhibit 7-2 for sample subpoena language).

Exhibit 7-2 Sample Language for Subpoena for Medical Records

Any and all medical, billing, and insurance records related to your admission, diagnosis, evaluation, and/or treatment of [NAME OF PLAINTIFF], SSN: _____, DOB: _____. This request includes, but is not limited to, any and all intake documents, patient questionnaires, patient history notes, clinical notes, results, surgical records, radiology reports, laboratory test results, therapy notes, treatment records, medications administered and/or prescriptions written, insurance records, billing records, medical-legal reports, correspondence with attorneys for the patient, records relating to referrals to this patient to other health care providers, reports and records of other health care providers relied upon by you in diagnosing and treating this patient, and any other records or reports pertaining to the treatment and/or evaluation of this patient.

Prior medical records are essential for determining whether the physical and mental symptoms attributed by the plaintiff to the workplace are in fact the result of other causes. For example, many plaintiffs claim that workplace events caused them to suffer depression and/or anxiety. Yet depression and anxiety are often chronic conditions that existed prior to and apart from any specific workplace events. The best evidence of a preexisting depression or anxiety consists of prior medical records reflecting treatment for those conditions. In many cases, such treatment is provided by a primary care physician (family practitioner or internist) or gynecologist. Records from those providers may contain references to patient complaints of depression or anxiety, to referrals to mental health professionals, or to prescriptions for antidepressant or antianxiety medications. Lists of common antidepressant and antianxiety medications are set forth in Tables 7-1 and 7-2. Medical records also sometimes contain indications of earlier and ongoing personal and family problems that are causing psychological symptoms.

Table 7-1 Common Antidepressant Medications

Brand Name	Generic Name
Prozac	fluoxetine
Paxil	paroxetine
Zoloft	sertraline
Serzone	nefazodone
Wellbutrin	buprorion
Desyrel	trazodone
Elavil	amitriptyline

continued

Table 7-1 Continued.
Common Antidepressant Medications

Brand Name	Generic Name
Effexor	venlafaxine
Tofranil	imipramine
Pamelor	nortriptyline
Sinequan	doxepin
Luvox	fluvoxamine
Anafranil	clomipramine

Table 7-2 Common Antianxiety Medications

Brand Name	Generic Name
Buspar	buspirone
Xanax	alprazolam
Ativan	lorazepam
Librium	chlordiazepoxide
Valium	diazepam
Klonopin	clonazepam
Serax	oxazepam
Tranxene	clorazepate

Another type of preexisting depressive condition is Bipolar Disorder (formerly known as manic-depressive disorder), which is characterized by periods of depression punctuated by episodes of mania. It is commonly treated with lithium carbonate, Eskalith, Tegretol, or Depakote.

These (and other) medications may often cause side effects that a plaintiff may misattribute to the workplace. For example, a common side effect of popular antidepressant medications such as Prozac, Paxil, and Zoloft is diminished libido. Often, plaintiffs in employment cases claim that being fired or harassed caused them to lose interest in sex. In such situations, it should be determined whether diminished libido may in fact be attributable to side effects of antidepressant or other medications.

Plaintiffs in employment cases often complain of insomnia as a result of job difficulties or termination. An examination of the plaintiff's medical records should be conducted to determine whether such insomnia preexisted the workplace events at issue. Medications commonly prescribed for insomnia include Halcion, Ambien, Dalmane, ProSom, and Restoril.

Finally, the plaintiff may have a medical disorder that produces psychological symptoms.[5] One such disorder that sometimes appears in employment cases is hyperthyroidism, which is also known as Graves' Disease. Hyperthyroidism, which occurs predominantly in women, results from an overactive thyroid

---

[5] *See* E. KLONOFF & H. LANDRINE, PREVENTING MISDIAGNOSIS OF WOMEN (1997).

gland and is characterized by symptoms such as tension, agitation, irritability, insomnia, anxiety, and emotional lability. The opposite condition, hypothyroidism, is characterized by symptoms such as fatigue, weakness, depression, and impaired memory and concentration. These conditions are diagnosed via a series of blood tests known as a thyroid panel. Results of these thyroid panels may be found in the records of a plaintiff's primary care physician, gynecologist, internist, or endocrinologist. There are three main tests in the thyroid panel—T3, T4, and TSH (thyroid stimulating hormone). The thyroid panel report is easy to interpret, as most reports indicate the normal range for each test and indicate when a score is out of range. An abnormally high T3 or T4 score, or an abnormally low TSH score, may indicate hyperthyroidism. An abnormally low T3 or T4 score, or an abnormally high TSH score, may indicate hypothyroidism. Any thyroid panel results in a plaintiff's medical records thus should be examined closely, in consultation with a qualified medical practitioner, to determine whether the plaintiff's reported psychiatric symptoms may actually be attributable to a thyroid condition.

Another common condition in women is mitral valve prolapse, which is a heart valve abnormality that causes the heart to race and the person to experience anxiety and even panic attacks. As one authority recently noted, "every patient who presents with panic or generalized anxiety disorder should be asked about prior cardiac history."[6] Thus, where a plaintiff complains that the workplace caused her to suffer anxiety or "panic attacks," her medical records should be examined for evidence of mitral valve prolapse.

Records of prior hospitalizations should also be examined to determine whether the plaintiff suffered a prior trauma or serious illness that may have produced lingering emotional symptoms. Hospitalizations resulting from prior sexual assaults or domestic violence ordinarily would be extremely relevant in a sexual harassment lawsuit. Hospitalizations resulting from prior drug overdoses or substance abuse would be extremely relevant where a possible personality disorder on the part of the plaintiff is at issue. Hospitalizations resulting from a violent physical assault or serious bodily injury would be relevant where a plaintiff is claiming to suffer from Posttraumatic Stress Disorder as a result of something that happened at work Certainly, records of any prior psychiatric hospitalizations should be scrutinized carefully for evidence of suicidal behavior, psychotic episodes, chronic depressive conditions, Axis II pathology, and substance abuse.

Occasionally a plaintiff will object to subpoenas for his or her medical records on the ground that they are overbroad or unduly intrusive. It is impossible in most cases to know in advance, however, just which records may be relevant. A gynecologist's records may reveal a prescription for antidepressant medication that preceded the workplace events in question, or a biopsy and attendant cancer scare that occurred at the same time the plaintiff claims to have suffered anxiety from an abusive boss. A urologist's records may reveal sexual dysfunction in a male plaintiff that would contradict his claim in the lawsuit that his

---

[6]*Id.* at 81.

sex life was fine until he lost his job. An endocrinologist's records may reveal a thyroid dysfunction or a hormonal deficiency that may produce an emotional disturbance. A limitation on records to be subpoenaed to include only those "directly relevant to the emotional distress alleged in the action" thus is superficially appealing, but it begs the question of what is truly relevant. All records containing evidence of preexisting or concurrent stressors that could rationally have caused or contributed to the emotional symptoms of which the plaintiff is complaining are relevant.

C. PERSONNEL RECORDS The plaintiff's personnel files from current and prior employers should be obtained and provided to the expert (see Exhibit 7-3 for sample subpoena language). Personnel files frequently contain valuable information concerning the plaintiff's behavior in other workplaces that might provide clues to the existence of a personality disorder or other preexisting psychopathology. Performance evaluations from prior employers, for example, might contain admissions by the plaintiff concerning certain personality traits relevant to the instant litigation, such as difficulty getting along with coworkers and supervisors. Multiple complaints of harassment or unfair treatment in prior jobs may indicate hypersensitivity or a "victimlike" mentality. Varying employment histories given on different employment applications may evidence a deceptive or evasive quality. Multiple job terminations for misconduct might reveal an antisocial personality, whereas an unstable pattern of moving from job to job in a variety of industries may suggest an identity disturbance characteristic of a Borderline Personality Disorder.

Exhibit 7-3   Sample Language for Subpoena for Personnel Records

All documents contained in the personnel file of [NAME OF PLAINTIFF], SSN: _____, DOB: _____, including, but not limited to, all documents reflecting terms of employment, employment applications, resumes, documents reflecting compensation and earnings, benefits, job duties, discipline, reasons for leaving, internal complaints or grievances, and any claims or lawsuits filed against your organization by this individual.

D. EDUCATIONAL RECORDS The plaintiff's school and college records, including any current school records, should be obtained (see Exhibit 7-4 for sample subpoena language). Sometimes emotional difficulties date back to the elementary or high school years. Dropouts, disciplinary problems, and teenage substance abuse may be evidence of a personality disorder. For example, *DSM-IV-TR* notes that "[i]ndividuals with Borderline Personality Disorder may have a pattern of undermining themselves at the moment a goal is about to be realized (e.g., dropping out of school just before graduation)."[7] Similarly, diagnosis of Antisocial Personality Disorder requires evidence of a Conduct Disorder (such

---

[7]DSM-IV-TR, *supra* note 1, at 708.

as aggression to people or animals, destruction of property, deceitfulness or theft, or serious rule violations) prior to age 15.[8] Although subpoenas for such records sometimes will draw an objection that a plaintiff's educational records are too remote in time to be relevant to the issues in an employment lawsuit later in adult life, it is precisely because they are so remote that they are so relevant. Personality disorders, by definition, begin in adolescence or early adulthood.[9] Although educational records are not by any means the only vehicle for diagnosing personality disorders, they can provide a key form of confirmation that a plaintiff's dysfunctional behavior and psychiatric symptomatology are the result of a personality disorder that long preexisted the plaintiff's entry into the defendant employer's workplace.

Further, some individuals are in school during the time period where they claim to have suffered serious emotional difficulties. Indications of a downturn in performance during this time would offer support for their complaints. Conversely, indications of high functioning in school could indicate an individual who is able to concentrate and is not hampered by symptoms of anxiety or depression. High functioning in classwork can also belie a plaintiff's claim of being psychologically disabled from working.

Exhibit 7-4 Sample Language for Subpoena for School Records

Any and all academic records pertaining to [NAME OF PLAINTIFF], SSN: _____, DOB: _____, including, but not limited to, academic transcripts, disciplinary records, counseling records, and attendance records.

E. RECORDS OF DIVORCE AND CHILD CUSTODY PROCEEDINGS Court files in divorce cases may contain relevant information on the plaintiff's background, such as financial problems, prior mental health treatment, and even criminal activity. Affidavits given in support of motions for protective orders may contain information about the other spouse's violent tendencies, emotional instability, or substance abuse problems. Of course, the source of such information must be taken into account. Accusations launched in the midst of a bitter divorce may not be the most reliable source of information on a plaintiff, but they might at least provide valuable leads for further investigation.

Information relating to a plaintiff's ex-spouse's violent or abusive behavior also might reveal that the plaintiff is displacing the undesirable traits of the ex-spouse onto an accused harasser in the workplace.

Records of contested child custody proceedings, although sealed in some jurisdictions, may contain considerable detail of a plaintiff's prior emotional and substance abuse problems. They also may contain reports of formal psychiatric or psychological evaluations performed to determine the plaintiff's fitness as a parent. These reports also may contain valuable information about a plaintiff's mental health treatment history.

---

[8]*Id.* at 706.
[9]*Id.* at 685.

Divorce and related court records are accessible to the public in most jurisdictions, so all that is required to obtain them is to send a copy service to the courthouse to copy them.

F. Prior Court Cases Civil and criminal index searches ordinarily should be run on a plaintiff. A criminal history not only may be relevant to possible impeachment of the plaintiff's trial testimony, but it may also suggest the existence of a personality disorder, particularly where theft, violence, or substance abuse is involved.

A plaintiff's prior civil lawsuits may reveal a pattern of similar behavior with other employers. A plaintiff who claims to have experienced the same kind of harassment or discrimination at the hands of several unrelated employers may suffer from more than just unfortunate coincidence. In addition, transcripts of the plaintiff's depositions in other recent lawsuits should be subpoenaed from the court reporting service or one of the lawyers involved. Such transcripts not only may reveal a fact pattern similar to that in the instant litigation, but they may also contain sworn testimony that the plaintiff suffered severe and debilitating emotional distress as a result of the acts of another defendant, thus constituting fairly potent evidence of alternative causation.

A prior bankruptcy case involving the plaintiff may be relevant in a number of respects. Obviously, it is evidence of a potential alternative stressor. It may also reflect spending habits or attitudes toward money and responsibility indicative of a personality disorder.

G. Workers' Compensation Files A number of employment lawsuits are preceded by, or proceed concurrently with, a workers' compensation case involving some of the same issues of emotional injury. The file relating to the workers' compensation proceeding may include psychiatric reports on the plaintiff, including psychological test results. Also, the plaintiff may have given testimony at a hearing or deposition in the workers' compensation case that may be inconsistent with the theory of the plaintiff's case in the subsequent lawsuit. If the plaintiff has initiated a workers' compensation proceeding, all files relating to that proceeding therefore should be obtained.

CASE EXAMPLE

The plaintiff in a sexual harassment lawsuit claimed to have suffered severe emotional injuries causing her to be unable to work for two years, to be hospitalized in a psychiatric institution, and even to attempt suicide. Yet a review of the records of her most recent psychiatric hospitalization revealed that the plaintiff told intake personnel that "family problems" were the cause of her most recent suicide attempt. The court file relating to her prior divorce and child custody case contained an affidavit of her ex-husband that described an earlier suicide attempt and psychiatric hospitalization, as well as her participation in a drug rehabilitation program. Records of her gynecologist revealed that she suffered two miscarriages during the preceding 18 months. Her high school records indicated that she dropped out during her freshman year after failing every class but one. Personnel files from her prior employers revealed that she had been fired from several jobs, that she misrepresented her academic and work history on several employment applications, and that she had filed a sexual harassment charge against a prior employer. Court records revealed prior convictions for prostitution and passing bad checks. All of these factors would suggest, at the very least, that the plaintiff's current emotional condition is not wholly the result of what happened to her at her last job.

3. Information to Obtain During the Plaintiff's Deposition

Defense counsel can assist the expert by obtaining some basic background information on the plaintiff during the plaintiff's deposition. This not only provides the expert with a "base" of information on the plaintiff prior to conducting the Rule 35 mental examination, but it elicits the information at a stage in the litigation where the plaintiff is not as likely to have been coached. The following questions might be asked, depending upon the nature of the plaintiff's claims.

Symptoms Suffered

1. **What specific symptoms of emotional distress have you suffered?**
2. [For each symptom:] **When did you begin experiencing the symptom?**
3. [For each symptom:] **When did you stop experiencing the symptom?**
4. [For each symptom:] **How often did you experience the symptom?**
5. [For each symptom:] **Is there anyone who can verify that you experienced the symptom?**
6. [For each symptom:] **Did you ever experience that symptom prior to [the workplace incident that led to the lawsuit]?**
7. [For each symptom:] **Did this symptom prevent you from working? How? For how long? Did it affect your life in any other way? How? For how long?**

Medical Treatment Received

1. [For each symptom:] **Did you receive any treatment for it? From whom?**
2. [For each doctor:] **What was the doctor's full name and office address? What kind of doctor?** [e.g., psychiatrist, psychologist, counselor, internist, chiropractor]
3. [For each doctor:] **When did you first see this doctor? Are you still seeing him/her? When was your last visit? How many times did you see him/her?**
4. [For each doctor:] **Who referred you to this doctor?**
5. [For each doctor:] **Who is paying this doctor?** [e.g., private health insurance, workers' compensation, lien against lawsuit proceeds]
6. [For each psychiatrist/psychologist/marriage/family therapist (MFT):] **Did you fill out a questionnaire during your first visit? Did you answer the questions honestly?**
7. [For each psychiatrist/psychologist/MFT:] **Did you take any psychological tests? Did you take a test of about 500 true-false questions?** [MMPI] **Did you take it home with you to fill out or did you do it in the doctor's office? Did the doctor show you a series of ink blots and ask you what you saw?** [Rorschach]

8. [For each psychiatrist/psychologist/MFT:] **Did the doctor interview you during your first visit? For how long? What kinds of questions did he/she ask? Was anyone else present? Did the doctor take notes?**
9. [For each psychiatrist/psychologist/MFT:] **Did the doctor arrive at a diagnosis? What was it? Did the doctor prescribe a treatment plan? What was it?**
10. [If treatment involved counseling:] **How many counseling sessions did you attend? Who conducted them? Were they group or individual? Did the doctor take notes during the session? Did the doctor ask you to keep a diary or take notes of any kind?**
11. [If treatment involved counseling:] **Did you talk about [the workplace incident] with the doctor during counseling? What did the two of you discuss about it? What other issues did you talk about in counseling?**
12. [If treatment involved counseling:] **Are you still going to counseling? When was your last visit? Did the counseling help? Has the doctor told you how long you will need to continue counseling?**
13. [For each psychiatrist:] **Did the doctor prescribe any medicines? Which ones?**
14. [For each medication:] **When did you start taking it? Are you still taking it? When did you last take it? Did it help? Did it produce any side effects? Describe.**
15. [For each medical doctor:] **Did you fill out a questionnaire during your first visit? Did you answer the questions honestly?**
16. [For each medical doctor:] **Did the doctor run any tests? Which ones? Do you know what the results were?**
17. [For each medical doctor:] **Did the doctor prescribe any medicines? Which ones?**
18. [For each medication:] **When did you start taking it? Are you still taking it? When did you last take it? Did you stop taking it on your own, or at your doctor's direction? Did it help? Did it produce any side effects? Describe.**
19. [For each medical doctor:] **How many times did you see the doctor for this condition? Did you get better? Are you still seeing the doctor for this condition?**

Medical History

1. Have you ever been hospitalized? When? What for?
2. Were you ever treated at a psychiatric institution? When? What for? Inpatient? Outpatient?
3. Have you ever received treatment or counseling from a psychiatrist? From a psychologist? From any other mental health professional? Identify each doctor, including office address.
4. [For each period of treatment:] Why did you seek treatment? What was the diagnosis? What treatment did you receive? How long did you receive treatment? Were you given medication? What kinds? Did you take them? For how long? Any side effects?
5. Have you ever suffered from:
   —depression?
   —anxiety?

—panic attacks?
—manic-depressive disorder?
—nervous condition?
—heart disease (including, for women, mitral valve prolapse)?
—cancer?
—high blood pressure?
—thyroid problems?
—sexual difficulties?
—alcoholism? (ever go to Alcoholics Anonymous?)
—drug addiction?
—eating disorders (anorexia or bulimia)?
—head injury?
6. Has anyone in your family suffered from:
—depression?
—manic-depressive disorder?
—alcoholism?
—drug addiction?
—Has anyone attempted suicide? Did they succeed?
7. Identify all doctors seen, for whatever reason, during your period of employment. Include type of doctor, office address, and what prompted the visit.
8. Identify (including office address) all doctors who served as your personal physician (general practitioner/family doctor) for the ten years prior to the start of your employment.

Relevant Social History

1. **Have you ever been divorced?** [If so, get:]
   —name of spouse
   —date of divorce
   —court in which divorce decree was entered
   —who got custody of children. (Was it contested?)
2. **Have you ever applied for a restraining order against anyone?** [Get details.]
3. **Are your parents living? Where?** [If deceased:] **When did they die?** [If deceased after plaintiff began working for defendant:] **How did the death affect you?**
4. **Have you ever had a spouse die? A child?**
5. [For women, in a sexual harassment case:] **Have you ever been raped or sexually assaulted?**
6. [For women, in a sexual harassment case:] **Were you ever molested by your father or a male relative? Were you a victim of incest?** [Get details.]
7. [If incest or molestation:] **Did you ever receive counseling or treatment?** [Get details.]
8. **Have you ever been fired from a job?** [Get details.]
9. **Did you ever feel harassed or discriminated against in previous jobs? Did you file a complaint, either internally or with an outside agency? Did you file a lawsuit?**
10. [If married:] **Have you ever been separated? Have you ever received marriage counseling?**

11. Have you ever sued anyone? Have you ever been sued by anyone?
12. Have you ever been convicted of or pled guilty to a crime?
13. Have you ever filed for bankruptcy?

E. Setting the Stage for the Mental Examination of the Plaintiff

It is counsel's responsibility to make arrangements for the expert to conduct a forensic mental examination of the plaintiff. This is typically more complicated than simply making an appointment.

It is sometimes difficult to arrive at an agreed-upon date for the mental examination. Sometimes experts are asked to block out several dates on their calendars. A comprehensive mental examination is typically an all-day event. Therefore, it is unfair to expect a busy mental health professional to reserve these dates indefinitely. It is counsel's responsibility to do what is necessary to obtain confirmation of a date. Further, it is helpful for all involved to ensure that there are no last minute cancellations or failures to appear at the designated time.

In most jurisdictions, a motion and court order may be required for a mental examination of the plaintiff.[10] While such a motion will not be required if the plaintiff's counsel agrees to produce the plaintiff for an examination, in the event an agreement is not made, defense counsel must allow enough time for a noticed motion to be heard and for the examination to proceed prior to the discovery cutoff. Sometimes a plaintiff's attorney may agree to produce the plaintiff for an examination, but on terms—a limitation on time or questions to be asked, or having an attorney present—that defense counsel and/or the expert may find unacceptable. In such an event, a motion will have to be brought and the same time considerations will have to be taken into account. Counsel should never just wait until the last minute and assume that the plaintiff will be produced by agreement.

No matter what the parameters that are to apply to the examination, they should be worked out well before the individual arrives for the scheduled appointment. It is extremely difficult for the mental health expert to establish the necessary rapport with the plaintiff if the examination begins with a series of desperate phone calls because the expert and the plaintiff have totally different ideas about what is about to occur. Additional pragmatic issues to be addressed before the exam date include determining whether the plaintiff requires an interpreter, needs any accommodations for a physical disability, or should be reminded to bring reading glasses in order to complete the psychological testing.

---

[10]The legal standards that govern such motions are discussed in Chapter 9.

Table 7-3 Checklist for Preparation of Case for the Expert

- [ ] Select expert early, so as to allow expert to participate in the development of the theory of the case.
- [ ] Check to ensure that expert has no issues in his or her background that might be exploited on cross-examination.
- [ ] Ensure that expert is familiar with the litigation process and will have the time and flexibility necessary to perform well as an expert.
- [ ] If expert will be examining the plaintiff and/or giving testimony in a jurisdiction where he or she is not licensed, ensure that local practice requirements of that jurisdiction's regulatory authority, if any, are satisfied.
- [ ] If expert will have to address issues outside his or her expertise, ensure that a suitable consultant with the requisite training and expertise is located.
- [ ] Arrive at an understanding with expert as to what his or her fees and expenses are likely to be, as well as an agreement that the expert will notify counsel in advance if it appears that the estimated budget will be exceeded.
- [ ] Provide expert with complaint, transcripts of the depositions of the plaintiff and key defense witnesses, any other written discovery responses relating to alleged emotional injuries, and transcripts of the depositions of opposing medical and psychological treatment providers and experts.
- [ ] Provide expert with plaintiff's personnel file.
- [ ] Obtain and provide expert with the plaintiff's psychotherapy records.
- [ ] Obtain and provide expert with the plaintiff's medical records.
- [ ] Obtain and provide expert with the plaintiff's personnel records from previous employers.
- [ ] Obtain and provide expert with the plaintiff's school and college records.
- [ ] Obtain and provide expert with court records of any divorce and/or child custody proceedings involving plaintiff.
- [ ] Obtain and provide expert with court records of any prior lawsuits in which plaintiff was involved, especially documents relating to claims for mental or emotional injuries.
- [ ] Obtain and provide expert with court records of any bankruptcy involving plaintiff.
- [ ] Obtain and provide expert with records relating to workers' compensation proceedings initiated by the plaintiff, especially documents relating to alleged mental or emotional injuries.
- [ ] Question plaintiff at deposition concerning symptoms of mental or emotional injury, treatment received, medical and mental health history, social history, family background, prior criminal and civil cases, bankruptcies, divorces, and child custody disputes.
- [ ] If expert will be performing mental examination of plaintiff out of town, ensure that an adequate facility (another clinician's office or a hotel conference room) is secured for that purpose.
- [ ] Ensure that all arrangements and conditions for mental examination of plaintiff are understood and established in advance of examination.
- [ ] Ensure that expert is paid all fees and expenses accrued to date before trial.

CHAPTER 8

THE RIGHT TO PRIVACY VERSUS THE NEED FOR DISCOVERY

James J. McDonald, Jr., J.D.

The right of plaintiffs to privacy and the right of defendants to due process are frequently in tension in employment litigation. Plaintiffs have increasingly raised privilege and privacy issues in employment lawsuits as defendants, in the course of defending emotional damage claims, have sought to conduct discovery into personal matters such as medical and psychological treatment, marital and relationship history, work history, and prior traumas. The courts have struggled to establish boundaries for permissible discovery designed to allow defendants to obtain the discovery they need—albeit sometimes intrusive—while at the same time preventing defendants from conducting searching inquiries of little relevance that serve mostly to embarrass a plaintiff.

The California Supreme Court put this issue in focus in the case of *Vinson v. Superior Court*,[1] where it explained:

> In the case at bar, plaintiff haled defendants into court and accused them of causing her various mental and emotional ailments. Defendants deny her charges. As a result, the existence and extent of her mental injuries is indubitably in dispute. In addition, by asserting a causal link between her mental distress and defendants' conduct, plaintiff implicitly claims it was not caused by a preexisting mental condition, thereby raising the question of alternative sources for the distress.[2]

The *Vinson* court went on to maintain that "plaintiff cannot be allowed to make her very serious allegations without affording defendants an opportunity to put their truth to the test."[3] Courts are usually faced with the challenge, therefore, of balancing a plaintiff's various privileges and privacy rights against a defendant's

---

[1] 43 Cal. 3d 833, 239 Cal. Rptr. 292, 44 FEP Cases 1174 (1987).
[2] *Id.* at 839–40, 239 Cal. Rptr. at 297, 44 FEP Cases at 1176.
[3] *Id.* at 842, 239 Cal. Rptr. at 298, 44 FEP Cases at 1177.

need to obtain discovery of potential causes of the plaintiff's mental and emotional condition that may have nothing to do with the workplace events that are the subject of the lawsuit.

Two key legal developments in the last decade have generated considerable litigation regarding the employer's right to discovery versus the employee's right to privacy. One is the U.S. Supreme Court's recognition, in *Jaffee v. Redmond*,[4] of a federal common law psychotherapist-patient privilege. This set the stage for considerable debate over whether and to what extent a plaintiff alleging emotional injury will be deemed to have waived this privilege, which in turn defines the permissible scope of an employer's discovery of the mental health records of a plaintiff in an employment lawsuit. The other key development was the amendment of Federal Rule of Evidence 412 to restrict discovery into the sexual behavior of plaintiffs in sexual harassment cases. This amendment triggered substantial controversy over whether a defendant in a sexual harassment lawsuit may discover and use evidence of a plaintiff's sexual conduct and comments inside and outside the workplace, as well as any history of sexual abuse suffered by the plaintiff. This chapter will examine the rapidly developing law in these areas.

I. Scope and Waiver of Privileges

A. Medical and Psychotherapy Records

Subpoenas or requests for a plaintiff's medical and psychotherapy records are frequently countered with the claim that the records are covered by the physician-patient or psychotherapist-patient privilege. In *Jaffee v. Redmond*,[5] the U.S. Supreme Court recognized a federal common law psychotherapist-patient privilege. Noting that all 50 states and the District of Columbia recognize such a privilege,[6] the Court held that the privilege will extend in federal cases to communications between a psychiatrist, psychologist, or licensed social worker and a patient in the course of psychotherapy. Courts have recently extended the *Jaffee* privilege to other types of records as well, such as unlicensed employee assistance program (EAP) records,[7] and records of a general practitioner who was consulted for mental health concerns.[8] The *Jaffee* Court noted, however, that "[l]ike other testimonial privileges, the patient may of course waive the protection."[9] This has produced considerable litigation over whether and to

---

[4]518 U.S. 1 (1996).
[5]*Id.*
[6]*Id.* at 12 n.11.
[7]Oleszko v. State Comp. Ins. Fund, 243 F.3d 1154, 85 FEP Cases 483 (9th Cir. 2001).
[8]Finley v. Johnson Oil Co., 199 F.R.D. 301, 85 FEP Cases 117 (S.D. Ind. 2001).
[9]518 U.S. at 15 n.14.

what extent a plaintiff waives the psychotherapist-patient privilege by asserting a claim for psychological injuries in an employment lawsuit.

1. Cases Viewing Waiver Broadly

One line of cases holds that a plaintiff waives the physician-patient or psychotherapist-patient privilege in litigation by asserting a claim for physical or mental injuries. For example, in *Sarko v. Penn-Del Directory Co.*,[10] the plaintiff sued, alleging that her discharge violated Title VII, the Age Discrimination in Employment Act (ADEA), and the Americans With Disabilities Act (ADA). She claimed an ADA violation in that she was suffering from clinical depression at the time of her termination. The defendant sought records of each of the plaintiff's medical providers identified in interrogatory responses, including those of her psychiatrist. The court rejected the plaintiff's claim of privilege, holding that a plaintiff waives the psychotherapist-patient privilege recognized in *Jaffee* by placing her mental condition at issue in a case. The *Sarko* court thus ordered the production of all the plaintiff's medical and psychiatric records, emphasizing that to allow a plaintiff to hide behind a claim of privilege when the condition is placed directly at issue in a case would be contrary to the most basic sense of fairness and justice.[11]

Courts that view the waiver of the psychotherapist-patient privilege broadly typically hold that once a plaintiff has put her mental condition at issue by alleging that the defendant caused her to suffer emotional distress, the defendant may explore the plaintiff's psychological history to determine whether alternative causes of the plaintiff's psychological condition may exist. In *Cleveland v. International Paper Co.*,[12] for example, the plaintiff sought to prevent discovery of her medical history by arguing that she suffered only "ordinary" stresses and psychological injury as a result of discrimination and harassment, and by pointing out that she did not seek treatment for any of the matters raised in her lawsuit. The court rejected this rationale, holding that where a plaintiff seeks to recover damages for mental anguish and emotional distress, the defendant is entitled to conduct discovery into the plaintiff's medical history to show that

---

[10] 170 F.R.D. 127, 7 AD Cases 195 (E.D. Pa. 1997).

[11] *Accord* EEOC v. St. Michael Hosp., 74 FEP Cases 993, 994 (E.D. Wis. 1997) (ordering disclosure of marriage counseling records where plaintiff claimed that workplace discrimination disrupted her marriage; "it is axiomatic that a plaintiff cannot brandish a sword and deny the defense a shield"); EEOC v. Kidder, Peabody & Co., 62 FEP Cases 899 (S.D.N.Y. 1993) (ordering production of records of plaintiff's medical doctors where plaintiff claimed that the workplace caused her to suffer various medical conditions); Ferrell v. Glen-Gery Brick, 678 F. Supp. 111, 46 FEP Cases 502 (E.D. Pa. 1987) (holding that right to privacy in medical records is waived by plaintiff's placing her mental state in issue, and noting that "an individual who wishes to receive the benefits of the judicial system should not be allowed to impose an additional burden on the system by withholding necessary information central to her claim").

[12] 74 FEP Cases 1661 (N.D.N.Y. 1997).

the claimed emotional distress "was caused at least in part by events and circumstances that were not job related."[13]

The plaintiffs in *Lanning v. Southeastern Pennsylvania Transportation Authority*[14] similarly sought to bar the defendant from gaining access to their psychiatric and gynecological records by arguing that they were not seeking damages for any specific psychiatric injury, they did not plan to offer expert witness testimony on their emotional damage claim, they did not seek to recover the costs of mental health treatment, and they were not pursuing a separate claim for intentional infliction of emotional distress. The court nonetheless held that the plaintiffs had waived the psychotherapist-patient privilege, and that in spite of their attempts "to limit damages regarding emotional distress, the claim for emotional distress remains a part of plaintiffs' action."[15] Further, reasoned the court, the defendant's right to discovery does not depend upon the manner in which the plaintiffs choose to present their claim. As long as they seek to recover damages for emotional distress, "[d]efense counsel has a right to inquire into plaintiffs' pasts for the purpose of showing that their emotional distress was caused at least in part by events and circumstances that were not job related."[16]

Likewise, in *Miranda v. Mount Sinai School of Medicine*,[17] the court rejected the plaintiff's argument that the defendant should be able to discover only those medical records that related to the issue of whether and to what extent the defendant's discrimination caused the plaintiff to suffer emotional harm. The court refused to impose such a narrow limitation. It maintained that the defendant is entitled to explore other possible stressors that are not job related that could have caused the plaintiff's emotional distress.[18]

In *Gatewood v. Stone Container Corp.*,[19] the plaintiff in a race discrimination action attacked the defendant's subpoena for his medical and psychiatric records as overbroad, irrelevant, and an invasion of privacy and stressed that he did not receive any treatment for the emotional distress allegedly resulting from discrimination. Noting that the defendant was seeking $100,000 in damages for mental and emotional anguish, the court narrowed the scope of the subpoena somewhat but permitted the discovery. It remarked:

---

[13]*Id.* at 1664 (quoting Bridges v. Eastman Kodak Co., 850 F. Supp. 216, 223, 64 FEP Cases 1100, 1104 (S.D.N.Y. 1994)).

[14]1997 WL 597905 (E.D. Pa. Sept. 17, 1997).

[15]*Id.* at *2.

[16]*Id.* (citing Lowe v. Philadelphia Newspapers, Inc., 101 F.R.D. 296, 298, 44 FEP Cases 1224, 1225 (E.D. Pa. 1983)).

[17]68 FEP Cases 546 (S.D.N.Y. 1995).

[18]*Id.* at 547. *But see* Pasternak v. Texaco Inc., 1997 WL 621267 (S.D.N.Y. Oct. 7, 1997) (denying motion to compel plaintiff's preinjury medical records, on the ground that speculation that plaintiff might have suffered some unknown physical condition that might have in turn caused a psychological injury was insufficient to justify intrusive discovery).

[19]170 F.R.D. 455, 78 FEP Cases 1251 (S.D. Iowa 1996).

> Generally, a defendant is entitled to discover whether there have been other stressors relating to plaintiff's mental and physical health during the relevant time period which may have contributed to the claimed emotional distress. This is not diminished by the fact [that] plaintiff has not sought medical or mental health care for the emotional distress resulting from the claimed discrimination.[20]

In *Fritsch v. City of Chula Vista*,[21] the district court overruled a magistrate judge's ruling that a plaintiff did not waive the psychotherapist-patient privilege by asserting a claim for emotional distress. The court opined that, if presented with the question, the Supreme Court would adopt a broad view of the waiver. It noted that the Supreme Court had submitted a proposed Rule of Evidence, Rule 504(d)(3), stating that the psychotherapist-patient privilege would not apply to communications regarding a patient's emotional condition if the patient relied upon that condition as an element of a claim in litigation. The court also observed that California has a similar psychotherapist-patient privilege,[22] accompanied by a statutory patient-litigant exception,[23] and that the California Supreme Court had ruled that a patient seeking damages for severe emotional distress waives the privilege.[24] Noting that the plaintiff sought $1 million in damages for emotional distress, the court held:

> Fritsch can testify to her emotions near the incident, and defendant is free to cross examine her about the depth of her emotional damage and other factors in her life at the time. But to insure a fair trial, particularly on the element of causation, the court concludes that defendants should have access to evidence that Fritsch's emotional state was caused by something else.[25]

The courts have allowed discovery into a variety of potential alternative stressors. In *Alden v. Time Warner, Inc.*,[26] noting that by seeking $2 million in damages for emotional distress allegedly caused by age discrimination, the plaintiff "clearly placed his emotional health at issue," the court compelled disclosure of the plaintiff's marriage counseling records. It explained: "Marital difficulties significant enough to prompt counseling are likely to have been an independent cause of emotional distress."[27] The court also ordered production of the plaintiff's substance abuse treatment records, noting that "drug and alcohol abuse surely contribute to emotional distress."[28] The court did not permit discovery of the plaintiff's family doctor's records, however, pointing out that

---

[20]*Id.* at 460.
[21]196 F.R.D. 562 (S.D. Cal. 1999).
[22]CAL. EVID. CODE §1010.
[23]CAL. EVID. CODE §1016.
[24]In re Lifschutz, 2 Cal. 3d 415, 85 Cal. Rptr. 829 (1970).
[25]196 F.R.D. at 568.
[26]1995 WL 679238 (S.D.N.Y. Nov. 14, 1995).
[27]*Id.* at *2. *But see* Tylo v. Superior Ct., 55 Cal. App. 4th 1379, 64 Cal. Rptr. 2d 731 (1997) (limiting deposition questioning of plaintiff concerning prior marital difficulties pursuant to California's constitutional right to privacy).
[28]*Id.* at *3.

the plaintiff was not claiming to have suffered any physical injury as a result of discrimination and that the defendant did not identify any physical condition that might have been an independent cause of the plaintiff's emotional distress. Conversely, in *Workman v. Carolina Freight Carriers Corp.*,[29] the court permitted discovery of medical records indicating that the plaintiff had been diagnosed with a sexually transmitted disease, because "the revelation that a person had a sexually transmitted disease would cause considerable emotional distress."[30]

Courts that view the waiver broadly also reject attempts by plaintiffs to limit a defendant's access to evidence of potential alternative stressors via manipulative litigation tactics. For example, in *Vann v. Lone Star Steakhouse*,[31] the court ordered disclosure of the plaintiff's psychotherapist's records where the plaintiff was seeking damages for emotional distress allegedly resulting from sexual harassment. In *Vann*, the plaintiff designated her treating psychiatrist as a testifying expert but then sought to prevent the disclosure of the psychiatrist's records on the ground that they were exempt from discovery under a state law providing that personal notes of a therapist are exempt from discovery. The court held that state law exemptions from discovery do not apply in nondiversity cases and that there is no similar exemption under federal law.[32]

Similarly, in *Doolittle v. Ruffo*,[33] the plaintiff initially claimed that her psychological condition was entirely the fault of defendants. When it was discovered that the plaintiff had suffered some significant childhood traumas, she attempted to limit discovery into those matters by changing her claim to exclude damage from childhood incidents and arguing that defendants should be barred from discovery into those matters. The court rejected that argument and maintained that the defendants were entitled to explore other potential stressors.

In *Sidor v. Reno*,[34] the court rejected the plaintiff's challenge to the defendant's subpoena for her treating psychologist's records. The plaintiff argued that since she did not plan to call her psychologist to testify at trial (but planned to designate a different clinician as her expert) there was no waiver of the psychotherapist-patient privilege. The court observed: "[P]laintiff may not in fairness select from the psychiatric testimony available and preclude defendant from learning the content of other records."[35] Similarly, the court in *EEOC v.*

---

[29] 65 FEP Cases 1209 (M.D. Ala. 1994).

[30] *Id.* at 1210.

[31] 967 F. Supp. 346, 75 FEP Cases 1131 (C.D. Ill. 1997).

[32] *Accord* Wynne v. Loyola Univ. of Chicago, 1999 WL 759401 (N.D. Ill. Sept. 3, 1999) (following *Vann*).

[33] 1997 WL 151799 (N.D.N.Y. Mar. 31, 1997).

[34] 8 AD Cases 18 (S.D.N.Y. 1998).

[35] *Id.* at 20. *See also* Adams v. Ardcor, 196 F.R.D. 339 (E.D. Wis. 2000) (plaintiff cannot avoid producing earlier psychological records involving a child custody dispute by retaining a different psychologist to testify at trial without consulting those earlier records); Kirchner v. Mitsui & Co., 184 F.R.D. 124 (M.D. Tenn. 1998) (district court reversed magistrate judge's ruling that the plaintiff was required to produce only the

Danka Industries, Inc.[36] rejected the plaintiffs' attempt to bar discovery of the records of their prior psychotherapists. It observed: "[F]airness requires a waiver of privilege. Plaintiffs cannot rely on advice given by certain psychotherapists to support their claims while at the same time expect to keep confidential advice given by other psychotherapists that may weaken their claims."[37]

Likewise, in *Sanchez v. U.S. Airways*,[38] the court rejected the plaintiffs' attempts to prevent discovery of psychotherapy records and ordered that the records be produced or the plaintiffs' claims for emotional damages be stricken. In that case a former airline employee and his wife sought emotional damages over his firing, which he alleged was discriminatory. Upon the defendant's request for their psychotherapy records, the plaintiffs' attorney reviewed the records and asserted that their "relevance to this case was quite limited and that they primarily contained other communications." The court rejected this assertion, noting that "[i]t is not for a party to determine, by a unilateral review of documentation, whether information is relevant to the case."[39] The court found the fact that the plaintiffs' therapy addressed other matters was a key reason for disclosure of the records. It explained:

> Essentially . . . what the Plaintiffs ask the Court to do is to allow them to make a claim for emotional and mental distress, but disallow the Defendant from discovering information about the myriad causes of their distress. Plaintiffs admit that factors unrelated to this action were involved in their decision to seek psychotherapy. The exact nature of these factors is presently unknown, but, their existence may serve to undercut or extinguish Plaintiffs' claims for emotional distress. If the records show that certain stress factors pre-dated Mr. Sanchez's termination, or that other factors unrelated to this litigation occurred after the termination, then Defendant could show that Plaintiffs' claims are either baseless, overblown or insubstantial.[40]

The court refused the plaintiffs' request that the defendant be limited to asking them whether they obtained treatment and what the causes of the unrelated emotional distress were, and that the defendant be prohibited from deposing their therapist or examining his records:

> Though it is true that this approach would protect the sanctity of the records, it would allow the Plaintiffs to proceed with a claim on unequal terms. Plaintiffs would be allowed to divulge what they wanted, and to independently assess the quantum of harm caused by Defendant's actions and the other, unrelated stress factors. Though convenient to Plaintiffs, this approach is unsatisfactory to our adversarial system of justice. It would be unfair to allow Plaintiffs to unilaterally

---

medical, psychological, and social worker records that would be relied upon by her expert at trial).

[36]990 F. Supp. 1138, 75 FEP Cases 685 (E.D. Mo. 1997).
[37]*Id.* at 1142, 75 FEP Cases at 688.
[38]2001 WL 311271 (E.D. Pa. Mar. 29, 2001).
[39]*Id.* at *3.
[40]*Id.*

determine the amount of harm Defendant caused, without allowing the Defendant or the fact-finder to argue, consider and weigh other relevant factors of emotional stress.[41]

The court also rejected the plaintiffs' argument that the records should not be discovered because the plaintiffs were not planning to put on expert testimony regarding their emotional injuries. It maintained that "just because Plaintiffs do not choose to use an expert does not mean that Defendant cannot use an expert to discredit Plaintiffs' claim," and in any event the plaintiffs' plans not to use an expert do not make their psychotherapy records "inviolable."[42]

In *Jackson v. Chubb Corp.*,[43] the court, applying a broad reading of the waiver, rejected the plaintiff's argument that disclosure of her psychotherapy records would interfere with her ongoing mental health treatment. In that race discrimination case, the plaintiff conceded that she had placed her mental condition in issue by alleging that she suffered specific psychiatric disorders as a result of workplace events, as well as including claims for intentional and negligent infliction of emotional distress. Yet she moved to bar the discovery of her treatment records and submitted an affidavit from her therapist claiming that disclosure of her records would compromise the effectiveness of her treatment. The court explained:

> While this Court recognizes the fundamental principle that effective psychotherapy is largely dependent on confidentiality between therapist and patient, it is similarly cognizant that a defendant against whom a claim of emotional distress has been asserted is helpless in mounting an adequate defense without all the relevant evidentiary materials.[44]

The court continued:

> [A] plaintiff in need of continuing psychotherapy will be forced to make the unenviable choice between seeking damages for his/her ongoing emotional distress and thereby waiving the privilege as to ongoing treatment, or forego recovering damages for the ongoing distress. The Court is certainly not insensitive to the Hobson's choice visited upon such a plaintiff. While there are undoubtedly elements of unfairness when a plaintiff who has allegedly suffered emotional or mental harm at the hands of a defendant is forced to choose between either unfettered psychotherapy or the right to claim relief for all harm continuing into the future, it would nonetheless prove more inequitable to permit a plaintiff to recover damages for a claim based upon selective disclosure, and bar a defendant from gathering the necessary evidence with which to present a defense.[45]

The *Jackson* court found especially significant the fact that the plaintiff wished to introduce evidence of recently diagnosed conditions such as Posttraumatic

---

[41]*Id.* at *4.
[42]*Id.* at n.7.
[43]193 F.R.D. 216 (D.N.J. 2000).
[44]*Id.* at 225.
[45]*Id.* at 226.

Stress Disorder, yet sought to prevent discovery of the records documenting such diagnoses. It remarked that the plaintiff could protect her current therapy records from disclosure by abandoning her claim for current emotional distress.[46]

One court has held that a defendant may conduct discovery of a plaintiff's psychiatric history even where the plaintiff is not seeking damages for emotional distress. In *Covell v. CNG Transmission Corp.*,[47] the plaintiff in a sexual harassment case withdrew her claims for emotional distress. Yet the court still ordered her to submit her psychiatric records to the court for in camera inspection to determine if they might be relevant to the issue of liability. Specifically, the *Covell* court, citing a previous case in which a witness's mental illness affected his "interpretation of reality,"[48] noted that "[r]eports concerning plaintiff's mental condition might be relevant to her subjective perceptions [of an abusive working environment], and would rebut her contention that the allegedly hostile work environment altered the conditions of her employment."[49]

Continued refusal of a plaintiff to cooperate in the production of psychotherapy records can lead to dismissal of the plaintiff's emotional damage claims. In *Schoffstall v. Henderson*,[50] the Eighth Circuit affirmed the district court's dismissal of the plaintiff's emotional distress claims in a sexual harassment suit where she repeatedly attempted to thwart the production of her medical and psychological records. Counsel for the defendant had requested that she sign releases for the records. She first refused and then later consented to only a limited production. The defendant filed a motion to compel, which was granted, and the plaintiff signed the releases. When the defendant subpoenaed the records, however, the treatment providers refused to produce them—indicating that the plaintiff had directed them not to do so. The defendant then moved to dismiss the claims for emotional damages as a discovery sanction, which the court granted.

2. Cases Viewing Waiver Narrowly

Other courts have taken a much more restrictive view of the waiver of the psychotherapist-patient privilege. In *Vanderbilt v. Town of Chilmark*,[51] the defendant in a discrimination and retaliation case argued that by seeking damages for emotional distress, the plaintiff put her emotional state at issue and therefore waived any privilege in her psychotherapy records that might exist. The court disagreed, holding that subsequent to the Supreme Court's *Jaffee* decision, a plaintiff does not waive the privilege simply by putting his or her emotional state at issue. Instead, according to the *Vanderbilt* court, a plaintiff must use the privileged communication as evidence herself before she waives

---

[46]*Id.* at 227.
[47]863 F. Supp. 202, 70 FEP Cases 914 (M.D. Pa. 1994).
[48]United States v. Diamond (*In re* Doe), 964 F.2d 1325 (2d Cir. 1992).
[49]863 F. Supp. at 206, 70 FEP Cases at 916.
[50]223 F.3d 818, 84 FEP Cases 1411 (8th Cir. 2000).
[51]174 F.R.D. 225, 74 FEP Cases 685 (D. Mass. 1997).

the privilege: "Were she to introduce evidence regarding the substance of her conversations with her psychotherapist in order to further her claim of emotional damage, this court would agree that she could not shield the communication from others. She has, however, done no such thing."[52] The *Vanderbilt* court concluded that the privilege would be waived if the plaintiff called her psychotherapist as a witness, or if she testified herself about the substance of her discussions with her therapist.[53] The court also emphasized that the mere fact that the plaintiff had therapy and the dates of such therapy (including therapy that preexisted the injury at issue) are not privileged.

In *Vasconcellos v. Cybex International, Inc.*,[54] the court quashed as overbroad a subpoena for all of the plaintiff's psychiatrist's records. Although noting that the plaintiff was pursuing a separate claim for intentional infliction of emotional distress as well as damages for emotional distress flowing from her other employment claims, the court held that the plaintiff "has a right to have discovery limited to information that is directly relevant to the lawsuit."[55] The court did not define just what it considered to be "directly relevant," although it quoted the following passage from an earlier case:

> [A]lthough the defendants will be permitted to inquire into plaintiff's personal histories, it must be emphasized that defendants may not engage in a fishing expedition by inquiring into matters totally irrelevant to the issue of emotional distress. In other words, the scope of the inquiry must be limited to whether, and to what extent, the alleged harassment caused plaintiffs to suffer emotional harm.[56]

The *Vasconcellos* court also suggested that the defendant could issue a new, narrower subpoena, and that the plaintiff was free to withdraw her claims for emotional injury if she wanted to avoid discovery into that area.[57]

In *Bottomly v. Leucadia National*,[58] a sexual harassment case, the court similarly narrowed the scope of the defendant's discovery of the plaintiff's psychotherapy records, noting that although a plaintiff "waives privacy claims as to those matters which are related to causation and damages as to her claim, plaintiff does not waive privacy interests on matters unrelated to the case or not calculated to lead to admissible evidence."[59] The court's application of this principle was somewhat muddled, however. It held that discovery must be allowed as to (1) all material the plaintiff's experts could reasonably rely on

---

[52]174 F.R.D. at 230, 74 FEP Cases at 688. *Accord* Booker v. City of Boston, 1999 WL 734644 (D. Mass. Sept. 10, 1999).

[53]*See also* Burrell v. Crown Cent. Petroleum, Inc., 177 F.R.D. 376 (E.D. Tex. 1997) (medical and psychological records need not be produced where plaintiff will not present medical evidence or rely on medical records to assist in proving claim).

[54]962 F. Supp. 701, 4 WH Cases 2d 1446 (D. Md. 1997).

[55]*Id.* at 708.

[56]*Id.* at 709, 4 WH Cases at 1452 (citing Bridges v. Eastman Kodak Co., 850 F. Supp. 216, 223 (S.D.N.Y. 1994)).

[57]962 F. Supp. at 709, 4 WH Cases 2d at 1452.

[58]163 F.R.D. 617 (D. Utah 1995).

[59]*Id.* at 619.

to address the relevant issues in the case and (2) information needed by the defendants' experts to form a basis for any counteropinion. The *Bottomly* court then gave conflicting directives, however. First, it said that

> matter that is not related to causation and extent of damage, but which merely goes to the plaintiff's character[,] is outside of proper bounds of discovery. Matters that are remote to what an expert may legitimately use for foundation for an expert opinion but which may be helpful in a clinical treatment mode or for a psychoanalytic personality analysis are too broad and intrusive and not needed for an expert opinion on the issues. A clinical whole person approach is not especially functional in the legal context of the case and is unjustifiably intrusive. A full personality inventory is not necessary for an expert witness to address the relevant issues of damages and causation.[60]

The court then said, however, that the defense expert's opinion must be "founded on what an expert in the discipline would reasonably rely on given the issues in the case," and that the defendants may have access to material that is related and relevant to what is appropriate for an expert to give or base an opinion on.[61] The problem with this formulation is that psychiatric and psychological experts in sexual harassment cases must consider whether the plaintiff has one or more personality disorders that may be relevant not only to causation of damages but to the very genesis of the workplace dispute at issue.[62] The *Bottomly* court seemed to at least partially recognize the importance of this inquiry by noting that it had permitted extensive questioning of the plaintiff concerning her prior sexual harassment claims against other employers. It acknowledged that "if a modus operandi of sexual harassment claims can be shown, such evidence may be admissible on whether the harassment alleged in this case really occurred."[63] In light of this concession to the relevance of the plaintiff's personality structure in a sexual harassment case,[64] the *Bottomly* court's prior

---

[60] *Id.* at 620.

[61] *Id.* at 621.

[62] *See* Chapter 6, Personality Disorders in Employment Litigation. *See also* James J. McDonald, Jr. & Paul R. Lees-Haley, *Personality Disorders in the Workplace: How They May Contribute to Claims of Employment Law Violations*, 22 EMPL. REL. L.J. 57 (1996). The court in *Covell v. CNG Transmission Corp.*, 863 F. Supp. 202, 70 FEP Cases 914 (M.D. Pa. 1994), recognized this point in holding that psychiatric records would be discoverable if they bore on the plaintiff's subjective perceptions in the workplace, even where the plaintiff had withdrawn her claim for emotional distress damages. *Id.* at 206, 70 FEP Cases at 916.

[63] 163 F.R.D. at 622 n.3.

[64] A history of sexual harassment claims brought against a variety of employers may be evidence of hypersensitivity to sexual cues or a repetition compulsion, each of which may be related to a personality disorder, and each of which is relevant to whether actionable sexual harassment occurred. *See* Sara P. Feldman-Schorrig & James J. McDonald, Jr., *The Role of Forensic Psychiatry in the Defense of Sexual Harassment Cases*, 20 J. PSYCHIATRY & L. 5 (1992); James J. McDonald, Jr. & Sara P. Feldman-Schorrig, *The Relevance of Childhood Sexual Abuse in Sexual Harassment Cases*, 20 EMPL. REL. L.J. 221 (1994).

comments on the inappropriateness of such discovery seem particularly difficult to reconcile.

3. Cases Taking a Balanced View

Some courts have attempted to avoid the extremes presented by the opposing lines of cases construing the waiver of the psychotherapist-patient privilege and have instead taken a more balanced and pragmatic approach.

In *Fox v. Gates Corp.*,[65] the plaintiff alleged a violation of the ADA, claiming that she was not hired on account of her two disabled sons and that she suffered emotional distress as a result. The defendant sought to discover her psychotherapy records covering the five years before and after the incident at issue. The court adopted an "applicable time period test," holding that the defendant was entitled to the plaintiff's therapy records preceding the incident because those records might reveal that the cause of the plaintiff's emotional distress was some other stressor in her life. As the plaintiff admitted that her emotional distress ceased before she obtained additional therapy after the incident, the court held that the defendants were not entitled to disclosure of the postincident therapy records. The court cautioned, however, that if the plaintiff subsequently claimed that her emotional distress was continuing, the defendant would be entitled to discovery of those records.

In *Santelli v. Electro-Motive*,[66] the plaintiff testified at deposition that she was seeing a psychotherapist for emotional distress allegedly suffered as a result of sex discrimination. Upon the defendant's seeking disclosure of her psychotherapy, alcohol and drug treatment, and HIV testing records, the plaintiff changed course and represented that she would seek damages only for humiliation and embarrassment, not for emotional distress. The court ruled that the plaintiff's narrowing of her claim made her psychotherapy records irrelevant, but the court also precluded the plaintiff at trial from introducing evidence of any symptoms (such as sleeplessness, nervousness, or depression), or of any medical or psychological diagnosis. Rather, the court maintained, the plaintiff would be allowed to testify only that she felt humiliated, embarrassed, angry, or upset. The court went on to say, "This may be a meager victory for [the plaintiff]. Bare testimony of humiliation or disgust may prevent her from fully recovering for her alleged emotional distress. She may be better off disclosing her psychological records, which would allow her to make a broader damage claim."[67]

4. Cases Applying a Rule 35 Analysis

A few courts have applied to discovery of psychotherapy records an analysis similar to that used by many courts in determining whether a mental examination

---

[65] 179 F.R.D. 303 (D. Colo. 1998).
[66] 188 F.R.D. 306 (N.D. Ill. 1999).
[67] *Id.* at 309.

of the plaintiff will be ordered under Rule 35 of the Federal Rules of Civil Procedure.[68] *Stevenson v. Stanley Bostitch, Inc.*[69] is one example. In that case, in which the plaintiff sued for sex discrimination, sexual harassment, and intentional infliction of emotional distress, she sought to block production of her psychotherapists' records on the ground of privilege. The court, after discussing various cases that had taken a broad view as well as a narrow view of the waiver of the psychotherapist-patient privilege, declared that "determining whether the plaintiff has placed her mental condition at issue so as to waive the privilege is analogous to, and should be generally consistent with, the analysis conducted when a Rule 35(a) examination is requested."[70] The court went on to note that while the plaintiff placed her mental condition at issue via her claim for intentional infliction of emotional distress, as to her discrimination claim she was not claiming anything other than "garden variety emotional distress damages." Finding that the plaintiff's claim for intentional infliction of emotional distress might not survive summary judgment, the court ruled that the plaintiff's therapy records did not have to be produced at that time, but that the defendant could renew its efforts to obtain the records should the claim for intentional infliction of emotional distress survive summary judgment or should the plaintiff seek recovery for more than just "garden variety" emotional distress damages.[71]

Similarly, *Ruhlmann v. Ulster County Dept. of Social Services*,[72] was an ADA case in which the plaintiff did not claim to be disabled but rather claimed that his employer *perceived* him to be disabled on account of his Bipolar Disorder and discriminated against him, and that he suffered mental and emotional distress as a result. He opposed the defendant's attempt to obtain his medical and psychiatric records, and the court barred their release, maintaining that "a party does not put his or her emotional condition in issue by merely seeking incidental, 'garden variety,' emotional distress damages, without more."[73] The court also rejected the argument that the defendant needed access to the records to defend against the ADA claim. It found no need to "explore plaintiff's psychiatric history in order to defend against an allegation of perceived disability."[74]

---

[68]*See* Chapter 9, The Mental Examination.

[69]2001 WL 812310 (N.D. Ga. Mar. 21, 2001).

[70]*Id.* at *4. The court cited, inter alia, Jackson v. Chubb Corp., 193 F.R.D. 216, 221–27 (D.N.J. 2000) (noting that waiver should not found where only a "garden variety" claim is presented); Santelli v. Electro-Motive, 188 F.R.D. 306, 308–09 (N.D. Ill. 1999) (privilege not waived where plaintiff limits her testimony to common humiliation and embarrassment, versus clinical diagnosis of depression and sleeplessness); Hucko v. City of Oak Forest, 185 F.R.D. 526, 529–31 (N.D. Ill. 1999) (no waiver of privilege where plaintiff not planning to offer evidence of psychotherapy or put on expert testimony to prove claim of emotional harm).

[71]*Stevenson* at *5. The court held that the privilege applied only to communications between the plaintiff and her therapists, however, and not to such other information as billing statements or dates of therapy. *Id.* at *6.

[72]194 F.R.D. 445, 449–51 (N.D.N.Y. 2000)

[73]*Id.* at 450.

[74]*Id.* at 448.

Not all courts take this view, however. In *LeFave v. Symbios, Inc.*,[75] the court denied the defendant's motion for a Rule 35 mental examination of the plaintiff, finding that the plaintiff's claim for damages for "pain and suffering, emotional trauma and humiliation" suffered as a result of discrimination and harassment amounted only to a "garden variety" claim for damages. Yet the court ordered production of the plaintiff's medical records (the plaintiff had voluntarily produced her psychological records) for the period from five years prior to the events at issue in the lawsuit through the present time. Finding no physician-patient privilege under federal law, the court applied the relevancy standard of Rule 26 of the Federal Rules of Civil Procedure and held:

> Medical records information is relevant to plaintiff's claim for emotional distress damages. The information is further relevant to the preparation of defendant's defenses against plaintiff's emotional distress damages claim, because her medical records may reveal stressors unrelated to defendants which may have affected plaintiff's emotional well being.[76]

The court in *McKenna v. Cruz*[77] rejected the "garden variety" test altogether. Although it noted that the plaintiff in that case was seeking to recover for more than a garden variety injury because he planned to introduce testimony that he was diagnosed with Posttraumatic Stress Syndrome, the court maintained that even if the plaintiff

> were to seek damages solely for generalized anxiety and emotional upset, plaintiff's argument is still unpersuasive because it fails to explain why waiver of the privilege should turn on the existence (or assertion) of a specific, diagnosable condition. If a plaintiff in an auto accident case alleged non-specific back pain as a result of the accident, there would be no serious argument that his assertion of such a claim waives any claim of physician-patient privilege he might otherwise have had with respect to the condition of his back. The waiver results from the plaintiff's putting his physical condition in issue, not the specificity of the diagnosis. Similarly, a plaintiff who chooses to put his psychiatric or emotional condition in issue should be found to have waived his psychotherapist-patient privilege. Whether or not there is a specific diagnosis, the plaintiff has put his emotional condition in issue, and it is that fact that gives rise to the waiver.[78]

B. Discovery of Other Records

Courts typically have permitted discovery of other types of records pertaining to plaintiffs in employment cases. In *EEOC v. Danka Industries*,[79] the court rejected the plaintiffs' motion to quash the defendant's subpoenas for records of a former employer of one plaintiff, the high school and college records of

---

[75] 2000 WL 1644154 (D. Colo. Apr. 14, 2000).
[76] *Id.* at *2.
[77] 1998 WL 809533 (S.D.N.Y. Nov. 19, 1998).
[78] *Id.* at *2.
[79] 990 F. Supp. 1138, 75 FEP Cases 685 (E.D. Mo. 1997).

three other plaintiffs, and even the medical examiner's records relating to the death of the boyfriend of one of the plaintiffs. The court maintained that because the plaintiffs had no claim of privilege in any of the subpoenaed documents, they had no standing to request that the subpoenas be quashed.

C. Depositions

Plaintiffs, their therapists, and others[80] ordinarily may be deposed concerning the nature and causation of the plaintiff's emotional distress.[81] Controversies sometimes arise, however, over whether and to what extent a defendant may question a plaintiff or the plaintiff's therapist about the plaintiff's psychological history.

In *Bridges v. Eastman Kodak Co.*,[82] the court rejected the plaintiffs' motion for a protective order restricting the defendant's questioning of the plaintiffs and their therapists about the plaintiffs' psychological histories. It explained:

> Although having to answer questions about their personal histories is to some extent an intrusion into their privacy, and may in fact inhibit some plaintiffs from proceeding with their claims, such an inquiry is warranted since plaintiffs are seeking compensation for their mental anguish. Moreover, since plaintiffs seek to prove that they have suffered emotional distress as a result of the sexual harassment through their testimony and the testimony of their therapists, defense counsel has a right to inquire into plaintiffs' pasts for the purpose of showing that their emotional distress was caused at least in part by events and circumstances that were not job related. Indeed, as far as the testimony of their therapists is concerned, defendants must be allowed to inquire into all relevant information upon which the therapists' opinions [are] based, not necessarily only information directly related to their employment.[83]

The only limitation on deposition questioning imposed by the *Bridges* court was that defendants could not engage in a "fishing expedition" by inquiring into matters "totally irrelevant" to the issue of emotional distress.[84]

In *Allen v. Cook County Sheriff's Department*,[85] the court refused to compel the depositions of the plaintiff's psychotherapists. While it took a narrow view

---

[80]*See* Alden v. Time Warner Inc., 1995 WL 679238 (S.D.N.Y. Nov. 14, 1995) (holding that plaintiff's wife may be deposed regarding manifestations of plaintiff's emotional distress).

[81]*But see* Allen v. Cook County Sheriff's Dep't, 1999 WL 168466 (N.D. Ill. Mar. 17, 1999) (defendant may not depose plaintiff's psychotherapists unless she designates them as expert witnesses).

[82]850 F. Supp. 216, 64 FEP Cases 1100 (S.D.N.Y. 1994).

[83]*Id.* at 216, 64 FEP Cases at 1104–05.

[84]*Id.* at 223, 64 FEP Cases at 1105. As an example, the *Bridges* court stated that "it would be inappropriate for defendants to question plaintiffs about their past sexual histories in order to show that sexually promiscuous people are less likely to be offended, and thus less damaged, than those who are not as sexually active." *Id.* at n.5.

[85]1999 WL 168466 (N.D. Ill. Mar. 17, 1999).

of the waiver of the psychotherapist-patient privilege, finding that the plaintiff had not placed her communications with the therapists into issue, it warned that a different result would apply in the event the plaintiff decided to have the therapists testify at trial. The court explained: "Fundamental fairness demands that the defendants should have ample opportunity to scrutinize the basis for the opinions of Allen's therapists if she attempts to elicit therapist testimony or evidence to prove her damages caused by her alleged emotional distress."[86]

In *Pfeifer v. State Farm*,[87] the court granted the defendant's motion to compel the plaintiff to answer questions regarding his illegal drug use while an employee of the defendant. The court noted that the answers to such questions could be relevant to the cause of the plaintiff's claimed mental illness, and it rejected the plaintiff's invocation of a Fifth Amendment privilege against self-incrimination.

In *Martinez v. Bally's Louisiana, Inc.*,[88] the plaintiff in a sexual harassment case brought under the Jones Act,[89] refused on the advice of her counsel to answer deposition questions regarding her physical condition. She insisted she was not making any physical injury claims. She later attempted to defeat the employer's motion for summary judgment (as purely emotional injuries are not compensable under the Jones Act) by asserting that she suffered from physical manifestations of harm such as sleeplessness, nervousness, inability to focus, and dependence on antidepressant medication. The district court nonetheless granted the motion and the Fifth Circuit affirmed, refusing to draw a distinction between physical injuries and physical manifestations of emotional injuries. It maintained that the plaintiff's attorney's representation at the deposition that a claim for physical injuries was not being made constituted a judicial admission that could not be contradicted later in the case.

4. Interrogatories

In *Hilt v. SFC Inc.*,[90] the court ruled insufficient a plaintiff's answer to an interrogatory asking her to list all physicians, psychologists, and counselors who had treated or consulted with her. The plaintiff listed the requested information for only a five-year period and referred the defendant to her medical records for further information. The court ordered the plaintiff to submit a complete response to the interrogatory, noting that it was relevant to the extent and causation of her damages. The court also maintained that an interrogatory "is not necessarily overly broad or unduly burdensome simply because it is unlimited in time and scope."[91]

---

[86]*Id.* at *2.
[87]1997 WL 276085 (E.D. La. May 22, 1997).
[88]244 F.3d 474, 85 FEP Cases 537 (5th Cir. 2001).
[89]46 U.S.C. App. §688.
[90]170 F.R.D. 182 (D. Kan. 1997).
[91]*Id.* (citing Lowe v. Philadelphia Newspapers, Inc., 101 F.R.D. 296, 298, 44 FEP Cases 1224, 1225 (E.D. Pa. 1983)).

In *Stevenson v. Stanley Bostitch, Inc.*,[92] the court held that an interrogatory was proper that asked the plaintiff to list all medications she took as a result of the workplace events at issue in the litigation. On the other hand, the same court ruled an interrogatory asking the plaintiff to list every medical diagnosis she had ever received was overbroad.

II. Discovery of Plaintiff's Sexual History

With the dramatic increase in the number of sexual harassment claims litigated over the past decade has come a new source of controversy over the discoverability and admissibility of evidence of the plaintiff's prior sexual experiences. On the extremes of this controversy lie one view that to inquire into such topics is unfairly "blaming the victim" and subjecting the plaintiff to further harassment, and the opposite view that if the plaintiff possesses "loose morals," such evidence should get to the jury to undercut the credibility of the plaintiff's claim that she was offended by harassment in the workplace.

In between these extremes, however, lies an issue that cannot be easily dismissed if notions of due process and litigation as a search for truth are to be taken seriously. A sexual harassment plaintiff's sexual conduct with others, particularly with persons in or connected with the workplace, is often quite relevant to the central issues in a harassment lawsuit of whether the plaintiff was subjectively offended by—or, put differently, whether she welcomed—the conduct alleged to be harassment.[93] A plaintiff's intimate relationship with a spouse or lover also may become relevant to a harassment plaintiff's claim for damages—especially if she claims that workplace events disrupted her personal relationships or caused her to shun intimacy.

Whether the plaintiff suffered prior sexual abuse is also crucially relevant to the plaintiff's claim for emotional distress damages, as the plaintiff may well be in a state of genuine emotional turmoil that is attributable not entirely to events at work but rather to the unresolved psychological effects of childhood sexual abuse or prior sexual assault as an adult. As one plaintiff's attorney recently conceded,

> many victims of sexual harassment have been sexually harassed or abused earlier in life. This history will probably be in the clinician's medical records and may be admitted to show that the past harassment or abuse contributed to, or caused, the plaintiff's emotional distress. Revealing this history can be devastating to a plaintiff and extremely prejudicial to a case.[94]

---

[92]201 F.R.D. 551 (N.D. Ga. 2001).

[93]In *Henson v. City of Dundee*, 682 F.2d 897, 29 FEP Cases 787 (11th Cir. 1982), the court maintained that sexual harassment must be *unwelcome* (that is, the employee did not solicit or incite it) to be actionable. This principle was endorsed by the Supreme Court in *Meritor Savings Bank v. Vinson*, 477 U.S. 57, 68, 40 FEP Cases 1822, 1826 (1986).

[94]Ellen Simon, *Experts in Employment Cases*, TRIAL, Oct. 1997, at 48, 49.

Unresolved effects of prior sexual abuse may even have caused a sexual harassment plaintiff to have been hypersensitive to sexual cues in the workplace (and thus to have responded other than as a nonhypersensitive, "reasonable woman" would have responded), or even to have "welcomed" the conduct now characterized as harassment.

Deciding on the correct approach, therefore, is not as simple as just decreeing that evidence of a plaintiff's prior sexual experiences always should or should not be considered in a sexual harassment lawsuit. It is necessary to strike a balance between the plaintiff's right to privacy and the defendant's right to a fair trial. Congress attempted such a balance in its 1994 amendment of Rule 412 of the Federal Rules of Evidence, but some uncertainty still remains as this area of the law continues to develop.

A. Amendments to Rule 412 of the Federal Rules of Evidence

The original version of Federal Rule of Evidence 412, enacted by Congress in 1978, limited the admissibility of a victim's past sexual behavior or conduct, but it applied only in criminal prosecutions for rape and similar sexual offenses. Its prohibition against the introduction of evidence of a victim's sexual history and conduct was not applicable to civil cases. The Rule's legislative history stated that its purpose was to protect rape victims from needless inquiries into their prior sexual conduct, particularly when such conduct might have little or no bearing on or relevance to the offense for which the defendant was being tried.[95] Rule 412, as originally enacted, was a legislative attempt to balance a rape victim's interest in protecting her private life from needless public exposure against the defendant's interest in being able to present a defense by offering relevant evidence that might prove exculpatory.

As civil claims for sexual harassment became more popular, a movement began to amend Rule 412 to provide some protections for sexual harassment plaintiffs analogous to those provided to rape victims. This drive to amend Rule 412 to include civil actions involving sexual misconduct originated in Congress in 1991.[96] The Advisory Committee on Evidence of the Judicial Conference of the United States began considering amending Rule 412 shortly thereafter.[97]

The ultimate adoption of the amended Rule 412 involved some controversy. The Supreme Court declined to forward to Congress the amendments proposed by the Judicial Conference. As discussed below, the amendments generally restricted use of evidence of a victim's sexual history. In a letter to the Chairman of the Advisory Committee of the Judicial Conference, Chief Justice Rehnquist

---

[95] *See* 124 CONG. REC. H11944 (daily ed. Oct. 10, 1978).

[96] *See* 137 CONG. REC. S9610 (daily ed. July 10, 1991) (proposal to amend Rule 412 as part of the Violence Against Women Act of 1991).

[97] Minutes of the Advisory Committee on the Federal Rules of Criminal Procedure (Apr. 23–24, 1992).

noted that some members of the Supreme Court were of the view that the amendments exceeded the Court's authority under the Rules Enabling Act, which forbids the enactment of rules that "abridge, enlarge or modify any substantive right."[98] The Supreme Court was concerned, according to the Chief Justice, that the amended Rule 412 might encroach upon the right of defendants in sexual harassment cases, recognized in *Meritor Savings Bank v. Vinson*,[99] to introduce evidence of a plaintiff's "sexually provocative speech or dress." In spite of the Supreme Court's objections, however, Congress enacted the amendments to Rule 412 into law on December 1, 1994, as part of the Violent Crime Control and Enforcement Act of 1994. Parts of amended Rule 412 are quoted and discussed below.[100]

The amended Rule 412 begins with a general prohibition against the admission of evidence of a victim's sexual history:

> (a) Evidence generally inadmissible.—The following evidence is not admissible in any civil or criminal proceeding involving alleged sexual misconduct except as provided in subdivisions (b) and (c):
> (1) Evidence offered to prove that any alleged victim engaged in other sexual behavior.
> (2) Evidence offered to prove any alleged victim's sexual predisposition.

Rule 412(b) then goes on to state some exceptions to this general prohibition. Rule 412(b)(1) sets forth exceptions that apply to criminal cases. Rule 412(b)(2) sets forth the exception that applies to civil cases:

> In a civil case, evidence offered to prove the sexual behavior or sexual predisposition of any alleged victim is admissible if it is otherwise admissible under these rules and its probative value substantially outweighs the danger of harm to any victim and of unfair prejudice to any party. Evidence of an alleged victim's reputation is admissible only if it has been placed in controversy by the alleged victim.

The Amended Rule 412 also mandates a specific procedure for the introduction of evidence of the victim's sexual history:

> (c) Procedure to determine admissibility—
> (1) A party intending to offer evidence under subdivision (b) must—(A) file a written motion at least 14 days before trial specifically describing the evidence and stating the purpose for which it is offered unless the court, for good cause requires a different time for filing or permits filing during trial; and (B) serve the motion on all parties and notify the alleged victim or, when appropriate, the alleged victim's guardian or representative.
> (2) Before admitting evidence under this rule the court must conduct a hearing in camera and afford the victim and parties a right to attend and be heard.

---

[98] *Supreme Court's Amendments to Fed. R. Ev. 412 Deletes "Rape Shield" Rule in Civil Cases,* 2 Emp. Disc. Rep. 624 (May 18, 1994).
[99] 477 U.S. 57, 40 FEP Cases 1822 (1986).
[100] The full text of amended Rule 412 is reprinted in Appendix 5.

The motion, related papers, and the record of the hearing must be sealed and remain under seal unless the court orders otherwise.

The Notes of the Advisory Committee of the Judicial Conference of the United States that drafted the amendments to Rule 412 are rather extensive and provide further gloss on the meaning of the amendments. For example, the Advisory Committee Notes make it clear that Rule 412 is to apply to sexual harassment lawsuits as well as other civil claims for sexual misconduct.[101] The Committee goes on to state that a balancing test was adopted for civil cases because "[g]reater flexibility is needed to accommodate evolving causes of action such as claims for sexual harassment." The Committee explains the test it adopted:

> This test for admitting evidence offered to prove sexual behavior or sexual propensity in civil cases differs in three respects from the general rule governing admissibility set forth in Rule 403. First, it Reverses [sic] that [sic] usual procedure spelled out in Rule 403 by shifting the burden to the proponent to demonstrate admissibility rather than making the opponent justify exclusion of the evidence. Second, the standard expressed in subdivision (b)(2) is more stringent than in the original rule; it raises the threshold for admission by requiring that the probative value of the evidence substantially outweigh the specified dangers. Finally, the Rule 412 test puts "harm to the victim" on the scale in addition to prejudice to the parties.[102]

Consideration of the application of Rule 412 requires that a distinction be drawn between volitional and nonvolitional sexual conduct. Although the Rule does not explicitly draw such a distinction, it does so implicitly by placing restrictions only on evidence that an alleged victim "engaged in" other sexual behavior.[103] Moreover, case law to date suggests that the Rule should apply to conduct in which the plaintiff was a voluntary participant but not to prior incidents in which the plaintiff was an unwilling victim of assault or abuse.

B. Application of Rule 412 to Volitional Conduct

A variety of issues have arisen concerning the application of the amended Rule 412 to prior volitional sexual conduct on the part of a sexual harassment plaintiff. These include just what kinds of "sexual behavior" are covered by the rule, application of Rule 412 to the "welcomeness" issue, application of the Rule to damages issues, whether Rule 412 applies at the discovery stage, and to what extent it applies to third-party witnesses.

---

[101] *See also* Wolak v. Spucci, 217 F.3d 157, 160, 83 FEP Cases 253, 256 (2d Cir. 2000) (expressly holding that Rule 412 applies to sexual harassment cases).

[102] Advisory Committee Notes to Amendment of FED. R. EVID. 412 (1994) [hereinafter Advisory Committee Notes].

[103] FED. R. EVID. 412(a)(1).

1. Types of Sexual Behavior Covered

The Advisory Committee Notes to the 1994 Amendments to Rule 412 assert that "sexual behavior connotes all activities that involve actual physical conduct, i.e., sexual intercourse or sexual contact."[104] The Notes then cite illustrative examples from prior case law such as use of contraceptives,[105] birth of an illegitimate child,[106] and evidence of venereal disease.[107] The Notes go on to state, "In addition, the word 'behavior' should be construed to include activities of the mind, such as fantasies or dreams."[108]

The courts to date, however, have not applied Rule 412 in quite so broad a fashion. In *Judd v. Rodman*,[109] the plaintiff claimed that the defendant wrongfully transmitted genital herpes to her. After the jury issued a verdict against her, the plaintiff on appeal invoked Rule 412 to attack the district court's admission of evidence of her breast augmentation surgery, her prior sexual history, and her career as a nude dancer. Noting that the plaintiff had failed to preserve an objection under Rule 412 to the admission of her breast augmentation surgery, the Eleventh Circuit sidestepped the issue of whether Rule 412 applied to such evidence. The plaintiff then argued that her prior sexual history should have been excluded under Rule 412 because its probative value did not substantially outweigh the unfair prejudice toward her. The Eleventh Circuit rejected this argument, finding that the plaintiff's sexual history was highly relevant:

> A central issue in this case . . . is whether Judd contracted genital herpes from Rodman. Expert testimony revealed that the herpes virus can be dormant for long periods of time and the infected person can be asymptomatic. Consequently, evidence of prior sexual relationships and the type of protection used during sexual intercourse was highly relevant to Rodman's liability. The court did not abuse its discretion in admitting evidence of Judd's prior sexual history.[110]

Finally, the Eleventh Circuit affirmed the district court's admission of the plaintiff's employment as a nude dancer. The plaintiff had challenged admission of this evidence, too, under Rule 412. As the court explained:

> Judd testified that she felt "dirty" after she contracted herpes. The court determined that Judd's employment as a nude dancer before and after she contracted herpes was probative as to damages for emotional distress because it suggested an absence of change in her body image following the herpes infection.[111]

Thus, even if activities such as nude dancing are considered "sexual behavior," they may still be admissible under Rule 412.

---

[104] See Advisory Committee Notes, *supra* note 102.
[105] United States v. Galloway, 937 F.2d 542 (10th Cir. 1991). *See also* Alberts v. Wickes Lumber Co., 1995 WL 117886 (N.D. Ill. Mar. 15, 1995).
[106] United States v. One Feather, 702 F.2d 736 (8th Cir. 1983).
[107] State v. Carmichael, 727 P.2d 918 (Kan. 1986).
[108] See Advisory Committee Notes, *supra* note 102.
[109] 105 F.3d 1339 (11th Cir. 1997).
[110] *Id.* at 1343.
[111] *Id.*

Other courts have also read Rule 412 somewhat narrowly. In *Janopoulos v. Harvey L. Walner & Associates*,[112] the plaintiff filed a motion in limine under Rule 412 to exclude mention of her marital history at the trial of her sexual harassment claim. The court held that the Rule did not apply because one's marital history is not the kind of "sexual behavior" it contemplates, but the court excluded the plaintiff's marital history nonetheless under Rules 401 and 402 as being irrelevant to any issue at trial. Similarly, in *Adams v. Goodyear Tire & Rubber Co.*,[113] the court held that Rule 412 did not apply to references in a defendant's summary judgment motion papers to the fact that the plaintiff was divorced and that her ex-husband and her current boyfriend physically abused her.

In *Barta v. City & County of Honolulu*,[114] the court in a sexual harassment lawsuit declined to apply Rule 412 to discovery of the identity of the plaintiff's social acquaintances, including those with whom she might have gone on dates. The court recognized that such individuals might have information relevant to defenses or damages. The court drew the line, however, at discovery into whether the plaintiff had had sexual relations with those acquaintances.[115] *Barta* thus makes it clear that although Rule 412 will protect a plaintiff's privacy as to her intimate sexual affairs, it cannot be invoked so broadly as to prevent a defendant from conducting discovery of spouses and past or present lovers as to other relevant issues in the case merely on the ground that the plaintiff may have had sexual relations with them.

2. Application of Rule 412 to the Welcomeness Issue

In *Meritor Savings Bank v. Vinson*,[116] the Supreme Court maintained that sexual conduct in the workplace must be "unwelcome" to be actionable as sexual harassment. Previously, in *Henson v. City of Dundee*,[117] the Eleventh Circuit had defined "unwelcome" sexual conduct as that which is not "solicited or incited" by the plaintiff. Thus, the plaintiff's role in the events that culminated in the claim of harassment is often a central issue in a sexual harassment lawsuit. Even evidence of the plaintiff's dress and personal thoughts may be relevant to the issue of welcomeness, in the *Vinson* Court's view.[118] As one commentator has observed: "*Henson* and *Meritor* thus establish that the plaintiff's invitation to or provocation of the alleged harassment is of central if not determinative importance to the disposition of her claim."[119]

---

[112]1995 WL 107170 (N.D. Ill. Mar. 7, 1995).
[113]184 F.R.D. 369 (D. Kan. 1998).
[114]169 F.R.D. 132 (D. Haw. 1996).
[115]*Id.* at 137.
[116]477 U.S. 57, 68, 40 FEP Cases 1822, 1826 (1986).
[117]682 F.2d 897, 903, 29 FEP Cases 787, 791 (11th Cir. 1982).
[118]477 U.S. at 68–69, 40 FEP Cases at 1826.
[119]Paul N. Monnin, *Proving Welcomeness: The Admissibility of Evidence of Sexual History in Sexual Harassment Claims Under the 1994 Amendments to Federal Rule of Evidence 412*, 48 VAND. L. REV. 1155, 1166–67 (1995).

Welcomeness can be a difficult concept with which to contend, however. The *Vinson* court could be no more precise than to say that the "totality of the circumstances" must be considered when considering welcomeness.[120] Sometimes, welcomeness evidence may be straightforward, such as where a plaintiff dresses provocatively or initiates sexual banter with coworkers and then complains of harassment when coworkers respond. More often, however, welcomeness issues are considerably more subtle, and their resolution often requires an understanding of the context of the relationship of the parties involved. For example, welcomeness issues often arise where the plaintiff and the accused harasser once were involved in a consensual relationship, or where the plaintiff willingly participated in sexual joking and horseplay in an effort to "fit in."

Yet, as Chief Justice Rehnquist predicted when the Supreme Court declined to forward the amended Rule 412 to Congress, the Rule may have a direct impact on the admissibility of evidence of welcomeness. The Advisory Committee Notes are somewhat ambiguous in this regard. At one point they warn: "[U]nless the (b)(2) exception is satisfied, evidence such as that relating to the alleged victim's mode of dress, speech, or life-style will not be admissible."[121] At another point, however, they point out that the term "other sexual behavior" is used "to suggest some flexibility in admitting evidence 'intrinsic' to the alleged sexual misconduct."[122] As welcomeness is undoubtedly "intrinsic" to a claim of sexual harassment, such flexibility would appear to be warranted.

In *Socks-Brunot v. Hirschvogel, Inc.*,[123] the court explicitly held that Rule 412 is applicable to evidence of welcomeness sought to be admitted at trial, and it awarded a new trial to the plaintiff because of the defendant's failure to comply with Rule 412's requirements prior to introducing evidence of the plaintiff's role in the creation of the hostile work environment she alleged. In that case, the plaintiff alleged that her supervisor made repeated comments about the size of her breasts, asked her what size condoms she used, asked her to sit on his lap, said he thought she could not go without sex for more than a few days, said her lipstick made her look like a whore, and told her that a coworker wanted to have sex with her. He also allegedly asked her to bring him a videotape of her delivering her son so he could "see another side" of her. The defendant, for its part, put on evidence that the plaintiff spoke to coworkers about an affair she had had with a prior supervisor, that she discussed oral sex with a female coworker, that a coworker observed the plaintiff flirting with the alleged harasser, and that the plaintiff liberally used profanity at work. In a pretrial hearing, the court held that Rule 412 would not govern introduction of evidence of welcomeness.

Following the trial, however, the *Socks-Brunot* court reversed itself and held that the defendant's evidence of welcomeness should have been sifted through the screening process required by Rule 412 before being submitted to

---

[120] 477 U.S. at 69, 40 FEP Cases at 1826.
[121] *See* Advisory Committee Notes, *supra* note 102.
[122] *Id.*
[123] 184 F.R.D. 113 (S.D. Ohio 1999).

the jury. The court rejected the defendant's argument that welcomeness evidence is not the kind of evidence of sexual behavior or sexual predisposition covered by Rule 412. Morever, the court noted that it would have excluded under Rule 412 most of the evidence of welcomeness offered by the defendant at trial. For example, the court noted that the plaintiff's discussion of her affair with a prior supervisor was irrelevant because there was no evidence that she discussed the affair with the alleged harasser. Similarly, the court noted that the alleged harasser was not a part of the plaintiff's discussion of oral sex. The court indicated that it likely would exclude evidence of the plaintiff's flirting with the alleged harasser because he never claimed the plaintiff was flirtatious. Finally, as to the plaintiff's use of profanity, the court noted that the plaintiff was not complaining that her supervisor used profanity in her presence but rather that he directed sexually explicit and degrading comments toward her.

A court took a more liberal approach in a case involving the plaintiff's own blatant sexual antics in the workplace in *Sublette v. Glidden Co.*[124] In that case alleging a hostile work environment, the plaintiff sought to exclude under Rule 412 and the defendant sought to admit evidence of the plaintiff's wearing a sign saying "Best Blow Jobs on the #8 line," offering to give oral sex to a coworker, ripping her T-shirt to expose her breasts, wetting her T-shirt and standing in front of a large fan to show off her breasts, touching male employees on their thighs and buttocks, allowing a male coworker to place his handprint in paint on her buttocks, and discussing with coworkers her intimate relations with her husband. The court remarked that it had "little difficulty" in finding such evidence to be relevant to welcomeness.[125]

Similarly, in *Fedio v. Circuit City Stores, Inc.*,[126] another hostile environment case wherein the plaintiff alleged that sexual propositions and crude comments were made to her, the court admitted evidence of the plaintiff's own conversations in the workplace about sex. Specifically, the court admitted testimony that the plaintiff told coworkers she was going to wear a finger ring until she "got laid" and that she subsequently removed the ring, and that she told them she had kept a delivery driver waiting outside her apartment while she had sexual intercourse with her roommate. The court also admitted testimony that the plaintiff has been the victim of date rape before she came to work for the defendant. The court maintained that the evidence was "highly" probative of how little Plaintiff would be offended by [a supervisor's] sexual innuendoes when she in fact felt comfortable publicizing information regarding her sex life."[127] The court further observed: "Plaintiff volunteered to her co-workers information regarding her sexual proclivities. To allow an alleged victim to publicly flaunt her sexual behaviors and yet remain protected by Rule 412 would be tantamount to a complete disregard of the rule's purpose."[128]

---

[124] 1998 WL 964189 (E.D. Pa. Oct. 1, 1998).
[125] *Id.* at *3.
[126] 1998 WL 966000 (E.D. Pa. Nov. 4, 1998).
[127] *Id.* at *6.
[128] *Id.*

Likewise, in *Woodard v. Metro I.P.T.C.*,[129] the court overruled the plaintiff's objections under Rule 412 to consideration of her blatant sexual activities at work in connection with the defendant's motion for summary judgment. The evidence included the plaintiff's posting flyers in the workplace showing her modeling lingerie, inviting coworkers to come and watch her private modeling shows for a $40 fee, distributing nude and topless photos of herself to coworkers, talking with coworkers about how "hot" her body looked, dressing in provocative clothing, and talking with coworkers about sex. The court found this evidence relevant to the issue of whether the plaintiff subjectively considered her working environment to be hostile.

Between these extremes—although the cases are not uniform—the rule that seems to be emerging from the developing case law is that evidence of a plaintiff's sexual conduct in the workplace and/or with individuals subsequently alleged to be her harassers ordinarily will not be barred by Rule 412, while evidence of a plaintiff's sexual activities with persons unconnected with the workplace will be excluded.[130] The application of Rule 412 to evidence of a plaintiff's actions with respect to others in the workplace who are not accused harassers remains unsettled.

For example, in *Herchenroeder v. Johns Hopkins University*,[131] the court permitted questioning of the plaintiff[132] as to whether she and her accused harasser had ever discussed having sexual relations.[133]

In *Rodriguez-Hernandez v. Miranda-Velez*,[134] the First Circuit affirmed the district court's allowing the defendant to introduce evidence that the plaintiff behaved flirtatiously toward the defendant and that her relationship with a man outside the workplace was interfering with her work. Also affirmed were the district court's exclusion of evidence attacking the plaintiff's moral character, characterizing her as promiscuous, and revealing that her boyfriend was married.

In *Dufresne v. J.D. Fields & Co.*,[135] the court denied the plaintiff's Rule 412 motion seeking to exclude evidence that she viewed Internet sex scenes

---

[129] 2000 WL 684101 (S.D. Ind. Mar. 16, 2000).

[130] *See* Holt v. Welch Allyn, Inc., 2000 WL 98118 (N.D.N.Y. Jan. 11, 2000) ("evidence governed by Rule 412 regarding either plaintiff's workplace conduct or conduct with a named defendant will be admissible; evidence of non work-related conduct will not be admissible"). This view is supported by the statement in the Advisory Committee Notes that in a sexual harassment case, "while some evidence of the alleged victim's sexual behavior and/or predisposition in the workplace may perhaps be relevant, non-workplace conduct will usually be irrelevant." The Advisory Committee then cited Burns v. McGregor Elec. Indus., Inc., 989 F.2d 959, 962–63, 61 FEP Cases 592 (8th Cir. 1993) (holding that plaintiff's posing nude for magazine outside work hours is irrelevant to issue of welcomeness). *See* Advisory Committee Notes, *supra* note 102.

[131] 171 F.R.D. 179 (D. Md. 1997).

[132] The court directed that this questioning be done in the form of written interrogatories and that the plaintiff's answers be subject to a confidentiality agreement/protective order. *Id.* at 182.

[133] *Id.* at 180. The plaintiff had previously testified, without objection, that she had not actually had sexual relations with the accused.

[134] 132 F.3d 848, 75 FEP Cases 1228 (1st Cir. 1998).

[135] 85 FEP Cases 25 (E.D. La. 2001).

on her office computer and on at least one occasion e-mailed a copy of one such scene to a manager at his home. The court found this evidence "relevant and probative both to the issue of hostile work environment and damages," but it would not allow the defendant to introduce the actual content of the pornography the plaintiff downloaded. The court also permitted the defendant to introduce evidence that the plaintiff was having an intimate relationship with a California man (though the court did not allow introduction of the details of that intimacy) to show that the plaintiff's real reason for resigning was not sexual harassment but her desire to move to California to pursue that relationship.

In *Sheffield v. Hilltop Sand & Gravel Co.*,[136] the court permitted the accused harasser to testify that the plaintiff participated in sexually provocative discussions and activities in the workplace.[137] It barred introduction of evidence that the plaintiff used "vulgar language" in the workplace and discussed with coworkers her sexual relationship with her husband, however. Although noting that such evidence "might be relevant," the court excluded it as a sanction against defendants for their failure to file their Rule 412 motion under seal as required by Rule 412(c).[138]

In *Barta v. City & County of Honolulu*,[139] the court ruled that discovery into evidence of the plaintiff's sexual conduct with the named defendants while on duty would be permitted under Rule 412 as evidence of possible welcomeness.[140] It barred discovery, however, of the plaintiff's sexual activities off-duty and outside the workplace with coworkers who were not defendants in the lawsuit.[141]

In *Excel Corp. v. Bosley*,[142] the Eighth Circuit affirmed the district court's exclusion of evidence of sexual relations that occurred between the plaintiff and her alleged harasser (who was also her ex-husband) during the same period as the alleged workplace harassment (which largely consisted of degrading sexual epithets and threats to kill her boyfriend). Part of the defendant's proffer was the testimony of a psychologist who treated both the plaintiff and her ex-husband and who indicated that the plaintiff acknowledged sending her ex-husband "mixed signals." While the court of appeals found that the district court did not "manifestly err" in excluding the evidence, it emphasized that the sexual activity occurred outside the workplace and that the corporate employer was not aware of it when it addressed the plaintiff's complaint of harassment.

---

[136] 895 F. Supp. 105, 68 FEP Cases 930 (E.D. Va. 1995).

[137] *Id.* at 109, 68 FEP Cases at 932.

[138] *Id.*, 68 FEP Cases at 933. *But see* Beard v. Flying J, Inc., 116 F. Supp. 2d 1077 (S.D. Iowa 2000) (finding admission of plaintiff's sexual conversations at work to be harmless error in spite of defendant's failure to follow Rule 412 procedure); Fedio v. Circuit City Stores, Inc., 1998 WL 966000 (E.D. Pa. Nov. 4, 1998) (admitting evidence of plaintiff's sexual history and conduct even though defendant did not comply with Rule 412's procedural requirements).

[139] 169 F.R.D. 132 (D. Haw. 1996).

[140] *Id.* at 135.

[141] *Id.* at 136.

[142] 165 F.3d 635, 78 FEP Cases 1844 (8th Cir. 1999).

In *Truong v. Smith*,[143] the court barred discovery of the plaintiff's extramarital affairs but noted that "evidence that a sexual assault victim has engaged in consensual sexual relations with the defendant in the past under similar conditions may have some logical relevance to the question of consent to the act charged."[144]

In *Ratts v. Board of County Commissioners*,[145] the court permitted deposition questioning of the plaintiff concerning her sexual activities with one of the defendants that had occurred before the period in which she claimed that defendant sexually harassed her, but it blocked questioning about her sexual activities with individuals other than the defendant.

In *Sanchez v. Zabihi*,[146] the court permitted a broader range of discovery under Rule 412 relating to a welcomeness defense. It permitted questioning of the plaintiff as to whether she had made any romantic or sexual advances toward a coworker, had been the subject of any romantic or sexual advances by a coworker, or had a romantic or sexual relationship with any coworker (except her spouse) within the three years prior to the alleged incidents of sexual harassment.[147]

In contrast, in *Howard v. Historic Tours of America*,[148] the court prohibited discovery of plaintiffs' sexual affairs with nonharassing coworkers, which the defendants sought to offer as evidence of welcomeness. The court remarked: "[I]t is absurd to think that any man in 1997 can be justified in believing that a woman who engages in [extramarital sex] is so degraded morally that she will welcome his sexual advances without protest."[149]

Finally, in the most permissive reading of Rule 412 to date, the court in *Holt v. Welch Allyn, Inc.*[150] permitted discovery of photographs showing the plaintiff at a party with a male exotic dancer. The court noted testimony by a coworker that the plaintiff had seen the photographs in the workplace and was not offended, and it upheld the magistrate judge's ruling that the plaintiff's behavior in the workplace "may be relevant to whether or not those co-workers perceived their workplace behavior toward her to be 'unwanted harassment.' "[151]

C. Application of Rule 412 to Emotional Damages Issues

In *Alberts v. Wickes Lumber Co.*,[152] Rule 412 was applied in a number of respects to damages issues. The plaintiff claimed that she had been sexually

---

[143] 183 F.R.D. 273 (D. Colo. 1998).

[144] *Id.* at 275.

[145] 189 F.R.D. 448 (D. Kan. 1999).

[146] 166 F.R.D. 500, 71 FEP Cases 835 (D.N.M. 1996).

[147] *Id.* at 502, 71 FEP Cases at 837. The *Zabihi* court also required that this information be obtained via interrogatory and be maintained under seal by defendants' counsel.

[148] 177 F.R.D. 48 (D.D.C. 1997).

[149] *Id.* at 52.

[150] 3 WH Cases 2d 1622 (N.D.N.Y. 1997).

[151] *Id.* at 1628.

[152] 1995 WL 117886 (N.D. Ill. Mar. 15, 1995).

assaulted by a coworker. Although the court excluded evidence of whether or not the plaintiff was using birth control on the night of the alleged assault, it permitted discovery into whether she kept contraceptives in the glove compartment of her car. This evidence was allowed because the alleged assailant testified that, a few weeks after the alleged assault, the plaintiff invited him into her car, which was parked in the garage of her home, and while showing him the car's stereo system, opened the glove compartment to reveal contraceptives. The court observed about this evidence:

> Proof of this evidence would allow the defendants a strong argument to the jury that the plaintiff ... could not possibly have been as traumatized as she now claims to be by the experience she had with this very same person just a few weeks before. A person so traumatized would not place herself in such a position. The behavior is not what one would expect if the plaintiff's claims of emotional trauma are true.[153]

The court went on to point out that the plaintiff claimed that the sexual assault and harassment by the assailant caused her to suffer lasting emotional impairment, yet for her later to invite her alleged assailant to be alone with her in the front seat of her car in the presence of condoms "could very well be significant evidence tending to rebut her claim of severe emotional trauma."[154] *Alberts* thus suggests that a plaintiff's sexual conduct with an alleged harasser subsequent to the alleged harassment may be admissible under Rule 412.

The next issue addressed in *Alberts* was the ability of the defendant to ask the plaintiff about affairs she had had with men other than the alleged harasser, in order to show that the plaintiff's emotional distress was caused by bad relationships with these other men rather than by the defendant. Although the court foreclosed such an inquiry under Rule 412, it did so not because the inquiry is inherently impermissible but because the defendant had failed to lay a sufficient predicate. The court noted that the defendant had sought to justify such questioning by arguing that the plaintiff had failed to tell her psychologist (who would testify as to her emotional distress) about these relationships, but it pointed out that the defendant had not questioned the psychologist on deposition about whether such information would be useful to him or would in any way change his opinion or alter his analysis of the plaintiff's emotional damages.[155] *Alberts* suggests, therefore, that, upon a proper showing, discovery of a plaintiff's other romantic relationships, particularly bad ones, may be permissible under Rule 412 as evidence of alternate causation of emotional distress. As the *Alberts* court suggests, an admission from the plaintiff's psychological expert that such information may be relevant to his analysis is one way to lay the predicate for such discovery. Another way might be testimony from the defendant's psychological expert to the same effect.

Finally, the court in *Alberts* permitted questioning of a sexual harassment plaintiff about the specifics of her claim that the harassment caused her to

---

[153]*Id.* at *3.
[154]*Id.* at *4.
[155]*Id.*

experience problems in achieving sexual intimacy. The court first noted that "it is doubtful that this conduct falls under the prohibition of Rule 412" because that rule prohibits only evidence offered to prove that a plaintiff engaged in other sexual behavior, yet the plaintiff in *Alberts* testified that she did not—and indeed could not—engage in other sexual behavior.[156] Even if Rule 412 were to apply, reasoned the court, the evidence would be admissible. The court explained:

> [H]ere it is the plaintiff who has, by her pleadings, injected into the very heart of her damages claim her inability to engage in intimate sexual relationships after the complained of occurrence. To allow [the plaintiff] to use these alleged experiences as evidence of her damages, but at the same time deny [the defendant] the opportunity to prove that these claims are not true, would be to turn the rape "shield" law into a sword solely for the plaintiff's benefit. If [the plaintiff] chooses to base her case for damages on her inability to engage in sexual behavior subsequent to the date of the alleged offense, then Rule 412 cannot be deemed to bar [the defendant] from mounting a defense against such a claim by the most direct and traditional of methods, i.e., proof that such a claim is simply not true.[157]

Similarly, the court in *Sublette v. Glidden Co.*[158] denied the plaintiff's motion to exclude evidence that after she left her job with the defendant (and then left a similar job with another employer), she took a job massaging men at a health club. The court held that the evidence was relevant to counter the plaintiff's claim that she suffered such severe emotional damage from sexual harassment by the defendant that she was unable to work around men.

Conversely, the Second Circuit in *Wolak v. Spucci*[159] held that evidence of the plaintiff's watching pornography and live sex performances away from work should have been excluded. The defense sought to justify this questioning as showing that the plaintiff was not subjectively offended by pornographic posters, videos, and magazines in the workplace and suffered no damages as a result. The district court admitted the evidence, noting that "[a]t least for purposes of computing her damages for shame and humiliation and the like, no plaintiff should be permitted to portray herself to the trial jury falsely, as some sort of shrinking violet or as a novice in a nunnery." The Second Circuit rejected that view, however. It explained:

> We conclude that the evidence was of, at best, marginal relevance. Whether a sexual advance was welcome, or whether an alleged victim in fact perceived an environment to be sexually offensive, does not turn on the private sexual behavior of the alleged victim, because a woman's expectations about her work environment cannot be said to change depending on her sexual sophistication. Even if a woman's out-of-work sexual experiences were such that she could perhaps be expected to suffer less harm from viewing run-of-the-mill pornographic images

---

[156]*Id.* at *5.
[157]*Id.*
[158]1998 WL 964189 (E.D. Pa. Oct. 1, 1998).
[159]217 F.3d 157, 83 FEP Cases 253 (2d Cir. 2000).

displayed in the office, pornography might still alter her status in the workplace, causing injury, regardless of the trauma inflicted by the pornographic images alone.[160]

The Second Circuit found that the probative value of the evidence of the plaintiff's sexual activities outside work did not substantially outweigh the danger of harm and unfair prejudice.[161]

D. Application of Rule 412 to Summary Judgment Motions

At least one court has held that Rule 412 applies to summary judgment motions. In *Dunegan v. City of Council Grove*,[162] the defendant filed a motion for summary judgment on the plaintiff's hostile environment harassment claim. It submitted evidence that the plaintiff sunbathed in the nude on the roof of the building while on duty, told sexual jokes in the workplace, talked about her sex life, pinched male employees on their buttocks, had sex with a coworker while on duty, and simulated fellatio with a candy bar in front of employees and a vendor, among other things. The plaintiff then filed a motion to exclude this evidence as inadmissible under Rule 412. The defendant argued that Rule 412 does not apply to summary judgment proceedings. Although the court noted that a reading of the rule and the Advisory Committee Comments suggested some merit to that argument (in that the rule addresses only the use at trial of evidence of a plaintiff's sexual conduct), it held that Rule 412 does apply to summary judgment proceedings. It remarked, "Rule 412 was designed to protect the privacy interests of victims of sexual misconduct. An interpretation of the rule that would allow the parties to expose this evidence in a summary judgment motion without the safeguards of Rule 412 would circumvent the purpose of the rule."[163]

E. Application of Rule 412 in Discovery

The Advisory Committee Notes to the 1994 Amendments to Rule 412 provide that the procedures set forth in subdivision (c) of that Rule "do not apply to discovery of a victim's past sexual conduct or predisposition in civil cases, which will continue to be governed by Fed. R. Civ. P. 26,"[164] which requires only "relevance" as a prerequisite to discovery. The Notes go on to suggest

---

[160]*Id.* at 160–61, 83 FEP Cases at 256 (citations omitted).

[161]*Id.* at 161, 83 FEP Cases at 256. The Second Circuit did not reverse, however, because it found the error to be harmless in that the plaintiff failed to put on evidence that she suffered damage as a result of a hostile environment at work. *Id.* at 161–62, 83 FEP Cases at 257.

[162]189 F.R.D. 649 (D. Kan. 1999).

[163]*Id.* at 652.

[164]*See* Advisory Committee Notes, *supra* note 102.

that courts should issue appropriate orders under Rule 26(c) to "protect the victim against unwarranted inquiries and to ensure confidentiality."[165] The Notes to Rule 412 thus suggest a different standard for discovery of information covered by Rule 412 than for its admissibility. In the Advisory Committee's view, a protective order should issue "unless the party seeking discovery makes a showing that the evidence sought to be discovered would be relevant under the facts and theories of a particular case, and cannot be obtained except through discovery."[166] Accordingly, only relevance need be shown for discoverability, not that the "probative value substantially outweighs the danger of harm to any victim and of unfair prejudice to any party," as is required by Rule 412(b)(2) for admissibility.

Some courts have held that Rule 412 does not apply at all in discovery. For example, in *Holt v. Welch Allyn, Inc.*,[167] the defendant sought production of a photograph of one of the plaintiffs at a party where a male exotic dancer performed. The plaintiffs cited Rule 412 in their attempt to bar the discovery, but the court remarked that the plaintiffs "have . . . overstated the protections of Rule 412."[168] The court pointed out that the photograph had been taken to the workplace and passed around, about which the plaintiff did not seem offended. The court felt that the photograph "may be relevant to show the perception of [plaintiff's] co-workers regarding her workplace behavior," although it also noted that the admissibility of the photograph at trial was "a matter for another day."[169]

In *Ramirez v. Nabil's, Inc.*,[170] the court similarly declined to apply Rule 412 to discovery, noting that the rule is "a rule of admissibility." In a sexual harassment case, the defendant sought production of medical records pertaining to psychiatric treatment received by two of the plaintiffs when they were adolescents. While those plaintiffs did not expressly indicate that the treatment involved sexual matters, they raised Rule 412 in an attempt to bar the discovery. The court applied Federal Rule of Civil Procedure 26 instead and ordered the records produced. It stated that the discovery sought appeared "reasonably calculated to lead to the discovery of admissible evidence regarding the claims of emotional distress by Cook and Boden and possibly the sexual propensities of Cook."[171] Thus, the ruling in *Ramirez* suggests that evidence of prior sexual abuse may be discoverable as to potential sexual propensities of a plaintiff as well as to possible alternative causation of damages.

Other courts that have addressed the issue have held that Rule 412's principles must at least guide courts in determining what is discoverable under Rule 26. In *Barta v. City & County of Honolulu*,[172] the court noted that Rule 412 "must inform the discovery process." Accordingly, a court "must impose

---

[165] *Id.*
[166] *Id.*
[167] 3 WH Cases 2d 1622 (N.D.N.Y. 1997).
[168] *Id.* at 1628.
[169] *Id.*
[170] 1995 WL 609415 (D. Kan. Oct. 5, 1995).
[171] *Id.* at *3.
[172] 169 F.R.D. 132, 135 (D. Haw. 1996).

certain restrictions on discovery to preclude inquiry into areas which will clearly fail to satisfy the balancing test of Rule 412(b)(2), although the trial judge will render the decisions on what evidence is ultimately admitted."[173]

In *Giron v. Corrections Corp. of America*,[174] a Section 1983 action by a former prison inmate alleging that a guard had raped her, the court, citing *Barta*, applied Rule 412 to bar discovery of the plaintiff's prior sexual partners. The defendant had sought the identity of those persons purportedly in an attempt to learn what preexisting psychological and medical conditions the plaintiff might have had. The court ruled that such information would be outside the expertise of a plaintiff's prior sexual partners. The court did, however, order the plaintiff to provide information regarding prior sexual contacts that were "violent or damaging to her in any way," and it specifically rejected a proposed time limitation of five years preceding the event at issue in the litigation.[175] The court reasoned that evidence of prior sexual abuse might be relevant to the causation of plaintiff's emotional damages.

In *Truong v. Smith*,[176] a sexual assault case brought by a nurse against a doctor under the Violence Against Women Act, the court applied Rule 412 to the defendant's attempt to discover the plaintiff's history of extramarital affairs, which he argued were relevant to his defenses of a consensual relationship and the initiation of contact by the plaintiff. The court denied the discovery, noting that Rule 412 prohibits use of a plaintiff's past sexual behavior to attack her credibility. The court explained:

> While evidence that a sexual assault victim has engaged in consensual sexual relations with the defendant in the past under similar circumstances may have some logical relevance to the question of consent to the act charged, and evidence of prior sexual activity with the defendant under dissimilar circumstances may also have some logical relevance, . . . "(w)hen both identity of persons and similarity of circumstances are removed, probative value all but disappears."[177]

---

[173]*Id. See also* Herchenroeder v. Johns Hopkins Univ., 171 F.R.D. 179, 182 (D. Md. 1997) (court must look to both Rule 26 and Rule 412 in discovery); Sanchez v. Zabihi, 166 F.R.D. 500, 502, 71 FEP Cases 835 (D.N.M. 1996) (Rule 412 "is applicable and has significance" in discovery).

[174]981 F. Supp. 1406 (D.N.M. 1997).

[175]*Id.* at 1408. As to each such encounter, the plaintiff was ordered to:
describe the manner and type of each sexual contact; the date and location of each sexual contact; all persons present during the contact; how the event occurred; the type of medical treatment received; the name, address and phone number of each treating physician; address of each hospital at which treatment was received; the other person who participated in the sexual contact and committed the abuse, touching or injury, and if such event was reported to a government agency, plaintiff is to identify that agency.

Id.

[176]183 F.R.D. 273 (D. Colo. 1998).

[177]*Id.* at 275 (quoting Andrea P. Ordover, *Admissibility of Patterns of Similar Sexual Conduct: The Unlamented Death of Character for Chastity*, 63 CORNELL L. REV. 90, 106 (1977)).

Similarly, the court in *Robinson v. Canon U.S.A.*[178] relied on Rule 412 to bar discovery of any extramarital affairs the plaintiff might have had with coworkers or customers. It rejected the defendant's argument that extramarital affairs might constitute alternative sources of emotional distress the plaintiff claimed to have suffered at the hands of the defendants. The court maintained that "it is a leap to argue that extramarital affairs are per se a source of stress. Second, Defendants suggest no way in which they can satisfy their obligation to segregate the 'harassment-induced stress' from the 'extramarital affair-induced stress.' "[179] The court did not specifically address the applicability of Rule 412 to discovery. It simply declared, without any analysis or explanation, that "evidence regarding Plaintiff's sexual conduct—regardless of what it may be—will not be admissible in this case, so discovery requests on the subject are not likely to lead to the discovery of admissible evidence."[180]

In *Williams v. Board of County Commissioners of Wyandotte County*,[181] the plaintiff in a lawsuit under the Violence Against Women Act alleging rape by a police officer objected under Rule 412 and Federal Rule of Civil Procedure 26 to an interrogatory asking her to state whether she had ever had any sexually transmitted diseases, the age at which she first had sexual intercourse, and the names and addresses of all persons with whom she had been sexually active in the previous five years. The defendant argued the interrogatory was necessary to help determine the cause of the emotional distress the plaintiff claimed to have suffered. The defendant also argued that Rule 412 was not applicable to discovery. The court found the interrogatory improper primarily under Rule 26, noting that the marginal relevance of the questions was outweighed by the potential harm to the plaintiff. Without specifically deciding that Rule 412 applies to discovery, the court maintained that the result would have been the same under that rule.

In *Fitzpatrick v. QVC, Inc.*,[182] a sexual harassment case in which a male plaintiff complained of advances by his male supervisor, the defendant's attorney asked the plaintiff during deposition whether he was a homosexual and about his last sexual relationship. In denying the defendant's motion to compel, the court applied Rule 412 and explained:

> [T]he Court rejects any suggestion that [the plaintiff's] private sexual conduct outside the workplace is relevant to the question of whether he was offended by [his supervisor's] conduct. With respect to the claim of emotional distress, courts generally deem evidence of a plaintiff's sexual orientation relevant only in limited circumstances such as where the defendant seeks to rebut the plaintiff's allegations that workplace harassment was the sole source of stress in his or her life by showing

---

[178]82 FEP Cases 1129 (W.D. Mo. 2000).

[179]*Id.* at 1130. The court maintained that apportionment of emotional distress is an affirmative defense upon which the defendant bears the burden of proof (citing Jenson v. Eveleth Taconite Co., 130 F.3d 1287, 75 FEP Cases 852 (8th Cir. 1997)).

[180]82 FEP Cases at 1130.

[181]192 F.R.D. 698 (D. Kan. 2000).

[182]1999 WL 1215577 (E.D. Pa. Dec. 7, 1999).

that at the time of the alleged harassment, the plaintiff had been experiencing some domestic upheavals.[183]

Finding that the plaintiff's sexual orientation "would have no probative value at all" in determining whether he was offended by his supervisor's conduct and only minimal probative value in terms of emotional distress, the court denied the motion to compel.

F. Application of Rule 412 to Nonparty Witnesses

In spite of the fact that the language of Rule 412 indicates that it applies only to alleged victims of sexual misconduct, the Committee Notes state that Rule 412 extends to "pattern" witnesses "whose testimony about other instances of sexual misconduct by the person accused is otherwise admissible."[184] This seems to mean that Rule 412 would apply to the sexual history of nonparty witnesses who testify that they also were harassed by the defendant, although at least two courts have taken somewhat contrary approaches.

In *Biggs v. Nicewonger Co.*,[185] the plaintiff filed a Rule 412 motion to exclude evidence regarding "any alleged victim's sexual predisposition," apparently referring to evidence concerning the types of clothing worn by another female employee expected to testify that she, too, had been sexually harassed while in the defendant's employ. The defendant opposed the motion, arguing that if the plaintiff raised the issue of the coworker's harassment, the defendant should be permitted to demonstrate that it took corrective action, which included counseling the coworker about her inappropriate style of dress. Although the court withheld ruling until such point as the plaintiff might attempt to introduce the alleged harassment of the co-worker, it noted that "evidence of the responses to and the actions taken by [the employer] to the complaints of [the coworker] is relevant evidence."[186]

In *Stalnaker v. K-Mart Corp.*,[187] the court declined to apply Rule 412 to nonparty witnesses who might testify that the alleged harasser also harassed them. Although holding that Rule 412 did not apply because the witnesses were not themselves victims of alleged sexual misconduct, the court barred inquiries to the nonparty witnesses about their sexual activities unconnected to the workplace. The court did allow discovery, however, into the witnesses' "voluntary romantic or sexual activities with [the alleged harasser] to the extent they show any conduct on his part to encourage, solicit, or influence any employee of defendant to engage or continue in such activities."[188]

---

[183]*Id.* at *3 (citation omitted).
[184]*See* Advisory Committee Notes, *supra* note 102.
[185]897 F. Supp. 483, 68 FEP Cases 1771 (D. Or. 1995).
[186]*Id.* at 484, 68 FEP Cases at 1772.
[187]71 FEP Cases 705 (D. Kan. 1996).
[188]*Id.* at 707.

On the other hand, in *Burger v. Litton Industries, Inc.*,[189] the court applied Rule 412 to a nonparty witness who was being deposed by the plaintiff. The witness testified to the sexual activity of others while she worked at Litton and to being sexually harassed by the plaintiff's supervisor. On cross-examination, the defendant's counsel asked the witness whether she had a sexual relationship with any other Litton employee while she worked at Litton. Noting that Rule 412 places the burden on the defendant to prove that the probative value of the evidence sought to be admitted substantially outweighs the invasion of privacy engendered by the admission of such evidence, the court determined that the value of the nonparty witness' answers to questions about her sexual conduct were substantially outweighed by the invasion of her privacy, and it thus barred the questioning.

G. Application of Rule 412 to Prior Sexual Abuse

Most of the cases interpreting Rule 412 have involved volitional sexual conduct on the part of the plaintiff (i.e., consensual sexual relationships). Also of extreme significance in sexual harassment cases, however, is the existence of any prior nonvolitional sexual experiences in the plaintiff's lifetime (i.e., sexual abuse or assault). Molestation as a child or sexual assault as an adult can have a profound and lasting impact on the psychological condition of the victim.

Numerous courts have considered a plaintiff's history of childhood sexual abuse as an alternative cause of emotional distress.[190] In *McCleland v. Montgomery Ward & Co.*,[191] the court admitted evidence of the plaintiffs' prior childhood and adolescent abuse, including sexual abuse, as evidence of a potential alternative cause for their emotional injuries. The court rejected the plaintiffs' motion in limine to exclude such evidence, in spite of the plaintiffs' argument that because they were not seeking damages for aggravation of preexisting mental or psychological conditions, any evidence of their prior childhood and adolescent sexual abuse was irrelevant and prejudicial.

The court in *McCleland* found that Rule 412 did not apply to childhood sexual abuse because the defendant did not seek to introduce the prior abuse as evidence of the plaintiffs' sexual behavior or predisposition.[192] Nonetheless,

---

[189]1995 WL 476712 (S.D.N.Y. Aug. 10, 1995).

[190]*E.g.,* McKinnon v. Kwong Wah Rest., 83 F.3d 498, 70 FEP Cases 1037 (1st Cir. 1996) (affirming award of $2,500 in emotional distress damages to sexual harassment plaintiff, noting the relevance of plaintiff's having been sexually abused by her stepfather from age 5 to age 17); Hurley v. Atlantic City Police Dep't, 933 F. Supp. 396, 72 FEP Cases 1828 (D.N.J. 1996) (in reducing jury award of $575,000 for emotional distress to $175,000, noting plaintiff's history of childhood molestation and two abusive marriages). *See also* Giron v. Corrections Corp. of Am., 981 F. Supp. 1406 (D.N.M. 1997) (permitting discovery of prior sexual abuse, noting possible relevance re causation of emotional damages).

[191]1995 WL 571324 (N.D. Ill. Sept. 25, 1995).

[192]*Id.* at *4 n.1.

the court noted, even if Rule 412 were to be applicable, the probative value of the evidence substantially outweighed the danger of harm or undue prejudice.[193] The court noted, among other things, that while the plaintiffs received extensive psychological treatment, their focus during that treatment was on their childhood abuse; neither mentioned to her therapist that she was being sexually harassed at work.[194]

In *Delaney v. City of Hampton*,[195] the court granted the defendant's Rule 412 motion to admit evidence of the plaintiff's history of prior sexual abuse as a potential alternative cause of her emotional damages. The plaintiff alleged that as a result of sexual harassment she suffered Posttraumatic Stress Disorder requiring numerous hospitalizations and long-term psychiatric treatment. The court noted that the defendant's experts planned to testify that the plaintiff's prior sexual abuse contributed to her psychiatric problems.

These cases demonstrate that Rule 412 will not necessarily bar the admission of evidence of the plaintiff's prior sexual abuse in a sexual harassment case.[196] An argument can be made that because Rule 412(a)(1) addresses evidence that the plaintiff "engaged in"[197] other sexual behavior, it does not apply to prior sexual experiences in which the plaintiff was an unwilling participant.[198]

The existence and impact of a plaintiff's prior sexual abuse are therefore important issues in sexual harassment litigation. One plaintiff's lawyer recently observed that although approximately 25 percent of all adult women in the United States were sexually abused as children, "there is strong evidence that the percentage is higher among sexual harassment plaintiffs."[199] That author actually discusses ways in which a plaintiff's childhood sexual abuse might be exploited to her tactical advantage in a sexual harassment lawsuit.[200] As another authority has observed, "Encountering a history of childhood sexual abuse in a plaintiff should constitute a red flag for the forensic psychiatrist: the possibility that the plaintiff has been instrumental in the events of which she complains must be carefully considered."[201]

---

[193]*Id.*

[194]*Id.* at *2.

[195]999 F. Supp. 794 (E.D. Va.), *aff'd*, 135 F.3d 769 (4th Cir. 1998) (table).

[196]*But see* Knoettgen v. Superior Ct., 224 Cal. App. 3d 11, 273 Cal. Rptr. 636 (1990) (barring deposition questioning of a plaintiff concerning her history of childhood sexual abuse under California counterpart to Rule 412).

[197]BLACK'S LAW DICTIONARY (5th ed.) defines "engage" as "[t]o employ or involve one's self; to take part in; to embark on."

[198]The court made just this distinction in *Giron v. Corrections Corporation of America*, 981 F. Supp. 1406 (D.N.M. 1997). *See also* Fedio v. Circuit City Stores, Inc., 1998 WL 966000 (E.D. Pa. Nov. 4, 1998) (admitting evidence, over Rule 412 objection, that plaintiff was the victim of a date rape prior to becoming employed by the defendant).

[199]Lisa Bloom, *Gretel Fights Back: Representing Sexual Harassment Plaintiffs Who Were Sexually Abused as Children*, 12 BERKELEY WOMEN'S L.J. 1, 2–3 (1997).

[200]*Id.* at 16–18.

[201]Sara P. Feldman-Schorrig, *Need for Expansion of Forensic Psychiatrists' Role in Sexual Harassment Cases*, 23 BULL. AM. ACAD. PSYCHIATRY & L. 513, 517 (1995).

Prior sexual abuse may bear upon any or all of the following issues in litigation: (1) alternative causation of damages, (2) the plaintiff's credibility, (3) the "reasonable woman" or "reasonable person" standard, and (4) the defense of "welcomeness."[202]

1. Alternative Causation of Damages

Prior sexual abuse can cause a whole range of chronic psychopathology later in life that the abuse victim may misattribute to more contemporary events, such as workplace harassment or discrimination.[203] Thus, although a sexual harassment plaintiff may exhibit genuine symptoms of depression or other types of emotional distress and attribute those symptoms to workplace events, it must be determined whether an alternative explanation of the causation of those symptoms is more plausible.

For example, there is substantial medical evidence indicating that childhood sexual abuse can cause depressive symptoms in adult life.[204] Moreover, it is commonly accepted within the psychiatric community today that childhood sexual abuse may cause a Borderline Personality Disorder to develop,[205] and many individuals with Borderline Personality Disorder are chronically depressed. As one authority puts it, the Borderline patient's "[r]epeated interpersonal, vocational, and academic failures lead to states of demoralization with overtones of anger, which sooner or later become clinically indistinguishable from chronic depression."[206] Therefore, where a sexual harassment claimant

---

[202] *See* James J. McDonald, Jr. & Sara P. Feldman-Schorrig, *The Relevance of Childhood Sexual Abuse in Sexual Harassment Cases*, 20 EMPL. REL. L.J. 221 (1994).

[203] See discussion in Chapter 14, Special Issues in Sexual Harassment Cases.

[204] *See, e.g.,* Diane K. Schetky, *A Review of the Literature on the Long-Term Effects of Childhood Sexual Abuse, in* INCEST-RELATED SYNDROMES OF ADULT PSYCHOPATHOLOGY 41 (Richard Kluft ed., 1990) ("Depression, low self-esteem, and feelings of being damaged are commonly reported among adults who experienced childhood sexual abuse."); Catherine G. Fine, *The Cognitive Sequelae of Incest, in* INCEST-RELATED SYNDROMES OF ADULT PSYCHOPATHOLOGY 163 (Richard Kluft ed., 1990) ("Feelings of depression and anxiety are by far the more common emotions described by these victims."); John G. Gunderson, *Borderline Personality Disorder, in* COMPREHENSIVE TEXTBOOK OF PSYCHIATRY 1390 (Harold I. Kaplan & Benjamin J. Sadock eds., 5th ed. 1989) ("unipolar depressions of variable severity are very characteristic of borderline patients"); GLEN O. GABBARD, PSYCHODYNAMIC PSYCHIATRY IN CLINICAL PRACTICE 339 (1990) ("The clinical observation that many patients with borderline personality disorder also have an Axis I diagnosis of major depression has been increasingly substantiated by research.").

[205] *See* JOEL PARIS, BORDERLINE PERSONALITY DISORDER: ETIOLOGY AND TREATMENT 7 (1993) ("The evidence that borderline patients have a high rate of physical abuse, childhood sexual abuse, and other traumatic experiences during childhood has been reported from so many sources and samples by now that it is overwhelming"). *See also* Mary Zanarini et al., *Childhood Experiences of Borderline Patients*, 30 COMPREHENSIVE PSYCHIATRY 18 (1989). A general discussion of Borderline Personality Disorder appears in Chapter 6, Personality Disorders in Employment Litigation.

[206] JEROME KROLL, THE CHALLENGE OF THE BORDERLINE PATIENT 62 (1988).

complains of depression, there is at least the possibility that the depression is a feature of a personality disorder and not the result of the alleged harassment.

Similarly, some plaintiffs in sexual harassment cases will claim that their depression over events in the workplace caused them to attempt suicide. Prior childhood sexual abuse of the plaintiff is relevant because studies have linked such abuse to subsequent suicidal behavior.[207] It is therefore necessary to determine whether suicidal behavior by a plaintiff in a sexual harassment case is accurately attributable to workplace events or to a chronic pattern of behavior originating from childhood trauma.

A sexual harassment plaintiff may also claim that workplace events disrupted her marriage or other intimate relationships. Chronic chaos in personal relationships, however, is a common characteristic of victims of childhood sexual abuse and persons with Borderline Personality Disorder.[208] As the authors of one study observe:

> Even years after the abuse, the attitudes of victims in relationships were masked by an inability to trust, by a fear of commitment and at the same time a tendency to cling to the partner, and by a passive helpless behavior as an expression of persistent emotional deficit. . . . Nearly half of the patients were living in a mostly unhappy relationship (marriage or companionship) or alone with an illegitimate child.[209]

Marital or relationship problems following a workplace incident may thus be just one example of a long history of such problems, which may well have occurred regardless of workplace events.

In *Giron v. Corrections Corp. of America*,[210] a sexual assault case brought under Section 1983, the court permitted discovery into prior incidents of sexual abuse involving the plaintiff. It reasoned that such incidents might be relevant to the issue of causation regarding plaintiff's emotional damages claim.

2. Impact on Plaintiff's Credibility

Although different jurisdictions take varying approaches to the issue, use of evidence of a mental condition may be permitted as a means of attacking a witness's credibility. As one California court explained:

---

[207]*See, e.g.*, Amy W. Wagner & Marsha M. Linehan, *Relationship Between Childhood Sexual Abuse and Topography of Parasuicide Among Women With Borderline Personality Disorder*, 8 J. PERSONALITY DISORDERS 1, 2 (1994); Schetky, *supra* note 204, at 42; John N. Briere & Lisa Y. Zaidi, *Sexual Abuse Histories and Sequelae in Female Psychiatric Emergency Room Patients*, 146 AM. J. PSYCHIATRY 1602, 1604–05 (1989).

[208]*See* AMERICAN PSYCHIATRIC ASSOCIATION, DIAGNOSTIC AND STATISTICAL MANUAL OF MENTAL DISORDERS 706 (4th ed. text rev. 2001) ("The essential feature of Borderline Personality Disorder is a pervasive pattern of instability of interpersonal relationships.").

[209]Johannes Kinzl & Wilfried Biebl, *Sexual Abuse of Girls: Aspects of the Genesis of Mental Disorders and Therapeutic Implications*, 83 ACTA PSYCHIATRICA ET NEUROLOGICA SCANDINAVICA 429 (1991).

[210]981 F. Supp. 1406 (D.N.M. 1997).

A witness may be cross-examined about her mental condition or emotional stability to the extent it may affect her powers of perception, memory or recollection, or communication. Expert psychiatric testimony may be admissible to impeach the credibility of a ... witness where the witness' mental or emotional condition may affect the ability of the witness to tell the truth.[211]

Prior sexual trauma may affect a plaintiff's credibility in a number of respects.

A. BORDERLINE RAGE One feature of Borderline Personality Disorder is rage. Individuals with this disorder will often have rapid mood shifts, in which they overreact emotionally to perceived slights by others, especially those upon whom the borderline previously depended. The anger may be interpreted as unresolved resentment that a victim of childhood sexual abuse feels toward her father or other male figure who abused her, but it is directed at whomever in her present life might serve as a convenient target.

Individuals with Borderline Personality Disorder are especially sensitive to rejection. They react with rage against whomever they perceive as having somehow rejected them, and they often look for ways in which to obtain revenge. This helps to explain why an employee with Borderline Personality Disorder who previously acted friendly and flirtatious with supervisors and coworkers and who may even have initiated sexually related conversations in the workplace, might suddenly change her mind and angrily accuse her colleagues of harassing her.

Borderline rage may even manifest itself in the filing of false accusations in a lawsuit. As one authority has observed, "the patient with borderline personality disorder may express rage in a vengeful manner by filing a specious suit."[212]

B. DISSOCIATION Even absent conscious lying, childhood sexual abuse may still affect a sexual harassment plaintiff's credibility in that many victims of such abuse suffer from a type of psychopathology known as dissociation. Dissociation refers to a disruption in the usually integrated functions of consciousness, memory, identity, or perception of the environment. Dissociation protects the ego by keeping traumatic experiences from conscious awareness, in effect "splitting off" affect and memory from the self.[213]

Incest victims may exhibit a variety of dissociative symptoms, including cognitive distortions such as misassuming causality, distortions of self-

---

[211]People v. Herring, 20 Cal. App. 4th 1066, 1072, 25 Cal. Rptr. 2d 213 (1993) (citation omitted). *But see* Doyle v. Superior Ct., 50 Cal. App. 4th 1878, 58 Cal. Rptr. 2d 476 (1996) (mental examinations are not authorized for purpose of testing a person's credibility).

[212]Thomas G. Gutheil, *Borderline Personality Disorder, Boundary Violations and Patient-Therapist Sex: Medicolegal Pitfalls,* 146 AM. J. PSYCHIATRY 597, 598 (1989).

[213]David A. Sandberg et al., *Sexual Abuse and Revictimization: Mastery, Dysfunctional Learning, and Dissociation, in* DISSOCIATION: CLINICAL AND THEORETICAL PERSPECTIVES 257 (Steven J. Lynn & Judith W. Rhue eds., 1994).

perception, time distortion, and dichotomous thinking (in which a person or situation is viewed as all good or all bad).[214] Most significantly, however, dissociative disorders are often characterized by memory dysfunctions, including difficulty in determining whether a given memory reflects an actual event or information acquired through a nonexperiential source (e.g., reading or hearing about the event).[215] Persons with dissociative disorders also often have difficulty distinguishing between fantasy and reality. As one leading authority on these disorders has observed, "The individual may report that memories have a dreamlike quality and at times cannot be distinguished from fantasy, so that the person becomes unsure of whether or not something actually occurred."[216] The fact that a dissociative personality might have such difficulty in being an accurate historian has significant implications for the credibility of such a person as a plaintiff in a sexual harassment lawsuit. Evidence of dissociative disorders may be uncovered by a thorough review of a plaintiff's history of mental health treatment. Multiple Personality Disorder is considered an extreme form of dissociative disorder, so any evidence in a plaintiff's mental health history of diagnosis or treatment of multiple personalities would likely be evidence of a dissociative disorder. There is also a testing instrument known as the Dissociative Experiences Scale (DES), which is used to detect and measure a subject's dissociative experiences. An effort should be made to determine whether a plaintiff was administered the DES, and the answer sheet should be obtained, as many of the questions on the instrument gauge the extent of the subject's contact with reality.[217]

3. The Reasonable Woman/Reasonable Person Standard

Not all harassment of a sexual nature is actionable. The Supreme Court, in *Harris v. Forklift Systems, Inc.*,[218] decreed that to violate Title VII, harassing conduct must be "severe or pervasive enough to create an objectively hostile or abusive work environment."[219] The Ninth Circuit provided a precursor to this notion in *Ellison v. Brady*,[220] when it stated:

---

[214] Frank Putnam, *Dissociative Disorders in Children and Adolescents, in* DISSOCIATION: CLINICAL AND THEORETICAL PERSPECTIVES 175 (Steven J. Lynn & Judith W. Rhue eds., 1994).

[215] *Id.* at 176.

[216] FRANK PUTNAM, DIAGNOSIS AND TREATMENT OF MULTIPLE PERSONALITY DISORDER 15 (1989).

[217] In one sexual harassment lawsuit tried by this author, the plaintiff had been administered the DES. Her answer to one question read:
> 18. Some people sometimes feel that they become so involved in a fantasy or daydream that it feels as though it were really happening to them.
> Percentage of the time this happens to you: *90*

Obviously, this portion of the test became an important trial exhibit.

[218] 510 U.S. 17, 63 FEP Cases 225 (1993).

[219] *Id.* at 21, 63 FEP Cases at 227.

[220] 924 F.2d 872, 54 FEP Cases 1346 (9th Cir. 1991).

In order to shield employers from having to accommodate the idiosyncratic concerns of the rare hyper-sensitive employee, we hold that a female plaintiff states a prima facie case of hostile environment sexual harassment when she alleges conduct which a reasonable woman would consider sufficiently severe or pervasive to alter the conditions of employment and create an abusive working environment.[221]

Thus, if a sexual harassment plaintiff is a "hypersensitive" individual who, because of her psychological history or makeup, is offended by workplace conduct that a "reasonable" woman (or person of the same gender as the plaintiff) of normal sensitivity would not find offensive, such a plaintiff cannot prevail on a sexual harassment claim.[222]

Considerable evidence has been developed in the field of psychiatry suggesting that women with a history of childhood sexual abuse display clinical symptoms that are consistent with a type of Posttraumatic Stress Disorder that becomes chronic and integrated into the victim's personality structure. Memory of the original stressor may be partially or completely repressed, but fear and hypervigilance resulting from the original trauma usually persist.[223] As one authority has pointed out, "[t]he most benign touch to someone who has been sexually abused can be experienced as sexual assault."[224]

This fear and hypervigilance may be manifest as a form of hypersensitivity to perceived sexual cues in the workplace. As the author of one study of the characteristics of sexually abused women observes, "a woman who has been [victimized] is likely to have a heightened response to harassing remarks at work." She states, "What is trivial to one person may trigger PTSD [Posttraumatic Stress Disorder] or a stress-response syndrome in another."[225] As one leading authority on trauma observes, "Chronic physiologic hyperarousal to stimuli reminiscent of the trauma is a cardinal feature of the trauma response, well documented in a large variety of traumatized individuals, including victims of child abuse."[226]

For example, one woman, with no history of victimization, might not be troubled by a sexual proposition of a coworker and in fact might laugh it off or even find it flattering. Another woman, with a prior history of sexual abuse, would be more likely to react to the same proposition with anger or fear. It is essential, therefore, to know whether a sexual harassment plaintiff was the

---

[221]*Id.* at 879.

[222]*See* Zabkowicz v. West Bend Co., 589 F. Supp. 780, 784 (E.D. Wis. 1984) ("Title VII does not serve as a vehicle for vindicating the petty slights suffered by the hypersensitive").

[223]Judith L. Herman et al., *Long-Term Effects of Incestuous Abuse in Childhood,* 143 AM. J. PSYCHIATRY 1293, 1293 (1986).

[224]Feldman-Schorrig, *supra* note 201, at 519.

[225]Jean A. Hamilton, *Emotional Consequences of Victimization and Discrimination in "Special Populations" of Women,* 12 PSYCHIATRIC CLINICS N. AM. 35, 42 (1989).

[226]Bessel A. van der Kolk, *The Compulsion to Repeat the Trauma,* 12 PSYCHIATRIC CLINICS N. AM. 389, 395 (1989).

victim of childhood sexual abuse to determine whether her response to the workplace events at issue was that of a hypersensitive or a reasonable person.

This point was highlighted by the court in *Blankenship v. Parke Care Centers, Inc.*[227] With respect to the subjective and objective tests set forth by the Supreme Court in *Harris v. Forklift Systems, Inc,*[228] the court observed, "Factors to be considered in making both the objective and subjective evaluations include the nature of the alleged harassment, the alleged victim's background and experience, the atmosphere of the workplace and the plaintiff's reasonable expectations regarding the workplace."[229] The court then observed, in awarding summary judgment for the defendant, that both plaintiffs were only 17 years old and had each been the victim of childhood sexual abuse. It stated, "The Court believes that Plaintiffs' youth, their relative inexperience in dealing with issues in any workplace environment, and their history of sexual victimization are all relevant factors to be considered in gauging their likely subjective reaction to the sexually-charged conduct of an over-40 male coworker."[230] The court opined that "although the facts herein weigh in favor of concluding that these particular Plaintiffs subjectively would perceive the alleged conduct to affect the conditions of their employment, the likely reaction of a hypothetical reasonable person is less clear."[231]

The court in *Sudtelgte v. Reno*[232] also took into account the plaintiff's psychological history (although it did not apparently involve childhood sexual abuse) in applying the "reasonable person" test. In that case, the court admitted psychiatric testimony in a sexual harassment lawsuit concerning the fact that the plaintiff suffered from a paranoid personality disorder that adversely affected her ability to get along with supervisors and coworkers and that caused her to feel persistently "picked on." The court held that although the plaintiff might have felt subjectively harassed, her reaction was the result of abnormal sensitivity caused by her personality disorder and she could not show that a reasonable woman would have been similarly offended.

4. Repetition Compulsion and the Welcomeness Defense

As noted previously, in *Meritor Savings Bank v. Vinson,*[233] the Supreme Court maintained that sexual conduct in the workplace must be unwelcome to be actionable. In *Henson v. City of Dundee,*[234] the Eleventh Circuit defined "unwelcome" sexual conduct as that which is not "solicited or incited" by the plaintiff. Thus, even though a plaintiff may have regarded workplace conduct of a sexual

---

[227]913 F. Supp. 1045 (S.D. Ohio 1995), *aff'd,* 123 F.3d 868, 75 FEP Cases 1351 (6th Cir. 1997), *cert. denied,* 118 S. Ct. 1039, 77 FEP Cases 64 (1998).
[228]510 U.S. 17, 63 FEP Cases 225 (1993).
[229]913 F. Supp. at 1051.
[230]*Id.* at 1055.
[231]*Id.*
[232]63 FEP Cases 1257 (W.D. Mo. 1994).
[233]477 U.S. 57, 40 FEP Cases 1822 (1986).
[234]682 F.2d 897, 903, 29 FEP Cases 787, 791 (11th Cir. 1982).

nature as undesirable or offensive, if she consciously or even unconsciously incited the conduct, her harassment claim may not be viable.

Women who have histories of sexual abuse and/or who have a Borderline Personality Disorder may interact with others in eroticized or seductive ways. In the workplace, such a woman may behave in a sexually provocative manner with supervisors or coworkers. This is in part attributable to the fact that, because of her history of abuse, she may expect abuse, set herself up for it, and then find her worst fears confirmed. As one authority has observed, "Most sexual harassment cases of the "hostile environment" type involve a complex relationship between two individuals, the plaintiff and the defendant; that relationship must of necessity be carefully analyzed."[235]

With respect to the relevance of an abuse history to sexual harassment claims, this authority notes, "Not only does a history of childhood sexual abuse make a woman particularly vulnerable to various forms of revictimization such as sexual harassment in adult life, but it may also affect her personality so that she provokes behavior that, in retrospect, she will probably perceive as abusive."[236] This is what is known as "repetition compulsion," and in a sexual harassment lawsuit it is relevant to the issue of whether the plaintiff, by her words or actions welcomed the conduct of which she later complained.

Repetition compulsion often causes a person to seek out or create situations in which she will be victimized. As a leading expert has observed:

> It is the playing out of these themes of victimization that produces in large part the intense and unstable interpersonal relationships so characteristic of the borderline. I would stress again that the victimization is seen mainly in the borderlines' ability to get others to do things to them, or upon them. . . . Their abilities to get others to do things to them are often dramatic and obvious.[237]

This commentator explains how a woman with a Borderline Personality Disorder might instigate sexual conduct in the workplace that might then become the basis of a sexual harassment complaint:

> The borderline performs an initial action to which others respond. The response may be predictable and within proportion to the seriousness of the initiating act, but often it is unpredictable and excessive, except in the sense that, predictably, others will take over and things may happen to the borderline to reinforce the victimization theme. In essence, the situation escalates rapidly. Often it is no longer the borderline who is out of control; it is the others. The borderline is then the indignant and hapless recipient of others' anger, irrationality, or inept attempts to help or rescue, or worse, the true victim of another's aggressiveness. Often the borderline need do no more than initiate a series of actions; sometimes, when the tempest begins to settle down, the borderline may provoke a little more, in order to heat the situation up again.[238]

---

[235] Feldman-Schorrig, *supra* note 201, at 517.
[236] *Id.* (emphasis in original omitted).
[237] KROLL, *supra* note 206, at 46.
[238] *Id.* at 50–51.

Evidence of a sexual harassment plaintiff's history of prior sexual abuse, therefore, may assist a qualified mental health expert to demonstrate to the fact finder how and why a plaintiff might have contributed significantly to the chain of events that ultimately led to the filing of the harassment claim.

CHAPTER 9

THE MENTAL EXAMINATION

James J. McDonald, Jr., J.D.
Francine B. Kulick, Ph.D.

I. Introduction

The mental examination of the plaintiff is in many ways the centerpiece of the inquiry into the nature and cause of emotional damages allegedly suffered by the plaintiff. The examination provides an opportunity for the defendant's mental health expert[1] to interview the plaintiff in a nonadversarial clinical setting to determine the existence and severity of any emotional injury and to gather clues as to the cause of such injury.[2] It also provides an opportunity for the examiner—or another qualified professional—to administer various forms of psychological testing. The examiner then integrates the findings from the mental examination with the results of the psychological testing and the information obtained in the records review to formulate opinions concerning the various psychological issues in the case.

Mental examinations in federal cases are governed by Rule 35 of the Federal Rules of Civil Procedure, which provides as follows:

> a. Order for Examination
> When the mental or physical condition . . . of a party . . . is in controversy, the court in which the action is pending may order the party to submit to a physical or mental examination by a suitably licensed or certified examiner. . . . The order may be made only on motion for good cause shown . . . and shall specify the

---

[1] In addition to examinations by psychiatrists and psychologists, plaintiffs may also be compelled to undergo evaluations by vocational experts pursuant to Rule 35. *E.g.,* Douris v. County of Bucks, 2000 WL 1358481 (E.D. Pa. Sept. 21, 2000); Smolinsky v. State Farm Ins. Co., 1999 WL 1285824 (E.D. Pa. Dec. 22, 1999); Jeffrys v. LRP Publications, Inc., 1999 WL 79058 (E.D. Pa. Feb. 16, 1999).

[2] Of course, the plaintiff may retain a mental health expert to conduct such an examination as well, but plaintiff's examination does not require court involvement.

time, place, manner, conditions, and scope of the examination and the person or persons by whom it is to be made.

b. Report of Examiner

(1) If requested by the party against whom an order is made under Rule 35(a) ... the party causing the examination to be made shall deliver to the requesting party a copy of the detailed written report of the examiner setting out the examiner's findings, including results of all tests made, diagnoses and conclusions, together with like reports of all earlier examinations of the same condition. After delivery, the party causing the examination shall be entitled upon request to receive from the party against whom the order is made a like report of any examination, previously or thereafter made, of the same condition. ... The court on motion may make an order against a party requiring delivery of a report on such terms as are just, and if an examiner fails or refuses to make a report the court may exclude the examiner's testimony if offered at trial.

(2) By requesting and obtaining a report of the examination so ordered or by taking the deposition of the examiner, the party examined waives any privilege the party may have in that action or any other involving the same controversy, regarding the testimony of every other person who has examined or may thereafter examine the party in respect of the same mental or physical condition.

(3) This subdivision applies to examinations made by agreement of the parties, unless the agreement expressly provides otherwise. This subdivision does not preclude discovery of a report of an examiner or the taking of a deposition of the examiner in accordance with the provisions of any other rule.

Until recently, virtually any claim for emotional distress was considered to constitute good cause for the plaintiff to be required to undergo a mental examination as part of the pretrial discovery process. As the California Supreme Court explained in *Vinson v. Superior Court*:[3]

> In the case at bar, plaintiff haled defendants into court and accused them of causing her various mental and emotional ailments. Defendants deny her charges. As a result, the existence and extent of her mental injuries is indubitably in dispute. In addition, by asserting a causal link between her mental distress and defendants' conduct, plaintiff implicitly claims it was not caused by a preexisting mental condition, thereby raising the question of alternative sources for the distress.[4]

The early view was that the plaintiff placed his or her mental state into controversy by bringing a claim for emotional distress damages, regardless of whether emotional damages are the entirety of the relief sought (as in the case of a claim for intentional or negligent infliction of emotional distress) or are simply a portion of the damages available (as in, for example, a claim of defamation or a claim for employment discrimination).[5]

---

[3] 43 Cal. 3d 833, 239 Cal. Rptr. 292, 44 FEP Cases 1174 (1987).
[4] *Id.* at 839–40, 239 Cal. Rptr. at 297, 44 FEP Cases at 1174.
[5] *E.g.,* Smedley v. Capps, Staples, Ward, Hastings & Dodson, 820 F. Supp. 1227, 61 FEP Cases 1360 (N.D. Cal. 1993) (employee suing for discrimination in violation

More recently, however, plaintiffs have contested defendants' demands for mental examinations with greater frequency, and a growing jurisprudence has developed as a result that has defined the circumstances under which such examinations may be compelled. This chapter will first explore this body of law, including the law affecting issues such as whether psychological testing may be included in the examination and whether observers may be permitted to attend. The chapter will then describe the clinical process by which the examination proceeds.

II. When Is a Mental Examination Available?

The showing necessary for an order compelling a Rule 35 mental examination was set forth by the U.S. Supreme Court in *Schlagenhauf v. Holder*.[6] The Court in *Schlagenhauf* established that a party seeking a mental examination under Rule 35 must demonstrate both that the other party's mental condition is in controversy and that good cause exists for conducting such an examination.[7] This determination must be made on a case-by-case basis, keeping in mind that these requirements are not simply a formality and are not met by mere conclusory allegations of the pleadings or by mere "relevance" to the case. Rather, there must be an affirmative showing that each condition as to which the examination is sought is genuinely in controversy and that good cause exists for ordering the examination.[8] The Court went on to state, however, that a plaintiff who claims to have suffered a mental or physical injury places his or her mental or physical state in controversy and provides the defendant with good cause for an examination to determine the existence and extent of such asserted injury.[9]

Schlagenhauf has received varied interpretations in employment cases. Consequently, the nature of the showing that a defendant must make to meet the "in controversy" and "good cause" prerequisites for a mental examination of a plaintiff in an employment lawsuit remains unsettled in a number of respects. As will be discussed subsequently, a number of conflicting federal court decisions have come down in recent years. Most of the conflict has been over whether the mental condition of a plaintiff who claims to have suffered emotional distress as a result of harassment or discrimination, but who does not plan to put on expert testimony or assert a separate claim for intentional

---

of California statute protecting political activities must undergo mental examination even after dropping her claims for intentional and negligent infliction of emotional distress, because "normal" emotional distress damages are still part of her claim for political discrimination).

[6] 379 U.S. 104 (1964).
[7] *Id.* at 117–19.
[8] *Id.* at 118–19.
[9] *Id.* at 119.

infliction of emotional distress, has been placed "in controversy" for purposes of Rule 35.

A. The "In Controversy" Requirement

Some courts have either explicitly or implicitly adopted the rationale of *Schlagenhauf* and found that mere allegations of mental or emotional distress place a plaintiff's mental condition in controversy. For example, in *Ali v. Wang Laboratories*,[10] the court ordered a discrimination plaintiff to undergo a mental examination in spite of the fact that he apparently was not asserting a separate claim for intentional infliction of emotional distress and he did not plan to offer expert testimony at trial. The court nonetheless held that in light of the fact that the plaintiff was seeking "substantial" emotional distress damages, the defendant should not be limited to merely cross-examining the plaintiff on his emotional distress damages. The court maintained: "The testimony of an expert is a well recognized and reasonable way" of challenging a plaintiff's claim of emotional damages, "and an examination of plaintiff by that expert is necessary for the expert to form a meaningful opinion."[11]

Similarly, a mental examination was ordered in *Smedley v. Capps, Staples, Ward, Hastings & Dodson*,[12] even though the plaintiff indicated that she would not call any mental health experts at trial. The court noted that the plaintiff planned to present evidence of her "normal" emotional distress, and it agreed with the defendants' argument that they needed a Rule 35 mental examination to refute such evidence. The court was not deterred by the fact that the plaintiff had previously dismissed her claim for intentional infliction of emotional distress.

In *Carrier Corp. v. New York State Division of Human Rights*,[13] a New York state appellate court reversed an administrative law judge's refusal to order a complainant in a sexual harassment and retaliation case to undergo a psychiatric examination. The complainant in that case was awarded $100,000 in emotional distress damages in a state administrative proceeding largely on the basis of the testimony of her own psychiatrist. The appellate court maintained that because of the seriousness of the emotional injuries alleged, the complainant should have been subject to a psychiatric examination to aid the defendant employer in rebutting the testimony of the complainant's psychiatrist.

Other courts, without extensive analysis, have found plaintiffs to have put their mental conditions in controversy in employment cases where they sought to recover damages for emotional injuries.[14]

---

[10]162 F.R.D. 165, 4 AD Cases 520 (M.D. Fla. 1995).
[11]*Id.* at 168, 4 AD Cases at 522.
[12]820 F. Supp. 1227, 61 FEP Cases 1360 (N.D. Cal. 1993).
[13]224 A.D.2d 936, 637 N.Y.S.2d 877 (1996).
[14]*E.g.,* Ford v. Contra Costa County, 179 F.R.D. 579, 76 FEP Cases 1849 (N.D. Cal. 1998); Large v. Our Lady of Mercy Med. Ctr., 76 FEP Cases 1054 (S.D.N.Y. 1998); Jansen v. Packaging Corp. of Am., 158 F.R.D. 409, 410, 66 FEP Cases 556, 557 (N.D. Ill. 1994); Zabkowicz v. West Bend Co., 585 F. Supp. 635, 636, 35 FEP

In contrast, still other courts have declined to find a plaintiff's mental condition to be in controversy where the plaintiff made only simple allegations of mental or emotional distress.[15] Some of these cases predate the Civil Rights Act of 1991. For example, in *Cody v. Marriott Corp.*,[16] the court in an employment discrimination case denied the defendants' Rule 35 motion but noted that the plaintiff did not claim to have suffered a psychiatric disorder and did not undergo psychiatric or psychological counseling as a result of the emotional distress she suffered. In *Robinson v. Jacksonville Shipyards*,[17] the court denied a Rule 35 motion in a sexual harassment case, but, significantly, the plaintiff was not seeking damages for emotional distress. She sought only back pay and declaratory and injunctive relief. In *Bridges v. Eastman Kodak Co.*,[18] a sexual harassment case, the defendants' Rule 35 motion was denied where the plaintiffs did not claim that they suffered any ongoing mental injuries and did not assert a separate claim for intentional infliction of emotional distress. The court suggested, however, that had the plaintiffs claimed ongoing mental illnesses, mental examinations would have been warranted.

Courts have offered additional rationales for finding that the mental condition of a plaintiff in employment litigation was not in controversy. Some courts maintain that "emotional distress" is not synonymous with "mental injury" as that term was used by the Supreme Court in *Schlagenhauf*.[19] Other courts point out that a party may suffer compensable "emotional distress" without having a "mental condition."[20] Still other courts have expressed a fear that allowing mental examinations whenever there is a claim of mental or emotional distress would "open the floodgates" to requests for such examinations.[21] One court concluded that "basic complaints" of emotional distress are within the understanding of the jury, making a mental examination unnecessary.[22]

Cases 209 (E.D. Wis. 1984); Ryzlak v. McNeil Pharm. Co., 38 Fed. R. Serv. 2d 443, 444 (E.D. Pa. 1982).

[15]*E.g.,* Neal v. Siegel-Robert, Inc., 171 F.R.D. 264, 266, 73 FEP Cases 637, 638 (E.D. Mo. 1996); Lahr v. Fulbright & Jaworski, L.L.P., 164 F.R.D. 204, 210–11 (N.D. Tex. 1996); Morton v. Haskell Co., 5 AD Cases 272, 274 (M.D. Fla. 1995); Turner v. Imperial Stores, 161 F.R.D. 89, 97 (S.D. Cal. 1995); Robinson v. Jacksonville Shipyards, Inc., 118 F.R.D. 525, 531, 54 FEP Cases 83, 88 (M.D. Fla. 1988); Cody v. Marriott Corp., 103 F.R.D. 421, 422–23, 44 FEP Cases 1228, 1229 (D. Mass. 1984).

[16]103 F.R.D. 421, 44 FEP Cases 1228 (D. Mass. 1984).

[17]118 F.R.D. 525, 54 FEP Cases 83.

[18]850 F. Supp. 216 (S.D.N.Y. 1994).

[19]*E.g., Neal,* 171 F.R.D. at 266, 73 FEP Cases at 638; *Turner,* 161 F.R.D. at 97.

[20]*See, e.g., Lahr,* 164 F.R.D. at 211; *Morton,* 5 AD Cases at 274.

[21]*See, e.g., Turner,* 161 F.R.D. at 97 n.4; O'Quinn v. New York Univ. Med. Ctr., 163 F.R.D. 226, 228 n.2, 68 FEP Cases 1798, 1800 n.2 (S.D.N.Y. 1995); Cody v. Marriott Corp., 103 F.R.D. 421, 422, 44 FEP Cases 1228, 1229 (D. Mass. 1984).

[22]*Neal,* 171 F.R.D. at 267, 73 FEP Cases at 638. *See also* Hardy v. ESSROC Materials, Inc., 1998 WL 103306 (E.D. Pa. Feb. 18, 1998)(motion to compel mental examination denied where it was based solely upon plaintiff's claim that discrimination caused her to feel anxious and have trouble sleeping).

1. "Garden Variety" Emotional Damages Claims

Recently, some courts have come to use the term "garden variety" to describe the types of emotional damage claims that do not warrant a Rule 35 mental examination. This term dates back to *Turner v. Imperial Stores*,[23] where the court denied the defendants' Rule 35 motion, in spite of the fact that the plaintiff was seeking more than $1 million in emotional distress damages. The court pointed out that the plaintiff was not asserting a separate claim for intentional infliction of emotional distress, she did not claim to suffer from a specific psychiatric injury or disorder, she did not claim to suffer "unusually severe" emotional distress, and she did not plan to offer expert testimony on her claim of emotional distress. The *Turner* court held that "emotional distress" is not the same as a "mental injury" and that a mere garden variety claim for emotional distress is not sufficient to justify a Rule 35 mental examination.[24]

In *Fox v. Gates Corp.*,[25] the court similarly denied the defendant's motion to compel a mental examination. In noting that the plaintiff was asserting only a garden variety claim for emotional distress damages resulting from the defendant's refusal to hire her, the court pointed out that the plaintiff was not asserting a separate cause of action for intentional or negligent infliction of emotional distress, was not claiming to have suffered a specific psychiatric injury, and was not claiming to have suffered "unusually severe" emotional distress.[26]

In *Lahr v. Fulbright & Jaworski, L.L.P.*,[27] the court maintained that where a garden variety claim is involved, the actual amount of emotional distress suffered by the plaintiff is not at issue. That court explained:

> Like the personal injury claimant who sues to recover damages for mental anguish associated with an injury, a Title VII claimant may seek compensatory damages for emotional pain, suffering, inconvenience, mental anguish, and loss of enjoyment of life. Because this is an assessment of the pain that in reasonable probability results from discrimination, and not that which actually resulted, the defendant in such a suit is not entitled to a compelled mental examination.[28]

In *Ricks v. Abbott Laboratories*,[29] the court denied the defendant's motion to compel a mental examination of the plaintiff where the plaintiff sought to

---

[23] 161 F.R.D. 89.

[24] *See also* Sabree v. Carpenters Local No. 33, 126 F.R.D. 422, 426 (D. Mass. 1989) (plaintiff making a garden variety claim of emotional distress did not place his mental condition at issue in the context of a request for production of documents pursuant to FED. R. CIV. P. 34).

[25] 179 F.R.D. 303 (D. Colo. 1998).

[26] *Id.* at 307.

[27] 164 F.R.D. 204 (N.D. Tex. 1996).

[28] *Id.* at 446. In *EEOC v. Old Western Furniture Corp.*, 173 F.R.D. 444 (W.D. Tex. 1996), the court relied on this language from *Lahr* in denying the defendant's Rule 35 motion.

[29] 198 F.R.D. 647 (D. Md. 2001).

recover damages for "the emotional distress, humiliation and personal indignity resulting from . . . loss of employment and loss of her good name,"[30] and where she stipulated that she would not offer psychiatric testimony in support of her claim. In denying the motion, the court observed:

> When emotional distress is unusually severe or alleged in clinical terms, or when another party intends to offer expert testimony about the distress, the testimony of the expert would help the trier of fact understand the nature, severity, and characteristics of the emotional distress. A trier of fact, however, does not need help understanding the ordinary grief, anxiety, anger, and frustration that any person feels when something bad occurs. . . . Because laypersons can understand this kind of ordinary emotional distress without the help of an expert, there is no need for an expert to conduct a mental examination of the plaintiff who claims only ordinary and uncomplicated emotional distress.[31]

The problem with this concept of garden variety emotional distress is that it may work well with respect to pain and suffering attendant to a physical injury such as a broken leg, but it is virtually impossible to measure when there is no physical injury and the harm is purely intangible. There is no garden variety or "standard" amount of emotional distress that automatically flows from workplace incidents. The psychological impact of a stressor such as a wrongful termination or sexual harassment may differ vastly, depending upon a variety of factors, including the frequency and severity of the stressor and the plaintiff's psychological history and functioning.

Courts have rejected the garden variety label, moreover, where the plaintiff claims to have suffered more specific types of mental or emotional distress. For example, in *Thiessen v. General Electric Capital Corp.*,[32] the court initially denied the defendant's Rule 35 motion based upon the plaintiff's general prayer in his complaint for emotional distress damages, noting that the plaintiff had asserted only a garden variety emotional distress claim, "one which amounted to no more than an attempt to recover for the generalized insult, hurt feelings and lingering resentment which anyone could be expected to feel if he or she were the recipient of an adverse employment action attributed to discrimination."[33] The court denied the motion without prejudice, however, and the defendant brought the motion again and submitted excerpts of the plaintiff's deposition wherein he claimed to have suffered specific ailments, including water in his lungs, congestive heart failure, and "periods of great sadness and depression." He also claimed that he had not slept well, that he had become very tired, and that he had nearly broken up with his fiancée as the result of workplace events. The court granted the renewed motion, observing that the plaintiff no longer was asserting simply a garden variety claim. The court also noted that

---

[30]*Id.* at 648.
[31]*Id.* at 649.
[32]178 F.R.D. 568 (D. Kan. 1998).
[33]*Id.* at 569.

the fact that the plaintiff offered not to present any expert or medical testimony at trial would not bar the defendant's motion for a mental examination.[34]

Similarly, in *Dahdal v. Thorn Americas, Inc.*,[35] the plaintiff resisted the defendant's Rule 35 motion by arguing that it constituted harassment of her and by offering not to present medical testimony at trial or the bills she paid for psychological counseling. The court rejected the argument that the motion was motivated by harassment and granted the motion in reliance on matters revealed in the plaintiff's deposition and in the records of the psychiatrist who had treated her. Her testimony and the records indicated that the plaintiff was claiming that workplace events had caused her to suffer flashbacks to sexual abuse she had suffered prior to going to work for the defendant and that as a result, she suffered severe depression and suicidal thoughts. The court found that the plaintiff had gone beyond alleging a mere garden variety injury and ordered her to submit to a mental examination, remarking that the defendant was entitled to pursue discovery designed to determine whether the distress the plaintiff claimed to have suffered was the result of sexual harassment and discrimination, her prior life experiences, or a combination of both.[36]

2. Factors Likely to Lead to a Finding of "In Controversy"

Although, as discussed below, there is some disagreement as to what additional showing is necessary to establish that a plaintiff's mental condition is in controversy, one or some combination of the following factors has led courts to conclude a controversy exists: (1) a separate tort claim for intentional infliction of emotional distress, (2) an allegation that the plaintiff suffers from a specific psychiatric disorder, (3) the plaintiff's plan to offer the testimony of his or her own psychiatric or psychological expert at trial, (4) allegations of continuing mental or emotional injury, (5) allegations of "severe" emotional injury, or (6) plaintiff's concession that his or her mental condition is in controversy.[37]

A. SEPARATE CLAIM FOR INTENTIONAL INFLICTION OF EMOTIONAL DISTRESS A plaintiff's mental condition is unquestionably placed in controversy where a separate claim of intentional or negligent infliction of emotional distress is brought.[38] The rationale for this universal rule was explained in *Lahr*

---

[34]*Id.* at 571.
[35]76 FEP Cases 88 (D. Kan. 1998).
[36]*Id.* at 89.
[37]*See* Sarko v. Penn-Del Directory Co., 170 F.R.D. 127, 131 (E.D. Pa. 1997); Turner v. Imperial Stores, 161 F.R.D. 89, 95 (S.D. Cal. 1995). *See also* LeFave v. Symbios, Inc., 2000 WL 1644154 (D. Colo. Apr. 14, 2000) (denying mental examination where none of these factors was present and plaintiff asked only for damages for "pain and suffering, embarrassment and humiliation").
[38]*E.g.*, Bethel v. Dixie Homecrafters, Inc., 192 F.R.D. 320, 82 FEP Cases 345 (N.D. Ga. 2000); *Sarko,* 170 F.R.D. at 131; Lahr v. Fulbright & Jaworski, L.L.P., 164 F.R.D. 204, 209 (N.D. Tex. 1996); *Turner,* 161 F.R.D. at 95; Ragge v. MCA/Universal Studios, 165 F.R.D. 605, 608–09 (C.D. Cal. 1995); Hirschheimer v. Associated Minerals & Minerals Corp., 1995 WL 736901, at *2 (S.D.N.Y. Dec. 12, 1995); Curtis v. Express,

v. *Fulbright & Jaworski, L.L.P.*[39] In *Lahr*, the plaintiff filed suit after her termination, claiming sexual harassment, retaliation, and intentional infliction of emotional distress. During discovery, the magistrate judge ordered the plaintiff to submit to a Rule 35 mental examination, finding that the plaintiff had placed her mental condition in controversy by making a claim of intentional infliction of emotional distress.

In upholding the magistrate judge's ruling, the district court explained that, unlike in most cases, where the question is how much mental anguish the plaintiff has suffered as a result of the defendant's wrongful action, "[i]n an action for intentional infliction of emotional distress, the injury that forms the basis of the claim is the severe emotional distress that accompanies the Defendant's outrageous conduct."[40] Therefore, "[a] claimant for intentional infliction of emotional distress does not ask a jury to value the suffering that would ordinarily accompany a wrong. Instead, she raises mental anguish as the essence of the wrong, thereby making her mental condition an issue in the case."[41] The *Lahr* court further explained that this is precisely the type of tort claim that the Supreme Court found in *Schlagenhauf* would satisfy the "in controversy" requirement of Rule 35. Accordingly, "[a] plaintiff who alleges an action for intentional infliction of emotional distress asserts a mental or emotional injury, and thereby places her mental condition in controversy on the basis of the pleadings alone."[42]

B. ALLEGED PRESENCE OF A SPECIFIC PSYCHIATRIC DISORDER

Courts routinely have found that a plaintiff's mental condition is in controversy when the plaintiff claims to have suffered a specific psychiatric disorder. In *Morton v. Haskell Co.*,[43] the plaintiff claimed that he had suffered a clinical depression and was discriminated against in violation of the Americans with Disabilities Act and denied leave in violation of the Family and Medical Leave Act. The court granted the defendant's motion to compel a mental examination under Rule 35. In reaching its conclusion, the court reasoned:

> The Court agrees with those cases which hold that plaintiff's "mental condition" within the meaning of Rule 35 is not necessarily placed in controversy merely because Plaintiff seeks recovery for "emotional distress." A person with no "mental condition" may still suffer emotional distress which is compensable. Plaintiff, however, has gone beyond a mere claim for emotional distress as a component for damages in the intentional infliction of emotional distress count. The crux of plaintiff's claims relate to the existence and severity of his clinical depression.

Inc., 868 F. Supp. 467, 469, 66 FEP Cases 449, 450 (N.D.N.Y. 1994); Bridges v. Eastman Kodak Co., 850 F. Supp. 216, 222, 64 FEP Cases 1100, 1104–05 (S.D.N.Y. 1994); Everly v. United Parcel Serv., Inc., 1991 WL 18429, at *1 (N.D. Ill. Feb. 5, 1991).

[39] 164 F.R.D. 204 (N.D. Tex. 1996).
[40] *Id.* at 209.
[41] *Id.*
[42] *Id.*
[43] 5 AD Cases 272 (M.D. Fla. 1995).

Plaintiff's mental condition has thus clearly been placed in controversy since it forms the foundation for most of his claims. If plaintiff did not suffer from this mental condition, or if it was insufficiently severe, he will not prevail on the bulk of his claims. This is clearly sufficient to place plaintiff's mental condition in controversy.[44]

Similarly, in *Ziemann v. Burlington County Bridge Commission*,[45] the plaintiff claimed that she had a depressive disorder resulting in a 60 percent permanent psychiatric disability, half of which she attributed to alleged sexual harassment in the workplace. The court granted the defendant's motion to compel a psychiatric examination pursuant to Rule 35, finding that the plaintiff's mental condition was clearly placed in controversy "because [her] allegations of distinct psychological injuries comprise the almost-exclusive element of damages."[46]

Other courts have also ordered Rule 35 mental examinations without offering any significant analysis of the issue, where the plaintiff has alleged a specific psychiatric disorder.[47]

C. PLAINTIFF'S USE OF A MENTAL HEALTH EXPERT A plaintiff is also generally considered to have put his or her mental condition in issue by indicating that he or she will call a mental health professional to testify at trial either in the capacity of expert witness or as treating physician or therapist.[48] In *Shepherd v. American Broadcasting Cos.*,[49] two plaintiffs claimed that the defendants had engaged in various racially discriminatory practices and retaliatory acts in connection with the plaintiffs' employment. The court entered a default judgment for the plaintiffs because of the defendants' misconduct during the litigation of the suit. In their proposed order of relief, both plaintiffs requested compensatory damages for emotional pain and suffering. Defendants opposed plaintiffs' claims for compensatory damages and sought a Rule 35 mental examination for each plaintiff. The court, in granting the defendants' request, found that both plaintiffs had definitely placed their mental conditions in controversy. The court's conclusion was based, in substantial part, on the fact that one of the plaintiffs had submitted the full text of her treating physician's

---

[44]*Id.* at 274.
[45]155 F.R.D. 497 (D.N.J. 1994).
[46]*Id.* at 501 n.1.
[47]*See, e.g.,* Shepherd v. American Broadcasting Cos., 151 F.R.D. 194, 212 (D.D.C. 1993), *rev'd in part and vacated in part on other grounds,* 62 F.3d 1469 (D.C. Cir. 1995); Little v. Edgington, 53 FEP Cases 1061 (D. Or. 1990); Kresko v. Rulli, 432 N.W.2d 764 (Minn. Ct. App. 1988); Sarko v. Penn-Del Directory Co., 170 F.R.D. 127, 131 (E.D. Pa. 1997); Turner v. Imperial Stores, 161 F.R.D. 89, 95 (S.D. Cal. 1995); Cody v. Marriott Corp., 103 F.R.D. 421, 423, 44 FEP Cases 1228, 1229 (D. Mass. 1984).
[48]*See Sarko,* 170 F.R.D. at 131; *Turner,* 161 F.R.D. at 95; Chaparro v. IBP, Inc., 1994 WL 714369, at *3 (D. Kan. Dec. 7, 1994); *Ziemann,* 155 F.R.D. at 501 n.1.
[49]151 F.R.D. 194 (D.D.C. 1993), *rev'd in part and vacated in part on other grounds,* 62 F.3d 1469 (D.C. Cir. 1995).

deposition in support of her claim that she was suffering from Posttraumatic Stress Disorder.

The court in *Ziemann v. Burlington County Bridge Commission*,[50] a sexual harassment case, also found that the plaintiff had placed her mental condition in controversy by retaining her own psychiatric expert, who was likely to testify on her behalf at trial. As the court noted, "[t]he decisions sanctioning evaluation by defense experts have generally entailed the plaintiff's introduction of psychiatric testimony at trial, which the defense is then permitted to rebut by testimony as to its own mental evaluation."[51]

In *Chaparro v. IBP, Inc.*,[52] the plaintiff identified an expert witness who was expected to testify about the emotional impact of the allegedly discriminatory and retaliatory termination of her employment, as well as her treating physician, who was expected to testify about her treatment for depression. The court ordered a Rule 35 mental examination, finding that the plaintiff's intention to call an expert and her treating physician to testify on her behalf at trial indicated that she had affirmatively put her mental condition in controversy.[53]

By the same token, evidence that an expert will not be called may be used to show that a plaintiff's mental condition is not in controversy. For example, in *Borquez v. Ozer*,[54] the Colorado Court of Appeals held that the plaintiff's general allegations of mental suffering and emotional distress in his wrongful discharge suit did not place his mental condition in controversy where he did not intend to make his mental state a matter of genuine controversy, did not intend to call a psychiatric expert witness at trial, and did not intend to present any medical evidence of his mental suffering.[55]

D. ALLEGATION OF CONTINUING EMOTIONAL INJURY Absent one of the other aforementioned factors discussed thus far, some courts have adhered to the notion that there must be allegations of continuing mental or emotional distress or injury before a plaintiff's mental condition is considered to be in controversy.[56]

---

[50] 155 F.R.D. 497.

[51] *Id.* at 501 n.1.

[52] 1994 WL 714369 (D. Kan. Dec. 7, 1994).

[53] *Id.* at *3.

[54] 923 P.2d 166, 69 FEP Cases 1415, 11 IER Cases 496 (Colo. App. 1995), *aff'd in part and rev'd in part on other grounds*, 940 P.2d 371, 12 IER Cases 1665 (Colo. 1997).

[55] *Id.* at 176, 69 FEP Cases at 421, 11 IER Cases at 503–04. *See also* Neal v. Siegel-Robert, Inc., 171 F.R.D. 264, 267, 73 FEP Cases 637, 638 (E.D. Mo. 1996) (age discrimination plaintiff's deposition testimony that he did not intend to see a psychiatrist or psychologist was evidence that his mental condition had not been placed in controversy).

[56] *See, e.g.,* O'Quinn v. New York Univ. Med. Ctr., 163 F.R.D. 226, 228, 68 FEP Cases 1798, 1800 (S.D.N.Y. 1995); Curtis v. Express, Inc., 868 F. Supp. 467, 469, 66 FEP Cases 449, 450 (N.D.N.Y. 1994); Bridges v. Eastman Kodak Co., 850 F. Supp. 216, 222, 64 FEP Cases 1100, 1104 (S.D.N.Y. 1994). *See also* Sarko v. Penn-Del Directory Co., 170 F.R.D. 127, 131 (E.D. Pa. 1997) (recognizing that courts tend to

For example, in *Doyle v. Superior Court*,[57] a California appellate court held that claims of only past mental and emotional suffering were insufficient to put a plaintiff's mental condition at issue. It distinguished the California Supreme Court's decision in *Vinson v. Superior Court*[58] in that there were allegations of continuing emotional distress in *Vinson*.[59] The *Doyle* court took a very narrow view of the definition of "in controversy." It explained:

> The mental condition of a person who is suffering ongoing mental distress is clearly "in controversy" in an action seeking damages for that ongoing mental distress. The "controversy" surrounding such a person's mental condition includes not only the nature and extent of the person's current mental injury but also the actual cause of this injury. In contrast, where a plaintiff alleges that she is not suffering any current mental injury but only that she has suffered emotional distress in the past arising from the defendant's misconduct, a mental examination is unnecessary because such an allegation alone does not place the nature and cause of the plaintiff's current mental condition "in controversy."[60]

In placing so much emphasis on the fact that the plaintiff's current mental condition was not in dispute, the *Doyle* court seemed to miss the point that the plaintiff there was not suing for current emotional injuries, but rather for past emotional injuries, the causation of which the defendant disputed. Although the plaintiff's past emotional condition was in controversy, the defendant was prevented by the court's decision from defending itself in that dispute via a mental examination of the plaintiff.

One issue that arises with respect to claims of emotional injury that is not continuing is the reliability of medical or psychological opinions concerning whether or not the plaintiff suffered emotional injury in the past. At least one court has indicated its belief that a physician conducting a Rule 35 examination is able to provide a "retrospective opinion" of the plaintiff's condition during the relevant time period, although in that case, the plaintiff alleged ongoing as well as prior mental injuries.[61] In *Jenson v. Eveleth Taconite Co.*,[62] moreover, the Eighth Circuit referred to as "questionable" the lower court's finding that there is no scientifically developed psychiatric model or procedure for determining whether a particular stressor caused a particular symptom or mental state and noted that several courts "have noted the probative value of expert psychological proof regarding causation of the claimant's depression and emotional distress."[63]

---

order mental examinations where "the plaintiff alleges that he suffers a severe ongoing mental injury").

[57]50 Cal. App. 4th 1878, 58 Cal. Rptr. 2d 476 (1996).

[58]43 Cal. 3d 833, 239 Cal. Rptr. 292, 44 FEP Cases 1174 (1987).

[59]*Vinson* also involved a separate claim for intentional infliction of emotional distress.

[60]50 Cal. App. 4th at 1887, 58 Cal. Rptr. at 482.

[61]Morton v. Haskell Co., 5 AD Cases 272, 274 (M.D. Fla. 1995).

[62]130 F.3d 1287 (8th Cir. 1997).

[63]*Id.* at 1297 (citing Karcher v. Emerson Elec. Co., 94 F.3d 502, 71 FEP Cases 1651 (8th Cir. 1996)); Webb v. Hyman, 861 F. Supp. 1094 (D.D.C. 1994); Alberts v.

Thus, for example, if a plaintiff were to claim that she was "severely depressed" following an episode of sexual harassment but is no longer depressed, a skilled forensic psychiatrist or psychologist could still elicit from the plaintiff a description of her symptoms and functioning during the period of her claimed depression, and compare such an account with the diagnostic criteria contained in the American Psychiatric Association's *Diagnostic and Statistical Manual of Mental Disorders (DSM-IV-TR)*.[64] If such a plaintiff claimed to have been severely depressed and unable to work but did not describe having suffered a sufficient number of symptoms for a diagnosis of depression, and if she related that during the same period she was able to care for herself and her family, apply successfully for disability benefits, and assist her attorney with the prosecution of her lawsuit, a qualified mental health expert might question whether the plaintiff met the diagnostic criteria for a severe and disabling depression.

Accordingly, the distinction between past and current mental condition seems an artificial one, albeit one that some courts are willing to recognize. Conversely, courts have routinely found a plaintiff's mental condition to be in controversy where there were allegations of ongoing mental or emotional distress.[65]

E. ALLEGATION OF SEVERE EMOTIONAL INJURY Claims of severe emotional distress alone may be sufficient to place a plaintiff's mental condition "in controversy." For example, in *Chaparro v. IBP, Inc.*,[66] the plaintiff asserted claims of employment discrimination and retaliatory discharge, alleging "grievous emotional injury." She also indicated that her treating physician as well as an expert would testify on her behalf at trial. The defendant then moved to compel a mental examination under Rule 35, arguing that the plaintiff's claim of severe emotional distress and the designation of the two expert witnesses placed her mental condition in controversy. The court granted the motion, noting that although the mere assertion of a claim for emotional distress does not by itself put the plaintiff's mental condition in controversy, here the plaintiff had identified two experts who would testify about her emotional condition and treatment, and more important, "[b]eyond a more conventional claim of emotional distress, she has alleged her distress to be 'severe and extreme.' "[67]

Wickes Lumber Co., 69 FEP Cases 304 (N.D. Ill. 1995); Hurley v. Atlantic City Police Dep't, 933 F. Supp. 396 (D.N.J. 1996).

[64]AMERICAN PSYCHIATRIC ASSOCIATION, DIAGNOSTIC AND STATISTICAL MANUAL OF MENTAL DISORDERS [hereinafter DSM-IV-TR] (4th ed. text rev. 2000).

[65]*E.g.,* Sarko v. Penn-Del Directory Co., 170 F.R.D. 127 (E.D. Pa. 1997); Hirschheimer v. Associated Minerals & Minerals Corp., 1995 WL 736901 (S.D.N.Y. Dec. 12, 1995); Ali v. Wang Labs., 162 F.R.D. 165, 4 AD Cases 520 (M.D. Fla. 1995); Ragge v. MCA/Universal Studios, 165 F.R.D. 605 (C.D. Cal. 1995); Jansen v. Packaging Corp. of Am., 409, 66 FEP Cases 556 (N.D. Ill. 1994); Ryzlak v. McNeil Pharm. Co., 38 Fed. R. Serv. 2d 443 (E.D. Pa. 1982).

[66]1994 WL 714369 (D. Kan. Dec. 7, 1994).

[67]*Id.* at *3.

Although the severity of the emotional injury allegedly suffered by the plaintiff was not the only factor that the court looked at in determining whether plaintiff's mental condition had been placed in controversy, the *Chapparo* court suggested that such allegations alone may be enough to meet the "in controversy" requirement.[68]

Other courts have not made this point as strongly. In *Ali v. Wang Laboratories*,[69] the court held that the "in controversy" requirement was satisfied by allegations of severe and ongoing emotional distress, but it did not indicate whether allegations of severe emotional distress alone would have produced the same result.[70] In *Turner v. Imperial Stores*,[71] the court observed that other courts have ordered Rule 35 mental examinations when the plaintiff alleged unusually severe emotional distress, but it went on to hold that there was no claim for severe emotional distress in this particular case even though the plaintiff was seeking more than $1 million in damages for "humiliation, mental anguish, and emotional distress."[72]

F. PLAINTIFF CONCEDES THAT MENTAL CONDITION IS IN CONTROVERSY The "in controversy" requirement is easily satisfied when a plaintiff concedes that his or her mental condition has been placed at issue.[73] When this occurs, the only issue for the court is whether there is good cause to order a Rule 35 mental examination.[74] The "good cause" requirement is discussed in detail below.

B. The Good Cause Requirement

In addition to showing that a plaintiff's mental condition is in controversy, a defendant also must show that there exists good cause for conducting a mental examination before one will be ordered pursuant to Rule 35. The Supreme

---

[68]*See also* Shepherd v. American Broad. Cos., 151 F.R.D. 194, 212–13 (D.D.C. 1993), *rev'd in part and vacated in part on other grounds*, 62 F.3d 1469 (D.C. Cir. 1995); Lowe v. Philadelphia Newspapers, Inc., 101 F.R.D. 296, 298–99; 44 FEP Cases 1224, 1225–26 (E.D. Pa. 1983).

[69]162 F.R.D. 165, 4 AD Cases 520.

[70]*Id.* at 168, 4 AD Cases at 522.

[71]161 F.R.D. 89 (S.D. Cal. 1995).

[72]*Id.* at 97. *But see Shepherd*, 151 F.R.D. at 212–13 (holding that plaintiffs placed their mental conditions "in controversy" by demanding close to $2 million in compensatory damages for emotional distress).

[73]*E.g.,* Shirsat v. Mutual Pharm. Co., 169 F.R.D. 68, 70 (E.D. Pa. 1996) (wrongful discharge); Ferrell v. Shell Oil Co., 1995 WL 688795, at *1 (E.D. La. Nov. 20, 1995) (sex discrimination, sexual harassment, intentional infliction of emotional distress). *See also* Sarko v. Penn-Del Directory Co., 170 F.R.D. 127, 131 (E.D. Pa. 1997) (recognizing that plaintiff's mental condition has been put in controversy where plaintiff concedes the issue); *Turner*, 161 F.R.D. at 95 (same).

[74]*Shirsat*, 169 F.R.D. at 70; *Ferrell*, 1995 WL 688795, at *1.

Court commented in *Schlagenhauf v. Holder*[75] that in a negligence action, allegations of mental or emotional injuries alone are enough to demonstrate good cause. In the arena of employment litigation, a few courts have followed this reasoning and found good cause to exist based entirely upon allegations of mental or emotional distress.[76]

"Good cause" has been held to require a showing that "the party seeking the medical examination has exhausted other discovery procedures before seeking such examination."[77] This can be demonstrated through the affidavit of an expert attesting that the discovery materials available to the defendant are inadequate by themselves from a psychiatric or psychological standpoint for the expert to formulate an opinion concerning the existence, nature, and cause of the plaintiff's emotional injury.[78]

"[S]ometimes the two requirements of Rule 35 are merged,"[79] however, and the presence of some other factors beyond a mere allegation of mental or emotional distress, such as those required by some courts for a plaintiff's mental condition to be "in controversy," may also satisfy the good cause requirement. For example, a number of courts will find good cause for ordering a mental examination upon allegations of ongoing emotional distress.[80] Similarly, a separate tort claim of intentional or negligent infliction of emotional distress also may provide good cause.[81]

A common basis for finding "good cause," whether or not other discovery methods have been exhausted, is the defendant's need to rebut the plaintiff's claims for damages for mental or emotional distress. This is especially true when plaintiffs plan to offer the testimony of their own experts or treating physicians or therapists to support their claims.[82]

---

[75] 379 U.S. 104, 119 (1964).

[76] *E.g.*, Jansen v. Packaging Corp. of Am., 158 F.R.D. 409, 410, 66 FEP Cases 556, 557; Smedley v. Capps, Staples, Ward, Hastings & Dodson, 820 F. Supp. 1227, 1232, 61 FEP Cases 1360, 1364 (N.D. Cal. 1993); Zabkowicz v. West Bend Co., 585 F. Supp. 635, 636, 35 FEP Cases 209, 209 (E.D. Wis. 1984).

[77] Everly v. United Parcel Serv., Inc., 1991 WL 18429, at *1 (N.D. Ill. Feb. 15, 1991). *Accord* Lahr v. Fulbright & Jaworski, L.L.P., 164 F.R.D. 204, 211–12 (N.D. Tex. 1996); Ragge v. MCA/Universal Studios, 165 F.R.D. 605, 609 (C.D. Cal. 1995).

[78] *See, e.g., Everly*, 1991 WL 18429, at *1; *Lahr*, 164 F.R.D. at 211–12.

[79] *Ragge*, 165 F.R.D. at 609. *Accord* Bethel v. Dixie Homecrafters, Inc., 192 F.R.D. 320, 82 FEP Cases 345 (N.D. Ga. 2000).

[80] *See, e.g.*, Sarko v. Penn-Del Directory Co., 170 F.R.D. 127, 131 (E.D. Pa. 1997); Hirschheimer v. Associated Minerals & Minerals Corp., 1995 WL 736901, at *2 (S.D.N.Y. Dec. 12, 1995); *Ragge*, 165 F.R.D. at 609; *Jansen*, 158 F.R.D. at 410, 66 FEP Cases at 557; Vinson v. Superior Court, 43 Cal. 3d 833, 839–40, 239 Cal. Rptr. 292, 297–98, 44 FEP Cases 1174, 1176 (1987).

[81] *See, e.g., Hirschheimer*, 1995 WL 736901, at *2.

[82] *See, e.g.*, Ferrell v. Shell Oil Co., 1995 WL 688795, at *1 (E.D. La. Nov. 20, 1995); Morton v. Haskell Co., 5 AD Cases 272, 274 (M.D. Fla. 1995); Chaparro v. IBP, Inc., 1994 WL 714369, at *3 (D. Kan. Dec. 7, 1994); Shepherd v. American Broad. Cos., 151 F.R.D. 194, 213 (D.D.C. 1993), *rev'd in part and vacated in part on other grounds,* 62 F.3d 1469 (D.C. Cir. 1995); Lowe v. Philadelphia Newspapers,

Even when the plaintiff does not plan to use an expert, a court may still find that the defendant has good cause for a Rule 35 mental examination to permit it to rebut the plaintiff's claims for mental or emotional damages. As the court in *Ali v. Wang Laboratories*[83] explained:

> While plaintiff may be content to offer only his own testimony to a jury, defendant is not compelled to limit its case to mere cross examination. Since plaintiff's mental condition is in controversy and substantial damages are asserted, it is essential for defendant to have the reasonable opportunity to challenge plaintiff's claim and testimony. The testimony of an expert is a well recognized and reasonable way of doing so, and an examination of plaintiff by that expert is necessary for the expert ... to form a meaningful opinion.[84]

Similarly, the California Supreme Court in *Vinson v. Superior Court*[85] observed, with respect to the plaintiff's claim for emotional distress damages in that case, "[P]laintiff cannot be allowed to make her very serious allegations without affording defendants an opportunity to put their truth to the test."

In *Douris v. County of Bucks*,[86] the court found good cause to order a mental examination in an Americans With Disabilities Act case to determine whether the plaintiff was disabled. It rejected the plaintiff's assertion that an examination was not necessary because the defendants had been given access to all the plaintiff's medical records.

A contrary result was reached, however, in *Shumaker v. West*,[87] a case in which the plaintiff claimed the defendant had discriminated against her in violation of the Rehabilitation Act of 1973 on account of her Posttraumatic Stress Disorder. The court observed that the defendant already possessed ample medical evidence that the plaintiff suffered from PTSD. The court also found that the defendant's seeking to obtain a mental examination was untimely in that it came only days before the defendant's expert disclosures were due under Federal Rule of Civil Procedure 26(a)(2)(B), which requires that the expert's report accompany the disclosure.

Occasionally, a plaintiff will object to a Rule 35 mental examination on the grounds that a prior examination has already been conducted and that a second examination would subject the plaintiff to unnecessary harassment. Courts have found good cause to order the second examination where there

---

Inc., 101 F.R.D. 296, 298–99, 44 FEP Cases 1224, 1226 (E.D. Pa. 1983); Ryzlak v. McNeil Pharm. Co., 38 Fed. R. Serv. 2d 443, 444 (E.D. Pa. 1982). *See also* Kresko v. Rulli, 432 N.W.2d 764, 770 (Minn. Ct. App. 1988) (not expressly addressing "good cause" but recognizing that a mental examination was appropriate where, among other things, plaintiff listed and called two expert witnesses to testify as to her psychological status).

[83]162 F.R.D. 165, 4 AD Cases 520 (M.D. Fla. 1995).

[84]*Id.* at 168, 4 AD Cases at 522 (citations omitted).

[85]Vinson v. Superior Court, 43 Cal. 3d 833, 842, 239 Cal. Rptr. 292, 298, 44 FEP Cases 1174, 1177 (Cal. 1987).

[86]2000 WL 1358481 (E.D. Pa. Sept. 21, 2000).

[87]196 F.R.D. 454 (S.D. W.Va. 2000).

was a change of circumstances warranting a new examination,[88] where the prior examination did not address all the issues being litigated,[89] or where the prior examination was conducted by the plaintiff's psychologist or psychiatrist.[90]

III. Terms Under Which a Mental Examination Shall Proceed

A. Timing of the Examination

Although typically the mental examination of the plaintiff is scheduled toward the end of the case just before trial, counsel must be mindful of two important deadlines. As the examination is a type of discovery, it must ordinarily occur prior to the discovery cutoff date. In addition, in federal cases, the examination must occur sufficiently in advance of the expert disclosure deadline that the expert can produce a report to accompany the expert designation. Federal Rule of Civil Procedure 26(a)(2)(B) provides, with respect to expert disclosures:

> Except as otherwise stipulated or directed by the court, this disclosure shall, with respect to a witness who is retained or specially employed to provide expert testimony in the case or whose duties as an employee of the party regularly involve giving expert testimony, be accompanied by a written report prepared and signed by the witness. The report shall contain a complete statement of all opinions to be expressed and the basis and reasons therefor; the data or other information considered by the witness in forming the opinions; any exhibits to be used as a summary of or support for the opinions; the qualifications of the witness; including a list of publications authored by the witness within the preceding ten years; the compensation to be paid for the study and testimony; and a listing of any other cases in which the witness has testified as an expert at trial or by deposition within the preceding four years.

Rule 26(a)(2)(C) goes on to provide that unless the court establishes a different due date, the parties' expert disclosures are due 90 days before trial. Rule 37(c)(1), in turn, provides that any party who fails to make such a disclosure "without substantial justification," unless the failure is "harmless," will be prevented from introducing the expert testimony at trial. This rule has been described by one court as an "automatic sanction" for failure to make timely and complete expert disclosures, which must include a "*complete* statement of *all* opinions to be expressed and the *basis* and *reasons* therefor;" not just "sketchy and vague" expert information.[91]

---

[88]*See* Ziemann v. Burlington County Bridge Comm'n, 155 F.R.D. 497, 501–02 (D.N.J. 1994).
[89]*See* Little v. Edgington, 53 FEP Cases 1061, 1062 (D. Or. 1990).
[90]*See* Shirsat v. Mutual Pharm. Co., 169 F.R.D. 68, 70 (E.D. Pa. 1996).
[91]Giladi v. Strauch, 2001 WL 388052, at *3, *5 (S.D.N.Y. Apr. 16, 2001).

In *Shumaker v. West*,[92] the court denied the defendant's motion to compel a mental examination of the plaintiff, in part because the motion was brought only six days before the expert disclosure deadline. The court maintained that the defendant should have sought to obtain the examination "well before" this deadline.[93]

B. Presence of Observers

In employment cases, plaintiffs ordered to submit to a Rule 35 mental examination will often request the presence of a third party. The trial court typically has broad discretion in deciding whether to allow a third-party observer.

Concerning the presence of third parties, one leading forensic psychiatrist has observed:

> The presence of third parties is fraught with difficulties. Sometimes, such "observers" are converted into witnesses that are used against the examiner, usually criticizing the method of the examination. When the claimant's attorney is present, the claimant's psychological symptoms may appear worse, even if the attorney does not directly interfere with the examination. The attorney's presence highlights the adversarial context of the examination, usually contributing to additional anxiety and a focus on symptomatology by the claimant. The presence of supportive family members and friends may cause the claimant to appear less symptomatic than previously reported. Emotional support can have a very quieting and soothing influence on the claimant.[94]

In an early case, the California Supreme Court echoed many of the same concerns. In *Edwards v. Superior Court*,[95] the court refused to allow the plaintiff's attorney to attend the plaintiff's mental examination. The plaintiff had argued that her attorney's presence was necessary to protect her from improper questioning, to make the examination a more comfortable experience for her, and to ensure accurate reporting. The court rejected all three arguments. Concerning the plaintiff's claim that she needed counsel to protect her from improper questions, the court remarked:

> The analyst in a psychiatric examination seeks by careful direction of areas of inquiry to probe, possibly very deeply, into the psyche, measuring stress, seeking origins, tracing aberrations, and attempting to form a professional judgment or interpretation of the examinee's mental condition. Given such techniques and purposes we do not think that an attorney, no matter how well intentioned, can fairly and objectively monitor such an examination. Psychiatry is a discipline requiring highly specialized skills. Further, while properly objecting to a question

---

[92]196 F.R.D. 454 (S.D. W.Va. 2000).
[93]*Id.* at 456.
[94]Robert I. Simon, *The Credible Forensic Psychiatric Evaluation in Sexual Harassment Litigation*, 26 PSYCHIATRIC ANNALS 139, 142 (1996).
[95]16 Cal. 3d 905, 130 Cal. Rptr. 14 (1976).

on legal grounds, counsel does not necessarily possess the ability to define the psychiatric relevance of elicited answers. Many questions which would be legally objectionable, if posed in a courtroom, might be very relevant in the formulation of a sound psychiatric judgment.[96]

In answer to the plaintiff's argument that her counsel's presence was necessary for her comfort and emotional support, the *Edwards* court expressed its concern that the presence of others during the examination would be "distracting, if not disrupting," and noted that an examination must proceed free of such disruptions if it is to be valid.[97] Finally, the court held that a verbatim account of all of the questions and answers at a mental examination is not necessarily desirable, as it might cause the examinee to react defensively and inhibit the "free, open and objective communication essential to an effective psychiatric examination."[98]

In *Reyes v. City of New York*,[99] the court maintained that the party seeking the attendance of a third party at a Rule 35 examination bears the burden under Rule 26(c)[100] of showing "good cause" for such attendance. It noted that where third parties have been excluded, courts have usually relied on affidavits or other statements by the examiner explaining how and why the presence of a third party would interfere with the examination.[101] In *Abduwali v. WMATA*,[102] the court cited such an affidavit in denying the plaintiff's request to have her attorney present and have the examination recorded. The affidavit of the examining psychiatrist averred:

> To the greatest extent possible, the examination should be conducted in a private, quiet and comfortable setting free from distractions and interference. The presence

---

[96] *Id.* at 911, 130 Cal. Rptr. at 17. In *Tirado v. Erosa*, 158 F.R.D. 294 (S.D.N.Y. 1994), the court similarly rejected the plaintiff's argument that the presence of her counsel and a stenographer was necessary because of the sensitive nature of the allegations in the case (unconsented sexual touching). It observed:

> Plaintiff also asserts that the subject matter is especially sensitive, but this consideration cuts both ways. On the one hand, plaintiff might not feel comfortable discussing intimate matters with defendants' psychiatric expert, but on the other it is not clear that having four people in the room rather than two will improve this situation. Plaintiff has made no showing that the presence of her male attorney and a complete stranger (male or female) taking down every word would make her any more comfortable.

Id. at 296.

[97] 16 Cal. 3d at 911, 130 Cal. Rptr. at 18.

[98] *Id.* at 911–12, 130 Cal. Rptr. at 18.

[99] 2000 WL 1528239 (S.D.N.Y. Oct. 16, 2000).

[100] FED. R. Civ.P. 26(c) provides in relevant part that "[u]pon motion by a party ... the court ... may make any order which justice requires to protect a party or person from annoyance, embarrassment, oppression, or undue burden or expense, including ... (5) that discovery be conducted with no one present except persons designated by the court."

[101] 2000 WL 1528239, at *3.

[102] 193 F.R.D. 10 (D.D.C. 2000).

of a third party during the examination or of camera/video equipment or of recording devices is inimical to the success of such an examination because it/they distort psychological openness and spontaneity. Consequently, such interfering variables may invalidate the examination findings and [any] inference that may be drawn therefrom.[103]

A majority of courts in employment cases have disallowed the presence of plaintiff's counsel during the Rule 35 mental examination. Justifications advanced for this view include the need (1) to conduct the examination without the distractions of a third person in order to obtain a valid psychiatric profile; (2) to provide the defendant with a "level playing field" because the plaintiff's physician would have examined the plaintiff without the presence of the defendant's attorney; (3) to prevent a more adversarial atmosphere during such examinations than is already unavoidably present; (4) to avoid the possible conflict of interests created by the fact that the presence of the plaintiff's attorney during the examination makes the attorney a potential witness at trial; and (5) the availability of other less obtrusive devices to protect the interests of the plaintiff.[104]

On the other hand, a minority of courts have allowed plaintiffs' attorneys to be present during Rule 35 mental examinations, reasoning that plaintiffs' interest in protecting themselves from unsupervised interrogation by an agent of their opponents outweighs defendants' interests in making the most effective use of their experts.[105] Some states also specifically authorize the presence of counsel during a mental examination in their state versions of Rule 35.[106]

For reasons similar to those given for prohibiting the presence of the plaintiff's attorney, most courts have prohibited other third parties from being

---

[103]*Id.* at 13. Similarly, in *Tirado v. Erosa,* 158 F.R.D. 294, 295 (S.D.N.Y. 1994), the court, in denying the plaintiff's request to have her attorney and a stenographer present during her mental examination, cited an affidavit submitted by the examiner stating that the presence of third parties "could impede the effectiveness of my examination, as well as potentially hinder my ability to fully and fairly evaluate whether, and the extent to which, a mental illness and/or emotional disturbance may or may not exist."

[104]*See, e.g.,* Bethel v. Dixie Homecrafters, Inc., 192 F.R.D. 320, 324, 82 FEP Cases 345, 347 (N.D. Ga. 2000); Breda v. Wolf Camera, Inc., 78 FEP Cases 433, 435 (S.D. Ga. 1998); Haensel v. Chrysler Corp., 1997 WL 537995 (E.D. La. 1997); Ferrell v. Shell Oil Co., 1995 WL 688795, at *2 (E.D. La. 1995); Hirschheimer v. Associated Minerals & Minerals Corp., 1995 WL 736901, at *3 (S.D.N.Y. Dec. 12, 1995); Vinson v. Superior Court, 43 Cal. 3d 833, 239 Cal. Rptr. 292, 44 FEP Cases 1174 (Cal. 1987); Lowe v. Philadelphia Newspapers, Inc., 101 F.R.D. 296, 299, 44 FEP Cases 1224, 1226 (E.D. Pa. 1983). *See also* Wheat v. Biesecker, 125 F.R.D. 479, 480 (N.D. Ind. 1989) (noting that majority rule is that plaintiff's attorney may not attend a Rule 35 examination).

[105]Zabkowicz v. West Bend Co., 585 F. Supp. 635, 636, 35 FEP Cases 209, 209–10 (E.D. Wis. 1984). *See also* Vreeland v. Ethan Allen, Inc., 151 F.R.D. 551, 551–52 (S.D.N.Y. 1993) (upholding a magistrate's ruling that allowed the presence of the plaintiff's attorney).

[106]*E.g.,* ARIZ. R. CIV. P. 35(a) (2000); 735 ILL. COMP. STAT. ANN. 5/2-1003 (West 2000); MICH. CT. R. 2.311(a) (2001).

present during a Rule 35 mental examination.[107] A few courts, however, have allowed the plaintiff's treating physician or psychotherapist to be present.[108]

C. Recording the Examination

There is a split of authority regarding whether the mental examination may be recorded by videotape or audiotape. Some courts prohibit the practice for many of the same reasons that the presence of the plaintiff's attorney has been disallowed.[109] One denied the plaintiff's request for tape recording, maintaining that the presence of a tape recorder "may invalidate the results of the examination, as it may consciously or unconsciously influence plaintiff to exaggerate or diminish her reactions to the examination."[110] Other courts permit tape recording, which, according to one court, is a less obtrusive means of preserving evidence of abuse by the examining physician.[111] California has a statute expressly permitting a plaintiff (as well as the examiner) to audiotape the mental examination.[112] As a matter of practice, if the plaintiff audiotapes the examination, the examiner should audiotape it as well.

---

[107]*E.g.*, Haensel v. Chrysler Corp., 1997 WL 537995 (E.D. La. Aug. 25, 1997) (psychologist and attorney); Hlinko v. Virgin Atlantic Airways, 1997 WL 68560 (S.D.N.Y. Feb. 19, 1997) (female nurse); Gavenda v. Orleans County, 174 F.R.D. 272 (W.D.N.Y. 1996) (court reporter); Shirsat v. Mutual Pharm. Co., 169 F.R.D. 68, 70–71 (E.D. Pa. 1996) (third-party observers in general and court reporters in particular); Ali v. Wang Labs., 162 F.R.D. 165, 168, 4 AD Cases 520, 523 (M.D. Fla. 1995) (wife and court reporter); Ragge v. MCA/Universal Studios, 165 F.R.D. 605, 609–10 (C.D. Cal. 1995) (third-party observers in general); Galieti v. State Mut. Auto. Ins. Co., 154 F.R.D. 262, 263–65 (D. Colo. 1994) (third-party observers in general). *See also* Lahr v. Fulbright & Jaworski, L.L.P., 164 F.R.D. 204, 212 n.5 (N.D. Tex. 1996) (crediting the magistrate's finding that the presence of an observer would disrupt the examination).

[108]*E.g.*, Morton v. Haskell Co., 1995 WL 819182, at *3, 5 AD Cases 272, 275 (M.D. Fla. Sept. 12, 1995); *Lowe*, 101 F.R.D. at 299, 44 FEP Cases at 1226–27. *See also Zabkowicz*, 585 F. Supp. at 636, 35 FEP Cases at 209–10 (allowing the presence of any third-party observer).

[109]*E.g.*, Abduwali v. WMATA, 193 F.R.D. 10, 14 (D.D.C. 2000); *Shirsat*, 169 F.R.D. at 70; *Hirschheimer*, 1995 WL 736901, at *4; *Ali*, 162 F.R.D. 165, 4 AD Cases at 523.

[110]Hertenstein v. Kimberly Home Health Care, Inc., 80 FEP Cases 355, 363 (D. Kan. 1999).

[111]Vinson v. Superior Court, 43 Cal. 3d 833, 845–46, 239 Cal. Rptr. 292, 300–02, 44 FEP Cases 1174, 1179 (Cal. 1987). *See also* Gavenda v. Orleans County, 174 F.R.D. 272 (W.D.N.Y. 1996) (permitting tape recording of examination); *Zabkowicz*, 585 F. Supp. at 636, 35 FEP Cases at 209–10 (allowing the use of a tape recording device or the presence of any third-party observer to protect the plaintiff from "unsupervised interrogation").

[112]CAL. CODE OF CIV. PROC. §2032(g)(2).

D. Limitations on the Duration of the Examination

A frequent issue surrounding Rule 35 mental examinations is the amount of time to be allowed for the examination. A properly conducted mental examination, including the administration of psychological testing, typically lasts for the better part of a day. Some courts have specifically approved of this time frame.[113] Other courts have either approved or specifically ordered a maximum of three hours to conduct the examination plus the time needed to administer any psychological tests.[114] In *Shepherd v. American Broadcasting Cos.*,[115] the court limited the psychiatric examinations of the race discrimination plaintiffs to five hours each, with no mention of psychological testing.[116] Further, in *Morton v. Haskell Co.*,[117] the court rejected the plaintiff's request to limit the mental examination to one hour, reasoning that there was "no basis to conclude that a one-hour examination will necessarily fit the circumstances of this case."[118] Notably, the court in that case did not impose any time restrictions for the examination.[119]

E. Restrictions on the Scope of the Examination

Rule 35 and most of its state counterparts require the party seeking a mental examination to specify the scope of the examination. In employment litigation, defendants naturally desire wide latitude in the scope of the examination to determine both the extent and the cause of the plaintiff's alleged mental or

---

[113]Bethel v. Dixie Homecrafters, Inc., 192 F.R.D. 320, 323 n.2, 82 FEP Cases 345, 348 n.2 (N.D. Ga. 2000)(imposed eight-hour limitation on duration of exam); Ragge v. MCA/Universal Studios, 165 F.R.D. 605, 610 (C.D. Cal. 1995) (ordered seven hours total including time needed for psychological tests); Chaparro v. IBP, Inc., 1994 WL 714369 at *4 (D. Kan. Dec. 7, 1994) (approved one day or two half-day sessions if the defendant pays for the plaintiff's expenses incurred because the examination was not conducted in a single day).

[114]*See, e.g., Hirschheimer,* 1995 WL 736901, at *5 (ordered maximum of two 90-minute sessions in addition to the time needed to administer the Minnesota Multiphasic Personality Inventory-2 (MMPI-2)); Burger v. Litton Indus., Inc., 1995 WL 363741, at *2, 68 FEP Cases 737, 739 (S.D.N.Y. June 19, 1995) (ordered maximum of three hours for the examination plus the time necessary to administer the MMPI-2, which is approximately four hours); Lowe v. Philadelphia Newspapers, Inc., 101 F.R.D. 296, 300, 44 FEP Cases 1224, 1228 (E.D. Pa. 1983) (ordered no more than two sessions lasting 90 minutes each); Ryzlak v. McNeil Pharm. Co., 38 Fed. R. Serv. 2d 443, 444 (E.D. Pa. 1982) (approved two 90-minute sessions).

[115]151 F.R.D. 194 (D.D.C. 1993), *rev'd in part and vacated in part on other grounds,* 62 F.3d 1469 (D.C. Cir. 1995).

[116]*Id.* at 215.

[117]5 AD Cases 272 (M.D. Fla. 1995).

[118]*Id.* at 275.

[119]*See also* Gavenda v. Orleans County, 174 F.R.D. 272 (W.D.N.Y. 1996) (court refused to place time limit on examination).

emotional distress or injury. Plaintiffs, on the other hand, want to limit the scope of the examination as much as possible.

From a clinical standpoint, the examiner must have wide latitude to conduct a thorough inquiry of the plaintiff's family and educational background, employment history, prior traumatic events (including sexual abuse), prior medical and psychiatric treatment, marital and relational history, and possible alternative sources of distress. These areas are important to consider in arriving at an informed psychiatric or psychological assessment of the plaintiff, whether conducted by plaintiff's or defendant's expert.

Yet, with increasing frequency, plaintiffs and their attorneys attempt to restrict the defense examiner's areas of inquiry on privacy or relevancy grounds, often seeking to shield from disclosure other significant traumas or life events that might bring into question the validity of the assertion that the employer is wholly to blame for the plaintiff's psychological condition. Prior sexual trauma is an area frequently sought to be shielded from inquiry,[120] as well as prior mental health treatment, prior or concurrent medical conditions, family dysfunction, and developmental difficulties.

The American Psychiatric Association (APA) recently published its *Practice Guideline for Psychiatric Evaluation of Adults*.[121] Although stressing that the *Practice Guideline* is not intended to serve as a standard of care,[122] the APA[123] sets forth a systematic outline of what it considers the appropriate scope of a clinical psychiatric evaluation. This *Guideline* may be useful in educating courts and discovery referees and in resisting attempts by plaintiffs' counsel to restrict the scope of inquiry during the mental examination of the plaintiff. It might be cited as evidence that certain types of inquiries need to be made, not in an attempt to embarrass or harass the plaintiff, but because the psychiatric profession, in its considered judgment, holds that such inquiries ordinarily must be made for a valid evaluation to occur.

The *Practice Guideline* divides the clinical evaluation process into a series of "domains," or areas of inquiry, as follows:

- The first two domains are the reason for the evaluation and the history of the present illness. This essentially involves the examiner's eliciting from the patient a description of the symptoms suffered and their history, including the patient's description of any precipitating or aggravating factors.[124]

---

[120]*See* Knoettgen v. Superior Court, 224 Cal. App. 3d 11, 273 Cal. Rptr. 636 (1990) (prohibiting discovery into plaintiff's prior sexual abuse in sexual harassment case).

[121]AMERICAN PSYCHIATRIC ASSOCIATION, *Practice Guideline for Psychiatric Evaluation of Adults, in* PRACTICE GUIDELINES (1996).

[122]*Id.* at ix.

[123]Although the *Practice Guideline* is published by the APA, a wide variety of other medical and mental health organizations had input into its drafting, including the American Psychological Association, the American Medical Association, the American Nurses Association, the American Psychoanalytic Association, and the American Academy of Psychiatry and the Law. *Id.* at 31.

[124]*Id.* at 14.

- The next domain is the past psychiatric history. This includes "a chronological summary of all past episodes of mental illness and treatment, including psychiatric syndromes not formally diagnosed at the time, previously established diagnoses, treatments offered, and responses to treatment."[125] This history should also include prior episodes of serious emotional distress or functional impairment even though no formal treatment was procured. The *Practice Guideline* suggests that the patient be asked about "the past use of psychotropic drugs prescribed by a nonpsychiatric physician, prior suicide attempts or other self-destructive behavior."[126] It suggests that past medical records might be consulted to obtain relevant data.[127]
- The next domain involves a general medical history. This should include an inquiry into "known general medical illnesses (e.g., hospitalizations, procedures, treatments, and medications) and undiagnosed health problems that have caused the patient major distress or functional impairment." It should also include inquiry into any episodes of important physical injury or trauma, as well as a sexual and reproductive history.[128]
- The next domain involves a history of the patient's substance use. This is to include both illegal and legal substances, such as alcohol, caffeine, and nicotine.[129]
- The next domain is an inquiry into the patient's psychosocial and development history, also known as the "personal history." This includes obtaining information about the person's formal education, religious, and cultural influences; contacts with the criminal justice system; sexual history; marriage and parenting; as well as "any history of physical, emotional, sexual, or other abuse or trauma."[130]
- The next two domains are a social history and an occupational history. The social history involves a consideration of relationships, familial and otherwise, that may serve as stressors or provide support. The occupational history involves a consideration of jobs held, reasons for job changes, and whether any of those jobs involved unusual amounts of stress.[131]
- Next is a family history, which explores the existence of medical or psychiatric illness in close relatives, including mood disorders, psychosis, suicide, and substance abuse.[132]
- Next is a review of symptoms, such as lack of sleep, loss of appetite, pain and discomfort, fatigue, and the like, and a mental status examination, which is not so much a separate area of inquiry as a "systematic collection of data based on observation of the patient's behavior during the interview" and at other

---

[125]*Id.*
[126]*Id.* at 15.
[127]*Id.* at 14.
[128]*Id.* at 15.
[129]*Id.*
[130]*Id.* at 15–16.
[131]*Id.* at 16.
[132]*Id.*

times while in the examiner's view.[133] Here, a functional assessment of the patient's ability to carry out activities of everyday living is usually conducted,[134] and depending upon the circumstances, a physical examination also may be conducted.[135]

The *Practice Guideline* advises that "the psychiatrist should always consider using collateral sources of information," such as records of prior medical and/or psychiatric treatment. It stresses that "[c]ollateral information is particularly important for patients with impaired insight,"[136] which, it could be argued, might include plaintiffs seeking to recover substantial damages for emotional distress.

The APA is not alone in maintaining that a comprehensive inquiry is necessary for a valid psychiatric evaluation to occur. As one prominent commentator similarly observes:

> Whether the examiner is retained by the plaintiff or defense attorney, it should be obvious that he or she must perform a complete psychiatric evaluation of the examinee. Nevertheless, some forensic reports do not contain any past psychiatric history of the examinee. It is as if the life of the examinee began with the litigation. Particularly in sexual harassment litigation, the prior history of the examinee is extremely important in the evaluation of psychic injury claims. . . . The longitudinal perspective of child and adolescent development and psychopathology is critical in making correct diagnosis and treatment assessments.[137]

Most courts to date have been reluctant to limit the scope of questioning during a mental examination. In *Bethel v. Dixie Homecrafters, Inc.*,[138] the court suggested that the parties submit an order defining the scope of the Rule 35 mental examination as follows:

> The scope of the examination shall be limited to information that reasonably may relate to the issues of causation and the assessment of damages for alleged psychological injuries and any alleged mental stress suffered by Plaintiff as an element of her claimed damages in the instant case and may include recognized and appropriate psychological testing.[139]

Similarly, in a gender discrimination and sexual harassment case, the court permitted the defendant's examiner a broad range of inquiry:

> The scope of the examination will be: a full history of plaintiff's entire mental history and its causes; all psychological problems and/or damages that she may

---

[133]*Id.* at 17–18.

[134]*Id.* at 19.

[135]*Id.* at 17. Physical examinations are not common during forensic mental examinations.

[136]*Id.* at 21.

[137]Simon, *supra* note 94, at 142.

[138]192 F.R.D. 320, 82 FEP Cases 345 (N.D. Ga. 2000).

[139]*Id.* at 324 n.3, 82 FEP Cases at 349 n.3.

have experienced in the past, is currently experiencing or may continue to experience in the future; and the extent of and causes of any such problems.[140]

In *Morton v. Haskell Co.*,[141] the plaintiff claimed that the employer discriminated against him on account of his clinical depression. The court refused to limit questioning during the mental examination to the year of the alleged adverse employment action, concluding that such a limitation was unwarranted, particularly in light of the plaintiff's own allegation that he had suffered a continuing history of clinical depression.[142]

In *Hertenstein v. Kimberly Home Health Care, Inc.*,[143] the court refused the plaintiff's request to forbid the examiner from questioning her about her sexual history, explaining:

> This is a sexual harassment case. [The plaintiff's psychological expert] has opined that alleged actions or inactions of defendant proximately caused the emotional distress of plaintiff. To validly assess her emotional state, the examiner must have leave to make relevant inquiries. To prohibit inquiry into private sexual activities may unreasonably restrict exploring the history of plaintiff relevant to this case.[144]

A more narrow approach was adopted by the court in *Sarko v. Penn-Del Directory Co.*[145] In *Sarko*, the plaintiff alleged that her employer had discriminated against her by failing to accommodate her clinical depression, which she claimed had a long-term impact on her mental state.[146] The court held that the defendant was entitled to conduct a mental examination because the plaintiff's allegation placed her current mental condition in controversy, but it specifically limited the scope of the examination to the long-term impact that the depression had on the plaintiff's current mental state.[147]

F. Conduct of Psychological Testing As Part of the Examination

Standardized psychological testing instruments are commonly administered in the course of mental examinations of plaintiffs in employment lawsuits.[148] Some plaintiffs have challenged the use of psychological tests during the Rule 35

---

[140]Ferrell v. Shell Oil Co., 1995 WL 688795, at *2 (E.D. La. Nov. 20, 1995).
[141]5 AD Cases 272 (M.D. Fla. 1995).
[142]*Id.* at 275.
[143]80 FEP Cases 355 (D. Kan. 1999).
[144]*Id.* at 359. Federal Rule of Evidence 412 may impact the scope of permissible questioning about a plaintiff's sexual history during the mental examination. For a detailed discussion of this issue, see Chapter 8, The Right to Privacy Versus the Need for Discovery.
[145]170 F.R.D. 127 (E.D. Pa. 1997).
[146]*Id.* at 131.
[147]*Id.*
[148]Psychological testing is discussed in detail in Chapter 10, Psychological Testing.

mental examination, however. Specifically, some plaintiffs have attempted to argue that a defendant should not be able to subject them to psychological testing in addition to a psychiatric examination. In one case, *Burger v. Litton Industries, Inc.*,[149] the court held that only the defendant's psychiatrist would be allowed to conduct an examination, rather than both a psychiatrist and a psychologist as originally proposed by the defendant. In other cases, however, courts have permitted psychological testing in addition to a psychiatric examination.

In *Ziemann v. Burlington County Bridge Commission*,[150] the court reasoned that the use of multiple examiners was appropriate because psychiatry and psychology are different disciplines, focusing on "different areas of thought and behavior."[151] In *Jackson v. Entergy Operations, Inc.*,[152] the plaintiff in a sexual harassment case objected to having to undergo psychological testing in addition to a psychiatric examination. The court overruled her objection, noting that Rule 35 does not limit the number of examinations a party may be required to undergo. It also observed that "psychological testing is a routine component of a complete psychiatric examination," a fact that provides sufficient basis to order such testing.[153]

In *Jaqua v. Furr's/Bishop's Cafeterias, L.P.*,[154] the court rejected the plaintiff's argument that the defendant had improperly subjected him to psychological testing where the defense psychiatric expert retained a psychologist to interpret psychological testing administered by the plaintiff's own psychologist. The court maintained that reviewing psychological tests obtained by someone else is not the same as performing one's own psychological testing. It also pointed out that it would have allowed the defense to conduct its own psychological testing of the plaintiff had such a request been made.

In *Chiperas v. Rubin*,[155] the court rejected the plaintiff's request that the defendant's expert not be permitted to administer psychological tests that previously had been administered to her. The court observed: "I would be loath to interfere with a conscientious determination by a medical professional that a test should be repeated to reach a sound scientific conclusion."[156]

1. Limitations on Tests That May Be Used

Some courts require that psychological tests conducted during a mental examination be shown to be reliable and offer probative evidence.[157] Other courts require that such tests be limited to those generally recognized in the mental

---

[149] 68 FEP Cases 737, 739 (S.D.N.Y. 1995).
[150] 155 F.R.D. 497 (D.N.J. 1994).
[151] *Id.* at 502.
[152] 76 FEP Cases 85 (E.D. La. 1998).
[153] *Id.* at 87.
[154] 175 F.R.D. 688, 75 FEP Cases 737 (D. Kan. 1997).
[155] 1998 WL 765126 (D.D.C. Nov. 3, 1998).
[156] *Id.* at *4.
[157] *See, e.g.,* Lahr v. Fulbright & Jaworski, L.L.P., 164 F.R.D. 204, 212 (N.D. Tex. 1996).

health professions.¹⁵⁸ The Minnesota Multiphasic Personality Inventory-2 (MMPI-2), for example, is one test that is generally accepted and commonly used by mental health professionals.

Results of the MMPI have been admitted into evidence by many state and federal courts,¹⁵⁹ and both the MMPI and MMPI-2 have been the subject of extensive validation studies. In employment litigation, the MMPI-2 also is routinely allowed during Rule 35 mental examinations.¹⁶⁰ For example, in *Burger v. Litton Industries*,¹⁶¹ over the plaintiff's claim that the action amounted to "harassment," the court ordered the plaintiff in an age and sex discrimination case to take the MMPI-2, which it described as a "generally accepted and commonly used test to obtain a psychological profile and history of the subject."¹⁶² Similarly, in *Hirschheimer v. Associated Minerals & Minerals Corp.*,¹⁶³ the court ordered the plaintiff in an age and disability discrimination lawsuit to take the MMPI-2, observing that even if, as the plaintiff argued, it provided only a "snapshot" of the plaintiff's personality at the time the test is taken, it was "still useful as part of a psychological examination."¹⁶⁴ Courts have ordered psychological testing as part of the Rule 35 mental examination in other cases as well.¹⁶⁵

In *Breda v. Wolf Camera, Inc.*,¹⁶⁶ the plaintiff moved for a protective order seeking to prevent the defendant's psychologist from performing psychological testing on her. Specifically, she sought to avoid the MMPI-2 and the Rorschach Ink Blot test, arguing that the tests were overly invasive and unreliable. The court rejected her request. It observed that "[e]ven a cursory scan of the caselaw reveals that both the MMPI-2 and Rorschach are acceptable diagnostic indicators in a mental examination."¹⁶⁷ With respect to the plaintiff's argument that the Rorschach is not sufficiently accurate to be reliable, the court noted that such an argument should be brought in a challenge to admissibility under *Daubert v. Merrill Dow Pharmaceuticals, Inc.*,¹⁶⁸ not in an attempt to prevent discovery.

---

¹⁵⁸*See, e.g.*, Ragge v. MCA/Universal Studios, 165 F.R.D. 605, 609 (C.D. Cal. 1995); Chaparro v. IBP, Inc., 1994 WL 714369, at *4 (D. Kan. Dec. 7, 1994).

¹⁵⁹For a general discussion of the admissibility of the MMPI, as well as a listing of federal and state cases in which MMPI test results were admitted, see KENNETH POPE ET AL., THE MMPI, MMPI-2 AND MMPI-A IN COURT 39–46 & Appendix E (1993).

¹⁶⁰*See, e.g.*, Shirsat v. Mutual Pharm. Co., 169 F.R.D. 68, 71–72 (E.D. Pa. 1996); Hirschheimer v. Associated Minerals & Minerals Corp., 1995 WL 736901, at *4–5 (S.D.N.Y. Dec. 12, 1995); Burger v. Litton Indus., Inc., 68 FEP Cases 737, 739 (S.D.N.Y. 1995).

¹⁶¹68 FEP Cases 737 (S.D.N.Y. 1995).

¹⁶²*Id.* at 739.

¹⁶³1995 WL 736901 (S.D.N.Y. Dec. 12, 1995).

¹⁶⁴1995 WL 736901, at *4.

¹⁶⁵*E.g.*, Workman v. Carolina Freight Carriers Corp., 65 FEP Cases 1209 (M.D. Ala. 1994); Chaparro v. IBP, Inc., 1994 WL 714369 (D. Kan. Dec. 7, 1994).

¹⁶⁶78 FEP Cases 433 (S.D. Ga. 1998).

¹⁶⁷*Id.* at 434.

¹⁶⁸509 U.S. 579 (1993).

Only one court has refused to allow such an administration of the MMPI-2. In a peculiar opinion in which the court referred to psychological tests as "mind control" devices, the court in *Usher v. Lakewood Usher Engineering & Manufacturing Co.*,[169] denied the defendant's motion to have the plaintiff undergo a battery of psychological tests, including the MMPI-2, during the Rule 35 mental examination. The *Usher* court did not provide any extensive analysis in support of its decision; it indicated merely that it felt that the questions on some of the tests were intrusive and of limited relevance to the issues in the litigation. At this point, however, the *Usher* decision is in the distinct minority.

2. Obligation to Identify Tests in Advance

An issue that is becoming more frequently litigated is whether the defense examiner must identify the psychological tests to be administered during the Rule 35 mental examination in advance of the examination. The obvious problem with advance disclosure is that the testing process becomes compromised; it cannot be known whether the plaintiff rehearsed the answers in advance, with the aid of counsel and/or therapist.[170]

The few cases decided to date are in conflict. In *Ragge v. MCA/Universal Studios*,[171] for example, the court refused to order the defense examiner to disclose in advance the specific psychological tests to be administered. An opposite conclusion was reached by the court in *Hirschheimer v. ASOMA Corp.*,[172] which limited the use of testing during the Rule 35 mental examination to the one test, the MMPI-2, that had been identified previously by the defense. The court commented: "[R]equiring Mr. Hirschheimer to undergo unidentified testing would deprive him of the opportunity to seek an order precluding those tests that may be irrelevant to this litigation."[173]

IV. Conducting the Clinical Interview

The purpose of the clinical interview is to complete the process started with record review by answering five basic questions:

- Does the plaintiff have one or more mental disorders that can be diagnosed in *DSM-IV-TR*[174] terminology?
- If the plaintiff has one or more such disorders, did any of them develop as a result of the workplace events at issue in the litigation?

---

[169] 158 F.R.D. 411, 66 FEP Cases 558 (N.D. Ill. 1994).
[170] Psychologists are ethically bound to maintain the integrity and security of psychological tests. *See* AMERICAN PSYCHOLOGICAL ASSOCIATION, *Ethical Principle No. 8*, *in* CASEBOOK ON ETHICAL PRINCIPLES OF PSYCHOLOGISTS 109 (1987).
[171] 165 F.R.D. 605 (C.D. Cal. 1995).
[172] 1995 WL 736901 (S.D.N.Y. Dec. 12, 1995).
[173] *Id.* at *4.
[174] DSM-IV-TR, *supra* note 64.

- With respect to each diagnosis on Axis I,[175] is it an acute condition or another episode of a chronic condition?
- What stressful events—both within and outside the workplace—seem to be linked to the diagnosable condition?
- Does the plaintiff also have an Axis II personality disorder,[176] and if so, to what extent did it affect the plaintiff's perception of the environment in the workplace and the plaintiff's relationships with supervisors and coworkers?

A. The Examiner's Approach

As has been outlined in the Chapter 7, Preparing the Case for the Expert, the examiner should review all pertinent documents and records prior to the examination. The clinical interview is typically a one-time contact for which the examiner must be well prepared. It is important for the examiner to be informed about the nature and extent of the alleged events that underlie the litigation before the interview begins. This is typically accomplished by reviewing the complaint in the lawsuit, the plaintiff's deposition testimony, and summaries of events often found in reports from other mental health professionals. A basic knowledge of the incidents that have been described previously paves the way for a more comprehensive examination. It is also critical for the examiner to be fully acquainted with all diagnoses of the plaintiff that have been given by other mental health professionals. Further, it is important to be well versed about the plaintiff's medical situation and the status of treatment for any ongoing conditions. It is also important to have an overall understanding of events claimed to have occurred in the workplace, as well as other stressful events in plaintiff's life. The examiner should review personnel records from past employers so as to obtain a comprehensive job history, as well as other background information on the plaintiff.

Mental health examinations are done at the request of both plaintiff and defense attorneys. The examiner should take the same approach to preparing for and conducting the examination no matter which side has made the referral. Although it would be difficult to argue that a mental examination is entirely scientific in nature, it can be standardized so that the same procedures are used by the examiner in every instance. Different findings can then more confidently be attributed to clinical observations about the plaintiff rather than to inconsistencies in the examiner's approach.

Most clinical interviews in employment lawsuits are conducted after the litigation has been in progress for a while. Efforts to resolve the matter earlier have failed. Numerous depositions have probably been taken. Dispositive motions may have been filed and may be pending. In this context, the plaintiff is

---

[175] Axis I disorders are discussed in detail in Chapter 5, Mental Disorders Commonly Encountered in Employment Litigation.

[176] Axis II disorders are discussed in detail in Chapter 6, Personality Disorders in Employment Litigation.

ordinarily not eager to participate in a mental examination conducted by an examiner retained by the employer's attorney, and it is important for the examiner to bear this in mind. The mental examination should be conducted in a clinical environment, in an atmosphere that gives the plaintiff every opportunity to provide a complete history and express fully his or her perception of events that occurred in the workplace.

The initial part of the interview process is designed to establish some degree of rapport with the plaintiff. This is typically accomplished by establishing a tone that is appropriately clinical in nature and does not resemble the formal environment of a deposition. The plaintiff must be treated with respect and with some acknowledgment of the adversarial and tedious nature of litigation. The plaintiff must be informed about the limits of confidentiality attaching to matters communicated during the interview. The examiner should ensure that the clinical interview is not like a typical therapy session with a psychologist or psychiatrist. Rather, the information elicited during the interview might be discussed in the future with the referring attorney, at a deposition, or as part of trial testimony.

In those jurisdictions where audiotaping of the interview is allowed, it is important to deal with any "technical difficulties" involving the equipment being used before the interview begins. Otherwise, there can be frequent interruptions to the flow of the discussion. If there is an interpreter present, it is important to ask for verbatim translations of the examinee's words. Otherwise there may be a tendency on the part of the interpreter to express things more clearly or in a more organized fashion than the examinee is capable of doing. Whether or not an interpreter's assistance is required, the clinician should bring to the situation a knowledge of cultural differences. This is essential in order to understand fully what the plaintiff is trying to communicate.

B. The Components of the Mental Examination

There are standard components to any mental exam in employment litigation. These features will be described below.

1. Mental Status Examination

The psychologist or psychiatrist brings a trained eye to the mental examination. The mental status examination includes all observations that have been made about plaintiff during the time spent with the examiner. Its purpose is to collect information about the plaintiff's current symptoms, as well as such matters as an individual's ability to reason abstractly and his or her capacity for insight and good judgment. Notes are taken of all behaviors that may later prove to be of clinical importance.

The clinical observations begin with the first moments of the encounter, including an assessment of plaintiff's dress and grooming. The clinician will attend to features of physical behavior, including the speed of the examinee's movements and any limitations in mobility. Ability to maintain eye contact and overall energy level are noted as well. These would include observations about concentration, use of speech, and quality of thought processes. Since accurate diagnosis is one of the goals of the exam, it is important to determine the presence of any delusional thinking or any evidence of auditory or visual hallucinations.

In all mental examinations there will be reference to whether the examinee is oriented to time, place, and person. Observations are made about ability to recall recent as well as past events.

Often the plaintiff will complain of depression or anxiety. Mental status observations would include any displays of behavior consistent with such symptoms. These might include sad expressions, crying, an inability to sit still, or trouble providing a coherent history. Assessment is made of the examinee's affect, such as whether it is flat or inappropriate to the thoughts being expressed. In appropriate situations it would be important to assess any degree of suicidal or homicidal thinking.

Sometimes plaintiffs will present different levels of emotional expression at different points in the examination. It is important to note when increased upset is expressed, in terms of the content being discussed at the time. Further, the clinician notes any points in the discussion where the patient becomes more evasive and seems more reluctant to provide detailed information.

It is also important for the examiner to assess intellectual level. In this area there would be observations about use of vocabulary, capacity for abstract reasoning and the ability to provide a logical and clear history. Standardized intelligence tests typically are not administered in employment lawsuits. However, the clinician is interested in the plaintiff's overall level of intellectual functioning, the consistency between presentation in the interview and level of formal education, and any indications of neurological difficulties. Psychiatrists will sometimes use a more formal means of assessing mental status. Such measures might be referred to in a written report using terminology such as "serial sevens" or "proverbs." These are specific questions posed to determine how clearly the patient is thinking and at what intellectual level he or she is functioning.

It is also important to note how the plaintiff approaches the idea of taking psychological tests, if such tests are part of the examination, including the degree of cooperation that is obtained. The clinician will typically maintain accurate notes about the length of time it took the individual to complete psychological tests, and any complaints that were voiced about the content of the tests or difficulty in understanding the questions.

Mental status observations are typically noted in the examiner's report apart from the actual history being taken. They are descriptions about the individual rather than a narrative of the historical information that has been gathered.

2. *Past History*

Claims of emotional injury made in employment litigation typically refer to the development of acute mental problems in response to specific alleged events in the workplace. To assess whether such a mental condition is present, it is critical to determine a baseline of the patient's emotional functioning. That is, the clinician must determine how well the individual functioned overall from a mental perspective before work was identified as a problem. This task is accomplished in part by the taking of a past history.

The history must be comprehensive, dating back to childhood. Information is gathered about early development, including data about adjustment at school, academic performance, and any early behavioral difficulties. Questions are asked about family life, including positive memories as well as any disruptive experiences in the early years. Inquiry is made as to episodes of medical illness, psychological difficulties, or any type of abuse or mistreatment. Questions are posed about any contacts with the criminal justice system, including juvenile delinquency.

It is important for the examiner to obtain a comprehensive history of any past medical or psychological problems. This would include information about any diagnoses, the treatment rendered for any condition, and the patient's response to that treatment. Details are gathered about past medications taken and any of their side effects. Further, it is important to account for any periods of exacerbation or remission of illness, particularly in the mental health area. As part of this area of history, questions are asked about any chronic medical or mental illnesses among family members.

The taking of an academic history leads chronologically to information about higher education as well as a detailed job history. The job history is particularly important in order to determine if there is any pattern of maladjustment in different workplaces.

Other relevant historical information would concern a history of important relationships, marriages, and difficulties created by excessive drug or alcohol use.

Data collected in the taking of a thorough past history are used in part to determine whether the examinee has ever had an acute mental condition prior to the time period that encompasses alleged adverse events at work. The history may also indicate the appropriateness of a diagnosis of a personality disorder. Since personality traits and disorders are in place by late adolescence or early adulthood, they are difficult to diagnose without historical detail covering that time period.

Sometimes the clinician is aware of a pertinent historical detail that the patient has omitted from the history. This might involve a prior medical problem or a past difficulty at another job or in a relationship. If a good rapport has been established and the examinee seems generally forthcoming, this can be explored in chronological fashion at the appropriate point in the history taking. If the plaintiff has been evasive or hostile to the process, it may be better to wait until the end of the interview to confront topics that may lead to further resistance or expressions of anger.

3. Account of Events in the Workplace

The plaintiff has filed a lawsuit alleging that some upsetting events occurred on the job, typically in the form of discriminatory treatment, sexually harassing behavior, or an unjust termination. Although the examiner conducting a mental examination is not a finder of fact, it is important as part of the assessment to understand how the plaintiff describes what occurred in the workplace. In conjunction with this area of discussion will be inquiry about the various psychological symptoms the plaintiff claims to have experienced as a result. The examiner will also need to inquire about all psychological or psychiatric treatment that was sought in this time period. This would include the duration and extent of therapeutic interventions, including any medication that has been prescribed. Some plaintiffs have actually had a period of psychiatric hospitalization in a time period concurrent with employment or after departure from a job. It is important to assess the patient's functioning in everyday life throughout this relevant time period.

Obviously, this part of the exam will differ from one case to the next. Some plaintiffs will describe a series of negative events taking place over several decades. In those instances, the past history and this portion of the examination will overlap, as events in the workplace took place concurrently throughout the years along with other life developments. In other cases, the plaintiff may have worked at a job for only a few months and will typically provide a much shorter narrative of disturbing experiences. Although it is not necessary to cover each situation in exhaustive detail, it is important to ensure that the major allegations in the lawsuit have been discussed during the interview.

It is often at this time that plaintiffs vent feelings of anger and frustration about the litigation process. They may have already attended several deposition sessions that they found to be extremely unpleasant. Plaintiffs frequently complain that during the litigation they are treated much worse than the coworkers about whom they originally complained. They often have not been warned in advance that litigation is lengthy, time-consuming, and intrusive. They are surprised to learn that because of their claims of emotional injury, past medical and mental health records will be reviewed. It is often appropriate in this clinical interaction for the examiner to empathize with the plaintiff's plight. Although it does not alter the extent of the information the examiner will gather or the opinions that are reached, it can be an appropriately respectful response and will certainly enhance rapport.

4. Assessment of Current Functioning

Part of the clinician's role is to determine if there is a diagnosable mental disorder at the time the plaintiff is being seen for the evaluation. This section of the interview involves a comprehensive discussion of different parts of an individual's functioning so that accurate diagnostic impressions can be reached.

Certainly it is important to assess all current psychological complaints. Although some mental status *observations* will be made throughout the exam, it is important to question the plaintiff about his or her experience of current symptoms. This would include the severity of current symptoms of depression or anxiety. If such symptoms are described, it is important to determine their impact in areas such as sleep patterns, appetite, energy level and general interest in activities, and the ability to concentrate. It is important to determine if therapy and/or a medication regimen are ongoing.

Questions are posed as to the plaintiff's current medical condition. This would include an exploration of acute medical conditions as well as those that are more chronic in nature (e.g., hypertension, diabetes, thyroid condition). It is important to be aware of all medications being taken and their side effects. If an examinee has a serious medical condition, his or her understanding of the prognosis should be explored, as depression is often present when one has a debilitating condition.

Part of understanding a plaintiff's current emotional functioning is an exploration of current activities, both job-related and personal. It is important to obtain information about a person's routine and how well he or she feels he or she is fulfilling major life roles, such as wage earner or parent. Information about the current financial situation is also relevant to understanding the level of stress the plaintiff may be experiencing. It is important to explore current relationships with partners, children, extended families, and friends. Further, it is necessary to inquire about any problems in the lives of those close to the plaintiff.

Certainly the examiner must inquire about the extent of any drug or alcohol use, as well as any current or historical substance abuse problems. It is also important to inquire about other concurrent legal involvement, in matters such as divorce, custody, or other prior or ongoing lawsuits. Such inquiry will not only furnish information about concurrent stressful events; it will also help to identify the occasional individual who is chronically litigious and may be involved in lawsuits only for secondary gain.

5. Psychological Testing

A forensic examination typically involves the administration of one or more psychological tests. These are objective, standardized instruments that may assess personality or intelligence. The most highly regarded tests have been researched extensively to help establish their levels of both validity and reliability.

This topic is addressed in detail in a Chapter 10, Psychological Testing. For purposes of this discussion it is important to note that the clinician should administer the tests using standard instructions. The test materials should never be taken home by the examinee, and no other individuals should be permitted to assist an examinee in the completion of paper-and-pencil tests. Testing should be done in a comfortable, quiet environment where the examinee can concentrate. Observations should be made of the time it takes for the examinee to complete the test and any evident difficulties that might be experienced.

C. Forming a Clinical Opinion

A great deal of information is gathered about an individual through a review of records, a thorough clinical interview, and the results of psychological testing. Each element plays a role in the formation of a clinical opinion. The goal is to determine the most cohesive explanation for what the patient has experienced.

Some information is used primarily to reach conclusions about whether the plaintiff has a current diagnosable mental disorder. Of great importance in forming that part of the opinion are the mental status observations, psychological test results, and the data gathered about the individual's current functioning.

This information is used in conjunction with historical detail and the medical records to determine how long a condition has been present and to what degree it may now be resolved or in remission.

Diagnostic conclusions are reached about the presence or absence of Axis II personality disorders. The diagnosis of an Axis II personality disorder will ordinarily require the clinician to comment about the plaintiff's perception of the workplace environment.

Reaching conclusions about the cause of any mental disorder is a complex matter. It requires a thorough understanding of the plaintiff's history to determine whether the individual suffers from chronic mental problems that predate workplace events. The clinician must also be fully informed about other stressful events in the person's life and any negative impact these have created. Consideration must be given to all complaints about the workplace and any impact these have had on the plaintiff's functioning.

A clinical evaluation can play an integral part in the determination of the extent of emotional distress. When it is done with the right amount of preparation and under the right conditions, it will enable the mental health expert to provide both consultation to the referring party and instructive testimony at time of trial.

CHAPTER 10

THE USE AND MISUSE OF PSYCHOLOGICAL TESTING

Paul R. Lees-Haley, Ph.D., ABPP
David D. Fox, Ph.D.

I. Introduction

The availability of emotional distress damages in employment lawsuits has resulted in a dramatic increase in the use of mental health experts by both sides in wrongful discharge, employment discrimination, and sexual harassment cases. Many of these experts use a variety of psychological testing instruments in the course of evaluating the plaintiff's mental condition. Properly administered and interpreted, these instruments can provide assistance to the expert in determining the existence and severity of a psychological injury. They can also enhance the credibility of the expert's opinion in the eyes of the fact finder, as they can be used to bring an element of objectivity to the diagnosis of mental illness—a process that is largely unfamiliar to most laypeople.

Psychological testing has significant potential for assisting with objective evaluation of plaintiffs in employment litigation. A substantial literature has developed indicating that psychiatric and psychological interviews may be unreliable in and of themselves in diagnosing mental disorders in the forensic context.[1] Actuarial methods have proved to be at least equal and usually superior to clinical judgment in almost all the relevant research studies in the history of psychology. Paul Meehl has pointed out that using clinical judgment instead of actuarial methods is analogous to eyeballing a pile of groceries in a grocery store and saying, "In my clinical experience that is about $50 worth," instead

---

[1] Much of this research is summarized in JAY R. ZISKIN, COPING WITH PSYCHIATRIC AND PSYCHOLOGICAL TESTIMONY 327–494 (5th ed. 1995).

of using the systematic method of adding up the individual prices.[2] Used properly, therefore, psychological tests can provide an important adjunct to the clinical interview to enhance the overall reliability of the forensic evaluation. They can add objectivity that is not influenced by factors such as charm, appearance, or persuasive interpersonal skills, all of which may bias an interview. Some tests can also help detect malingering (i.e., the fabrication or exaggeration of symptoms), and a few do so in a manner which produces useful exhibits for courtroom use.

Certain psychological tests can also provide valuable clues to a subject's long-term character and functioning. One type of long-term psychopathology that almost always predates the individual's entry into the workplace is the personality disorder, and as demonstrated elsewhere in this volume, personality disorders not only may be relevant to damages issues but may even affect liability in some workplace harassment and discrimination lawsuits.[3]

Unfortunately, however, psychological tests may sometimes be misused in employment lawsuits. They may be administered carelessly by clinicians who lack the requisite training. They may be scored inaccurately or in an idiosyncratic fashion. Instruments may be used that lack proper validation, or validated tests may be used for purposes for which they were never designed. Instruments may be used that, because of the leading nature of the inquiries they make, are far too prone to exaggeration or fabrication of symptoms to be suitable for use in a forensic context. As a result, the fact finder may be misled to believe that test results provide scientific proof in support of a litigant's position when in fact they do no such thing.

It is important for attorneys faced with prosecuting or defending a claim for psychological injury to have a basic understanding of the value—and the limits—of psychological testing. The goal of this chapter is to describe the nature and limits of the psychological tests likely to be encountered in employment litigation in terms that make sense to individuals who are not psychologists.

The chapter will begin with an introduction to some of the basic nomenclature of psychological testing. It will then describe in some detail the psychological tests that are found most frequently in employment lawsuits—the Minnesota Multiphasic Personality Inventory-2 (MMPI-2), the Millon Clinical Multiaxial Inventory-III (MCMI-III), and the Wechsler Adult Intelligence Scale-III (WAIS-III). These tests have been extensively validated and accepted for use in forensic settings. The chapter will also describe more briefly a variety of other tests that appear less frequently in employment cases. Many of these tests have not been validated (or are not capable of being validated) and therefore are not appropriate for use in a forensic context, although they may have value

---

[2]PAUL E. MEEHL, CLINICAL VERSUS STATISTICAL PREDICTION: A THEORETICAL ANALYSIS AND A REVIEW OF THE EVIDENCE (1954); William M. Grove & Paul E. Meehl, *Comparative Efficiency of Informal (Subjective, Impressionistic) and Formal (Mechanical, Algorithmic) Prediction Procedures: The Clinical-Statistical Controversy*, 2 PSYCHOL. PUB. POL'Y & L. 293 (1996).

[3]See Chapter 6, Personality Disorders in Employment Litigation.

in a therapeutic setting. Finally, the chapter will address some of the problems that can result when psychological tests are not administered or interpreted properly.

II. Testing Terminology

Some familiarity with testing terminology is helpful for understanding issues relating to psychological testing. Many of the more commonly encountered terms are defined below.

Ability Test: A general term for standardized tests that determine how well an individual can perform specific types of skills. Tests are available to measure intellectual skills such as vocabulary and mathematics, dexterity, and even emotional states and interpersonal skills.

Abstract Reasoning Test: A general term for tests of the ability to form concepts, figure out solutions, reason logically, infer patterns from a few examples, or recognize similarities and differences between things. In analyzing intelligence, psychologists make a distinction among concrete, functional, and abstract ways of describing phenomena. For example, an apple might be characterized (1) in terms of tangible characteristics, e.g., red and juicy (concrete); or (2) in terms of what one does with it—its use or function—e.g., something to eat (functional); or (3) as a member of a general class or category, e.g., fruit (abstract). A penchant for abstract thinking is associated with high IQ scores.

Achievement Test: A general term for any test used to measure the extent of learning in an educational subject. For example, achievement tests measure the extent of learning of reading, writing, and mathematics.

Aptitude Test: A generic term for tests of ability in specific areas of cognitive or psychomotor functioning. For example, there are numerous tests of aptitude (proficiency) in math, word usage, and other ability areas. Although most psychologists make some distinction between aptitude and achievement (what one is capable of versus what one does with one's abilities), the term "aptitude" tends to be used generally and inconsistently.

Inventory: A general term for a questionnaire, checklist, list of true-false questions, or other written survey of feelings, symptoms, beliefs, interests, or other characteristics of the person completing the inventory.

IQ Test: An intelligence test.

Likert Scale: A general term for a technique for making subjective ratings in questionnaires or interviews. For example, a subject may be asked to rate statements in terms of how true each statement is as applied to the subject's condition, on a scale ranging from 1 = "Not True at All" to 5 = "Very True."

Malingering Test: Any test of intentional exaggeration or faking of pathology for the purpose of obtaining an external gain.

Mental Status Examination: A mental status examination is not actually a test or examination in the usual sense of the word. Rather, it is an evaluation of the subject by a clinician during a clinical interview that is conducted by observing the subject in person and recording observations such as how the subject expresses emotion, motor behavior, language comprehension and expression, self descriptions of mental and emotional functioning, behaviors suggesting the presence or absence of psychopathology, interpersonal style, and behaviors that provide evidence related to cognitive functioning.

Objective Test: Any test administered and scored according to standardized procedures. Psychologists often use the word "objective" in a misleading fashion. In normal usage in the English language and in other professional fields, objective events are tangible, observable phenomena capable of independent study by other persons. However, psychologists use the term to refer to tests that a subject completes in a systematic, standardized manner, even if the subject is only making a systematic description of purely subjective impressions not observable by anyone but the subject. The objective aspect of the test is that the answers are represented in an observable form such as a true-false answer sheet that can be scored reliably by different experts. Thus a paper-and-pencil true-false test is objective even if the person taking the test is lying, delusional, joking, or illiterate but pretending to be able to read and marking answers at random.

Projective Test: A general term for tests in which the subject is asked to respond to vague stimuli based on the notion that the subject's responses will be something projected from the person because the stimuli are so ambiguous or vague that they possess no significant objective characteristics themselves. For example, the Rorschach Test, Thematic Apperception Test, and Human Figure Drawing Tests supposedly sample the personality or psychodynamics of the examinee. Projective tests are unreliable procedures when used by experts who confuse their subjective impressions and speculations with scientific measurement.

Psychodiagnostic Test: A general term for any psychological test used to assist in formulating a diagnosis of a mental disorder.

Psychological Test: Any one of numerous standardized procedures for sampling behaviors of individuals or groups. Psychological tests are used to help diagnose mental disorders, evaluate prospects for educational and vocational functioning in the future, measure the extent of disability or employability, and determine the level of an individual's functioning in cognitive and emotional and interpersonal domains, as well as for other purposes.

Psychomotor Test: Any test that measures one's coordination or ability to integrate movement and perception or thought. For example, a psychomotor test may measure how quickly one performs tasks with one's hands.

Scales: Also known as subtests or subscales, these are tests within a larger test. For example, one of the scales/subtests within a widely used intelligence test is the vocabulary subtest.

Self-Administered Test: Any test taken by the subject with little or no interaction with the examiner after the introduction and directions for taking the test. The subject may complete the test alone in a testing room.

Self-Report Inventory: Any questionnaire or test in which one describes data about oneself. For example, complaints of subjective symptoms, feelings, and thoughts are all based on self-report. A self-report inventory is a systematic collection of what the subject tells the examiner.

Symptom Validity Test: A generic term for malingering tests and related procedures.

Test Battery: A general term for a group of tests administered as part of one evaluation.

III. Psychological Tests Most Frequently Found in Employment Lawsuits

A. Minnesota Multiphasic Personality Inventory-2

The MMPI-2 is the revised edition of the most widely used objective personality test in the world. Its original edition (the MMPI) was released in 1943, and it underwent a substantial revision in 1989. The MMPI-2 assesses a variety of characteristics of the subject that are relevant to assessing the nature and extent of emotional injuries, if any, and the subject's ability to function in society. It is also helpful in assessing malingering. It additionally may help clarify whether the plaintiff's problems are chronic (and thus probably preexisting), or the result of some workplace incident. The MMPI-2 may shed light on problems that affect interactions with fellow employees, supervisors, and customers, and psychopathology that may affect performance on the job.

The MMPI-2 consists of 567 true-false items. The examinee reads items in a test booklet and answers on a separate answer sheet. Unlike the original MMPI, on which 16 items were repeated, no item in the MMPI-2 is repeated verbatim, but the content of some items is similar. A tape-recorded version is available for persons who for various reasons cannot read the test. Administration requires approximately one to one and a half hours of the examinee's time and little or no professional psychological time to administer (it can be administered in a few minutes by a carefully trained, properly supervised clerk). The test should not be sent home with the examinee, however. Such will typically invalidate the administration of the test.

The MMPI-2 is scored on a variety of scales, separated into basic, content, and supplementary types. The raw scores obtained from a particular examination of the MMPI-2 are converted statistically to what is known as a T-score, which permits comparison of scores across all of the scales. For virtually all MMPI-2 scales, the more items endorsed, the greater the "elevation" of the resulting T score and the greater the likelihood of having the characteristics associated with that scale. The basic scales were part of the original validation of the test and have received the vast majority of the empirical research. They are composed of validity and clinical scales and are intended to serve as the basis for describing an individual's psychological condition. The validity scales provide information about the test-taking attitude the examinee had in answering the items, and their configuration can indicate how much faith can be put in the results of the remainder of the test.

The basic clinical scales were developed to describe important areas of psychopathology such as the level of emotional distress, the presence of psychosis (e.g., schizophrenia), and long-term personality problems. The content and supplementary scales typically have been constructed on their "face validity" to address specific areas of interest and usually have less established empirical validity. These scales include those measuring depression, irrational fears, self-esteem, and the source of stress, among others. Such scales have no correction for symptom exaggeration and are particularly susceptible to malingering.

1. MMPI-2 Validity Scales

The MMPI-2 contains several useful validity scales that determine whether the results of a particular administration of the test are valid. Indication from these scales that a test administration is invalid may be evidence that the test subject is not being truthful.

A. L Scale The L scale measures the subject's willingness to underreport psychopathology by, for example, refusing to admit to ordinary human shortcomings. Conversely, examinees who are faking bad or overemphasizing psychopathology on the MMPI-2 often score in the low range on the L scale. One commentator has noted that scores equal to or below T = 44 may be associated with deliberate attempts to create a pathological picture of oneself.[4] The MMPI-2 manual identifies possibly faking bad as one of the interpretive implications of scores equal to or below T = 49.[5] Other possible interpretations of low scores include the hypothesis that the examinee is self-confident and independent or is cynical and sarcastic. Although historically this scale was intended to catch subjects who were not responding straightforwardly, its items are so obvious to most people that it primarily raises questions about invalidity in naive test takers.

B. F Scale The F scale measures the subject's tendency to overreport psychopathology. It consists of unusual items that are infrequently answered in the scored direction by either genuinely disturbed patients or members of the normal population. Fewer than 10 percent of the MMPI-2 normative population answered these items in the scored direction.[6] Because elevated F scores indicate that the patient is responding to the test with answers that are unusual even for genuinely psychologically disturbed patients, malingering becomes a possible hypothesis. As one authority notes, "[t]he F Scale was devised as a measure of the tendency to admit to a wide range of psychological problems or to fake bad. An individual who scores high on the F Scale is admitting to a wide range of complaints that are infrequently endorsed by the general population and reflect a tendency to exaggerate problems."[7]

There are reasons other than malingering for elevation of an F scale. A subject who is unable to read and thus answers test questions randomly will obtain a high F score. A grossly psychotic patient may have a high F scale score. The presence of such a degree of pathology can be ruled out by clinical observation, however, because these people are so disturbed that they do not appear normal during the interview. Yet another cause of a high F score can

---

[4]Roger L. Greene, The MMPI-2/MMPI: An Interpretive Manual 109 (1991).

[5]James N. Butcher et al., MMPI-2 Manual for Administration and Scoring 23 (1989).

[6]Greene, *supra* note 4, at 109.

[7]James N. Butcher, The MMPI-2 in Psychological Treatment 28–29 (1990).

be a subject's refusal to cooperate by merely answering the questions at random. A review of other portions of the test permits the examiner to rule out this possibility. Sometimes examiners interpret F scale elevations as a "cry for help," but the examiner should be cautious not to confuse motive with accuracy. That is, exaggeration by another name is still exaggeration and thus a false measurement of the true extent of pathology.

Personal injury claimants malingering emotional distress tend to produce elevated scores on the F scale. In general, when the F scale exceeds a T score of 65, exaggeration of emotional distress should be considered. The *MMPI-2 Manual* indicates malingering as one of the potential explanations for F scale scores that exceed 70.[8] However, the content of some items on the F scale includes material that personal injury claimants may be reluctant to report, so there is reason to suspect that the F scale may be less sensitive to personal injury malingering than to litigants attempting to appear extremely psychotic. For example, some of the items that increase F scale scores require the subject to admit being dishonest or in trouble or peculiar in ways that personal injury malingerers usually wish to avoid. As a general rule of thumb, personal injury malingerers tend to attempt to present themselves as credible and reasonable or normal, with the exception of the emotional distress they suffer as a result of their injury. However, answering some of the items on the F scale would suggest that they steal, drink excessively, do not love their mothers, do not care if animals suffer, do not believe in law enforcement, or are attracted to other people's shoes to such an extent that they want to steal them.

C. K Scale The K scale measures the subject's defensiveness. It was developed when early research on the MMPI suggested that the L Scale was easy for intelligent fakers to fool because its items were so obvious.[9] The K scale was designed to be a more subtle index of a subject's attempts to pretend to be healthier ("faking good") or less healthy ("faking bad") psychologically than he or she really is. A low K score is associated with deliberate efforts to fake psychopathology. For example, the *MMPI-2 Manual* suggests that K scores of 40 and below may be due to fake-bad responding,[10] and another authority notes that K scores below 40 may be due to a deliberate attempt to present oneself in an unfavorable light.[11]

D. F Minus K Index The F and K scales are significant not only in themselves but also in relation to each other. The "F minus K" index is a comparison of a measure of the tendency to present oneself as disturbed or psychotic with a measure of the tendency to present oneself as normal or

---

[8]Butcher et al., *supra* note 5, at 26.

[9]J. Charnley McKinley, Starke R. Hathaway & Paul E. Meehl, *The MMPI: VI. The K Scale*, 12 J. Consulting Psychol. 20 (1948); Paul E. Meehl & Starke R. Hathaway, *The K Factor As A Suppressor Variable in the MMPI*, 30 J. Applied Psychol. 525 (1946).

[10]Butcher et al., *supra* note 5, at 26.

[11]John R. Graham, MMPI-2: Assessing Personality and Psychopathology, 29 (2d ed. 1993).

without pathology. It measures the difference between the raw score on the F scale and the raw score on the K scale. The F minus K index has been used on the MMPI since the 1940s,[12] and it continues to be used on the MMPI-2.

Where the F minus K value is positive, there is a greater likelihood of malingering.

As one authority has noted, "[a]lthough a single cutoff score cannot be established for all settings, whenever the F-scale raw score is greater than the K-scale raw score, the possibility of faking bad should be considered; and as the difference becomes greater, the likelihood of a fake bad profile becomes greater."[13] A variety of cutoffs have been suggested for the F minus K index for purposes of detecting malingering in personal injury claimants. These cutoff scores include 0, 7, 9, and 11; and as noted above, any F minus K greater than 0 needs to be reviewed in terms of potential malingering. As a point of comparison, on the MMPI-2 the difference between the average F and K scores for the normative group is minus 11. Note that a malingerer in an employment case will not ordinarily produce as high an F minus K value as a malingerer in a criminal setting, since some of the items that increase the F minus K require the subject to admit to being dishonest or peculiar in ways that most plaintiffs in employment litigation prefer to avoid. Because this measure is based in part on the F Scale, the concern that personal injury malingerers may avoid some items because of their content applies to F minus K as well as to the F Scale.

E. WEINER-HARMON SUBTLE-OBVIOUS SUBSCALES Another means of detecting malingering on the MMPI-2 is by use of the Weiner-Harmon Subtle-Obvious Subscales. This measure groups questions relating to various types of psychopathology on scales 2 (*D*), 3 (*Hy*), 4 (*Pd*), 6 (*Pa*), and 9 (*Ma*) into "obvious" and "subtle" categories. An untrained lay subject will be able to fake psychopathology with respect to the obvious questions, but faking is more difficult with respect to the subtle questions, whose relevance to psychopathology is generally known only by trained psychologists. A difference of 20 or more between the obvious and subtle T scores on one of the Weiner-Harmon subscales (for example, depression) may suggest malingering, as does a total difference of 100 or greater between the obvious and subtle T scores on all of the five Weiner-Harmon subscales. The original concept was that the differential ability of laypeople to fake obvious and subtle items provided measures of exaggeration on specific scales. More recent research has suggested that the subtle scales should not be interpreted as independent measures of the same construct as the obvious scales.[14] However, the total obvious-minus-subtle score serves as a useful measure of exaggeration.

---

[12]Harrison G. Gough, *The F minus K Dissimulation Index for the MMPI*, 14 J. CONSULTING PSYCHOL. 408 (1950); Harrison G. Gough, *Simulated Patterns on the MMPI*, 42 J. ABNORMAL & SOC. PSYCHOL. 215 (1947).

[13]GRAHAM, *supra* note 11, at 42.

[14]Linda D. Nelson, David Pham & Craig Uchiyama, *Subtlety of the MMPI-2 Depression Scale: A Subject Laid to Rest?* 8 PSYCHOL. ASSESSMENT 331-33 (1996);

F. DISSIMULATION SCALE-REVISED The Dissimulation Scale (Ds) was created in 1954[15] and later revised from 74 items to 40 items as the Dissimulation Scale-Revised (Dsr).[16] This scale was created by asking normal persons to pretend to be disturbed in a neurotic fashion. The items on the MMPI were then identified that differentiate normal people faking disturbance from genuinely disturbed patients. A high score on the dissimulation scale means that the person taking the test resembles the fakers as opposed to the truly disturbed patients. During the conversion from the MMPI to the MMPI-2 many test scales were changed. Because 6 of the 40 items from the MMPI Dsr scale were omitted on the MMPI-2, the score on the MMPI-2 is based on the 34 remaining items.

As one authority has pointed out, a high dissimulation scale score points to malingering and serves as an independent measure not particularly correlated with other validity indicators such as the F scale and the F minus K index.[17] Thus, it is useful to examine this score as independent evidence of possible malingering. An elevation on the Dsr in a personal injury claim raises concern that the patient is simulating or exaggerating psychopathology. The higher the score, the greater the concern. T scores above 74 are of some concern, and scores above 84 are strongly suggestive of symptom exaggeration.

G. FAKE BAD SCALE The Fake Bad Scale (FBS) was designed to assist in the detection of personal injury malingering.[18] Although originally oriented toward emotional distress injuries, research suggests that it is useful in the detection of somatic malingering, i.e., cases reporting physical injuries or pain.[19] One commentator suggested that "somatic malingering should be considered whenever elevations on scales 1 and 3 exceed T=80, accompanied by a significant elevation on the FBS."[20] He went on to observe that the FBS was superior to "traditional MMPI/MMPI-2 malingering scales, such as F, in 12 litigants, with no electrophysiologic or neuroradiologic evidence of brain damage, who had objective evidence of malingering on neuropsychological tests (e.g., worse-than-chance performance)."[21]

Daniel Boone, *Reliability of the MMPI-2 Subtle and Obvious Scales with Psychiatric Inpatients*, 62 J. PERSONALITY ASSESSMENT 346 (1994).

[15]Harrison G. Gough, *Some Common Misconceptions About Neuroticism*, 18 J. CONSULING PSYCHOL. 287 (1954).

[16]HARRISON G. GOUGH, CALIFORNIA PSYCHOLOGICAL INVENTORY MANUAL (1957).

[17]ALEX B. CALDWELL, MMPI SUPPLEMENTAL SCALE MANUAL 90 (1988).

[18]Paul R. Lees-Haley, Lue T. English & Walter J. Glenn, *A Fake Bad Scale on the MMPI-2 for Personal Injury Claimants*, 68 PSYCHOL. REPS. 203 (1991).

[19]Glenn J. Larrabee, *Somatic Malingering on the MMPI and MMPI-2 in Personal Injury Litigants*, 12 CLINICAL NEUROPSYCHOLOGIST 179 (1998).

[20]Glenn J. Larrabee, *Neuropsychological Outcome, Post Concussion Symptoms, and Forensic Considerations in Mild Closed Head Trauma*, 2 SEMINARS IN CLINICAL NEUROPSYCHIATRY 196, 203 (1997).

[21]*Id.*

Another authority has reported that the FBS "already has demonstrated efficacy in discriminating personal injury litigants who are malingering from other groups" and concluded: "Hence, in reports or expert testimony, forensic psychologists who use the FBS as one of a number of validity measures have a reasonable scientific basis for doing so."[22] In a study oriented toward potential utility for detecting invalid emotional distress claims, data from 119 personal injury claimants were examined. In this emotional distress sample, a cutoff of >23 for men and >25 for women correctly classified 75 percent of male and 74 percent of female spurious Posttraumatic Stress Disorder (PTSD) claimants and 96 percent of male and 92 percent of female controls. In that study, pseudo-PTSD patients were defined as those who (1) claimed to be suffering a psychological injury (2) that was so severe that it was disabling, (3) due to an experience that was entirely implausible for a candidate for PTSD criterion A in DSM-III-R, and (4) scored T = 65 or higher on both PK and PS, the PTSD subscales of the MMPI-2.[23]

H. F BACK SCALE The F Back (Fb) scale was developed in a manner similar to that used to develop the F scale; i.e., these items were answered in the scored direction by fewer than 10 percent of the normal subjects on which the MMPI-2 was normed.[24] Items for the standard F scale appear early in the test booklet, and there was interest in similar data for validity for the latter part of the test. The items included on the Fb scale appear in the latter part of the test booklet, almost all in the second half.

Fb appears to be sensitive to random responding.[25] Profiles in which the F scale appears valid and Fb is elevated suggest that the patient stopped paying attention to the items in the latter part of the test or shifted to a random response pattern. In this situation, a clinician could interpret the standard scales that are scored with items which appear earlier in the test booklet; however, supplementary and content scales based on items that appear later in the test booklet should not be interpreted.

Personal injury claimants malingering emotional distress tend to produce elevated scores on the Fb scale. As one authority notes: "The levels of *Fb* scale elevation and their interpretation should be very similar to the standard *F* scale since the items were selected by the same criterion. Consequently, the same interpretive statements are suggested for both *Fb* and *F* scales."[26]

---

[22]Allan B. Posthuma & James F. Harper, *Comparison of MMPI-2 Responses of Child Custody and Personal Injury Litigants*, 29 PROF. PSYCHOL.: RES. & PRAC. 437, 440 (1998).

[23]Paul R. Lees-Haley, *Efficacy of MMPI-2 Validity Scales and MCMI-II Modifier Scales for Detecting Spurious PTSD Claims: F, F-K, Fake Bad Scale, Ego Strength, Subtle-Obvious Subscales, DIS, and DEB*, 48 J. CLINICAL PSYCHOL. 681 (1992).

[24]Greene, *supra* note 4, at 4.

[25]Anthony M. Paolo & Joseph J. Ryan, *Detection of Random Response Sets on the MMPI-2*, 11 PSYCHOTHERAPY IN PRIVATE PRAC. 1 (1992); David T.R. Berry et al., *Detection of Random Responding on the MMPI-2: Utility of F, Back F, and VRIN Scales*, 3 PSYCHOL. ASSESSMENT 418, 423 (1991).

[26]Greene, *supra* note 4, at 113.

I. VARIABLE RESPONSE INCONSISTENCY SCALE The Variable Response Inconsistency scale (VRIN) is a validity scale that appeared with the publication of the MMPI-2. VRIN consists of 67 pairs of items with similar or opposite content.[27] Each inconsistent answer counts as one point on the raw score for VRIN. Certain characteristics of the VRIN scale are interpretable with regard to the issue of malingering. For example, VRIN appears to be sensitive to random responding.[28] One study found that VRIN was elevated in random responding but not in malingering, thus implying that the origins of a high F or Fb may be clarified with a normal VRIN, while elevations on both strongly suggest the possibility of random responding.[29] Subjects with brain injuries so severe they cannot read or who are so severely disturbed (for example, disorganized psychotics) that they answer the profile in an incoherent manner that is essentially random produce highly elevated VRIN T scores; e.g., a random score will exceed 100. However, examinees who are careful to answer consistently while faking emotional distress injuries in an organized manner will not produce random scores on the MMPI-2 or highly elevated VRIN scores.

A score in the average or below-average range suggests that the subject answered the test in a deliberate, consistent fashion; thus if other indicators of faking are elevated, it is not because the subject was answering chaotically as a result of incapacitation by emotional distress injuries, brain injuries, or other impairment.

J. TRUE RESPONSE INCONSISTENCY SCALE The True Response Inconsistency scale (TRIN) is another of the validity scales developed for the MMPI-2. A TRIN scored response consists of answering true or false to both of a pair of inconsistent items. The scale consists of 23 pairs with contradictory content—14 true-answer pairs and 9 false-answer pairs. The examinee who is faking bad (faking emotional distress or psychological disturbance) by paying attention to the items and answering in a consistent manner will tend to obtain a TRIN scale that is not extremely high or low, even though he or she obtains elevations on other scales ostensibly associated with psychopathology.[30]

2. MMPI-2 Clinical Scales

The results of the MMPI-2 are reported on ten clinical scales (see Table 10-1). These scales provide an overview of the psychological problems of the subject and assess common problems such as hypochondriasis, depression, and anxiety, as well as more disruptive problems such as Schizophrenia, Bipolar (manic-depressive) Disorder, and paranoia.

---

[27]Graham, *supra* note 11, at 31.
[28]Paolo & Ryan, *supra* note 25; Berry et al., *supra* note 25.
[29]Margaret W. Wetter et al., *Sensitivity of MMPI-2 Validity Scales to Random Responding and Malingering*, 4 PSYCHOL. ASSESSMENT 369 (1992).
[30]Greene, *supra* note 4, at 113.

Table 10-1   MMPI-2 Clinical Scales

Number	Scale	Abbreviation
1	Hypochondriasis	Hs
2	Depression	D
3	Hysteria	Hy
4	Psychopathic Deviate	Pd
5	Masculinity-Femininity	Mf
6	Paranoia	Pa
7	Psychasthenia	Pt
8	Schizophrenia	Sc
9	Hypomania	Ma
0	Social Introversion	Si

A description of each clinical scale follows.

A. HYPOCHONDRIASIS (*Hs*) SCALE   The *Hs* scale is composed of a variety of items reflecting vague and nonspecific concerns about bodily functioning and neurotic worry about health. High scorers tend to have many physical complaints and do not respond well to psychological treatment. Typically, such people are seen as unhappy, whiny, hostile, and demanding of attention. Those with genuine physical illnesses produce only slightly elevated scores, and elevations above T = 65 are likely to reflect psychological factors in their complaints regardless of any organic contribution.[31] High scores are also found in those intentionally overreporting medical problems and psychological distress.

B. DEPRESSION (*D*) SCALE   The *D* scale is a multidimensional measure of the various symptoms associated with clinical depression. In addition to the usual symptoms—pessimism, low self-esteem, dysphoria—are items addressing physical symptoms, lack of sociability, and excessive sensitivity. Scores can be elevated from recent stressors as well as from long-term depressive tendencies and usually indicate, when valid, that the examinee is moody, shy, distressed, and guilt-prone.[32] It is frequently elevated in patients seen for psychotherapy as well as in those who overreport symptoms.

C. HYSTERIA (*Hy*) SCALE   As with many of the basic clinical scales, the *Hy* scale is complex. It is composed of items that address specific somatic complaints and those in which examinees indicate they are well adjusted, characteristics typically associated with having a hysterical (histrionic) personality. Such people are prone to developing specific physical problems when

---
[31]*Id.* at 137.
[32]*Id.* at 139.

under stress.³³ Often elevated along with the Hypochondriasis scale, the Hysteria scale usually indicates the presence of various neurotic characteristics. Subjects with elevated scores on this scale are seen as naïve, immature, dependent, insightless, and self-centered. Social relationships can be surprisingly good, although usually at a very superficial level. When validly elevated, this scale usually indicates long-standing adjustment problems rather than a response to a recent stress.

D. PSYCHOPATHIC DEVIATE (PD) SCALE The *Pd* scale covers a variety of maladjusted behaviors that are associated with many personality disorders. Groups of items address problems within the family, conflicts with authority, and general social difficulties. Roughly correlated with anger, this scale gives an indication as to the extent an examinee acts out behavior overtly or in passive-aggressive ways. Those who score highly on this scale are usually described as being friendly and outgoing but rebellious, unreliable, egocentric, and irresponsible.³⁴ Such elevations often indicate a susceptibility to substance abuse. Typically, those involved in making civil claims will try to deny these traits, which suggests that even a minor elevation on this scale has significance in such cases. In employment situations, subjects with elevated scores on this scale usually have chronic conflicts with supervisors and chafe under the normal restrictions of the workplace.

E. MASCULINITY-FEMININITY (MF) SCALE Scale *MF* is essentially a heterogeneous-interest scale. Originally intended to identify homosexuals with feminine identification, today it is largely used to describe the extent to which an individual identifies with the masculine or feminine stereotype. High scores indicate deviance from this stereotype (i.e., women who score high are described as having masculine traits such as being aggressive and tough while men with elevated scores are described as having feminine traits such as being sensitive and passive). Level of education and sophistication can strongly influence the results, particularly among men.³⁵ This scale is not usually considered in reaching conclusions about the current psychological state of an individual.

F. PARANOIA (PA) SCALE The *Pa* scale is made up of items that measure interpersonal sensitivity, moral self-righteousness, and suspiciousness, as well as delusions. When valid among clinical patients, elevations can indicate the presence of disturbed thinking (psychosis) or a marked tendency to blame others, hold a grudge, and be distrustful of people's motives.³⁶ In the medical-legal context, elevations on this scale usually indicate a subject's long-standing

---

[33] KENNETH S. POPE, JAMES N. BUTCHER & JOYCE SEELEN, THE MMPI, MMPI-2, AND MMPI-A IN COURT: A PRACTICAL GUIDE FOR EXPERT WITNESSES AND ATTORNEYS 258 (1993).
[34] Greene, *supra* note 4, at 147.
[35] *Id.* at 154.
[36] *Id.* at 161.

problems trusting other people, oversensitivity to minor criticisms, and a tendency to blame his or her employer for all problems and to be argumentative. Usually such people wish to pursue claims, at least in part, to right all the wrongs committed against them.

G. PSYCHASTHENIA (PT) SCALE   The *Pt* scale is focused on a variety of neurotic symptoms. Manifestations of anxiety, worry, and sometimes obsessive-compulsive behavior are usually detected by this scale. This scale also addresses difficulties with concentration, irrational fears and feelings of guilt. It is often elevated in conjunction with the Depression scale and, when valid, can indicate the presence of general psychological distress. Although elevation on the *Pt* scale may sometimes be in response to a specific stress, it usually means the examinee has a premorbid tendency toward anxiety.[37] Like the *D* scale, the *Pt* scale will typically be elevated in those people exaggerating their emotional problems.

H. SCHIZOPHRENIA (SC) SCALE   Despite its name, the *Sc* scale is sensitive to many conditions other than schizophrenia. Items on this scale concern difficulties with family and social relationships, problems with concentration and impulse control, and sexual troubles as well as bizarre thought patterns. Interpretation of this scale is strongly dependent on the overall pattern of results, and there are many possible diagnoses associated with elevated scores. Usually people with high scores on the *Sc* scale are described as being unconventional and alienated from others.[38] This scale is not particularly common in medical-legal cases, but it can be elevated when an examinee exaggerates overall symptomatology.

I. HYPOMANIA (MA) SCALE   Items on the *Ma* scale cover elated and unstable mood, increased psychomotor activity, and disturbed thinking processes. High scorers can vary from being enthusiastic, optimistic, and outgoing to being impulsive, irritable, out-of-control, or grandiose. Low scorers may have a low level of energy.[39] As with most of the MMPI scales, the precise interpretation depends upon the overall pattern of scores. This scale is rarely elevated among those making claims for damages because it typically indicates the presence of a long-standing pattern of inappropriate behavior, something most claimants deny.

J. SOCIAL INTROVERSION (SI) SCALE   This scale is concerned with an individual's comfort and preference for social contact. Those who score high on this scale tend to be shy and uncomfortable in social situations and thus generally keep to themselves. In contrast to most other MMPI scales, low scores are meaningful and suggest the examinee is an outgoing, friendly, and

---

[37]*Id.* at 160.
[38]*Id.* at 167.
[39]POPE ET AL., *supra* note 33, at 260.

socially engaged person. The presence of elevation on this scale does not necessarily indicate the presence of psychopathology and instead may be suggestive of a long-standing personality preference.

3. MMPI-2 Content Scales

As an adjunct to the basic clinical scales, a series of scales based on the overt content of the items has also been developed. These scales purportedly measure the characteristics associated with the scale name but have had fairly minimal empirical validation. They depend upon the examinee's accurately reporting symptoms and thus are subject to distortion, intentional or not. The most popular of the content scales for the MMPI-2 have been developed by James Butcher and colleagues. The content scales are set forth in Table 10-2.[40]

Table 10-2 MMPI-2 Content Scales

Internal Symptom Content Scales

Anxiety *(ANX)*
     Fears *(FRS)*
     Obsessiveness *(OBS)*
     Depression *(DEP)*
     Health Concerns *(HEA)*
     Bizarre Mentation *(BIZ)*

External Aggressive Tendency Content Scales

Anger *(ANG)*
     Cynicism *(CYN)*
     Antisocial Practices *(ASP)*
     Type A Behavior *(TPA)*

Negative Self-Views Content Scale
Low Self-Esteem *(LSE)*
General Problem Content Scales

Family Problems *(FAM)*
     Social Discomfort *(SOD)*
     Work Interference *(WRK)*
     Negative Treatment Indicators *(TRT)*

4. MMPI-2 Supplementary Scales

To further measure various symptoms, a large number of supplementary scales have been developed. Depending upon the relevant clinical question, these

---

[40] JAMES N. BUTCHER ET AL., DEVELOPMENT AND USE OF THE MMPI-2 CONTENT SCALES 5 (1990).

scales can assist in measuring important characteristics not necessarily covered by the basic or content scales. Their major drawback is that they typically have had very little validation research and usually have inadequate norms. Developed by many different researchers and clinicians in a variety of settings, these scales should be used only as supplements to the basic scales, and hypotheses based upon them should be considered tentative.

Frequently scored supplementary scales are set forth in Table 10-3.

Table 10-3 MMPI-2 Supplementary Scales

Welsh Anxiety (*A*)
Welsh Repression (*R*)
Ego Strength (*Es*)
MacAndrew Alcoholism-Revised (*MAC-R*)
Over-Controlled Hostility (*OH*)
Dominance (*Do*)
Social Responsibility (*Re*)
College Maladjustment (*Mt*)
Gender Role—Masculine (*GM*)
Gender Role—Feminine (*GF*)
Addiction Admission (*AAS*)
Addiction Potential (*APS*)
Marital Distress (*MDS*)
Personality Disorder Scales[41]

5. Interpretation of the MMPI-2

The MMPI items are arranged into a large number of scales, with some items appearing on more than one scale. Each item is scored in a "pathological" direction based upon the normative data and the ability of the item to discriminate between normals and various diagnostic groups. For each scale the total number of items endorsed in the pathological direction is tallied. The obtained raw score is then translated into a standardized score (T score) for the appropriate gender based upon the normative sample. Each scale's T score has a mean of 50 and a standard deviation of 10 in the normal population. These T scores thus provide a basis for comparing scores from diverse scales as to the degree of abnormality. Scores from some of the basic clinical scales undergo a further normalization such that each T score from these scales falls at the identical percentile. The T scores are then plotted on a graph to illustrate patterns. Often this scoring process is accomplished via computer program. Figure 10-1 represents a typical MMPI-2 profile for a 42-year-old male complaining of job stress.

---

[41]*See* Leslie C. Morey & Marcia R. Smith, *Personality Disorders*, *in* THE MMPI: USE WITH SPECIFIC POPULATIONS 110 (Roger L. Greene ed., 1988).

Figure 10-1 MMPI-2 Profile

T scores	L	F	K	HS	D	HY	PD	MF	PA	PT	SC	MA	SI
	47	68	50	79	89	75	62	51	56	69	61	48	63

MMPI-2 SCALES
Scores above 64 are abnormal.

Often, the MMPI-2 is scored and interpreted via computer. The two major providers of such services are National Computer Systems (NCS) and the Caldwell Report. Although computers have the cachet of scientific objectivity, in fact they merely represent a routinized procedure based on the opinions of one or more psychologists. Computerization does not imply any empirical basis for conclusions. Further, these interpretive programs make (unstated) assumptions as to the appropriateness of the interpretation for any particular population. On the other hand, if the test is hand-scored, there may be errors that could dramatically undermine the validity of any interpretation. Careful questioning as to the scoring and interpretation procedures is recommended to ascertain that accurate scoring took place as well as to identify the sources for interpretation.

6. MMPI-2 Code Types

With the T scores, a psychologist can then determine the examinee's test-taking attitude and any limitations in validity. The most salient psychological characteristics can then be gleaned, estimated from the clinical and supplementary scales. Usually this is accomplished by considering the overall pattern of results or particular pairing of scales ("code types"). Basing an interpretation on individual scales, considered either sequentially or in decreasing order of elevation, is usually considered inadequate. By using all the empirically derived data, however, hypotheses can be generated on the most prominent symptoms, probable diagnoses, and recommended treatment approaches.

A code type represents the highest and second-highest T scores on the MMPI-2's clinical scales. Thus, an individual who scores highest on scale 2 (depression) and scale 6 (paranoia) would produce a "2-6/6-2" code type. One author writing on MMPI interpretation describes this code-type:

> Touchy, moody, depressed, and oversensitive to criticism, these persons have a strong underlying anger and most often a long history of interpersonal difficulties.

Paranoid trends are usually evident. They read malevolent meaning into neutral situations, and jump to conclusions based on insufficient data. Resentfulness, agitation, fatigue, and aggressiveness are usually marked. Often these persons adopt a "chip on the shoulder" attitude in an attempt to reject others before they are rejected, or as a means to avoid becoming dependent.[42]

As such a description might tend to fit a good number of plaintiffs in employment litigation, the MMPI-2's code types can be a useful tool in the defense of such cases. Among those making worker's compensation claims, nearly 40 percent of the profiles have as their highest scores combinations of scales *Hs*, *D*, and *Hy*. The mean profile for workers' compensation cases has been found to include Depression, Hypochondriasis, and Hysteria as the highest scales with significant secondary elevations on Psychasthenia and Schizophrenia.[43]

B. Millon Clinical Multiaxial Inventory-III

The Millon Clinical Multiaxial Inventory-III (MCMI-III) is a 175-item objective personality test. The third edition of the test replaced its predecessor, the MCMI-II, in 1994. This test is particularly useful for evaluating the possible existence of personality disorders that reflect lifelong problems rather than new emotional distress injuries. Like the MMPI-2, the MCMI-III contains scales that help to assess the level of cooperation of the examinee in taking the test.

The MCMI-III includes measures of various personality disorders as well as clinical scales that measure pathology such as Anxiety Disorder, Somatoform Disorder, Dysthymic Disorder, Major Depression, and Delusional Disorder, among others. Interpretation of the MCMI-III can be difficult and must be done by an examiner who is trained and experienced in interpretation of this instrument. In addition, the MCMI-III is prone to produce false positives, so its results cannot always be taken at face value but instead must be integrated with information taken from the clinical interview and from collateral sources.

The MCMI-III is not meant to be used with normal populations, as the normative data are based on clinical samples of individuals with psychological problems or who are in therapy. However, the creator of the test indicates that it is appropriate for use in forensic settings—for example, in personal injury cases.[44]

The MCMI-III contains 24 clinical scales and three correction scales (see Table 10-4). These scales are divided into five categories to reflect the distinction between relatively enduring personality features and acute symptoms. In addition to the three validity scales Millon refers to as correction scales (Disclosure,

---

[42]ALAN F. FRIEDMAN, JAMES T. WEBB, & RICHARD LEWAK, PSYCHOLOGICAL ASSESSMENT WITH THE MMPI 167 (1989).

[43]Glenn Repko & Robert Cooper, *A Study of the Average Workers' Compensation Case*, 39 J. CLINICAL PSYCHOL. 287 (1983).

[44]THEODORE MILLON, MILLON CLINICAL MULTIAXIAL INVENTORY-III MANUAL 5 (1994).

Desirability, and Debasement) the MCMI-III includes a Validity Index, Scale V, that has been shown to be sensitive to careless, confused, or random responding.

Table 10-4 MCMI-III Scales

Clinical Personality Pattern Scales (Axis II)

Scale 1	Schizoid
Scale 2A	Avoidant
Scale 2B	Depressive
Scale 3	Dependent
Scale 4	Histrionic
Scale 5	Narcissistic
Scale 6A	Antisocial
Scale 6B	Aggressive (Sadistic)
Scale 7	Compulsive
Scale 8A	Passive-Aggressive
Scale 8B	Self-Defeating

Severe Personality Pathology Scales

Scale S	Schizotypal
Scale C	Borderline
Scale P	Paranoid

Clinical Syndrome Scales (Axis I)

Scale A	Anxiety Disorder
Scale H	Somatoform Disorder
Scale N	Bipolar: Manic Disorder
Scale D	Dysthymic Disorder
Scale B	Alcohol Dependence
Scale T	Drug Dependence
Scale R	Posttraumatic Stress Disorder

Severe Clinical Syndrome Scales

Scale SS	Thought Disorder
Scale CC	Major Depression
Scale PP	Delusional Disorder

Modifying Indices

Scale X	Disclosure
Scale Y	Desirability
Scale Z	Debasement

Validity Index

Scale V	Validity

On the MCMI-III, for the fourteen personality disorder scales, BR (Base Rate) scores of 75 suggest the presence of a *trait*, and scores at BR 85 or above suggest the presence of a *disorder*. For Scales A through PP relating to clinical syndromes, BR 75 points to the *presence* of a syndrome, and BR 85 is associated with the *prominence* of a syndrome.[45]

A computerized scoring and interpretation system is available with this test (provided through National Computer Systems in Minneapolis). This software permits the examiner to print out scores with or without accompanying narrative interpretation and suggested diagnoses. These computerized interpretations are hypotheses, not conclusions. They are designed to assist the clinician with recognizing problems, making a differential diagnosis, and evaluating motivation (including malingering and faking good).

The scale that leads the computerized scoring and interpretation system to designate an administration of the test as "valid" is composed of three rather obvious items that really identify only subjects who did not even read the test, answered so carelessly that they might as well not have read it, or are so confused or psychotic that they are answering in a bizarre manner. The designation of valid on the printout therefore should *not* be construed to mean that the profile on the whole is valid or that the scores are a valid reflection of the subject's condition. For example, someone pretending to be healthier than he or she really is by denying real psychological problems could easily obtain a valid profile. On the validity scale, one answer in the scored direction raises questions about the validity of the profile, and two are enough to designate the test as invalid.

In forensic settings the debasement index (Scale Z), desirability index (Scale Y), and disclosure index (Scale X) are more useful than the three-item validity index as indicators of problematic response styles. Scale X measures a subject's level of disclosure, or willingness to be frank and self-revealing. According to the MCMI-III manual, a subject who obtains a BR score on Scale X greater than 85 is said to be "very self-disclosing," 75–84 is "moderately disclosing," 60–74 is "slightly disclosing," 36–59, "slightly non-disclosing," and less than 35, "moderately to very nondisclosing."[46] Scale X assists the clinician in the interpretation of clinical scale scores. A subject who shows few elevations on clinical scales and has a low BR score on Scale X may be defensively denying the presence of difficulties.

The debasement measure (Scale Z) of the MCMI-III is a scale designed to detect the extent of examinees' efforts to play up their emotional vulnerability or make themselves appear mentally anguished. Generally, a BR score above 75 on the MCMI-III Debasement Index indicates an effort to present more troublesome emotional and personal difficulties than are suggested by an objective assessment. If the subject is in a setting where malingering of emotional

---

[45]THEODORE MILLON, ROGER D. DAVIS, & CARRIE MILLON, MILLON CLINICAL MULTIAXIAL INVENTORY-III MANUAL 61 (2d ed. 1997).
[46]*Id.* at 46.

distress needs to be ruled out (for example, in personal injury or employment litigation), this is the most useful scale on the MCMI-III for this purpose.

The desirability index (Scale Y) is associated with efforts to appear normal, socially acceptable, or psychologically healthy. There is less forensic research on applications of Scale Y.

It is important to keep in mind that the computer-generated statements based on this test are hypotheses, not firm conclusions. They are intended for the clinician to use in formulating diagnoses and conclusions about the personality of the patient under consideration.

C. Wechsler Adult Intelligence Scale-III

The Wechsler Adult Intelligence Scale-III (WAIS-III) is perhaps the most sophisticated of intelligence tests. It measures vocabulary, general knowledge, certain aspects of memory, judgment, and other aspects of intelligence relevant to job performance. The WAIS-III is a particularly useful test in assessing a claim of vocational disability. A relatively high score on this instrument might belie a plaintiff's claim of being mentally or emotionally unable to work.

The WAIS-III requires the examinee to respond to numerous problems and questions involving words, recall of information, arithmetic, working puzzles, and other matters. The eleven tests (also referred to as "subtests"—parts of a larger test) that comprised the original Wechsler-Bellevue Scale were retained, with revision, in the Wechsler Adult Intelligence Scale (1955), the Wechsler Adult Intelligence Scale-Revised (1981), and the WAIS-III that is in current use. Three new subtests were added to the WAIS-III—Letter-Number Sequencing, Matrix Reasoning, and Symbol Search. These subtests are classified into two types of intelligence—verbal and performance.

The Verbal scale comprises seven of the eleven tests: Information, Digit Span, Vocabulary, Arithmetic, Comprehension, Letter-Number Sequencing, and Similarities. The Performance scale is also comprised of seven subtests: Picture Completion, Symbol Search, Picture Arrangement, Block Design, Matrix Reasoning, Object Assembly, and Digit Symbol.

1. WAIS-III Verbal Tests

The *Information Test* includes 28 items that sample the subject's range of general information. The items are related to intellectual alertness, motivation, and retention of information.

The *Digit Span Test* measures memory for series of digits, forward and backward, increasing in difficulty up to nine digits forward and eight digits backward. This procedure is related to auditory recall, attention, and freedom from distractibility.

The *Vocabulary Test* consists of 33 words to be defined by the examinee. This test is considered an excellent measure of general intelligence.

The *Arithmetic Test* includes 20 problems presented orally and timed. It is a measure of arithmetic reasoning, ability to comprehend verbal instructions, concentration, and freedom from distractibility.

The *Comprehension Test* consists of 18 questions about aspects of everyday living and social situations and is a measure of judgment and abstract reasoning. It requires evaluation of past experience, application of judgment to practical situations, and ability to verbalize.

The *Similarities Test* requires the examinee to abstract and articulate what is similar about 19 paired items. This task measures abstract reasoning, associative thinking, and conceptual judgment.

Letter-Number Sequencing is a new verbal subtest that assesses working memory, attention, and concentration. In this subtest, the examinee is required to order sequentially a series of letters and numbers that are presented in a specified random order. The examinee must recall the numbers while simultaneously sequencing them.

2. WAIS-III Performance Tests

The *Picture Completion Test* consists of 25 color pictures in which some important feature is missing. The examinee is required to identify that picture. It requires the ability to recognize familiar objects and to differentiate essential from nonessential details.

The *Digit Symbol-Coding Test* requires the subject to draw symbols quickly in a series of empty boxes according to the way they are paired with numbers 1 through 9 in the key at the top of the page. The examinee is allowed 120 seconds to complete as many as possible. This subtest measures psychomotor speed and accuracy, ability to learn an unfamiliar task, and visual-motor dexterity.

In the *Block Design Test*, nine designs are to be constructed from red and white blocks following patterns presented on cards. It measures form perception, problem solving, visual-motor integration, and speed of performance.

The *Matrix Reasoning Test* measures abstract reasoning and visual information processing. This subtest is comprised of four types of items for a total of 26 items. Each item consists of a stimulus matrix in which a section is missing. The examinee chooses from five response alternatives the choice that best completes the matrix.

The *Picture Arrangement Test* is made up of 11 items consisting of sets of pictures that tell a story presented in a random order. The subject is required to arrange the pictures in the proper sequence so the story makes sense. This test measures social judgment and visual sequencing ability.

The *Symbol Search Test* requires the examinee to visually scan the target and search group of symbols. The examinee marks either yes or no to indicate whether either of the target symbols appears in the search group.

The *Object Assembly Test* is an optional test that consists of five puzzles with large pieces that the examinee is required to put together as quickly as possible. This subtest is a measure of visual analysis, ability to synthesize parts into wholes, and assembly skill.

3. Scoring

With the exception of the Symbol Search, Letter-Number Sequencing, and Object Assembly tests, scores on the remaining subtests are combined to produce a Verbal IQ (VIQ), a Performance IQ (PIQ), a Full Scale IQ (FSIQ), and index scores for Verbal Comprehension and Perceptual Organization. With the administration of Symbol Search and Letter-Number Sequencing, index scores for Working Memory and Processing Speed can be calculated.

IQ scores are characterized as follows:

> 130+ is very superior
> 120 to 129 is superior
> 110 to 119 is high average
> 90 to 109 is average
> 80 to 89 is low average
> 70 to 79 is borderline
> 69 and below is extremely low

In addition to traditional IQ scores, the WAIS-III also includes four factor indexes:

> Verbal Comprehension
> Perceptual Organization
> Working Memory
> Processing Speed

WAIS-III IQ scores range from about 1.2 to 4.8 points lower than the WAIS-R IQ scores. This difference is relevant when comparisons are made between pre- and postinjury scores.

Differences between Performance IQ scores and Verbal IQ scores are common. For example, about one-fourth of the standardization sample produced VIQ-PIQ differences of 15 or more points. About one-fourth also obtained differences of 15 or more points between the Verbal Comprehension Index (VCI) and POI Perceptual Organization Index (POI) scores.[47] Also, performance declines with age on the performance subtests, especially tests where speed is a factor.

While there is no validity scale per se on the WAIS-III, a procedure has been proposed, known as the Reliable Digits Procedure (greatest number of digits forward plus greatest number of digits backward) for the detection of malingering.[48] A score of 7 or less suggests the possibility of malingering. A validation study for this measure found that probable malingerers scored worse (mean = 6.6, SD = 1.83) than severe brain injury patients scored (mean = 8.75 and SD = 1.87).[49]

---

[47]DAVID WECHSLER, WAIS-III MANUAL 207 (1997).

[48]Manfred F. Greiffenstein, Walter J. Baker, & Thomas Gola, *Validation of Malingered Amnesia Measures with a Large Clinical Sample*, 6 PSYCHOL. ASSESSMENT 218 (1994).

[49]Manfred F. Greiffenstein, Walter J. Baker & Thomas Gola, *MMPI-2 Validity Scales Versus Domain Specific Measures in Detection of Factitious Traumatic Brain Injury*, 9 CLINICAL NEUROPSYCHOLOGIST 230 (1995).

IV. Other Testing Instruments That May Appear in Employment Lawsuits

A. Beck Anxiety Inventory

The Beck Anxiety Inventory (BAI) is a 21-item self-report inventory that provides some measure of the level of anxiety. Reported on a 4-point scale (0 to 3), the items involve ratings of symptoms associated with various anxiety disorders. Although it has been shown to have some ability to describe the degree of anxiety in clinical patients, when the BAI is used in the medical-legal context, the results can be quite misleading because there is no correction for symptom exaggeration. It is similar in design and format to the Beck Depression Inventory, with similar limitations.

B. Beck Depression Inventory

The Beck Depression Inventory (BDI) is a 21-item self-report inventory designed to measure the severity of depression in patients already diagnosed by other means as depressed. It nonetheless is sometimes applied in the forensic context as a screening instrument for detecting the presence of depressive symptoms.

Each question on the BDI has four multiple choice answers that are scored 0 to 3. The items were originally based on clinical observations and symptoms frequently reported by depressed psychiatric patients (e.g., depressed mood, suicidal ideation, crying, etc.).

A revised BDI was introduced at the University of Pennsylvania Medical School Center for Cognitive Therapy in 1971 to replace the original BDI developed in 1961. However, the 1971 version of the BDI was not called the BDI-Revised or BDI-II. The revised BDI is sometimes referred to as the BDI-IA. The term "BDI-II" is used for the BDI-II released in 1996. In the most recent revision, four items were dropped and replaced by new items, two items were revised, and many statements were reworded.

Administration of this test takes approximately five to ten minutes. The subject typically reads and responds to the questionnaire alone, but the questions can also be administered orally. The test is scored by adding the sum of the numbers beside the answers, with a range of 0 to 63. Separate scores can be calculated for the items reflective of cognitive-affective symptoms (Items 1 to 13) and for the items reflective of somatic-vegetative symptoms (Items 14 to 21).

Scores on the BDI are interpreted as follows:

    0 to 13 = minimal depression
    14 to 19 = mild depression
    20 to 28 = moderate depression
    29 to 63 = severe depression[50]

---

[50] AARON T. BECK, ROBERT A. STEER, & GREGORY K. BROWN, BECK DEPRESSION INVENTORY MANUAL 8 (2d ed. 1996).

Note that by this interpretation system it is impossible for a patient to score in a range of "no depression."

The BDI score does *not* provide a sufficient basis for diagnosing a mental disorder listed in the *Diagnostic and Statistical Manual of Mental Disorders*.[51] The BDI, moreover, addresses only *the previous two weeks* before the subject takes the test. To conclude, therefore, on the basis of the BDI that the subject has been depressed in the past or will continue to be depressed in the future is speculative and unfounded.

Although the BDI is useful in nonforensic clinical settings, it is easily manipulated by malingerers because it essentially asks: "How depressed are you?" It is simple for untrained laypersons to pretend to be more or less depressed than they really are when taking this test.[52] Because the BDI *presumes* that the subject is depressed, reliance upon this test as a basis for diagnosis of a mental disorder, or for the opinion that the patient is permanently disabled, is a scientific error.

C. Beck Hopelessness Survey

The Beck Hopelessness Survey (BHS) is a 20-item, true-false questionnaire that purports to measure three aspects of hopelessness—feelings about the future, expectations, and loss of motivation. Its purpose is to assess aspects of hopelessness and potential for suicide.

The test takes about five to ten minutes to administer. Subjects complete a self-report questionnaire. The test can also be verbally administered by a trained administrator. Scoring is accomplished by adding the sum of the numbers beside the answers.

There are no standardized norms of interpretation. The test creator notes that cutoff scores need to be based on the decisions or purpose for which the test is being employed, but general guidelines for interpretation are as follows:

> 0–3 = Minimal
> 4–8 = Mild
> 9–14 = Moderate
> >14 = Severe[53]

A number of studies have evaluated the relationship between BHS scores and suicidal ideation or prediction of eventual suicide. Several studies have found a positive relationship. For example, one study of 73 psychiatric inpatients found that suicide intent correlated more with hopelessness than with depres-

---

[51] AMERICAN PSYCHIATRIC ASSOCIATION, DIAGNOSTIC AND STATISTICAL MANUAL OF MENTAL DISORDERS (4th ed. text rev. 2000) [hereinafter DSM-IV-TR].

[52] *See* Paul R. Lees-Haley, *Malingering Traumatic Mental Disorder on the Beck Depression Inventory*, 65 PSYCHOL. REPS. 623 (1989).

[53] AARON T. BECK, BECK HOPELESSNESS SCALE (1993).

sion.⁵⁴ When hopelessness was covaried out, there was no relationship between depression and suicidal intent. In another study, 91 percent of eventual suicides were correctly identified (during the 5–20 year follow-up) by scores of 10 or higher on the BHS in a sample of 207 patients who had been evaluated during hospitalization for suicidal ideation.⁵⁵ In yet another study, it was found that a cutoff score of 9 or higher identified 16 of 17 outpatient subjects who eventually committed suicide.⁵⁶ In contrast, other studies have found that other variables are better predictors of suicide potential or that the BHS is not a reliable predictor.⁵⁷ Finally, one commentator has pointed out that BHS scores are not necessarily a direct measure of suicidality, as test-takers can fake good if they do not want their suicidal plans to be discovered.⁵⁸

Accordingly, any expert who claims to be able to predict suicide attempts by a plaintiff should be asked to produce scientific evidence to support the claim. The claim may be based on speculation rather than reliable methodology. The expert should be asked to disclose true and false positive and true and false negative rates or error rates for the methodology used to support such a prediction.

D. Hamilton Anxiety Rating Scale

The Hamilton Anxiety Rating Scale (HARS) is designed to assess severity of anxiety in individuals who have already been diagnosed as suffering from an anxiety disorder. The most common application of this test is in the evaluation of treatment outcome. A rating scale is completed by the clinician based on observations and a clinical interview of the subject. A structured interview guide for the test, called the Hamilton Anxiety Rating Scale Interview Guide (HARS-IG), has been developed for the purpose of standardizing clinical probe questions.⁵⁹ The clinician indicates the level of severity of 14 symptoms

---

⁵⁴Richard D. Wetzel et al., *Hopelessness, Depression, and Suicide Intent*, 41 J. CLINICAL PSYCHIATRY 159 (1980).

⁵⁵Aaron T. Beck et al., *Hopelessness and Eventual Suicide: A 10-year Prospective Study of Patients Hospitalized with Suicidal Ideation*, 142 AM. J. PSYCHIATRY 559 (1985).

⁵⁶Aaron T. Beck et al., *Relationship Between Hopelessness and Ultimate Suicide: A Replication with Psychiatric Outpatients*, 147 AM. J. PSYCHIATRY 190 (1990).

⁵⁷*E.g.*, Aaron T. Beck et al., *Suicide Ideation At Its Worst Point: A Predictor of Eventual Suicide in Psychiatric Outpatients*, 29 SUICIDE & LIFE-THREATENING BEHAVIOR 1 (1999); Anders Nimeus, Lil Traeskman-Bendz, & Margot Alsen, *Hopelessness and Suicidal Behavior*, 42 J. AFFECTIVE DISORDERS 137 (1977).

⁵⁸Ephrem Fernandez, *Review of the Beck Hopelessness Scale (Revised)*, in THE THIRTEENTH MENTAL MEASUREMENTS YEARBOOK 123 (James C. Impara & Barbara S. Plake eds., 1997).

⁵⁹Gunter S. Bruss et al., *Hamilton Anxiety Rating Scale Interview Guide: Joint Interview and Test-Retest Methods for Interrater Reliability*, 53 PSYCHIATRY RES. 191 (1994).

associated with anxiety, based on subjective responses elicited from the subject. These items include somatic, intellectual, emotional, and behavioral complaints. Each item is rated on a scale from 0 to 4. This scale is defined as follows:

    0 = None
    1 = Mild
    2 = Moderate
    3 = Severe
    4 = Severe, grossly disabling

This is an inappropriate test to use in forensic settings. The answers are transparent to an examinee who wishes to portray an inaccurate picture of his or her mental condition.

E. Hamilton Depression Rating Scale

The Hamilton Depression Rating Scale (HDRS) was designed to assess the severity of depression in individuals who have already been diagnosed with a depressive illness. It is a rating scale completed by the clinician based on observations and clinical interview of the subject. The scale includes 17 items, and each item is scored 0 to 4 or 0 to 2, for a possible total of 52 points. There are four additional items that are rated, but these are not added to the total score. There is also a 24-item version of the test that includes items on helplessness, worthlessness, and hopelessness.

Administration of this test takes about 20 to 30 minutes. The clinician typically begins the clinical interview in a more open-ended fashion, allowing the subject to discuss symptoms and to ask questions. It may then be necessary for the clinician to ask more specific questions in order to complete the rating instrument. The clinician is also allowed to use other sources of information when they are vailable (e.g., observations by nurses).

For items rated on a scale of 0–4, a score of 2 represents mild, 3 is moderate, and 4 is severe. For items scored on a scale of 0–2, a score of 0 is for absent, 2 is for present, and 1 is for equivocal. Note that these are not strictly defined (i.e., specific criteria are not indicated), which introduces a degree of subjectivity of the clinician in scoring the items. These scores are summed to compute a total severity score. Suggested cutoff scores for psychiatric patients are as follows:

    25 Severe Depression
    18–24 Moderate Depression
    7–17 Mild Depression
    0–6 No Depression[60]

The HDRS was not designed as a primary diagnostic tool, and the inappropriateness of its use in the forensic context should be apparent. Nonetheless,

---

[60]Jean Endicott et al., *Hamilton Depression Rating Scale*, 38 ARCHIVES GEN. PSYCHIATRY 98 (1981).

one study examined articles on the HDRS in five major psychiatry journals and found that "there was considerable evidence that the instruction that the HDRS was only to be used in situations where the patient had received a diagnosis of primary depressive illness had been ignored."[61] Another study found that the HDRS, BDI, and the Brief Symptom Inventory depression scale could identify major depression and depressive disorder not otherwise specified (NOS), but none of the three scales were consistently sensitive for identifying dysthymia, which is frequently an issue in the forensic context in employment cases.[62]

F. Hamilton Depression Inventory

The Hamilton Depression Inventory (HDI) is a paper-and-pencil self-report version of the HDRS. It is available in a 23-item full form, a 17-item form (HDI-17), and a 9-item short form (HDI-SF). The HDI-17 corresponds in content and scoring to the 17-item HDRS (the HDI includes six additional items besides the original 17 on the HDRS, to reflect *DSM-IV-TR* diagnostic criteria). There is an associated Major Depression Checklist to assist with evaluation of symptoms of Major Depression as defined in *DSM-IV-TR*. Some of the items have multiple components. For example, with regard to sleep problems, there are questions about both frequency (how often they occur) and duration (e.g., how long it takes to fall asleep). Therefore, the HDI has a total of 38 questions, the HDI-17 has 31 questions, and the HDI-SF has 15 questions. Each item is scored from 0–2 or 0–4 to be consistent with the original scoring format of the HDRS.

G. Human Figure Drawing

This test, also known as the Human Figure Drawing Test, House-Tree-Person Test, and Draw-a-Person Test, is used for personality assessment and psychodiagnostic assessment. In a typical administration of this test the examinee is instructed to draw a person, not a stick figure, on an 8 1/2" x 11" sheet of white paper. When finished, the examinee is told to turn over the page and draw a person of the opposite sex. In some procedures the examinee is instructed to draw a house, a tree, and a person.

The interpretation of the test is highly subjective and speculative. Some examiners believe that the way a patient draws persons, houses, trees, and so

---

[61] Ronald P. Snaith, *Present Use of the Hamilton Depression Rating Scale: Observation on Method of Assessment in Research of Depressive Disorders*, 168 BRIT. J. PSYCHIATRY 594 (1996).

[62] Karl W. Stukenberg, J.R. Dura & Janice Kiecolt-Glaser, *Depression Screening Scale Validation in an Elderly, Community-Dwelling Population*, 2 PSYCHOL. ASSESSMENT 134 (1990).

on provides a measure of psychological functioning, but the scientific research has not supported this view. Human figure drawing testing is extremely controversial and not generally accepted as a basis for the diagnosis of mental disorders or disability evaluation. As one observer has noted, "[p]rojective techniques . . . do not deserve to be called scientific at all."[63] Other observers suggest that the evidence for the validity of Human Figure Drawing testing is so low that such testing may be contrary to the American Psychological Association Code of Ethics.[64] Another study reviewed the diagnoses of 20 Draw-a-Person experts and found that they were able to identify "mental defectives" at a level better than chance but could not tell the difference between schizophrenics, neurotics, and normals, even after being given a second chance to make a correct diagnosis.[65]

Use of Draw-a-Person tests for forensic purposes is therefore inappropriate, and any expert who attempts to use it nonetheless will be vulnerable to severe cross-examination.

H. Impact of Event Scale

The Impact of Event Scale (IES) was designed to assess posttraumatic stress—specifically, intrusion and avoidance symptoms. It is a self-report measure used to assess the impact of any specific life event on psychological functioning. This test grew out of the work of researchers seeking to develop a questionnaire to evaluate human responses to stressful events and the cumulative subjective impact of stressors on individuals and groups.[66] These researchers observed that in studies of responses to stressful life events, common reports were heard from patients with different personality styles. These researchers abstracted two types of responses, *intrusion* and *avoidance,* from studies of treatment and evaluation of stressed patients. *Intrusion* was defined in terms of recurring experiences such as waking and sleeping thoughts and feelings that intruded upon the patient. *Avoidance* responses included constriction or blunting of ideas, sensations, behaviors, and emotions; denial; and, counterphobic activity

---

[63]Paul Meehl, *What Social Scientists Don't Understand*, in METATHEORY IN SOCIAL SCIENCE 313, 316 (Donald W. Fiske & Richard A. Shweder eds., 1986).

[64] Robert W. Motta, Steven G. Little, & Michael I. Tobin, *A Picture Is Worth Less Than a Thousand Words: Response to Reviewers*, 8 SCH. PSYCH. Q. 197 (1993).

[65]Z. W. Wanderer, *Validity of Clinical Judgments Based on Human Figure Drawings*, in ADVANCES IN PROJECTIVE DRAWING INTERPRETATION 301 (Emanuel F. Hammer ed., 1997).

[66]Mardi J. Horowitz, Nancy Wilner, & William Alvarez, *Impact of Event Scale: A Measure of Subjective Stress*, 41 PSYCHOSOMATIC MED. 209 (1979). *See also* Mardi J. Horowitz et al., *Life Event Questionnaires for Measuring Presumptive Stress*, 39 PSYCHOSOMATIC MED. 413 (1997); STRESSFUL LIFE EVENTS: THEIR NATURE AND EFFECTS (Barbara S. Dohrenwend & Bruce P. Dohrenwend eds., 1974); LIFE STRESS AND ILLNESS (Eric Gunderson & Richard Rahe eds., 1974).

(doing the opposite of what is feared). A 1997 revision of the test, the IES-R, added hyperarousal symptoms (e.g., trouble falling asleep, feeling jumpy).[67]

The IES lists 15 symptoms; seven tap intrusive symptoms and eight tap avoidant symptoms. The IES-R lists 22 symptoms, adding seven hyperarousal symptoms. Subjects are asked to rate the frequency of occurrence of each symptom during the last seven days on a rating scale marked 0 (not at all), 1 (rarely), 3 (sometimes), and 5 (often).

The IES administration time is approximately 10–15 minutes. Respondents are asked to read the instructions at the top of the IES form. They are then asked to list the stressful event (e.g., rape, motor vehicle accident) and the date that it occurred at the top of the questionnaire. The contents of the IES were derived from statements used by persons who had experienced recent life changes to describe their distress. The subject is asked to answer each question by selecting the category that best describes how distressing it was to experience each of the 15 symptoms during the last seven days (not at all, rarely, sometimes, often). Note that if the IES is being used as a screening instrument, the stressful event need not be specified; however, if a respondent endorses multiple symptoms, the clinician should inquire about stressors.

Scores on the IES are computed for the Intrusion and the Avoidance subscales. The total score is the sum of the Intrusion and Avoidance subscales. The Intrusion subscale is made up of items 1, 4, 5, 6, 10, 11, and 14. The Avoidance subscale is made up of items 2, 3, 7, 8, 9, 12, 13, and 15. Interpretation guidelines for the IES total score are as follows:

> Low = below 8.5
> Medium = in between
> High = 19 or more

The IES-R adds a subscale for hyperarousal symptoms as well. Note that no correlation has been established between any IES or IES-R score and a threshold sufficient for diagnosis of Posttraumatic Stress Disorder as defined by *DSM-IV-TR*.[68]

Occasionally examiners misinterpret this test as measuring periods other than the past seven days. For example, it is purely speculative to presume that answers concerning the past seven days predict future or permanent functioning. Also, examiners sometimes administer this instrument inappropriately by asking the subject to recall how he or she felt on each item during a week six months

---

[67]The creator of the IES does not advocate use of the IES-R and considers the IES a better instrument, stating that the IES-R hyperarousal items are "not as sensitive and specific to the PTSD diagnosis, or to stress response syndromes in general as are the intrusions and avoidance items that exist in the IES. [The] hyperarousal symptoms are important in many stress response syndromes, but they are relatively non-specific and often not present." He also points out that the instructions differ for the IES-R, which emphasizes level of distress rather than frequency of occurrence, and notes that distress "is often colored by a number of other motives and qualities." Mardi J. Horowitz, personal communication, May 19, 1999.

[68]DSM-IV-TR, *supra*, note 51, at 1424.

previously. In addition, untrained individuals can fake this test quite simply,[69] which makes the test inappropriate for use in most forensic contexts.

I. Posttraumatic Stress Diagnostic Scale

The Posttraumatic Stress Diagnostic Scale (PDS) was designed to assist with diagnosis of Posttraumatic Stress Disorder (PTSD) and quantification of the severity of symptoms. The PDS is a 49-item self-report survey designed to correspond to *DSM-IV* diagnostic criteria for PTSD. The first 21 items provide a list of traumatic events and ask whether the examinee has witnessed or lived through the events and which one "bothers you the most." The PDS also collects descriptive data about the event and the examinee's thoughts and feelings at the time. The next 19 items ask about problems associated with PTSD. The last nine items ask whether the problems specified have interfered with areas of life such as work, household chores, fun and leisure, etc. The test requires 10 to 15 minutes to administer.

The PDS produces six results:

- PTSD diagnosis
- Symptom Severity Score
- Number of Symptoms Endorsed
- Specifiers related to onset and duration of symptoms (if appropriate)
- Symptom Severity Rating
- Level of Impairment in Functioning

The *PTSD diagnosis* result reveals whether the subject responded affirmatively when provided with a list of PTSD symptoms and asked if he or she had them. The diagnosis is given only if the patient meets all six *DSM-IV* criteria.

The *Symptom Severity* score measures how often the examinee reports having symptoms. The score is based on the weighted sums of items 22–38. The response weights range from 0 (not at all or only one time) to 3 (five or more times a week/almost always).

The *Number of Symptoms Endorsed* is a count of how many symptoms the examinee reported having more than one time (items number 22–38).

The *Specifiers related to onset and duration of symptoms* classify the PTSD as acute (less than three months), chronic (three months or longer), or delayed (onset at least six months after the traumatic event). This measure should be used only when a diagnosis of PTSD is rendered.

The *Symptom Severity Rating* is derived solely from the test creator's "clinical judgment and experience."[70] These categories were derived from a sample consisting of 376 female assault victims. The test creator advises PDS users that the following cutoff scores should be used with caution because their

---

[69]Paul R. Lees-Haley, *Malingering Mental Disorder on the Impact of Event Scale: Toxic Exposure and Cancerphobia*, 3 J. TRAUMATIC STRESS 315 (1990).

[70]EDNA B. FOA, POSTTRAUMATIC STRESS DIAGNOSTIC SCALE MANUAL 10 (1995).

reliability and validity have not yet been examined and their applicability to trauma populations other than female assault victims is unknown:

≤ 10	Mild
≥ 11 and ≤ 20	Moderate
≥ 21 and ≤ 35	Moderate to Severe
≥ 36	Severe

The *Level of Impairment in Functioning* is a count of how many areas the examinee says have been affected by PTSD complaints. With no basis specified, the test creator suggests the following labels for the number of such complaints:

No impairment	0 Yes Responses
Mild	1–2 Yes Responses
Moderate	3–6 Yes Responses
Severe	7–8 Yes Responses or Yes to Item 49

Not one validation study is cited in the manual for the PDS. Validity claims in the manual are in essence based on the finding that patients who complain of PTSD symptoms do so when surveyed with leading questions. For example, the PTSD diagnosis of "Yes" or "No" reveals only whether the subject responded to a set of leading questions with no distractors by claiming to have the problems listed. To claim that this scale provides the basis for a valid diagnosis of PTSD in a forensic setting, especially with no symptom validity checks or review of alternative sources of data, is naive at best, and decidedly unscientific. Note also that if an examinee circles "Y" for Yes on *one* item saying that the problems interfered during the past month with "overall level of functioning in all areas of your life," then the examinee is classified as having severely impaired functioning due to PTSD symptoms.

J. Profile of Mood States

The primary use of the Profile of Mood States (POMS) is assessing change in mood states in outpatient psychiatric patients, as described in its manual.[71] Subjects are asked to rate themselves on 65 adjectives or "scales," using a five-point rating system, as to how they have been feeling "during the past week including today." The rating system is as follows: 0 = not at all; 1 = a little; 2 = moderately; 3 = quite a bit; 4 = extremely. These responses are scored and provide information about mood status along six dimensions: Tension-Anxiety, Depression-Dejection, Anger-Hostility, Vigor-Activity, Fatigue-Inertia, and Confusion-Bewilderment.

The *Tension-Anxiety* factor is "defined by adjective scales descriptive of heightened musculoskeletal tension," including observable and less overt

---

[71]Douglas M. McNair, Maurice Lorr, & Leo F. Droppleman, Manual for the Profile of Mood States (1971).

symptoms. The *Depression-Dejection* factor is thought to represent "a mood of depression accompanied by a sense of personal inadequacy." The *Anger-Hostility* factor is defined by symptoms of "anger and antipathy towards others." The *Vigor-Activity* factor is "defined by adjectives suggesting a mood of vigorousness, ebullience, and high energy." The *Fatigue-Inertia* factor "represents a mood of weariness, inertia, and low energy level." The *Confusion-Bewilderment* factor is thought to be "characterized by bewilderment and muddleheadedness." The test manual indicates that for the Confusion-Bewilderment factor it is unclear if this measures "a trait of cognitive inefficiency, a mood state, or both."

The test manual indicates that rating periods shorter or longer than one week should not be used because the procedure would be inconsistent with that used to develop the normative data. The examiner is allowed to assist the examinee if the meaning of a word is unclear, but the instructions clearly state that the examiner should not define one item by referring to another.

A score for each factor is computed by summing the ratings for each item in the factor, with the exception of two scales (one in the Tension-Anxiety scale and one in the Confusion scale) that are negatively weighted in determining the factor score. A global "Total Mood Disturbance Score" (TMD) can be computed by summing the scores of the six factors (the Vigor factor is negatively weighted).

Malingering emotional distress is easy for untrained persons on the POMS. The items are common-language phrases, and an untrained individual can readily determine which direction to respond if attempting to over- or under-emphasize psychopathology.

K. Rorschach Inkblot Test

The Rorschach Inkblot Test is a test in which the subject is shown a series of ten cards containing black-and-white or colored inkblots and asked to describe what the image might be. The cards are presented in the same order to each subject. Subjects indicate what they see, and the examiner records the subject's responses. Later, the examiner inquires about each response to determine where in the ink blot the response was seen and what aspect of the ink blot led the individual to perceive it that way. The subject's responses are then interpreted according to various protocols.

The Rorschach is a "projective" test because the inkblots are so ambiguous that the subject's personality characteristics and psychopathology, not characteristics of the inkblot, are assumed to be the source of the descriptions provided by the subject. When Hermann Rorschach developed this test in 1921, he intended the inkblots and system for coding responses to lead to a method for detecting schizophrenia, not to describe personality or provide a general diagnostic instrument, as the Rorschach has since been used.

During the three decades following Rorschach's introduction of the inkblot test, five separate systems were developed for interpreting the test. More recently, the system developed by John Exner[72] has dominated the Rorschach

---

[72]JOHN EXNER, THE RORSCHACH: A COMPREHENSIVE SYSTEM VOLUME ONE (1974).

scene. As noted by some observers, however, the differences between these systems are so great as to make it virtually impossible to consider the Rorschach a single test.[73]

Exner attempted to correct these problems by developing a comprehensive system, and his system quickly became widely adopted as the standard. However, this complex system is time-consuming to score, and in fact it is commonly not followed. In 1986, in introducing a new guide for the interpretation of the Rorshach, Exner himself remarked that his first system had "become woefully outdated."[74] He thus has presented yet another Rorschach. Exner has continued to revise his system and disseminate data through workshops and to some extent through publicly available publications. Thus a critical question to ask of the examiner who claims to have used the Exner system is "*Which* Exner system?" Likewise, such examiners should be asked, "Which of Exner's norms did you use as a basis for your decision making and how do you justify the use of these particular norms as opposed to others distributed by Dr. Exner in his more recent workshops?"

The claim that the Rorschach produces scientific evidence of psychopathology, disability, or specific impairments is a dubious proposition. An early observer referred to the "grim picture of the reliability and validity of the Rorschach procedure" and says that "the monotonous overall conclusions have been that there is little evidence to support the claims made for the technique by its proponents."[75] The Rorschach is so controversial that even its defenders admit "[c]urrent literature reflects a persistent inclination in some quarters to denigrate the Rorschach Inkblot Method as an invalid and useless instrument for assessing personality functioning."[76] Other commentators attack the practice of circulating Rorschach validity data in workshops without publishing that data for rebuttal in the peer-reviewed literature.[77] Work that is not exposed for peer review cannot be rebutted in the scientific forum.

Moreover, while some experts claim the Rorschach cannot be faked, the empirical research suggests otherwise. For example, in one study, experts were unable to detect faking of psychosis by normal individuals who had no previous experience with the Rorschach and who knew relatively little about psychosis.[78] The protocols from these individuals received as many psychotic diagnoses as did the actual psychotic protocols. An additionally significant result of that

---

[73]Julia R. Vane & Vincent J. Guarnaccia, *Personality Theory and Personality Assessment Measures: How Helpful to the Clinician?* 45 J. CLINICAL PSYCHOL. 5 (1989).

[74]JOHN EXNER, THE RORSHACH: A COMPREHENSIVE SYSTEM VOLUME ONE: Basic Foundations ix (2d ed. 1986).

[75]Leonard D. Eron, *Review of the Rorschach,* SIXTH MENTAL MEASUREMENTS YEARBOOK 495 (1965).

[76]Irving B. Weiner, *Some Observations on the Validity of the Rorschach Inkblot Method,* 8 PSYCHOL. ASSESSMENT 206 (1996).

[77]James M. Wood, M. Teresa Nezworski & William J. Stejskal, *The Comprehensive System for the Rorschach: A Critical Examination,* 7 PSYCHOL. SCI. 3 (1996).

[78]Samuel Albert, Hayward M. Fox & Marvin W. Kahn, *Faking Psychosis on the Rorschach: Can Expert Judges Detect Malingering?* 44 J. PERSONALITY ASSESSMENT 115 (1980).

study is that the expert judges rated 24 percent of the "normal" protocols as psychotic while correctly identifying psychosis in only 48 percent of the actual psychotic protocols. This indicates a high false positive rate (calling normals psychotic—24 percent) and an even higher false negative rate (calling psychotics normal—52 percent).[79] Thus, even under nonfaking conditions the Rorschach judges made significant errors.

Defenders of the Rorschach need to make a distinction between (1) what the Rorschach *might* be capable of if handled carefully and consistently according to one of the methods proposed by Exner, on the one hand, and (2) what people actually do in clinical practice, which is not to administer and score the Rorschach according to an empirically validated system proposed by Exner. Use of the Rorschach in forensic cases is an invitation to a *Daubert* challenge.[80] The test is so controversial and so widely rebutted by scientists that it is not suitable to offer as evidence in court.[81]

L. Sentence Completion Test

This refers to any of a number of tests in which the patient is provided with the first few words of a sentence and instructed to make up an ending. This is a "projective test" in which the endings created supposedly reveal the subject's personality functioning. Sentence completion tests are subjective techniques in which clinicians infer unreliable conclusions based on their personal feelings and idiosyncratic experience. Interpretations vary from one clinician to the next in a capricious, unreliable fashion. Consequently, these tests are unsuitable for use in the forensic context.

M. Shipley Institute of Living Scale

The Shipley Institute of Living Scale is a brief test of intelligence that is sometimes given in place of the longer WAIS. The test consists of two subtests—a 40-item vocabulary test and a 20-item test of abstract thinking. These two subtests are presented on opposite sides of an 8½" x 11" sheet. The subject reads instructions at the top of each side and then has ten minutes to complete that side of the test.

IQs are defined in the Shipley manual[82] as follows:

130+	Very Superior Range
120–129	Superior Range

---

[79]*Id.* at 117.

[80]Daubert v. Merrill Dow Pharm., Inc., 509 U.S. 579 (1993).

[81]*See* Scott O. Lilienfeld, James M. Wood, & Howard N. Garb, *The Scientific Status of Projective Techniques*, 1 PSYCHOL. SCI. IN PUB. INT. 22 (2000).

[82]ROBERT A. ZACHARY, SHIPLEY INSTITUTE OF LIVING SCALE REVISED MANUAL (1986).

110–119	High Average Range
90–109	Average Range
80–89	Low Average Range
70–79	Borderline Range
69 and below	Mentally Retarded Range

A variety of studies have suggested that the Shipley is a useful instrument for estimating full-scale IQ on the WAIS. The Shipley is not appropriate for assessing intellectual functioning in individuals with borderline or retarded intelligence, and it underestimates intelligence in individuals whose true score lies in the superior to very superior intellectual range. As with intellectual tests generally, education and motivation affect performance on the Shipley.

N. State-Trait Anxiety Inventory

The State-Trait Anxiety Inventory (STAI) is a test for measuring current (state) and long-term (trait) anxiety. The STAI is a paper-and-pencil test consisting of two 20-item self-descriptive scales. It is used in clinical settings and as a research instrument. This test is inappropriate for forensic settings because it is so easily manipulated. However, it is occasionally offered as alleged "objective" evidence that a plaintiff feels whatever he or she claims to feel.

O. Symptom Checklist 90-R

The Symptom Checklist 90-R (SCL-90-R) is used to determine self-reported psychological complaints experienced in the last seven days. According to its author, the SCL-90-R is designed for "a broad spectrum of individuals, ranging from non-patient "normal" respondents through medical patients of various types to individuals with psychiatric disorders."[83]

The SCL-90-R (the revised version of the earlier SCL-90) is a paper-and-pencil checklist on which the subject reviews a list of 90 problems and complaints and describes how much discomfort each problem has caused during the last seven days, including the day of testing. The test's creator notes that the instrument was designed to have some flexibility to measure other periods of time but provides no validity or reliability data for this assertion and cautions that "time windows" longer than 14 days introduce "noticeable distortions."[84] The examinee rates how much discomfort each of the 90 items has caused during the last seven days with the following scale:

0 = Not at all
1 = A little bit
2 = Moderately

---

[83]LEONARD R. DEROGATIS, SCL-90-R MANUAL-II 5 (1983).
[84]Id. at 4.

3 = Quite a bit
4 = Extremely

The SCL-90-R is scored on nine primary symptom dimensions and three global indices of distress. The nine primary symptom dimensions are:

Somatization (SOM)
Obsessive-Compulsive (O-C)
Interpersonal Sensitivity (I-S)
Depression (DEP)
Anxiety (ANX)
Hostility (HOS)
Phobic Anxiety (PHOB)
Paranoid Ideation (PAR)
Psychoticism (PSY)

The three global indices of distress are:

Global Severity Index (GSI)
Positive Symptom Distress Index (PSDI)
Positive Symptom Total (PST)

Empirical research has suggested, however, that the SCL-90-R primary dimensions probably do not exist and that the instrument may be more appropriately considered a measure of general distress.[85] SCL-90-R validity studies for the most part demonstrate correlations of the SCL-90-R with other self-report measures. The discussion of "validation" studies in the SCL-90-R manual provides a fascinating illustration of the cat-chasing-its-tail method of validation seen in psychological research on self-report inventories. For example, the SCL-90-R's written method for portraying self-descriptions by subjects is occasionally referred to by experts as a demonstration by claimants of psychological distress. This merely echoes what the claimant alleges without adding any scientific value.

SCL-90-R normative data also provide a good illustration of the need to consider base rates when interpreting psychological complaints—i.e., the need to consider how often *average* or *normal* people make the same complaints. For example, consider the percentages of adult *nonpatients* who reported the following symptoms on the SCL-90-R:[86]

Headaches	54.8%
Nervousness or shakiness inside	39.4%
Unwanted thoughts	39.4%
Trouble remembering things	42.3%
Feeling low in energy	51.5%
Temper outbursts	25.3%

---

[85] J. Cyr, J. M. McKenna-Foley & E. Peacock, *Factor Structure of the SCL-90-R: Is There One?* 49 J. PERSONALITY ASSESSMENT 571 (1985).

[86] Derogatis, *supra* note 83, at 40.

Pains in lower back	37.0%
Feeling lonely	24.9%
Feeling blue	32.6%
Worry too much about things	55.7%
Feel no interest in things	19.3%
Feelings easily hurt	37.4%
Have to do things slowly	26.2%
Trouble falling asleep	31.3%
Double-check what you do	28.2%
Difficulty making decisions	28.8%
Trouble concentrating	27.2%
Feeling tense	47.8%
Thoughts of death or dying	19.9%
Awakening in early morning	30.4%
Sleep restless or disturbed	35.5%
Feeling everything is an effort	19.1%

Finally, the SCL-90-R does not incorporate formal scales to detect faking or other response distortions. The test creator states: "In developing the SCL-90-R, I ultimately decided to forego formal validity scales. The primary reason for this decision rested with *the additional time* such scales would add to the administration of the instrument."[87] Unfortunately, however, untrained persons can simulate psychopathology on the SCL-90-R without difficulty. In one study, literally 100 percent of 52 untrained examinees were able to fake psychopathology at a level comparable to the average range for psychiatric patients.[88] For this reason, the SCL-90-R is not appropriate for forensic use.

P. Thematic Apperception Test

The Thematic Apperception Test (TAT) is a projective test in which a patient is asked to make up a story about poor-quality black-and-white drawings. The person administering the test records the stories for later consideration. For example, the patient may be asked to make up stories about ten of the cards, describing what is happening, how the people feel, and the outcome of the story. Among the purported purposes of the TAT are the measurement of temperament, level of emotional maturity, observational ability, intellectuality, imagination, psychological insight, creativity, sense of reality, and factors of family and psychic dynamics.

Although the normal practice is to require a trained examiner for administration of the TAT, one has to wonder why, because no two people seem to administer it the same way. Scoring of the test is also conspicuously nonstandardized. When Henry Murray first produced the TAT at Harvard in the late

---

[87]*Id.* at 35 (original emphasis).
[88]Paul R. Lees-Haley, *Malingering Mental Disorder on the SCL-90-R: Toxic Exposure and Cancerphobia,* 65 PSYCHOL. REPS. 1203 (1989).

1930s, he provided a scoring system. Thereafter, however, psychologists spontaneously developed their own idiosyncratic systems of scoring and interpretation. A good illustration of how remarkably idiosyncratic TAT interpretations are is found in one study that had 22 psychologists analyze a single TAT protocol. Each of the 22 was found to have used a different system for scoring and interpretation.[89]

As noted by more recent observers, not only do psychiatric diagnoses in general have reliability problems, but the TAT in particular was not designed with psychiatric diagnostic criteria in mind, and it does not predict psychiatric diagnostic criteria effectively.[90] The claim that the TAT offers reliable or valid test evidence that the subject is suffering from either a mental disorder or a psychiatric disability is speculative and inconsistent with the scientific literature.

Q. Other Instruments

Occasionally, other testing instruments appear in employment cases that are merely inventories of symptoms purporting to measure the quality of a plaintiff's life but that by their nature are so subjective and prone to manipulation that they are scientifically useless. Many of these instruments carry impressive-sounding titles such as "Emotional Distress Rating Scale" or "Loss of Enjoyment of Life Quantitative Scale," but these questionnaires are often written by the clinicians who administer them, and they have virtually no scientific basis. Many of these questionnaires in fact are merely checklists that suggest the existence of symptoms the plaintiff might not otherwise list. Unfortunately, many judges do not appreciate the complete lack of scientific basis inherent in these instruments. They may conclude that if the examiner felt the instrument to have been helpful in reaching a diagnosis, the test result should be admitted. This sort of an approach is dangerous in that a jury may believe that what in reality is just a description of the plaintiff's self-reported symptoms carries the mantle of scientific proof derived from a methodologically sound test.

V. Misuse of Psychological Testing

Psychological tests are commonly misused in employment litigation today. The expert on the stand, addressed as "doctor" and possessing a long resume of apparently valid credentials, may opine that psychological testing "proves" that the plaintiff suffered severe emotional injury at the hands of the defendant employer. Such testimony often sounds impressive and can be difficult to rebut. A thorough grasp of the methods and limits of psychological testing, however, can assist counsel in preventing the trier of fact from being deluded by what is essentially scientific nonsense.

---

[89]EDWIN S. SCHNEIDMAN, THEMATIC TEST ANALYSIS (1951).
[90]Vane & Guarnaccia, *supra* note 73.

Psychological testing may be misapplied in a number of ways. Some of the more common examples are explored further here.

A. Lack of Examiner Qualifications

In order for a psychological test to be valid, the examiner must be qualified to administer and interpret it. Psychologists typically are the most highly qualified experts in psychological testing. Every psychologist has a unique pattern of professional training, however, so competency cannot be presumed. For example, many psychologists whose primary interest is in psychotherapy or research do not maintain their proficiency in psychological testing (in some cases, they never developed expertise in the first place).

Most psychiatrists, social workers, marriage and family counselors, and pastoral counselors have little or no expertise in psychological testing. At least one recent case decided under *Daubert v. Merrill Dow Pharmaceuticals, Inc.*[91] holds that an expert's qualifications may properly be the subject of a *Daubert* challenge. In *Isley v. Capuchin Province*,[92] the court held that a party seeking to introduce expert psychological testimony must, as a foundational prerequisite, establish that the proffered expert is qualified by virtue of education and training to give the opinions at issue. A clinician who lacks training and expertise in psychological testing may thus be prevented from testifying about psychological test results via a *Daubert* motion.

It is not uncommon, moreover, for psychiatrists and other clinicians who are not experts in test interpretation to administer the MMPI-2 and the MCMI-III and have them interpreted by a commercial scoring service that provides them with interpretive reports. While the mere use of a commercial scoring service will not invalidate a test administration, experts who rely solely upon them are vulnerable to cross-examination over a lack of understanding of test methodology, unfamiliarity with the contents of the test, misunderstanding of the meaning of the interpretive report, inability to answer questions about the significance of specific scores, and the like.

Some clinicians will attempt to circumvent such cross-examination by claiming that these tests are analogous to a laboratory test. They will assert that they know how to interpret the results of the tests even if they are not familiar with the manner in which the tests are scored and interpreted. An enterprising opponent might obtain the plaintiff's raw test data from such a clinician, submit it to several different scoring services, and point out that the interpretations vary depending on which scoring service is used. Experts who rely on external scoring and interpretation services are often at a loss when confronted with such results and unable to explain contradictory interpretations.

---

[91] 509 U.S. 579 (1993).
[92] 877 F. Supp. 1055 (E.D. Mich. 1995).

B. Test Administration

The fact that almost everyone is familiar with tests in school creates a deceptive impression that psychological tests can be validly administered by virtually anyone, or in a casual fashion. Correct administration of psychological tests, however, requires control over how, where, and when the test is administered. Psychological tests should be administered in a clinical setting under the examiner's supervision.

Psychological tests should never be sent home with the subject for completion. The subject may become distracted while taking the test, may receive assistance with the test from family or friends, or may even be coached by the subject's own therapist or attorney. A plaintiff whose own expert or treating therapist has conducted psychological testing should be questioned closely in discovery concerning the conditions under which the test was administered. If the test was not properly administered in a clinical setting, a challenge to the admissibility of the test result might be considered.

Correct instructions are also essential if test results are to be valid. For example, when administering the MMPI-2, the correct procedure is to instruct the subject to answer in terms of his or her current condition at the time of testing, not his or her condition during or immediately after the events that led to the litigation. For the MMPI-2 it is important for the length of completion time to be recorded because either too rapid (less than 45 minutes) or too lengthy (more than three hours) administration may indicate an aberrant test-taking attitude.

Finally, some experts give only portions of tests instead of the entire test. Although there are certain circumstances in which this may be appropriate, some experts engage in highly questionable practices such as testing only for their predetermined conclusions and omitting the parts of the test that address malingering or preexisting conditions. An example would be the expert who administers only the Posttraumatic Stress Disorder scale of the MMPI-2, omitting the validity scales and questions dealing with chronic personality problems. These practices produce results that are highly vulnerable to attack.

C. Scoring

Psychological tests sometimes are scored in a manner analogous to grading an academic test. For example, an intelligence test, much like an academic test, tends to consist of correct and incorrect answers. However, in personality testing, there is no correct answer. Rather, the appropriate answer is the one most consistent with one's own character or behavior. These tests are scored in terms of the patterns of the subject's responses. Instead of producing one overall score like a school grade of 100 or 90, or a letter grade like A or B, a number of smaller tests within the test are scored.

Scorings are done either by hand or by computer. Either method of scoring is prone to error, however. It is therefore recommended that the opponent obtain the raw test data and have it rescored by a reliable scoring method. Should such a rescoring reveal errors in the original scoring, the opposing expert's conclusions based upon those erroneous scores would obviously be vulnerable.

D. Interpretation

Interpretation is the process of determining what test scores mean. It takes place at two levels. The first step is a hypothetical interpretation that is relatively independent of context. For example, a pattern of MMPI-2 scores may be interpreted as potentially indicative of certain emotional problems such as depression or Posttraumatic Stress Disorder (PTSD). The second step in interpretation is to consider the context, such as other data that are known about the examinee. For example, elevated scores may be produced by illiteracy, failure to cooperate with the test, or malingering, in which case the superficial evidence of PTSD produced by testing would be disregarded.

Test interpretations for a particular individual are based on the assumption that the subject's history is accurate and thorough. Conclusions based on inaccurate or incomplete histories are little more than conjecture. A useful approach to impeachment of unreliable test findings is to demonstrate that regardless of how reliable the tests may be in general, the data were interpreted in the absence of critically important data or were based on false assumptions. For example, it is not uncommon to discover that the psychologist interpreting the test data was unaware of chronic alcoholism, drug abuse, powerful stressors unrelated to the cause of action, prior traumas, or other factors that may have dramatic impact on test data.

Occasionally, an expert is encountered whose interpretations of psychological testing uniformly point to the conclusion that the plaintiff has been injured. For this reason, transcripts of the expert's deposition or trial testimony in prior cases should be obtained. For example, one psychologist, in three different cases, might testify that (1) a high score on the Beck Depression Inventory is evidence of depression, (2) a moderate score on the BDI is evidence of depression, and (3) a low score on the BDI is evidence that the plaintiff was in a state of denial (of depression). No matter what the test result, the conclusion is the same! If such information can be placed before the court, the expert's credibility is likely to be diminished substantially.

Some experts arbitrarily ignore evidence inconsistent with their general impression. A useful avenue of questioning in an expert's depositions is as follows:

- "Doctor, are all of the test results in your battery 100 percent consistent with your conclusion that the plaintiff has Posttraumatic Stress Disorder and not some other diagnosis?"
- "Which results are inconsistent?"
- "What are the implications of the inconsistent results?"
- "How do you justify discounting these alternative findings?"
- "Could reasonable experts reach different conclusions than those you have reached?"
- "What are some other possible explanations for these data?"

In addition, some experts—particularly those lacking sufficient training in interpretation of the MMPI-2—will attempt to interpret each clinical scale by itself, or even look at only selected scales such as the depression scale. This kind of select interpretation is unscientific and improper. For a valid interpretation of the MMPI-2 to occur, its clinical scales must be interpreted together.

In deposing and cross-examining experts who use psychological tests, it is important to ask not only about the abnormal scores upon which psychologists tend to focus, but also about the normal scores. Questions about what is normal can be phrased in several ways helpful to the trier of fact. For example, rather than asking if the score is normal or abnormal, ask what percentage of the normal population would produce an equivalent or higher score. Many psychological experts will include a substantial percentage of the population in their definition of "abnormal." To demonstrate the weakness of their reasoning, point out that by their logic a similar percentage of the members of the jury would be abnormal, too. For example, some experts have testified that anyone scoring in the lower one-third of the normative group is abnormal. By this logic, one-third of the jury is abnormal if they are typical Americans.

It is important to note that many psychological tests do not clarify whether the subject's condition is the result of workplace events or instead is preexisting. Psychological testing cannot prove causation. An MMPI-2 result indicating that the plaintiff is depressed, for example, does not constitute proof that being fired or harassed caused the depression. It is just as reasonable to assume that the plaintiff suffers from a chronic and preexisting depression.

Psychopathology revealed on psychological tests, moreover, is not equivalent to vocational impairment. The fact that a plaintiff may have a number of psychological problems does not necessarily mean that the plaintiff is disabled from working. There are many individuals with serious psychological problems who work full time, often at a high level of performance. Psychopathology may affect the subjective happiness and personal relationships of a person without preventing that person from working. Although there are a number of tests that measure vocational abilities, for an expert to testify that, based upon test results indicating the presence of psychopathology, the plaintiff is unable to work is scientifically suspect.

E. Validity Issues

In order to be scientifically valid, a test must be proven capable of accurately measuring what it purports to measure. Tests are statistical in nature, but they are neither absolute nor perfect. They produce false positive (indicating injury when there is none) and false negative (an incorrect finding of no injury) results. An expert should be asked on cross-examination about the error rate of each test relied upon. Self-proclaimed experts in psychological testing often are unable to provide this information.

Some tests, such as the MMPI-2, contain their own validity scales to ensure that a particular administration of the test is valid. There are numerous influences that may cause tests to produce invalid results. Lack of cooperation, drug or alcohol intoxication, medical illnesses, psychological disorders interfering with test performance, malingering, illiteracy, cultural characteristics, improper test administration, and inappropriate testing conditions may each possibly lead to an invalid test administration. Some experts will either disregard validity scale results on the MMPI-2 indicating an invalid profile or even characterize an invalid profile as a "cry for help" and attempt to use a malingered profile as evidence of injury. There is no empirical research in the scientific literature supporting the "cry for help" hypothesis; it is merely the product of clinical folklore.[93]

F. Coaching

It is becoming increasingly apparent that coaching by attorneys is interfering with validity of psychological assessment. For example, one recent survey found that 63 percent of attorneys surveyed felt they should provide clients with information about psychological test validity measures (47 percent of attorneys surveyed believe they should "always or usually" provide such information to their clients before the testing, and another 16 percent said they should "sometimes" do so). Of the 63 percent of attorneys who believe they should provide such information, 42 percent said they should provide as much as possible and another 42 percent said they believed they should provide a "moderate" amount of information.[94] Sometimes this preparation for testing by the claimant can take the form of outright cheating in which an already prepared answer sheet is substituted or copied during the actual testing. Thus, those who administer the test should also, at least periodically, monitor it as well.

Attorney coaching may compromise the validity of psychologists' expert opinions by directly affecting the test data or by indirectly invalidating the interview, which affects the expert's interpretation of the test data. The outcome of coaching may be that the expert's results mislead rather than inform the trier of fact.

Coaching of plaintiffs by their attorneys prior to a mental examination or psychological testing is unethical.[95] It is no less an example of tampering with evidence than altering a document or contaminating a blood sample. Coaching may be prevented to an extent by refusing to divulge in advance the identity

---

[93] *See* Roger L. Greene, *Assessment of Malingering and Defensiveness by Multiscale Personality Inventories, in* CLINICAL ASSESSMENT OF MALINGERING AND DECEPTION 194–95 (Richard Rogers ed., 2d ed. 1997).

[94] Martha Wetter & Susan Corrigan, *Providing Information to Clients About Psychological Tests: A Survey of Attorneys' and Law Students' Attitudes*, 26 PROF. PSYCHOL.: RES. & PRAC. 474 (1995).

[95] *See* MODEL CODE OF PROF'L RESPONSIBILITY DR-7-102(A)(4)&(6) (a lawyer shall not "knowingly use . . . false evidence" or "participate in the creation" of false evidence); CAL. RULES OF PROF'L CONDUCT Rule 5-200(B)(A lawyer "shall not seek to mislead the judge, judicial officer, or jury by an artifice or false statement of fact or law").

of the tests to be administered during the Rule 35 mental examination. In *Ragge v. MCA/Universal Studios*,[96] for example, the court refused to order the defense examiner to disclose in advance the specific psychological tests to be administered. Certainly, requests by plaintiffs' counsel for copies of tests to be administered during the Rule 35 examination must be vigorously resisted; the defense examiner may cite in support the ethical requirement of psychologists to maintain the integrity and security of psychological tests.[97]

VI. Conclusion

Psychological testing can be a valuable asset to attorneys seeking a scientific means of assessing psychological injuries. The improper use of psychological tests may mislead the trier of fact, however. *Daubert* may provide some potential protection from the misuse of psychological testing in employment litigation, but perhaps the best safeguard is a modicum of knowledge of scientific principles. It is important that attorneys understand the difference between proper and improper use of psychological testing so that courts and juries do not confuse sloppy or dishonest practices with legitimate science.

---

[96] 165 F.R.D. 605 (C.D. Cal. 1995).
[97] AMERICAN PSYCHOLOGICAL ASSOCIATION, ETHICAL PRINCIPLES OF PSYCHOLOGISTS AND CODE OF CONDUCT §2.10 (1992).

CHAPTER 11

MALINGERING: DISTORTION AND DECEPTION IN EMPLOYMENT LITIGATION

Jonathan P. Rosman, M.D.

And, after all, what is a lie? 'Tis but the truth in masquerade.

—Lord Byron

I. Introduction

It has been said that the aim of the justice system is to arrive at the truth underlying a dispute. Because of the adversarial nature of any civil legal procedure in which a plaintiff is pitted against a defendant, there are two sides to every legal story. One of these sides will prevail, but the truth, objectively, may be found on either side, on both sides, or on *neither* side. The story told by either side is not necessarily a true one, and there is an obvious incentive to distort the facts to arrive at a favorable judgment.

When a case involves psychiatric symptoms, there may be a temptation to distort facts by the manner in which these symptoms are portrayed. This is especially prevalent in employment litigation because of the broad scope of discrimination, harassment, and disability law and the remedies provided; the important role that work plays in a person's life; and the perception that most employer-defendants have "deep pockets." In order to present an objective view of the plaintiff's symptoms to a judge or a jury, a mental heath expert is often needed who knows how the presentation of psychiatric symptoms and illnesses can be distorted.

This chapter will discuss the nature of malingering, how it may occur in the context of employment litigation, and how it may be detected.

II. Definition of Terms: Classification of Distortion

There are several different forms in which distortion of psychiatric symptoms can occur. Some forms of distortion are conscious and willful, while others are unintended. It is important to distinguish between the different forms of distortion in order to both accurately identify the willful prevaricator and avoid an incorrect pejorative labeling of someone as a liar.

A. Conscious Distortion

Conscious distortion may be further subdivided into two forms, evasion and deception.

1. Evasion

Evasion is the willful refusal to admit adverse, yet objective, facts. It results in the presentation of partial truths, rather than the whole truth. This is probably the most common way in which facts are distorted, and it is extremely common in the realm of employment litigation.

For example, a plaintiff complaining of harassment from a supervisor may develop symptoms of depression. It is discovered during the course of examining the plaintiff, however, that the plaintiff's husband left her around the same time as the alleged harassment occurred. However, the plaintiff refuses to consider or acknowledge any strong feelings engendered by the loss of the marriage. The plaintiff thus evades the importance of a personal loss and presents an exaggerated view of the impact of the harassment on her life.

Evasion of the context is another way in which facts may be distorted. Sometimes a plaintiff will take a remark, a joke, or a gesture out of context and claim that it represented an instance of harassment or discrimination. For example, a manager may tell an off-color joke to his staff as a way of trying to keep the atmosphere in the office cordial and not unduly stiff or formal. An employee may drop the context in which the joke was told—for instance, to a group of people, with no reference to that particular employee—and conclude that the joke was directed at her specifically, rather than just being a bad joke told in bad taste at a bad time.

Evasion can often be detected if the examiner is well prepared prior to interviewing the plaintiff. By presenting for the plaintiff's consideration facts that the examiner knows the plaintiff has left out of his account, the examiner can test how the plaintiff processes the omitted information. The plaintiff's refusal to consider material that can be easily corroborated suggests evasion of those facts.

For example, a plaintiff in a lawsuit was invited by a manager to apply for a better-paying position. However, she was not selected for that job, and she alleged that the reason she did not get the job was racial discrimination on the part of the manager. The examiner, knowing that she had been invited to apply for the promotion, was able to ask the plaintiff why, if she was being discriminated against, the manager would have invited her to apply for the job, rather than just not considering her for it. The plaintiff refused to consider that the manager's invitation suggested a motive other than discrimination for failing to promote her.

2. Deception

While evasion is the willful omission of facts, deception is the willful falsifying of facts. A deceiver purposely makes up facts or exaggerates facts. There are three different psychiatric forms of deception that may occur in the context of employment litigation.

Malingering is the feigning or exaggeration of symptoms of mental illness for obvious gain, such as for monetary awards in a lawsuit. There are always two components to malingering: first, symptoms must be invented or exaggerated, and second, this must be done deliberately to gain something. The forms of malingering commonly encountered in employment litigation will be discussed in greater detail in Section IV below.

Dissimulation is the feigning or exaggeration of health for obvious gain. It is malingering in reverse. Dissimulation may be encountered in fitness-for-duty evaluations, in which an employee wants to get back to work. For example, a paranoid individual may deny that he feels the need to defend himself with physical force against perceived threats by others in the workplace. Dissimulation may also occur in situations in which a plaintiff does not wish a preexisting mental illness to be discovered so that all of the plaintiff's symptoms can be claimed to have developed as a result of the issue in litigation. In such a case, a plaintiff may simply lie by denying that he has ever been treated for mental illness before. The key to detecting dissimulation lies in obtaining as many past medical and treatment records as possible. Clues to the existence of preexisting conditions may also be found in divorce records, prior litigation records, and high school and military records.

Factitious disorder is the feigning or exaggeration of symptoms of mental illness in order to be a patient. The motivation of a patient with factitious disorder is different from that of a malingerer. While a malingerer lies for the purpose of clear gain—for example, to win money in a lawsuit—a patient with factitious disorder lies in order to have others treat him or her as a patient. In other words, a person with factitious disorder wants health care professionals to devote time and energy to looking after him or her. This kind of patient often wants treatment and needs to be dependent on health care providers because being a patient provides him or her with a feeling of being special and worthy, i.e., of being worthy of the attention of the treatment team. Factitious disorder may arise in the context of employment litigation in more than one way.

First, a relatively minor work-related injury may continue to get worse, ultimately developing a life of its own. For example, an employee hurts his back on the job and files a workers' compensation claim. He then develops an addiction to the painkillers used to treat his back pain and is admitted to the hospital to be detoxified from the painkillers. Then he complains of worsening back pain and resumes using narcotics to control the pain. He then complains of depression and suicidal ideas stemming from his inability to work, his chronic pain, and the depressant effects of the painkillers. He is admitted to a hospital several times for treatment. Each time, his mood and functional ability improve markedly within a day or two of admission to the hospital, but soon after discharge he complains of new symptoms and worries that, he claims, cause a relapse of his initial presenting complaints. He enjoys being in the hospital, where he begins to feel quite at home. It is only when contacts are made between his attending psychiatrist and the large number of other specialists he has seen that it is discovered that he has been grossly exaggerating the impact of all his numerous complaints.

Another way in which factitious disorder can arise in the context of employment litigation is that an employee who suffers from already-established conditions or symptoms may assert a claim of discrimination, either on the basis of having a disability or on the refusal of the employer to reasonably accommodate the employee's disability. For example, an employee may complain of severe, intractable migraine headaches that cause her to miss work frequently and to be unable to complete her assigned duties at work. She also may complain of severe anxiety and panic attacks over the possibility of losing her job, and depression as a result of the combination of these symptoms and the pressures to which she is being subjected at her job. She is being treated by both a psychiatrist and a neurologist. She develops a pattern of consistently overusing narcotics prescribed for her migraines, claiming that the severity of her headaches has worsened, thus necessitating the use of extra medication. However, when her supply of medication is severely restricted by her neurologist, she somehow manages to function adequately until the time her next refill of medication is due. The same pattern of behavior emerges with respect to her anxiety and depressive symptoms. She enjoys the large amounts of attention she receives from her doctors, and she solicits their help in communicating her severe levels of distress to her employer to support her attempt to avoid discipline for her job performance problems and obtain a "reasonable accommodation" instead.

Because persons with a factitious disorder present themselves to health care providers with claims of very serious symptoms, they tend to build up large and complex medical dossiers, which they can then offer as proof that they have conditions that warrant serious attention by the employer. Because the symptoms have been grossly exaggerated or even completely fabricated, the employer may have quite reasonably assessed the employee to be able to perform the job without any special accommodations.

Persons with factitious disorder typically have multiple treatment providers, and they try to keep their treatment fragmented—that is, they try to keep one doctor from discovering just what their other doctors are thinking or recommending. They prefer to have each doctor rely on the history that they proffer of their treatment at the hands of their other doctors. The detection of factitious disorder is usually made by a careful gathering of all available treatment records on the patient, which then exposes the inconsistencies between the patient's account of her symptoms and her actual status.

B. Subconscious Distortion

Subconscious distortion is the distortion of facts without conscious intent or evasion. Subconscious distortion is done unwittingly. It may result from distortions of thinking or perception caused by episodes of psychiatric illness (*Diagnostic and Statistical Manual of Mental Disorders* (*DSM-IV-TR*) Axis I conditions),[1] from ingrained or automated mental habits or defense mechanisms (including *DSM-IV-TR* Axis II conditions),[2] or from a psychological reaction to major life events.

1. Subconscious Distortion Due to Axis I Conditions

Distortions due to *DSM-IV-TR* Axis I conditions occur because of problems with a plaintiff's thinking that are caused by the Axis I condition. In other words, the condition causes a plaintiff to lose objectivity with regard to his employment. Symptoms that may give rise to distortions include delusions or paranoid misperceptions, depression, mania, and anxiety.

For example, if an employee is paranoid and believes that a particular supervisor is out to get him and ruin his life, his symptoms of paranoia may generate charges of discrimination or harassment. Similarly, if an employee exhibits manic grandiosity, her illness may cause her to overestimate her own abilities and value to the workplace, and she may be less careful and make costly mistakes. If she fails to be promoted, or if she is terminated, her grandiosity may lead her to conclude that she is the obvious victim of discrimination or unfair treatment, and thus to file a lawsuit against her employer.

Someone who is depressed typically has a negative view of the world, including the workplace environment. This may cause an employee to latch on to the worst possible (i.e., most discriminatory) explanation for workplace events. Additionally, employees who are depressed may struggle to work at their usual efficiency or pace, causing them to receive negative feedback about their work performance from their superiors, which sometimes just further demoralizes them.

Anxiety disorders, such as social phobia or panic disorder, may lead to distortions. Persons with social phobias may have great difficulty making presentations in front of groups or dealing with the public. If their employers set expectations for doing tasks that require them to perform in front of other people, they may blame the work environment rather than their anxiety disorder for their worsening discomfort on the job. Similarly, persons suffering from

---

[1] AMERICAN PSYCHIATRIC ASSOCIATION, DIAGNOSTIC AND STATISTICAL MANUAL OF MENTAL DISORDERS (4th ed. text rev. 2000) [hereinafter, DSM-IV-TR]. See Chapter 5, Mental Disorders Commonly Encountered in Employment Litigation, for a detailed discussion of Axis I conditions.

[2] See Chapter 6, Personality Disorders in Employment Litigation, for a detailed discussion of Axis II disorders.

panic disorder, which is characterized by severe anxiety attacks, may misattribute the cause of their panic to the workplace environment. A preexisting Posttraumatic Stress Disorder (PTSD) may cause an individual to reexperience the emotional effects of an earlier trauma if an otherwise innocuous workplace event serves as a trigger for those symptoms.

Thus, there are numerous Axis I conditions that may cause people difficulty in performing their work duties and that may even cause them to be disabled from working. Owing to the nature of the symptoms themselves, plaintiffs may incorrectly regard and present the symptoms of these conditions and the disability that may result as being caused by a workplace injustice.

2. Subconscious Distortion Due to Axis II Conditions

Personality disorders are maladaptive styles of relating to others, consisting of numerous ingrained habits formed during a person's developmental years. The fact that these habits are so ingrained and are so much a part of a person's makeup causes the person exhibiting them to be unaware of them and to regard them as a perfectly natural way of functioning. However, personality disorders, while they may seem normal to the persons who have them, are pathological because, among other things, they typically cause problems in interacting with others. Thus, persons suffering from personality disorders typically distort the nature of their relationships with others but see nothing wrong with their own way of functioning. They are therefore primed to blame their work environment or others at work for their own maladaptive functioning.

For example, an employee with a Histrionic Personality Disorder may dramatize small incidents and turn molehills into mountains by claiming that a few flirtatious remarks made by a coworker constitute harassment. Or an employee with a Borderline Personality Disorder may be sexually provocative without realizing it, and then react with outrage when the provocative behavior evokes a response. (Further examples of the mechanism by which each personality disorder may cause factual distortions are discussed in Section III.A.3 below.)

The presence of a personality disorder may be detected in an interview with a plaintiff by noting the style of interaction the plaintiff adopts with respect to the examiner, as well as by a history of maladaptive relationships with others. Prior treatment records, divorce records, and employment records may all provide important information in this regard. Additionally, the use of psychological testing such as the Minnesota Multiphasic Personality Inventory-2 (MMPI-2) may help to assess an individual's characteristic method of responding to his or her environment.

3. Subconscious Distortion Due to Emotionally Charged Life Events

Major life events, such as sexual traumas, near-death experiences or major losses, may have a very strong impact on an individual, and the intensity of the emotional experience associated with life events may color the way an individual responds to events that provoke similar emotions later in life.

For example, a victim of childhood sexual abuse may tend to place herself in situations that could lead to her being abused without realizing her provocative role. This is termed a "repetition compulsion."[3] Another example might be a homosexual who has had trouble feeling comfortable in a heterosexual world, and for whom normal heterosexual advances by another provoke discomfort, leading the homosexual individual to raise charges of harassment.

The presence of trauma in an individual's past, such as a history of sexual molestation during childhood, does not by itself, however, mean that an individual is distorting the truth (for example, with respect to allegations of sexual harassment in the workplace). The key to detecting a repetition compulsion lies in finding that a plaintiff has a history of reacting to similar situations or relationships repetitively or in a habitual manner. For example, in the case of a victim of childhood sexual molestation, a finding that the plaintiff had a history of involvement in multiple relationships with abusive men, or that she was frequently flirtatious with authority figures, would suggest the presence of a repetition compulsion.

III. Opportunities for Distortion and Deception in Employment Litigation

Distortion may arise from several quarters in employment litigation, including from plaintiffs themselves or from experts for the plaintiff or for the defense. On the other hand, deception with regard to psychiatric symptoms typically stems from the plaintiffs themselves.

A. Distortion by a Plaintiff

Distortion by a plaintiff can include the areas of distortion mentioned in the previous sections. The following are the major ways in which a plaintiff may distort facts.

1. Downplaying Alternative Causes of Symptoms

A plaintiff's focus in a lawsuit is on the alleged wrong that he perceives has been done to him. A plaintiff may consciously lie about (dissimulate) other problems in his life, or he may simply not see the relevance of an expert's questions about areas that seem to be far afield from the issues at hand in the

---

[3] *See* Sara P. Feldman-Schorrig & James J. McDonald, Jr., *The Role of Forensic Psychiatry in the Defense of Sexual Harassment Cases*, 20 J. PSYCHIATRY & L. 5, 13–16 (1992); Jonathan P. Rosman & James J. McDonald, Jr., *Forensic Aspects of Sexual Harassment*, 22 PSYCHIATRIC CLIN. OF N. AM. 129, 138 (1999).

lawsuit, and thus he may be reluctant to talk about problems in other areas of his life.

For example, a plaintiff may deny any relationship problems, but she may have undergone a messy divorce and custody battle at the same time that workplace harassment occurred. It may be quite conceivable in such a case that the stress caused by the messy divorce and custody battle caused the plaintiff to have difficulty tolerating and coping with normal workplace stresses, and that the stress of the divorce and custody battle caused symptoms that were then attributed to events at work.

2. Distortion of the Nature of the Work Environment

It is to the advantage of a plaintiff to present the work environment as hostile, intimidating, and uncongenial. A plaintiff may give the impression that every minute at work during the period of alleged harassment was unpleasant and that selected superiors were uniformly hostile or discriminating against the plaintiff. A common way in which this distortion is carried out is by giving the impression that a relatively few incidents occurred continuously.

One way to identify this distortion is to compare the plaintiff's characterization of the workplace environment with that of coworkers. It may be found that the plaintiff presents a much more hostile picture of the work environment than do the coworkers. If it is not feasible for the examiner to interview coworkers, their impressions of the workplace might be obtained by counsel via deposition.

Another clue to distortion by the plaintiff of the nature of the work environment can be found by taking a careful chronological history of that environment. What will often be found is that the plaintiff describes the work environment as extremely pleasant and congenial up until the time at which she alleges that harassment took place. At that time, the plaintiff may exaggerate the changes that occurred in the workplace, claiming that it turned into a place with no redeeming features. The plaintiff may condemn, from that moment on, every feature of her workplace as hostile or offensive. Such a total makeover of the workplace is extremely unlikely to have actually occurred, unless there was a concerted effort by everyone surrounding the plaintiff to make the plaintiff's life miserable.

A more sophisticated plaintiff, however, does not claim that the entire workplace changed. Rather, she claims that from the time of the alleged harassment, things became unbearable for her because of the changes that did take place. Here, too, it is important to obtain from the plaintiff a clear idea of when she claims the workplace changed into a hostile environment. The reason is that by the time the expert gets to evaluate a plaintiff, the lawsuit has usually evolved quite a bit from the time of its filing. For example, the claims of harassment that are related this late in the lawsuit may differ from the claims that were originally asserted. In keeping with the changes in the plaintiff's claims, her account of the nature of the workplace may also have changed.

For example, if a plaintiff originally claims that there were five incidents of harassment over a period of five months, through various legal motions and maneuvers those claims may be reduced to incidents 3, 4, and 5 (particularly if the statute of limitations prevents the earlier claimed incidents from being litigated). If so, the plaintiff may tell an evaluator that the nature of the workplace changed at the time of incident 3, whereas previously the plaintiff had claimed the environment had changed at the time of incident 1 (which is no longer a part of the lawsuit). The reason the plaintiff is motivated to change her account of when the workplace became hostile is that if she continues to claim that it became hostile at an earlier date, then she can be viewed as an employee who was already disgruntled and unhappy at work at the time of the first litigated incident (number 3 in this example). This would weaken her case because if she was already unhappy by the time any alleged harassment occurred, it could look as if she fabricated her allegations of harassment, or else that the harassment did not have much further effect on her.

3. The Plaintiff's Misconstruing Normal Behaviors As Sexual and/or Harassing

It is a fact that not all people think and act reasonably. There are certain psychiatric factors that predispose some plaintiffs to think unreasonably and to be hypersensitive to others. Examples include a history of prior sexual abuse and the presence of a personality disorder.

A person who has been the victim of sexual abuse may later become abnormally sensitive to any remark or contact from someone of the same gender as the abuser, or who is perceived to be similar to the abuser in some way. Frequently, authority figures, such as managers or other superiors in the workplace, take the place of the abuser in the victim's mind, and any contact from those persons is tainted thereafter. The plaintiff thereafter labels the manager or superior as abusive, rejecting, or discriminating. A victim of prior abuse can in this way present a distorted view of her relationship with her superior(s). A plaintiff's past history and history of relationships, as well as an evaluation of coworkers' responses to similar interactions with the alleged harasser, may provide clues to this form of distortion.

The presence of a personality disorder also may predispose a plaintiff to misconstrue occurrences at work. A personality disorder represents a pathological (and maladaptive) style of functioning and manifests itself particularly in the way a person interacts with others. When evaluating someone for the presence of a personality disorder, it is important to take a detailed early life history because a person's personality develops in the formative years of life. Psychological testing, such as the MMPI-2, also can be helpful in detecting the presence of a personality disorder.

The following are ways in which various personality disorders may cause an individual to distort events in the workplace.

- *Paranoid Personality Disorder.* A healthy person assumes that a supervisor is benevolently motivated toward him unless he has good reason to think otherwise. However, a person with a Paranoid Personality Disorder may assume that a supervisor is out to get him. Such a plaintiff may then proceed to gather "evidence" to support that viewpoint, selecting out only incidents that seem to prove his premise of discrimination.

- *Borderline Personality Disorder.* A healthy person regards other human beings as having virtues and flaws and can accept that most people are not all good or all bad. However, a person with a Borderline Personality Disorder has very poor self-esteem and has a need to involve herself with someone whom she can regard as all good. This kind of person begins a relationship with another by putting the other person on a pedestal, so to speak; that is, she overidealizes the other person, which allows her to feel initially that everything is wonderful in the relationship. This is the "honeymoon" phase. However, when the other person is unable to live up to her distorted, idealized expectations, she feels rejected and abandoned, and her view of the other person is shattered; that is, she knocks the other person off the pedestal and often seeks revenge. When this kind of interaction occurs in the workplace between a plaintiff and her boss, the plaintiff cannot understand how her boss (or her work environment) could have changed so radically from being ideal to being intolerable, and she may conclude that she is being harassed or discriminated against.
- *Histrionic Personality Disorder.* A healthy person accepts facts for what they are and deals with life's ups and downs with equanimity. However, a person with a Histrionic Personality Disorder dramatizes facts in order to bolster her self-esteem, believing that if she is at the center of a large-scale drama, she must be important, and the issues she is dealing with must be important. A histrionic personality turns ordinary events into major dramatic epics and places herself in a sympathetic role at the center of the epic. In the workplace, an employee with a Histrionic Personality Disorder may blow up relatively minor remarks or gestures into a large-scale conflict. Allegations of harassment or discrimination trigger large-scale investigations and the creation of just the kind of dramatic conflict a histrionic needs in order to feel worthwhile. The ensuing drama of the courtroom provides a further opportunity for a histrionic to play a part, except that she is not playing, as the role is ingrained into her personality. Drama for a histrionic is a way of life, and this kind of person is thus never out of role. This means that an evaluator may detect a histrionic by her manner and mannerisms while interviewing her, including the way in which a histrionic describes events. A histrionic's nonverbal behavior in depositions or in the courtroom is also often quite revealing, and where a Histrionic Personality Disorder is suspected, it may be helpful diagnostically to videotape the plaintiff's deposition.
- *Schizoid Personality Disorder.* A healthy person enjoys the company of others, whereas someone with a Schizoid Personality Disorder prefers to be alone. Although a healthy person enjoys being alone, too, a schizoid person derives no emotional nourishment from contact with others. A schizoid's desire to stay alone is not motivated by fear, as in an Avoidant Personality Disorder. A job that requires a lot of contact with other people is not well suited to someone with Schizoid Personality Disorder because such a person may perceive the need to connect with others as an intrusion and as unwelcome. For example, normal comments and compliments from a member of the opposite sex may be construed as unwelcome advances.
- *Narcissistic Personality Disorder.* A healthy person is able to view a situation from a variety of standpoints and can understand that persons with different contexts of knowledge may come to different conclusions about many things,

rightly or wrongly. A healthy person is always open to considering reasonable alternatives. However, a narcissist locks himself into a particular viewpoint that portrays him as virtuous in all circumstances, no matter what the facts are, in order to prop up his fragile self-esteem. When facts are brought to his attention that do not fit his rigid, self-aggrandizing viewpoint, a narcissist's pseudo-self-esteem is threatened. However, instead of questioning his original conclusions, the narcissist questions the person who brought the unwanted facts to his attention. He experiences a sense of being aggrieved or emotionally wounded by that individual, what is often referred to as "narcissistic injury." If he can shift blame to the other person, he can salvage his pseudo-self-esteem. His view of his interactions with others is skewed by his need to feel virtuous at all times. In the workplace, a narcissist may be difficult to get along with and may be very resistant to accepting criticism of his work. If he is criticized, he may not accept responsibility for his errors, and may try to turn the facts around so as to blame someone else—for example, the boss who criticized him—for his own errors. He might, for instance, feel that the boss must have been discriminating against him by not recognizing his talents enough and constantly putting him down. When he does feel aggrieved, an individual with a Narcissistic Personality Disorder is remarkably resilient and will bounce back very quickly from a perceived personal attack or injury, once he has been able to latch on to an explanation of events that reestablishes his previous sense of self. Thus, a clue to the presence of a Narcissistic Personality Disorder is a claim of being grievously wounded, emotionally, by a wrong in the workplace, but a remarkably quick restitution to the level of functioning that existed prior to the injury. Other clues to the presence of narcissism would be evidence that an individual does not take well to criticism—as noted, for example, in personnel records—or that a person goes to exceptional lengths to justify every action, even when this is totally unnecessary. This is sometimes also reflected in personnel files by means of an employee's responses to work performance evaluations. In interviews with an employee, with careful questioning one can detect how rigidly the person clings to a personal frame of reference when considering questions, or whether the person is able to entertain various hypotheses reasonably. The use of psychological testing, such as the MMPI-2, can also indicate whether a person is portraying himself as excessively virtuous.

- *Antisocial Personality Disorder.* In contrast with a healthy individual who faces facts honestly and who acts conscientiously according to moral principles, an individual with an Antisocial Personality Disorder (also known as a "sociopath") tries habitually to get away with ignoring facts. When he deals with others, a sociopath tries to put something over on them and to get something for nothing, such as their respect or a financial reward. A sociopath does not care about telling lies or about the effects of his actions on others. Rather, he cares about getting caught in a lie or being made to take responsibility for his actions. He seeks to manipulate others to get his own way. A sociopath is obviously prone to engage in outright malingering, that is, lying about his case and his symptoms for financial gain, not caring about what this does to others. He may also lie out of revenge or retaliation—for example if his employment is terminated and he wants to take revenge on those he did not like at the workplace. A sociopath is likely to be a "pathological liar." This means that a sociopath has such an ingrained habit of lying to manipulate others that he lies even when it is totally unnecessary to do so because it is too much a part of his personality to do otherwise. This personality trait often enables one to detect the presence of an Antisocial Personality Disorder because an individual may lie far too much, even about issues for which there is ample evidence to the contrary. For example, an employee may assert the presence of a company policy that never existed and then claim that when he followed the policy, he was nevertheless discriminated against by a supervisor. Or he may claim that all persons of his race were passed over for promotion, when company records may show the exact opposite. Clues to the presence of an Antisocial Personality Disorder may be obtained from an individual's past history. For example, one may discover that the individual had prior run-ins with the law, a spotty work history, disciplinary problems in school records, a history of substance abuse, or other childhood indicators of chronic dishonesty and a lack of regard for social norms.

4. Avoidance of Responsibility

Wishing to avoid responsibility for their actions may lead plaintiffs to blame others for the results of their own errors, laziness, or incompetence. This may result from immaturity, a defect in character, or just plain dishonesty.

For example, if a plaintiff is not meeting the performance goals expected of her, she may seek to avoid responsibility for her inadequate performance by trying to lay blame on others for creating an environment in which she was unable to adequately perform. She may blame her own incompetence on a bad manager who she claimed singled her out for discrimination, or, if she was treated well, for a failure to promote her to a job where her "true talents" would have been recognized. If actions are initiated against her for failing to perform, she may retaliate by claiming that she was wrongfully terminated or that the criticisms leveled against her were discriminatory.

Plaintiffs may also project blame onto others for behaviors they themselves engaged in or encouraged. For example, a plaintiff may consciously or subconsciously incite sexual comments from coworkers by dressing or acting in a sexually provocative manner and then blame those coworkers for their responses.

If harassment did in fact occur, a plaintiff may try to impose on the harasser and the employer more than their fair share of the blame, even though she may have unreasonably failed to complain about harassment, or unreasonably failed to take action to mitigate the harm she did suffer. In the case of an injured plaintiff who fails to act to mitigate her damages, she may reason that since the defendants should have acted differently in a particular situation, she can relinquish any responsibility in any subsequent situation, since everything that happens thereafter is, according to her, still the responsibility of the defendants.

A refusal to consider objective facts is called denial. Denial is an extremely common psychological defense mechanism, which may be seen in all psychiatric conditions. Avoidance of responsibility goes hand in hand with denial, and it should be looked for in all clinical situations. In the medicolegal context of detecting distortion, it is typically not psychiatric symptoms that are denied but rather the responsibility of managing one's own life (including one's symptoms).

B. Distortion by an Expert

1. Distortion by Plaintiff's Expert

Distortion by a plaintiff's expert occurs especially in cases where such an expert is also the plaintiff's treating clinician, as a result of a so-called therapeutic bias.[4] A treating clinician is likely to accept at face value the history of a patient, but in a legal context, which is necessarily adversarial, there are always two sides to a story. A clinician treating a patient may not have access to the "other side" of the story. Additionally, the roles of clinician and expert are totally different,[5] and a clinician may be unable to critique his or her patient openly without fear of jeopardizing the clinician-patient relationship, whereas an independent expert is not so constrained. Thus, not only may a clinician's view of the case be distorted by a lack of collateral information, but the clinician's ability to deliver an objective opinion of the case may be constrained by the therapeutic relationship.

There are several ways in which a plaintiff's expert may cause a distortion of the facts.

A. EXAGGERATION OF THE DIAGNOSIS Although the formulation of a psychiatric diagnosis does not usually itself provide the answer to any legal test or issue, a psychiatric diagnosis does carry weight in the eyes of a judge or jury. Because there often is an overlap of symptoms between diagnostic categories, the symptoms claimed by a plaintiff can be construed by different experts to be indicative of a more or less serious condition.

For example, a mild depression that might ordinarily be diagnosed as a Dysthymic Disorder can be "upgraded" by an expert to the more serious diagnosis of a Major Depressive Disorder. Or, mild symptoms of isolated panic attacks may be characterized by an expert as a full-blown Panic Disorder. Yet another common area of overdiagnosis occurs in cases of postconcussion syndrome, in which relatively mild cognitive, emotional, and behavioral deficits may be characterized as "severe brain injury."

Two areas of particular relevance to employment litigation are the overdiagnosis of Posttraumatic Stress Disorder (PTSD) and the elevation of symptoms to the level of a "mental impairment" under the Americans With Disabilities Act (ADA).

I. OVERDIAGNOSED PTSD Symptoms of Posttraumatic Stress Disorder are often claimed by plaintiffs to have arisen as a result of a perceived traumatic event. It has been shown in veterans that the availability of compensation for these symptoms resulted in a dramatically higher level of symptoms of PTSD

---

[4]THOMAS G. GUTHEIL, THE PSYCHIATRIST IN COURT 93–116 (1998).

[5]Larry H. Strasburger, Thomas G. Gutheil & Archie Brodsky, *On Wearing Two Hats: Role Conflict in Serving as Both Psychotherapist and Expert Witness*, 154 AM. J. PSYCHIATRY 448, 448–56 (1997).

claimed by the veterans.[6] If a clinician is sympathetic to a plaintiff's plight, the clinician may overrate the severity of a stressful event (which for PTSD has to be the equivalent of a life-threatening situation) and elevate to the status of PTSD what would otherwise be diagnosed either as a normal reaction to stress or as an Adjustment Disorder, which is a milder condition that is alleviated once the person is removed from the stressful situation that triggered it.

The actual symptoms of PTSD can easily be faked by a sophisticated litigant who has done his or her homework. If an expert is not careful to assess properly the severity of the alleged stressful traumatic event, the expert's subjective identification with the plight of the plaintiff may lead him to make a diagnosis of PTSD. However, in employment litigation it is rare for a traumatic event to rise to the level needed to diagnose PTSD. For example, in sexual harassment cases, it is unusual for a plaintiff to allege actual rape, a trauma that certainly could be life-threatening and could lead to PTSD. Most sexual harassment cases involve innuendoes, gestures, touches, or the creation of an alleged hostile environment—all of which are far short of anything as dangerous as rape.

Additionally, since forensic psychiatric evaluations are often performed at a considerable time after the stress has occurred, a plaintiff alleging ongoing symptoms who is diagnosed by an expert as having PTSD will often be diagnosed as having chronic PTSD. The label of "chronic" carries an implication that the condition is there to stay and that it has a poor prognosis. Such a conclusion may have a significant impact on the amount of damages sought in a case. In fact, however, a diagnosis of a chronic condition under *DSM-IV-TR* criteria simply means that the condition has existed for a specified period of time—for example, longer than six months. If a plaintiff has not received appropriate treatment for a condition, or if other factors such as protracted litigation have contributed to the length of time that symptoms have been present, the prognosis for recovery may in fact be very good despite the chronicity of the symptoms.

II. The Existence of a "Mental Disability" Under the ADA

The definition of "mental impairment" under the Americans with Disabilities Act (which is the first step toward determining whether a person has a covered "disability")[7] is extremely broad. The Equal Employment Opportunity Commission's (EEOC) regulations have defined mental impairment to include "any mental or psychological disorder, such as mental retardation, organic brain syndrome, emotional or mental illness, and specific learning disabilities."[8] Although the EEOC's Technical Assistance Manual on the ADA recognizes that

---

[6]B. Christopher Frueh, Paul B. Gold & Michael A. de Arellano, *Symptom Overreporting in Combat Veterans Evaluated for PTSD: Differentiation on the Basis of Compensation Seeking Status,* 68 J. Pers. Assess. 369, 380 (1997).

[7]See Chapter 16, Mental Disabilities Under the Americans with Disabilities Act, for a detailed discussion of the ADA.

[8]29 C.F.R. §1630.2(h)(2).

mere stressful life situations do not constitute impairments under the ADA, if the stress causes a diagnosable mental disorder, then it may be covered under the ADA.[9] Thus, if an expert fails to distinguish between a normal reaction to job stress and a diagnosable mental disorder, the expert may incorrectly diagnose an individual as having a condition that constitutes a mental impairment under the ADA.

Additionally, there is a danger that treating physicians or psychotherapists or mental health experts may use a number of "soft" diagnoses to elevate a plaintiff into the realm of the ADA. These include conditions whose very existence is in controversy, or those for which there is little objective physical evidence and for which the diagnosis must rely heavily on the self-report of the patient/plaintiff. Examples of controversial "syndromes" include Chronic Fatigue Syndrome (CFS), Chronic Fatigue Immune Deficiency Syndrome (CFIDS), and Multiple Chemical Sensitivities. Examples of conditions with little or no objective physical evidence other than the patient's self-report include chronic pain syndromes, fibromyalgia, irritable bowel syndrome (IBS), chronic migraines, Posttraumatic Stress Disorder, and emotional changes in the absence of neuro-vegetative or behavioral signs.

For example, a patient/plaintiff may manifest a reaction to stress in the form of headaches or other symptoms, such as diarrhea, muscle tension and spasms, vague aches and pains, fatigue or jumpiness, to name but a few. Her treating clinician, erring on the side of caution so as not to miss a significant diagnosis, may diagnose her with one or more soft syndromes, such as those mentioned above. Since stress always manifests itself in a person in some form, a person under stress will always have at least one symptom of stress. If a clinician elevates isolated symptoms or a normal stressful response into a formal diagnosis, a mere stressful life situation may become a mental impairment under the ADA. When the diagnosis is of a soft syndrome, it may become very difficult for an independent evaluator to refute it because of the problem inherent in trying to prove the nonexistence of something for which the only evidence is the patient/plaintiff's self-reported symptom(s).

B. DOWNPLAYING THE IMPORTANCE OF ALTERNATIVE CAUSES OF SYMPTOMS To an aggrieved plaintiff, the cause-and-effect relationship between what she perceived happened to her and the onset of symptoms seems clear. For example, consider a plaintiff who claimed she was sexually harassed on the job and who then developed symptoms of depression. To her, it was clear that the depression arose from the harassment, and it is likely that she will present this conclusion about the cause of her symptoms to an evaluator, even if she does not engage in any malingering. Such a plaintiff will usually be quite focused on the alleged wrongdoing she suffered, which is typically an emotionally charged experience or set of experiences, and this will be the center of the history she will relate. As a result, any other significant history will tend to be overlooked or downplayed.

---

[9]EEOC TECHNICAL ASSISTANCE MANUAL ON TITLE I OF THE AMERICANS WITH DISABILITIES ACT, *reprinted in* FEP Manual (BNA) 405:6988 (1992).

If an expert accepts uncritically the plaintiff's conclusions about cause and effect, the expert may easily fall prey to the logical fallacy of *post hoc ergo propter hoc*. An expert is especially prone to fall into this trap if the expert is accustomed to the workers' compensation no-fault system because under those rules, the causal connection between symptoms and work is very loose indeed, such that as long as the symptoms arose out of, or in the context of, an employment situation, an injured worker is eligible to receive compensation. In the typical workers' compensation legal framework it is often not necessary to probe for alternative causes with respect to liability, and experts may become lax in probing into alternative causes even in the area of the apportionment of damages.

To avoid this kind of bias, an expert has to be vigilant for the presence of alternative explanations for the plaintiff's symptoms and frequently has to probe in depth into seemingly unrelated areas of the plaintiff's life. For example, a plaintiff with a history of prior episodes of a Major Depressive Disorder would be expected to have further episodes of severe depression in her lifetime even without any environmental stresses, and so the natural history of her condition would need to be considered as a possible alternative cause for her symptoms.

C. EXAGGERATING THE SEVERITY OF THE PROGNOSIS AND THE EXPECTED DURATION OF FURTHER TREATMENT As noted above, labeling a condition as chronic imputes a negative prognosis to the condition, even though this conclusion is not necessarily justified. The reasons that symptoms arise (the originating cause) may be quite different from the reasons that symptoms persist (the maintaining cause). For example, in most cases of sexual harassment, by the time a plaintiff is evaluated by plaintiff's expert, the plaintiff has long since been removed from any harassing environment, so that contact with the alleged harasser or hostile environment may no longer be a causal agent in the perpetuation of the plaintiff's symptoms.

If an expert, however, uncritically assumes that a plaintiff's continuing symptoms are maintained by the same factors that led to their development in the first place—for example, an incident of harassment—the expert may be exaggerating the causal significance of the harassment and may be ignoring other factors that could be maintaining the symptoms.

Other factors that commonly lead to the maintenance of chronic symptoms that should be examined by an expert include the psychological and financial effects of unemployment, the stress of litigation (including the exposure of previously private life history), the failure of a plaintiff to obtain adequate treatment for his symptoms, the presence of preexisting psychopathology such as personality disorders, marital or family problems, chronic physical conditions, and the exaggeration of symptoms by a plaintiff for the purposes of the lawsuit.

D. DISTORTING THE EXPERT'S OWN ROLE Cases in which a plaintiff's expert is also the plaintiff's treating clinician are especially prone to distortion on the part of the expert. All of the aforementioned kinds of distortion may occur. However, there are particular kinds of distortion that occur as a result of the blurring of the roles of the expert.

For example, an expert who is also the treating therapist may take on the role of plaintiff's advocate and try to win the case for the plaintiff. If so, the expert is less inclined to present facts that detract from the plaintiff's theory of the case. An expert may acquiesce to a plaintiff's (or the plaintiff's attorney's) request not to record information in the clinical record that deals with alternative causes for the plaintiff's symptoms. Or else, even when the clinical record is replete with references suggesting that the chief focus of treatment is on matters not directly connected to the workplace—marital problems, for example—an expert may nonetheless insist in deposition or in a medicolegal report that marital issues were an insignificant factor in the maintenance of the plaintiff's symptoms. In extreme cases, an expert might even alter clinical records in order to present the plaintiff in a more favorable light to the court.

An expert who is also the treating therapist might also come to view a successful resolution of a patient's symptoms as synonymous with a favorable outcome of the lawsuit, which leads the expert to present an unfavorable prognosis for the plaintiff as long as the lawsuit is unresolved in favor of the plaintiff.

A treating expert who has a financial incentive in the case, such as one who treats the plaintiff on a lien, has a vested interest in providing very intensive treatment to the patient. Additionally, a clinician may come to believe that it is only his or her special brand or intensity of treatment that is preventing a plaintiff from being even more symptomatic, since even with intensive treatment the plaintiff may continue to present the same severity of symptoms. This may result in an iatrogenic (clinician-caused) component to a plaintiff's symptoms. A clue to this distortion is finding that a plaintiff has undergone inordinately costly and intensive treatment sessions by one clinician/expert. Transferring the treatment of the plaintiff to another, independent clinician who has no expert witness role in the plaintiff's case may often result in a dramatic improvement in the patient's symptoms and in the clinician's prognosis.

2. Distortion by a Defense Expert

Except for the case of therapeutic bias, the same distortions that can be generated by a plaintiff's expert can also be caused by an expert who is hired by the defense. A defense expert may be prone to distort facts in the same ways but in the opposite direction to that of the plaintiff's expert. A defense expert's distortions might show plaintiffs to be healthier than they really are. Thus, a defense expert may underdiagnose a plaintiff or overrate the importance of alternative stresses. A defense expert may also label a plaintiff as a malingerer without sufficient evidence for malingering.

IV. Malingering in the Workplace

Malingering is the conscious fabrication or exaggeration of symptoms—in this context, for the purpose of winning a lawsuit. Malingering may involve any psychiatric symptom or collection of symptoms. The form in which malingering occurs depends upon the setting. For example, on the part of a criminal defendant awaiting trial, malingering often takes the form of feigned psychotic symptoms, such as hallucinations or delusions (fixed, false beliefs), with the aim of convincing the court that the defendant is insane so that he may avoid punishment.

In the context of civil employment litigation, however, malingering usually takes on more subtle forms. These include feigned disability, fabricated claims of harassment or discrimination, exaggerated effect of a medical or psychological condition upon "major life activities," exaggerated symptoms, misattribution of causes, and the reversal of cause and effect.

A. Malingering of a Psychiatric Disability to Avoid Work

The desire to obtain disability benefits so as not to have to work for a living is a strong motivating factor for some individuals to exaggerate the extent of their emotional distress.

Clues to the malingering of disability include the following:

- The nature of the condition claimed to be disabling is not normally disabling. Examples include migraine headaches and the chronic, low-grade depression known as Dysthymic Disorder.
- An employee claims to be disabled despite little evidence of disabling symptoms. For example, although the plaintiff may claim that a depressive condition causes him to be unable to work, he does not present symptoms that would support a diagnosis of a depressive disorder or that would prevent him from fulfilling his job duties.
- An employee is capable of performing actions outside work that require the same skills as do work-related tasks. For example, a plaintiff may indicate that he cannot concentrate on his job, but he is able to spend hours at a time on his computer at home developing a day-trading business for himself.
- An employee claims that he will be disabled indefinitely. It is not possible to predict a poor prognosis in many cases, and claims of indefinite disability may contradict the natural history of many conditions.
- Where an employee has applied for Social Security Disability Insurance (SSDI) benefits, the possibility of malingered disability should be considered. The reason is that Social Security rules typically preclude an individual from obtaining benefits unless there is a determination that the individual will in all probability be disabled for a period of at least two years. Thus, if someone has filed for SSDI benefits, until those benefits are granted that person has a pecuniary interest in remaining sick. Even if he has shown dramatic improvement in his symptoms, he may not admit to any improvement for fear that his application for SSDI benefits will be denied.
- Notes in the medical records of a plaintiff indicate a level of improvement that the plaintiff does not endorse. For example, repeated notations to the effect that the plaintiff was "doing much better" or that specific life functions, such as sleep, had normalized, while the plaintiff claims to have experienced no improvement in the same life functions during that period of time, suggest the presence of malingering.

- The disability is attributed to a personality conflict with a superior. For example, a plaintiff may claim that her relationship with a particular superior is so bad that she cannot function on the job because she is so distraught and upset, and her symptoms are triggered only when she has to deal, or anticipate having to deal, with that particular superior. She may claim to be unable to work even after that boss has been removed or she has been transferred to a different department under a different boss. Disability, however, refers to a person's ability to perform a job, rather than to work under a specific boss or in a specific environment.
- A plaintiff creates a novel syndrome that applies only to his particular kind of work. For example, an anesthesiologist may claim to have an "operating room phobia" that prevents him from entering an operating room and therefore from engaging in his occupation. This kind of malingering is likely to be found in persons who carry insurance policies that contain "own occupation" riders providing for payment of disability benefits when the person is unable to perform his previous principal occupation, irrespective of whether he is able to work in any other capacity.

B. Fabrication of Harassment or Discrimination Claims

Sexual harassment law introduced a new element into the definition of a civil wrong—the state of mind of the plaintiff. In other kinds of torts, it is the state of mind of the tortfeasor that defines the wrong. But in harassment cases, the presence or absence of harassment hinges on whether or not the plaintiff perceived the relevant events as a "reasonable woman" (or a reasonable person of the same gender) would have,[10] and whether or not the plaintiff "welcomed" the conduct in question.[11] This subjective test of the victim opens up a whole new area to a malingerer, who may allege that events were unwelcome when, in fact, at the time he or she did not experience them as such.

A common scenario for this kind of malingering occurs in instances of retaliation after an employee was somehow rebuffed by a supervisor, or when a preexisting relationship between them has been downgraded in some way. For example, if an employee had a welcome, consensual sexual affair with her manager, and the manager later decided to terminate the relationship, the employee might retaliate in anger by claiming that the manager made unwelcome advances to her and that she felt helpless to resist him for fear of losing her job. Or if a man was attracted to a female supervisor who was not similarly attracted to him, he may allege sexual (or other) discrimination by the supervisor when she failed to promote him over other employees.

In such cases, as in cases of genuine harassment or discrimination, a plaintiff may experience real emotions of hurt, anger, and sadness, among others, in response to the situation at work. However, a clue to detecting this

---

[10]Ellison v. Brady, 924 F.2d 872, 879 (9th Cir. 1991).
[11]Meritor Sav. Bank v. Vinson, 477 U.S. 57, 67 (1986).

kind of malingering lies in identifying the source and nature of the emotions experienced by the plaintiff. The reason is that many plaintiffs think that all expressions of anger, hurt, depression, and other emotions are the same—that is, generic in nature—and they do not understand that an emotional response is generated by an identification and evaluation of particular facts. In other words, not all anger is alike, and the same is true of all other emotions.

For example, if there is evidence that an employee was flirtatious toward a superior and that the superior did not play along with her, then an evaluation of the context at work might suggest that the employee's hurt resulted from the defendant's lack of responsiveness to her overtures rather than from discrimination on the part of the defendant toward her. Although the plaintiff would experience the emotion of hurt from either cause, the two experiences would be significantly different, and it would be important to distinguish the two in any clinical evaluation.

Another clue to the possible fabrication of a discrimination claim can be found by studying the development of a plaintiff's allegations of discrimination. In some cases, a relatively naïve plaintiff may initially allege one form of discrimination but later in the litigation allege a completely different form. Although there is a certain amount of legal posturing that is legitimate and normal in the course of a lawsuit's development, a plaintiff may create a problem for herself if she does this in a harassment case. This is because of the subjective arm of the test for harassment. The very fact that it is the mental state of the plaintiff that in part defines whether or not unlawful harassment has occurred makes it hard for a plaintiff to change the character of her complaint, because she is then claiming to have had a different mental state than previously alleged.

For example, suppose an African-American female plaintiff alleges that her Caucasian male supervisor passed her up for a promotion because she did not respond to his sexually charged overtures. She initially files a complaint with the EEOC or equivalent state agency alleging that she was the victim of sexual harassment, which has caused her severe mental distress and anguish. She then hires an attorney to represent her. However, when her attorney reviews the facts, he does not feel that she has a strong case for her sexual harassment allegations, but he does think that she may prevail on the grounds that she was discriminated against because of her race. The plaintiff then files a complaint for racial discrimination. The inconsistency lies in the fact that the plaintiff's perception of the workplace events at the time they occurred was one of discrimination on the basis of gender. Her attorney's subsequent interpretation of the workplace events is one of discrimination on the basis of race. When the plaintiff, after the fact, changes her perception and interpretation of what took place, this draws into serious question the credibility of both her original and her subsequent claims, because if her initial perceptions were truly of being discriminated against on the basis of sex, then no other perceptions are legitimate.

A more sophisticated plaintiff may claim instead, "Well, at first I knew that something wrong was being done to me, but I did not know in what way," and then she may claim to have subsequently discovered in what way she was being discriminated against. However, this more subtle attempt to hedge her bets is also problematic, because it means that she did not actually perceive the nature of the wrong that she later figured out "must have" occurred, which suggests that she may not have perceived anything wrong at the time. Again, such a plaintiff could fail the subjective perception test of harassment.

Additionally, as discussed above, similar emotions are not identical emotions. The hurt, anger, and other emotions that one may experience as a result of a situation involving sexual harassment are not the same ones that result from a situation involving racial or other kinds of discrimination, and thus the emotional response to one kind of discrimination is not transferable to other kinds.

A malingerer may of course exaggerate the severity and pervasiveness of any harassment that in fact did take place. A clue that there is exaggeration of the extent of the harassment is to find that, as the causes of action in the case grow, so do the symptoms of which the plaintiff complains. For example, it is common for a sexual harassment lawsuit to include multiple causes of action, such as wrongful termination, intentional infliction of emotional distress, breach of contract, and so forth. It may be tempting for a plaintiff to try to expand the account of the symptoms she experienced to fit into all the categories of legal actions. For instance, if a sexual harassment claim grows into an action for wrongful termination, a plaintiff's complaints may grow from a hypersensitivity to men and authority figures, to depression over being fired and unemployed, to total disability and the inability to hold any job indefinitely.

Another clue to the exaggeration of the severity or pervasiveness of discrimination or harassment is a tendency of some plaintiffs to expand discrete incidents of discrimination into an allegation of pervasive, continuous discrimination. It is important for an evaluator not to accept vague, general statements about discrimination at face value, but to obtain a detailed account of the alleged events, and to pin down the time of occurrence and the nature of the events as accurately as possible. For example, a plaintiff may claim repeatedly that a manager made lewd remarks to her "all the time" or "on a daily basis," or that he disparaged her "constantly" in front of others, whereas in fact there may be only two or three actual instances that the plaintiff herself can recollect when such remarks were alleged to have been made.

Similarly, in sexual harassment cases not involving actual physical assault, it may be to a plaintiff's advantage to create the impression that the reason she was traumatized as severely as she was, was not merely because of a few specific remarks or actions of the defendant but rather because those remarks or actions in effect poisoned her work environment, such that from that time on the whole workplace became a hostile and offensive place to her.

For example, if a plaintiff complains that a supervisor made an unwelcome advance toward her, although the supervisor is transferred out of her department by upper management, the plaintiff may continue to complain of severe symptoms of anxiety and panic at the prospect of running into the supervisor, of depression that the supervisor is still employed there, of anger that upper management failed to take her complaints seriously enough, and of inability to function effectively on the job because the whole company now seems to have turned from a safe environment into a hostile one. While in some cases these complaints that the environment at work has turned hostile are credible, in other cases they may be a deliberate attempt by a plaintiff to exaggerate the severity of the alleged trauma and of the symptoms alleged to have resulted from it.

An important clue that the environment at work is not as hostile as a plaintiff claims is where a plaintiff's behavior at work does not mesh with her complaints. For example, if a plaintiff appears to interact quite normally with other coworkers and managers and shows a pattern of normal interactions with those in her immediate work environment, this would suggest that the environment has not really been poisoned for the plaintiff. A plaintiff's view of the nature of the work environment can be cross-checked against the perceptions of her coworkers, in order to evaluate the reasonableness of her claims.

Another clue to this form of malingering is the finding that a plaintiff's symptoms appear to take on a life of their own, independent of the work environment. For example, if a plaintiff is no longer working in the alleged offensive environment and thus is no longer subject to its toxic effects, one would expect the symptoms derived from the direct exposure to the poisoned environment to improve (taking into account the presence of other factors that could maintain the symptoms, such as unemployment and continued litigation stresses). However, if a plaintiff's complaints of symptoms continue to grow and worsen, and the picture presented is one of symptoms that grow as the legal case grows, it suggests that the plaintiff may be malingering.

C. Exaggerated Effect of Medical or Psychological Condition on "Major Life Activities"

In cases invoking the protection of the Americans with Disabilities Act, a plaintiff has to show, among other things, that his symptoms cause a "substantial limitation" on some "major life activity."[12] What constitutes a major life activity is open to considerable interpretation. For example, both the EEOC and the Ninth Circuit have even suggested that sleep—a form of *in*activity—be considered a major life activity.[13] The vagueness of the term "substantial limitation" presents a ripe opportunity for plaintiffs to exaggerate the effects of their symptoms in the hope of qualifying for ADA coverage. In this form of malingering, it is not the presence or severity of symptoms per se, but rather the impact or effect that the symptoms have on the person's life, that is exaggerated.

A clue that an employee may be exaggerating the impact of his symptoms on his life activities can be found in the way the employee describes his symptoms. For example, a person may claim to have migraine headaches that are so severe that they interfere with his concentration and ability to think, such that he cannot read or work, and that force him to lie down in a darkened room to minimize nausea. This person may indicate that it is impossible to work with this severity of migraine unless he is provided with a place to lie

---

[12] 42 U.S.C. §12102(2)(A).
[13] McAlindin v. County of San Diego, 192 F.3d 1226 (9th Cir. 1999).

down at work. While his medical records may indeed confirm the diagnosis of severe migraine headaches, they may be found to occur relatively infrequently and to be responsive to treatment. Thus, although an individual headache may impair the plaintiff's ability to work for the rest of that day, the frequency of the headaches may be insufficient to cause such a global problem with concentration and thinking that there would be a "substantial limitation" within the meaning of the ADA.

Similarly, virtually every psychiatric condition described in *DSM-IV-TR* must have some significant impact upon a person's functioning for the diagnosis to be made. Yet there are many people who are very successfully employed despite carrying psychiatric diagnoses. One example is a person who is chronically depressed. Although such a person is "substantially impaired" in his ability to achieve happiness in one or more areas of his life, his condition may be irrelevant to his job performance. However, once a lawsuit has been initiated, such a person may claim that his condition, which prior to the lawsuit had no or little impact on his work, now substantially impacts his work.

D. Exaggeration of Symptoms

Plaintiffs may exaggerate their symptoms in several ways. The following are some of the ways in which symptoms can be exaggerated.

1. The Nature and Severity of the Impairment

Typically, the more severe a plaintiff's symptoms are, the better his or her case. Psychotic symptoms are the most severe of psychiatric symptoms, because to the extent one has them, one is not in contact with reality and cannot function. The malingering of psychotic symptoms, in which persons present themselves as "insane," is less common in employment litigation than in criminal cases. However, malingered psychosis may be seen in fitness-for-duty evaluations in which an employee is trying to avoid work or qualify for disability benefits.

Clues to the malingering of psychotic symptoms include the following:[14]

- The person claims to experience a psychotic symptom in isolation, without any other associated symptoms of psychosis. For example, a person may claim to hear voices, with absolutely no other indications of a psychotic mental process.
- The claimed symptom does not conform to the usual way psychotic symptoms present themselves. Essentially, the person simply does not know enough about how psychosis works to make his act convincing. For example, someone may claim to hear voices telling him to do things and claim that he always does what the voices tell him to do, whereas in fact, psychotic individuals give in to command hallucinations only a very small percentage of the time.

---

[14]Phillip J. Resnick, *Malingered Psychosis*, in CLINICAL ASSESSMENT OF MALINGERING AND DECEPTION 47–67 (Richard J. Rogers ed., 2d ed. 1997); Phillip J. Resnick, *The Detection of Malingered Psychosis*, 22 PSYCHIATRIC CLINIC OF N. AM. 159 (1999).

- A psychotic individual does not think in the same way as a nonpsychotic individual. It is not only the content but also the form of the thoughts that differs. It is much harder to simulate the form of psychotic thinking than it is to simulate the content of a delusion. For example, a psychotic individual often makes identifications and conclusions not by logic but "loosely," according to his emotional state, and it is very difficult for someone who is not in the same state of mind to come up with similar identifications.

2. The Duration of the Impairment

Another common method of malingering is for plaintiffs to exaggerate the length of time that they have remained impaired from their symptoms. As mentioned before, many work-related symptoms improve considerably when the triggering stress is removed. For example, if an employee is transferred to a department under a different manager, the stress of the previous manager's "harassment" is removed, and symptoms triggered by that manager's actions should be expected to improve considerably.

Litigation by its nature, however, is a drawn-out process, and it can take years to reach a resolution of a case. If a plaintiff appears before a jury and declares that she was severely emotionally damaged from an alleged work injury two years before, but at the time of the trial the plaintiff states that she has recovered fully, the jury, seeing a plaintiff who looks totally normal, may be more likely to conclude that the plaintiff never did suffer much emotional harm from the injury, and the plaintiff's credibility may be called into question. Thus, there is an inherent incentive for plaintiffs to want to present themselves to juries in a manner that portrays them in the worst possible condition by exaggerating the duration of their symptoms as extending up until the time of trial, when in fact their symptoms had resolved quite some time earlier.

A clue that a plaintiff may be malingering ongoing severe symptoms may be obtained from the nature of the symptoms themselves. For example, symptoms that meet the criteria of Adjustment Disorder but that are not severe enough to meet the criteria for Posttraumatic Stress Disorder would be expected to ameliorate and resolve within six months after the precipitating stress is removed. Other examples of conditions that usually resolve within a few weeks to months include soft tissue injuries, such as whiplash, as well as cases of mild postconcussional syndrome.

In evaluating a case in which a plaintiff alleges continuing symptoms, it is thus very important for an evaluator to take a careful history of the progression of each symptom and to compare the plaintiff's account with the account given in his or her medical or psychiatric records. It is common for the records to indicate significant improvement in symptoms during a time frame in which the plaintiff alleges no improvement. It also is common for a plaintiff to acknowledge that symptoms responded to treatment—for example, an antidepressant—but then have no explanation as to why she did not resume treatment after the symptoms were alleged to have returned.

Another clue that a plaintiff may be malingering about the duration of his or her impairment is the failure of the plaintiff to seek treatment despite claims of very severe symptoms. If someone were suffering, one would expect that person to seek help to relieve the suffering. For example, if a plaintiff who claims to have become severely depressed after being sexually harassed on the job does not seek treatment until shortly before trial, this may suggest to an evaluator that the plaintiff is seeking treatment now to bolster her claim of impairment rather than to obtain relief for genuinely distressing symptoms.

3. The Permanent or Long-Term Impact of an Impairment

A related type of malingering is the attempt to show that symptoms are permanent and that the plaintiff is doomed to suffer from them indefinitely, when this prediction is not supportable in fact. For example, a plaintiff might indicate that she has suffered from a severe depression since being sexually harassed and claim that the alleged incident has irreversibly tainted her trust of men and thus her ability to form new relationships. She might claim that the harassment destroyed her sex life and caused her ability to work with any authority figures to be impaired for life. She might further claim to have chronic thoughts of suicide, to be unable to derive any enjoyment from life, and that she is barely existing, having withdrawn into a shell. Her therapist may confirm this history and conclude that the plaintiff's prognosis is very poor for recovery and that she is unlikely ever to be able to work again.

A look at such a plaintiff's past psychiatric treatment records, however, may indicate that she had episodes of severe depression previously that were triggered by stressors just as severe as the alleged incidents of harassment, and from which she recovered very well in a few months with standard therapy. The history of a good response to treatment for the same condition belies the poor prognosis given her by her current therapist and suggests that the examiner should look further for other evidence of malingering. The examiner might then discover that the plaintiff had a history of unstable relationships and a mistrust of male authority figures since childhood, and yet that this had never before caused her to be unable to work. This history suggests the possibility of malingering a poor prognosis so as to maximize the gain from a lawsuit.

Cases such as these, in which a plaintiff's prognosis is given an overly pessimistic outlook, often arise when the case has already worked its way through the workers' compensation system. In order for a workers' comp case to proceed, a determination typically must be made by the treating physician that an injured worker is "permanent and stationary" before a formula can be applied to determine the amount of benefits the worker is to receive. The determination that a worker is permanent and stationary is a term peculiar to the workers' compensation system and does not apply in any other context. It means, basically, that a worker's condition has stabilized enough that significant further improvement is not expected within the short term, given the current treatment program. It specifically does not mean that the worker cannot improve further, nor does it mean that the symptoms the worker has at that point are permanent. It is merely a specific time in a worker's treatment that is used to calculate benefits.

Two points are important to note in this process, however: (1) it is the treating clinician who submits a permanent and stationary report on the worker's behalf, and (2) at that point, workers' compensation benefits are cut off until a determination is made in the case. If the worker's symptoms resolve fully and quickly, the worker receives fewer benefits. Thus, a worker who malingers ongoing symptoms may receive benefits longer because the clinician may delay calling him permanent and stationary. When the doctor does finally make such a determination, the permanent and stationary report may provide a falsely pessimistic view of the worker's condition. Additionally, it is a natural tendency for a clinician to become invested in his own brand of treatment and to feel that if his patient is not responding to his treatment, he will not respond to any other. He may therefore conclude that because the worker is still symptomatic at the time he declares the worker to be permanent and stationary, the worker will not improve at all in the future. A treating clinician's opinion is given great weight in the workers' compensation system despite the obvious potential for therapeutic bias. A worker may latch onto his clinician's permanent and stationary findings and conclude that they mean that his symptoms are permanent and that he cannot improve. He may then use this conclusion in other legal causes of action related to the events at the workplace to show that he is permanently impaired. Clues that a plaintiff is using the findings of the workers' compensation system to create an impression that his symptoms are untreatable and permanently disabling can be found by examining the records of the clinician who treated the plaintiff for the workers' compensation injury, as well as by looking at the workers' compensation file regarding the injury.

In order for an injured worker to delay the finding that he is permanent and stationary, he must be showing some improvement in the records. However, if he shows too much improvement, his condition will not be ongoing. Thus, an examiner should be suspicious if there is a mismatch between a worker's symptoms noted in the records and the clinician's opinion at the time regarding improvement. For example, if the treating clinician's notes indicate that a worker's depression is improving but the clinician indicates on updates to the workers' compensation carrier that the worker's symptoms have not changed in severity, this would indicate such a mismatch. If the worker's condition had been improving, the worker would have had fewer symptoms. If the worker's symptoms had remained the same, the clinician should have made a permanent and stationary finding.

Moreover, if a clinician is overly invested in his own therapeutic approach, he may contribute to this mismatch by claiming improvements that are not evident in the history recorded from his patient and also by failing to alter the therapy or to refer his patient for other therapies. For example, a psychologist who feels overconfident of his own therapy style may be convinced his therapy is working when in fact the patient's symptoms remain unchanged, and the psychologist may fail to refer the patient for medication even when it is indicated. A malingerer may be quite comfortable with this therapist because he can pretend to be engaged in therapy without showing any improvement, knowing he has a staunch ally on his side.

E. Misattribution of the Cause of Symptoms to the Workplace

A very common form of malingering in employment litigation is the attempt to link symptoms caused outside the workplace to "causes" within the workplace. In this way, a plaintiff does not have to make up symptoms out of whole cloth but merely has to present symptoms that actually exist in such a way as to suggest that they resulted from a workplace incident. The plaintiff's symptoms are indeed genuine, but the true origins of the symptoms are obscured.

There are several ways in which a plaintiff may attempt to obscure the true cause(s) of his symptoms.

1. The Use of the Logical Fallacy of Post Hoc Ergo Propter Hoc

In the misuse of the logical fallacy of *post hoc ergo propter hoc*, a plaintiff gives a history of various symptoms that all supposedly began shortly after the alleged incident at work and that the plaintiff claims had never previously been experienced. For instance, a plaintiff may claim that a serious depression started after he was allegedly discriminated against at work, stating that he had never before had problems with sleeping, headaches, dizziness, and so forth. The idea is that if the symptoms can be shown to have originated after the alleged incident, then they must have originated because of the alleged incident.

In evaluating a plaintiff, it is therefore very important to attempt to discover whether the plaintiff had any prior treatment, medical or psychiatric, that may indicate the presence of symptoms that predate the alleged incident. It may be found that while some of the symptoms did indeed begin after the incident, several others had been present for a long time previously and were lumped together by the plaintiff as all occurring after the incident. For example, if it is found that a plaintiff suffered from chronic migraines, had sleep problems suggestive of obstructive sleep apnea, and had dizzy spells suggestive of an inner ear problem, then the plaintiff's complaints of headaches, disrupted sleep, and dizziness should be subtracted from the other symptoms the plaintiff complained of to give a more realistic picture of the plaintiff's current problem of anxiety and depression.

If a plaintiff becomes very defensive or vague in talking about prior medical or psychiatric treatment, or in discussing prior problems in general, this suggests the possibility that the plaintiff is trying to hide or minimize the impact of past pathology in order to create the impression that all of his problems relate to the one cause.

Another clue to this form of malingering may be roadblocks put in the way of discovery of past treatment records by plaintiff and her counsel, such as forgetting or being unwilling to provide the names of prior treating clinicians, or moving to quash subpoenas or medical or psychotherapy records, which may suggest an effort to hide or cover up pertinent data related to the origin of symptoms.

2. Reversal of Cause and Effect

Another important way in which causes of symptoms may be misattributed to the workplace is by means of a complete reversal of cause and effect, in situations in which workplace problems are not the cause, but the effect, of an employee's psychiatric symptoms.

Psychiatric problems arising from other causes frequently affect a person's ability to work, including the person's relationships with coworkers and supervisors. For example, someone who is depressed may be irritable and short-tempered at work, which may cause a deterioration of that person's relationship with others on the job. Such an employee may worry that he will not be able to do his work or that he will be fired. If severe enough, the expression of psychiatric symptoms in the workplace may lead to an employee's receiving a negative job or performance evaluation, being subjected to heightened supervision or scrutiny of his work by his superiors, receiving lower bonuses, being passed over for promotion, and even being subject to disciplinary actions and termination. This resultant "negative feedback" causes the employee to feel even worse than before.

A person who is experiencing emotional distress often wishes to receive a caring response from the significant people in his environment. If such a person is not receiving care or nurturance at home (which is where many psychiatric problems originate) or from friends or family, he may be desperate for support at work. He may either conceal his need as a secret craving for a kind word from his boss, or he may openly discuss his problems in the workplace, trying to solicit some sympathy. His superiors at work may, quite appropriately, limit their focus and support strictly to his on-the-job performance, and they may purposefully ignore any signs of mental problems or instability, because such issues are a part of the employee's personal life and may be none of the employer's business. An employee who is experiencing emotional distress may regard such a dispassionate, professional response from a superior as cold, uncaring, and rejecting. The employee's feelings may be hurt, and he may attribute his hurt feelings to his perceived abandonment by those in positions of authority at work.

If an employee sees that there is a way to claim compensation for his hurt feelings from his employer, he may see this as a solution that is satisfying both emotionally and financially. The employee may then engage in malingering by claiming that it was problems at work that caused his depression, rather than the other way around.

This form of malingering involves denial and avoidance of responsibility, as well the misattribution of symptoms. First, the employee refuses to confront the actual source of his problems (denial). Second, he avoids the responsibility both of facing the true cause of his symptoms (such as problems at home) and of not saddling his employer with his psychological problems. Finally, he cashes in by projecting blame for his emotional predicament onto his employer (misattribution).

V. Dissimulation in the Workplace

It is generally appropriate for an employee to conceal her psychological symptoms from her employer, because there is a job that needs to be done, and professionalism on any level requires that an individual keep any internal turmoil out of the work environment. Professionalism requires that an individual not let her emotions interfere with the application of her reasoning mind to the actions that her job description requires of her.

However, there are situations in which employees conceal their problems from their employers when it is not appropriate to do so, that is, they feign being healthy. The conscious feigning of health for a conscious purpose is called dissimulation. Dissimulation can arise when an employee wishes to return to work in order to earn money even though he is too sick to do his job properly. If the employee then decompensates in reaction to normal stresses at work, he may blame those stresses for causing his symptoms, rather than attributing them to the preexisting illness that he concealed.

Another situation involving dissimulation involves the employee who wants to return to work to seek revenge on someone in the workplace. He may pretend he is fine even though he is seething with rage.

Clinicians may encounter these situations when asked by a patient to write a return-to-work note after a period of disability, or these situations may be encountered by evaluators who conduct formal fitness-for-duty evaluations for employers. An employee being seen by an evaluator conducting a fitness-for-duty evaluation may be particularly on his guard, because the evaluator is in a sense an agent of the employer, even though there are limitations as to what may be reported to the employer as a result of such an evaluation. With the rise in workplace violence, an evaluator conducting a fitness-for-duty examination must often do a careful evaluation of dangerousness, because an employee's denial of intent to hurt others may not be truthful.

Dissimulation, which is a conscious concealment of symptoms, must be distinguished from the minimization of symptoms that may be displayed by someone as a manifestation of the person's actual illness. For example, a paranoid or narcissistic person will complain about others while believing there is nothing wrong with him. Depressed individuals may not realize how depressed they are. People with anxiety disorders may think they have cardiac problems. While these individuals distort their accounts of themselves by minimizing the significance of their symptoms, they generally do give a fair history of those symptoms, and the examiner can then put the symptoms together in his own mind to arrive at a clinical diagnosis.

VI. The Detection of Distortion and Deception in Employment Litigation

In 1973, David Rosenhan published a new classic study in which eight people pretending to be patients were admitted to a psychiatric hospital.[15] In order to gain admission, they all alleged that they heard voices, but once they were admitted, the eight pseudo-patients stopped reporting the symptoms they had

---

[15]David Rosenhan, *On Being Sane in Insane Places*, 172 SCIENCE 250 (1973). *See* David Faust, *The Detection of Deception*, 13 NEUROLOGIC CLINS. 255 (1995).

feigned. All of them were diagnosed as schizophrenic and were hospitalized for 9 to 52 days. Rosenhan concluded that mental health professionals could not tell the difference between health and mental illness. The corollary of his conclusions is that mental health professionals cannot distinguish between real and feigned psychosis (although patients with genuine psychosis were able to identify the fakers). In a clinical setting, such as the inpatient setting utilized by Rosenhan, it is far worse to overlook a disorder than to overdiagnose it, and thus there is often a tendency for a physician in doubt to presume dysfunction. However, in a legal setting, exaggerating the presence of illness may be just as harmful as understating it, and in a legal context a physician has to have a much higher index of suspicion for the presence of distortion than in a clinical setting. It is therefore very important for attorneys, both for the plaintiff and for the defense, who are involved in employment litigation not to rely solely on the view of a treating physician or therapist, and when malingering is suspected, to utilize the services of an independent forensic expert.

A. The Use of Collateral Sources of Information

For the same reason that one should not rely on the self-report of a plaintiff alone, the use of collateral sources of information by a forensic examiner is essential in employment litigation. The kinds of information that may be helpful in detecting distortion and malingering are varied, and thus an evaluator may need to cast a broad net, so to speak. There are factors that should be taken into account by experts for both sides to ensure that they maintain as much objectivity as possible.

It is important for an evaluator to try to understand the theories of the case put forth by both sides, so as not to fixate on a version of events that is given to the evaluator by the side that retained him. For example, if an evaluator is retained by the defense, it is very helpful to obtain a copy of the plaintiff's complaint and deposition transcripts. While a frequently changing story by a plaintiff may suggest malingering, a consistently told story that is congruent with the psychiatric picture presented may militate against a conclusion of malingering.

Each of the following collateral sources may be helpful in the detection of malingering in employment litigation:

- *Past medical and psychiatric records*. Medical and psychiatric records may provide evidence of preexisting conditions and may allow the evaluator to gauge the severity and the natural history of those conditions. For example, if a plaintiff has a recurring depressive condition, he may be distorting the facts by claiming his depression was caused solely by work conditions. An evaluator also should look for evidence of personality disorders, which might predispose a plaintiff to being hypersensitive to events in the workplace.
- *Divorce records*. Plaintiffs may not wish to reveal or may seek to minimize (dissimulate) the extent of acrimony and stress from prior or contemporaneous divorce and custody battles, yet court records often contain information about

stresses in a plaintiff's life that were unrelated to work, and that need to be accounted for to understand the plaintiff's present symptoms.
- *Treatment and perceptions of other employees.* Statements by other employees may reveal that the discrimination that a plaintiff has alleged was not perceived by others who were in situations similar to that of the plaintiff. Or the responses of similarly situated employees may indicate that a plaintiff's reactions were not those of a reasonable person.
- *Past criminal records.* Criminal records may reveal evidence of a preexisting mental illness, or they may shed light on the credibility of a plaintiff's claims of damages. For example, a record of a prior arrest for exposing himself in a public place diminished the credibility of a plaintiff who alleged that he suffered severe emotional distress from sexual gestures from a supervisor.
- *Litigation records.* Prior suits for alleged harassment may indicate a hypersensitive plaintiff who distorts the facts, particularly where similar allegations were raised in prior suits at unrelated workplaces.
- *Current and prior personnel files.* These records may indicate whether a person has a history of being a good worker or a troublemaker, or whether or not a person accepts responsibility for his mistakes. They can also provide a means of checking a plaintiff's account of job promotions, absences from work, company policies, and circumstances surrounding termination.
- *Depositions of key witnesses.* Depositions of witnesses other than the plaintiff may assist an evaluator to detect malingering in several ways. First, a plaintiff may have given a relatively "mild" account of allegedly discriminatory incidents to others, but then later exaggerated or changed the account for the lawsuit. Second, witnesses may corroborate or deny that an environment was hostile or offensive. Third, the perception of events reported by coworkers may suggest distortion on the part of the plaintiff.
- *Investigators' reports and other interviews of third parties.* A forensic evaluator typically does not have the time or the resources to track down and interview third-party witnesses who could shed light on a plaintiff's story or psychiatric history. However, attorneys routinely employ investigators to collect witness statements and to conduct background investigations. The reports of investigators may help to broaden the context of knowledge about a plaintiff, and such reports can point to inconsistencies within a plaintiff's account. Reports from investigators may also indicate whether a plaintiff is engaging in activities that are at odds with his claims of disability. Examples might include working at another job, playing sports, performing household chores, or engaging in hobbies.

B. The Use of Psychological Testing

Psychological tests may be useful adjuncts in the assessment of malingering, but they should not be relied upon as the primary evidence to support a conclusion of malingering because a psychological test cannot replace an interview and a reasoned analysis of factual data.

The MMPI-2 is probably the best and most widely used psychological test to aid in the detection of malingering.[16] The test is standardized, it is easily administered, and the scoring is objective.[17]

It may be very helpful to compare the data from MMPI-2 tests completed by the same individual at different times. In comparing MMPI test results, however, it is very important to obtain the raw data of previous tests, i.e., the actual answers that were given by the person who took the test. It is important to have the raw data to avoid having to rely on the interpretation of the person who administered the previous test, who may have been the treating clinician with a different agenda than a forensic examiner, or who may not have been very skilled in interpreting the test, or who may have made erroneous interpretations from the data.

For psychological tests that require training to administer properly, an attorney should use the services of a psychologist who is familiar with the testing as well as the application of the testing to the forensic setting. For example, if a plaintiff claims a loss of intellectual functioning, intelligence and other neuropsychological tests may be useful to determine whether the plaintiff indeed is functioning at the level he claims.

C. Understanding Normal Responses to Traumatic Events

While a plaintiff who is involved in employment litigation may have suffered real stress, such a plaintiff may nonetheless exaggerate the emotional effects that the stress is having on him. A clinician evaluating a plaintiff may mistakenly conclude that because the stress was real, the plaintiff's emotional responses to that stress must necessarily constitute a pathological process or condition that requires intensive treatment. Moreover, if the clinician is also treating the plaintiff, third-party insurance requirements may demand from the clinician some kind of diagnosis in order to qualify for reimbursement. This increases the possibility of therapeutic bias, in that the clinician may be tempted to "stretch" the patient's symptoms to fit a diagnosis.

A plaintiff's emotional responses to a traumatic stressful event may constitute a normal reaction to stress that requires little or no specialized treatment. In fact, most people do not develop a mental illness after being exposed to trauma,[18] even though there may be a high level of distress associated with the trauma. Even when victims of violent crime as a whole were studied, the lifetime prevalence rates for PTSD varied considerably, between 19 percent and 75 percent, and current PTSD rates varied between 5 percent and 39 percent.[19] Thus, just because a person is distressed following trauma, it does

---

[16]Kenneth S. Pope, James N. Butcher & Joyce Seelen, The MMPI, MMPI-2 and MMPI-A in Court 5,13 (1997).

[17]For a detailed discussion of the MMPI-2, see Chapter 10, The Use and Misuse of Psychological Testing.

[18]L. Stephen O'Brien, Traumatic Events and Mental Health 44 (1998).

[19]*Id.* at 68.

not follow that the trauma has caused the person to suffer a diagnosable mental disorder.

There are several symptoms that may arise as a normal reaction to trauma. These include symptoms of anxiety and depression, insomnia and nightmares, and symptoms of increased arousal (for example, increased vigilance and hypersensitivity). A normal response to trauma may extend over a lengthy period of time, and symptoms may fluctuate for several months without becoming chronic.[20]

Because the symptoms that can result from trauma vary widely, each case must be evaluated individually to assess whether a plaintiff is exhibiting a normal, as opposed to a pathological, response. One criterion that may help to distinguish between a normal and a pathological response to trauma is the presence or absence of disability, that is, whether the symptoms that result from a trauma significantly affect the person's ability to function.

For example, a female employee alleged that she had been sexually assaulted by a coworker, but she had no problems in continuing to work, and she even received an award for high performance for the months after the alleged rape. The fact that she was not disabled suggested that her emotional responses to the alleged trauma were normal and adaptive, rather than constituting a chronic, unremitting PTSD.

D. The Forensic Interview of the Plaintiff

The principles of how to interview a plaintiff are essentially the same in all psychiatric medicolegal evaluations.[21] The focus of this section is the application of the standard forensic psychiatric interview to the detection of malingering and distortion.

1. Know the Collateral Data

The more sources of data an examiner has been able to study prior to interviewing a plaintiff, the better such an examiner will be able to focus the questions in the interview, and the less he or she will be led astray by a plaintiff. It is helpful for the examiner to have prior knowledge of discrepancies between various versions of the events, as this knowledge can help the examiner to probe into dubious areas during the interview. For example, knowing from her medical records that a plaintiff had gone skiing and gambling shortly after an alleged rape, an examiner would be able to catch the plaintiff in a definite lie if she were to claim that she was left totally debilitated following the assault.

---

[20]*Id.* at 48.
[21]For a detailed general discussion of this subject, see Chapter 9, The Mental Examination.

2. Obtain a Thorough Background History to Establish a Pattern of Behavior and Reaction to Various Kinds of Stresses

Plaintiffs and their counsel may object to detailed questioning about the plaintiff's background, but such an inquiry is essential to the evaluation of distortion and deception. For example, one plaintiff had a history of two prior marriages to men she had met at work, yet she claimed that a coworker's advances towards her were unwelcome because she would never date a coworker. Her pattern of prior relationships belied her reason for rejecting the coworker's advances.

Plaintiffs often do not understand the relevance of an inquiry into their backgrounds, which makes it harder for them consciously to distort that earlier life history. If anything, they will seek instead to have their background histories suppressed as an irrelevant invasion of their privacy.

3. Ask Open-Ended Questions

Just as an expert assesses the plaintiff, so a plaintiff who is malingering assesses the expert, trying to figure out what is safe to reveal and what the expert is looking for. A malingering plaintiff will exaggerate a symptom when he thinks it safe to do so. An expert should ask open-ended questions that do not reveal how the plaintiff should answer. Leading questions should normally be avoided because a plaintiff is likely to endorse items that indicate a greater severity of illness. For example, an expert should avoid asking, "Have you been sleeping well over the last week?" Instead, a better question would be, "How many hours' sleep a night have you had in the last week, and how long did it take you to fall asleep?"

4. Ask Leading Questions in the Wrong Direction

When one suspects that a plaintiff may be malingering, however, it can be very helpful to ask leading questions in the *wrong* direction. The questions should be designed to lead a person into an answer that is incompatible with what he or she is claiming. A well-known ploy, for example, is to ask someone who is claiming to hear voices whether he hears them better from the left ear or from the right ear. A plaintiff who is trying to lie thinks that he ought to endorse the voices as coming more from one side of the head, whereas a plaintiff who really is hallucinating simply reports that they are equal on both sides. If a plaintiff answers that she is hearing the voices equally, the examiner may express surprise. He may say, for example, "Really?! So there's no difference at all between how you hear them on the left or on the right?" If the malingerer had thought that voices should be heard symmetrically between left and right but wasn't too sure of that fact, the examiner's show of surprise may shake him into modifying his account, as, for example, "Well, sometimes I hear them more from the left."

5. Ask Detailed Questions, Particularly When Responses Are Vague and Generalized

It is important to elucidate each traumatic incident in detail. Especially in harassment cases, plaintiffs may claim that certain harassing behavior occurred "all the time," or "constantly." While in fact there may have been only two or three specific incidents of harassment, unless a careful history is taken of each incident, the impression may be gained that the harassment was more pervasive than it actually was.

6. Evaluate Every Symptom in Detail

A plaintiff may link symptoms to a workplace cause in his own mind when in fact a detailed evaluation of the symptoms shows them to be unrelated to the workplace. For example, a plaintiff may link complaints of tiredness and fatigue to depression caused by workplace discrimination, when in fact a detailed history of the symptoms may show that the plaintiff has symptoms of an unrelated sleep disorder that causes daytime fatigue and sleepiness, or that the plaintiff had requested to work a lot of overtime, which caused him to become excessively fatigued.

Plaintiffs may allege the presence of serious symptoms when in fact such symptoms are minor or are normal reactions to events. One reason for this is that many plaintiffs do not fully understand how symptoms actually manifest themselves, and because they are upset by what has happened to them, they dramatize the importance of their responses and they may elevate minor complaints to the status of major symptoms. (This is analogous to the patient with indigestion who presents to an emergency room with a "heart attack.") For example, a plaintiff who has vivid memories of a workplace incident may claim to have "flashbacks" of it. A flashback, however, is not simply a vivid memory of an event; it is an episode of reexperiencing it. This means that the person actually believes the event is being reenacted in the present and that she is actually back in that situation. If one does not take a detailed history of the person's experience, one may elevate a vivid memory—which is a normal reaction to an upsetting event—to the status of a serious symptom of PTSD.

An evaluator should ask about symptoms that commonly occur together with the ones presented by the plaintiff. Plaintiffs may allege the presence of some symptoms of PTSD (for example, flashbacks), but not others, such as a heightened startle response or the avoidance of situations associated with the trauma. Plaintiffs who endorse too few or too many symptoms of any condition may thereby raise the suspicion of malingering to an evaluator—too few, because the symptoms then do not add up to a disorder the plaintiff may be alleging she has; too many, because psychiatric conditions present with different symptom patterns in different individuals, and most patients do not exhibit every symptom or manifestation of a condition.

An evaluator should evaluate the progression of each symptom from its onset until the present. Thus, each symptom should have its own timeline. This will help the expert to assess the credibility of a plaintiff, according to how well the timelines of all the symptoms comport with one another. For example, one plaintiff said that his depression was still quite severe at the time of the evaluation. However, he (and his treatment records) indicated at least partial resolution of several of his symptoms (such as sleep disturbance, nightmares, etc.) only a few weeks after the workplace event in question, even with minimal treatment. A careful history of each individual symptom in this case belied his claim of a persistent severe depression.

7. Look for Verbal Cues of Vagueness and Evasiveness

Evasiveness is a common form of defense to probing questions. Vague, nonresponsive replies to questions can indicate that a plaintiff wishes to avoid a direct, straightforward answer that might disadvantage his case. Thus, it is important for an examiner not to be satisfied with approximate answers and to bring a plaintiff back to the question at hand if the plaintiff wanders off topic. It is also important for an examiner to note what subject areas a plaintiff avoids, as this may present clues as to how the plaintiff is trying to distort the facts.

Another strategy used by plaintiffs to avoid committing themselves to definite answers is to use ambiguous language. For example, a plaintiff, when she answered a question affirmatively, repeatedly used the phrase, "I believe I did," or "I believe so," rather than a more unequivocal statement such as, "Yes, I did," or "Yes." The ambiguous language that she used left it unclear in the examiner's mind as to whether something actually did happen, or whether she merely thought that something had happened and wasn't quite sure. (In this case, the examiner was able to clarify her answers by asking her, "When you say 'I believe,' is that a 'yes,' or are you uncertain?")

8. Look for Nonverbal Cues

Look for how and when emotions are displayed in the interview. A display of strong emotions in an interview is indicative of how important the particular subject matter under discussion is to a plaintiff. Comparing a plaintiff's responses to alleged workplace events with responses the plaintiff has shown to other significant life events can provide a gauge of the relative significance of the events. For example, if a plaintiff is claiming severe emotional distress from harassment and her only display of emotion in the interview occurs while discussing the death of her father some years previously, this suggests that the intensity of the emotional distress from the harassment may be overstated.

The manner in which a plaintiff displays her emotions may be significant. For example, if a plaintiff dramatically (or melodramatically) breaks down sobbing over some relatively minor sexual innuendoes made to her at work, yet she is far more composed and sedate regarding the effects of a prior, violent rape, this would suggest that the plaintiff may be exaggerating the intensity and effect of the workplace trauma.

Look for other behavioral signs. A plaintiff's behavior on the day of the interview may provide helpful clues to the presence of malingering. It is important to evaluate how a plaintiff dresses and behaves both in the interview and in arriving for and leaving the interview. For example, if a plaintiff walks normally in the parking lot but initiates a limp once inside the examiner's offices, obviously the change in gait would be suspicious. A plaintiff's ability to tolerate a lengthy interview without requesting breaks and without lapses of focus and attention may draw into question claims of disability or poor attention span.

How a plaintiff dresses for an interview may be significant. For example, a plaintiff in a sexual harassment lawsuit who appears for an evaluation dressed in a tight-fitting, revealing dress suggests she could have been sexually provocative at work toward the male defendant.

9. Look for Inconsistencies in the Interview

A plaintiff may give a different history to an evaluator than the plaintiff has given to others on previous occasions. Changing versions of events detracts from a plaintiff's credibility, but an evaluator has to be careful not to make too much of insignificant changes in a plaintiff's story. Giving a plaintiff some opportunity to explain inconsistencies in data may help to avoid this mistake.

A plaintiff may also present inconsistencies within the forensic interview itself that may show her to be lying. For example, in the course of describing her past relationships, a plaintiff indicated that her relationship with her husband had been wonderful and passionate from the moment they met, and that they had a frequent sex life, starting from their first date. However, later in the interview, when the effects of the alleged workplace sexual harassment were discussed, she said that she had been so traumatized that she had not been able to have sex with her husband until three months after they were married.

A plaintiff may also show inconsistencies in the mental status examination. For example, a plaintiff may correctly answer more difficult items and incorrectly answer simpler items. By correctly answering more difficult items, a plaintiff shows that he is not very impaired in the area being tested. However, by answering simple items wrongly, he tries to give the examiner the impression that he has serious deficits in that area. He is inconsistent because he does not know the relative difficulty of the items, and he may figure that to answer all the questions wrongly would look suspicious.

In cases in which plaintiffs claim to be unable to work, it is important to look for inconsistencies between their claimed inability to work and their performance in the interview. For example, a plaintiff may claim to be too irritable to deal with others at work, yet the same plaintiff may show a calm demeanor, with few signs of irritability throughout a whole day's stressful evaluation.

10. Evaluate the Impact of the Legal Process

Litigation is a very stressful process that may affect the severity and duration of a plaintiff's symptoms, even if the plaintiff does not consciously fake symptoms in order to win the case. A lawsuit often contributes so significantly to a plaintiff's level of distress that many potential plaintiffs decide not to file one because they are not prepared to put themselves through the additional stress that litigation necessarily involves.

Most plaintiffs complain that their symptoms are exacerbated whenever they have to deal with their cases in some way, because the adversarial process brings into sharp focus the very symptoms from which they are trying to escape. For example, even when their symptoms are minimal or absent by the time the litigation gets underway, when they have to appear for depositions or other legal proceedings, their symptoms may be rekindled. In this way, litigation may cause plaintiffs' symptoms to endure far longer than they would have otherwise.

A frequent form of distortion used by plaintiffs is to minimize the impact of a lawsuit on their symptoms, or to blur the distinction between the effects of the alleged traumas and the effects of the litigation. It is therefore crucial for an evaluator to try to distinguish what effects the lawsuit is having on them and on their symptoms from the effects of other alleged traumas.

An examiner can approach this task simply by asking a plaintiff how the lawsuit is affecting him. Another way to assess the effects of a lawsuit is to ask a plaintiff what it would be like if there were no suit—i.e., if a decision or settlement had already been reached in the case. One can assess a plaintiff's responses to different potential outcomes of the case. For example, if a plaintiff believed that all of her symptoms would resolve were she to prevail in the case but that she would be permanently crippled if she were to lose her case, this would suggest a strong motivation to exaggerate her symptoms in order to win her case.

A plaintiff's demeanor in a psychiatric interview can be measured against her demeanor in a deposition. Typically, a deposition is a much more stressful, tense, dramatic, and adversarial process than a psychiatric evaluation in which only the plaintiff and the evaluator are present. A plaintiff is more likely to be on her guard in a deposition, which is conducted in an adversarial manner, whereas she may be much more relaxed in a one-to-one interview setting. A plaintiff may present as much sicker in her deposition, which may suggest that she is exaggerating her symptoms "for the cameras," so to speak. Or she may be much more guarded in the deposition, giving out little information, prompted by her attorney to be as reticent as possible. However, a plaintiff who present the same degree of pathology in the same manner in both settings may be much more credible as a result.

11. Evaluate Plaintiffs' Attitudes Toward Their Alleged Emotional Distress

If someone sustains a physical injury, he will normally take steps to obtain treatment for the injury so as to heal himself. One expects the person to do the same if he sustains an emotional injury. If a person claims severe distress but takes no steps to obtain any relief for the distress, his inaction may call into question the severity of the distress.

For example, a plaintiff claimed to have suffered from a severe depression after being discriminated against at work, but she did not seek treatment until many months later when her attorney referred her to a therapist. Her failure to seek help sooner suggested that she had not been as depressed as she had claimed.

12. Look for Alternative Motives for the Lawsuit

Malingering is the feigning or exaggeration of illness for a conscious purpose or motive. The proper motive for a lawsuit is a desire to right a wrong done to the plaintiff. The presence of alternative motives for a lawsuit may be indicative of malingering.

Every lawsuit carries with it the desire on the part of the plaintiff to be made whole by means of some sort of monetary award. Although this obviously does not imply that every plaintiff is a malingerer, it does mean that gaining an undeserved money award is always one alternative motive that should be considered.

It is important to look beyond the possible desire for money, however, because there are several other motives that are frequently found in plaintiffs that also cause them to lie or to otherwise distort the facts. These alternative motives may include revenge (including revenge for being fired or passed over for promotion), retaliation for being rejected sexually, and envy of the success of others. While revenge and retaliation are conscious motives, they may result from anger that is caused by a peculiar sensitivity of a plaintiff that stems from a personality disorder—such as so-called narcissistic rage or the rage found in persons with Borderline Personality Disorder.

VII. Problems and Pitfalls in the Detection of Distortion and Deception

There are many reasons why distortion and deception may go undetected in employment litigation. Being aware of how plaintiffs' distortions may manifest themselves enables an examiner to detect the distortions. Conversely, a lack of understanding of the ways in which plaintiffs can distort the truth will cause an examiner to fail to assess for the presence of distortion. Anyone can be fooled, including experts, but by paying attention to some common pitfalls, an expert can increase the objectivity of his or her opinions.

A. Inadequate or Blocked Discovery

Experts may be consulted relatively late in a case, when discovery cutoff dates are close at hand. There may be insufficient time left to obtain adequate collateral sources of information. Alternatively, counsel for either side may seek to limit an expert's access to certain information, sometimes for legitimate legal reasons and sometimes to hide highly relevant and damaging data from an expert. An expert should therefore try to obtain a broad understanding of the case as soon as possible so that he can advise the party retaining him as to what kinds of discovery documents he wishes to review. The sooner this is done, the more time the attorney who retains the expert then has to track down and subpoena any relevant material, and the more time there is for the expert to prepare declarations for counsel to move to unblock the discovery of important material. An expert should review complete, and not partial, records.

There are times, of course, when records are simply unavailable or when a judge rules that they are not discoverable or admissible. In such situations, an expert should indicate in his report that the pertinent records were requested but that they were not made available for review.

If an expert is limited only to an examination of a plaintiff, and there are records in existence that clearly would impact on the objectivity of his opinion, the expert may be unable to form an opinion in the case and should not feel obligated to do so. (In some cases, such as with disability evaluations, there may not be much in the way of collateral records, and this limitation may not be significant. However, more complex cases, such as those involving sexual harassment, may require a broader inquiry.)

B. Failure to Recognize Therapeutic Bias

Most mental health professionals take the histories of their patients at face value and they do not easily believe that their patients may be lying to them or that they may be distorting the truth. Also, therapists typically do not have access to collateral sources of data against which to check the stories of their patients. In a legal setting, these factors lead to so-called therapeutic bias, in which therapists become attached to their patients and become advocates for their patients' legal cases. Therapists sometimes may go to great lengths to demonstrate that their patients were wronged.

Most mental health professionals are not trained to provide forensic (legal) opinions, and they feel uncomfortable in the adversarial process of the legal system. Therapists may be loath to antagonize their patients by rendering an opinion that their patients are lying or distorting the truth, on the grounds that this would destroy the therapeutic alliances they have established with their patients. (Of course, it is questionable whether any genuine therapeutic alliance can be founded on lies and deception.)

For all these reasons, it is preferable for a forensic expert not to wear a "therapeutic hat," and for a treating clinician not to offer a forensic opinion. This may be hard to avoid in some circumstances. For example, the workers' compensation system actually promotes therapeutic bias because it encourages the treating clinician to adopt a duality of roles. Additionally, therapists who accept cases on lien may have a financial bias in the outcome of their patients' cases. Extraordinarily high clinical fees may be a tip-off to the presence of therapeutic bias because the sicker a patient, the more intensive the treatment, and a therapist may be tempted to exaggerate the intensity of the treatment required.

C. Failure to Evaluate a Plaintiff Adequately

1. Failure to Establish the Appropriate Parameters for an Evaluation

Evaluating a plaintiff adequately requires that the evaluator have enough leeway to conduct an adequate examination. Sometimes attorneys will attempt to prevent an adequate examination by trying to limit the amount of time a plaintiff will be made available for it, by trying to limit the scope of questions that may be asked, or by otherwise trying to set up conditions that make an objective assessment impossible, such as having third parties sit in on the psychiatric interview. The ostensive reasons given for these limitations include protecting the plaintiff's privacy and protecting an already abused plaintiff from an abusive interview. A skilled interviewer should have no difficulty accessing needed information without invading any protected privacy areas and should be able to interview a plaintiff without anything remotely approaching abuse. Thus an evaluator should not give in to this kind of pressure to conduct an interview under conditions that render an objective assessment impossible. This kind of problem can usually be preempted by working with the party employing the expert to establish reasonable parameters for the interview, if necessary with the court's imprimatur.

2. Failure to Evaluate the Effects of Major Life Events

Whether or not a plaintiff has a prior history of mental illness, all people are affected emotionally by major events in their lives. These include career changes, marriages, divorces, breaking up of the family unit, and death or serious illness in the family, as well as traumatic events such as physical or sexual abuse. It is important to gauge the effects of major life events on plaintiffs in order to understand how they cope with normal and abnormal stresses. Without evaluating a plaintiff's responses to other major life events, an examiner loses an important context in which to evaluate the credibility of a plaintiff's present injury claim.

Some plaintiffs attempt to whitewash the past, claiming that events that would have an emotional impact on anyone did not really affect them. Or else plaintiffs may exaggerate the impact of workplace stresses as being greater than the impact of far more traumatic events from their past. Some plaintiffs present a workplace stress as if it were the last straw that broke them, emotionally, after being weakened by repeated stresses. However, an evaluation of their responses to major life events may show that instead of being weakened by repetitive stresses, they become hardened, more resilient, and better able to cope with stress.

For example, a professional woman claimed that she was totally and permanently disabled from working because the stresses of her job were too much for her to cope with in her clinically depressed state. However, her history revealed that she had suffered from severe depression all her life in response to multiple losses and other negative life events. Her work was the one thing that invariably helped her out of her depression, gave her a sense of purpose and self-esteem, and made her more resilient to the next bout of depression.

3. Failure to Evaluate for Personality Defects, Poor Judgment, or Short Temper

Mental health clinicians are trained to assess patients primarily for *DSM-IV-TR* Axis I conditions, which are clinical syndromes consisting of a collection of symptoms—for example, anxiety or depression. However, the presence or absence of a clinical syndrome does not constitute a full description of an individual. People have different personality traits, quirks, and temperaments. For example, one person may have a short temper, whereas another is even-tempered; one person may characteristically exercise good judgment in certain situations, whereas another may show poor judgment when placed in similar situations; or one person may typically depend on others to make decisions, whereas another may be a very independent thinker.

The characteristics of individuals known as personality traits may or may not be pathological. However, their personality traits influence how people respond to or evaluate a given situation. For example, if an employee with a short temper and a sense of entitlement provokes his coworkers, he may easily feel harassed or discriminated against if they shun him because of his temperament.

Personality traits (noted on Axis II in *DSM-IV-TR*) are particularly important to take note of in employment litigation for several reasons. First, they can affect the objectivity with which an individual assesses and responds to a given situation, and thus they can cause a plaintiff to be unusually sensitive to normal or relatively minor aggravations that would not so affect others. In cases such as sexual harassment cases that are tested according to a "reasonable person" standard, a personality disorder (constituting a collection of personality traits) may result in a plaintiff's being unreasonable, or "hypersensitive." Second, personality traits may lead a plaintiff into seeking revenge or retaliation, as discussed above, which can in turn lead a plaintiff into a conscious distortion of the facts. Third, the presence of a personality disorder may draw into question a plaintiff's credibility.

For example, an individual with an Antisocial Personality Disorder has a track record of dishonesty and character defects that affects his credibility. An individual with a Borderline Personality Disorder may have a track record of manipulating her relationships with others, of dishonesty, and of overreacting by perceiving abandonment when she does not get her way. Thus, just as character evidence may bolster an individual's credibility by showing a track record of honesty and reliability, so character pathology may undercut an individual's credibility.

However, while positive character traits in healthy individuals do not require expert testimony to be presented before the court, character pathology, which is subtle and is not within the ken of ordinary laypersons does require assessment by an expert to be detected and presented before the court.

D. Over- or Underdiagnosing Malingering

Obviously, not all plaintiffs malinger or distort the truth. Even those who do malinger do not lie all of the time, or else nobody would believe them. Since even a malingerer does not lie all of the time, an evaluator has to constantly assess the credibility of what is being told to her by a plaintiff. A conclusion that a plaintiff is malingering should be made with a good amount of evidence to support it.

There is no specific test for malingering, because malingering is simply a particular form of lying, and there is no foolproof way to detect lying. The failure of an examiner to look for the presence of malingering, however, may cause it to be either overdiagnosed or undetected. Malingering will be undetected if an examiner does not look for, and therefore misses, clues that facts are being distorted. However, an examiner may also overdiagnose malingering if he accepts at face value not the plaintiff's version of the facts but the defendant's version. He may conclude without justification that the plaintiff is a "bad actor."

For example, many defendants simply deny outright all allegations put forth by plaintiffs because, after all, the burden of proof is on a plaintiff to show that what she alleged took place did in fact happen. Since an examiner's job is to evaluate a plaintiff and not the defendant in the case, he may be lulled into accepting the defendant's version of the facts too uncritically. Against this version, the plaintiff's account may seem far-fetched. However, if the examiner scrutinizes the defendant's story more closely, the defendant's blanket denial of everything may appear less than credible.

Furthermore, in many cases, particularly sexual harassment cases, there are no witnesses to the alleged harassing events. In such cases, it may be tempting for an examiner simply to dismiss a plaintiff's story because she does not have collateral evidence to back it up. However, it is not the examiner's role to try the case. It is helpful in such cases to begin one's analysis of the case by assuming that the fact pattern presented by the plaintiff is true and then to assess the credibility of the plaintiff's claims of psychological injury using the plaintiff's own fact pattern. If there is more than one plausible explanation for the facts, the various possible explanations can be laid out separately for the trier of fact to consider.

Even when an expert adequately evaluates a plaintiff, it is important that he substantiate his conclusions regarding malingering and distortion. If an expert has sufficient data to conclude that a plaintiff is malingering, it is a good idea for the expert to prepare a written report in which he can present all the evidence in support of malingering (which ought to be considerable). A failure to consider malingering when performing a forensic evaluation can decrease the credibility of an expert.

E. Failing to Evaluate the Ability to Work in Other, Similar Job Environments

Plaintiffs in employment litigation frequently allege that they are disabled and unable to return to their jobs. In many cases involving allegations of workplace harassment or discrimination, plaintiffs will choose never to return to their former positions. Many plaintiffs, quite understandably, do not wish to return to a work environment in which they feel they have been wrongly treated, but they claim that they cannot work at all and are totally disabled. Since litigation typically is protracted, there is an incentive for a plaintiff not to return to any work prior to the resolution of the lawsuit because the plaintiff will look worse off to a jury, judge, or arbitrator. However, it is important for an evaluator to determine whether a plaintiff truly is unable to return to her job or whether she simply does not wish to return to a job where she feels she was wronged.

One of the best ways to determine whether a person can perform the duties of a particular job is to assess whether the person can perform those or similar tasks in other, similar situations. Additionally, in many cases it is essential to assess a plaintiff's ability to work in positions other than the one the plaintiff held previously. For example, under the ADA, if a person is limited only from performing a particular job, or from working under a particular supervisor, he is not considered "substantially limited" in working. In a harassment suit, if a person is fully able to work in a similar job away from the alleged harasser, then the person may not have suffered as severe an emotional trauma as she alleges. Thus, as a part of assessing a plaintiff's limitations, it is important to look for areas in which the plaintiff is able to function adequately.

F. Working with Outdated Knowledge

Limitations in knowledge can make it difficult to determine whether a plaintiff's presentation makes sense medically. A plaintiff may complain of multiple symptoms, both physical and psychological in nature, which affect multiple organ systems and areas of medical subspecialty. Many of the symptoms, such as pain, may be purely subjective. Malingerers may be very artful in the presentation of subjective complaints that are hard to measure objectively. For all these reasons, it may be necessary for an examiner to review the literature regarding the symptoms and syndromes a plaintiff presents.

For example, one plaintiff presented with symptoms of a postconcussional syndrome after a blow to the head. Among other symptoms, he complained of headaches, dizziness, dry eyes, depression, and anxiety. He had been treated with high doses of multiple medications prior to being evaluated by a psychiatrist hired by the defense team. The plaintiff claimed that all his symptoms had been caused by the blow to his head. In order to sort out the cause-and-effect relationships between the plaintiff's symptoms and the blow to the head, the examiner had to research the literature on postconcussional syndrome, understand that the causes of dry eyes do not include a concussion, and know enough about headaches to tell that the plaintiff had suffered "rebound" headaches caused by the medication he had been taking. Only then could he sort out the relative importance of these medical factors in causing the plaintiff's anxiety and depression.

Although plaintiffs frequently present with a combination of physical and psychological symptoms, they might present with psychological symptoms only. For example, a woman claimed that she had been "date raped" by a coworker during working time. She explained her amnesia for the alleged rape by asserting that he had slipped her a drug commonly used in date rapes. Her claimed symptoms thus consisted of amnesia for the rape and numerous symptoms of Posttraumatic Stress Disorder (PTSD) as a result. However, her account of the events surrounding the alleged amnesia, taken at face value, was not consistent with the known pharmacology of drugs commonly used in date rapes. Further, her allegation of amnesia for the alleged traumatic event was not consistent with PTSD. Thus, knowledge of psychopharmacology and of PTSD was necessary to assess her complaints.

VIII. Conclusion

In any litigation, there is a possibility that a plaintiff will lie to win a lawsuit or to obtain a larger damage award. However, employment litigation in particular offers a plaintiff numerous ways to distort facts and to lie about the psychiatric aspects of his case to his advantage. The assessment of malingering is a complex task that requires an expert to apply an understanding of normal responses to trauma, of psychopathology and its treatment, and of personality, character, and temperament to an analysis of the assertions made by a plaintiff. An expert must, in addition to this vast body of knowledge, have an understanding of the issues involved in employment litigation, because the manner in which a plaintiff will distort the truth depends on the setting in which the distortion occurs. Though there is no foolproof method to detect lying, a careful gathering of data, together with a reasoned analysis of that data, often allows an expert to assist both counsel and the court to arrive at a more objective understanding of the facts.

CHAPTER 12

PHARMACOLOGY AND PSYCHOPHARMACOLOGY

Daniel P. Greenfield, M.D., M.P.H., M.S.

In a thought-provoking essay entitled "How Prozac Slew Freud,"[1] Edward Shorter, historian of science at the University of Toronto, asserted that the psychoanalytic orientation in psychiatry is outmoded and ineffective, and that psychopharmacology is the proper orientation and basic skill set for psychiatry. Shorter's opinion is an accurate depiction of the current state of psychiatry as a branch of medicine,[2] and his assertion highlights the importance of understanding the complexity of psychopharmacology as applied not only in clinical contexts but in forensic contexts as well.[3]

The field of psychopharmacology is broad, detailed, technical, and constantly changing and evolving. This chapter will present a summary and overview of psychopharmacology, emphasizing for the nonphysician and nonscientist practical aspects of the basic principles of psychiatry and pharmacology, and classification of psychopharmacologic drugs and medications. The broad intent of this chapter is to present and discuss principles of pharmacology and psychopharmacology that will be useful to the employment law practitioner who encounters a case in which psychiatric and psychopharmacologic issues are present. These issues may be relevant to liability *and* damages aspects of a case.

To present an accurate and current overview of pharmacology in the context in which psychopharmacologic agents are used generally, and in the context of employment law issues, this chapter will address several broad areas relevant to these aspects of psychopharmacology.

---

[1]Edward Shorter, *How Prozac Slew Freud*, AMERICAN HERITAGE, Sept. 1998, at 52.

[2]*See* Daniel P. Greenfield & Frederick A. Russell, *A Modest Proposal*, 1 ADDICTION INSIGHT 1, 3 (1999).

[3]*See* JOHN R. LION, THE ART OF MEDICATING PSYCHIATRIC PATIENTS (1978).

First, it will utilize an "epidemiologic triangle," or interactive model of host, agent, and environment.[4] The "host" in this model is the patient/litigant who is taking or has taken psychotropic medications. The "agent" is that pharmacologically or chemically active compound, or medication, that the host has taken—licitly or illicitly.[5] The "environment" for the purposes of this chapter is the employment law context in which issues pertaining to psychopharmacology occur.

Additional definitions involving concepts in psychiatry, pharmacology, psychopharmacology, physiology, toxicology, and related topics will be presented and discussed, as a prelude to a more detailed review and discussion of pharmacology and psychopharmacology. This more detailed review will cover uses and classes of psychoactive ("affecting the mind") or psychotropic ("moving the mind")[5] drugs, as well as psychiatric aspects of nonpsychotropic drugs and related topics.

The second broad area of psychopharmacology to be discussed in this chapter concerns classes and properties of psychotropic agents. Both *licit* (i.e., prescribed by a physician and taken as prescribed) and *illicit* (i.e., "street drugs," or prescription drugs illegally diverted and abused) will be considered. The licit psychotropic agents will be further categorized into "fourteen antis,"[6] according to the clinical psychiatric conditions that these various medications are intended to treat. In addition, four other types of pharmacologic agents will be discussed—antiparkinsonian agents, anticholinergic agents, over-the-counter (OTC) medications (a heterogeneous group of pharmacologic and psychopharmacologic agents), and nonpharmaceutical preparations such as herbal medicines, dietary supplements, vitamins, and related compounds.

The final section of the chapter will pull together material previously presented as well as review the relevance of psychopharmacologic issues in the employment law context, using five reported employment law cases as reference points.

Although this chapter is not intended as a comprehensive or definitive treatise on psychopharmacology, the approach it takes in the employment law context and the information contained in it are intended to provide the legal practitioner, researcher, and scholar with a basic understanding of this area, and with a reference source for further research.

---

[4] JUDITH S. MAUSNER AND SHIRA KRAMER, MAUSNER AND BAHN EPIDEMIOLOGY–AN INTRODUCTORY TEXT 33 (2d ed. 1985) ("The Epidemiologic Triangle is considered to consist of three components–host, environment, and agent. The model implies that each must be analyzed and understood for comprehension and predictions of patterns of a disease. A change in any one of the components will alter an existing equilibrium to increase or decrease the frequency of a disease.").

[5] *See* Daniel P. Greenfield, *Prescription Drug Abuse and Dependence: An Introduction, in* PRESCRIPTION DRUG ABUSE AND DEPENDENCE: HOW PRESCRIPTION DRUG ABUSE CONTRIBUTES TO THE DRUG ABUSE EPIDEMIC 3 (Daniel P. Greenfield, ed. 1995).

[6] See Table 12-5 below.

I. Basic Principles of Psychopharmacology

Excerpts from the following reported legal cases give examples of how concepts of psychopharmacology may be encountered in employment law.

- *Lowe v. Philadelphia Newspapers:*[7] The defense put on medical testimony as to how the antidepressant and other medications the plaintiff was taking, some of which had soporific side effects, affected the plaintiff's dependability, quality of work, and attitude in the work environment.[8] This testimony applied to both the liability and damages aspects of the case. It illustrates how side effects of a psychotropic medication can actually produce psychiatric symptomatology (such as fatigue or sedation) that may be confused with symptoms of a psychiatric disorder such as depression and that may affect an employee's performance in the workplace.
- *EEOC v. Amego, Inc.:*[9] The employee's depression rendered her unqualified to perform the essential job function of administering and monitoring residents' medication, and her termination based on her suicide attempts via medication overdoses was not discharge "because of" her depression.[10] Although she had a psychiatric disorder (depression) that might have qualified her for coverage under the Americans with Disabilities Act (ADA), her abuse of medications in response to that condition (i.e., suicide attempts by means of medication overdoses) were considered by the court in disqualifying her from ADA coverage, as she was determined unqualified to perform her essential job functions.
- *Brown v. Northern Trust Bank:*[11] The plaintiff was diagnosed with Major Depression, Single Episode and declared unable to work. After a course of treatment with Prozac and Desyrel, along with psychotherapy, the plaintiff returned to work and her psychiatric treatment terminated. The court therefore held that she did not meet the definition of disabled under the Americans with Disabilities Act because of her admitted improvement and the absence of a recurring symptoms following her return to work. This excerpt illustrates the differentiation between *diagnosis* and *disability*, in that the plaintiff's diagnosis of Major Depression did not disable her to the point of her permanently not being able to return to work and was managed via a combination of psychotherapy and pharmacotherapy.
- *Blakey v. Continental Airlines Inc.:*[12] The plaintiff was prescribed psychotropic medication for a period of time and treated by a psychologist as a result of sexual harassment in the workplace. As an indication of the severity of the plaintiff's psychiatric symptomatology, she required pharmacotherapy with psychotropic medications following a period of stress-related problems caused by the harassment.

---

[7]594 F. Supp. 123, 54 FEP Cases 167 (E.D. Pa. 1984).
[8]*Id.* at 125, 54 FEP Cases at 169.
[9]110 F.3d 135, 6 AD Cases 997 (1st Cir. 1997).
[10]*Id.* at 135–36, 6 AD Cases at 999.
[11]1997 WL 543098 (N.D. Ill. Sept. 2, 1977).
[12]992 F. Supp. 731, 76 FEP Cases 280 (D.N.J. 1998).

To understand the basics of psychiatric and psychopharmacologic concepts discussed in these and other cases, the fundamentals of psychiatric diagnoses as applied to the individual patient or litigant—the host in the epidemiologic triangle model—must first be understood. These fundamentals will be discussed briefly in the framework of the widely used *Diagnostic and Statistical Manual of Mental Disorders, Fourth Edition—Text Revision*, or *DSM-IV-TR*, of the American Psychiatric Association.[13]

A. Fundamentals of Psychiatric Diagnosis

Mental disorders are described in *DSM-IV-TR* in the broad categories of *thought disorders* or *psychoses* (Schizophrenia; Delusional Disorders; paranoid disorders; others); *mood* or *affective* disorders (Major Depression, Dysthymia, Bipolar or manic-depressive disorders); *anxiety disorders* (Panic Disorder, Phobias, Generalized Anxiety Disorder, Posttraumatic Stress Disorder); and *organic brain disorders* (delirium, dementia, and toxin-induced syndromes such as drug overdoses or workplace exposures). These four broad categories (in addition to other substance abuse disorders, somatoform disorders, factitious disorders, dissociative disorders, sexual and gender identity disorders, eating disorders, sleep disorders, impulse-control disorders, and adjustment disorders) constitute the types of Axis I disorders[14] that would generally come to the attention of a mental health professional for evaluation and treatment and would be considered amenable to psychopharmacologic treatment, depending on symptom severity. Axis II disorders, or personality disorders,[15] on the other hand, are not typically amenable to pharmacotherapy unless they include symptoms such as anxiety, depression, or psychosis that are more characteristic of Axis I disorders and are amenable to such treatment.

It is additionally necessary to distinguish between *diagnosis*, on one hand, and level of functioning, symptomatology, and/or disability on the other hand.[16] An alleged accident victim, for example, or an alleged victim of wrongful discharge or sexual harassment in the employment law context, may satisfy *DSM-IV-TR* diagnostic criteria for the diagnosis of a depressive disorder but may not be *disabled.* In such a situation, the determination of disability or a reduced level of functioning must be made following a clinical evaluation.

Finally, an individual's mental disorder does not exist in isolation from other aspects of his or her life. In this regard, the multiaxial diagnostic system of *DSM-IV-TR* takes into account five "axes" to be used in diagnosing an

---

[13]AMERICAN PSYCHIATRIC ASSOCIATION, DIAGNOSTIC AND STATISTICAL MANUAL OF MENTAL DISORDERS (4th ed. text rev. 2000) [hereinafter *DSM-IV-TR*].

[14]For a detailed discussion of Axis I disorders, see Chapter 5, Mental Disorders Commonly Encountered in Employment Litigation.

[15]For a detailed discussion of Axis II disorders, see Chapter 6, Personality Disorders in Employment Litigation.

[16]Jeffrey A. Brown & Daniel P. Greenfield, *Weighing Psychiatric Claims in P.I. Cases*, 124 N.J.L.J. 52, 53 (1989).

individual in order to describe that individual in a broad-based and comprehensive way.[17] Similarly, the overall clinical picture of the individual must always be taken into account when assessing issues of psychopharmacology.

B. Fundamentals of Pharmacology and Psychopharmacology

In the broad fields of pharmacology and psychopharmacology, medicine, and psychiatry, the most fundamental life science may be considered to be *physiology* (from the Greek "physio," or "nature," and "logia," or "study of"). This basic clinical science encompasses the physical and chemical functioning of the normal human organism, unchanged and uninfluenced by chemicals or substances.

In contrast, *pharmacology* (from the Greek "pharmakon," or "drug") refers to the science of the effects on the human organism of foreign substances (i.e., not normally found within the organism or in any of its organ systems or subsystems).

Toxicology (from the Greek "toxikon," or "poison") is generally considered a parallel science, or subscience, of pharmacology. Its relationship to pharmacology was captured some 500 years ago in the words of Paracelsus (1493–1541), the "father of toxicology," who said that "all substances are poisons; there is none which is not a poison. The right dose differentiates a poison from a remedy."[18]

Finally, *psychopharmacology* (from the Greek "psyche," or "soul") is that branch of pharmacology that deals with pharmacologic agents, drugs, or medications that act upon ("psychoactive") or influence ("psychotropic") the mind—or in more current terminology, the central nervous system.

In the fields of pharmacology and psychopharmacology, three fundamental concepts are of considerable practical importance in understanding basic principles of these fields. These concepts are the *dose-response relationship*, *desired-undesired ("side") effects*, and *pharmacologic interactions*.[19]

1. Dose-Response Relationship

The first fundamental concept involves the dose-response relationship of a drug and its graphic representation in the form of the dose-response curve (see Figure 12-1). This describes the reaction, or response, of an organism to a dose of an active pharmacologic agent. Typically, the response follows a predictable pattern with changes in the dose. In many instances, this response pattern will demonstrate a greater response to an increased dose after an initial lag, or

---

[17] For a detailed discussion of the five axes in *DSM-IV-TR*, see Chapter 4, The Diagnostic and Statistical Manual of Mental Disorders.

[18] Curtis D. Klaasen, *Introduction*, in CASARETT AND DOULL'S TOXICOLOGY 5 (Curtis D. Klaasen, Mary K. Amdur & John Doull eds., 4th ed. 1990).

[19] Jonathan E. Alpert, Jerrold G. Bernstein & Jerrold F. Rosenbaum, *Psychopharmacologic Issues in the Medical Setting*, in MASSACHUSETTS GENERAL HOSPITAL HANDBOOK OF GENERAL HOSPITAL PSYCHIATRY 249–303 (Ned H. Cassem ed., 4th ed. 1997).

induction phase, and will plateau in its response at the end of the maximal beneficial dose. The "s-shaped" or "sigmoid" dose response curve characterizes this type of response, and is illustrated in Figure 12-1 below.

In other instances, the dose-response curve for a pharmacologic agent may follow a bell-shaped curve pattern, with a maximal response from the organism following an initial lag (induction) phase followed by a slowing response phase, followed by a plateau phase, followed finally by a declining response phase. This response pattern is seen, for example, with certain types of antidepressant medications, such as nortriptyline. The effective dose range in this dose-response paradigm is often referred to as a "therapeutic window," which is also illustrated in Figure 12-1.

The development of *tolerance* to a drug—a state of diminished responsiveness as a consequence of prior exposure—may change the dose-response relationship of a person to a particular drug. This phenomenon is particularly characteristic of depressant medications and of alcohol.[20]

Figure 12-1 Theoretical Dose-Response Curves

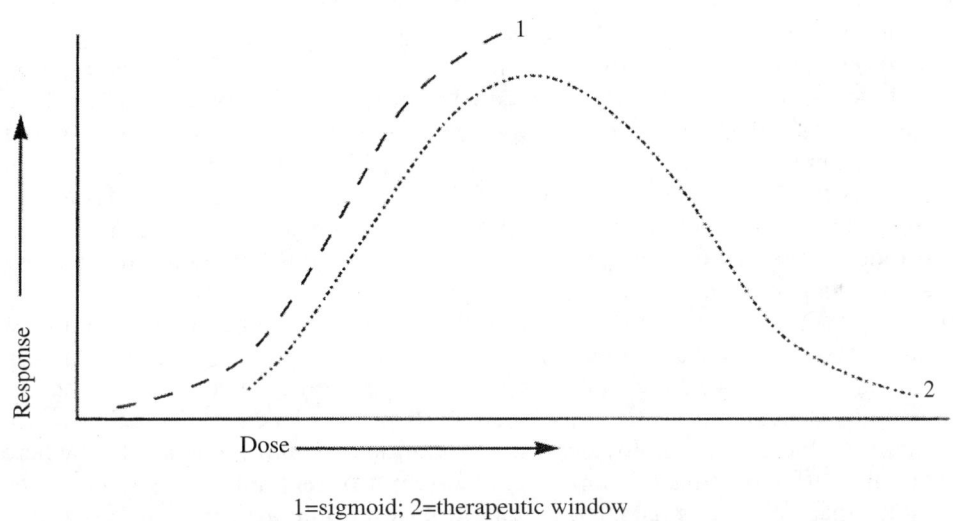

1=sigmoid; 2=therapeutic window

Adapted with permission from David R. Price and Paul R. Lees-Haley, *The Insurer's Handbook of Psychological Injury Claims* (The National Underwriter Co. 1995).

2. Desired Versus Undesired Effects

The second fundamental concept involves *desired* (target) effects versus *undesired* (side) effects of psychopharmacologic agents. Simply stated, no pharmacologic agent exhibits only the beneficial, or desired, effects for which it is

---

[20]Jerrold C. Winter, *Tolerance, Physical Dependence, and Drug Abuse, in* TEXTBOOK OF PHARMACOLOGY 37 (Cedric M. Smith & Alan M. Reynard eds., 1992).

intended. Rather, all active pharmacologic agents will manifest some undesirable effects to a greater or lesser extent. These side effects may be dose-related themselves (as in the dose-response relationship just described), or they may be "idiosyncratic" (i.e., not dose-related) and occur if a threshold dose is reached. Allergic reactions are good examples of these. In addition, these side effects may be *specific* (i.e., related to the desired effects of the pharmacologic agents given—for example, excessive sedation from hypnotic, sleep-inducing medications) or may be *non-specific* (i.e., unrelated to the desired effect of the pharmacologic agent—for example, subjective feelings of malaise and lethargy caused by some antibiotics).[21] The term commonly applied to situations in which a medication produces an undesired effect ("response") is "adverse drug reaction," or "ADR."

3. Pharmacologic Interactions

The third fundamental concept in pharmacology recognizes that chemical interactions of pharmacologic agents with other substances in the body can influence their actions and effectiveness and may require changes (upward or downward) in doses of a medication for it to have its desired effect. The two most commonly described interactions are interactions of drugs with other drugs (called "drug-drug interactions" or "DDIs") and interactions of drugs with food (called "drug-food interactions," or "DFIs"). The practical implications of these interactions include the potential need for adjustment in doses of a medication for it to have its desired and expected response. For example, there is an increased dose requirement for antiseizure drugs when cimetidine (Tagamet®), an antiulcer drug, is taken. Similarly, ingestion of certain types of foods (e.g., tyramine-containing foods such as cheeses, chocolate, fava beans, and lime) should be avoided when certain medications are taken (e.g., anti-depressant medications known as MAOIs).

Awareness of these interactions will allow the employment law practitioner to understand better the potential issues involved in employment law cases in which litigants have psychiatric disorders that are being treated by psychopharmacologic medications. In a case such as *Brown v. Northern Trust Bank*,[22] for example, the astute employment law practitioner would be aware that where the plaintiff's pharmacotherapy included two different anti-depressant agents, issues that must be considered include drug-drug interactions, dose effectiveness, the presence and severity of the plaintiff's underlying depressive order, the possible effects of all these factors on the plaintiff's clinical psychiatric condition, and the possible attribution of symptomatology to the workplace experience rather than to the medications. These points will be discussed in more detail subsequently.

---

[21]Daniel P. Greenfield & Jeffrey A. Brown, *Psychopharmacology*, in THE INSURER'S HANDBOOK OF PSYCHOLOGICAL INJURY CLAIMS 133 (David R. Price & Paul R. Lees-Haley eds., 1995).
[22]1997 WL 543098 (N.D. Ill. Sept. 2, 1977).

C. Classes of Pharmacologic Agents

For present purposes, pharmacologic agents may be broadly divided into *nonpsychotropic* and *psychotropic* types, recognizing that a variety of undesired side effects of a psychiatric, neuropsychiatric, or neurologic nature (e.g. dizziness, fatigue, lethargy, transient sensory disturbances, malaise, depression, and others) may be seen from both of these types of pharmacologic agents. The vast majority of both nonpsychotropic and psychotropic medications are prescribed by nonpsychiatric physicians (family physicians, internists, pediatricians, other primary care physicians, obstetricians-gynecologists, surgeons and surgical subspecialists, orthopedists, and other specialists).[23]

Nonpsychotropic classes of pharmacologic agents may be described in terms of both the organ system they are intended to affect and the disease or condition they are intended to treat. Tables 12-1 and 12-2 below give examples of these types of classes of nonpsychotropic pharmacologic agents.[24]

Table 12-1   Examples of Nonpsychotropic Medications Classified by Organ System Affected

Organ System	
Cardiovascular	Digitalis preparations (cardiac):
	- Digoxin (various preparations)
	Antihypertensives:
	- Atenolol (Tenormin®)
	- Alphamethyldopa (Aldomet®)
	- Beta-propranolol (Inderal®)
Gastrointestinal	Motility agents:
	- Metoclopramide (Reglan®)
	Antacids:
	- Maalox®
	- Mylanta®
	Histamine blockers:
	- Cimetidine (Tagamet®)
	- Ranitidine (Zantac®)
Endocrine/metabolic	Diabetes mellitus preparations:
	- Humulin®
	- NPH
	- Oral hypoglycemics

continued

---

[23]Lynn A. Cunningham, *Depression and Anxiety in the Primary Care Setting*, 23 COMPREHENSIVE THERAPY 400 (1997).

[24]In this chapter, the generic, or chemical (pharmacologic) designations of medications will be given first, followed by the trade (brand) name and trademark symbol, in parentheses.

Table 12-1 Continued.
Examples of Nonpsychotropic Medications Classified by Organ System Affected

Organ System	
Endocrine/metabolic *continued*	Thyroid replacement preparations: - Cytomel®, - Synthroid®
Pulmonary	Bronchodilators: - Isoproterenol (Isuprel®) - Epinephrine
Integumentary (skin)	Topical steroids: - Retin-A® - Cortisone ®

Adapted with permission from David R. Price & Paul R. Lees-Haley, *The Insurer's Handbook of Psychological Injury Claims* (The National Underwriter Co. 1995).

Table 12-2 Examples of Nonpsychotropic Medications Classified by Disease Treated

Disease Affected	Agent (Medication)
Infectious diseases (pneumonia, meningitis, AIDS)	Antibiotics and Antivirals: - Penicillins - Cephaloxin [Keflex®] - Erythromycin - Zidovudine [Retrovir®]
Neoplastic disease (cancers)	Methotrexate; Steroids; Cisplatinum
Rheumatoid diseases	Steroids; Aspirin; Nonsteroidal anti-inflammatory drugs (NSAIDs)
Immunological diseases	Steroids; Azulfidine; Immuran®
Degenerative Central Nervous System (CNS) diseases	L-Dopa, Sinemet® (for Parkinson's Disease)
Poisoning	Syrup of ipecac; Chelating agents - EDTA - Penicillamine

Adapted with permission from David R. Price & Paul R. Lees-Haley, *The Insurer's Handbook of Psychological Injury Claims* (The National Underwriter Co. 1995).

These medications have side effects that may be relevant in the employment law context:

- Bronchodilators are stimulating agents that may produce dysphoria, irritability, anxiety, tension, and excitement; these symptoms may be erroneously attributed to a plaintiff's employment experience rather than to the medication.
- Metoclopramide (Reglan®) may have side effects of confusion, forgetfulness, memory disturbances, and other such cognitive disturbances. Like agitation and irritability, these may also be mistaken for symptoms arising from workplace experiences in the context of employment litigation rather than from the medication.
- Hypoglycemia (too low blood sugar) and hyperglycemia (too high blood sugar) may be associated with inadequate pharmacologic management of diabetes mellitus. Like agitation and confusion resulting from psychostimulants and Reglan,® these symptoms may be mistakenly attributed to workplace experiences in the context of employment litigation.
- Thyroid replacement medications and thyroid blocking agents may be associated, respectively, with agitation, excitement, irritability, and other such stimulated ("hyper") symptomatology; or with depression, dullness, forgetfulness, apathy, and other such depressed ("down") symptomatology. As with symptoms and side effects associated with other classes of nonpsychotropic drugs, these symptoms may be incorrectly associated with workplace experiences rather than with the medications themselves.
- Anti-hypertensive agents may also cause depression, lethargy, malaise, and dullness, which may be erroneously associated with and attributed to workplace experiences in the context of employment litigation, rather than to the agents.
- Steroids may be associated with both agitation and depression, depending on a variety of circumstances and conditions. As a practical matter, in assessing the psychiatric/psychological condition of any litigant on steroids, both the circumstances and dose of the steroid medication and the underlying condition for which the steroid medication is prescribed (e.g., systemic lupus erythematosis, neoplastic (cancer) conditions) need to be known, since both the medication treatment and the underlying condition may cause psychiatric/ psychological symptomatology.
- L-Dopa (Sinemet®), as well as the underlying Parkinson's Disease treated with L-Dopa, may be associated with confusion, emotional lability, agitation, mania, forgetfulness, excitement, apathy, and a variety of other such nonspecific psychiatric and psychological symptoms. As with steroids and many other classes of nonpsychotropic and psychotropic medications, both the medication treatment and the underlying condition may cause relevant psychological/psychiatric symptomatology erroneously attributed to workplace experiences.

These are just some examples; many other nonpsychotropic pharmacologic agents are associated with side effects that, as in the above examples, may be erroneously attributed to past workplace experiences in the context of employment litigation. The employment law practitioner should be certain to determine whether a plaintiff may have used any such agents during the relevant period in question.

Psychotropic classes of pharmacologic medications may be described in a variety of ways. For present purposes, these agents are divided into two subtypes—licit and illicit agents. They may also be classified as *stimulants*, *depressants*, and *hallucinogens*. The former subtypes delineate the legally acceptable and unacceptable uses of these agents, and the latter categories delineate their three major psychoactive effects.

Table 12-3 illustrates these points.

Table 12-3   Licit and Illicit Psychotropic Agents

Licit Psychotropic Agents	*Illicit Psychotropic Agents*
Fourteen "antis" (see Table 12-5)	Stimulants Depressants Hallucinogens ("psychotomimetics")

Adapted with permission from David R. Price & Paul R. Lees-Haley, *The Insurer's Handbook of Psychological Injury Claims* (The National Underwriter Co. 1995).

1. Classification According to Lawfulness of Use

Licit agents are those that may be taken legally (such as prescription medications and over-the-counter medications), and illicit agents are those that may not—typically drugs of abuse, or "street drugs." However, areas of overlap may be found between these two categories. An example of such overlap is abuse or diversion of prescribed analgesic (anti-pain) medications, such as Demerol® (an opioid analgesic) or Dilaudid® (another opioid analgesic) for their euphorigenic ("high"-producing) properties. Awareness of these categories and of the areas of overlap between them may be very important to the employment law practitioner in situations, for example, in which a plaintiff being treated pharmacologically for workplace-induced symptoms may be misusing, abusing, or otherwise noncompliant with prescribed or OTC medications and not responding to pharmacotherapy as expected.

Examples of these agents are given in Table 12-4 and are discussed in further detail below.

Table 12-4   Examples of Illicit Psychotropic Agents

Stimulants
- Amphetamines and related compounds (sympathomimetics)
- Cocaine

Depressants
- Alcohol (ethanol)
- Heroin and other opioids
- Sedative-hypnotics
- Anxiolytics (including benzodiazepines)

Hallucinogens
- Inhalants (especially nitrates)
- Lysergic acid diethylamide (LSD)
- Marijuana (cannabinol and related compounds)
- MDMA ("Ecstasy") and other "designer drugs"
- Phencyclidine (PCP)

Adapted with permission from David R. Price & Paul R. Lees-Haley, *The Insurer's Handbook of Psychological Injury Claims* (The National Underwriter Co. 1995).

The psychoactive effects of these illicit or illicitly used drugs may be incorrectly attributed to workplace events by a plaintiff in an employment lawsuit. The excitement, agitation, and irritability associated with cocaine and the amphetamines ("stimulants"); the depression, fatigue, and apathy associated with sedative-hypnotics, alcohol, and opioids ("depressants"); and the confusion, memory disturbances, and disorganized and violent behaviors associated with PCP and LSD ("hallucinogens") are all examples of symptoms that may erroneously be attributed to workplace experiences.

2. Classification According to Effect

Psychotropic agents may also be divided into three generally accepted broad categories of their psychoactive effects—namely, stimulants (which excite, stimulate, and otherwise "speed up" the user), depressants (which dull, depress, and otherwise "slow down" the user), and hallucinogens (otherwise known as "psychotomimetics," or "psychedelics"). Hallucinogens induce a state of psychosis, or break with reality, often characterized by vivid hallucinations, such as the vivid visual hallucinations often seen with LSD ingestion.

3. Classification According to Clinical Purpose

A third classification system for psychotropic agents divides them into fourteen classes, or categories, according to the clinical psychiatric condition they are intended to treat—i.e., their clinical indications. Overlap exists among the various psychotropic medications in the fourteen categories in this scheme (because some medications have more than one clinical indication and may be found in more than one category), although the categories of conditions treated are considered reasonably distinct from one another and are generally treated differently from one another pharmacologically.

Table 12-5 summarizes this system of classification of psychotropic medications. The groups of medications in these fourteen classes will be discussed in detail later in this chapter.

Table 12-5   Licit Psychotropic Agents: The Fourteen "Antis"

- Anti-Addiction agents
- Anti-Anxiety agents (anxiolytics or minor tranquilizers)
- Anti-Appetite agents (anorexiants)
- Anti-Convulsant agents (anti-seizure agents and anti-epileptic drugs)

continued

Table 12-5 Continued.
Licit Psychotropic Agents: The Fourteen "Antis"

- Anti-Dementia agents (cognition enhancers)
- Anti-Depressant agents (mood elevators and thymoleptics)
- Anti-Hyperactivity agents (psychostimulants)
- Anti-Insomnia agents (sedative-hypnotics)
- Anti-Manic agents (mood stabilizers and thymoleptics)
- Anti-Obsessive-Compulsive Disorder (OCD) agents
- Anti-Pain agents (analgesics)
- Anti-Panic agents
- Anti-Psychotic agents (neuroleptics and major tranquilizers)
- Anti-Sex agents

Adapted with permission from David R. Price & Paul R. Lees-Haley, *The Insurer's Handbook of Psychological Injury Claims* (The National Underwriter Co. 1995).

4. Four Additional Classes

Another set of four heterogeneous types of drugs and medications that have psychoactive effects but do not "fit" conveniently into the broad categories presented above are (1) anti-Parkinsonian agents, (2) anti-cholinergic agents, (3) OTC agents, and (4) nonpharmaceutical preparations such as herbal medicines, dietary supplements, vitamins, and related compounds. These will be discussed next.

Anti-Parkinsonian medications are often used in psychiatric practice to treat the acute movement disorders (uncoordinated, spasmodic, and jerky involuntary movements, called "extra-pyramidal movements," or "EPS," or "Parkinsonian side effects," or "Parkinsonism") associated with the use of certain antipsychotic medications. These medications are also sometimes used in neurologic practice to treat Parkinson's Disease as a primary condition. At this time, nine such medications in three pharmacologic classes are licensed by the Food and Drug Administration for such use, as set forth in Table 12-6 below.

Table 12-6 Anti-Parkinsonian Medications

Anti-cholinergic Compounds
- Benztropine mesylate (Cogentin®)
- Biperiden (Akineton®)
- Ethopropazine (Parsidol®)
- Orophenarine (Banflex®; K-Flex®; others)
- Trihexylphenidyl (Artane®)

Antihistaminic Compounds
- Diphenhydramine (Benadryl®; others)

Dopamine Agonist Compounds
- Amantadine (Symadine®; Symmetrel®)
- Pramipexole (Mirapex®)
- Ropinirole (Requip®)

Adapted with permission from David R. Price & Paul R. Lees-Haley, *The Insurer's Handbook of Psychological Injury Claims* (The National Underwriter Co. 1995).

Somatic (related to the body, as opposed to psychic, or related to the mind) side effects commonly seen with the anti-cholinergic anti-parkinsonian agents include dry mouth, blurry vision, constipation, urinary hesitancy, and tachycardia (rapid heart rate). Central nervous system (neurologic and neuropsychiatric) side effects include organic brain disorder symptomatology (memory impairment, disorientation, acute confusional state, and delirium, among others). Such symptomatology may be confusing to the observer, by virtue of the medication taker's underlying psychosis, symptoms of which may overlap with side effect symptomatology from these agents. Side effects attributable to amantadine (Symmetrel®) include gastrointestinal upset, anxiety, lethargy, and ataxia (a broad-based gait), among others.

In the context of employment litigation, the feelings of discomfort, dysphoria, and irritability resulting from movement disorders may be incorrectly attributed to unpleasant workplace experiences rather than to the condition for which the anti-parkinsonian medication is prescribed. As with all classes of psychopharmacologic agents, the employment law practitioner should be aware of the plaintiff's past as well as present medication regimens.

Anti-cholinergic medications, which as a larger class of pharmacologic agents include most of the anti-parkinsonian agents, also include a wide variety of medications used for treating many conditions in many different organ systems (examples are anti-spasmodic gastrointestinal agents and genitourinary agents, and agents for treating glaucoma), and they have a variety of properties and side effects.[25]

OTC medications are a heterogeneous collection of medications, many of which have psychoactive properties and some of which are marketed as psychotropics. The only feature common to these agents is that they are available without prescription. The regulation of these preparations by the Food and Drug Administration (FDA) periodically permits what the National Drug Manufacturers Association calls a "prescription-to-OTC switch." This switch process changes the status of a medication from being available only by prescription to being available over the counter, and it is generally of tremendous financial benefit to the pharmaceutical company that manufactures the switched medication.[26] Since these switches occur frequently with medications that may have psychoactive effects and interactive effects with both psychotropic and nonpsychotropic agents, it behooves counsel or other reviewers of medical records to be aware of the potentially confounding symptomatic effects OTC medications may have on a plaintiff in an employment lawsuit.[27]

---

[25]BERNARD G. KATZUNG, BASIC AND CLINICAL PHARMACOLOGY 105–17 (7th ed. 1998). For further discussion of these medications, properties, and side effects, the reader may refer to a standard textbook of pharmacology; for example, GOODMAN AND GILMAN'S THE PHARMACOLOGICAL BASIS OF THERAPEUTICS (Joel G. Hardman et al. eds., 9th ed. 1996).

[26]Katherine Gannon, *Prescription to OTC Switches,* 17 DRUG TOPICS 25 (1991).

[27]For a detailed discussion of these medications, the reader is referred to the PHYSICIANS' DESK REFERENCE FOR NONPRESCRIPTION DRUGS AND DIETARY SUPPLEMENTS (2001).

Herbal medicines, vitamins, dietary supplements, and other such nonpharmaceutical preparations constitute the fourth heterogeneous collection of pharmacologic agents that do not fit conveniently into the other categories. Considerable interest in these preparations has been shown over the past several years, with sales of herbal remedies doubling every four years.[28] These preparations include a wide variety of compounds, with a wide variety of therapeutic and adverse effects. Some, such as St. John's Wort (for the treatment of depression), have been carefully studied and well characterized from clinical and pharmacologic perspectives; others have not. None of these compounds is regulated by the FDA, leaving their consumer faced with uncertain claims by the manufacturers.

Without reviewing details of the classes, indications, contents, and other such features of these preparations, a point needs to be made about them in the context of employment litigation, analogous to the points made for the other three types of heterogeneous compounds discussed in this section of the chapter. Counsel should be aware that these compounds and agents exist, that they may exert interactive effects and side effects on a plaintiff who uses them, and that they may present confounding and confusing symptomatology with respect to the issue of alleged psychiatric damages in a lawsuit. Counsel therefore should include exploration and review of these compounds during interviews, depositions, and record reviews.

II. Classes and Properties of Psychotropic Medications

For present purposes, psychotropic agents—whether licit or illicit—may be divided, with some overlap, into stimulants, depressants, hallucinogens, and the fourteen "antis." Each of these groups will be discussed in turn.

A. Stimulants

Stimulants—also called "psychostimulants" and "uppers"—are psychopharmacologic agents that accelerate or excite the user in both physical (e.g., increased heart rate and blood pressure) and psychological (e.g., a sense of excitement or restlessness) ways. Examples include amphetamines and related compounds, cocaine, methylphenidate (Ritalin®), anorexiant agents (appetite suppressants), caffeine and related thioxanthines, and others. These agents are good examples of the overlap between licit and illicit designations for psychotropic drugs, in that all of them have legitimate clinical indications as well as illegitimate and abusive uses. All of them can be obtained legitimately through physicians' prescriptions, illegitimately through purchase on the street, and illegitimately through diversion from legitimate physician prescription ("prescription drug abuse").[29]

---

[28] PHYSICIANS' DESK REFERENCE FOR HERBAL MEDICINES ii (1998).

[29] Kenneth J. Weiss & Daniel P. Greenfield, *Prescription Drug Abuse*, 9 PSYCHIATRIC CLINICS OF N. AM. 475 (1986).

B. Depressants

Depressants—also called "downers"—are psychopharmacologic agents that dull, slow, lower, or decelerate the user in both physical (e.g., decreased heart rate and blood pressure) and psychological (e.g., a sense of dullness, despair, slowness, uncertainty, inactivity) ways. Examples include alcohol (the most commonly used depressant in this country), opiates and opioids (narcotics), benzodiazepines, barbiturates, nonbenzodiazepine and nonbarbiturate sedatives-hypnotics, and others. Like stimulants, many of these agents such as heroin and hydromorphone (Dilaudid®) (diverted from a physician's prescription) are popular street drugs, and they have the same implication for the employment law practitioner as do stimulants. Counsel should become familiar with the plaintiff's drug and medication history, as they may produce potentially confounding factors in the context of evaluating causation and psychiatric damages in an employment law case.

C. Hallucinogens

Hallucinogens—also called "psychotomimetics," or "psychedelics"—are different from stimulants and depressants in that with very few exceptions, they do not have acceptable or legitimate clinical indications or uses in medical or psychiatric care.[30] As such, from the regulatory perspective, these agents come under the "Controlled Dangerous Substance" designation of Schedule I in the classification of illegal substances of the U.S. Drug Enforcement Administration. Drugs in this classification are tightly regulated, with potentially serious criminal consequences for abusers and suppliers. As their name suggests, hallucinogens produce active psychotic states, characterized by such symptomatology as hallucinations, delusions, paranoia, incoherent and loose speech, bizarre ideas, and other indications of a loss of contact with reality. Examples of drugs of this type include LSD (lysergic acid diethylamide), PCP (phencyclidine), marijuana (cannabinols), volatile inhalants (glue, toluene, nitrites), psilocybin and psilocin ("magic mushrooms"), and "designer drugs" (Ecstasy, or MDMA), among others. Unlike stimulants and depressants, these agents do not overlap in the licit and illicit categories of psychotropic agents (since they are almost always illicit as a class), nor do they demonstrate overlap among the fourteen antis (since they have almost no accepted medical use). Nevertheless, as they may present potentially confounding factors in the context of psychiatric damages in litigation, a plaintiff's use of these substances during the period relevant to the litigation must be explored.

---

[30]One such exception is the use of marijuana (cannabinols), either smoked or in oral preparations (e.g., Dronabinol®), as an anti-emetic (anti-nausea agent) for treating chronic and intractible nausea and vomiting associated with cancer, cancer chemotherapy, and HIV/AIDS. *See Principles of Cancer Therapy in* THE MERCK MANUAL OF DIAGNOSIS AND THERAPY 986–95 (17th ed. 1999).

D. The Fourteen "Antis"

The fourteen antis are a classification system for psychotropic drugs and medications based on the clinical diagnoses, or conditions, which these agents are intended to treat (they were presented in an overview in Table 12-5 above). Some of these anti designations (such as anti-anxiety, anti-manic, anti-depressant, anti-convulsant, and anti-psychotic) are well recognized and frequently encountered as terms of art in the medical literature. Others (such as anti-addiction, anti-appetite, anti-dementia, and anti-hyperactivity) are not, but they are included in this classification system as a means to continue the analogy and to present a complete and comprehensive schema of pharmacologic agents that affect the central nervous system.[31]

1. Anti-Addiction Agents

The first of the fourteen "anti's" are called *anti-addiction agents*. As a treatment modality in medicine, addiction medicine, and psychiatry, pharmacologic approaches to the treatment and management of addiction, substance abuse, and chemical dependency (which terms are used interchangeably here) are relatively young, having begun with the use of disulfiram (Antabuse®) as an aversive agent in the pharmacologic treatment of alcoholism in the 1950s.[32] This was followed by methadone as a blocking agent to the euphorigenic effects of heroin and other opiates in the 1960s,[33] followed by similar blocking or aversive approaches to a variety of addictions and dependencies, such as nicotine addiction, addiction to heroin and other opioids, cocaine addiction, and alcoholism, among others, in the 1980s and 1990s.

The rationale behind pharmacotherapy for the addictions involves the use of psychotropic agents as a substitute (a pharmacologic *agonist*) for the addictive substance, with a more desirable side effect and main effect profile than of the substance of abuse. Substituting methadone for street heroin is one example. Such drugs may also serve as a *partial* substitute (a *partial agonist*) for the addictive substance, such as nicotine replacement polacrilex gum. They might also serve as an *antagonist* (to counter undesirable effects of the addictive substance, induce withdrawal or a withdrawal-like state, initiate detoxification, and produce an aversive experience for the user); one example is Antabuse® for alcoholism and haloxone for opioid use. They might also serve as an anti-withdrawal agent (to reduce the discomfort and likelihood of convulsions, seizures, and delirium tremens); examples include benzodiazepines and anti-

---

[31]This system is derived from several sources, including the author's own experience, PHYSICIANS' DESK REFERENCE PSYCHOTROPIC PRESCRIBING GUIDE (1999), and Charles DeBattista & Alan F. Schatzberg, *Current Psychotropic Dosing and Monitoring Guidelines*, 7 PRIMARY PSYCHIATRY 26 (2000).

[32]E. Mansell Pattison, *The Selection of Treatment Modalities for the Alcoholic Patient, in* JACK H. MENDELSON & NANCY K. MELLO, THE DIAGNOSIS AND TREATMENT OF ALCOHOLISM 125 (1979).

[33]Vincent P. Dole, *Implications of Methadone Maintenance for Theories of Narcotics Addiction*, 260 JAMA 3025, 3029 (1988).

anxiety drugs and anti-convulsants to treat alcohol and other sedative-hypnotic withdrawal. Another use is as an *anti-craving agent* to reduce the drive and compulsion of an addict to seek the desired drug or medication. Finally, they might serve as a psychotropic medication or drug to treat comorbid psychiatric disorders in the substance-abusing patient with coexisting psychiatric disorders.

Table 12-7 summarizes the types and reasons for medications used as anti-addiction drugs, and gives examples where such examples exist.[34]

Table 12-7   Anti-Addiction Agents

Drug of Addiction	Pharmacologic Property	Examples of Medication
Alcohol	Agonists (substitute)	None
	Partial agonists	None
	Antagonists	Disulfiram (Antabuse®)
	Anti-withdrawal (detoxification) agents	Benzodiazepines; anti-convulsants
	Anti-craving agents	Naltrexone (Revia®)
	Concomitant treatment agents	Acamprosate, varies (Table 5)
Cocaine	Agonists (substitute)	None
	Partial agonists	None
	Antagonists	None
	Anti-withdrawal (detoxification) agents	None (not a major clinical problem)
	Anti-craving agents	None
	Concomitant treatment agents	Varies (Table 5)
Nicotine	Agonists (substitute)	Nicotine substitution, gum, patch, aerosol
	Partial agonists	None
	Antagonists	Mecamylamine
	Anti-withdrawal (detoxification) agents	Bupropion (Zyban®)
	Anti-craving agents	Nicotine substitution, Bupropion
	Concomitant treatment agents	Varies (Table 5)
Opiates / Opioids	Agonists (substitute)	Methadone, LAAM
	Partial agonists	Buprenorphine
	Antagonists	Naltrexone, Naloxone
	Anti-withdrawal (detoxification) agents	Methadone, Clonidine, Buprenorphine

---

[34]The table is adapted from Herbert D. Kleber, *Overview of Drug Addiction Treatment*, presented at a Symposium on Drug Addiction Treatment: New Research Findings, Columbus-Presbyterian Medical Center, New York, April 24, 1999.

Anti-craving agents	Clonidine, Lofexidine

In terms of the applicability of this class of psychotropic agents to the employment litigation context, the following points should be noted:

- The heterogeneous agents and medications that comprise this class vary widely in their own pharmacologic actions and properties, and they may be associated with initially any side effect that can affect the central nervous system (CNS). The employment law practitioner should know if the plaintiff is taking or has taken any of these medications in order to assess whether symptoms attributed to workplace experiences may in fact be due to medications.
- A plaintiff taking these medications for treatment of addiction may or may not be compliant with the treatment regimen. Depending on the extent of such compliance, nonspecific CNS symptomatology (such as discomfort, depression, agitation, excitement, irritability, and so forth) may be the result of complete or partial noncompliance and may erroneously be attributed to workplace experiences. It behooves the employment law practitioner not only to inquire about *whether* the plaintiff is taking prescribed anti-addiction medications, but also about the *extent* to which the plaintiff is taking the medication as prescribed.
- Finally, given the chronic and relapsing nature of the addictions and the nonspecific psychological/psychiatric symptomatology associated with relapses, such symptomatology in those situations may be erroneously attributed by the plaintiff to workplace events, to prescribed medications, or to a combination of both, rather than to the true cause of such symptomatology—namely a relapse into active addiction and its accompanying symptoms.

2. Anti-Anxiety Agents

Also known as "anxiolytics," or "minor tranquilizers," *anti-anxiety agents* comprise the second of the fourteen "antis" in this chapter's classification system for psychotropic drugs and medications. These agents are widely used, are subject to abuse and have addictive properties, and are made up of several subtypes of compounds. Their main clinical applications are the treatment of anxiety disorders and related conditions, such as Panic Disorder. The principal undesirable side effects associated with these medications derive primarily from their desired effects—sedation and tranquilization—and consist of excessive sedation, drowsiness, and sleepiness, as well as possible drug dependency.

Additional clinical applications of anti-anxiety agents for other disorders and conditions include, among others, seizures, muscle spasms (as in low back pain syndrome), insomnia, and withdrawal from alcohol and other depressants. Anti-anxiety agents may be divided into several subclasses: (1) benzodiazepines (the largest number of medications and drugs, the most commonly used, and the safest type of medication used for anxiety and related disorders, in terms of toxicity),[35] (2) nonbenzodiazepines, (3) ataractics (antihistamines, with sedating and anxiety-reducing side effects), and (4) combination preparations.

---

[35] C. Barr Taylor, *Treatment of Anxiety Disorders*, in TEXTBOOK OF PSYCHOPHARMACOLOGY 641 (Alan F. Schatzberg & Charles B. Nemeroff eds., 1955).

Table 12-8 presents anti-anxiety medications currently approved by the Food and Drug Administration, grouped by these subtypes.

Table 12-8 Anti-Anxiety Agents

Benzodiazepines
- Alprazolam (Xanax®)
- Chlordiazepoxide (Librium®)
- Clorazepate dipotassium (Tranxene®)
- Diazepam (Valium®)
- Lorazepam (Ativan®)
- Oxazepam (Serax®)
- Clonazepam (Klonopin®)

Nonbenzodiazepines
- Amobarbital (Amytal®)
- Buspirone (Buspar®)
- Mephobarbital (Mebaral®)
- Meprobamate (Miltown®, Equanil®)

Antihistamines
- Diphenhydramine (Benadryl®)
- Hydroxyzine HCl (Atarax®)
- Hydroxyzine pamoate (Vistaril®)

Combination Preparations
- Limbitol® (Chlordiazepoxide and amitiptyline (Elavil®), an antidepressant)

As with all sedating medications, or depressants, the main side effects of all these agents are excessive sleepiness, apathy, lack of energy, dullness, and depression. These may also be symptoms associated with discouraged and demoralized feelings on the part of a plaintiff in employment litigation. The employment law practitioner should be aware of these potential effects, as well as the present and past medication history of the plaintiff, in order to identify possible incorrect attribution of present symptomatology to workplace experiences.

3. Anti-Appetite Agents

Appetite suppressants are the third of the fourteen antis in this classification system; they are called, for present purposes, *anti-appetite agents*. As the name suggests, this type of medication is intended for use in weight loss and for weight management. Within this anti class are different subclasses of medications, some of which are stimulants (amphetamine and methamphetamine, for example). The use of these medications for weight management and control has been controversial over the years in medicine and clinical nutrition. However, to the extent that they are used for this purpose, current professional sentiment in these fields dictates that these medications be used on a short-term basis as part of a comprehensive, balanced clinical progression of diet, exercise, good sleep routines, and other such healthy practices.[36]

Table 12-9 below lists anorexiant drugs currently available in some states.

Table 12-9   Anti-Appetite Agents

- Amphetamine (Biphetamine®)
- Fenfluramine (Pondimin®) (removed from the market in 1998)
- Mazindol (Mazanor®, Sanorex®)
- Methamphetamine (Desoxyn®)
- Orlistat (Xenical®)
- Phendimetrazine (various brands)
- Phentermine (Adipex -P®; various brands)
- Sibutramine (Meridia®)

Since a common feature of all these drugs is their stimulating ("speeding") quality, they may produce irritability that may lead to workplace conflicts or symptoms of anxiety that may be mistaken for job stress. In addition, the employment law practitioner should be aware of the legal status and availability of anti-appetite medications taken by a plaintiff, as their availability without a prescription varies among jurisdictions, and it may be that the plaintiff obtained the drug inappropriately or illegally.

4. Anti-Convulsant Agents

The fourth category in this classification system consists of *anti-convulsant agents*. Although more widely used in the practice of neurology for treating patients with seizure disorders of a variety of types, recent developments in psychiatric research have recognized the usefulness of some of these medications (also called "anti-seizure" medications) as mood stabilizers in the treatment of mood disorders such as Bipolar Disorder.[37] Such disorders are characterized by wide and extensive mood changes ranging from manicky, uncontrollable behaviors on the one hand to depressed, withdrawn behaviors on the other.

The anti-convulsant agents most often used in the treatment of mood disorders are set forth in Table 12-10.

---

[36] James Kolanowski, *A Risk-Benefit Assessment of Anti-Obesity Drugs*, 56 DRUG SAFETY 1093 (1998).

[37] Jonathan F. Goldberg, *The Use of Anti-Convulsants in Mood Disorders*, presented at a Symposium on Advances in Neuropsychiatry and Epilepsy: Millennium 2000, Weill Medical College of Cornell University, New York, February 5, 2000.

Table 12-10 Anti-Convulsant Agents

- Valproic acid; valproate (Depakote®; Depakene®)
- Carbamazepine (Tegretol®; Carbatrol®)
- Gabapentin (Neurontin®)
- Lamotrigine (Lamictal®)
- Topiramate (Topimax®)
- Gabitril (Tiagabine®)

In the context of employment litigation, the fact that the plaintiff is taking or has taken an anti-convulsant agent may be significant because it may signal the existence of a serious mood disorder that preceded the workplace events at issue. In the event treatment with anti-convulsants appears in a plaintiff's medical records, counsel should determine whether the treatment was for Bipolar Disorder or some other mood disorder or for a seizure disorder.

5. Anti-Dementia Agents

In the fifth category are medications intended to improve cognitive functioning in individuals with cognitive impairment, or dementia, especially of the Alzheimer's type. Called *anti-dementia agents*, or "cognition enhancers," they presently consist of two FDA-approved medications, both "cholinesterase inhibitors" by chemical class; other agents are under development. The two presently approved anti-dementia agents are Donazepil (Aricept®) and Tacrine (Cognex®). They are believed to exert their beneficial effects on cognition by making more of the neurotransmitter acetylcholine available to brain cells responsible for cognition, memory, and other higher intellectual functions (a deficiency of this neurotransmitter is believed to be responsible for the decline in cognitive functioning associated with dementing conditions, such as Alzheimer's Disease). Undesirable side effects associated with these two medications are those characteristic of their drug class (cholinesterase inhibitors), namely nausea and vomiting, myalgia (muscle aches), anorexia, and rashes. As this class of medications is prescribed primarily for the generally nonworking elderly, they are unlikely to appear often in employment litigation.

6. Anti-Depressant Agents

A large number of medications comprise the sixth of the fourteen antis— namely, *anti-depressant agents*. These are also known as "mood elevators," and "thymoleptics," and consist of five subclasses: (1) cyclic compounds (tricyclic, tetracyclic, heterocyclic, polycyclic), (2) Monoamine Oxidase Inhibitors (further divided into $MAOI_A$'s and $MAOI_B$'s, depending on pharmacologic properties), (3) Selective Serotonin Reuptake Inhibitors (SSRI's), (4) other miscellaneous agents, and (5) combination preparations. The main clinical application of these medications is the treatment of unipolar depression.

The mechanisms of action of these medications vary according to their subclass and chemical type; their undesired side effects are also largely a function of their subclass and clinical type. In terms of their side effects, those of the cyclic compounds (especially tricyclic antidepressants) largely occur by virtue of the anticholinergic properties of these agents. These side effects may include dry mouth, blurry vision, constipation, urinary retention, rapid heart rate, memory impairment, confusion, nausea, dizziness, weakness and asthenia, tremors, weight gain, somnolence or insomnia, headache, diaphoresis (sweating), palpitations, sedation, and sexual disturbances (including decreased libido), among others. Side effects of the other major class of antidepressants in common use—the SSRIs—are less troublesome and prevalent than those of the older cyclic compounds (especially tricyclic antidepressants, or TCAs), and include nausea and vomiting, headache, dry mouth, excessive sedation, nervousness and restlessness, dizziness, insomnia, and diaphoresis (sweating), among others.

Table 12-11 lists the FDA-approved antidepressant medications, according to these several subtypes.

Table 12-11   Anti-Depressant Agents

Cyclic Compounds
  A. Tricyclics (TCAs)
   - Amitriptyline (Elavil®, Etrafon®, and others)
   - Clomipramine (Anafranil®)
   - Desipramine (Norpramin®, and others)
   - Doxepin (Sinequan®, and others)
   - Imipramine (Tofranil®, and others)
   - Nortriptyline (Pamelor®, Aventyl®; and others)
   - Protriptyline (Vivactil®, and others)
   - Trimipramine (Surmontil®, and others)

  B. Other cyclic compounds (tetracyclic, bicyclic, heterocyclic, polycyclic)
   - Amoxapine (Asendin®)
   - Maprotiline (Ludiomil®)
   - Miratazapine (Remeron®)
   - Venlafaxine (Effexor®)

Monoamine Oxidase Inhibitors (MAOI's)
  - Isocarboxazid (Marplan®)
  - Phenylzine (Nardil®)
  - Selegeline (Eldepryl®)
  - Tranylcypramine (Parnate®)

Selective Serotonin Reuptake Inhibitors (SSRI's)
  - Citalopram (Celexa®)
  - Fluoxetine (Prozac®)
  - Paroxetine (Paxil®)
  - Sertraline (Zoloft®)

Other (Miscellaneous) Agents
- Bupropion (Wellbutrin®)
- Nefazodone (Serzone®)
- Trazodone (Desyrel®)

Combination Preparations
- Amitriptyline (Elavil®) and perphenazine (Trilafon® —an antipsychotic): Triavil® and Etrafon®
- Amitriptyline (Elavil®) and Chlordiazepoxide (Librium®, an anti-anxiety agent): Limbitrol®

The medications in this class of psychotropic drugs vary widely in their own pharmacologic actions and properties, and they may be associated with a wide variety of side effects. These side effects, in turn, may be incorrectly attributed to workplace experiences rather than to the antidepressant medication. In addition, of course, any evidence in a plaintiff's medical records of treatment with antidepressant medication may suggest that the source of a depression at issue in the litigation might lie outside the workplace.

7. Anti-ADHD Agents

The seventh type of anti is the *anti-Attention Deficit Hyperactivity Disorder (ADHD) agent*. Attention Deficit Hyperactivity Disorder, as currently viewed, is the most commonly diagnosed behavioral disorder of childhood, estimated to affect 3 to 5 percent of school-age children. Its core symptoms include developmentally inappropriate levels of attention, concentration, activity, distractibility, and impulsivity.[38] The condition may continue through adulthood, leading to long-term adverse effects on academic performance, vocational success, and social-emotional development.

The mainstay medications for this condition are psychostimulants. These medications are beneficial for individuals with ADHD—both children and adults—because of their paradoxical calming and organizing effects on the aggressive, irritable, distracted, inattentive, and disorganized features of ADHD. This phenomenon is the *opposite* of what would intuitively be expected of psychostimulants. Although prone to abuse and still controversial in their use for this condition, stimulants are nevertheless considered the initial drug of choice for individuals with this ADHD.

Other medications used for this condition include Clonidine (Catapres®, an anti-hypertensive agent also used for opioid detoxification), several tricyclic antidepressants, and bupropion (Wellbutrin® or Zyban®).

Table 12-12 below lists the psychostimulants currently used in child, adolescent, and adult psychiatry in pharmacotherapy for ADHD.

---

[38]*Diagnosis and Treatment of Attention Deficit Hyperactivity Disorder*, 16 NIH CONSENSUS STATEMENT 1 (1998).

Table 12-12 Anti-Attention Deficit Hyperactivity Disorder [ADHD] Agents (Stimulant Class)

- Dextroamphetamine (Dexedrine®)
- Dextroamphetamine and Amphetamine (Adderal®)
- Methamphetamine (Desoxyn®)
- Methylphenidate (Ritalin®)
- Pemoline (Cylert®)

As these agents are psychostimulants, they may produce agitation, jitteriness, excitement, anxiety, irritability, manicky behaviors, and similar effects. These effects may be misinterpreted in the employment law context as psychological responses to adverse workplace experiences. In addition, such medications may make interactions between an employee and supervisors or coworkers difficult, in turn leading the employee to feel ostracized or harassed.

8. Anti-Insomnia Agents

Part of the class of medications more conventionally known as "sedative-hypnotics," those in the eighth class of the fourteen antis are called the *anti-insomnia agents*. These medications are similar to the daytime sedatives discussed earlier as anti-anxiety agents. From a practical clinical pharmacologic perspective, no real distinction between the two exists; the only differences are in the times they are administered—during the day for daytime sedatives, and at night for nighttime hypnotics. Otherwise, these two types of medications—mostly benzodiazepines—are virtually identical in terms of mechanisms of action, pharmacologic properties, undesired side effects, abuse potential, etc. Like the daytime sedatives (anxiolytics), nighttime hypnotics as a class of medications consist mainly of benzodiazepines to be taken at night, with two relatively new agents (zolpiden, or Ambien®, and zaleplon, or Sonata®), and one old one (chloral hydrate, or Noctec®) also commonly used.

Table 12-13 lists nighttime hypnotics in this class.

Table 12-13 Anti-Insomnia Agents

Benzodiazepines
- Estazolam (Prosom®)
- Flurazepam (Dalmane®)
- Quazepam (Doral®)
- Temazepam (Restoril®)
- Triazolam (Halcion®)

Others
- Chloral hydrate (Noctec®, Aquachloral Supprettes®)
- Zalaplon (Sonata®)
- Zolpidem (Ambien®)

Since benzodiazepines make up many of the medications in this class as well as in the class of anti-anxiety agents, and since the main effects of all agents in this class—excessive sedation, apathy, sleepiness, dullness, and depression—also overlap with this class, anti-insomnia agents may have the same relevance in the context of employment litigation as anti-anxiety agents. Specifically, feelings of sleepiness, dullness, and apathy may be misattributed to negative workplace events rather than to the effects of these medications.

9. Anti-Manic Agents

Anti-manic agents consist of one group of several different lithium compounds plus six anti-convulsants (described earlier) utilized primarily for mood stabilization. As with the other several classes of anti agents, the adverse side effects of these medications depend on the pharmacologic properties of the medications themselves.

The side effects of lithium compounds are generally divided into mild and common (fine tremors, drowsiness and fatigue, memory problems, and excessive urination); moderate and less common (diarrhea, thirst, hypothyroidism, and more severe symptomatology of the mild type); and severe and unusual (cardiac electrical disturbances, hypothyroidism, and inappropriate anti-diuretic hormone syndrome and resulting fluid and electrolyte disturbances, among others). Severe or unusual side effects are often associated with inadvertent or deliberate overdose of lithium preparations.

Lithium levels typically are monitored via periodic lithium-level serum-blood-level determinations, and additional studies including periodic electrocardiograms, complete blood counts, thyroid function testing, liver function testing, urine studies, and others may also be done on an ongoing basis while an individual is taking this medication. In that way, both a patient's compliance with medication and the possible development of side effects and undesired complications associated with chronic and ongoing lithium pharmacotherapy can be detected, tracked, and treated.

Anti-convulsants, mentioned earlier, are used primarily for the treatment of individuals with different types of seizure disorders. However, beginning with carbamazepine (Tegretol®) and valproate (valproic acid; Depakote® and Depakene®) as early as the 1960s, the mood-stabilizing effects of these drugs on individuals with bipolar disorder were recognized, and clinical research and practice into the mechanisms of action and usefulness of anti-convulsants in this area began and has continued. Since these medications presently are FDA-approved as anti-convulsants, their use by physicians as anti-manic drugs is an off-label use, even though it is commonly done in current psychiatric practice. As is the case with any class of medications, the side effects of these mood-stabilizing anti-convulsants are based on their pharmacologic properties, and may include dizziness, drowsiness, ataxia, somnolence, nausea, and vomiting, psychomotor slowing and dullness, decreased concentration, nervousness, tremor, and depression, among others.

Table 12-14 lists the mood-stabilizing anti-manic medications by "general" and "anti-convulsant" subclass.

Table 12-14 Anti-Manic Agents

General Subclass
- Lithium preparations (lithium carbonate, Eskalith®, Lithobid®)

Anti-Convulsant Subclass
- Valproic acid, valproate (Depakote®, Depakene®)
- Carbamazepine (Tegretol®, Carbatrol®)
- Gabapentin (Neurontin®)
- Lamotrigine (Lamictal®)
- Topiramate (Topimax®)
- Gabitril (Tiagabine®)

10. Anti-Obsessive Agents

The five drugs used for amelioration or management of obsessive-compulsive symptoms and Obsessive-Compulsive Disorder (OCD) are called *anti-obsessive agents*. They are all antidepressant medications by drug class, with relief of depressive symptomatology as their principal desired effect. Relief of obsessive symptomatology has been observed as a side effect of medications that are potent selective serotonin reuptake inhibitors (SSRIs), as well as clomipramine (Anafranil®), an older tricyclic antidepressant agent.

Table 12-15 lists those medications currently used, as an "off-label" indication, to treat OCD symptomatology.

Table 12-15 Anti-Obsessive Agents

Selective Serotonin Reuptake Inhibitors (SSRIs)
- Fluvoxamine (Luvox®)
- Paroxetine (Paxil®)
- Fluoxetine (Prozac®)
- Sertraline (Zoloft®)

Tricyclic Antidepressant
- Clomipramine (Anafranil®)

Since all anti-obsessive agents are anti-depressants by class, the same direct and side effects apply as would apply to anti-depressants. They may include vivid dreams or even nightmares, sometimes associated with fluoxetine (Prozac®), as well as agitation and excitement, gastrointestinal symptomatology (pains and cramps, bloating, dyspepsia, and others), and headaches and dizziness sometimes associated with the SSRIs.

11. Anti-Pain Agents

Anti-pain ("analgesic") agents comprise the eleventh of the fourteen classes of psychotropic medications. For these purposes, "pain" is defined as an unpleasant sensation localized to a part of the body, often described in terms of a penetrating or tissue-destructive process and/or of a bodily or emotional reaction accompanied by anxiety and the urge to escape or terminate the feeling.[39] This broad and comprehensive definition includes both physical and emotional or psychological aspects of pain—the latter of which are often encountered in psychiatric practice—and lends itself to a distinction between acute and chronic pain. Acute pain generally resolves relatively quickly and completely, without enduring consequences. Chronic pain, by contrast, does not resolve quickly.

Anti-pain agents come from several different pharmacologic drug classes, some of which are not analgesic (painkiller) agents as such, but are so-called co-analgesic agents such as anti-depressant medications, used as adjuvant medications along with analgesics in the treatment of chronic pain. Some anti-pain agents (such as the opioids and benzodiazepines) have both dependence and addiction potential as well as the potential to aggravate, modify, or otherwise affect individuals with chronic pain who have comorbid psychiatric conditions.[40]

For classification purposes, anti-pain agents may be divided into *primary analgesics* (nonnarcotic and narcotic drugs) and *secondary analgesics*, or *co-analgesics*, examples of which are given in Table 12-16.

Table 12-16   Anti-Pain ("Analgesic") Agents

Primary Analgesics
1. Narcotic analgesics
   - Methadone
   - Meperidine (Demerol®)
   - Hydromorphone (Dilaudid®)
   - Fentanyl (Duragesic®)

2. Nonnarcotic analgesics
   - Aspirin
   - Acetaminophen (Tylenol®)

Secondary Analgesics ("Co-analgesics")
- Anti-convulsants
- Anti-depressants
- Anti-histamines
- Local anesthetics, such as lidocaine (Novocaine®)
- Nonsteroidal anti-inflammatory drugs, such as ibuprofen (Motrin®)

Anti-pain medication may be relevant in employment litigation in two respects. On the one hand, a plaintiff may be abusing pain medications, thereby

---

[39] *See* Harold L. Fields & James B. Martin, *Pain: Pathophysiology and Management, in* HARRISON'S PRINCIPLES OF INTERNAL MEDICINE 53 (Anthony S. Fauci et al. eds., 14th ed. 1998).

[40] Daniel P. Greenfield, *Psychiatric and Psychological Aspects of Chronic Pain,* 4 CNS SPECTRUMS 53, 59 (1999).

producing symptoms that might be incorrectly attributed to the workplace. On the other hand, the side effects of prescribed medications taken properly may also produce symptomatology that might be inappropriately attributed to workplace events. For example, an individual with chronic pain who is taking prescribed opioids for reasons unrelated to the pending lawsuit may complain of depression and malaise and attribute those symptoms to the workplace, whereas the opioid medications themselves may actually be producing such symptomatology. In this sense, the effects of the plaintiff's medication for pain may be a confounding factor in determining the cause of the psychiatric damages claimed by the plaintiff.

12. Anti-Panic Agents

Anti-panic agents, like other types of psychotropic medications, are drawn from other classes of medications—specifically, anti-anxiety agents, anti-depressant agents, and anti-insomnia agents. Like medications in these other classes, anti-panic agents may be associated with abuse, misuse, and adverse side effects. These in turn may complicate the clinical presentation of a plaintiff seeking emotional distress damages in litigation.

Anti-panic agents are used to treat panic disorders, which are a subset of anxiety disorders, in which the panicky symptomatology is time-limited and circumscribed and occurs in bursts. "Panic attacks" are the hallmark of these psychiatric disorders. These attacks are characterized by palpitations, pounding heart, or accelerated heart rate, sweating, trembling or shaking, sensations of shortness of breath or smothering, feeling of choking, chest pain, nausea or abdominal distress, dizziness, derealization (feelings of unreality) or depersonalization (detached from oneself), fear of losing control or going crazy, fear of dying, paresthesias (numbness or tingling sensations), and chills or hot flushes.[41]

Psychotropic medications used for panic and panic-phobic disorders consist of antidepressants (tricyclics, SSRIs, and others) and anti-anxiety agents (benzodiazepines). Of these, four presently are FDA-approved for use in treating panic disorders; these are clonazepam (Klonopin®) and alprazolam (Xanax®)—both benzodiazepines—and paroxetine (Paxil®) and sertraline (Zoloft®)—both SSRI antidepressants.

These agents, especially paroxetine (Paxil®), are increasingly being used to treat social phobia, which involves fear of social or performance situations in which the person is exposed to unfamiliar people or to possible scrutiny by others. Exposure to the feared situation almost invariably provokes anxiety, which may take the form of a situationally bound or situationally predisposed panic attack.[42] Considering the prevalence of this disorder (approximately 12 percent of the general population),[43] pharmacologic treatment of this condition

---

[41]*See* DSM-IV-TR at 432.
[42]*Id.* at 456.
[43]Joseph K. Myers, et al., *Six-Month Prevalence of Psychiatric Disorders in Three Communities: 1980-1982*, 41 ARCH. GEN. PSYCHIATRY 959 (1984).

may potentially affect a large number of individuals, including those involved in employment and other litigation.

Table 12-17 below lists the four FDA-approved medications and other off-label medications prescribed for panic and panic-phobic disorders.

Table 12-17   Anti-Panic Agents

FDA-Approved
1. Benzodiazepines (anti-anxiety agents)
   - Alprazolam (Xanax®)
   - Clonazepam (Klonopin®)

2. SSRI Antidepressants
   - Paroxetine (Paxil®)
   - Sertraline (Zoloft®)

Off-label Uses (Other antidepressants)
   - Amitriptyline (Elavil®)
   - Fluoxetine (Prozac®)
   - Imipramine (Tofranil®)
   - Phenylzine (Nardil®)

In the context of employment litigation, not only might the side effects of these medications complicate the clinical picture presented by a plaintiff in litigation, but counsel should not just assume that the fact that a plaintiff is taking medication that might ordinarily be used for treatment of depression means that the plaintiff actually suffers from depression. The multiple indications of these medications make it necessary to examine in more detail the condition being treated.

13. Anti-Psychotic Agents

Anti-psychotic agents are also known as "neuroleptics" and "major tranquilizers," although the old term "major tranquilizer" is inaccurate, since it suggests that the main effect of these medications is to sedate the patient taking them, as opposed to reducing or eliminating psychotic symptomatology. These medications are for the treatment of thought disorders or psychoses (schizophrenia, delusional disorders, paranoid disorders, etc.), the hallmark of which is symptomatology that is out of contact with reality. Such symptoms include delusions (false ideas that cannot be altered by persuasion), hallucinations (perceptual distortions in which a perception is created without a stimulus for it), agitation, paranoia, social withdrawal, occupational deterioration, and other such symptomatology. Anti-psychotic agents are among the oldest and largest single group of psychotropic medications in current use and are among the most widely used for individuals with severe psychotic symptoms.

As is generally the case in pharmacology, since the desired antipsychotic effect for all these medications is the same, the choice of a particular agent for a particular individual is based on optimizing this desired effect and minimizing the undesired effects. In that sense, and in terms of the side effect profile of these agents, this profile depends on the pharmacologic properties of the antipsychotic drug itself. These profiles of these drugs may be divided, broadly, into (1) those that tend to induce movement disorders (short-term involuntary jerky and twitching movements and motor restlessness and long-term disorders, called "tardive dyskinesia," consisting of involuntary writhing, oral, and ongoing uncontrollable movements associated with long-term use of certain antipsychotic medications); and (2) those that tend not to induce movement disorders but do tend to induce sedation, hypotension (lowered blood pressure), dry mouth and blurry vision, constipation, urinary retention, reduced libido, weight gain, retrograde ejaculation, photosensitivity, liver abnormalities and jaundice, white blood cell abnormalities, cardiotoxicity, and neuroleptic malignant syndrome, among others.

Medications in the former group of antipsychotic medications are prescribed in low-dose ranges, whereas members in the latter are prescribed in high-dose ranges; all are intended to produce the same anti-psychotic effects. The former group are called "high-potency, low-dose neuroleptics," and the latter are called "low-potency, high-dose neuroleptics."

Table 12-18 lists typical neuroleptic medications in current use, displayed by chemical (pharmacologic) type and by the dose-potency classification system.

Table 12-18 Anti-Psychotic Agents I: Traditional Medications

Drug Class	High-Potency, Low-Dose	Low-Potency, High-Dose
Phenothiazines		
- Aliphatic subclass		chlorpromazine (Thorazine®) triflupromazine (Vespril®) promazine (Sparine®)
- Piperidine subclass		thioridazine (Mellaril®) mesoridizine (Serentil®)
- Piperazine subclass	trifluoperazine (Stelazine®) fluphenazine (Prolixin®)	prochlorperazine (Compazine®)
Thioxanthines	thiothixene (Navane®)	chlorprothixene (Taractan®; no longer manufactured)
Dibenzoxapines	loxapine (Loxitane®)	
Dihydroindoles	molindone (Moban®)	
Butyrophenones	haloperidol (Haldol®) droperidol (Inapsine®)	
Diphenylperidine	pimozide (Orap®)	

Within the past ten years, a series of "atypical antipsychotics" has been developed with novel pharmacologic properties, including a low likelihood of movement disorders as undesirable effects. This subclass of medications has been developed specifically to avoid the types of side effects seen in the traditional neuroleptics, and these medications have come to be widely accepted and used in psychiatric practice, both inpatient and outpatient. The side effect profile of these drugs includes sedation, weight gain, hypotension, and such anticholinergic symptoms as dry mouth, blurry vision, urinary retention, constipation, and others.

Table 12-19 lists the atypical antipsychotic agents currently used.

Table 12-19   Anti-Psychotic Agents II: "Atypical" Anti-Psychotic Medications

- Clozapine (Clozaril®)
- Risperidone (Risperdal®)
- Olanzepine (Zyprexa®)
- Quietapine (Seroquel®)
- Ziprasidone (Geodon®)

As with all psychotropic medications, the underlying symptomatology of the psychiatric condition (in this instance, a psychotic disorder) for which these drugs are prescribed, as well as side effects from the drugs themselves, may otherwise alter the clinical condition and presentation of a party in a lawsuit for reasons unrelated to the circumstances leading to the lawsuit itself, and may thereby complicate the determination of causation of a plaintiff's emotional condition.

14. Anti-Sex Agents

Although not generally considered a distinct class of psychotropic medications, *anti-sex agents* are included as the fourteenth and last group of antis. This is because some of the medications in this class are traditional psychotropic agents and the goal of this class of agents is to influence, control, and reduce particular types of behaviors—namely sexual behaviors and paraphilias—in the sense of limiting, reducing, or even eliminating the drives associated with sexually offensive behaviors, and therefore the behaviors themselves. From the pharmacologic perspective, theories of sexually offensive behaviors have focused traditionally on the arousing role of androgens and male hormones, and more recently, on the role of CNS neurotransmitters in influencing or reducing sexual arousal and interest.[44] The translation of these theories into clinical practice

---

[44]JOHN K. CORNWELL, JOHN JACOBI, PHILIP H. WITT, & DANIEL P. GREENFIELD, REPORT TO THE GOVERNOR: NEW JERSEY SEXUALLY VIOLENT PREDATOR ACT: ANALYSIS AND RECOMMENDATIONS FOR THE TREATMENT OF SEX OFFENDERS IN NEW JERSEY 9 (1999).

has resulted in the use of two types of pharmacologic agents for sex offenders, namely (1) anti-androgenic compounds (most commonly medroxyprogesterone acetate, or Depo-Provera®, and leuprolide, or Lupron®, more commonly used for the treatment of prostate cancer); and (2) SSRI antidepressants.[45] Although none of these medications has current FDA approval for use in treating sexual disorders and paraphilias, their use in this area is not unusual among practitioners with pharmacotherapeutic orientations (especially psychiatrists) as an off-label clinical indication for these agents.

As with the other thirteen anti drugs in this classification scheme, both side effects and desired effects (e.g., amelioration of depressive symptomatology to the point of excitement, or mania) of these drugs may be mistaken for effects of past workplace experience in the context of employment litigation. Since the SSRIs, the second major type of medication used as anti-sex agents, are also widely used for other clinical indications (depressive disorders, OCD, eating disorders, and others), the employment law practitioner should know the current medications and past medication history of the plaintiff in order to assess these diagnostic possibilities.

III. Psychiatric Aspects of Nonpsychotropic Agents

Nonpsychotropic medications sometimes have psychiatric or behavioral features. Two such frequently encountered psychiatric features of nonpsychotropic agents are (1) the treatment of primary psychiatric conditions and side effects of psychotropic agents, and (2) the potential to cause psychiatric symptoms.

Common examples of nonpsychotropic drugs used to treat the side effects of psychotropic medications and psychiatric disorders are presented in Tables 12-20 and 12-21.

Table 12-20 Nonpsychotropic Agents Used To Treat Side Effects of Psychotropic Agents

Non-Psychotropic Agent Class	Example(s)	Psychotropic Agent Side Effect(s)
Anti-parkinsonian / anticholinergic agents	Benztropin (Cogentin®) Biperiden (Akineton®) Biperiden (Artane®) Amantadine (Symmetrel®)	Movement disorders (dystonias; EPS; See Table 17)

---

[45]Frederick S. Berlin, *The Paraphilias and Depo-Provera: Some Medical, Ethical, and Legal Considerations*, 17 BULL. AM. ACAD. PSYCHIATRY & L. 233 (1989). Martin P. Kafka, *Current Concepts in the Drug Treatment of Paraphilias and Paraphilia-Related Disorders*, 3 CNS DRUGS 9–21 (1995).

Beta-adrenergic blocking medications	Beta-propranolol (Inderal®); Atenolol (Tenormin®); Pindolol (Visken®); Pimozide (Orap®) (also a dopamine blockade agent)[44]	Movement disorders: - Tremors (lithium-induced) - Jitteriness (anti-depressant-induced)
Diuretics	Chlorothiazide (Diuril®); Spironolactone (Aldactone®)	Polyuria (excessive urination) (lithium-induced)
Anti-emetics (anti-nausea)	Prochlorperazine (Compazine®); Trimethobenzamide (Tigan®)	Nausea and vomiting (caused by several classes of psychotropic agents)

Table 12-21 Nonpsychotropic Medications Used to Treat Psychiatric Conditions and Signs/Symptoms of Psychiatric Disorders

Specific Agent	*Psychiatric Disorder(s) Treated*
Clonidine (Catapres®)	Opioid detoxification Movement disorders Aggressiveness Attention Deficit Hyperactivity Disorder (ADHD)
Calcium Channel Blockers: - Nifedipine (Procardia®) - Verapamil (Calan®) - Diltiazem (Cardizem®)	Tourette's Syndrome Premenstrual Syndrome Migraine headaches
Dopamine agonists: - bromocryptine(Parlodel®) - apomorphine - dopamine - Selegeline®	Parkinson's Disease Refractory depression
Thyroid hormone (Synthroid®, Cytomel®)	Refractory depression (augment anti-depressant medication)
Vitamins: - E (tocopherol) - B_6 (nicotinic acid) - Folate (folic acid)	Tardive dyskinesia Paresthesias caused by MAOIs Depression caused by oral contraceptives Psychotropic-induced folate deficiency anemia

IV. Synthesis and Summary

A comprehensive review of the desired effects (including those that are excessive) and undesired effects of all the nonpsychotropic and psychotropic medications covered in this chapter is beyond the scope of the chapter. However, the important point brought out by this discussion bears repeating: all the drugs in all the classes and categories reviewed in this chapter have side effects as well as desired effects, any or all of which are prone to be confused by plaintiffs in employment litigation with symptoms believed to have resulted from adverse workplace events. Mood disturbances, sexual inhibition and loss of libido, gastrointestinal symptomatology, vivid dreams and nightmares, irritability and dysphoria, and myriad other specific and nonspecific symptoms may be caused by the medications described in this chapter, and not necessarily by workplace events that are the subject of litigation. This is especially so when the medications are being taken currently and the workplace experiences occurred in the past.

A summary of the principal side effects of many of the medications discussed herein appears in Table 12-22.

Table 12-22 Summary of Medication Side Effects

Class of Medication	Side Effects: Examples
By Organ System Affected	
• Cardiovascular: Antihypertensives	Depression, lethargy, hopelessness, dullness, malaise, fatigue, weakness
• Gastrointestinal: Motility Agents	Cognitive disturbances, forgetfulness, irritability
• Endocrine/metabolic: Hypoglycemics Thyroid Preparations	Agitation, confusion, psychiatric-like states, excitement, irritability, anger, emotional liability
• Pulmonary: Bronchodilators	Irritability, agitation, rapid and pressured speech, fearfulness
By Disease Treated	
• Rheumatoid Diseases: Steroids	Agitation, psychosis, confusion, depression, "steroid rage"
• Neoplastic Disease (cancers): Antimetabolites	Nausea and vomiting, depression, cognitive impairment, demoralization
• Degenerative CNS Diseases: L-DOPA	Emotional lability, confusion, mania, memory disturbances
Drugs Often Abused	
• Stimulants: Cocaine, Amphetamines	Agitation, dysphoria, irritability, anger, anxiety, panicky feelings

- Depressants: Benzodiazepines, Sedative-Hypnotics — Lethargy; malaise, apathy, lack of energy, demoralization
- Hallucinogens — Psychosis, delusional ideas, bizarre presentation

Four Additional Classes
- Antiparkinsonian Medications — Agitation, confusion, depression, delirium, mania, excitement
- Anticholinergic Medications — Urinary hesitancy, confusion, blurry vision
- OTC Medications — Stimulant, depressant, and cognitive effects, depending on ingredients
- Herbal Medicines, Dietary Supplements, Vitamins — Wide range of side effects, depending on ingredients and pharmacology

The Fourteen "Antis"
- Anti-Addiction Agents — Lethargy, depression, hopelessness, excessive sleep (opioids); agitation, confusion (anti-nicotine preparations)
- Anti-Anxiety Agents — Lethargy, excessive sedation, depression, confusion; withdrawal "rage" and anger, rebound tension and anxiety
- Anti-Appetite Agents — Agitation, stimulation ("speeding"), sleeplessness, anxiety, irritability, dysphoria, mania, psychosis
- Anti-Convulsant Agents — Primary indications are for seizure disorders, *not* mood disorders or psychiatric indications
- Anti-Dementia Agents — Not prominent in employment litigation
- Anti-Depressant Agents — Agitation, confusion, mania, anxiety, excessive sedation, cognitive disturbances, nightmares
- Anti-ADHD Agents — Stimulant effects: Racing thoughts, irritability, anxiety, dysphoria, agitation, stimulation ("speeding")
- Anti-Insomnia Agents — Excessive sedation, rebound insomnia, poor concentration, dullness, depression, slowing of faculties

continued

**Table 12-22 Continued.
Summary of Medication Side Effects**

Class of Medication	Side Effects: Examples
• Anti-Manic Agents	Lethargy, malaise, irritability, cognitive impairment; agitation and mania if not well controlled
• Anti-Obsessive Agents	Same side effect profile as for Anti-Depressant Agents
• Anti-Pain Agents	Sedation, drug withdrawal, drug dependence, overdose, depression, agitation, anxiety
• Anti-Panic Agents	Same side effect profiles as for Anti-Anxiety Agents and Anti-Depressant Agents
• Anti-Psychotic Agents	Movement disorders, stiffness, dysphoria, agitation, excessive sedation, cardiac problems, blood dyscrasias
• Anti-Sex Agents	Same side effect profile as for SSRIs; hormonal and endocrine abnormalities and symptomatology

In addition, it should be borne in mind that a plaintiff's compliance with, or adherence to, his or her medication schedule is likely not to be complete (as is the case generally with patients). As a result, psychiatric symptomatology attributed presumably either to workplace experience or to current medications may, in fact, be caused by untreated or insufficiently treated preexisting psychiatric disorders or conditions.

It is essential, therefore, that the employment law practitioner be thoroughly familiar with a plaintiff's medical history, including all medications currently being taken and all medications taken during any period relevant to the litigation. Counsel should obtain as many of the plaintiff's medical records as possible—not just those of the plaintiff's current treating psychotherapist but those of current and former general practitioners, internists, gynecologists (for women), endocrinologists, surgeons, and mental health professionals.[46] These records should be carefully reviewed for prior medications that have been prescribed for the plaintiff.

To assist in the identification of such medications, Table 12-23 lists the prescription medications discussed in this chapter by generic name, and Table 12-24 lists them by brand names.

---

[46]The topic of obtaining a plaintiff's medical records is treated in more detail in Chapter 7, Preparing the Case for the Expert.

Table 12-23 Alphabetical Listing of Medications by Generic Name

Generic Name	Brand Name	Purpose
Acetaminophen	Tylenol®	Anti-pain
Alphamethyldopa	Aldomet®	Cardiovascular/anti-hypertensive
Alprazolam	Xanax®	Anti-anxiety
Amantadine	Symandine®, Symmetrel®	Anti-Parkinsonian/Anti-cholinergic
Amitriptyline + perphenazine	Triavil®, Etrafon®	Anti-depressant
Amitriptyline	Elavil®	Anti-depressant
Amitriptyline + chlordiazepoxide	Limbitrol®	Anti-depressant
Amobarbital	Amytal®	Anti-anxiety
Amoxapine	Asendin®	Anti-depressant
Amphetamine	Biphetamine®	Anti-appetite
Atenolol	Tenormin®	Cardiovascular/anti-hypertensive; beta-adrenergic blocking
Benztropin	Cogentin®	Anti-Parkinsonian/anti-cholinergic
Beta-propranolol	Inderal®	Cardiovascular/anti-hypertensive; beta-adrenergic blocking
Biperiden	Artane®, Akineton®	Anti-Parkinsonian/anti-cholinergic
Buprenorphine		Anti-addiction (opiates)
Bupropion	Wellbutrin®, Zyban®	Anti-depressant; anti-addiction (nicotine)
Buspirone	Buspar®	Anti-anxiety
Carbamazepine	Carbatrol®, Tegretol®	Anti-manic, anti-convulsant
Cephaloxin	Keflex®	Antibiotic/antiviral
Chloral hydrate	Noctec®, Aquachloral Supprettes®	Anti-insomnia
Chlordiazepoxide + amitiptyline	Limbitol®	Anti-anxiety
Chlordiazepoxide	Librium®	Anti-anxiety
Chlorothiazide	Diuril®	Diuretic
Chlorpromazine	Thorazine®	Traditional anti-psychotic
Cimetidine	Tagamet®	Gastrointestinal/histamine blocker
Citalopram	Celexa®	Anti-depressant
Clomipramine	Anafranil®	Anti-depressant

continued

Table 12-23 Continued.
Alphabetical Listing of Medications by Generic Name

Generic Name	Brand Name	Purpose
Clonazepam	Klonopin®	Anti-anxiety
Clonidine		Anti-addiction (opiates)
Clorazepate dipotassium	Tranxene®	Anti-anxiety
Clozapine	Clozaril®	Atypical anti-psychotic
Desipramine	Norpramin® and others	Anti-depressant
Dextroamphetamine	Dexedrine®	Anti-Attention Deficit Hyperactivity Disorder
Dextroamphetamine + amphetamine	Adderal®	Anti-Attention Deficit Hyperactivity Disorder
Diazepam	Valium®	Anti-anxiety
Diphenhydramine	Benadryl®	Anti-Parkinsonian, anti-anxiety
Disulfiram	Antabuse®	Anti-addiction (alcohol)
Doxepin	Sinequan® and others	Anti-depressant
Droperidol	Inapsine®	Traditional anti-psychotic
Epinephrine		Pulmonary/bronchodilator
Erythromycin		Antibiotic/antiviral
Estazolam	Prosom®	Anti-insomnia
Ethopropazine	Parsidol®	Anti-Parkinsonian
Fenfluramine (removed from the market in 1998)	Pondimin®	Anti-appetite
Fentanyl	Duragesic®	Anti-pain
Fluoxetine	Prozac®	Anti-depressant
Fluphenazine	Prolixin®	Traditional anti-psychotic
Flurazepam	Dalmane®	Anti-insomnia
Gabapentin	Neurontin®	Anti-convulsant, anti-manic
Gabitril	Tiagabine®	Anti-manic, anti-convulsant
Haloperidol	Haldol®	Traditional anti-psychotic
Hydromorphone	Dilaudid®	Anti-pain
Hydroxyzine HCl	Atarax®	Anti-anxiety
Hydroxyzine pamoate	Vistaril®	Anti-anxiety
Ibuprofen (nonsteroidal anti-inflammatory)	Motrin®	Anti-pain
Imipramine	Tofranil® and others	Anti-depressant
Isocarboxazid	Marplan®	Anti-depressant
Isoproterenol	Isuprel®	Pulmonary/bronchodilator
Lamotrigine	Lamictal®	Anti-convulsant, anti-manic
Lithium preparations	Eskalith®, Lithium Carbonate, Lithobid®	Anti-manic

Lofexidine		Anti-addiction (opiates)
Lorazepam	Ativan®	Anti-anxiety
Loxapine	Loxitane®	Traditional anti-psychotic
Maprotiline	Ludiomil®	Anti-depressant
Mazindol	Sanorex®, Mazanor®	Anti-appetite
Mecamylamine		Anti-addiction (nicotine)
Meperidine	Demerol®	Anti-pain
Mephobarbital	Mebaral®	Anti-anxiety
Meprobamate	Equanil®, Miltown®	Anti-anxiety
Mesoridzine	Serentil®	Traditional anti-psychotic
Methadone		Anti-addiction (opiates)
Methamphetamine	Desoxyn®	Anti-Attention Deficit Hyperactivity Disorder, anti-appetite
Methylphenidate	Ritalin®	Anti-Attention Deficit Hyperactivity Disorder
Metoclopramide	Reglan®	Gastrointestinal/motility agent
Mirtazapine	Remeron®	Anti-depressant
Molindone	Moban®	Traditional anti-psychotic
Naltrexone	Revia®	Anti-addiction (alcohol)
Naloxone		Anti-addiction (opiates)
Nefazodone	Serzone®	Anti-depressant
Nortriptyline	Aventyl®, Pamelor® and others	Anti-depressant
Olanzepine	Zyprexa®	Atypical anti-psychotic
Orlistat	Xenical®	Anti-appetite
Orophenarine	Banflex®, K-Flex®	Anti-Parkinsonian
Oxazepam	Serax®	Anti-anxiety
Paroxetine	Paxil®	Anti-depressant
Pemoline	Cylert®	Anti-Attention Deficit Hyperactivity Disorder
Penicillin		Antibiotic
Phendimetrazine	various brands	Anti-appetite
Phentermine	Adipex-P®, various brands	Anti-appetite
Phenylzine	Nardil®	Anti-depressant
Pimozide	Orap®	Traditional anti-psychotic
Pindolol	Visken®	Beta-adrenergic blocking
Pramipexole	Mirapex®	Anti-Parkinsonian
Prochlorperazine	Compazine®	Traditional anti-psychotic; anti-nausea
Promazine	Sparine®	Traditional anti-psychotic
Protriptyline	Vivactil® and others	Anti-depressant

continued

**Table 12-23 *Continued.*
Alphabetical Listing of Medications by Generic Name**

Generic Name	Brand Name	Purpose
Quazepam	Doral®	Anti-insomnia
Quietapine	Seroquel®	Atypical anti-psychotic
Ranitidine	Zantac®	Gastrointestinal/histamine blocker
Risperidone	Risperdal®	Atypical anti-psychotic
Ropinirole	Requip®	Anti-Parkinsonian
Selegeline	Eldepryl®	Anti-depressant
Sertraline	Zoloft®	Anti-depressant
Sibutramine	Meridia®	Anti-appetite
Spironolactone	Aldactone®	Diuretic
Temazepam	Restoril®	Anti-insomnia
Thioridazine	Mellaril®	Traditional anti-psychotic
Thiothixene	Navane®	Traditional anti-psychotic
Topiramate	Topimax®	Anti-manic, anti-convulsant
Tranylcypramine	Parnate®	Anti-depressant
Trazodone	Desyrel®	Anti-depressant
Triazolam	Halcion®	Anti-insomnia
Trifluoperazine	Stelazine®	Traditional anti-psychotic
Triflupromazine	Vespril®	Traditional anti-psychotic
Trihexylphenidyl	Artane®	Anti-Parkinsonian
Trimethobenzamide	Tigan®	Anti-nausea
Trimipramine	Surmontil® and others	Anti-depressant
Valproic acid; valproate	Depakote®, Depakene®	Anti-convulsant, anti-manic
Venlafaxine	Effexor®	Anti-depressant
Zalaplon	Sonata®	Anti-insomnia
Zidovudine	Retrovir®	Antibiotic/antiviral
Ziprasidone	Geodon®	Atypical anti-psychotic
Zolpidem	Ambien®	Anti-insomnia

Table 12-24 Alphabetical Listing of Medications by Brand Name

Brand Name	Generic Name	Purpose
Adderal®	dextroamphetamine + amphetamine	Anti-Attention Deficit Hyperactivity Disorder
Adipex-P®, various brands	phentermine	Anti-appetite
Akineton®	biperiden	Anti-Parkinsonian/Anti-cholinergic
Aldactone®	spironolactone	Diuretic

Aldomet®	alphamethyldopa	Cardiovascular/anti-hypertensive
Ambien®	zolpidem	Anti-insomnia
Amytal®	amobarbital	Anti-anxiety
Anafranil®	clomipramine	Anti-depressant
Antabuse®	disulfiram	Anti-addiction (alcohol)
Aquachloral Supprettes®	chloral hydrate	Anti-insomnia
Artane®	biperiden, trihexylphenidyl	Anti-Parkinsonian/anti-cholinergic
Asendin®	amoxapine	Anti-depressant
Atarax®	hydroxyzine HCl	Anti-anxiety
Ativan®	lorazepam	Anti-anxiety
Aventyl® and others	nortriptyline	Anti-depressant
Banflex®	orophenarine	Anti-Parkinsonian
Benadryl®	diphenhydramine	Anti-Parkinsonian, anti-anxiety
Biphetamine®	amphetamine	Anti-appetite
Buspar®	buspirone	Anti-anxiety
Carbatrol®	carbamazepine	Anti-convulsant, anti-manic
Celexa®	citalopram	Anti-depressant
Clozaril®	clozapine	Atypical anti-psychotic
Cogentin®	benztropin, benztropine mesylate	Anti-Parkinsonian/anti-cholinergic
Compazine®	prochlorperazine	Traditional anti-psychotic, anti-nausea
Cylert®	pemoline	Anti-Attention Deficit Hyperactivity Disorder
Dalmane®	flurazepam	Anti-insomnia
Demerol®	meperidine	Anti-pain
Depakene®	valproic acid; valproate	Anti-convulsant, anti-manic
Depakote®	valproic acid; valproate	Anti-convulsant, anti-manic
Desoxyn®	methamphetamine	Anti-Attention Deficit Hyperactivity Disorder, anti-appetite
Desyrel®	trazodone	Anti-depressant
Dexedrine®	dextroamphetamine	Anti-Attention Deficit Hyperactivity Disorder
Dilaudid®	hydromorphone	Anti-pain
Diuril®	chlorothiazide	Diuretic
Doral®	quazepam	Anti-insomnia
Duragesic®	fentanyl	Anti-pain
Effexor®	venlafaxine	Anti-depressant
Elavil®	amitriptyline	Anti-depressant
Eldepryl®	selegeline	Anti-depressant
Equanil®	meprobamate	Anti-anxiety

continued

Table 12-24 Continued.
Alphabetical Listing of Medications by Brand Name

Brand Name	Generic Name	Purpose
Eskalith®	lithium preparations	Anti-manic
Etrafon®	amitriptyline + perphenazine	Anti-depressant
Geodon®	ziprasidone	Atypical anti-psychotic
Halcion®	triazolam	Anti-insomnia
Haldol®	haloperidol	Traditional anti-psychotic
Inapsine®	droperidol	Traditional anti-psychotic
Inderal®	beta-propranolol	Cardiovascular/anti-hypertensive, beta-adrenergic blocking
Isuprel®	isoproterenol	Pulmonary/bronchodilator
K-Flex®	orophenarine	Anti-Parkinsonian
Keflex®	cephaloxin	Antibiotic/antiviral
Klonopin®	clonazepam	Anti-anxiety
Lamictal®	lamotrigine	Anti-manic, anti-convulsant
Librium®	chlordiazepoxide	Anti-anxiety
Limbitol®	chlordiazepoxide + amitiptyline	Anti-anxiety
Limbitrol®	amitriptyline + chlordiazepoxide	Anti-depressant
Lithium Carbonate	lithium preparations	Anti-manic
Lithobid®	lithium preparations	Anti-manic
Loxitane®	loxapine	Traditional anti-psychotic
Ludiomil®	maprotiline	Anti-depressant
Marplan®	isocarboxazid	Anti-depressant
Mazanor®	mazindol	Anti-appetite
Mebaral®	mephobarbital	Anti-anxiety
Mellaril®	thioridazine	Traditional anti-psychotic
Meridia®	sibutramine	Anti-appetite
Miltown®,	meprobamate	Anti-anxiety
Mirapex®	pramipexole	Anti-Parkinsonian
Moban®	molindone	Traditional anti-psychotic
Motrin®	ibuprofen (nonsteroidal anti-inflammatory)	Anti-pain
Nardil®	phenylzine	Anti-depressant
Navane®	thiothixene	Traditional anti-psychotic
Neurontin®	gabapentin	Anti-manic, anti-convulsant
Noctec®	chloral hydrate	Anti-insomnia
Norpramin®	desipramine	Anti-depressant
Orap®	pimozide	Traditional anti-psychotic
Pamelor® and others	nortriptyline	Anti-depressant
Parnate®	tranylcypramine	Anti-depressant

Parsidol®	ethopropazine	Anti-Parkinsonian
Paxil®	paroxetine	Anti-depressant
Pondimin®	fenfluramine (removed from the market in 1998)	Anti-appetite
Prolixin®	fluphenazine	Traditional anti-psychotic
Prosom®	estazolam	Anti-insomnia
Prozac®	fluoxetine	Anti-depressant
Reglan®	metoclopramide	Gastrointestinal/motility agent
Remeron®	mirtazapine	Anti-depressant
Requip®	ropinirole	Anti-Parkinsonian
Restoril®	temazepam	Anti-insomnia
Retrovir®	zidovudine	Antibiotic/antiviral
Revia®	naltrexone	Anti-addiction (alcohol)
Risperdal®	risperidone	Atypical anti-psychotic
Ritalin®	methylphenidate	Anti-Attention Deficit Hyperactivity Disorder
Sanorex®	mazindol	Anti-appetite
Serax®	oxazepam	Anti-anxiety
Serentil®	mesoridzine	Traditional anti-psychotic
Seroquel®	quietapine	Atypical anti-psychotic
Serzone®	nefazodone	Anti-depressant
Sinequan®	doxepin	Anti-depressant
Sonata®	zalaplon	Anti-insomnia
Sparine®	promazine	Traditional anti-psychotic
Stelazine®	trifluoperazine	Traditional anti-psychotic
Surmontil®	trimipramine	Anti-depressant
Symandine®	amantadine	Anti-Parkinsonian
Symmetrel®	amantadine	Anti-Parkinsonian/Anti-cholinergic
Tagamet®	cimetidine	Gastrointestinal/histamine blocker
Tegretol®	carbamazepine	Anti-convulsant, anti-manic
Tenormin®	atenolol	Cardiovascular/anti-hypertensive; beta-adrenergic blocking
Thorazine®	chlorpromazine	Traditional anti-psychotic
Tiagabine®	gabitril	Anti-manic, anti-convulsant
Tigan®	trimethobenzamide	Anti-nausea
Tofranil®	imipramine	Anti-depressant
Topimax®	topiramate	Anti-manic, anti-convulsant
Tranxene®	clorazepate dipotassium	Anti-anxiety
Triavil®	amitriptyline + perphenazine	Anti-depressant
Tylenol®	acetaminophen	Anti-pain
Valium®	diazepam	Anti-anxiety

continued

Table 12-24 Continued.
Alphabetical Listing of Medications by Brand Name

Brand Name	Generic Name	Purpose
Vespril®	triflupromazine	Traditional anti-psychotic
Visken®	pindolol	Beta-adrenergic blocking
Vistaril®	hydroxyzine pamoate	Anti-anxiety
Vivactil®	protriptyline	Anti-depressant
Wellbutrin®	bupropion	Anti-depressant
Xanax®	alprazolam	Anti-anxiety
Xenical®	orlistat	Anti-appetite
Zantac®	ranitidine	Gastrointestinal/histamine blocker
Zoloft®	sertraline	Anti-depressant
Zyban®	bupropion	Anti-addiction (nicotine)
Zyprexa®	olanzepine	Atypical anti-psychotic

Counsel should also inquire of the plaintiff's medication history as a part of taking a larger medical history during the plaintiff's deposition. It is insufficient, for example, for deposing counsel simply to inquire of the plaintiff whether he or she "is taking any medication that might affect today's deposition."

Table 12-25 suggests some areas of deposition inquiry concerning a plaintiff's medical history.

Table 12-25 Deposition Questions Concerning Past Medical History

- **Hospitalizations** (Give the dates, reasons for hospitalization, name of attending physicians, surgical procedures performed, if any, and results/outcome of hospitalization.)
- **Operations** (Give the dates, reasons for operations, name of attending physician, adverse outcomes.)
- **Transfusions** (List the dates, reasons, names of attending physicians, adverse outcomes.)
- **Trauma** (If any; list the motor vehicle accidents, slips and falls, and so forth; dates, treatments, results/outcome of traumas.)
- **Allergies** (List all known allergies to food, pollen, dust, pollutants and chemicals, ragweed, hay fever, medications, other known allergies, if any; indicate treatment, name of attending physicians, outcome/result of treatment, if any.)
- **Medications** (List any and all medications, including psychotropics, taken under a physician's supervision for more than two weeks; give name of treating physician for each medication.)
- **Pregnancy History** (Age of first menstruation, frequency of periods, regularity of periods, amount of bleeding during periods, pain syndromes during

periods; number of times pregnant, number of living children, number of miscarriages and/or therapeutic abortions.)
- **Substance Use** (Including drug and alcohol history, cigarette history, and other addictions; include age of first use, frequency and amount of use, treatment programs for drug and/or alcohol use, and adverse consequences of drug/alcohol use).
- **Illnesses** (List any and all illnesses that have required treatment, bed rest, hospitalizations, or a physician's care that have lasted more than two weeks; list names of all treating physicians for these illnesses.)
- **Growth and Development** (List and describe any deviations from developmental milestones, such as age of walking, talking, speaking difficulties in school, repeating of grades in school, and so forth.)
- **Family History** (List and describe any family members/blood relatives who have or have had a history of psychiatric disorder, emotional problems, or mental illnesses; include the date of onset of problems, or mental nature and duration of treatment of problems, the names of attending physicians, and the result/outcome of treatment.)
- **Personal History** (Indicate any psychiatric, alcohol/drug abuse, or related history not already described above.)
- **Employment History** (Include workers' compensation claims filed and all medical, traumatic, and exposure-related events during all jobs and positions.)
- **Criminal/Legal History** (List types and dates of charges, outcome and disposition and any charges pending, especially involving drug or alcohol use or possession, domestic violence, and sexual crimes.)

The following points should be borne in mind by the employment law practitioner in considering the role and significance of pharmacology issues in an employment lawsuit and in reviewing medical records:

1. Nonspecific responses may be seen for any active pharmacological agent in an apparently random way.
2. Be aware of the broad range of possible side effects from any active pharmacological agent, and investigate medical records carefully for a complete drug and medication history. Look for illicit drug and alcohol histories as well.
3. Be aware of the wide range of types of physicians—not just psychiatrists—who prescribe psychotropic medications.
4. Be attentive to the possible excessive, inappropriate, or illicit use of licit (prescribed) medications.
5. Pharmacology references should be available to consult. Examples are given below (Suggestions for Further Reading and Research).
6. Attention should be paid to identifying patterns of prescription of psychotropic medication before the alleged incident in question. Identify the psychotropic medications prescribed in terms of the classes presented in this chapter and consult pharmacology reference sources for further information.
7. Look for indications of change (improvement) in the plaintiff's clinical condition, and look for changes in psychotropic medication prescribing patterns over three- to six-month periods.

8. Look for the presence (or absence) of prior psychiatric history or treatment (inpatient or outpatient).
9. Look for the presence (or absence) of prior chemical dependency history, rehabilitation or treatment in reviewing medical records.
10. Be attentive to all aspects of the patient's drug history, including licit, illicit, and OTC agents.

Careful review and consideration of these points and a general awareness and knowledge of the information presented in this chapter should help the legal professional review medical records, understand potential contributing and confounding pharmacologic factors, and work productively with his or her consulting psychiatrist or psychopharmacologist.

V. Suggestions for Further Reading and Research

For most cases, the level of information and detail presented in this chapter should be sufficient for the legal professional's needs. But for some cases, additional and more specific information may be needed. For that purpose, a list of references follows that will provide the interested reader with additional information.

Jonathan E. Alpert, Jerrold G. Bernstein & Jerrold F. Rosenbaum, *Psychopharmacologic Issues in the Medical Setting*, in MASSACHUSETTS GENERAL HOSPITAL HANDBOOK OF GENERAL HOSPITAL PSYCHIATRY 249–303 (Ned H. Cassem ed., 4th ed. 1997).

AMERICAN PSYCHIATRIC ASSOCIATION, DIAGNOSTIC AND STATISTICAL MANUAL OF MENTAL DISORDERS (4th ed. text rev. 2000).

CASARETT AND DOULL'S TOXICOLOGY (Curtis Klaasen, Mary Amdur & John Doull eds., 4th ed. 1990).

DOMENIC A. CIRAULO ET AL., DRUG INTERACTIONS IN PSYCHIATRY (2d ed. 1995).

JEFFREY L. CUMMINGS & MICHAEL R. TRIMBLE, NEUROPSYCHIATRY AND BEHAVIORAL NEUROLOGY (1995).

Dominic M.H. DeBattista & Alan F. Schatzberg, *Current Psychotropic Dosing and Monitoring Guidelines*, 7 PRIMARY PSYCHIATRY 26 (2000).

Drugs for Psychiatric Disorders, 36 MEDICAL LETTER ON DRUGS AND THERAPEUTICS 89 (1994).

Drugs That Cause Psychiatric Symptoms, 35 MEDICAL LETTER ON DRUGS AND THERAPEUTICS 65 (1993).

JERROLD P. GOLDSTEIN, HANDBOOK OF DRUG THERAPY IN PSYCHIATRY (3d ed. 1995).

GOODMAN AND GILMAN'S THE PHARMACOLOGICAL BASIS OF THERAPEUTICS (Joel G. Hardman et al. eds., 9th ed. 1996).

PHILIP G. JANICAK ET AL., PRINCIPLES AND PRACTICE OF PSYCHOPHARMACOTHERAPY (2d ed. 1997).

HAROLD I. KAPLAN & BENJAMIN J. SADOCK, POCKET HANDBOOK OF PSYCHIATRIC DRUG TREATMENT (2d ed. 1996).

BERNARD KATZUNG, BASIC AND CLINICAL PHARMACOLOGY (7th ed. 1998).

THE MEDICAL LETTER, INC., THE MEDICAL LETTER HANDBOOK OF ADVERSE DRUG INTERACTIONS (1998).

Physicians' Desk Reference (56th ed. 2001).
Physicians' Desk Reference for Herbal Medicines (1998).
Physicians' Desk Reference for Nonprescription Drugs and Dietary Supplements (1999).
Physicians' Desk Reference Psychotropic Prescribing Guide (2d ed. 1999).
Prescription Drug Abuse and Dependence: How Prescription Drug Abuse Contributes to the Drug Abuse Epidemic (Daniel P. Greenfield ed., 1995).
Some Drugs That Cause Psychiatric Symptoms, 40 Medical Letter on Drugs and Therapeutics 21 (1998).
Textbook of Psychopharmacology (Alan F. Schatzberg & Charles B. Nemeroff eds., 1995).
Textbook of Pharmacology (Cedric M. Smith & Alan M. Reynard eds., 1992).

CHAPTER 13

POSTTRAUMATIC STRESS DISORDER IN EMPLOYMENT CASES

Liza H. Gold, M.D.
Robert I. Simon, M.D.

I. Introduction

The diagnosis of Posttraumatic Stress Disorder (PTSD) has had a profound influence in the law since it was first included in the third edition of the American Psychiatric Association's *Diagnostic and Statistical Manual*[1] in 1980. PTSD has been associated with litigation with such increasing frequency in the past 20 years that it has been referred to as both "a cottage industry"[2] and "a forensic minefield."[3] This diagnosis is often found in the context of employment litigation. In actions resulting from physical injury due to accident or assault, for example, a diagnosis of PTSD might seem straightforward. However, diagnoses of PTSD are also encountered in lawsuits where the nature of the injury is less tangible, such as wrongful discharge, discrimination, or sexual harassment. In the context of such litigation, a diagnosis of PTSD provides the semblance of a medically sanctioned expression of proximate cause since an external injury is by definition the explicit cause of the disorder.

The concept of a mental disorder that results from an external physical or emotional traumatic event has existed in some form for well over a century. The earliest formulations of posttraumatic emotional injuries date back over 100 years. Since that time, the medical and legal contexts in which the concept of an emotional injury following trauma has been used have had areas of overlap as well as areas of conflict. This has resulted in a certain amount of confusion for both clinicians and the legal system.

---

[1] AMERICAN PSYCHIATRIC ASSOCIATION, DIAGNOSTIC AND STATISTICAL MANUAL OF MENTAL DISORDERS (3d ed. 1980).
[2] Alan A. Stone, *Post-traumatic Stress Disorder and the Law: Critical Review of the New Frontier,* 21 BULL. AM. ACAD. PSYCHIATRY & L. 23 (1993).
[3] Landy F. Sparr & James K. Boehnlein, *Posttraumatic Stress Disorder in Tort Actions: Forensic Minefield,* 18 BULL. AM. ACAD. PSYCHIATRY & L. 283 (1990).

Paradoxically, PTSD is often overdiagnosed in situations involving litigation, and often underdiagnosed in purely clinical settings. The recently revised edition of the *Diagnostic and Statistical Manual of Mental Disorders (DSM-IV-TR)*[4] provides the current medical definition of PTSD and forms the basis of the medical context used by clinicians. The editors of *DSM-IV-TR* have recognized that the process of making any diagnosis is not necessarily straightforward and requires more than the mechanical application of *DSM-IV-TR* diagnostic criteria.[5] However, in practice, many clinicians make idiosyncratic diagnoses of PTSD, often as a result of lack of familiarity with the *DSM-IV-TR* definition and the clinical presentation of PTSD. In contrast, the lay concept of "stress," which is often used synonymously with the word "trauma," often forms the basis for the overdiagnosis of PTSD following adverse events. This has resulted in the increased presence and use of the diagnosis of PTSD in litigation.

The editors of *DSM-IV-TR* recognized that the overlap between the clinical and legal use of all psychiatric diagnoses, including PTSD, is limited. They explicitly warn against the dangers of the misuse or misunderstanding of diagnoses that "arise because of the imperfect fit between the questions of ultimate concern to the law and the information contained in a clinical diagnosis." They go on to state: "In determining whether an individual meets a specified legal standard . . . additional information is usually required beyond that contained in the *DSM-IV-TR* diagnosis."[6] This caveat was added to emphasize the fact *DSM-IV-TR* is a tool devised to assist clinicians, not the legal system, and the diagnoses described therein can be used accurately only in the context of clinical experience.

In addition, the definition of PTSD and the question of what constitutes a traumatic stressor have been the subject of much research and debate over the years. Severe emotional upset due to stress can result in the development of a number of psychological symptoms that sometimes reach the level of diagnosable mental disorders. However, emotional stress or distress not due to actual witnessed or threatened physical injury is unlikely, by itself, to result in PTSD. Certainly, exposure to true trauma such as serious accidents and violence does occur in the workplace, and it can unquestionably result in the development of PTSD in nonvulnerable individuals. Vulnerable individuals can and do develop PTSD as a result of exposure to less severe stressors. The evaluation of the events in question, the individual's psychiatric response to those events, and the variety of factors that influence that response form the crux of forensic evaluation of PTSD.

The assessment of claims of PTSD creates a number of diagnostic dilemmas for the forensic clinician. An understanding of the clinical disorder of PTSD as well as the forensic issues such a diagnosis raises is essential in such

---

[4]AMERICAN PSYCHIATRIC ASSOCIATION, DIAGNOSTIC AND STATISTICAL MANUAL OF MENTAL DISORDERS (4th ed. text rev. 2000) [hereinafter *DSM-IV-TR*].
[5]*Id.* at xxxii.
[6]*Id.* at xxiii.

evaluations. The forensic clinician must be familiar with the clinical definition of PTSD and with the research on its etiology, course, treatment, and prognosis. To provide clarification of how these matters may affect issues in employment litigation, the forensic clinician must also understand the legal questions a claim of PTSD raises. This chapter will review the clinical aspects of PTSD, suggest guidelines for a forensic evaluation of the disorder, and discuss clinical issues specific to employment litigation that arise in the course of that evaluation.

II. PTSD in the Clinical Context

An understanding of the nature of emotional distress and its relationship to PTSD is crucial to understanding the clinical description of PTSD. Most people will normally experience a certain amount of emotional distress following exposure to a traumatic stressor. The typical pattern for individuals exposed to even the most catastrophic experiences, however, typically includes at least a partial resolution of that distress. The development of PTSD as a result of a traumatic exposure, whether it occurs in individuals with preexisting vulnerabilities or in individuals with no previously recognized risk factors, is a pathological process. Only a minority of the individuals exposed to traumatic events will go on to develop PTSD, and with the passage of time the symptoms will resolve in approximately two-thirds of these cases.[7]

The symptoms do not present immediately after exposure to a traumatic event, although some may begin at that time. PTSD is a disorder that develops over time as a mechanism to cope with the distress triggered by the event. The basis of the disorder is a dysfunction of psychological and biological processes that results in the dominance, rather than diminishment, of the trauma in memory. The attempts to contain the effects of the trauma on the individual's life that characterize PTSD result in the maintenance of the traumatic memories over time rather than their psychological integration and resolution.

A. Diagnostic Criteria

DSM-IV-TR sets forth the diagnostic criteria for PTSD, which are divided into six categories (see Table 13-1). These criteria have been extensively researched and validated, and each criterion forms an integral part of the clinical presentation of PTSD. Taken together, they describe a significant and severe disorder.

Table 13-1 *DSM-IV-TR* Diagnostic Criteria for Posttraumatic Stress Disorder

A. The person has been exposed to a traumatic event in which both of the following were present:

---

[7]Ronald C. Kessler et al., *Posttraumatic Stress Disorder in the National Comorbidity Survey*, 52 ARCHIVES GEN. PSYCHIATRY 1048 (1995).

(1) the person experienced, witnessed, or was confronted with an event or events that involved actual or threatened death or serious injury, or a threat to the physical integrity of self or others.
(2) the person's response involved intense fear, helplessness, or horror.

B. The traumatic event is persistently reexperienced in one (or more) of the following ways:
   (1) recurrent and intrusive distressing recollections of the event, including images, thoughts or perceptions.
   (2) recurrent distressing dreams of the event.
   (3) acting or feeling as if the traumatic event were recurring (includes a sense of reliving the experience, illusions, hallucinations, and dissociative flashback episodes, including those that occur on awakening or when intoxicated).
   (4) intense psychological distress at exposure to internal or external cues that symbolize or resemble an aspect of the traumatic event.
   (5) physiological reactivity on exposure to internal or external cues that symbolize or resemble an aspect of the traumatic event.

C. Persistent avoidance of stimuli associated with the trauma and numbing of general responsiveness (not present before the trauma), as indicated by three (or more) of the following:
   (1) efforts to avoid thoughts, feelings or conversations associated with the trauma
   (2) efforts to avoid activities, places or people that arouse recollections of the trauma
   (3) inability to recall an important aspect of the trauma
   (4) markedly diminished interest or participation in significant activities
   (5) feeling of detachment or estrangement from others
   (6) restricted range of affect (e.g., unable to have loving feelings)
   (7) sense of a foreshortened future (e.g., does not expect to have a career, marriage, children, or a normal life span)

D. Persistent symptoms of increased arousal (not present before the trauma), as indicated by two (or more) of the following:
   (1) difficulty falling or staying asleep
   (2) irritability or outbursts of anger
   (3) difficulty concentrating
   (4) hypervigilance
   (5) exaggerated startle response

E. Duration of the disturbance is more than 1 month.

F. The disturbance causes clinically significant distress or impairment in social, occupational, or other important areas of functioning.

Acute: if duration of symptoms is less than 3 months
Chronic: if duration of symptoms is 3 months or more
With Delayed Onset: if onset of symptoms is at least 6 months after the stressor

Source: Reprinted with permission from the *Diagnostic and Statistical Manual of Mental Disorders, Fourth Edition, Text Revision,* 467–68. Copyright 2000 American Psychiatric Association.

1. Criterion A: The Traumatic Stressor

Criterion A has been the subject of much clinical and forensic debate, and it is primarily responsible for the favor this diagnosis has found among plaintiff's attorneys. It is often referred to as the "gateway criterion" for PTSD because it defines both a traumatic stressor and a traumatic stress response, that is, the external precipitating event and the individual's subjective response to that event. An individual cannot be diagnosed as having PTSD without meeting criterion A, which emphasizes the causal factor of the disorder without mentioning any predisposing characteristics or vulnerabilities in the individual. Criterion A is misinterpreted by both clinicians and the legal system more than any other aspect of PTSD. Despite the explicit parameters described in *DSM-IV-TR*, events that cause distress and events that are traumatic stressors are frequently considered one and the same.

Criterion A describes a traumatic stressor as an event in which the person experienced, witnessed, or was confronted with an event or events that involved actual or threatened death or serious injury, or a threat to the physical integrity of self or others. In addition, it specifies that the person's subjective response involved intense fear, helplessness, or horror. *DSM-IV-TR* offers examples of events that meet Criterion A, including direct traumatic events, witnessed traumatic events, and traumatic events experienced by others that are learned about by the patient (see Table 13-2). Traumatic events that are commonly acknowledged to potentially result in PTSD are all capable of inducing extreme fear and the perception of absolute helplessness.

Table 13-2 Examples of Traumatic Events That Qualify as a Criterion A Stressor Under *DSM-IV-TR*

Events which are experienced directly:
  Military combat
  Violent personal assault (sexual assault, physical attack, robbery, mugging)
  Being kidnapped
  Being taken hostage
  Terrorist attack
  Torture
  Incarceration as a prisoner of war or in a concentration camp
  Natural or manmade disasters
  Severe automobile accidents
  Being diagnosed with a life-threatening illness
Events which are witnessed:
  Observing the serious injury or unnatural death of another person due to violent assault, accident, war or disaster
  Unexpectedly witnessing a dead body or body parts
Events experienced by others that are learned about:
  Violent personal assault, serious accident, or serious injury experienced by a family member or a close friend
  Learning that one's child has a life-threatening disease.

Source: Reprinted with permission from the *Diagnostic and Statistical Manual of Mental Disorders, Fourth Edition, Text Revision*, 463–64. Copyright 2000 American Psychiatric Association.

Devastating single occurrence events such as serious accidents or violent assaults are sometimes encountered in employment litigation. In addition, non-traumatic but distressful events, such as unexpected job termination, racial or sexual discrimination or harassment, or interpersonal conflict between an employee and supervisor are often claimed to constitute a qualifying traumatic stressor. Typically, such events do not meet Criterion A. They may be associated with the development of PTSD or other psychiatric disorders for reasons other than the severity of the stress, however. These reasons include the exposed individual's psychological vulnerability or the meaning of the upsetting event to that individual. Individuals may have increased psychological vulnerability to the development of a variety of mental disorders due to previous traumatic exposure or previous psychiatric history. The development of new onset PTSD in an individual without such predisposing factors, however, can be reliably diagnosed only when an individual has been exposed to a valid traumatic stressor.

Many have argued that the *DSM*'s definition of traumatic stressors, which is based on combat, assault, or disaster experiences, does not adequately encompass the range of traumatic events that can induce PTSD. *DSM-IV-TR* did not intend its list of traumatic stressors to be exclusive, however, and it explicitly states that traumatic events are not limited to the examples given.[8] Other types of events, such as miscarriage, surgery, and poisoning, have also been associated with PTSD, as have exposures to long-term multiple traumatic events such as domestic violence or occupations that include routine, frequent exposure to trauma (e.g., paramedics or police officers). PTSD related to multiple-exposure events of either high or low intensity has never been satisfactorily differentiated from PTSD resulting from time-limited, high-intensity traumatic exposure; multiple-exposure events are not included in *DSM-IV-TR*'s descriptions of the Criterion A stressors. However, the further the traumatic event strays from acknowledged traumatic stressors, the greater the burden of demonstrating both the subjective and objective traumatic nature of the exposure. Any diagnosis of PTSD based on a reported traumatic exposure that falls outside the *DSM-IV-TR* parameters should be well supported by literature and research to avoid idiosyncratic application of the definition of a traumatic stressor.

Events alleged to be traumatic stressors that are not described in *DSM-IV-TR* often need to be evaluated in employment-related claims of PTSD. Multiple exposures to lower-intensity stressors are often alleged in employment litigation involving sexual harassment, discrimination, and various types of interpersonal conflict. Because the *DSM*'s list of traumatic stressors was not meant to be exclusive, the forensic evaluator should be able to evaluate such claims. However, the purpose of having criteria defining a traumatic stressor is to prevent the inclusion of idiosyncratic definitions of stressors as legitimate traumatic events. The forensic evaluator can assess traumatic stressors not included in the *DSM-IV-TR* list with more accuracy by dividing them into three different types.[9] These are:

---

[8]DSM-IV-TR, *supra* note 4, at 463.
[9]Alexander C. McFarlane & Giovanni De Girolamo, *The Nature of Traumatic Stressors and the Epidemiology of Posttraumatic Reactions*, in TRAUMATIC STRESS:

Type 1: Time-limited events, such as an aircraft accident or rape. This type of traumatic stressor is characterized by the unpreparedness of the victim and the high intensity of the event. These events tend to be more typical of the Criterion A stressors described in *DSM-IV-TR*.

Type 2: Sequential stressors, which in contrast to time-limited events can have a cumulative effect. These are particularly relevant for emergency service workers, such as police, firefighters, or paramedics. These are individuals who may cope with a large number of high- or low-intensity stressors on a daily basis and may ultimately develop PTSD. The precipitating traumatic exposure in these cases may not be of high intensity.

Type 3: Stressors characterized by long-lasting exposure to danger, which can evoke uncertainty and helplessness and typically involve multiple exposures. These are discussed in *DSM-IV-TR* as torture, hostage, or prisoner-of-war scenarios. However, this type of stressor is also representative of events such as childhood abuse or domestic violence. In contrast to torture or prisoner-of-war experiences, these types of social violence usually occur in the context of a significant relationship.

All three types of traumatic stressors vary within their category and across categories in multiple ways. Research has identified certain factors inherent to the stressor that must be considered in assessing its nature and the exposed individual's response. These include duration, complexity, content, qualities, and kinds and amounts of associated losses. Numerous studies have demonstrated the existence of a directly proportional dose-response relationship between stressor magnitude and subsequent risk of developing PTSD. The likelihood of developing PTSD may increase as the intensity of and physical proximity to the stressor increase. The dimensions of threat to life, severe physical harm or injury, exposure to grotesque death and loss, or the injury of a loved one are at least modestly correlated to the likelihood of developing PTSD. In addition, although the initial traumatic response is predicated on the severity of the stressor, the subsequent adaptational response can vary according to the subjective psychological meaning of the experience and the external support available rather than the precise nature of the traumatic event.

Experiencing stress and exposure to trauma can result in a variety of psychiatric symptoms and disorders. However, any event alleged to result in the development of PTSD must still meet the subjective arm of the Criterion A definition of a traumatic stressor. This standard specifies that the person's response must involve fear, helplessness, or horror. Such reactions in nonvulnerable individuals typically occur only in the event of the perception of threat to life, the perceived potential for physical violence, and the experience of extreme fear and attribution of personal helplessness. Studies have demonstrated that higher levels of perceived threat, perception of suffering, and cognitive perception of control over the situation, as well as coping styles dominated by emotional responses or denial, increase the risk of developing PTSD. Research further suggests that longer and more complex traumatic stress experiences tend to produce more severe or longer-lasting PTSD. However, without the subjective experience of fear, helplessness, or horror that may trigger the development of a pathological posttraumatic process, an individual's clinical presentation of symptoms is not likely to meet criteria for a diagnosis of PTSD.

2. Criteria B, C, and D: The Symptoms of PTSD

Unlike people who are temporarily distressed after exposure to adverse events, individuals who develop PTSD begin to organize their lives around the trauma. The persistence of intrusive and distressing recollections, rather than the direct experience of the traumatic event itself, drives the biological and psychological dimensions of PTSD. The most chronic forms of PTSD represent the failure of healing and the failure of modulation of the acute response to traumatic exposure. In the chronic forms of PTSD, the associated disability and impairments are primarily responses to the distress and disruption caused by the symptoms of the disorder rather than primary reactions to the experiences of the traumatic event.

Individuals who are unable to integrate a traumatic experience over time start developing the specific symptom patterns of *reexperiencing, avoidance*, and *hyperarousal* associated with PTSD, described by Criteria B, C, and D in the *DSM-IV-TR* definition of PTSD (see Table 13-3).

Table 13-3 The Clinical Symptoms of PTSD

Criterion B: Persistent reexperiences of the traumatic event:
    (1) Preoccupation with the trauma, including recurrent and intrusive distressing recollections, images, thoughts or perceptions
    (2) Recurrent distressing dreams
    (3) Acting or feeling as if the traumatic event were recurring, including a sense of reliving the experience, illusions, hallucinations and dissociative flashback episodes
    (4) Intense physiological and/or psychological distress at exposure to internal or external cues that remind the individual in some way of the traumatic event

Criterion C: Persistent avoidance of stimuli associated with the trauma and general numbing of emotional responsiveness:
    (1) Phobic avoidance of activities, places or people associated with the trauma
    (2) Efforts to avoid thoughts, feelings or conversations associated with the trauma
    (3) Inability to recall an important aspect of the trauma
    (4) Diminished interest or participation in significant activities
    (5) Feelings of detachment and estrangement from others
    (6) Constriction of emotional responses, such as the ability to experience pleasure or the ability to have loving feelings

continued

Table 13-3 Continued.
The Clinical Symptoms of PTSD

(7) Sense of foreshortened future
(8) Fearfulness

Criterion D: Persistent symptoms of increased arousal not present before the trauma:
(1) Difficulty falling and staying asleep, often with nightmares
(2) Irritability or outbursts of anger
(3) Difficulty concentrating
(4) Hypervigilance, fearfulness and tenseness
(5) Exaggerated startle reactions

Source: Reprinted with permission from the *Diagnostic and Statistical Manual of Mental Disorders, Fourth Edition, Text Revision,* 468. Copyright 2000 American Psychiatric Association.

Criterion B describes symptoms that can cause an individual to feel as if he or she is reexperiencing the traumatic event. To meet the diagnostic criteria for PTSD, an individual must experience at least one type of persistent reexperiencing phenomenon. For example, a claimant may have depersonalization symptoms in which he or she sees and relives a traumatic event in vivid detail, as if watching a film. Reexperiencing symptoms such as those involved in flashbacks or nightmares are recurrent, intrusive, and distressing. Merely thinking or anxiously reflecting about a traumatic event usually is not sufficient to meet reexperiencing criteria, however. Most often, individuals with PTSD find the reexperiencing of feelings associated with traumatic events, such as terror and helplessness, rather than the content of the memory itself, to cause the most pain. Generally, the more numb or dissociative the quality of the reexperiencing phenomenon described by the claimant, the more solidly it meets criterion B for PTSD.

Some reexperiencing symptoms are more resistant than others to distortion over time. Flashback symptoms tend to replay traumatic events with accuracy over long periods of time, although the intensity of the flashbacks may decrease. On the other hand, the content of recurrent nightmares typically changes over time. The intensity of the emotions associated with the trauma may persist, but within days to a few weeks after the event the content changes.[10] Reports that an individual is experiencing recurrent dreams of the traumatic events in exact detail months later through the entire sleep cycle should raise suspicions regarding the validity of the report.

Criterion C symptoms describe the phenomenon of persistent avoidance and generalized numbing associated with PTSD. A generalized numbing of responsiveness and withdrawal alternating with irritability and increased anxiety responses is the avoidance symptom most commonly observed. In contrast to the symptoms involving the reexperiencing of the trauma, symptoms of avoid-

---

[10]The exception to this is combat-related trauma, where dream content may retain accuracy of the event.

ance tend to worsen over time. Symptoms of avoidance and numbing are likely to evolve into long-term personality change if the initial psychological impact of the trauma is left untreated.[11] Criterion D symptoms are those that indicate a persistent state of arousal also characteristic of this disorder. The individual must have at least three symptoms of avoidance of stimuli associated with the trauma, and at least two symptoms of increased arousal not present before the trauma.

Overall, the symptom presentation of PTSD is characterized by a combination of *tonic* and *phasic* reexperiencing, avoidance, numbing, and hyperarousal features. Tonic symptoms or features are those that the patient manifests all or most of the time and that constitute a part of baseline mental functioning. These are most often perceived by others as changes in the individual's personality. The patient may be less interested in activities that were previously a significant part of his life and in which he took pleasure, such as hobbies or sports. He may be more withdrawn, isolated, moody, and irritable. He may actively avoid people or places that create distress, to the point of constricting his ability to function. He may also be more emotionally reactive and be prone to unprovoked bursts of anger or episodes of tearfulness. In addition, he may demonstrate more overall fearfulness, anxiety, and pessimism about the future. Tonic arousal symptoms include insomnia and hypervigilance.

Phasic features are symptoms that are intermittent. At some times, they occur quite frequently; however, there may also be long periods where such symptoms are relatively rare or absent. Phasic symptoms include nightmares, flashbacks, intrusive recollections, exaggerated startle response and physiological reactivity upon exposure to events that symbolize or resemble an aspect of the traumatic event and are evoked by an environmental event or reminder. Tonic symptoms result from the painful phasic recollections triggered by reminders of the traumatic event. Patients typically complain most often about the frequency and intensity of intrusive phasic symptoms. However, the tonic avoidance symptoms such as numbness, withdrawal, and diminished interests typically produce the most dysphoria and functional impairment. These symptoms may not be mentioned by the patient unless the evaluator specifically asks about them.[12]

3. Criteria E and F: Duration of Symptoms and Functional Impairment

Criterion E addresses the length of time symptoms must be present for a diagnosis of PTSD to be made. One month is considered the minimum time requirement. The definition of subtypes of PTSD described in the *DSM-IV-TR* is dependent on the length of time symptoms are present and the length of

---

[11] Richard G. Honig et al., *Assessing Long-Term Effects of Trauma: Diagnosed Symptoms of Avoidance and Numbing*, 156 AM. J. PSYCHIATRY 483–85 (1999).

[12] Roger K. Pitman, *Biological Findings in Posttraumatic Stress Disorder: Implications for DSM-IV-TR Classification*, in POSTTRAUMATIC STRESS DISORDER: DSM-IV AND BEYOND 173, 174 (Jonathan R. T. Davidson & Edna B. Foa eds., 1993).

time before symptom onset. On the basis of duration of symptoms, *DSM-IV-TR* describes acute PTSD, which has a duration of symptoms of less than three months. Another acknowledged subtype is PTSD with delayed onset, where symptoms first occur at least six months after the stressor. The assessment of the duration of symptoms is a significant factor in the determination of prognosis, and as such is an integral factor in the assessment of damages.

Criterion F addresses the critical issue of degree of distress or impairment. PTSD is known to be associated with significant risk of impaired functioning and diminished quality of life. However, if there is no significant distress or impairment in social, occupational, or other important areas of functioning, a diagnosis of PTSD cannot be made, even if all other criteria are met. Criterion F is another type of gatekeeper. It distinguishes between individuals who are temporarily distressed but able to recover and individuals who demonstrate objective changes in functional and relational capacity that persist over time. Besides prognosis, the degree of functional impairment is the most significant clinical issue in the legal determination of damages. As with Criterion A, objective evidence that facilitates accurate assessment is often available to support or refute claims of distress or impairment.

Scales for assessment of functional impairment are widely available and should be used in forming an opinion about degree of impairment. Both *DSM-IV-TR* and the American Medical Association's *Guide to the Evaluation of Permanent Impairment*[13] offer scales for structured assessments of functioning. *DSM-IV-TR* uses the Global Assessment of Functioning (GAF) Scale, which considers psychological, social, and occupational functioning on a hypothetical continuum of mental health and illness.[14] Instructions for the use of the GAF Scale specifically state that impairment in functioning due to other limitations, such as physical illness or environmental problems, should not be included. This scale assigns a numerical value from 1 to 100 to rate degree of functioning. Higher ratings indicate less impairment; lower ratings indicate more severe impairment. Examples are given to assist the evaluator in determining level of function for each ten-point range. This scale can be utilized to assess functioning at different points in time. Often, ratings are given for current functioning and highest functioning in the past year.

DSM-IV-TR also includes a new scale, the Social and Occupational Functioning Assessment Scale (SOFAS), which can be used specifically for the assessment of occupational functioning.[15] It differs from the GAF Scale in that it focuses exclusively on the individual's level of social and occupational functioning. In the GAF scale, the overall severity of the individual's psychological symptoms must be considered in assigning a value, whether these symptoms

---

[13] AMERICAN MEDICAL ASSOCIATION, GUIDES TO THE EVALUATION OF PERMANENT IMPAIRMENT (5th ed. 2000).
[14] DSM-IV-TR, *supra* note 4, at 32–34.
[15] *Id.* at 817–18.

impair functioning or not. In addition, other conditions, such as medical disorders, that affect functional capacity are not taken into consideration in assigning a GAF score. Unlike the GAF scale, the rating system of the SOFAS scale is not directly influenced by the overall severity of the individual's psychological symptoms; it considers only degree of functional impairment, whether related to psychiatric or medical conditions. Like the GAF scale however, the SOFAS scale retains the environmental stress exclusion, such as the stress of litigation, and can also be utilized to assess both past and present functioning.

Another set of guidelines for the assessment of functional impairment is provided in the American Medical Association's *Guide to the Evaluation of Permanent Impairment*. These have been adapted in part from Social Security Administration regulations. The AMA guidelines are based on four aspects of functional limitation and are rated on a scale of 1 through 5, with 1 indicating no impairment and 5 indicating extreme impairment that precludes useful functioning. The four aspects assessed are:

- *Activities of daily living*: activities such as self-care, personal hygiene, communication, ambulation, travel, sexual function, sleep, and social and recreational activities. Assessment is based on the number of activities restricted, and the overall degree of restriction or combination of restrictions.
- *Social functioning*: an individual's capacity to interact appropriately and communicate effectively with other individuals. Impairment may be demonstrated by a history of altercations, evictions, firings, avoidance of interpersonal relationships, or similar events and characteristics. Social functioning in work situations may involve interactions with the public, responding to persons in authority such as supervisors, or being part of a team. Assessment is based on the number of aspects of social functioning impaired, and on the overall degree of interference with a particular aspect of functioning, such as functioning in work situations or personal relationships.
- *Task completion*: the ability to sustain focused attention long enough to permit the timely completion of tasks commonly found in work settings; includes assessment of concentration, persistence, and pace. This assessment may involve both formal testing, as in a mental status examination, or psychological testing, but instructions in the use of this guideline specifically include consideration of aspects of functioning in a work rather than a testing environment.
- *Deterioration or decompensation in work or worklike settings*: an assessment of an individual's stress tolerance in a work environment. Stresses common to the work environment include attendance, decision making, scheduling, task completion, and interacting with peers and supervisors. Repeated failure to adapt to stressful circumstances may result in an exacerbation of a mental disorder, withdrawal from the workplace, and overall decompensation of the individual in other areas of functioning.[16]

---

[16]GUIDES TO THE EVALUATION OF PERMANENT IMPAIRMENT, *supra* note 13, at 361–64.

B. Epidemiology

The development of PTSD following a traumatic exposure has often been considered a normal physiological response to exposure to an abnormal stress.[17] Recent traumatic stress studies indicate that this is not the case. Recent epidemiologic studies have demonstrated that approximately 40 percent to 90 percent of adult community samples have been exposed to trauma. By contrast, PTSD has an estimated prevalence of 1 percent to 9 percent in the general population in the United States, with higher rates of 12 percent to 14 percent in women.[18] The limited prevalence of PTSD compared with the prevalence of traumatic exposure indicates that the development of PTSD is not the inevitable outcome of such events. The incidence of development of PTSD after exposure to specific types of trauma appears to depend to a large degree on the nature and severity of the traumatic event and on the individual's risk factors for developing this disorder. Higher rates of PTSD are associated with life-threatening traumatic events such as rape, assault, or motor vehicle accidents. However, with the exception of sexual assault, research indicates that even extremely traumatic events usually do not lead to the development of PTSD in more than 25 percent of the exposed population.[19]

The forensic clinician must not assume that a stressor will necessarily produce PTSD simply because it meets Criterion A parameters. Available epidemiologic data show that PTSD—and certainly chronic PTSD—is a more uncommon development following exposure to a variety of acknowledged traumatic events than previously thought. The incidence of PTSD after less-well-acknowledged traumatic stressors, such as those often alleged in employment litigation, is likely to be even lower than the rates found after exposure to more typical traumatic stressors.

1. Factors Predictive of the Development of PTSD

Whether an individual goes on to develop PTSD following exposure to a traumatic event is affected by that individual's preexisting vulnerabilities, degree of perceived threat from the event, and duration of exposure to the event. The development of PTSD following exposure to truly traumatic events, especially certain types of traumatic stressors, is a real possibility even for those without identifiable prior histories of psychiatric problems. However, the epidemiological studies indicate that certain risk factors are associated with an increased risk of the development of PTSD.[20] Factors predictive of the develop-

---

[17] Naomi Breslau, *Epidemiology of Trauma and Posttraumatic Stress Disorder*, in PSYCHOLOGICAL TRAUMA 1 (Rachel Yehuda ed., 1998).

[18] Rachel Yehuda & Cheryl M. Wong, *Etiology and Biology of Post-Traumatic Stress Disorder: Implications for Treatment*, 8 PSYCHIATRIC CLINICS OF N. AM. 109 (2001).

[19] *Id.* at 111; Naomi Breslau et al., *Traumatic Events and Posttraumatic Disorder in an Urban Population of Young Adults*, 48 ARCHIVES GEN. PSYCHIATRY 216 (1991).

[20] Yehuda & Wong, *supra* note 18, at 111.

ment of PTSD, identified through research and clinical experience, are a critical part of an evaluation and are summarized in Table 13-4. In light of the epidemiologic data indicating a typically low incidence of actual PTSD, the evaluation of the likelihood or severity of a diagnosis of PTSD in any individual who has been exposed to a traumatic stressor must include an assessment of these factors.

Table 13-4 Factors Predictive of the Development of PTSD

- Pretrauma vulnerabilities
- Magnitude of the stressor
- Preparedness for the event
- Immediate and short-term responses
- Postevent "recovery" factors

A. Pretrauma Vulnerabilities These include risk factors related to genetics, biology, life course, childhood environment, mental health, and personality. The more of these factors that are present, the greater the likelihood of developing PTSD following a traumatic exposure, even if the exposure itself was of relatively low magnitude and intensity. Pretrauma risk factors include:

- Being female[21]
- Family history of psychiatric illness, particularly major depression and anxiety
- Personal experience of and/or exposure to childhood abuse or sexual assault
- Childhood behavior disorder
- Childhood separation from parents
- Parental divorce in early childhood
- Family adversity, such as severe poverty

B. Magnitude of the Stressor The rates of development of PTSD increase with increasing magnitude and intensity of the stressor. Generic dimensions of traumatic stressors include:

- Threat to one's life and bodily integrity
- Severe harm or injury
- Receipt of intentional injury or harm
- Exposure to the grotesque
- Witnessing or learning of violence to loved ones
- Learning of exposure to a noxious agent
- Causing death or severe harm to another
- Whether the stressor was manmade or an event of nature

The risk of developing PTSD varies by type of trauma but is increasingly likely as the magnitude and intensity of the traumatic exposure increase. The highest risk is associated with some types of assaultive violence, primarily rape, sexual

---

[21]*Id.*; Breslau, *supra* note 17, at 19–20.

assault, and severe physical beating. As a class, assaultive violence can result in the development of PTSD in approximately 20 percent of individuals exposed. Rape, however, confers the highest risk as a single type of traumatic exposure, variously estimated at between 50 and 94 percent.[22] The composite class of other injury or shocking experiences is associated with a relatively low risk of PTSD, at a rate of 6.1 percent. Learning about a sudden unexpected death of a loved one confers a moderate risk of PTSD, 14.3 percent. In one community sample, about one-third of the total PTSD cases were attributable to the sudden unexpected death of a loved one.[23] The prominence of this type of trauma as a cause of PTSD in the general population reflects its high prevalence in the community. Sudden unexpected death of a loved one was by far the single most important trauma as a cause of PTSD. Other trauma types, such as rape or severe physical assault, which confer higher risks of PTSD, account for smaller proportions of the total burden of PTSD, because of their relatively rare occurrence in the general population.[24]

C. PREPAREDNESS FOR THE EVENT Adequate preparation has been demonstrated to protect individuals from the effects of stress. This factor is particularly important in the evaluation of psychological injury due to trauma in individuals whose occupations routinely include multiple exposures to trauma. Police offices or paramedics, for example, are trained and prepared for exposure to many types of trauma. This often protects them from the psychological effects of routine exposure to certain types of trauma. In an untrained individual, even a single exposure to the same type of trauma, such as witnessing the aftermath of a motor vehicle accident, might result in an extreme psychological response. Trained professionals may cope very well with "routine" trauma but may develop PTSD after exposure to an unexpected traumatic stressor for which they are unprepared. In addition, depending on the adequacy of their coping mechanisms, their threshold for developing PTSD may be lower because of the cumulative effects of multiple exposure. An exposure to a traumatic stressor that is of less intensity than those with which they routinely cope well may result in the development of PTSD if that lesser exposure is unexpected, the individual is unprepared, and his or her resiliency has been decreased over time by compromised coping with multiple traumatic exposures.

D. IMMEDIATE AND SHORT-TERM RESPONSES An individual's "peri-traumatic" responses, those that occur during and immediately after the traumatic exposure, have been found to be highly predictive of the development of PTSD. The immediate or short-term response most highly predictive of the later development of PTSD is dissociation. Dissociation is a way of organizing

---

[22]*Id.* at 17–18; Barbara O. Rothbaum et al., *A Prospective Examination of Posttraumatic Stress Disorder in Rape Victims,* 5 J. TRAUMATIC STRESS 455 (1992).

[23]Breslau, *supra* note 17, at 17–18.

[24]*Id.* at 18.

information that involves compartmentalization of experience. Individuals describe dissociative experiences with statements such as, "I felt myself leaving my body and watching what was happening as if I was floating on the ceiling or outside the window," or "I felt like I was watching characters in a movie, even though I knew it was happening to me." This defensive coping mechanism allows individuals to separate from the overwhelming physical and emotional aspects of a traumatic experience.

Dissociation is listed among the diagnostic criteria for Acute Stress Disorder, a disorder that was defined for the first time in *DSM-IV*.[25] Despite the fact that it is not listed in the diagnostic criteria for PTSD, research has consistently demonstrated that a dissociative response at the time of the trauma is more highly correlated with later development of PTSD than the effects of gender, age, and event severity.[26] Factors that have been found to be associated with the greater levels of dissociation at the time of trauma include:

Younger age
Higher levels of exposure
Greater subjective perceived threat
Poorer general psychological adjustment
Poorer identity formation
Greater external locus of control
Greater use of escape/avoidance to cope with the trauma
Greater use of emotional rather than cognitive or behavioral coping strategies

People with less work experience, more vulnerable personality structures, greater reliance on the external world for a sense of security, and greater use of maladaptive coping strategies are more vulnerable to dissociative responses. Other immediate or short-term responses that have been associated with later development of psychiatric illness, including but not limited to PTSD, are conversion reactions, severe agitation, stupor, anxiety and panic, numbing, and confusion. Studies indicate that the effects of stress are ultimately moderated more by successful coping, rather than by any particular coping strategy.

E. POSTEVENT "RECOVERY" FACTORS External support to counteract the severity and emotional effects of the trauma is the most significant postevent factor in the later development of PTSD. Initially this may take the form of tending to physical needs and assuring safety. However, once these needs are addressed, the presence or absence of emotional support addressing the intensity of and the individual's response to the trauma is critical in the psychological outcome for that individual. Extensive research supports these findings in

---

[25]AMERICAN PSYCHIATRIC ASSOCIATION, DIAGNOSTIC AND STATISTICAL MANUAL OF MENTAL DISORDERS (4th ed. 1994).
[26]Randall D. Marshall, Jonathan R.T. Davidson & Rachel Yehuda, *Pharmacotherapy in the Treatment of Posttraumatic Stress Disorder and Other Trauma-Related Syndromes*, in PSYCHOLOGICAL TRAUMA 134 (R. Yehuda ed., 1998).

victims of sexual assault. Literature relating to the clinical assessment and treatment of gender discrimination and sexual harassment also describes the impact of external support or lack thereof in later development of psychological symptoms. The lack of belief and support demonstrated by those to whom an individual appropriately turns for assistance is referred to as "second injury." Clinicians have found that the damaging psychological effects of second injury at times can be more profound than those of the initial injury itself.

2. Subthreshold PTSD

The *DSM-IV-TR* criteria for the diagnosis of PTSD have been extensively researched and validated. However, it is well documented that individuals can develop many of the symptoms of PTSD after exposure to a traumatic event without meeting the *DSM-IV-TR*'s requisite number of symptoms for a formal diagnosis of PTSD. Such individuals may be diagnosed with "subthreshold PTSD."[27] A recent large epidemiologic study found significant impairment in individuals meeting partial as well as full criteria for PTSD.[28] This condition may be particularly common the first year after a traumatic exposure but may also persist over many years. Assuming a lifetime prevalence of PTSD of 9 percent, as indicated in one epidemiological study,[29] the addition of such subthreshold cases would increase the estimated lifetime prevalence to 14–15 percent.[30]

The diagnosis of a subthreshold condition requires careful evaluation and consideration, and it must be well justified. *DSM-IV-TR* stresses that the diagnostic criteria for any disorder are meant to serve as guidelines to be informed by clinical judgment and training in the diagnosis of psychiatric illness.[31] It allows that the exercise of clinical judgment may justify giving a certain diagnosis to an individual even though the clinical presentation falls just short of meeting the full criteria for the diagnosis as long as the symptoms that are present are persistent and severe.[32] A classification system based on categories with static definitions works best when all members of a diagnostic

---

[27]Matthias Schutzwohl & Andreas Maercker, *Effects of Varying Diagnostic Criteria for Posttraumatic Stress Disorder Are Endorsing the Concept of Partial PTSD*, 12 J. TRAUMATIC STRESS 155–65 (1999); Daniel S. Weiss et al., *The Prevalence of Lifetime and Partial Posttraumatic Stress Disorder in Vietnam Theater Veterans*, 5 J. TRAUMATIC STRESS 365 (1992).

[28]Murray B. Stein et al., *Full and Partial Posttraumatic Stress Disorder: Findings From a Community Survey*, 154 AM. J. PSYCHIATRY 1114 (1997).

[29]Breslau, *supra* note 17, at 10–11.

[30]Barbara O. Rothbaum & Edna B. Foa, *Cognitive Behavioral Therapy for Posttraumatic Stress Disorder*, in TRAUMATIC STRESS: THE EFFECTS OF OVERWHELMING EXPERIENCE ON MIND, BODY AND SOCIETY 491 (Bessel A. van der Kolk, Alexander C. McFarlane & Lars Weisaeth eds., 1996).

[31]DSM-IV-TR, *supra* note 4, at xxxii.

[32]*Id.*

class are homogeneous and when there are clear boundaries between classes. *DSM-IV-TR* acknowledges that psychiatric disorders do not always meet these optimal conditions:

> There is no assumption that each category of mental disorder is a completely discrete entity with absolute boundaries dividing it from other mental disorders or from no mental disorders. There is also no assumption that all individuals described as having the same mental disorder are alike in all important ways. The clinician using the *DSM-IV* should therefore consider that individuals sharing a diagnosis are likely to be heterogeneous even in regard to the defining features of the diagnosis.[33]

Subthreshold PTSD is the type of condition to which this statement in the *DSM* refers. However, the use of a diagnosis of subthreshold PTSD should be limited to deviations in Criteria B, C, and D, which define the number and kind of symptoms associated with PTSD. For example, an individual who demonstrates only two Criterion C avoidance symptoms, rather than the requisite three, or who complains of prominent nightmares, increased arousal, heightened startle responses and poor concentration, but who demonstrates minimal avoidance behavior, may be considered to have subthreshold PTSD if he or she meets all the other criteria. Deviations from typical Criterion A stressors and Criterion F regarding degree of impairment are not appropriately the basis for a diagnosis of subthreshold PTSD.

Where subthreshold PTSD has been diagnosed, the forensic evaluator should carefully assess whether the individual meets the criteria for other *DSM* diagnoses, particularly anxiety disorder not otherwise specified (NOS) and whether these diagnoses are more appropriate and accurate. A number of the symptoms of PTSD overlap considerably with the symptoms of certain other mood and anxiety disorders. These disorders can also be influenced by external events, and many have a higher incidence following a traumatic exposure than does PTSD. In addition, they may exist comorbidly with PTSD.

Most important, *DSM-IV-TR* also warns that "lack of familiarity with *DSM-IV-TR* or excessively flexible and idiosyncratic application of *DSM-IV-TR* criteria or conventions substantially reduces its utility as a common language for communication."[34] Any assessment of PTSD, even one that concludes in a diagnosis of subthreshold PTSD, must adhere to *DSM* criteria to be credible. The further a diagnosis of subthreshold PTSD deviates from the diagnostic criteria of PTSD—particularly from Criteria A and F—the less likely it is to be accurate. A diagnosis of subthreshold PTSD cannot be made only on the basis of clinical judgment; it must be supported by research and literature, and the clinician must demonstrate that he carefully considered the *DSM* diagnostic criteria. In such cases, the claimant bears the burden of proof for establishing the validity of the PTSD diagnosis in a particular case.

---

[33]*Id.* at xxxi.
[34]*Id.*

C. PTSD and Comorbidity

PTSD has been consistently associated with an increased current and lifetime incidence of other psychiatric disorders, including depression, anxiety, and substance abuse.[35] This results in additional challenges in the assessment of a claim of PTSD. Most individuals with PTSD have at least one other psychiatric disorder in their lifetime. The lifetime prevalence of any psychiatric disorder comorbid with PTSD was six times greater in persons with PTSD than in those without. One study found that between 79 percent and 88 percent of individuals with PTSD met criteria for at least one other disorder.[36]

Comorbid disorders may arise independently from the same traumatic stressor or may be a complication of PTSD.[37] PTSD is known to increase the risk of first onset major depression and substance abuse disorders. One study of comorbidity found that PTSD was the primary (i.e., earliest onset) disorder in 30 percent to 58 percent of cases and generally preceded any comorbid affective or substance abuse disorder. The authors of that study estimated PTSD to be primary with respect to all other comorbid disorders between 29.3 percent and 51.3 percent of the time among men and between 40.8 percent and 57.6 percent of the time among women.[38] New psychiatric illnesses may result from a prolonged PTSD syndrome, perhaps reflecting the effects of a chronic illness.[39] A comorbid condition, however, may exist prior to the development of PTSD and result in an increased vulnerability to subsequent development of PTSD following a traumatic exposure. Preexisting major depression and anxiety disorders increase the vulnerability to PTSD following trauma, and they increase the risk for the development of a chronic rather than acute course.[40] An individual exposed to a traumatic event may develop any of a variety of psychiatric disorders, of which PTSD is only one, and not the most common. Table 13-5 contains a list of *DSM-IV-TR* diagnoses other than PTSD that have been found to be caused by or associated with trauma.

---

[35] Kessler et al., *supra* note 7; John E. Helzer, Lee N. Robins & Larry McEvoy, *Post-Traumatic Stress Disorder in the General Population*, 317 NEW ENG. J. MED. 1630 (1987).

[36] Breslau et al., *supra* note 19.

[37] Terence M. Keane & Jessica L. Wolfe, *Comorbidity in Posttraumatic Stress Disorder: An Analysis of Community and Clinical Studies*, 20 J. APPLIED SOC. PSYCHOL. 1776 (1990).

[38] Kessler, *supra* note 7; Avi Bleich et al., *Post-Traumatic Stress Disorder and Depression*, 170 BRIT. J. PSYCHIATRY 479 (1997).

[39] Thomas Mellman et al., *Phenomenology and Course of Psychiatric Disorders Associated with Combat-Related Posttraumatic Stress Disorder*, 149 AM. J. PSYCHIATRY 1568 (1992).

[40] Breslau, *supra* note 17; Alexander C. McFarlane & Peter Papay, *Multiple Diagnoses in Posttraumatic Stress Disorder in the Victims of a Natural Disaster*, 180 J. NERVOUS & MENTAL DISORDERS 498 (1992).

Table 13-5 *DSM-IV-TR* Diagnoses Associated with Trauma Responses

Acute Stress Disorder
Posttraumatic Stress Disorder
Major Depression
Generalized Anxiety Disorder
Substance Abuse Disorder
Adjustment Disorder
Somatization Disorder
Conversion Disorder
Dissociative disorders, including Dissociative Identity Disorder
Brief Reactive Psychosis
Simple Phobia

The most common disorders comorbid with PTSD in the general population are major depression, anxiety disorders, and substance abuse disorders. Drug and alcohol abuse or dependence is common in all posttrauma populations and may mask an underlying PTSD. The development of substance abuse problems appears to be the result of the individual's efforts to self-regulate excessive arousal and other PTSD symptoms. One study found that among treatment-seeking patients, from 60 to 80 percent suffer from alcohol or drug abuse or dependence. Opioids, alcohol, and benzodiazepines are the substances most frequently utilized.[41] Studies have also found significant comorbidity of somatization disorder, panic disorder, social phobia, and dissociative disorders.[42] Finally, dissociative disorders and antisocial, borderline, and mixed personality disorders also commonly coexist with PTSD.

The high incidence of the comorbidity of other psychiatric illnesses with PTSD raises questions regarding the increased vulnerability to PTSD and the increased likelihood of developing chronic PTSD. Alternatively, it is possible that secondary depression and other psychiatric complications might arise from a secondary pathological process caused by the distressing symptoms of PTSD. It is also possible that individuals with comorbid disorders may have preexisting vulnerabilities to the development of any psychiatric disorder, including PTSD. An increased incidence of first onset major depression and substance abuse disorders has been found in persons with PTSD but not in persons with a history of exposure to trauma alone. If this is true, then in some individuals PTSD would not be the cause of subsequent disorders but instead a marker of

---

[41]Jonathan R. T. Davidson & Bessel A. van der Kolk, *The Psychopharmacological Treatment of Posttraumatic Stress Disorder, in* TRAUMATIC STRESS: THE EFFECTS OF OVERWHELMING EXPERIENCE ON MIND, BODY AND SOCIETY 510 (Bessel A. van der Kolk, Alexander C. McFarlane & Lars Weisaeth eds., 1996).

[42]Jonathan R. T. Davidson et al., *Posttraumatic Stress Disorder in the Community: An Epidemiological Study*, 21 PSYCHOL. MED. 713 (1991).

preexisting vulnerability to psychopathology. Research data do exist that support this hypothesis.[43]

The forensic examiner must consider whether other psychiatric diagnoses exist comorbidly with a diagnosis of PTSD and identify them if they are present. A clinical assessment of the etiology and relative contribution of comorbid disorders to the claimant's presentation requires careful evaluation of symptoms and history. Many, if not most, individuals who meet the diagnostic criteria for PTSD also meet diagnostic criteria for another psychiatric disorder. Comorbid disorders can result from the development of PTSD, and the presence of a comorbid disorder clinically complicates and worsens the symptoms and prognosis of PTSD. However, comorbid disorders may also preexist and contribute to the development of a new onset PTSD. It may be difficult to distinguish whether the comorbid disorder preexisted the development of PTSD. Nevertheless, this can be significant in the litigation of claims of PTSD, particularly in arguments regarding causation and damages.

D. Course and Prognosis

1. Acute Stress Disorder

In response to research describing immediate posttraumatic symptoms, *DSM-IV-TR* defines Acute Stress Disorder (ASD) as a disorder occurring within the first four weeks following exposure to a traumatic stressor.[44] This diagnosis represents an attempt both to describe an acute traumatic syndrome and to identify those individuals who are likely to go on to develop PTSD after exposure to a traumatic event. Individuals who meet the criteria for ASD following exposure to a traumatic stressor are at higher risk for developing PTSD than individuals who do not. The diagnostic criteria for ASD are similar to those for PTSD. The notable differences are the presence of dissociative symptoms among the diagnostic criteria for ASD and the length of time involved. In ASD, symptoms occur within four weeks of the event and last from two days to four weeks. In contrast, acute PTSD is defined to be present no earlier than four weeks after traumatic exposure. After four weeks of experiencing symptoms and meeting the other *DSM-IV-TR* diagnostic criteria, the clinical diagnosis changes by definition to PTSD if the other *DSM-IV-TR* criteria for PTSD are met.

2. Chronic PTSD

Since PTSD is a disorder related to attempts to cope with the consequences of exposure, it usually develops some time after the trauma. The delay before symptoms actually develop can be as short as one week or as long as thirty years. PTSD becomes chronic by definition when the symptoms persist for more than three months. Symptoms can fluctuate over time and may be most

---

[43]Breslau, *supra* note 17.
[44]*DSM-IV-TR*, *supra* note 4, at 469.

intense during periods of stress. In general, longitudinal studies indicate that many individuals with PTSD recover or improve over time, although their symptoms do not necessarily disappear.[45] It is not unusual to find cases of PTSD where symptoms are said to have persisted for many years.

The development of a chronic PTSD is a significant factor in litigation. The presence of a chronic illness may potentially affect both prognosis and the level of functional impairment. These in turn raise issues regarding assessment of damages. The forensic clinician must therefore carefully evaluate a claim of chronic PTSD and understand the risk factors associated with its development. A checklist of factors associated with and predicting a chronic course of PTSD has been proposed.[46] Not surprisingly, some of these factors overlap with those that render an individual more vulnerable to the initial development of PTSD. The risk factors for the development of a chronic course of PTSD are summarized in Table 13-6, and are reviewed below.

Table 13-6   Factors Associated with Chronic PTSD

- Severity of PTSD stressors
- Severity of PTSD symptoms
- Current comorbidity of psychiatric and medical illnesses
- Lifetime comorbidity of psychiatric illness
- Childhood separation from a parent
- Childhood physical and/or sexual abuse
- Demographics: female sex, marital status, education level
- Concurrent life stressors
- Family history of psychiatric illness
- External support
- Treatment
- Functional impairment

1. *Severity of the traumatic exposure.* High stressor dose or severity of the stressor has been positively correlated with a higher risk of developing PTSD as well as developing chronic PTSD.
2. *Number and severity of PTSD symptoms.* People with chronic PTSD have, on average, significantly more symptoms and symptoms that are more severe than do those with acute PTSD. Dissociation during the event is correlated with long-term PTSD symptoms. Overreactivity to stimuli that symbolized the stressor and interpersonal numbing are the two specific symptoms that have been found to occur more frequently in persons with chronic versus nonchronic PTSD.
3. *Current comorbidity.* Individuals with chronic PTSD are more likely than those with acute PTSD to have comorbid psychiatric disorders and medical

---

[45]Robert I. Simon, *Chronic Posttraumatic Stress Disorder: A Review and Checklist of Factors Influencing Prognosis*, 6 HARV. REV. PSYCHIATRY 304 (1999).
[46]*Id.* at 309–10.

conditions. The comorbid psychiatric disorders most commonly found in individuals with chronic PTSD are anxiety and affective disorders, and they are often characterized by symptoms of avoidance. Drug and alcohol abuse are often found comorbidly as well.

4. *Lifetime comorbidity.* This refers to the presence of preexisting psychiatric or medical illnesses, which unlike current comorbid conditions, may not be present at the time the symptoms of PTSD are active. Lifetime rates of psychiatric disorders and medical conditions are higher among persons with chronic PTSD than among those with acute PTSD.

5. *Childhood separation and abuse.* Exposure to stress early in life increases an individual's vulnerability to mental illness due to stress later in life. Separation from a parent in childhood, for example, quadruples a person's odds for PTSD. A history of childhood physical and sexual abuse is strongly associated with the development of psychopathology and is often a forerunner of a variety of adult mental disorders, including PTSD.

6. *Demographics.* These include factors such as female sex, marital status, and education level. Women have a significantly higher lifetime prevalence of PTSD than do men and appear to be twice as likely as men to have a chronic course.[47] Among both men and women lifetime prevalence of PTSD is significantly higher among the separated, divorced, or widowed than among the currently married. Education level has been noted as a measure of an individual's coping ability by PTSD researchers. In addition, frequency of exposure to traumatic events has been found to vary inversely with educational level. Accordingly, the lifetime prevalence of PTSD significantly decreases as educational level increases.

7. *Concurrent life stressors.* All individuals face a variety of stressors at any given time in their lives. The correlation between current stressful life events and illness is well known. Current life stressors, such as marital, family, employment or financial difficulties can promote the persistence of symptoms in persons with PTSD. Involvement in litigation itself is a widely acknowledged major stressor. Litigation can stir up painful memories, flashbacks, or nightmares of the traumatic event. On the other hand, secondary gain can also be a significant factor in maintaining PTSD chronicity over an extended period of litigation.

8. *Family history.* A family history of psychiatric illness, in particular a history of antisocial behavior and anxiety, increases an individual's risk for the development of a chronic course of PTSD.

9. *Support.* The availability of external support is an important factor in the prognosis of individuals with PTSD. Both the initial onset of PTSD and the development of a chronic course is associated with lower levels of perceived and received social support.

10. *Treatment.* The effects of treatment can be a major factor in the establishment of a chronic course of illness. Appropriate treatment can be beneficial and help avoid or minimize a prolonged course of PTSD. However, when no treatment is obtained, or treatment is ineffective, improper, or harmful, an

---

[47]Breslau, *supra* note 17, at 21.

individual can suffer detrimental effects that can lead to the development of chronic PTSD.
11. *Functional impairment.* Current functional impairment is a good predictor of future impairment. Treatment and rehabilitation can significantly improve the degree of functioning. Additional stressors, such as chronic medical illness that will cause progressive deterioration in physical health, can result in a deterioration in functioning. Higher levels of functional impairment are associated with a more chronic course of illness. However, the evaluator must bear in mind that the degree of functional impairment may not parallel the severity of PTSD, and conversely, that an individual with symptoms of PTSD that do not meet full criteria for the disorder may nevertheless manifest significant functional impairment. The development of a chronic course of PTSD is a significant factor in the assessment of prognosis. However, the prognostic significance of these chronic risk factors is not known. Although they are associated with the risk of developing a chronic course of PTSD, they are not necessarily predictive of chronicity. In addition, some factors are more significant than others, both as a general rule and in specific cases.

3. Prognosis

The assessment of prognosis is a critical part of the evaluation of PTSD. The relationship between prognosis and functional impairment involves complex issues, including secondary gain, malingering, and lifestyle. When making prognostic assessments, the clinician must bear in mind that no diagnosis inherently correlates with a specific degree of functional impairment. Although PTSD is known to be associated with significant risk of impaired functioning and diminished quality of life, prognosis and degree of functional impairment are not necessarily equivalent. The degree of functional impairment is not necessarily directly proportional to the severity of PTSD, and even a poor prognosis should not be assumed to imply a specific level of functioning. The forensic clinician must be careful to separately assess prognosis and level of present and future functional impairment. Factors that are both predictive of the development of PTSD (Table 13-4) and those associated with the development of chronic PTSD (Table 13-6) must also be evaluated. The presence or severity of these factors can significantly worsen prognosis.

The assessment of prognosis must also be informed by a thorough clinical evaluation and the natural history of PTSD, as demonstrated by epidemiological data regarding the course of this disorder. A good prognosis is predicted by a rapid onset of symptoms, short duration of symptoms (less than six months), good premorbid functioning, strong social supports, and the absence of other psychiatric, medical, or substance-related disorders. Most prospective studies suggest that after a traumatic experience, many individuals show a spontaneous, gradual diminution of symptoms over months to years. One study found that the average duration of PTSD symptoms was 36 months in those who received treatment and 64 months in untreated individuals.[48] In addition, the study found

---

[48]Kessler et al., *supra* note 7.

that a rapid rate of spontaneous recovery often occurred in the first year, followed by a more gradual pattern of improvement over the next six years. An earlier study demonstrated similar findings. Although 94 percent of women met criteria for PTSD within two weeks of suffering a rape, only 47 percent continued to meet these criteria after three months.[49] As the traumatic event becomes more remote in time, the rate of recovery declines, often reaching a plateau between one and six years following the trauma.[50]

These studies suggests that improvement is common, for both chronic and acute PTSD. In general, 30 percent of patients diagnosed with PTSD recover completely, 40 percent continue to have mild symptoms, 20 percent continue to have moderate symptoms, and 10 percent remain unchanged or become worse.[51] There are, of course, many variations of this general tendency toward recovery, and each individual must be carefully assessed to determine the prognosis associated with his clinical condition. For example, at some point during recovery, an individual may no longer meet criteria for PTSD but still remain symptomatic and distressed. Individuals with chronic PTSD may experience a decrease in the intensity of intrusive PTSD symptoms and the dysfunction associated them. However, avoidance and withdrawal symptoms and the distress and dysfunction associated with them may increase over time. Such individuals may present as flattened, withdrawn, and isolative, and have at times been misdiagnosed as schizophrenic.

The most significant link between impairment and disability is an individual's motivation for recovery. An assessment of motivation is a key factor in any prognostic assessment. The best available treatment will not be effective for an individual who refuses it or who is unmotivated to participate in that treatment. Poor motivation in and of itself can be a major cause of poor functioning in some individuals. An individual's underlying character may be important in determining whether he or she is motivated to benefit from treatment and rehabilitation. Personality characteristics usually remain unchanged throughout life but are often strongly influenced by external events and psychological reactions. These in turn have a strong influence on the course of an illness. The presence of a pathological character trait and its exacerbation during a course of PTSD may be more significant than the illness in negating motivation for improved function.[52] For example, an individual who tends to be dependent may become more dependent as an illness proceeds and less motivated to take steps to ameliorate the effects of the illness.

The clinical assessment of motivation is difficult because lack of motivation may be difficult to distinguish from mental impairment. In addition, in a forensic setting, motivation for recovery may be reduced by an individual's belief that

---

[49]Rothbaum et al., *supra* note 22.

[50]Ari Shalev & Rachel Yehuda, *Longitudinal Development of Traumatic Stress Disorders, in* PSYCHOLOGICAL TRAUMA 35 (Rachel Yehuda ed., 1998).

[51]HAROLD I. KAPLAN & BENJAMIN J. SADOCK, SYNOPSIS OF PSYCHIATRY 622 (8th ed. 1998).

[52]GUIDES TO THE EVALUATION OF PERMANENT IMPAIRMENT, *supra* note 13, at 298.

maintaining a symptomatic state will benefit his litigation interests. Ultimately, making a determination regarding motivation requires clinical judgment, aided by a careful investigation of the individual's efforts, accomplishments, and functional capacities both before and after the onset of the disorder.

E. Treatment and Treatment Outcomes

Many cases of PTSD demonstrate significant improvement, with and without treatment. Treatment can have a major effect on prognosis and functional impairment. However, the effect of treatment can vary widely. Appropriate treatment can shorten the course of illness.[53] Nevertheless, in one-third of individuals diagnosed with PTSD, the disorder fails to remit regardless of treatment.[54]

The forensic evaluator must therefore assess each case in detail. Good treatment responses significantly improve prognosis. Although many cases remit over time independent of treatment, this is unlikely to be true for more severe, complicated, or chronic cases. An individual who is quite symptomatic and impaired but has not obtained treatment may be someone whose condition will improve with appropriate treatment, and thus have a good prognosis. An individual who has not responded well to appropriate treatment typically has a poorer prognosis. However, if an individual has been in treatment and has not improved or has deteriorated, the forensic evaluator should determine whether the treatment has been adequate or appropriate. Patients with PTSD often receive ineffective or inadequate treatment, which can exacerbate PTSD symptoms and can result in a chronic course of illness and permanent functional impairment. Poor treatment is a significant factor in worsening prognosis.

Effective treatment of PTSD typically requires a combination of psychotherapy and psychotropic medication. The goal of treatment in PTSD is to help patients sustain or recover the capacity to engage in satisfying relationships and to regain or maintain previous levels of functioning. Symptoms and functional impairment are often the result of a loss of control over emotional responses related to intrusive reexperiencing of the traumatic event. Treatment should enable individuals with PTSD to regain control of their responses rather than to suffer an uncontrolled and terrifying reexperiencing of the past trauma in present events and feelings. Good responses to the use of medication in combination with psychosocial treatments over several months have been described in the open-treatment literature. At present however, no systematic data exist that address such fundamental clinical issues as optimum length of treatment, long-term treatment response, relapse rates after treatment is discontinued, or clinical approaches to relapse. In addition, there are no studies that compare or combine pharmacologic and psychosocial treatments for PTSD, in spite of the fact that the two modalities are often combined in clinical practice, particularly in chronic PTSD.

---

[53]Kessler et al., *supra* note 7.
[54]Simon, *supra* note 45.

Psychotherapy is needed in many cases to address the problems associated with PTSD. Individuals often have a need to find a larger or new perspective on their traumatic experience. In addition, psychotherapy can help people address and manage the core symptoms of PTSD, ranging from intrusive thoughts and anxiety to beliefs about the self as defective and fragile and about the world as unsafe and exploitative. Cognitive behavioral therapies for PTSD have been the subject of the greatest number of empirical studies with the tightest controls. Prolonged exposure therapy is the treatment most tested in these studies and has demonstrated significant efficacy. In this form of treatment, individuals are provided with education about the disorder, breathing training, and repeated exposure to imaginal and in vivo cues which symbolize the trauma and stimulate intrusive reexperiencing and avoidance symptoms. This treatment has been demonstrated to have a success rate of about 65 percent.[55] Treatment methods such as stress inoculation training, cognitive restructuring, and cognitive processing therapy have also demonstrated positive benefits in treating PTSD. Other treatments found to be useful include hypnotherapy, psychodynamic treatment, cognitive behavioral treatments, systematic desensitization, eye movement desensitization and retraining (EMDR), cognitive therapy, and anxiety management training.[56]

Medication, however, is typically needed to stabilize the symptoms of PTSD before psychotherapy can be effectively undertaken. Trauma-focused psychotherapy can be extremely overwhelming for some patients and can interfere with their recovery.[57] Failure to stabilize the patient with medication can and often does result in the worsening of symptoms and functioning during such therapy and can contribute to the development of a chronic course of illness with significant functional impairment. Moreover, individuals who have been exposed to trauma or who have developed PTSD as a result of exposure to lower-level stressors often have other psychiatric problems besides PTSD that require treatment before specific trauma treatment can begin. These problems may include substance abuse, depression, or panic disorder, and may preclude effective treatment for PTSD unless they are treated with appropriate medication first.

There are no drugs specific to the treatment of PTSD or trauma-related disorders. Drug therapy is aimed at the reduction of PTSD symptoms and symptoms of comorbid disorders. Although the use of medication will not cure PTSD, the symptom relief that results from effective drug therapy enables patients to regain areas of functioning and to participate more effectively in other forms of therapy. Symptoms can be grouped into clusters, and medications can be selected accordingly. Symptom clusters found in PTSD and the medications used to treat symptoms of PTSD are listed in Tables 13-7 and 13-8,

---

[55]Yehuda & Wong, *supra* note 18, at 116.

[56]*Id.* at 117; Edna B. Foa & Elizabeth A. Meadows, *Psychosocial Treatments for Posttraumatic Stress Disorder*, in PSYCHOLOGICAL TRAUMA 179 (Rachel Yehuda ed., 1998).

[57]Yehuda & Wong, *supra* note 18, at 117.

respectively. For example, severe anxiety symptoms should be treated with antianxiety agents. Depressive symptoms can be treated with antidepressants.

Table 13-7 Symptom Clusters in PTSD

Intrusive symptoms, including
- flashbacks
- somatic sensations
- nightmares

Interpretation of incoming stimuli as a recurrence of the trauma
Conditioned and generalized hyperarousal, including
- loss of affect regulation
- sleep difficulties
- fear of traumatic nightmares
- anxiety
- panic attacks

Avoidance behavior
Depression and numbing
Psychotic or dissociative symptoms
Impulsive aggression against self and others

Table 13-8 Medications Used in the Treatment of PTSD

SSRI antidepressants
- fluoxetine
- paroxetine
- sertraline
- fluvoxamine

Tricyclic antidepressants
- imipramine
- amitriptyline

Atypical antidepressants
- nefazadone
- trazadone

Other serotonergic agents
- buspirone
- cyproheptadine

Benzodiazepines
- clonazepam
- alprazolam

Mood stabilizers
- valproic acid
- carbamazepine

Beta adrenergic blockers
- propanolol

Alpha adrenergic agents
- clonidine

Opioid antagonists
- naltrexone

Typical and atypical neuroleptics
- thorazine
- risperidone
- olanzapine

General guidelines for medication selection suggest that once an individual has developed PTSD, the clinician should initially select an antidepressant. Selective serotonin reuptake inhibitors (SSRIs) are currently considered the first line of medication treatment and have been reported to be very effective in reducing the symptoms of PTSD. This class of medication has come the closest to targeting the whole syndrome of PTSD and not just discrete symptom clusters. Tricyclic antidepressants (TCAs) have been found to be more helpful for hyperarousal and intrusive symptoms. A variety of other antidepressants are available, but data regarding their efficacy is limited.[58]

Typically individuals with PTSD need to utilize more than one medication, and studies have demonstrated the efficacy of using combinations of medication to obtain symptom relief. A second medication, such as an anticonvulsant, mood stabilizer, or benzodiazepine, is often introduced after a few weeks if the response to an antidepressant is only partial. The choice of a second drug should be guided by the symptom profile.[59] Mood stabilizers have some efficacy in the treatment of chronic PTSD and are frequently used in conjunction with antidepressants. Beta-blockers, alpha-adrenergic agents, opioid antagonists, and atypical neuroleptics have also been used effectively in combination pharmacotherapy.[60] In cases of chronic PTSD in which comorbid psychopathology may be prominent, these medications have been found to be effective for symptoms such as self-destructive behavior, impulsivity, and depression.

Acute trauma is best treated with any of the drugs that decrease autonomic arousal, such as benzodiazepines or clonidine. Effective use of medications at this early stage of response may prevent the development of nightmares and other intrusive symptoms. The entrenchment of these and other dysfunctional trauma responses can result in the development of chronic PTSD, an intractable, debilitating disorder. Early identification of individuals at risk for the development of chronic PTSD can facilitate appropriate treatment and management of remediable risk and associated factors, and may help to prevent chronicity in individuals with PTSD.

Treatment of factors associated with chronic PTSD such as major depression and alcohol and drug abuse may remove a stressor that can also contribute to the development of chronic PTSD. Inadequate, improper, or harmful treatment can result in the intensification and prolongation of PTSD symptom, and a chronic course of illness. Chronic PTSD is unlikely to improve without treatment. In severe cases, even appropriate medication treatment may result in only modest levels of symptom reduction and improved interpersonal and occupational functioning. A well-established legal principle holds that a litigant claiming emotional damages has a duty to try to mitigate those damages. Claimants may resist obtaining psychiatric treatment because of a fear of worsening their symptoms by talking about the traumatic event. Research has found that among individuals with Axis I psychiatric disorders, those most resistant to treatment are individuals with PTSD and substance abuse disorders. A variety of other reasons may also exist for not obtaining appropriate treatment, including concerns regarding legal strategy. Attorneys and their clients may believe that a more severe clinical presentation will support their legal claims. It is not unusual for the forensic examiner

---

[58]*Id.* at 117–18.
[59]Marshall, Davidson, & Yehuda, *supra* note 26, at 156.
[60]Yehuda & Wong, *supra* note 18, at 117–18.

to be confronted with an evaluation of an individual who has not obtained recommended treatment or who has been noncompliant with treatment recommendations.

III. The Forensic Evaluation of PTSD

The forensic evaluation and clinical evaluation of PTSD differ significantly. In a clinical evaluation, the clinician listens closely to the complaints of symptoms as well as the patient's version of events, which is considered the "narrative" truth. The patient's presence implies a desire for treatment, and so the treating psychiatrist adopts a neutral or supportive stance. The purpose of this nonjudgmental stance is to enhance the formation of a therapeutic treatment alliance, which forms the basis of the treatment relationship. The treating therapist does not initially question the patient's version of events even if he doubts their accuracy, for fear of jeopardizing the nascent therapeutic alliance. As treatment progresses over time, the patient's distortions and misperceptions of events, if any, will usually become clear and can be addressed as part of the treatment.

The forensic evaluator approaches his evaluation from a very different perspective. Although part of his or her task is also to determine diagnosis, the forensic clinician attempts to establish "historical truth." The claimant's version of events is only one piece of data to be considered. The forensic clinician, unlike the treating therapist, must gather relevant data from as many sources as possible and consider that the claimant's presentation may be driven by considerations other than those of amelioration of symptoms. Clinical and research data demonstrate that only a minority of individuals exposed to traumatic events will develop the debilitating symptoms of PTSD. Therefore, the forensic clinician cannot infer a diagnosis of PTSD on the basis an individual's exposure to a documented traumatic event. He or she must be even more cautious in the assessment of a claim of PTSD in which the criteria for a traumatic exposure are not met.

Issues of exposure, diagnosis, and disability are usually present in litigation in which PTSD is claimed by the plaintiff. In order to provide an accurate assessment of such a claim, the forensic evaluation must integrate multiple sources of information, including the claimant's report of traumatic exposure, symptoms and level of functioning, corroborating evidence gathered by the clinician's own evaluation and the reports of others, and the scientific data regarding PTSD. No formal or official guidelines for the assessment of PTSD in litigation exist. The forensic clinician, however, does follow certain procedures and relies on certain types of evidence and data to form his or her opinion. Guidelines for the forensic assessment of PTSD claims have been proposed, based on the accepted system of psychiatric diagnoses and the procedures, evidence, and data commonly used by forensic psychiatrists. This section will review these guidelines, as well as the evidence and usefulness of other data in the forensic assessment of claims of PTSD.

A. Guidelines for the Forensic Assessment of PTSD

A claim of PTSD in litigation raises questions that the forensic evaluator must address as part of his or her assessment. These questions form the basis of the forensic evaluation:

- Does the claim of PTSD meet the Axis I diagnostic criteria for this disorder?
- Is the traumatic stressor that is alleged to have caused PTSD of sufficient severity to meet the stressor severity criteria for this disorder?
- What is the pre-incident psychiatric history of the claimant?
- Is the PTSD diagnosis based exclusively on the subjective reporting of symptoms by the claimant?
- What is the claimant's current level of functional impairment?

The forensic evaluation begins by following general guidelines for forensic psychiatric evaluations. Such guidelines have been proposed, and are widely acknowledged to provide structure for forensic psychiatric evaluations.[61] Some of these principles have been incorporated into the ethical guidelines of the American Academy of Psychiatry and Law.[62] Guidelines that have been proposed for the forensic assessment of PTSD are based on the multiaxial diagnostic system. This system is the standard from of diagnostic assessment of any psychiatric condition used by all mental health professionals. The multiaxial system of diagnosis and its use are explained in detail in *DSM-IV-TR*.[63] The multiaxial system of diagnostic assessment is the clinical basis of any forensic psychiatric evaluation. The use of this system encourages a comprehensive and systematic evaluation of mental and physical disorders, psychosocial and environmental problems, and level of functioning. In addition, it provides a standardized format for organizing and communicating complicated clinical information. Failure to follow the general guidelines for forensic evaluation without reasonable grounds for departure from them raises questions regarding the integrity of the forensic evaluation.

General guidelines for forensic assessment do not address the specific issues raised by the above questions in regard to the assessment of claims of PTSD, however. The Program in Psychiatry and Law at the Georgetown University School of Medicine has developed and proposed specific guidelines for the assessment of PTSD in litigation based on these questions.[64] They are as follows:

---

[61] Robert I. Simon & Robert M. Wettstein, *Toward the Development of Guidelines for the Conduct of Forensic Psychiatric Examinations*, 25 J. AM. ACAD. PSYCHIATRY & L. 17 (1997).

[62] AMERICAN ACADEMY OF PSYCHIATRY AND LAW, ETHICAL GUIDELINES FOR THE PRACTICE OF FORENSIC PSYCHIATRY (1995), reprinted in Appendix 2.

[63] DSM-IV-TR, *supra* note 4, at 27–37.

[64] Robert I. Simon, *Toward the Development of Guidelines in the Forensic Psychiatric Examination of Posttraumatic Stress Disorder Claimants*, in POSTTRAUMATIC STRESS DISORDER IN LITIGATION: GUIDELINES FOR FORENSIC ASSESSMENT 31 (Robert I. Simon ed., 1995).

- The diagnosis of PTSD should be based on current *DSM* criteria. In general, the forensic examiner should be guided by the official diagnostic manuals, the professional literature, and current research. Idiosyncratic definitions of PTSD should not be used. If the official diagnostic criteria are not used, the burden of proof should be on the forensic examiner to provide scientific evidence for the diagnosis of PTSD.
- In assessing the sufficiency of a traumatic stressor for the diagnosis of PTSD, the forensic examiner should be guided by official diagnostic manuals, the professional literature, and current research. The possible contributions of multiple stressors to the PTSD claimant's clinical picture should be evaluated.
- A credible forensic psychiatric evaluation of a PTSD claimant requires a thorough examination of the claimant's psychiatric and medical history, including review of prior medical, psychiatric, and other pertinent records. The presence of Antisocial Personality Disorder should raise the suspicion of malingering.
- Relying solely on subjective reporting of symptoms by PTSD claimants without considering additional sources of information is insufficient. As a corollary, treater and forensic roles should not be mixed in the forensic examination of a PTSD claimant.
- Standard assessment methods should be used in evaluating the level of functional psychiatric impairment of PTSD claimants. Relying solely on clinical experience or on strictly subjective or idiosyncratic criteria in assessing psychiatric impairment should be avoided.

These guidelines provide the forensic examiner with a framework specifically for the assessment of PTSD. By following these guidelines, the forensic examiner can provide a complete and accurate assessment of the complex issues related to PTSD that arise at the interface between clinical evaluation and litigation.

B. Importance of Review of Records

An extensive review of records is essential in the assessment of PTSD claims in employment litigation. The Georgetown Guidelines emphasize the need for the review of the claimant's psychiatric and medical history, and the need to include sources of information other than the subjective reports of the claimant to provide an accurate assessment. Previous trauma history, previous or current psychiatric or medical diagnosis, previous history of interpersonal or legal difficulties, and documentation of traumatic exposure and effect on function if any, all may be revealed in documentation. Every effort should be made to provide the forensic evaluator with the most detailed documentation available in order to provide a complete evaluation of a plaintiff's claims. These records should include not only events prior to and concurrent with the alleged traumatic exposure, but any records subsequent to the time of the alleged injury as well. These are important for the evaluation of subsequent adjustment and to assess the impact of alleged retaliation against the plaintiff by the defendant.

The process of complaint, litigation, and evaluation often takes months or years. When there is documentation of ongoing psychological difficulties from the time of the alleged incident up to the time of evaluation, and the same symptoms are revealed by examination, the assessment is relatively straightforward. However, even when the plaintiff has developed PTSD, it is not unusual for the disorder to have remitted by the time of the evaluation. In such a case, the evaluation itself, including psychological testing, may provide little information regarding the occurrence or absence of psychological damage. The mental health expert may conclude on the basis of the evaluation that clinical symptoms are not present, and that the claimant is not functionally impaired or in need of treatment. Documentation of prior symptoms, treatment, and impairment is essential in such cases to establish whether a clinically significant level of psychological symptoms existed, and if so, for how long.

When possible, the documentation described in Table 13-9 should be furnished to the examiner evaluating a claim of PTSD in litigation.

Table 13-9 Documentation Requirements for the Forensic Evaluation

Employment records
Mental health records
Medical records
Depositions
Complaint and other significant legal filings
Financial records
Records from any other criminal or civil litigation
Military records
Personal records

1. *Employment records from current and previous employment.* Performance reviews, records of promotions and raises, and records of previous problems, periods of probation or employee grievances are particularly valuable to help establish the level of performance and functioning prior to the alleged incidents.
2. *Mental health records.* Records of any prior mental health treatment as well as treatment that occurred during the period in question or afterwards should be obtained.
3. *Medical records.* Many individuals experiencing psychological or emotional distress may be more aware of physical symptoms than psychological ones. They often seek treatment from their primary care physicians or other medical providers rather than from a mental health provider. Conversely, if individuals who have claimed long-standing physical stress symptoms have not sought medical treatment, this can relate to issues of credibility. Extensive medical records that contain no mention of any physical or psychological distress during or after the time in question raise doubt about the existence or severity of the alleged symptoms.
4. *Depositions of all parties.* These should be reviewed prior to the evaluation if possible. If depositions are taken after the expert performs the examination, the forensic evaluator may want to do a follow-up interview to address additional issues raised in the depositions.

5. *Legal filings.* The complaints, the response to complaints, interrogatories and answers, filings with the Equal Employment Opportunity Commission (EEOC) and/or state human rights agency, and relevant correspondence should be reviewed by the expert for additional information and consistency with the evaluation findings.
6. *Financial records.* Evidence of financial problems, such as bankruptcy, may indicate another source of significant stress or may reveal a motive for seeking a large cash award.
7. *Records from other criminal or civil litigation,* such as divorce proceedings, child custody, or other employment litigation. These records should include litigation prior and subsequent to alleged events, and can reveal a number of relevant personal, medical, and psychiatric issues.
8. *Military records, if any.* These often contain critical information regarding previous traumatic exposures and the individual's responses to them.
9. *Personal records of the plaintiff.* These may include school records, diaries, calendars, correspondence, and e-mail, and may also contain information relating to previous level of functioning, the presence of previous psychiatric history, or alternate sources of stress.

C. Testing in the Diagnosis of PTSD

Diagnostic tests specific to the assessment of PTSD are not available. However, certain types of psychological and physiological testing can be of use in the assessment of claims of PTSD, depending on the circumstances of the case. A forensic evaluator may suggest that such testing be obtained to clarify or support the diagnosis of either a major psychiatric illness, such as PTSD or depression, or the diagnosis of a personality disorder or malingering.

1. Physiological Testing

Various psychophysiologic tests have focused on the heightened reactivity of individuals with PTSD to trauma-related stimuli. Studies have examined the exaggerated startle responses found in PTSD through the measurement of eye blinking, electromyography, heart rate, and skin conductance responses to intense auditory stimuli. Such tests have typically found increased responsiveness in these physiologic measurements in individuals with PTSD. In one study, psychophysiologic testing correctly diagnosed 61–88 percent of previously identified PTSD subjects and correctly identified 79–100 percent of non-PTSD subjects.[65] However, another study found that 25 percent of previously identified

---

[65]Roger K. Pitman & Scott P. Orr, *Psychophysiologic Testing for Post-Traumatic Stress Disorder: Forensic Psychiatric Application*, 21 BULL. AM. ACAD. PSYCHIATRY & L. 37 (1993).

non-PTSD subjects who were asked to simulate the physiologic responses of PTSD were able to do so.[66] Other forms of psychophysiologic testing that are being investigated include acoustic startle response, neuroendocrine alterations, and neuroimaging.[67]

Psychophysiological testing may confirm the physiologic reactivity criteria of PTSD, thus adding an objective dimension to this diagnosis. However, the fact that up to 25 percent of individuals may be able to simulate PTSD responses raises doubts about the value of positive test results. In addition, when evidence clearly points to a diagnosis of PTSD but test results are inconclusive or negative, the validity of these results becomes even less clear. Although psychophysiological testing can support the presence of some symptoms, no one test is currently available that can conclusively diagnose PTSD. Psychophysiological testing has been used in court to prove that a specific trauma precipitated or caused PTSD. Some experts believe that psychophysiological testing as a means of assessing the physiologic reactivity criteria of PTSD is supported by much peer-reviewed research.[68] However, questions concerning the admissibility of psychophysiological testing as evidence in civil cases have arisen. Despite its scientific usefulness and the intriguing possibilities of finding an objective measurement to confirm a diagnosis of PTSD, the usefulness in of psychophysiological testing in litigation may be limited.

2. Psychological Testing

In contrast to psychophysiological testing, psychological testing has an established value in the diagnostic assessment of PTSD and other psychiatric disorders. A psychological test is a standardized and objective measure of a sample of verbal or nonverbal behavior. Standardization ensures that procedures for collecting, recording, organizing, and synthesizing information are held constant. The overall performance of a psychological test is evaluated by applying the concepts of reliability and validity. Reliability refers to the consistency of test scores, that is, the extent to which they are free of measurement error. Validity is the extent to which a test measures what it purports to measure.

---

[66]Scott P. Orr & Danny G. Kaloupek, *Psychophysiological Assessment of Posttraumatic Stress Disorder*, in ASSESSING PSYCHOLOGICAL TRAUMA AND PTSD 69 (John P. Wilson & Terence M. Keane eds., 1997).

[67]Charles A. Morgan & Christian Grillon, *Acoustic Startle in Individuals with Posttraumatic Stress Disorder*, 28 PSYCH. ANNALS 430 (1998); Steven M. Southwick, Rachel Yehuda, & Shiela Wang, *Neuroendocrine Alterations in Posttraumatic Stress Disorder*, 28 PSYCH. ANNALS 436 (1998); J. Douglas Bremner, *Neuroimaging of Posttraumatic Stress Disorder*, 28 PSYCH. ANNALS 445 (1998).

[68]Pitman & Orr, *supra* note 65; CHESTER B. SCRIGNAR, POSTTRAUMATIC STRESS DISORDER: DIAGNOSIS, TREATMENT AND LEGAL ISSUES 186 (3d ed.1996).

Certain psychological tests measure personality traits and characteristics that are often of significance in evaluating claims of emotional injury in employment litigation. The nature and severity of the plaintiff's mental condition, the plaintiff's capacity for adaptive functioning, and the credibility of information supplied by the plaintiff may be able to be assessed by such testing. Psychological test data may provide objective evidence in the formulation of a diagnostic assessment, particularly when the forensic evaluator suspects the presence of a personality disorder or malingering. Test results alone cannot produce a complete and accurate assessment. However, the integration of test results, interview findings, and document review can lead to a forensic assessment of an individual's symptoms, personality, and coping styles that is supported by the objective data provided by testing. Psychological testing is of the most use in cases where diagnostic issues of personality disorders and malingering are considered.

As with any type of scientific testing, psychological testing has certain weaknesses. The tests are typically designed to evaluate an individual's general psychological responses rather than specific disorders such as PTSD. In addition, regardless of the disorder in question, a respondent may have difficulty with a particular test format, may experience fatigue or attention difficulties at one testing occasion, or may demonstrate response bias on a particular test. Another weakness of such testing lies in the fact that various assessment formats have different relative strengths. An interviewer format may be influenced by how the interviewer asks questions, and tests based on self-report rely on purely subjective perceptions.

Personality inventories, projective techniques, and tests of intellectual and cognitive functioning are the three major types of psychological tests with potential relevance to employment litigation. Personality inventories are standardized measures of psychological symptoms and personality traits in normal and pathological personalities assessed through subject self-report. They are often called "objective personality tests" because clinical judgment plays no role in their administration or scoring. The results are interpreted according to preestablished standards and therefore have limited susceptibility to examiner bias. In addition, personality inventories often use validity scales to address one of the most significant problems in data collected by self-report: bias in how individuals present themselves. The use of such validity scales thus increases the value of these tests.

The second edition of the Minnesota Multiphasic Personality Inventory (MMPI-2) is the personality inventory most widely used in forensic contexts. In the context of employment litigation, an MMPI-2 can illuminate certain personality features of a litigant that either may have contributed to the events in the workplace that are the focus of litigation or may demonstrate preexisting vulnerabilities that influence the degree of damages. It is most useful in identifying subjects who are malingering or exaggerating their symptoms. Features of these problems might not have been immediately apparent or demonstrable in the interview, or the litigant may have attempted to deny or rationalize them. The MMPI-2 has been problematic in the specific assessment of PTSD, as individuals with clinically diagnosed PTSD in nonforensic settings typically demonstrate profiles consistent with exaggeration of symptoms or a wide variety of other disorders, including anxiety, psychosis, and depression. A profile suggestive of PTSD has been developed.[69] However, no specific MMPI-2 profile exists for the definitive assessment of PTSD.

Projective techniques are designed to assess personality under relatively constant conditions without relying on self-report. The Rorschach Ink Blot Test is the most standardized and validated of the projective techniques.[70] The comprehensive system developed by John Exner for administering, scoring, and interpreting data is generally accepted as the system having the greatest reliability, normative data, and validity. The Rorschach can compensate for some of the limitations of a self report format such as the MMPI-2, where subjects may attempt to manage the impression of themselves by answering questions based on their understanding of how the responses will be evaluated.

Rorschach tests can provide standardized information on psychological functions about which individuals may be unable to report, such as illogical thought process, oversimplified perceptions, or grossly misperceived stimuli. This can be useful in elucidating paranoid thinking or psychotic thought processes. Rorschach testing can also reveal an individual's stress tolerance and capacity for controlled implementation of coping efforts, characteristic thought patterns, perceptual accuracy, self-image, and concepts of interpersonal relationships.

Cognitive testing to assess overall intellectual ability and specific cognitive functions can also have several potential uses in evaluating claims of emotional injury. Cognitive complaints differ from most other functional complaints in that they are more accurately measured through performance tests than through self-report. Cognitive tests provide well-standardized and objective information about the presence of symptoms such as impairment in memory and concentration, which frequently form part of the diagnostic criteria for Axis I psychiatric disorders.

Cognitive tests also provide an opportunity to observe problem-solving behavior that correlates with occupational and social effectiveness. This can provide information about the individual's future capacity for adaptive functioning that might affect the determination of damages. Assessment of cognitive functions such as memory and concentration are an essential aspect of the evaluation of a claim of disability based on emotional symptoms. Difficulties with concentration and memory are frequently reported in claims of emotional and psychological injury, but such self-reported complaints of cognitive dysfunction are often overestimated. Valid objective evidence of such cognitive symptoms can affect how subjective cognitive complaints are weighted. Cognitive test evidence of adequate concentration in an individual who reports poor concentration will likely have a mitigating effect on how the subjective com-

---

[69]John P. Wilson & Alison J. Walker, *Toward an MMPI Trauma Profile*, 3 J. TRAUMATIC STRESS 151 (1990).

[70]Patti Levin & Bruce Reis, *Use of the Rorshach in Assessing Trauma*, in ASSESSING PSYCHOLOGICAL TRAUMA AND PTSD 529 (John P. Wilson & Terence M. Keane eds., 1997).

plaint is viewed by the trier of fact. By contrast valid observations of impaired concentration tend to enhance the impact of a subjective complaint.

The Wechsler Adult Intelligence Scale-Revised (WAIS-R) is the cognitive test best standardized and most widely used in clinical practice.[71] This test measures intelligence as well as the consistency and efficiency of an individual's cognitive functioning. The WAIS-R can measure a variety of cognitive functions and detect relative strengths and weaknesses. One weakness of the WAIS-R, however, is that anxiety and depression often affect measures of attention, concentration, memory, and speed and efficiency of psychomotor functioning in a testing situation. Thus a person with such a disorder may demonstrate more impaired function than he is experiencing as a result of the interference of his symptoms with his test-taking ability.

Psychological testing can be particularly helpful in the detection of malingering or exaggerating traumatic reactions to stress. Personality inventories with validity scales identify subjects who may be malingering by identifying individuals who report overall levels of symptoms that appear unrealistic and excessive. In general, exaggerating individuals have higher elevations on validity scales than truly disturbed individuals. The MMPI-2's malingering indexes have excellent sensitivity to dissimulation. In the Rorshach, the most important variables of the test are much less susceptible than self-report to impression-management strategies, and they can also identify those individuals who are subjectively reporting disturbances that cannot be validated by their test responses. Intelligence tests can provide a behavioral record of efforts to feign impairment of cognitive function.

D. Bias and the Misdiagnosis of PTSD

The diagnosis of PTSD may sometimes be the subject of manipulation in litigation. Indeed, PTSD is a diagnosis that lends itself well to litigation. Unlike other *DSM* diagnoses, PTSD contains within its criteria the causative trauma. This results in the appearance of a straightforward relationship between a cause and an effect that is typically welcomed by plaintiff's attorneys. However, lawyers cannot introduce a PTSD diagnosis into evidence except through the testimony of a clinical expert. The misdiagnosis of PTSD by clinicians is in part responsible for the appearance of its abuse and the skeptical response it receives when it arises in litigation. PTSD is frequently misdiagnosed: overdiagnosis often occurs in cases involving litigation, and underdiagnosis in purely clinical situations is common.[72]

An inspection of the frequency of misdiagnosis must focus on the clinicians making the diagnostic evaluation. Misapplication of the diagnosis of PTSD

---

[71]Kaplan & Sadock, *supra* note 51, at 194.

[72]Roger K. Pitman et al., *Legal Issues in Posttraumatic Stress Disorder, in* TRAUMATIC STRESS: THE EFFECTS OF OVERWHELMING EXPERIENCE ON MIND, BODY AND SOCIETY 393 (Bessel A. van der Kolk, Alexander C. McFarlane & Lars Weisaeth eds., 1996).

may result from lack of knowledge and expertise. The underdiagnosis of PTSD may result from:

- Characterization of PTSD symptoms as merely understandable, normal reactions to the traumatic event
- Basing opinion on superficial, open-ended interviews, without an adequate attempt to explore details of the traumatic event and subsequent symptomatology
- Idiosyncratic thresholds for diagnosis
- Failure to acknowledge that the diagnosis of PTSD may be made despite the presence of major vulnerability factors
- Mistaking predisposition for preexisting psychopathology
- False attribution of the evaluee's symptoms to other life events
- Espousal of narrow or outdated theories of etiology that may play on popular prejudices (e.g., "All mental illness results from early childhood experiences" or "All mental illness is inherited")
- Failure to consider relevant, supportive PTSD literature
- Absence of PTSD symptoms at the time of evaluation due to the phasic nature of the illness
- Denial of symptoms by the individual due to avoidance, shame, or the fear of stigmatization associated with the diagnosis of a mental illness

Overdiagnosis of PTSD, however, is more common in cases involving litigation. Some psychiatrists erroneously believe that any psychiatric disturbance that occurs after a stressful experience qualifies as PTSD, applying a type of *post hoc, ergo propter hoc* reasoning. The overdiagnosis of PTSD in contexts of litigation was demonstrated by a study of a boating disaster in which a number of people died. Of the 22 survivors, 20 brought suits against their employer. Eighty-six percent of the survivors were diagnosed with PTSD by either treating clinicians or clinicians retained to perform forensic evaluations. In contrast, the defense evaluator found that only 26 percent of the survivors involved in the litigation had firm or provisional diagnoses of PTSD.[73] Epidemiological studies have revealed that no traumatic exposure results in this high an incidence of PTSD except in cases of severe sexual assault. This indicates a significant overdiagnosis of PTSD. The defense evaluator's findings are in agreement with epidemiological estimates of approximately 25 percent incidence of PTSD following traumatic exposure, and are likely to be a more realistic figure.

The overdiagnosis of PTSD can arise from:

- Failure to separate nonpathological emotional distress following an adverse event from a mental disorder
- Application of fewer criteria than are required to meet the *DSM-IV-TR* diagnostic definition

---

[73]Gerald M. Rosen, *The Aleutian Enterprise Sinking and PTSD: Misdiagnosis in Clinical and Forensic Settings*, 26 PROF. PSYCHOLOGY: RES. & PRAC. 82 (1995).

- Failure to consider the contribution of earlier, unrelated traumatic events to the subject's illness, resulting in the false attribution of current pathology to the traumatic event being litigated
- Failure to diagnose preexisting psychopathology
- Failure to identify a positive family history of mental disorder that may point to another etiology
- Failure to consider a differential diagnosis[74]

In addition to lack of experience and familiarity with PTSD, the clinician's own biases may play a major role in the misdiagnosis of PTSD. The ethical guidelines of the American Academy of Psychiatry and Law (AAPL) acknowledge the existence of bias in any human endeavor.[75] These guidelines direct forensic psychiatrists to address such biases and strive for honesty and objectivity in the course of all forensic evaluations. Some of the biases found in the evaluation of PTSD are common to all forensic evaluations, such as advocacy bias and bias due to the double role of treating clinician and forensic examiner. Other biases are particular to the social and political issues that the diagnosis of PTSD and its use in litigation raise.

The effects of advocacy bias in the misdiagnosis of PTSD were demonstrated in a study comparing the diagnostic conclusions of plaintiff's and defense experts in regard to sexual harassment cases.[76] The diagnosis of PTSD was predominantly used by plaintiff's experts or treating clinicians. In the same cases, experts retained by the defense typically made other diagnoses, including a significant number of personality disorder diagnoses. The study found little to no overlap between plaintiff's experts' diagnoses of PTSD and defense experts' diagnoses of personality disorder in the same cases. In instances where a defense expert diagnosed a personality disorder, the plaintiff's expert did not, and where the plaintiff's expert diagnosed PTSD, the defense expert did not.

Such a wide discrepancy between experts' findings are the result of a number of factors. Nevertheless, this study demonstrates that the side that retains the expert often has a significant influence in the development of the expert's conclusions. This influence is termed advocacy bias. Legal ethics require that an attorney be a passionate advocate for his or her client's position. However, a forensic evaluator is ethically bound to attempt to provide a neutral and objective evaluation. It is not uncommon for this objectivity to give way to the conscious or unconscious pressures of advocacy bias, in which the forensic evaluator renders an opinion most favorable to the side that retains him or her.

Advocacy bias can be further compounded when the treating clinician is retained as the forensic evaluator, typically by the plaintiff's attorney. The fourth of the Georgetown Guidelines for the assessment of PTSD claims contains a corollary statement advising that the two roles of forensic evaluator and

---

[74]Pitman et al., *supra* note 72, at 393.

[75]See Appendix 2.

[76]Barbara L. Long, *Psychiatric Diagnoses in Sexual Harassment Cases*, 22 BULL. AM. ACAD. PSYCHIATRY & LAW 195 (1994).

treating clinician not be assumed by the same individual. This recommendation results from the observation and experience that these two roles are not compatible with each other. The assumption of both by one individual inevitably results in compromising the psychiatrist's capacity to fulfill either role effectively.[77] In fact, the conflict between these two roles is the reason that attorneys often find treating clinicians unwilling to be drawn into a role in their patient's litigation, even as a fact witness. The methods, forms of alliance, type of assessments, interpretations of data, and ethics of the forensic evaluator and the treating clinician differ significantly. Treating clinicians are necessarily biased in favor of their patients, rely only their patients' subjective reports to formulate their opinions, and often do not systematically assess other factors involved in the patients' presentation or level of functional impairment. Treating clinicians who offer expert forensic opinions often find their testimony discredited by the opposing side as a result of these factors.

Finally, bias may also arise specifically around the PTSD diagnosis and its use in litigation. Sympathy with, or antipathy toward, the "sociopolitical ideology of victimization"[78] can result in the misdiagnosis of PTSD. A misapplied PTSD diagnosis at times represents a vehicle for what one commentator has termed "bootlegging humanistic values through psychiatry."[79] A bias toward a "victims' rights" ideology can result in the application of PTSD as a way of compensating an individual who may have suffered some adverse event for which the evaluator feels he or she should be compensated. Conversely, an expert's negative feelings regarding the victims' rights ideology can result in the reluctance to use this diagnosis even when clinically indicated. The diagnosis of PTSD should not be made in order to facilitate or thwart a legal, social, or political agenda.

The forensic evaluation of PTSD is a complicated task that requires the systematic and neutral evaluation of many sources of information. The Georgetown Guidelines for the assessment of claims of PTSD, general guidelines for forensic assessment, and the multiaxial system of psychiatric diagnosis provide a structure for such assessments that increases their accuracy and effectiveness in litigation. The inability of the forensic evaluator to provide a comprehensive structured and neutral assessment of claims of PTSD leads not only to the misdiagnosis of PTSD, but to significant problems for an attorney whose expert may be easily discredited. Adherence to the Georgetown Guidelines in particular will help prevent the misdiagnosis of PTSD due to the common error of stretching the criteria of PTSD to fit a particular situation, as well as other types of errors that arise through lack of systematic assessment. In addition, the Georgetown Guidelines can help the forensic evaluator address and minimize

---

[77]Larry H. Strasburger, Thomas G. Gutheil & Archie Brodsky, *On Wearing Two Hats: Role Conflict in Serving as Both Psychotherapist and Expert Witness*, 154 AM. J. PSYCHIATRY 448 (1997); Stuart A. Greenberg & Daniel W. Shuman, *Irreconcilable Conflict Between Therapeutic and Forensic Roles,* 28 PROF. PSYCHOLOGY: RES. & PRAC. 50 (1997).

[78]Stone, *supra* note 2.

[79]Pitman et al., *supra* note 72, at 393.

the types of error that arise from an examiner's bias in the review or interpretation of all relevant data in a claim of PTSD in litigation.

IV. Special Issues in the Forensic Assessment of PTSD

The methodology and guidelines discussed in the previous section provide a framework for the assessment of PTSD in litigation. A credible and informed evaluation of a claim of PTSD requires that the forensic evaluator apply these methods in the context of legal and clinical issues specific to such claims. These issues include:

- Frequent comorbidity of PTSD with other psychiatric disorders
- Contribution of preexisting psychiatric disorders, prior trauma history and personality disorders to the development of PTSD
- Difficulties in quantifying the severity of functional impairment resulting from PTSD
- Possibility of malingering for financial gain

These issues correspond with legal issues of proximate cause, alternate causation, preexisting vulnerabilities (including personality disorders), functional impairment, prognosis, damages, and malingering. The following discussion illustrates the evaluation of these issues.

A. Trauma History, Comorbid Disorders, and Proximate Cause

CASE EXAMPLE

Mr. A, a 35-year-old office manager, worked on the eighth floor of a ten-story office building. One day, the fire alarm went off. Mr. Smith was responsible for evacuating all office personnel and discharged his obligations calmly and competently. He spoke with the fire department and was assured that the situation was not dangerous. He directed the other employees as they evacuated the building by going down the staircase. Although the staircase was dark, the emergency lights were on and the amount of smoke was minimal. Everyone got outside quickly and safely, and the fire was extinguished. No one was hurt and no property was lost. After the situation was resolved, Mr. Smith appeared calm, in a good mood, and was seen joking with employees.

About one week later, Mr. A developed trouble sleeping. Over the next week, he became increasingly agitated, irritable, and unable to concentrate on his work. His sleep became increasingly fitful, and he began to experience nightmares of being trapped in various situations. He became unable to discuss the events of the fire and was particularly distressed when the company wanted to give him a commendation for his performance that day. He had sudden fits of rage, after which he became withdrawn. He began to isolate himself from his colleagues and family. Two months after the fire, Mr. A was diagnosed as having PTSD. He brought a suit against his employer in which he identified the fire as the proximate cause of his emotional injury.

The forensic evaluator determined that Mr. A met the diagnostic criteria for PTSD and Major Depression. However, it did not appear that the traumatic exposure was of sufficient magnitude to be responsible for the severity of Mr. A's PTSD symptoms. Evaluation of Mr. A's psychiatric history revealed that when he was fifteen, his home was destroyed in a fire that also resulted in the death of his grandmother. Although Mr. A was physically unharmed, he developed PTSD. He was treated with medication and psychotherapy, and his PTSD symptoms resolved within 18 months of treatment. He had, however, been treated with medication and psychotherapy on and off in the intervening years for a diagnosis of recurrent depression. At the time of the recent fire, Mr. A was on antidepressant medication.

Mr. A had a previously resolved PTSD, which was reactivated by exposure to a less intense but similar stressor. This is more likely to occur if the previous trauma was of greater magnitude than the recent exposure. In addition, Mr. A had a recurrent and recent history of depression, further increasing his vulnerability. As a victim's psychological vulnerability increases, the intensity or magnitude of the stressor needed to precipitate PTSD decreases. Conversely, when risk factors are low, a more intense stressor is required to precipitate PTSD. In Mr. A's case, a relatively low-intensity stressor triggered a recurrence of a previously existing PTSD in the context of an ongoing depressive illness. Although the recurrence of PTSD was precipitated by a recent low-level exposure, it was actually caused by a previous trauma, the disastrous fire of many years before.

CASE EXAMPLE

Ms. B was a 23-year-old woman who was working full-time as a waitress in a restaurant and attending college part-time. The restaurant manager frequently made remarks about her appearance, and questioned her about personal matters, including her sexual activities. He often suggested that she would be more satisfied sexually if she engaged in a relationship with him. He often touched her and rubbed up against her. He engaged in this behavior both when alone with her and in front of others, and she repeatedly asked him to stop. She reported him to his supervisor. The supervisor assured her that he would take care of the problem, but the manager's behavior continued. One day, in front of coworkers, the manager grabbed Ms. B as she walked past him. He took her hand, placed it on his penis, and said "Think about it. I'm free tonight." She became very upset, left the restaurant, and was unable to return to work.

During the months before this incident, Ms. B reported that she had become more withdrawn and depressed. She had developed difficulty sleeping and concentrating and dreaded going into work. She did not quit because she needed to pay her tuition and also was trying to save enough money to move out of her parents' home. She did not want to tell her parents what was going on at work because she feared her father would lose his temper and assault the manager. After the final incident, she reported having nightmares and panic attacks. Her father figured prominently in the nightmares. She denied any psychiatric history. She was diagnosed with PTSD and panic disorder without agoraphobia. She brought a sexual harassment complaint against her employer, alleging that her manager's behavior was the proximate cause of her injuries.

Ms. B's clinical condition met the diagnostic criteria for PTSD and panic disorder. However, as in the case of Mr. A, the intensity of the traumatic exposure seemed *insufficient for the development of PTSD in the absence of a preexisting vulnerability. Since Ms. B had no preexisting psychiatric or medical history that would account for such a vulnerability, the forensic evaluator needed to search elsewhere for data that might explain Ms. B's clinical presentation. Interviews with Ms. B's coworkers and with her father, Mr. B, revealed a long history on the part of Mr. B of unemployment, alcoholism, and domestic violence. Mr. B had been violent with Ms. B and her mother on at least three occasions in the past year. During this time, Mr. B was arrested twice for his assaultive behavior, and Ms. B on one occasion had required treatment at a local emergency room. Examination of Ms. B's childhood medical records revealed numerous injuries, which strongly suggested a pattern of domestic violence and physical assault for many years.*

Although Ms. B did not have a preexisting diagnosis of PTSD, she had a documented history of exposure to trauma that raised questions about both preexisting PTSD and alternate causation of current clinical presentation. The forensic evaluation determined that the proximate cause of her PTSD and panic disorder was more likely to be her repeated traumatic exposure to domestic violence rather than her manager's behavior.

The evaluation of a diagnosis of PTSD in the context of litigation should include consideration of whether the condition:

- Is a new disorder caused by recent trauma
- Is a previously undiagnosed or undetected PTSD caused by a previous trauma
- Has been precipitated by recent trauma but caused by a previous trauma
- Has been caused by interactions of both recent and previous trauma.[80]

An assessment of a traumatic exposure and a diagnosis of PTSD cannot be made with certainty in the absence of an evaluation of psychiatric and trauma history. The information gained by an evaluation of this history affects issues related to proximate cause and assessment of damages. Although the proximate cause of the PTSD is identified by definition to be a specific traumatic exposure, the claimant may have other life problems that are causing mental distress independent of the events identified in litigation. PTSD has a high current and lifetime comorbidity with a number of psychiatric disorders. Determination of proximate cause can be affected by establishing that a prior or current PTSD coexisted with another psychiatric disorder, or that preexisting PTSD has been exacerbated by a current stressor. In such cases, a claimant's PTSD may be unrelated to the current claim, and the exposure in question may not be the proximate cause of the claimant's current psychological state.

A detailed assessment of Criterion A, the traumatic stressor, including the review of as much collateral information as possible, is essential in the evaluation of PTSD claims. In litigation, the event alleged to be the Criterion A stressor is typically considered the proximate cause. Therefore, the presence or absence of a valid Criterion A stressor must be well established by the forensic clinician. If the reported stressor is not equivalent in intensity and

---

[80]Stuart B. Kleinman, *Trauma Induced Psychiatric Disorders and Civil Law*, in PRINCIPLES AND PRACTICE OF FORENSIC PSYCHIATRY 243 (Richard Rosner ed., 1994).

magnitude to the examples cited in the *DSM-IV-TR*, its relationship to an exposed individual's subsequent development of PTSD must be particularly well supported by clinical experience, research, and sources of information other than the claimant. If the stressor is of insufficient magnitude to result in the claimant's clinical condition, alternate causes of the emotional injury, such as a preexisting diagnosis of PTSD or alternate traumatic exposures, must be considered. It is not unusual to find that the events at issue in the lawsuit have provided a "convenient focus" for distress that has been caused by other traumatic experiences.

The lifetime prevalence of PTSD in the general population is approximately 10 percent. Although this may seem high, clinical experience, research, and national crime statistics establish that more individuals are exposed to childhood and adult trauma than is commonly recognized. At least 20 percent of American women and 5–10 percent of American men have experienced some form of sexual abuse as children. Around 20–25 percent of child sexual abuse cases involve penetration or oral genital contact.[81] The statistics regarding adult victimization are equally distressing. Thirteen to 23 percent of adult women will be the victims of completed rape, and 24–53 percent of adult women will experience some type of sexual assault. Between 21 percent and 34 percent of all women will be physically assaulted by an intimate male sometime during their adulthood. Between 20 percent and 50 percent of all murders in this country occur within the family, often in the context of previous domestic violence that is typically witnessed by children.[82]

An individual with a prior trauma history may have a preexisting PTSD regardless of whether he or she received treatment. This raises the issue of whether the more recently identified stressor is indeed the trauma to which the individual is reacting or has merely triggered reactions to the earlier trauma. Even if an individual has not developed PTSD, prior trauma exposure increases vulnerability to the development of PTSD following a new exposure. Research has suggested that early severe trauma, especially childhood sexual and physical abuse, may induce neurophysiologic changes that predispose an individual to the development of PTSD and other psychiatric disorders.[83] The *DSM-IV-TR* formulation of PTSD does not take into account individual vulnerabilities such as previous exposures to trauma, preexisting PTSD, or other preexisting psychiatric disorders. In the past, clinicians were able to distinguish diagnosti-

---

[81]David Finkelhor, *Current Information on the Scope and Nature of Child Sexual Abuse*, 4 THE FUTURE OF CHILDREN 31 (1994).

[82]Deborah S. Rose, *Sexual Assault, Domestic Violence, and Incest*, in PSYCHOLOGICAL ASPECTS OF WOMEN'S HEALTH CARE 447 (Donna E. Stewart & Nada L. Stotland eds., 1993).

[83]Rachel Yehuda, *Neuroendocrinology of Trauma and Posttraumatic Stress Disorder*, in PSYCHOLOGICAL TRAUMA 97 (R. Yehuda ed., 1998); Bessel A. van der Kolk, *The Body Keeps Score: Approaches to the Psychobiology of Posttraumatic Stress Disorder*, in TRAUMATIC STRESS: THE EFFECTS OF OVERWHELMING EXPERIENCE ON MIND, BODY AND SOCIETY 214 (Bessel A. van der Kolk, Alexander C. McFarlane & Lars Weisaeth eds., 1996).

cally between the presentation of posttraumatic syndromes in vulnerable individuals, referred to as "traumatic neurosis," and a posttraumatic reaction in a psychologically healthy individual. Despite the absence of this diagnostic distinction in the *DSM-IV-TR* formulation of PTSD, individual vulnerabilities play a significant role in the development and severity of PTSD. The forensic evaluator should always assess significant prior and current traumatic exposures and psychiatric vulnerabilities affecting an individual's claim of PTSD since they can affect issues in the litigation of such claims.

In the above case examples, Mr. A's previous history of traumatic exposure and PTSD and Ms. B's alternate exposure to trauma can have significant implications on the issues of proximate cause and the ultimate award of damages. The importance of an evaluation of past psychiatric history and trauma history in light of these forensic issues cannot be overstated. Attorneys for such plaintiffs may argue that the prior or current exposure to trauma made the plaintiff more vulnerable to other stressors in his environment. The defense might argue that the prior exposure was in fact the proximate cause, and that the workplace events represented a coincidental problem or a convenient focus rather than a traumatic exposure.

The forensic examiner must begin his or her evaluation with the understanding that although a PTSD claimant has had an exposure to a traumatic event, that event may or may not be directly related to the claimant's clinical presentation. The variables involved in the development of any psychiatric disorder, including PTSD, are such that it cannot be assumed that a traumatic exposure is always relevant to the development and/or maintenance of a psychological disorder. Traumatic experiences may be entirely unrelated to the psychopathology in question or be related to preexisting PTSD or a comorbid disorder. The evaluation of a current claim of PTSD must include an evaluation of previous traumatic exposure and previous psychiatric history. Opinions regarding proximate cause cannot be supported without assessment of these factors.

B. Personality Disorders and PTSD

CASE EXAMPLE

Ms. C was a 32-year-old woman who worked at a large corporation as a computer systems analyst. Her office space consisted of one cubicle in a series of rows of cubicles. Each workspace was equipped with its own computer monitor. Ms. C had a clear view of the monitor belonging to a coworker. Because of the construction of the office space, Ms. C was unable to avoid seeing her coworker's monitor when she entered or left her cubicle, and came to realize that he spent a good deal of time downloading pornography from the Internet. He invited Ms. C as well as other coworkers to view what he considered the most interesting pictures. Ms. C declined, but she frequently saw coworkers gathering around her coworker's monitor and heard their comments.

Ms. C asked her coworker to stop looking at pornography while at work and reminded him it was against company policy. He ignored her requests. He stated that she was oversensitive, since other coworkers enjoyed the photographs and had not complained. Ms. C reported him to their supervisor, who assured her that the problem would be addressed, but the coworker's activities continued unchanged. Ms. C reported the coworker and her supervisor to the division vice president. Shortly thereafter, she was moved to a less desirable office location, with less access to resources and personnel. Ms. C had begun to experience symptoms of depressed mood and social withdrawal when she first became aware of her coworker's activities. As the activities continued, she became increasingly distressed. She began to experience marked instability of mood, swinging between rage and depression. She began to lash out at coworkers who would gather around her coworker's monitor, and became the object of derisive humor regarding her "prudish" nature. By the time she reported her complaints to the vice president, she had developed paranoid thoughts about other employees watching her and talking about her. After being relocated, she became suicidal and had to be hospitalized. She was diagnosed with PTSD and Borderline Personality Disorder (BPD). She quit her job and brought a suit against her employer for sexual harassment.

Ms. C had a history of childhood physical and sexual abuse, which had resulted in the development of BPD. She had been in psychiatric treatment for many years. Her BPD had resulted in functional difficulties in her personal life, which she was able to separate from her work, and she had done well professionally. Ms. C had been psychiatrically hospitalized twice in her early twenties for suicidal thoughts, but she had not been suicidal or hospitalized since then. She had never been diagnosed as having PTSD. Her coworkers confirmed that she had not had interpersonal difficulties at her job until the events in question began. Review of her employment records during her nine years at the company revealed outstanding work reviews and consistent pay raises and promotions.

CASE EXAMPLE

Ms. D was a 32-year-old woman who worked in a government office for two years as a clerical assistant. She had been noted by others to dress provocatively in revealing clothing, but not outside the accepted office dress code. Coworkers also noticed that she was more friendly with male coworkers and supervisors than with females. She made a point of letting everyone she worked with know that she was single and was interested in "partying" rather than in finding a long-term relationship. She fulfilled her employment obligations adequately, but when corrected or reprimanded after making an error, she would typically blame someone else for the problem.

Mr. D's supervisor was a 35-year-old married, middle manager in the office. He often commented in a lighthearted way about Ms. D's appearance. He began to ask her to do extra work for him, sometimes after regular hours. On some of these occasions, he offered to buy her dinner after work. Ms. D had always cheerfully agreed to his requests and appeared to enjoy his attention. This continued for several months until the supervisor was unexpectedly transferred to another project at a different, but nearby, location. Ms. D was assigned a new on-site supervisor. Ms. D contacted her former supervisor and wanted to continue seeing him. She suggested that they meet for a date, although she knew he was married. He told her that a date was not possible and that he was not interested in a social relationship. He stated that although he had *enjoyed working with her, he considered theirs to be only a business relationship, that he was no longer her supervisor and that given this reassignment, he would no longer be working with her.*

Ms. D became enraged and accused her former supervisor of leading her on. She told him that he was just like all the other men she had known, who had exploited her and then "thrown me away like trash." She quit her job, with no notice, and within days filed a complaint of sexual harassment. She alleged that everyone in the office knew that her former supervisor had been pursuing a sexual relationship with her. She alleged that he insisted that she work extra hours for him and go out to dinner with him. She further charged that he pressured her to engage in a physical relationship with him and that on two occasions he had attempted to grab her breasts. She claimed that she developed PTSD as a result of his behavior. A forensic psychiatrist retained by Ms. D's attorney diagnosed PTSD; the forensic psychiatrist retained by the defense diagnosed Borderline and Histrionic Personality Disorder.

A review of Ms. D's records disclosed multiple workplace problems. She had had four similar jobs in the past six years, and had left each after alleging that she had been treated unfairly by a supervisor or coworkers. Typically these allegations involved accusations of sexual harassment, although she had not brought a lawsuit before. She had been divorced twice, and arrested on three occasions for driving while intoxicated. Although previous employers had referred her to EAP services, she had refused counseling, because she stated, "I am not the one with the problem." She had presented herself to the local emergency room twice in the previous year, claiming that she had taken overdoses of over-the-counter medication, but none had been detected and she was discharged. She had no other documented psychiatric history.

Office coworkers confirmed that Ms. D's behavior was often provocative and bordering on inappropriate. They stated that she seemed to enjoy her former supervisor's attention and often talked about how special it made her feel. No one witnessed any inappropriate sexual activity on the part of her former supervisor, who was known as a congenial and friendly person. The supervisor denied Ms. D's allegations, and her claims could not be substantiated in any way. She did not meet the symptom or stressor criteria for PTSD. The diagnosis of BPD, in conjunction with her employment history and observed behavior, offered an alternative hypothesis for her distorted perception of the workplace events and the distress she associated with these perceptions.

The diagnosis of personality disorder in an individual with a claim of PTSD can become a central issue in cases of employment litigation. A plaintiff's credibility, the course of litigation, and the assessment of damages can be significantly affected by a diagnosis of personality disorder. Such a diagnosis raises several legal and clinical issues most often but not exclusively found in sexual harassment litigation. These include hypersensitivity, the "reasonable woman" concept, and welcomeness of the conduct. However, a forensic evaluator may often have difficulty making a diagnosis of a personality disorder in the course of an evaluation interview. In addition, the diagnoses of BPD and PTSD share certain clinical features, and both conditions may be present in the same individual, further complicating assessment.

Nevertheless, a careful assessment of the presence or absence of a personality disorder in a litigant claiming PTSD is essential in the forensic evaluation of such claims. To provide such an assessment, the forensic psychiatrist must have both a clinical understanding of the nature of personality disorders and their relationship to PTSD and an understanding of the legal issues a diagnosis of personality disorder raises.[84]

Assessment of a personality disorder requires an understanding of relevant definitions. *Personality* can be described as the combined total of an individual's emotional and behavioral traits, which form a characteristic pattern of functioning and relating to others. This pattern is usually stable and predictable in ordinary life circumstances. *Personality traits* are individual components of personality. These are identifiable, specific, and consistent patterns of perceiving, relating to, and thinking about the environment and oneself that are exhibited in a wide range of social and personal contexts. A *personality disorder* is a psychiatric diagnosis applied to a pathological deviation from the norm that consists of pervasive, inflexible, and maladaptive personality traits. These enduring pathological patterns are present across a broad range of important personal and occupational areas of functioning and cause significant distress and functional impairment. Deviations in emotional experience and behavior must be manifested in at least two areas, including cognition, mood and emotional responses, interpersonal functioning, and impulse control, in order to meet diagnostic criteria. Personality disorders appear in adolescence or early adulthood and are stable over time.

Laypersons often mistakenly refer to an individual's irritating or difficult personality traits as a personality disorder. A personality disorder, however, is more than a collection of irritating or difficult traits; it is a type of pathology. It is composed of those aspects of an individual that cause the person to engage in self-defeating and/or manipulative behaviors, and it creates turmoil in most of that individual's occupational and social relationships. Typically, individuals with personality disorders have little or no understanding of the dysfunctional nature of their responses and behavior, and they blame others when things go wrong.

Borderline, Histrionic, and Narcissistic Personality Disorders are those most typically found in cases associated with employment litigation. Narcissistic Personality Disorder is characterized by a pattern of grandiosity, need for admiration, and lack of empathy. These individuals expect to be given whatever they want or feel they need, regardless of the realistic limitations of the environment or the needs of others. When their sense of entitlement is not gratified or they feel slighted or rejected, they often become enraged and devalue those whom they hold responsible. Histrionic Personality Disorder is a pattern of excessive emotionality and attention seeking. Individuals with this disorder tend to draw attention to themselves and feel unappreciated when they are not the center of attention and are often inappropriately sexually provocative or seductive and often consider relationships to be more intimate than they really are. When confronted with their behavior, they often feel victimized and blame others.

---

[84]See Chapter 6, Personality Disorders in Employment Litigation.

1. Borderline Personality Disorder: Clinical Presentation

BPD is the most controversial and complicated of the personality disorder diagnoses. Its clinical importance and forensic implications are such that the forensic clinician must be familiar with its diagnostic criteria (Table 13-10) and clinical presentation.

Table 13-10 *DSM-IV-TR* Diagnostic Criteria for Borderline Personality Disorder

A pattern of instability of interpersonal relationships, self-image and affects, and marked impulsivity beginning by early adulthood and present in a variety of contexts, as indicated by five or more of the following:
(1) frantic efforts to avoid real or imagined abandonment
(2) a pattern of unstable and intense interpersonal relationships characterized by alternating between extremes of idealization and devaluation
(3) identity disturbance: markedly and persistently unstable self-image or sense of self
(4) impulsivity in at least two areas that are potentially self-damaging, such as spending, substance abuse, reckless driving, binge eating
(5) recurrent suicidal behavior, gestures, threats, or self-mutilating behavior
(6) affective instability due to marked reactivity of mood (e.g. intense episodic dysphoria, irritability, or anxiety usually lasting a few hours and rarely more than a few days)
(7) chronic feelings of emptiness
(8) inappropriate, intense anger or difficulty controlling anger (e.g. frequent displays of temper, constant anger, recurrent physical fights)
(9) transient, stress related paranoid ideation or severe dissociative symptoms.

Source: Reprinted with permission from the *Diagnostic and Statistical Manual of Mental Disorders, Fourth Edition, Text Revision,* 710. Copyright 2000 American Psychiatric Association.

BPD is estimated to occur in about 2 percent of the general population.[85] Women typically constitute about 75 percent of individuals diagnosed with the disorder.[86] It is associated with a high degree of comorbidity with Axis I psychiatric disorders, including mood disorders, substance-related disorders, eating disorders, PTSD, and other personality disorders.[87] However, while these Axis I disorders may be adequately treated or may resolve, BPD, an Axis II diagnosis, typically remains unchanged over time.

The clinical presentation of individuals with BPD is notable primarily in the dysfunction of their relationships. Individuals with BPD often have significant

---

[85] DSM-IV-TR, *supra* note 4, at 708.

[86] Jessica Wolfe & Rachel Kimerling, *Gender Issues in the Assessment of Posttraumatic Stress Disorder, in* ASSESSING PSYCHOLOGICAL TRAUMA AND PTSD 204 (John P. Wilson & Terence J. Keane eds., 1997).

[87] Mary C. Zanarini et al., *Axis I Comorbidity of Borderline Personality Disorder,* 155 AM. J. PSYCHIATRY 1733 (1998).

distortions in their perceptions of themselves and their relationships with others, and typically have patterns of unstable and intense relationships. They may, however, function adequately and appropriately in interpersonal relationships, and even excel in various areas of personal and professional endeavors, until they experience some form of stress. Actual or perceived stress results in a worsening of perceptual distortions, leading to a deterioration of function usually across a number of areas of social functioning.

Individuals with BPD are very sensitive to environmental circumstances, and small events or changes can be stressful for them. Their reactions to events in their emotional and interpersonal world are often disproportionate to the magnitude of the event. For example, they may interpret the annoyance of others or the cancellation of an appointment as rejection, and respond with inappropriate anger and fury. Individuals with BPD typically make frantic efforts to avoid rejection and abandonment, often with impulsive and ill-considered behaviors, which may include suicidal gestures or attempts. These extreme reactions to what others perceive as minor or neutral events often provoke confusion and angry responses in others. The actual loss of a relationship or job, which most people would consider extremely stressful, can result in extreme changes in self-image, mood, cognition, and behavior. These extreme responses can result in unstable behavior that at times appears psychotic.

Individuals with BPD often have a pattern of provoking the events that cause them stress. Typically, however, individuals with BPD have little insight into how they provoke the stress and distress they experience. For example, they often idealize important figures in their lives. When these persons disappoint them in some way, idealization may quickly change to angry devaluation, and the formerly idealized person is now perceived as cruel or punitive. Impulsivity coupled with emotional reactivity and instability often results in episodes of inappropriate, intense anger that individuals with BPD have difficulty controlling. The object of these storms often has no idea why such an abrupt change in the individual's demeanor has occurred. When the formerly valued individual responds to this anger by getting angry himself, the individual with BPD believes that his or her assessment of this person as cruel or malicious was justified. Persons with this disorder typically do not take responsibility for their own behaviors and responses.

In the workplace, this maladaptive behavior may appear as impulsive and self-destructive choices regarding career, coworkers, supervisors, and job responsibilities. Interpersonal stressors may provoke verbal outbursts, displays of extreme sarcasm or bitterness, or impulsive responses such as walking out of a job at a critical moment or suddenly quitting. Inappropriate interpersonal behavior often occurs at the moment a goal is about to be attained, resulting in a loss of opportunity or desired relationship. When such events occur, these individuals rarely recognize their own contribution to the negative turn of events. In such circumstances, they often feel victimized and hold others responsible for their distress.

The perceptual distortions and extreme responses found in individuals with BPD are closely connected with the etiology of the disorder. Research has found a high correlation between histories of childhood trauma and a diagnosis of BPD. Approximately 80 percent of individuals with BPD have histories of significant childhood physical or sexual abuse.[88] Individuals with BPD who have been traumatized in childhood typically experience current stressors with an intensity of emotion that belongs to the past. The feelings that were generated by and are connected to the earlier trauma are continually reexperienced on an interpersonal level. These intense responses are inappropriately attributed to present events and are often destructive to the current relationships the individual most values.

Individuals with BPD tend to experience their own extremes of response as well as the emotional reactions and behavioral responses of others as retraumatizing and have little insight into the cause of these extreme reactions. As a result, they lead traumatizing and traumatized lives. Many individuals with BPD become involved in social situations that bear a striking similarity to the circumstances in which they were first traumatized, and they are rarely consciously aware that they are repeating earlier life experiences. In such reenactments, the individual with BPD may alternately play the role of the victim or victimizer.

A. BPD AND TRAUMA BPD and PTSD often exist comorbidly in individuals with histories of trauma. One recent study found that 56 percent of individuals diagnosed with BPD also met the criteria for the diagnosis of PTSD.[89] Given the statistics on the incidence of trauma in the etiology of BPD, it is not surprising to find the occurrence of such a large overlap in diagnoses. This overlap is the source of many of the clinical and forensic complications a diagnosis of BPD generates. Research has also demonstrated that a history of previous victimization during childhood, with or without accompanying borderline symptomatology, increases the risk of revictimization and the likelihood of developing PTSD.[90]

B. THE "SITTING DUCK" SYNDROME An individual with BPD, who is symptomatic even when stable and has compromised ego strengths, is clearly at risk for further misadventure. Childhood abuse has been recognized as a high predictor of sexual exploitation, second only to prior sexual victimization. The risk of repeated rape and battering is approximately doubled for survivors of childhood abuse. In one study, women who had been victims of childhood incest had far higher rates of adult sexual assault than women who had no incest history (65 percent vs. 36 percent). Types of revictimization noted in this study were marital physical and sexual abuse, being sexually approached

---

[88]Wolfe & Kimerling, *supra* note 86, at 204; James A. Chu, *The Revictimization of Adult Women with Histories of Childhood Abuse*, 1 J. PSYCHOTHERAPY PRAC. & RES. 259 (1992); Judith L. Herman, J. Christopher Perry & Bessel A. van der Kolk, *Childhood Trauma in Borderline Personality Disorder*, 146 AM. J. PSYCHIATRY 490 (1989); Susan N. Ogata et al., *Childhood Sexual and Physical Abuse in Adult Patients with Borderline Personality Disorder*, 147 AM. J. PSYCHIATRY 1008 (1990).

[89]Zanarini et al., *supra* note 87.

[90]Wolfe & Kimerling, *supra* note 86.

by an authority figure, or being asked to pose for pornography.[91] Similar claims of increased risk for sexual harassment have been made for women with histories of victimization.

One author has referred to this increased potential for revictimization as the "Sitting Duck" Syndrome.[92] He explains the increased incidence of revictimization in this population as a result of a combination of several factors, all of which result from prior trauma exposure, including:

- Active psychiatric symptoms
- Dysfunctional individual dynamics
- Pathological interpersonal functioning
- Distortions in perception and decreased cognitive capabilities

Dissociation is one of the criteria in the diagnosis of BPD. Although not a criterion for PTSD, it has been widely associated with the development of PTSD following a traumatic exposure. Dissociative episodes, during which individuals feel numb and detached from their environment, increase the risk of victimization. A person in a threatening situation who dissociates is unable to bring his or her experience and cognitive processes to bear on a potentially dangerous situation. The individual may be unaware of the potential threat in the environment and as a result, not respond in ways that minimize the danger. Indeed, the individual's judgment may be so impaired by a dissociative response that the choices he or she makes may seem paradoxical or complicit.[93]

In addition, the disruption of early attachments that occurs in abusive family environments has a profound impact on normal ego development. Individuals with such experiences have difficulty forming psychologically healthy bonds with others. They anticipate that intimate relationships, which they desperately crave, will be an unavoidable source of pain, and often approach them anticipating the worst. Another common result of such abuse experiences is self-hatred and negative self-esteem. These individuals often cannot conceive of situations in which they would be treated kindly and with respect. As a result, they may feel compelled to engage with others in ways that are hostile, dependent, and even abusive to others or to themselves. They often allow themselves to become involved in or remain in situations in which they are revictimized, feeling that they deserve nothing better.

It has been proposed by one author that BPD be considered a form of complex posttraumatic syndrome, and that the term "BPD" itself be eliminated because of its negative gender bias and clinical inaccuracy.[94] This proposition is based on the argument that the current formulation of PTSD, based largely

---

[91]Chu, *supra* note 88.

[92]Richard P. Kluft, *Incest and Subsequent Revictimization: The Case of Therapist-Patient Sexual Exploitation, With a Description of the Sitting Duck Syndrome, in* INCEST RELATED SYNDROMES OF ADULT PSYCHOPATHOLOGY 263 (Richard P. Kluft ed., 1990).

[93]Chu, *supra* note 88.

[94]JUDITH L. HERMAN, TRAUMA AND RECOVERY 123 (1992).

on the study of Type 1 trauma, ignores the probable posttraumatic responses of earlier or more chronic traumatic exposure such as childhood abuse. This author argues that the lack of more precise, descriptive terminology for PTSD encompassing this type of traumatic exposure results in the mistaken primary psychiatric diagnosis of BPD in this population.[95]

C. REPETITION COMPULSION Another behavioral phenomenon that contributes to increased rates of revictimization was originally described by Freud, who observed that severe abusive experiences at a young age overwhelm a child's limited ego capacities and defenses. As a result, these experiences are often repressed and dissociated from consciousness. They do not remain unconscious but emerge both covertly and overtly into current experience. Because the individual cannot consciously remember and work through the past experience, he or she becomes unconsciously obliged to repeat or reenact the repressed material in the present. Freud referred to this as the repetition compulsion.

Freud believed that the repetition compulsion involved an unconscious need for the person to rework the original experience in an attempt to gain mastery over it by taking an active rather than passive role. In addition, Freud noted that repetitions allow the repeated expressions of emotions associated with the repressed experience, particularly sadism and hostility.[96] These two dynamic issues—the active mastery of previous, passively experienced unpleasant events and the expression of emotions associated with past events—result in the symptoms and behaviors in which the repetition compulsion is manifested.[97]

Freud's observations about the repetition compulsion are remarkably accurate in the clinical setting. Patients with histories of childhood abuse commonly reexperience the repressed traumatic events of the past in a variety of symptomatic and behavioral ways. Repetition symptoms, such as sensory and emotional flashbacks reexperienced in intrusive and uncontrolled episodes, are passive reexperiences of past events. Symptom induction is an active form of repetition compulsion and is seen in the behavior of individuals who are unconsciously drawn to expose themselves to stimuli that are certain to trigger flashback responses and other symptoms.

Behavioral reenactments are a common form of the unconscious compulsion to repeat or reenact previous traumatic experiences. Poor personal and interpersonal choices or provocative or manipulative behavior often results in re-creation of aspects of the original traumatic experience. An example of this form of reenactment would be the decision of a woman who was physically abused by an alcoholic father to marry a man who is alcoholic and violent. Inappropriate boundaries and feelings of abandonment are integral parts of

---

[95]*Id.* at 126.

[96]Sigmund Freud, *Beyond the Pleasure Principle*, in 18 COMPLETE PSYCHOLOGICAL WORKS OF SIGMUND FREUD 7 (James Strachey ed., 1955).

[97]Chu, *supra* note 88, at 260–61.

abuse experiences in childhood and are often an essential emotional aspect of the repetition compulsion. This results in unstable, intense, and ultimately nonviable relationships with others in which the individual feels trapped or helpless to effect change without experiencing abandonment. Attempts by the other participant to leave or alter the situation may also result in rage and feelings of abandonment.

Unfortunately, the unconscious attempts to undo or master past trauma through present repetition are usually doomed to failure. In attempting to ward off feelings of abandonment, such individuals provoke others to reject them. In trying to undo past physical or sexual exploitation, they often make choices that increase the likelihood of repeated exploitation. In addition, such individuals may experience an event as traumatic because of distorted perceptions or emotional responses related to the dynamics of a repetition compulsion. Their perception of rejection, abandonment, and exploitation are often hypersensitive distortions of present events based on past emotional experiences. The perpetrators of emotional, physical, or sexual exploitation are of course responsible for their own behavior. However, individuals who unconsciously orchestrate repetition of past experiences play active roles in their present experiences of trauma and revictimization that may significantly affect aspects of litigation associated with these events.

2. Forensic Assessment of Personality Disorders

BPD and PTSD share numerous common symptoms, such as emotional instability, dissociation, impulsivity, self-injurious behavior, and severe disruptions in relationships. This requires the forensic evaluator to look beyond symptom presentation as a primary method of diagnosis. In addition, episodes of actual or perceived retraumatization create new psychological damage and can result in significant deterioration in mental health.[98] Further, individuals with histories of childhood abuse and BPD are at increased risk of exposure to new trauma and often experience severe reactions to lower-intensity traumatic exposures. The presentation of this population after new traumatic exposures is typically more complex as well as more severe. This results in part from the decreased ability to adapt to and defend themselves against aversive experiences. Finally, they may also experience severe reactions to perceived rather than actual traumatic reexposure, which can present as new-onset PTSD. These factors require that an assessment of Axis II pathology be as accurate and complete as possible in order to address forensic issues such as proximate cause, damages, and plaintiff credibility.

Individuals with personality disorders typically come into psychiatric treatment for complaints of depression and anxiety. They rarely, if ever, present themselves as suffering from a personality disorder. In a treatment setting, this diagnosis is made over time in the course of the patient's relationship with the

---

[98]*Id.* at 262–65.

clinician. Clinicians are aware that the diagnosis of a personality disorder often takes more time to become evident than most other psychiatric disorders. The treating clinician has the diagnostic advantage of an ongoing relationship with his patient, during which he can evaluate the patient's interpersonal functioning over an extended period of time. The forensic clinician, however, does not have this opportunity, and often must formulate an opinion after one or two interviews, without the benefit of a long-term therapeutic relationship in which the salient features of an individual's personality disorder are revealed. Thus, the diagnostic complexity of cases with issues of both PTSD and BPD is further complicated by the forensic clinician's limited interaction with the individual. The forensic clinician must be prepared to use methods of assessment other than those primarily relied on in a clinical setting in making a determination of the presence of a personality disorder.

The forensic evaluator must also distinguish the personality traits characteristic of a personality disorder from coping styles or behaviors that emerge from transient mental states or in response to specific situational stressors. Both preexisting PTSD and personality disorders can be exacerbated by social stressors. In addition, other temporary problems related to an external precipitant, such as brief reactive psychosis or adjustment disorder, may resemble either a personality disorder or PTSD. The response to severe social stressors, such as domestic violence or discrimination or harassment in employment, is known to include a presentation of paranoid thinking and periods of extreme emotional reactivity alternating with numbing and withdrawal even in individuals with no significant preexisting psychiatric history.

The diagnosis of personality disorders requires an evaluation of an individual's long-term patterns of functioning as revealed through a variety of sources. By definition, diagnostic features must be evident by early adulthood, and the clinician should assess the stability of personality traits over time and across different situations. It may be helpful for the forensic evaluator to conduct more than one interview and to space successive interviews over time. Even when this is possible, however, the time frame involved is still relatively brief, usually consisting of days or one or two weeks. An initial determination may be possible by obtaining a detailed trauma history with respect to symptom onset. Symptoms that predate the alleged traumatic exposure would be more supportive of a diagnosis of personality disorder or prior PTSD rather than a new onset PTSD. In addition, a severe clinical presentation following a low-level traumatic exposure or environmental stress should raise suspicion of the possibility of a personality disorder, even if PTSD is diagnosed.

Ultimately, supplementary sources of information are essential in making the diagnosis of a personality disorder in a forensic evaluation. Review of those records suggested previously can provide information supporting a diagnosis of PTSD or BPD. A history of relatively healthy relationships and stable functioning prior to stressor exposure might support a diagnosis of PTSD. A history of notable characterological problems in multiple areas of functioning would, by contrast, support a diagnosis of a personality disorder. Record review in individuals with BPD often reveals histories of recurrent job losses, interrupted education, and broken marriages. In addition, reports of misinterpretation of comments and prior unsubstantiated claims of inappropriate behavior might support a diagnosis of personality disorder. Other indications of the presence of a personality disorder found in documents might include:

- Multiple employers
- The use of sick time for illnesses that do not merit extensive use of sick time
- Disability claims for illnesses that are often considered psychosomatic. An individual may report that she has no prior psychiatric history and may never have been in psychiatric treatment, but may have manifested psychiatric disturbances in the psychosomatic conditions.
- Prior lawsuits, claims, or grievances with current or previous employers

The evaluation of an individual with a personality disorder is further complicated by his lack of insight, perceptual distortion, and conscious or unconscious need to present himself in a certain manner. Often the individual does not consider the characteristics that define his personality disorder to be problematic, and if acknowledged, is likely to rationalize them or attribute them to other causes. As a result, interviews with other individuals who have had relationships with the claimant, such as family members and coworkers, may also be helpful in the determination of a diagnosis of personality disorder. Significant discrepancies between the claimant's description of himself and events and the reports of others could indicate the presence of the perceptual distortion found in individuals with personality disorders.

Psychological testing will often provide an invaluable alternate source of information regarding patterns of coping and response. Testing data, when integrated with the data obtained from interviews and document review, can provide objective results that support the presence of a personality disorder. The MMPI-2 is the favored personality assessment instrument for evaluating individuals in forensic settings, particularly if there is a question of personality disorder or malingering.

3. *The Interplay of Personality Disorders and PTSD*

The distinction between the diagnosis of PTSD and a personality disorder may be critical in a case of employment litigation. A diagnosis of PTSD confers upon the sufferer a "victim" status that focuses attention on external events and the responsibility of others. A diagnosis of a personality disorder, particularly Borderline or Histrionic Personality Disorder, undermines the claimant's credibility and focuses attention primarily on the claimant. On the other hand, the presence of BPD can legitimately result in increased vulnerability to the development of PTSD and a more severe and complicated traumatic response following a low-magnitude traumatic exposure.

Proximate cause, damage assessments, and liability are all affected by the assessment of the issues raised by a diagnosis of personality disorder, especially the possibility that the plaintiff was hypersensitive or welcomed the conduct at issue. Hypersensitivity is an extreme response to a relatively mild stimulus. Such extreme responses are often caused by the perceptual distortion of a stimulus or the misattribution of feelings generated by past events to events occurring in the present. For example, an individual who interprets a casual compliment regarding personal appearance as an intrusive sexual proposition and has an extreme emotional response to the statement might be demonstrating hypersensitivity. Welcomeness relates to whether the event in question was acceptable or desired by the individual. The effects of social interactions based on mutual attraction and choice differ significantly from those resulting from the imposition of unwanted behavior on an unwilling individual.

These possibilities must be evaluated in the context of a thorough assessment of diagnosis, history, and functioning. An individual with a personality disorder may have more impairment of function in some areas than others, and thus might appear asymptomatic if the evaluation fails to encompass all areas of function. In addition, many individuals with a history of childhood abuse generally associated with BPD do not have personality disorders or the pathology often inferred or imputed to them and may be genuinely stable or asymptomatic. Finally, individuals with a severe personality disorder may undergo traumatic experiences entirely unrelated to their personality disorder that result in severe psychological damage.

However, individuals with personality disorders do bring complaints and undergo events that are the result of aspects of their character pathology and directly affect issues involved in litigation. Their perceptions and responses may be unreasonable or hypersensitive and their reports of events distorted. Their claims may indeed not be credible. The diagnosis of a personality disorder or a history of abuse, in and of itself, does not reveal specifics about the events in question or how the individual responded to those events. The forensic evaluation should place the diagnosis and history in the context of the specific events in question and attempt to understand the relationships between them.

The forensic assessment of the case examples of Ms. C and Ms. D demonstrates the value of this approach. Both women had preexisting personality disorders. The effect of this preexisting condition on the events and injuries in question differed markedly, however. Ms. C's prior traumatic exposures and preexisting diagnosis of BPD rendered her vulnerable to the development of PTSD. Her development of PTSD in response to events that would not typically meet the criteria for a traumatic exposure or result in suicidal thoughts and hospitalization raised the issue of preexisting vulnerability or alternate causation. Her diagnosis of PTSD are valid. However, the traumatic stressors responsible for the development were not the workplace events but her previous trauma history. Her preexisting Borderline Personality Disorder increased her vulnerability to the development of PTSD as a result of a stressing and distressing event and also made her symptomatic presentation more complex and severe.

The presence of the personality disorder was critical in understanding the degree of emotional harm and impairment of function that resulted from Ms. C's workplace experience. The forensic evaluator would expect Ms. C to have both a lower threshold for the development of PTSD following a stressful experience—particularly one that triggered recollections of her earlier trauma—

and a more severe, or "hypersensitive," reaction to such an exposure. The defense attorneys could argue that she was hypersensitive and that the degree of her reaction was "unreasonable." Her suicidal thoughts and need for hospitalization were related to her preexisting pathology and history of abuse and were not the result of the workplace events. Ms. C's attorneys would argue that despite her preexisting BPD and her trauma history, the events of the workplace were the proximate cause of Ms. Brown's injuries. To support their arguments, they would point to her level of functioning in the workplace and the onset of her symptoms following the events. The trier of fact would of course make the final determination, but neither legal argument can be supported without a comprehensive forensic assessment beyond the determination of the presence of a personality disorder.

In the case of Ms. D, the presence of the personality disorder was again critical in the evaluation of her allegations. Ms. D's evaluation revealed hypersensitivity, unreasonable responses, and elements of a repetition compulsion. In addition, Ms. D appeared to welcome behavior that she later characterized as offensive. She was not uncomfortable with her supervisor's attention until she felt rejected by him. Following this distorted perception, Ms. D became driven by a need for acknowledgment of emotional harm and perhaps even revenge. Ms. D was undoubtedly experiencing emotional pain, but this pain was not the result of the workplace events, as she claimed.

Ms. D's counsel might argue that Ms. D was more vulnerable to victimization and exploitation as a result of her history, and that her unconscious need for special attention was not responsible for her supervisor's exploitative behavior. Defense counsel would argue that Ms. D's distorted perceptions and mischaracterization of behavior resulted in a hypersensitive, unreasonable response to conduct that she initially welcomed but later claimed to be sexual harassment. Again, the final determination of Ms. D's credibility would be the province of the court. The forensic evaluation, however, might provide information that could be used by the court in coming to a conclusion regarding the credibility of her claims, including an explanation of why Ms. D would make such claims and an understanding of how she would indeed be vulnerable to repeated exploitation.

Each of these cases demonstrates that individuals with personality disorders or a history of childhood abuse often make identifications in the present that are powerfully influenced by their past experiences. Plaintiff's attorneys often file motions to bar discovery of such histories based on rules of evidence even when the plaintiff is claiming emotional injury. Defense attorneys must attempt to provide this information to the forensic psychiatrist because it is directly relevant to issues of hypersensitivity, reasonableness of response, welcomeness, credibility, proximate cause, prognosis, and damages. However, the forensic evaluator must make a careful assessment of the relevance of each of these issues in each case. For example, to attack Ms. C's credibility on the basis of hypersensitivity or reasonableness of response might create sympathy for her given the specifics of her case. In contrast, the issues of welcomeness and repetition compulsion would likely play a significant and justified role in the defense against Ms. D's claims. Counsel for either defense of plaintiff can strengthen their case by using a forensic evaluation that places histories and diagnoses in context.

C. Functional Impairment and the Assessment of Damages

CASE EXAMPLE

Mr. E was a 42-year-old construction worker. One day, the scaffolding upon which he was standing collapsed. Mr. E and a coworker fell 30 feet to the ground, and the scaffolding fell on top of them. Mr. E's coworker died as others were extricating them. Mr. E had not been seriously injured, but he feared that he too would die if not extricated quickly. Medical examination revealed that Mr. E had suffered some bone fractures in his legs, and he was admitted to the hospital for treatment. He was discharged to his home after a two-day admission. Mr. E brought a workers' compensation claim against his employer. He claimed that he had PTSD and would never be able to work again as a result of the accident and the ensuing emotional injury.

A forensic evaluation determined that Mr. E met the criteria for a diagnosis of PTSD but that he did not have the degree of functional impairment he claimed. Although not working, he continued to engage in other physical activities that he enjoyed, such as playing softball and bowling. He had not become socially isolated, and his wife reported that she had not noticed any major personality changes. She did report that Mr. E occasionally had nightmares, but overall he was able to sleep quite well. He did demonstrate severe anxiety when he returned to the scene of the accident or when he was exposed to heights, and he tried to avoid these two situations. He had no other anxiety or avoidance symptoms. Despite meeting the criteria for PTSD, Mr. E had minimal functional impairment, which was limited to certain situations. His prognosis, particularly with appropriate treatment, was quite good. Accommodations such as change in work site and job assignments would likely result in good functional recovery even if he were to experience some residual PTSD symptoms.

CASE EXAMPLE

Mr. F was a 35-year-old steel worker. He was severely burned on his back, groin, and legs by molten steel in an accident caused by a coworker. As the molten steel was falling toward him, Mr. F believed he was going to die. His recovery was long and painful, and he developed a chronic pain syndrome from scar tissue and nerve damage. His physical pain triggered flashbacks of the accident on a daily basis. He was diagnosed with PTSD, and he filed a workers' compensation claim against his employer. He claimed complete functional impairment as a result of his physical and emotional injuries, and stated he did not believe he would ever be able to work again.

Forensic evaluation of Mr. F revealed that he had become a social recluse. He stayed at home much of the time and avoided contact with others. Exacerbations of his chronic pain, which occurred frequently, brought on flashbacks of the accident.

He had given up most of his previous social and physical activities. He no longer communicated with his family or friends. He considered attempts to engage him in conversation or activities as intrusions, and such attempts frequently provoked outbursts of anger. He had received appropriate psychiatric and medical treatment but without significant improvement. He received vocational rehabilitation training, but after a few hours, he was unable to participate because of pain. His functional impairment was severe and resulted from the effects of his chronic pain syndrome and PTSD.

The presence of a physical injury complicated and exacerbated Mr. F's PTSD symptoms and recovery of function. Despite appropriate medical and psychiatric treatment, his chronic pain syndrome and PTSD symptoms had become so enmeshed that he was not able to overcome either. As a result, Mr. F's prognosis for improvement was quite poor.

Mr. E and Mr. F were both exposed to traumatic events, and both were diagnosed with PTSD. The assessment of damages in litigation is closely associated with the psychiatric assessment of the level of an individual's impairment. Often, simply assigning a psychiatric diagnosis to an individual gives the impression that the individual is of necessity functionally impaired. PTSD is indeed known to be associated with a significant risk of impaired functioning and diminished quality of life. However, a diagnosis of PTSD, like other psychiatric diagnoses, does not of itself establish the degree of an individual's functional impairment. The loss of function may be greater or less than a given diagnosis might imply, and the individual's performance may fall short of, or exceed, that usually associated with a diagnosis.

Because of the importance of an individual's present and future functioning in litigation, the forensic evaluator is obligated to give this aspect of the assessment careful consideration. Conclusions regarding functional impairment should be supported with data collected from a variety of sources of information. The evaluation should include an assessment of the severity of symptoms and the effect of these symptoms in all spheres of the claimant's functioning. This will determine whether the symptoms truly interfere specifically with occupational functioning.

The use of standard assessment scales rating levels of psychological, social, and occupational functioning indicates a thoughtful evaluation of functional impairment that can be communicated in a standardized format. As discussed previously, the forensic examiner should consider using the Global Assessment of Functioning (GAF) Scale set forth in the *DSM-IV-TR* or the scale described in the American Medical Association's *Guide to the Evaluation of Permanent Impairment*. The use of these standardized scales helps the examiner avoid evaluations of psychological damage based solely on his or her clinical experience and helps ensure that all areas of functioning are assessed and rated.

In addition, the PTSD claimant's pre-incident and post-incident functional status must be determined and compared. A review of records is often essential is this aspect of the evaluation. Employment, school, police, military, medical, and psychiatric and other pertinent records should be reviewed if they are available. When possible, persons who have known the claimant both before and after the events in question should be interviewed. Psychological testing may also be of use if claims include problems with memory or other cognitive functions due to psychiatric symptoms. Present level of functioning is more accurately determined when this information is available for review.

Forensic evaluators are also frequently asked to assess prognosis and future level of function in individuals with PTSD. The likelihood of improvement or deterioration of function due to the future course of the illness can vary widely among individuals and is based on a number of factors. Predictive risk factors for chronic PTSD have been identified on the PTSD prognostic checklist (see Table 13-6) and may assist clinicians and forensic examiners in evaluating the future course of this disorder.[99] In general, current functional impairment is a good predictor of future impairment. The inability to return to work by the time of a legal settlement, for whatever reason, is indicative of a poor prognosis. As with diagnosis, however, an explicit and specific connection between prognosis and functional impairments should be made for each PTSD claimant. In addition, other factors besides chronicity of illness are of considerable importance in the assessment of prognosis and future level of functional impairment.

Treatment and motivation for recovery are major factors in such assessments. The forensic psychiatrist must evaluate the adequacy and effects of a PTSD claimant's treatment. Effective treatment can result in significant symptom relief and improvement of function. Even if an individual is not able to function in one area of employment, treatment that includes rehabilitation and vocational training may result in a return to function in another area. Individuals with PTSD often receive poor treatment, which can result in an exacerbation of symptoms and a deterioration of functioning. The harm caused by poor or inadequate treatment can be as severe as the original injury itself and may be irreparable. The effects of such treatment must be addressed separately from the impairment in function directly attributable to the original injury itself, since an employer is not typically liable for damages related to poor treatment.

For some individuals, lack of motivation for recovery is the major feature of continuing impairment. Lack of motivation can result from depression and may be difficult to distinguish from mental impairment. An individual's underlying personality characteristics, however, may be important in determining whether he is motivated to benefit from treatment or rehabilitation. For example, an individual who tends to be dependent may become more dependent as the illness proceeds. The exacerbation of a pathological character trait may be more significant than symptoms of the illness in negating motivation for improved function. Ultimately, making this distinction requires a clinical judgment, which should be aided by a careful investigation of the individual's efforts and accomplishments before and after the onset of the alleged impairment. Since a claimant is legally required to mitigate his damages, his adherence to treatment recommendations and compliance with treatment should be evaluated, as well as his reasons for either complying with or refusing treatment suggestions.

The forensic evaluation must also consider the role of litigation in the clinical presentation and assessment of functional impairment of a PTSD claimant. Involvement in the litigation process is an extremely stressful experience

---

[99]Simon, *supra* note 45.

regardless of the outcome and is widely acknowledged to exacerbate a plaintiff's psychological symptoms regardless of the diagnosis.[100] Clinicians frequently observe exacerbations of PTSD symptoms in their patients during periods of intense litigation activity. These clinical exacerbations can result from the inevitable reexperiencing of aspects of the traumatic event as well as the exposure to an intrusive and often invalidating adversarial process. They often result in disruption of current functioning and relationships in the claimant's present employment and personal life. In addition, the litigation can reinforce the need to hold onto or exaggerate symptoms. Finally, litigation often results in severe financial stress, which can further exacerbate symptoms and cause a deterioration in function. The effects of the stress of litigation, like other environmental stressors, are expressly excluded in the standardized rating scale assessments of functioning. Those aspects of functional impairment related to the stress of litigation must be assessed and identified separately from those related to the PTSD injuries.

Continued incapacity despite apparent medical recovery after an injury may be due to several factors, one of which may be malingering. The pursuit of a financial award can induce individuals to avoid treatment and maintain a symptomatic state as a part of legal strategy. However, other factors may play a role. Physical injury and pain often produce regression, characterized by a breakdown of mature coping mechanisms. Injured patients may become totally dependent on their families. In these individuals, the gratification of dependency needs is an unconscious secondary gain that leads to resistance to recovery and improved functioning. Often such a situation is accompanied by depression. This may further decrease an individual's motivation and interest in what happens to him and result in a more delayed recovery. In addition, certain secondary detrimental psychological effects occur as a result of an unoccupied individual's lack of access to the beneficial psychological, social, and financial rewards derived from productive occupational functioning. The examiner must distinguish the functional impairment that is a response to PTSD from impairment as a result of the secondary consequences of not working.

The two cases described above demonstrate how widely functional impairment can vary in diagnoses of PTSD. The use of a standardized rating scale in the evaluation of these cases demonstrates the usefulness of such a tool in the evaluation and communication of level of functioning. Mr. E would be given a comparatively high GAF score, and Mr. F would receive a much lower rating. When a claimant receives a high GAF score and appears able to function effectively in all areas of endeavor except work, issues of motivation to return to work, secondary gain, or malingering must be considered. When physical injury and PTSD coexist, a low GAF score reflects the conclusion that chronic pain or physical incapacity combined with emotional injury may prevent return to a functional level required for a work situation.

Claims regarding emotional harm form the bulk of employer liability in employment litigation and are critical in the determination of damages and

---

[100]Larry H. Strasburger, *The Litigant-Patient: Mental Health Consequences of Civil Litigation*, 27 J. AM. ACAD. PSYCHIATRY & L. 203–12 (1999).

awards. The presence of psychological symptoms does not necessarily equate with level of disability or functional impairment. The forensic psychiatrist must evaluate evidence of impairment found in the claimant's psychiatric history, behavior, examination, and documentation. The accurate evaluation of functional impairment can mitigate or substantiate damage assessments.

D. PTSD Used as Syndrome Evidence

CASE EXAMPLE

Ms. G was a 26-year-old assembly line worker in an electrical factory. One day, toward the end of the late shift, her supervisor asked her to come to his office. When she arrived, he appeared to be intoxicated. He closed and locked the door, and sexually assaulted her. The assault included vaginal intercourse and oral sex over three hours. Ms. G attempted to stop him, begged him to let her go, and tried to flee, but he successfully persisted in his assault. When he did finally allow her to leave, he said he would deny the assault if she attempted to report it, and that no one would believe her word against his. Because the assault occurred after hours, there were no witnesses.

Ms. G was stunned and overwhelmed. In a dissociated state, she drove herself home. Feeling shamed and dirty, she showered repeatedly during the next 48 hours. She called in sick to work and would not leave her room. She did not tell anyone what had happened. Her roommate noticed that something was wrong, and on the third day after the assault heard Ms. G sobbing uncontrollably. She confronted Ms. G, who related the details of the assault to her. The roommate convinced Ms. G to go to the police and bring a complaint against the supervisor.

The supervisor denied Ms. G's allegations. Since there were no witnesses and no physical evidence of assault, no criminal charges were filed. Ms. G retained a lawyer and brought a lawsuit against the supervisor and her employer. She was evaluated by two psychiatrists, one retained by her attorney and one retained by the defense. The plaintiff's expert made a diagnosis of rape trauma syndrome and identified the traumatic exposure and proximate cause to be the workplace assault. The defense expert also concluded that Ms. G had a diagnosis of PTSD. He found no evidence of traumatic exposure other than the reported assault, nor did he find preexisting psychiatric history or personal vulnerabilities. The defense objected to the admission of the plaintiff's expert's testimony on the grounds that it was not probative. The defense argued that in inferring that the rape had occurred as the plaintiff alleged from testimony indicating the presence of PTSD, the plaintiff's expert was usurping the role of the jury, and thus his testimony should not be admitted.

Employment litigation related to claims of sexual harassment and assault frequently must be litigated in the absence of corroborative witness testimony and physical evidence. Such cases often come down to a "he said, she said" situation. In recent years, various syndromes relating to traumatic exposure have been identified and widely publicized. Such syndromes may be offered as evidence during litigation. Examples of this include battered woman syndrome, battered child syndrome, and rape trauma syndrome. These syndromes are not psychiatric diagnoses. They are descriptions of symptom clusters based on a common traumatic exposure.

Expert testimony about various trauma syndromes has been offered in both civil and criminal cases to establish that a specific traumatic exposure has occurred. Because such syndromes are not enumerated as diagnostic entities in the *DSM-IV-TR*, they are more susceptible to idiosyncratic or biased use. It has been argued that the use of syndrome evidence should be clearly stated to be such and differentiated from formal *DSM-IV-TR* diagnoses supported by clinical and scientific research.

Courts have been cautious in approaching the use of such syndromes as evidence that an alleged event occurred. Among other problems related to the use of such evidence, the symptoms reported may have resulted from a traumatic event other than the one alleged. For these and other reasons, courts have both allowed and rejected syndrome evidence testimony. Some courts have held that an expert may testify that the victim's behavior and symptoms follow a pattern seen in persons suffering a particular type of traumatic exposure. Others have held that such testimony is inadmissible.[101] However, more extensive diagnostic evaluation often reveals that individuals described as having a trauma-related syndrome actually meet the *DSM-IV-TR* criteria for a diagnosis of PTSD.

A court may nevertheless consider a diagnosis of PTSD equivalent to syndrome evidence when no other evidence of the alleged traumatic exposure exists. Thus, a diagnosis of PTSD may be disallowed as a means of proving the occurrence of any specific traumatic exposure. The vignette of Ms. G resembles the facts of *Spencer v. General Electric Co.*,[102] In *Spencer*, a female worker brought a tort action alleging that her supervisor had sexually harassed, assaulted, and raped her. The supervisor denied that any rape had taken place. The plaintiff offered into evidence a forensic psychiatrist's opinion that the plaintiff suffered from PTSD whose symptoms were consistent with exposure to the trauma of assault and rape. The court rejected the evidence, noting that authorities were divided regarding the admissibility of PTSD testimony to prove that the disorder's triggering event, in this case a rape, had occurred. The court stated: "PTSD is simply a diagnostic category created by psychiatrists, to help identify, predict, and treat emotional problems experienced by the counselors, clients or patients. It was not developed or devised as a tool for ferreting out the truth in cases where it is hotly disputed whether the rape occurred." The court concluded that evidence of PTSD is not a scientifically reliable means of proving that a rape occurred, and testimony regarding PTSD was disallowed on this basis.

A forensic psychiatrist can clinically determine the presence of PTSD in an individual who cannot legally prove that a reported traumatic exposure has occurred. Extensive investigation by the evaluator may fail to find any evidence

---

[101]GARY B. MELTON ET AL., PSYCHOLOGICAL EVALUATION FOR THE COURTS 209–10 (1997).

[102]697 F. Supp. 204 (E.D. Va. 1988), *aff'd*, 894 F.2d 651 (4th Cir. 1990).

of an alternate traumatic exposure or individual vulnerability to the development of PTSD. In the absence of evidence of other traumatic exposure, the evaluator should maintain his honest opinion that PTSD is present and that the traumatic exposure alleged could result in the development of PTSD. If questioned, he might also have to allow that no diagnosis establishes etiology. Neither clinical experience nor research has ever demonstrated that the cause of any disorder can be determined on the basis of its clinical presentation. The court will make its own determination regarding the admissibility and probative value of such evidence. However, retaining counsel should be aware that the use of syndrome evidence and the diagnosis of PTSD to prove that a specific traumatic exposure occurred is legally problematic.

E. Malingering

CASE EXAMPLE

Mr. H was a 36-year-old man who worked as a security guard at a large metropolitan hospital. One day, an angry patient with a gun entered the clinic where Mr. H was on duty. Without warning, the patient began shooting at people in the clinic. Mr. H did not have a gun but was able to approach the gunman from behind and disarm and restrain him. Other security staff soon arrived and assisted in restraining the gunman. Mr. H took disability leave due to his reported emotional distress over the incident. He did not return to work and filed a workers' compensation claim against the hospital. He claimed that he had developed PTSD, which was diagnosed by a forensic evaluator retained by his attorney.

On evaluation by the forensic psychiatrist retained by the defense, Mr. H was hostile and challenging. He reported that he was experiencing every PTSD symptom listed in the DSM-IV-TR. He claimed to be completely incapacitated, insisting that he was unable to leave his home and was unable to engage in social activities. In contrast, he described his pre-exposure functioning as extraordinarily good. He repeatedly stated that he had been treated unfairly by the hospital. He reported that he had not obtained treatment because he couldn't afford it.

Mr. H reported that he had been divorced two years prior to the incident. Court documents from the divorce were obtained and revealed that Mr. H had a criminal history, which included selling drugs and fencing stolen merchandise. These records also included an account of a workers' compensation claim brought against a previous employer, in which Mr. H also alleged he had PTSD. A review of documents related to that litigation revealed similar allegations of negligence and an almost identical report of PTSD symptoms.

The case of Mr. H exemplifies a presentation that strongly suggests pure malingering for financial gain. The behaviors discovered by reviewing documents relating to his divorce suggested the presence of an antisocial personality disorder, which should in and of itself raise the suspicion of malingering. Mr. H's demeanor and report of his symptoms during his evaluation also led the examiner to suspect malingering. Other factors in this case that raise the index of suspicion regarding malingering include Mr. H's avoidance of treatment despite his complaints of severe symptoms, the presence of an almost identical complaint in litigation some years before, and his resentment toward his employer.

CASE EXAMPLE

Ms. I was a 32-year-old administrative assistant in a financial corporation. As she was leaving work one day, a slow-moving car in the company garage narrowly avoided hitting her. Ms. I became quite upset. She acknowledged that the car did not hit her, but said that she had sprained her ankle in attempting to avoid it. She was shaking and could not stop crying. She refused offers to transport her to the local emergency room, stating she needed to go home. She walked unassisted to her car and drove herself home. Ms. I did not return to work, stating that she was continuing to experience severe distress as a result of this event and that she could not function. She claimed that as a result of the incident, she had to seek medical attention for her emotional distress, which was diagnosed by the treating clinician as PTSD. Ms. I brought a suit against the operator of the garage for negligence, alleging that poor lighting and traffic signs resulted in the incident in the garage, which was the proximate cause of her injury and her current disability.

On examination, Ms. I reported that she was experiencing some, but not all, of the PTSD symptoms listed in DSM-IV-TR. She did demonstrate impaired concentration and heightened startle responses. She appeared to be genuinely experiencing symptoms and functional impairment associated with PTSD and had no preexisting psychiatric history. Interviews with coworkers, however, revealed that Ms. I was married to an abusive, alcoholic husband. She had told coworkers over the previous months that his drinking and abusive behavior had escalated since he lost his last job. Two months prior to the incident in the garage, Ms. I had reported increasing anxiety, insomnia, and nightmares as a result of her husband's behavior to her primary care physician, who documented this in her medical records. Ms. I's work performance had noticeably deteriorated, and she had been given a documented warning regarding her performance.

Further information obtained from coworkers revealed that one month prior to the mugging, Ms. I's husband threatened her with a gun and had pushed her down ten stairs. She was seen in an emergency room, where she was diagnosed with fractured ribs. She was out of work for one week, and when she returned, coworkers noticed a change in her personality. She stopped talking about her domestic problems and became withdrawn and isolated. She seemed anxious and jumped at any noise or sudden movement. She was unable to concentrate on her work or to complete tasks that she had previously done without difficulty.

Ms. I's evaluation also raised suspicions for the forensic examiner and proved to be an example of the false-attribution form of malingering. A minor traffic mishap in which no significant harm is incurred is unlikely to result in the severity of symptoms Ms. I displayed, particularly in an individual with no preexisting psychiatric history or vulnerability. Evaluation revealed both a diagnosis of PTSD and an exposure to at least one recent and more severe traumatic event. Psychologically, Ms. I was demonstrating displacement of her feelings regarding her husband and her increasingly difficult domestic situation onto her minor accident and employment situation. In addition, financial stress due to her husband's unemployment and her own increasing difficulty coping with her marital problems provided motives for not returning to work and for seeking a financial award.

The possibility of malingering must always be considered in a forensic setting. Malingering is defined in *DSM-IV-TR* as "the intentional production of false or grossly exaggerated physical or psychological symptoms motivated by external incentives, such as avoiding military duty, avoiding work, obtaining financial compensation, evading criminal prosecution, or obtaining drugs."[103] Malingering differs from fictitious disorders, where the motivation for the intentional production of symptoms is to assume the role of a patient. The sick role is itself the goal, whereas the production of symptoms in malingering is a temporary means to reach another, usually financial, goal. There are several types of malingering. Pure malingering is the feigning of disease when it does not exist at all. Partial malingering is the conscious exaggeration of existing symptoms or the fraudulent allegation that prior genuine symptoms are still present. Another type of malingering is false imputation, in which the patient ascribes actual symptoms to a cause that he consciously recognizes has no relationship to the symptoms. The motivation for malingering is usually financial gain but may also be sympathy and social support.

The incidence of malingered psychological symptoms after injury is unknown, but estimates of malingered illness range from 1 to 50 percent.[104] The types of psychiatric disorders that most commonly occur after a traumatic experience include PTSD, depressive disorders, postconcussion syndromes, and, occasionally, psychosis. Plaintiffs are most likely to malinger concussion or depression. Pure malingering is uncommon in PTSD cases, but it is possible to find exaggeration of symptoms. Since descriptions of symptoms of various disorders are easily accessible to the resourceful individual, and a diagnosis of PTSD is often based primarily on subjective reports of symptoms, the forensic evaluator must consider the possibility that an individual, if not engaging in pure malingering, may be engaging in partial malingering or in false imputation for personal gain.

The clinician's index of suspicion regarding the malingering of psychological distress or PTSD following a traumatic exposure should rise when the following facts are observed or reported:

- A malingerer may assert an inability to work but retain the capacity for recreation, such as enjoyment of movies or sports activities. In contrast, the genuine PTSD patient is more likely to withdraw from recreational activities as well as work.
- A malingerer may have a history of spotty employment and drifting, and may have been a marginal member of society for many years. A person who has

---

[103]DSM-IV-TR, *supra* note 4, at 739.
[104]Phillip J. Resnick, *Guidelines for the Evaluation of Malingering in Posttraumatic Stress Disorder*, in POSTTRAUMATIC STRESS DISORDER IN LITIGATION: GUIDELINES FOR FORENSIC ASSESSMENT 117 (Robert I. Simon ed., 1995).

always been a responsible, honest member of society is less likely to feign illness.
- A malingerer may seem evasive during the interview and be unwilling to make definite statements about returning to work, financial gain, or other expectations.
- A malingerer may be sullen, ill at ease, or resentful.
- A malingerer may have a history of previously incapacitating injuries and extensive absences from employment.
- A malingerer is unlikely to volunteer information regarding sexual dysfunction, although he is generally eager to emphasize his physical complaints.
- A malingerer's personality is more likely to be greedy, dishonest, unpleasant, or demanding.
- A malingerer is unlikely to volunteer information about nightmares unless she has read the diagnostic criteria for PTSD.
- A malingerer may depict himself and prior functioning in exclusively complimentary terms.
- A malingerer may pursue a claim tenaciously, although she alleges that she is depressed or incapacitated by symptoms of PTSD.
- A malingerer may refuse employment of which he is capable in spite of some disability.
- A malingerer focuses on the symptoms of PTSD related to reexperiencing the traumatic event, rather than psychic numbing symptoms.
- A malingerer is more likely to present the symptoms very neatly, as if reciting from a textbook.[105]

The clinical assessment of malingering requires a detailed history of symptoms and treatment efforts, accompanied by careful corroboration of the information collected. Clinicians who simply inquire about specific symptoms of PTSD and other *DSM-IV-TR* diagnostic criteria are more likely to miss this malingering or exaggeration of symptoms. It has been demonstrated that it is easy to endorse the symptoms of PTSD to the point of meeting the *DSM-IV-TR* criteria,[106] and the accessibility of the criteria permits the resourceful malingerer to report the "right" symptoms. It is critical to get corroboration for these reports, whenever possible, by others who have heard the examinee discuss them outside the context of the litigation.

On examination, the clinician should also insist on a detailed illustration of PTSD symptoms. Coached PTSD claimants may know which PTSD symptoms to report but may not be able to elaborate on them with convincing personal life details. Invented symptoms are more likely to have a vague or stilted quality. The examiner should see whether claimants minimize other causes of their symptoms or exaggerate the severity of the traumatic exposure.

---

[105]Phillip J. Resnick, *Malingering of Posttraumatic Psychiatric Disorders*, 4 J. PRAC. PSYCHOL. & BEHAV. HEALTH 329 (1998); Phillip J. Resnick, *Malingering of Posttraumatic Disorders, in* CLINICAL ASSESSMENT OF MALINGERING AND DECEPTION 130 (Richard Rogers ed., 2d ed. 1997).

[106]Resnick, *Malingering of Posttraumatic Psychiatric Disorders*, *supra* note 105, at 331.

Clinicians should also look for actual evidence in the mental status exam of irritability, difficulty concentrating, and exaggerated startle responses. Malingerers are also unlikely to volunteer information about nightmares unless they have read the diagnostic criteria for PTSD. In addition, genuine nightmares in PTSD show variations on the theme of the traumatic event.[107] The malingerer who does not know the expected dream patterns may claim that he has repetitive dreams that always reenact the traumatic event in exactly the same way.

The forensic clinician also must obtain a detailed history of the claimant's living patterns preceding the stressor. For example, symptoms such as difficulty concentrating or insomnia may have been present before the traumatic event. Baseline activity in a typical week before the stressor should be compared with reported impairment at the time of the evaluation. The clinician must carefully examine the reasonableness of the relationship between the symptoms and the traumatic exposure, the time elapsed between the traumatic exposure and symptoms development, and the relationship between any prior psychiatric symptoms and current impairment.

An exaggerated sense of self-importance or of the importance of the traumatic exposure and its consequences is often present in malingered cases of PTSD. Certainly, individuals with narcissistic or other types of personality disorders may be exposed to traumatic events. However, such persons also on occasion attach themselves to salient events in the press or current fads in the popular culture. Such individuals may also suffer from identity confusion. For example, a number of men who claimed to have been traumatized in Vietnam were discovered not to be veterans, to be veterans but never to have served in Vietnam, or to be veterans who had served in Vietnam but in a noncombatant capacity. Financial gain was not always the obvious motivation behind their claims. Some appeared to want only to be a part of the Vietnam veterans groups and to gain the social status derived from such membership. In these cases, the gain produced by malingering seemed to lie in establishing a new "enhanced" identity.

The issue of malingering frequently arises in the assessment of sexual harassment claims. Women can and sometimes do make false claims of PTSD in the context of allegations of sexual harassment. It is probable that many of these women, like those who falsely accuse their therapists of sexual misconduct, suffer from Borderline Personality Disorder. The forensic examiner should attempt to understand the psychological dynamics of each individual case in order to provide an effective explanation for the malingering of the claim in question. The examiner should be reluctant to conclude that a sexual harassment claim is false without having arrived at an alternative explanation for the plaintiff's actions that can be substantiated with data from the evaluation.

False or exaggerated sexual harassment claims may result from phenomena other than outright lying or from pathology other than Borderline Personality Disorder. "Pseudologica fantastica," commonly referred to as pathological lying, is rare, but it may also result in false claims. In such cases, the evaluator

---

[107]*Id.* at 333.

often finds that the essence of the accusation is a product of the individual's imagination, but some actual details, such as dates or locations where meetings took place, are added to give a semblance of truth to the lie. The psychological defense of displacement, where a person projects his or her feelings about one individual or situation onto another, can also result in the misattribution of feelings. The person or situation onto whom the feelings are projected is usually less threatening to the claimant than the true object of the feelings. Displacement is a common psychological phenomenon and not necessarily pathological, but in certain individuals it can result in distorted perceptions that lead to false claims of harassment. Such claims are most often seen in women who are victims of abuse by a partner or spouse and who have displaced the feelings related to these events onto another individual, such as a supervisor, or a work-related situation.

Some women file sexual harassment claims in retribution for a perceived wrong, such as a missed promotion or termination, that in actuality did not include sexual harassment. Occasionally, feelings of rejection at the end of consensual affair may trigger such a claim as well. Whereas most women would not react to such a situation with enough anger to drive them to make false accusations, some women with Borderline or Narcissistic Personality Disorder may experience sufficient rage to take such a course of action. Finally, an obsessional erotic fixation can result in the claimant's belief that she has been involved in a true romantic relationship with a coworker or employee. Individuals with borderline erotomania view separation as abandonment, and rejection by the object of affection evokes abandonment rage and may precipitate a claim of sexual harassment in revenge. Although rare, the forensic examiner should consider this possibility in his assessment of such claims. The clinical assessment of malingering can be quite difficult. Drugs such as sodium amytal, which are used to assist in recovering genuinely repressed memories, are not reliable in unmasking malingering.[108] Studies have found that persons simulating traumatic neurosis retained or further exaggerated their malingered symptoms upon receiving sodium amytal. One study found that half of such individuals were able to maintain a lie under the influence of the drug. Psychological tests, in particular the MMPI-2, can be of value in determining untruthful patterns of response and should be obtained whenever there is a suspicion of malingering.

Mental health professionals are often reluctant to give an individual a diagnosis that is the equivalent of calling the person a liar. Forensic psychiatrists may have concerns regarding liability in such cases, even though they are usually protected by immunity.[109] One state court ruled that an action for defamation against a forensic psychiatrist could be brought, even though an action for malpractice could not.[110] One author has suggested that there are only two situations in which a diagnosis of malingering can be confirmed with

---

[108]Resnick, *supra* note 104, at 143.

[109]Robert Weinstock & Thomas Garrick, *Is Liability Possible for Forensic Psychiatrists?* 23 BULL. AM. ACAD. PSYCHIATRY & L. 183 (1995).

[110]Rand v. Miller, 408 S.E.2d 655 (W. Va. 1991).

certainty: when malingerers are caught in the act while they think they are unobserved and when malingerers actually confess to their behavior.[111] Unless a clinician has very strong evidence, he will generally state that a firm conclusion is not possible. Nevertheless, the clinician's suspicions and data supporting them may be crucial in the ultimate outcome of litigation. An individual consciously making a false claim may withdraw when faced with evidence that will demonstrate that he is being less than truthful or is making a false imputation.

V. Conclusion

The diagnosis of PTSD is made upon the finding of certain characteristic symptoms combined with the presence of or perception of an extreme stressor. Although symptoms may start while the traumatic event is still taking place, particularly if the event is of long duration, posttraumatic responses emerge when the immediate threat is over. PTSD is a psychiatric disorder that results from behavioral and biological attempts to cope with the consequences of exposure to extreme stressors. The psychiatric illness of PTSD is not equivalent to the direct responses to adverse experiences or to the normal, transient periods of distress that typically follow adverse events. Unfortunately, both clinicians and the legal system frequently confuse these responses. This confusion is partially responsible for the increased frequency of the association between the diagnosis of PTSD and all types of litigation, including employment litigation.

All parties involved benefit when forensic examiners perform credible psychiatric examinations of PTSD claimants. A credible forensic evaluation strengthens a plaintiff's genuine PTSD claims and allows a defendant to fairly compensate a truly injured individual while defending vigorously against the fabricated or exaggerated claim. Adherence to the general principles of forensic assessment and to the Georgetown Guidelines for the assessment of claims of PTSD in litigation provides a structure and methodology that assist the forensic evaluator in making the complex assessments involved in legal claims involving PTSD. The forensic issues involved in such claims require both a structured evaluation and the knowledgeable consideration of legal and clinical issues specific to PTSD. The combination of a thorough evaluation and knowledge of the complicated issues related to employment litigation and claims of PTSD will inform the psychiatric conclusions required by counsel in advocating for their clients.

---

[111]Resnick, *Malingering of Posttraumatic Psychiatric Disorders*, *supra* note 105.

CHAPTER 14

SPECIAL ISSUES IN SEXUAL HARASSMENT CASES

Mae F. Keller, Ph.D.
Elissa P. Benedek, M.D.

I. History and Legal Context

The behaviors that may constitute sexual harassment have a history as long as that of the workplace. Legal definitions have developed only over the course of the last few decades, however, and the parameters of such definitions are by no means static or uniform. Further, it is important to note that legal definitions may vary from those used in academic research, clinical evaluations, and ordinary social discourse.

Behaviors that may be characterized as sexual harassment span an enormous range—suggestive verbal comments and demeaning, gender-related jokes and remarks; requests for dates, intrusive questions, and unsolicited touching; and pressure for sexual contact and even physical or sexual assault.[1]

Such behaviors may be initiated by a supervisor, instigated by a workplace peer, or perpetrated by a group. The victims may be one, several, or many. They may be male or female. The context of complaints may vary: the workplace may be pervasively aggressive or inappropriately friendly and intrusive. The interpersonal relationship between victim and harasser may range from shared employment only to a romantic relationship that has soured. Compliance with the harassing behavior may or may not be directly linked to continuation in the job, pay raises, or performance reviews. Rejection or reporting of the harassment may be followed by retaliation against the victim. The duration of harassment may vary, but in general the more enduring, severe, or egregious the behavior, the more likely it is to be regarded as harassment.

---

[1]Diane K. Shrier, *Introduction and Brief Overview*, in SEXUAL HARASSMENT IN THE WORKPLACE AND ACADEMIA 3 (Diane K. Shrier ed., 1996).

A. Legal Definitions and Milestones

As noted previously, there are many definitions of sexual harassment, which may vary in important ways. For example, the U.S. Merit Systems Protection Board, in its most recent study, investigated a spectrum of behaviors associated with sexual harassment, such as uninvited letters or materials of a sexual nature; deliberate touching; suggestive looks or gestures; pressure for sexual favors or dates; and sexual teasing, remarks, or questions.[2] The definition focuses on sexual behavior rather than discriminatory acts, and the study expressly acknowledges that many of these behaviors do not meet the legal definition. The various definitions used in the empirical literature and the implications for their application to litigated cases will be discussed further below. For now, it may simply be noted that the law's interest in sexual harassment is not in the regulation of sexuality in the workplace or the enforcement of good manners (though some would argue the courts have overshot the mark and this indeed has become the effect). Rather, the law is intended to address the discriminatory aspects of sexual harassment. It has gradually come to be accepted that such behavior may disrupt equal access to and participation in the workplace. This was not always so.

Current definitions of sexual harassment are rooted in Title VII of the Civil Rights Act of 1964[3] and in Title IX of the Educational Amendments of 1972.[4] Title VII provides that it is illegal to discriminate against employees on the basis of race, color, religion, sex, or national origin. Title IX prohibits discrimination in educational programs that are recipients of federal monies. These statutes themselves did not address the concept of harassment, however. A number of legal milestones shaped the current trends, and since this area of the law is continuing to evolve, any account of it can only be a snapshot in time.

The first cases of sexual harassment brought under Title VII in the early 1970s were dismissed by federal courts, which held that the conduct alleged did not constitute sexual discrimination. For instance, in *Barnes v. Train*,[5] the court viewed a case in which a supervisor retaliated against a female employee who refused his advances as "underpinned by the subtleties of an inharmonious personal relationship."[6] Employers typically were not held liable for the acts of individual employees. In *Corne v. Bausch & Lomb, Inc.*,[7] two women reportedly quit because of a supervisor's verbal and physical abuse. The court held that Title VII might have been applicable had the company's policies been

---

[2]U.S. MERIT SYSTEM PROTECTION BOARD, SEXUAL HARASSMENT IN THE FEDERAL WORKPLACE: TRENDS, PROGRESS, AND CONTINUING CHALLENGES (1995).

[3]2 U.S.C. §§2000e et seq.

[4]*Id.* §§1681 et seq.

[5]13 FEP Cases 123 (D.D.C. 1974), *rev'd sub nom.* Barnes v. Costle, 561 F.2d 983, 15 FEP Cases 345 (D.C. Cir. 1977).

[6]*Id.* at 124.

[7]390 F. Supp. 161, 10 FEP Cases 289 (D. Ariz. 1975), *vacated,* 562 F.2d 55 (9th Cir. 1977) (table).

discriminatory but the law did not apply to the supervisor's "personal urge." Further, the court held that a finding favorable to the plaintiff might lead to a result in which all "amorous or sexually oriented advances" in the workplace were actionable.[8]

Sexual harassment was first recognized by a federal court as a form of discrimination under Title VII in 1976, in *Williams v. Saxbe*,[9] a case involving sexual advances and supervisory retaliation against a female employee who had complained about annoying comments, unfavorable reviews, and unwarranted reprimands. In 1977, the U.S. Court of Appeals for the District of Columbia Circuit found in favor of a plaintiff whose government job had been eliminated after she refused her supervisor's demands for sexual favors.[10] Such cases began to establish acceptance by the courts of quid pro quo harassment as a legitimate basis for claims under Title VII.

Perhaps the most widely known definition of sexual harassment in the workplace was developed by the Equal Employment Opportunity Commission (EEOC) in 1980. The EEOC defined sexual harassment as:

- Unwelcome sexual advances, request for sexual favors, and other verbal or physical conduct of a sexual nature when
- Submission to such conduct is made either explicitly or implicitly a term or condition of an individual's employment,
- Submission to or rejection of such conduct by an individual is used as the basis for employment decisions affecting such individual, or
- Such conduct has the purpose or effect of unreasonably interfering with an individual's work or creating an intimidating, hostile, or offensive working environment.[11]

This definition guides the EEOC in its enforcement activities. In general, cases involving the first three elements have been categorized as *quid pro quo* harassment, and cases involving the fourth element have been described as *hostile environment* harassment. In a quid pro quo case, the victim's submission to unwanted sexual behavior is linked to keeping a job, obtaining a promotion, etc. Power differences between harasser and victim are typically present, and strict liability may apply to employers.

Hostile environment cases have been harder to define and were more slowly accepted by the courts, with a range of outcomes in terms of employer liability. These cases followed in the 1980s after the EEOC guidelines were established. Again, the first cases tended to be unsuccessful. In 1981, the District of Columbia Circuit first found that a harassing work environment

---

[8]*Id.* at 163, 10 FEP Cases at 291.
[9]Williams v. Saxbe, 413 F. Supp. 654, 12 FEP Cases 1093 (D.D.C. 1976), *rev'd on other grounds sub nom.* Williams v. Bell, 587 F. 2d 1240, 17 FEP Cases 1662 (D.C. Cir. 1978).
[10]Barnes v. Costle, 561 F.2d 983, 15 FEP Cases 345 (D.C. Cir. 1977).
[11]29 C.F.R. §1604.11 (1980).

could constitute sex discrimination,[12] following earlier court decisions regarding racial discrimination.[13] Then in 1986, the U.S. Supreme Court upheld the concept of environmental harassment in *Meritor Savings Bank v. Vinson*.[14]

Vinson involved a female bank employee who alleged that her supervisor had made sexual advances and pressured her for sexual relations during her four-year employment. She claimed she resisted at first but then complied for fear of losing her job. The allegations included intercourse between 40 and 50 times, fondling in front of other employees, and several incidents of rape. During the same time, the plaintiff was promoted from teller to assistant branch manager, which the court found to be merit-based. The plaintiff did not avail herself of the bank's complaint procedure, reportedly from fear of her supervisor.

Although *Vinson* has some similarities to typical quid pro quo cases, the Court's specific findings have generally been viewed as defining environmental harassment. Largely tracking the EEOC's definition, the Court held such harassment occurs when "conduct has the purpose or effect of unreasonably interfering with an individual's work performance or creating an intimidating, hostile or offensive work environment." Only harassing conduct that is sufficiently severe or pervasive as to so alter the work environment is unlawful, maintained the *Vinson* Court. In addition, the employer in *Vinson* argued that because the plaintiff suffered psychologically but not economically, Title VII was inapplicable. The Court disagreed, asserting that economic loss was not an essential element of hostile environment harassment. Further, the employer argued that the plaintiff had complied voluntarily with her supervisor's sexual advances. The Court established that the central question was not the voluntary nature of the plaintiff's compliance, but rather the unwelcome nature of the supervisor's conduct.

The elements of a claim of hostile environment harassment have been defined through court decisions since 1986. In general, the following five elements must be present:

- *The victim is a member of a protected class under Title VII.* Title VII applies to both women and men.
- *The victim was subjected to unwelcome harassment.* Factors relevant to establishing unwelcomeness have included the victim's response and his or her characteristic workplace behavior, sexual history, and personality structure.
- *The harassment was related to the victim's gender.* Proof of this element may be relatively straightforward when the alleged harassment is overtly sexual but may be less clear when it is not. Some courts have held a variety of behaviors may constitute sexual harassment.
- *The harassment was so severe or pervasive as to affect a term, condition, or privilege of employment.* Evidence regarding severity/pervasiveness is to be based on the totality of circumstances, and may include psychological damages.

---

[12]Bundy v. Jackson, 641 F.2d 934, 24 FEP Cases 1155 (D.C. Cir. 1981).
[13]Rogers v. EEOC, 454 F.2d 234, 4 FEP Cases 92 (5th Cir. 1971).
[14]477 U.S. 57, 40 FEP Cases 1822 (1986).

- *The employer should be held liable.* Questions regarding this element often revolve around whether the employer knew or should have known of the alleged misconduct and took appropriate action in response.[15]

Defenses to environmental harassment claims typically involve assertions that one or more of these elements is not present.

The early 1990s were a particularly critical time in the history of sexual harassment. Public awareness of harassment and the number of complaints increased markedly after Anita Hill's testimony before Congress during Clarence Thomas's confirmation hearings. Enactment in the same year of the Civil Rights Act of 1991 raised the stakes of harassment litigation by permitting the recovery of compensatory and punitive damages. The "reasonable woman," rather than "reasonable person" standard, was applied for the first time by the Ninth Circuit in *Ellison v. Brady*,[16] as the court noted that women are disproportionately the victims of sexual harassment and may find offensive conduct that men regard as unobjectionable. This standard is also used by the EEOC but has not been adopted uniformly. Pornography in the workplace was first held to constitute harassment for which an employer may be held liable in *Robinson v. Jacksonville Shipyards*.[17]

In 1993, the issue of psychological injury and damages in sexual harassment cases was addressed by the Supreme Court in *Harris v. Forklift Systems, Inc.*[18] This was an environmental harassment case involving repeated demeaning comments and sexual suggestions toward the plaintiff and other female employees by a supervisor, with other males joining in. The plaintiff experienced a range of stress-related symptoms and received medication as a result, but a lower court ruled that the harassment did not seriously compromise her work performance or emotional well-being. The case was eventually heard by the Supreme Court, which held unanimously that a sexual harassment plaintiff need not prove psychological injury in order to recover monetary damages. The Court held that psychological harm was but one sort of evidence relevant to the question of whether the harassment had been so severe or pervasive as to alter the conditions of the plaintiff's employment. As in *Vinson*, the Court found that an abusive, hostile work environment involving "discriminatory intimidation, ridicule, and insult" could, in and of itself, be evidence of such severity/pervasiveness as to constitute a violation of Title VII.

Regarding the bases for legal action in sexual harassment cases, the most common basis currently is Title VII or Title IX. In addition, such complaints may be pursued as common-law torts. Tort actions provided for punitive damages and damages for pain and suffering before similar remedies became available under

---

[15] Ramona L. Paetzold & Anne M. O'Leary-Kelly, *The Implications of U.S. Supreme Court and Circuit Court Decisions for Hostile Environment Sexual Harassment Cases*, in SEXUAL HARASSMENT IN THE WORKPLACE 93 (Margaret S. Stockdale ed., 1996).

[16] 924 F.2d 872, 54 FEP Cases 1346 (9th Cir. 1991).

[17] 760 F. Supp. 1486, 57 FEP Cases 971 (M.D. Fla. 1991).

[18] 510 U.S. 17, 63 FEP Cases 225 (1993).

the Civil Rights Act of 1991. Tort claims may include intentional or negligent infliction of emotional distress, negligence, violation of public policy, assault and battery, and loss of consortium. Workers' compensation claims may also be pursued in sexual harassment cases in many states.[19]

Criminal proceedings are relatively rare in sexual harassment cases, although allegations of criminal sexual misconduct are not particularly unusual. Such allegations range from low-level sexual assaults, such as unwanted touching, to forcible rape. Other criminal allegations may involve stalking, vandalism, etc.

B. Developments in Sexual Harassment

Some of the questions about the legal definition of sexual harassment and the scope of Title VII and Title IX were addressed by the U.S. Supreme Court, following a number of years of considerable variation in courts' rulings. Beginning in 1998, after a period of relative silence following *Harris* in 1993, the Court heard several cases that will clearly shape developments for some time.

1. Sexual Harassment in School Settings

Recent court decisions have extended application of many of the legal principles developed in sexual harassment cases in adult employment settings to schools, based upon a view of schools as the "workplaces" of children and adolescents.

In *Davis v. Monroe County Board of Education*,[20] the U.S. Supreme Court held in a 5–4 decision that schools may be held liable for sexual harassment by students. The reasoning followed an earlier decision regarding schools' liability for teacher-student nonconsensual sex and harassment.[21] The case involved events beginning when the female victim was in the fifth grade. A male classmate reportedly began taunting her, asking her for sex in crude terms, and touching her breast and genital area. On one occasion, the boy put a doorstop in his pants and behaved in a sexually suggestive manner. Despite repeated complaints by the girl's mother, the school did not intervene. The girl's grades dropped and she wrote a suicide note. The family eventually pressed criminal charges, and the boy pleaded guilty in juvenile court to sexual battery. The family subsequently sued the school. The lower court held Title IX did not apply to student-on-student sexual harassment. The case was later appealed to the Supreme Court.

---

[19]For further discussion of legal bases for harassment lawsuits, see Elissa P. Benedek, *Forensic Aspects of Sexual Harassment*, in SEXUAL HARASSMENT IN THE WORKPLACE AND ACADEMIA, *supra* note 1, at 116.

[20]526 U.S. 629 (1999).

[21]Gebser v. Lago Vista Ind. Sch. Dist., 524 U.S. 274 (1998) (school district not liable for teacher-student sexual harassment under Title IX, unless an official in a position to take corrective action knew of and was deliberately indifferent to the misconduct).

The majority opinion held that, in order to be liable for harassment under Title IX, schools must know of the harassment and respond with "deliberate indifference" to behavior "so severe, pervasive and objectively offensive that it denies its victims the equal access to education" guaranteed by Title IX.[22] Ordinary "acts of teasing and name calling among school children" are not cause for action, according to the Court.[23] The dissent argued that the decision represented an unwarranted federal intrusion into the everyday affairs of local schools. The reported harassment was described as merely "immature, childish behavior," and the dissent cautioned against applying the norms of the adult workplace to peer relationships in schools.[24]

The *Davis* Court's decision occurred in a cultural context in which prohibitions against sexual harassment have come to be more broadly applied, while at the same time, overtly sexual speech and behavior have become more and more mainstream, among children, adolescents, and adults. *Davis*, though controversial, may be regarded as relatively straightforward in that the behavior was specifically sexual and the harasser was readily identifiable. In other instances, the distinction between adolescent cruelty, peer dynamics, and overt sexual harassment may often be more difficult to define.

2. Same-Sex Harassment

The majority of sexual harassment cases involve female plaintiffs and male defendants. Complaints of women harassing men are relatively infrequent, but it has been generally understood that Title VII is applicable in such cases. However, for a number of years courts ruled inconsistently on the issue of sexual harassment allegations between same-sexed persons. In some instances, it was concluded that same-sex harassment was not covered by Title VII's prohibition against discrimination based on sex. In others, courts concluded that harassment linked to homosexuality was covered, but not harassment involving two same-sex heterosexuals.

In 1998 the U.S. Supreme Court ruled unanimously in *Oncale v. Sundowner Offshore Services, Inc.*[25] that employers could be held liable for same-sex harassment involving heterosexuals. The plaintiff in *Oncale* worked on an oil rig and reported taunts, threats of rape, and sexual abuse while showering. He complained to supervisory personnel and ultimately left his job. The federal district court, affirmed by the circuit court, held that same-sex harassment is not prohibited by Title VII. In reversing the earlier decisions, the Supreme Court affirmed that Title VII addresses discrimination based upon sex. Sexual desire need play no role; harassing actions motivated by gender and expressed in terms consistent with gender-based discrimination are sufficient. The Court also addressed concerns that Title VII would be used as a sweeping standard

---

[22]526 U.S. at 650.
[23]*Id.* at 652.
[24]*Id.* at 674 (Kennedy J., dissenting).
[25]523 U.S. 75, 76 FEP Cases 221 (1998).

of workplace civility, stating that the statute does not require asexuality and is not concerned with ordinary horseplay or flirtation; rather, it prohibits behavior so objectively offensive as to alter the conditions of employment.

3. Employer Precautions and Employee Responsibility

In a departure from lower court rulings, the U.S. Supreme Court in 1998 held in *Burlington Industries, Inc. v. Ellerth* [26] and *Faragher v. City of Boca Raton*[27] that employers may be vicariously liable for harassment that had no tangible adverse effects, and of which they were ignorant, unless they can offer an affirmative defense showing that (1) reasonable care was exercised to prevent and correct sexual harassment, and (2) the employee unreasonably failed to take advantage of the corrective opportunities offered by the employer. Both cases involved female plaintiffs who left their jobs and pursued litigation without pursuing internal complaint procedures. These rulings established a shared responsibility among employers and employees for preventing and correcting harassment. Employers are held responsible for maintaining strict policies against harassment and an effective mechanism for employees to use to report harassment. Employees are now held responsible in most instances for availing themselves of the employer's preventive and corrective mechanisms rather than just quitting and suing.

C. Alternatives to Litigation: Complaint Procedures, Mediation, and Arbitration

Many sexual harassment complaints never reach the litigation stage. Most employers now have some form of internal complaint procedure by which sexual harassment claims may be addressed, and, as noted, the Supreme Court in *Ellerth* and *Faragher* decreed that a sexual harassment complainant who "unreasonably" fails to take advantage of such internal complaint procedures might be barred from litigating in court. Those involved in psychiatric assessment in sexual harassment cases should have some familiarity with complaint processes, since a historical account of these processes may figure in the litigation, especially if postreporting retaliation or inadequate investigation and intervention by the employer are alleged.

Various kinds of internal complaint procedures exist. Many large employers have a centralized equal employment office or human resources department to investigate and make recommendations. In such systems, reporting of all suspected incidents of harassment is often mandatory, and the investigation procedures may be uniform, with formal adjudication as the outcome. Ordinary supervisory staff may have little formal role in the process beyond reporting. In a decentralized system, managers and supervisors may be responsible for

---

[26] 524 U.S. 742, 77 FEP Cases 1 (1998).
[27] 524 U.S. 775, 77 FEP Cases 14 (1998).

investigating complaints of discrimination and sexual harassment along with their other supervisory responsibilities. Various arrangements may be made for reporting, investigating, and addressing complaints, but the process typically involves local supervision, perhaps in concert with human resources.

One commentator has addressed the relative advantages and disadvantages of these two models.[28] A centralized system may provide greater consistency in how complaints are handled, greater expertise on the part of the EEO officer who typically serves as the investigator, and more complete recordkeeping with a corresponding increase in the ability to identify patterns or repeated problems. However, some employees, depending upon the nature of the complaint, may be uncomfortable with formal, win-lose procedures. A decentralized system may provide for more rapid and flexible resolution of complaints, and employees may more readily report difficulties to someone they know, but it may be difficult to clearly delineate responsibility in such a system, and a local supervisor may be or appear to be, more vulnerable to conflicts of interest.

Hybrid models combining features of both approaches can also be adopted. Some studies have addressed questions of the relative efficacy of various organizational models in terms of accessibility to complainants and cost-effectiveness.[29] Dissatisfaction with harassment policies and procedures is not proof they failed or were poorly designed, however. There are no perfect policies and procedures; such systems must be tailored to the overall organization's mission and structure. Further, as one commentator has observed, once a complaint has arisen, "it is difficult to bring about any resolution that is wholly positive. This virtually guarantees that harassment policies and complaint systems have an unsatisfactory reputation."[30]

In assessing the efficacy of employer policies and procedures, it may be tempting to conclude that organizations should be able to prevent harassment and the associated complaints. As will be discussed further in this chapter's review of empirical studies, however, social science models of sexual harassment see it as a function of both individuals' behavior and features of organizations. While some organizations may be viewed as more or less tolerant of harassment, individual employee action is still an important variable. Some employees may be prone to engaging in harassing behavior regardless of the strictness or leniency of the employer's policies. Another measure of efficacy of employer policies might well be that the organization has a complaint procedure that is actually actively utilized.

Even where internal complaint procedures fail to resolve a harassment complaint, such a complaint may still be successfully resolved via mediation

---

[28]Mary P. Rowe, *Dealing with Harassment: A Systems Approach*, in SEXUAL HARASSMENT IN THE WORKPLACE, *supra* note 15, at 241.

[29]*Id.*; Deborah Erdos Knapp & Gary A. Kustis: *The Real "Disclosure": Sexual Harassment and the Bottom Line*, in SEXUAL HARASSMENT IN THE WORKPLACE, *supra* note 15, at 197; Kathy A. Hanisch: *An Integrated Framework for Studying the Outcomes of Sexual Harassment: Consequences for Individuals and Organizations*, in SEXUAL HARASSMENT IN THE WORKPLACE, *supra* note 15, at 174.

[30]Rowe, *supra* note 28, at 234.

or other form of alternative dispute resolution before any lawsuit is filed. The Supreme Court's decision in *Circuit City Stores, Inc. v. Adams*[31] confirms that employers may require binding arbitration as a means of settling disputes and avoiding litigation. The impact of this decision may be varied, but it is likely to encourage further the use of arbitration and mediation.

An article published in the aftermath of *Ellerth* and *Faragher* but before *Adams* discusses alternative dispute resolution methods such as mediation and arbitration in sexual harassment cases.[32] The article points out that although mediation and arbitration are not associated with large monetary awards, these alternative approaches may be more accessible to many workers, in contrast to expensive, time-consuming litigation. Mediation involves facilitating communication to support the process of reaching a settlement, and mediators often may also provide opinions, predictions, and evaluations about the likely outcome of a case if it is taken to the lawsuit stage. Arbitration in sexual harassment cases is more potentially problematic, in the author's view, because of concerns that nonvoluntary arbitration favors employers since they are able to establish many of the rules, avoid jury trials, and have an advantage as "repeat players"; thus she underscores the importance of due process safeguards. Nonetheless, neither the EEOC nor the courts resolve the majority of sexual harassment complaints, and many disputes lend themselves to local solutions and alternative methods of dispute resolution.

Psychiatrists and psychologists may be involved in mediation and arbitration proceedings. They may serve as evaluators to the extent that the procedures are concerned with issues of credibility, emotional impact, personality factors, and other issues that might be addressed by psychological assessment. They may also have the potential to serve as mediators, as mental health professionals do currently in, for instance, child custody matters.

D. Intellectual History and Controversies in Sexual Harassment

The history of sexual harassment is antidote for anyone who believes that ideas have no practical impact upon American culture. The passage of Title VII in 1964 and Title IX in 1972 occurred as part of a broad approach to discrimination and civil rights. More specifically, sexual harassment law owes much to feminism and feminist scholars. Perhaps best known among these is Catharine MacKinnon, whose work in the 1970s contributed significantly to the shift from viewing sexualized workplace behavior as a private and personal matter to recognizing quid pro quo and hostile environment harassment as a form of gender discrimination.[33] In addition, MacKinnon argued that sex for women

---

[31] 532 U.S. 105, 85 FEP Cases 266 (2001).

[32] Susan A. FitzGibbon *Arbitration, Mediation, and Sexual Harassment*, 5 Psychol., Pub. Pol'y & L. 693 (1999).

[33] Catharine MacKinnon, Sexual Harassment of Working Women: A Case of Sex Discrimination (1979).

cannot be genuinely consensual in a patriarchal culture. In her view, sexual relations become the means of constructing and maintaining female subordination. This view provides little basis for distinguishing between sexual behavior that is harassing and discriminatory and sexual behavior that is not, however.

In recent years it has been argued that the focus on overtly sexual behavior in sexual harassment cases has distracted the courts, and indeed the entire society, from the original issue of gender discrimination. For instance, one commentator has argued, in the wake of the Thomas/Hill hearings, that it is the prevention of discrimination that ought to be the focus for the courts rather than regulating sex.[34] She notes that the "sexual desire-dominance" paradigm of sexual harassment, advanced by feminists, was useful in identifying certain types of discriminatory activity. However, she raises a concern that courts have come to rely too narrowly on evidence of direct sexual behavior, such as lewd comments or unwanted touching, rather than upon other sorts of evidence that might address gender-based discrimination, such as treating a female manager differently from male managers of comparable status. She cites the practice of disaggregation, in which allegations of discriminatory acts and sexual acts are dealt with separately, as evidence that courts have, perhaps inadvertently, adopted a sexual desire-dominance paradigm as a means of analyzing claims of sexual harassment.

The emphasis on regulating sexual behavior may also be seen in an increase in employers' policies and training regarding sexual harassment. It is an increasingly common practice for employers to discourage or prohibit dating and sexual relationships between employees, especially those who are not workplace peers. This represents an attempt to avoid litigation and liability, but the aforementioned commentator considers such developments to represent an erosion of women's independence and choice with regard to their own sexual behavior, noting that this encourages employers and the courts to adopt a rather paternal, protective role. It is likely that this tension will continue to be reflected not only in the courts, but, especially in the aftermath of *Ellerth*, *Faragher*, and *Davis*, in the policies and approaches adopted in the American workplace.

II. Social Science Perspectives and Selected Empirical Studies: Uses and Limitations

It should be noted at the outset that the applicability of much of the social science and the empirical literature to litigated cases in general and forensic assessment in the individual case is limited. First, as noted earlier, definitions of sexual harassment vary. Legal definitions are not consistently used in the empirical literature. Indeed, numerous studies use a broad continuum of behav-

---

[34]Vicki Schultz, *Reconceptualizing Sexual Harassment*, 107 YALE L.J. 1762 (1998).

iors, including many that clearly would not meet the legal criteria. This naturally limits their applicability to litigated cases, and it also makes comparisons among studies quite difficult. Second, most studies take a broad, demographic approach. A number of issues that are central in forensic psychological and psychiatric practice receive little attention in the social science literature, such as diagnostic questions, claimant credibility, assessment methods, and feigning or exaggerating. Third, there is little information on how cases resulting in complaint or litigation vary from those that do not. Are they distinctive because of the nature of the harassing behavior? On account of certain victim characteristics? In the absence of such information, it cannot be concluded that broad studies of societal patterns of sexual harassment cast much light on litigated cases. No particular pattern of empirical findings or school of thought should be taken as a definitive guide to understanding harassment in general, and certainly not in assessing any given case. Sexual harassment cases and claims are diverse, and there is simply no substitute for careful clinical assessment of the individual case.

Nonetheless, social science perspectives and research are pertinent to our knowledge and understanding of sexual harassment. Legal developments shape areas of research, and, in turn, empirical studies are seen as having implications for policy and practice in the workplace and interpretation of legal standards.[35] The following studies concern prevalence, types of harassment, range of possible effects, and victim, perpetrator, and organizational characteristics. In light of the breadth of this literature and the overall purpose of this chapter, this section will not attempt to provide a comprehensive review of the range of findings and methodological issues. Rather, the discussion will be selective, providing a sampling of some particular areas of investigation and related research findings.

A. Types of Sexual Harassment

A number of authors have offered categories of sexual harassment, typically arranged along a continuum of severity. These are summarized by one observer as follows:

- *Gender harassment:* generalized comments and behavior that convey insulting, degrading, and/or sexist attitudes
- *Unwanted sexual attention:* behavior ranging from inappropriate, offensive, physical or verbal sexual advances to assault or rape
- *Sexual coercion:* the solicitation/coercion of sexual activity in the context of promises of reward or the threat of punishment or retaliation.[36]

Other commentators have proposed a model of sexual harassment liking types and severity of impact in terms of the following factors: source, frequency

---

[35]*See* Richard L. Wiener & Barbara A. Gutek, *Advances in Sexual Harassment Research, Theory, and Policy,* 5 PSYCHOL., PUB. POL'Y & L. 507 (1999).

[36]Margaret S. Stockdale, *What We Know and What We Need to Learn about Sexual Harassment, in* SEXUAL HARASSMENT IN THE WORKPLACE 7 (Margaret S. Stockdale ed., 1996).

or duration, directness, averseness, and threat. They propose that these factors have implications for the development of policy and legal standards.[37]

B. Prevalence of Sexual Harassment

The U.S. Merit Systems Protection Board conducted a national survey regarding sexual harassment among federal employees in 1981,[38] with follow-up surveys in 1987[39] and 1995.[40] These stand as among the largest such surveys; the most recent involved over 8,000 federal employees, with a 61 percent response rate to a survey. The survey inquired about a range of behaviors, asked respondents if they believed the conduct constituted sexual harassment, and inquired about their own experiences. The study found that uninvited sexual remarks, jokes, and teasing were most common, with 37 percent of women and 14 percent of men reporting some experience of this behavior in the preceding two years. Pressure for sexual favors, stalking, and sexual assault were reported by between 4 percent and 7 percent of the women and 2 percent of the men. Harassment by supervisors was reported to be less frequent than that by others—77 percent of women and 79 percent of men identified the sources of the unwelcome behavior as coworkers. Twelve percent of the victims reported the harassment to a supervisor or other official.

Other studies have addressed sexual harassment in specific professions or work settings. One found 20 percent to 30 percent of female undergraduates and 30 percent to 40 percent of female graduate students reported some form of harassment, ranging from sexual jokes and innuendo to unwanted physical contact with male faculty. However, only 2 percent reported coercive behavior such as bribes or threats in exchange for sexual activity. Fifty percent of female faculty and staff reported sexual harassment. In contrast, less than 5 percent of male students reported sexual harassment by either females or other males.[41]

Findings regarding the medical profession are similar to those in other work settings. Female physicians reported experiences ranging from actual harassment (27 percent) to unwanted sexual attention (79 percent). Such experiences were more common during training but persisted into practice. Twenty-two percent of male residents reported sexual harassment. Most incidents involved verbal harassment or offensive materials. Physical harassment, threats,

---

[37] James E. Gruber, Michael Smith & Kaisa Kauppinen-Toropainen, *Sexual Harassment Types and Severity: Linking Research and Policy*, in SEXUAL HARASSMENT IN THE WORKPLACE, *supra* note 15, at 151.

[38] U.S. MERIT SYSTEM PROTECTION BOARD, SEXUAL HARASSMENT IN THE FEDERAL WORKPLACE: IS IT A PROBLEM? (1981).

[39] U.S. MERIT SYSTEM PROTECTION BOARD, SEXUAL HARASSMENT IN THE FEDERAL WORKPLACE: AN UPDATE (1987).

[40] U.S. MERIT SYSTEM PROTECTION BOARD, SEXUAL HARASSMENT IN THE FEDERAL WORKPLACE: TRENDS, PROGRESS, AND CONTINUING CHALLENGES (1995).

[41] Shrier, *supra* note 1.

or bribes for sexual favors were more common among the women. Women also were more likely than men to be harassed by supervisors; though reported harassers also included peers, patients, and their families.[42]

It has been suggested that women who are also members of racial/ethnic minorities may be more likely to be sexually harassed as a result of stereotyped views of sexual availability and relative power and status. Empirical findings have been mixed, with some studies providing support for this hypothesis and others showing no differences.[43]

Given the relative paucity of information on litigated cases as opposed to broader studies of sexual harassment, it is worth noting the findings of a review of hostile environment harassment cases in U.S. Courts of Appeals.[44] The most frequent allegations concerned unwelcome, nonviolent touching and offensive language specifically addressed to the plaintiff. Sexual propositions were reported in 44 percent of the cases and sexual assaults of various degrees in 22 percent. In 73 percent of the cases a harasser was the plaintiff's supervisor; in 42 percent a harasser was a coworker (in a number of cases there was more than one harasser).

Some authors suggest that the reported rates of sexual harassment may underestimate the actual incidents of such behaviors. It has been reported that women may fail to identify harassment as such,[45] and even if they do identify it, they may not report it for reasons similar to those underlying the underreporting of rape. Victims of sexual harassment may fear embarrassment, ostracism, or reprisals; or they may just hope the problems will go away.[46]

Overall, research suggests that experiences of sexual harassment are much more common than are formal complaints and litigation. However, it is difficult to extrapolate from the empirical literature to conclusions about the incidence of legally actionable sexual harassment. Many studies include behaviors that may indeed be inappropriate in the workplace. However, many of the definitions used provide no measure of repetition or severity that might correspond to the legal importance of the notion of impact upon the conditions of employment. The U.S. Merit Protection Board survey provides some measure of severity, albeit defined by respondents' self-report: 21 percent of victims said they suffered a decline in productivity; 7 percent said they would have found medical

---

[42]Leah J. Dickstein, *Sexual Harassment in Medicine*, in SEXUAL HARASSMENT IN THE WORKPLACE AND ACADEMIA supra note 1, at 223.

[43]Audrey J. Murrell, *Sexual Harassment and Women of Color: Issues, Challenges, and Future Directions*, in SEXUAL HARASSMENT IN THE WORKPLACE, supra note 15, at 51.

[44]Ramona L. Paetzold & Anne M. O'Leary-Kelly, *The Implications of U.S. Supreme Court and Circuit Court Decisions for Hospital Environment Sexual Harassment Cases*, in SEXUAL HARASSMENT IN THE WORKPLACE, supra note 15, at 89.

[45]For a summary, see Stockdale, *supra* note 36.

[46]Barbara A. Gutek & Mary P. Koss, *How Women Deal with Sexual Harassment and How Organizations Respond to Reporting*, in SEXUAL HARASSMENT IN THE WORKPLACE AND ACADEMIA, supra note 1, at 39.

or emotional help beneficial, and 2 percent transferred to a new job.[47] However, in a number of studies, it would appear that one incident of offensive speech might be identified as sexual harassment, so the studies should be considered in that context.

C. Gender Differences in Perceptions Related to Sexual Harassment

Gender differences have consistently been found regarding the perception of sexual harassment. Women are more inclined to identify sexual harassment than are men, with the differences being more marked in more ambiguous cases.

The U.S. Merit Protection Board asked respondents if they would "probably" or "definitely" consider a range of behaviors from supervisors or coworkers to be sexual harassment. Ninety-nine percent of women and 97 percent of men reported that pressure for sexual favors from a supervisor would be harassment; 77 percent of women and 64 percent of men would define sexual teasing by coworkers as harassment. In short, the more serious the behavior, the more agreement across genders that it constitutes harassment. Also, although the overall results of the Board's finding in the multiple studies since 1980 have shown little change, there is a trend toward greater agreement between male and female subjects.[48]

Men have also been found to perceive evidence of sexual interest in behaviors that women see as friendly or outgoing.[49] One study hypothesizes that these differences might lead men to engage in harassing behaviors; that is, men might believe women are signaling sexual interest, and the men's response might result in their engaging in or tolerating harassment.[50] Predictably, men and women differed in perceptions of signals of sexual interest. Men could be further subgrouped in terms of their propensity to view women as behaving flirtatiously or seductively. However, these differences did not predict men's tolerance of or likelihood to engage in sexual harassment, as measured by these studies. A number of researchers have investigated the possible correlations between such factors as hostile sexism[51] and LSH (likelihood to sexually harass)[52] and sexual harassment as a means of more clearly identifying variables

---

[47]U.S. MERIT SYSTEM PROTECTION BOARD, *supra* note 40.

[48]*Id.*

[49]Frank E. Saal, Catherine B. Johnson, & Nancy Weber, *Friendly or Sexy? It May Depend on Whom You Ask*, 13 PSYCHOL. OF WOMEN Q. 263 (1989).

[50]Frank E. Saal, *Men's Misperceptions of Sexual Harassment*, in SEXUAL HARASSMENT IN THE WORKPLACE, *supra* note 15, at 67.

[51]Peter Glick & Susan T. Fiske, *The Ambivalent Sexism Inventory: Differentiating Hostile and Benevolent Sexism*, 70 J. PERS. & SOC. PSYCHOL. 491 (1996); Susan T. Fiske & Peter Glick, *Ambivalence and Sterotypes Cause Sexual Harassment: A Theory with Implications for Organizational Change*, 51 J. SOC. ISSUES 97 (1995).

[52]John B. Pryor, *Sexual Harassment Proclivities in Men*, 17 SEX ROLES 269 (1987).

that might distinguish men prone to engage in sexual harassment from men who are not.[53]

D. Victim Characteristics and Patterns of Sexual Harassment

There appears to be agreement that younger, unmarried women are most likely to be sexually harassed. There also appear to be broad commonalities in the range of behaviors associated with sexual harassment. Some commentators deny that there is any "blue collar sexual harassment" that might be distinguished from that found in "white collar" or clerical occupations.[54] On the other hand, it has been found that certain occupational and organizational characteristics, such as the ratio of women to men, tend to be correlated with some features of sexual harassment. For instance, women in either nontraditional occupations (e.g., a skilled female factory worker) or traditional "feminine" occupations (e.g., secretaries or nurses) may be more likely to experience harassment than those in occupations with both sexes more evenly represented.[55]

In recent years a number of issues regarding victim characteristics, in terms of personality or historical factors, have been raised in litigated cases. These issues will be addressed more fully later in this chapter.

E. Offender and Organizational Characteristics

Some research findings address the association of offender and organizational characteristics with sexual harassment, with varying degrees of emphasis upon either individual or organizational factors. One study indicates that a combination of individual characteristics and situational context might be correlated with harassing behavior. Specifically, it found that men who subscribe to traditional or adversarial views of sex roles combined with negative attitudes toward women are more likely to engage in sexual harassment under particular circumstances, such as when a male experimenter models such behavior or when engaging in a task with a woman that involves some physical contact.[56] This supports the view that some sexual harassment may be understood as an interaction of individual and organizational characteristics; that is, men with a high potential for engaging in harassment may be especially likely to do so in an organizational context that models or tolerates such actions. A somewhat

---

[53]Barbara A. Gutek & Bruce Morasch, *Sex Ratios, Sex Role Spillover, and Sexual Harassment of Women at Work*, 38 J. Soc. Issues 55 (1982).

[54]Gruber, Smith & Kauppinen-Toropainen, *supra* note 37.

[55]Gutek & Morasch, *supra* note 53.

[56]John B. Pryor, Christine M. LaVite & Lynnette M. Stoller, *A Social Psychological Analysis of Sexual Harassment: The Person/Situation Interaction*, 42 J. Vocational Behav. 38 (1993); John B. Pryor & Jeanne D. Day, *Interpretations of Sexual Harassment: An Attributional Analysis*, 18 Sex Roles 405 (1988).

different approach is taken by others.[57] They emphasize a view of sexual harassment as a function of the degree to which a work group is predominately male, plus the degree to which an organization is tolerant of harassing behaviors. Though they do not deny individual factors, they see them as being less critical.

Employee perceptions of workplace practices and attitudes have also been studied. One study developed an experimental measure to assess perceptions that sexual harassment would result in, for instance, risks to the complainant and consequences for the harasser.[58] Factors accounting for some of the variance included job level of the harasser and the nature or seriousness of the allegation. Women, in general, reported viewing organizations as more tolerant of harassing behaviors than did male respondents.

Studies have also addressed the differences between employees reporting some experience of sexual harassment and those who did not. One analysis reviewed data regarding the experience of workers in the U.S. Department of Defense and a large organization.[59] Women who felt management made good faith efforts to stop harassment were less likely to report having been harassed; women who reported they had been harassed had a more negative view of management in this regard. This finding may suggest that women who have not been harassed may have a more benign view of the workplace. However, women who reported they had been harassed did not differ from those reporting no harassment in their ratings of the degree to which various scenarios constituted sexual harassment. The author of the study suggests it speaks against a general view of sexual harassment complaints as a reflection of hypersensitivity.

The notion that an interaction of individual and organizational factors is relevant to understanding some incidents of sexual harassment may certainly have some validity, since taking into account the social context frequently enriches our understanding of individual behavior. Again, however, it should be noted that general findings have little predictive value in assessing any individual case.

F. Individual Responses and the Effects of Harassment

Responses to sexual harassment vary considerably, from indirect or passive strategies to direct confrontation or complaint.[60]

Victims' indirect responses may range from doing nothing to passive acceptance to mild rebuff ("I'm not your type"). They may joke and banter in return, sometimes to defuse the situation and become "one of the boys," and

---

[57]Charles L. Hulin, Louise F. Fitzgerald & Fritz Drasgow, *Organizational Influences on Sexual Harassment*, in SEXUAL HARASSMENT IN THE WORKPLACE, *supra* note 15, at 127; Louise F. Fitzgerald, Charles L. Hulin & Fritz Drasgow, *The Antecedent and Consequences of Sexual Harassment in Organizations: An Integrated Model*, in JOB STRESS IN A CHANGING WORKFORCE: INVESTIGATING GENDER 55 (Gwendolyn P. Keita & Joseph J. Hurrell eds., 1995).
[58]Hulin, Fitzgerald & Drasgow, *supra* note 57.
[59]Pryor, LaVite & Stoller, *supra* note 56.
[60]Gutek & Koss, *supra* note 46.

sometimes in a more attacking or insulting manner. Avoiding the harasser is common, sometimes to the point of leaving a job. Direct strategies include telling the harasser clearly the behavior is unwelcome, either verbally or in writing; telling or threatening to tell others; and, of course, formal complaint or litigation.

Indirect responses have been reported to be relatively ineffective.[61] They are thought to be preferred, however, because (1) the nature of the offending behavior may be somewhat ambiguous; (2) the victim may wish to avoid public knowledge of the behavior; (3) the victim may fear retaliation; or (4) the victim may be concerned about repercussions for the offender or his family.

Direct responses, such as confronting the harasser, are reported to be more effective.[62] However, formal complaints can result in repercussions ranging from interpersonal tension to outright reprisals.

The literature suggests that many people, both men and women, believe sexual harassment can be handled effectively and promptly on an individual level. For instance, 88 percent of all respondents in the U.S. Merit Protection Board's 1995 study said they believed asking or telling the person to stop would be effective. Thirty-five percent of the victims reported they did so: 60 percent of those said it made things better, 8 percent of women and 15 percent of men reported it made it worse, and 32 percent of women and 25 percent of men said it made no difference. Regarding complaints to supervisors, 66 percent of all respondents said they believed this would be effective in stopping the harassment. Twelve percent of victims reported they made such a complaint. Of those victims, 58 percent of women and 33 percent of men said this made things better, 13 percent of women and 16 percent of men reported it made things worse, and 29 percent of women and 52 percent of men said it made no difference.[63]

The literature regarding the range of responses to sexual harassment has relevance to some of the issues encountered in forensic assessment. Some cases involve a long history of allegations. The forensic evaluator may encounter disputes about whether a claimant actually interpreted past behaviors as harassing or not. A part of the evaluation may involve distinguishing between active, voluntary participation in sexualized workplace banter (which is not uncommon), and defensive attempts by a victim to give as good as she gets to ward off further intimidation. Where the allegations involve a series of behaviors over an extended period, the claimant often has resorted to various response strategies at different stages during the harassment.

Victims of sexual harassment are reported to experience a range of emotional, psychological, physical, and interpersonal effects. The harassment may be a mild life stressor or a severe one, comparable to such life crises as major illness or divorce.[64] One observer summarizes the possible emotional and

---

[61]*Id.*

[62]*Id.* at 44.

[63]U.S. MERIT SYSTEM PROTECTION BOARD, *supra* note 40.

[64]Sharyn Lenhart, *Physical and Mental Health Aspects of Sexual Harassment, in* SEXUAL HARASSMENT IN THE WORKPLACE AND ACADEMIA, *supra* note 1, at 21.

psychological effects as including sadness, depression, pessimism, irritability, mood swings, loss of energy, anxiety, guilt and shame, anger, fear, humiliation, self-doubt, diminished self-confidence, poor concentration, and alienation.[65] Physical symptoms may also occur, including fatigue, weight loss or gain, decreased libido, gastrointestinal problems, generalized tension (jaw tightening, teeth grinding, muscle spasms), and sleep problems.[66]

The effects of sexual harassment may range from strong, unpleasant feelings to symptoms warranting a diagnosis of a mental disorder. In some cases, the sense of loss and disillusionment with others is an important factor and a contributor to the individual's distress. The victim may feel betrayed by previously trusted or important coworkers, colleagues, or supervisors. Family and friends may react supportively, or they may contribute to the individual's feeling misunderstood and frustrated as a result of their reactions. In forensic psychiatric and psychological assessment, it should be understood that not all stressors result in symptoms warranting a diagnosis. The impact on the individual may be expected to vary depending upon the nature, duration, and severity of the harassment; the victim's history; and the response of both the workplace and the victim's family.

G. The Effects of Harassment Upon Organizations

Various studies have proposed possible models for assessing the organizational cost of sexual harassment, not solely in relation to litigation but with regard to sick leave, job turnover, and individual and work group productivity.[67] Other aspects of the impact on organizations have also been noted. Sexual harassment victims have been described as losing commitment to their jobs; experiencing reduced self-esteem, productivity, and motivation; and experiencing poor interpersonal relationships. The organization may be faced with similar negative repercussions, with increased workplace tensions, polarization, blame, and anxiety affecting any number of people.[68] However, it does not appear that empirical findings provide a decisive basis for determining the appropriateness or effectiveness of various antiharassment policies and procedures.

H. Legal Standards: Reasonable Victim/Woman/Person

Some studies have examined how the use of various standards might affect the assessment of sexual harassment. These studies present findings and arguments

---

[65]*Id.* at 29.
[66]*Id.*
[67]Knapp & Kustis, *supra* note 29. *See also* Hanisch, *supra* note 29.
[68]Hanisch, *supra* note 29. *See also* Barbara A. Gutek, *Sexual Harassment at Work: When an Organization Fails to Respond*, in SEXUAL HARASSMENT AND THE WORKPLACE, *supra* note 15, at 272.

regarding the use of the "reasonable victim," "reasonable woman," and "reasonable person" standards.

One commentator recommends use of the "reasonable victim" standard in part to avoid the gender bias of the reasonable woman standard. She argues a standard should avoid errors based upon a threshold that is too stringent, which may fail to identify harassment as such, and errors based upon a threshold that is too low or subjective, which may overidentify harassment.[69] Another study examined contrasts in the use of the reasonable person and reasonable woman standards, and analyzed differences in how male and female subjects reason about and define sexual harassment. That study found that both men and women were more inclined to see sexual harassment when using the reasonable woman standard, offsetting other factors that contributed to variability in their judgments.[70] A third study specifically assessed use of the reasonable woman and reasonable person standards in hostile environment scenarios. It found the legal standard used accounted for 2 percent of the variance at most, and so had very little impact on subjects' judgments regarding hostile environment, plaintiff credibility, predictions of jurors' reactions, issues of responsibility, and amount of damages.[71]

I. Integrating Social Science Perspectives and Legal Issues

As noted, the study of sexual harassment might generally be expected to have implications for policy and legal practice. However, some commentators have acknowledged that the sophistication of sexual harassment research and it applicability to legal issues are highly variable.[72] Further, social science approaches are strongly influenced by differing feminist viewpoints. There is no single feminist perspective.[73] Rather, a range of such perspectives exists. One extreme is expressed in views that all sexual behavior in the workplace may constitute harassment and discrimination. As noted earlier, such views provide little basis for distinctions between consensual and nonconsensual sexual interactions, and they lead to proposals to ban all sexual contact between coworkers. Other approaches view social interactions and perceptions as consistently shaped by gender and the fact that sexual expression and relationships are inevitable.

The social psychological and empirical literature provides a broad portrayal of the incidence of sexual harassment, its effects, and possible explanations

---

[69]Jane Goodman-Delahunty, *Pragmatic Support for the Reasonable Victim Standard in Hospital Workplace Sexual Harassment Cases*, 5 PSYCHOL., PUB. POL'Y & L. 519 (1999).

[70]Richard L. Wiener & Linda E. Hurt, *An Interdisciplinary Approach to Understanding Social Sexual Conduct at Work*, 5 PSYCHOL., PUB. POL'Y & L. 556 (1999).

[71]Barbara A. Gutek et al., *The Utility of the Reasonable Woman Legal Standard in Hostile Environment Sexual Harassment Cases: A Multimethod, Multistudy Examination*, 5 PSYCHOL., PUB. POL'Y & L. 596 (1999).

[72]Wiener & Gutek, *supra* note 35.

[73]Wiener & Hurt, *supra* note 70.

and associated factors. Just as court decisions often provide inconsistent and haphazard messages regarding sexual harassment, social science has not yet produced a model of sexual harassment that sufficiently integrates legal issues and the focus of research in a way that might come to be relied upon by the courts.

III. Special Issues in Sexual Harassment Cases: Selected Literature

A. Background and Overview

As the legal context of sexual harassment cases has changed and evolved, the clinical issues faced in assessment of sexual harassment plaintiffs have changed as well. Selected forensic psychiatric and psychological literature regarding the appropriate focus and scope of forensic assessment in sexual harassment cases will be reviewed here. In contrast to the more demographic approach of social science literature, the clinical literature approaches sexual harassment with a focus upon the appropriate roles of mental health professionals within the legal system, the process of clinical assessment, and related special issues in sexual harassment. This will be followed by discussion of a range of issues commonly raised in sexual harassment litigation and related case examples.

One caveat may be in order. Sexual harassment cases do not always involve competing "he said/she said" claims of indeterminate validity and severity. There are many cases in which the allegations are neither ambiguous nor sharply contested. The behavior at issue may be egregious and reasonably well substantiated. In other cases the allegations may be trivial, self-serving, or both. In short, it is important to avoid overgeneralization; all sorts of cases can and do occur. However, the more subjective, gray-area cases rightly are the focus of much discussion and appear to be on the increase, and so it is such cases that are most relevant to this discussion.

What are the distinctive features of sexual harassment cases, how do these features shape forensic evaluations, and how should these the clinical issues be brought to bear on legal questions? In this section, the contributions of some prominent contributors to the literature are reviewed. These authors represent various points of view, in part because their work is shaped by differing concerns regarding the special features of sexual harassment cases and the uses, misuses, scope, and limits of forensic assessment.

B. The Extent of the Expert's Role in Sexual Harassment Cases

Margaret Jensvold objects particularly to the practice of requiring that sexual harassment complainants be seen for mental health evaluation or treatment absent a lawsuit.[74] Robert Simon agrees that psychiatrists should not participate

---

[74]Margaret F. Jensvold, *Potential for Misuse and Abuse of Psychiatry in Workplace Sexual Harassment, in* SEXUAL HARASSMENT IN THE WORKPLACE AND ACADEMIA, *supra* note 1, at 153.

in "specious forced fitness-for-duty examinations," and other roles that constitute "abuse of psychiatric expertise."[75] It should be noted that little data exist regarding the prevalence of this practice; to the extent that it occurs, Jensvold addresses its improprieties and potential for abuse. She argues that the assessment process is highly likely to have adverse results for the examinee regardless of the merit of her claims. Jensvold suggests "several factors make psychiatric assessments attractive to harassers. Psychiatry's tendency to focus on the individual's own contribution to problems and individual vulnerabilities as opposed to what is being done to a person is complementary to the harasser's viewpoint. Psychiatric truth which focuses on the intrapsychic experience and 'legal truth,' which focuses on what is being done by the harasser, may be different."[76] Jensvold expresses concern that the potential for abuse exists whenever mental health professionals are not in roles directly linked to serving patients, even if the practitioner attempts to work responsibly and ethically.

Despite these concerns, Jensvold sees appropriate roles for mental health professionals in sexual harassment cases, including:

- Serving as treating therapists,
- Performing psychological evaluations of plaintiffs for court purposes in lawsuits claiming emotional damages, and
- Functioning as expert witnesses in court, providing expertise on issues other than the plaintiff's mental status per se.[77]

However, Jensvold also points out "alleged harassers never undergo court-ordered psychiatric assessment. Their psychotherapy records are never opened up in court."[78] She notes that the claim of emotional damages opens the issue of the examinee's mental status, with the result that psychological evaluation may be required and past records of treatment released. Jensvold argues in favor of reform in sexual harassment cases, with restrictions that are similar to rape shield laws, to avoid revictimization of the claimant. She suggests possible corresponding changes in how damages are assessed and awarded; a plaintiff who prevails in litigation would be provided damages based upon the distress expectable for a "reasonable person" or "reasonable woman" in like circumstances.[79]

Sara Feldman-Schorrig and James McDonald's work occurs in the context of expanding bases for environmental harassment claims and the increasingly adversarial nature of much sexual harassment litigation in the wake of the 1991 Civil Rights Act, and focuses upon particular uses of forensic assessment by the defense.[80] They note that some sexual harassment allegations may be highly

---

[75]Robert I. Simon, *The Credible Forensic Psychiatric Evaluation in Sexual Harassment Litigation*, 26 PSYCHIATRIC ANNALS 140 (1996).

[76]Jensvold, *supra* note 74, at 167.

[77]*Id.* at 155.

[78]*Id.* at 174.

[79]*Id.* at 174–75.

[80]Sara P. Feldman-Schorrig & James J. McDonald, Jr., *The Role of Forensic Psychiatry in the Defense of Sexual Harassment Cases*, 20 J. PSYCHIATRY & L. 5 (1992).

subjective, that conflicting accounts often exist, and that sexual harassment complaints may be subject to distortion or exaggeration. They argue that examiners are in a position to offer explanations of the basis and credibility of the allegation based upon assessment of the plaintiff's history and personality.[81] Feldman-Schorrig and McDonald describe evaluation in sexual harassment cases as a defensive tool for detecting exaggeration or fabrication and observe that examinations "can provide valuable material to bring into question the causation of a plaintiff's alleged emotional injuries."[82] They enumerate a number of factors that may contribute to exaggerated claims:

- A characterological hypersensitivity to sexual cues,
- The operation of a repetition compulsion,
- The presence of a personality disorder,
- The displacement of anger toward a currently abusive partner or spouse,
- A wish to avenge or punish an unrelated wrong, and
- An expectation of financial reward.[83]

In particular, Feldman-Schorrig and McDonald depict the victim of childhood sexual abuse as likely to be flirtatious but hypersensitive, provoking a sexualized response from others that is then experienced as harassment.[84]

In another article, Feldman-Schorrig posits that forensic examiners should move beyond the assessment of damages into assessment of "whether the plaintiff's own emotional condition contributed to the alleged harassment."[85] In many cases, such contribution may have occurred unconsciously; that is, the plaintiff may not have been aware of her true role in the events as they unfolded (or she may not be willing to admit it even if she recognizes it).[86] Feldman-Schorrig notes that history of childhood sexual abuse may particularly contribute to claims of sexual harassment as a result of repetition compulsion—that is, the notion that a traumatized individual is likely to re-create trauma in order to master it. Repetition compulsion on the part of a plaintiff may not constitute a complete legal defense; this would be a question for the court.

Questions of personality disorder, a history of trauma—including sexual trauma—and issues pertinent to the credibility of the claimant's clinical presentation should routinely be addressed in forensic evaluation in sexual harassment cases, along with other diagnostic and historical issues. However, no particular diagnosis or historical event, in and of itself, provides the basis for conclusions about the merit of sexual harassment claims. In addition, forensic examiners

---

[81] *Id.* at 7.
[82] *Id.* at 12.
[83] *Id.* at 13.
[84] *Id.* at 14. *See also* James J. McDonald, Jr. & Sara P. Feldman-Schorrig, *The Role of Childhood Sexual Abuse in Sexual Harassment Cases*, 20 EMPL. REL. L.J. 221 (1993).
[85] Sara P. Feldman-Schorrig, *Expansion of Forensic Psychiatrists' Role in Sexual Harassment Cases*, 23 BULL. AM. ACAD. PSYCHIATRY & L. 513 (1995).
[86] *Id.* at 517.

should not offer opinions as to whether the alleged harassment did or did not occur; this is outside the scope of examiner expertise.

Feldman-Schorrig's work provides little guidance as to how clinical assessment could distinguish between the claimant with a history of childhood sexual abuse or personality problems who may have contributed to the circumstances of the harassment and/or is hypersensitive, and a claimant who has not. Both exist. Feldman-Schorrig was more interested in exploring an area of relevance for the defense of sexual harassment claims than in providing a comprehensive overview of all sides of the issues. However, some of her assertions also call for critique on theoretical and clinical grounds.

First, Feldman-Schorrig uses the psychodynamic ideas of unconscious processes and the role of repetition compulsion to explain how some claimants may contribute to or orchestrate harassment. It is widely accepted within psychiatry and psychology that early experiences shape personality and that some portion of an individual's motives and emotions may be unconscious; these concepts have a place in clinical practice. However, psychodynamic notions about unconscious motives have long been criticized as not subject to meaningful proof or disproof.[87] Although extensive discussion of this issue is outside the scope of this chapter, important distinctions between psychic meaning and causation are worth noting. The sexual harassment claimant with a history of childhood sexual abuse is very likely to construe *meanings* about the alleged harassment in relation to her earlier history, but that history, in and of itself, does not justify a conclusion that it caused the alleged harassment.

Second, repetition compulsion is only one possible outcome of trauma and childhood sexual abuse. The impact of stress and trauma varies enormously and must be assessed in each individual case. Trauma in childhood may influence later personality structure, but how and to what extent will depend on many factors. Trauma in adulthood may result not only in repetition but also in withdrawal and avoidance; one might hypothesize that some traumatized individuals, rather than being hypersensitive and overreactive, might be especially passive if harassed or subjected to abuse.

Third, in the absence of a direct report by the claimant or compelling collateral information, it is highly problematic to infer that childhood sexual abuse occurred. It became common in the 1980s and early 1990s to suspect repressed childhood sexual abuse based upon broad, nonspecific symptoms. This occurred in the context of an upsurge of interest in trauma and its effects, and in repressed memory and victimization. The associated works included

---

[87]*See, e.g.,* Stephen J. Morse, *Law and Mental Health Professionals: The Limits of Expertise*, 9 PROF. PSYCHOL. 389 (1978); Stephen J. Morse, *Failed Explanations and Criminal Responsibility: Experts and the Unconscious*, 68 VA. L. REV. 971 (1982). Morse argues that mental health professionals' testimony should include observation of specific symptoms and hard data but not psychodynamic formulations or diagnoses. See GARY B. MELTON ET AL., PSYCHOLOGICAL EVALUATIONS FOR THE COURTS: A HANDBOOK FOR MENTAL HEALTH PROFESSIONALS AND LAWYERS 18–20 (2d ed. 1997), for a discussion of Morse's views.

Judith Herman's highly regarded contributions.[88] However, a politicized movement also developed. Some observers, for instance, argued that vast numbers of women had been sexually abused by family members and/or satanic cults as children and repressed it.[89] It became somewhat common for counselors to actively cultivate this understanding on the part of their clients, to accompany diagnoses of Multiple Personality Disorder and Posttraumatic Stress Disorder (PTSD).

Louise Fitzgerald and her colleagues have criticized Feldman-Schorrig and McDonald.[90] They argue the data do not support the contention that victims of childhood sexual abuse are hypersensitive, and, more broadly, they take a markedly different approach to the role of mental evaluations in sexual harassment cases. They compared women with a self-reported history of childhood sexual abuse and women with no such history with regard to their reactions to stimuli depicting potentially sexually harassing situations of varying severity and found that subjects with a history of childhood sexual abuse did not differ from control subjects. The authors defined childhood sexual abuse as "the experience of unwanted sexual touching (e.g., breasts, genitals) as a child or young adolescent by someone at least 5 years older,"[91] and they describe this as a conservative definition of abuse. All unwanted sexual contact in childhood is inappropriate; however, it should be noted that this definition would apparently include individuals with one experience of unwelcome sexual contact with an older child, and that these subjects may not be differentiated from, for instance, victims of long-standing incestuous abuse. As acknowledged by Fitzgerald et al., the impact of childhood sexual abuse may vary greatly.

With regard to mental evaluations in sexual harassment cases, Fitzgerald and colleagues argue that research has consistently shown that sexual harassment is emotionally damaging to the physical and emotional health of victims. Given the robustness of this general finding, they note it seems "reasonable to argue that when a plaintiff proves her facts, she in essence proves that she was damaged, at least to some degree."[92] The authors see mental evaluations as largely irrelevant to this determination. "As long as the plaintiff's injury, rather than the egregiousness of the harasser's conduct, remains the heart of the damages determination, women will continue to be tried and found wanting."[93] They suggest that scientific opinion in such cases should focus on social framework data rather than clinical evaluation.

While it may be the case, in general, that experiences of sexual harassment are associated with emotional distress, the impact may vary considerably depending upon a variety of factors, as noted earlier. The nature and degree of

---

[88] JUDITH L. HERMAN, TRAUMA AND RECOVERY (1992).

[89] ELLEN BASS & LAURA DAVIS, THE COURAGE TO HEAL: A GUIDE FOR WOMEN SURVIVORS OF SEXUAL ABUSE (1998).

[90] Louise F. Fitzgerald et al., *Junk Logic: The Abuse Defense in Sexual Harassment Litigation*, 5 PSYCHOL., PUB. POL'Y & L. 730 (1999).

[91] *Id.* at 737.

[92] *Id.* at 755.

[93] *Id.*

the distress are frequently at issue. Courts currently do not confine themselves exclusively to the use of broad statistical data in determining the outcome of the specific case, as Fitzgerald et al. suggest they should do. To do so would require extensive changes in how damages tend to be assessed and awarded. Moreover, there are sexual harassment cases in which the allegations are subjective, the evidence conflicting, and "facts" very difficult to establish. Such cases pose challenges to the legal system and to forensic evaluators as well, and they would be poorly suited to a statistical method of calculation of damages.

C. Issues of Scope, Focus, and Assessment Practices in Sexual Harassment Cases

Simon has approached sexual harassment cases from the vantage point of credible and appropriate psychiatric practice.[94] He outlines special features of these cases and the issues that arise for the psychiatric expert. He discusses potential difficulties for maintaining objectivity in sexual harassment cases. For instance, he notes that if retained by the plaintiff, the expert may be inclined to view the claimant as a patient, with the attendant wishes to help and perhaps rescue. Conversely, experts retained by defense may be tempted to view the claimant in terms of negative stereotypes of sexual harassment plaintiffs, or be inclined to regard the allegations as fantasy. The goal, of course, is to guard against possible bias and to maintain objectivity and sound practice.

Simon also describes the typical paradigms regarding psychiatric issues underlying sexual harassment litigation. He notes that Posttraumatic Stress Disorder "has found favor in sexual harassment cases brought by plaintiffs."[95] The plaintiff paradigm underscores the multiple losses associated with sexual harassment and stresses the aims of achieving justice and overcoming helplessness as the goals of litigation. Simon portrays the defense paradigm as focusing upon the plaintiff and likely her history prior to the alleged harassment. The defense may offer alternative explanations of any symptoms, such as childhood sexual abuse or a personality disorder, and argue that these conditions are especially prevalent in sexual harassment claimants. The defense paradigm emphasizes such factors as revenge and financial gain as motives for pursuing litigation.

Within this context, Simon describes the forensic expert as appropriately offering information regarding diagnosis, credibility, damages, trauma reactions, and typical patterns of behavior associated with sexual harassment. He notes that the symptoms associated with sexual harassment, if they constitute a diagnosable mental disorder, may range from adjustment disorders to depressive and anxiety disorders to PTSD. He cites some special concerns regarding PTSD, emphasizing the importance of adhering to the diagnostic criteria outlined in the *Diagnostic and Statistical Manual of Mental Disorders* (*DSM-IV-*

---

[94]Simon, *supra* note 75.
[95]*Id.* at 144.

TR)⁹⁶ and stressing that PTSD should not be diagnosed in order to further legal or political agendas. At the same time, he notes that experts have valid roles in describing the range of victim behaviors that may be associated with sexual harassment. In assessment relevant to damages, he also underscores the importance of distinguishing between diagnosis and damages, with a focus on functional impairment and recognition that sexual harassment may be associated with a range of psychic losses.

Finally, Carl Malmquist approaches the issue of sexual harassment with an emphasis upon the pitfalls for experts who blur appropriate role boundaries, and the invalid clinical material that may be elicited by distorted interview techniques.[97] He notes that many sexual harassment cases are difficult to either prove or disprove. Such cases may "devolve to assessments of the credibility of the allegations. It often becomes a matter of recruiting witnesses from each side of the workplace to support or negate the credibility" of the claimant."[98] For the forensic expert, the boundaries of questions related to damages, preexisting conditions, credibility, and reasonable person exceptions may become unusually vague, and the expert may overstep his or her appropriate boundaries out of ignorance, hubris, or a combination of the two. The assessment of claimant credibility may give way to offering opinions about whether or not the alleged behavior occurred or whether it constituted harassment. Malmquist comments: "Because sexual harassment cases are not going to disappear from courtrooms and the revolution in the American workplace is likely to continue, it is important for psychiatrists to delineate their roles carefully. Otherwise, they extend themselves beyond their expertise and pretend to an exactness that is not achievable."[99]

With regard to assessment techniques, Malmquist cautions that examiners may elicit reports of symptoms that distort the examinee's condition, and he focuses on PTSD as an illustration. Malmquist notes that the examiner preoccupied with gathering information relevant to a particular diagnosis may conduct an interview guided by diagnostic criteria rather than the examinee's self-report. This may result in leading, persistent, and overly detailed questions that may not be justified by the examinee's presentation, such as: "It sounds like you thought you were at risk of being seriously injured at that time," or "Do you feel detached from others and quite different from how you used to be when socializing?" or "How often do you try to block out thoughts about what happened at your job?"[100] Such questions may ultimately yield results, albeit misleading. For instance, Malmquist notes that many people, with prompting, may report some degree of social discomfort, sleep disturbance, relationship

---

[96] AMERICAN PSYCHIATRIC ASSOCIATION, DIAGNOSTIC AND STATISTICAL MANUAL OF MENTAL DISORDERS (4th ed. text rev. 2000) [hereinafter DSM-IV-TR].

[97] Carl P. Malmquist, *The Use and Misuse of Psychiatry in Sexual Harassment Cases*, 26 PSYCHIATRIC ANNALS 149 (1996).

[98] *Id.* at 150.

[99] *Id.* at 155.

[100] *Id.* at 154–55.

problems, etc., but that the examiner who gains such information in the context of leading questions is apt to misconstrue it.

IV. Forensic Assessment in Sexual Harassment Cases

A. The Role of the Forensic Expert

Sexual harassment evaluations present some particular assessment questions, and they sometimes raise special concerns as to the appropriate boundaries of expert opinion, as will be discussed further below. Many aspects of the roles of psychiatric and psychological experts in sexual harassment cases are not vastly different from those in in other types of litigation, however. The expert may provide consultation, clinical evaluation, or both. Consultation may revolve around diagnostic questions or research findings. As evaluators, psychiatrists and psychologists conduct assessments and may provide reports and testimony. Simon summarizes the range of potential functions as follows:

- Expert witness vs. forensic consultant (or both)
- Evaluating diagnosis, treatment, and prognosis
- Evaluating trauma responses and victim behaviors
- Evaluating causation of alleged psychic injury
- Evaluating factors influencing severity of trauma response
- Assessing psychological damages
- Assessing credibility of litigant[101]

The roles of consultant and evaluator may be combined in most cases. However, the forensic evaluator should not also serve as therapist, as will be discussed further below.

B. Ground Rules

Before describing some of the particular assessment questions that arise in sexual harassment cases, it may be useful to review general guidelines to sound forensic practice. The clinician should establish the ground rules for appropriate assessment during the initial referral from an attorney or a court. The following should be addressed prior to the evaluation:[102]

- The clinician should be expected to evaluate the plaintiff in a neutral and objective manner, reporting things as he or she sees them, regardless of which side has requested the assessment. A forensic evaluator should be an advocate for his or her professional opinion, not for one side or another in a particular case.

---

[101]Simon, *supra* note 75.

[102]With slight differences, this list also appears in Benedek, *supra* note 19.

- The clinician should be provided with all relevant, reasonably available documents. Attorneys should not be permitted to sift or select the information to be provided to the clinician, as such a practice may compromise the validity and credibility of the overall assessment.
- If the clinician will be asked to offer an opinion regarding a mental status of a particular person, it is essential that the clinician have the opportunity for an in-person clinical interview. Diagnosis should not be offered in the absence of such an interview; document review in itself is inadequate for diagnostic purposes. On occasions when an expert is asked to provide information, consultation, or testimony about a general issue,[103] clinical assessment of the individual may not be necessary.
- Cases outside the clinician's area of expertise should be referred or declined. The clinician must assume responsibility for this judgment, rather than relying upon the attorney. Short of this, some cases call for research in particular areas, consultation with other professionals, or a team approach if broad expertise is needed, as will be discussed further below.
- Arrangements that may alter the typical conditions of clinical assessment should be discussed in advance if at all possible. These include limitations on the time allotted for the evaluation or upon the scope of the assessment. Also, it is not uncommon for attorneys to expect to be present or to want the evaluation recorded. While courts may allow such arrangements, the evaluation is nearly always compromised to some degree by such departures from typical clinical practice. If a clinician can predict in advance that the proposed arrangements represent such a constraint upon or deviation from sound clinical practice that a valid assessment most likely cannot be conducted, the referral should, of course, be declined or the court should be requested to intervene.

C. Relevant Areas of Expertise

The evaluator in a sexual harassment case should have expertise in areas generally pertinent to forensic assessment. Forensic assessment in general rests upon sound diagnostic skills, including use of the *DSM-IV-TR*. Assessment should include special attention to the detection of exaggeration and malingering, as indicated. Evaluations often include both clinical interview and psychological testing, as will be discussed further below.

In addition, there are particular issues of relevance to sexual harassment. The evaluator should have knowledge of the sexual harassment literature and familiarity with the range of clinical reactions that may occur in response to trauma, for example. This might include not only the literature concerning the aftermath of childhood sexual abuse, but also work delineating the various reactions and stages of responses to trauma encountered in adult life. However,

---

[103]General issues that arise in sexual harassment cases might include such topics as trauma and its range of sequelae, why sexual harassment victims may not immediately report or complain, and standards for conducting forensic evaluations.

it should be noted that sexual harassment cases may involve a range of issues, and that the related literatures may be vast. Thus, forensic examiners should expect to research new areas, obtain consultation as needed, and, in some cases, decline a referral. For example, if a particular case involved allegations that the stress of harassment contributed to the development of a specific medical condition, a clinician lacking the background to assess this question should decline the case, consult with an appropriate specialist, or function as part of a team. Or a case might involve the argument that a plaintiff was not harassed but rather, had misrepresented her background upon hiring, and lacked the intellectual abilities to perform certain tasks. This situation would call for formal intellectual assessment. Some cases present a range of psychological and/or medical issues that call for expertise from multiple sources.

D. Examiner Objectivity and Possible Bias

Clinicians engaged in forensic practice must be cognizant of potential sources of bias. Simon has argued that special concern regarding bias is appropriate in sexual harassment cases because of the strong feelings and opinions these cases may evoke.[104] He describes several possible sources of bias. First, the clinicians who conduct forensic assessments have typically also been trained as therapists. This may broaden and enrich their overall clinical skills, but it can also be a possible source of role confusion. Second, forensic clinicians should guard against an excessively ideological or politicized approach to sexual harassment cases. Third, forensic clinicians bring their own personal histories to their work, and in some cases this may interfere with their functioning.

1. The Distinction Between Therapist and Evaluator

The forensic examiner should not also function as a treatment provider; similarly, therapists should refrain from serving as forensic examiners. Commentators have addressed dual professional roles, noting the inherent potential conflicts in attempting to combine the central aims of forensic assessment and therapeutic work.[105] They emphasize that in forensic evaluation, the goal is to provide information to the legal system; one cannot predict whether or not the assessment will be helpful to the plaintiff. In order to avoid the examinee's participating in the assessment process with any false assumptions, forensic evaluators should specifically inform the examinee of the purpose of the contact and the limits upon confidentiality. Professionals in treatment roles should avoid serving as forensic evaluators whenever possible. Therapeutic work is based upon a helping posture on the part of the clinician, an alliance that evolves over time, and confidentiality. Similarly, Simon emphasizes that forensic evaluators should not serve as dual agents and that the claimant must be

---

[104]Simon, *supra* note 75.
[105]MELTON ET AL., *supra* note 87, at 84–87.

informed that no doctor-patient relationship exists.[106] Of course, in the event the examiner discovers a plaintiff is acutely psychotic, a risk to self or others, or otherwise in need of emergency treatment, responsible action must be taken.

On occasion, a treatment relationship is established after a forensic evaluation. This may not always be inappropriate—for instance, in small, rural communities where mental health professionals may be scarce. Dual-role conflicts may arise, however, if a formal or informal arrangement exists in which it can be anticipated that evaluation will lead to treatment. The *Specialty Guidelines for Forensic Psychologists* state that forensic psychologists should avoid dual roles; if dual roles become inevitable, the psychologists should seek to minimize the effects.[107]

Therapists may inevitably become involved in the legal process when treating a patient who is also involved in litigation. The therapist's records may be disclosed and/or the therapist's testimony may be required. Under these circumstances the clinician can and should preserve appropriate role boundaries by testifying as a fact witness rather than a forensic evaluator.

2. *The Importance of Avoiding Ideology*

Ideological or political beliefs have been noted as a possible source of bias. Simon suggests the risk of bias may be particularly salient in sexual harassment cases, given the strong ideological views held by many with respect to this subject.[108] He observes that strongly held political or feminist beliefs need not necessarily interfere with assessment in sexual harassment cases, but he warns that they may represent a source of bias that might preclude participation in such evaluations. It should be underscored that a forensic examiner need not be apolitical or lacking in strong personal views, in sexual harassment cases or other areas of practice, but it is important that an examiner not reflexively frame the issues in a particular case in terms of personal ideology. This is not an impossible task; it rests upon a commitment to professionalism and the simple recognition that personal values and broad generalities are not a good guide to understanding the specific case. Cases range from malingered disorders and relatively trivial claims of sexual harassment to severely damaged victims who are apt to have long-term difficulties with depression and posttraumatic symptoms following extreme harassment.

3. *The Examiner's History*

Simon also notes that forensic examiners who have a history of being abused or who have been victims of harassment themselves may have difficulties performing evaluations as they may either overidentify with the plaintiff or, if they are relatively unscarred, be inclined to dismiss claims of distress.[109] The

---

[106] Simon, *supra* note 75.
[107] The *Specialty Guidelines* are reproduced in Appendix 3.
[108] Simon, *supra* note 75, at 141–42.
[109] *Id.* at 141.

general point that examiners should not overgeneralize from their own experience is well taken. However, care should be used not to draw too sweeping a conclusion about the impact of any particular experience upon professional functioning, including sexual abuse or harassment. If one considers the spectrum of behavior associated with sexual harassment, some experience of it may hardly be unremarkable among female forensic examiners; indeed, one of the present authors has published an account of such experiences.[110] This need not be an insurmountable source of bias. Again, bias may be offset by a commitment to professionalism and experiences over time in a variety of cases.

V. The Evaluation Process

A. The Forensic Interview in Sexual Harassment Cases: Content and Process

The forensic interview includes most features of a standard psychiatric or psychological interview, with specific attention given to issues relevant to the litigation. The forensic interview in a sexual harassment case must review the allegations, gather information about the claimant's personal history, and assess areas of symptomatic impairment, if any. Although sexual harassment cases often pose special assessment questions, it is important that such questions not undermine attention to the broad areas that form the foundation of much diagnostic and forensic work. In the long run, the questions particular to sexual harassment cases will be best addressed in this broader diagnostic context.

In general, the forensic interview in a sexual harassment case should include a review of the individual's history, the alleged events that led to the litigation, and an assessment of the litigant's mental status. Historical factors may include the following:

- Family history
- Academic history
- Job history
- Marital and relationship history
- Substance abuse history
- Medical history
- History of treatment for psychological problems or substance abuse (in both the litigant and family members)
- Legal history (other litigation, criminal convictions)
- History of suicidality, self-destructive, or self-mutilating acts
- Issues related to culture, religious beliefs, or ethnicity
- Interests, hobbies, social activities
- Sources of stress or life trauma (history of sexual or physical abuse, losses, illnesses, etc.)
- Other relevant factors

---

[110]Elissa P. Benedek, C.J. Voigt & Diane E. Heisel, *Brief Personal Reflections of Sexual Harassment*, 26 PSYCHIATRIC ANNALS 128 (1996).

Mental status testing typically consists of both structured questions and observations made during the course of the interview. Mental status testing provides information regarding:

- Cognitive functioning (attention, concentration, and memory)
- Evidence of any thought disorder or psychosis (delusions, paranoia, hallucinations, or other deficits in reality testing)
- Evidence of mood disturbance (depression, manic depressive disorder, anxiety disorders, etc.)

From the content of this information and the manner in which it is provided, the experienced examiner may derive information and hypotheses regarding aspects of the litigant's psychological functioning, such as:

- Quality of interpersonal relationships both in and outside the workplace
- Typical psychological defenses (intellectualization, projection, denial, rationalization, etc.)
- Mood/affect
- Cognitive style and level of functioning
- Core features of personality structure

General issues regarding diagnostic assessment are addressed elsewhere in this book.[111] For present purposes, it is helpful to note the differentiation between two broad categories of disorders, designated in *DSM-IV-TR* as Axis I and Axis II disorders.[112] Axis I concerns broad categories of clinical disorders that may be a focus of clinical attention. It includes schizophrenia and other psychotic disorders, substance-related disorders, mood disorders, anxiety disorders, etc. The Axis I conditions most commonly encountered in sexual harassment litigation include the following:

- Mood disorders, such as major depression or less severe depressive disorders
- Anxiety disorders (including Posttraumatic Stress Disorder)
- Somatoform disorders
- Adjustment disorders

Also, *DSM-IV-TR* includes a number of other conditions (V-codes) that are coded on Axis I, such as relational problems, occupational problems, etc. These conditions are defined as warranting clinical attention under the following conditions—the individual has no diagnosable mental disorder, a mental disorder exists but is unrelated to the problem, or a mental disorder exists but the problem is sufficiently severe to warrant independent attention.

Questions about distortion, exaggeration, and malingering of symptoms should always be addressed in sexual harassment cases, not because of any special features of these claims, but because such questions should always be

---

[111] See Chapter 4, The Diagnostic and Statistical Manual of Mental Disorders.

[112] For a detailed explanation of this area, see Chapter 5, Mental Disorders Commonly Encountered in Employment Litigation, and Chapter 6, Personality Disorders in Employment Litigation.

considered when a clinical evaluation might be associated with real and serious consequences and/or significant monetary gain.[113] In addition, litigants claiming emotional distress may be motivated to minimize past difficulties or problematic behaviors, such as substance abuse.

Axis II includes the personality disorders. Personality disorders involve fixed and maladaptive character traits that are related to long-standing patterns of perceiving, relating to, and thinking about the environment and oneself. These disorders are evident in a broad range of the individual's functioning. It should be noted that they very often involve a combination of traits, rather than "pure" types. Thus, a person who does not meet the full criteria for personality disorder may nonetheless have a number of problematic personality traits or features. Personality disorders or traits that may occur with some frequency in sexual harassment cases include a broad range—borderline, dependent, paranoid, histrionic, narcissistic, and antisocial.

An important issue in sexual harassment and many other forensic evaluations involves the differentiation between personality disorder or other problematic character traits (i.e., Axis II disorders) and distressing symptoms that represent a change in the claimant's usual functioning, which may be a response to life stressors (i.e., Axis I disorders). In short, the first question is whether or not the individual appears to be experiencing some impairment or serious psychological symptoms. If so, the next question is whether these are best attributed to enduring personality traits or whether they represent some other, more acute disturbance. If the interview and other information suggest the individual does not suffer from a personality disorder, the question remains whether the symptoms might be more readily attributable to the reported harassment than to other stressors and factors in the individual's life. Thus, the interview should also involve careful exploration of additional sources of difficulty, such as family problems, illness, loss, domestic abuse, or other stressors. It should be noted that the distinction between personality problems and more acute disturbance may be difficult even under ordinary circumstances, and it may be further complicated by the adversarial context of the forensic evaluation. One can also find a combination of the two, in which long-standing characterological problems have been exacerbated by more recent stress. In addition, conclusions that a plaintiff meets diagnostic criteria for a personality disorder should not be based solely on information about circumstances related to the alleged sexual harassment. A personality disorder, if appropriately diagnosed, should be evident in various areas of the individual's history and functioning.

In sexual harassment evaluations, special attention is given to such topics as relationship history, sexual history, any history of childhood sexual abuse, or other adverse sexual experiences. In addition, the examiner should explore in detail the reported harassment. This should not be simply a recitation by the claimant of the events but also her thoughts and feelings about those events. It is useful to explore the course of the complaint process, whether the complaint

---

[113]See Chapter 11, Malingering: Distortion and Deception in Employment Litigation.

occurred prior to litigation, and any complaints of retaliation. It is important to gather information about the responses of significant others in the claimant's life, not only in the workplace but also among friends and family members. Support and understanding may mitigate the impact of harassment and litigation, or their absence may intensify the claimant's psychological difficulties.

One common pitfall in conducting an evaluation of a sexual harassment plaintiff is adopting a clinical stance that is either overly confrontational or overly solicitous of symptomatic complaints. It is important in a forensic assessment, as in any clinical endeavor, to establish rapport and ask a number of open-ended questions to elicit the claimant's thoughts, feelings, and perspective. When possible, the examiner should take an inquiring, neutral stance, regardless of which side retained the examiner's services, and regardless of whether the examiner is skeptical of or inclined to credit the claimant's self-report. This position may be difficult to maintain in an adversarial context. Some claimants may be angry and hostile, especially if the evaluation has been requested by the defense. Further, in all forensic assessment there may be times when the examiner must ask difficult, personal, and even directly challenging questions. This may be essential for exploring and clarifying the issues. On the other hand, the examiner who falls into a pattern of conducting evaluations as if they were depositions is apt to emerge less well informed about important aspects of the claimant's history and mental state than the examiner who generally maintains an inquiring tone, with some variations in approach as indicated. This may be especially important in sexual harassment cases, which require attention to relationship history, sexual history, and other potentially sensitive topics.

Conversely, some examiners, whether as a result of a misplaced attempt to be thorough or from some other motive, may ask leading, repetitious, or overly specific questions. Such an approach is likely to affect all aspects of the evaluation, but it is especially harmful to the examiner's ability to establish an accurate diagnosis as it may significantly distort the symptoms reported.

The claimant's account of the harassment and the litigation can often be long, detailed, and complex. It is essential to explore this information, but it should not eclipse assessment of other aspects of the claimant's history and functioning. Claimants vary in their willingness to discuss the full range of relevant topics. Some readily provide detailed, emotional accounts of the harassment but are reluctant to provide any other personal information. Others, especially if the litigation is far advanced, may provide rote, mechanical recitations of the allegations as if it were the fourth day of their deposition; some claimants have been instructed by their attorneys not to discuss the facts of the case at all. The examiner must be prepared to work with the claimant in order to elicit balanced information in all the relevant areas. Again, questions of diagnosis (preexisting disorders, personality disorders, etc.), the existence and/or extent of emotional damages, and credibility are best evaluated in the context of broad information about many aspects of the individual's history, personality, and functioning.

On very rare occasions, evaluation of both the complainant and the alleged perpetrator or harasser might occur. Similar evaluation procedures should be utilized in order to obtain a comparable range of data. The evaluator may compare and contrast versions of the alleged harassment. This may, or may not, provide a basis from which to address issues of relative credibility. At the very least, assessment of an alleged harasser may provide information regarding his mental state and possible psychopathology; however, the examiner should bear in mind that there is no psychological profile of likely or unlikely perpetrators of harassment. It is unclear whether or not evaluations of alleged harassers will become more common; it is certainly an atypical practice at present. When such evaluations occur, the examiner must avoid conclusions that intrude upon the province of the trier of fact.

B. Psychological Testing: Uses and Limitations

Psychological testing can be a useful tool in sexual harassment evaluations, though testing alone is insufficient for establishing a diagnosis or serving as a basis for conclusions about preexisting disorders or damages. It should be used in conjunction with the clinical interview and review of available collateral information. Psychological tests are best used to generate hypotheses that may be assessed, elaborated, or refined when considered in concert with other aspects of the assessment. Psychological testing tends to be a less flexible technique than clinical interviewing, but it is valuable in providing a means to assess an individual's functioning in relation to standardized norms. Chapter 10 provides an overview of psychological testing, including specific features of tests commonly used in forensic assessment. Some issues unique to psychological testing in sexual harassment cases will be discussed briefly here. In particular, testing is often employed in assessing the overall credibility of the claimant's clinical presentation, and it may also be useful in assessing the relative weights of long-standing personality traits and more acute or recent symptoms.

1. Issues of Test Validity and Claimant Credibility

Psychological test results may bear on questions of the claimant's credibility. Attorneys may sometimes ask whether psychological testing can show whether a plaintiff is being honest about the specific allegations. The answer is nearly always no. However, psychological tests can shed light on factors relevant to assessing an examinee's self-presentation, typical problem areas, degree of psychological disturbance, and, in some cases, whether problems are long-standing or attributable to more recent events, such as the alleged harassment.

A number of instruments, for example, the Minnesota Multiphasic Personality Inventory-2 (MMPI-2) and Millon Clinical Multiaxial Inventories (MCMI-II and III),[114] have validity scales or modifying indexes, respectively, that

---

[114] For discussions of the uses and limitations of the MCMI inventories, see James W. Schutte, *Using the MCMI-III in Forensic Evaluations*, 19 AM. J. FORENSIC PSYCHOL. 5 (2001); Richard Rogers et al., *Validation of the Millon Clinical Multiaxial Inventory for Axis II Disorders: Does It Meet the Daubert Standard?* 23 LAW & HUM. BEHAV. 425 (1999); Robert J. Craig, *Testimony Based on the Millon Clinical Multiaxial Inventory: Review, Commentary, and Guidelines,* 73 J. PERSONALITY ASSESSMENT 290 (1999).

provide information about the examinee's approach to the task and whether the clinical results provide a valid picture of the examinee's personality traits and psychological symptoms. Such scales generally tap into the examinee's tendency to endorse unusual symptoms, willingness to acknowledge problems and flaws, whether he or she approaches the test consistently, and other factors. Claimants may exaggerate or deny problems for a variety of reasons. Broadly stated, exaggeration or denial may be a function of a claimant's personality or a more specific reaction to the litigation and the evaluation.

Test validity and claimant credibility are not synonymous. Validity refers to the extent to which a test measures what it is intended to measure. Credibility refers to overall integrity and believability. In general, of course, valid test results and a credible clinical presentation tend to occur together. However, valid test results do not automatically imply the claimant is credible. Conversely, some degree of minimizing or overendorsing symptoms does not necessarily discredit the claimant's clinical presentation. An example of straightforwardly valid results and a generally credible claimant follows.

CASE EXAMPLE

Ms. A reported a coworker at a small company had hugged and kissed her on two occasions and once unzipped his fly and joked he would expose himself; the latter occurred with witnesses. Indignant, Ms. A complained. The investigation was cursory and no action was taken. The investigator reportedly gossiped about the case and appeared to ridicule the claimant. During the evaluation the claimant reported only feeling anxious and said she remained angry and upset, but she denied any notable depression and described her overall functioning as "pretty good." The results of psychological testing appeared valid; they suggested some tension and anxiety but no diagnosable mental disorder.

In this case example, the testing results parallel the claimant's account. The results are relevant in an assessment of credibility as well as the extent of emotional damages, which appear to be minimal to none.

It is not unusual in sexual harassment cases, however, as in other litigation involving claims of emotional distress, to find test results suggestive of a tendency to overendorse problems and symptoms. The interpretation of such results should be based upon the particular pattern and values of the validity scales and other contextual clinical information. Mild overemphasis of problems does not preclude the existence of genuine distress. However, a tendency to emphasize symptoms on psychological testing that are not readily explicable in terms of other aspects of the claimant's reported history and clinical presentation should raise useful questions about the nature of the discrepancies.

CASE EXAMPLE

Ms. B, a sexual harassment plaintiff, described herself during the interview as very depressed and anxious. Asked to describe those feelings, she was vague and inconsistent.

In contrast, her spontaneous descriptions of her day-to-day functioning and her relationships suggested little distress or impairment. The test results were suggestive of overendorsing or exaggeration of symptoms.

In such a case, the examiner must weigh the question of whether the claimed depression and anxiety are genuine or whether the plaintiff is opportunistically overendorsing symptoms when asked explicit questions in the interview or through the test items. Psychological test findings consistent with outright malingering should of course raise doubts about other aspects of the claimant's clinical presentation.

In addition, it is not unusual for sexual harassment plaintiffs to produce defensive testing results, which may typically be associated with a tendency to underreport problems. It initially seems counterintuitive that a claimant alleging emotional distress would produce a defensive profile. Extreme versions of this approach are known as "fake good" in the MMPI-2 literature. A milder version of faking good is a tendency to present oneself in the best possible light and minimize or deny symptoms and problems. Such an approach is not unusual in, for example, child custody evaluations, as one might expect. In general, a defensive approach means that both personal flaws and psychological symptoms are minimized or denied. However, in some cases, a defensive minimization of flaws and shortcomings may be accompanied by strongly endorsing psychological symptoms and distress. Defensive profiles may coexist with elevated clinical scales, especially where the claimant attempts to create a particular "pattern of disability."[115] In sexual harassment cases, this often may be attributed to a combination of somewhat conflicting factors. On the one hand, the claimant may wish to portray herself or himself as emotionally distressed (whether this report is genuine or not). On the other hand, the scrutiny that may be brought to bear upon the claimant's history and background may also result in a wish to minimize any historical problems or personal faults.

CASE EXAMPLE

Ms. C, who alleged harassment by a coworker, also had a history of exotic dancing and probable substance abuse. She described herself as depressed, socially withdrawn, and anxious as a result of the harassment, and she sought to avoid discussion of her past during the interview. The results of testing suggested a defensive approach along with extreme elevations on scales associated with depression and anxiety.

Defensive results should, of course, prompt review by the examiner of other information and history in order to assess other possible areas in which information was withheld by the claimant or difficulties minimized. However, it should be noted that mildly defensive profiles do not necessarily imply that the

---

[115]KENNETH S. POPE, JAMES N. BUTCHER & JOYCE SEELEN, THE MMPI, MMPI-2, AND MMPI-A IN COURT: A PRACTICAL GUIDE FOR WITNESSES AND ATTORNEYS 101 (1993).

underlying difficulties are severe or significantly contributed to the claimant's current condition. In some circumstances, claimants may become guarded, apprehensive, and wary as a result of the stress and lack of privacy associated with being involved in a lawsuit, and this may contribute to a defensive profile. The correlation of clinical data with collateral information is of course crucial in assessing the range of possible explanations.

2. Psychological Tests and Assessment of Personality and Symptoms

Psychological testing may also be useful in sexual harassment cases in addressing the question of whether a personality disorder exists. As will be discussed further below, the presence of a personality disorder has been held to bear upon the question of the claimant's credibility, causation of the events at issue and/or the claimant's injury, and the extent of emotional damages. A number of psychological tests provide information relevant to the differentiation of acute symptoms (typical of many depressive disorders, adjustment disorders, etc.) versus enduring problematic personality traits. Personality disorders or problematic traits may, of course, coexist with genuine symptoms. However, the presence of some personality disorders may suggest a claimant is knowingly endorsing exaggerated symptoms. In others, personality factors may cause the claimant to misattribute long-standing problems to the alleged harassment, or to distort interpersonal events relevant to the alleged harassment.

CASE EXAMPLE

Ms. D reported having become isolated and excluded as one of the few women on a management team in the wake of a reorganization at her company. In her lawsuit, she claimed gender discrimination and some harassing behaviors, mainly in the form of patronizing jokes. Some collateral information and Ms. D's presentation in the interview suggested that the new management team was more efficiency- and performance-oriented than the previous regime, and Ms. D felt this undermined the friendly, supportive workplace atmosphere that had existed previously. She described herself as having become severely depressed, with a number of related symptoms. Her psychological testing results appeared valid, despite some tendency to overendorse symptoms and difficulties. The results also suggested significant personality problems. For instance, on the MMPI-2, Ms. D produced a marked "conversion V," a pattern of results associated with somatic complaints, the use of defenses such as denial and projection, immaturity and strong dependency needs, unacknowledged hostility, and a lack of willingness to acknowledge fault or psychological problems.

In this case example, the psychological test results as well as other sources of information strongly suggested problematic personality traits that intensified and perhaps distorted the plaintiff's reaction to the changes in her work environment.

It should be borne in mind, however, that personality disorders and more acute pathology, such as depression and anxiety, are not mutually exclusive. Indeed, as noted above, symptoms that emerge under stress often represent exacerbation of the vulnerabilities and liabilities of the individual's personality structure. Thus, the task in forensic assessment, assisted by psychological testing, is to offer information that assists the court in weighing personality problems on the one hand and symptoms attributable to the alleged harassment and/or the stress of litigation on the other.

C. The Forensic Examiner's Testimony in Sexual Harassment Cases

The forensic expert has the task of presenting the results of a clinical evaluation in a legal, adversarial context. This is not always an easy task, as psychiatry and the legal system are based upon different paradigms, and this tends to complicate communication.[116] There are several issues unique to the forensic examiner's expert testimony in sexual harassment cases.

1. The Obligation to Provide Complete and Balanced Information

Experts must account for the bases of their opinion and sum up evaluation findings. As often as not, the evaluation will reveal some mix of factors, rather than being entirely favorable or unfavorable to either plaintiff or defense, even if the bottom-line opinion is ultimately favorable to one side or the other. The adversarial legal system often seeks polarized, black or white portrayals of people and situations rather than the shades of gray often found in clinical assessment. This may be accentuated in sexual harassment cases that hinge on the plaintiff's history and credibility. Attorneys may quite naturally wish to highlight information favorable to their client, and on occasion this may clash with the clinician's obligation to report all areas relevant to the assessment.

CASE EXAMPLE

Ms. E was evaluated at the request of her attorney following a well-substantiated claim of sexual harassment. Her history was relatively unremarkable, but in response to standard questions she forthrightly acknowledged a brief period of alcohol abuse a few years previously, near the end of college but prior to the alleged harassment. In describing the impact of the harassment, she described herself as upset, anxious, more wary of others, and prone to see the world somewhat differently, but her distress did not seem to rise to the level of a diagnosable disorder. Her account of the harassment was consistent and credible. A report was requested after the evaluation. Her attorney protested the inclusion of her substance abuse history in the report. It remained because the clinician felt it was standard practice to inquire about and summarize information in various areas of the plaintiff's history. The case went to trial and despite the report of past substance abuse and the lack of serious symptomatic impairment, the plaintiff

---

[116]MELTON ET AL., *supra* note 87, at 3–25.

received a substantial damage award. The clinician testified regarding the plaintiff's overall credibility and the validity of her subjective distress.

2. Avoiding Excessive Inference

Clinical practice, including forensic practice, can never be entirely atheoretical. Assessment is not a completely empirical exercise; some degree of inference is always involved, for instance, in assessing how a reported cluster of symptoms best fit a particular diagnosis, or how personality may have been shaped by history. However, the forensic examiner should be cognizant of these underlying assumptions and avoid highly intuitive or inferential leaps, speculation, or far-reaching conclusions based on ambiguous information. During the clinical interview, it is appropriate for the examiner to listen for underlying themes, to explore hypotheses about an individual, and to elicit new information. However, when issuing a report or testifying, the forensic clinician is obliged to offer opinions based upon a careful weighing of all available information with conclusions that are best supported by that information and the relevant literature, and to avoid being excessively swayed by a particular theory, ideology, or diagnostic fad. For instance, there are periodic claims that a disorder is vastly more prevalent than has been previously recognized. This has occurred in recent years with both Posttraumatic Stress Disorder and dissociative disorders, especially in connection with the notion that many people have been sexually abused but do not directly recall the experience. While debates about various disorders may raise useful questions, forensic examiners should exercise caution in the absence of clearly established diagnostic criteria and methods.

3. Assessing Credibility Versus Usurping the Role of the Trier of Fact

The uses and limitations of psychiatric reports and testimony in the courts have been the topic of considerable debate. The typical view is that experts may appropriately offer testimony relevant to a range of legal questions, but they should refrain from testimony that threatens to usurp the role of the trier of fact. Thus, forensic experts should not offer conclusions as to whether or not the alleged events did or did not occur. This may seem to be a subtle distinction, given that it is common to offer opinions as to a claimant's overall credibility, but it is a critical and important distinction nonetheless. The following vignette may illustrate the appropriate boundary.

CASE EXAMPLE

Ms. F claimed harassment and retaliation by a supervisor over a number of months. During the course of the interview she was difficult to follow as she presented information chaotically, often drawing conclusions about the supervisor's meaning or intention that were not readily apparent to the examiner. Her account of her personal history was somewhat dramatic, and it was difficult to get a picture of important events and relationships in her life, although she did not seem evasive. Psychological testing appeared valid and suggested histrionic personality structure and a rather haphazard, imprecise cognitive style. The examiner noted it was beyond the scope of clinical practice to determine whether or not the harassment had occurred. The evaluation noted features of the claimant's clinical presentation that suggested a general potential for error in judgment based upon her imprecise, emotion-driven style, and also noted that the test results were valid and did not suggest any deliberate attempt to be misleading.

The appropriate focus is to offer an overall assessment of the claimant's clinical presentation, including credibility, grounded in sound diagnostic practice, with special consideration of psychological factors related to the legal issues. Such psychological findings may be varied, with some favorable to the plaintiff and others favorable to the defense; the expert should include and address both. It will ultimately be up to a judge or jury to assess both the expert's opinion and the facts.

VI. Special Assessment Issues in Sexual Harassment Cases

A. Overview

Assessment in sexual harassment cases involves multiple factors. The claimant's personality structure, past level of functioning, and characteristic defenses form a context for reported symptoms. Preexisting personality disorders, deficits in reality testing, mood disorders, and other relevant factors should be noted. Conditions that might predispose an individual to feel harassed or victimized should be carefully assessed. The possibility of exaggerated, feigned, or malingered psychological complaints should always be considered and assessed. In addition, features of the environment and interpersonal relationships can be significant factors, as they might either ameliorate or intensify the psychic impact of the alleged harassment. The evaluator should consider that plaintiffs have a variety of reactions and engage in a range of coping behaviors. These might include ignoring offensive or harassing behaviors, deflecting these behaviors through avoidance and changes in personal appearance, minimizing the emotional impact of harassment by joking or other verbal repartee, or setting verbal limits. Decisions about whether or not to report alleged harassment might be influenced by a wide variety of factors. These might include the claimant's preferred coping style as well as her perception about how a report might be viewed by others. If the harassment has been of sufficient severity or duration, it may be expected that the plaintiff will have experienced a range of emotions that might include guilt, embarrassment, anger, and helplessness. An assessment may make significant clinical findings about any of these factors. Selected vignettes below illustrate some of the particular issues regarded as relevant in sexual harassment assessment. They are necessarily brief and are intended to highlight the range of clinical findings one may encounter. It should be noted that many cases present multiple issues for consideration.

B. Childhood Sexual Abuse

A history of childhood sexual abuse has been regarded as pertinent to a wide variety of questions in sexual harassment cases, including damages, welcomeness, and heightened sensitivity to sexual remarks or conduct. As noted, it has been proposed that persons with a history of childhood sexual abuse may recreate their earlier circumstances through repetition compulsion. While this may occur in some instances, there is a broad range of outcomes in individuals with such a history.

CASE EXAMPLE

Ms. G presented a history of childhood sexual abuse, according to her own report and past treatment records, by both an uncle and an older stepbrother. Nonetheless, she had done reasonably well in school and had sought psychotherapy in early adulthood. Her appearance, since early adolescence, was noteworthy for her short hair, shapeless clothing, and lack of makeup. She was active in sports and was an avid carpenter. Despite these "masculine" trappings, she was heterosexual and had a long-term boyfriend. Ms. G obtained a job on a building crew. She fielded the sexual banter by responding in kind, drank occasionally with the crew after work, and was gradually accepted. However, a former crew member returned from medical leave and rejoined the group. He began hiding her equipment, pressing against her when working in close quarters, and asking for sex, and several times followed her home from work or from the bar. The others were aware of some of his behavior and neither joined in nor interfered with his conduct. After several months, he attempted to assault Ms. G, and she formally complained.

In this case, what was the contribution of the claimant's history of childhood sexual abuse? One might suggest that her job choice reflected a wish to recreate, in disguised form, the circumstances of her earlier trauma by giving her an opportunity to function as something other than a vulnerable young girl. However, rather than behave flirtatiously, she renounced some aspects of an outwardly feminine appearance and became invested in a defensive strategy of "passive into active," which may have played a role in her choice of employment. There would also appear to be little information to suggest hypersensitivity; indeed, such a claimant may feel humiliated by the prospect of complaining and resist doing so as it would undermine her sense of her own competence.

CASE EXAMPLE

Ms. H had a history of sexual abuse by her stepfather, who threatened to do the same to her younger sister if she told. After a phase of adolescent sexual promiscuity and substance abuse, Ms. H had achieved a reasonably stable marriage and a fairly good work history. She presented as shy and nondescript, but her competence earned her a promotion. A new manager in her workplace presented as loud and prone to make sexual jokes, and he occasionally hugged women in the office. Others regarded him as annoying. Ms. G had a number of conflicts with him and eventually filed a lawsuit. During her mental evaluation, it became clear that a number of her conflicts with the manager had been prompted by her perception that he was picking on other people, and her language as she described her interactions with him was similar to her description of her situation as an abused child.

The question to be considered is whether this plaintiff has some features of a hypersensitive plaintiff, or whether she is merely vigilant on behalf of others because of her history. In this case, her history of sexual abuse may have played a role in her depiction of and reactions to the circumstances surrounding the allegations. Such a clinical finding does not obviate the question of whether or not the alleged behaviors constitute harassment, but may be weighed, especially in gray-area cases, as a possible contributing factor, and may be considered in addressing damages.

In both of the above examples, the plaintiffs appeared to have a number of strengths, along with some problematic personality traits. The following vignette concerns a claimant whose overall level of functioning is poor.

CASE EXAMPLE

Ms. I had a history of sexual abuse by her brother and his adolescent friend in late childhood and early adolescence. Her work history was rocky, but she had achieved a fairly good record in her current job until about a year before the complaint. However, the collateral information obtained described her as dependent and needy with her supervisors, easily angered and hurt, and often flirtatious, engaging in and initiating sexual banter. About a year before the complaint, Ms. I's work assignment had been changed, and her performance declined as she found the new assignments difficult. Practical jokes, sexual e-mails, and the like continued to be a part of the workplace, but Ms. I became more withdrawn and sporadically upset in response. She was frequently tearful when her supervisor spoke to her about her job performance, and she said she felt left out by the other workers in her area. She eventually pursued sexual harassment litigation. The clinical assessment strongly supported a diagnosis of Borderline Personality Disorder. For instance, she had a history of treatment for episodes of impulsively cutting herself. She also reported a long-standing pattern of the unstable, intense, all-or-nothing relationships that are characteristic of this personality disorder.

This claimant's presentation appears to be typical of what would be expected from a sexual harassment complainant with a history of childhood sexual abuse.[117] Her flirtatious, sexualized self-presentation may be infused with underlying dependence. The change in the plaintiff's work assignment and her diminished sense of her own worth may bear on her finding offensive interactions that she had participated in previously.

---

[117] *See* McDonald & Feldman-Schorrig, *supra* note 84.

In short, it may be expected that childhood sexual abuse will have an impact upon an individual's functioning, but that impact must be carefully assessed in any given case. The severity, nature, and duration of the original abuse are relevant. Attention must also be given to the claimant's general level of adjustment. Although there may be a statistical association between a history of childhood sexual abuse and such diagnoses as Borderline Personality Disorder, this association is never a foregone conclusion in any particular case.

C. Personality Disorders

The assessment of underlying personality structure and the existence of a possible personality disorder is central in sexual harassment cases, as in other types of forensic assessment. Personality disorders may be pertinent to questions of damages, as a number of symptoms may be, in some cases, attributable to long-standing problems rather than to the effects of the alleged harassment. In addition, some personality traits or disorders (such as Antisocial, Narcissistic, Histrionic, or Borderline) may especially raise concerns about dramatizing, exaggerating, or feigning symptoms. The interpersonal patterns and perceptions associated with personality disorders may also be deemed relevant as contributors to the events culminating in the litigation. For example, in *Pascouau v. Martin-Marietta Corp.*,[118] the court found that the plaintiff had a personality disorder with Borderline, Histrionic, and Narcissistic features and agreed with expert testimony that the disorder led to her perceiving others in a highly personal and overemotional fashion, with little sense of responsibility for the events around her. A case with a somewhat different diagnostic picture follows.

CASE EXAMPLE

Ms. J complained of harassment by a coworker. Investigation by the company had found some improper behavior, and the coworker was transferred. Ms. J saw him only every several months at large quarterly meetings. But it made her increasingly angry, and she pursued litigation. She was also angry about the referral for evaluation. Despite this, she spoke freely and with evident pleasure about aspects of her own history. She presented herself as a special, sensitive, and gifted person. She had few friends, and her relationships with acquaintances and family members were marked with conflicts over favoritism and perceived slights. In describing her feelings at work, she did not depict herself as fearful or traumatized. Rather, she expressed indignation that some coworkers continued to have cordial contact with the harasser.

This plaintiff might well be judged to have a personality disorder characterized by a combination of Narcissistic and Borderline traits, evident in a range of

---

[118] 994 F. Supp. 1276, 76 FEP Cases 651 (D. Colo. 1998), *aff'd in relevant part*, 185 F.3d 874 (10th Cir. 1999) (table).

areas of her functioning. Her reaction to the limited continued contact with the coworker and her anger at the company's response may be consistent with her character structure, in the absence of other explanations.

Personality disorders also may coexist with symptomatic difficulties that represent a blend of long-standing difficulties and distress attributable to the alleged harassment. The examiner should be aware that the distinction between personality disorder and problems attributable to situational stress may be a difficult one to make. Sexual harassment claimants are usually evaluated during a period of considerable stress. Further, the existence of problematic personality traits does not preclude the existence of symptoms or distress that might be attributed, at least in part, to alleged harassment. Personality traits or disorders are best assessed through a multipronged approach, using interview data (both the content and the style of presentation), historical and collateral information, and psychological testing.

CASE EXAMPLE

Ms. K, a female factory worker, alleged sexual harassment and gender discrimination following a transfer. She claimed that her equipment had been destroyed and other workers had refused to work with her in tasks requiring a partner for safety reasons. She indicated she had been taunted and intruded upon while going to the bathroom and that pornography was repeatedly left in her locker. She claimed that these incidents had occurred frequently over a period of many months and that complaints to management had resulted in little change. Ms. K's history was remarkable for a tumultuous and somewhat abusive family. She was divorced, with adolescent children who had a number of behavioral problems. She had a history of periods of excessive drinking. She initially described the alleged harassment but revealed little about her subjective state. However, over the course of the interview it emerged that she had lost weight, had difficulty sleeping, became sick to her stomach on her way to work, and had episodes of both rage and crying.

In the above case, the plaintiff had a number of problematic personality patterns and traits, although she would not neatly fit into any category of personality disorder. However, her past problems and personality traits may account for relatively little in terms of her current symptoms and difficulties, given the nature of the allegations.

D. Reasonable Person/Woman Exceptions: The "Hypersensitivity" Issue

In *Ellison v. Brady*,[119] the Ninth Circuit provided some basis for distinguishing between objectively hostile or abusive environments and overly subjective claims:

---

[119] 924 F.2d 872, 54 FEP Cases 1346 (9th Cir. 1991).

> In order to shield employers from having to accommodate the idiosyncratic concerns of the rare hypersensitive employee, we hold that a female plaintiff states a prima facie case of hostile environment sexual harassment when she alleges conduct which a reasonable woman would consider sufficiently severe or pervasive to alter the conditions of employment and create an abusive working environment.[120]

As noted, past experiences of sexual trauma, abuse, or earlier harassment have been offered as evidence of a plaintiff's "hypersensitivity" to events that would not ordinarily be regarded as distressing by another person. It has been argued that such a history results in fear and hypervigilance.

In addition to childhood sexual abuse, emotional conditions other than traumatic sexual history have been offered as evidence of hypersensitivity. For instance, in *Sudtelgte v. Reno*,[121] psychiatric evidence was admitted diagnosing the plaintiff as having a Paranoid Personality Disorder that affected her workplace relationships and her perceptions of being "picked on." Hypersensitivity may occur in the context of various diagnostic pictures.

CASE EXAMPLE

Ms. L brought a sexual harassment suit after a single incident at work, which she described as deliberate and quite traumatic. She began to fall near some steps, whereupon a male colleague grabbed her and fell with her. In the end, he wound up holding her breast, and there were several onlookers. The colleague said he was trying to assist Ms. L and lost his balance; the onlookers' accounts supported him. The collateral information revealed no history of workplace disputes involving Ms. L. Upon evaluation, there was no evidence of exaggeration or malingering. However, Ms. L appeared to have a schizotypal personality. For example, she avoided contact with others and expressed long-standing concerns about her neighbors' habits, which she believed represented veiled communications to her.

In general, clinical information related to hypersensitivity should not rest solely on the account of the alleged harassment and the plaintiff's reaction. Factors that might plausibly be associated with hypersensitivity should be discernible in other aspects of the plaintiff's history, relationships, or functioning.

E. Welcomeness and Plaintiff Response

Regarding the issue of welcomeness, the Supreme Court maintained in *Meritor Savings Bank v. Vinson*[122] that sexual conduct must be unwelcome if it is to

---

[120]*Id.* at 879, 54 FEP Cases at 1350.
[121]63 FEP Cases 1257 (W.D. Mo. 1994).
[122]477 U.S. 57, 40 FEP Cases 1822 (1986).

be actionable as sexual harassment. In *Henson v. City of Dundee*,[123] the Eleventh Circuit defined "unwelcome" conduct as conduct not "solicited or incited" by the plaintiff. Thus, the plaintiff's behavior or role in the events at issue in litigation may be relevant at trial and during the forensic examination. If a plaintiff is shown to have elicited or freely participated in sexualized conduct later alleged to be harassing, the allegations may be refuted. Courts have admitted evidence regarding dress and even personal thoughts on the part of the plaintiff as being relevant to the issue of welcomeness. Developing case law suggests that evidence regarding a plaintiff's sexual conduct, broadly defined, with alleged harassers will be held to be admissible, but evidence regarding a plaintiff's sexual activities unconnected with the workplace will be excluded.[124]

Questions of welcomeness can be among the most subtle and difficult issues to arise in sexual harassment cases. These questions require an understanding of the social and interpersonal context of the behaviors. For instance, it is not uncommon to find that a plaintiff once participated in sexual banter that was commonplace in a particular work setting but was later alleged to be part of a pattern of harassment. From a clinical perspective, such past behavior may have a variety of meanings. It may have been genuinely volitional and raise doubts about later claims of emotional distress; changes in the workplace may have occurred that changed the interpersonal meaning of the banter; or the plaintiff may have participated in order to appear tough and invulnerable. Welcomeness must be evaluated on a case-by-case basis.

Disputes about the welcomeness/unwelcomeness of the alleged behaviors and the nature of the plaintiff's reactions are common. The related assessment questions are usually addressed within the context of the plaintiff's account of her past feelings and reactions, collateral information regarding those reactions, and consideration of what may have been typical within the workplace in question. If a plaintiff did not pursue a complaint promptly, as is often the case, the reasons for the delay may be considered potentially relevant to the question of welcomeness. Assessment of this issue should involve consideration of the range of possible responses suggested by the literature.

CASE EXAMPLE

Ms. M had been employed for a number of years in a small company. She reported good work relationships, including that with her boss (the owner), and many of the employees were personal friends. The owner divorced, and during this time he was described as noticeably distraught or depressed. Ms. M had sought him out on a number of occasions to inquire about how he was doing and to offer encouragement and support. Shortly after, he told her he loved her and invited her to have an affair. She said she did not wish to do so, noted she was married, and told him he was simply

---

[123]682 F.2d 897, 29 FEP Cases 787 (11th Cir. 1982).
[124]See Chapter 8, The Right to Privacy Versus The Need for Discovery.

upset because of his recent circumstances. She said he persisted, pursuing her both verbally and physically on many occasions when they were alone. This went on for a number of months before she even considered the possibility of complaining, as she regarded his feelings as misguided but genuine and defined it as a personal problem. When she reached the point of wanting to complain, she noted that it was a small company and he was the owner. She eventually quit her job and initiated litigation.

In this example, a workplace that might be described as warm and friendly under some circumstances turns out to be a place with poor boundaries between the professional and the personal, and little recourse in the event of trouble. Features of the workplace, the past relationship, and typical factors that affect responses to sexual harassment should be considered. The plaintiff's lack of formal action for a number of months does not necessarily suggest welcomeness so much as confusion, self-doubt, and concern for someone she once regarded as a friend.

Another example illustrates some of the reactions that may occur over time.

CASE EXAMPLE

Ms. N described feeling initially flattered by the flirtatious attention of a handsome supervisor. She said she became alarmed when he began pressuring her to see him outside work. She declined repeatedly, and he became angry and reproachful and eventually began spreading vulgar rumors about her that, she believed, had affected the projects she was involved in. She spoke of having felt for some time that she was to blame for his behavior, and she described feeling regretful and ashamed that she had ever felt gratified by his attention.

The forensic examiner should weigh such an account in the context of the range of reactions plaintiffs might well have over the course of time and communicate information about these reactions to the attorneys and/or court as well.

In contrast, there may be instances in which the evaluation does not provide an alternative explanation for past, apparently voluntary, participation in sexualized behavior. The examiner may also find that the question of when and why a complaint was pursued coincides with other personal or workplace factors.

CASE EXAMPLE

Ms. O had been employed on a part-time basis at a company while also being involved in a personal relationship with one of the managers. They socialized and occasionally traveled to conferences together; Ms. O acknowledged the manager sometimes paid her expenses. Others in the company were aware that the two were a couple. Ms. O then obtained a higher, more responsible position that she had wanted for some time at the company, with the support of the manager. Other employees reported they did not believe she would have obtained the position without his support, and there were questions about her qualifications. She then began to complain about a series of incidents in which her recommendations were not heeded and she was not included in meetings. She filed a complaint, including allegations that the manager's past conduct was sexual harassment. Her predominant affect in describing what occurred during the evaluation was controlled anger. She was reluctant to provide much detail about her past contacts with the manager. They both said the relationship had ended sometime after her promotion, but their accounts differed as to when and why.

Cases presenting such an array of factors and multiple, conflicting accounts are not rare. In this case, the plaintiff's relationship with the manager is characterized by poorly defined personal and professional boundaries. The overall context and plaintiff's presentation provide little clinical support for a conclusion that the manager's behavior in the past was unwelcome.

F. Assessment of Severity of Emotional Damages

Numerous factors may be pertinent to questions of emotional damages. These include the severity, nature, and duration of the alleged harassment, preexisting conditions, additional stressors, and responses of significant others. In general, one expects proportionality between the magnitude of the alleged harassment and the severity of the symptoms presented. The more severe the behavior, the more severe the symptoms may be expected to be. The more protracted the harassment, the more apt the plaintiff is to become symptomatic, sometimes as a result of distressing and conflicting feelings of anger, guilt, and helplessness. If proportionality between the stressor and the symptom is absent, an explanation should be sought. This explanation may range from exaggeration and malingering to a range of factors that help account for the clinical picture.

CASE EXAMPLE

Ms. P alleged stalking and then sexual assault by a coworker. She complained during the stalking, but no action was taken. Collateral information from a criminal complaint supported her claim. She met the criteria for Major Depression, with many features of Posttraumatic Stress Disorder. Personal historical information included the death of a parent, a divorce, and the serious illness of one of her children five years previously. She had a history of a few periods of some depressive symptoms.

Such extreme allegations do indeed occur. In this case, there would be little reason to regard historical factors as contributory to the plaintiff's current distress. A history of transient depressive symptoms is not uncommon and appears commensurate to the past stressors she had experienced.
On the other hand, disproportionate symptoms may have multiple possible explanations.

CASE EXAMPLE

Ms. Q asserted that a coworker in her new job at a furniture store put his arm around her and joked on several occasions about how they should try out the mattresses together. She quit the job and claimed during the evaluation that she was anxious about his following her, was easily startled, and had bad dreams about the event.

This report might be assessed differently depending on the plaintiff's history. Suppose additional information suggested the plaintiff was an isolated, obsessive person with a history of anxiety symptoms. This might be considered in assessing damages—her self-report of symptoms might be credible, but her strong reaction might be partly the result of long-standing difficulties. Or, as an alternative, suppose the plaintiff had a history of substance abuse, no stable past employment, and hopes of leaving her husband. One might suspect feigning or malingering for financial gain, with no real emotional distress.

In addition to personal historical factors, cultural issues and/or the response of others may play a role in the severity of the symptoms presented.

CASE EXAMPLE

Ms. R, a religious woman from a conservative immigrant community, was harassed by her supervisor via sexual jokes and unwanted touching. She confided in a friend, who reported the harassment out of concern. The company investigated and said it found no evidence of wrongdoing. Hurt and humiliated, Ms R. pursued litigation. She then found herself the subject of gossip in her community, and her family was embarrassed and angry with her. She presented as severely depressed with her day-to-day functioning seriously compromised.

Of course, the contrasting scenario may occur, in which a plaintiff feels understood and supported by those close to her, and this may ameliorate distress. Such differences sometimes are especially clear in cases involving multiple plaintiffs with similar allegations but different personal histories and different responses from important others.

CASE EXAMPLE

Multiple plaintiffs alleged harassment by a coworker that included sexual comments, rubbing against them, and following them to their cars, ostensibly as an escort, but in a manner the plaintiffs uniformly described as "creepy." The alleged harasser had been disciplined previously and referred for treatment but the behavior recurred, and the plaintiffs felt their subsequent complaints had been ignored. The women had communicated with one another about the harassment and provided mutual support. They all presented as angry with management. None of them had particularly serious preexisting conditions. Clinically, they ranged from having mild Adjustment Disorder to Major Depression. The plaintiff suffering from Major Depression noted that her brother worked at the same company, and he and other family members were angry with her for pursuing the complaint.

Differences in emotional support may therefore lead to different clinical outcomes. Plaintiff and defense may likely differ in how such differences should be considered in assessing damages, with the plaintiff arguing, for instance, that the depression was inextricably linked to the harassment. The defense would argue that it is separate and less relevant.

To summarize, sexual harassment cases and their associated clinical outcomes vary greatly. The task of the forensic evaluator, as in assessment more generally, is an integrative one. No single diagnostic, historical, or situational factor can be expected to guide assessment generally. Indeed, most cases have a range of issues to consider before an expert opinion can be formulated.

VII. Psychological Treatment in Sexual Harassment Cases

This section will explore the various issues involved in treating the patient/litigant in sexual harassment cases, with attention to two general themes: (1) the impact of litigation upon treatment, and (2) the role of therapist in the legal system.

In general, litigation or other significant intrusions on confidentiality significantly undermine the conditions of psychotherapeutic treatment. This does not mean that a claimant suffering psychological distress cannot receive some support from treatment during litigation, but the extent of that support and the scope of the treatment may be compromised. Therapists and attorneys vary in their perspectives on these difficulties, and therapists vary widely in their understanding of and sophistication regarding the legal system. In general, attorneys tend to believe that therapists will function unreservedly as advocates for their patients in litigation. It is not uncommon for attorneys to refer sexual harassment claimants to therapy, and some therapists readily enter the legal arena. In some such cases, it is legitimate to wonder if the treatment is largely a means of substantiating an emotional distress claim. Other therapists and patients are appropriately concerned about the erosion of confidentiality and the potential impact upon the treatment, and rightly regard litigation as an unpredictable and stressful undertaking.

A. The Decision to Litigate

The legal system is not designed to be responsive to victims' emotional needs or support a process of healing and recovery. One commentator observes:

> It would be difficult to imagine two disciplines more antithetical to one another than therapy and litigation. Therapy takes place in an atmosphere of confidentiality, trust, and support, with the goal of healing. Litigation takes place in the public arena of the courts and, contrary to popular mythology and the hopes of litigants, its goal is not to find out the truth and obtain justice but rather to resolve disputes.[125]

---

[125] Lynne H. Schafran, *Sexual Harassment Cases in the Courts, or Therapy Goes to War: Supporting a Sexual Harassment Victim During Litigation*, in SEXUAL HARASSMENT IN THE WORKPLACE AND ACADEMIA, *supra* note 1, at 133.

Some therapists may encourage patients to pursue litigation, believing it will be helpful to them in resolving the distress and symptoms attributable to sexual harassment, or other forms of victimization. The expectation that litigation will be a psychologically healing or helpful experience for the patient may be quite naive, however.

Certainly victims of sexual harassment may choose to pursue litigation for any of a wide variety of reasons. They may feel angry, betrayed, humiliated, or powerless. They may be motivated by the hope of financial gain, a determination not to tolerate victimization, or a feeling of obligation that others should be protected from similar experiences. Persons considering litigation may certainly ponder the question of how they will feel about themselves in the long run if they do not sue, fearing that they will feel they failed to stand up for themselves. But even if one judges a particular claimant's motives for bringing litigation as being well founded, it is only sensible to regard litigation as a potentially bruising and stressful experience.

One author suggests that the question of whether or not to pursue litigation be considered in terms of the patient's ability to withstand the demands of the process—the lack of closure, the time involved, and the ruthless discovery process.[126] Others note that, despite the warlike nature of litigation, it is the only acceptable choice for some patients, for realistic or irrational reasons.[127] They note that patients fare best when they:

- Set realistic goals,
- Maintain a sense of control of the litigation process,
- Seek out adequate support from at least one significant source (family, therapist, peers, attorney),
- Appreciate and focus energy on restoring the original equilibrium of their lives independent of the litigation process, and
- Adequately acknowledge and grieve the losses inevitably involved even when litigation has a favorable outcome. Implementing all of these steps is easier said than done.[128]

B. Confidentiality Issues

It is typical to expect that communications between therapist and patient are confidential. When a patient, either at his or her own initiative or at the suggestion of an attorney, enters treatment with the expectation that it will buttress the claims in a case, there may be little expectation of confidentiality from the outset. However, there are also many occasions when a troubled and distressed claimant enters treatment with motives and concerns more typical of therapy patients, or when a patient in ongoing treatment becomes a plaintiff. In such

---

[126]*Id.* at 146–47.

[127]Sharyn Lenhart & Diane K. Shrier: *Potential Costs and Benefits of Sexual Harassment Litigation*, 26 PSYCHIATRIC ANNALS 132 (1996).

[128]*Id.* at 133.

cases, it is often nearly impossible to safeguard the boundaries of treatment from developments in the litigation.

A claimant alleging emotional distress, in a sexual harassment case or in other cases, should routinely expect that any and all records of mental health treatment will be subpoenaed and ultimately released. Many subpoenas are not sufficient for the release of records in the absence of explicit authorization to do so by the patient or some other notice procedure,[129] though the therapist must, of course, respond to the subpoena. Subpoenas for mental health records should prompt the therapist to review the pertinent laws, consult the patient and/or the patient's attorney regarding authorization for release, and obtain legal or professional consultation as needed.

Theoretically, a plaintiff may be able to refuse to authorize release of therapy records. Such a refusal likely will significantly compromise any claim for emotional damages, however. In short, the patient/litigant cannot both allege pain and suffering and simultaneously expect to prevent disclosure of records pertinent to those claims. Furthermore, the therapist-patient privilege typically cannot be only partially waived. Ordinarily, if release of information is authorized, all records and notes may be obtained. The therapist may also be required to testify. As noted, it is most appropriate for the therapist to do so as a fact witness; however, this designation is ultimately in the hands of others.

C. The Therapist/Evaluator Distinction Revisited

In an earlier section, it was noted that forensic examiners should not also function as treatment providers in the same case. This issue will now be revisited, with the focus upon the role of the therapist treating a patient who is also a sexual harassment litigant. It has become commonplace to regard therapeutic and evaluative roles as distinct and even mutually exclusive. While this is helpful as a general guideline, it may also be something of an oversimplification.

In a given case, evaluators should not function as therapists, but all therapeutic work involves evaluation. The difficulty lies in the common failure to distinguish between general diagnostic assessment and forensic assessment. It has been argued that the roles of therapist and evaluator are mutually exclusive in part because therapists are seen as the patient's natural ally, accepting her representations of her experience and circumstances relatively uncritically.[130] However, in good psychotherapeutic treatment, there should be a distinction between an interest in the patient's welfare and reflexive acceptance of the patient's view of reality. Therapeutic work involves evaluation, not only during the initial stages of treatment, which are aimed explicitly at assessment, but in later stages as well. Rather than accepting a patient's representations

---

[129]*See, e.g.,* CAL. CIV. PROC. CODE §1985.3 (providing for "notice to consumer" and opportunity to object prior to production of records in lieu of patient release).
[130]Simon, *supra* note 75, at 141.

uncritically, a good therapist suspends judgment to some degree, expecting that as treatment proceeds new information will emerge, and the therapist also knows that the patient's history and psychological dynamics may affect his/her presentation of information. Such assessment is not adequate for forensic purposes, however.

Forensic evaluation involves diagnostic assessment but goes beyond it as well. Forensic assessment typically involves more active review of information from multiple sources, and to a different end. Thus, therapists asked to testify in harassment lawsuits typically should refrain from offering expert opinions on the forensic issues, even if encouraged to do so, and even if the therapist has worked as a forensic examiner in other contexts. Even if designated as an expert witness, the therapist may rightly decline to offer opinions on specific forensic questions. The following vignette provides a view of the possible pitfalls.

CASE EXAMPLE

The therapist treating Ms. S, a plaintiff in a sexual harassment case, was subpoenaed for a deposition. Ms. S, a young woman, reported that she had been harassed along with several coworkers by a supervisor who was verbally demeaning, showed them pornography, and repeatedly attempted to grope Ms. S. The company had been unresponsive to complaints. Ms. S had no history of psychological problems, and her background suggested a hardworking, eager-to-please person. During deposition, the therapist reported a diagnosis of major depression. Asked about the cause, the therapist said the only apparent precipitant was the sexual harassment. The therapist was then asked if she was aware that Ms. S's husband reportedly had had an affair. Ms. S had apparently confided this to a coworker a couple of years before, and the coworker had been deposed. The therapist's unawareness of this potentially significant alternative stressor greatly undermined her credibility and effectiveness as a witness.

In this example, the therapist did nothing improper; therapists will, of course, testify about diagnosis, reported history, course of treatment, etc. Rather, this vignette underscores the fact that even a cooperative, motivated patient may not provide the sort of information that might become available through a forensic assessment, and it highlights the distinctions between general diagnostic assessment and forensic work. It is not unusual for patients to withhold some information over the course of treatment, either because trust in the therapist is still being established or because they are not yet ready to deal with certain issues. Of course, the affair does not necessarily mean the sexual harassment did not also contribute to the patient's depression, but the therapist is hardly in the best position to testify regarding the relative weights of these different precipitants.

D. Treatment Approaches with Sexual Harassment Claimants

Few meaningful, broadly general statements are possible regarding the most appropriate treatment modalities with sexual harassment claimants. The acts associated with sexual harassment are simply too diverse, with an enormous range of possible effects upon the victim. Symptoms will be shaped by personality structure, life history, the nature of the harassment, workplace dynamics, and family and social supports. However, a few recurring concerns in treating sexual harassment claimants might be noted.

First, treatment should attend to all aspects of the patient's life circumstances and functioning. This may be particularly difficult to do when litigation is especially consuming or the harassment was especially severe. These topics may crowd out other concerns. However, it is obviously important to attend to other areas because additional sources of difficulty will impede the patient's progress.

CASE EXAMPLE

Ms. T, a patient with a history of sexual harassment, presented in therapy with symptoms of major depression. She improved somewhat in response to therapy and medication. With considerable ambivalence, she decided to initiate a lawsuit. The initial phases of contact with her attorney, which involved pulling together documentation for the case, seemed to energize her, despite her continued difficulties. The lawsuit became the predominant topic of the therapy. Eventually, the therapist inquired about the Ms. T's family, since she had discussed them more in the past. It emerged that her husband, who had been quite concerned and caretaking when she was more overtly depressed, had become more withdrawn. After exploring this, the therapist recommended some marital sessions. Ms. T's husband had reacted to the litigation by becoming somewhat jealous, feeling it signified Ms. T's reinvolvement with the harasser. Also, he was disappointed that her mild symptomatic improvement had not led more directly to her putting the harassment behind her and returning to their prior life.

Therapists treating sexual harassment claimants should also be aware of the likely impact of the compromises in confidentiality. Once the patient realizes that treatment records are likely to be released and/or the therapist deposed, communication in the therapy sessions will almost inevitably be affected. In effect, the treatment will take place with a potential audience. Some patients may become constricted, even if they consciously wish to avoid doing so. In other cases, the material presented in the sessions may become a rehearsal for the lawsuit, as the patient catalogs symptoms and difficulties related to the harassment.

If records are released or the therapist is deposed, there will likely be consequences for the treatment. In many cases, therapists typically have documentation or ideas they have not communicated to the patient because it was not yet appropriate in the context of the therapy. These may end up being disclosed in testimony, with negative effects on the treatment alliance. Even if this does not occur, it may be jarring for patients to hear or read about themselves in clinical language. On the other hand, the therapist who attempts to safeguard the treatment from litigation and expresses reluctance about releasing records or being deposed is apt to find the patient feels unsupported and abandoned as a result.

Third, patients involved in litigation inevitably have strong hopes, wishes, and fears regarding what the litigation might achieve. These may shift over the course of time and should be addressed in treatment. Patients may be interested in reestablishing their self-respect, in monetary gain, or in forcing the employer to deal differently with harassment in the future. While some hopes may be inflated, they may not be entirely unrealistic. More specific and quite unrealistic hopes and wishes may also exist. These may be difficult for the patient to recognize or articulate, but they may nonetheless influence his or her behavior and should be explored when possible.

CASE EXAMPLE

Ms. U and two coworkers had been harassed by a supervisor, Ms. U especially severely. She had felt helpless and guilty about her inability to protect the other women. Before the supervisor was hired, she felt she had been well regarded and had enjoyed a good relationship with her superiors. However, her complaints about the supervisor's behavior had been disregarded. Once she initiated the lawsuit, Ms. U spoke repeatedly of her hope not only that the supervisor would be dismissed, but also that the company would acknowledge it had been wrong and apologize to her and the other women. The therapist noted that although such an outcome might not be absolutely impossible, it would certainly not be typical, and she questioned Ms. U about how she would feel if either the case were dismissed or she received an offer of some monetary settlement. For a time Ms. U avoided these questions, and then she became increasingly depressed, explaining that the possible monetary offer made her feel like a "whore."

Finally, the supportive and empathic therapist may find himself or herself overidentifying with the patient, with the result that the focus of the therapeutic session becomes discussion of legal issues rather than exploration and interpretation of thoughts and feelings. In the long run, this blurs the distinction between therapy and the litigation. A patient may find it difficult to discuss the full range of his or her feelings if the therapist is perceived as overly interested in the legal process or invested in a particular outcome. It likely will be easier for the patient to express and work through the vicissitudes of his/her emotions and experiences with a therapist who preserves a balanced approach.

CHAPTER 15

AVOIDING AND ATTACKING "JUNK SCIENCE" IN EMPLOYMENT LITIGATION

Jane M. McFetridge, J.D.

The testimony of psychiatric or psychological experts on emotional distress damages issues has become a prominent part of most employment lawsuits in recent years. Although expert testimony is not necessarily a prerequisite for the recovery of emotional distress damages,[1] emotional damage claims are often buttressed by testimony offered by a psychiatrist, psychologist, or other mental health professional concerning the nature and extent of the plaintiff's psychological injuries. Mental and emotional injury is a difficult phenomenon to detect and measure with precision, however, and some "expert" opinions offered in support of such injury claims amount to little more than unsubstantiated conjecture, or "junk science."[2] Recent developments in the law of evidence provide a means to prevent an opponent's introduction of junk science into the emotional damages aspect of employment litigation, however.

As discussed below, in 1993 the U.S. Supreme Court in *Daubert v. Merrill Dow Pharmaceuticals*[3] established a new standard for the admissibility for scientific evidence. Then, in 1999, the Court in *Kumho Tire v. Carmichael*[4] expanded the applicability of the *Daubert* standard to nonscientific or technical evidence. Also in 1999, Federal Rule of Evidence 702 was modified to more directly reflect the Supreme Court's intent in *Daubert* and its progeny, including *Kumho Tire*.[5] Overall, the courts appear to view psychiatric and psychological

---

[1] *See* discussion in Chapter 1, The Legal Context.
[2] This term was popularized in P. HUBER, GALILEO'S REVENGE: JUNK SCIENCE IN THE COURTROOM (1991).
[3] 509 U.S. 579 (1993).
[4] 526 U.S. 137 (1999).
[5] Revised Rule 702 provides:
If the scientific, technical, or other specialized knowledge will assist the trier of fact to understand the evidence or to determine a fact in issue, a witness qualified as an expert by knowledge, skill, experience, training, or education, may testify thereto in the form of an opinion or otherwise, if (1) the testimony is based upon

testimony as scientific, and thus not subject to an alternative *Kumho Tire* analysis. While testimony of other experts such as family therapists, which is often based more on experience than scientific principles, may have previously avoided scrutiny under a strict *Daubert* standard, it will now be subject to a *Kumho Tire*/revised Rule 702 analysis. Under either standard, as will be seen, reliability is the key to admissibility of expert testimony.

I. The Development of the Law Against Junk Science

In 1923, the U.S. Court of Appeals for the District of Columbia established the first standard for the admissibility of expert evidence. This rule, created in *Frye v. United States*,[6] is known as the "general acceptance" test. The test allows expert testimony into evidence only if such testimony is generally accepted in the scientific community. In the *Frye* case, the defendant unsuccessfully attempted to admit expert testimony concerning the defendant's results on a lie detector test. The court rejected the expert testimony, holding that the systolic blood pressure deception test, or lie detector, had not yet gained sufficient "standing and scientific recognition" to justify its admission.[7] "[W]hile courts will go a long way in admitting expert testimony deduced from a well-recognized scientific principle or discovery, the thing from which the deduction is made must be sufficiently established to have gained *general acceptance* in the particular field in which it belongs."[8]

The *Frye* general acceptance test was the prevailing rule regarding the admissibility of expert testimony until the U.S. Supreme Court's decision in *Daubert v. Merrill Dow Pharmaceuticals, Inc.*, seventy years later.

A. *Daubert*

In 1993, the U.S. Supreme Court established a new standard for the admissibility of scientific evidence in federal court cases. In *Daubert v. Merrill Dow Pharmaceuticals, Inc.*,[9] the Court rejected the *Frye* rule, which had required that scientific evidence be generally accepted as reliable in the relevant scientific community as a prerequisite to its admissibility into evidence. Although the standard adopted by the *Daubert* Court—and based on Federal Rule of Evidence 702—superficially appears more permissive than the *Frye* rule, it actually

---

sufficient facts or data, (2) the testimony is the product of reliable principles and methods, and (3) the witness has applied the principles and methods reliably to the facts of the case.

FED. R. EVID. 702.
[6]293 F. 1013 (D.C. Cir. 1923).
[7]*Id.* at 1014.
[8]*Id.* (emphasis added).
[9]509 U.S. 579 (1993).

provides trial judges with an important tool to prevent the introduction of conjecture and junk science under the guise of expert scientific testimony.

Daubert involved the attempt by a plaintiff in a products liability case to introduce expert testimony that the drug at issue, Benedictin, could cause birth defects. The district court ruled such testimony inadmissible because all prior published studies had concluded that Benedictin did *not* cause birth defects. The court reasoned that the lack of published studies supporting the plaintiff's experts' position indicated that their position was not generally accepted within the scientific community. The court of appeals affirmed.

The Supreme Court reversed, holding that the proper standard for admissibility is contained in Federal Rule of Evidence 702, which superseded *Frye*. Whether a proffered expert's theory or test is generally accepted within the relevant scientific community is one factor to be considered by the court in applying Rule 702, according to *Daubert*, but it is no longer the only criterion. The *Daubert* Court read Rule 702 to require that an expert's testimony must amount to "scientific knowledge" to be admissible. It went on to specify that "scientific" implies a grounding in the methods and procedures of science, and "knowledge" means "more than subjective belief or unsupported speculation."[10]

The *Daubert* Court further maintained that in cases involving scientific evidence, evidentiary reliability (for the purposes of admissibility under Rule 702) will be based on scientific validity. Scientific validity, according to the *Daubert* Court, means that the theory or technique that is at the root of the expert's opinion can be tested. Moreover, there must be a valid scientific connection to the pertinent inquiry as a precondition to admissibility.[11]

Daubert thus requires that when faced with the proffer of expert scientific testimony, the trial judge must determine (1) whether the proffered testimony is scientifically valid, and (2) whether it will assist the trier of fact to understand or determine a fact in issue.[12] As the *Daubert* Court put it: "This entails a preliminary assessment of whether the testimony is scientifically valid and of whether the reasoning and methodology properly can be applied to the facts in issue."[13] These preliminary matters must be established by a preponderance of the evidence prior to the introduction of such expert testimony before the jury.[14]

As one commentator has observed:

Before *Daubert*, the trial judge had to ask: What do the relevant scientists think about this? The judge had to decide: "Has the proponent of this evidence shown me that scientists agree with her?" After *Daubert*, the trial judge has to decide: "Is this good science?"[15]

---

[10]*Id.* at 589–90.
[11]*Id.* at 591–92.
[12]*Id.* at 592.
[13]*Id.* at 592–93.
[14]In *General Electric Co. v. Joiner*, 522 U.S. 136 (1997), the Supreme Court held that an abuse of discretion standard applies to this determination by the district court.
[15]G. Michael Fenner, *The Daubert Handbook: The Case, Its Essential Dilemma, and Its Progeny*, 29 CREIGHTON L. REV. 939, 948 (1996). This commentator further ob-

Daubert thus places the trial judge in the role of "gatekeeper" charged with verifying the scientific validity of expert testimony before such testimony is permitted to reach the jury. This gatekeeper role of the trial court is designed to prevent juries from being swayed by "expert" testimony that may sound quite impressive but that may be scientifically meaningless. Although the Supreme Court in *Daubert* vested trial judges with this new gatekeeper role, it did not provide them with much detailed guidance on how to perform this new function. The *Daubert* Court provided a nonexclusive list of factors for trial courts to consider—whether the expert's methodology can be tested, whether it has been subject to peer review and publication, the known or potential rate of error of the methodology, and whether a methodology is "generally accepted" within the relevant scientific community[16]—but it did not provide a mandate as to which of these factors is most important or whether any or all of them must be satisfied in every case.

More detailed guidance is provided to trial courts and advocates in the Ninth Circuit's decision on remand in *Daubert*,[17] authored by Judge Alex Kozinski. Judge Kozinski begins by summarizing the trial court's task under *Daubert*:

> First, we must determine nothing less than whether the experts' testimony reflects "scientific knowledge," whether their findings are "derived by the scientific method," and whether their work product amounts to "good science." Second, we must ensure that the proposed expert testimony is "relevant to the task at hand," i.e., that it logically advances a material aspect of the proposing party's case.[18]

Judge Kozinski debunks the notion that expert testimony is necessarily scientific just because it may come from a scientist. He observes: "[S]omething doesn't become 'scientific knowledge' just because it's uttered by a scientist; nor can an expert's self-serving assertion that his conclusions were 'derived by the scientific method' be deemed conclusive."[19] The court's task, then, "is to analyze not what the experts say, but what basis they have for saying it."[20] As Judge Kozinski explains: "[T]he expert's bald assurance of validity is not enough. Rather, the party presenting the expert must show that the expert's findings are based on sound science, and this will require some objective, independent validation of the expert's methodology".[21]

---

serves:
> The irony of the federal judge crafting the edifice of scientific evidence in the courtroom is that, in my experience, a chief reason many of us went to law school is that the other choices all seemed to involve science: we fled science; we fled any profession that uses numbers in any more complex way than as volume, page, or section references.

Id. at 954.
[16] 509 U.S. at 593–94.
[17] 43 F.3d 1311 (9th Cir. 1995).
[18] *Id.* at 1315 (citations omitted).
[19] *Id.* at 1315–16.
[20] *Id.* at 1316.
[21] *Id.*

According to Judge Kozinski, "one very significant fact to be considered" by a court in determining whether expert testimony will be admissible is "whether the experts are proposing to testify about matters growing naturally and directly out of research they have conducted independent of the litigation, or whether they have developed their opinions expressly for purposes of testifying."[22] He concludes: "That the testimony proffered by an expert is based directly on legitimate, preexisting research unrelated to the litigation provides the most persuasive basis for concluding that the opinions he expresses were 'derived by the scientific method.' "[23]

Of course, particularly in employment cases involving claims of emotional injury, most experts' testimony will not be based wholly upon prior research conducted by that expert. Such testimony will still be admissible, however, provided that the proffering party comes forward with "other objective, verifiable evidence that the testimony is based on 'scientifically valid principles.' "[24] One means of showing this, according to the Ninth Circuit, is by proof that the research and analysis supporting the proffered conclusions have been subject to normal scientific scrutiny through peer review and publication.[25]

In the absence of prior research or publication in peer-reviewed journals, the proponent of expert scientific testimony may attempt to satisfy its burden through the testimony of its own experts, but, according to the Ninth Circuit,

> [f]or such a showing to be sufficient, the experts must explain precisely how they went about reaching their conclusions and point to some objective source—a learned treatise, the policy statement of a professional association, a published article in a reputable scientific journal or the like—to show that they have followed the scientific method, as it is practiced by (at least) a recognized minority of scientists in their field.[26]

Thus, the proponent of expert testimony must "explain the expert's methodology and demonstrate in some objectively verifiable way that the expert has both chosen a reliable scientific method and followed it faithfully."[27] The opposing party must then be afforded the opportunity to challenge the showing. This could be done by presenting evidence (including expert testimony) that the opposing expert either employed unsound methodology or "failed to assiduously follow an otherwise sound protocol."[28] The court must then hold an *in limine* hearing outside the presence of the jury to consider the conflicting evidence and to make findings about the soundness and reliability of the methodology employed by the proffered experts.[29]

Applying these standards to the evidence before it, the Ninth Circuit in *Daubert* held that the plaintiffs' expert testimony was inadmissible. The court

---

[22]*Id.* at 1317.
[23]*Id.*
[24]*Id.* at 1317–18.
[25]*Id.* at 1318.
[26]*Id.* at 1319.
[27]*Id.* at 1319 n.11.
[28]*Id.* at 1319 n.10.
[29]*Id.*

observed that "plaintiffs rely entirely on the experts' unadorned assertion that the methodology they employed comports with standard scientific procedures." It continued: "We've been presented with only the experts' qualifications, their conclusions and their assurances of reliability. Under *Daubert*, that's not enough."[30]

The Ninth Circuit's decision on remand in *Daubert* therefore provides important guidance on the admissibility of expert psychiatric or psychological testimony in employment cases, testimony that is often lacking in scientific basis.[31] A useful comparison may be drawn between the testimony of one of the proffered experts in *Daubert* (that Benedictin caused the plaintiff's birth defects) with the testimony of many experts in employment cases (that being fired or harassed caused the plaintiff to suffer severe psychiatric injury). As the Ninth Circuit in *Daubert* observed:

> Dr. Palmer asserts only that Benedictin is a teratogen and that he has examined the plaintiffs' medical records, which apparently reveal the timing of their mothers' ingestion of the drug. Dr. Palmer offers no tested or testable theory to explain how, from this limited information, he was able to eliminate all other potential causes of birth defects, nor does he explain how he alone can state as a fact that Benedictin caused plaintiffs' injuries.[32]

After concluding that "[p]ersonal opinion, not science, is testifying here," the Ninth Circuit rejected this expert's testimony under *Daubert*. The opinion of a psychiatric or psychological expert—given without considering the possible role of alternative stressors—that a particular workplace event caused a plaintiff to suffer severe psychological injury may similarly be vulnerable to a *Daubert* challenge.

As discussed in more detail below, the Ninth Circuit in *Daubert* went on to reject testimony from other experts that Benedictin is "capable of causing" birth defects. The court observed that "what plaintiffs must prove is not that Benedictin causes some birth defects, but that it caused *their* birth defects."[33] An analogy also might be drawn between this principle and proffered expert testimony in many employment cases to the effect that merely being fired is

---

[30]*Id.* at 1319.

[31]The law professor who argued the *Daubert* case on behalf of the plaintiffs in the Supreme Court and in the Ninth Circuit on remand argues that psychiatric and psychological evidence should not be subject to *Daubert* because psychiatric diagnosis is not "testable." *See* Michael H. Gottesman, *Admissibility of Expert Testimony After Daubert: The "Prestige" Factor*, 43 EMORY L.J. 867 (1994). Courts *have* applied *Daubert* to psychiatric and psychological evidence, as well as to other types of medical evidence, however. *See* Tyus v. Urban Search Mgmt., 102 F.3d 256, 263 (7th Cir. 1996) (*Daubert* "is applicable to social science experts, just as it applies to experts in the hard sciences"). *See also* Kumho Tire v. Carmichael, 526 U.S. 137 (1999) (solidifying the application of the *Daubert* standard to "soft sciences" and technical evidence).

[32]43 F.3d at 1319.

[33]*Id.* at 1322.

capable of causing depression or that sexual harassment is capable of causing Posttraumatic Stress Disorder.

The *Daubert* decision therefore should have a profound impact on the admissibility of scientific expert testimony offered to prove that workplace incidents caused significant psychological injury, in a number of respects. First, it may prevent testimony from "experts" who lack sufficient training and experience in clinical diagnosis of mental illness. Second, it may bar testimony from experts who, while possessing the requisite training and experience, fail to employ standard diagnostic principles derived through application of the scientific method, such that their testimony is little more than unsupported conjecture.

B. *Kumho Tire*

One of the questions left open by *Daubert* was whether its standards applied to expert testimony that is not scientifically based. The lack of authority in this area often caused unreliable testimony to be admitted into evidence simply *because* it was not scientific. In *United States v. Starzecpysel*,[34] for example, the court concluded that "forensic document examination could not satisfy the *Daubert* reliability standard because the process relied on subjective factors and the expert's practical experience rather than upon any scientific method."[35] For this reason—because *Daubert* was not applicable and thus did not exclude such unreliable "nonscientific" testimony—the court found the testimony admissible.

In *United States v. Webb*,[36] the Ninth Circuit similarly recognized this loophole caused by *Daubert*. The trial court below had permitted a law enforcement officer to testify as an expert on why a person would conceal a weapon in the engine compartment of a car. On appeal, the Ninth Circuit reversed, observing the incongruity in failing to apply *Daubert* to nonscientific evidence:

> In saying that the *Daubert* standards for admission simply do not apply to specialized knowledge of law enforcement, we cannot be suggesting that the district court examine less rigorously the specialized knowledge underlying proffered non-scientific testimony, or that the district court may abdicate its role as gatekeeper where the subject matter does not depend on the scientific method. The trial court's role as gatekeeper concerning nonscientific "specialized knowledge" proves equally crucial to the integrity of the trial process, particularly where, as here, the proffered testimony's potential for prejudice to the defendant runs so high.[37]

---

[34] 880 F. Supp. 1027 (S.D.N.Y. 1995).
[35] FED. R. EVID. 702 advisory committee's note.
[36] 115 F.3d 711, 713 (9th Cir. 1997).
[37] *Id.* at 716. *See also* Advisory Committee's Note to FED. R. EVID. 702 (citing Watkins v. Telsmith, 121 F.3d 984 (5th Cir. 1997) (unless the trial court's gatekeeping function applies to nonscientific expert testimony, "experts who purport to rely on general engineering principles and practical experience might escape screening by the

In 1999, the U.S. Supreme Court resolved this anomaly by taking the *Daubert* standard a step further. In *Kumho Tire v. Carmichael*,[38] the Court announced that the *Daubert* evidentiary standard is not limited just to scientific testimony but instead extends to all expert testimony.[39] In *Kumho Tire*, a tiremaker and its distributor were sued after a tire blowout caused a vehicle crash. The plaintiffs proffered expert testimony that a defect in the manufacture or design of the tire caused the tire to blow out. In reaching this conclusion, the expert testified that if the age and history of the tire had caused the blowout, the tire should have shown signs of distress or misuse, known as "overdeflection." The expert added that he had inspected the tire in question and conceded that the tire showed some signs of wear and misuse, but explained that since this tire exhibited only two of the four signs of overdeflection, the blowout must have been due to a defect. The trial court determined that it should act as a *Daubert*-type gatekeeper with technical as well as scientific evidence, and it thus applied the *Daubert* factors to the expert testimony and excluded the expert testimony as unreliable. The Eleventh Circuit reversed, holding that the *Daubert* analysis applies strictly to scientific evidence.[40]

The U.S. Supreme Court disagreed with the Eleventh Circuit and agreed with the trial court's holding that a trial judge may screen nonscientific expert testimony. The Supreme Court further held that the factors determining the reliability of expert testimony should be applied liberally. All these factors do not necessarily apply in every instance where scientific testimony is challenged, let alone nonscientific testimony. For instance, scientific expert testimony on a particular topic may never have been the subject of peer review, not because the topic is not reliable but because it previously "never interested any scientist."[41] These factors were "meant to be helpful, not definitive."[42] The U.S. Supreme Court in *Kumho Tire* also affirmatively stated that the *Daubert* gatekeeping function should apply to technical, or nonscientific, testimony, as well as to scientific testimony. "[I]t will at times be useful to ask even of a witness whose expertise is based purely on experience, say, a perfume tester able to distinguish among 140 odors at a sniff, whether his preparation is of a kind that others in the field would recognize as acceptable."[43] The factors used to determine the admissibility of expert testimony should be applied to this type of nonscientific evidence. The perfume tester should not be held to any lesser or heightened degree of scrutiny than a scientist. The testimony of both experts should be evaluated in the same manner.

---

district court simply by stating that their conclusions were not reached by any particular method or technique. The moral of this approach would be the less factual support for an expert's opinion, the better.")).

[38] 526 U.S. 137 (1999).
[39] *Id.* at 141.
[40] Carmichael v. Samyang Tire, Inc., 131 F.3d 1433 (11th Cir. 1997).
[41] 526 U.S. at 151.
[42] *Id.*
[43] *Id.*

A few courts have relied upon *Kumho Tire* to admit nonscientific expert testimony in employment cases. In *Adams v. Ameritech Services*,[44] a sex discrimination case, the Seventh Circuit held that the trial court should have admitted the plaintiff's expert testimony on statistical evidence of disparate treatment and a pattern or practice of discrimination. In reaching its decision, the court applied the *Kumho Tire* framework to determine that the nonscientific expert testimony was both relevant and reliable. Conversely, courts have used the same reasoning set forth in *Kumho Tire* to exclude technical expert testimony. For instance, in *Lang v. Kohl's Food Stores, Inc.*,[45] the plaintiff brought a sex discrimination lawsuit based on the fact that pay in the defendant's produce department was higher than in its bakery and deli departments, and workers were not distributed uniformly by sex. In support of her case, the plaintiff proffered expert testimony by a consultant, with a Ph.D. in labor relations and economics, who taught a class at the University of Pennsylvania. The report consisted of a job evaluation system supporting the plaintiff's position that bakery and deli duties require as much skill as produce duties. The report, however, did not explain how the job evaluation system worked. Reliable scientific methodologies were not used to construct the report. Anyone reading the report would have to take "everything on faith, and that alone would be good reason to exclude [the expert's] conclusion."[46] The court excluded this "expert" testimony pursuant to *Kumho Tire*, finding that the report contained "unreasoned assertions" and "did little more than parrot [the plaintiff's] belief that bakery and deli duties require [the same] skill as produce duties."[47]

C. Revised Federal Rule of Evidence 702

On December 1, 2000, the Advisory Committee on Evidence Rules amended Federal Rule of Evidence 702 in light of *Daubert* and *Kumho Tire*. Revised Rule 702 provides:

> If the scientific, technical, or other specialized knowledge will assist the trier of fact to understand the evidence or to determine a fact in issue, a witness qualified as an expert by knowledge, skill, experience, training, or education, may testify thereto in the form of an opinion or otherwise, if (1) the testimony is based upon sufficient facts or data, (2) the testimony is the product of reliable principles and methods, and (3) the witness has applied the principles and methods reliably to the facts of the case.

The amended rule essentially codifies the principles enunciated in *Daubert* and *Kumho Tire* and subsequent cases, requiring that expert testimony be both reliable and helpful to the jury in order to be admissible. Rule 702 now formally

---
[44] 231 F.3d 414 (7th Cir. 2000).
[45] 217 F.3d 919 (7th Cir. 2000).
[46] *Id.* at 924.
[47] *Id.* at 923–24.

empowers the trial judge to act as gatekeeper—screening the expert testimony to determine if it is sufficiently reliable and helpful to the trier of fact. The role of the trial court as gatekeeper differs from the role of the trier of fact because the court's focus is on the "principles and methodology" of the expert's testimony, not on whether or not the conclusion is correct.[48] Judicial screening of expert testimony is required because of the wide latitude given to expert witnesses, as opposed to lay witnesses, to offer opinions.

This screening process is in no way intended to replace thorough cross-examination, however. As one court recently noted, "[t]he rejection of expert testimony is the exception rather than the rule, and the trial court's role as gatekeeper is not intended to serve as a replacement for the adversary system."[49] Rather, "vigorous cross-examination, presentation of contrary evidence, and careful instruction on the burden of proof are the traditional and appropriate means of attacking shaky but admissible evidence."[50] If a party fails to make a timely objection before the expert testimony is admitted, then that party forfeits the opportunity to subject the reliability or usefulness of the expert testimony to a *Daubert* challenge:[51] "[A] decision to admit expert opinion evidence will only be reviewed for plain error when objections under *Daubert/Kumho* are not timely made."[52] The court will not make such an objection on behalf of an unsuspecting party simply because the expert testimony appears incorrect or an expert's credentials are shaky. The court's role is limited to screening to ensure that the expert's testimony rests on reliable methodology and is relevant to the matter at hand. The trial court's decision to admit expert opinion testimony "will be reviewed only for plain error when objections under *Daubert/Kumho* are not timely made."[53] When a party has properly objected to the admissibility of expert testimony, the proper standard of review is "abuse of discretion."[54]

---

[48]Rudd v. General Motors Corp., 127 F. Supp. 2d 1330 (M.D. Ala. 2001).

[49]Spearman Indus. v. St. Paul Fire & Marine Ins. Co., 128 F. Supp. 2d 1148, 1150 (N.D. Ill. 2001).

[50]*Id.*; *see also* Smith v. Ford Motor Co., 215 F.3d 713 (7th Cir. 2000) (The court's gatekeeping function focuses on the expert's methodology; the "soundness of the factual underpinnings of the expert's analysis and the correctness of the expert's conclusions based on that analysis are factual matters to be determined by the trier of fact").

[51]Macsenti v. Becker, 237 F.3d 1223, 1230 (10th Cir. 2001).

[52]*Id.* at 1232.

[53]*Id.* In a prior case, *Goebel v. Denver & Rio Grande W. R.R. Co.*, 215 F.3d 1083, 1088 (10th Cir. 2000), the Tenth Circuit held that when a district court is faced with a party's objection, it must "adequately demonstrate by specific findings on the record that it has performed its duty as gatekeeper."

[54]General Elec. Co. v. Joiner, 522 U.S. 136 (1997). In *Joiner*, the Supreme Court rejected the "hard look" standard—somewhere between de novo and abuse of discretion—for the abuse of discretion standard traditionally applied to evidentiary rulings. The court further eliminated any distinction between "rulings admitting and excluding evidence, and likewise rejected a more searching standard of review for evidentiary rulings that are 'outcome-determinative.'" It is now clear that the only

The amended Rule 702 resolves the confusion, subsequent to *Daubert*, regarding the application of the rule to nonscientific expert testimony. The advisory committee stressed several points about this new rule. First, the gatekeeper function of the trial court must apply to all expert testimony.[55] "If scientific testimony is singled out for special scrutiny, proponents would have an incentive to argue that their expert should not be regulated because he is not scientific. That kind of race to the bottom should be discouraged."[56]

Second, the reliability standards "must apply not only to the theory or methodology used by the expert, but also to the application of that theory or methodology in the specific case."[57] The advisory committee sought to prevent situations in which an expert might attempt to misuse a reliable theory by improperly applying it to the facts of the case.

Third, the factors listed for trial judges to use in assessing the reliability of expert testimony are meant to be broad and used only as a guidepost.[58] Testimony does not necessarily have to meet all or even most of these factors to be admissible. The advisory committee explained that:

> It does not pay to get too detailed about the factors that a trial judge should use in assessing reliability. The more detailed the factors, the more likely it is that some will be left out. The risk of leaving out important reliability factors is especially great because experts in different fields use different methodologies, and it would be very difficult to describe an all inclusive list of reliability factors that would cover the testimony of all experts.[59]

Kumho Tire and the new Rule 702 therefore establish a more flexible standard for admissibility of technical expert testimony that is not based on pure science. To view *Kumho Tire* and the new Rule 702 as permitting trial judges to admit speculative, questionable, or shaky expert testimony under this flexible standard would be a mistake, however. Always underlying this more flexible standard is the requirement that expert testimony be reliable in order to be admissible.

II. Junk Science in Employment Cases

Daubert, Kumho Tire, and the new Rule 702 may be relevant in a number of respects to a mental health expert's testimony in an employment case.

---

standard of review where a party has made a timely *Daubert* objection is abuse of discretion. *Joiner* suggests that a trial judge's *Daubert* rulings will rarely be reversed.
[55] FED. R. EVID. 702 Advisory Committee's Note.
[56] *Id.*
[57] *Id.*
[58] *Id.*
[59] *Id.*

A. The Expert's Training and Experience

If a mental health professional attempts to base on his or her clinical skills and experience an opinion that employment-related conduct such as discrimination or harassment caused significant psychological injury, the opinion may be inadmissible if the expert lacks the proper clinical training or the requisite clinical experience with such cases. Under *Kumho Tire*, the court would apply the same screening method to a nonscientific or technical expert. For some experts, experience may be a crucial component for admissibility, whereas academic training may be more essential for another.[60]

Courts have applied *Daubert* specifically to the qualifications of a proffered psychological expert. In *Isley v. Capuchin Province*,[61] the court set forth two prerequisites that a psychological expert must meet before being found qualified to testify. First, the expert must demonstrate that he or she has education and training in the discipline at issue "sufficient to give him/her expertise or special knowledge such that any opinions that the expert has will be of assistance to the jury in its fact-finding responsibilities."[62] Second, the expert must show that he or she has personal experience in treating patients with the condition at issue.[63] For example, a licensed clinical psychologist who has never treated patients with personality disorders would have the requisite training and education but would lack the requisite clinical experience to qualify to give an opinion as to whether a plaintiff in an employment lawsuit does or does not suffer from a personality disorder.

1. Education and Training

Case law construing *Daubert* appears to require that psychological experts possess sufficient education and training such that their opinions will carry a measure of scientific reliability. With respect to psychiatrists and clinical psychologists, this should not ordinarily be a problem, provided that the expert testifies about a subject within the scope of his or her expertise. Psychiatrists and clinical psychologists receive rigorous training in the use of scientific principles in diagnosing mental illness. Although the nature of the training varies somewhat between the two professions, its substance is essentially the same. The psychiatrist or clinical psychologist is trained in the process of differential diagnosis, by which mental illness is diagnosed by posing and ruling out a number of alternative hypotheses based on the symptoms presented before arriving at a final diagnosis. For example, when diagnosing Posttraumatic

---

[60]*Id.* (discussing Berry v. City of Detroit, 25 F.3d 1342 (6th Cir. 1994); an expert could testify to principles on the basis of training with no experience, but testimony as to the effect of applying those principles requires a basis in experience).

[61]877 F. Supp. 1055 (E.D. Mich. 1995).

[62]*Id.* at 1063.

[63]*Id. See also* Berry v. Crown Equip. Corp., 108 F. Supp. 2d 743, 749 (E.D. Mich. 2000) (in order to qualify under Rule 702, an expert's training must "relate to the subject matter of his testimony," and the expert must have "first hand familiarity with the subject of the testimony").

Stress Disorder (PTSD), it is the normal standard of practice in forensic evaluations to first rule out Acute Stress Disorder, adjustment disorders, anxiety disorders, personality disorders, and malingering before settling on a diagnosis of PTSD.[64]

Other mental health professionals who may seek to give expert testimony in employment lawsuits, such as marriage and family counselors, social workers, and educational psychologists, typically lack this training in scientifically based diagnosis. These professionals may have a nominal clinical orientation but lack the rigorous training in scientific principles of diagnosis that competent psychiatrists and clinical psychologists possess. The focus of many of these professionals' practices is on counseling and assisting clients with situational difficulties, such as marital discord, which ordinarily do not involve the diagnosis of mental disorders. Moreover, the licensure statutes governing these classes of professionals may limit the scope of their practice in a way that would prevent them from testifying in court as forensic experts.[65]

In cases preceding *Kumho Tire*, some courts refused to allow these mental health professionals to give expert testimony. For example, in *Jackson v. Bayou Industries*,[66] the court in a race discrimination case refused to allow testimony from a "licensed professional counselor" that the plaintiffs suffered PTSD as a result of race discrimination, although it allowed her to testify about her interviews with the plaintiffs, any behavioral characteristics she observed during those interviews, and the course of counseling she pursued with the plaintiffs. In refusing to allow the counselor to testify that discrimination caused the plaintiffs to suffer PTSD, the court observed that the counselor was not a psychiatrist or a licensed psychologist, nor had she ever practiced in the field of psychology. She testified that she had a master's degree in psychology and was in the process of getting a doctorate degree in social work. The witness stated that she had only had one formal course at the noncollege level in Diagnostic and Statistical Manuals in addition to one three-hour afternoon seminar on Diagnostic and Statistical Manuals. Finally, she stated that she did not specialize in psychological testing and did not administer psychological tests to the plaintiffs.[67]

Other courts took a contrary view. For example, in *Sanfelice v. Dominick's Finer Foods*,[68] the court permitted expert testimony from a psychotherapist in

---

[64]James J. McDonald, Jr. & Paul R. Lees-Haley, *Avoiding "Junk Science" in Sexual Harassment Litigation*, 21 EMPL. REL. L.J. 51, 59 (1995).

[65]For example, in California, marriage and family therapists are authorized to treat marital and family problems but not to diagnose mental illness. *See* CAL. BUS. & PROF. CODE §4980.02.

[66]1995 WL 143538 (E.D. La. Mar. 29, 1995).

[67]*Id.* at *1. *See also* Karlin v. Foust, 975 F. Supp. 1177 (W.D. Wis. 1997) (rejecting, pursuant to *Daubert*, proffered testimony by Ph.D. in "family social science" that abortion causes PTSD); State v. Willis, 256 Kan. 837, 888 P.2d 839 (1995) (reversing trial court's admission of testimony from social worker diagnosing rape victim with PTSD; social worker lacked qualifications to make medical diagnosis of PTSD).

[68]1995 WL 608602 (N.D. Ill. Oct. 13, 1995).

spite of the fact that he did not have a degree in psychology.[69] The court emphasized, however, that the expert was "trained extensively in the area of psychotherapy" and had been performing therapy and counseling continuously since 1956. After *Kumho Tire*, more of these types of mental health professionals may be expected to seek to testify as experts. The main inquiry for the court will be to determine if nonscientific expert testimony is both reliable and relevant. If it is, the fact that a social worker, for example, lacks rigorous training in the scientific principles of diagnosis may be irrelevant.

On the other hand, the diagnostic process is inherently scientific—hypothetical diagnoses are considered and ruled out until the proper diagnosis is settled upon. Marriage counselors and social workers may quite effectively perform therapy without necessarily determining the proper diagnosis, but arriving at the proper diagnosis is essential in the forensic context. The testimony of an expert who does not have sufficient training and/or experience in diagnosis would therefore almost always be unreliable.

In addition, there is an ever-growing class of "experts" in employment cases, such as social psychologists, organizational psychologists, sociologists, and so-called "victimologists" and "discriminatologists," who may not possess any clinical orientation at all, but who come from a more general social science or human resources background. Some may attempt to offer diagnoses of psychological disorders, while others may seek to offer opinions on such issues as whether a particular workplace was a "hostile working environment" or that the plaintiff's failure to complain contemporaneously is consistent with the profile of a "typical victim" of harassment (and thus should not undercut her credibility).[70] Although some courts have admitted this kind of testimony,[71] an increasing number are refusing to do so.[72]

For example, in *Lipsett v. University of Puerto Rico*,[73] the court disallowed testimony from a social worker and a social psychologist who sought to testify that unlawful sexual harassment existed in the defendant's workplace. The

---

[69] It is not clear from the court's opinion in just which field, if any, the therapist was degreed.

[70] *See* Karibian v. Columbia Univ., 930 F. Supp. 134, 71 FEP Cases 325 (S.D.N.Y. 1996).

[71] For example, in *Flavel v. Svedala Indus., Inc.*, 1994 WL 761447 (E.D. Wis. Oct. 25, 1994), the court permitted an industrial psychologist to testify regarding "stereotypes in the employment context and management conduct and practices which reflect age consciousness and age stereotypes" to establish the motive for the actions taken by the defendant.

[72] *See, e.g.*, United States v. Rouse, 111 F.3d 561, 571 (8th Cir. 1997) (assessing the reliability or credibility of a victim's accusations is the exclusive function of the jury; psychological expert's opinions about witness credibility are properly excluded); *Karibian*, 930 F. Supp. at 140 (excluding testimony of social worker that plaintiff's failure to complain of sexual harassment was attributable to "reluctance of people to complain about sexual harassment;" noting that this is "such an oversimplification of the issue that it would be of no real help to the jury and could be misleading").

[73] 740 F. Supp. 921 (D.P.R. 1990).

court held both that the proffered experts could not qualify as experts and that their testimony would not assist the jury. With respect to an expert's qualifications, the *Lipsett* court ruled that an expert must be a member of a traditional profession that maintains ethical standards and requires extensive education and mastery of a specialized field of knowledge. Absent these qualifications, a proffered expert's testimony "would not possess the professional safeguards ensuring objectivity."[74]

The *Lipsett* court additionally maintained that testimony of a social worker or social psychologist to the effect that sexual harassment existed in a workplace "would not bring to the jury anything more than the lawyers can offer in argument." *Lipsett* is an important step toward eliminating so-called expert testimony that involves more advocacy than true expertise and that addresses matters more appropriately within the province of the jury to decide.[75] Thus, neither the status of "professional" nor the title "doctor" necessarily makes an expert witness. Although a proffered psychological expert's various credentials may sound impressive, what matters from an evidentiary standpoint is whether that expert's training included adequate training in clinical diagnostics. For experts who are not licensed clinical psychologists or board-certified psychiatrists,[76] this threshold may be difficult to meet, even after *Kumho Tire*.

2. Clinical Experience

Even if a proffered expert has had the requisite basic clinical training in diagnosing mental disorders, that expert's testimony still may not be admissible unless it can be shown that the expert additionally has sufficient personal experience in the diagnosis of patients with the type of condition at issue in the lawsuit.[77]

Courts have used *Daubert* as a basis for excluding testimony by medical experts grounded solely in the expert's clinical experience where the expert lacks extensive experience in diagnosing the condition at issue. For example, in *O'Conner v. Commonwealth Edison Co.*,[78] the Seventh Circuit affirmed the

---

[74]*Id.* at 924.

[75]Similarly, in *United States v. Whitted*, 11 F.3d 782 (8th Cir. 1993), a sexual abuse case, the court permitted a physician to testify about the alleged victim's bedwetting, nightmares, and inability to sleep at night, but it refused to allow the physician to testify that the alleged victim had suffered "repeated sexual abuse." The court explained that because the physician's diagnosis rested solely on his acceptance of the victim's account, his testimony amounted to nothing more than an invitation to the jury to believe his assessment of the victim's truthfulness.

[76]Upon the completion of a psychiatric residency, a physician is eligible to sit for the certification examination in psychiatry administered by the American Board of Psychiatry and Neurology. Although in most jurisdictions a physician need not be board-certified to practice psychiatry, only board certification in psychiatry will guarantee that the physician has received the proper clinical training in psychiatry.

[77]Isely v. Capuchin Province, 877 F. Supp. 1055, 1063–64 (E.D. Mich. 1995).

[78]13 F.3d 1090 (7th Cir. 1994).

trial court's exclusion of the testimony of the plaintiff's medical expert, who sought to testify that he could simply look at a cataract and determine whether it was caused by radiation exposure. The court began by rejecting the plaintiff's argument that the testimony of a treating physician is not governed by *Daubert*.[79] The court went on to note that the expert was basing his opinion on his prior experience with radiation-induced cataracts, but then observed: "However, Dr. Scheribel has treated only five patients with radiation-induced cataracts in his 20 years of practice. We do not believe that this limited exposure to radiation-induced cataracts qualifies as a basis for a scientifically sound opinion."[80] The Seventh Circuit took a similar position in rejecting testimony of a physician who sought to testify that in his experience, ibuprofen can cause a type of kidney failure known as anti-GBM RPGN.[81] The court noted that the testimony failed to satisfy the *Daubert* standards because the physician "has encountered only about five cases of anti-GBM RPGN in his career."[82] Again, in *Wintz v. Northrop Corp.*,[83] the Seventh Circuit affirmed the trial court's decision to exclude expert testimony regarding the likelihood that the chemical bromide would cause birth defects.[84] The Court found that although the expert was generally qualified as a toxicologist, he was lacking personal experience with bromide and birth defects. This lack of experience disqualified the expert's testimony.[85]

Thus, in the mental health context, an expert who seeks to testify that workplace incidents caused a plaintiff to become depressed may have to demonstrate sufficient personal experience in diagnosing not only patients complaining of depression but also patients who claim to have been the victims of similar workplace conduct in order for such testimony to be deemed reliable. Although most mental health professionals will have sufficient experience in diagnosing and treating depressed patients, for example, relatively few will have diagnosed and treated a sufficient number of sexual harassment victims suffering from depression to reach this threshold. Moreover, even clinicians who have previously treated a few harassment victims likely would not have treated a sufficient number of victims of the type of conduct alleged in the instant case to permit meaningful clinical comparisons and generalizations to be drawn.

The following example illustrates this problem. Suppose a plaintiff seeks to have her treating psychologist testify that, in his opinion, her depressed

---

[79]*Id.* at 1105 n.14.
[80]*Id.* at 1107 n.19.
[81]Porter v. Whitehall Labs., Inc., 9 F.3d 607 (7th Cir. 1993).
[82]*Id.* at 614 n.6.
[83]110 F.3d 508 (7th Cir. 1997)
[84]*Id.* at 510.
[85]*Id.* at 514; *see also* Antoine-Tubbs v. Local 513, Transport Workers Union, 50 F. Supp. 2d 601 (N.D. Tex. 1998) (excluding testimony of physician that an argument between plaintiff and a manager caused plaintiff to develop pre-eclampsia and lose her unborn baby; where physician had never personally treated a pre-eclampsia case previously and was unable to identify any research indicating that job stress causes pre-eclampsia).

condition is attributable solely to sexual harassment (in the form of repeated sexual joking and horseplay by coworkers) suffered at the defendant's workplace. Voir dire questioning of the psychologist indicates that although he is properly licensed and received the requisite general training in diagnostics, he has treated only two victims of sexual harassment previously—one patient who was raped by a coworker and who did exhibit symptoms of a clinical depression, and one patient who was fired after ending a consensual affair with her boss and who felt angry and betrayed but did not suffer a diagnosable mental disorder. If such an expert seeks to base his opinion on his clinical skills and experience, he may well lack the requisite clinical experience with sexual harassment victims to support an opinion as to causation.

B. The Expert's Diagnostic Technique

To the extent that a psychological expert fails to follow standard clinical protocols and principles in reaching a diagnosis, that expert's opinion may be inadmissible under *Daubert* and *Kumho Tire*. Although the diagnosis of mental illness is not as precise a science as "hard" sciences such as chemistry and physics, a number of diagnostic protocols and principles have been developed through application of the scientific method. These have been validated through testing in field trials, and they are generally accepted by the psychiatric and psychological professions.

An expert's attempt to use *Daubert* or *Kumho Tire* to justify a departure from mainstream diagnostic protocols and principles on the ground that the cases no longer absolutely require that an expert's theories be generally accepted by the relevant scientific community would be misplaced. *Kumho Tire* still requires that an expert's methodologies be reliable in order to be admissible, and as noted above, diagnosis is an inherently scientific process. Where an expert's chosen methodologies are not be based on the scientific method and lack sufficient other indicia of reliability, the *Daubert and Kumho Tire* standards will not be met. Revised Rule 702 requires that expert testimony be "the product of reliable principles and methods that are reliably applied to the facts of the case."[86] Although the "principles" and "methods" applied to scientific testimony may be very different from the principles and methods applied to technical or other specialized knowledge, the requirement of reliability is no less applicable.

In employment cases, experts most frequently fail to use standard clinical protocols and principles by failing to apply the diagnostic criteria set forth in the American Psychiatric Association's *Diagnostic and Statistical Manual of Mental Disorders* (the current edition of which is known as *DSM-IV-TR*),[87] failing to apply principles of differential diagnosis, or failing to administer and interpret psychological testing properly.

---

[86] FED. R. EVID. 702 Advisory Committee's Note.
[87] AMERICAN PSYCHIATRIC ASSOCIATION, DIAGNOSTIC AND STATISTICAL MANUAL OF MENTAL DISORDERS (4th ed. text rev. 2000) [hereinafter DSM-IV-TR].

1. Failure to Use DSM-IV-TR

DSM-IV-TR is the only generally accepted diagnostic manual of the mental health professions in the United States. It contains objective diagnostic criteria for each of the recognized mental disorders, criteria that were formulated after lengthy study and debate among psychiatrists and psychologists and that have been subjected to extensive field testing.[88] Although no compendium of diagnostic criteria could be perfect, *DSM-IV-TR* provides an essential measure of objectivity to the rather slippery subject matter of diagnosing mental illness.

Numerous plaintiffs' experts fail to follow *DSM-IV-TR* in rendering a diagnosis, however. Instead, they employ subjective, idiosyncratic diagnostic criteria not found in any manual. Although at times this may be for the expedient purpose of maximizing the value of the plaintiff's claim, more often it is due to the fact that many plaintiffs' experts also serve as the plaintiffs' treating therapists, and strict adherence to standard diagnostic criteria is less important in the therapeutic context than in the forensic. Nonetheless, to the extent an expert's diagnosis of a plaintiff fails to conform with *DSM-IV-TR* criteria, there is an issue as to whether that diagnosis will be admissible under either *Daubert* or *Kumho Tire*.

One court has held that a psychologist's failure to utilize *DSM* diagnostic criteria is not grounds to exclude her testimony under *Daubert*. In *Mancuso v. Consolidated Edison Co. of New York*,[89] the defendant sought to exclude the testimony of a psychologist diagnosing the plaintiffs' child as having a learning disorder. The defendant argued that the child could not have had a learning disorder as defined by *DSM-IV* criteria because none of her scores were two standard deviations below her overall intelligence score, as required by *DSM-IV* for such a diagnosis.[90] The court refused to exclude the testimony. It first noted that it could find no case law requiring that an expert use *DSM-IV* criteria to qualify to testify. It then observed that it appeared that the psychologist's diagnosis could nonetheless fit within the *DSM-IV* category of "Learning Disorder Not Otherwise Specified,"[91] that the diagnosis was based upon the administration of several well-recognized intelligence tests, and that it conformed with the diagnostic criteria in another authoritative text on learning disabilities.[92] The court maintained that the defendant's attack on the psychologist's failure to adhere to *DSM-IV* diagnostic criteria was an issue as to the weight, but not the admissibility, of the evidence.

Mancuso appears to be inconsistent with the Ninth Circuit's mandate on remand in *Daubert* that a scientific expert "assiduously follow" scientific protocol.[93] Several courts in the wake of *Daubert*, moreover, have noted that even though clinical practitioners such as psychiatrists and psychologists need

---

[88] *See id.* at xviii–xix for a discussion of these field tests.
[89] 967 F. Supp. 1437 (S.D.N.Y. 1997).
[90] *See* DSM-IV-TR, *supra* note 87, at 46–47.
[91] *Id.* at 53.
[92] 967 F. Supp. 1454–57.
[93] 43 F.3d 1311, 1319 n.10 (9th Cir. 1995).

not be held to the same rigorous scientific standards as are researchers in the "hard" sciences, they must nonetheless utilize the methodologies and protocols commonly utilized in their field. For example, in *Moore v. Ashland Chemical, Inc.*,[94] the court addressed the applicability of *Daubert* to a clinical physician's expert opinion on the cause of the plaintiff's respiratory disease. It maintained that although the *Daubert* standards for determining the evidentiary reliability of scientific evidence are not appropriately applied to clinical medicine (as opposed to research or laboratory medicine), Federal Rule of Evidence 702, as interpreted by *Daubert*, still requires that the district court examine the soundness of the evidence involved prior to admitting it. As the *Moore* court explained:

> [U]nder Rule 702, an opinion based on other technical or specialized knowledge must be grounded in the principles, methods and procedures of the particular field of knowledge involved. Every discipline employs a body of methods, rules and postulates, i.e., methodology, both in its ordinary functions and in developing and adopting new concepts, techniques and analogues. . . . Thus, the proffered opinion of any expert in a field of knowledge, in order to be evidentiarily reliable, must either be based soundly on the current knowledge, principles and methodology of the expert's discipline or be soundly inferred or derived therefrom.[95]

Then, in a subsequent appeal in the same case, the Fifth Circuit again found that it was proper for the trial court to exclude expert testimony because of Rule 702:

> That the Frye test was displaced by the Rules of Evidence does not mean, however, that the Rules themselves place no limits on the admissibility of purportedly scientific evidence. Nor is the trial judge disabled from screening such evidence. To the contrary, under the Rules the trial judge must ensure that any and all scientific testimony or evidence admitted is not only relevant, but reliable.[96]

As a precursor to *Kumho Tire* and the revised Rule 702, the *Moore* court expanded the *Daubert* principle to testimony that is based on clinical experience as opposed to pure science, finding that "an opinion is governed by Fed. R. Evid. 702 and *Daubert*, even though the opinion is not grounded in 'hard sciences,' assuming a distinction exists."[97]

Thus, as the current edition of the *DSM* is the only commonly accepted diagnostic manual of the mental health professions, an expert's failure to adhere to the *DSM*'s diagnostic criteria would make that expert's methodology highly vulnerable to a *Daubert/Kumho Tire* challenge.

---

[94] 126 F.3d 679 (5th Cir. 1997).

[95] *Id.* at 686–87. *Accord* Watkins v. Telsmith, Inc., 121 F.3d 984, 991 (5th Cir. 1997) (trial court must ensure that expert's opinion comports with applicable professional standards outside the courtroom); Tyus v. Urban Search Mgmt., 102 F.3d 256, 263 (7th Cir. 1996) (social science testimony must adhere to same standards of intellectual rigor that apply in expert's professional field).

[96] 151 F.3d 269, 274–75 (5th Cir. 1998).

[97] *Id.* at 275.

One common situation in which a plaintiff's expert may fail to adhere to standard diagnostic protocols occurs where the expert evaluated the plaintiff prior to the commencement of litigation, with an eye toward prescribing treatment rather than toward giving testimony in court. For example, in *Gier v. Educational Service Unit No. 16*,[98] the court excluded expert testimony from various mental health professionals seeking to demonstrate that the plaintiffs had been sexually and emotionally abused. The court explained:

> Plaintiffs have failed to demonstrate by a preponderance of the evidence that their experts' methodologies for evaluating the plaintiffs in this particular case are reliable for the investigative purposes plaintiffs now seek to use them. The witnesses all testified that their purposes in evaluating plaintiffs were for the provision of therapy, not investigation. The methods used here may well have been sufficiently reliable for purposes of choosing a course of psychotherapy for these disturbed children, a course which must, to some extent, rely upon perception as well as reality, and upon the subjective reports of parents and others. However, the methodologies have not been shown to be reliable enough to provide a sound basis for investigative conclusions and confident legal decision-making.[99]

The *Gier* court quoted *Daubert* for the point that "scientific validity for one purpose is not necessarily scientific validity for other, unrelated purposes."[100] Diagnostic practice in the therapeutic setting tends to be less precise than in the forensic setting. In the therapeutic context, determining the cause and even the precise identity of a mental disorder is often less important than prescribing an effective treatment. If a patient consults a psychiatrist, complaining of being depressed, the psychiatrist can prescribe a course of medication or counseling therapy without necessarily determining whether the patient's condition would fall within the specific *DSM-IV-TR* category of Major Depression, Dysthymic Disorder, Adjustment Disorder with Depressed Mood, or Depressive Disorder Not Otherwise Specified. The fact that the clinician may have applied idiosyncratic diagnostic criteria is not as important as whether he or she has prescribed the right treatment.

In court, by contrast, the cause of a particular mental disorder is usually a central issue in the litigation. It also may be important to determine whether the patient suffers from Dysthymic Disorder (a chronic depressed state that often precedes the workplace events at issue in litigation),[101] or Adjustment Disorder with Depressed Mood (a short-term condition that is triggered by an identifiable stressor and resolves within six months).[102] In the litigation context, therefore, where a claim for substantial money damages is usually at stake, *Daubert* would appear to require faithful adherence to the rigorous diagnostic

---

[98] 845 F. Supp. 1342 (D. Neb. 1994), *aff'd*, 66 F.3d 940 (8th Cir. 1995).

[99] *Id.* at 1353. *Accord* Isely v. Capuchin Province, 877 F. Supp. 1055, 1059 (E.D. Mich. 1995).

[100] 845 F. Supp. at 1353 (quoting Daubert v. Merrill Dow Pharm., Inc., 509 U.S. 579, 591 (1993)).

[101] *DSM-IV-TR, supra* note 87, at 376–81.

[102] *Id.* at 679–83.

standards set forth in *DSM-IV-TR*, at least in the absence of some other indicia carrying a similarly high degree of scientific reliability.

One common example of the application of idiosyncratic diagnostic criteria in employment cases is found in the diagnosis of PTSD in a plaintiff in a sexual harassment case where the alleged harassment did not involve a sexual assault. *DSM-IV-TR* sets forth precise diagnostic criteria for PTSD.[103] One key criterion is that the person must have been subject to "an extreme traumatic stressor" of such a dramatic and profound nature that it involved "actual or threatened death or serious injury, or other threat to one's physical integrity."[104] *DSM-IV-TR* provides the following examples of qualifying stressors: rape, robbery, mugging, kidnapping, being taken hostage, torture, incarceration as a prisoner of war, and natural or man-made disasters. Without such a stressor, a PTSD diagnosis will not be valid under *DSM-IV-TR*. Stressors of a less serious nature—no matter how annoying, unpleasant, or persistent—simply do not qualify. For example, *DSM-IV-TR* expressly provides that "being fired" is not a stressor sufficiently serious to justify a PTSD diagnosis.[105] Moreover, although *DSM-IV-TR* loosens the diagnostic criteria for PTSD a bit over the previous edition of the manual, it does *not* recognize a "cumulative trauma" stressor for PTSD.[106]

Nonetheless, many plaintiffs' experts will insist that their patients suffered PTSD as a result of sexual harassment. They may attempt to justify this position by noting that rape is a qualifying stressor for PTSD, and by then asserting that because sexual harassment is "like rape," sexual harassment must similarly constitute a qualifying stressor for PTSD. This position is wrong on a number of counts. First, sexual harassment is *not* like rape. Such an imprecise comparison is based in ideology, not science. Second, nothing in *DSM-IV-TR* suggests that such incidents as a boss's sexual proposition, a coworker's unwanted kiss or hug or pat on the buttocks, overhearing dirty jokes, viewing pinup posters, or even being called foul and insulting names are sufficient to cause PTSD. A plaintiff's expert who nonetheless diagnoses PTSD in cases involving nonassaultive sexual harassment[107] therefore cannot be relying on the *DSM-IV-TR* diagnostic criteria. There are no other generally accepted diagnostic criteria for PTSD, however, so such an expert must be relying on his or her own idiosyncratic diagnostic criteria that, ordinarily lacking any grounding in the scientific method and incapable of being tested, may be inadmissible under *Daubert*.

---

[103] *Id.* at 463–68.

[104] *Id.* at 424.

[105] *Id.* at 427.

[106] *See* Robert I. Simon, *Toward the Development of Guidelines in the Forensic Psychiatric Examination of Posttraumatic Stress Disorder Claimants, in* POSTTRAUMATIC STRESS DISORDER IN LITIGATION 31, 51–52 (Robert I. Simon ed., 1995) ("Stressor research has not clarified whether a minor stress, if experienced long enough, can produce sufficient traumatic stress to cause PTSD.").

[107] Of course, where the alleged sexual harassment involved actual rape, a diagnosis of PTSD could be appropriate if the *DSM-IV-TR* criteria are otherwise met.

Other diagnoses that frequently appear in discrimination and harassment cases—such as major depression and panic disorder—similarly carry strict diagnostic criteria that are set forth in *DSM-IV-TR*. To the extent that a plaintiff seeks to introduce evidence of a diagnosis of one of these conditions in court where the *DSM-IV-TR* diagnostic criteria have not been met, such a diagnosis may be vulnerable to a Rule 702 challenge.

2. Failure to Conduct Differential Diagnosis

It is fundamental precept of forensic psychiatry and psychology that any mental evaluation must include an exploration of significant prior and concurrent events in the plaintiff's life to determine whether there may be an alternative cause—besides the alleged acts or omissions of the defendant—for the mental condition at issue in the litigation. Specifically, the examining clinician must probe the plaintiff's prior psychological history for evidence of preexisting mental disorders (for example, bipolar disorder or chronic depression), personality disorders,[108] or significant prior traumas such as sexual assault[109] or childhood sexual abuse.[110] The clinician also must explore whether concurrent stressors exist in the plaintiff's personal life that may have affected that person's psychological condition, such as marital problems or substance abuse.

The clinician must not only ask questions of the plaintiff about these matters during the clinical interview but also review all available records pertaining to the plaintiff. This records review should include medical and psychological records, employment records, criminal records, divorce records, and school records. Such a records review is essential because the plaintiff's own account of his or her history may at best be subject to memory lapses, and at worst be intentionally misrepresented.

Only after a comprehensive review of the plaintiff's prior psychological history and potential concurrent stressors can a clinician render an objective opinion as to the causation of the plaintiff's current condition. The clinician must rule out preexisting mental or personality disorders, prior traumas, and concurrent stressors as potential causes of the plaintiff's current condition to render any scientifically valid opinion that sexual harassment caused the plaintiff's current psychopathology.

Numerous courts have excluded expert testimony under *Daubert* because the clinician failed to conduct such a process of differential diagnosis.

A leading case on this subject is *In re Paoli Railroad Yard PCB Litigation*,[111] in which the Third Circuit affirmed exclusion of expert testimony of

---

[108] For a detailed discussion of personality disorders, see Chapter 6, Personality Disorders in Employment Litigation.

[109] Sara P. Feldman-Schorrig & James J. McDonald, Jr., *The Role of Forensic Psychiatry in the Defense of Sexual Harassment Cases*, 20 J. PSYCHIATRY & L. 5, 13 (1992).

[110] *See* James J. McDonald, Jr. & Sara P. Feldman-Schorrig, *The Relevance of Childhood Sexual Abuse in Sexual Harassment Cases*, 20 EMPL. REL. L.J. 221 (1994).

[111] 35 F.3d 717 (3d Cir. 1994).

two physicians who failed to employ differential diagnosis. The court remarked that "at the core of differential diagnosis is a requirement that experts at least consider alternative causes—this almost has to be true of any technique that tries to find a cause of something."[112] The court went on to state:

> Defendants' experts explained that a reliable differential diagnosis generally requires a physical examination of the patient, a review of medical records, taking a history and conducting of laboratory tests, and always requires careful consideration of alternative causes. We agree with the defendants that performance of physical examinations, taking of medical histories, and employment of laboratory tests all provide significant evidence of a reliable differential diagnosis, and that their absence makes it much less likely that a differential diagnosis is reliable.[113]

The *Paoli* court noted that a clinician does not have to employ *all* these techniques for a differential diagnosis to be reliable, however. The court held that where one of the plaintiff's experts had either examined the plaintiff or reviewed the plaintiff's medical records and considered alternative causation, her testimony would be admissible.

The *Paoli* court was emphatic, however, that a medical expert may not rely simply upon a plaintiff's own self-report of symptoms and causation. It affirmed the exclusion of the testimony of one physician who had simply given the plaintiffs a written questionnaire and based his diagnosis on the answers given by the plaintiffs. It described such questionnaires as "an unreliable source of information."[114] Other courts similarly have condemned plaintiffs' experts' failure to employ differential diagnosis to take into account the potential impact of alternative psychosocial stressors on a plaintiff's mental condition.[115]

Nonetheless, many plaintiffs' experts—particularly those who were initially engaged to provide therapy—fail to take a comprehensive patient history or to review records. They may diagnose the plaintiff as suffering from one or more mental disorders based upon the plaintiff's self-report of symptoms and then simply endorse the plaintiff's view that workplace events were the

---

[112]*Id.* at 759.
[113]*Id.* at 758.
[114]*Id.* at 762–63.
[115]*E.g.,* Mancuso v. Consolidated Edison Co., 967 F. Supp. 1437, 1451 (S.D.N.Y. 1997) (failure of plaintiffs' expert to employ differential diagnosis "is particularly disturbing in light of the common nature of many of the plaintiffs' complaints"); Alberts v. Wickes Lumber Co., 69 FEP Cases 304, 306 (N.D. Ill. 1995) (condemning plaintiff's expert's acceptance of plaintiff's version of events as true and failing to consider other possible causes of plaintiff's condition). *See also* Borawick v. Shay, 68 F.3d 597, 609 (2d Cir. 1995) (in part because there was no record of the procedures that the plaintiff's expert used, the expert's testimony was excluded because the court had no means, independent of the expert's testimony, to determine whether or not appropriate methodology was applied); Sanfelice v. Dominick's Finer Foods, Inc., 1995 WL 608602 (N.D. Ill. Oct. 13, 1995) (court considered *Daubert* challenge to expert's alleged failure to follow accepted methodology for diagnosis of PTSD but found that expert followed methodology).

sole cause of the emotional difficulties, without conducting any independent inquiry into alternative causation. There is nothing at all scientific about such an approach, however, and it is highly vulnerable to attack under *Daubert*.

C. Misuse of Psychological Testing

An increasing number of mental health experts on both sides in wrongful discharge, employment discrimination, and sexual harassment cases use a variety of psychological testing instruments in the course of evaluating a plaintiff's mental condition. Psychological tests are commonly *mis*used in employment litigation, however. Expert testimony regarding psychological testing may suggest a level of scientific "proof" that the plaintiff suffered emotional damage as the result of workplace events. Such testimony often may impress a jury and be difficult to rebut. A thorough grasp of *Daubert* and an understanding of the methods and limits of psychological testing, however, can assist counsel in preventing the trier of fact from being misled by testimony that is in fact scientifically worthless.

Some of the more common ways in which psychological testing is misapplied are explored below.

1. Lack of Expert's Qualifications in Testing

For a psychological test to be valid, the examiner must be qualified to administer and interpret the test. Psychologists typically are the most highly qualified experts with respect to psychological testing. Every psychologist has a unique pattern of professional training, however, so competency cannot be presumed. For example, many psychologists whose primary interest is in psychotherapy or research do not maintain their proficiency in psychological testing (in some cases, they never developed expertise in the first place). Most psychiatrists, social workers, marriage and family counselors, and pastoral counselors have little or no expertise in psychological testing. Because courts have held that an expert's qualifications may properly be the subject of a *Daubert* challenge,[116] a clinician who lacks training and expertise in psychological testing might be prevented from testifying about psychological test results.[117]

Psychiatrists and other clinicians who are not experts in test interpretation might nonetheless administer psychological testing and have it interpreted by a commercial scoring service that provides them with an interpretive report. These experts are vulnerable to cross-examination because they may be unfamil-

---

[116]*E.g.*, Isely v. Capuchin Province, 877 F. Supp. 1055, 1063 (E.D. Mich. 1995).

[117]In *Gier v. Educational Service Unit No. 16*, 845 F. Supp. 1342, 1351 (D. Neb. 1994), *aff'd*, 66 F.3d 940 (8th Cir. 1995), the court excluded testimony about the results of psychological testing in part because the examiners lacked adequate training in the tests administered.

iar with test methodology, unfamiliar with the contents of the test, or unfamiliar with the significance of specific scores.

Experts who rely on external scoring and interpretation services without having undergone training in the interpretation of the tests administered may be quite vulnerable to cross examination.

2. Lack of Scientific Basis in the Test

Although some tests such as the MMPI are grounded in the scientific method and have been validated extensively, many other psychological testing instruments used in employment litigation are of dubious scientific validity. Examples of tests that have little or no scientific basis in the forensic context are the so-called projective tests—Human Figure Drawings, the Thematic Apperception Test, Sentence Completion Tests, and the Rorschach Ink Blot Test. Examiners using these instruments have plaintiffs draw pictures of houses or people or trees, or make up sentences and stories, or describe what they see in a series of ambiguous ink blots, and then claim that they can reliably and validly measure emotional distress by interpreting this material. These tests are so subjective in nature, however, that they permit the examiner to base virtually any opinion upon results of the test.

Other instruments are merely inventories of symptoms that purport to measure the quality of a plaintiff's life but which by their nature are so subjective and prone to manipulation that they are scientifically worthless. Many of these questionnaires are merely checklists that ask leading questions suggesting the existence of symptoms that the plaintiff might not otherwise list. Unfortunately, many courts fail to appreciate the complete lack of scientific or technical basis inherent in these instruments. They may conclude that if the examiner felt the instrument to have been helpful in reaching a diagnosis, the test result should be admitted. This sort of an approach is not only inconsistent with *Daubert* and *Kumho Tire*, but it is highly dangerous in that a jury may be led to believe that a mere description of the plaintiff's self-reported symptoms is the equivalent of a methodologically sound test.

One case in which such a self-report inventory was rejected as inconsistent with *Daubert* is *McGuire v. City of Santa Fe*.[118] In that case, a psychologist designed and administered a "Lost Pleasure of Life Scale" to a plaintiff in an employment lawsuit and, in conjunction with an economist, determined that the defendants' harassment and termination of the plaintiff had caused between $1,430,000 and $2,300,000 worth of "lost enjoyment of life." The court noted that *Daubert* requires that any methodology that lies at the root of expert testimony must have an acceptable error rate, and then observed of the test instrument at issue:

> Dr. Murphy's report states the "Lost Pleasure of Life Scale," which she used to calculate the relevant percentages to be attributed to Plaintiff's hedonic losses,

---

[118] 954 F. Supp. 230 (D.N.M. 1996).

"has been found to be moderately reliable and that moderate reliability and validity means that results are greater than chance." This is hardly a quantifiable error rate and it hardly seems useful to provide the fact finder with "expert" testimony on figures that are only touted as slightly more reliable than those which might be drawn out of a hat.[119]

A *Daubert* challenge therefore may be raised with regard to an opponent's attempted use of instruments that do not constitute scientifically valid tests. Should the court reject such a challenge and allow the results of such instruments to be admitted, the examiner should be vigorously cross-examined so that the instruments may be demystified for the jury. For example, the actual ink blots used in the Rorschach or the pictures of houses or trees drawn by the plaintiff might be shown to the jury at the same time the expert is questioned closely about how he or she was able to reach diagnostic conclusions from such materials. The speculative nature of such testimony soon should become apparent. Similarly, symptom checklists completed by the plaintiff should be shown to the jury to demonstrate that they consist largely of leading questions and to make it obvious how any plaintiff seeking to obtain emotional distress damages in a lawsuit might answer them.

3. Improper Test Administration

For the results of a psychological test to be valid, the test must be administered correctly. Correct administration of a psychological test requires careful control over how, where, and when the test is taken.

A psychological test should be administered in a clinical setting under the examiner's supervision; it should never be sent home with the subject for completion. The subject may become distracted while taking the test, may receive assistance with the test from family or friends, or may even be coached by the subject's own therapist or attorney. A plaintiff whose own expert or treating therapist has conducted psychological testing should be questioned closely in discovery concerning the conditions under which the test was administered. If the test was not properly administered in a clinical setting, a *Daubert* challenge to the admissibility of the test result should be considered.[120]

Correct instructions also are essential if test results are to be valid. For example, in administering the MMPI-2, the correct procedure is to instruct the subject to answer in terms of his or her current condition at the time of testing, not his or her condition during or immediately after the events that led to the litigation.

Finally, some examiners give only portions of a test instead of the entire test. Although there are certain circumstances in which this may be appropriate,

---

[119]*Id.* at 233.

[120]See Chapter 10, The Use and Misuse of Psychological Testing, for further discussion of proper test administration.

some experts engage in highly questionable practices, such as testing only for their predetermined conclusions, and omitting the parts of the test that address malingering or preexisting conditions. An example would be the expert who administers only the PTSD scale of the MMPI-2, omitting the validity scales and questions dealing with chronic personality problems. These practices produce results that are scientifically dubious.

4. Improper Scoring of Tests

Psychological test scoring is done either by hand or via computer. Either method of scoring is prone to error, however. Counsel therefore should obtain the raw test data and have it rescored by a reliable scoring method. If a rescoring reveals errors in the original scoring, the opposing expert's conclusions based upon those erroneous scores obviously would be suspect.

5. Improper Interpretation of Tests

Psychological test scores are sometimes misinterpreted in employment cases.

For example, some experts—particularly those lacking sufficient training in interpretation of the MMPI-2—may attempt to interpret each clinical scale by itself or may interpret only selected scales, such as the depression scale. This kind of select interpretation is unscientific and improper.[121] For a valid interpretation of the MMPI-2 to occur, its clinical scales must be interpreted together.

It is important to note that many psychological tests do not clarify whether the subject's condition is the result of workplace events or instead is preexisting. Psychological testing may indicate the presence of one or more mental disorders but it cannot prove what caused them. An MMPI-2 result indicating that the plaintiff is depressed, for example, does not constitute proof that a workplace incident caused the depression. It is just as reasonable to assume that the plaintiff suffers from a chronic and preexisting depression. Attempts by litigants to use psychological test results as proof that a workplace incident caused the plaintiff to suffer a mental disorder are scientifically invalid.

Some tests, such as the MMPI-2, contain validity scales to ensure that a particular administration of the test is valid. There are a number of factors that may cause tests to produce invalid results. Lack of cooperation, drug or alcohol intoxication, medical illnesses, psychological disorders interfering with test performance, malingering, illiteracy, cultural characteristics, improper test administration, and inappropriate testing conditions may each possibly lead to an invalid test administration. Some experts will disregard validity scale results on the MMPI-2 indicating an invalid profile. Others might characterize an

---

[121]Paul R. Lees-Haley & James J. McDonald, Jr., *The Use (and Misuse) of Psychological Testing in Employment Litigation*, 23 EMPL. REL. L.J. 37, 49 (1997).

invalid profile as a "cry for help" and attempt to use a malingered profile as evidence of injury. There is no empirical research in the scientific literature supporting this "cry for help" notion, however.[122]

---

[122] See Roger L. Greene, *Assessment of Malingering and Defensiveness by Multiscale Personality Inventories*, in CLINICAL ASSESSMENT OF MALINGERING AND DECEPTION 194–95 (Richard Rogers ed., 2d ed. 1997).

CHAPTER 16

MENTAL DISABILITIES UNDER THE AMERICANS WITH DISABILITIES ACT

Myra K. Creighton, J.D.

I. Introduction

One area of employment law in which mental health issues have gained prominence in recent years is the application of the Americans with Disabilities Act (ADA) to persons with mental disabilities. In the decade following the enactment of the ADA in 1990, mental impairments have come to account for the largest category of ADA discrimination charges filed with the Equal Employment Opportunity Commission (EEOC).[1] Given that much of the structure of the ADA was designed to apply to persons with physical disabilities, the rapidly increasing number of mental disability claims creates new challenges for employers, attorneys, and the courts. This is attributable to a number of factors.

First, providing a reasonable accommodation for a physically disabled employee—while not necessarily inexpensive—is often a rather straightforward process. Wheelchair ramps can be installed, doorways can be widened, ergonomic aids can be furnished. The process of accommodation becomes much more difficult, however, in the case of an employee who, because of a psychological condition, may be unable to cope with workplace stress or supervisory criticism.[2] Moreover, mental disabilities are much more difficult to discern than

---

[1] In the most recent fiscal year (1998–99) for which statistics are available, mental impairment claims accounted for the greatest percentage (19.4%) of ADA claims filed with the EEOC. *Source:* http://www.eeoc.gov/stats/ada-receipts.html.

[2] During congressional debate of the ADA, at least one senator expressed concern about the difficulty in determining accommodations for the mentally ill. Senator Humphrey stated: "While the committee report gives examples of clear-cut accommodations for the [physically disabled] it studiously avoids the more bizarre accommodation requirements imposed by the bill. What are employers expected to do to accommodate alcoholics, the mentally retarded, or persons with neurotic or psychotic disorders? This Senator has no idea, and I doubt that other Senators do either." 135 CONG. REC. S10,785 (daily ed. Sept. 8, 1989) (statement of Senator Humphrey).

physical disabilities. Unlike physical disabilities, which are generally fairly apparent, mental disabilities can go undetected, even by the person suffering from the condition. Often individuals with a mental disorder delay seeking help until some adverse incident, such as the loss of a job, occurs on account of the stigma that may accompany mental health treatment and the tendency of health plans not to provide full coverage for psychiatric treatment.

Second, some mental disabilities may be difficult to distinguish from a simple inability to perform the job or to get along with supervisors and coworkers. The employer may perceive that the employee has poor people or managerial skills[3] or cannot manage time well. More and more employees are attempting to characterize their poor job performance or workplace misconduct as a product of a mental disorder. Employers are often at a loss to determine whether a difficult or disruptive employee should be disciplined or instead must be accommodated.

Third, the business of diagnosing mental disorders is not perfectly objective. The fourth edition text revision of the American Psychiatric Association's *Diagnostic and Statistical Manual of Mental Disorders (DSM-IV-TR)*,[4] which sets forth diagnostic criteria for mental disorders, is continually being revised.[5] With every new edition of the manual, new mental disorders are added and others are deleted, and diagnostic criteria for others are revised. Moreover, diagnosis of mental disorders largely depends upon the patient's subjective report of symptoms experienced; there is ordinarily no X-ray or blood test to objectively confirm a diagnosis. In addition, mental health professionals generally owe a duty of loyalty to their patients, not to their patients' employers, and the professionals' primary focus is on assisting the patient in coping with his perception of reality rather than upon a precise diagnosis. Thus, if a patient complains to a therapist about feeling depressed, he is likely to be diagnosed as suffering from clinical depression. Liability may be imposed or accommodation obligations created, therefore, based on conditions that may be subjectively perceived and difficult to define.

II. The Definition of "Mental Disability" Under the ADA

Not all mental disorders are disabilities covered by the ADA. The determination of whether a particular condition is covered is quite complex and requires a multistep analysis. Unless a mental disorder meets the criteria for coverage

---

[3]*See* Webb v. Mercy Hosp., 102 F.3d 958, 6 AD Cases 333 (8th Cir. 1996).
[4]AMERICAN PSYCHIATRIC ASSOCIATION, DIAGNOSTIC AND STATISTICAL MANUAL OF MENTAL DISORDERS (4th ed. text rev. 2000) [hereinafter DSM-IV-TR].
[5]*See* Chapter 4, The Diagnostic and Statistical Manual of Mental Disorders.

under the ADA, an employer has no obligation to "reasonably accommodate" or avoid discriminating against an individual with such a condition.[6]

The ADA defines a covered "disability" as (1) a physical or mental impairment that substantially limits one or more of the major life activities of such individual; (2) a record of such impairment; or (3) being regarded as having such impairment.[7] In order to determine whether a particular mental or emotional condition is covered by the ADA, therefore, the following inquiries must be made:

- Is it a mental impairment?
- Does it substantially limit a major life activity of the individual?
- Is it a condition that may meet the preceding two criteria but is nonetheless expressly excluded from coverage by the terms of the ADA?

A. Mental Impairment That Substantially Limits a Major Life Activity

1. What Constitutes an Impairment

Although many courts just assume that an impairment exists and immediately move to address the issue of substantial limitation,[8] the first issue that must be determined is whether a particular condition qualifies as an impairment. The EEOC's regulations implementing the ADA define "mental impairment" to include any "mental or psychological disorder, such as mental retardation, organic brain syndrome, emotional or mental illness, and specific learning disabilities."[9] Mental disorders are the psychiatric equivalent of a physical illness. That is, they are patterns of symptoms that have been observed to repeatedly occur together, across cultures, socioeconomic classes, time, and ethnicities. The word "disorder" is employed instead of "disease" because the etiologic agents that cause various mental disorders have not yet been definitively identified.

A. MENTAL DISORDERS LISTED IN THE *DSM* The *DSM-IV-TR* defines a mental disorder as:

> A clinically significant behavioral or psychological syndrome or pattern that occurs in an individual and that is associated with present distress (e.g., a painful

---

[6]This chapter addresses mental disabilities under the ADA. State laws, however, may define disability differently. *E.g.*, CAL. GOV'T CODE §12926(i). *See* James J. McDonald, Jr., *I'm Disabled, You're Disabled, We're All Disabled Now*, 26 EMPL. REL. L.J. 141 (2001).

[7]42 U.S.C. §12102(2).

[8]*See, e.g.*, Amir v. St. Louis Univ., 184 F.3d 1017, 9 AD Cases 999 (8th Cir. 1999); O'Neill v. Atlanta Gen. & Light Co., 968 F. Supp. 721 (S.D. Ga. 1997) (expressing doubt whether plaintiff with stress disorder has impairment but assuming he does).

[9]29 C.F.R. §1630.2(h)(2).

symptom) or disability (i.e., impairment in one or more areas of functioning) or with significantly increased risk of suffering death, pain, disability, or an important loss of freedom.[10]

While diagnosable mental disorders will most likely qualify as impairments under the ADA, it is important to understand that not all conditions listed in the DSM-IV are mental *disorders*. The *DSM-IV-TR* utilizes a "multi-axial" system of classifying mental disorders.[11] While there are five separate axes for assessment, the two most important for ADA purposes are Axis I and Axis II. Clinical disorders and other conditions that may be a focus of clinical attention are diagnosed on Axis I. Personality disorders and mental retardation are diagnosed on Axis II. Axis I clinical disorders include the following:

- *Developmental and Learning Disorders* (with the exception of mental retardation), such as reading and communication disorders, autism, Attention Deficit Disorder, conduct disorders, and tic disorders);
- *Delirium, Dementia, Amnestic, and Other Cognitive Disorders*;
- *Mental Disorders Due to a General Medical Condition*, where the mental symptoms are a direct physiological consequence of a medical illness;
- *Substance-Related Conditions*, including drug and alcohol abuse and withdrawal;
- *Schizophrenia and Other Psychotic Disorders*, which are usually characterized by delusions and/or hallucinations;
- *Mood Disorders*, including major depression, dysthymia, and manic-depressive illness;
- *Anxiety Disorders*, including phobias, panic disorders, Posttraumatic Stress Disorder, and Obsessive-Compulsive Disorder;
- *Somatoform Disorders*, including Hypochondriasis, Conversion Disorder, and Somatization Disorder;
- *Factitious Disorders*, which involve physical or psychological symptoms that are intentionally produced or feigned in order to assume the sick role;
- *Dissociative Disorders*, including depersonalization and multiple personality disorder;
- *Sexual and Gender Identity Disorders*, including sexual dysfunction, fetishism, exhibitionism, and transvestism;
- *Eating Disorders*, including anorexia and bulimia;
- *Sleep Disorders*, such as insomnia and narcolepsy;
- *Impulse Control Disorders*, such as kleptomania, pyromania, and pathological gambling; and

---

[10]DSM-IV-TR, *supra* note 4, at xxxi.
[11]These are:
Axis I   Clinical Disorders
           Other Conditions That May Be a Focus of Clinical Attention
Axis II   Personality Disorders
           Mental Retardation
Axis III General Medical Conditions
Axis IV Psychosocial and Environmental Problems
Axis V   Global Assessment of Functioning
Id. at 27.

- *Adjustment Disorders*, which involve symptoms that develop in response to an identifiable stressor and resolve within six months.[12]

B. OTHER CONDITIONS DESCRIBED IN THE *DSM* The other conditions that may be a focus of clinical attention that are diagnosed on Axis I include adverse effects of medication (not including substance abuse) and "V-codes." V-codes pertain to a variety of relational, abuse, behavioral, academic, and occupational problems that do not themselves amount to diagnosable mental disorders but may be the focus of consultation or treatment by a mental health professional. Those conditions given V-codes include the following:

- Relational Problem Related to a Mental Disorder or General Medical Condition
- Parent-Child Relational Problem
- Partner Relational Problem
- Sibling Relational Problem
- Physical Abuse of Child
- Sexual Abuse of Child
- Neglect of Child
- Physical Abuse of Adult
- Sexual Abuse of Adult
- Adult Antisocial Behavior
- Child or Adolescent Antisocial Behavior
- Academic Problem
- Occupational Problem
- Identity Problem
- Religious or Spiritual Problem
- Phase of Life Problem

Because V-code conditions are not considered mental disorders and Congress intended only mental disorders defined in the *DSM* to qualify as mental impairments potentially covered by the ADA,[13] V-codes are not likely to qualify as impairments under the ADA.[14] Simple bereavement and malingering (the intentional production of false or grossly exaggerated physical or psychological symptoms) are also assigned V codes,[15] and grief is not considered a disabling condition.[16]

C. CONDITIONS NOT CONTAINED IN THE *DSM* In its *Technical Assistance on Title I of ADA Manual* (*EEOC Technical Assistance Manual*) the EEOC recognized that mere stressful life situations, which are not disorders

---

[12]*Id.* at 27–28.

[13]*See* CONG. REC. S10772 (Sept. 7, 1989) (statement of Senator Armstrong).

[14]Equal Employment Opportunity Commission, *Enforcement Guidance on the Americans With Disabilities Act and Psychiatric Disabilities* (Mar. 25, 1997), *reprinted in* 8 FEP Manual 405:7461, 7462 [hereinafter *EEOC Guidance on Psychiatric Disabilities*].

[15]DSM-IV-TR, *supra* note 4, at 739–41.

[16]*See* Johnson v. Boardman Petroleum, 923 F. Supp. 1563, 5 AD Cases 983 (S.D. Ga. 1996) (grief not a disability).

recognized in the *DSM,* do not constitute impairments under the ADA.[17] As the EEOC explained, "A person suffering from general 'stress' because of job or personal life pressures would not be considered to have an impairment."[18] The courts have concurred.[19] The EEOC introduced some confusion on the issue, however, in its *Enforcement Guidance on the Americans with Disabilities Act and Psychiatric Disabilities* (*EEOC Guidance on Psychiatric Disabilities*), wherein it described the *DSM* as merely "relevant" for identifying mental disorders that may qualify for coverage under the ADA.[20]

The notion that the *DSM* may only be relevant creates some problems. If only the *DSM-IV-TR* conditions are impairments under the ADA, then an employer need not accommodate an individual who has not been diagnosed by a qualified mental health professional as suffering from a mental disorder, using the diagnostic criteria prescribed in the *DSM-IV-TR*. Creatively diagnosed conditions that do not appear in the *DSM-IV-TR*, such as "chronic lateness syndrome," or only generally described conditions, such as "stress," would not qualify for ADA coverage.[21] The EEOC's seeming equivocation in its Guidance makes it more difficult for employers to determine what conditions legally require accommodation.

The courts to date have drawn distinctions between diagnosed mental disorders and other, less-defined, conditions. For example, in *Duda v. Board of Education of Franklin Park Public Schools,*[22] the court noted that "our cases have distinguished between claims of personal conflicts with supervisors or mere temperament and irritability, which do not amount to disabilities under the ADA, and medically diagnosed conditions like the [manic depression] from

---

[17]Equal Employment Opportunity Commission, *Technical Assistance on Title I of ADA Manual* (Jan. 27, 1992) *reprinted in* 8 FEP Manual 405:6981, 6988 [hereinafter *EEOC Technical Assistance Manual*].

[18]*Id.*

[19]*See, e.g.,* Miller v. National Cas. Co., 61 F.3d 627, 4 AD Cases 1089 (8th Cir. 1995) (stressful family situation not a disability under the ADA); Mundo v. Sanus Health Plan of Greater N.Y., 966 F. Supp. 171, 8 AD Cases 937 (E.D.N.Y. 1997) (inability to tolerate stressful situations not an impairment under ADA); DeWitt v. Carsten, 941 F. Supp. 1232, 6 AD Cases 1255 (N.D. Ga. 1996) (plaintiff's job-related stress caused by working in a correctional institution was not a disability because it would disqualify the plaintiff only from working in one particular job); *see also* Alexandru v. North E. Util. Serv. Co., 1996 WL 684421 (D. Conn. Oct. 10, 1996) (engineer who suffered miscarriages from job-related stress not substantially limited in reproduction; impairment had no permanent or long-term effects, and since she was no longer in job, she should be able to reproduce).

[20]*EEOC Guidance on Psychiatric Disabilities, supra* note 14, at 7463. The EEOC based this statement on *Boldini v. Postmaster General,* 928 F. Supp. 125, 130, 5 AD Cases 11, 14 (D.N.H. 1995), which states "in circumstances of mental impairment, a court may give weight to a diagnosis of mental impairment which is described in the [*DSM*]...."

[21]*EEOC Guidance on Psychiatric Disabilities, supra* note 14, at 7463.

[22]133 F.3d 1054, 8 AD Cases 99 (7th Cir. 1998).

which plaintiff suffers, which are recognized 'disabilities' under the ADA."[23] Likewise, in *Paleologos v. Rehab Consultants, Inc.*,[24] the plaintiff claimed she had a stress-related mental condition caused by her work. She claimed she suffered from stress, anxiety, and depression and had been treated by a doctor for those conditions. The court noted that stress and depression could qualify as impairments if they resulted from a documented physiological or mental disorder, but that the plaintiff's conclusory statements did not establish such an impairment.[25]

Contrary to *Duda* and *Paleologos*, however, is *Leisen v. City of Shelbyville*.[26] In that case, the court held that a firefighter who allegedly suffered from stress-related depression but who was never diagnosed with a specific disorder nonetheless had a qualifying impairment because her doctor testified that she suffered from sleep and memory problems, crying, anxiety, suicidal ideation, and depression. *Leisen* is troubling because there is a difference between mere *symptoms* of depression and a clinically diagnosable depressive disorder.

D. PERSONALITY DISORDERS AND PATHOLOGICAL PERSONALITY TRAITS The *EEOC Guidance on Psychiatric Disabilities* excludes from the ADA's coverage certain common personality traits such as poor judgment or a quick temper, at least where those traits are not symptoms of a mental disorder.[27] The *EEOC Technical Assistance Manual* adds "irresponsible behavior" to the list of traits not covered.[28]

---

[23]*Id.* at 1059, 8 AD Cases at 103. *See also* Fromm-Vane v. Longwood Med. Ctr., Inc., 995 F. Supp. 1471 (S.D. Fla. 1997) (court rejects defendant's argument that neither job stress nor stress from divorce rose to level of disability based on doctor's diagnosis of depressive disorder); Adams v. Rochester Gen. Hosp., 977 F. Supp. 226, 8 AD Cases 1143 (W.D.N.Y. 1997) (plaintiff who claimed he had depression, manic depression, and psychosis did not establish impairment; he presented no evidence of an expert medical opinion, medical affidavit, or any other medical evidence that he had a mental impairment).

[24]990 F. Supp. 1460 (N.D. Ga. 1998).

[25]*See also* Adams v. Rochester Gen. Hosp., 977 F. Supp. 226, 8 AD Cases 1143 (W.D.N.Y. 1997) (plaintiff who said he had depression, manic depression, and psychosis did not establish impairment; he presented no expert medical opinion, medical affidavit, or any other medical evidence).

[26]968 F. Supp. 409 (S.D. Ind. 1997), *aff'd,* 153 F.3d 805, 8 AD Cases 892 (7th Cir. 1998).

[27]29 C.F.R. §1630.2(h) app. (1995). *See, e.g.*, Daley v. Koch, 892 F.2d 212, 1 AD Cases 1549 (2d Cir. 1989) (employee not disabled simply because he had poor judgment and a lack of impulse control); Greenberg v. New York State Dep't of Corr. Servs., 919 F. Supp. 637, 5 AD Cases 1851 (E.D.N.Y. 1996) (employer's perception that employee was unable to make appropriate decisions concerning safety in emergencies, to perform well under stressful conditions, and to recognize potentially disruptive situations was essentially conclusion that he had poor judgment, which is not protected under ADA); Watson v. City of Miami Beach, 177 F.3d 932, 934, 9 AD Cases 760, 762 (11th Cir. 1999) (defendant's view that plaintiff was "paranoid, disgruntled, oppositional, difficult to interact with, unusual, suspicious, threatening and distrustful" was perception of behavior and not an impairment).

[28]*EEOC Technical Assistance Manual, supra* note 17, at 6988.

On the other hand, the EEOC takes the position that personality disorders fall within the ADA's protective ambit.[29] This is unsurprising given that the EEOC's regulations implementing the ADA define covered "mental disorders" to include "emotional illnesses,"[30] and many personality disorders can most aptly be described as emotional illnesses.

A personality disorder is a learned pathological and enduring maladaptive pattern of perceiving, relating to, and thinking about the environment and oneself, which is exhibited in a wide range of social and personal contexts and which causes either significant functional impairment or subjective distress in the individual.[31] Personality disorders typically become manifest in adolescence or earlier and continue throughout most of an adult's life. They can profoundly and adversely affect a person's interpersonal relations, including those with supervisors and coworkers.[32] Management of employees with personality disorders can be extremely difficult because such individuals generally have engaged in the same dysfunctional patterns of behavior for a long period of time and generally lack insight into how their behavior affects others.

The *DSM-IV-TR* lists ten specific types of personality disorders, which are briefly described below, plus a condition known as "Personality Disorder Not Otherwise Specified":

- *Paranoid Personality Disorder*—a pattern of distrust and suspiciousness such that others' motives are interpreted as malevolent
- *Schizoid Personality Disorder*—a pattern of detachment from social relationships and a restricted range of emotional expression
- *Schizotypal Personality Disorder*—a pattern of acute discomfort in close relationships, cognitive or perceptual distortions, and eccentricities of behavior
- *Antisocial Personality Disorder*—a pattern of disregard for, and violation of, the rights of others
- *Borderline Personality Disorder*—a pattern of instability in interpersonal relationships, self-image, and affects, and marked impulsivity
- *Histrionic Personality Disorder*—a pattern of excessive emotionality and attention seeking
- *Narcissistic Personality Disorder*—a pattern of grandiosity, need for admiration, and lack of empathy
- *Avoidant Personality Disorder*—a pattern of social inhibition, feelings of inadequacy, and hypersensitivity to negative evaluation
- *Dependent Personality Disorder*—a pattern of submissive and clinging behavior related to an excessive need to be taken care of
- *Obsessive-Compulsive Personality Disorder*—a pattern of preoccupation with orderliness, perfectionism, and control[33]

---

[29] *EEOC Guidance on Psychiatric Disabilities, supra* note 14, at 7462.
[30] 29 C.F.R. §1630.2(h)(2).
[31] *See* Chapter 6, Personality Disorders in Employment Litigation.
[32] *See* James J. McDonald, Jr. & Paul R. Lees-Haley, *Personality Disorders in the Workplace: How They May Contribute to Claims of Employment Law Violations*, 22 EMPL. REL. L.J. 57 (1996).
[33] DSM-IV-TR, *supra* note 4, at 685.

Even if a personality disorder qualifies as an impairment for ADA purposes, it must still substantially limit one or more major life activities in order to qualify for ADA coverage, and personality disorders often fall short in this regard. The "substantial limitation" requirement is addressed below.

2. Substantial Limitation

The diagnosis of a mental disorder that qualifies as an impairment, standing alone, is insufficient to establish that an individual has an ADA-covered disability. The impairment must also substantially limit one or more of the individual's major life activities.[34] The EEOC has implied that some mental conditions are inherently substantially limiting, such as Bipolar Disorder and alcoholism.[35] The courts, by contrast, after reviewing the statutory language and stressing that impairments must be evaluated on a case-by-case basis,[36] have not agreed that Bipolar Disorder[37] and alcoholism[38] are inherently substantially limiting. Indeed, impairments such as depression,[39]

---

[34] 42 U.S.C. §12102(2).

[35] *EEOC Definition of the Term "Disability,"* reprinted in 8 FEP Manual 405:7265.

[36] *E.g.*, Sutton v. United Airlines, Inc., 527 U.S. 471, 502, 9 AD Cases 673, 685–86 (1999); Murphy v. United Parcel Serv. Inc., 527 U.S. 516, 523, 9 AD Cases 691, 692 (1999).

[37] *See, e.g.*, Hoeller v. Eaton Corp., 149 F.3d 621, 8 AD Cases 537 (7th Cir. 1998); Klein v. Florida Dep't of Family Affairs & Child Servs., 34 F. Supp. 2d 1367 (S.D. Fla. 1998); Witter v. Delta Air Lines, Inc., 138 F.3d 1366, 8 AD Cases 747 (11th Cir. 1998); Bergsrud v. Columbia-Lee Reg'l Med. Ctr., 2000 WL 33287447 (D.N.M. June 24, 2000).

[38] Burch v. Coca-Cola, 119 F.3d 305, 7 AD Cases 241 (5th Cir. 1997) (holding employee failed to establish that alcoholism was a disability); Wallin v. Minnesota Dep't of Corrs., 153 F.3d 681, 8 AD Cases 1012 (8th Cir. 1998) (alcoholism analyzed on case-by-case basis); Martin v. Barnesville Exempted Village, 35 F. Supp. 2d 1038, 9 AD Cases 46 (S.D. Ohio 1999) (holding that there was no evidence alcoholism made employee disabled for ADA purposes).

[39] Spades v. City of Walnut Ridge, 186 F.3d 897, 9 AD Cases 1015 (8th Cir. 1999); Cody v. Cigna Healthcare of St. Louis, Inc., 139 F.3d 595, 7 AD Cases 1716 (8th Cir. 1998); Siemon v. AT&T Corp., 113 F.3d 1175, 6 AD Cases 1249 (1st Cir. 1997); Soileau v. Guilford of Maine, Inc., 105 F.3d 12, 6 AD Cases 437 (1st Cir. 1997); Sanders v. Arneson Prods., Inc., 91 F.3d 1351, 5 AD Cases 1292 (9th Cir. 1996); Williams v. Healthreach Network, 2000 WL 760742 (E.D. Mo. Feb. 22, 2000); Nweke v. Prudential Ins. Co., 25 F. Supp. 2d 203, 82 FEP Cases 1621 (S.D.N.Y. 1999); Polderman v. Northwest Airlines, Inc., 40 F. Supp. 2d 456 (N.D. Ohio 1999); Bowers v. Multimedia Cablevision, Inc., 1998 WL 856074 (D. Kan. Nov. 3, 1998); Hill v. Metropolitan Rapid Transit Auth., 77 F. Supp. 2d 1291 (N.D. Ga. 1998); Erjavac v. Holy Family Health Plus, 13 F. Supp. 2d 737 (N.D. Ill. 1998); Formosa v. Miami Dade Cmty. Coll., 990 F. Supp. 1433, 7 AD Cases 1768 (S.D. Fla. 1997); Brown v. Northern Trust Bank, 7 AD Cases 548 (N.D. Ill. 1997); Sarko v. Penn-Del Directory Co., 968 F. Supp. 1026, 7 AD Cases 1201 (E.D. Pa. 1997); Wheelock v. Philip Morris, USA, 1997 WL 45292 (E.D. La. Feb. 5, 1997); Johnson v. New York Med. Coll., 1997 WL 580708 (S.D.N.Y. Sept. 18, 1997); Wisiewski v. Ameritech, 1996 WL 501737 (N.D. Ill. Sept. 3, 1996).

agoraphobia,[40] panic disorder,[41] paranoia,[42] Posttraumatic Stress Disorder (PTSD),[43] and Tourette's Syndrome[44] have been held not to be substantially limiting. Thus, the name of a condition, no matter how disabling it may sound, is never dispositive.[45]

A person is substantially limited who is unable to perform a major life activity that the average person in the population can perform or who is significantly restricted as to the condition, manner, or duration of performing a major life activity as compared with the average person in the population.[46] The difficulty in determining whether an individual with a mental impairment is substantially limited in a major life activity, of course, is that there is ordinarily no objective test for this kind of limitation. Furthermore, according to the EEOC, expert testimony is not necessary for a plaintiff to establish a substantial limitation.[47] Rather, the plaintiff's own testimony or the testimony of family and friends will satisfy the EEOC.[48]

---

[40]Reeves v. Johnson Controls World Servs., 140 F.3d 144, 7 AD Cases 1675 (2d Cir. 1998) (plaintiff's agoraphobia not substantially limiting).

[41]Zirpel v. Toshiba Am. Info. Sys., Inc., 111 F.3d 80, 81, 6 AD Cases 929, 930 (8th Cir. 1997); Mistrella v. Volusia County Dep't of Corrs., 61 F. Supp. 2d 1255 (M.D. Fla. 1999); Jerina v. Richardson Auto., 960 F. Supp. 106 (N.D. Tex. 1997).

[42]Schwartz v. Comex, 8 AD Cases 1223 (S.D.N.Y. 1997) (plaintiff's paranoid thought disorder not substantially limiting).

[43]Patterson v. Chicago Ass'n for Retarded Citizens, 150 F.3d 719, 8 AD Cases 983 (7th Cir. 1998); Hamilton v. Southwestern Bell Tel. Co., 136 F.3d 1047, 8 AD Cases 1219 (5th Cir. 1998); Dupre v. Harris County Hosp., 8 F. Supp. 2d 908 (S.D. Tex. 1998); Glowacki v. Buffalo Gen. Hosp., 2 F. Supp. 2d 346 (W.D.N.Y. 1998); Gazaway v. Makita USA, Inc., 11 F. Supp. 2d 1281 (S.D.N.Y. 1998); Seamon v. C.S.P. Eight, Inc., 1997 WL 538751 (N.D. Tex. Aug. 25, 1997); Mastio v. Wausau Serv. Corp., 948 F. Supp. 1396 (E.D. Mo. 1996).

[44]Lanci v. Arthur Anderson, 10 AD Cases 1004 (S.D.N.Y. 2000) (Tourette's Syndrome not a disability per se).

[45]29 C.F.R. §1630.2(j) app. (1995) ("The determination of whether an individual has a disability is not necessarily based on the name or diagnosis of the impairment the person has, but rather on the effect of that impairment on the life of the individual."). *See also* Bragdon v. Abbott, 524 U.S. 624, 8 AD Cases 239 (1998) (asymptomatic HIV not per se disability); Tice v. Centre Area Transp. Auth., 247 F.3d 506, 11 AD Cases 1185 (3d Cir. 2001) (particular diagnosis no matter how severe, standing alone is not sufficient to establish a disability).

[46]29 C.F.R. §1630.2(j)(i),(2) (1995). *See also* Maynard v. Pneumatic Prods., 233 F.3d 1344, 11 AD Cases 295 (11th Cir. 2000); Gonzales v. National Bd. Med. Exam'rs, 225 F.3d 620, 10 AD Cases 1575 (6th Cir. 2000); Doyal v. Oklahoma Heart, Inc., 213 F.3d 492, 10 AD Cases 991 (10th Cir. 2000); Colwell v. Suffolk County Police Dep't, 158 F.3d 635, 8 AD Cases 1232 (2d Cir. 1998); Soileau v. Guilford of Maine, Inc., 105 F.3d 12, 6 AD Cases 437 (1st Cir. 1997).

[47]*EEOC Guidance on Psychiatric Disabilities, supra* note 14, at 7463–64.

[48]*See id.*; *Maynard*, 233 F.3d 1344, 11 AD Cases 295 (average person in population may testify concerning abilities), *vacated on other grounds,* 256 F.3d 1259, 11 AD Cases 1790 (11th Cir. 2001).

The substantial limitation on the major life activity may be direct or indirect.[49] In determining whether an individual's impairment substantially limits a major life activity, courts evaluate the nature and severity of the impairment, its expected duration, and its expected impact, whether permanent or long-term.[50]

A. TEMPORARY NONCHRONIC IMPAIRMENTS Temporary, nonchronic impairments that do not last for a long time and that have little or no long-term impact typically are not covered by the ADA. The EEOC gives as examples broken bones that heal normally or a bad case of the flu.[51] Similarly, a mental impairment that is only temporary and nonchronic in nature generally will not constitute a covered disability under the ADA.[52]

There is a whole class of diagnosable mental disorders described in the *DSM-IV-TR* known as Adjustment Disorders that by definition are temporary and nonchronic in nature. As the *DSM-IV-TR* describes it, "[t]he essential feature of an Adjustment Disorder is the development of clinically significant

---

[49]*See* Equal Employment Opportunity Commission, *Instructions for Field Offices: Analyzing ADA Charges After Supreme Court Decisions Addressing "Disability" and "Qualified"* (July 26, 1999), *reprinted in* 2 ADA Manual 70:1441 [hereinafter *EEOC Instructions for Field Offices*]. *See, e.g.*, Christian v. St. Anthony Med. Ctr., 117 F.3d 1051, 6 AD Cases 1665 (7th Cir. 1997) (attorney with an impairment that is not disabling but requires treatment that is disabling, is disabled under the ADA); Fehr v. McLean Packaging Co., 3 AD Cases 798 (E.D. Pa. 1994) (plaintiff entitled to jury trial on issue of whether his breathing was substantially limited by medication he was taking for depression).

[50]29 C.F.R. §1630(j)(2) (1995).

[51]*EEOC Technical Assistance Manual, supra* note 17, at 405:6968.

[52]*See, e.g.*, Spades v. City of Walnut Ridge, 186 F.3d 897, 9 AD Cases 1015 (8th Cir. 1999) (police officer who attempted suicide was not disabled because the evidence showed that he took medication and received counseling for his depression and it ended); Hamilton v. Southwestern Bell Tel. Co., 136 F.3d 1047, 8 AD Cases 1219 (5th Cir. 1998) (summary judgment for employer where plaintiff's PTSD triggered by rescuing a drowning woman was temporary); Soileau v. Guilford of Maine, Inc., 105 F.3d 12, 6 AD Cases 437 (1st Cir. 1997) (no disability because plaintiff's episodic depression did not substantially limit any major life activity); Sanders v. Arneson Prods., Inc., 91 F.3d 1351, 5 AD Cases 1292 (9th Cir. 1996) (plaintiff's psychological impairment, which lasted approximately three months with no residual effect, was of insufficient duration to be protected); Glowacki v. Buffalo Gen. Hosp., 2 F. Supp. 2d 346 (W.D.N.Y. 1998) (plaintiff with Bipolar Disorder not substantially limited because condition varied in intensity and was sporadic); Cutler v. Jewel Food Stores, Inc., 1998 WL 895453 (N.D. Ill. Dec. 14, 1998) (employee with adjustment disorder whose entire treatment consisted of four appointments with two therapists, three of which were in one month, and who was able to function normally again within two months not disabled); Muller v. Automobile Club of S. Cal., 897 F. Supp. 1289, 5 AD Cases 1997 (S.D. Cal. 1995) (plaintiff with PTSD whose condition improved and who was subsequently diagnosed with adjustment disorder with anxiety and depression in remission and atypical panic disorder in remission had impairment of limited duration that did not substantially limit a major life activity).

emotional or behavioral symptoms in response to an identifiable psychosocial stressor or stressors," such as divorce, marital problems, occupational failure, or financial difficulties.[53] The *DSM-IV-TR* further provides: "By definition, an Adjustment Disorder must resolve within 6 months of the termination of the stressor (or its consequences)."[54] The types of adjustment disorders described in the *DSM-IV-TR* are as follows:

- Adjustment Disorder With Depressed Mood
- Adjustment Disorder With Anxiety
- Adjustment Disorder With Mixed Anxiety and Depressed Mood
- Adjustment Disorder With Disturbance of Conduct
- Adjustment Disorder With Mixed Disturbance of Emotions and Conduct
- Adjustment Disorder Unspecified.[55]

Adjustment Disorders account for many of the stressful and upsetting emotional reactions that follow fairly common life events. This includes stressful workplace events such as layoffs or terminations, and altercations with supervisors, coworkers, or customers. The mere fact, therefore, that an employee is under stress or is temporarily feeling depressed as a result of some identifiable incident does not necessarily make such an employee disabled within the meaning of the ADA.[56]

The EEOC takes the position that an impairment that lasts several months is not short-term and temporary.[57] Most courts, however, have held that conditions that have no residual effects are short-term and temporary even if they last several months.[58] The mere possibility that the impairment might reoccur is insufficient to establish a substantial limitation.[59] The same principle applies

---

[53]DSM-IV-TR, *supra* note 4, at 679.

[54]*Id.*

[55]*Id.* at 679–80.

[56]Stauffer v. Bayer Corp., 1997 WL 588890 (N.D. Ind. July 21, 1997).

[57]*EEOC Definition of the Term "Disability," supra* note 35, at 7271. *See also* Clemente v. Executive Airlines, Inc., 215 F.3d 25, 10 AD Cases 996 (1st Cir. 2000) (severe condition that lasts for several months may be a disability); Aldrich v. Boeing Co., 146 F.3d 1265, 8 AD Cases 424 (10th Cir. 1998) (condition need not be permanent to be a disability).

[58]Burch v. Coca Cola, 119 F.3d 305, 7 AD Cases 1241 (5th Cir. 1997) (permanency of condition is touchstone); Goodwin-Haulmark v. Menninger Clinic, Inc., 76 F. Supp. 2d 1235, 5 WH Cases 2d 1548 (D. Kan. 1999) (plaintiff who suffered from depression, anxiety, and insomnia was unable to establish substantial limitation on working because impairment was neither permanent nor severe and she was expected to recover within a few weeks); Paegle v. Department of Interior, 813 F. Supp. 61, 2 AD Cases 482 (D.D.C. 1993) (back impairment lasting nine months not substantially limiting); Rakestraw v. Carpenter Co., 898 F. Supp. 386, 5 AD Cases 622 (N.D. Miss. 1995) (plaintiff's back impairment was temporary because it resolved within 18 months of his injury).

[59]Roush v. Weastec, Inc., 96 F.3d 840, 5 AD Cases 1713 (6th Cir. 1996) (plaintiff with lifelong congenital kidney problem had a temporary nonchronic condition; mere possibility that kidney blockage might reoccur was insufficient to establish a substantial limitation).

to mental impairments that are only temporary in nature. For example, in *Edmond v. Fujitsu-ICL Systems, Inc.*,[60] the court held that a plaintiff who suffered anxiety and depression, which required her to take a two-week leave and to work limited hours when she returned, was not disabled because there was no evidence of any permanent long-term effects resulting from her condition. The court stated, "Such short term interruption of work with little or no long-term impact or restriction fails as a matter of law to establish that plaintiff is limited in the major life activity of working."[61]

Short-term psychological impairments may qualify for ADA coverage if they are caused by a more serious, long-term physical impairment. For example, in *Vande Zande v. Wisconsin Department of Administration*,[62] the court held that the plaintiff's pressure ulcers were an extension of her underlying mobility impairment. The same argument could be used to cover temporary or episodic depression caused by cancer, quadriplegia, etc.[63]

Some mental impairments are permanent[64] or are at least chronic in nature. If the impairment is chronic, the episodes must be substantially limiting during the recurrence of the symptoms in order to qualify for ADA coverage.[65] In *Taylor v. Phoenixville School District*,[66] a plaintiff who suffered a psychotic episode was hospitalized for Bipolar Disorder. She was successfully treated with medication and returned to work but was subsequently fired for poor job performance. In affirming the lower court's denial of the employer's motion for summary judgment, the Third Circuit found that even with medication, the plaintiff continued to suffer chronic but episodic difficulties in thinking; the

---

[60]1997 WL 118406 (N.D. Tex. Mar. 5, 1997).

[61]*Id.* at *3. *But see* Cehrs v. Northeast Ohio Alzheimer's Research Ctr., 155 F.3d 775, 8 AD Cases 825 (6th Cir. 1998) (plaintiff with psoriasis that periodically flared up had substantially limiting impairment); Lanci v. Arthur Andersen, 10 AD Cases 1004 (S.D.N.Y. 2000) (genuine issue whether plaintiff's exacerbated symptoms during his acute phase of Tourette's Syndrome lasted sufficiently long to be substantially limiting; condition not temporary impairment because the acute symptoms waxed and waned over eight months and were chronic; the acute phase occurred when his Tourette's interacted with his Obsessive-Compulsive Disorder); Shannon v. City of Philadelphia, 1999 WL 1065210 (E.D. Pa. Nov. 23, 1999) (plaintiff possibly substantially limited in working where she required between 6 and 12 months' leave after 12-day hospitalization and doctor said she could not do any work).

[62]851 F. Supp. 353, 2 AD Cases 1846 (W.D. Wis. 1994).

[63]Whitney v. Greenberg, Rosenblatt, Kull & Bitsoli, 258 F.3d 30, 12 AD Cases 18 (1st Cir. 2001) (plaintiff argued she had dementia caused by chemotherapy and that it was a qualified impairment because it was listed in the DSM-IV). *But see* Sanders v. Arneson Prods., Inc., 91 F.3d 1351, 5 AD Cases 1292 (9th Cir. 1996) (rejecting argument that depression caused by underlying cancer is a disability).

[64]*See* Criado v. International Bus. Mach. Corp., 145 F.3d 437, 8 AD Cases 336 (1st Cir. 1998) (finding Attention Deficit Disorder to be a permanent impairment).

[65]Branch v. City of New Orleans, 1995 WL 295320 (E.D. La. May 5, 1995) (plaintiff's Crohn's disease, which resulted in intermittent flare-ups of limited duration, deemed too episodic to constitute disability).

[66]184 F.3d 296, 9 AD Cases 1187 (3d Cir. 1999).

absence of a daily difficulty did not undermine her claim. The court explained: "Chronic, episodic conditions can easily limit how well a person performs an activity as compared to the rest of the population; repeated flare-ups of poor health can have a cumulative weight that wears down a person's resolve and continually breaks apart long term projects."[67]

B. MITIGATING MEASURES In two 1999 decisions, *Sutton v. United Airlines*[68] and *Murphy v. United Parcel Service*,[69] the Supreme Court held that an impairment corrected by mitigating measures cannot constitute a disability under the ADA even if the impairment is substantially limiting absent such ameliorative measures. Specifically, the Court explained, "if a person is taking measures to correct for, or mitigate, a physical or mental impairment, the effects of those measures—both positive and negative—must be taken into account when judging whether a person is 'substantially limited' in a major life activity and thus 'disabled' under the Act."[70]

In *Sutton*, the Supreme Court concluded that two airline pilots with severe myopia whose vision was normal when they wore corrective lenses were neither actually disabled nor "regarded as disabled" for purposes of the ADA. The two had applied for airline jobs but were rejected because their uncorrected vision was not 20/100 or better. In *Murphy*, the plaintiff was hired as a truck mechanic. His blood pressure was approximately 250/160 without medication but with medication was only slightly higher than normal and he was able to function normally. The employer required mechanics to have commercial driver's licenses and to make test drives and emergency road calls. Although Department of Transportation (DOT) regulations banned drivers with "high blood pressure likely to interfere with his/her ability to operate a commercial vehicle safely,"[71] the DOT erroneously issued the plaintiff a medical certificate. The plaintiff was fired after the error was discovered.

In affirming the Tenth Circuit's rejection of both cases, the Supreme Court pointed to the ADA requirement that a plaintiff currently be substantially limited in a major life activity. In *Sutton,* the Court concluded that the EEOC's regulation that the disability determination had to be made without regard to mitigating measures such as medication or assistive devices was an impermissible interpretation of the ADA for three reasons. First, "[l]ooking at the Act as a whole, it is apparent that if a person is taking measures to correct for, or mitigate, a physical or mental impairment, the effects of those measures—both positive and negative—must be taken into account when judging whether that person is 'substantially limited' in a major life activity and thus 'disabled' under the Act."[72] In reaching this conclusion, the majority ignored the legislative history

---

[67]*Id.* at 308, 9 AD Cases at 1196.
[68]527 U.S. 471, 9 AD Cases 673 (1999).
[69]527 U.S. 516, 9 AD Cases 691 (1999).
[70]*Sutton*, 527 U.S. at 482, 9 AD Cases at 678.
[71]49 C.F.R. §391.41(b)(6).
[72]527 U.S. at 482, 9 AD Cases at 678.

and focused solely on the statutory language of the ADA. Noting that Section 12102(2)(a) contains the phrase "substantially limits" in the present indicative verb form, the Court required that a person be "presently—not potentially or hypothetically—substantially limited in order to demonstrate a disability."[73] The Court concluded that a corrected impairment does not substantially limit a major life activity.

Second, the *Sutton* Court concluded that the EEOC's guidelines conflicted with the ADA's mandate to make individualized inquiries concerning an individual's status. The Court stated that "the EEOC's approach would often require courts and employers to speculate about a person's condition and would, in many cases, force them to make a disability determination based on general information about how an uncorrected impairment usually affects individuals, rather than on the individual's actual condition."[74]

Third, the *Sutton* Court found that Congress's reference to "43 million Americans" with disabilities[75] was inconsistent with the EEOC's definition of disability. The Court concluded that the number in the statute "reflects an understanding that those whose impairments are largely corrected by medication or other devices are not 'disabled' within the meaning of the ADA."[76]

While the Supreme Court's decisions in *Sutton* and *Murphy* could have been viewed as bringing about the demise of the ADA, subsequent court decisions have proven otherwise.[77] Moreover, on July 27, 1999, the EEOC

---

[73]*Id.* at 482–83, 9 AD Cases at 678.
[74]*Id.* at 483, 9 AD Cases at 678.
[75]*Id.* at 484, 9 AD Cases at 679.
[76]*Id.* at 483, 9 AD Cases at 678–79.
[77]*See, e.g.,* Taylor v. Phoenixville Sch. Dist., 184 F.3d 296, 9 AD Cases 1187 (3d Cir. 1999) (school secretary who took lithium to control her Bipolar Disorder presented sufficient evidence that the drug did not perfectly control her symptoms, leaving her substantially limited in her ability to think); McAlindin v. County of San Diego, 192 F.3d 1226, 10 AD Cases 252 (9th Cir. 1999) (plaintiff with panic and anxiety disorders for which he took several medications, which made him drowsy and sexually impotent, and who was in psychotherapy, presented evidence he was substantially limited in sleeping, interacting with others, and sexual relations); Lemire v. Silva, 104 F. Supp. 2d 80, 11 AD Cases 141 (D. Mass. 2000) (plaintiff on antidepressants for panic disorder and agoraphobia presented evidence she was substantially limited in interacting with others and working). *But see* Spades v. City of Walnut Ridge, 186 F. 3d 897, 9 AD Cases 1015 (8th Cir. 1999) (plaintiff with depression who testified he could function without limitation if he took his medication and underwent counseling not substantially limited); Krocka v. City of Chicago, 203 F.3d 507, 10 AD Cases 289 (7th Cir. 2000) (plaintiff's severe depression not substantially limiting where he exhibited no symptoms when taking Prozac and could perform police officer job); Todd v. Academy Corp., 57 F. Supp. 2d 448, 9 AD Cases 1306 (S.D. Tex. 1999) (epileptic plaintiff on medication who continued to have one small approximately 15-second seizure per week, during which plaintiff's thinking was "cloudy," was not substantially limited in a major life activity); Robb v. Horizon Credit Union, 66 F. Supp. 2d 913, 9 AD Cases 1365 (D.C. Ill. 1999) (plaintiff with chronic depression who could function and work with antidepressant medication was not substantially limited).

issued *Instructions for Field Offices: Analyzing ADA Charges After Supreme Court Decisions Addressing "Disability" and "Qualified"* (*EEOC Instructions for Field Offices*).[78] In that directive, the EEOC pointed out that in *Bragdon v. Abbott*,[79] the Supreme Court broadly interpreted the terms "impairment," "major life activity," and "substantial limitation," and the agency stated its intent to give a broad interpretation to those terms.[80] The EEOC also noted that the Supreme Court had emphasized that the determination of whether an individual was disabled had to be based on the individual's actual condition at the time of the alleged discrimination.[81] The EEOC's directive therefore focuses primarily on questions of the effectiveness and the adverse consequences of the mitigating measure.

With respect to mental impairments, the *EEOC Instructions for Field Offices* gives several examples of situations where an individual would be substantially limited as a result of medication he was using. In discussing the combination of two or more mitigating measures that create a substantial limitation, the EEOC gives the following example:

> A [charging party] with attention deficit disorder (ADD) and depression may take medications to treat each condition. Each medication, by itself, affects the ability to sleep (a major life activity), but is not substantially limiting. However, the combined effect of the two medications substantially limits the charging party's ability to sleep.[82]

When discussing other major life activities that may be adversely affected by mitigating measures relevant to mental disabilities, the EEOC's directive mentions thinking, concentrating, and other cognitive functions, pointing out that they may be substantially limited as a result of the individual's response to certain drugs used to treat psychiatric illness.[83] For example, an individual with a mental impairment who is taking psychotropic medication may be required to exert greater effort to engage in cognitive functions if the medication causes the person to feel groggy, disoriented, or slow.[84] A person may also have difficulty with memory because of certain medications.[85]

The *EEOC Instructions for Field Offices* also mentions eating as a major life activity that can be affected by the use of mitigating measures because certain medications can cause nausea.[86] Conversely, an individual who has to

---

[78] *EEOC Instructions for Field Offices*, supra note 49, at 1441.
[79] 524 U.S. 624, 8 AD Cases 239 (1998).
[80] *EEOC Instructions for Field Offices*, supra note 49, at 1442.
[81] *Id.* at 1441.
[82] *Id.* at 1443.
[83] *Id.*
[84] *Id.*
[85] *Id.*
[86] *See, e.g.,* Lawson v. CSX Transp., Inc., 245 F.3d 916, 10 AD Cases 832 (7th Cir. 2001) (diabetic with severe eating restrictions presented evidence of substantial limitations); Amir v. St. Louis Univ., 184 F.3d 1017, 9 AD Cases 999 (8th Cir. 1999) (plaintiff possibly substantially limited in his ability to eat).

maintain a rigid eating schedule because of certain medications or impairments would not seem to be limited in any major life activities.[87]

Most troubling is the EEOC's example concerning a mitigating measure that substantially limits caring for oneself:

> It may also be a significant impact on the ability to care for oneself as a result of experiencing a medical episode. The inability of a mitigating measure to prevent such an episode may cause so much fear that it seriously affects a [Charging Party's] ability to care for himself. For example, a [Charging Party] with epilepsy may have had traumatic experiences having a seizure in public where strangers reacted badly. As a result, he may not be able to go out alone to run routine errands or buy groceries and may require that someone familiar with his epilepsy always accompany him. Alternatively, a [Charging Party] may fear possible injury from a seizure, and therefore may be unable to engage in basic activities of caring for oneself, such as cooking and bathing unless another person is present.[88]

This same example can easily be applied to individuals who suffer panic or anxiety attacks or who have phobias. The EEOC is essentially saying that fear about what might happen can create a substantial limitation.

3. Major Life Activities

The EEOC's regulations promulgated under the ADA describe "major life activities" as those basic activities that the average person in the general population can perform with little or no difficulty.[89] Such activities include caring for oneself, performing manual tasks, walking, seeing, hearing, speaking, breathing, reading,[90] learning, and working.[91] The EEOC later added sitting, standing, lifting, reaching,[92] mental and emotional processes such as thinking, concentrating, interacting with others,[93] sleeping,[94] and eating.[95]

The Supreme Court addressed the issue of what constitutes a major life activity for the first time in *Bragdon v. Abbott*.[96] *Abbott* was an ADA Title III

---

[87]*See* Weber v. Strippit, 186 F.3d 907, 9 AD Cases 961 (8th Cir. 1999) (unspecified dietary restrictions imposed by heart condition not a substantial limitation on eating). *See also* Popko v. Pennsylvania State Univ., 84 F. Supp. 2d 589, 10 AD Cases 1404 (M.D. Pa. 2000) (plaintiff's need to get seven to eight hours' sleep per night did not substantially limit her in sleeping).

[88]*EEOC Instructions for Field Offices, supra* note 49, at 1443.

[89]29 C.F.R. §1630.2(i) (1995).

[90]*See* Gonzales v. National Bd. Med. Exam'rs, 225 F.3d 620, 10 AD Cases 1575 (6th Cir. 2000) (reading and writing are major life activities); Bartlett v. New York State Bd. L. Exm'rs, 226 F.3d 69, 10 AD Cases 1687 (2d Cir. 2001) (reading is a major life activity).

[91]29 C.F.R. §1630.2(i).

[92]29 C.F.R. §1630.2(i) app.

[93]*EEOC Definition of the Term "Disability," supra* note 35, at 7261.

[94]*EEOC Guidance on Psychiatric Disabilities, supra* note 14, at 7466–67.

[95]*EEOC Instructions for Field Offices, supra* note 49, at 1443.

[96]524 U.S. 624, 638, 8 AD Cases 239, 244–45 (1998).

case involving an asymptomatic HIV-infected individual. The plaintiff contended that her HIV infection constituted a substantial limitation on her ability to reproduce. The defendant argued that the ADA was intended to cover only those "aspects of a person's life which have a public, economic, or daily character."[97] In rejecting the defendant's argument, the Court noted that the ADA had to be construed to be consistent with the Rehabilitation Act, which sets forth a representative list of major life activities. The Supreme Court then stated that "the plain meaning of the word 'major' denotes comparative importance and suggests that the touchstone for determining an activity's inclusion under the statutory rubric is its significance."[98]

While courts generally agree on those major life activities that primarily relate to physical impairments—e.g., sitting, standing, walking, etc.—they disagree on whether certain activities that often relate to mental impairments are major life activities. Generally, the major life activities claimed to be limited by a mental impairment are far more amorphous and less discernible than those limited by a physical impairment. The major life activities often cited in mental disability cases include, for example, learning, concentrating, sleeping, getting along with others, and thinking.[99]

Major life activities frequently claimed by individuals with mental impairments are discussed in the following sections.

A. INTERACTING WITH OTHERS Initially, the ability to get along with others was not considered a major life activity. For example, in *Adams v. Alderson*,[100] the plaintiff claimed to be handicapped in that he suffered from a "maladaptive reaction to psychosocial stressor," i.e., his allegedly antagonistic supervisor, whom he physically assaulted. The court rejected the claim, observing that the plaintiff's condition was "hardly an impairment which substantially limits one or more . . . major life activities."[101]

In *Soileau v. Guilford of Maine*,[102] an engineer claimed that his dysthymia (a depressive disorder) interfered with his ability to interact with others. The First Circuit rejected interacting with others as a major life activity, stating:

> The concept of "ability to get along with others" is remarkably elastic, perhaps so much so as to make it unworkable as a definition. While such an ability is a skill to be prized, it is different in kind from breathing or walking, two examples

---

[97]*Id.* at 625, 8 AD Cases at 245.

[98]*Id.* at 638, 8 AD Cases at 245.

[99]*See, e.g.*, Davidson v. Midelfort Clinic, Ltd., 133 F.3d 499, 8 AD Cases 77 (7th Cir. 1998) (plaintiff, diagnosed with Attention Deficit Disorder (ADD), claimed she was substantially limited in learning because her disorder interfered with cognitive processes involving the ability to concentrate, learn, organize thoughts, verbalize them, and formulate explanations); Amir v. St. Louis Univ., 184 F.3d 1017, 9 AD Cases 999 (8th Cir. 1999) (a former medical student presented evidence that his Obsessive Compulsive Disorder substantially limited his ability to eat and drink without vomiting, his ability to concentrate and learn, and his ability to get along with others).

[100]723 F. Supp. 1531, 51 FEP Cases 647 (D.D.C. 1989).

[101]*Id.* at 1531, 51 FEP Cases at 648.

[102]105 F.3d 12, 6 AD Cases 437 (1st Cir. 1997).

which are used in the regulations. Further, whether a person has such an ability is a subjective judgment, and the ability may or may not exist depending on the context."[103]

Other courts have reached similar conclusions.[104]

The EEOC took the position, in its *Guidance on Psychiatric Disabilities*, that interacting with others is a major life activity.[105] The Commission maintained that "some unfriendliness" with coworkers or supervisors, standing alone, is insufficient to constitute a substantial limitation on interacting with others. Rather, in order to show a substantial limitation on this activity, an employee must show that his/her "relations with others were characterized on a regular basis by severe problems, for example, consistently high levels of hostility, social withdrawal, or failure to communicate when necessary."[106] As two commentators have observed about this rather amorphous standard, "Aside from raising the obvious question of where to draw the line, what this means is that the occasionally irascible employee is not protected but the consistently obnoxious employee qualifies for the law's protection."[107]

The Ninth Circuit found interacting with others to constitute a major life activity, in *McAlindin v. County of San Diego*.[108] In *McAlindin*, the plaintiff, who suffered from anxiety disorders, panic disorders, and somatoform disorders, alleged that he was substantially limited in sleeping, sexual relations, and interacting with others. Dismissing the defendant's argument that interacting with others is too vague a concept, the court remarked:

> We see nothing in the statutory text that makes vagueness the test for determining what is a major life activity. We do not think any vagueness in the term rises to the level of making it unworkable as a major life activity. . . . Recognizing

---

[103]*Id.* at 15, 6 AD Cases at 440. Notwithstanding this pronouncement, the First Circuit left the door open on the issue of communication as a major life activity by stating, "a more narrowly defined concept going to essential attributes of human communication could, in a particular setting, be understood to be a major life activity." *Id.* A year later, the First Circuit in *Criado v. International Business Machines Corp.*, 145 F.3d 437, 8 AD Cases 336 (1st Cir. 1998), concluded that a plaintiff with ADD, anxiety disorder, and depression was substantially limited in her ability to relate to others.

[104]*E.g.*, Breiland v. Advance Circuits, Inc., 976 F. Supp. 858, 7 AD Cases 619 (D. Minn. 1997) (plaintiff diagnosed with major depression, schizoid personality disorder, and psychosocial distress not disabled because ability to get along with coworkers is not a major life activity); Kiphart v. Saturn Corp., 74 F. Supp. 2d 769, 9 AD Cases 1650 (M.D. Tenn. 1999) (interacting with others not a major life activity), *rev'd on other grounds*, 251 F.3d 573, 11 AD Cases 1473 (6th Cir. 2001). *See also* Davis v. University of N.C., 263 F.3d 95, ___ n.4, 12 AD Cases 243, ___ n. 4 (4th Cir. 2001) (expressing doubt that socializing is a major life activity); Horwitz v. L&J.G. Stickley, Inc., 122 F. Supp. 2d 350, 354 n.3 (N.D.N.Y. 2000) (same).

[105]*EEOC Guidance on Psychiatric Disabilities, supra* note 14, at 7463.

[106]*Id.* at 7465–66.

[107]James J. McDonald, Jr. & Jonathan P. Rosman, *EEOC Guidance on Psychiatric Disabilities: Many Problems, Few Workable Solutions*, 23 EMPL. REL. L.J. 5, 13 (1997).

[108]192 F.3d 1226, 9 AD Cases 1217 (9th Cir. 1999).

interacting with others as a major life activity . . . does not mean that any cantankerous person will be deemed substantially limited in a major life activity. Mere trouble getting along with other co-workers is not sufficient to have a substantial limitation. Here there are clinical findings indicating that one of the effects of [plaintiff's] mental illness is a pattern of withdrawal from public places and family members.[109]

The court ultimately concluded the plaintiff presented a genuine issue of fact concerning his limitation because he put forth documentation showing that after a panic attack he "became increasingly more withdrawn and his ability to deal with people and stress has seriously diminished."[110] Furthermore, the plaintiff's doctor testified that the plaintiff stayed around the house about 20 hours a day, limited his social activities to his family, and had no political or religious affiliations.[111] The court concluded that such evidence suggested that the plaintiff "suffers from a total inability to communicate at times, in addition to a more subtle impairment in engaging in meaningful discussion. His alleged 'fear reaction' and 'communicative paralysis' are sufficiently severe to raise a genuine issue of fact."[112]

Other courts similarly have found interacting with others to be a major life activity.[113] The difficulty with regarding interaction with others as a major life activity is where to draw the line.[114] For example, in *Garvey v. Jefferson Smurfit Corp.*,[115] an employee with hypertension claimed that he was substantially limited in his major life activities of interpersonal relations and socializing. After concluding that both are major life activities, the court explained:

> There is evidence that anytime Garvey becomes involved in a stressful social situation or argument, his blood pressure will rise to a dangerous level. Thus, Garvey must avoid stressful situations, argument, heated debates, and emotional conversation at all costs. Consequently, a question of fact exists whether plaintiff's ability to enter into stressful situations, interpersonal or otherwise, is a substantial limitation on his ability to interact with others.[116]

In *Lemire v. Silva*,[117] the plaintiff, who suffered from a panic disorder with agoraphobia, claimed she was substantially limited in interacting with

---

[109] *Id.* at 1235, 9 AD Cases at 1222.

[110] *Id.*, 9 AD Cases at 1222.

[111] *Id.*

[112] *Id.* at 1235–36, 9 AD Cases at 1222.

[113] Amir v. St. Louis Univ., 184 F.3d 1017, 9 AD Cases 999 (8th Cir. 1999); Olson v. Dubuque Cmty. Sch. Dist., 137 F.3d 609, 7 AD Cases 1598 (8th Cir. 1998); Garvey v. Jefferson Smurfit Corp., 11 AD Cases 154 (E.D. Pa. 2000); Lemire v. Silva, 104 F. Supp. 2d 80, 11 AD Cases 141 (D. Mass. 2000); Krocka v. Bransfield, 969 F. Supp. 1073, 8 AD Cases 707 (N.D. Ill. 1997) *aff'd*, 203 F.3d 507, 10 AD Cases 289 (7th Cir. 2000); Sherback v. Wright Auto. Group, 987 F. Supp. 433 (W.D. Pa. 1997).

[114] *See* Stauffer v. Bayer Corp., 1997 WL 588890 (N.D. Ind. July 21, 1997) (episodic inability to interact with others insufficient to constitute substantial limitation).

[115] 11 AD Cases 154.

[116] *Id.* at 156.

[117] 104 F. Supp. 2d 80, 11 AD Cases 141 (D. Mass. 2000).

others. In finding such interaction to be a major life activity, the court remarked:

> The ability to interact with others, if defined broadly to include the most basic types of interactions, is a major life activity. Human beings are fundamentally social beings. The ability to interact with others is an inherent part of what it means to be human. Even if we had the capacity to live without any human interaction, that capacity is immaterial in view of the highly interactive society in which we live. The ability to interact is thus both fundamental in itself and also essential to contemporary life.[118]

The *Lemire* court concluded that although the plaintiff's prognosis was good concerning her ability to interact with her immediate family, she might be substantially limited in her ability to interact with others because the evidence showed her ability to interact with others in crowded places was impaired.[119]

In *Gilday v. Mecosta County*,[120] the court affirmed denial of summary judgment for the employer where a diabetic employee had established that his diabetes caused his blood sugar levels to fluctuate, which in turn caused him to become so irritable that he could not get along with coworkers and customers. The court maintained that the ability to get along was necessary for almost all jobs, and the plaintiff had presented evidence that his fluctuating blood sugar levels substantially limited his ability to work.

These cases teach that a plaintiff needs to be specific concerning the precise limitation imposed on the major life activity of interacting with others. The question is also raised of how a defendant counters testimony concerning a plaintiff's alleged difficulties. Difficulties interacting with supervisors and coworkers often precede the termination of employment of an employee who might later attribute such problems to a disability. Ironically, the employer that relies on the employee's interpersonal difficulties as a basis for termination also lays the groundwork for the employee to claim to be substantially limited in the major life activity of getting along with others. While discovery can be conducted into the nature of a plaintiff's relations with others outside work, it might be difficult and time-consuming for an employer to refute a plaintiff's claim of having difficulty interacting with others in a broad range of contexts.

B. ENGAGING IN SEXUAL RELATIONS In *Bragdon v. Abbott*,[121] the Supreme Court maintained that "reproduction falls well within the phrase 'major life activity.' Reproduction *and the sexual dynamics surrounding* it are central to the life process itself."[122] Relying on this statement, courts have held that

---

[118]*Id.* at 80–82, 11 AD Cases at 146–47.
[119]*Id.* at 89, 11 AD Cases at 148.
[120]124 F.3d 760, 7 AD Cases 1268 (6th Cir. 1997).
[121]524 U.S. 624, 8 AD Cases 239 (1998).
[122]*Id.* at 637, 8 AD Cases at 244–45 (emphasis added). The legislative history of the ADA supports the Court's conclusion. *See* H.R. REP. NO. 101-485, pt. 2, at 52 (1990), *reprinted in* 1990 U.S.C.C.A.N. 267, 324–34 ("a person infected with [HIV] is covered under the first paragraph of the definition of the term disability because of a substantial limitation to procreation and intimate sexual relationships").

having sexual relations is a major life activity. In *McAlindin*, the plaintiff testified that he experienced impotence as a result of the medication he took for his mental impairment. Reasoning that "sexuality is important in how we define ourselves and how we are perceived by others and is a fundamental part of how we bond in intimate relationships,"[123] the Ninth Circuit held that having sexual relations is a major life activity.[124]

The question, as always, is how much evidence is needed to establish a substantial limitation. The courts have held, for example, that the inability to have unprotected sex, to utilize a favored position, or to achieve the level of sexual performance desired does not constitute a substantial limitation on the major life activity of having sex.[125] In *Bragdon* the plaintiff presented no evidence that she was physically unable to have sexual intercourse. Instead, she argued that she could not reproduce because she could not become pregnant while having safe sex, i.e., using a condom. The Supreme Court discussed the harmful legal and health consequences of an HIV-infected individual's engaging in sexual relations, but it did not specifically address the *inability* to have sex. Arguably, the diminution of the desire to engage in a major life activity is not a substantial limitation on the *ability* to do so.[126] The counter to this argument, however, is the manner in which courts view interacting with others. In *McAlindin*, where the plaintiff withdrew from others, the court treated a lack of desire to interact the same as an inability to interact. Therefore, arguably, the lack of desire to engage in a major life activity is equivalent to an inability to do so.

---

[123]McAlindin v. County of San Diego, 192 F.3d. 1226, 1234, 9 AD Cases 1217, 1221 (9th Cir. 1999).

[124]*Id.* at 1234, 9 AD Cases at 1221.

[125]*See, e.g.,* Taylor v. Nimock's Oil Co., 214 F.3d 957, 10 AD Cases 1069 (8th Cir. 2000) (plaintiff who admitted she could have sex "in moderation" not substantially limited); Reese v. American Food Serv., 2000 WL 1470212 (E.D. Pa. Sept. 29, 2000) (plaintiff with Hepatitis C who testified he and his spouse had not altered their sexual precautions since his diagnosis and that he did not regularly use a condom during sex is not substantially limited); Buskirk v. Apollo Metals, 116 F. Supp. 2d 591, 11 AD Cases 178 (E.D. Pa. 2000) (plaintiff with back injury who testified along with his wife that his sexual performance "had changed" not substantially limited); Qualls v. Lack's Stores, Inc., 1999 WL 731758 (N.D. Tex. Mar. 31, 1999) (the use of a condom during intercourse, at least without more, does not constitute a substantial limitation on one's sex life); Hoskins v. Oakland County Sheriff's Dep't, 44 F. Supp. 2d 882, 890 (E.D. Mich. 1999) (plaintiff's inability to utilize the same position during intercourse that her husband favored before her accident was not a substantial limitation on a major life activity); Francis v. Chemical Banking Corp., 62 F. Supp. 2d 948 (E.D.N.Y. 1999) (plaintiff with panic disorder not substantially limited in socializing simply because he cannot ejaculate with partner as hard as he would like and because he cannot leave the state with a woman because he would not know where a hospital was in the event of a panic attack).

[126]*See* Johnson v. New York Med. Coll., 1997 WL 580708 (S.D.N.Y. Sept. 18, 1997) (depressed plaintiff's lack of interest in sexual relations was not a substantial limitation on a major life activity).

C. REPRODUCTION In analyzing whether an HIV-infected asymptomatic plaintiff was substantially limited in a major life activity of reproduction because she could not become pregnant practicing safe sex, the Supreme Court in *Bragdon* noted that the infection affected the plaintiff's ability to reproduce because she could infect both a child and her sexual partner with the virus.[127] Although the defendant presented evidence that antiretroviral therapy could reduce the risk of transmission from 25 percent to 8 percent, the Supreme Court, sidestepping the issue of mitigating measures, stated, "It cannot be said as a matter of law that an 8% risk of transmitting a dread and fatal disease to one's child does not represent a substantial limitation on reproduction."[128]

The *Bragdon* Court further noted that the decision to reproduce carries legal and economic consequences—specifically, the cost of treating a child with HIV and the fact that five states apply criminal penalties to an HIV-infected individual who has intercourse (the plaintiff lived in none of those states).[129] The Court then declared: "In the end, the disability definition does not turn on personal choice. When significant limitations result from the impairment, the definition is met even if the difficulties are not insurmountable."[130] The notion that disability does not turn on personal choice with respect to a major life activity voluntarily not done is consistent with the EEOC's position that the voluntariness of a condition is irrelevant—i.e., it does not matter that the impairment was caused by a volitional act.[131] The difficulty with this position in some circumstances, however, is that an individual may decide not to utilize a mitigating measure to control the limitation imposed by the impairment, which may render him disabled under the ADA. Some courts have held that such a choice puts the individual outside the ADA's protection.[132]

Bragdon raises a number of issues concerning the type of evidence to present outside the HIV context to demonstrate a substantial limitation on reproduction. For example, the *EEOC Instructions for Field Offices* directs investigators to inquire whether the mitigating measure the charging party

---

[127] 524 U.S. at 625, 8 AD Cases at 245.
[128] *Id.* at 626, 8 AD Cases at 246.
[129] *Id.*
[130] *Id.* at 625–26, 8 AD Cases at 246.
[131] *EEOC Definition of the Term "Disability," supra* note 35, at 7261. *See also* Cook v. Rhode Island Dep't of Mental Health, 10 F.3d 17, 2 AD Cases 1476 (1st Cir. 1993) (mutability of plaintiff's morbid obesity irrelevant to determination of disability).
[132] *See, e.g.*, Hein v. All Am. Plywood, 232 F.3d 482, 11 AD Cases 308 (6th Cir. 2000) (plaintiff who voluntarily failed to maintain appropriate supply of blood pressure medication, which if he took controlled his disability, not substantially limited); Van Stan v. Family Colours & Co., 125 F.3d 563, 570, 7 AD Cases 426, 431 (7th Cir. 1997) ("A plaintiff cannot recover under the ADA if through his own fault he fails to control an otherwise controllable disability"); Tangires v. Johns Hopkins Hosp., 79 F. Supp. 2d 587, 10 AD Cases 215 (D. Md. 2000); Spradley v. Custom Campers, 68 F. Supp. 2d 1225 (D. Kan. 1999). *But see* Finical v. Collections Unlimited, Inc., 65 F. Supp. 2d 1032, 9 AD Cases 1162 (D. Ariz. 1999) (plaintiff's unwillingness to wear a hearing aid is irrelevant to determination of whether she is substantially limited).

utilizes imposes a substantial limitation on any major life activity.[133] With respect to reproduction, the EEOC advises: "Many medications prescribed to control seizures or psychiatric illnesses cause birth defects, thus creating a substantial limitation in procreation."[134] The question is whether the mere chance of such a result is sufficient to be a substantial limitation. For example, what if the chance is 1 percent or less than 8 percent? Presumably, a plaintiff will need to present expert medical evidence concerning the likelihood that a birth defect will result. Even assuming, however, the probability is 50 percent, will the courts then evaluate whether the type of potential birth defect is "dread and fatal"?

Moreover, with respect to certain mental impairments that appear to run along family lines, a child may eventually suffer from the same mental impairment as the parent. Arguably, an individual who inherited a mental impairment from a parent and decides he does not want to have children for fear his child will suffer from the same condition is substantially limited in reproduction. On the other hand, when the prospect is one of passing down to one's children less serious conditions than HIV that may be controlled by a number of medications (if taken) and that do not necessarily impose devastating financial consequences, the individual's decision not to have children might simply be viewed as a personal choice. In such case, the best defense might be to establish that the plaintiff never planned on having children,[135] that the risk of communicating the condition is minimal or highly speculative, that the condition does not impose devastating financial consequences, or that it does not impose the drastic consequences that AIDS does.

D. SLEEPING The EEOC takes the position that sleeping is a major life activity[136] and the courts have agreed.[137] A person is not substantially limited in sleeping if he has some trouble falling asleep or sometimes sleeps fitfully.[138]

---

[133] *EEOC Instructions for Field Offices, supra* note 49, at 1442, 1443.

[134] *Id.* at 1443.

[135] *See* Qualls v. Lack's Stores, Inc., 1999 WL 731758 (N.D. Tex. Mar. 31, 1999) (plaintiff who voluntarily had a vasectomy after he and his wife decided not to have children could not claim Hepatitis C substantially limited him in reproduction). *But see* Hernandez v. Prudential Ins. Co., 977 F. Supp. 1160 (M.D. Fla. 1997) (court rejected defendant's argument that HIV did not substantially limit plaintiff in reproduction because plaintiff was in exclusive homosexual relationship); Hiller v. Runyon, 95 F. Supp. 2d 1016 (S.D. Iowa 2000) (defendant's contention that plaintiff who had a testicular cancer was not substantially limited in reproduction because he and his wife had decided not to have children was irrelevant).

[136] *EEOC Guidance on Psychiatric Disabilities, supra* note 14, at 7463.

[137] *See, e.g.*, Pritchard v. Southern Co., 102 F.3d 1118, 6 AD Cases 206 (11th Cir. 1996); Pack v. K-Mart Corp., 166 F.3d 1300, 8 AD Cases 1880 (10th Cir. 1999); McAlindin v. County of San Diego, 192 F.3d 1226, 9 AD Cases 1217 (9th Cir. 1999); Baulos v. Roadway Express, Inc., 139 F.3d 1147, 7 AD Cases 1753 (7th Cir. 1998); Colwell v. Suffolk County Police Dep't, 158 F. 3d 635, 8 AD Cases 1232 (2d Cir. 1998).

[138] *EEOC Guidance on Psychiatric Disabilities, supra* note 14, at 7467.

Rather, the individual should be compared with the average person in the general population.[139] The EEOC cites a *Washington Post* article reporting that of 1,000 adults, 71 percent averaged five to eight hours of sleep on weeknights. Although the EEOC did not state whether it considered this the "national sleep standard" such that anyone who sleeps more or less than five or eight hours a night would be considered disabled, the courts have viewed it as such. The problem is that some individuals' normal sleep patterns may not fall within the five-to-eight-hour range. For example, would an individual who slept ten hours per night for years and then began sleeping only seven have a significant restriction on his ability to sleep? Arguably, because the substantial limitation evaluation is an individualized inquiry, the individual should be viewed as substantially limited in sleeping. On the other hand, when compared with the average person in the population, the individual is not limited.

In *Kvintus v. RL Polk & Co.*,[140] the plaintiff, who suffered from Posttraumatic Stress Disorder and Adjustment Disorder with mixed anxiety and depressed mood, proffered evidence that he had slept an average of less than four hours a night for the last 30 years. The court, while acknowledging that sleeping is a major life activity, concluded that neither the plaintiff nor his doctor had demonstrated how his lack of sleep interfered with the plaintiff's work or any other activities. In *Pack v. K-Mart Corp.*,[141] the Tenth Circuit held that the plaintiff's depression did not substantially limit her in sleeping even though she had episodes of sleep disruption and waking without feeling rested. The court found no evidence that her sleep problems were severe or long-term or had a permanent impact. Similarly, the courts have held that simply suffering from insomnia, restlessness, fitful sleeping, or discomfort during sleep is not a substantial limitation on sleeping.[142]

---

[139]*Id.* at 7466.

[140]3 F. Supp. 2d 788 (E.D. Mich. 1998).

[141]166 F.3d 1300, 8 AD Cases 1880 (10th Cir. 1999).

[142]*See, e.g.*, Doyal v. Oklahoma Heart, Inc., 213 F.3d 492, 10 AD Cases 991 (10th Cir. 2000) (plaintiff not substantially limited in sleeping where medication allowed her to sleep 14 hours per night); Popko v. Pennsylvania State Univ., 84 F. Supp 2d 589, 10 AD Cases 1404 (M.D. Pa. 2000) (fact that plaintiff with epilepsy required to get seven to eight hours' sleep per night to prevent seizures did not establish substantial limitation on sleeping); Hawkins v. Trustees of Ind. Univ., 83 F. Supp. 2d 987, 10 AD Cases 819 (S.D. Ind. 1999) (testimony that plaintiff slept too much or too little is insufficient to create issue of fact on whether sleeping is substantially limited); Marcum v. Consolidated Freightways, 48 F. Supp. 2d 721, 9 AD Cases 1494 (N.D. Ohio 1999) (discomfort during sleep is not substantial limitation); Kiphart v. Saturn Corp., 74 F. Supp. 2d 769, 9 AD Cases 1650 (M.D. Tenn 1999) (testimony that plaintiff took medication and that he usually got a "tough night's sleep" is insufficient to establish substantial limitation); Stauffer v. Bayer Corp., 1997 WL 588890 (N.D. Ind. July 21, 1997) (testimony that plaintiff suffered from insomnia is insufficient to show that plaintiff is substantially limited in sleeping) *Compare* Franklin v. Consolidated Edison Co. of New York, Inc., 1999 WL 796170 (S.D.N.Y. Sept. 30, 1999) (plaintiff presented evidence that her sleeping was substantially limited).

E. COGNITIVE FUNCTIONS Many plaintiffs with mental disabilities claim that their impairment substantially limits them in learning, thinking, or concentrating.[143] These activities are hard to define with any precision, however. In *Taylor v. Phoenixville School District*,[144] the Third Circuit noted that given the breadth of the activity of thinking, there was a valid objection to its recognition as a major life activity. Nonetheless, the court concluded the "most objections about the broadness of thinking as a life activity can be captured in an analysis of *when* the activity is substantially limited."[145] Cognitive functions may be affected by the impairment itself or by the medication used to treat it. For example, lithium, which is used to treat individuals with Bipolar Disorder, may cause the individual to feel mentally slow.[146]

The Third Circuit in *Taylor* considered whether the plaintiff was actually substantially limited in her thinking. The court noted the following evidence in concluding that she was: (1) lithium, which the plaintiff took every day, had a narrow therapeutic range and did not control all her symptoms; (2) the medication's side effects could indirectly affect her thinking; (3) the plaintiff still experienced paranoia and distorted mood that could affect her thinking even if it did not reach the level that would force hospitalization; (4) she sought treatment 25 days during the year; (5) she had good performance reviews before she was hospitalized but had problems after she returned. The court explained:

> That [the plaintiff] may not have experienced problems every day does not defeat her claim. Chronic, episodic conditions can easily limit how well a person performs an activity as compared to the rest of the population: repeated flare-ups of poor health can have a cumulative weight that wears down a person's resolve and continually breaks apart longer-term projects.[147]

In *Doyal v. Oklahoma Heart, Inc.*,[148] the court held that the plaintiff was not substantially limited in thinking just because she had problems making simple decisions and that she was not limited in learning simply because she forgot names and had difficulty learning a new computer system. Similarly, in *Bowen v. Income Producing Management of Oklahoma*,[149] a plaintiff with a

---

[143]The Fifth Circuit declined to find that "awareness" is a major life activity. Deas v. River W., 152 F.3d 471, 8 AD Cases 989 (5th Cir. 1998).

[144]184 F.3d 296, 9 AD Cases 1187 (3d Cir. 1999).

[145]*Id.* at 307 (emphasis added). *Compare* Doyal v. Oklahoma Heart, Inc., 213 F.3d 492, 10 AD Cases 991 (10th Cir. 2000) (thinking not a major life activity), *with* Bergsrud v. Columbia-Lee Reg'l Med. Ctr., 2000 WL 33287447 (D.N.M. June 24, 2000) (assuming for purposes of motion that thinking was a major life activity).

[146]Taylor v. Phoenixville Sch. Dist., 184 F.3d 296, 308, 9 AD Cases 1187, 1195 (3d Cir. 1999) (lithium's side effects may impair ability to think, concentrate, and remember).

[147]*Id.* at 308–09, 9 AD Cases at 1196.

[148]213 F.3d 492, 10 AD Cases 991 (10th Cir. 2000).

[149]202 F.3d 1282, 10 AD Cases 296 (10th Cir. 2000). *See also* Leison v. City of Shelbyville, 153 F.3d 805, 8 AD Cases 892 (7th Cir. 1998) (depressed firefighter who had problems passing one course not substantially limited in learning).

brain injury asserted that he was substantially limited in learning because he had suffered a memory loss, had an inability to concentrate, and had problems doing basic math. The court concluded he was not disabled because his skills and abilities were still above those of the average person.

At least one court has found that concentration is a major life activity.[150] The Tenth Circuit has stated that concentration is not a separate activity but is a "significant and necessary" aspect of other activities like working, speaking, or learning.[151] Another court rejected concentration as a major life activity because of the difficulty in defining it with enough specificity to prevent merely tailoring the definition of the activity to fit the impairment.[152] In *Cody v. Cigna Healthcare of St. Louis*,[153] the plaintiff claimed that diagnosis of schizotypal personality disorder created a genuine issue of fact as to whether she was substantially limited in the major life activity of "interpretation of events." The court rejected the plaintiff's argument because she presented no evidence that she actually misperceived reality.

F. CARING FOR ONESELF As with thinking and other cognitive functions, the courts have not yet laid out the parameters for the major life activity of caring for oneself.[154] The EEOC has provided some guidance and said that in assessing whether or not an employee is substantially limited in caring for oneself, a number of considerations need to be taken into account, including (1) whether medication or prosthetic devices cause extreme fatigue that affects the ability to care for oneself, (2) whether failure of a mitigating measure to prevent a "medical episode" creates so much fear that the individual will not go out alone and to buy groceries, and (3) whether the fear prevents the individual from cooking and bathing unless another individual is present.[155]

The limited number of cases addressing this activity provide some definition to it. In *EEOC v. Sara Lee Corp.*[156] the EEOC sued for violation of the ADA on behalf of an employee with a seizure disorder. The defendant shut down a factory and offered the employees the opportunity to transfer to another plant. The defendant had an internal seniority policy that was unrelated to a collective bargaining agreement. A worker from the closed plant with more seniority than the plaintiff wanted to work on the first shift, which would bump the plaintiff to the second or third shift. When the employee learned she would be displaced she informed the employer that transferring her to the other

---

[150]Humphrey v. Memorial Hosp. Ass'n, 239 F.3d 1128, 11 AD Cases 765 (9th Cir. 2001).

[151]Pack v. K-Mart Corp., 166 F.3d 1300, 1305, 8 AD Cases 1880, 1883 (10th Cir. 1999). *But see* Bergsrud v. Columbia-Lee Reg'l Med. Ctr., 2000 WL 33287447 (D.N.M. June 24, 2000) (distinction between thinking and concentrating not apparent).

[152]Lemire v. Silva,104 F. Supp. 2d 80, 87, 11 AD Cases 141, 147 (D. Mass. 2000).

[153]139 F.3d 595, 7 AD Cases 1716 (8th Cir. 1998).

[154]One court has held that caring for another is not a major life activity. Kravel v. Iowa Methodist Med. Ctr., 95 F.3d 674, 5 AD Cases 1503 (8th Cir. 1996).

[155]*EEOC Instructions for Field Offices*, *supra* note 49, at 1443.

[156]237 F.3d 349, 11 AD Cases 595 (4th Cir. 2001).

shifts would disturb her sleep pattern and exacerbate her seizure disorder. The company's doctor, however, found that a change in shift would not disrupt the employee's sleep patterns as long as she worked a nonrotating shift. The employer accordingly refused to allow the employee to circumvent the normal seniority policy and subsequently gave her three options, one of which was to take a severance package, which she did.

The EEOC sued, asserting that the employee was substantially limited in, among other things, caring for herself. In support of this contention the EEOC pointed out that the employee's husband assisted her during her seizures and sometimes after her seizures. The Fourth Circuit rejected this argument, citing other evidence indicating that the seizures were relatively infrequent and that the employee performed multiple tasks despite her seizures, such as caring for her son, driving a car, and performing her job effectively. Consequently, the plaintiff was found not substantially limited in caring for herself.[157]

Likewise, in *Ouzts v. USAir, Inc*,[158] the plaintiff alleged that her physical impairments substantially limited her ability to care for herself. The court rejected her assertion, noting that she was able to prepare meals for herself and her daughter, to go shopping and run errands, to drive, to exercise, to fix her hair, to houseclean, and to enjoy her boat on good weather weekends.[159] These cases, therefore, indicate that it may be difficult for a plaintiff to establish a substantial limitation in caring for herself if she has been able to perform basic daily activities.

Conversely, in *Bilodeau v. Mega Industries*,[160] the plaintiff claimed that her alcoholism substantially limited her in taking care of herself. She testified that during the months preceding her treatment she suffered from chronic diarrhea, did not eat properly, did not take care of her appearance, did not sleep well, and cried all the time. The court noted that the "[p]laintiff has presented evidence of symptoms resulting from her alcoholism that are more severe than an inability to get along with others, including difficulty sleeping, difficulty eating, difficulty concentrating and being severely emotional. The Court finds that a jury may conclude from this evidence that [p]laintiff is unable to carry on the normal activities of daily life as well as an average person."[161] The court ultimately concluded that the plaintiff had presented sufficient evidence that she was substantially limited in the ability to care for herself.[162]

Finally, in *Humphrey v. Memorial Hospital Association*,[163] a plaintiff with Obsessive-Compulsive Disorder argued that she was substantially limited in

---

[157] *Id.* at 353, 11 AD Cases at 597.

[158] 1996 WL 578514 (W.D. Pa. July 26, 1996).

[159] *Id.* at *14.

[160] 50 F. Supp. 2d 27, 9 AD Cases 850 (D. Me. 1999).

[161] *Id.* at 36, 9 AD Cases at 857.

[162] *See also* Ryan v. Grae & Rybicki P.C., 135 F.3d 867, 7 AD Cases 1387 (1st Cir. 1998) (finding that an impairment that caused periodic limitation on the ability to care for oneself was not a substantial limitation where the plaintiff was able to get dressed and groomed and go to work).

[163] 239 F.3d 1128, 11 AD Cases 765 (9th Cir. 2001).

the ability to care for herself. The plaintiff and her physician testified that it took the plaintiff significantly more time than the average person to bathe and get dressed. For example, the process of washing and doing her hair could take several hours. Her physician testified that the plaintiff took three times as long as most people to shower, wash her hands, fix her hair, or handle food. The Ninth Circuit found her substantially limited in the activity of caring for herself, remarking that "an individual who has a physical or mental impairment that causes him to take inordinately more time than others to complete a major life activity, is substantially limited as to that activity under the ADA."[164]

G. TRAVELING In *Reeves v. Johnson Controls World Services, Inc.*,[165] a plaintiff with agoraphobia and panic disorder argued that he was limited in the major life activity of "everyday mobility" because he was assertedly unable to travel over bridges or through tunnels.[166] The court, however, held that "everyday mobility" was not a major life activity as a matter of law and indicated that if mobility had been defined more broadly, such as the ability to leave his home or go to work, a different result would have applied. Similarly, in *Lemire v. Silva*,[167] a plaintiff with agoraphobia asserted that she was substantially limited in her ability to travel. The court held that the ability to travel is a major life activity if defined to include basic mobility such as leaving home.[168] The court then found the plaintiff not substantially limited in this activity because her physician's report stated her impairment interfered with her ability to travel far away from home and she testified that she could travel to buy groceries and other errands.[169]

H. WORKING The question of whether a person is substantially limited in working is considered only when the individual is not substantially limited in any other major life activity.[170] In *Sutton v. United Airlines*[171] the Supreme Court explained:

> When the major life activity under consideration is that of working the phrase "substantially limits" requires, at a minimum, that plaintiffs allege they are unable

---

[164]*Id.* at 1235, 11 AD Cases at 770.

[165]140 F.3d 144, 7 AD Cases 1675 (2d Cir. 1998).

[166]*Id.* at 152, 7 AD Cases at 1681. *See also* Sinkler v. Midwest Property Mgmt. Ltd., 209 F.3d 678, 11 AD Cases 677 (7th Cir. 2000) (court rejected plaintiff's claim that her phobia of driving in unfamiliar places substantially limited her in her ability to think and concentrate and "in basic personal mobility"). *Compare* Kralik v. Durbin, 130 F.3d 76, 7 AD Cases 1040 (3d Cir. 1997) (not disputing lower court's implication that traveling is a major life activity); Anderson v. General Manager Boston Star, 924 F. Supp. 763, 5 AD Cases 673 (E.D. Tex. 1996) (suggesting travel is major life activity).

[167]104 F. Supp. 2d 80, 11 AD Cases 141 (D. Mass. 2000).

[168]*Id.* at 87, 11 AD Cases at 147.

[169]*Id.* at 88, 11 AD Cases at 148.

[170]29 C.F.R. Pt. 1630 §1630.2(j) app. ("Working should be analyzed only if no other major life activity is substantially limited by an impairment.")

[171]527 U.S. 471, 9 AD Cases 673 (1999).

to work in a broad class of jobs. . . . To be substantially limited in the major life activity of working, then, one must be precluded from more than one type of job, a specialized job, or a particular job of choice. If jobs utilizing an individual's skills (but perhaps not his or her unique talents) are available, one is not precluded from a substantial class of jobs. Similarly, if a host of different types of jobs are available, one is not precluded from a broad range of jobs. [172]

Although in *Sutton* the Supreme Court questioned whether working was a major life activity,[173] the circuit courts have expressed no such reservations.[174] In *EEOC v. R.J. Gallagher*,[175] the court addressed this question. Relying on the Supreme Court's statement in *Bragdon v. Abbott* that "major" denotes the comparative importance and significance of the activity,[176] the Fifth Circuit concluded:

[F]or many, working is necessary for self-substance or to support an entire family. The choice of an occupation often provides the opportunity for self-expression and for contribution to productive society. Importantly, most jobs involve some degree of social interaction, both with co-workers and with the public at large, providing opportunities for collegial collaboration and friendship. For those of us who are able to work and choose to work, our jobs are an important element of how we define ourselves and how we are perceived by others. The inability to access the many opportunities afforded by working constitutes exclusion from many of the significant experiences of life. Without doubt, then, working is a major life activity.[177]

For an individual to be considered substantially limited in working, his or her impairment must disqualify him or her from a broad range of jobs or a class of jobs.[178] The relevant factors to consider in assessing such a limitation

---

[172]*Id.* at 491–92, 9 AD Cases at 682–83. *See also* 29 C.F.R. §1630.2(j)(3)(i) (inability to perform a particular job is not a substantial limitation; rather, the individual must be significantly restricted in the ability to perform an entire class of jobs or a wide range of jobs).

[173]*Id.* at 492–93, 9 AD Cases at 682.

[174]Mullins v. Crowell, 228 F.3d 1305, 11 AD Cases 38 (11th Cir. 2000); Dovoll v. Webb, 194 F.3d 1116, 9 AD Cases 1533 (10th Cir. 1999); Heyman v. Queens Village Comm. for Mental Health, 198 F.3d 68, 110 AD Cases 27 (2d Cir. 1999).

[175]181 F.3d 645, 9 AD Cases 917 (5th Cir. 1999).

[176]*Id.* at 654, 9 AD Cases at 923.

[177]*Id.* at 654–55, 9 AD Cases at 923.

[178]29 C.F.R. §1630.2(j)(3); Davis v. University of N.C., 263 F.3d 95, 12 AD Cases 243 (4th Cir. 2001) (student with dissassociative identity disorder at best "perceived as unable to perform a single job—teaching, or perhaps a very narrow range of jobs—those that require unsupervised contact with children"); Webb v. Choate Mental Health & Dev. Ctr., 230 F.3d 991, 11 AD Cases 97 (7th Cir. 2000) (psychologist with condition that precluded interaction with infectious or violent patients not precluded from class of jobs); Sandford v. Stearn, 2 AD Cases 491 (N.D. Ohio 1992) (plaintiff not substantially limited in working simply because he could not participate in self-defense course); Mackie v. Runyon, 804 F. Supp. 1508, 2 AD Cases 260 (M.D. Fla. 1992) (plaintiff's inability to work night shifts because of Bipolar Disorder not substantially limiting).

include (1) the geographical area to which the individual has access, (2) the jobs from which the individual has been disqualified because of the impairment, (3) the number and types of jobs utilizing similar training and skills, and (4) the jobs from which the individual has been disqualified and the number and types of jobs not using similar skills and training. The question is what kind of evidence a plaintiff needs to survive summary judgment.

The courts are split on the issue of whether plaintiffs must provide evidence of jobs they can perform versus jobs they cannot perform. The Eighth Circuit appears to consider the jobs the individual cannot perform.[179] In contrast, the Sixth and Seventh Circuits consider whether the individual is generally excluded from any form of employment by looking at whether there are a number of jobs the individual can perform.[180]

Most plaintiffs with mental disabilities who have claimed to be substantially limited in working have not survived summary judgment.[181] However, in

---

[179]Webb v. Garelick Mfg. Co., 94 F.3d 484, 6 AD Cases 127 (8th Cir. 1996) (court would not analyze whether plaintiff could perform other jobs in the labor pool, looking instead at the class of jobs he could not perform, considering his "expertise, background and job expectations").

[180]McKay v. Toyota Motor Mfg. USA, 110 F.3d 369, 6 AD Cases 933 (6th Cir. 1997); Skorup v. Modern Door Corp., 153 F.3d 512, 8 AD Cases 808 (7th Cir. 1998).

[181]See, e.g., Patterson v. Chicago Ass'n for Retarded Citizens, 150 F.3d 719, 8 AD Cases 983 (7th Cir. 1998) (teacher with paranoia that prevented her from working with special needs children was not substantially limited in working because she could work in other teaching jobs); Champagne v. Servister Corp., 138 F.3d 7, 7 AD Cases 1685 (1st Cir. 1998); Hamilton v. Southwestern Bell Tel. Co., 136 F.3d 1047, 8 AD Cases 1219 (5th Cir. 1998) (manager with Posttraumatic Stress Disorder not substantially limited in working); Simeon v. AT&T Corp., 117 F.3d 1173 (10th Cir. 1997) (plaintiff with stress and depression not substantially limited in working); Weiler v. Household Fin. Corp., 101 F.3d 519, 6 AD Cases 106 (7th Cir. 1996); Lusk v. Christ Hosp. & Med. Ctr., 2000 WL 263975 (N.D. Ill. Mar. 6, 2000) (nurse with history of breast cancer and depression not substantially limited in working because she obtained employment after employer terminated her); Cook v. Cub Foods, Inc., 99 F. Supp. 2d 945, 83 FEP Cases 536 (N.D. Ill. 2000) (maintenance manager with history of depression not substantially limited in working because he did job with defendant while he had part-time job too); Hawkins v. Trustees of Ind. Univ., 83 F. Supp. 2d 987, 10 AD Cases 819 (S.D. Ind. 1999) (depressed electrician was not substantially limited in working; evidence showed he moved from custodial position to skilled position); Gazaway v. Makita USA, Inc., 11 F. Supp. 2d 1281 (S.D.N.Y. 1998) (plaintiff with PTSD who was able to return to his job and who got another job when let go not substantially limited in working; loss of "competitive edge" because of PTSD only disqualified him from particular job); Martin v. General Mills, Inc., 1996 WL 648721 (N.D. Ill. Nov. 5, 1996) (accountant's depression and anxiety did not substantially limit him in working); Muller v. Automobile Club of S. Cal., 897 F. Supp. 1289, 5 AD Cases 1997 (S.D. Cal. 1995) (employee with Posttraumatic Stress Disorder was not substantially limited in working); Hatfield v. Quantum Chem. Corp., 920 F. Supp. 108, 5 AD Cases 765 (S.D. Tex. 1996) (process technician's depression did not substantially limit him in working).

Criado v. International Business Machines Corp.,[182] the court concluded that the plaintiff's depression substantially limited her ability to work because it caused her difficulty in relating to coworkers, as well as sleep deprivation, which affected her ability to report to work on time. Similarly, in *Bilodeau v. Mega Industries*,[183] the court held that an alcoholic employee was substantially limited in working because when she suffered relapses, she was able to work only in unskilled labor jobs though she was trained as an electrician.[184]

In recent years, the courts have focused on certain limitations imposed by various impairments in determining whether a person is substantially limited in working.

(i) Inability to Tolerate Stress

The courts have almost uniformly rejected claims that a person is substantially limited in working because he cannot tolerate stress on the job.[185] For example, in *Silver v. Engelman Securities, Inc.*,[186] a floor trader argued that his disability was an emotional and mental ailment caused by increasing levels of, and decreasing tolerance for, stress. The court held that even assuming that the plaintiff's stress was a disabling condition, the most he could show was that it impaired his ability to perform his job. Likewise, in *Marschand v. Norfolk*

---

[182]145 F.3d 437, 8 AD Cases 336 (1st Cir. 1998).

[183]50 F. Supp. 2d 27, 9 AD Cases 850 (D. Me. 1999).

[184]*Id.* at 36–37, 9 AD Cases at 858. *See also* Lemire v. Silva, 104 F. Supp. 2d 80, 11 AD Cases 141 (D. Mass. 2000) (plaintiff who suffered panic attacks presented sufficient evidence that she was substantially limited in working by testifying that in the past she had to quit a job because she suffered panic attacks at work and that her fear of similar attacks precluded her from making other efforts at such employment).

[185]*See, e.g.,* Schneiker v. Fortis Ins. Co., 200 F.3d 1055, 10 AD Cases 75 (7th Cir. 2000) (plaintiff who argued stress triggered her depression was not substantially limited in working because there was no evidence that the inability to work in stressful situations precluded her from a class or broad range of jobs; plaintiff needed to provide evidence of the job requirements that were problematic); Colwell v. Suffolk County Police Dep't, 158 F.3d 635, 8 AD Cases 1232 (2d Cir. 1998) (plaintiffs not substantially limited in working merely because they had medical restrictions limiting them to jobs without confrontation or stress); Gaul v. AT & T, Inc., 955 F. Supp. 346, 6 AD Cases 705 (D.N.J. 1997) (employee with stress disorder and major depression not substantially limited in working because of his inability to work in stressful position), *aff'd sub nom.* Gaul v. Lucent Tech. Inc., 134 F.3d 576, 7 AD Cases 1223 (3d Cir. 1998); Mundo v. Sanus, 966 F. Supp. 171, 8 AD Cases 937 (E.D.N.Y. 1997) (plaintiff not perceived as disabled simply because employer perceived her as unable to tolerate the stress of her job); Sherman v. New York Life Ins. Co., 1997 WL 452024 (S.D.N.Y. Aug. 7, 1997) (employee with Obsessive-Compulsive Disorder did not have disability because he alleged only that he was unable to tolerate the stress of his job); Stauffer v. Bayer Corp., 1997 WL 588890 (N.D. Ind. July 21, 1997) (stress-inducing and stressful jobs do not constitute a class of jobs or broad range of jobs under the ADA); Martin v. General Mills, Inc., 1996 WL 648721 (N.D. Ill. Nov. 5, 1996) (the ADA does not protect employees from the general stress of the workplace and the inability to work for certain people because they cause an employee depression and anxiety).

[186]1995 WL 413456 (N.D. Ill. July 11, 1995).

& Western Ry. Co.,[187] a railroad engineer was diagnosed with Posttraumatic Stress Disorder after being involved in an accident that killed an entire family. He offered evidence that his condition prevented him from working in any position that required him to be responsible for the safety of others. The court held that his ability to work was not substantially limited because there were jobs he could perform that did not have such a requirement.

In contrast, in *Presta v. Southeastern Pennsylvania Transportation Authority*,[188] the court held that there was a genuine issue whether the plaintiff, who had adjustment and anxiety disorders with PTSD symptoms, was substantially limited in working because his physician testified that although the only job that the plaintiff could not perform at the defendant's company was the job he held, he would also be unable to do jobs with similar stressful conditions, such as those requiring him to handle several tasks at the same time, those that significantly affected the safety of others, and those that involved working in a room where he continuously used communication equipment.

(ii) Personality Conflicts with Supervisors

Courts consistently have held that mental impairments triggered or exacerbated by personality conflicts with supervisors or coworkers do not substantially limit an individual in the activity of working.[189] In *Weiler v. Household Finance Corp.*,[190] the plaintiff alleged that her depression and anxiety were triggered by stress caused by her supervisor. The district court granted summary judgment for the employer and the Seventh Circuit affirmed. It declared, "[T]he ADA

---

[187] 876 F. Supp. 1528, 4 AD Cases 1099 (N.D. Ind. 1995).

[188] 1998 WL 310735 (E.D. Pa. 1998).

[189] *Schneiker*, 200 F.3d 1055, 10 AD Cases 75 (plaintiff with stress-induced depression not substantially limited in working because it affected only her interactions with supervisor); *Gaul*, 134 F.3d 576, 7 AD Cases 1223 (employee's depression and anxiety did not substantially limit him in working); Siemon v. AT & T Corp., 113 F.3d 1173, 6 AD Cases 1249 (10th Cir. 1997) (plaintiff who suffered intermittent episodes of depression not substantially limited in working simply because he could not work under his supervisor or anyone in supervisor's chain of command); Dunegan v. City of Council Grove, 77 F. Supp. 2d 1192 (D. Kan. 1999) (plaintiff with PTSD not substantially limited in working when she was unable to work only for a particular supervisor because of the stress and anxiety associated with that supervisor); Cook v. Cub Foods, Inc., 99 F. Supp. 2d 945, 83 FEP Cases 536 (N.D. Ill. 2000) (plaintiff with depression not limited in working because he had difficulty working with supervisor); Osika v. Board of Educ. for Bremen Cmty. High Schs., 1999 WL 1044838 (N.D. Ill. Nov. 16, 1999) (clinically depressed teacher's inability to work at a certain school because of "bad vibes" between herself and school administrators did not make her substantially limited in working); Stauffer v. Bayer Corp., 1997 WL 588890 (N.D. Ind. July 21, 1997) (the inability to work a job with one supervisor is not substantially limiting in working); Langford v. County of Cook, 965 F. Supp. 1091 (N.D. Ill. 1997) (inability to work with particular supervisor due to stress and anxiety is not substantially limiting); Hatfield v. Quantum Chem. Corp., 920 F. Supp. 108, 5 AD Cases 765 (S.D. Tex. 1996) (inability to work with particular supervisor due to stress and anxiety is not substantially limiting in working).

[190] 101 F.3d 519, 6 AD Cases 106 (7th Cir. 1996).

does not protect people from the general stresses of the workplace. . . . Being unwilling or even unable to work with a particular individual simply is not the equivalent of being substantially limited in working."[191] In another case, *Palmer v. Circuit Court of Cook County*,[192] the Seventh Circuit reached a similar result, noting that "a personality conflict with a supervisor or coworker does not establish a disability within the meaning of the disability law, even if it produces anxiety and depression, as such conflicts often do."[193]

(iii) Shift Work and Overtime

Individuals with mental disabilities may also claim they are substantially limited in working because they cannot work a night or a rotating shift or work overtime. For example, In *Mackie v. Runyon*,[194] the court held that the inability of a plaintiff with Bipolar Disorder to work a night shift did not substantially limit him in working.

Likewise, most courts have been unreceptive to claims that an inability to work overtime substantially limits the ability of an employee to work.[195] At least one court, however, has taken the opposite position.[196]

---

[191]*Id.* at 524, 6 AD Cases at 109.
[192]117 F.3d 351, 6, AD Cases 1569 (7th Cir. 1997).
[193]*Id.* at 352, 6 AD Cases at 1570.
[194]804 F. Supp. 1508, 2 AD Cases 260 (M.D. Fla. 1992).
[195]Taylor v. Nimock's Oil Co., 214 F.3d 957, 10 AD Cases 1069 (8th Cir. 2000) (although overtime may be required for many jobs, inability to work overtime not a substantial limitation); Berg v. Norand Corp., 169 F.3d 1140, 9 AD Cases 207 (8th Cir. 1999) (diabetic employee not substantially limited by inability to work 40–50-hour workweek); Doren v. Battle Creek Health Sys., 187 F.3d 595, 9 AD Cases 1115 (6th Cir. 1999) (nurse not substantially limited because she could not work 12-hour shift); Tardie v. Rehabilitation Hosp. of R.I., 168 F.3d 538, 9 AD Cases 155 (1st Cir. 1999) (plaintiff not substantially limited because there were "various" opportunities to work jobs that required only 40-hour weeks); Kellogg v. Union Pac. R.R. Co., 2000 WL 766281 (D. Neb. Jan. 28, 2000) (senior manager with history of anxiety and depression not disabled by inability to work more than 40 hours per week); Muthler v. Ann Arbor Mach. Inc., 18 F. Supp. 2d 722, 9 AD Cases 365 (E.D. Mich. 1998) (heart impairment that limited plaintiff to 40-hour week did not substantially limit plaintiff in working); Kolpas v. G.D. Searle & Co., 959 F. Supp. 525, 8 AD Cases 1285 (N.D. Ill. 1997) (accounting supervisor with a heart condition who was required to work 60–70-hour weeks and who could work only 40 hours a week was not substantially limited in working); Overton v. Tar Heel Farm Credit, 942 F. Supp. 1066, 9 AD Cases 547 (E.D.N.C. 1996) (obsessive-compulsive employee's inability to work more than a 40-hour week was not a substantial limitation on his ability to work): Brennan v. National Tel. Directory Corp., 850 F. Supp. 331, 4 AD Cases 76 (E.D. Pa. 1994) (inability to work overtime does not render plaintiff disabled).
[196]Fjellestad v. Pizza Hut of Am., Inc., 188 F.3d 944, 9 AD Cases 1153 (8th Cir. 1999) (plaintiff who was limited to 35–40 hours per week and to working no more than three consecutive days presented sufficient evidence that he was substantially limited in working).

B. Conditions Excluded From Coverage

As a matter of public policy, the ADA specifically excludes from its coverage a number of conditions that may both constitute diagnosable mental disorders and substantially limit one or more life activities. Conditions that are expressly not covered include transvestism,[197] homosexuality and bisexuality,[198] transsexualism,[199] pedophilia, exhibitionism, voyeurism, gender identity disorders not resulting from physical impairments or other sexual behavior disorders,[200] compulsive gambling, kleptomania, and pyromania.[201]

Moreover, sexual harassers are not entitled to the protection of the ADA. In *Blanton v. AT&T Communications*,[202] the court rejected the claim that an individual terminated for sexually harassing female employees was handicapped because his conduct "constituted an aberration from his normal behavior." Similarly, in *Winston v. Maine Technical College*,[203] the Maine Supreme Judicial Court held that a teacher discharged for kissing a student was not handicapped under the Rehabilitation Act even though he was diagnosed by two mental health professionals as suffering from "sexual impulse control disorder."

C. Record of Disability

An individual who has a record of a disability or who has been misclassified as having a mental or physical impairment that substantially limits a major life activity is also protected under the ADA.[204] If a condition was not an impairment

---

[197] 42 U.S.C. §12208.

[198] *Id.* §12211(a).

[199] This condition and gender identity disorder may be covered under state antidiscrimination laws, whether under sex, gender, or disability. *See, e.g.,* Enriquez v. West Jersey Health, 11 AD Cases 1810 (N.J. Super. Ct. 2001) (transsexualism may be handicap under state law); Goins v. West Group, 619 N.W. 424, 426 (Minn. Ct. App. 2000) (individual born male who changed legal name to female name and took female hormones protected under MINN. STAT. §363.01 subd. 45 even though he did not have sex change); Rentos v. OCE Office Sys., 72 FEP Cases 1717 (S.D.N.Y. 1996) (New York State and New York City law protects transsexuals); Doe v. Boeing Co., 846 P.2d 531, 2 AD Cases 548 (Wash. 1996) (transsexual not protected but only because he was not discriminated against on that basis). *But see* Doe v. Yuntis, 2000 WL 33162199 (Mass. Super. Ct. Oct. 11, 2000) (student with gender identity disorder not likely to succeed on disability discrimination claim); Holt v. Northeast Pa. Training P'ship Consortium, Inc., 694 A.2d 1134 (Pa. Commw. Ct. 1997) (transsexualism not a disability under state law because plaintiff did not contend it substantially limited any major life activity); Sommers v. Iowa Civil Rights Comm'n, 337 N.W.2d 470 (Iowa 1993).

[200] 42 U.S.C. §12211(b)(1).

[201] *Id.* §12211(b)(2).

[202] 1 AD Cases 1552 (D. Mass. 1990).

[203] 631 A.2d 70, 2 AD Cases 1228 (Me. 1993).

[204] 29 C.F.R. §1630.2(k).

or was not substantially limiting, it is not protected under the "record of" prong, however.[205] The question is what creates the record of such an impairment. This question is particularly important given that an individual may be classified as disabled under other laws. Generally, it is easier to determine what does *not* constitute a record of impairment. Certainly, one brief hospital stay does not create a record of impairment under the ADA.[206] As with a current disability that substantially limits a major life activity, the employer must have known that the employee had a record of a disability in order to have acted on it.[207]

The record or misdiagnosis/misclassification must be related to an impairment that substantially limited a major life activity.[208] For example, in *Olson v. General Electric Astrospace*,[209] a rejected applicant who had been hospitalized for depression and who was diagnosed with Multiple Personality Disorder and Posttraumatic Stress Disorder failed to demonstrate that he had a record of disability. The plaintiff's evidence of his diagnosis and evidence that he had been tested for sleeping disorders did not establish that he was substantially limited while his impairment was active.[210]

---

[205]*EEOC Definition of the Term "Disability,"* supra note 35, at 7276.

[206]Gutridge v. Clure, 153 F.3d 898, 8 AD Cases 705 (8th Cir. 1998) (hospital stay does not necessarily mean plaintiff has record of disability); Burch v. Coca-Cola Co., 119 F.3d 305, 7 AD Cases 241 (5th Cir. 1997) (absent a history of substantial limitation of a major life activity, hospitalization is insufficient to establish a record of disability); Byrne v. Board of Educ., 979 F.2d 560, 2 AD Cases 284 (7th Cir. 1992) (single hospital stay for allergy tests not evidence of record of disability); Colwell v. Suffolk County Police Dep't, 158 F.3d 635, 8 AD Cases 1232 (2d Cir. 1998) (plaintiff must show more than mere hospitalization). *But see* School Bd. of Nassau County v. Arline, 480 U.S. 273, 1 AD Cases 1026 (1987) (plaintiff's extended hospital stay for tuberculosis established record of a disability); EEOC v. Gallagher Co., 181 F.3d 645, 9 AD Cases 917 (5th Cir. 1999) (plaintiff may have record of disability considering effect of cancer on vision, 30-day hospitalization for treatment, which prevented plaintiff from caring for himself, and isolation from others because of weak immune system, which affected his ability to work); Wheaton v. Ogden Newspapers, Inc., 9 AD Cases 1456 (N.D. Iowa 1999) (hospitalization for 10 days, plus 15 years of reasonable accommodations at work and a note from physician indicating condition is permanent constitutes record of disability).

[207]Grinstead v. Pool Co. of Texas, 3 AD Cases 9 (E.D. La. 1994), *aff'd*, 26 F.3d 1118, 4 AD Cases 160 (5th Cir. 1994).

[208]29 C.F.R. §1630.2(l) app.

[209]101 F.3d 947, 6 AD Cases 270 (3d Cir. 1996).

[210]*Accord* Pryor v. Trane Co., 138 F.3d 1024, 8 AD Cases 271 (5th Cir. 1998) (employee with back impairment that restricted her ability to lift, pull, and push and perform repetitive lifting did not have a record of a disability because restrictions limiting an ability to perform a particular job did not establish a substantial limitation on working); Mastio v. Wausau Serv. Corp., 948 F. Supp. 1396 (E.D. Mo. 1996) (plaintiff suffering from PTSD from sexual harassment did not present evidence of record of disability; plaintiff's evidence consisted of two leaves of absence and an e-mail to her supervisor telling him the problems she was experiencing and that she had been diagnosed with clinical depression).

In *Davidson v. Midelfort Clinic, Ltd.*,[211] a psychotherapist with a learning disability claimed that she was terminated because of her record of a disability. The court allowed her claim to proceed because she presented evidence of how her learning disorder manifested itself and how she compensated for its limitations, thereby demonstrating that she had a history of being substantially limited in her ability to learn. Finally, in *Pritchard v. Southern Co.*,[212] a plaintiff who could not return to the nuclear plant where she worked because of Posttraumatic Stress Syndrome survived summary judgment because the defendant's actions were evidence that the plaintiff had a record of a disability.[213]

D. Being Regarded as Disabled

Under the ADA, an employer regards an employee as having an impairment when (1) the employer treats an impairment as substantially limiting when it is not, (2) the employer's attitude concerning an impairment creates a substantial limitation, or (3) the employer treats an employee as having an impairment when the employee does not.[214] Generally, the key evidence that enables a plaintiff to survive summary judgment is testimony concerning statements the employer made or the employer's beliefs, feelings, or actions taken in response to information concerning the impairment.[215]

---

[211] 133 F.3d 499, 8 AD Cases 77 (7th Cir. 1998).

[212] 92 F.3d 1130, 5 AD Cases 1480 (11th Cir. 1996).

[213] *Id.* at 1134, 5 AD Cases at 1483.

[214] 29 C.F.R. §1630.2(l)(1) app. ("regarded as" is not limited to major life activity of working). *But see* Taylor v. Dover Elevator Sys., 917 F. Supp. 455, 5 AD Cases 616 (N.D. Miss. 1996) (under the ADA, "regarded as" means that the employer regards the employee as substantially limited in working).

[215] *See, e.g.*, McInnis v. Alamo Cmty. College, 207 F.3d 276, 10 AD Cases 597 (5th Cir. 2000) (summary judgment denied where defendant's ADA coordinator said she could tell from plaintiff's file he might be disabled and letter stated transfer was "accommodation for handicap"); Riemer v. Illinois Dep't of Transp., 148 F.3d 800, 807, 8 AD Cases 440, 445 (7th Cir. 1998) (employer's misperception about the effects of plaintiff's asthma led it to exclude plaintiff from class of jobs); Sanders v. City of Chicago, 2000 WL 198901 (N.D. Ill. Feb. 15, 2000) (court denied defendant's motion to dismiss plaintiff's ADA claim even though plaintiff's alleged impairment, "emotional stress syndrome," had not been recognized as a disability in any case, because plaintiff alleged "perceived as" claim based on employer's reassignment of plaintiff to another position because of impairment); Haiman v. Village of Fox Lake, 79 F. Supp. 2d 949, 10 AD Cases 57 (N.D. Ill. 2000) (supervisor's comment that "she did not want anybody dropping dead in my office and me paying for it" and that plaintiff was causing everybody's insurance rates to increase created a genuine issue of fact on issue of "regarded as" disabled); Dipol v. New York Transit Auth., 999 F. Supp. 309 (S.D.N.Y. 1999) (evidence that defendant regarded plaintiff as disabled because after defendant received information from plaintiff's physician defendant immediately placed plaintiff on no-work status); Bicknell v. Thomas Tile & Carpet, Inc., 45 F. Supp. 2d 538, 9 AD Cases 481 (S.D. W.Va. 1999) (employer who believed plaintiff could not lift more than seven pounds for an indefinite duration perceived plaintiff was disabled);

For example, in *Olson v. General Electric Astrospace*,[216] the plaintiff survived summary judgment because a supervisor who knew that he had previously been hospitalized for depression interviewed him and asked him a number of questions about his depression. Additionally, the supervisor had previously prepared a written evaluation of the plaintiff that made several references to the plaintiff's depression-related absences, which caused the supervisor to question his commitment to the job. Similarly, in *McKenzie v. Davala*,[217] a deputy sheriff who suffered from PTSD, Adjustment Disorder, Borderline Personality Disorder, and Major Depressive Disorder resigned to seek medical treatment after she had begun to miss work, fired her gun into her father's grave, and took drug overdoses. After approximately one month of treatment, her physician released her to return to work. She thereafter reapplied at the sheriff's department but was rejected. She eventually was rejected at every agency where she applied. A year later, she asked the sheriff's department to consider her for any job in the department. The sheriff told the plaintiff he was unwilling to consider her application because of liability concerns and fear of public uneasiness concerning her past problems. He further admitted he had passed over her application and had not ordered a psychological exam as provided by state law to determine her fitness. Moreover, the sheriff had asked the state to revoke plaintiff's certification as a peace officer soon after she resigned because he believed she should no longer be a law officer.

The plaintiff sued, arguing that the defendant treated her as if she had a substantially limiting impairment when she did not. The Tenth Circuit reversed the district court's grant of summary judgment for the sheriff, noting that although the sheriff said he was worried about liability, he never ordered a psychiatric exam pursuant to state law. The rejection of the plaintiff's application without doing so was evidence that his concerns were based on myths, fears, and stereotypes rather than an individualized inquiry concerning plaintiff's qualifications. Moreover, according to the court, the sheriff's refusal to consider the plaintiff for less sensitive posts in the department suggested that he regarded the plaintiff as substantially limited in a class of jobs, as did his request to have plaintiff decertified.

Similarly, in *Stradlay v. LaFourche Communications, Inc.*,[218] a plaintiff diagnosed with Adjustment Disorder with Mixed Emotional Features survived summary judgment because the supervisor who terminated his employment

---

Coleman v. Keeble Co., 997 F. Supp. 1102 (N.D. Ill. 1998) (employer's belief that plaintiff was unable to do any production jobs in plant created issue of fact as regarded claim); Weissman v. Dawn Joy Fashions, Inc., 7 AD Cases 365 (S.D.N.Y. 1997) (court denied summary judgment because the defendant's office manager had prepared an application for disability benefits for plaintiff who had heart attack, there was a notation in the employee's personnel file that he "was not able to hold a job," and the supervisor believed the employee was bedridden at the time of the termination and had commented that the employee might be out a long time).

[216] 101 F.3d 947, 6 AD Cases 270 (3d Cir. 1996).
[217] 242 F.3d 967, 11 AD Cases 936 (10th Cir. 2001).
[218] 869 F. Supp. 442, 3 AD Cases 1507 (E.D. La. 1994).

testified that it was his understanding that the plaintiff suffered from acute anxiety and depression, which made him potentially violent and hostile in the workplace. In *Cline v. WalMart Stores, Inc.*,[219] the plaintiff was a maintenance supervisor who took medical leave to have surgery on a brain tumor; when he returned, the defendant demoted him to a nonsupervisory position. A short time later, the plaintiff was terminated for allegedly stealing time. He claimed that the defendant perceived him as disabled, offering evidence that his supervisors had told his wife he could work only a couple of days a week and could not take the stress of being a supervisor, and that his job had been given to someone else in case he did not have the mental capacity to do it after surgery. The court held that the defendant regarded the plaintiff as substantially limited in working.

With respect to a plaintiff's allegation that the employer regarded him as substantially limited in the major life activity of working, the employer must believe that the impairment generally forecloses the type of employment involved, not just a narrow range of job tasks.[220] The mere fact that an employer considers an employee unable to perform a particular job does not establish that the employer regarded the employee as substantially limited in working.[221] Similarly, the employer's belief that an employee is not qualified to serve in a supervisory capacity does not establish that the employer perceived him or her as substantially limited in working.[222]

---

[219]144 F.3d 294, 8 AD Cases 154 (4th Cir. 1998).

[220]Gordon v. E.L. Hamm & Assocs., Inc., 100 F.3d 907, 6 AD Cases 282 (11th Cir. 1996). *See also* Sutton v. Lader, 185 F.3d 1203, 9 AD Cases 1182 (11th Cir. 1999) (employer who believes employee has temporary inability to do job does not perceive employee as disabled).

[221]Sutton v. United Airlines, 527 U.S. 471, 473, 9 AD Cases 673, 677 (1999); Witter v. Delta Air Lines, Inc., 138 F.3d 1366, 8 AD Cases 747 (11th Cir. 1998) (airline did not violate ADA by permanently grounding pilot with Bipolar Disorder because piloting was too narrow a range of jobs for airline to have regarded him as substantially limited in working); Miller v. City of Springfield, 146 F. 3d 612, 8 AD Cases 321 (8th Cir. 1998) (plaintiff denied employment as police officer because she scored above average for depression was not perceived as substantially limited in working because overall employment opportunity not limited); Bicknell v. Thomas Tile & Carpet, Inc., 45 F. Supp. 2d 538, 9 AD Cases 481 (S.D. W.Va. 1999) (employer who believed plaintiff could not lift more than seven pounds for an indefinite duration perceived plaintiff as disabled); Hanna v. Santa Rosa Mem'l Hosp., 1997 WL 446231 (N.D. Cal. July 29, 1997) (hospital that revoked job offer after an examination revealed nurse was at high risk for lumbar injuries and recommended that she not lift patients did not perceive her as substantially limited in working); Marschand v. Norfolk & Western Ry. Co., 876 F. Supp. 1528, 4 AD Cases 1099 (N.D. Ind. 1995), *aff'd on other grounds*, 81 F.3d 714, 5 AD Cases 1184 (7th Cir. 1996) (defendant did not regard train engineer with PTSD caused by a fatal train accident as substantially limited in working because the defendant perceived only that the plaintiff's impairment prevented him from working in train or engine service).

[222]Mundo v. Sanus Health Plan of Greater N.Y., 966 F. Supp. 171, 8 AD Cases 937 (E.D.N.Y. 1997). *But see* Cline v. Wal-Mart, Inc., 144 F.3d 294, 8 AD Cases 154 (4th Cir. 1998) (supervisory jobs are a class of jobs).

Set forth below are various scenarios claimed by employees to indicate that their employers regarded them as disabled.

1. Referrals to Counseling or to an Employee Assistance Program

Generally, an employer's referral of an employee to, or the suggestion an employee utilize, an employee assistance program (EAP) does not establish that the employer perceived the employee to be substantially limited in a major life activity.[223] However, a referral to an EAP, standing alone, may result in a denial of summary judgment to the employer. In *Holihan v. Lucky Stores, Inc.*,[224] a store manager who was suffering from depression, anxiety, and stress survived summary judgment by proffering evidence that the employer had received doctors' reports showing his diagnosis and that during meetings with supervisors to discuss his aberrant behavior, which included throwing food on the floor and ordering employees to clean it up and repeatedly threatening to fire his entire staff, his supervisors asked if he was having any problems and strongly encouraged him to seek counseling through the company's EAP.

Likewise, in *Miners v. Cargill Communications, Inc.*,[225] an employer who was concerned that an employee was violating the company's alcohol policy gave the employee the option of either being terminated or enrolling in a chemical dependency program with no loss of pay or rank. The employee

---

[223]Krocka v. City of Chicago, 203 F.3d 507, 10 AD Cases 289 (7th Cir. 2000) (neither referring police officer to EAP nor placement in Personal Concerns Program was evidence that defendant perceived plaintiff as disabled when plaintiff was allowed to continue working as police officer without restriction); Burch v. Coca-Cola, 119 F.3d 305, 7 AD Cases 241 (5th Cir. 1997) (referral to EAP of alcoholic employee who engaged in misconduct was way to assist employee to continue working, not regarding the employee as unable to work); Webb v. Mercy Hosp., 102 F.3d 958, 6 AD Cases 333 (8th Cir. 1996) (defendant who ordered plaintiff to participate in EAP program or be fired because the plaintiff was difficult and insubordinate did not perceive plaintiff as disabled); Chamberlain v. McNeil Consumer Prods. Co., 1998 WL 42271 (N.D. Ill. Jan. 29, 1998) (plaintiff's supervisor's encouragement to utilize the EAP and a statement that her impairment might be affecting her performance did not evidence that employer perceived plaintiff as disabled); Lippman v. Sholom Home, Inc., 945 F. Supp. 188, 6 AD Cases 1389 (D. Minn. 1996) (court rejected plaintiff's argument that the defendant's letter, which suggested that employee "take advantage of assessment services . . . and see if there are any medical or psychological concerns that affect your ability to do your work," showed either that the defendant knew about plaintiff's alleged disability or that the defendant perceived plaintiff as disabled). *But see* Pouncy v. Vulcan Materials Co., 920 F. Supp. 1566, 7 AD Cases 1621 (N.D. Ala. 1996) (court assumed defendant perceived plaintiff as disabled because employer had encouraged plaintiff to get long-term counseling and inquired whether plaintiff had done so); Fenton v. Pritchard Corp., 926 F. Supp. 1437, 7 AD Cases 1109 (D. Kan. 1996) (employer's perception that plaintiff was a violent person in absence of evidence that defendant encouraged plaintiff to seek counseling not perception that plaintiff was mentally disabled).

[224]87 F.3d 362, 5 AD Cases 1068 (9th Cir. 1996).

[225]113 F.3d 820, 6 AD Cases 1229 (5th Cir. 1997).

refused to enter treatment and was fired. The Eighth Circuit held that the order to attend the substance abuse program was evidence that the employer perceived the employee as an alcoholic.[226]

Conversely, in *Fenton v. Pritchard Corp.*,[227] the employer failed to refer a plaintiff employee to counseling who had a history of violent and obsessive behavior. Instead, the employer terminated his employment for misconduct. The court concluded that although the employer perceived the plaintiff as having violent inclinations, absent evidence that the employer encouraged the plaintiff to seek counseling or considered him mentally impaired, there was no evidence that it perceived him as disabled. The court also held that coworkers' opinions that the plaintiff was unstable or would "go postal" could not be imputed to the employer.

2. Expression of Concern

The mere expression of concern about an employee's emotional state does not establish that the employer regards the employee as disabled. In *Johnson v. Boardman Petroleum, Inc.*,[228] the defendant terminated the plaintiff because of ongoing major cash shortages at the store she supervised. The plaintiff argued that the defendant perceived her as disabled because her manager told her to seek professional help after her husband died, required a release before allowing her to return to work, and told her that he believed she was physically and mentally incapable of continuing her job as a district supervisor. The court held that the manager's suggestions to seek help merely showed his concern for her emotional state, observing, "This suit flies in the face of policy concerns underlying the ADA because it encourages employers to dehumanize their relationships with their employees for fear that showing concern for and recognizing their employees' emotional problems would land them in court facing a claim based on a perceived disability."[229]

3. Perception of Personality Traits

As indicated previously, personality traits are not considered impairments under the ADA.[230] Thus, an employer's perception that an employee has certain undesirable personality traits has not been equated to the perception of a

---

[226]This case is interesting in that it presumably falls under the prong of perceiving the employee to have an impairment when the employee does not. In contrast, in *Cody v. Cigna Healthcare of St. Louis, Inc.*, 139 F.3d 595, 7 AD Cases 1716 (8th Cir. 1998), the Eighth Circuit held that an employer that asked a nurse who was suffering from depression and behaving erratically to take medical leave and to see a psychologist before returning to work did not regard the employee as disabled because employers have the right to discover the origin of the inappropriate employee behavior.
[227]926 F. Supp. 1437, 7 AD Cases 1109 (D. Kan. 1996).
[228]923 F. Supp. 1563, 5 AD Cases 983 (S.D. Ga. 1996).
[229]*Id.* at 1568, 5 AD Cases at 986.
[230]29 C.F.R. §1630.2(h) app.

disability.[231] For example, in *Stewart v. County of Brown*,[232] the court held that the defendant's opinion that a suspended deputy sheriff was excitable, psychologically unbalanced, and temperamentally unfit for the position and the defendant's instructions for the employee to undergo psychological evaluations did not demonstrate that the defendant perceived the plaintiff as having a mental impairment that substantially limited a major life activity but only as having a personality problem. Likewise, in *Greenberg v. New York State*,[233] an applicant was not hired after he failed a psychological examination that indicated he had poor judgment in certain situations. The court concluded that poor judgment is a personality trait and not protected by the ADA. In contrast, in *Does v. District of Columbia*,[234] the court denied the defendant summary judgment because it had administered the Minnesota Multiphasic Personality Inventory, sentence completion test, figure drawing test, and clinical interviews to the plaintiffs, which resulted in the defendant's deeming the plaintiffs "psychiatrically disqualified" from employment. These cases suggest that an employer may make employment decisions based on general personality traits without violating the ADA, but that attempts to determine whether such traits might constitute a diagnosable mental disorder are unlawful.

4. Knowledge of Symptoms

An employer's knowledge that an employee exhibits symptoms that may be associated with a particular impairment or that an employee has a particular impairment does not necessarily establish that the employer regarded the employee as disabled.[235] Also, an employer's perception that an employee cannot

---

[231]Duncan v. State of Wisconsin Dep't of Health & Family Servs., 166 F.3d 930, 8 AD Cases 1800 (7th Cir. 1999) (court upheld employer's refusal to allow a youth counselor to return to work until he completed a recommended treatment for anger management and alcohol use after a psychiatrist concluded that he was prone to episodic temper outbursts, which seriously restricted his ability to be a youth counselor); Webb v. Mercy Hosp., 102 F.3d 958, 6 AD Cases 333 (8th Cir. 1996) (plaintiff perceived as difficult and insubordinate does not establish that employer perceived her as disabled); Daley v. Koch, 892 F.2d 212, 1 AD Cases 1549 (2d Cir. 1989) (employer's belief that plaintiff had poor judgment and impulse control did not show employer perceived him as disabled).

[232]86 F.3d 107, 5 AD Cases 1018 (7th Cir. 1996).

[233]919 F. Supp. 637, 5 AD Cases 1851 (E.D.N.Y. 1996).

[234]10 NDLR ¶14 (D.D.C. 1997).

[235]Cody v. Cigna Healthcare of St. Louis, 139 F.3d 595, 599, 7 AD Cases 1716, 1719 (8th Cir. 1998) ("mere knowledge of behavior that could be associated with an impairment" does show that the employer perceived the employee as disabled); Olson v. Dubuque Cmty. Sch. Dist., 137 F.3d 609, 7 AD Cases 1598 (8th Cir. 1998) (defendant's awareness of plaintiff's depression and that she had sought medical treatment for it did not support "perceived as" claim); Roberts v. Unidynamics Corp., 126 F.3d 1088, 7 AD Cases 1867 (8th Cir. 1997) (supervisor's knowledge of employee's deteriorating physical condition along with coworker's jokes that plaintiff looked like he had AIDS insufficient to create an issue of fact on "perceived as" issue); Kelly v. Drexel Univ.,

tolerate the stress of the job does not demonstrate that the employee was perceived as having a mental impairment that is substantially limiting.[236]

5. Offer of Accommodation

An employer's willingness to offer an accommodation to an employee or to provide an accommodation does not establish that the employer perceives the employee as disabled.[237] In *Colwell v. Suffolk County Police Department*,[238] the Second Circuit rejected the plaintiff's reliance on the defendant's open-ended light-duty policy to establish a record of disability. It explained:

> An employer that accedes to minor and potentially debatable accommodations (a feasible way to avoid litigation, liability, and confrontation) does not thereby stipulate to the employer's record of a chronic and endless disability. Otherwise, costless accommodations to physical complaints ... would entail large future costs, would discourage the employment of persons with minor limitations and

---

94 F.3d 102, 5 AD Cases 1353 (3d Cir. 1996) (mere knowledge of impairment is insufficient to demonstrate that employer regarded plaintiff as disabled); Hamm v. Runyon, 51 F.3d 721, 4 AD Cases 357 (7th Cir. 1995) (employer's knowledge that an employee exhibits symptoms that may be associated with an impairment does not necessarily establish a "perceived as" claim). *But see* McInnis v. Alamo Cmty. Coll. Dist., 207 F.3d 276, 10 AD Cases 597 (5th Cir. 2000) (summary judgment denied to employer given testimony of ADA compliance coordinator that she could discern from plaintiff's file that he was disabled or was perceived as disabled); Olson v. General Elec. Astrospace, 101 F.3d 947, 6 AD Cases 270 (3d Cir. 1996) (summary judgment denied to employer who knew about plaintiff's hospitalizations for depression, referred to absences as related to illness in evaluations, and who spent a significant amount of time talking to plaintiff about illness and related absences); Testerman v. Chrysler Corp., 1997 WL 820934 (D. Del. Dec. 30, 1997) (defendant's knowledge of plaintiff's inpatient treatment and DUIs raised genuine issue of material fact on "perceived as" claim).

[236]Mundo v. Sanus, 966 F. Supp. 171, 8 AD Cases 937 (E.D.N.Y. 1997).

[237]Cody v. Cigna Healthcare of St. Louis, 139 F.3d 595, 7 AD Cases 1716 (8th Cir. 1998) (offer of medical leave did not show defendant perceived plaintiff as disabled); Huff v. UARCO, Inc., 122 F.3d 374, 74 FEP Cases 879 (7th Cir. 1997) (defendant did not regard employee with herniated disc as disabled merely because it provided him with an electric cart to travel around his workplace); Jones v. Men's Wearhouse, 1999 WL 134210 (N.D. Tex. Mar. 10, 1999) (plaintiff could not show defendant regarded him as having Attention Deficient Disorder because it reduced him from 40 to 32 hours per week to accommodate his college schedule); Kvintus v. R.L. Polk & Co., 3 F. Supp. 2d 788 (E.D. Mich. 1998) (court refused to infer perception of disability from defendant's offer to plaintiff of medical leave because "to hold otherwise would necessarily inhibit employers from any inquiry regarding the status of behavior of employee that the employer may deem inappropriate"); Nave v. Woolridge Const. of Pa., Inc., 8 AD Cases 1351 (E.D. Pa. 1997) (evidence that employer offered reduced work hours to an employee with a history of Hodgkins Disease and depression did not establish that he was perceived as disabled).

[238]158 F.3d 635, 8 AD Cases 1232 (2d Cir. 1998).

would promote litigation without assisting persons entitled to protection under the ADA.[239]

At least one court, however, has held that an employer's placing an employee on *mandatory* leave gives rise to an inference of disability.[240]

6. Safety Concerns

An employer does not perceive an employee as disabled simply because the employer believes the employee cannot safely perform a particular job.[241] In *Margeson v. Springfield Terminal Railway Co.*,[242] the plaintiff claimed that his employer perceived him as disabled, reassigning him from a train dispatcher position to a less stressful dispatcher position because the plaintiff's doctors' notes indicated he was suffering from work-related stress and because of his agitated behavior in his conversation with his supervisor. The court held that the defendant's conclusion that plaintiff was unsuited for a "critical, public safety sensitive, high pressure position" was not a perception that he was substantially limited in working. Rather, it was simply a decision that the plaintiff's "temperament and stress level would be better suited for a different job."[243]

7. Request for Medical Evaluation

Courts generally have held that an employer's request for a medical examination is not tantamount to regarding an employee as disabled.[244] The courts recognize that employers should and must be able to determine the cause of problematic conduct without exposing themselves to liability under the ADA.[245] Neverthe-

---

[239]*Id.* at 646, 8 AD Cases at 1240.

[240]Pilman v. New York City Housing Auth., 2000 WL 236322 (S.D.N.Y. Feb. 25, 2000) (evidence that employer perceived plaintiff with mental impairment as disabled because it put her on leave against her will when other accommodations might have existed).

[241]Chandler v. City of Dallas, 2 F.3d 1385, 2 AD Cases 1326 (5th Cir. 1993). *See also* Miller v. City of Springfield, 146 F.3d 612, 8 AD Cases 321 (8th Cir. 1998) (plaintiff rejected for police office position because of score on psychological test not regarded as substantially limited in working; plaintiff was already working for defendant). *But see EEOC Definition of the Term "Disability," supra* note 35, at 7282 ("if an employer believes that a person poses a safety risk even though his blood pressure is at the normal range, the employer may regard the employee as disabled").

[242]2 AD Cases 1240 (D. Mass. 1993).

[243]*Id.* at 1243–44.

[244]Wright v. Illinois Dep't of Corrs., 204 F.3d 727, 10 AD Cases 408 (9th Cir. 2000); Krocka v. Chicago, 203 F.3d 507, 10 AD Cases 289 (7th Cir. 2000); Sullivan v. River Valley Sch. Dist., 197 F.3d 804, 9 AD Cases 1711 (6th Cir. 1999); Cody v. Cigna Healthcare of St. Louis, 139 F.3d 595, 7 AD Cases 1716 (8th Cir. 1998).

[245]Tice v. Centre Area Transp. Auth., 247 F.3d 506, 11 AD Cases 1185 (3d Cir. 2001); *Krocka*, 203 F.3d 507, 10 AD Cases 289 (employer was reasonable and responsible in sending plaintiff with mental difficulties for fitness-for-duty exam); *Sullivan*,

less, medical inquiries may provide evidence that an employer perceived a plaintiff as disabled. For example, in *Emberger v. Deluxe Check Printers*,[246] an employee who suffered from depression and anxiety attacks developed an infatuation for a coworker who eventually severed all ties with the employee. The employee left his coworker romantic letters and voice mails and talked to other coworkers about her. The coworker subsequently complained about harassment. Although suspended and warned to stop, the employee resumed his behavior when he returned. The defendant eventually terminated him and he sued. The court concluded the plaintiff could establish a prima facie case of disability discrimination because the plaintiff's supervisor had discussions with him about his mental state and requested permission to contact his psychiatrist.[247] Moreover, his supervisor's notes said that the plaintiff appeared to have a mental disorder.[248]

III. Qualified Individual with a Disability

Even if an individual has an impairment that substantially limits some major life activity, he or she must still be qualified for the job in question in order to be covered by the ADA. A qualified individual with a disability is one who—with or without reasonable accommodation—currently can perform the essential functions of the job the individual holds or the job for which he or she has applied.[249] In order to be protected by the ADA, a disabled individual must meet the requisite skill, experience, education, and other job-related requirements of the position desired.[250] All qualification standards that tend to

---

197 F.3d 804, 9 AD Cases 1711 ("an employer needs to be able to determine the cause of an employee's aberrant behavior"); *Cody*, 139 F.3d 595, 7 AD Cases 1716.

[246] 1997 WL 677149 (E.D. Pa. Oct. 30, 1997).

[247] *Id.* at *4.

[248] *Id.*

[249] 42 U.S.C. §12111(9)(A); 29 C.F.R. §1630.2(m) app.

[250] 29 C.F.R. §1630.2(M). *See, e.g.,* Christopher v. Adam's Mark Hotels, 137 F.3d 1069, 7 AD Cases 1537 (8th Cir. 1998) (termination of secretary with Bipolar Disorder upheld when secretary did not have the word processing skills entry-level secretaries were required to have and she had misrepresented her skills and was unwilling to learn the necessary skills); Williams v. Anheuser-Busch, Inc., 957 F. Supp. 1246, 6 AD Cases 905 (M.D. Fla. 1997) (genuine issue of material fact whether alcoholic brewery worker who told bar patrons he urinated in beer was otherwise qualified because he had been employed four years before his termination); Kemer v. Johnson, 900 F. Supp. 677, 4 AD Cases 1832 (S.D.N.Y. 1995), *aff'd,* 101 F.3d 683, 5 AD Cases 1536 (2d Cir. 1996) (applicant with depressive neurosis and Schizotypal Personality Disorder who failed to complete employment application as instructed was not otherwise qualified); Lassiter v. Reno, 885 F. Supp. 869, 4 AD Cases 609 (E.D. Va. 1995) (deputy marshal with Paranoid Personality Disorder was not qualified because under U.S. Marshals Service medical qualifications a person with mental instability or a history of a personality disorder was disqualified), *aff'd,* 86 F.3d 1151, 5 AD Cases 1343 (4th Cir. 1996).

screen out disabled individuals must be job related and consistent with business necessity.[251]

An employee may be terminated for failure to perform the essential functions of his or her job even if the inability to do so arises from the employee's mental health condition.[252] Employers, however, may not make decisions concerning terminations, demotions, or hiring based on the assumption that a mental health condition will make an employee unable to perform the job sometime in the future.[253] The decision must be made on the individual's current ability to perform the job.[254] However, "the ADA does not limit the employer's ability to establish or change the content, nature, or functions of a job."[255] Employers also may establish, enforce, and change uniform production standards, which do not have to be lowered for disabled individuals,[256] so long as the change is not implemented to discriminate against the disabled employee.[257]

When determining whether a particular function is essential, there is a distinction between tasks that are functions of the position and the way the function is performed. If the task is actually a function of the job, the employer must determine whether it is an essential or a marginal function.[258] A function may be essential because (1) the position exists to perform the function,[259] (2) there are a limited number of employees available who could perform the

---

[251] 42 U.S.C. §12112(b)(6); 29 C.F.R. §1630.10.

[252] *See* McDaniel v. Allied Signal, Inc., 896 F. Supp. 1482, 4 AD Cases 1471 (W.D. Mo. 1995) (employee who lost security clearance because of mental illness and alcohol-related arrests not qualified individual).

[253] 29 C.F.R §1630.2(m) app.; Duda v. Board of Educ. of Franklin Park Public Sch. Dist. No. 84, 133 F.3d 1054, 8 AD Cases 99 (7th Cir. 1998) (determination whether person qualified must be based on employee's capabilities at the time decision made, not on speculation about the future).

[254] 29 C.F.R. §1630.2(m); Holiday v. City of Chattanooga, 206 F.3d 637, 10 AD Cases 501 (6th Cir. 2000) (verdict upheld for HIV-positive applicant whom defendant rejected as not sufficiently strong to do job based on doctor's recommendation because plaintiff passed agility test and had experience as police officer; doctor did not make individual inquiry and there was evidence that defendant was afraid of transmittal).

[255] 42 U.S.C. §12111(8); *EEOC Technical Assistance Manual*, *supra* note 17, at 6996.

[256] Gaston v. Bellinggrath Gardens & Home, 167 F.3d 1361, 8 AD Cases 1862 (11th Cir. 1999).

[257] Milton v. Scrivner, 53 F.3d 1118, 1124, 4 AD Cases 432, 436 (10th Cir. 1995).

[258] For example, if an employer advertises for a "floating supervisor" to substitute for supervisors on varying shifts, the ability to work any time is an essential function because the purpose of the position is to have a person who can work any shift. *EEOC Technical Assistance Manual*, *supra* note 17, at 6994.

[259] 29 C.F.R §1630.2(m) app.; Mackie v. Runyon, 804 F. Supp. 1508, 2 AD Cases 260 (M.D. Fla. 1992) (plaintiff suffered from mental illness that precluded her from working at night, which was an essential function of an automated letter-sorting machine operator).

function,²⁶⁰ or (3) the function is highly specialized and the individual was hired because of his or her expertise.²⁶¹

In *Benson v. Northwest Airlines*,²⁶² the Eighth Circuit held that the plaintiff bears the burden of proving he can perform the essential functions of the job, but that the employer bears the burden of production as to which functions are essential. In determining whether a function is essential, the evidence may include the employer's judgment, preemployment written job descriptions,²⁶³ the amount of time spent on the job performing the function, the consequences of not performing the function,²⁶⁴ the terms of a collective bargaining agreement, the work experience of former and other employees in the same position²⁶⁵ or employees in similar positions,²⁶⁶ and the employer's treatment of the employee who cannot perform the function as qualified or not.²⁶⁷ A function is not essential simply because it logically would seem to be so. For example, in *Hamlin v.*

---

²⁶⁰A function, however, is not made marginal merely because other employees are available to perform it. EEOC CASE STUDY TRAINING MANUAL 8 (1996).

²⁶¹29 C.F.R. §1630.2(n); Robertson v. Neuromedical Ctr., 161 F.3d 292 (5th Cir. 1998) (neurologist's administrative duties were major reason his position existed; he was one of few employees who could do them because the duties were highly specialized).

²⁶²62 F.3d 1108, 4 AD Cases 1234 (8th Cir. 1995).

²⁶³42 U.S.C. §12111(8).

²⁶⁴29 C.F.R. §1630.2(m). *See, e.g.,* Martinson v. Kinney Shoe, 104 F.3d 683, 6 AD Cases 434 (4th Cir. 1997) (epileptic shoe salesman's unpredictable seizures rendered him not otherwise qualified because he could not keep the store secure when left on his own); EEOC v. Amego, Inc., 110 F.3d 135, 6 AD Cases 997 (1st Cir. 1997) (behavioral therapist whose duties included administration of medication not qualified by virtue of her own medication overdoses); Maurio v. Borgess Med. Ctr., 886 F. Supp. 1349, 4 AD Cases 737 (W.D. Mich. 1995) (surgical technician with HIV who occasionally had to place his hands into an incision during surgery to make room and give visibility to the surgeon was not entitled to have this duty eliminated as reasonable accommodation because it was an essential function of the job). *But see* Garvey v. Jefferson Smurfit Corp., 11 AD Cases 154 (E.D. Pa. 2000) (where evidence showed that not all production supervisors worked a three-shift rotation, rotation was not an essential function); Oswald v. LaRoche Chems., Inc., 894 F. Supp. 988, 5 AD Cases 401 (E.D. La. 1995) (telephone repairman who was afraid of heights after a fall survived summary judgment on otherwise-qualified issue even though the job required the ability to work at high altitudes by offering evidence that repairmen worked in groups of three and each did only two of the four essential functions; others in plaintiff's group could have performed climbing work).

²⁶⁵Overton v. Reilly, 977 F. 2d 1190, 2 AD Cases 254 (7th Cir. 1992).

²⁶⁶42 U.S.C. §211(8); 29 C.F.R. §1630.2(m)(3); Depaoli v. Abbott Labs., 140 F.3d 668, 7 AD Cases 1828 (7th Cir. 1998) (court would consider whether other employees in position were actually required to perform alleged essential function but would otherwise not second-guess employer).

²⁶⁷Timbol v. Commercial Bank of Kuwait, 2000 WL 282886 (S.D.N.Y. Mar. 15, 2000) (bank that did not terminate plaintiff who engaged in observable psychotic behavior and then rehired him after he resigned cannot claim he was not otherwise qualified).

Township of Flint[268] the assistant fire chief filed a lawsuit after the defendant terminated him because he was physically unable to engage in firefighting. The court denied summary judgment to the defendant because the plaintiff proffered evidence that the key functions of his job were administrative and supervisory in contrast to the firefighter's key tasks of responding to emergencies and frontline fire suppression. He testified that even if he went to the fire scene, he would supervise rather than actually fight fires. A plaintiff, however, may not attack an essential function by arguing that it is not a fair requirement or not justified.[269]

In *Simmerman v. Hardee's Food Systems, Inc.*,[270] a fast-food manager who could not work nights or more than 40 hours a week because of his clinical depression was found not otherwise qualified for his job. The employer's job description demonstrated that the ability to work 50 hours per week and work occasional night shifts was an essential function of the managerial position. In contrast, in *Overton v. Reilly*,[271] a chemist suffering from depression avoided summary judgment by showing that contact with the public was not an essential function of his job because it was not part of his official job description and a similarly situated employee was not required to deal with the public.

While written job descriptions prepared in advance of advertising or interviewing are relevant, they are not dispositive,[272] and job descriptions prepared after the alleged discriminatory incident will not be considered as evidence.[273] It is not necessary to list all the essential functions of a job in the description. For example, in *EEOC v. Amego, Inc.*,[274] a behavioral therapist who was depressed and suicidal was held not qualified to work at a residential care facility for individuals with mental disorders because she had twice attempted suicide with medications. Her job duties included dispensing medication, although that function was not expressly set forth in her job description. Nevertheless, the court found administration of medication to be an essential function because mishandling medication would have serious consequences for facility residents, regardless of the amount of time the therapist spent giving out medication.[275]

Thus, in establishing that a function is essential, the work of other employees in the same position should be examined, as it may provide more relevant evidence than a job description. Furthermore, the fact that a function is performed infrequently should not be taken as conclusive evidence that it is not

---

[268] 165 F.3d 426, 8 AD Cases 1688 (6th Cir. 1999).

[269] 29 C.F.R. §1630.2(m) app.

[270] 7 AD Cases 887 (E.D. Pa. 1996), *aff'd*, 118 F.3d 1578, 8 AD Cases 480 (3d Cir. 1997).

[271] 977 F.2d 1190, 2 AD Cases 254 (7th Cir. 1992).

[272] *See, e.g.*, Echazabel v. Chevron, 226 F.3d 1063 (9th Cir. 2000); Deane v. Pocono Med. Ctr., 142 F.3d 138, 7 AD Cases 1809 (3d Cir. 1998) (court did not apply "conclusive effect" to job description to determine essential function).

[273] 42 U.S.C. §2111 (8); 29 C.F.R. §1630.2(m) app.; Muller v. Hotsy Corp., 917 F. Supp. 1389, 6 AD Cases 35 (N.D. Iowa 1996).

[274] 110 F.3d 135, 6 AD Cases 997 (1st Cir. 1997).

[275] *Id.* at 148, 6 AD Cases at 1006–07.

an essential function. Rather, the focus is on whether there are any adverse consequences if the function is not performed.[276] Finally, an employer should make sure that if it determines an individual is not qualified on the basis of a physician's report, the physician performed an individualized inquiry and did not just take into account generalizations about the condition.[277]

Job requirements that an employee may be unable to meet because of a mental disability are discussed in Section III.A–G.

A. Attendance

The EEOC takes the position that regular attendance is not an essential function of a job.[278] The courts, however, generally have held that regular and predictable attendance is an essential function of an employee's position.[279] In *Kotlowski*

---

[276]*See, e.g.,* Lenkar v. Methodist Hosp., 210 F.3d 792, 10 AD Cases 782 (7th Cir. 2000) (nurse's inability to lift left other nurses without assistance in lifting); Kees v. Wallerstein, 161 F.3d 1196, 8 AD Cases 1629 (9th Cir. 1998) (direct interactive contact with prisoners is an essential function because it was in job description and done by other officers, jail safety would be jeopardized if it could not occur when required in emergency situation, and collective bargaining agreement required rotation to jobs that required such contact).

[277]Holiday v. City of Chattanooga, 206 F.3d 637, 10 AD Cases 501 (6th Cir. 2000) (verdict upheld for HIV-positive applicant whom defendant rejected as not sufficiently strong to do job based on doctor's recommendation because plaintiff passed agility test and had experience as police officer; doctor did not make individual inquiry).

[278]Equal Employment Opportunity Commission, *Enforcement Guidance on Reasonable Accommodation and Undue Hardship Under the ADA* (Mar. 1, 1999), *reprinted in* 8 FEP Manual 405:7601 (1999) [hereinafter *EEOC Guidance on Reasonable Accommodation*]. Some courts apply a reasonable accommodation analysis to attendance cases where unpaid leave is involved. *See* Cehrs v. Northeast Ohio Alzheimer's Research Ctr., 155 F.3d 775, 8 AD Cases 825 (6th Cir. 1998) (rejecting regular attendance as an essential function to the extent that taking medical leave makes employee unqualified).

[279]*E.g.,* Jovanovic v. In-Sink-Erator, 201 F.3d 894, 899, 10 AD Cases 193, 197 (7th Cir. 2000) ("Common sense dictates that regular attendance is usually an essential function . . . , if one is not present, he is usually unable to perform his job."); Greer v. Emerson Elec. Co., 185 F.3d 917, 9 AD Cases 1100 (8th Cir. 1999) (employee who missed 67 days in 1993, 65 in 1994, and 100 in first 9 months of 1995 was not otherwise qualified because regular and reliable attendance is an essential function); Nesser v. Trans World Airlines, 160 F.3d 442, 8 AD Cases 1348 (8th Cir. 1998) (attendance is essential function as evidenced by defendant's consistent enforcement of its attendance policy); Hypes v. First Commerce Corp., 134 F.3d 721, 7 AD Cases 1546 (5th Cir. 1998) (plaintiff who missed 23 full and 16 half days in six-month period not qualified because "regular and reliable attendance is essential function in most jobs"); Morgan v. Hilti, Inc., 108 F.3d. 1319, 4 WH Cases 2d 1226 (10th Cir. 1997) (employer did not violate ADA when it fired employee with an emotional impairment, depression, and anorexia nervosa who came late, left early, or missed 30 working days in a year; inability to return to work after a seven-month leave of absence made plaintiff not otherwise qualified); Leatherwood v. Houston Post Co., 59 F.3d 533, 4 AD Cases 1091 (5th Cir. 1995) (plaintiff with Bipolar Disorder who missed three to four months in

v. *Eastman Kodak, Co.*,[280] the court held that an employee with clinical depression with attendance and tardiness problems was not qualified for a job because she could not maintain a regular and reliable level of attendance. The court pointed out that the ADA does not require an employer to accommodate an employee who cannot get to work.[281]

Employers have not always prevailed on their arguments that the plaintiff was not qualified because of attendance issues,[282] however, because there is a difference between sporadic and unreliable attendance, which is unacceptable, and periodic absenteeism of short duration, which may require a reasonable accommodation.[283] For example, in *Vera v. Williams Hospitality*

---

nine-month period not qualified); Daddazio v. Kathrine Gibbs Sch. Inc., 9 AD Cases 585 (D.S.D. 1999) (court upheld failure to renew employment contract of teacher hospitalized for PTSD because he was not able to regularly attend work); Tumbler v. American Trading & Prod. Corp., 6 AD Cases 1439 (E.D. Pa. 1997) (employee terminated after ten-month leave not otherwise qualified); Formosa v. Miami Date Cmty. Coll., 990 F. Supp. 1433, 7 AD Cases 1768 (S.D. Fla. 1997) (depressed employee with excessive absenteeism not otherwise qualified); Mears v. Gulfstream Aerospace Corp., 905 F. Supp. 1075, 5 AD Cases 1295 (S.D. Ga. 1995) (dysthymic and agoraphobic employee was not qualified for her job because attendance is an essential function and plaintiff stated that she could not attend work because of her disability); Matzo v. Postmaster General, 685 F. Supp. 260, 1 AD Cases 1137 (D.D.C. 1987), *aff'd*, 861 F.2d 1290, 1 AD Cases 1399 (D.C. Cir. 1988) (manic depressive plaintiff who had poor attendance record in a preceding year and who failed to remain on duty for the duration of the workday was not otherwise qualified).

[280]922 F. Supp. 790, 6 AD Cases 609 (W.D.N.Y. 1996).

[281]*Id.* at 798, 6 AD Cases at 613.

[282]*See, e.g.*, Fritz v. Mascotech Auto. Sys. Group, 914 F. Supp. 1481, 6 AD Cases 1103 (E.D. Mich. 1996) (although the employer demonstrated that regular attendance was an essential function of the plaintiff's position, the plaintiff presented evidence that the employer rejected plaintiff's suggested accommodations and worsened the plaintiff's attendance problem by requiring him to obtain a doctor's note each time his diabetes caused him to miss work and that there was a jury issue whether the employer could have accommodated the plaintiff's disability to improve his attendance); Carlson v. Inacom Corp., 885 F. Supp. 1314, 4 AD Cases 600 (D. Neb. 1995) (secretary who missed approximately nine days a year because of migraine headaches not considered unqualified because employer failed to show attendance was an essential function given its lack of a policy on unscheduled absenteeism and its failure to show that the secretary's absences caused essential work not to be done in a timely and efficient manner).

[283]*Compare* Waggoner v. Olin Corp., 169 F.3d 481, 484, 9 AD Cases 88, 91 (7th Cir. 1999) ("in most instances the ADA does not protect persons who have erratic, unexplained absences even when these absences are the result of a disability"); Brundage v. Hahn, 66 Cal. Rptr. 2d 830, 7 AD Cases 286 (Ct. App. 1997) (absence of several weeks not protected by ADA or state law even though it was the result of employee's Bipolar Disorder), *with* Garcia-Ayala v. Lederle Parenterals, Inc., 212 F. 3d 638, 10 AD Cases 865 (1st Cir. 2000) (genuine issue of fact whether employee's request for additional four months of leave beyond one year was a reasonable accommodation that would enable plaintiff to do job); Rascon v. U.S. W. Communications, Inc. 143

Group, Inc.,[284] the defendant argued that an employee who had missed 41 days, which included a 10-day stay for hospitalization after he expressed suicidal and homicidal thoughts, was not otherwise qualified because of his absenteeism. The court rejected the employer's argument because the employer had included days the employee was not scheduled to work as well as vacation days.[285] Furthermore, the plaintiff's longest absence was the uninterrupted hospitalization, which indicated that his absenteeism was neither unpredictable nor intermittent.[286]

Likewise, in *Bultemeyer v. Fort Wayne Community Schools*,[287] a mentally disabled school custodian was terminated after he failed to report to work at his assigned school, which he claimed was too stressful for his condition. The court held that he stated a genuine issue of material fact as to whether he was able to perform the essential function of reporting to work. It maintained that a reasonable accommodation might have enabled the custodian to overcome his fear of working in a school larger than those in which he had previously worked.[288]

The Family and Medical Leave Act (FMLA)[289] may also provide entitlement to leave. Although the ADA allows disabled employees to be terminated for excessive absenteeism, if the FMLA applies to the employer and the employee's condition qualifies as a "serious health condition" as defined under the FMLA, the employee has 12 weeks of job-protected leave whether used at once or intermittently,[290] which could protect an employee prone to sporadic unpredictable absences. For example, suppose an employee has a mental disorder that causes him to leave work early, erratically, or to miss work altogether. Such absences may be covered by the FMLA. While such an employee could be

---

F.3d 1324, 8 AD Cases 541 (10th Cir. 1998) (jury issue whether employee with PTSD, which caused him to fight with coworkers, was otherwise qualified because his physician testified that he could perform the essential functions of his job if the company allowed him leave for counseling and inpatient treatment); Haschmann v. Time Warner Entm't Co., 151 F.3d 591, 8 AD Cases 692 (7th Cir. 1998) (court held that plaintiff with lupus could meet the essential job function of attendance even though she needed a two-to-four-week medical leave because short-term absences do not render an employee incapable of performing the essential function of attendance); Criado v. International Bus. Machs. Corp., 145 F.3d 437, 445, 8 AD Cases 336, 341 (1st Cir. 1998) ("allowing a disabled employee a one-month leave of absence does not absolve an employer's duty to accommodate, especially where the extra leave requested is not expected to be prolonged or perpetual"); Cehrs v. Northeast Ohio Alzheimer's Research Ctr., 155 F.3d 775, 8 AD Cases 825 (6th Cir. 1998) ("no presumption should exist that uninterrupted attendance is an essential job requirement" because leave is a reasonable accommodation).

[284]73 F. Supp. 2d 161, 9 AD Cases 1626 (D.P.R. 1999).
[285]*Id.* at 167, 168, 9 AD Cases at 1631.
[286]*Id.* at 168, 9 AD Cases at 1632.
[287]100 F.3d 1281, 6 AD Cases 67 (7th Cir. 1996).
[288]*Id.* at 1286, 6 AD Cases at 72.
[289]29 U.S.C. §§2601 et seq.
[290]*Id.* §2612.

terminated without incurring liability under the ADA, the employer could potentially be liable under the FMLA. The employer may, however, count FMLA leave as part of the unpaid leave provided as a reasonable accommodation under the ADA.[291]

Finally, whether attendance is an essential function will depend on the actual job. In *Ward v. Massachusetts Health Research Institute*,[292] an arthritic data entry assistant worked a flextime schedule, which allowed him to work 7.5 hours, but he had to start between 7:00 and 9:00 a.m. The plaintiff experienced severe pain and stiffness in the morning, which caused him frequently to be late. The employer terminated him, and the plaintiff argued he would be qualified if he had an open-ended schedule. The court rejected the employer's argument that attendance was an essential job function because although regular and reliable attendance was an essential element of most jobs, there was no evidence that the data entry position required the plaintiff to be present certain hours of the day. The evidence showed that plaintiff's work had to be done before the next day and that plaintiff's schedule did not interfere with other employees' ability to do their jobs.[293]

B. Punctuality

Employees with mental disabilities may also, because of medication or the symptoms of the condition itself, have difficulty getting up in the morning and getting to work on time.[294] Although an employer must attempt to accommodate employees with such problems, courts generally have held that punctuality is an essential function of the job.[295]

---

[291]*EEOC Guidance on Reasonable Accommodation*, supra note 278, at 7617.

[292]209 F.3d 29, 10 AD Cases 776 (1st Cir. 2000).

[293]*Id.* at 35, 10 AD Cases at 780. Accord Humphrey v. Memorial Hosp. Ass'n, 239 F.3d 1128, 11 AD Cases 765 (9th Cir. 2000) (regular attendance not an essential function for medical transcriptionist who could work at home).

[294]Again, the FMLA may protect an employee who is tardy as a result of a mental disorder that also constitutes a serious health condition under the FMLA. For example, an employee with Obsessive-Compulsive Disorder who is intermittently late for work because of his condition is no different from the pregnant employee who is late because of morning sickness or an epileptic employee who is late because of a seizure. There is no counterpart in the FMLA to the ADA concept of undue hardship; the term "incapacitated" under the FMLA means the complete inability to perform the functions of one's job and does not take reasonable accommodation into consideration. *See* 29 C.F.R. §825.115. Thus, the FMLA may provide greater protection than the ADA to an employee with a mental disorder who has problems getting to work on time, albeit only until the maximum 12 weeks of leave are exhausted.

[295]*See, e.g.*, Guice-Mills v. Derwinski, 967 F. 2d 794, 2 AD Cases 187 (2d Cir. 1992) (head nurse who could not start her 8:00 a.m. shift until 10:00 a.m. because of the medication she was taking for depression was not otherwise qualified because an essential function of being head nurse required that management personnel be present from 8:00 to 10:00 a.m.); Kotlowski v. Eastman Kodak Co., 922 F. Supp. 790, 6 AD Cases 609 (W.D.N.Y. 1996) (clerical employee with depression who had a well-

In certain situations a reasonable accommodation may not be possible because the specific schedule itself is an essential function of the position.[296] Whether or not the schedule is an essential function will most likely depend on the type of job plaintiff has. For example, in *Earl v. Mervyns, Inc.*,[297] the plaintiff, a store area coordinator, was given a second warning after she was late 29 times in 365 days. She subsequently advised the employer that she suffered from Obsessive-Compulsive Disorder, which caused her to be late. Within approximately three and one-half months, she was late four more times. She was again warned, and she submitted verification from her doctor concerning her condition. The employer offered to allow her to clock in fifteen minutes ahead of her shift, but she requested to be allowed to clock in whenever she arrived and make it up at the end of her shift. The plaintiff's doctor asserted that no reasonable accommodation could enable the plaintiff to arrive at work on time. The court concluded that punctuality was an essential function of the job because the defendant placed a high premium on punctuality as evidenced by its handbook rules and system of warnings, and because of the nature of the plaintiff's job, which required specific duties to be performed at certain times. The court noted, "if [plaintiff] were tardy in the morning, her area would not be ready for the usual influx of morning customers. If [plaintiff] were tardy in the afternoon or evening, the Area Coordinator from the previous shift would be forced to work a longer shift."[298] Likewise, in *Guice-Mills v. Derwinski*,[299] a head nurse who could not start her 8:00 a.m. shift until 10:00 a.m. because of the medication she was taking for depression was held not otherwise qualified because an essential function of being head nurse, and part of management, was being present from 8:00 a.m. to 10:00 a.m.

In contrast, *Humphrey v. Memorial Hospital Association*[300] involved a medical transcriptionist who had difficulty getting to work on time, if at all. The employer offered her the accommodation of arriving any time within a 24-hour period on days she was scheduled to work, which she accepted. Unfortunately, this accommodation did not seem to work, and the plaintiff continued to arrive late. The plaintiff's subsequent request to work at home was denied. When the employer terminated her, she asked for a leave of absence. The Ninth Circuit concluded there was a genuine issue of fact whether plaintiff was qualified because she could perform the essential functions at home and that while regular and reliable attendance was an essential function, her actual physical presence was not. The court held that either requested accommodation could have made her otherwise qualified and reversed summary judgment for the employer.

---

documented tardiness problem was not qualified for her job because she could not maintain a regular and reliable level of attendance).

[296]*See* Ward v. Massachusetts Health Research Inst., 209 F.3d 29, 10 AD Cases 776 (1st Cir. 2000).
[297]207 F.3d 1361, 10 AD Cases 673 (11th Cir. 2000).
[298]*Id.* at 1366, 10 AD Cases at 675.
[299]967 F. 2d 794, 2 AD Cases 187 (2d Cir. 1992).
[300]239 F.3d 1128, 11 AD Cases 765 (9th Cir. 2001).

C. Shifts/Hours Worked

Whether overtime or a particular shift is an essential job function will largely depend on the job in question. For example, in *Simmerman v. Hardee's Food Systems, Inc.*,[301] the court held that a fast-food manager who could not work nights or more than 40 hours a week was not otherwise qualified because the ability to work 50 hours per week and occasional night shifts was an essential function of his job. In *Tardie v. Rehabilitation Hospital of Rhode Island*,[302] the court held that working more than 40 hours was an essential function of a director of human resources job.[303] Overtime also may be an essential function of an employee's position,[304] which an employee with a mental impairment may be unable to meet, and the time during which a position is performed can be essential.[305]

In certain cases the courts have agreed that working a particular shift is an essential function of a job. In *Laurin v. Providence Hospital*,[306] the court held that a "rotating shift" was an essential function of a nursing position. Because the hospital had structured the jobs to ensure that it could meet its 24-hour coverage needs, the court found that any other conclusion "would be tantamount to maintaining that night work is not an 'essential function' of a night watchman's job, even though that is the only time the premises are not otherwise occupied."[307] Similarly, in *Turco v. Hoechst Celanese Chemical Corp.*,[308] the court held that the employer did not have to modify a rotating shift for a diabetic employee so that it was a straight day shift position. In *Gile v. United Airlines, Inc.*,[309] a plaintiff who suffered from depression, which prevented her from being able to work nights, was held to be unable to perform

---

[301] 7 AD Cases 887 (E.D. Pa. 1996), *aff'd*, 118 F.3d 1578, 8 AD Cases 480 (3d Cir. 1997).

[302] 168 F.3d 538, 9 AD Cases 155 (1st Cir. 1999).

[303] The fact that an employee is restricted to a 40-hour workweek does not mean that the employer has no reasonable accommodation obligation if the job normally entails more hours than those the employee is allowed to work, since transfer to a vacant 40-hour-per-week position may be a reasonable accommodation. Gile v. United Airlines, Inc., 95 F.3d 492, 5 AD Cases 1466 (7th Cir. 1996); Kolpas v. G.D. Searle & Co., 959 F. Supp. 525, 8 AD Cases 1285 (N.D. Ill. 1997).

[304] Davis v. Florida Power & Light Co., 205 F.3d 1301, 10 AD Cases 492 (11th Cir. 2000) (overtime is an essential function of job involving reconnection of electric power because of need for same-day connection; employment application said overtime was part of job, employees regularly worked overtime, and the collective bargaining agreement required involuntary overtime); Violette v. International Bus. Machs. Corp., 962 F. Supp. 446, 7 AD Cases 395 (D. Conn. 1996) (a depressed employee who was restricted to 8-hour workdays was not otherwise qualified for a position requiring 12-hour shifts), *aff'd*, 116 F.3d 466, 7 AD Cases 544 (2d Cir. 1997).

[305] *EEOC Guidance on Reasonable Accommodation*, *supra* note 278, at 7618.

[306] 150 F.3d 52, 8 AD Cases 768 (1st Cir. 1998).

[307] *Id.* at 52, 8 AD Cases at 773.

[308] 101 F.3d 1090, 6 AD Cases 278 (5th Cir. 1996).

[309] 95 F.3d 492, 5 AD Cases 1466 (7th Cir. 1996).

the essential functions of the job because working the night shift was an essential function of a night shift data entry operator. Conversely, in *Garvey v. Jefferson Smurfit Corp.*,[310] the court held that where not all production supervisors worked a three-shift rotation, such rotation was not an essential function.

D. Ability to Get Along with Coworkers and Supervisors

While it might be assumed that the ability to get along with coworkers and supervisors is an essential function of virtually any job, some employees with mental disorders may argue that it is not. Indeed, the EEOC has taken the position that positive interaction with coworkers is not necessarily an essential job function.[311] Nonetheless, generally the courts have recognized that getting along with others is an essential job function.[312]

For example, in *Mancini v. General Electric Co.*,[313] the plaintiff had numerous altercations with his bosses and was ultimately terminated for refusing a work assignment. The court rejected his disability claim, maintaining that "the ability to follow the orders of superiors is an essential function of any position. In other words, employees who are insubordinate are not otherwise qualified for the position."[314]

In *Palmer v. Circuit Court of Cook County*,[315] an employee who had been diagnosed as paranoid and delusional was suspended after telling a coworker that she was going to "kick her ass." Upon her return she was suspended for telling her boss to "go to hell." Again she returned to work, only to say of her boss, "Her ass is mine. She needs her ass kicked and I'm going to do it. . . . I want her dead." In a telephone call to her boss, the employee said, "Your ass is mine, bitch." After being fired, the employee sued. She claimed she was fired on account of her mental disability. The Seventh Circuit found otherwise: "She was fired because she threatened to kill another employee. . . . [I]f an employer fires an employee because of the employee's unacceptable behavior, the fact that that behavior was precipitated by a mental illness does not present an issue under the Americans with Disabilities Act."[316] The court went on: "The Act protects only 'qualified' employees, that is, employees qualified to do the job for which they were hired; and threatening other employees disqualifies one."[317]

---

[310]11 AD Cases 154 (E.D. Pa. 2000).

[311]*EEOC Guidance on Psychiatric Disabilities*, *supra* note 14, at 7461.

[312]*E.g.*, Grenier v. Cyanamid Plastics, 70 F.3d 667, 5 AD Cases 75 (1st Cir. 1995) (ability to get along with others essential to most jobs); Pesterfield v. Tennessee Valley Auth., 941 F.2d 437, 1 AD Cases 1858 (6th Cir. 1991) (ability to get along with others was an essential function of plaintiff's job).

[313]820 F. Supp. 141, 2 AD Cases 764 (D. Vt. 1993).

[314]*Id.* at 147, 2 AD Cases at 768.

[315]117 F.3d 351, 6 AD Cases 1569 (7th Cir. 1997).

[316]*Id.* at 352, 6 AD Cases at 1570.

[317]*Id. See also* Boldini v. Postmaster Gen., 928 F. Supp. 125, 5 AD Cases 11 (D.N.H. 1995) (although court found that the plaintiff was psychiatrically disabled, it

E. Interacting with Customers or General Public

Sometimes employees with mental disorders will encounter difficulties dealing with customers or members of the public, and litigation under the ADA will ensue. Often the issue is whether dealing with customers or the public is truly an essential function of the position.[318] In *Overton v. Reilly*,[319] the court found a genuine issue of fact whether dealing with the public was an essential function of the job of a chemist with depression. The plaintiff presented evidence that only 5 percent of his time was spent dealing with the public in person, that he was able to handle written correspondence, and that any telephone contact could be handled by another employee. Likewise, in *Taylor v. Food World, Inc.*,[320] the Eleventh Circuit held that there was a genuine issue of material fact whether a salesclerk with Asperger's Disorder, which caused him to speak loudly and repetitively and to ask personal questions of others, was otherwise qualified for a position that required customer service. The court noted that a reasonable jury could find that the plaintiff could perform his job without offending customers, since he received no more customer complaints than other salesclerks and there was testimony that his behavior was not inappropriate.[321]

In contrast, in *Smith v. Blue Cross Blue Shield of Kansas, Inc.*,[322] a customer service representative with a panic disorder was held not to be a qualified because her condition prevented her from performing the essential function of talking on the phone with customers who were often angry and verbally abusive. In *Johnson v. Morrison, Inc.*,[323] a waitress was held to be unable to perform the essential functions of her job when the stress of serving customers during busy periods in the restaurant caused her to "melt down" and be unable to perform her duties. In *Larkins v. CIBA Vision Corp.*,[324] a customer service representative whose panic attacks prevented her from answering telephone calls was held to be unable to perform the essential function of her job.

---

determined that she was not otherwise qualified for her position because of her repeated defiance of her supervisors' directives and her numerous altercations with coworkers and customers).

[318] *See* Durning v. Duffens Optical, Inc., 1996 WL 67640 (E.D. La. Feb. 14, 1996) (epileptic salesman who had seizures in presence of customers was not otherwise qualified because effective communication with customers of the employer's products and services, in-person sales calls to customers, and presentation of workshops were essential functions of sales representative job).

[319] 977 F. 2d 1190, 2 AD Cases 254 (7th Cir. 1992).
[320] 133 F.3d 1419 (11th Cir. 1998).
[321] *Id.* at 1424.
[322] 894 F. Supp. 1463, 4 AD Cases 1378 (D. Kan. 1995).
[323] 849 F. Supp. 777, 3 AD Cases 259 (N.D. Ala. 1994).
[324] 858 F. Supp. 1572, 3 AD Cases 715 (N.D. Ga. 1994).

F. Security Clearance

Courts have upheld terminations of employees whose mental condition prevented them from obtaining a security clearance.[325] Likewise, some individuals with mental impairments may be screened out of certain jobs by virtue of federal regulations.[326]

G. Other Essential Functions

Courts have also held that the ability to work independently,[327] concentration,[328] and licensure[329] are essential functions with respect to certain jobs.

---

[325]Lassiter v. Reno, 885 F. Supp. 869, 4 AD Cases 609 (E.D. Va. 1995) (deputy marshal with paranoid personality disorder was not otherwise qualified because his condition prevented him from carrying a firearm, which was an essential function of his position, and there was no reasonable accommodation that would allow the employee to return to his former position or to carry a firearm despite the plaintiff's physician's statement that the plaintiff could return to general employment with follow-up treatment); McDaniel v. Allied Signal, 896 F. Supp. 1482, 4 AD Cases 1471 (W.D. Mo. 1995) (electrician who lost his security clearance because of his mental impairment and arrests for alcohol incidents not a qualified individual with a disability); Hogarth v. Thornburgh, 833 F. Supp. 1077, 2 AD Cases 1777 (S.D.N.Y. 1993) (FBI communication officer with Bipolar Disorder was not otherwise qualified despite his and his psychiatrist's claims that there was a minimal possibility of relapse and disclosure of classified information); Swann v. Walters, 620 F. Supp. 741, 35 FEP Cases 1246 (D.D.C. 1984) (paranoid schizophrenic convicted of child abuse was not otherwise qualified because his mental condition undermined his stability, rendering him unsuitable for a security clearance, as did his criminal misconduct).

[326]*See, e.g.*, 14 C.F.R. §§67.107, 67.207, 67.307 (first-, second- and third-class airmen may not have medical history or clinical diagnosis of personality disorder that has manifested itself by overt acts, psychosis, or Bipolar Disorder); 32 C.F.R. §§147.2, 147.6, 147.11 pt. 154 app. H (adjudicative guidelines for determining eligibility for access to classified information; disqualifying behaviors include mental or emotional illness or condition that could result in significant defect in judgment or reliability).

[327]Webster v. Methodist Occupational Health Ctrs., Inc., 141 F.3d 1236, 8 AD Cases 33 (7th Cir. 1998) (nurse with continuing attention and concentration difficulties because of a stroke was not otherwise qualified because she could not work unsupervised); Bolstein v. Reich, 1995 WL 686236 (D.D.C. Oct. 4, 1995) (attorney with depression who could not do work independently and perform complex assignments not otherwise qualified).

[328]Turco v. Hoechst Celanese Chem. Corp., 101 F.3d 1090, 6 AD Cases 278 (5th Cir. 1996).

[329]Jacobsen v. Tillmann, 17 F. Supp. 2d 1018, 8 AD Cases 913 (D. Minn. 1998) (dyslexic teacher licensure candidate who took math portion of standardized licensure exam with government-approved accommodations not otherwise qualified).

IV. Reasonable Accommodation

Failure to provide a reasonable accommodation to a disabled individual[330] is a form of discrimination under the ADA.[331] Although the ADA does not specifically define the term "reasonable accommodation," "[i]n general, an accommodation is any change in the work environment or in the way things are customarily done that enables an individual with a disability to enjoy equal employment opportunities."[332] Reasonable accommodations fall into three categories:

- Modifications or adjustments to the job application process that enable a qualified applicant with a disability to be considered for the position the applicant desires
- Modifications or adjustments to the work environment or to the manner or circumstances in which the position held or the position desired is customarily performed that enable a qualified disabled individual to perform the essential functions of that position
- Modifications or adjustments that enable a covered entity's employee with a disability to enjoy the same benefits and privileges of employment that are provided to the entity's other similarly situated employees without disabilities[333]

Reasonable accommodations for persons with mental disabilities may include job restructuring, part-time or modified work schedules, acquiring or modifying equipment, changing test or training materials, or policies, training, reassignment to a vacant position, or unpaid leave.[334] The reasonable accommodation obligation attaches from the application process forward[335] and is continuing in nature.[336] It is irrelevant whether an employee who requests an accommodation is still in his probationary period or simply works part-time.[337]

---

[330] An employer is not required to accommodate a perceived disability or a record of a disability. Although the EEOC neatly sidestepped this question in its *Guidance on Reasonable Accommodation,* its training manual for investigators states that employers do not have to accommodate a perceived disability. EEOC ADA CASE STUDY TRAINING MANUAL 6 (1996). The courts have reached the same conclusion. *See, e.g.,* Weber v. Strippit, Inc., 186 F.3d 907, 9 AD Cases 961 (8th Cir. 1999) (holding that an employer need accommodate only actual disabilities); Workman v. Frito-Lay, Inc., 165 F.3d 460, 8 AD Cases 1761 (6th Cir. 1999) (noting that an employer does not need to accommodate a person "regarded as" having a disability); Newberry v. East Texas State Univ., 161 F.3d 276, 8 AD Cases 1595 (5th Cir. 1998) (noting an employer need not provide reasonable accommodation to an employee perceived to be impaired). *But see* Taylor v. Pathmark Store, Inc., 177 F.3d 180, 9 AD Cases 497 (3d Cir. 1999) (open issue in Third Circuit); Katz v. City Metal Co., 87 F.3d 26, 5 AD Cases 1120 (1st Cir. 1996) (those perceived to be disabled may bring failure-to-accommodate claims).

[331] 42 U.S.C. §12112(b)(5)(A).

[332] 29 C.F.R. §1630.2(o) app.

[333] *Id.* §1630.2(o)(1)(i–iii).

[334] 42 U.S.C. §12111(9); 29 C.F.R. §1630.2(o)(2)(i).

[335] *EEOC Guidance on Reasonable Accommodation, supra* note 278, at 7602.

[336] Ralph v. Lucent Techs., 135 F.3d 166, 7 AD Cases 1345 (1st Cir. 1998).

[337] *EEOC Guidance on Reasonable Accommodation, supra* note 278, at 7602.

A. Defining "Reasonable" Accommodations

There currently is a split of authority on the issue of what constitutes a reasonable accommodation. The EEOC takes the position that a modification or adjustment satisfies the accommodation obligation if it is "effective," i.e., it enables an employee to perform the essential functions of his job or enables an applicant to participate equally in the application process and to be considered for an available position, or allows the disabled employee to enjoy the same benefits and privileges in employment as nondisabled employees.[338] Some courts, however, in determining the reasonableness of accommodations have also employed a cost-benefit analysis.[339] Under this analysis, a court weighs the cost of a suggested accommodation against the perceived benefit to the employer and employee.[340] The EEOC has explicitly rejected the latter position.[341]

B. Burden of Proof in Establishing That Accommodation Is Reasonable

Although the EEOC takes the position that a plaintiff need show only that the requested accommodation would enable him or her to do the job and the

---

[338]*Id.* at 7603. *See also* Mustafa v. Clark County Sch. Dist., 157 F.3d 1169, 1176, 8 AD Cases 1119, 1124 (9th Cir. 1998) (plaintiff must show that the "suggested accommodation would, more probably than not, have resulted in his ability to perform the essential functions of his job"); Evans v. Federal Express Corp., 133 F.3d 137, 142, 8 AD Cases 151, 153 (1st Cir. 1998) (one element of reasonable accommodation is "likelihood of success"); Bryant v. Better Bus. Bureau of Greater Md., 923 F. Supp. 720, 736, 5 AD Cases 625, 634 (D. Md. 1996) (issue is whether accommodation "would address the job-related difficulties presented by the employee's disability and would allow the employee to attain an 'equal' level of achievement, opportunity and participation" with that of a nondisabled employee in the same position); Dutton v. Johnson County Bd. of Comm'rs, 859 F. Supp. 498, 507, 3 AD Cases 808, 815 (D. Kan. 1994) ("[f]or an accommodation to be reasonable, it must be effective in permitting a disabled worker to perform the essential job functions"); Davis v. York Int'l., Inc., 2 AD Cases 1810 (D. Md. 1993) (actual effect of accommodation is key in determining whether it is reasonable); Lewis v. Zilog. Inc., 908 F. Supp. 931, 4 AD Cases 1787 (N.D. Ga. 1995) (request of plaintiff with Bipolar Disorder to be transferred to California not a reasonable accommodation because plaintiff presented no evidence it would enable her to do her job).

[339]*See, e.g.,* Walsh v. United Parcel Serv., 201 F.3d 718, 10 AD Cases 161 (6th Cir. 2000); Kennedy v. Dresser Rand, 193 F.3d 120, 9 AD Cases 1335 (2d Cir. 1999); Walton v. Mental Health Ass'n of Southeastern Pa., 168 F.3d 661, 9 AD Cases 34 (3d Cir. 1999); Woodman v. Runyon, 132 F.3d 1330, 7 AD Cases 1189 (10th Cir. 1997); Monette v. Electronic Data Sys. Corp., 90 F.3d 1173, 1184 n.10, 5 AD Cases 1326, 1335 n.10 (6th Cir. 1996); Vande Zande v. Wisconsin Dep't of Admin., 44 F.3d 538, 543, 3 AD Cases 1636, 1638 (7th Cir. 1995); Borkowski v. Valley Cent. Sch. Dist., 63 F.3d 131, 4 AD Cases 1264 (2d Cir. 1995).

[340]Walsh v. United Parcel Serv., 201 F.3d 718, 727–28 n.5, 10 AD Cases 161, 166–67 n.5 (6th Cir. 2000).

[341]*EEOC Guidance on Reasonable Accommodation, supra* note 278, at 7603 n.11.

employer has the burden of showing that it is too difficult or expensive, no circuit court has adopted this position. Courts to date have taken two different approaches.[342] Some consider the burden of identifying a reasonable accommodation to be one of production; they then shift the burden of persuasion from plaintiff to defendant. If the plaintiff can proffer a plausible accommodation the benefits of which do not exceed its cost, the plaintiff has established a prima facie case and the defendant must offer evidence that the accommodation is not reasonable.[343] Other courts put all the burden of proving reasonable accommodation on the plaintiff.[344]

C. What Triggers the Accommodation Obligation

An employer's duty to accommodate an employee applies only where:

- The employer knows of the disability;
- The individual requests an accommodation;
- The individual satisfies all the skill, experience, education, and licensing requirements of the job;

---

[342]*See* Reed v. LePage Bakeries, Inc., 244 F.3d 254, 11 AD Cases 1150 (1st Cir. 2001) (discussing split of authority).

[343]*See, e.g.*, Fjellestad v. Pizza Hut, 188 F.3d 944, 9 AD Cases 1153 (8th Cir. 1999); *Walton,* 168 F.3d 661, 9 AD Cases 34; *Borkowski,* 63 F.3d 131, 4 AD Cases 1264; Benson v. Northwest Airlines, Inc., 62 F.3d 1108, 4 AD Cases 1234 (8th Cir. 1995); White v. York Int'l Corp., 45 F.3d 357, 3 AD Cases 1746 (10th Cir. 1995).

[344]*Reed*, 244 F.3d at 259, 11 AD Cases at 1155 ("In order to prove 'reasonable accommodation,' a plaintiff needs to show not only that the proposed accommodation would enable her to perform the essential functions of her job, but also that, at least on the face of things, it is feasible for the employer under the circumstances."); Barth v. Gelb, 2 F.3d 1180, 2 AD Cases 1180 (D.C. Cir. 1993) (reasonable accommodation is a method of accommodation that is reasonable in the run of cases, whereas the undue hardship inquiry focuses on the hardships imposed by the preferred accommodations in the context of the [employer's] operations"); Willis v. Conopco, Inc., 108 F.3d 282, 6 AD Cases 806 (11th Cir. 1997); Riel v. Electronic Data Sys., 99 F.3d 678, 6 AD Cases 26 (5th Cir. 1996); Vande Zande v. State of Wis. Dep't of Admin., 44 F.3d 538, 3 AD Cases 1636 (7th Cir. 1995); *see also* Monette v. Electronic Data Sys. Corp., 90 F.3d 1173, 1184 n.10, 1187, 5 AD Cases 1326, 1335 n.10 (6th Cir. 1996) (the language of §12112 states that although an "employer has the burden of persuasion on whether an accommodation would impose an undue hardship," a disabled individual has the initial and separate burden of showing a purposed accommodation is objectively reasonable); Walsh v. United Parcel Serv., Inc., 201 F.3d 718, 726 n.3, 10 AD Cases 161, 165 n.3 (6th Cir. 2000) (the determination whether an accommodation is reasonable requires "a factual determination untethered to the defendant employer's particularized situation," while the determination of whether a reasonable accommodation imposes an undue burden is evaluated with regard to "the employer's specific situation").

- The individual can perform the essential functions of the job if a reasonable accommodation is made; and
- The accommodation does not impose an undue hardship.[345]

The obligation to accommodate a disabled employee generally is triggered when an employee or his representative (e.g., a physician, family member, or friend), advises the employer that the employee requires an adjustment or change at work because of a disability.[346] An individual is not required to mention the ADA or use the phrase "reasonable accommodation."[347] Indeed, the EEOC's position is that an employee's request for time off because he is "depressed and stressed" is sufficient to put the employer on notice that a reasonable accommodation is being requested.[348] The EEOC, however, also maintains that an employer is obligated to initiate the interactive process even absent a request if the employer (1) knows the employee has a disability, (2) knows or has reason to know the employee's disability is causing the employee to have problems at work, and (3) knows or has reason to know that the employee's disability prevents the employee from asking for an accommodation.[349] The courts have differed over what constitutes sufficient information to put the employer on notice that a request has been made.[350] The issue is

---

[345] *EEOC Technical Assistance Manual, supra* note 17, at 6992–7005.

[346] *EEOC Guidance on Reasonable Accommodation, supra* note 278, at 7602–04; Gaston v. Bellingrath Gardens & Home, Inc., 167 F.3d 1361, 8 AD Cases 1862 (11th Cir. 1999) (initial burden of requesting accommodation on employee); Robin v. Espo Eng'g., 200 F.3d 1081, 81 FEP Cases 1332 (7th Cir. 2000) (absent request, employer has no obligation to accommodate); Smith v. Midland Brake, Inc., 180 F.3d 1154, 9 AD Cases 738 (10th Cir. 1999) (en banc) ("The interactive process must ordinarily begin with the employee providing notice to the employer of the employee's disability and any resulting limitations."); Gantt v. Wilson Sporting Goods, 143 F.3d 1042, 8 AD Cases 308 (6th Cir. 1998) ("[An] employer is not required to speculate as to the extent of the employee's disability or the employee's need or desire for an accommodation"). *But see* Dovoll v. Webb, 194 F.3d 1116, 1133, 9 AD Cases 1533 (10th Cir. 1999) (employee does not have to request accommodation if employee is aware request will be denied).

[347] *EEOC Guidance on Reasonable Accommodation, supra* note 278, at 7604–05; Taylor v. Phoenixville Sch. Dist., 184 F.3d 296, 9 AD Cases 1187 (3d Cir. 1999) (employee does not need to use words "reasonable accommodation" or make request in writing); Schmidt v. Safeway, Inc., 864 F. Supp. 991, 997, 3 AD Cases 1141, 1146 (D. Or. 1994) ("The statute does not require the plaintiff to speak any magic words . . . the employee need not mention the ADA or even the term 'accommodation.' "). *But see* Hammon v. DHL Airways, Inc., 165 F.3d 441, 8 AD Cases 1707 (6th Cir. 1999) (court held that the plaintiff failed to make a prima facie case; plaintiff informed his employer that he had "lost his confidence" but never suggested that his emotional problems stemmed from a condition of disability).

[348] *EEOC Guidance on Psychiatric Disabilities, supra* note 14, at 7471.

[349] *EEOC Guidance on Reasonable Accommodation, supra* note 278, at 7628.

[350] *Taylor,* 184 F.3d 296, 9 AD Cases 1187 (employer put on notice employee required accommodations when it learned she was in hospital for mental condition); Cannice v. Norwest Bank Iowa N.A., 189 F.3d 723, 9 AD Cases 1103 (8th Cir. 1999)

whether the employee has given the employer sufficient information for the employer to know the employee has a disability and needs an accommodation.

First, the employer must know about the limitations a disability imposes before it can be held liable for failure to accommodate.[351] Some circuits have required more information than others. For example, in *Taylor v. Principal Financial Group, Inc.*,[352] an office manager suffered from bipolar and anxiety disorders. After a five-month probation period and repeated counseling concerning his declining work performance, the plaintiff advised his manager that he had been diagnosed with "bipolarism." The manager said that he did not know what that was, and the plaintiff asked him to talk to a doctor to learn about the disorder. The plaintiff subsequently requested a reduction in his objectives and job pressure. When his supervisor asked the plaintiff if he was all right, however, the plaintiff responded affirmatively.[353] The supervisor extended the plaintiff's probationary period for six months and gave him a memorandum listing the objectives he had to meet to continue working. Approximately one

---

(employee who told human resources that he had "stress syndrome" and needed a private phone line so he could talk to his "support network" made request when he had a panic attack in supervisor's office; employer knew employee was on medication and that he cried at work); Hendricks-Robinson v. Excel Corp., 154 F.3d 685, 694, 8 AD Cases 875, 882 (7th Cir. 1998) ("a request as straightforward as asking for continued employment is a sufficient request for accommodation"); Fliss v. Movado Group, Inc., 10 AD Cases 1524 (N.D. Ill. 2000) (plaintiff's note from physician, which set forth restrictions, was request for reasonable accommodation); McGinnis v. Wonder Chem. Co., 5 AD Cases 219 (E.D. Pa. 1995) (employer on notice that employee had requested accommodation because employee told supervisor his pain prevented him from working and employee requested leave under the FMLA). *But see* Hammon v. DHL Airways, Inc., 165 F.3d 441, 8 AD Cases 1707 (6th Cir. 1999) (plaintiff failed to establish that his employer should have known about this disability; he never suggested that his emotional problems stemmed from a condition of disability).

[351]Hunt-Golliday v. Metropolitan Water Reclamation Dist., 104 F.3d 1004, 6 AD Cases 725 (7th Cir. 1997) (obligation to accommodate restricted to employer's knowledge of disability and employee must tell defendant of disability; no duty to accommodate plaintiff with mental disability who never mentioned it or need for accommodation); Beck v. University of Wis. Bd. of Regents, 75 F.3d 1130, 1134, 5 AD Cases 304, 305 (7th Cir. 1996) ("an employee has the initial duty to inform the employer of a disability before ADA liability may be triggered for failure to provide accommodation"); Morisky v. Broward County, 80 F.3d 445, 448, 5 AD Cases 737, 739 (11th Cir. 1996) ("vague or conclusory statements revealing an unspecified incapacity are not sufficient to put an employer on notice of its obligations" under ADA; fact that plaintiff disclosed that she had taken special education courses did put employer on notice she had a disability); Stola v. Joint Indus. Bd., 889 F. Supp. 133, 4 AD Cases 1018 (S.D.N.Y. 1995) (employer did not have notice of plaintiff's mental disability because of plaintiff's workplace misconduct; employer must accommodate only obvious disability).

[352]93 F.3d 155, 5 AD Cases 1653 (5th Cir. 1996).

[353]*Id.* at 159, 5 AD Cases at 1655.

week later, the plaintiff was hospitalized and never returned to work. The Fifth Circuit specifically rejected the plaintiff's argument that the defendant had an affirmative obligation to make a reasonable accommodation simply because the plaintiff had disclosed that he was bipolar and suffered from an anxiety disorder. Rather, the court found that it is the employee's responsibility to advise the employer of the need for an accommodation.[354]

The *Taylor* court distinguished between an employer's knowledge of an employee's impairment and the limitations it imposes and simply knowing that the employee has an impairment.[355] The court emphasized that "employers are obligated to make reasonable accommodations only to the physical or mental limitations resulting from the disability that is known to the employer."[356] Furthermore, courts have required that in the instance of a mental disability where limitations and accommodations are not obvious to the employer, the employee must disclose any such limitations and suggest possible or reasonable accommodations.[357]

Similarly, in *Miller v. National Casualty Co.*,[358] the plaintiff had worked for the defendant for ten years without ever telling anyone that she suffered from a mental disorder or that she needed any special accommodation. Near the end of her employment, she asked a supervisor for a few days off to deal with stress, which the employer granted. When the plaintiff requested an extension of her leave, she was told that she needed to return to work as scheduled unless she provided documentation concerning her illness. She failed to do either. Sometime during that same week the plaintiff's sister called the plaintiff's supervisor and said that the plaintiff was "mentally falling apart" and that the family was trying to get her into a hospital. The defendant subsequently terminated the plaintiff, and she filed a lawsuit. The court held that the plaintiff had not adequately informed the defendant that she suffered from a mental impairment and that her sister's statement merely that the plaintiff was falling apart was insufficient to alert the employer that the plaintiff suffered from a mental disability.[359] The court rejected the argument that the plaintiff's symptoms were such obvious manifestations of an underlying disability that the employer should have inferred from them that she had a disability.[360] The court held that because the employer did not know about the disability, it did not

---

[354]*Id.* at 165, 5 AD Cases at 1659.

[355]*Id.* at 164, 5 AD Cases at 1659.

[356]*Id.*

[357]*Id.* at 165, 5 AD Cases at 1660. *See also* Hammon v. DHL Airways, Inc., 980 F. Supp. 919, 7 AD Cases 900 (S.D. Ohio 1997), *aff'd,* 165 F.3d 441, 8 AD Cases 1707 (6th Cir. 1999) (pilot who suffered emotional problems after traumatic experience during flight simulator drill and resigned because he "lost all confidence" did not put employer on notice that he had a disability by saying that he was "going backwards," and "this is not working").

[358]61 F.3d 627, 4 AD Cases 1089 (8th Cir. 1995).

[359]*Id.* at 630, 4 AD Cases at 1091.

[360]*Id.*

have a duty to accommodate the plaintiff and the termination could not have been based on her disability.[361]

Finally, in *Seaman v. C.S.P.H, Inc.*,[362] a pizza store manager who allegedly had Bipolar Disorder claimed that the defendant had failed to provide an accommodation. The Fifth Circuit affirmed dismissal of his claim because he had not produced any evidence that his request was denied. In fact, the defendant had given him two days off per week, had not disciplined him for unexcused absences, and did not require him to wear a pager. The court explained that in cases involving a mental disability "in which the resulting limitations are not obvious to the employer, an employee cannot remain silent and expect his employer to bear the burden of identifying the need for and suggesting appropriate accommodation."[363]

In contrast, other circuits have held that where the employer knows about the disability and the need for accommodation, the employer must provide an accommodation if the employee's disability is such that he cannot request it. In *Bultemeyer v. Fort Wayne Community Schools*,[364] the plaintiff was a custodian who suffered from Bipolar Disorder, anxiety attacks, and Schizophrenia. After several disability leaves, he indicated that he was able to return to work, and the defendant offered him a job at a high school. The defendant also advised him that he was required to undergo a fitness-for-duty examination before he could return from disability leave. The plaintiff met with the maintenance director at the high school and as they were walking through the school, the director remarked that if the plaintiff moved as slowly as he was walking, he would never get his work done. The plaintiff later informed the defendant that the high school job was too much for him to handle and he did not undergo the physical because he was afraid that if he passed he would have to work at the high school. The defendant fired him for failing to report to work. On the same day the defendant made that decision, the plaintiff delivered a doctor's note requesting a less stressful position, to which the defendant never responded. The plaintiff subsequently filed a lawsuit and the trial court granted the defendant's motion for summary judgment.

The Seventh Circuit reversed, citing the fact that the plaintiff had advised the defendant that the high school job was too much for him and submitted a doctor's note requesting a less stressful position. The court maintained that when an employee has a mental illness, the employer must "meet the employee halfway" and that when "it appears that the employee may need accommodation but doesn't know how to ask for it, the employer should do what it can to help."[365] The court noted that the plaintiff's fear about working at the high school was understandable and stated that an employer "cannot place the whole burden of interactive process on the shoulders of [an employee], who

---

[361] *Id.*
[362] 179 F. 3d 297, 5 WH Cases 2d 673 (5th Cir. 1999).
[363] *Id.* at 301, 5 WH Cases at 675.
[364] 100 F.3d 1281, 6 AD Cases 67 (7th Cir. 1996).
[365] *Id.* at 1285, 6 AD Cases at 71.

is admittedly suffering mental problems."[366] The court concluded that the defendant should have met with the plaintiff to discuss why he felt the high school position was stressful or asked his doctor to provide more information.

According to *Bultemeyer*, therefore, when dealing with an employee who suffers from a mental disability who may not know how or whom to ask for accommodation, an employer has a greater responsibility to initiate the interactive process.[367] The Seventh Circuit reiterated its position in *Miller v. Illinois Department of Corrections*,[368] holding that if the employee's disability impairs his ability to communicate, such as a mental disability might, and if the employer knows the employee has a disability, the employer must make an effort to understand what the employee needs even absent clear communication from the employee.[369] If an employee declines an accommodation in such a situation, however, the employer will be deemed to have complied with the ADA.[370]

D. The Interactive Process

Once an applicant or employee makes a request for an accommodation, the employer[371] must engage in an "interactive process" to clarify what the disabled individual needs and to identify the appropriate reasonable accommodation.[372] The employer must respond to a request for reasonable accommodation as quickly as possible.[373] Any unnecessary delay may create liability.[374]

---

[366] *Id.* at 1286, 6 AD Cases at 72.

[367] *See also* Walsted v. Woodbury County, 113 F. Supp. 2d 1318, 11 AD Cases 20 (N.D. Iowa 2000) (employer should have recognized that borderline mentally retarded custodian required an accommodation).

[368] 107 F.3d 483, 6 AD Cases 678 (7th Cir. 1997).

[369] *Id.* at 486, 6 AD Cases at 681.

[370] *EEOC Guidance on Reasonable Accommodation, supra* note 278, at 7628.

[371] Gile v. United Airlines, 213 F.3d 365, 10 AD Cases 968 (7th Cir. 2000) (once employee with psychiatric disorder initiates accommodation process, employer has obligation to seek plaintiff out and try to develop reasonable accommodation); Woodman v. Runyon, 132 F.3d 1330, 7 AD Cases 1189 (10th Cir. 1997) (employer has role in finding accommodation once employee requests one). *But see* Willis v. Conopco, Inc., 108 F.3d 282, 6 AD Cases 806 (11th Cir. 1997) (plaintiff must produce evidence that she requested specific accommodation that would work and must show that it is reasonable).

[372] *EEOC Guidance on Reasonable Accommodation, supra* note 278, at 7606. *See* 29 C.F.R. §1630.2(o)(3); 29 C.F.R. §§1630.2(o), 1630.9 app.

[373] *EEOC Guidance on Reasonable Accommodation, supra* note 278, at 7610; Dalton v. Subaru-Isuzu Auto., Inc., 141 F.3d 667, 7 AD Cases 1872 (7th Cir. 1998).

[374] *EEOC Guidance on Reasonable Accommodation, supra* note 278, at 7610–11. The EEOC takes the position that in determining whether an unnecessary delay has occurred in providing an accommodation, the relevant factors include (1) the reason(s) for the delay, (2) the length of the delay, (3) how much the individual with the disability and the employer each contributed to the delay, (4) what the employer was doing during the delay, and (5) whether the required accommodation was simple or complex to provide. *Id.*

1. Steps in the Process

The interactive process should identify the precise limitations resulting from the disability and potential reasonable accommodations that should overcome those limitations.[375] The EEOC's Technical Assistance Manual sets forth four steps in the interactive process:

- Identifying the essential functions of the specific job;
- Consulting with the employee to determine his specific physical or mental limitations;
- Consulting with the employee and identifying potential accommodations and assessing each accommodation's effectiveness; and
- Selecting the accommodation that best serves the need of the employer and the employee.[376]

Although the employer has the discretion to choose among various effective accommodations[377] it may not require a disabled individual to accept a reasonable accommodation.[378] However, an employee who is unable to perform the essential functions of the position or is a direct threat absent a reasonable accommodation—yet refuses to accept one—may not be qualified for the job.[379]

Moreover, an employer does not have to provide an accommodation that is not necessitated by the employee's disability. For example, in *Gaines v. Runyon*,[380] the court held that the employer did not violate the ADA by not transferring an epileptic employee to another shift because his epilepsy did not mandate the transfer. Indeed, his medical information supported keeping him on the straight shift he was on.

2. Liability for Failure to Engage in the Process

The EEOC has taken the position that an employer's failure to participate in the interactive process may result in liability for failure to provide a reasonable accommodation.[381] Most circuits, by contrast, have held that the mere failure to engage in the interactive process will not result in liability under the ADA absent evidence the employer could have provided a reasonable accommoda-

---

[375] 29 C.F.R. §1630.2(o)(3); *EEOC Guidance on Reasonable Accommodation*, supra note 278, at 7606. An employer's participation in the interactive process can serve as evidence of good faith, if the employer subsequently does not provide an accommodation for reasons of undue hardship, which may allow it to avoid punitive and compensatory damages. *See* 42 U.S.C. §1981a(a)(3).

[376] 29 C.F.R. §1630.9 app.; Taylor v. Phoenixville Sch. Dist., 184 F.3d 296, 9 AD Cases 1187 (3d Cir. 1999); Fjellestad v. Pizza Hut of Am., Inc., 188 F.3d 944, 9 AD Cases 1153 (8th Cir. 1999).

[377] 29 C.F.R. §1630.9 app.

[378] *EEOC Guidance on Reasonable Accommodation*, supra note 278, at 7611.

[379] *See* 29 §1630.9 app.; *see also* Hankins v. Gap, Inc., 84 F.3d 797, 5 AD Cases 924 (6th Cir. 1996).

[380] 107 F.3d 1171, 6 AD Cases 688 (6th Cir. 1997).

[381] *EEOC Guidance on Reasonable Accommodation*, supra note 278, at 7608.

tion.[382] The courts typically will assess who is responsible for the breakdown in the accommodation process[383] and whether the parties even engaged in the interactive process when a possible reasonable accommodation existed that was not provided.[384]

---

[382]*See, e.g.,* Earl v. Mervyns, Inc., 207 F.3d 1361, 10 AD Cases 673 (11th Cir. 2000) (employer not obligated to engage in interactive process when no reasonable accommodation exists); Rehling v. City of Chicago, 207 F.3d 1009, 10 AD Cases 589 (7th Cir. 2000) (interactive process not an end in itself; plaintiff must show the employer did not provide a reasonable accommodation, not simply that the employer did not engage in the interactive process); Cannice v. Norwest Bank Iowa N.A., 189 F.3d 723, 9 AD Cases 1103 (8th Cir. 1999) (no per se liability for not engaging in interactive process); Fjellestad v. Pizza Hut of America, 188 F.3d 944, 9 AD Cases 1153 (8th Cir. 1999) (no per se liability for not engaging in interactive process); Taylor v. Phoenixville Sch. Dist., 184 F.3d 296, 318, 9 AD Cases 1187, 1201–02 (3d Cir. 1999) (only if the employer could have provided a reasonable accommodation will the failure to engage in the interactive process in good faith result in liability); Smith v. Midland Brake, Inc. 180 F.3d 1154, 9 AD Cases 738 (10th Cir. 1999) (employer liable for failure to provide accommodation but not for failure to engage in interactive process); Loulseqed v. Akzo Nobel, Inc., 178 F.3d 731, 9 AD Cases 783 (5th Cir. 1999) (interactive process not an end in itself); Willis v. Conopco, Inc., 108 F.3d 282, 285, 6 AD Cases 806, 808–09 (11th Cir. 1997) ("the ADA ... is not intended to punish employers for behaving callously if, in fact, no accommodation for the employees' disability could reasonably have been made"); Moses v. American Nonwovens, Inc., 97 F.3d 446, 5 AD Cases 1651 (11th Cir. 1996) (employer had no obligation to engage in an interactive process once it determined that there were no possible accommodations to plaintiff's uncontrolled epilepsy in factory environment involving high temperatures and exposure to machinery); Jacques v. Clean-Up Group, Inc., 96 F.3d 506, 515, 5 AD Cases 1594, 1601 (1st Cir. 1996) (whether employer's failure to engage in interactive process violates the ADA turns on facts and whether parties were reasonable).

[383]*E.g.,* Stewart v. Happy Herman's Cheshire Bridge, Inc., 117 F.3d 1278, 6 AD Cases 1834 (11th Cir. 1997) (employee who rejected five possible accommodations was responsible for the breakdown of the accommodation process); Hennenfant v. Mid Dakota Clinic, 164 F.3d 419, 8 AD Cases 1537 (8th Cir. 1998) (employee cannot support failure-to-accommodate claim when he refused defendant's request for independent medical examination); Templeton v. Neodata Servs., 162 F.3d 617, 8 AD Cases 1615 (10th Cir. 1998) (accommodation claim fails when plaintiff does not provide requested medical information); Steffes v. Stepan Co., 144 F.3d 1070, 8 AD Cases 352 (7th Cir. 1998) (plaintiff who failed to provide medical documentation on type of work she could do caused breakdown); Davis v. Guardian Life Ins. Co. of Am., 11 AD Cases 550 (E.D. Pa. 2000) ($1.5 million verdict overturned where plaintiff refused to participate in the interactive process).

[384]*See, e.g.,* Barnett v. U.S. Air, Inc., 228 F.3d 1105, 10 AD Cases 1761 (9th Cir. 2000) (en banc) (employer denied plaintiff's three suggested accommodations without discussion; summary judgment reversed); Cravens v. Blue Cross & Blue Shield of Kans., 214 F.3d 1011, 10 AD Cases 1057 (8th Cir. 2000) (failure to engage in interactive process is prima facie evidence of bad faith); Rehling v. City of Chicago, 207 F.3d 1009, 10 AD Cases 589 (7th Cir. 2000) (summary judgment may be denied when evidence suggests employer failed to engage in interactive process or caused it to break down); Taylor v. Phoenixville Sch. Dist., 184 F.3d 296, 9 AD Cases 1187 (3d Cir.

For example, in *Beck v. University of Wisconsin Board of Regents*,[385] the Seventh Circuit addressed an employee's responsibility for the breakdown of the interactive process. The plaintiff was a secretary who suffered from recurring major depression. The university reassigned her to a less stressful job after her first leave of absence. After her second leave of absence, the university requested more information from her physician, but she refused to sign the required medical release. Following her third leave, she gave the university a letter from her doctor, which requested "appropriate assistance with her workload," and that her workload be tailored to a level she and management believed she could do. The university asked the plaintiff to provide more information regarding the specific accommodation required. While waiting for that information, the university moved her desk to a quieter office and significantly decreased her workload. After several weeks, the plaintiff went on another medical leave without having provided the additional requested information, and the university terminated her employment. The district court granted summary judgment to the defendant on the plaintiff's claim of failure to accommodate.

The Seventh Circuit addressed whether the employer or the employee bore the ultimate burden to ascertain what accommodations were required. The court maintained that an employee first must advise the employer of her disability. Once she has done so, "the employer has at least some responsibility in determining the necessary accommodation . . . [T]he regulations envision an interactive process that requires participation by both parties."[386] The court concluded, however, that the interactive process had broken down because the plaintiff had failed to provide the defendant with additional information about her medical condition in response to the employer's request.[387] The court explained: "[B]ecause the University was never able to obtain an adequate understanding what action it should take, it cannot not be held liable for failure to make a reasonable accommodation."[388]

The *Beck* court noted that in determining the cause of the breakdown, the courts should look for evidence of failure to participate in good faith or evidence that one of the parties failed to help the other determine what specific accommodations were required.[389] The court explained that such evidence could include obstructing the interactive process, failing to initiate communication, failing to respond to communication, or failing to provide requested information—e.g., the nature of the disability, limitations imposed by the disability, and information about available equipment or work site modifications.[390]

1999) (genuine issue of material fact whether employer engaged in interactive process in good faith; plaintiff required to request specific accommodation); Bultemeyer v. Fort Wayne Cmty. Schs., 100 F.3d 1281, 6 AD Cases 67 (7th Cir. 1996) (summary judgment denied because employer failed to engage in interactive process).

[385]75 F.3d 1130, 5 AD Cases 304 (7th Cir. 1996).
[386]*Id.* at 1135, 5 AD Cases at 308.
[387]*Id.* at 1136, 5 AD Cases at 310.
[388]*Id.* at 1137; 5 AD Cases at 310.
[389]*Id.* at 1135, 5 AD Cases at 308.
[390]*Id.* at 1135–36, 5 AD Cases at 308.

E. Common Forms of Accommodation Requested by Mentally Disabled Individuals

The forms of reasonable accommodation that may be most applicable to employees with mental disabilities include unpaid leave, a flexible or modified work schedule, working at home, shift changes, and transfer to another job.

1. Unpaid Leave

Reasonable accommodation may include providing an employee with unpaid leave[391] for treatment or recovery related to a disability "unless (or until) the employee's absence imposes an undue hardship on the operation of the employer's business."[392]

Although the *EEOC Guidance on Psychiatric Disabilities* is ambiguous regarding whether indefinite leave is required as an accommodation and seems to place on the employer the burden of proving that provision of an indefinite leave would constitute an "undue hardship,"[393] the EEOC confirmed its position in its *Guidance on Reasonable Accommodation,* stating that an employer may deny leave to an employee who cannot provide a definite[394] date to return only if the employer can show undue hardship based on the employer's inability to provide a date of return.[395] The courts, however, have almost uniformly held that indefinite leave need not be provided as a reasonable accommodation, noting that the purpose of an accommodation is to assist the employee in doing the job as opposed to protecting an employee who cannot perform the job.[396]

---

[391] Such leave may also be required under the FMLA. *See* 29 U.S.C. §§2601 et seq.

[392] *EEOC Guidance on Reasonable Accommodation, supra* note 278, at 7473.

[393] This allocation of the burden of proof is at odds with the Eleventh Circuit's decision in *Willis v. Conopco, Inc.,* 108 F.3d 282, 6 AD Cases 806 (11th Cir. 1997), in which the court held that the plaintiff in an ADA case has the burden of proving that his proposed accommodation is reasonable. The employer may assert undue hardship as an affirmative defense, according to the Eleventh Circuit, but the initial burden remains on the plaintiff. *Id.* at 286, 6 AD Cases at 806–07.

[394] *EEOC Guidance on Reasonable Accommodation, supra* note 278, at 7632. For example, if the employee's inability to give a date of return "disrupt[s] the operation of the entity . . . because the employer can neither plan for the employee's return nor fill the position." *Id.*

[395] An employer cannot deny leave simply because the employee provides an approximate date of return. *Id.* at 7632.

[396] *E.g.,* Parker v. Columbia Pictures Indus., 204 F.3d 326, 10 AD Cases 396 (2d Cir. 2000) (employer not required to hold position indefinitely for employee); Walsh v. United Parcel Serv., 201 F.3d 718, 727, 10 AD Cases 161, 166 (6th Cir. 2000) (employee whose doctor said he could return in one to three years made request for indefinite leave; "when the requested accommodation has no reasonable prospect of allowing the individual to work in the identifiable future, it is objectively not an accommodation the employer should be required to provide"); Taylor v. Pepsi-Cola Co., 196 F.3d 1106, 9 AD Cases 1731 (10th Cir. 1999) (plaintiff who failed to present evidence of the projected duration of condition not entitled to medical leave because indefinite leave is not a reasonable accommodation); Mitchell v. Washington Cent.

For example, in *Myers v. Hose*,[397] and *Hudson v. MCI Telecommunications Corp.*,[398] the courts held that the ADA does not require indefinite leave because the concept of reasonable accommodation refers to steps that presently, or in the immediate future, enable the employee to perform the essential functions of the job in question. Moreover, repeated requests for extension of leave may be held unreasonable.[399] An employer, however, may not assume that the leave is indefinite.[400]

Generally, where plaintiffs have requested medical leaves of absence stretching beyond a year, the courts have held that the employee is not otherwise qualified as a matter of law.[401] The question then is whether there is an amount of time under one year that is unreasonable. For the most part, the courts have held that in cases involving less than one year of leave, the accommodation

---

Sch. Dist., 190 F.3d 1, 9 AD Cases 1123 (2d Cir. 1999) (indefinite leave not required); Nowak v. St. Rita High Sch., 142 F.3d 999, 1004, 8 AD Cases 106, 109 (7th Cir. 1998) ("[T]he ADA does not require an employer to accommodate an employee who suffers a prolonged illness by allowing him an indefinite leave of absence"); Monette v. Electronic Data Sys. Corp., 90 F.3d 1173, 1187, 5 AD Cases 1326, 1338 (6th Cir. 1996) ("[E]mployers simply are not required to keep an employee on staff indefinitely in the hope that some position may become available sometime in the future."); Smith v. Blue Cross & Blue Shield of Kans., 102 F.3d 1075, 6 AD Cases 367 (10th Cir. 1996) (employer not required to provide continued leave to employee with panic disorder when she had not provided any evidence of the expected duration of her disability); Johnson v. Foulds, Inc., 5 AD Cases 1635 (N.D. Ill. 1996) (indefinite leave for employee with depression not reasonable). *But see* Cehrs v. Northeast Ohio Alzheimers Research Ctr., 155 F.3d 775, 8 AD Cases 825 (6th Cir. 1998) (suggesting that indefinite unpaid leave could be a reasonable accommodation.)

[397]50 F.3d 278, 4 AD Cases 391 (4th Cir. 1995).

[398]87 F.3d 1167, 5 AD Cases 1099 (10th Cir. 1996).

[399]Walton v. Mental Health Ass'n of S. Pa., 168 F.3d 661, 9 AD Cases 34 (3d Cir. 1999) (employer not required to grant repeated extensions of requested leave).

[400]Haschmann v. Time Warner Entm't, 151 F.3d 591, 8 AD Cases 692 (7th Cir. 1998) (employer's argument that plaintiff requested indefinite leave rejected because company did not confirm leave was indefinite with plaintiff's doctor or have plaintiff submit to independent medical examination. *Accord* Powers v. Polygram Holding, Inc., 40 F. Supp. 2d 195, 9 AD Cases 1370 (S.D.N.Y. 1999) (failure to give absolute return date does not make plaintiff not qualified).

[401]Taylor v. Pepsi-Cola Co., 196 F.3d 1106, 9 AD Cases 1731 (10th Cir. 1999) (plaintiff who was out for 10.5 months and requested additional one-year leave was not otherwise qualified); Nowak v. St. Rita High Sch., 142 F.3d 999, 8 AD Cases 106 (7th Cir. 1998) (plaintiff missed approximately 18 months of work before being terminated); Courder v. Lucent Techs., Inc., 162 F.3d 924, 8 AD Cases 1611 (7th Cir. 1998) (plaintiff who had received 43 weeks of leave in 1991, 19 weeks in 1992, and 9 weeks in 1993 before her termination not otherwise qualified); Duckett v. Dunlop Tire Corp., 120 F.3d 1222, 7 AD Cases 572 (11th Cir. 1997) (plaintiff who received approximately 10 months of leave and requested two more not otherwise qualified); Rogers v. International Marine Terminals, Inc., 87 F.3d 755, 5 AD Cases 1115 (5th Cir. 1996) (requested accommodation would have been an approximately one year's leave of absence). *But see* Garcia-Ayala v. Parentals, Inc., 212 F.3d 638, 10 AD Cases 865 (1st Cir. 2000) (genuine issue whether leave extending beyond one year imposed

was reasonable or at least there was a genuine issue of material fact as to its reasonableness.[402]

There are two other types of requests for leaves that the courts have found unreasonable as a matter of law. The first involves leave that is so erratic that the employer does not know from one day to the next whether the employee will be returning to work or what time the employee might arrive.[403] The second involves requests for leave where the employee would still not be qualified upon returning from leave.[404]

The EEOC takes the position that during unpaid leave, an employer must hold open an employee's job as a reasonable accommodation unless the employer can show that holding the position open would impose an undue hardship.[405] The EEOC further maintains that if during an employee's medical leave the employer realizes it can no longer hold the employee's job open, the employer must evaluate whether there are available positions for which the employee is qualified and to which the employee can be transferred at the end of the leave.[406] The EEOC provides the following example:

---

undue hardship); Ralph v. Lucent Techs., Inc., 135 F.3d 166, 7 AD Cases 1345 (1st Cir. 1998) (request for 4 additional weeks' leave totaling a 52-week leave not unreasonable).

[402]Cehrs v. Northeast Ohio Alzheimers Research Ctr., 155 F.3d 775, 8 AD Cases 825 (6th Cir. 1998) (finding a genuine issue of fact as to whether an eight-week leave of absence followed by a request for an additional one-month leave was a reasonable accommodation under the ADA); Criado v. IBM Corp., 145 F.3d 437, 8 AD Cases 336 (1st Cir. 1998) (genuine issue of material fact whether a one-month disability leave followed by a request for a leave of an unspecified duration rendered the employee unqualified for her position); Rascon v. U.S. W. Communications, Inc., 143 F.3d 1324, 8 AD Cases 541 (10th Cir. 1998) (finding that the employee's request for a leave of absence after having been granted and taken three separate leaves of absence each for 30 days was a reasonable accommodation); Powers v. Polygram Holding, Inc., 40 F. Supp. 2d 195, 9 AD Cases 1370 (S.D.N.Y. 1999) (17-week leave of absence not too long to render employee legally unqualified for job); Shannon v. City of Philadelphia, 1999 WL 1065210 (E.D. Pa. Nov. 23, 1999) (jury question whether request by plaintiff with major depression for three months' leave after she exhausted FMLA leave was a reasonable accommodation).

[403]*See, e.g.*, Waggoner v. Olin Corp, 169 F.3d 481, 9 AD Cases 88 (7th Cir. 1999) (plaintiff missed work or was late for work 40 times during the 20 months she worked for defendant); Smartt v. Charlotte Housing Auth., 1998 WL 760866 (W.D.N.C. Apr. 7, 1998) (plaintiff could not report to work on time because she alleged that her medication made her drowsy); Scott v. American Airlines, Inc., 1997 WL 278129 (N.D. Tex. May 15, 1997) (employee's request to "arrive late whenever she so chooses and however late she so chooses" is not a reasonable accommodation).

[404]Tyndall v. National Educ. Ctrs. Inc., 31 F.3d 209, 3 AD Cases 868 (4th Cir. 1994) (accommodation of plaintiff's disability would not have improved plaintiff's attendance level because the majority of her absences were unrelated to her own disability); Allen v. GTE Mobile Cmty. Serv. Corp., 6 AD Cases 1063 (N.D. Ga. 1997) (plaintiff and her physician agreed that she could not return to work because the work environment contributed to the emotional problems that caused her disability).

[405]*EEOC Guidance on Reasonable Accommodation, supra* note 278, at 7615.
[406]*Id.*

An employee needs eight months of leave for treatment and recuperation related to a disability. The employer grants the request, but after four months the employer determines that it can no longer hold open the position for the remaining four months without incurring undue hardship. The employer must consider whether it has a vacant equivalent position to which the employee can be reassigned for the remaining four months of leave, at the end of which time the employee would return to work in a new position. If an equivalent position is not available, the employer must look for a vacant position at a lower level. Continued leave is not required as a reasonable accommodation if a vacant position at a lower level is also unavailable.[407]

The EEOC also holds that an employer may not apply to a disabled employee a "no fault" leave policy under which employees are automatically terminated after they have been on leave for a certain period of time.[408] According to the EEOC, the employer must modify a no-fault leave policy to provide a disabled employee with additional leave unless it can show either that (1) there is another effective accommodation that would enable the employee to perform the essential functions of the position or (2) granting additional leave would cause an undue hardship.[409]

2. Modified Work Schedule

Employees with mental disabilities may require a modified or flexible work schedule as a reasonable accommodation.[410] This includes adjusting arrival or departure times, providing periodic breaks, altering when certain functions are performed, or allowing an employee to use accrued paid leave for time missed.[411] The fact that an employer may not provide such modified or

---

[407] *EEOC Guidance on Reasonable Accommodation, supra* note 278, at 7615–16. Additionally, the employer may be required to reinstate the employee to the same or an equivalent position if the employee's disability also qualifies as a serious health condition under the FMLA and the employee has not exhausted his 12 weeks of leave under the Act. *See* 29 U.S.C. §2614(b)(1).

[408] *EEOC Guidance on Reasonable Accommodation, supra* note 278, at 7615. *See also* Garcia-Ayala v. Lederle Parenterals, Inc., 212 F.3d 638, 10 AD Cases 865 (1st Cir. 2000) (rejecting employer's argument that it could not be required to extend leave as an accommodation beyond one year because employer presented no evidence that it was an undue hardship to hold employee's position open); Gantt v. Wilson Sporting Goods, 143 F.3d 1042, 8 AD Cases 308 (6th Cir. 1998) (uniformly applied one-year leave of absence policy did not violate ADA but employer may be required to grant additional leave under ADA as a reasonable accommodation).

[409] *EEOC Guidance on Reasonable Accommodation, supra* note 278, at 7615. *See also* Ralph v. Lucent Techs., Inc., 135 F.3d 166, 7 AD Cases 1345 (1st Cir. 1998) (modified schedule is a form of reasonable accommodation). Again, if the employee's disability also qualifies as a serious health condition under the FMLA, the employer may not count the days missed under its no-fault attendance policy. 29 C.F.R. §825.220. Indeed, even if the leave causes an undue hardship for the employer under the ADA, the employee may not be terminated if he has not exhausted his FMLA allotment.

[410] *EEOC Guidance on Reasonable Accommodation, supra* note 278, at 7618.

[411] *Id.* at 7614–25.

flexible schedules for other employees is irrelevant to a reasonable accommodation analysis.[412]

Accommodations relating to attendance or punctuality involve an intertwining of the notions of "essential function" and "reasonable accommodation." In *Ward v. Massachusetts Health Research Institute*,[413] the First Circuit identified three different analyses used in cases dealing with requests for modified schedules: (1) whether a fixed schedule is an essential function of the specific job;[414] (2) if it is, whether there is a reasonable accommodation;[415] and (3) whether a modified schedule is a reasonable accommodation to allow an employee to perform the essential functions of the job.[416] The First Circuit in *Ward* adopted a two-prong analysis to determine whether attendance is an essential function and if it is, whether a modified schedule is a reasonable accommodation.[417]

In *Ward*, an employee with inflammatory arthritis, which caused swelling and pain in his joints, requested a modified work schedule. The employer, which had a flextime schedule that allowed all employees to start work anytime between 7:00 and 9:00 and leave after they had worked 7.5 hours, denied the request on the ground that the ADA did not require an accommodation that would permit the employee to start work later than other employees. The district court granted summary judgment for the employer. The First Circuit reversed, finding insufficient evidence in the record that a regular and predictable schedule was an essential function of the data entry position, that an open-ended schedule would be an undue hardship, or that the employee had a constant need for supervision. Furthermore, there was no evidence that the position required the employee to be present during certain hours of the working day. The court noted that the data had to be entered only before the next morning. The court further noted that the employer had failed to offer any evidence of undue hardship, other than asserting that such an accommodation would eliminate its control over the workplace and ability to maintain standards.[418]

---

[412]*Id.* at 7618.

[413]209 F.3d 29, 10 AD Cases 776 (1st Cir. 2000).

[414]*See, e.g.*, Laurin v. Providence Hosp., 150 F.3d 52, 8 AD Cases 768 (1st Cir. 1998) (shift rotation an essential function in 24-hour marketing unit because some shifts are less desirable than others); Tyndall v. National Educ. Ctrs., Inc., 31 F.3d 209, 3 AD Cases 868 (4th Cir. 1994) (instructor at business college required to teach and see students on campus during scheduled class times); Salmon v. Dade County Sch. Bd., 4 F. Supp. 2d 1157, 1162–63 (S.D. Fla. 1998) ("guidance counselor must counsel students at the school during the hours in which the children are in attendance"); EEOC v. AIC Sec. Investigation Ltd., 820 F. Supp. 1060, 2 AD Cases 561 (N.D. Ill. 1993) (denying summary judgment due to question of fact whether regular attendance is an essential function of job).

[415]Jacques v. Clean-Up Group, Inc., 96 F.3d 506, 5 AD Cases 1594 (1st Cir. 1996); Carr v. Reno, 23 F.3d 525, 3 AD Cases 434 (D.C. Cir. 1994).

[416]*Ward*, 209 F.3d at 33, 10 AD Cases at 780–81.

[417]*Id.*, 10 AD Cases at 780–81.

[418]*Id.* at 35–37, 10 AD Cases at 780–81. *But see* Soto-Ocasio v. Federal Express Corp., 150 F.3d 14, 20, 8 AD Cases 1067, 1072 (1st Cir. 1998) (employer could not grant requested accommodation because it would have required other employees to do plaintiff's data entry work so that she met her deadlines); *Laurin*, 150 F.3d 52, 8 AD

In contrast, in *Earl v. Mervyns, Inc.*,[419] the defendant fired an employee with Obsessive-Compulsive Disorder after she was late for work 33 times in a 365-day period because of her disability. Her psychiatrist testified that nothing

---

Cases 768 (shift rotation is an essential function of a day nurse position in a hospital maternity unit); *Jacques*, 96 F.3d 506, 5 AD Cases 1594 (jury reasonably found that accommodating the plaintiff by allowing him to start working later in the day would be unreasonable when 8:00 a.m. start time was essential function); *Tyndall*, 31 F.3d at 213–14, 3 AD Cases at 871 (regular and reliable level of attendance is a necessary element of most jobs; plaintiff, a college professor, "held a job that could not be performed away from. . . . campus, her position required that she teach the assigned courses during the scheduled class times"); Carr v. Reno, 23 F.3d 525, 3 AD Cases 434 (D.C. Cir. 1994) (employer's 4:00 p.m. deadline rendered a flexible schedule an undue hardship where employee requested a flexible arrival time that would allow her to arrive between 8:00 a.m. and noon and even with a flexible schedule, plaintiff was unable to work a full eight-hour day); Wojciechowski v. Emergency Technical Servs. Corp., 6 AD Cases 1290 (N.D. Ill. 1997) (an essential function of inside sales representative position was regular attendance during normal working hours; employer not obligated to allow plaintiff to work at home because she could not show that such an accommodation would allow her to regularly and predictably work full-time); Aquinas v. Federal Express Corp., 940 F. Supp. 73, 79, 6 AD Cases 485, 488 (S.D.N.Y. 1996) (plaintiff's proposed accommodation to work a flexible work schedule, "which amounts to a request for permission to work only when her illness permits, necessarily undermines the policy of regular attendance that is essential to her job"); Fritz v. Mascotech Auto. Sys. Group, Inc., 914 F. Supp. 1481, 6 AD Cases 1103 (E.D. Mich. 1996) (keeping of regular hours was an essential function of designer's job, but summary judgment denied because defendant failed to prove that it could not reasonably accommodate plaintiff's disability); Vorhies v. Pioneer Mfg., Co., 906 F. Supp. 578, 6 AD Cases 572 (D. Colo. 1995) (plaintiff was the only employee assigned certain tasks, his job description included attendance as an essential function of the job, and plaintiff failed to show a reasonable accommodation was possible); Hendry v. GTE, N., Inc., 896 F. Supp. 816, 6 AD Cases 451 (N.D. Ind. 1995) (regular attendance is a necessary element of the service clerk position where position was essentially a "one person operation" and use of substitute employee during plaintiff's illness was not a reasonable accommodation); Barfield v. BellSouth Telecomms., Inc., 886 F. Supp. 1321, 1325–27, 4 AD Cases 1159, 1163–64 (S.D. Miss. 1995) ("regular and predictable attendance is an essential function of the job of service representative" where one important facet of the job is dealing with customers' complaints and inquiries, so plaintiff's "open-ended work when able schedule" request was unreasonable); Heise v. Genuine Parts Co., 900 F. Supp. 1137, 4 AD Cases 1551 (D. Minn. 1995) (question of fact existed as to the amount and timing of customer contact that is an essential function of the job); Dutton v. Johnson County Bd. of County Comm'rs, 859 F. Supp. 498, 3 AD Cases 808 (D. Kan. 1994) (employer failed to establish that plaintiff's use of unscheduled vacation to cover his disability-related absences was an unreasonable accommodation); Kennedy v. Applause, Inc., 3 AD Cases 1734 (C.D. Cal. 1994), *aff'd*, 90 F.3d 1477, 5 AD Cases 1249 (9th Cir. 1996) (work-when-able schedule not a reasonable accommodation for time sensitive job); Guice-Mills v. Derwinski, 772 F. Supp. 188, 199, 1 AD Cases 1886 (S.D.N.Y. 1991) (administrative workweek tour of duty was a critical requirement for head nurse; employer therefore had no duty to grant plaintiff's request for late start time).

[419]207 F.3d 1361, 10 AD Cases 673 (11th Cir. 2000).

could be done to help her get to work on time. The court held that the employer was not required to allow the plaintiff to start work once she arrived without reprimanding her or to allow her to make up time at the end of her shift.[420]

Thus, in those situations where an employer can show attendance or attendance during particular hours is an essential function, courts most likely will conclude that the modified schedule sought is not reasonable. Likewise, when a shift accommodation would cause other employees to have to do the requesting employee's work, courts will likely find the request unreasonable.[421]

3. Part-Time Work

Generally, an employer is obligated to allow an employee to work part-time as a reasonable accommodation where the employee is returning from a leave of absence and the part-time schedule is not for an indefinite period of time or an undue hardship. For example, in *Ralph v. Lucent Technologies, Inc.*,[422] the First Circuit ruled that a plaintiff who suffered from depression was entitled to an accommodation that would allow him to work part-time for 4 weeks even though the employer had previously reassigned him and given him 52 weeks of paid medical leave. Additionally, in *Parker v. Columbia Picture Industries, Inc.*,[423] the court held that allowing an employee to work part-time for a finite period of time is a reasonable accommodation if the employee can perform the essential functions of the job on the reduced schedule. If an employee needs indefinite part-time work, however, the employee is essentially asking the employer to create a part-time position, which is not required as an accommodation.[424]

Finally, an employer is not obligated to pay full-time pay for a reduced-work-schedule employee,[425] and if an employee is given a part-time job as an accommodation and benefits are available only to full-time employees, the employee is not entitled to continued benefits.[426]

---

[420]*Id.* at 1367, 10 AD Cases at 676.

[421]*See Soto-Ocasio*, 150 F.3d 14, 8 AD Cases 1067 (requested accommodation would require an employer to reallocate appellant's data entry work to other employees to ensure that her deadlines were met); *Carr*, 23 F.3d 525, 3 AD Cases 434 (flexible schedule an undue hardship because others would have to regularly do plaintiff's work); *Guice-Mills*, 772 F. Supp. 188, 1 AD Cases 1886 (waiving start time of 10:00 a.m. for supervisor was unreasonable because her duties would have to be reassigned).

[422]135 F.3d 166, 7 AD Cases 1345 (1st Cir. 1998).

[423]204 F.3d 326, 335–36, 10 AD Cases 396, 401 (2d Cir. 2000).

[424]*See* Treanor v. MCI Telecomm. Corp., 200 F.3d 570, 10 AD Cases 80 (8th Cir. 2000); Terrell v. USAir, 132 F.3d 621, 8 AD Cases 529 (11th Cir. 1998); Burch v. Coca Cola, 119 F.3d 305, 7 AD Cases 241 (5th Cir. 1997); *Soto-Ocasio*, 150 F.3d 14, 8 AD Cases 1067.

[425]Roads v. Bob Florence Contractor, Inc., 890 F. Supp. 960, 4 AD Cases 1201 (D. Kan. 1995) (employee whose back impairment prevented him from working more than 30 hours a week was not entitled to be paid for 40 hours as a reasonable accommodation).

[426]*EEOC Guidance on Reasonable Accommodation, supra* note 278, at 7605; Tenbrink v. Federal Home Loan Bank, 920 F. Supp. 1156, 15 AD Cases 1283 (D.

4. Shift Changes

The EEOC has recognized that the ability to work a specific shift can be an essential function of a job.[427] In discussing the concept of essential functions, the EEOC's *Technical Assistance Manual* provides an example where a company has a floating supervisor who substitutes for the regular supervisors on various shifts.[428] Because the position exists to work on various shifts, it is an essential function of the job to be able to work any time of day.[429] If the shift is essential to the ability to perform the functions of the job, it does not have to be changed as a reasonable accommodation. For example, in *Turco v. Hoechst Celanese Chemical Corp.*,[430] the court held that the employer was not obligated to create a straight day-shift position for a diabetic employee who could not work a rotating shift, which was an essential job function.

5. Working at Home

Working at home may be a reasonable accommodation.[431] depending on the job at issue.[432]

Kan. 1996) (plaintiff with Chronic Fatigue Syndrome working on part-time schedule did not have to be provided with medical benefits as a reasonable accommodation).

[427]*EEOC Technical Assistance Manual*, *supra* note 17, at 6981, 6994.
[428]*Id.* at 6994.
[429]*Id.*
[430]101 F.3d 1090, 6 AD Cases 278 (5th Cir. 1996).
[431]*EEOC Guidance on Reasonable Accommodation*, *supra* note 278, 7626 (employer must modify policy concerning where work is performed to allow employee to work at home if doing so is effective and not an undue hardship); *see also* Carr v. Reno, 23 F.3d 525, 3 AD Cases 434 (D.C. Cir. 1994) (work at home may be a reasonable accommodation); Langon v. Department of Health & Human Servs., 959 F.2d 1053, 2 AD Cases 152 (D.C. Cir. 1992) (employer must consider accommodation of working at home). *But see* Vande Zande v. Wisconsin Dep't of Admin., 44 F.3d 538, 3 AD Cases 1636 (7th Cir. 1997) (work at home is not a reasonable accommodation as a matter of law).
[432]*EEOC Guidance on Reasonable Accommodation*, *supra* note 278, at 7626 (noting that certain jobs, like cashier and food service, must be performed on site while others, such as telemarketing and proofreading, may be done at home). *See also* Kvorjak v. State of Maine, 259 F.3d 48, 12 AD Cases 160 (1st Cir. 2001) (working at home not a reasonable accommodation for claims adjuster where essential job functions involved attending hearings, conducting training, and dealing with public); Waggoner v. Olin Corp., 169 F.3d 481, 9 AD Cases 88 (7th Cir. 1999) (working at home might be reasonable accommodation for some jobs but not production jobs); Hypes v. First-Commerce Corp., 134 F.3d 721, 7 AD Cases 1546 (5th Cir. 1998) (employer not required to permit loan review analyst with chronic lung disease, which limited his ability to travel regularly to the office, to work at home or part-time because regular attendance is an essential function and employers are not required to accept lowered productivity, especially where employee's presence is necessary to ensure efficient team functioning); Smith v. AmeriTech, 129 F.3d 857, 7 AD Cases 917 (6th Cir. 1997) (employer not required to permit sales representative to work at home because it would

For example, in *Humphrey v. Memorial Hospital Association*,[433] a medical transcriptionist with Obsessive-Compulsive Disorder, who was constantly late for work, if she arrived at all, requested to work at home when her prior accommodation of a flexible work schedule was not effective. The employer denied the request because the plaintiff had been disciplined for tardiness in the past, which made her ineligible under the employer's work-at-home policy. The Ninth Circuit found summary judgment inappropriate because the plaintiff's physician testified that working at home might accommodate the plaintiff's disability because her mental impairment did not interfere with her ability to type and transcribe; the plaintiff testified that her condition primarily interfered with her ability to leave her home.

In contrast, in *Vande Zande v. Wisconsin Department of Administration*,[434] the court held that a paraplegic employee was not entitled to the reasonable accommodation of working at home full-time because her job involved supervised teamwork rather than solitary unsupervised work and such work could not be done at home without a significant decline in the quality of the employee's performance. The court held that the ADA does not require an employer to permit disabled employees to work without supervision where their productivity would be greatly reduced.[435]

6. Transfer

Reassignment to a vacant position generally must be considered only when accommodation within the individual's current position would pose an undue hardship or when there is no accommodation that would enable the employee to perform his current job.[436] An employer is not required to transfer an employee

---

result in a productivity loss); *Langon*, 959 F.2d 1053, 2 AD Cases 152 (finding that there was a genuine issue about whether the plaintiff could perform her computer programmer job at home); Stanley v. Lester M. Pronje, Inc., 25 F. Supp. 2d 581, 8 AD Cases 1157 (E.D. Pa. 1998) (not reasonable accommodation for log clerk to work at office four hours a day and at home four hours a day when essential job functions included training and meeting with drivers); Wojciechowski Emergency Technical Servs. Corp., 6 AD Cases 1290, 1293 (N.D. Ill. 1997) (inside sales representative failed to "show that working at home would have allowed her to regularly and predictably work full-time, not to mention perform each of her other essential duties"); Whillock v. Delta Airlines, 926 F. Supp. 1555, 5 AD Cases 1027 (N.D. Ga. 1995) (airline reservation sales agent could not work at home because of necessity of monitoring, training, evaluating, and counseling); Anzalone v. Allstate, Ins. Co., 5 AD Cases 455 (E.D. La. 1995) (claim adjuster's request to work at home was not, per se, unreasonable because the employer had permitted other employees to work at home and there was no evidence that his productivity would decrease if he worked at home, considering a substantial part of his job was performed in the field rather than at the office).

[433] 239 F.3d 1128, 11 AD Cases 765 (9th Cir. 2001).
[434] 44 F.3d 538, 3 AD Cases 1636 (7th Cir. 1995).
[435] *Id.* at 545, 3 AD Cases at 1640.
[436] 29 C.F.R. §1630.20 app.; Vollmart v. Wisconsin Dep't of Transp., 197 F.3d 293, 9 AD Cases 1704 (7th Cir. 1999) (summary judgment denied to employer who

when no vacant positions are available.[437] Nor is an employer required to transfer an employee merely because of a conflict with a supervisor.[438] To be entitled to the transfer, the employee must be qualified for the position he or she desires.[439] If, however, the employee's disability prevents the employee from

---

transferred employee with a learning disability to another job when she had a problem learning new computer skills because evidence suggested that intensive training would have enabled her to learn them); Bryant v. Better Bus. Bureau, 923 F. Supp. 720, 5 AD Cases 625 (D. Md. 1996) (transfer of employee with a hearing problem to a different position, which received fewer telephone calls, instead of providing a TTY device in her prior position created a genuine issue of material fact as to whether the employer failed to reasonably accommodate employee's disability because the employer did not show that providing a TTY device would impose an undue hardship); Vazquez v. Bedsole, 888 F. Supp. 727, 4 AD Cases 970 (E.D.N.C. 1995) (deputy sheriff who could no longer drive a car, carry a weapon, or apprehend a criminal because of the symptoms of a depressed skull fracture was still qualified to perform various other sheriff deputy positions that did not require her to perform those duties and thus created a genuine issue of material fact whether the employer violated the ADA when it terminated her rather than reassigning her to a vacant position).

[437]Gonzagowski v. Widnall, 115 F.3d 744, 6 AD Cases 1559 (10th Cir. 1997) (military was not required to transfer computer programmer with anxiety disorder because there was no evidence that a position was open and the plaintiff did not establish that he had requested such transfer); Dalton v. Subaru-Isuzu Auto., Inc., 141 F.3d 667, 7 AD Cases 1872 (7th Cir. 1998) (employer did not have to reassign automobile workers to jobs occupied by temporary employees because even temporary employees do not have to be bumped out of job to make room for a disabled full-time employee).

[438]*EEOC Guidance on Reasonable Accommodation, supra* note 278, at 7625–26; Kennedy v. Dresser Rand Co., 193 F.3d 120, 9 AD Cases 1335 (2d Cir. 1999) (reassignment away from supervisor as reasonable accommodation is presumptively unreasonable and plaintiff must overcome presumption); Gaul v. Lucent Techs., Inc., 134 F.3d 576, 7 AD Cases 1223 (3d Cir. 1998) (proposed accommodation of being transferred away from supervisor would impose a wholly impractical obligation on any employer); Siemon v. AT&T Corp., 113 F.3d 1175, 6 AD Cases 1249 (10th Cir. 1997) (employer did not have to transfer employee with severe depression and anxiety, which employee said was brought on by working with particular supervisor, to another position); Weiler v. Household Fin. Corp., 101 F.3d 519, 6 AD Cases 106 (7th Cir. 1996) (employer did not have to transfer an allegedly disabled employee to work for a different supervisor or transfer the employee's current supervisor based on employee's allegations that her stress and related disorders were caused or exacerbated by the current supervisor); Mears v. Gulfstream Aerospace Corp., 905 F. Supp. 1075, 1080, 5 AD Cases 1295, 1300 (S.D. Ga. 1995) (court rejects proposed accommodation of not having contact with supervisor; "requiring a company to employ a person in a particular department while forbidding a supervisor from having any contact with her would be undue burden on the employer"); DeWitt v. Carsten, 941 F. Supp. 1232, 1236, 6 AD Cases 1255, 1257 (N.D. Ga. 1996) ("were an employee able to demand reassignment merely because her boss creates stress, entire business offices could go unstaffed").

[439]Jackan v. New York State Dep't of Labor, 205 F.3d 562, 10 AD Cases 497 (2d Cir. 2000); Davoll v. Webb, 194 F.3d 1116, 9 AD Cases 1533 (10th Cir. 1999); Dalton v. Subaru-Isuzu Auto., Inc., 141 F.3d 667, 7 AD Cases 1872 (7th Cir. 1998);

being able to perform the essential functions of the present position and he is qualified for the available position, the employer must transfer him to the available position.[440] An employee being accommodated by reassignment, however, cannot be required to compete for a new position.[441]

7. Accommodation of Employee Misconduct

Employers are often confronted with behavior that may be (or may be alleged to be) a manifestation of a mental disability covered by the ADA. According to various enforcement guidances issued by the EEOC, an employer may hold all employees to the same performance and conduct standards and is not required to waive or rescind discipline for a disabled employee as a reasonable accommodation in most circumstances—provided the workplace conduct standard is job related for the position in question and consistent with business necessity.[442] The EEOC reiterated this standard in its *Guidance on Reasonable Accommodation*, stating that an employer is not required to forgo discipline or termination of an employee who violates a workplace conduct standard that is job related and consistent with business necessity simply because the individual is disabled:

> An employer never has to excuse a violation of a uniformly applied conduct rule that is job related and consistent with business necessity. This means, for example, that an employer never has to tolerate or excuse violence, threats of violence, stealing or destruction of property. An employer may discipline an employee

---

Foreman v. Babcock & Wilcox, Co., 113 F.3d 1402, 6 AD Cases 1523 (5th Cir. 1997); Turco v. Hoechst Celanese Corp., 101 F.3d 1090, 6 AD Cases 278 (5th Cir. 1996).

[440]Gile v. United Airlines, Inc., 95 F.3d 492, 5 AD Cases 1466 (7th Cir. 1996) (depressed data entry operator with sleep disorder who could not work the night shift was possibly entitled to reinstatement to a vacant equivalent daytime position for which she was qualified); Benson v. Northwest Airlines, Inc., 62 F.3d 1108, 4 AD Cases 1234 (8th Cir. 1995) (concluding that reassignment to engineering positions comparable to jobs that the plaintiff performed previously or to another vacant job precluded summary judgment); Laurin v. Providence Hosp., 150 F.3d 52, 8 AD Cases 768 (1st Cir. 1998) (nurse with seizure disorder was not entitled to be assigned to permanent day shift even though the employer had done that on a temporary basis because the employer is not required to make a temporary position permanent under the ADA).

[441]Barnett v. U.S. Air, Inc., 228 F.3d 1105, 10 AD Cases 1761 (9th Cir. 2000) (en banc); Smith v. Midland Brake, Inc., 180 F.3d 1154, 9 AD Cases 738 (10th Cir. 1999) (en banc); Aka v. Washington Hosp. Ctr., 156 F.3d 1284, 8 AD Cases 1093 (D.C. Cir. 1998) (en banc). *But see* EEOC v. Humiston-Keeling Inc., 227 F.3d 1024, 10 AD Cases 1665 (7th Cir. 2000) (ADA does not obligate employers to reassign less qualified employee to vacancy when more qualified candidates exist; such is "affirmative action with a vengeance"); Foreman v. Babcock & Wilcox Co., 117 F.3d 800, 7 AD Cases 331 (5th Cir. 1997) (reassignment not required because ADA does not require affirmative action).

[442]*EEOC Guidance on Psychiatric Disabilities, supra* note 14, at 7476.

with a disability for engaging in such misconduct if it would impose the same discipline on an employee without a disability.[443]

Additionally, the EEOC has taken the position that if the punishment for the misconduct is not termination, the employer must reasonably accommodate the disabled employee who violates a conduct rule to assist the employee to comply with the conduct standard in the future, unless doing so would impose an undue hardship. An employer is not required to excuse past misconduct even if it is caused by the employee's disability, however,[444] nor are disabled employees terminated for misconduct or failure to perform entitled to a second chance as a reasonable accommodation.[445]

Courts have taken differing views of this issue.[446] In *EEOC v. Amego, Inc.*,[447] a behavioral therapist in a residential care facility for autistic and behavior-disordered adolescents and adults whose job duties included administering prescription medication to facility residents tried to kill herself (while off duty) by overdosing on medication. Her employer subsequently terminated her, and the EEOC filed a lawsuit alleging that the employer violated the ADA by doing so. The employer moved for summary judgment, arguing that the employee was not qualified for a position involving the handling of prescription medication, having disqualified herself by her two suicide attempts utilizing medication. The EEOC (taking a position that varied from that set forth in its enforcement guidance) argued that the suicide efforts were behavioral manifestations of the employee's disability and that firing her for such a reason was effectively firing her because she was disabled. The district court granted summary judgment for the employer. The EEOC appealed, and the First Circuit affirmed, observing: "To the extent that the EEOC is arguing a conduct connected to a disability must always be considered to be action 'because of' a disability, that is too broad a formulation."[448]

---

[443]*EEOC Guidance on Reasonable Accommodation*, supra note 278, 7627.
[444]*Id.* at 7627.
[445]*See, e.g.*, Hill v. Kansas City Area Transp. Auth., 181 F.3d 891, 9 AD Cases 833 (8th Cir. 1999) (plaintiff not entitled to second chance to control her controllable disability); Burch v. Coca-Cola, Co., 119 F.3d 305, 7 AD Cases 241 (5th Cir. 1997) (alcoholic's request to return to his old job not a request for a reasonable accommodation); Siefken v. Village of Arlington Heights, 65 F.3d 664, 4 AD Cases 1441 (7th Cir. 1995) (plaintiff not entitled to second chance to properly monitor medication); Zihala v. Illinois Dep't of Health, 1999 WL 116221 (N.D. Ill. Feb. 26, 1999) (second chance is not the same as a request for accommodation under the ADA); Green v. George L. Smith II World Cong. Ctr. Auth., 987 F. Supp. 1481, 7 AD Cases 1419 (N.D. Ga. 1997) (defendant not required to delete from records bipolar plaintiff's violation of a policy; retroactive reasonable accommodation not required); Flynn v. Raytheon Co., 868 F. Supp. 383, 3 AD Cases 1495 (D. Mass. 1994), *aff'd*, 94 F.3d 640 (1st Cir. 1996) (ADA does not require employer to rehire a former employee who was lawfully discharged for disability-related failure to meet its legitimate job requests).
[446]*See* James J. McDonald, Jr., *My Disability Made Me Do It!*, 27 EMPL. REL. L.J. 83 (2001).
[447]110 F.3d 135, 6 AD Cases 997 (1st Cir. 1997).
[448]*Id.* at 149, 6 AD Cases at 1009.

Conversely, in *Den Hartog v. Wasatch Academy*,[449] a teacher at a private school was fired because of his mentally ill son's physical attacks against a former schoolmate and threats against the headmaster and his children. The district court granted summary judgment for the school, drawing a distinction between disability and misconduct resulting from a disability and holding the latter to be unprotected by the ADA. The Tenth Circuit affirmed, albeit on different grounds, but it rejected the district court's distinction between disability and misconduct resulting from a disability. It explained:

> The text of the ADA makes only one specific reference to "disability-caused misconduct," where an employer is authorized to disregard the fact that the misconduct or prior performance may be caused by disability and where the employer can hold a disabled person to exactly the same conduct as a non-disabled person. It provides that an employer: may hold an employee who engages in illegal use of drugs or who is an alcoholic to the same qualification standards for employment or job performance and behavior that such entity holds other employees, even if any such unsatisfactory performance or behavior is related to the alcoholism or drug use of such employee.[450]

The *Den Hartog* court accepted the plaintiff's argument that the district court had erred by importing the distinction between "disability versus disability-caused misconduct into a case in which neither drugs nor alcohol were involved."[451] The court stated that the dichotomy between disability and disability-caused misconduct is unique to alcoholism and drugs. The *Den Hartog* court, however, did not suggest that disability-caused misconduct that caused a direct threat had to be accommodated.[452] Rather, the court maintained that, in light of the ADA's undue hardship and direct threat defenses:

> [T]here are certain levels of disability-caused conduct that need not be tolerated or accommodated by employers. However, the necessary corollary is that there must be certain levels of disability-caused conduct that have to be tolerated or accommodated. [But] appellee's effort to put all disability-caused conduct beyond the pale of ADA protection cannot be correct. Mental illness is . . . normally diagnosed on the basis of abnormal behavior. To permit employers carte blanche to terminate employees with mental disabilities on the basis of any abnormal behavior would largely nullify the ADA's protection of the mentally disabled.[453]

The Tenth Circuit in *Den Hartog* ultimately affirmed summary judgment for the employer because it found the plaintiff's son posed a direct threat to the safety of others.

Most courts to date have followed the First Circuit's approach. In *Adams v. Alderson*,[454] a computer programmer with a compulsive personality disorder

---

[449] 129 F.3d 1076, 7 AD Cases 764 (10th Cir. 1997).
[450] *Id.* at 1086, 7 AD Cases at 773 (citing 42 U.S.C. §12114(c)(4)).
[451] *Id.*
[452] *Id.* at 1087, 7 AD Cases at 774.
[453] *Id.* at 1087–88, 7 AD Cases at 774.
[454] 723 F. Supp. 1531, 51 FEP Cases 647 (D.D.C. 1989).

attacked a supervisor and destroyed office equipment. He requested reassignment to a different supervisor as a reasonable accommodation. The court held that the employer was not obligated to tolerate a propensity for violence and that reassignment away from a supervisor was not a reasonable accommodation. Likewise, in *Palmer v. Circuit Court of Cook County*,[455] an employee diagnosed with depression and a delusional paranoid disorder who threatened a supervisor that she would "kick her ass" and "throw her out a window" did not have to be accommodated.

In *Spath v. Hayes Wheels International—Indiana, Inc.*,[456] the employer terminated the plaintiff after he filed a false workers' compensation claim over an incident of horseplay. The plaintiff then sued, alleging that the employer failed to accommodate his organic brain syndrome, mild mental retardation, and dependent personality disorder, which he claimed caused him to deny involvement in the horseplay incident. The Seventh Circuit rejected this notion, remarking, "In essence, Spath is asking this Court to extend the ADA so as to prevent an employer from terminating an employee who lies, just because the lying is allegedly connected to a disability. We are of the opinion that the ADA does not require this."[457] Other courts have reached similar results.[458]

The Ninth Circuit, however, recently followed the *Den Hartog* approach in *Humphrey v. Memorial Hospital Ass'n,*[459] involving a medical transcriptionist with Obsessive-Compulsive Disorder who engaged in a series of obsessive rituals that prevented her from arriving at work on time if at all. After concluding that there was a genuine issue of material fact on whether the employer could have accommodated her by allowing her to work at home, the court held that the plaintiff's termination for absenteeism was unlawful if her Obsessive-Compulsive Disorder had caused her absences. It explained:

> For purposes of the ADA, with a few exceptions, conduct resulting from a disability is considered to be part of the disability, rather than a separate basis

---

[455]117 F.3d 351, 6 AD Cases 1569 (7th Cir. 1997).

[456]211 F.3d 392, 10 AD Cases 878 (7th Cir. 2000).

[457]*Id.* at 395 n. 5, 10 AD Cases at 880 n.5.

[458]*E.g.,* Sullivan v. River Valley Sch. Dist., 197 F.3d 804, 9 AD Cases 1711 (6th Cir. 1999) (threatening others disqualifies an employee from a job); Jones v. American Postal Workers Union Nat'l, 192 F.3d 417, 429, 9 AD Cases 1249, 1257 (4th Cir. 1999) (employer may terminate employee for threatening to kill his supervisor even if threat is disability-related; "the law is well-settled that the ADA is not violated when an employer discharges an individual based on the employee's misconduct, even if the misconduct is related to a disability"); Hamilton v. Southwestern Bell Tel. Co., 136 F.3d 1047, 8 AD Cases 1219 (5th Cir. 1998) (ADA does not protect employees who have violent or emotional outbursts on the job); Taylor v. Dover Elevator Sys., 917 F. Supp. 455 (N.D. Miss. 1996) (rejecting plaintiff's argument that medication that he took for epilepsy caused him to get into fight that resulted in his discharge); James v. James River Paper Co., 1995 WL 938383 (D. Or. Apr. 6, 1995), *aff'd,* 101 F.3d 705 (9th Cir. 1996) (epileptic plaintiff with anxiety and sleep disorder who became physically confrontational with coworker can be terminated even if conduct was disability-related).

[459]239 F.3d 1128, 11 AD Cases 765 (9th Cir. 2001).

for termination. The link between a disability and termination is particularly strong where it is the employer's failure to reasonably accommodate a known disability that leads to discharge for performance inadequacies resulting from a disability.[460]

The court further stated that "[t]he text of the ADA authorizes discharges for misconduct or inadequate performance that may be caused by a "disability" in only one category of cases—alcoholism and illegal drug use.[461]"

The *Den Hartog* and *Humphrey* line of cases therefore hold that an employer must accommodate inappropriate behavior even if it is job related, so long as it (1) is not the result of illegal drug use or alcohol abuse, (2) does not involve egregious or criminal conduct, (3) does not pose a direct threat to the health and safety of others, or (4) would not result in undue hardship. Whether other courts will follow this trend remains to be seen.

8. Requirement That Employee Obtain Treatment

An employer may not force or coerce an employee to accept a proffered accommodation.[462] Where misconduct or poor performance is involved, the question is whether the employer may offer an employee the option of treatment or termination without violating the ADA. As discussed below, a "treatment or termination" ultimatum most likely does not violate the ADA if, at the point the offer is made, the employer has communicated to the employee that he or she is about to be fired or disciplined for misconduct or performance issues and the employer has either exhausted its reasonable accommodation efforts or no accommodation is available.[463]

Courts have almost uniformly permitted employers to put admitted alcoholics or employees whose work performance deteriorates because of alcohol abuse to such an election.[464] For example, in *McKey v. Occidental Chemical Corp.*,[465] an employee was fired after he violated his "return to work" agreement that required him to seek treatment for alcoholism and attend therapy as designated by his EAP counselor and abstain from drinking alcohol. The employee was subsequently terminated for violating the no-alcohol provision in the agreement. The court upheld the plaintiff's termination, noting that he understood that "failure to comply with any of the . . . conditions [of his return to work agreement] would be cause for immediate termination."[466] The courts have not decided, however, whether an employer can put an employee who has a mental

---

[460]*Id.* at 1139–40, 11 AD Cases at 774.

[461]*Id.* at 1139 n.18, 11 AD Cases at 774 n. 18.

[462]42 U.S.C. §12201(d).

[463]*Id.* §12201(d); Roberts v. City of Fairfax, 937 F. Supp. 541, 548–49, 8 AD Cases 919, 926 (E.D. Va. 1996).

[464]*See* Fuller v. Frank, 916 F.2d 558, 1 AD Cases 1701 (9th Cir. 1990).

[465]956 F. Supp. 1313, 6 AD Cases 883 (S.D. Tex. 1997).

[466]*Id.* at 1318, 6 AD Cases at 887.

disability not involving abuse of drugs or alcohol to a treatment or termination election.[467]

Generally, monitoring an employee's medication is not a reasonable accommodation.[468] The EEOC's *Guidance on Psychiatric Disabilities* provides that in dealing with a disabled employee who is engaging in misconduct because he is not taking his medication, "[t]he employer should focus on the employee's conduct and explain . . . the consequences of misconduct in terms of uniform disciplinary procedures. It is the *employee's* responsibility to decide about medication and to consider the consequences of not taking the medication."[469] The EEOC's statement implies that if the individual does not take the medication and if such failure causes misconduct or poor performance to continue, the employer may terminate the employee. Courts have followed this reasoning.[470] Presumably, the same reasoning would apply to other forms of treatment, including psychological counseling.

If the employer may legally terminate the employee, then arguably the employer may, rather than terminating the employee, offer a treatment or termination option. *Equal Employment Opportunity Commission v. Hertz Corp.*,[471] provides support for this position. In *Hertz,* the court held that the defendant was not legally obligated to continue employing two mentally retarded employees after it dismissed their full-time job coaches, both of whom were provided by a federally funded entity. The EEOC argued that such dismissal violated the ADA. In rejecting the EEOC's position, the court noted that the employer should not be punished for its generosity. Likewise, employers who offer employees an alternative to legally imposed discipline or termination should not be penalized for, in effect, offering an employee a second chance,

---

[467]At least one court has upheld a last-chance agreement for an employee with a mental disability. *See* Franklin v. United States Postal Serv., 687 F. Supp. 1214, 1 AD Cases 1312 (S.D. Ohio 1988) (last-chance agreement for employee with paranoid schizophrenia).

[468]Robertson v. Neuromedical Ctr., 161 F.3d 292 (5th Cir. 1998) (employer is not obligated to require neurologist with ADHD who posed direct threat to take his medication because medication is a "personal choice"); Brookins v. Indianapolis Power & Light Co., 90 F. Supp. 2d 993, 1004 (S.D. Ind. 2000) (employer had no obligation to schedule an appointment for employee with anxiety and depression to see a psychiatrist who would prescribe medication for his condition).

[469]*EEOC Guidance on Psychiatric Disabilities, supra* note 14, at 7475.

[470]*Id. See, e.g.,* Siefken v. Village of Arlington Heights, 65 F.3d 664, 4 AD Cases 1441 (7th Cir. 1995) (police officer terminated when he experienced a diabetic reaction while driving on duty did not state a claim under the ADA because he failed to control a controllable disability by not taking his medication; employer not required to give him a second chance to properly monitor his medication); Franklin v. United States Postal Serv., 687 F. Supp. 1214, 1 AD Cases 1312 (S.D. Ohio 1988) (defendant's termination of plaintiff was not discriminatory because misconduct resulted from plaintiff's failure to take her medication); Hardy v. Sears, Roebuck & Co., 1996 WL735565 (N.D. Ga. Aug. 28, 1996) (defendant did not fail to accommodate plaintiff because plaintiff's failure to take lithium increased the risk of aggressive behavior).

[471]7 AD Cases 1097 (E.D. Mich. 1998).

which they have no obligation to do.[472] Conditioning continued employment on acceptance of a proposed course of treatment, however, is not without risk.[473]

F. Accommodations Not Required

Various sources have suggested a wide range of accommodations of mental disabilities that might be appropriate.[474] Many of these are aspirational as opposed to mandatory, however, at least under current case law. An employer's obligation to accommodate employees with mental disabilities is not unlimited. For example, the courts will not require employers to eliminate essential job functions in order to accommodate a mentally disabled employee. In *Hill v. Florida Department of Public Health*,[475] the court held that an employer did not have to eliminate the public contact function of a position to accommodate an employee with a depressive disorder who could not tolerate the stress of contact with the public, because such an accommodation would impose undue hardship by requiring a coworker to perform the employee's job. Similarly, in *Larkins v. CIBA Vision Corp.*,[476] the court held that an employer was not obligated to eliminate the telephone answering function from a job for an employee who was unable to field telephone calls because of panic attacks caused by Posttraumatic Stress Disorder.[477]

Additionally, an employer is not required to lower qualitative or quantitative production standards that are uniformly applied to employees with and without disabilities.[478] An employer, however, may be required to provide a

---

[472] "[I]f the employer ... bends over backwards to accommodate a disabled worker—goes farther than the law requires—it must not be punished for its generosity by being deemed to have conceded the reasonableness of so far reaching an accommodation. That would hurt rather than help disabled workers." Vande Zande v. Wisconsin Dep't of Admin., 44 F.3d 538, 545, 3 AD Cases 1636, 1640 (7th Cir. 1995).

[473] *See* Pettus v. Cole, 49 Cal. App. 4th 402, 12 IER Cases 74 (Ct. App. 1996) (employer violated employee's "autonomy privacy" interest in making intimate personal decisions about the appropriate course of medical treatment for his disabling stress condition when it terminated him after he refused to enter inpatient alcohol rehabilitation as a condition of continued employment).

[474] *See, e.g.*, Paul J. Carling, *Reasonable Accommodations in the Workplace for Individuals with Psychiatric Disabilities, in* IMPLICATIONS OF THE AMERICANS WITH DISABILITIES ACT FOR PSYCHOLOGY 103 (Suzanne M. Bruyere & Janet O'Keeffe eds., 1994); DEBORAH ZUCKERMAN, KATHLEEN DEBENHAM & KENNETH MOORE, THE ADA AND PEOPLE WITH MENTAL ILLNESS: A RESOURCE MANUAL FOR EMPLOYERS 15–52 (1992).

[475] 2 AD Cases 177 (M.D. Fla.1992).

[476] 858 F. Supp. 1572, 3 AD Cases 715 (N.D. Ga. 1994).

[477] *See also* Beaver v. Delta Air Lines, Inc., 43 F. Supp. 2d 685 (N.D. Tex. 1999) (high productivity can be an essential element of a position); Pikora v. Blue Cross/Blue Shield of Mich., 970 F. Supp. 591 (E.D. Mich. 1997) (phone usage was essential to customer service position).

[478] 29 C.F.R. §1630.2(n) app.

reasonable accommodation that enables an employee to meet the qualitative or quantitative production standards.[479]

Furthermore, employers are not required to provide treatment or monitoring of an employee's condition.[480] In *Gardner v. Morris*,[481] an employee with Bipolar Disorder was granted a transfer to Saudi Arabia. While en route, he had a severe episode and was hospitalized. His physician adjusted the amount of lithium prescribed and required that the employee's lithium level be monitored, which would have been difficult in a remote location. The court held that to require the employer to retain a physician and provide laboratory facilities for the monitoring of the employee's lithium level in Saudi Arabia would constitute an undue hardship. Similarly, in *Hogarth v. Thornburgh*,[482] an FBI communications operator was held to be not otherwise qualified for his job because his inability to perceive reality hampered his ability to send and receive confidential documents and could have produced dire consequences for the safety of others. The court also held that to require the FBI to monitor the employee's medication or alter his position so that he did not handle classified information would impose an undue hardship. Finally, in *Robertson v. Neuromedical Center*,[483] a neurologist with Attention Deficit Hyperactivity Disorder argued that the defendant failed to accommodate him because it could have monitored his medication intake. The court held that the accommodation proposed was not reasonable because the decision to take or not to take medication is a personal one, not an accommodation option for the employer.[484] Indeed, an employer may not require an employee to take medication or undergo treatment.[485] There are two exceptions to this prohibition: (1) when the employer does so in lieu of termination[486] and (2) when monitoring or treatment is job related and consistent with business necessity.[487]

Moreover, the ADA does not require an employer to eliminate stress from the work environment[488] or to alter a particular position as an accommodation

---

[479]*EEOC Guidance on Reasonable Accommodation*, supra note 278, at 7601.

[480]*Id.* at 7627.

[481]752 F.2d 1271, 1 AD Cases 673 (8th Cir. 1985).

[482]833 F. Supp. 1077, 2 AD Cases 1777 (S.D.N.Y. 1993).

[483]161 F.3d 292 (5th Cir. 1998).

[484]*Id.* at 296.

[485]Equal Employment Opportunity Commission, *Guidance on Disability Related Inquiries and Medical Examinations of Employee Under the Americans with Disabilities Act* (July 26, 2000), *reprinted in* 8 FEP Manual 405:7712 [hereinafter *EEOC Guidance on Disability Related Inquiries*].

[486]*Id.* at 7717.

[487]*Id.* at 7716–18.

[488]*See* Pesterfield v. Tennessee Valley Auth., 941 F.2d 437, 1 AD Cases 1858 (6th Cir. 1991) (plaintiff's inability to handle rejection or criticism made it impossible to perform the essential functions of his job, and it was not reasonable to require defendant to provide him with a stress-free environment to accommodate his disability); Potter v. Xerox Corp., 88 F. Supp. 2d 109, 82 FEP Cases 1116 (W.D.N.Y. 2000) (employer not obligated to provide plaintiff security investigator who suffered from anxiety and depression with stress-free work environment).

in order to eliminate stress.[489] An employer may be required, however, to *reduce* stress as a reasonable accommodation if such would not constitute an undue hardship.[490] For example, in *Kent v. Derwinski*,[491] the plaintiff's mental retardation and undefined emotional disability caused difficulties with interpersonal relationships, extreme sensitivity to derogatory comments and criticism, anxiety, and emotional outbursts. The court held that the employee was entitled to a reasonable accommodation in the form of sensitivity training of coworkers, which included training on appropriate and inappropriate remarks and jokes to make in the workplace to coworkers with disabilities.[492] The court additionally required the employee's supervisor to use care in discipline to avoid direct criticism or undue stress.[493]

G. Undue Hardship

An accommodation might constitute an undue hardship if it is "excessively costly, extensive, substantial or disruptive," or would "fundamentally alter the nature or operation of the business."[494] Although the financial condition of the employer may be taken into account, the financial difficulty involved in a particular accommodation will not be determinative in and of itself on the question of whether such an accommodation is reasonable.[495] Moreover, to the extent that the cost of providing an accommodation constitutes an undue hardship, the disabled employee must be given the option of helping pay the cost of the accommodation.[496]

---

[489]*See* Schmidt v. Bell, 1 AD Cases 491 (E.D. Pa. 1983) (plaintiff suffering from PTSD did not have to be accommodated by transfer to another supervisor; position of student loan collector is by its nature stressful, and evidence showed plaintiff reacted explosively when confronted by authority, criticized, or placed in a frustrating stressful situation).

[490]*See* Gonzagowski v. Widnall, 115 F.3d 744, 747–48, 6 AD Cases 1559, 1561 (10th Cir. 1997) (accommodation that plaintiff with anxiety disorder be put in work environment free from stress and criticism not reasonable; "[w]hile specific stressors in a work environment may in some cases be legitimate targets of accommodation, it is unreasonable to require an employer to create a work environment free of stress and criticism"). *But see* Arenson v. Sullivan, 946 F.2d 90, 2 AD Cases 31 (8th Cir. 1991) (defendant should have provided employee suffering from apraxia, which caused him difficulty in expressing ideas and in writing, with distraction-free environment of private work area, computer, and tape recorder).

[491]790 F. Supp. 1032, 2 AD Cases 947 (E.D. Wash. 1991).

[492]*Id.* at 1040, 2 AD Cases at 952.

[493]*Id.*

[494]29 C.F.R. §1630.2(p) app. (Interpretive Guidance).

[495]*Id.*; Muller v. Costello, 5 AD Cases 779 (N.D.N.Y. 1996) (reasonableness of accommodations depends on effectiveness and cost to employer); Garza v. Abbott Labs., 940 F. Supp. 1227, 6 AD Cases 1507 (N.D. Ill. 1996) (accommodation is reasonable if it is effective in enabling employee to do job and cost-effective to employer).

[496]*EEOC Technical Assistance Manual*, *supra* note 17, at 6999.

Furthermore, undue hardship is not limited to the economic cost of the accommodation.[497] It may also be found in the disruptive impact that a proposed accommodation would have on the employer's business operation. For example, if restructuring a job to accommodate a disabled individual creates a heavier workload for other employees, an undue hardship may result. On the other hand, an undue hardship would not exist merely because other employees complain about an employer's granting a disabled coworker unpaid leave or a more flexible work schedule, where such accommodation has no direct impact upon them.[498]

V. Drug and Alcohol Abuse

A. Drug Use

The ADA protects former drug addicts whose addiction constituted a substantially limiting impairment and individuals who are erroneously perceived as engaging in the current use of illegal drugs.[499] A former casual drug user who did not have an addiction is not covered under the ADA, however.[500] The ADA, moreover, specifically excludes individuals currently using illegal drugs from coverage,[501] whether or not they are addicted to drugs.

The illegal use of drugs includes the use of illegal drugs that are controlled substances and the illegal use of prescription drugs that are controlled substances.[502] If an employee tests positive for any illegal drugs such as marijuana or methadone, the employer should make sure that the employee is not using the drug under the supervision of a licensed health care professional. For example, an employee may use marijuana for glaucoma, and methadone may be used to treat a recovering heroin addict. Such use would be considered legal use.

"Current" drug use is illegal drug use that occurred recently enough to justify an employer's reasonable belief that the drug use is an ongoing prob-

---

[497]*EEOC Guidance on Reasonable Accommodation, supra* note 278, at 7604.

[498]*EEOC Technical Assistance Manual, supra* note 17, at 7006 n. 10.

[499]*See* 42 U.S.C. §12114(b); *EEOC Technical Assistance Manual, supra* note 17, at 6981, 7052–53; Zenor v. El Paso Healthcare Sys., Ltd., 176 F.3d 847, 9 AD Cases 609 (5th Cir. 1999) (recovering drug addict must show that his condition substantially limited him in a major life activity to qualify for ADA coverage).

[500]Buckley v. Consolidated Edison Co. of N.Y., Inc., 127 F.3d 270, 274, 7 AD Cases 794, 797 (2d Cir. 1997) ("past drug addiction, not merely past use, is required to make out a claim under the ADA"); Hartman v. City of Petaluma, 841 F. Supp. 946, 2 AD Cases 1860 (N.D. Cal. 1994) (there must be "some indicia of dependence" to be considered substantially limiting).

[501]42 U.S.C. §12114(a); 29 C.F.R. §1630.3(a).

[502]Nielson v. Moroni Feed Co., 162 F.3d 604, 611 n.12, 8 AD Cases 1553, 1559 n.12 (10th Cir. 1998); 29 C.F.R. §1630.3 app.

lem.⁵⁰³ The courts have held that an individual may be considered a current user even if he has not used drugs for a number of weeks or even months.⁵⁰⁴ In *Shafer v. Preston Memorial Hospital Corp.*,⁵⁰⁵ a nurse who was terminated after she stole medication to which she had become addicted filed an ADA claim against her employer. During the investigation of the theft, the nurse went into drug rehabilitation. The hospital terminated her the day after she completed her inpatient drug rehabilitation for "gross misconduct involving the diversion of controlled substances."⁵⁰⁶ The court concluded that the plaintiff was still a current illegal drug user, noting that "the ordinary or natural meaning of the phrase currently using drugs does not require that a drug user have a heroin syringe in his arm or a marijuana bong to his mouth at the exact moment contemplated."⁵⁰⁷ Rather, an individual is a current user if he illegally used drugs "in a periodic fashion during the weeks and months prior to discharge."⁵⁰⁸

In *McDaniel v. Mississippi Baptist Medical Center*,⁵⁰⁹ the plaintiff entered a drug treatment center before his termination. The court held he nonetheless was not protected by the ADA because he had not been drug free for a "considerable length of time since he had not used drugs for only a few weeks."⁵¹⁰ Similarly, in *Salley v. Circuit City Stores, Inc.*,⁵¹¹ the court held that a heroin addict who had a lengthy history of heroin addiction with intervening

---

⁵⁰³*See* 29 C.F.R. §1630.3 app.; Collins v. Longview Fibre Co., 63 F.3d 828, 4 AD Cases 1278 (9th Cir. 1995) (current use does not mean a certain number of days or weeks but means that the use occurred recently enough so plaintiffs were current users even though they had entered a rehabilitation program).

⁵⁰⁴*Zenor*, 176 F.3d 847, 9 AD Cases 609 (cocaine-using pharmacist who used cocaine five weeks before hospital notified him of termination was current user); Salley v. Circuit City Stores, Inc., 160 F.3d 977, 8 AD Cases 1407 (3d Cir. 1997) (drug use was current because not using for only three weeks was too current for plaintiff to be protected by safe harbor provision); Quigley v. Austeel Lemont Co., 79 F. Supp. 2d 941, 10 AD Cases 351 (N.D. Ill. 2000) (plaintiff who had been drug free only one month at time of his discharge was current user); Vedernikov v. West Virginia Univ., 55 F. Supp. 2d 518 (D. W.Va. 1999) (anesthesiologist who abused fentenyl in November and who denied it even while in employer-mandated treatment program was still current user in February); McDaniel v. Mississippi Baptist Med. Ctr., 877 F. Supp. 321, 4 AD Cases 241 (S.D. Miss. 1998), *aff'd*, 74 F.3d 1238, 6 AD Cases 800 (6th Cir. 1995) (employee who had been drug free only six weeks at time of termination was current user); Baustian v. Louisiana, 910 F. Supp. 274, 4 AD Cases 1692 (E.D. La 1995) (plaintiff who had abstained from using drugs for only seven weeks was not a recovered addict because testimony showed he had not abstained long enough to be stable recovering addict).

⁵⁰⁵107 F.3d 274, 6 AD Cases 682 (4th Cir. 1997).

⁵⁰⁶*Id.* at 275, 6 AD Cases at 683.

⁵⁰⁷*Id.* at 281, 6 AD Cases at 685.

⁵⁰⁸*Id.*

⁵⁰⁹877 F. Supp. 321, 4 AD Cases 241 (S.D. Miss. 1998), *aff'd*, 74 F.3d 1238, 6 AD Cases 800 (6th Cir. 1995).

⁵¹⁰*Id.*

⁵¹¹160 F.3d 977, 8 AD Cases 1407 (3d Cir. 1997).

periods of treatment who relapsed was still a current user because he had been drug free for only three weeks.

A drug addict who violates workplace rules cannot obtain the ADA's protection by enrolling in a supervised drug rehabilitation program. In *Zenor v. El Paso Healthcare System, Ltd.*,[512] a cocaine-addicted pharmacist entered a residential rehabilitation facility and was subsequently terminated. The employee objected to his termination because the company's drug policy stated that employees who self-reported their drug use would not be fired. The hospital was concerned, however, because pharmaceutical cocaine would be available to the pharmacist where he worked. Although the pharmacist offered to transfer to a day shift where he could be monitored or to a satellite pharmacy where pharmaceutical cocaine would be unavailable, the employer rejected his request. Following a jury trial, the district court granted the employer's motion for judgment as a matter of law on the plaintiff's disability discrimination claim.

In upholding the district court's decision, the Fifth Circuit court noted that the plaintiff had stopped using cocaine for only five weeks, during which time he was hospitalized or in a residential treatment program. The court explained:

> Such a short period of abstinence, particularly following such a severe drug problem, does not remove from the employer's mind a reasonable belief that the drug use remains a problem. [The plaintiff's] position as a pharmacist required a great deal of care and skill, and [plaintiff] admits that any mistakes could gravely injure [the employer's] patients. Moreover, [the employer] presented substantial testimony about the extremely high relapse rate of cocaine addiction. [The plaintiff's] own counselors, while supportive and speaking highly of [the plaintiff's] progress, could not say with any real assurance that [the plaintiff] wouldn't relapse. Finally, [the employer] presented substantial evidence regarding the on-going nature of cocaine-addiction recovery. The fact that [the plaintiff] completed the residential portion of his treatment was only the first step in a long-term recovery program. Based on these factors, [the employer] was justified in believing that the risk of harm from a potential relapse was significant, and that [the plaintiff]'s drug abuse remained an ongoing threat.[513]

The court further noted that the plaintiff's entry into a rehabilitation program did not bring him within the safe harbor of protection of 42 U.S.C. §12114(b), which provides that an individual who has successfully completed a supervised drug rehabilitation program and is no longer engaging in the illegal use of drugs, or who is participating in a supervised rehabilitation program and is no longer engaging in such use, may be a qualified individual with a disability. The court noted that the House Report on this provision stated that the safe harbor provision applied only to individuals who had been drug free for a significant period of time.[514] Moreover, the court rejected the plaintiff's argu-

---

[512] 176 F.3d 847, 9 AD Cases 609 (5th Cir. 1999).

[513] *Id.* at 857, 9 AD Cases at 615.

[514] *Id.* at 857, 9 AD Cases at 615. *See* H.R. CONF. REP. NO. 101-596, at 64 ("On the other hand, this provision recognizes that many people continue to participate in

ment that he was protected by the safe harbor provision because he self-reported his addiction and voluntarily entered a treatment program.[515]

B. Alcoholism

Alcoholism may be a disability under the ADA if it substantially limits an individual's major life activities. Employers nonetheless may prohibit the use of alcohol in the workplace, require that employees not be under the influence of alcohol in the workplace, and hold an alcoholic employee to the same job performance and behavioral standards to which it holds other employees even if unsatisfactory performance or inappropriate behavior is related to the employee's alcoholism.[516] An employer may not, however, apply its workplace rules more stringently to alcoholic employees.[517]

Generally a leave of absence to obtain medical treatment for alcoholism is reasonable accommodation.[518] The ADA legislative history, however, indicates that an employer is not obligated to pay for alcohol rehabilitation treatment. In Senate proceedings, when asked, "Is the employer under a legal obligation under the Act to provide rehabilitation for employee who is using . . . alcohol?" Senator Harkin responded, "No, there is no such legal obligation."[519] Furthermore, the Senate report states that a reasonable accommodation "does not affirmatively require that the covered entity must provide a rehabilitation program or an opportunity for rehabilitation . . . for any current employee who is [an] alcoholic against whom employment-related actions are taken" for performance or conduct reasons.[520] In *Schmidt v. Safeway, Inc.*,[521] the court stated that an employer is not required to give a leave of absence for an alcoholic employee to get treatment if such treatment would be futile.[522] Specifically, an employer is not required to "provide repeated leaves of absence (or perhaps

---

drug treatment programs long after they have stopped using drugs illegally, and that such persons should be protected under the Act").

[515]*See also* Quigley v. Austeel Lemont Co., Inc., 79 F. Supp. 2d 941, 10 AD Cases 351 (N.D. Ill. 2000); Shafer v. Preston Mem'l Hosp. Corp., 107 F.3d 274, 6 AD Cases 682 (4th Cir. 1997); Wormley v. Arkla, Inc., 871 F. Supp. 1079, 3 AD Cases 1703 (E.D. Ark. 1998).

[516]42 U.S.C. §12114(c); 29 C.F.R. §1630.16(b)(4).

[517]Miners v. Cargill Communications, Inc., 113 F.3d 820, 6 AD Cases 1229 (5th Cir. 1997) (evidence that employer inconsistently applied alcohol policy gave rise to perceived-as-disability claim); Flynn v. Raytheon Co., 868 F. Supp. 383, 3 AD Cases 1495 (D. Mass. 1994).

[518]Schmidt v. Safeway, Inc., 864 F. Supp. 991, 3 AD Cases 1141 (D. Or. 1994).

[519]135 Cong. Rec. S10777 (daily ed. Sept. 7, 1989).

[520]S. Rep. No. 101-116, at 41–42 (1989).

[521]864 F. Supp. 991, 3 AD Cases 1141 (D. Or. 1994).

[522]*Id.* at 991, 3 AD Cases at 1146.

even a single leave of absence) for an alcoholic employee with a poor prognosis for recovery."[523]

Finally, the courts have routinely upheld the termination of alcoholics for misconduct.[524]

VI. Benefit Plans

The ADA does not mandate that employers cover mental disabilities under their health care plans for employees. Although an employer may not discriminate on the basis of disability against a qualified individual with a disability in regard to fringe benefits available by virtue of employment,[525] such as employee health or long-term disability insurance plans, health plan distinctions that do not discriminate on the basis of disability do not violate the ADA. Although the EEOC initially stated that it is not a violation of the ADA to provide a lower

---

[523]*Id. See also* Evans v. Federal Express Corp., 133 F.3d 137, 140, 8 AD Cases 151, 153 (1st Cir. 1998) (employer not required to provide second leave of absence for substance abuse treatment because "it is one thing to say that further treatment made medical sense and quite another to say that the law required the company to accommodate [the employee] through a succession of efforts"); Corbett v. National Prods. Co., 4 AD Cases 987, 990 (E.D. Pa. 1995) (employer is not required to give "several leaves of absence [to] an alcoholic worker for whom a successful treatment is unlikely," but employer violated ADA when it refused to grant 28-day leave of absence for alcohol rehabilitation). Note that leave of absence may also be mandated by the FMLA, 29 U.S.C. §2601. *See* 29 C.F.R. §§825.114(d), 825.112(9).

[524]Renaud v. Wyoming Dep't of Family Servs., 203 F.3d 723, 5 WH Cases 2d 1505 (10th Cir. 2000) (ADA does not distinguish between alcoholism and alcoholism-related misconduct; therefore, employer could terminate school superintendent for reporting to work drunk); Barnsville Exempted Village Sch. Dist. Bd. of Educ., 209 F.3d 931, 10 AD Cases 787 (6th Cir. 2000) (employer did not discriminate against former custodian who had been disciplined for drinking on the job when it refused to hire him as a bus driver); Newland v. Dalton, 81 F.3d 904, 5 AD Cases 735 (9th Cir. 1996) (employee fired because of drunken rampage during which he attempted to fire an assault rifle at bar patrons was not discriminated against even if rampage was caused by his alcoholism); Maddox v. University of Tenn., 62 F.3d 843, 4 AD Cases 1253 (6th Cir. 1995) (employer properly terminated assistant football coach after his third arrest for DUI); Despears v. Milwaukee County, 63 F.3d 635, 4 AD Cases 1313 (7th Cir. 1995) (employer could legally demote employee after his fourth conviction for drunk driving); Murphy v. Village of Hoffman Estates, 1999 WL 160305 (N.D. Ill. Mar. 17, 1999) (employer did not violate the ADA by terminating recovering alcoholic employee for drinking at work even if unacceptable behavior was caused by disability); Williams v. Anheuser-Busch, Inc., 957 F. Supp. 1246, 6 AD Cases 905 (M.D. Fla. 1997) (alcoholic employee who told patrons at a bar that he urinated in beer was terminated for alcohol-related misconduct, not because he was an alcoholic).

[525]29 CFR §1630.4(f).

level of benefits for mental conditions than for physical conditions,[526] the agency eventually changed its position in regard to distinctions within long-term disability insurance plans.[527] The courts, however, have not been receptive.

Some courts have held that the ADA does not protect former employees (for example, those seeking long-term disability benefits) because the person does not qualify as a qualified individual with a disability.[528] Other courts that consider former employees as qualified individuals with a disability nonetheless have held that a shorter term of coverage for mental disabilities under an employer's long-term disability plan does not violate the ADA.[529]

VII. Medical Examinations and Inquiries

The ADA limits an employer's ability to make medical inquiries and to require employee applicants and employees to submit to medical examinations.[530] The restrictions differ at the various stages of the employment process. Congress based the parameters of medical examinations and inquiries under the ADA on Rehabilitation Act regulations.[531]

---

[526]Equal Employment Opportunity Commission, *Interim Guidance on Application of ADA to Health Insurance* (June 8, 1993), *reprinted in* FEP Manual 405:7115. *See also* Doe v. Colautti, 592 F.2d 704 (3d Cir. 1979) (Rehabilitation Act did not require Pennsylvania's medical assistance to provide the same level of benefits for inpatient hospital treatment of mental illness as for inpatient hospital treatment of physical illness); Doe v. Devine, 545 F. Supp. 576 (D.D.C. 1982) (Blue Cross cutbacks in mental health benefits for federal employees reasonable and did not discriminate on the basis of disability), *aff'd on other grounds*, 703 F.2d 1319 (D.C. Cir. 1983).

[527]Equal Employment Opportunity Commission, *Employee Benefits* (Oct. 3, 2000), *reprinted in* EEOC Compliance Manual, 627:0001, 0022.

[528]Weyer v. Twentieth Century Fox Film Corp., 198 F.3d 1104, 10 AD Cases 65 (9th Cir. 2000); EEOC v. CNA Ins. Cos., 96 F.3d 1039, 5 AD Cases 1769 (7th Cir. 1996); Gonzales v. Garner Food Servs., 89 F.3d 1523, 5 AD Cases 1202 (11th Cir. 1996).

[529]EEOC v. Aramark Corp., Inc., 208 F.3d 266, 10 AD Cases 798 (D.C. Cir. 2000); McNeil v. Time Ins. Co., 205 F.3d 179, 10 AD Cases 415 (5th Cir. 2000); Weyer v. Twentieth Century Fox Film Corp., 198 F.3d 1104, 1116–18, 10 AD Cases 65, 71–74 (9th Cir. 2000); Lewis v. K-Mart, 180 F.3d 166, 9 AD Cases 791 (4th Cir. 1999); Ford v. Schering-Plough Corp., 145 F.3d 601, 8 AD Cases 190 (3d Cir. 1998).

[530]42 U.S.C. §12112(d).

[531]"[A] review of the legislative history shows that the section on medical examinations and inquiries was included to parallel the same requirements and regulations under the Rehabilitation Act of 1973, and designed to prevent employers from using preemployment information obtained from forms and interviews to exclude applicants with disabilities, particularly persons with 'hidden' disabilities." Armstrong v. Turner Indus., Ltd., 950 F. Supp. 162, 167, 7 AD Cases 875, 879–80 (M.D. La. 1996), *aff'd*, 141 F.3d 554, 8 AD Cases 118 (5th Cir. 1998).

A. Preemployment Inquiries

1. General

The ADA prohibits preemployment inquiries (whether on an application or in an interview) concerning whether the applicant has a disability or concerning the nature or severity of such a disability[532] or seeking information about an individual's physical or psychological health.[533] It does, however, allow employers to ask questions concerning an applicant's ability to perform the essential functions of the job.[534] For example, an applicant may be asked, "How many days of work did you miss last year?" but not, "How many days were you sick last year?"[535] Inquiries about past treatment for mental health problems are also prohibited.[536]

Generally, there are three exceptions to the general rule prohibiting pre-offer medical inquiries: (1) when preemployment inquiries concern an applicant's ability to perform job-related functions,[537] (2) when an employer can reasonably believe that an applicant's known disability[538] will interfere with his performance of a job-related function,[539] and (3) when an applicant requests reasonable accommodation for the application process or for a job.[540]

Courts have permitted preemployment medical inquiries when the employer was aware of an applicant's disability. In *Grenier v. Cyanamid Plastics, Inc.*,[541] an employer asked a former employee who the employer knew suffered paranoia directed at its plant manager, whether he could effectively function at work and get along with his coworkers and management. The employer also requested a medical certification from the former employee's psychiatrist

---

[532] 42 U.S.C. §12112(d)(2)(A). In *Armstrong v. Turner Industries*, 141 F.3d 554, 8 AD Cases 118 (5th Cir. 1998), the Fifth Circuit held that a nondisabled job applicant who was subjected to preemployment medical inquiries but still hired had no standing because he had not suffered a compensable injury. *But see* Griffin v. Steeltek, Inc., 160 F.3d 591, 8 AD Cases 1249 (10th Cir. 1999) (nondisabled applicant subjected to preemployment medical inquiries who was not hired had standing under ADA).

[533] A disability-related inquiry is one that is likely to elicit information about a disability. *EEOC Guidance on Disability Related Inquiries*, supra note 485, at 7704.

[534] 42 U.S.C. §12112(c)(2)(B).

[535] Equal Employment Opportunity Commission, *EEOC Guidance on Pre-Employment Inquiries Under the ADA*, reprinted in 8 FEP Manual 405:7190, at 405:7194 [hereinafter *EEOC Guidance on Pre-Employment Inquiries*].

[536] *Id.* at 7192–93.

[537] 42 U.S.C. §12112(d)(2)(B).

[538] The disability may be known because it is obvious, e.g., blindness, or because the applicant voluntarily discloses an invisible disability. *EEOC Guidance on Pre-Employment Inquiries*, supra note 535, at 7193.

[539] 29 C.F.R. §1630.14(a); *EEOC Guidance on Pre-Employment Inquiries*, supra note 535, at 7193 (when an employer can reasonably believe that an applicant's known disability will interfere with the performance of a job-related function, the employer may ask the applicant to describe or demonstrate how he would perform the function with or without reasonable accommodation).

[540] *EEOC Guidance on Pre-Employment Inquiries*, supra note 535, at 7193.

[541] 70 F.3d 667, 5 AD Cases 75 (1st Cir. 1995).

confirming his ability to function at work. The First Circuit found that this did not violate the ADA's prohibition on preemployment medical inquiries. The court reasoned that an employer should be encouraged to engage in the interactive process with a disabled individual to determine a reasonable accommodation, and it rejected the plaintiff's argument that the employer was restricted to confirming his technical qualifications because such qualifications were not the only qualifications for the job.[542] The court held that an employer could also require medical certification about the applicant's mental and emotional state.[543] The court noted that the employer's belief that the former employee was not capable of performing the job was reasonable under the circumstances.[544]

Likewise, in *Harris v. Harris & Hart, Inc.*,[545] the Ninth Circuit held that an employer's refusal to rehire an employee with carpal tunnel syndrome, absent a medical release, did not violate the ADA. The plaintiff, a sheet metal worker, complained that the employer had failed to reasonably accommodate him and then resigned. Approximately 12 days later the union sent him back to work for the defendant and then sent him back again one year later. The court noted that the "[d]efendant had no reason to believe plaintiff's condition had cured itself, and no reason a year later to believe that the union's decision to send him out constituted a guarantee of his fitness to perform the essential functions of a sheet metal worker. In short, defendant knew of plaintiff's disability, knew the union had sent him out even while suffering from it, and had no evidence that he had recovered."[546] The court endorsed the premise that an employer may treat a former employee with a known disability like an injured employee returning to work.[547]

These cases are consistent with the EEOC's position.[548] In response to the inquiry "whether an employer may ask how an individual will perform job functions when the individual's known disabilities appear to interfere with or prevent the performance of job related functions," the EEOC's regulations state that an employer may make "pre-employment inquiries into the ability of an applicant to perform job related functions, and/or may ask an applicant to describe or to demonstrate how, with or without reasonable accommodation, the applicant will be able to perform job related functions."[549] The same is true if the applicant voluntarily discloses a disability.[550]

---

[542]*Id.* at 674–75, 5 AD Cases at 81.

[543]*Id.*, 5 AD Cases at 82.

[544]*Id.*, 5 AD Cases at 81.

[545]206 F.3d 838, 10 AD Cases 481 (9th Cir. 2000).

[546]*Id.* at 843, 10 AD Cases at 485.

[547]*Id.*

[548]*EEOC Guidance on Pre-Employment Inquiries, supra* note 535, at 7193.

[549]29 C.F.R. §1630.14(a). *See also* Brumley v. Pena, 62 F.3d 277, 4 AD Cases 1239 (8th Cir. 1995) (FAA allowed to require a former employee who wanted to return to work after he had been terminated for medical reasons to undergo an independent medical examination to find out whether the plaintiff had fully recovered from severe depression because he was still receiving disability payments).

[550]*See* Thomas v. Mississippi State Dep't of Health, 934 F. Supp. 768 (S.D. Miss. 1996) (former employee terminated for drug abuse and addiction could be questioned

2. Preemployment Psychological Testing

There are a variety of testing instruments available for personnel assessment. Some predict how well an applicant will get along in a particular work environment. Others describe more generally the personality traits possessed by an individual. Still others gauge an applicant's honesty.

Whether a preemployment test is permissible under the ADA depends upon whether it can be classified as a "medical examination," since the ADA prohibits pre-offer medical examinations.[551] Medical examinations are procedures or tests that seek information about an individual's physical or mental impairment or physical or psychological health. Psychological tests that discern an individual's skills or tastes are not considered medical, however.[552] The following factors are used to determine whether a test is medical in nature:

- Whether the test is administered by a health care professional or someone trained by a health care professional;
- Whether the results are interpreted by a health care professional or someone trained by a health care professional;
- Whether the test is designed to reveal the existence, nature, or severity of an impairment or the subject's physical or psychological health;
- Whether the employer is administering the test for the purpose of revealing the existence, nature, or severity of an impairment or the subject's physical or psychological health;
- Whether the test is invasive (e.g., whether it requires the drawing of blood, urine, breath, etc.);
- Whether the test measures physiological or psychological responses as opposed to the individual's performance of a task;
- Whether the test is normally administered in a medical setting (e.g., a health care professional's office, a hospital); and
- Whether medical equipment or devices are used for the test.[553]

Although the determination of whether a test is medical in nature is made on a case-by-case basis, psychological examinations will be considered medical in nature to the extent they provide evidence that an applicant has a mental disorder or impairment as set forth in the *DSM-IV-TR*.[554] Moreover, an employer who seeks to ascertain an applicant's tastes, habits, or attitudes with a psychological test designed to reveal mental illness and frequently used in a clinical setting to evaluate a test-taker's mental health, and who has the test interpreted by a psychologist will be considered to have administered a medical examination.[555]

---

about his drug use and treatment since such inquiries were relevant to the position for which he had applied).

[551]42 U.S.C. §12112(c)(2). The legislative history indicates that this prohibition applies to psychological examinations. *See* H.R. REP. NO. 101-485, at 46 (1990).

[552]*EEOC Guidance on Pre-Employment Inquiries*, *supra* note 535, at 7193.

[553]*Id.* at 7208.

[554]*Id.* at 7210.

[555]*Id. See also* Grenier v. Cyanamid Plastics, Inc., 70 F.3d 667 5 AD Cases 75 (1st Cir. 1995); Barnes v. Cochran, 944 F. Supp. 897, 5 AD Cases 1685 (S.D. Fla. 1996) (prohibition on pre-offer medical examinations "includes psychological examinations").

In light of these guidelines, administration to job applicants of tests such as the Minnesota Multiphasic Personality Inventory (MMPI) that not only assess personality traits but also reveal a variety of psychopathologies would be unlawful under the ADA.[556] On the other hand, tests that assess aptitude for a particular job or the ability of a person to get along in a particular work environment (for example, ability to work under pressure, ability to accept criticism, attitudes toward customer service, etc.) generally are permissible.[557]

3. Preemployment Drug Testing

Drug testing of job applicants is a key screening device that is not affected by the ADA. Drug tests used to determine current illegal drug use are not considered medical examinations under the ADA and may be administered at the preemployment stage.[558] Moreover, as the ADA expressly disqualifies current users of illegal drugs from its coverage,[559] an employer may lawfully refuse to hire a job applicant who tests positive for illegal drugs.

Sometimes an individual will test positive for illegal drugs when taking certain prescribed medications. If an applicant tests positive for illegal drugs, an employer may lawfully inquire about prescription drug use that could have caused the positive result.[560] An employer may not seek further information about current or prior lawful drug use, however, once the applicant or employee explains the positive test result by responding that he is lawfully using drugs.[561]

Prehire alcohol tests are not permitted if they require the drawing of blood, urine, or breath.[562] An employer is permitted to ask an applicant whether he drinks alcohol or whether he has ever been arrested for driving under the influence but may not make inquiries concerning how much the employee drinks or whether the employee has ever participated in alcohol rehabilitation.[563] Similarly, employers may ask, without violating the ADA, whether an applicant

---

[556]Does v. District of Columbia, 962 F. Supp 202, (D.D.C. 1997) (court denied summary judgment for defendant who had administered MMPI, sentence completion test, figure drawing test, and clinical interview on issue of violating prohibition in Rehabilitation Act concerning preemployment medical inquiries and noted such examinations would also violate the ADA).

[557]Thomas v. Borg-Warner Protective Servs., 1996 WL 162990 (N.D. Cal. Mar. 11, 1996) (evidence that a test is designed to reveal "behavioral problems" and "emotional instability" and lack of evidence that Pass-III D.A.T.A. survey reveals such information, when neither is a disability or characteristic that can lead to the identification of an applicant's mental impairment as defined by the *DSM* or by some other parameter, is insufficient to establish that survey is a medical examination).

[558]42 U.S.C. §12114(d); 29 C.F.R. §1630.16(c).

[559]42 U.S.C. §12114(a).

[560]*EEOC Guidance on Pre-Employment Inquiries, supra* note 535, at 7196.

[561]*Id.*

[562]*Id.*

[563]*Id.* Questions concerning the frequency or amount of use are prohibited. *Id.*

is currently using illegal drugs, whether the individual has ever used illegal drugs, and the date of the most recent use.[564]

C. Post-Offer Preemployment Examinations and Inquiries

The ADA permits medical examinations and inquiries after a conditional job offer[565] has been made but before the individual begins to work.[566] An examination or inquiries made to an individual with a conditional offer do not have to be related only to the individual's ability to perform the job that he has been offered.[567] For example, in *Norman-Bloodsaw v. Lawrence Berkeley Laboratory*,[568] the Ninth Circuit held that the plaintiffs, who were tested without their knowledge for such medical information as syphilis, sickle cell trait, and pregnancy, did not have a claim because the ADA does not restrict the scope of employee entrance health examinations to job-related matters.

While the examination or inquiry does not have to be job related, it is not without restriction. For example, the particular examination or inquiry must be made to all applicants in the same job category.[569] Consequently, if an employer knew that an individual to whom it had made a conditional job offer had a parent with Bipolar Disorder, it could not require that individual to undergo a psychological examination or ask whether that individual had Bipolar Disorder if the employer did not make the same inquiry of other job applicants entering the same job category. Furthermore, if a job applicant reveals a prior illness or medical condition in response to a medical inquiry, the employer cannot require the applicant to get a medical examination concerning that condition unless all applicants in the same job category are also required to do so.[570] Nonetheless, if a medical examination of an applicant discloses a medical condition that could affect the applicant's future job performance, the

---

[564]*Id.* at 7195; January 17, 1997 Informal Guidance Letter from Peggy Mastroiani (employers may ask applicants whether they have "ever personally smoked, or ingested by any means, marijuana without authorization and the date of the last such use").

[565]To be a bona fide job offer, the job offer must occur after the employer has "evaluated all relevant non-medical information which it reasonably could have obtained and analyzed prior to giving the offer." *EEOC Guidance on Pre-Employment Inquiries*, *supra* note 535, at 7200. *See* Buchanan v. City of San Antonio, 85 F.3d 196, 5 AD Cases 987 (5th Cir. 1996); Downs v. Massachusetts Bay Transp. Auth., 13 F. Supp. 2d 130, 8 AD Cases 447 (D. Mass. 1998) (offer made prior to completion of application, interview, drug exam, and background check was not bona fide); Doe v. City of Chicago, 883 F. Supp. 1126, 1135 n.2 (N.D. 1994) (question whether bona fide offer made when such was conditioned on a background check).

[566]42 U.S.C. §12112(d)(3).

[567]29 C.F.R. §1620 app., §1630 (commentary on §1630.14(b)); *EEOC Technical Assistance Manual*, *supra* note 17, at 7029.

[568]135 F.3d 1260, 7 AD Cases 1395 (9th Cir. 1998).

[569]29 C.F.R. §1620 app., §1630 (commentary on §1630.14(b)); *EEOC Technical Assistance Manual*, *supra* note 17, at 7029.

[570]*Id.* at 7038.

employer is permitted to have that particular applicant undergo a follow-up medical examination.[571]

Once the employer has made medical examinations and inquiries, it cannot withdraw the job offer unless it does so for reasons that are job related and consistent with business necessity.[572] According to the EEOC, in order to prove this, the employer must be able to show that there is no reasonable accommodation available that would have enabled the person to perform the job.[573] For example, in *Miller v. City of Springfield*,[574] a city dispatcher who applied for a police officer position was rejected because of her low score on a psychological test. The court found the defendant could not have screened her out on the basis of disability because it regarded her as nondisabled, as demonstrated by her continued employment as a city dispatcher.[575] The court further stated, "In any event, we easily conclude that appropriate psychological screening is job related and consistent with business necessity where the selection of individuals to train for the position of police officer is concerned."[576] Consequently, the results from medical examinations and inquiries may be used to withdraw a conditional job offer only if such results indicate that the applicant is unable to meet a legitimate physical or mental qualification standard.

An employer's reliance on a physician's opinion in deciding to withdraw a job offer will not protect an employer from incurring liability under the ADA, however. For example, in *Holiday v. City of Chattanooga*,[577] the defendant rejected the plaintiff for a police officer position after its contract physician concluded that the plaintiff was not able to withstand the rigors of police work. The district court granted summary judgment for the defendant because it had relied on the doctor's report. The Sixth Circuit reversed, noting that the plaintiff had passed the defendant's physical agility test and that he had served as a police officer in the past without limitation. The court ruled that the physician's conclusion was not supported by any definite medical findings and was at odds with the objective evidence.[578] The court admonished, "[E]mployers do not escape their legal obligations under the ADA by contracting out certain hiring and personnel functions to third parties. . . . Courts need not defer to an individual doctor's opinion that is neither based on an individualized inquiry

---

[571]*EEOC Guidance on Pre-Employment Inquiries, supra* note 535, at 7200; *EEOC Technical Assistance Manual, supra* note 17, at 7039.

[572]42 U.S.C. §12112 (b)(6); 29 C.F.R. §1630.10. The EEOC will closely scrutinize offers withdrawn for alleged nonmedical reasons. *EEOC Technical Assistance Manual, supra* note 17, at 7037.

[573]*EEOC Technical Assistance Manual, supra* note 17, at 7037. *But see* Willis v. Conopco, 108 F.3d 282, 6 AD Cases 806 (11th Cir. 1997) (employee has the burden of proof to identify an accommodation, and the burden of persuasion regarding its reasonableness.)

[574]146 F.3d 612, 8 AD Cases 321 (8th Cir. 1998).

[575]*Id.* at 615, 8 AD Cases at 322.

[576]*Id.*

[577]206 F.3d 637, 10 AD Cases 501 (6th Cir. 2000).

[578]*Id.* at 645, 10 AD Cases at 506.

mandated by the ADA nor supported by objective scientific and medical evidence."[579]

Finally, if a person to whom the employer has made a conditional offer requests an accommodation and the disability is not obvious, the employer may request reasonable documentation of the disability.[580] The request, however, must be limited to information necessary to establish the disability and need for accommodation.[581]

C. Postemployment Medical Inquiries

Generally, the ADA permits an employer to make medical inquiries of an employee[582] and to require employees to undergo fitness-for-duty examinations where job related and consistent with business necessity.[583] The EEOC has stated that this requirement "sometimes" may be met when the employer has a reasonable belief, based on objective evidence[584] that (1) an employee will pose a direct threat as a result of a medical condition; or (2) an employee's ability

---

[579]*Id. See also* Doe v. District of Columbia, 796 F. Supp. 559, 2 AD Cases 197 (D.D.C. 1992); EEOC v. Texas Bus Lines, 923 F. Supp 965, 5 AD Cases 878 (S.D. Tex. 1996).

[580]*EEOC Guidance on Pre-Employment Inquiries*, *supra* note 535, at 7201. EEOC ADA CASE STUDY TRAINING MANUAL 6 (1996) (employer may request such documentation if the disability is not obvious and there is a connection between the disability and the individual's limitation).

[581]*EEOC Guidance on Reasonable Accommodation*, *supra* note at 278, at 7607.

[582]The courts are split on the issue of whether a nondisabled employee would have standing to pursue a claim for illegal medical inquiries. *See* Krocka v. Bransfield, 969 F. Supp. 1073, 8 AD Cases 707 (N.D. Ill. 1997), *aff'd*, 203 F.3d 507, 10 AD Cases 289 (7th Cir. 2000) (protective ambit of the ADA extends only to individuals with disabilities so that an employee who was not disabled could not maintain an action against his employer for illegal medical inquiry). *But see* Fredenburg v. Contra Costa County Dep't of Health Serv., 172 F.3d 1176, 9 AD Cases 385 (9th Cir. 1999) (paranoid mental health specialist did not have to prove that she was a qualified individual with a disability to challenge the scope of medical examination under the ADA; ADA's restriction on medical examinations is to prevent employers from using tests to deter disabled persons from applying for positions); Adler v. L&M Rail Link, LLC, 13 F. Supp. 2d 912, 8 AD Cases 775 (N.D. Iowa 1998) (employees pursuing claims for violations of §102(d)(4) do not have to be disabled to maintain lawsuit).

[583]42 U.S.C. §12112(d).

[584]The evidence may come from the employer's observation or from a third party. *EEOC Guidance on Disability Related Inquiries*, *supra* note 485, at 7710–11. An employer should consider the following factors when seeking to determine whether the third-party information provided supports making a disability-related inquiry: (1) relationship of third party to employee, (2) seriousness of medical condition at issue, (3) possible motivation of third party in providing information, (4) how the third party has learned the information, and (5) other evidence concerning reliability. *Id.*

to perform essential job functions will be impaired by a medical condition.[585] A medical examination under (1) or (2) would include a mental examination conducted by a psychiatrist or clinical psychologist under at least two circumstances: (1) when, on account of a mental disability (or the treatment for such disability), the employee appears no longer able to perform the essential functions of the job;[586] and (2) when, on account of a mental disability (or the treatment for such disability), the employee behaves in an aberrant fashion or makes threats, suggesting that he may pose a danger to himself or others.[587] An examination for either reason must be tailored to seek only that information necessary to determine whether the employee can perform his job or whether he is a direct threat.[588]

---

[585]*EEOC Guidance on Disability Related Inquiries, supra* note 485, at 7713–14; 29 C.F.R. §1630.14(c) app. (Interpretive Guidance). Although the EEOC initially took the position that a medical examination was permissible when an employee sought an accommodation to determine whether the employee's condition was a disability under the ADA, it subsequently retreated from that position. Specifically, the EEOC stated that an employer may require an employee to go to an employer-chosen health care professional when the employee requests an accommodation only if the information the employee's physician provides is insufficient to show that the employee is disabled and requires a reasonable accommodation. Even then, an employer must advise the employee why the information is insufficient and give him an opportunity to provide the information required. The EEOC also states that the employer should possibly consult with the employee's physician before sending him to its physician. *Id.* Documentation may be considered insufficient when it does not indicate that the employee has an ADA disability and/or does not explain the need for accommodation. The EEOC gives the following examples:
1. The health care professional does not have the expertise to give an opinion about the employee's medical condition and the limitations imposed by it;
2. The information does not specify the functional limitations imposed by the disability; and,
3. Other functions indicate the information is not credible or fraudulent. If an employee provides sufficient information and the employer keeps asking for additional information or requires the employee to submit to a medical examination, such requirements may be viewed as retaliation.

EEOC Guidance on Disability Related Inquiries, supra note 485, at 7713–14.

[586]*See, e.g.,* Sullivan v. River Valley Sch. Dist., 197 F.3d 804, 9 AD Cases 1711 (6th Cir. 1999); Miranda v. Wisconsin Power & Light Co., 91 F.3d 1011, 5 AD Cases 1856 (7th Cir. 1996) (questions about an employee's ability to perform job-related functions are job related and consistent with business necessity).

[587]*EEOC Guidance on Psychiatric Disabilities, supra* note 14, at 7468–69; *EEOC Guidance on Disability Related Inquiries, supra* note 485, at 7708.

[588]Riechman v. Cutler-Hammer, Inc., 95 F. Supp. 2d 1171, 1186 (D. Kan. 2000) (summary judgment denied to employer accused of violating ADA prohibition on medical inquiries because questions concerning stroke victim's medication, dosage, and how physical impairment affected employee mentally/emotionally were overbroad in scope); *see also EEOC Guidance on Disability Related Inquiries, supra* note 485, at 7712–13 (employer may request only that documentation necessary to show employee has disability and needs accommodation requested in response to request for accommodation).

D. Performance-Related Concerns

Employers are permitted to require an employee to undergo a fitness-for-duty examination where the employee's performance has declined or where an employee, previously without a disability, develops a mental disability during the course of employment that affects the employee's ability to perform the essential functions of the job. In *Yin v. State of California*,[589] the Ninth Circuit held that the defendant did not violate the ADA by requiring an employee to submit to a medical examination. The court explained: "[W]hen health problems have had a substantial and injurious impact on an employee's job performance, the employer can require the employee to undergo a physical examination designed to determine his or her ability to work even if the examination might disclose whether the employee is disabled or the extent of any disability."[590]

In contrast to *Yin*, which involved objective evidence concerning an employee's ability to perform her job requirements, in *Gonzales v. Sandoval County*,[591] the court held that the defendant's medical inquiry concerning the plaintiff police officer's Chronic Fatigue Syndrome and Epstein-Barr virus violated the ADA because the plaintiff was not having any problems performing the essential functions of his job. The court rejected the employer's argument that New Mexico law, which made good health a requirement to be certified as a police officer, authorized the defendant's inquiry, stating that an employer's inquiry could not extend beyond that permitted by the ADA.[592]

A fitness-for-duty mental examination may also be required, for example, when an employee is disciplined for erratic attendance or for engaging in emotional outbursts with customers or coworkers, and when he discloses that his job performance problems are due to a mental disability. Such an examina-

---

[589] 95 F.3d 864, 5 AD Cases 1487 (9th Cir. 1996).

[590] *Id.* at 868, 5 AD Cases at 1489. *See also* Law v. Garden State Tanning, 2001 WL 322550 (E.D. Pa. Feb. 12, 2001) (employer who required employee in drug treatment program as a condition of continued employment to undergo a psychiatric examination after physician treating employee advised employer that, in his opinion, employee had a mental impairment impeding the employee's progress in the program did not violate the ADA); Fritsch v. City of Chula Vista, 11 AD Cases 273 (S.D. Cal. 2000) (defendant did not violate the ADA when it terminated assistant city attorney for refusing to submit to a psychiatric examination after she got into a verbal altercation with an opposing counsel in court even though the attorney had behaved properly the preceding nine years).

[591] 2 F. Supp. 2d 1442, 8 AD Cases 1337 (D.N.M. 1998).

[592] *See also* Roe v. Cheyenne Mountain Conference Resort, Inc.,124 F. 3d 1221, 7 AD Cases 779 (10th Cir. 1997) (policy requiring employees to disclose all legal prescription medications they used violated the ADA because it specifically elicited information about employees' disabilities); Lent v. Goldman Sachs & Co., 1998 WL 915906 (S.D.N.Y. Dec. 30, 1998) (if supervisor asked employee whether employee's seizures required medication only to discover whether he had a cavalier attitude about his medical condition, such inquiry was prohibited under the ADA); Doe v. Kohn Nast & Graf C.C., 866 F. Supp. 190, 3 AD Cases 1322 (E.D. Pa.1994) (employer's search through employee's office to confirm suspicion that he had AIDS prohibited by ADA).

tion can be used to determine whether a mental disorder really caused the performance problems at issue, or whether they were simply the result of carelessness or a poor attitude.

For example, in *Sullivan v. River Valley School District*,[593] a tenured teacher whose performance and behavior were satisfactory for nearly 20 years was asked to undergo a mental fitness-for-duty examination after several instances of erratic behavior. When he refused to comply with the school board's request, he was suspended for his conduct and refusal. The court found that the school board's request was job related and consistent with business necessity, stating that such standard was met where there is "significant evidence that could cause a reasonable person to inquire as to whether an employee is still capable of performing his job."[594] The court went on to state:

> The examinations ordered for Sullivan by defendants in this case meet the standard. Sullivan's behavior had given the school district reason to seek further information about his fitness for continued employment. Though we need not decide today whether advice from an outside health professional is always necessary, we note that the district's obtaining advice that further examination was needed to determine Sullivan's fitness for work buttresses the district's claim that it had reason to believe that Sullivan could not perform some essential aspects of his job. This court has upheld requiring a mental and physical exam as a precondition of returning to work.[595]

According to the EEOC, the job-related standard "sometimes" can be met when (1) "an employer knows what an employee's particular medical condition" is or (2) a credible third party has given an employer reliable information "that an employee has a medical condition, or the employer may observe symptoms indicating that an employee may have a medical condition that will impair his/her ability to perform essential job functions or will pose a direct threat."[596] The mental health professional conducting a fitness-for-duty examination may also be asked to evaluate whether the employee could perform the essential functions of the job with a reasonable accommodation, and which accommodations might be feasible.

In addition, a fitness-for-duty mental examination may be used to determine whether an employee is able to return to work following a disability-related

---

[593] 197 F.3d 804, 9 AD Cases 1711 (6th Cir. 1999).

[594] *Id.* at 811, 9 AD Cases at 1715. According to the Sixth Circuit, significant evidence must exist. Annoying or inefficient behavior is insufficient to justify an examination. *Id.*

[595] *Id.*, 9 AD Cases at 1715. *See also* Miller v. Champaign Cmty. Unit Sch. Dist. No. 4, 983 F. Supp. 1201, 8 AD Cases 1142 (C.D. Ill. 1997) (court concluded that where a teacher had exhibited erratic behavior, causing the school board to require a mental examination, "as a matter of law, a psychiatric examination is 'job-related and consistent with business necessity' when an elementary school employee shows even mild signs of 'schizophreniform' behavior").

[596] *EEOC Guidance on Disability Related Inquiries, supra* note 485, at 7708.

leave of absence.[597] In *Porter v. U.S. Alumoweld Co., Inc.*,[598] the employer terminated an employee who refused to submit to a return-to-work examination. The Fourth Circuit held that the employer's request for a fitness-for-duty examination after a work-related injury did not violate the ADA because the request was justified in light of the employer's valid concern about the plaintiff's functional capacity and that the employer was justified in terminating the plaintiff's employment.[599]

1. Direct Threat

A medical examination is appropriate "if there is a legitimate reason for believing that [an individual] might pose a direct threat, . . . [to determine whether the individual], in fact, poses a direct threat."[600] The degree of evidence necessary to support the fitness-for-duty examination may vary depending on the functions of the job. Jobs involving public safety—for example, police officers, firefighters, physicians, etc.—may require less evidence than less safety-sensitive jobs.

For example, in *Watson v. City of Miami Beach*,[601] the court upheld the termination of a police officer who refused to undergo a medical evaluation. The police department ordered the examination after the plaintiff overreacted in a situation and filed multiple grievances. The court stated that the defendant had good cause for concern whenever a police officer was perceived to be even mildly paranoid or hostile, and that the ADA did not require it to wait until the threat became real or the questionable behavior resulted in injuries.[602]

Likewise, in *Judice v. Hospital Service District No. 1*,[603] the court held that a hospital, relying on the opinions of two of its physicians, did not violate

---

[597]Any such requirement must be specific to the employee's condition and job requirements. *See* Norris v. Sysco Corp., 191 F.3d 1043, 9 AD Cases 1262 (9th Cir. 1994) (company policy requiring return without restrictions would violate ADA if actually enforced).

[598]125 F. 3d 243, 7 AD Cases 537 (4th Cir. 1997).

[599]Employers, however, must be careful when the employee is returning from an FMLA leave not to violate the FMLA. Under the FMLA an individual returning from FMLA leave need only provide a note stating that he is capable of returning to work in order to be reinstated. 29 C.F.R. §825.310. In *Albert v. Runyon*, 6 F. Supp. 2d 57, 4 WH Cases 2d 1128 (D. Mass. 1998), an employee was on FMLA leave for depression. When she was released by her physician to return to work without restriction, her employer asked her to undergo a psychological examination, which she refused to do. The employer terminated her employment. The district court held that the employer had violated the FMLA, which provides that an employer must return an employee to work if she presents a note from her physician stating that she is able to return. The court held that the FMLA does not permit an employer to request a medical examination merely because an employee is returning from leave absent independent grounds under the ADA. *Id.* at 66, 4 WH Cases 2d at 1139.

[600]EEOC CASE STUDY TRAINING MANUAL *supra* note 580, at 5; *EEOC Guidance on Disability Related Inquiries*, *supra* note 485, at 7708–10.

[601]177 F.3d 932, 9 AD Cases 760 (11th Cir. 1999).

[602]*Id.* at 935, 9 AD Cases at 762.

[603]919 F. Supp. 978, 7 AD Cases 825 (E.D. La. 1996).

the ADA by refusing to restore staff privileges to an alcoholic neurosurgeon who refused to submit to a four-day fitness-for-duty examination with an addictionologist. The state licensing board had reinstated the physician's license under certain conditions and said he was fit to return to work, as had the plaintiff's physician. Nevertheless, the court concluded that the hospital had a right to ensure that its physicians practiced safely and skillfully and to consider the plaintiff's history.[604] The court explained: "Certainly, a doctor working while severely depressed or impaired by alcohol poses a 'direct threat.' . . . Likewise, a doctor laboring under a high likelihood of relapse, based on specific prior history, might pose such a risk."[605] The court then noted that the hospital was aware of one suspicious death and that the doctor had relapsed more than once and had aborted a surgery because of alcohol in his bloodstream. The court concluded that the doctor posed a significant risk to public safety.[606] *Judice* demonstrates that an employer does not always have to accept the opinion of an employee's physician concerning the risk the employee poses where there is other objective evidence that an untenable risk exists.

Additionally, in *Reigel v. Kaiser Foundation Health Plan*,[607] the district court held that the defendant did not violate the ADA when it asked a physician with a physical impairment to submit to a mental evaluation before returning to work because her physical condition caused her pain, which would make concentration difficult, and because while on medical leave she had blamed and threatened others and was suspicious of the defendant's motives when questioned about her condition.[608] The plaintiff's personal physician had stated that the physical impairment was causing the plaintiff mental and emotional strain that could affect her performance.[609]

2. Disclosures of Prescription Medication Use

An employer generally may not ask employees to disclose the prescription medications they are taking.[610] According to the EEOC, however, in limited circumstances, "certain employers may be able to demonstrate that it *is* job related and consistent with business necessity to require employees in positions affecting public safety to report when they are taking medication that may

---

[604]*Id.* at 983, 7 AD Cases at 828.

[605]*Id.*, 7 AD Cases at 828.

[606]*See also* EEOC v. Prevo's Family Mkt., Inc., 135 F. 3d 1089, 8 AD Cases 401(6th Cir. 1998) (defendant's request for medical examination of produce employee who told manager he was HIV-positive did not violate ADA because he frequently cut his hands when he cut produce); Miller v. Champaign Cmty. Unit Sch. Dist., 983 F. Supp. 1201, 8 AD Cases 1142 (C.D. Ill. 1997) (school district-ordered psychological examination did not violate ADA where custodian engaged in paranoid and agitated conduct such as making unfounded accusations against coworkers and threatening to booby-trap the office).

[607]859 F. Supp. 963, 3 AD Cases 577 (E.D.N.C. 1994).

[608]*Id.* at 974–75, 3 AD Cases at 586.

[609]*Id.* at 978, 3 AD Cases at 587.

[610]*EEOC Guidance on Disability Related Inquiries, supra* note 485, at 7711.

affect their ability to perform an essential function. *Under these limited circumstances, an employer must be able to demonstrate that an employee's inability or impaired ability to perform essential functions will result in a direct threat.*"[611]

Nevertheless, in *Duda v. Board of Education*,[612] an alcoholic janitor with Bipolar Disorder who took medication for his condition was suspended after school officials found and read portions of his personal diary. The school agreed to return the employee to work if he would attend Alcoholics Anonymous, get counseling, and agree to keep taking his medication. Furthermore, he was also required to notify the school if any changes were made to his medication or counseling. The court held that the employee could state a claim for violation of the ADA's prohibition on medical examinations and inquiries that are not "job-related and consistent with business necessity."[613] In dicta, however, the court explained:

> We have no doubt that there are situations in which a prudent employer, concerned with the safety of its employees, would be justified in requiring information of this type from an employee suffering from a psychiatric illness, as long as the inquiries were related to his job and were necessary to the business. ... At a later stage in this litigation, the school district will have the opportunity to demonstrate that it was necessary to make such an inquiry in this situation.[614]

3. Monitoring and/or Requiring Medication or Treatment

Periodic medical examinations and other monitoring under specific circumstances may be job related and consistent with business necessity.[615] As an example, the EEOC's *Guidance on Disability Related Inquiries* refers to an employee who returns from leave from alcohol rehabilitation. In this circumstance, an employer can subject the employee to periodic alcohol testing if the employer has a reasonable belief, based on objective evidence, that the employee will pose a direct threat in the absence of such testing.[616] A "reasonable belief" requires an individualized assessment of the employee and his position, and it cannot be based on general assumptions.[617] Employers may also conduct periodic alcohol testing pursuant to a last-chance agreement and may terminate an employee who violates such an agreement.[618]

In determining whether to subject an employee to periodic alcohol testing (in the absence of a last-chance agreement), the employer should consider the

---

[611]*Id.* at 7711–12 (emphasis in original).
[612]133 F.3d 1054, 8 AD Cases 99 (7th Cir. 1998).
[613]*Id.* at 1060, 8 AD Cases at 104.
[614]*Id.*
[615]*EEOC Guidance on Disability Related Inquiries, supra* note 485, at 7716. *See* Roe v. Cheyenne Mountain Conference Resort, 124 F.3d 1221, 7 AD Cases 779 (10th Cir. 1997) (policy requiring employees to tell supervisors about prescription drugs unrelated to issue of safety risks violated ADA).
[616]*EEOC Guidance on Disability Related Inquiries, supra* note 485, at 7717–18.
[617]*Id.*
[618]*Id.*

safety risks associated with the employee's position, the consequences of the employee's inability to perform his job functions, and how recently the events that caused the employer to believe the employee will pose a direct threat occurred.[619] Furthermore, the duration and frequency of testing must be designed to address particular safety concerns and not used to harass the employee.[620]

For example, in *Hinnershitz v. Ortep of Pennsylvania, Inc.*,[621] an alcoholic employee requested vacation time to complete an inpatient treatment program of his own choice.[622] The employer conditioned the grant of this medical leave upon the employee's agreement to submit to substance abuse testing upon his return and to complete any ongoing treatment program recommended by the employee's treatment program.[623] The employee agreed to these terms and completed his inpatient treatment.[624] The inpatient treatment center recommended two continuing, outpatient treatment programs—counseling and attendance at Alcoholics Anonymous meetings four times per week. The employee quit attending counseling after only a few sessions and attended no AA meetings. The employee claimed that he no longer needed such treatment and that he desired to have his outpatient program reevaluated.[625] The defendant terminated the employee.[626] The court held that the defendant had satisfied its duty to provide a reasonable accommodation by allowing the plaintiff to keep his job if he attended counseling and AA meetings.[627] The court maintained "[t]hat plaintiff did not desire this accommodation is irrelevant," since the ADA requires only a reasonable accommodation, not necessarily the accommodation the employee prefers.[628] The court also found that plaintiff's breach of the return-to-work agreement was a legitimate, nondiscriminatory reason for his firing.[629]

In *Williams v. Houston Lighting & Power Co.*,[630] an employee was abusing prescription painkillers. After the employee completed treatment, the employer held a return-to-work meeting with her, during which it told her that she would thereafter be subject to an increased monitoring and testing program and regularly would have to meet with an EAP counselor for three years. The employer terminated the employee because she refused to sign an agreement containing these terms. The court held that the employee's refusal to sign the return-to-work agreement constituted a legitimate, nondiscriminatory reason for her termination.[631] It explained:

---

[619]*Id. See* Judice v. Hospital Serv. Dist. No. 1, 919 F. Supp. 978, 7 AD Cases 825 (E.D. La. 1996).
[620]*EEOC Guidance on Disability Related Inquiries, supra* note 485, at 7717.
[621]1998 WL 962096 (E.D. Pa. 1998).
[622]*Id.* at *1.
[623]*Id.*
[624]*Id.*
[625]*Id.*
[626]*Id.*
[627]*Id.* at *5.
[628]*Id.*
[629]*Id.* at *6.
[630]980 F. Supp. 879 (S.D. Tex. 1997).
[631]*Id.* at 884.

This Court has held such "return-to-work" agreements to be valid requirements for employment. . . . The company had a compelling reason for requiring plaintiff's compliance with the monitoring regimen: her doctor had diagnosed her as an abuser of prescription medication. [Defendant] clearly has a significant obligation to its employees and to the public as a whole to ensure compliance with the health and safety regulations at its nuclear power plant. . . . Once [defendant] has any suspicion, *however* raised, that one of its employees may have a drug problem, . . . it has an affirmative duty to act to prevent the problem from affecting its plant operations.[632]

4. Employee Refusal to Respond to Medical Inquiry or Submit to Medical Examination

An employee who might pose a direct threat may be terminated for refusing to submit to a fitness-for-duty examination.[633] Moreover, an employer may refuse to return an employee to work during the period in which the employee fails to cooperate in submitting to an examination. In *Davis-Durnil v. Village of Carpentersville*,[634] a police officer began suffering anxiety attacks after she shot a suspect. She sought help from the defendant's EAP, which referred her to a doctor who subsequently diagnosed her with Posttraumatic Stress Disorder and atypical depression and recommended that she take medical leave and receive treatment. The police officer did so for approximately five weeks, after which she received a medical release to return to work. Over two years later, she suffered an anxiety attack while taking part in a training exercise involving a simulated shooting. At that time, she advised the department she suffered from PTSD. The next day, the chief of police ordered her to meet with a psychologist and placed her on leave until the psychological evaluation was complete. The police department subsequently mailed her forms for her signature authorizing the release of her mental health records and consenting to an

---

[632]*Id.* (emphasis in original).

[633]EEOC v. Prevo's Family Mkt., Inc., 135 F.3d 1089, 8 AD Cases 401 (6th Cir. 1998). *See also* Yin v. State of California, 95 F.3d 864, 5 AD Cases 1487 (9th Cir. 1996) (employer can require employee to undergo fitness-for-duty mental examination). According to the EEOC, however, an employer may not terminate an employee who refuses to submit to an examination or inquiry motivated by performance issues, or in response to a request for a reasonable accommodation. *EEOC Guidance on Disability Related Inquiries, supra* note 485, at 7712; *EEOC Guidance on Reasonable Accommodation, supra* note 278, at 7608. Instead, when an employee with performance problems refuses to respond to the inquiry or submit to the examination, the employer may discipline the employee only for performance problems and not for the refusal. *EEOC Guidance on Disability Related Inquiries, supra* note 485, at 7712. Similarly, an employer may terminate an employee who requests an accommodation and then refuses to accept an effective accommodation, but only if the employee would be unqualified for the position without an accommodation. *EEOC Guidance on Reasonable Accommodation, supra* note 278, at 7611.

[634]128 F. Supp. 2d 575 (N.D. Ill. 2001).

independent psychological exam. Although the police officer signed the consent form, she added a long disclaimer stating that she was signing it under duress and reserving her right to take legal action against the defendant and the psychologist. The psychologist declined to meet with her because of the disclaimer.

About a month later, the police chief sent another letter to the police officer, again with a consent to examination for a different psychologist. The police officer again added disclaimer language and again the psychologist declined to meet with her. Three months later the police chief sent another consent form for yet another psychologist. This time, the police officer signed the form without the disclaimer language and met with the psychologist a week later. On the basis of the psychologist's report, the police chief returned the plaintiff to duty. She subsequently filed a lawsuit alleging violations of the ADA.

The court concluded that the defendant had a valid reason for putting her on leave after the training incident. The court stated that "[a]n employer is entitled to inquire into the mental health of its employees when there are legitimate concerns about employee and public safety. . . . Indeed, the ADA does not provide a shield from fitness for duty examinations for employees with jobs that affect public safety."[635]

VIII. Violence and Threats

A. Introduction

ADA issues are being implicated more frequently as employers seek to prevent or respond to threats and violence in the workplace. Under the ADA, an employer may require that an individual "not pose a direct threat to the health or safety of other individuals in the workplace"[636] as a qualification standard. A direct threat is "a significant risk to the health or safety of others that cannot be eliminated by reasonable accommodation."[637] In drafting this provision, Congress intended the determination whether an individual posed a direct threat to be based on an individualized inquiry.[638] Under such an approach, an employer cannot assume an employee with a mental disability poses a direct threat absent

---

[635]*Id.* at 580.

[636]42 U.S.C. §12113(b). Congress used *School Board of Nassau County v. Arline*, 480 U.S. 273, 1 AD Cases 1026 (1987), as the starting point for the direct threat provision. *See* S. REP. NO. 101-116, at 27, 40 (1989); H.R. REP. NO. 101-485, pt. 2, at 52-27; pt. 3, at 34, 45-42.

[637]42 U.S.C. §12111(3).

[638]S. REP. NO. 101-116, at 27 (1989) ("The determination that an individual with a disability will pose a direct threat to others must be made on a reasonable case basis and not be based on generalizations, misperceptions, ignorance, irrational fears, patronizing attitudes or pernicious mythologies").

objective evidence[639] based on the employee's behavior such as recent acts or threats that caused harm or threatened harm.[640] The EEOC expanded and clarified the issue of direct threat in its regulations by stating that direct threat means "a significant risk[641] of substantial harm to the health or safety of the individual or others that cannot be eliminated or reduced by reasonable accommodation."[642] In determining whether an individual poses a direct threat, the analysis must be based "on an individualized assessment of the individual's present ability to safely perform the essential functions of the job. This assessment shall be based on a reasonable medical judgment that relies on the most current medical knowledge and/or the best available objective evidence."[643]

Courts are split on the issue of whether the direct threat provision in the statute includes threats to self or just threats to others. In *Echazabel v. Chevron USA, Inc.*,[644] the Ninth Circuit held invalid the EEOC's regulation that includes threats to self as well as others. The court found that regulation to be inconsistent with the statutory language of the ADA.[645] Other courts have found the ADA's direct threat exception to apply to threats to self as well as to others.[646]

B. Burden of Proof

The ADA's language has caused some degree of confusion in the courts concerning whether the burden of proving direct threat rests upon the employee or the

---

[639]The type of objective evidence relevant to the determination includes input from the individual with a disability, the individual's past experience in similar jobs, and "opinions of medical doctors, rehabilitation counselors, or physical therapists who have expertise in the disability involved and/or direct knowledge of the individual with the disability." 29 C.F.R. §1630.2(r) app.

[640]H.R. REP. No. 101-485, pt. 3, at 45–46 (1990).

[641]A significant risk is a "high probability" of substantial harm. 29 C.F.R. §1630.2(r) app.

[642]29 C.F.R. §1630.2(r).

[643]*Id.*

[644]226 F.3d 1063 (9th Cir. 2000).

[645]*Id.* at 1069. The Ninth Circuit had previously upheld threat to self as a defense in Rehabilitation Act cases. *See* Mantolete v. Bolger, 767 F.2d 1416, 1 AD Cases 811 (9th Cir. 1985) (defendant who denied an epileptic a job at a multipurpose letter-sorter machine position did not violate Rehabilitation Act because plaintiff could seriously injure herself if she had a seizure while operating the machine).

[646]*E.g.*, Borgialli v. Thunder Basin Coal Co., 235 F.3d 1284, 11 AD Cases 484 (10th Cir. 2000) (direct threat includes threat to self as expanded under 29 C.F.R. §1630.2(r)); Moses v. American Nonwovens, 97 F.3d 446, 5 AD Cases 1651 (11th Cir. 1996) (holding, without explanation, that threat to self is a defense); *see also* EEOC v. Amego, Inc., 110 F.3d 135, 6 AD Cases 997 (1st Cir. 1997) (stating in dictum the defense covers threat to self); Daugherty v. El Paso, 56 F.3d 695, 4 AD Cases 993 (5th Cir. 1995) (same).

employer.[647] A number of courts have ruled that when an individual poses a direct threat to the health or safety of others, he is not "otherwise qualified for employment."[648] The EEOC, however, maintains that "with regard to safety requirements that screen out or tend to screen out an individual with disability or a class of individuals with disabilities, an employer must demonstrate that the requirement, as applied to the individual, satisfies the 'direct threat' standard."[649]

Current authority is weighted toward the principle that when essential job functions necessarily implicate the safety of others, the plaintiff bears the burden of proving that he can perform such functions in a manner that does not endanger others.[650] For example, in *EEOC v. Amego, Inc.*,[651] the court held that the depressed plaintiff who dispensed medication to mentally disabled residents in a group home was not otherwise qualified for her job after she tried to commit suicide by overdosing because she was a direct threat. The court further noted that a defendant would have the burden of proving a direct threat in situations where "the issue of direct threat is not tied to the issue of essential job functions but is purely a matter of defense."[652] Likewise, in *Robertson v. Neuromedical Center*,[653] the Fifth Circuit held that a neurologist with Attention Deficit/Hyperactivity Disorder (ADHD), who had made mistakes on patient charts and concerning medications and who admitted he was going to harm someone, was not a qualified individual under the ADA because his memory problems made him a direct threat to his patients' safety. Similarly, in *Bekker v. Humana Health Plan*,[654] the Seventh Circuit agreed with the district court that the allegedly alcoholic physician had the burden of proving she was not a direct threat and therefore qualified.

---

[647]The section concerning qualifications appears in a section titled "Defenses." See 42 U.S.C. §12113(b). As part of his prima facie case, however, a plaintiff must show that he is otherwise qualified, 42 U.S.C. §12111(8), which he cannot do if his disability is a direct threat to the health or safety of others. 42 U.S.C. §12113(b).

[648]*See, e.g.,* EEOC v. Amego, Inc., 110 F.3d 135, 6 AD Cases 997 (1st Cir. 1997); Siefken v. Arlington Heights, 65 F.3d 664, 4 AD Cases 1441 (7th Cir. 1995); Lassiter v. Reno, 885 F. Supp. 869, 4 AD Cases 609 (E.D. Va. 1995), *aff'd,* 86 F.3d 1151, 5 AD Cases 1343 (4th Cir. 1996); Mazzarolla v. United States Postal Serv., 849 F. Supp. 89 (D. Mass. 1994).

[649]29 C.F.R. §1630.15(b)–(c) app.

[650]Altman v. New York City Health & Hosp. Corp., 100 F.3d 1054, 6 AD Cases 73 (2d Cir. 1996); Doe v. University of Md. Med. Sys. Corp., 50 F.3d 1261, 1265, 4 AD Cases 379, 383 (4th Cir. 1995); Newman v. Chevron U.S.A., 979 F. Supp. 1085, 7 AD Cases 1821 (S.D. Tex. 1993) (plaintiff with PTSD not qualified to drive truck filled with highly flammable gasoline). The EEOC acknowledged the correctness of the standard during oral argument in *Rizzo v. Children's World Learning Centers, Inc.*, 213 F.3d 209, 213 n.4, 10 AD Cases 976, 978 n.4 (5th Cir. 2000) (the burden may be on the plaintiff to show she can perform those functions without endangering others").

[651]110 F.3d 135, 6 AD Cases 997 (1st Cir. 1997).

[652]*Id.* at 144, 6 AD Cases at 1005.

[653]161 F.3d 292 (5th Cir. 1998).

[654]229 F.3d 662, 10 AD Cases 1776 (7th Cir. 2000).

In *Rizzo v. Children's World of Learning Centers, Inc.*,[655] however, the Fifth Circuit held that when safety requirements screen out or tend to screen out an individual with a disability or a class or individuals with disabilities, the employer bears the burden of proof with respect to direct threat. In *Rizzo*, the plaintiff was a hearing-impaired administrative aide who regularly drove students in the school van. After parents complained, the defendant removed her from driving duties, which caused her to lose hours and forced her to work a split shift. Consequently, the plaintiff sued, alleging disability discrimination. The plaintiff prevailed at trial and the defendant appealed. The court rejected the defendant's argument that the burden concerning direct threat should have been placed on the plaintiff. The court noted that the defendant had imposed a safety requirement that any teacher who drove the van had to be able to distinguish spoken words, which screened out a class of hearing-impaired individuals.[656]

Other circuits vary. The Eleventh Circuit takes the position that "the employee retains at all times the burden of persuading the jury either that he was not a direct threat or that reasonable accommodations were available."[657] Conversely, the Ninth Circuit imposes on the employer the burden of proving that the employee is a direct threat.[658]

C. Magnitude of Threat

A determination of a direct threat must be based on a reasonable medical judgment that relies on the most current medical knowledge and/or on the best available objective evidence.[659] The evaluation cannot be based on subjective perceptions, irrational fears, patronizing attitudes, or stereotypes about the nature of the particular disability.[660] That is, the employer may not simply fear that harm will occur.

---

[655] 213 F.3d 209, 10 AD Cases 976 (5th Cir. 1999).

[656] This is consistent with *EEOC v. Exxon Corp*, 203 F.3d 871, 10 AD Cases 225 (5th Cir. 2000). In that case, the Fifth Circuit held that the employer could assert business necessity to establish the legality of its safety standard excluding employees who had undergone substance abuse treatment from working in safety-sensitive jobs without having to prove direct threat. The court stated that the direct-threat test "applies in cases in which an employer responds to an individual employee's supposed risk that is not addressed by an existing qualification standard." *Id.* at 875, 10 AD Cases at 228.

[657] Moses v. American Nonwovens, Inc., 97 F.3d 446, 477, 5 AD Cases 1651 (11th Cir. 1996) (citing Benson v. Northwest Airlines, Inc., 62 F.3d 1108, 1112 (8th Cir. 1995)). *Accord* Lachance v. Duffy's Draft House, Inc., 146 F.3d 832, 836, 8 AD Cases 652, 655 (11th Cir. 1998) (plaintiff has burden of persuasion that "he was not a direct threat or that reasonable accommodation was available").

[658] Nunes v. Wal Mart Stores, Inc., 164 F.3d 1243, 8 AD 1813 (9th Cir. 1999).

[659] 29 C.F.R. §1630.2(r).

[660] 29 C.F.R. §1630.2(r) app. (Interpretive Guidance). *See, e.g.*, Carter v. Casa Cent., 849 F.2d 1048, 1055, 1 AD Cases 1332, 1337 (7th Cir. 1988) (court rejected defendant's argument that nurse with multiple sclerosis posed direct threat because of

The risk of harm must be substantial and, where a mental or emotional disability is involved, the employer must identify the specific behavior on the part of the individual that would pose a direct threat.[661] The EEOC also suggests that an employer should look for guidance from a health care professional with "expertise in the employee's specific condition."[662] Indeed, the Supreme Court has specifically rejected the argument that a mere "good faith" belief that an individual poses a direct threat is a defense.[663]

In *Wallace v. Veterans Administration*,[664] the defendant rejected a nurse with a history of drug addiction who had applied for a job as an I.C.U. nurse and had asked the hospital to restrict her access to controlled substances for a 12–18-month period. The hospital claimed she could not do all her job duties because of her requested restriction concerning access to narcotics. The court rejected the defendant's argument, concluding that administering controlled substances was not job related and that the nurse's inability to do it would not harm patient care because the hospital offered no objective proof it would do so. In contrast, the plaintiff presented expert testimony that her restriction posed a very small likelihood that the restriction would hurt patients. Additionally, there was evidence the hospital previously had employed nurses who could not intravenously administer drugs and they had not hurt patients.[665]

Moreover, an employer may not deny employment to an individual with a disability because of a slightly increased risk of harm.[666] Rather, the risk may be considered only when it poses a *significant* risk, i.e., a high probability of substantial harm.[667] To date, neither the EEOC nor the courts have offered any real guidance as to how "significance" is measured. The relevant factors in determining whether an individual poses such a threat include (1) the duration of the risk, (2) the nature and severity of the potential harm, (3) the likelihood the potential harm will occur, and (4) the imminence of the potential harm.[668]

---

limitations on walking imposed by her doctor; court remarked, "It is precisely this type of uninformed generalization based on stereotypes and projections which the Rehabilitation Act is designed to counteract."); Mendez v. Gearon, 956 F. Supp. 1520, 8 AD Cases 1181 (N.D. Cal. 1997) (Peace Corps violated Rehabilitation Act because defendant failed to gather all relevant information concerning plaintiff's medical history and did not try to determine what accommodation plaintiff with depression needed before it denied her medical clearance and told her she would not be accepted until she could show there was no risk she would experience depression.).

[661] 29 C.F.R. §1630.2(r).
[662] *EEOC Guidance on Disability Related Inquiries*, *supra* note 485, at 7714.
[663] Bragdon v. Abbott, 524 U.S. 624, 649, 8 AD Cases 239, 249 (1998).
[664] 683 F. Supp. 758, 766, 1 AD Cases 1263, 1269 (D. Kan. 1988).
[665] *Id.* at 766, 1 AD Cases at 1270.
[666] 29 CFR §1630.2(r).
[667] *Id.* §1630.2(r) app. (Interpretive Guidance). *See also* Hamlin v. Township of Flint, 165 F.3d 426, 8 AD Cases 1688 (6th Cir. 1999) (significant risk is one that is highly probable); EEOC v. Kinney Shoe Corp., 917 F. Supp. 419, 428, 5 AD Cases 506, 513–14 (W.D. Va. 1996) *aff'd sub nom.* Martinson v. Kinney Shoe Corp., 104 F.3d 683, 6 AD Cases 434 (4th Cir. 1997).
[668] 29 C.F.R. §1630.2(r) app.

Some courts have used a balancing test—even when the risk is small, if the consequences would be catastrophic, there is a direct threat.[669]

For example, in *Altman v. NYC Health & Hospital Corp.*,[670] a hospital denied reinstatement to its chief of medicine after he was treated for alcoholism and enrolled in a recovery program. The court found that despite the plaintiff's treatment, he posed a direct threat because of the safety-sensitive nature of his duties, such as treating patients and making treatment decisions for other doctors.[671] The court noted that the plaintiff's proposed accommodation—monitoring him—would not reduce the risk of harm to "insignificant" because he had already demonstrated his ability to drink a large amount of alcohol without detection by his colleagues.[672]

Furthermore, in *Borgialli v. Thunder Basin Coal*,[673] a blaster who operated vehicles and other equipment in dangerous geographical areas sued his employer under the ADA. The plaintiff had taken a leave of absence when he began having problems with dizziness and blurred vision. The defendant allowed him to return to work once his doctor authorized him to do so. Approximately one month later, the plaintiff received a bad performance review. He called his former supervisor that night and expressed suicidal thoughts. The next day he communicated his feelings to the defendant's nurse and told her that the defendant should be concerned about his safety. The plaintiff missed the next day and then returned to work. At the end of his shift, the defendant told him he could not return to work until he was evaluated by a company-chosen psychiatrist. Approximately two weeks later, the plaintiff met with a psychiatrist, who concluded that he could not return to work as a blaster because he suffered major depression, anxiety and personality disorders, and physical impairments.

---

[669]*See, e.g.*, Donahue v. Consolidated Rail Corp., 224 F.3d 226, 10 AD Cases 1505 (3d Cir. 2000) (train dispatcher with heart problems that caused him to lose consciousness on rare occasions posed a direct threat because "[i]f the threatened harm is grievous . . . even a small risk may be 'significant' "); EEOC v. Exxon Corp., 203 F.3d 871, 875, 10 AD Cases 225, 228 (5th Cir. 2000) (when establishing business necessity for general safety-based qualification standard, "The acceptable probability of an incident will vary with the potential hazard posed by the particular position: a probability that might be tolerable in an ordinary job might be intolerable for a position involving atomic reactors, for example. In short, the probability of the occurrence is discounted by the magnitude of its consequences"); Onishea v. Hopper, 171 F.3d 1289, 1299 (11th Cir. 1999) (when transmission of a disease involves death, a significant risk is present if the evidence shows a certain event can occur and that according to reliable medical opinion, the event can transmit the disease); Huber v. Howard County, 849 F. Supp. 407, 3 AD Cases 262 (D. Md. 1994) (a firefighter with asthma posed a safety risk because there was a 10 percent chance he would become incapacitated during a fire, and given "the life and death circumstances facing firefighters," the employer "does not have to assume such a ten percent risk").

[670]903 F. Supp. 503, 4 AD Cases 1665 (S.D.N.Y. 1995), *aff'd*, 100 F.3d 1054, 6 AD Cases 73 (2d Cir. 1996).

[671]*Id.* at 508–09, 4 AD Cases at 1670–71.

[672]*Id.* at 511, 4 AD Cases at 1672.

[673]235 F.3d 1284, 11 AD Cases 484 (10th Cir. 2000).

The doctor recommended that he not interact with those individuals who exacerbated his symptoms. The plaintiff subsequently obtained a medical opinion that partially conflicted with the one from the company's chosen physician. The company asked the plaintiff to undergo a third psychiatric examination, and when he refused, the defendant terminated his employment. The plaintiff argued on appeal that regardless of the potential risk involved, the district court had failed to assess the likelihood of the harm's occurring, the duration of the risk, and the imminence of the potential harm. The Tenth Circuit disagreed, stating that given the conflicting medical opinions and the plaintiff's refusal to resubmit to a third examination, summary judgment was appropriate. It observed that "the ADA does not require employers to take unnecessary risks when dealing with mentally or physically impaired employees in an inherently dangerous job."[674]

Likewise, in *Layser v. Morrison*,[675] the plaintiff was a campus security officer who carried a weapon on duty. Following a bad evaluation and failure to be promoted, he dreamed about pointing a gun at the head of his supervisor. Disturbed by the dream, the plaintiff went to a psychologist, who warned the supervisor. The defendant made the plaintiff give up his weapon and go on paid leave until he was cleared to return to work. The defendant subsequently returned the plaintiff to work as a dispatcher without a weapon and required him to submit to a second psychological examination. Approximately one year later, the defendant returned him to work after it received the second psychological report. The plaintiff subsequently filed a lawsuit. Although the court granted summary judgment to the defendant on the grounds that the plaintiff's claim was untimely, it indicated in dicta that the defendant had sufficient evidence to establish "that a threat existed that [plaintiff] might have, acting under stress, anger, and depression, shot [his supervisor]."[676]

D. Suicide Threats

One question that sometimes arises is whether a suicide attempt makes an employee a direct threat to others. Generally, the answer will be no.[677] There can be a threat, however, depending on the essential functions of the position and the method the employee used in seeking to end his life. For example, in *Doe v. Region 13 Mental Health-Mental Retardation Commission*,[678] a severely depressed psychiatric worker alleged a violation of the Rehabilitation Act based on her discharge from a psychiatric hospital after she threatened to commit

---

[674]*Id.* at 1295, 11 AD Cases at 491; *see also* Donahue v. Consolidated Rail Corp., 224 F.3d 226 10 AD Cases 1505 (3d Cir. 2000) (train dispatcher whose heart impairment caused him to lose consciousness was a direct threat even though the event happened rarely).

[675]935 F. Supp. 562, 6 AD Cases 1295 (E.D. Pa. 1995).

[676]*Id.* at 569, 6 AD Cases at 1300.

[677]*EEOC Guidance on Psychiatric Disabilities supra* note 14, at 7480.

[678]704 F.2d 1402, 1 AD Cases 447 (5th Cir. 1983).

suicide. Although the plaintiff had undergone psychotherapy and been treated with psychogenic drugs, she told her psychiatrist, coworkers, and a friend that she intended to kill herself. The hospital placed her on a leave of absence after an expert concluded that the plaintiff could communicate to her patients her view that suicide was a reasonable alternative. The Fifth Circuit upheld the termination.

Similarly, in *Spades v. City of Walnut Ridge*,[679] the Eighth Circuit in dicta stated that even if the plaintiff police officer who had attempted suicide was disabled, the defendant had a legitimate reason for terminating him; i.e., the "increased potential liability associated with an employee's past activities is a legitimate concern . . . particularly when there is known violent behavior."[680]

E. Conflicting Medical Information

The EEOC's *Guidance on Disability Related Inquiries* provides that an employer may require that an employee who it reasonably believes poses a direct threat be examined by a health care provider of the employer's choice.[681] The EEOC warns, however:

> An employer should be cautious about relying solely on the opinion of its own health care professional that an employee poses a direct threat where that opinion is contradicted by documentation from the employee's own treating physician, who is knowledgeable about the employee's medical condition and job functions, and/or other objective evidence.[682]

In evaluating conflicting medical information, the employer may consider:

- The area of expertise of each medical professional who has provided information;
- The kind of information each person providing documentation has about the job's essential functions;
- Whether a particular opinion is based on speculation or on current, objectively verifiable information about the risks associated with a particular condition; and
- Whether the medical opinion is contradicted by information known to or observed by the employer (e.g., information about the employee's actual experience in the job in question or in previous jobs).[683]

Often, however, employers are faced with conflicting reports and recommendations from the employee's doctor and the employer's doctor. The Seventh

---

[679]186 F.3d 897, 9 AD Cases 1015 (8th Cir. 1999).

[680]*Id.* at 900, 9 AD Cases at 1017.

[681]*EEOC Guidance on Disability Related Inquiries*, *supra* note 485, at 7714.

[682]*Id. See also* Holiday v. City of Chattanooga, 206 F.3d 637, 10 AD Cases 501 (6th Cir. 2000) (physician made an unsubstantiated conclusion that applicant was automatically unqualified solely because of her HIV infection); EEOC v. Texas Bus Lines, 923 F. Supp. 965, 5 AD Cases 878 (S.D. Tex. 1996) (employer erroneously relied on its physician's opinion based on subjective stereotypes).

[683]*EEOC Guidance on Disability Related Inquiries*, *supra* note 485, at 7714.

Circuit, in a Rehabilitation Act case, recognized that employers have a certain amount of discretion:

> We do not believe that, in cases where medical experts disagree in their assessment of the extent of a real risk of serious harm or death, Congress intended that the courts—neutral arbiters but generally less skilled in medicine than the experts involved—should make the final medical decision. Instead, in the midst of conflicting expert testimony regarding the degree of serious risk of harm or death, the court's place is to ensure that the exclusion or disqualification of an individual was individualized, reasonably made, and based upon competent medical evidence.[684]

Similarly, in *Tokar v. City of Chicago*,[685] the plaintiff was a city garbage truck driver. After two psychiatrists diagnosed her with various psychological disorders and stated that a risk to the public existed if she continued driving, the city removed her from paid leave, placed her on unpaid leave, and asked her to submit any medical evidence she had that contradicted the psychiatrists' conclusions. The plaintiff subsequently began seeing her own psychiatrist, who diagnosed her with paranoid disorder and prescribed medications to control her symptoms. One month later, the plaintiff's psychiatrist wrote to the city requesting that the plaintiff be reinstated as he thought she might be "'fit to return to her employment responsibilities if certain accommodations for her personal difficulties [were] made.'"[686] The city responded that the psychiatrist's letters did not help it determine the plaintiff's fitness for duty because neither addressed which duties she could perform and what accommodations she would need. Four months later, the city had a different psychiatrist examine the plaintiff, who determined that she remained unfit to return to her job. The plaintiff's psychiatrist wrote several letters over the next months asking that the city reinstate the plaintiff, but it declined to do so.

The court found that although the city's initial placement of the plaintiff on paid leave might not have been justified by safety concerns, it made its subsequent decision to remove her from paid leave because

> multiple doctors concurred that [the plaintiff's] psychological condition rendered her unfit to resume her driving duties. . . . Although [the plaintiff] attempts to undermine the soundness of the City's expert opinions, she has not established that the City's asserted reasons for prohibiting her return to duty were pretextual. The question is whether [the City] honestly believed that [the plaintiff] posed a danger. The difference of opinion between the City's doctors and [the plaintiff's] physician does not mean [the City] did not honestly believe the [doctors to whom it referred the plaintiff], all of whom suggested that [the plaintiff] presented a risk to herself and others. [The plaintiff's physician] took a tenuous position in advocating for [her] return, and failed to provide support for his stance. Thus,

---

[684]Knapp v. Northwestern Univ., 101 F.3d 473, 485 (7th Cir. 1996).
[685]2000 WL 1230489 (N.D. Ill. Aug. 25, 2000).
[686]*Id.* at *10.

[the City's] refusal to rely on [his] opinion does not demonstrate that [its] articulated safety concerns were pretextual.[687]

These cases indicate that where there are conflicting medical recommendations the employer is not obligated to accept the employee's doctor's recommendation, so long as the employer relies upon a thorough and objective analysis by a qualified examiner.

---

[687]*Id.* at *8.

APPENDIX 1*

EEOC POLICY GUIDE ON COMPENSATORY AND PUNITIVE DAMAGES UNDER 1991 CIVIL RIGHTS ACT

Following is the text of relevant portions of an EEOC policy guide, issued July 7, 1992, setting forth the Commission's position on the availability of compensatory and punitive damages under the Civil Rights Act of 1991.

EEOC Policy Guide

Subject Matter

This enforcement guidance sets forth the Commission's position on how to assess compensatory and punitive damages under §102 of the Civil Rights Act of 1991, 105 Stat 1071, Pub. L. No. 102-166 (hereinafter referred to as §1981A).

* * *

II. Types and Extent of Recovery

Section 1981A(b) sets limitations on certain damages that complaining parties may recover. First, it specifies that punitive damages are available only if the complaining party demonstrates that the respondent engaged in discrimination "with malice or reckless indifference to the federally protected rights of an aggrieved individual." It also provides that punitive damages are not available against a governmental entity or political subdivision.

Second, §1981A(b) reiterates that compensatory damages do not include any relief authorized under §706(g) of Title VII. Third, it provides a limitation on the sum of punitive damages and compensatory damages for "future pecuniary losses, emotional pain, suffering, inconvenience, mental anguish, loss of enjoyment of life, and other nonpecuniary losses." The limitation on the amount

---

*Reprinted from Fair Employment Practices Manual (BNA).

of damages (caps) is based on the size (number of employees)[6] of the respondent. The limitations are stated as follows:

15 to 100 employees	$ 50,000
101 to 200 employees	$100,000
201 to 500 employees	$200,000
501 employees or more	$300,000

The limitations do not, on their face, apply to respondents who have fewer than fifteen employees, although labor organizations and employment agencies with fewer than fifteen employees may be subject to Title VII.[7] Basing a union's damage caps on its number of employees, rather than on the number of its members, may have been a drafting error. However, since §1981A(b)(3) specifically refers to the number of "employees," and since that is not inconsistent with the provision's purpose, the Commission interprets the statute to mean that the caps relate to the number of a union's employees, rather than to the number of its members. Thus, a literal interpretation of the provision would potentially subject them to unlimited damages. Such an interpretation would be inconsistent with Congress' clear intent to spare small respondents from large damage awards. The provision could also be read to mean that labor organizations and employment agencies with fewer than fifteen employees are not subject to any damages. The Commission rejects both interpretations and concludes that all covered employment agencies and labor organizations with 100 or fewer employees are subject to the $50,000 cap on damages.

* * *

A. *Compensatory Damages*

Compensatory damages are awarded to compensate a complaining party for losses or suffering inflicted due to the discriminatory act or conduct. *See*

---

[6]Part-time employees are included in this count. *See* EEOC Policy Guidance No. N-915-052, "Whether part-time employees are employees within the meaning of §701(b) of Title VII and §11(b) of the ADEA," April 20, 1990 [405:6857]. Two circuits have concluded that part-time employees are not counted as employees for jurisdictional purposes. *See, e.g., EEOC v. Garden and Associates,* 956 F.2d 842 [58 FEP Cases 136] (8th Cir. 1992) (ADEA); *Zimmerman v. North American Signal Corp.,* 704 F.2d 347, 354, 31 EPD ¶33,486 [31 FEP Cases 634] (7th Cir. 1983) (ADEA). However, the conclusions in these cases were based on the definitional requirement that employers have the requisite number of employees "for each working day in each of twenty or more calendar weeks." Because §1981A(b)(3) does not contain the "for each working day" requirement for counting employees to determine a respondent's cap, the rationale for a *Garden* or *Zimmerman* type of result appears to have been eliminated.

[7]*See* EEOC Compliance Manual, Volume II, §605, Appendix N [405:6607]. This guidance explains that both labor organizations and employment agencies with fewer than fifteen employees may be covered by Title VII, if they regularly deal with Title VII covered employers. Labor organizations need only operate a hiring hall which procures employees for an employer or have fifteen members to be covered by Title VII. *See* 42 U.S.C. §2000e(e).

Carey v. Piphus 435 U.S. 247, 254 (1978) (purpose of damages is to "compensate persons for injuries caused by the deprivation of constitutional rights"). Compensatory damages "may be had for any proximate consequences which can be established with requisite certainty." 22 Am Jur 2d Damages §45 (1965). Compensatory damages include damages for past pecuniary loss (out-of-pocket loss), future pecuniary loss, and nonpecuniary loss (emotional harm). Compensatory damages are allowed against federal, state, and local governments and private sector employers.

The following section sets forth the legal parameters for computing compensatory and punitive damages where appropriate.

* * *

2. Nonpecuniary Losses

Damages are available for the intangible injuries of emotional harm such as emotional pain, suffering, inconvenience, mental anguish, and loss of enjoyment of life. Other nonpecuniary losses could include injury to professional standing, injury to character and reputation, injury to credit standing, loss of health, and any other nonpecuniary losses that are incurred as a result of the discriminatory conduct. Nonpecuniary losses for emotional harm are more difficult to prove than pecuniary losses.[13] Emotional harm will not be presumed simply because the complaining party is a victim of discrimination.[14] The existence, nature, and severity of emotional harm must be proved. Emotional harm may manifest itself, for example, as sleeplessness, anxiety, stress, depression, marital strain, humiliation, emotional distress, loss of self esteem, excessive fatigue, or a nervous breakdown. Physical manifestations of emotional harm may consist of ulcers, gastrointestinal disorders, hair loss, or headaches.

An award for emotional harm is warranted only if there is sufficient causal connection between the respondent's illegal actions and the complaining party's injury. *See Gore v. Turner,* 563 F.2d 159, 164 (5th Cir. 1977). The discriminatory act or conduct must be the cause of the emotional harm. The claim of emotional harm will be seriously undermined if the onset of symptoms of emotional harm preceded the discrimination. However, if a complaining party had preexisting emotional difficulties and his mental health deteriorates as a result of the discriminatory conduct, the additional harm may be attributed to the respondent. The fact that the complaining party may be unusually emotionally sensitive

---

[13]Cases awarding compensatory and punitive damages under other civil rights statutes will be used for guidance in analyzing the availability of damages under §1981A. Section 1981 cases are particularly useful because Congress treated the §1981A damage provisions as an amendment to §1981.

[14]Complaining parties should be informed that if they claim emotional harm, respondents may be able to obtain records of medical and/or psychiatric treatments for conditions relevant to the complained of symptoms. A respondent may also obtain relevant information concerning the complaining party's private life.

and incur great emotional harm from discriminatory conduct will not absolve the respondent from responsibility for the greater emotional harm. *Williamson v. Handy Button Machine Company,* 817 F.2d 1290, 1294, 43 EPD ¶37,178 (7th Cir. 1987) ("perhaps [plaintiff] was unusually sensitive, but a tortfeasor takes its victims as it finds them"). For example, suppose the Commission finds that the respondent is liable for sexual harassment against three female employees, one of whom is an incest victim. The incest victim incurred much greater emotional harm from the sexual harassment than did her two co-workers. The respondent is liable for the greater emotional harm that the incest victim suffered.

For charges alleging emotional harm, consider factors that are directly relevant to whether and to what extent the employer caused the employee's emotional harm. For example, in *Cowan v. Prudential Insurance Co.,* 852 F.2d 688, 690-91, 47 EPD ¶38,167 (2d Cir. 1988), the court found that defendant's failure to promote the plaintiff caused him severe emotional distress, humiliation, loss of self esteem, marital problems, and heavy drinking. However, the court considered several factors to determine whether and to what extent the emotional harm was caused by the defendant or by other factors. The factors considered were that: 1) the plaintiff had not been subjected to overt racism or public humiliation; 2) upper management was not aware that race was a factor in the failure to promote the plaintiff, who had been offered three other less attractive positions; 3) the plaintiff had caused some of the humiliation and difficulties that he had with his co-workers because he told clients that he would be promoted and he criticized his co-workers in a newspaper article; and 4) the plaintiff had not sought counseling. The court found that these factors justified a lower amount than the plaintiff sought. In *Vance v. Southern Bell Telephone and Telegraph Company,* 863 F.2d 1503, 1516, 48 EPD ¶38,626 [50 FEP Cases 742] (11th Cir. 1989), the court found that an award of $500,000 in compensatory damages for mental distress, emotional harm, or humiliation resulting from racial discrimination was properly ruled excessive where there were other factors which probably contributed to the plaintiff's mental distress. The plaintiff had marital problems because her husband was named in a paternity suit by another woman, financial problems, problems resulting from an automobile accident, dietary problems, and family illnesses and deaths. Therefore, where a complaining party's emotional harm is due in part to personal difficulties, which were not caused or exacerbated by the discriminatory conduct, the employer is liable only for the harm resulting from the discriminatory conduct.

The Commission will typically require medical evidence of emotional harm to seek damages for such harm in conciliation negotiations. However, evidence of emotional harm may be established by testimony. *Gunby v. Pennsylvania Electric Company,* 840 F.2d 1108, 1121-22, 45 EPD ¶37,785 [45 FEP Cases 1818] (3d Cir. 1988), *cert. denied,* 492 U.S. 905, 50 EPD ¶39,201 [50 FEP Cases 96] (1989); *Cowan v. Prudential Insurance Co.,* 582 F.2d at 690-91. The "plaintiff's own testimony may be solely sufficient to establish humiliation or mental distress." *Williams v. TransWorld Airlines, Inc.,* 660 F.2d 1267, 1273, 27 EPD ¶32,174 [27 FEP Cases 487] (8th Cir. 1981). For example, a plaintiff was awarded $52,644.80 in damages for mental anguish and emotional distress resulting from losing his house and car, marital harmony, and the respect of his children, after he was discriminatorily discharged. *Muldrew v. Anheuser-Busch Inc.,* 728 F.2d 989, 33 EPD ¶34,187 [34 FEP Cases 93] (8th Cir. 1984). In *Block v. R.H. Macy & Co. Inc.,* 712 F.2d 1241, 1245, 32 EPD ¶33,730 [32 FEP Cases 609] (8th Cir. 1983), the plaintiff was awarded $12,402 for "mental anguish, humiliation, embarrassment and stress," $7,598 in backpay, and $60,000 in punitive damages. The evidence presented was that the supervisor openly manifested racial bias against Blacks by making racially offensive references to the plaintiff, another employee, and customers. On one occasion, the supervisor and plaintiff got into a dispute during which the supervisor berated the plaintiff in street language in front of coworkers and customers, although she never addressed White employees in this manner. The supervisor reported the dispute to management and told them that she wanted plaintiff "out of there." Management discharged the plaintiff without asking for her version of the incident, although they were well aware of the supervisor's racial bias. The plaintiff testified that she "cried and felt angry" with her supervisor after her discharge. Plaintiff further testified that she was unemployed for thirteen months and because of her financial dilemma, she suffered sleeplessness, anxiety, embarrassment, and depression. The jury found this evidence sufficient to award damages for mental distress.

Similarly, in *Stallworth v. Shuler,* 777 F.2d 1431, 38 EPD ¶35,806 [39 FEP Cases 983] (11th Cir. 1985), a case brought under §1983 and §1981, the court affirmed an award for $100,000 for humiliation and emotional distress. Over a period of years, the plaintiff was consistently passed over for administrative positions and principalships for racial reasons, while less qualified White persons were promoted. As a result, plaintiff suffered emotional stress, loss of sleep, marital strain, and humiliation. The defendant stated that there was no evidence that plaintiff missed work, received professional help, or slipped in his relationships with students or co-workers. Plaintiff countered that he was careful not to give the respondent a reason not to promote him. The court found that plaintiff's evidence was sufficient to award damages. However, for conciliation or settlement purposes, testimony solely by the complaining party may not be sufficient to establish emotional harm. There should be corroborating testimony by the complaining party's co-workers, supervisors, family, friends, or anyone else with knowledge of the emotional harm.

Damage awards for emotional harm vary significantly and there are no definitive rules governing the amounts to be awarded. However, compensatory damage awards must be limited to the sums necessary to compensate the plaintiff for actual harm, even if the harm is intangible. *Carter v. Duncan-Huggins, Ltd.,* 727 F.2d 1225, 33 EPD ¶34,187 [34 FEP Cases 25] (D.C. Cir. 1984). In *Williamson v. Handy Button Machine Company,* 817 F.2d at 1293-95, the court upheld a damage award of $10,000 for the psychological disability of a nervous breakdown after the following sequence of events. Plaintiff was discriminated against for over a decade. She was assigned unskilled work, although she was qualified for, and occasionally performed, skilled work. Plaintiff was passed over for numerous promotions, in favor of less qualified White employees with less seniority. Plaintiff was also demoted to a lower status department despite her protests and the seniority rule in the collective bargaining agreement. Finally, on one occasion, the plaintiff used an upstairs bathroom, where she had been assigned a locker by the company, and was loudly berated in scatological terms by a supervisor for using this particular bathroom. The psychiatrist characterized the bathroom incident as the straw that broke the camel's back. The plaintiff was never able to return to work. In addition to the award for emotional harm, plaintiff received $130,000 for backpay and frontpay, $10,000 for medical and psychological expenses, and $100,000 for punitive damages.

In comparison, in another case brought under §1981, the plaintiff received $123,000 for emotional distress. The plaintiff had been under stress continuously for fear of making a mistake on the job, because he was discriminatorily denied proper training which he needed for adequate performance. The plaintiff's White coworkers, both senior and junior to the plaintiff, regularly received formal training. He was denied pay raises equivalent to those of his White coworkers because of his poor evaluations, which stressed the need for training. When the plaintiff finally received training after numerous requests, it was superficial in nature. Plaintiff's stressful situation resulted in high absenteeism and he was placed on probation. He filed a complaint and was subsequently discharged. Plaintiff's psychiatrist testified that the plaintiff was suffering from nxiety, stress, and depression. The court found that this was an adequate basis for the award. Plaintiff also received $176,000 in backpay, and $300,000 in punitive damages. *Rowlett v. Anheuser-Busch,* 832 F.2d 194, 44 EDP ¶37,428 [44 FEP Cases 1617] (1st Cir. 1987).

The method for computing nonpecuniary damages during conciliation or settlement should typically be based on a consideration of the severity of harm and the time that the complaining party has suffered from the emotional harm.[15] To determine the severity of the harm consider, for example, whether the harm consisted of occasional sleeplessness, or a nervous breakdown resulting in years of psychotherapy. The length of time that the complaining party has suffered from the emotional harm is also relevant. Of course, a complaining party who has suffered from severe depression for two months will be awarded less money than a complaining party who has suffered from severe depression for a year. However, different methods of computing damage amounts for emotional harm may be appropriate in certain cases. Since medical evidence is important, a medical release should be obtained from the complaining party whenever emotional or physical harm is alleged.

* * *

---

[15]During litigation, the amount of damages will be decided by a jury if either party requests a jury. Jury trials will be available if a plaintiff seeks compensatory or punitive damages. Section 1981A(c).

APPENDIX 2

AMERICAN ACADEMY OF PSYCHIATRY AND THE LAW ETHICAL GUIDELINES FOR THE PRACTICE OF FORENSIC PSYCHIATRY

Adopted May, 1987; last revised 1995
Reprinted by permission

I. PREAMBLE

The American Academy of Psychiatry and the Law is dedicated to the highest standards of practice in forensic psychiatry. Recognizing the unique aspects of this practice which is at the interface of the professions of psychiatry and the law, the Academy presents these guidelines for the ethical practice of forensic psychiatry.

Commentary

Forensic Psychiatry is a subspecialty of psychiatry, a medical specialty. Membership in the American Psychiatric Association, or its equivalent, is a prerequisite for membership in the American Academy of Psychiatry and the Law. Hence, these guidelines supplement the Annotations Especially Applicable to Psychiatry of the American Psychiatric Association to the Principles of Medical Ethics of the American Medical Association.

The American Academy of Psychiatry and the Law endorses the Definition of Forensic Psychiatry adopted by the American Board of Forensic Psychiatry, Inc.

"Forensic Psychiatry is a subspecialty of psychiatry in which scientific and clinical expertise is applied to legal issues in legal contexts embracing civil, criminal, and correctional or legislative matters: forensic psychiatry should be practiced in accordance with guidelines and ethical principles enunciated by the profession of psychiatry." (Adopted May 20, 1985)

The forensic psychiatrist practices this subspecialty at the interface of two professions, each of which is concerned with human behavior and each of which has developed its own particular institutions, procedures, values, and vocabulary. As a consequence, the practice of forensic psychiatry entails inherent potentials for complications, conflicts, misunderstandings and abuses.

In view of the these concerns, the American Academy of Psychiatry and Law provides these guidelines for the ethical practice of forensic psychiatry.

II. CONFIDENTIALITY

Respect for the individual's right of privacy and the maintenance of confidentiality are major concerns of the psychiatrist performing forensic evaluations. The psychiatrist maintains confidentiality to the extent possible given the legal context. Special attention is paid to any limitations on the usual precepts of medical confidentiality. An evaluation for forensic purposes begins with notice to the evaluee of any limitations on confidentiality. Information or reports derived from the forensic evaluation are subject to the rules of confidentiality as apply to the evaluation, and any disclosure is restricted accordingly.

Commentary

The forensic situation often presents significant problems in regard to confidentiality. The psychiatrist must be aware of and alert to those issues of privacy and confidentiality presented by the particular forensic situation. Notice should be given as to any limitations. For example, before beginning a forensic evaluation, psychiatrists should inform the evaluee that although they are psychiatrists, they are not the evaluee's "doctor." Psychiatrists should indicate for whom they are conducting the examination and what they will do with the information obtained as a result of the examination. There is a continuing obligation to be sensitive to the fact that although a warning has been given, there may be slippage and a treatment relationship may develop in the mind of the examinee.

Psychiatrists should take precautions to assure that none of the confidential information they receive falls into the hands of unauthorized persons.

Psychiatrists should clarify with a potentially retaining attorney whether an initial screening conversation prior to a formal agreement will interdict consultation with the opposing side if the psychiatrist decides not to accept the consultation.

In a treatment situation, whether in regard to an inpatient or to an outpatient in a parole, probation, or conditional release situation, psychiatrists should be clear about any limitations on the usual principles of confidentiality in the treatment relationship and assure that these limitations are communicated to the patient. Psychiatrists should be familiar with the institutional policies in regard to confidentiality. Where no policy exists, psychiatrists should clarify these matters with the institutional authorities and develop working guidelines to define their role.

III. CONSENT

The informed consent of the subject of a forensic evaluation is obtained when possible. Where consent is not required, notice is given to the evaluee of the nature of the evaluation. If the evaluee is not competent to give consent, substituted consent is obtained in accordance with the laws of the jurisdiction.

Commentary

Consent is one of the core values of the ethical practice of medicine and psychiatry. It reflects respect for the person, a fundamental principle in the practices of medicine, psychiatry and forensic psychiatry. Obtaining informed consent is an expression of this request.

It is important to appreciate that in particular situations, such as court ordered evaluations for competency to stand trial or involuntary commitment, consent is not required. In such a case, the psychiatrist should so inform the subject and explain that the evaluation is legally required and that if the subject refuses to participate in the evaluation, this fact will be included in any report or testimony.

With regard to any person charged with criminal acts, ethical considerations preclude forensic evaluation prior to access to, or availability of legal counsel. The only exception is an examination for the purpose of rendering emergency medical care and treatment.

Consent to treatment in a jail or prison or other criminal justice setting must be differentiated from consent to evaluation. The psychiatrists providing treatment in these settings should be familiar with the jurisdiction's rules in regard to the patient's right to refuse treatment.

IV. HONESTY AND STRIVING FOR OBJECTIVITY

Forensic psychiatrists function as experts within the legal process. Although he may be retained by one party to a dispute in a civil matter or the prosecution or defense in a criminal matter, they adhere to the principle of honesty and they strive for objectivity. Their clinical evaluation and the application of the data obtained to the legal criteria are performed in the spirit of such honesty and efforts to obtain objectivity. Their opinion reflects this honesty and efforts to attain objectivity.

Commentary

The adversarial nature of our Anglo-American legal process presents special hazards for the practicing forensic psychiatrist. Being retained by one side in a civil or criminal matter exposes the forensic psychiatrist to the potential for unintended bias and the danger of distortion of their opinion. It is the responsibility of forensic psychiatrists to minimize such hazards by carrying out his responsibilities in an honest manner striving to reach an objective opinion.

Practicing forensic psychiatrists enhance the honesty and striving for objectivity of their work by basing their forensic opinions, forensic reports, and forensic testimony on all the data available to them. They communicate the honesty and striving for objectivity of their work, efforts to obtain objectivity, and the soundness of their clinical opinion by distinguishing, to the extent possible, between verified and unverified information as well as among clinical "facts," "inferences" and "impressions."

While it is ethical to provide consultation to an adversary in a legal dispute as a testifying or reporting expert, honesty and striving for objectivity are required. The impression that psychiatrists in a forensic situation might distort their opinion in the service of the party which retained them is especially detrimental to the profession and must be assiduously avoided. Honesty, objectivity and the adequacy of the clinical evaluation may be called into question when an expert opinion is offered without a personal evaluation. While there are authorities who would bar an expert opinion in regard to an individual who has not been personally examined, it is the position of the Academy that if, after earnest effort, it is not possible to conduct a personal examination, an opinion may be rendered on the basis of other information. However, under such circumstances, it is the responsibility of the forensic psychiatrist to assure that the statement of their opinion and any reports of testimony based on those opinions, clearly indicate that there was no personal examination and the opinions expressed are thereby limited.

In custody cases, honesty and striving for objectivity require that all parties be interviewed, if possible, before an opinion is rendered. When this is not possible, or, if for any reason not done, this fact should be clearly indicated in the forensic psychiatrist's report and testimony. Where one parent has not been interviewed, even after deliberate effort, it may be inappropriate to comment on that parent's fitness as a parent. Any comment on that parent's fitness as a parent should be qualified and the data for the opinion should be clearly indicated.

Contingency fees, because of the problems that these create in regard to honesty and efforts to obtain objectivity, should not be accepted. On the other hand, retainer fees do not create problems in regard to honesty and efforts to obtain objectivity and, therefore, may be accepted.

Treating psychiatrists should generally avoid agreeing to be an expert witness or to perform evaluations of their patients for legal purposes because a forensic evaluation usually requires that other people be interviewed and testimony may adversely affect the therapeutic relationship.

V. QUALIFICATIONS

Expertise in the practice of forensic psychiatry is claimed only in areas of actual knowledge and skills, training and experience.

Commentary

As regards expert opinions, reports and testimony, the expert's qualifications should be presented accurately and precisely. As a correlate of the principle that expertise may be appropriately claimed only in areas of actual knowledge, skill, training and experience, there are areas of special expertise, such as the evaluation of children or persons of foreign cultures, or prisoners, that may require special training and expertise.

VI. PROCEDURES FOR HANDLING COMPLAINTS OF UNETHICAL CONDUCT

Complaints of unethical conduct against members of the Academy will be returned to the complainant with guidance as to where the complaint should be registered. Generally, they will be referred to the local district branch of the American Psychiatric Association (APA). If the member does not belong to the APA, the complainant will be referred to the state licensing board or to the psychiatric association in the appropriate country. If either the APA, American Academy of Child and Adolescent Psychiatry, or the psychiatric association of another country should expel or suspend a member, AAPL will also expel or suspend the member upon notification of such action, regardless of continuing membership status in other organizations. AAPL will not necessarily follow the APA or other organizations in other actions.

Commentary

It is the present policy of the American Academy of Psychiatry and Law not to adjudicate questions of unethical conduct against members or nonmembers.

General questions in regard to ethical practice in forensic psychiatry are welcomed by the Academy and should be submitted for consideration to the Committee on Ethics.

The Committee will issue opinions on general or hypothetical questions but will not issue an opinion on the ethical conduct of a specific forensic psychiatrist or about an actual case.

Should a specific complaint against a member be submitted to the Academy, it will be referred to the Chair of the Ethics Committee. The Chair will, in turn, generally direct the complainant to the ethics committee of the local district branch of the American Psychiatric Association, to the state licensing board, or to the psychiatric organization of other countries for foreign members.

The Academy, through its Committee on Ethics or in any other way suitable, will assist the local or national committee on ethics of the American Psychiatric Association, state licensing boards or ethics committees of psychiatric organizations in other countries in the adjudication of complaints of unethical conduct or the development of guidelines of ethical conduct as they relate to forensic psychiatric issues.

APPENDIX 3

SPECIALTY GUIDELINES FOR FORENSIC PSYCHOLOGISTS

Prepared by the Committee on Ethical Guidelines for Forensic Psychologists, Division 41, American Psychological Association, and the American Board of Forensic Psychology. Reprinted by permission.

Introduction

The *Specialty Guidelines for Forensic Psychologists,* while informed by the *Ethical Principles of Psychologists* (APA, 1990) and meant to be consistent with them, are designed to provide more specific guidance to forensic psychologists in monitoring their professional conduct when acting in assistance to courts, parties to legal proceedings, correctional and forensic mental health facilities, and legislative agencies. The primary goal of the *Guidelines* is to improve the quality of forensic psychological services offered to individual clients and the legal system and thereby to enhance forensic psychology as a discipline and profession. The *Specialty Guidelines for Forensic Psychologists* represent a joint statement of the American Psychology-Law Society and Division 41 of the American Psychological Association and are endorsed by the American Academy of Forensic Psychology. The Guidelines do not represent an official statement of the American Psychological Association.

The Guidelines provide an aspirational model of desirable professional practice by psychologists, within any subdiscipline of psychology (e.g., clinical, developmental, social, experimental), when they are engaged regularly as experts and represent themselves as such, in an activity primarily intended to provide professional psychological expertise to the judicial system. This would include, for example, clinical forensic examiners; psychologists employed by correctional or forensic mental health systems; researchers who offer direct testimony about the relevance of scientific data to a psycholegal issue; trial behavior consultants; psychologists engaged in preparation of *amicus* briefs; or psychologists, appearing as forensic experts, who consult with, or testify before, judicial, legislative or administrative agencies acting in an adjudicative capacity. Individuals who provide only occasional services to the legal system and who do so without representing themselves as *forensic experts* may find these *Guidelines* helpful, particularly in conjunction with consultation with colleagues who are forensic experts.

While the *Guidelines* are concerned with a model of desirable professional practice, to the extent that they may be construed as being applicable to the advertisement of services or the solicitation of clients, they are intended to prevent false or deceptive advertisement or solicitation, and should be construed in a manner consistent with that intent.

I. Purpose and Scope

A. *Purpose*

1. While the professional standards for the ethical practice of psychology, as a general discipline, are addressed in the American Psychological Association's *Ethical Principles of Psychologists,* these ethical principles do not relate, in sufficient detail, to current aspirations of desirable professional conduct for forensic psychologists. By design, none of the *Guidelines* contradicts any of the *Ethical Principles of Psychologists;* rather, they amplify those *Principles* in the context of the practice of forensic psychology, as herein defined.
2. The *Guidelines* have been designed to be national in scope and are intended to conform with state and Federal law. In situations where the forensic psychologist believes that the requirements of law are in conflict with the *Guidelines,* attempts to resolve the conflict should be made in accordance with the procedures set forth in these *Guidelines* [IV(G)] and in the *Ethical Principles of Psychologists.*

B. *Scope*

1. The *Guidelines* specify the nature of desirable professional practice by forensic psychologists, within any subdiscipline of psychology (e.g., clinical, developmental, social, experimental), when engaged regularly as forensic psychologists.
    a. "Psychologist" means any individual whose professional activities are defined by the American Psychological Association or by regulation of title by state registration or licensure, as the practice of psychology.
    b. "Forensic psychology" means all forms of professional psychological conduct when acting, with definable foreknowledge, as a psychological expert on explicitly psycholegal issues, in direct assistance to courts, parties to legal proceedings, correctional and forensic mental health facilities, and administrative, judicial and legislative agencies acting in an adjudicative capacity.
    c. "Forensic psychologist" means psychologists who regularly engage in the practice of forensic psychology as defined in I(B)(1)(b).
2. The *Guidelines* do not apply to a psychologist who is asked to provide professional psychological services when the psychologist was not informed at the time of delivery of the services that they were to be used as forensic psychological services as defined above. The *Guidelines* may be helpful, however, in preparing the psychologist for the experience of communicating psychological data in a forensic context.
3. Psychologists who are not forensic psychologists as defined in I(B)(1)(c), but occasionally provide limited forensic psychological services, may find the

Guidelines useful in the preparation and presentation of their professional services.

C. Related Standards

1. Forensic psychologists also conduct their professional activities in accord with the *Ethical Principles of Psychologists* and the various other statements of the American Psychological Association that may apply to particular subdisciplines or areas of practice that are relevant to their professional activities.
2. The standards of practice and ethical guidelines of other relevant "expert professional organizations" contain useful guidance and should be consulted even though the present *Guidelines* take precedence for forensic psychologists.

II. Responsibility

A. Forensic psychologists have an obligation to provide services in a manner consistent with the highest standards of their profession. They are responsible for their own conduct and the conduct of those individuals under their direct supervision.

B. Forensic psychologists make a reasonable effort to ensure that their services and the products of their services are used in a forthright and responsible manner.

III. Competence

A. Forensic psychologists provide services only in areas of psychology in which they have specialized knowledge, skill, experience and education.

B. Forensic psychologists have an obligation to present to the court, regarding the specific matters to which they will testify, the boundaries of their competence, the factual bases (knowledge, skill, experience, training, and education) for their qualification as an expert, and the relevance of those factual bases to their qualification as an expert on the specific matters at issue.

C. Forensic psychologists are responsible for a fundamental and reasonable level of knowledge and understanding of the legal and professional standards which govern their participation as experts in legal proceedings.

D. Forensic psychologists have an obligation to understand the civil rights of parties in legal proceedings in which they participate, and manage their professional conduct in a manner that does not diminish or threaten those rights.

E. Forensic psychologists recognize that their own personal values, moral beliefs, or personal and professional relationships with parties to a legal proceeding may interfere with their ability to practice competently. Under such circumstances, forensic psychologists are obligated to decline participation or to limit their assistance in a manner consistent with professional obligations.

IV. Relationships

A. During initial consultation with the legal representative of the party seeking services, forensic psychologists have an obligation to inform the party of factors that might reasonably affect the decision to contract with the forensic psychologist. These factors include, but are not limited to:

1. the fee structure for anticipated professional services;
2. prior and current personal or professional activities, obligations and relationships that might produce a conflict of interest;
3. their areas of competence and the limits of their competence; and
4. the known scientific bases and limitations of the methods and procedures which they employ and their qualifications to employ such methods and procedures.

B. Forensic psychologists do not provide professional services to parties to a legal proceeding on the basis of "contingent fees," when those services involve the offering of expert testimony to a court or administrative body, or when they call upon the psychologist to make affirmations or representations intended to be relied upon by third parties.

C. Forensic psychologists who derive a substantial portion of their income from fee-for-service arrangements should offer some portion of their professional services on a *pro bono* or reduced fee basis where the public interest or the welfare of clients may be inhibited by insufficient financial resources.

D. Forensic psychologists recognize potential conflicts of interest in dual relationships with parties to a legal proceeding, and they seek to minimize their effects.

1. Forensic psychologists avoid providing professional services to parties in a legal proceeding with whom they have personal or professional relationships that are inconsistent with the anticipated relationship.
2. When it is necessary to provide both evaluation and treatment services to a party in a legal proceeding (as may be the case in small forensic hospital settings or small communities), the forensic psychologist takes reasonable steps to minimize the potential negative effects of these circumstances on the rights of the party, confidentiality, and the process of treatment and evaluation.

E. Forensic psychologists have an obligation to ensure that prospective clients are informed of their legal rights with respect to the anticipated forensic service, of the purposes of any evaluation, of the nature of procedures to be employed, of the intended uses of any product of their services, and of the party who has employed the forensic psychologist.

1. Unless court ordered, forensic psychologists obtain the informed consent of the client or party, or their legal representative, before proceeding with such evaluations and procedures. If the client appears unwilling to proceed after receiving a thorough notification of the purposes, methods, and intended uses of the forensic evaluation, the evaluation should be postponed and the psychologist should take steps to place the client in contact with his/her attorney for the purpose of legal advice on the issue of participation.
2. In situations where the client or party may not have the capacity to provide informed consent to services or the evaluation is pursuant to court order, the

forensic psychologist provides reasonable notice to the client's legal representative of the nature of the anticipated forensic service before proceeding. If the client's legal representative objects to the evaluation, the forensic psychologist notifies the court issuing the order and responds as directed.
3. After a psychologist has advised the subject of a clinical forensic evaluation of the intended uses of the evaluation and its work product, the psychologist may not use the evaluation work product for other purposes without explicit waiver to do so by the client or the client's legal representative.

F. When forensic psychologists engage in research or scholarly activities that are compensated financially by a client or party to a legal proceeding, or when the psychologist provides those services on a *pro bono* basis, the psychologist clarifies any anticipated further use of such research or scholarly product, discloses the psychologist's role in the resulting research or scholarly products, and obtains whatever consent or agreement is required by law or professional standards.

G. When conflicts arise between the forensic psychologist's professional standards and the requirements of legal standards, a particular court, or a directive by an officer or the court or legal authorities, the forensic psychologist has an obligation to make those legal authorities aware of the source of the conflict and to take reasonable steps to resolve it. Such steps may include, but are not limited to, obtaining the consultation of fellow forensic professionals, obtaining the advice of independent counsel, and conferring directly with the legal representatives involved.

V. Confidentiality and Privilege

A. Forensic psychologists have an obligation to be aware of the legal standards that may affect or limit the confidentiality or privilege that may attach to their services or their products, and they conduct their professional activities in a manner that respects those known rights and privileges.

1. Forensic psychologists establish and maintain a system of record keeping and professional communication that safeguards a client's privilege.
2. Forensic psychologists maintain active control over records and information. They only release information pursuant to statutory requirements, court order, or the consent of the client.

B. Forensic psychologists inform their clients of the limitations to the confidentiality of their services and their products (see also Guideline IV-E) by providing them with an understandable statement of their rights, privileges, and the limitations of confidentiality.

C. In situations where the right of the client or party to confidentiality is limited, the forensic psychologist makes every effort to maintain confidentiality with regard to any information that does not bear directly upon the legal purpose of the evaluation.

D. Forensic psychologists provide clients or their authorized legal representatives with access to the information in their records and a meaningful explanation of that information, consistent with existing federal and state statutes, the *Ethical Principles of Psychologists,* the *Standards for Educational and Psychological Testing,* and institutional rules and regulations.

VI. Methods and Procedures

A. Because of their special status as persons qualified as experts to the court, forensic psychologists have an obligation to maintain current knowledge of scientific, professional and legal developments within their area of claimed competence. They are obligated also to use that knowledge, consistent with accepted clinical and scientific standards, in selecting data collection methods and procedures for an evaluation, treatment, consultation or scholarly/empirical investigation.

B. Forensic psychologists have an obligation to document and be prepared to make available, subject to court order or the rules of evidence, all data that form the basis for their evidence or services. The standard to be applied to such documentation or recording *anticipates* that the detail and quality of such documentation will be subject to reasonable judicial scrutiny; this standard is higher than the normative standard for general clinical practice. When forensic psychologists conduct an examination or engage in the treatment of a party to a legal proceeding, with foreknowledge that their professional services will be used in an adjudicative forum, they incur a special responsibility to provide the best documentation possible under the circumstances.

1. Documentation of the data upon which one's evidence is based is subject to the normal rules of discovery, disclosure, confidentiality and privilege that operate in the jurisdiction in which the data were obtained. Forensic psychologists have an obligation to be aware of those rules and to regulate their conduct in accordance with them.
2. The duties and obligations of forensic psychologists with respect to documentation of data that form the basis for their evidence apply from the moment they know or have a reasonable basis for knowing that their data and evidence derived from it are likely to enter into legally relevant decisions.

C. In providing forensic psychological services, forensic psychologists take special care to avoid undue influence upon their methods, procedures and products, such as might emanate from the party to a legal proceeding by financial compensation or other gains. As an expert conducting an evaluation, treatment, consultation or scholarly/empirical investigation, the forensic psychologist maintains professional integrity by examining the issue at hand from all reasonable perspectives, actively seeking information which will differentially test plausible rival hypotheses.

D. Forensic psychologists do not provide professional forensic services to a defendant or to any party in, or in contemplation of, a legal proceeding prior to that individual's representation by counsel, except for persons judicially determined, where appropriate, to be handling their representation *pro se.* When the forensic services are pursuant to court order and the client is not represented by counsel, the forensic psychologist makes reasonable efforts to inform the court prior to providing the services.

1. A forensic psychologist may provide emergency mental health services to a pretrial defendant prior to court order or the appointment of counsel where there are reasonable grounds to believe that such emergency services are needed for the protection and improvement of the defendant's mental health and where failure to provide such mental health services would constitute a substantial risk of imminent harm to the defendant or to others. In providing such services the forensic psychologist nevertheless seeks to inform the defendant's counsel in a manner consistent with the requirements of the emergency situation.
2. Forensic psychologists who provide such emergency mental health services should attempt to avoid providing further professional forensic services to that defendant unless that relationship is reasonably unavoidable [see IV(D)(2)].

E. When forensic psychologists seek data from third parties, prior records, or other sources, they do so only with the prior approval of the relevant legal party or as a consequence of an order of a court to conduct the forensic evaluation.

F. Forensic psychologists are aware that hearsay exceptions and other rules governing expert testimony place a special ethical burden upon them. When hearsay or otherwise inadmissible evidence forms the basis of their opinion, evidence or professional product, they seek to minimize sole reliance upon such evidence. Where circumstances reasonably permit, forensic psychologists seek to obtain independent and personal verification of data relied upon as part of their professional services to the court or to a party to a legal proceeding.

1. While many forms of data used by forensic psychologists are hearsay, forensic psychologists attempt to corroborate critical data which form the basis of their professional product. When using hearsay data that have not been corroborated, but are nevertheless utilized, forensic psychologists have an affirmative responsibility to acknowledge the uncorroborated status of that data and the reasons for relying upon such data.
2. With respect to evidence of any type, forensic psychologists avoid offering information from their investigations or evaluations that does not bear directly upon the legal purpose of their professional services and that is not critical as support for their product, evidence or testimony, except where such disclosure is required by law.
3. When a forensic psychologist relies upon data or information gathered by others, the origins of those data are clarified in any professional product. In addition, the forensic psychologist bears a special responsibility to ensure that such data, if relied upon, were gathered in a manner standard for the profession.

G. Unless otherwise stipulated by the parties, forensic psychologists are aware that no statements made by a defendant, in the course of any (forensic) examination, no testimony by the expert based upon such statements, nor any other fruits of the statements can be admitted into evidence against the defendant in any criminal proceeding, except on an issue respecting mental condition on which the defendant has introduced testimony. Forensic psychologists have an affirmative duty to ensure that their written products and oral testimony conform to this Federal Rule of Procedure (12.2[c]), or its state equivalent.

1. Because forensic psychologists are often not in a position to know what evidence, documentation or element of a written product may be or may lead to a "fruit of the statement," they exercise extreme caution in preparing reports or offering testimony prior to the defendant's assertion of a mental state claim or the defendant's introduction of testimony regarding a mental condition. Consistent with reporting requirements of state or Federal law, forensic psychologists avoid including statements from the defendant relating to the time period of the alleged offense.
2. Once a defendant has proceeded to the trial stage, and all pretrial mental health issues such as competency have been resolved, forensic psychologists may include in their reports or testimony any statements made by the defendant that are directly relevant to supporting their expert evidence, providing that the defendant has "introduced" mental state evidence or testimony within the meaning of Federal Rule of Procedure 12.2.(c), or its state equivalent.

H. Forensic psychologists avoid giving written or oral evidence about the psychological characteristics of particular individuals when they have not had an opportunity to conduct an examination of the individual adequate to the scope of the statements, opinions or conclusions to be issued. Forensic psychologists make every reasonable effort to conduct such examinations. When it is not possible or feasible to do so, they make clear the impact of such limitations on the reliability and validity of their professional products, evidence or testimony.

VII. Public and Professional Communications

A. Forensic psychologists make reasonable efforts to ensure that the products of their services, as well as their own public statements and professional testimony, are communicated in ways that will promote understanding and avoid deception, given the particular characteristics, roles, and abilities of various recipients of the communications.

1. Forensic psychologists take reasonable steps to correct misuse or misrepresentation of their professional products, evidence and testimony.
2. Forensic psychologists provide information about professional work to clients in a manner consistent with professional and legal standards for the disclosure of test results, interpretation of data, and the factual bases for conclusions. A full explanation of the results of tests and the bases for conclusions should be given in language that the client can understand.
    a. When disclosing information about a client to third parties who are not qualified to interpret test results and data, the forensic psychologist complies with Principle 16 of the *Standards for Educational and Psychological Testing*. When required to disclose results to a non-psychologist, every attempt is made to ensure that test security is maintained and access to information is restricted to individuals with a legitimate and professional interest in the data. Other qualified mental health professionals who make a request for

information pursuant to a lawful order are, by definition, "individuals with a legitimate and professional interest."
   b. In providing records and raw data, the forensic psychologist takes reasonable steps to ensure that the receiving party is informed that raw scores must be interpreted by a qualified professional in order to provide reliable and valid information.

B. Forensic psychologists realize that their public role as "expert to the court" or as "expert representing the profession" confers upon them a special responsibility for fairness and accuracy in their public statements. When evaluating or commenting upon the professional work product or qualifications of another expert or party to a legal proceeding, forensic psychologists represent their professional disagreements with reference to a fair and accurate evaluation of the data, theories, standards and opinions of the other expert or party.

C. Ordinarily, forensic psychologists avoid making detailed public (out-of-court) statements about particular legal proceedings in which they have been involved. When there is a strong justification to do so, such public statements are designed to assure accurate representation of their role or their evidence, not to advocate the positions of parties in the legal proceeding. Forensic psychologists address particular legal proceedings in publications or communications only to the extent that the information relied upon is part of a public record, or consent for that use has been properly obtained from the party holding any privilege.

D. When testifying, forensic psychologists have an obligation to all parties to a legal proceeding to present their findings, conclusions, evidence or other professional products in a fair manner. This principle does not preclude forceful representation of the data and reasoning upon which a conclusion or professional product is based. It does, however, preclude an attempt, whether active or passive, to engage in partisan distortion or misrepresentation. Forensic psychologists do not, by either commission or omission, participate in a misrepresentation of their evidence, nor do they participate in partisan attempts to avoid, deny or subvert the presentation of evidence contrary to their own position.

E. Forensic psychologists, by virtue of their competence and rules of discovery, actively disclose all sources of information obtained in the course of their professional services; they actively disclose which information from which source was used in formulating a particular written product or oral testimony.

F. Forensic psychologists are aware that their essential role as expert to the court is to assist the trier of fact to understand the evidence or to determine a fact in issue. In offering expert evidence, they are aware that their own professional observations, inference and conclusions must be distinguished from legal facts, opinions and conclusions. Forensic psychologists are prepared to explain the relationship between their expert testimony and the legal issues and facts of an instant case.

APPENDIX 4

MODEL ENGAGEMENT LETTERS
FOR MENTAL HEALTH EXPERTS

Version for Use with Plaintiff's Counsel

[Attorney Name & Address]

Re: [Case Name]

Dear _____:

Thank you for engaging me to serve as an expert witness and/or consultant in the above-referenced matter. It is my practice to set forth the terms of my engagement in writing in order to avoid misunderstandings, and this letter will describe those terms. If these terms are acceptable, I will ask that you and your client indicate your agreement by executing the copy of this letter and returning it to me.

The services I may provide in this matter include review of records, conduct of a clinical interview of the plaintiff, administration of psychological testing, preparation of a written report, testimony at deposition and trial or arbitration, and conferences with counsel regarding my findings and conclusions. Since I do not have access to the court system except through counsel who retains me, it is important for you to note that I will have to depend upon you to obtain various records and to arrange for the mental examination of your client to occur under clinically acceptable conditions. I will furnish you separately with a list of records that I will need for you to obtain from your client, from your client's health care providers, or from third parties via subpoena. My effectiveness as an expert witness will depend to a great degree on my having access to these records. Similarly, I will need to depend upon you to arrange for me to meet with your client for the purpose of conducting a forensic mental examination. It is ordinarily my practice to conduct such an examination of the plaintiff outside the presence of third parties such as attorneys, relatives, therapists, etc.

As you may know, in some jurisdictions a written report from a mental health examiner is mandatory; in other jurisdictions it is merely optional. I will not write a formal report of my findings unless you specifically ask that I do so, but if you wish for me to produce such a report, please give me at least _____ days' notice of the due date.

The fees for my services are set forth on the attached fee schedule. My fees may change from time to time, and you will be notified in the event of a change in my fees. I also bill for out-of-pocket expenses, such as travel, conference room rental, telephone calls, overnight delivery and courier services, and the like. My ordinary practice is to charge for travel time unless other arrangements specifically have been agreed upon in advance, and please note that telephone or in-person conferences are considered billable time.

I will send you monthly invoices, which I will expect to be paid within 30 days of receipt. In the event an invoice is not paid within 30 days, I reserve the right to add an interest charge of _____% per year, compounded monthly, to all overdue amounts. Because of the potential for cross-examination on the grounds of financial bias, I require that all of my invoices be paid in full prior to my giving testimony at any hearing, trial, or arbitration. In the event of nonpayment of my invoices, you agree that I may withdraw my services regardless of whether or not I have been formally designated as an expert. It is also agreed that in the event I must initiate legal action to recover unpaid fees and expenses, the venue for such action shall be the courts of _____ County, _____ and that the prevailing party in such litigation shall also recover costs of litigation and reasonable attorney's fees.

[Optional: It is also my practice to require an initial retainer in the amount of $_____ to be applied to the final billing for my services in this matter. If any balance is remaining on this retainer at the conclusion of this case it will be refunded to you.]

I also require that your client execute this agreement and agree to be bound by it. Specifically, your client agrees that if my invoices are unpaid and legal action becomes necessary to obtain payment, such legal action may be brought directly against your client.

I apologize for the formal and legalistic tone of this letter, but I believe it best that we commence this engagement with a clear understanding of its terms and conditions. If these terms are acceptable to you and your client, please sign where indicated below on the enclosed copy of this letter and return it to me.

Thank you for your confidence in me and I look forward to working with you on this matter.

                          Sincerely,

                      [Name of Clinician]

On behalf of the below-named law firm, I accept the terms and conditions set forth in this letter and agree to be bound by them.

_____   _____
Signature of Attorney   Date

_____
Name of Law Firm

I accept the terms and conditions set forth in this letter and agree to be bound by them.

_____   _____
Signature of Client   Date

_____
Printed Name

_____
Address of Client

Version for Use with Defendant's Counsel

[Attorney Name & Address]

Re: [Case Name]

Dear _____:

    Thank you for engaging me to serve as an expert witness and/or consultant in the above-referenced matter. It is my practice to set forth the terms of my engagement in writing in order to avoid misunderstandings, and this letter will describe those terms. If these terms are acceptable, I will ask that you and your client indicate your agreement by executing the copy of this letter and returning it to me.

    The services I may provide in this matter include review of records, conduct of a clinical interview of the plaintiff, administration of psychological testing, preparation of a written report, testimony at deposition and trial or arbitration, and conferences with counsel regarding my findings and conclusions. Since I do not have access to the court system except through counsel who retains me, it is important for you to note that I will have to depend upon you to obtain various records and to arrange for the mental examination of the plaintiff to occur under clinically acceptable conditions. I will furnish you separately with a list of records that I will need for you to obtain from the plaintiff or from third parties via subpoena. My effectiveness as an expert witness will depend to a great degree on my having access to these records. Similarly, I will need to depend upon you to arrange for a mental examination of the plaintiff. As you may know, if the plaintiff does not agree to such an examination, a motion to the court will be necessary and such a motion will have to be brought far enough in advance of the discovery cutoff to permit an examination to occur within the discovery period. Also, sometimes opposing counsel or the court will attempt to place restrictions or conditions on mental examinations, such as time limits, limits on topics of inquiry, or requiring the presence of outsiders. Please do not agree to any such restrictions or conditions, or fail to oppose them in court, without my specific approval, as such restrictions or conditions can significantly impair my effectiveness as an examiner.

As you may know, in some jurisdictions a written report from a mental health examiner is mandatory; in other jurisdictions it is merely optional. I will not write a formal report of my findings unless you specifically ask that I do so, but if you wish for me to produce such a report, please give me at least _____ days' notice of the due date.

The fees for my services are set forth on the attached fee schedule. My fees may change from time to time, and you will be notified in the event of a change in my fees. I also bill for out-of-pocket expenses, such as travel, conference room rental, telephone calls, overnight delivery and courier services, and the like. My ordinary practice is to charge for travel time unless other arrangements specifically have been agreed upon in advance, and please note that telephone or in-person conferences are considered billable time.

I will send you monthly invoices, which I will expect to be paid within 30 days of receipt. In the event an invoice is not paid within 30 days, I reserve the right to add an interest charge of _____% per year, compounded monthly, to all overdue amounts. Because of the potential for cross-examination on the grounds of financial bias, I require that all of my invoices be paid in full prior to my giving testimony at any hearing, trial, or arbitration. In the event of nonpayment of my invoices, you agree that I may withdraw my services regardless of whether or not I have been formally designated as an expert. It is also agreed that in the event I must initiate legal action to recover unpaid fees and expenses, the venue for such action shall be the courts of _____ County, _____ and that the prevailing party in such litigation shall also recover costs of litigation and reasonable attorney's fees.

[*Optional*: It is also my practice to require an initial retainer in the amount of $_____ to be applied to the final billing for my services in this matter. If any balance is remaining on this retainer at the conclusion of this case it will be refunded to you.]

I also require that your client execute this agreement and agree to be bound by it. Specifically, your client agrees that if my invoices are unpaid and legal action becomes necessary to obtain payment, such legal action may be brought directly against your client. If an insurance carrier is obligated to cover the costs of defense of this action, then a representative of the insurance carrier may sign this agreement in the place of your client.

I apologize for the formal and legalistic tone of this letter, but I believe it best that we commence this engagement with a clear understanding of its terms and conditions. If these terms are acceptable to you and your client, please sign where indicated below on the enclosed copy of this letter and return it to me.

Thank you for your confidence in me and I look forward to working with you on this matter.

Sincerely,

[Name of Clinician]

On behalf of the below-named law firm, I accept the terms and conditions set forth in this letter and agree to be bound by them.

_____   _____
Signature of Attorney   Date

_____
Name of Law Firm

On behalf of the below-named client entity, I accept the terms and conditions set forth in this letter and agree to be bound by them.

_____   _____
Signature   Date

_____
Printed Name

_____
Title

_____
Name of Client Entity

_____
Address of Client Entity

APPENDIX 5

RULE 412, FEDERAL RULES OF EVIDENCE

(as amended in 1994)

Rule 412. Sex Offense Cases; Relevance of Alleged Victim's Past Sexual Behavior or Alleged Sexual Predisposition

(a) Evidence generally inadmissible.—The following evidence is not admissible in any civil or criminal proceeding involving alleged sexual misconduct except as provided in subdivisions (b) and (c):
   (1) Evidence offered to prove that any alleged victim engaged in other sexual behavior.
   (2) Evidence offered to prove any alleged victim's sexual predisposition.
(b) Exceptions.—
   (1) In a criminal case, the following evidence is admissible, if otherwise admissible under these rules:
      (A) evidence of specific instances of sexual behavior by the alleged victim offered to prove that a person other than the accused was the source of semen, injury or other physical evidence;
      (B) evidence of specific instances of sexual behavior by the alleged victim with respect to the person accused of the sexual misconduct offered by the accused to prove consent or by the prosecution; and
      (C) evidence the exclusion of which would violate the constitutional rights of the defendant.
   (2) In a civil case, evidence offered to prove the sexual behavior or sexual predisposition of any alleged victim is admissible if it is otherwise admissible under these rules and its probative value substantially outweighs the danger of harm to any victim and of unfair prejudice to any party. Evidence of an alleged victim's reputation is admissible only if it has been placed in controversy by the alleged victim.
(c) Procedure to determine admissibility.—
   (1) A party intending to offer evidence under subdivision (b) must—
      (A) file a written motion at least 14 days before trial specifically describing the evidence and stating the purpose for which it is offered unless the court, for good cause requires a different time for filing or permits filing during trial; and
      (B) serve the motion on all parties and notify the alleged victim or, when appropriate, the alleged victim's guardian or representative.

(2) Before admitting evidence under this rule the court must conduct a hearing in camera and afford the victim and parties a right to attend and be heard. The motion, related papers, and the record of the hearing must be sealed and remain under seal unless the court orders otherwise.

(As amended Pub.L. 100—690, Title VII, § 7046(a), Nov. 18, 1988, 102 Stat. 4400; Apr. 29, 1994, eff. Dec. 1, 1994; Pub.L. 103—322, Title IV, § 40141(b), Sept. 13, 1994, 108 Stat. 1919.)

ADVISORY COMMITTEE NOTES

1994 Amendments

Rule 412 has been revised to diminish some of the confusion engendered by the original rule and to expand the protection afforded alleged victims of sexual misconduct. Rule 412 applies to both civil and criminal proceedings. The rule aims to safeguard the alleged victim against the invasion of privacy, potential embarrassment and sexual stereotyping that is associated with public disclosure of intimate sexual details and the infusion of sexual innuendo into the factfinding process. By affording victims protection in most instances, the rule also encourages victims of sexual misconduct to institute and to participate in legal proceedings against alleged offenders.

Rule 412 seeks to achieve these objectives by barring evidence relating to the alleged victim's sexual behavior or alleged sexual predisposition, whether offered as substantive evidence of [sic] for impeachment, except in designated circumstances in which the probative value of the evidence significantly outweighs possible harm to the victim.

The revised rule applies in all cases involving sexual misconduct without regard to whether the alleged victim or person accused is a party to the litigation. Rule 412 extends to "pattern" witnesses in both criminal and civil cases whose testimony about other instances of sexual misconduct by the person accused is otherwise admissible. When the case does not involve alleged sexual misconduct, evidence relating to a third-party witness' alleged sexual activities is not within the ambit of Rule 412. The witness will, however, be protected by other rules such as Rules 404 and 608, as well as Rule 403.

The terminology "alleged victim" is used because there will frequently be a factual dispute as to whether sexual misconduct occurred. It does not connote any requirement that the misconduct be alleged in the pleadings. Rule 412 does not, however, apply unless the person against whom the evidence is offered can reasonably be characterized as a "victim of alleged sexual misconduct." When this is not the case, as for instance in a defamation action involving statements concerning sexual misconduct in which the evidence is offered to show that the alleged defamatory statements were true or did not damage the plaintiff's reputation, neither Rule 404 nor this rule will operate to bar the evidence; Rule 401 and 403 will continue to control. Rule 412 will, however, apply in a Title VII action in which the plaintiff has alleged sexual harassment.

The reference to a person "accused" is also used in a non-technical sense. There is no requirement that there be a criminal charge pending against the person or even that the misconduct would constitute a criminal offense. Evidence offered to prove allegedly false prior claims by the victim is not barred by Rule 412. However, the evidence is subject to the requirements of Rule 404.

Subdivision (a). As amended, Rule 412 bars evidence offered to prove the victim's sexual behavior and alleged sexual predisposition. Evidence, which might otherwise be admissible under Rules 402, 404(b), 405, 607, 608, 609 of [*sic*] some other evidence rule, must be excluded if Rule 412 so requires. The word "other" is used to suggest some flexibility in admitting evidence "intrinsic" to the alleged sexual misconduct. *Cf.* Committee Note to 1991 amendment to Rule 404(b).

Past sexual behavior connotes all activities that involve actual physical conduct, i.e. sexual intercourse or sexual contact. *See, e.g., United States v. Galloway,* 937 F.2d 542 (10th Cir. 1991), *cert. denied,* 113 S.Ct. 418 (1992) (use of contraceptives inadmissible since use implies sexual activity); *United States v. One Feather,* 702 F.2d 736 (8th Cir. 1983) (birth of an illegitimate child inadmissible); *State v. Carmichael,* 727 P.2d 918, 925 (Kan. 1986) (evidence of venereal disease inadmissible). In addition, the word "behavior" should be construed to include activities of the mind, such as fantasies of [*sic*] dreams. *See* 23 C. Wright and K. Graham, Jr., *Federal Practice and Procedure,* § 5384 at p. 548 (1980) ("While there may be some doubt under statutes that require 'conduct,' it would seem that the language of Rule 412 is broad enough to encompass the behavior of the mind.").

The rule has been amended to also exclude all other evidence relating to an alleged victim of sexual misconduct that is offered to prove a sexual predisposition. This amendment is designed to exclude evidence that does not directly refer to sexual activities or thoughts but that the proponent believes may have a sexual connotation for the factfinder. Admission of such evidence would contravene Rule 412's objectives of shielding the alleged victim from potential embarrassment and safeguarding the victim against stereotypical thinking. Consequently, unless the (b)(2) exception is satisfied, evidence such as that relating to the alleged victim's mode of dress, speech, or life-style will not be admissible.

The introductory phrase in subdivision (a) was deleted because it lacked clarity and contained no explicit reference to the other provisions of the law that were intended to be overridden. The conditional clause, "except as provided in subdivisions (b) and (c)" is intended to make clear that evidence of the types described in subdivision (a) is admissible only under the strictures of those sections.

The reason for extending the rule to all criminal cases is obvious. The strong social policy of protecting a victim's privacy and encouraging victims to come forward to report criminal acts is not confined to cases that involve a charge of sexual assault. The need to protect the victim is equally great when a defendant is charged with kidnapping, and evidence is offered, either to prove motive or as background, that the defendant sexually assaulted the victim.

The reason for extending Rule 412 to civil cases is equally obvious. The need to protect alleged victims against invasions of privacy, potential embarrassment, and unwarranted sexual stereotyping, and the wish to encourage victims to come forward when they have been sexually molested do not disappear because the context has shifted from a criminal prosecution to a claim for damages or injunctive relief. There is a strong social policy in not only punishing those who engage in sexual misconduct, but in also providing relief to the victim. Thus, Rule 412 applies in any civil case in which a person claims to be the victim of sexual misconduct, such as actions for sexual battery or sexual harassment.

Subdivision (b). Subdivision (b) spells out the specific circumstances in which some evidence may be admissible that would otherwise be barred by the general rule expressed in subdivision (a). As amended, Rule 412 will be virtually unchanged in criminal cases, but will provide protection to any person alleged to be a victim of sexual misconduct regardless of the charge actually brought against an accused. A new exception has been added for civil cases.

In a criminal case, evidence may be admitted under subdivision (b)(1) pursuant to three possible exceptions, provided the evidence also satisfies other requirements for admissibility specified in the Federal Rules of Evidence, including Rule 403. Subdivisions (b)(1)(A) and (b)(1)(B) require proof in the form of specific instances of sexual behavior in recognition of the limited probative value and dubious reliability of evidence of reputation or evidence in the form of an opinion.

Under subdivision (b)(1)(A), evidence of specific instances of sexual behavior with persons other than the person whose sexual misconduct is alleged may be admissible if it is offered to prove that another person was the source of semen, injury or other physical evidence. Where the prosecution has directly or indirectly asserted that the physical evidence originated with the accused, the defendant must be afforded an opportunity to prove that another person was responsible. See *United States v. Begay,* 937 F.2d 515, 523 n.10 (10th Cir. 1991). Evidence offered for the specific purpose identified in this subdivision may still be excluded if it does not satisfy Rules 401 or 403. *See, e.g., United States v. Azure,* 845 F.2d 1503, 1505—06 (8th Cir. 1988) (10 year old victim's injuries indicated recent use of force; court excluded evidence of consensual sexual activities with witness who testified at in camera hearing that he had never hurt victim and failed to establish recent activities).

Under the exception in subdivision (b)(1)(B), evidence of specific instances of sexual behavior with respect to the person whose sexual misconduct is alleged is admissible if offered to prove consent, or offered by the prosecution. Admissible pursuant to this exception might be evidence of prior instances of sexual activities between the alleged victim and the accused, as well as statements in which the alleged victim expresses an intent to engage in sexual intercourse with the accused, or voiced sexual fantasies involving that specific accused. In a prosecution for child sexual abuse, for example, evidence of uncharged sexual activity between the accused and the alleged victim offered by the prosecution may be admissible pursuant to Rule 404(b) to show a pattern of behavior. Evidence relating to the victim's alleged sexual predisposition is not admissible pursuant to this exception.

Under subdivision (b)(1)(C), evidence of specific instances of conduct may not be excluded if the result would be to deny a criminal defendant the protections afforded by the Constitution. For example, statements in which the victim has expressed an intent to have sex with the first person encountered on a particular occasion might not be excluded without violating the due process right of a rape defendant seeking to prove consent. Recognition of this basic principle was expressed on subdivision (b)(1) of the original rule. The United States Supreme Court has recognized that in various circumstances a defendant may have a right to introduce evidence otherwise precluded by an evidence rule under the Confrontation Clause. *See, e.g., Olden v. Kentucky,* 488 U.S. 227 (1988) (defendant in rape cases had right to inquire into alleged victim's cohabitation with another man to show bias).

Subdivision (b)(2) governs the admissibility of otherwise proscribed evidence in civil cases. It employs a balancing test rather than the specific exceptions stated in subdivision (b)(1) in recognition of the difficulty of foreseeing future developments in the law. Greater flexibility is needed to accommodate evolving causes of action such as claims for sexual harassment.

The balancing test requires the proponent of the evidence, whether plaintiff or defendant, to convince the court that the probative value of the proffered evidence "substantially outweighs the danger of harm to any victim and of unfair prejudice of any party." This test for admitting evidence offered to prove sexual behavior or sexual propensity in civil cases differs in three respects from the general rule governing admissibility set forth in Rule 403. First, it Reverses [*sic*] that [*sic*] usual procedure spelled out in Rule 403 by shifting the burden to the proponent to demonstrate admissibility rather than making the opponent justify exclusion of the evidence. Second, the standard expressed in subdivision (b)(2) is more stringent than in the original rule; it raises the threshold for admission by requiring that the probative value of the evidence *substantially* outweigh the specified dangers. Finally, the Rule 412 test puts "harm to the victim" on the scale in addition to prejudice to the parties.

Evidence of reputation may be received in a civil case only if the alleged victim has put his or her reputation into controversy. The victim may do so without making a specific allegation in a pleading. *Cf.* Fed.R.Civ.P. 35(a).

Subdivision (c). Amended subdivision (c) is more concise and understandable than the subdivision it replaces. The requirement of a motion before trial is continued in the amended rule, as is the provision that a late motion may be permitted for good cause shown. In deciding whether to permit late filing, the court may take into account the conditions previously included in the rule: namely whether the evidence is newly discovered and could not have been obtained earlier through the existence of due diligence, and whether the issue to which such evidence relates has newly arisen in the case. The rule recognizes that in some instances the circumstances that justify an application to introduce evidence otherwise barred by Rule 412 will not become apparent until trial.

The amended rule provides that before admitting evidence that falls within that prohibition of Rule 412(a), the court must hold a hearing in camera at which the alleged victim and any party must be afforded the right to be present and an opportunity to be heard. All papers connected with the motion must be kept and remain under seal during the course of trial and appellate proceedings unless otherwise ordered. This is to assure that the privacy of the alleged victim is preserved in all cases in which the court rules that proffered evidence is not admissible, and in which the hearing refers to matters that are not received, or are received in another form.

The procedures set forth in subdivision (c) do not apply to discovery of a victim's past sexual conduct or predisposition in civil cases, which will be continued to be governed by Fed. R. Civ. P. 26. In order not to undermine the rationale of Rule 412, however, courts should enter appropriate orders pursuant to Fed. R. Civ. P. 26 (c) to protect the victim against unwarranted inquiries and to ensure confidentiality. Courts should presumptively issue protective orders barring discovery unless the party seeking discovery makes a showing that the evidence sought to be discovered would be relevant under the facts and theories of the particular case, and cannot be obtained except through discovery. In an action for sexual harassment, for instance, while some evidence of the alleged victim's sexual behavior and/or predisposition in the workplace may perhaps be relevant, non-work place conduct will usually be irrelevant. *Cf. Burns v. McGregor Electronic Industries, Inc.,* 989 F.2d 959, 962—63 (8th Cir. 1993) (posing for a nude magazine outside work hours is irrelevant to issue of unwelcomeness of sexual advances at work). Confidentiality orders should be presumptively granted as well.

One substantive change made in subdivision (c) is the elimination of the following sentence: "Notwithstanding subdivision (b) of Rule 104, if the relevancy of the evidence which the accused seeks to offer in trial depends upon the fulfillment of a condition of fact, the court, at the hearing in chambers or at a subsequent hearing in chambers scheduled for such purpose, shall accept evidence on the issue of whether such condition of fact is fulfilled and shall determine such issue." On its face, this language would appear to authorize a trial judge to exclude evidence of past sexual conduct between alleged victim and an accused or a defendant in a civil case based upon the judge's belief that such past acts did not occur. Such an authorization raises questions of invasion of the right to a jury trial under the Sixth and Seventh Amendments. *See* 1 S. Saltzburg & M. Martin, *Federal Rules of Evidence Manual,* 396–97 (5th ed. 1990).

The Advisory Committee concluded that the amended rule provided adequate protection for all persons claiming to be the victims of sexual misconduct, and that it was inadvisable to continue to include a provision in the rule that has been confusing and that raises substantial constitutional issues.

[Advisory Committee Note adopted by Congressional Conference Report accompanying Pub.L. 103–322. See H.R. Conf. Rep. No. 103–711, 103rd Cong., 2nd Sess., 383 (1994).]

HISTORICAL NOTES

Subd. (b). Pub.L. 100–690, § 7046(a)(2), substituted "an offense under chapter 109A of title 18, United States Code" for "rape or of assault with intent to commit rape".

Subd. (b)(2)(B). Pub.L. 100–690, § 7046(a)(5), substituted "such offense" for "rape or assault".

Subd. (c)(1). Pub.L. 100–690, § 7046(a)(4), substituted "an offense under chapter 109A of title 18, United States Code" for "rape or assault with intent to commit rape".

Subd. (d). Pub.L. 100–690, § 7046(a)(4), substituted "an offense under chapter 109A of title 18, United States Code" for "rape or assault with intent to commit rape".

Legislative History

For legislative history and purpose of Pub.L. 100–690, see 1988 U.S. Code Cong. and Adm. News, p. 5937.

1994 Amendments

Pub.L. 103–322, § 40141(b), completely revised rule, substituting provisions relating to admissibility of evidence regarding relevance of alleged victim's past sexual behavior or alleged sexual predisposition in sex offense cases, for provisions relating to admissibility of evidence regarding relevance of victim's past sexual behavior in sex offense cases.

1988 Amendment

Heading. Pub.L. 100–690, § 7046(a)(1), substituted "Sex Offense" for "Rape".

Subd. (a). Pub.L. 100–690, § 7046(a)(2), (3), substituted "an offense under chapter 109A of title 18, United States Code" and "offense" for "rape or of assault with intent to commit rape" and "rape or assault", respectively.

(as enacted in 1978)

Rule 412. Rape Cases; Relevance of Victim's Past Behavior

(a) Notwithstanding any other provision of law, in a criminal case in which a person is accused of rape or of assault with intent to commit rape, reputation or opinion evidence of the past sexual behavior of an alleged victim of such rape or assault is not admissible.

(b) Notwithstanding any other provision of law, in a criminal case in which a person is accused of rape or of assault with intent to commit rape, evidence of a victim's past sexual behavior other than reputation or opinion evidence is also not admissible, unless such evidence other than reputation or opinion evidence is—

    (1) admitted in accordance with subdivisions (c)(1) and (c)(2) and is constitutionally required to be admitted; or

(2) admitted in accordance with subdivision (c) and is evidence of—

(A) past sexual behavior with persons other than the accused, offered by the accused upon the issue of whether the accused was or was not, with respect to the alleged victim, the source of semen or injury; or

(B) past sexual behavior with the accused and is offered by the accused upon the issue of whether the alleged victim consented to the sexual behavior with respect to which rape or assault is alleged.

(c)(1) If the person accused of committing rape or assault with intent to commit rape intends to offer under subdivision (b) evidence of specific instances of the alleged victim's past sexual behavior, the accused shall make a written motion to offer such evidence not later than fifteen days before the date on which the trial in which such evidence is to be offered is scheduled to begin, except that the court may allow the motion to be made at a later date, including during trial, if the court determines either that the evidence is newly discovered and could not have been obtained earlier through the exercise of due diligence or that the issue to which such evidence relates has newly arisen in the case. Any motion made under this paragraph shall be served on all other parties and on the alleged victim.

(2) The motion described in paragraph (1) shall be accompanied by a written offer of proof. If the court determines that the offer of proof contains evidence described in subdivision (b), the court shall order a hearing in chambers to determine if such evidence is admissible. At such hearing the parties may call witnesses, including the alleged victim, and offer relevant evidence. Notwithstanding subdivision (b) of rule 104, if the relevancy of the evidence which the accused seeks to offer in the trial depends upon the fulfillment of a condition of fact, the court, at the hearing in chambers or at a subsequent hearing in chambers scheduled for such purpose, shall accept evidence on the issue of whether such condition of fact is fulfilled and shall determine such issue.

(3) If the court determines on the basis of the hearing described in paragraph (2) that the evidence which the accused seeks to offer is relevant and that the probative value of such evidence outweighs the danger of unfair prejudice, such evidence shall be admissible in the trial to the extent an order made by the court specifies evidence which may be offered and areas with respect to which the alleged victim may be examined or cross-examined.

(d) For purposes of this rule, the term "past sexual behavior" means sexual behavior other than the sexual behavior with respect to which rape or assault with intent to commit rape is alleged.

(Added Pub.L. 95—540, § 2(a), Oct. 28, 1978, 92 Stat. 2046.)

APPENDIX 6

RULE 702, FEDERAL RULES OF EVIDENCE

Rule 702. Testimony by Experts

If scientific, technical, or other specialized knowledge will assist the trier of fact to understand the evidence or to determine a fact in issue, a witness qualified as an expert by knowledge, skill, experience, training, or education, may testify thereto in the form of an opinion or otherwise, if (1) the testimony is based upon sufficient facts or data, (2) the testimony is the product of reliable principles and methods, and (3) the witness has applied the principles and methods reliably to the facts of the case.

(Pub.L. 93-595, Jan. 2, 1975, 88 Stat. 1937; Apr. 17, 2000, eff. Dec. 1, 2000.)

ADVISORY COMMITTEE NOTES

1972 Proposed Rules

An intelligent evaluation of facts is often difficult or impossible without the application of some scientific, technical, or other specialized knowledge. The most common source of this knowledge is the expert witness, although there are other techniques for supplying it.

Most of the literature assumes that experts testify only in the form of opinions. The assumption is logically unfounded. The rule accordingly recognizes that an expert on the stand may give a dissertation or exposition of scientific or other principles relevant to the case, leaving the trier of fact to apply them to the facts. Since much of the criticism of expert testimony has centered upon the hypothetical question, it seems wise to recognize that opinions are not indispensable and to encourage the use of expert testimony in non-opinion form when counsel believes the trier can itself draw the requisite inference. The use of opinions is not abolished by the rule, however. It will continue to be permissible for the experts to take the further step of suggesting the inference which should be drawn from applying the specialized knowledge to the facts. See Rules 703 to 705.

Whether the situation is a proper one for the use of expert testimony is to be determined on the basis of assisting the trier. "There is no more certain test for determining when experts may be used than the common sense inquiry whether the untrained layman would be qualified to determine intelligently and to the best possible degree the particular issue without enlightenment from those having a specialized understanding of the subject involved in the dispute." Ladd, *Expert Testimony*, 5 Vand.L.Rev. 414,

418 (1952). When opinions are excluded, it is because they are unhelpful and therefore superfluous and a waste of time. 7 Wigmore §1918.

The rule is broadly phrased. The fields of knowledge which may be drawn upon are not limited merely to the "scientific" and "technical" but extend to all "specialized" knowledge. Similarly, the expert is viewed, not in a narrow sense, but as a person qualified by "knowledge, skill, experience, training or education." Thus within the scope of the rule are not only experts in the strictest sense of the word, e.g., physicians, physicists, and architects, but also the large group sometimes called "skilled" witnesses, such as bankers or landowners testifying to land values.

2000 Amendments

Rule 702 has been amended in response to *Daubert v. Merrell Dow Pharmaceuticals, Inc.*, 509 U.S. 579 (1993), and to the many cases applying Daubert, including *Kumho Tire Co. v. Carmichael*, 119 S.Ct. 1167 (1999). In Daubert the Court charged trial judges with the responsibility of acting as gatekeepers to exclude unreliable expert testimony, and the Court in Kumho clarified that this gatekeeper function applies to all expert testimony, not just testimony based in science. See also *Kumho*, 119 S.Ct. at 1178 (citing the Committee Note to the proposed amendment to Rule 702, which had been released for public comment before the date of the *Kumho* decision). The amendment affirms the trial court's role as gatekeeper and provides some general standards that the trial court must use to assess the reliability and helpfulness of proffered expert testimony. Consistently with *Kumho*, the Rule as amended provides that all types of expert testimony present questions of admissibility for the trial court in deciding whether the evidence is reliable and helpful. Consequently, the admissibility of all expert testimony is governed by the principles of Rule 104(a). Under that Rule, the proponent has the burden of establishing that the pertinent admissibility requirements are met by a preponderance of the evidence. See *Bourjaily v. United States*, 483 U.S. 171 (1987).

Daubert set forth a non-exclusive checklist for trial courts to use in assessing the reliability of scientific expert testimony. The specific factors explicated by the *Daubert* Court are (1) whether the expert's technique or theory can be or has been tested—that is, whether the expert's theory can be challenged in some objective sense, or whether it is instead simply a subjective, conclusory approach that cannot reasonably be assessed for reliability; (2) whether the technique or theory has been subject to peer review and publication; (3) the known or potential rate of error of the technique or theory when applied; (4) the existence and maintenance of standards and controls; and (5) whether the technique or theory has been generally accepted in the scientific community. The Court in *Kumho* held that these factors might also be applicable in assessing the reliability of non-scientific expert testimony, depending upon "the particular circumstances of the particular case at issue." 119 S.Ct. at 1175.

No attempt has been made to "codify" these specific factors. *Daubert* itself emphasized that the factors were neither exclusive nor dispositive. Other cases have recognized that not all of the specific *Daubert* factors can apply to every type of expert testimony. In addition to *Kumho*, 119 S.Ct. at 1175, see *Tyus v. Urban Search*

Management, 102 F.3d 256 (7th Cir. 1996) (noting that the factors mentioned by the Court in *Daubert* do not neatly apply to expert testimony from a sociologist). See also *Kannankeril v. Terminix Int'l, Inc.*, 128 F.3d 802, 809 (3d Cir. 1997) (holding that lack of peer review or publication was not dispositive where the expert's opinion was supported by "widely accepted scientific knowledge"). The standards set forth in the amendment are broad enough to require consideration of any or all of the specific *Daubert* factors where appropriate.

Courts both before and after *Daubert* have found other factors relevant in determining whether expert testimony is sufficiently reliable to be considered by the trier of fact. These factors include:

(1) Whether experts are "proposing to testify about matters growing naturally and directly out of research they have conducted independent of the litigation, or whether they have developed their opinions expressly for purposes of testifying." *Daubert v. Merrell Dow Pharmaceuticals, Inc.*, 43 F.3d 1311, 1317 (9th Cir. 1995).

(2) Whether the expert has unjustifiably extrapolated from an accepted premise to an unfounded conclusion. See *General Elec. Co. v. Joiner*, 522 U.S. 136, 146 (1997) (noting that in some cases a trial court "may conclude that there is simply too great an analytical gap between the data and the opinion proffered").

(3) Whether the expert has adequately accounted for obvious alternative explanations. See *Claar v. Burlington N.R.R.*, 29 F.3d 499 (9th Cir. 1994) (testimony excluded where the expert failed to consider other obvious causes for the plaintiff's condition). Compare *Ambrosini v. Labarraque*, 101 F.3d 129 (D.C. Cir. 1996) (the possibility of some uneliminated causes presents a question of weight, so long as the most obvious causes have been considered and reasonably ruled out by the expert).

(4) Whether the expert "is being as careful as he would be in his regular professional work outside his paid litigation consulting." *Sheehan v. Daily Racing Form, Inc.*, 104 F.3d 940, 942 (7th Cir. 1997). See *Kumho Tire Co. v. Carmichael*, 119 S.Ct. 1167, 1176 (1999) (*Daubert* requires the trial court to assure itself that the expert "employs in the courtroom the same level of intellectual rigor that characterizes the practice of an expert in the relevant field").

(5) Whether the field of expertise claimed by the expert is known to reach reliable results for the type of opinion the expert would give. See *Kumho Tire Co. v. Carmichael*, 119 S.Ct. 1167, 1175 (1999) (Daubert's general acceptance factor does not "help show that an expert's testimony is reliable where the discipline itself lacks reliability, as for example, do theories grounded in any so-called generally accepted principles of astrology or necromancy.")[;] *Moore v. Ashland Chemical, Inc.*, 151 F.3d 269 (5th Cir. 1998) (en banc) (clinical doctor was properly precluded from testifying to the toxicological cause of the plaintiff's respiratory problem, where the opinion was not sufficiently grounded in scientific methodology); *Sterling v. Velsicol Chem. Corp.*, 855 F.2d 1188 (6th Cir. 1988) (rejecting testimony based on "clinical ecology" as unfounded and unreliable).

All of these factors remain relevant to the determination of the reliability of expert testimony under the Rule as amended. Other factors may also be relevant. See *Kumho*, 119 S.Ct. 1167, 1176 ("[W]e conclude that the trial judge must have considerable leeway in deciding in a particular case how to go about determining whether particular expert testimony is reliable."). Yet no single factor is necessarily dispositive of the reliability of a particular expert's testimony. See, e.g., *Heller v. Shaw Industries, Inc.*, 167 F.3d 146, 155 (3d Cir. 1999) ("not only must each stage of the expert's testimony be reliable, but each stage must be evaluated practically and flexibly without bright-line exclusionary (or inclusionary) rules."); *Daubert v. Merrell Dow Pharmaceuticals, Inc.*, 43 F.3d 1311, 1317, n.5 (9th Cir. 1995) (noting that some expert disciplines "have the courtroom as a principal theatre of operations" and as to these disciplines "the fact that the expert has developed an expertise principally for purposes of litigation will obviously not be a substantial consideration.").

A review of the caselaw after *Daubert* shows that the rejection of expert testimony is the exception rather than the rule. *Daubert* did not work a "seachange over federal evidence law," and "the trial court's role as gatekeeper is not intended to serve as a replacement for the adversary system." *United States v. 14.38 Acres of Land Situated in Leflore County, Mississippi*, 80 F.3d 1074, 1078 (5th Cir. 1996). As the Court in *Daubert* stated: "Vigorous cross-examination, presentation of contrary evidence, and careful instruction on the burden of proof are the traditional and appropriate means of attacking shaky but admissible evidence." 509 U.S. at 595. Likewise, this amendment is not intended to provide an excuse for an automatic challenge to the testimony of every expert. See *Kumho Tire Co. v. Carmichael*, 119 S.Ct.1167, 1176 (1999) (noting that the trial judge has the discretion "both to avoid unnecessary 'reliability' proceedings in ordinary cases where the reliability of an expert's methods is properly taken for granted, and to require appropriate proceedings in the less usual or more complex cases where cause for questioning the expert's reliability arises.").

When a trial court, applying this amendment, rules that an expert's testimony is reliable, this does not necessarily mean that contradictory expert testimony is unreliable. The amendment is broad enough to permit testimony that is the product of competing principles or methods in the same field of expertise. See, e.g., *Heller v. Shaw Industries, Inc.*, 167 F.3d 146, 160 (3d Cir. 1999) (expert testimony cannot be excluded simply because the expert uses one test rather than another, when both tests are accepted in the field and both reach reliable results). As the court stated in *In re Paoli R.R. Yard PCB Litigation*, 35 F.3d 717, 744 (3d Cir. 1994), proponents "do not have to demonstrate to the judge by a preponderance of the evidence that the assessments of their experts are correct, they only have to demonstrate by a preponderance of evidence that their opinions are reliable. . . . The evidentiary requirement of reliability is lower than the merits standard of correctness." See also *Daubert v. Merrell Dow Pharmaceuticals, Inc.*, 43 F.3d 1311, 1318 (9th Cir. 1995) (scientific experts might be permitted to testify if they could show that the methods they used were also employed by "a recognized minority of scientists in their field."); *Ruiz-Troche v. Pepsi Cola*, 161 F.3d 77, 85 (1st Cir. 1998)

("*Daubert* neither requires nor empowers trial courts to determine which of several competing scientific theories has the best provenance.").

The Court in *Daubert* declared that the "focus, of course, must be solely on principles and methodology, not on the conclusions they generate." 509 U.S. at 595. Yet as the Court later recognized, "conclusions and methodology are not entirely distinct from one another." *General Elec. Co. v. Joiner*, 522 U.S. 136, 146 (1997). Under the amendment, as under *Daubert*, when an expert purports to apply principles and methods in accordance with professional standards, and yet reaches a conclusion that other experts in the field would not reach, the trial court may fairly suspect that the principles and methods have not been faithfully applied. See *Lust v. Merrell Dow Pharmaceuticals, Inc.*, 89 F.3d 594, 598 (9th Cir. 1996). The amendment specifically provides that the trial court must scrutinize not only the principles and methods used by the expert, but also whether those principles and methods have been properly applied to the facts of the case. As the court noted in *In re Paoli R.R. Yard PCB Litig.*, 35 F.3d 717, 745 (3d Cir. 1994), "any step that renders the analysis unreliable . . . renders the expert's testimony inadmissible. This is true whether the step completely changes a reliable methodology or merely misapplies that methodology."

If the expert purports to apply principles and methods to the facts of the case, it is important that this application be conducted reliably. Yet it might also be important in some cases for an expert to educate the factfinder about general principles, without ever attempting to apply these principles to the specific facts of the case. For example, experts might instruct the factfinder on the principles of thermodynamics, or bloodclotting, or on how financial markets respond to corporate reports, without ever knowing about or trying to tie their testimony into the facts of the case. The amendment does not alter the venerable practice of using expert testimony to educate the factfinder on general principles. For this kind of generalized testimony, Rule 702 simply requires that: (1) the expert be qualified; (2) the testimony address a subject matter on which the factfinder can be assisted by an expert; (3) the testimony be reliable; and (4) the testimony "fit" the facts of the case.

As stated earlier, the amendment does not distinguish between scientific and other forms of expert testimony. The trial court's gatekeeping function applies to testimony by any expert. See *Kumho Tire Co. v. Carmichael*, 119 S.Ct. 1167, 1171 (1999) ("We conclude that *Daubert*'s general holding—setting forth the trial judge's general 'gatekeeping' obligation—applies not only to testimony based on 'scientific' knowledge, but also to testimony based on 'technical' and 'other specialized' knowledge."). While the relevant factors for determining reliability will vary from expertise to expertise, the amendment rejects the premise that an expert's testimony should be treated more permissively simply because it is outside the realm of science. An opinion from an expert who is not a scientist should receive the same degree of scrutiny for reliability as an opinion from an expert who purports to be a scientist. See *Watkins v. Telsmith, Inc.*, 121 F.3d 984, 991 (5th Cir. 1997) ("[I]t seems exactly backwards that experts who purport to rely on general engineering principles and practical experience might escape screening by the district court simply by stating that their conclusions were not reached by any particular method or technique."). Some types of expert testimony will be more objectively verifiable, and subject to the expectations of falsifiability, peer review, and publication, than others. Some types of expert testimony will not rely on anything like a scientific method, and so will have to be evaluated by reference to other standard principles attendant to the particular area of expertise. The trial judge in all cases of proffered expert testimony must find that it is properly grounded, well-reasoned, and not speculative before it can be admitted. The expert's testimony must be grounded in an accepted body of learning or experience in the expert's field, and the expert must explain how the conclusion is so grounded. See, e.g., *American College of Trial Lawyers, Standards and Procedures for Determining the Admissibility of Expert Testimony after Daubert*, 157 F.R.D. 571, 579 (1994) ("[W]hether the testimony concerns economic principles, accounting standards, property valuation or other non-scientific subjects, it should be evaluated by reference to the 'knowledge and experience' of that particular field.").

The amendment requires that the testimony must be the product of reliable principles and methods that are reliably applied to the facts of the case. While the terms "principles" and "methods" may convey a certain impression when applied to scientific knowledge, they remain relevant when applied to testimony based on technical or other specialized knowledge. For example, when a law enforcement agent testifies regarding the use of code words in a drug transaction, the principle used by the agent is that participants in such transactions regularly use code words to conceal the nature of their activities. The method used by the agent is the application of extensive experience to analyze the meaning of the conversations. So long as the principles and methods are reliable and applied reliably to the facts of the case, this type of testimony should be admitted.

Nothing in this amendment is intended to suggest that experience alone—or experience in conjunction with other knowledge, skill, training or education—may not provide a sufficient foundation for expert testimony. To the contrary, the text of Rule 702 expressly contemplates that an expert may be qualified on the basis of experience. In certain fields, experience is the predominant, if not sole, basis for a great deal of reliable expert testimony. See, e.g., *United States v. Jones*, 107 F.3d 1147 (6th Cir. 1997) (no abuse of discretion in admitting the testimony of a handwriting examiner who had years of practical experience and extensive training, and who explained his methodology in detail); *Tassin v. Sears Roebuck*, 946 F.Supp. 1241, 1248 (M.D.La. 1996) (design engineer's testimony can be admissible when the expert's opinions "are based on facts, a reasonable investigation, and traditional technical/mechanical expertise, and he provides a reasonable link between the information and procedures he uses and the conclusions he reaches"). See also *Kumho Tire Co. v. Carmichael*, 119 S.Ct. 1167, 1178 (1999) (stating that "no one denies that an expert might draw a conclusion from a set of observations based on extensive and specialized experience.").

If the witness is relying solely or primarily on experience, then the witness must explain how that experience leads to the conclusion reached, why

F.3d 184 (1st Cir. 1997) (discussing the application of *Daubert* in ruling on a motion for summary judgment); *In re Paoli R.R. Yard PCB Litig.*, 35 F.3d 717, 736, 739 (3d Cir. 1994) (discussing the use of in limine hearings); *Claar v. Burlington N.R.R.*, 29 F.3d 499, 502-05 (9th Cir. 1994) (discussing the trial court's technique of ordering experts to submit serial affidavits explaining the reasoning and methods underlying their conclusions).

The amendment continues the practice of the original Rule in referring to a qualified witness as an "expert." This was done to provide continuity and to minimize change. The use of the term "expert" in the Rule does not, however, mean that a jury should actually be informed that a qualified witness is testifying as an "expert." Indeed, there is much to be said for a practice that prohibits the use of the term "expert" by both the parties and the court at trial. Such a practice "ensures that trial courts do not inadvertently put their stamp of authority" on a witness's opinion, and protects against the jury's being "overwhelmed by the so-called 'experts'." Hon. Charles Richey, *Proposals to Eliminate the Prejudicial Effect of the Use of the Word "Expert" Under the Federal Rules of Evidence in Criminal and Civil Jury Trials*, 154 F.R.D. 537, 559 (1994) (setting forth limiting instructions and a standing order employed to prohibit the use of the term "expert" in jury trials).

that experience is a sufficient basis for the opinion, and how that experience is reliably applied to the facts. The trial court's gatekeeping function requires more than simply "taking the expert's word for it." See *Daubert v. Merrell Dow Pharmaceuticals, Inc.*, 43 F.3d 1311, 1319 (9th Cir. 1995) ("We've been presented with only the experts' qualifications, their conclusions and their assurances of reliability. Under Daubert, that's not enough."). The more subjective and controversial the expert's inquiry, the more likely the testimony should be excluded as unreliable. See *O'Conner v. Commonwealth Edison Co.*, 13 F.3d 1090 (7th Cir. 1994) (expert testimony based on a completely subjective methodology held properly excluded). See also *Kumho Tire Co. v. Carmichael*, 119 S.Ct. 1167, 1176 (1999) ("[I]t will at times be useful to ask even of a witness whose expertise is based purely on experience, say, a perfume tester able to distinguish among 140 odors at a sniff, whether his preparation is of a kind that others in the field would recognize as acceptable.").

Subpart (1) of Rule 702 calls for a quantitative rather than qualitative analysis. The amendment requires that expert testimony be based on sufficient underlying "facts or data." The term "data" is intended to encompass the reliable opinions of other experts. See the original Advisory Committee Note to Rule 703. The language "facts or data" is broad enough to allow an expert to rely on hypothetical facts that are supported by the evidence. Id.

When facts are in dispute, experts sometimes reach different conclusions based on competing versions of the facts. The emphasis in the amendment on "sufficient facts or data" is not intended to authorize a trial court to exclude an expert's tes[timony on the] ground that the court b[elieves one ver]sion of the facts and n[ot another].

There has been s[ome confusion] over the relationship b[etween Rules] 702 and 703. The amen[dment makes] clear that the sufficiency [of the basis of] an expert's testimony is [to be decided] under Rule 702. Rule 702 [sets forth the] overarching requirement [of reliability,] and an analysis of the su[fficiency of] the expert's basis cannot b[e divorced] from the ultimate reliability [of the ex]pert's opinion. In contrast, th[e "reason]able reliance" requirement o[f Rule 703] is a relatively narrow inqui[ry. When] an expert relies on inadmissi[ble infor]mation, Rule 703 requires [the trial] court to determine whether th[at infor]mation is of a type reasonab[ly relied] on by other experts in the fiel[d. Whether] the expert can rely on the info[rmation] in reaching an opinion. Howe[ver, the] question whether the expert is [relying] on a sufficient basis of informa[tion—] whether admissible informati[on or] not—is governed by the require[ments] of Rule 702.

The amendment makes n[o at]tempt to set forth procedural req[uire]ments for exercising the trial co[urt's] gatekeeping function over expert te[sti]mony. See Daniel J. Capra, *The D[au]bert Puzzle*, 38 Ga.L.Rev. 699, [699] (1998) ("Trial courts should be [al]lowed substantial discretion in deali[ng] with *Daubert* questions; any attem[pt] to codify procedures will likely giv[e] rise to unnecessary changes in practic[e] and create difficult questions for appel[l]ate review."). Courts have shown considerable ingenuity and flexibility in considering challenges to expert testimony under Daubert, and it is contemplated that this will continue under the amended Rule. See, e.g., *Cortes-Irizarry v. Corporacion Insular*, 111

APPENDIX 7

SAMPLE CROSS-EXAMINATION OF PLAINTIFF'S EXPERT

The following is a simulated cross-examination of a plaintiff's psychological expert in a sexual harassment lawsuit.

QUALIFICATIONS

ATTORNEY: Doctor, you really are not a psychologist, are you?

EXPERT: I most certainly am.

ATTORNEY: Are you licensed to practice psychology in this state?

EXPERT: I'm licensed as a marriage and family counselor. And, as I said, I have a Ph.D. in psychology.

ATTORNEY: But you are not licensed to *practice* psychology, are you?

EXPERT: I am fully licensed for the kind of therapy I perform.

ATTORNEY: Doctor, are you a licensed psychologist?

EXPERT: No.

ATTORNEY: Is it not true, doctor, that the licensure statute for marriage and family therapists in this state provides that such therapists may provide counseling to assist persons with marital, family, and other relational difficulties?

EXPERT: Yes, I think so.

ATTORNEY: That statute does not authorize marriage and family therapists to diagnose mental illness, does it?

EXPERT: I'm not familiar with the specific language of the law.

ATTORNEY: Your Honor, I ask the Court to take judicial notice of the licensure statute for marriage and family counselors, and that I may approach the witness.

THE COURT: Judicial notice is taken. You may approach.

ATTORNEY: Doctor, would you please look at the statute that authorizes you to practice, and tell me where it authorizes you to diagnose mental illness.

EXPERT: Well, I guess it really doesn't.

ATTORNEY: Doctor, have you ever taken the examination for licensure as a psychologist?

EXPERT: No. I've been so busy with my practice that I have not had time.

ATTORNEY: Doctor, did you perform a clinical internship after you received your Ph.D.?

EXPERT: No.

ATTORNEY: Such an internship is a prerequisite to licensure as a psychologist in this state, is it not?

EXPERT: I'm really not sure.

ATTORNEY: You're really not sure because you're really not a psychologist, are you?

OPPONENT: Objection. Argumentative; asked and answered.

THE COURT: Sustained. Move on.

ATTORNEY: Doctor, are you a Diplomate of the American Board of Professional Psychology?

EXPERT: No.

ATTORNEY: Are you a member of the American Psychological Association?

EXPERT: No. I am a member of the American Association of Marriage and Family Therapists.

FAILURE TO CONSIDER ALTERNATIVE STRESSORS

ATTORNEY: Doctor, you testified that all of the plaintiff's emotional distress is the result of sexual harassment at my client's place of business, correct?

EXPERT: That and her being forced to quit her job as a result of the sexual harassment.

ATTORNEY: Did you consider any other stressors in her life that might have caused her to suffer emotional distress?

EXPERT: Well, she was so obviously upset about what happened to her at work, I really didn't have to consider anything else.

ATTORNEY: So your answer, doctor, is that you did not consider any other potential stressors, correct?

EXPERT: That's correct.

ATTORNEY: So you don't know whether any other stressors played a role in causing the plaintiff's present emotional condition, do you?

EXPERT: Well, I believe my patient when she tells me that the sexual harassment and loss of her job has had a devastating effect on her emotionally.

ATTORNEY: By the way, doctor, who referred the plaintiff to you?

EXPERT: Her attorney.

ATTORNEY: So she was already contemplating litigation when she came to see you?

EXPERT: I don't know. We did not discuss that initially.

ATTORNEY: Well, has her attorney referred other clients to you?

EXPERT: Yes.

ATTORNEY: How many?

EXPERT: I would estimate seven or eight.

ATTORNEY: Did all of those people file lawsuits?

EXPERT: I don't know for sure. Some of them did.

ATTORNEY: Did you testify for any of them?

EXPERT: Three, I think.

ATTORNEY: So the plaintiff was the eighth or ninth person referred to you by her attorney, right?

EXPERT: That's right.

ATTORNEY: Yet you feel you are able to be completely objective, right?

EXPERT: Yes.

ATTORNEY: But you did not consider any alternative causes of the plaintiff's emotional distress, did you?

OPPONENT: Objection. Asked and answered.

THE COURT: Sustained.

ATTORNEY: Well, did you know, for example, that the plaintiff was under a psychiatrist's care for anxiety and depression before she ever went to work for my client?

EXPERT: I do now.

ATTORNEY: But you did not know that until I informed you of that fact when I took your deposition, did you?

EXPERT: No, I did not.

ATTORNEY: And you did not know that when you wrote your report in this case giving your opinions, did you?

EXPERT: No.

ATTORNEY: Did you know that the plaintiff was involved in a physically abusive relationship during the time she was employed by my client?

EXPERT: She mentioned that.

ATTORNEY: Are you aware that her ex-husband had a severe drinking problem?

EXPERT: That's what she told me.

ATTORNEY: Are you aware that after a drinking binge, her ex-husband once beat her so severely that she spent three days in the hospital?

EXPERT: Yes.

ATTORNEY: And that she received that beating about a month before she left my client's employment?

EXPERT: Approximately.

ATTORNEY: And that while she was in the hospital, her ex-husband took her child and left the state?

EXPERT: I'm aware of that.

ATTORNEY: And that he had cleaned out their bank account, leaving her with no money?

EXPERT: She mentioned that.

ATTORNEY: And that she was evicted from the apartment she had shared with her ex-husband?

EXPERT: She mentioned that, too.

ATTORNEY: Did she also mention that a week before she complained of sexual harassment and walked off the job, she asked her supervisor, whom she is now accusing of harassment, for a loan?

EXPERT: She did tell me that.

ATTORNEY: Did she tell you that she told her supervisor that her life was a mess and she needed money badly?

EXPERT: She told me she had asked him for a loan so she could hire an attorney to help get her child back.

ATTORNEY: So the plaintiff told you that her ex-husband beat her, stole her child, and left her homeless with no money, is that right?

EXPERT: I'm not sure she put it quite that way, but . . .

ATTORNEY: But she told you about all of those things, did she not?

EXPERT: Yes.

ATTORNEY: Yet, you still feel that all of her emotional distress is the result of sexual harassment?

EXPERT: Well, I would have to say that it was the major cause.

ATTORNEY: Major cause? Meaning that you now concede that there may have been other causes as well?

EXPERT: Perhaps, but when she was in an especially vulnerable position, she looked to her employer for protection and all she got was harassment and abuse.

ATTORNEY: I'm sorry, doctor, I don't think you answered my question. Are you saying there were other causes of the plaintiff's emotional distress?

EXPERT: Yes, but sexual harassment was the major cause.

ATTORNEY: So are you changing your opinion, doctor? Are you now saying that sexual harassment was a major cause instead of the sole cause?

EXPERT: I would say major cause.

ATTORNEY: But at the time you wrote your report, doctor, you did not consider any other causes, did you?

EXPERT: No.

FAILURE TO CONSIDER PERSONALITY DISORDER

ATTORNEY: Doctor, did you find the plaintiff to be suffering from a personality disorder?

EXPERT: No.

ATTORNEY: Did you at least consider the possibility of a personality disorder?

EXPERT: I always consider the possibility of a personality disorder.

ATTORNEY: You consider yourself fully qualified to diagnose personality disorders?

EXPERT: Absolutely.

ATTORNEY: Well, how did you rule out a personality disorder in this case?

EXPERT: Based on my clinical experience, I just do not feel that the plaintiff has a personality disorder.

ATTORNEY: Before reaching that conclusion, did you examine any of the plaintiff's prior medical records?

EXPERT: No, I did not have those records.

ATTORNEY: So you did not know that five years ago, the plaintiff was admitted to a psychiatric hospital after trying to kill herself?

EXPERT: Well, I found out about that in the course of this lawsuit.

ATTORNEY: So the plaintiff did not tell you about that?

EXPERT: I did not ask her.

ATTORNEY: Doctor, did the plaintiff tell you that she had been admitted to a psychiatric institution five years ago after she tried to kill herself?

EXPERT: No.

ATTORNEY: Are prior suicide attempts not an indication that a personality disorder may be present?

EXPERT: They could be.

ATTORNEY: During your therapy sessions with the plaintiff, you and she discussed her cocaine addiction, did you not?

EXPERT: Well, yes. But as I said previously, oftentimes victims of sexual harassment will attempt to self-medicate their pain through drugs or alcohol.

ATTORNEY: But, doctor, your own notes indicate that the plaintiff's drug problems pre-dated her employment with my client, do they not?

EXPERT: Yes.

ATTORNEY: And is a history of substance abuse not another indication that a personality disorder might be present?

EXPERT: It could be.

ATTORNEY: Your notes also indicate that the plaintiff was sexually molested by her stepfather when she was young, do they not?

EXPERT: Yes.

ATTORNEY: And is there not a substantial body of medical evidence indicating that childhood sexual abuse can cause a personality disorder to develop later in life?

EXPERT: Well, I don't know if I agree with that. . . .

ATTORNEY: Doctor, my question was whether there is a substantial body of medical evidence indicating that childhood sexual abuse causes personality disorders to develop, not whether you agree or disagree with that evidence.

OPPONENT: Objection. Argumentative. No question pending.

ATTORNEY: OK. Once more. Doctor, is there not a substantial body of medical evidence indicating that childhood sexual abuse can cause a personality disorder to develop?

EXPERT: Yes.

ATTORNEY: In particular, it can cause what's known as a Borderline Personality Disorder to develop, can it not?

EXPERT: That's what the literature says.

ATTORNEY: And one feature of a Borderline Personality Disorder is a chaotic course of interpersonal relationships, is it not?

EXPERT: It can be.

ATTORNEY: And yet, you attribute the collapse of the plaintiff's relationship with her boyfriend solely to the events at work?

EXPERT: Well, it was after she was forced to quit that they broke up.

ATTORNEY: Do you know how many other times in the past the plaintiff has broken off a relationship?

EXPERT: No. I never asked her that.

ATTORNEY: In fact, doctor, people with personality disorders often have difficulty getting along with others, do they not?

EXPERT: It's possible.

ATTORNEY: Well, doctor, a personality disorder would affect a person's ability to get along with co-workers, would it not?

EXPERT: It could.

ATTORNEY: Personality disorders often affect a person's perceptions of the words or actions of others, correct?

EXPERT: That's correct.

ATTORNEY: So a person with a personality disorder may misinterpret the words or actions of co-workers, correct?

EXPERT: It's possible.

ATTORNEY: Doctor, you also are aware, are you not, that the plaintiff has suffered from bulimia off and on for the past 17 years?

EXPERT: That's what her medical records indicate.

ATTORNEY: Medical records that you did not review until you prepared to testify in this case?

OPPONENT: Objection. Argumentative.

THE COURT: Counsel?

ATTORNEY: I'm simply trying to find out when the doctor informed himself of the plaintiff's medical history. It goes to the basis of his opinion.

THE COURT: Overruled.

ATTORNEY: Bulimia is another indication that a personality disorder may be present, is it not, doctor?

EXPERT: It can be.

ATTORNEY: Doctor, you are also aware, are you not, that the plaintiff dropped out of high school in the 11th grade?

OPPONENT: Objection. Irrelevant. This has nothing to do with sexual harassment.

ATTORNEY: Your Honor, this witness has testified that he does not think the plaintiff has a personality disorder, yet he has admitted that the existence of such a personality disorder might constitute an alternative explanation for some of the problems the plaintiff seeks to blame on her employer. I'm just trying to determine how careful the doctor was in ruling out the possibility of a personality disorder here.

THE COURT: Overruled. But counsel, you seem to be reaching a bit far, and we need to move on.

ATTORNEY: Doctor, you are aware, are you not, that the plaintiff dropped out of high school in the 11th grade?

EXPERT: Yes.

ATTORNEY: And that's another indication that a personality disorder may be present, is it not?

EXPERT: Not necessarily. I don't think that's a valid statement.

ATTORNEY: Doctor, you relied on the American Psychiatric Association's *Diagnostic and Statistical Manual* in your diagnosis of the plaintiff, did you not?

EXPERT: Yes, basically.

ATTORNEY: In fact, the *DSM* is the standard diagnostic manual relied upon by the mental health professions, is it not?

EXPERT: Yes.

ATTORNEY: Did you bring your manual to court with you today?

EXPERT: Actually, no . . .

ATTORNEY: Here, doctor, you can use mine. Your Honor, may I approach?

THE COURT: You may.

ATTORNEY: Doctor, please turn to page 708 of the *DSM*. What do you find there?

EXPERT: Well, it's a description of Borderline Personality Disorder.

ATTORNEY: Doctor, please read the first full paragraph.

EXPERT: "Individuals with Borderline Personality Disorder may have a pattern of undermining themselves at the moment a goal is about to be realized. For example, dropping out of school just before graduation . . ."

ATTORNEY: Is there more?

EXPERT: "Or destroying a good relationship just when it is clear that the relationship could last."

ATTORNEY: Thank you, doctor. Doctor, in light of all of your answers to my questions about personality disorders today, is it still your belief that the plaintiff does not have a personality disorder?

MISDIAGNOSIS OF PTSD

ATTORNEY: Now, doctor, you said you diagnosed the plaintiff as suffering from Posttraumatic Stress Disorder, correct?

EXPERT: Yes.

ATTORNEY: Did you diagnose her based on the criteria set forth in *DSM-IV-TR*?

EXPERT: That and my clinical experience.

ATTORNEY: Well, did you rely on *DSM-IV-TR* or not?

EXPERT: I did.

ATTORNEY: So you are aware, are you not, doctor, that valid diagnosis of PTSD requires the occurrence of an event or events that involved actual or threatened death or physical injury or a threat to the physical integrity of oneself or others?

EXPERT: I'm familiar with the definition.

ATTORNEY: So, doctor, what traumatic event in the workplace did the plaintiff experience that you believe triggered her PTSD?

EXPERT: As I testified earlier, the sexual harassment.

ATTORNEY: Well, what incident or incidents specifically do you feel triggered PTSD?

EXPERT: The assault, for one.

ATTORNEY: You are referring to her boss putting his arm around her?

EXPERT: And suggesting that he would pay her to be his girlfriend.

ATTORNEY: Aren't you referring to the supervisor's testimony that when the plaintiff asked him for a loan, he said, "Well, it's not like you're my girlfriend or anything"?

EXPERT: That's his version. My patient perceived him to be pressuring her for sex.

ATTORNEY: Any other traumas that you believed triggered PTSD?

EXPERT: Well, she had to endure a daily barrage of off-color jokes and innuendo, and she ultimately lost her job, which was quite a serious trauma for her.

ATTORNEY: But doctor, doesn't *DSM-IV-TR*, at page 467, specifically state that being fired is not a sufficient trigger for PTSD?

EXPERT: But the plaintiff was not fired. She was forced to quit on account of the sexual harassment.

ATTORNEY: So, doctor, are you saying that overhearing some off-color jokes and comments is a trauma involving actual or threatened death or physical injury or a threat to her physical integrity?

EXPERT: Well, sexual harassment is like rape, and rape is certainly a recognized PTSD stressor.

ATTORNEY: Doctor, are you saying that what the plaintiff claimed happened to her was the equivalent of rape?

EXPERT: In her mind she certainly felt it was. Keep in mind, this woman has been in therapy for a year and a half as the result of what happened to her at work.

ATTORNEY: Therapy that you conducted, right, doctor?

EXPERT: That's right.

ATTORNEY: And after a year and a half, she's *still* in therapy?

EXPERT: This was a very traumatic experience for her.

ATTORNEY: And during that year and a half of therapy, doctor, did you ever suggest to her that maybe she was overreacting?

EXPERT: Oh, no. To have done so would have been very harmful to her.

ATTORNEY: So you just took her word for it, doctor?

EXPERT: Well, of course, she had no reason to lie to me.

ATTORNEY: No reason to lie?! She's suing for money, she was sent to you by her attorney, and you don't think she had any reason to lie?

OPPONENT: Objection. Argumentative.

THE COURT: Sustained. Move on.

ATTORNEY: Well, doctor, did you consider whether her being beaten, put in the hospital, and thrown out on the street by her ex-husband might have caused this so-called PTSD?

EXPERT: Yes, I considered it, but I think what finally made her snap was her supervisor sexually propositioning her when she turned to him for help.

ATTORNEY: Doctor, here, look at *DSM-IV-TR* and tell me where it says that having your boss make a pass at you can cause PTSD.

EXPERT: Well, it does not say that per se, but one might interpret it that way.

ATTORNEY: When the PTSD diagnosis was developed, it was designed to apply to war veterans, wasn't it?

EXPERT: Yes.

ATTORNEY: And the *DSM* says other people who might be expected to suffer from PTSD are prisoners of war and torture victims, does it not?

EXPERT: Yes.

ATTORNEY: And you equate the plaintiff's boss making a pass at her, even if he did, as being the same as being a POW or a torture victim?

EXPERT: Well, it did make her very uncomfortable.

FINANCIAL BIAS

ATTORNEY: Doctor, how many therapy sessions did you say you had with the plaintiff?

EXPERT: Well, twice a week for six months, and then about once a week for the last year.

ATTORNEY: So about 100 sessions?

EXPERT: Give or take a few; I'd say that sounds about right.

ATTORNEY: Did you charge her for those sessions?

EXPERT: Of course.

ATTORNEY: How much per session?

EXPERT: My normal rate is $100.

ATTORNEY: Well, is that what you charged her?

EXPERT: Yes.

ATTORNEY: So 100 sessions at $100—that comes to $10,000, correct?

EXPERT: Yes.

ATTORNEY: Have you been paid any of that money?

EXPERT: Her insurance covered part of it.

ATTORNEY: What part of it?

EXPERT: Ten sessions.

ATTORNEY: Do you expect to get any more insurance money?

EXPERT: No. I understand that 10 sessions is all her policy covers.

ATTORNEY: So she still owes you for 90 sessions, correct?

EXPERT: Correct.

ATTORNEY: Has she paid you anything?

EXPERT: No, she couldn't afford to after she was forced to quit her job with your client.

ATTORNEY: So the plaintiff now owes you $9,000?

EXPERT: Approximately.

ATTORNEY: Has she made any arrangements to pay you?

EXPERT: Not yet, but I trust her.

ATTORNEY: Doctor, you are testifying as the plaintiff's expert as well as her treating therapist in this case, are you not?

EXPERT: Yes.

ATTORNEY: And in your role as expert, you are trying to be objective, are you not?

EXPERT: Of course.

ATTORNEY: Yet, if the plaintiff does not win this lawsuit and collect some money, you are not likely to get paid, are you?

OPPONENT: Objection. Argumentative.

ATTORNEY: I'll withdraw it. No further questions.

TABLE OF CASES

References are to footnote numbers in the preface or chapters (e.g., 9: 102 refers to footnote 102 in chapter 9).

A

Abduwali v. WMATA, 193 F.R.D. 10 (D.D.C. 2000) **9:** 102, 103, 109

Abrams
—v. Kelsey-Seybold Med. Group, Inc., 178 F.R.D. 116 (S.D. Tex. 1997) **1:** 228
—v. Lightolier, 841 F. Supp. 584, 65 FEP Cases 1149 (D.N.J. 1994) **1:** 146

Adams
—v. Alderson, 723 F. Supp. 1531, 51 FEP Cases 647 (D.D.C. 1989) **16:** 100, 101, 454
—v. Ameritech Servs., 231 F.3d 414 (7th Cir. 2000) **15:** 44
—v. Ardcor, 196 F.R.D. 339 (E.D. Wis. 2000) **8:** 35
—v. Goodyear Tire & Rubber Co., 184 F.R.D. 369 (D. Kan. 1998) **8:** 113
—v. Rochester Gen. Hosp., 977 F. Supp. 226, 8 AD Cases 1143 (W.D.N.Y. 1997) **16:** 23, 25

Adler v. L&M Rail Link, LLC, 13 F. Supp. 2d 912, 8 AD Cases 775 (N.D. Iowa 1998) **16:** 582

Adriana Int'l Corp. v. Thoeren, 913 F.2d 1406 (9th Cir. 1990) **1:** 89

AIC Sec. Investigation, Ltd.; EEOC v.
—55 F.3d 1276, 4 AD Cases 693 (7th Cir. 1995) **1:** 152
—820 F. Supp. 1060, 2 AD Cases 561 (N.D. Ill. 1993) **16:** 414

Aka v. Washington Hosp. Center., 156 F.3d 1284, 8 AD Cases 1093 (D.C. Cir. 1998) **16:** 441

Albert v. Runyon, 6 F. Supp. 2d 57, 4 WH Cases 2d 1128 (D. Mass. 1998) **16:** 599

Alberts v. Wickes Lumber Co., 1995 WL 117886, 69 FEP Cases 304 (N.D. Ill. Mar. 15, 1995) **8:** 105, 152–57; **9:** 63; **15:** 115

Alden v. Time Warner, Inc., 1995 WL 679238 (S.D.N.Y. Nov. 14, 1995) **8:** 26–28, 80

Aldrich v. Boeing Co., 146 F.3d 1265, 8 AD Cases 424 (10th Cir. 1998) **16:** 57

Alexandru v. North East Util. Serv. Co., 1996 WL 684421 (D. Conn. Oct. 10, 1996) **16:** 19

Ali v. Wang Lab., 162 F.R.D. 165, 4 AD Cases 520 (M.D. Fla. 1995) **9:** 10, 11, 65, 69, 70, 83, 84, 107, 109

Allen
—v. Cook County Sheriff's Dep't, 1999 WL 168466 (N.D. Ill. Mar. 17, 1999) **8:** 81, 85, 86
—v. GTE Mobile Community Serv. Corp., 6 AD Cases 1063 (N.D. Ga. 1997) **16:** 404
—v. Jones, 104 Cal. App. 3d 207, 163 Cal. Rptr. 445 (1980) **1:** 103

Allison v. Citgo Petroleum Corp., 151 F.3d 402, 81 FEP Cases 501 (5th Cir. 1998) **1:** 221–27

Altman v. NYC Health & Hosp. Corp., 903 F. Supp. 503, 4 AD Cases 1665 (S.D.N.Y. 1995), *aff'd,* 100 F.3d 1054, 6 AD Cases 73 (2d Cir. 1996) **16:** 650, 670–72

Amego, Inc.; EEOC v., 110 F.3d 135, 6

Amego, Inc. (*cont.*)
AD Cases 997 (1st Cir. 1997) *12:* 9, 10; *16:* 264, 274, 275, 447, 448, 646, 648, 651, 652

Amir v. St. Louis Univ., 184 F.3d 1017, 9 AD Cases 999 (8th Cir. 1999) *16:* 8, 86, 99, 113

Anderson v. General Manager Boston Star, 924 F. Supp. 763, 5 AD Cases 673 (E.D. Tex. 1996) *16:* 166

Andrews v. City of Philadelphia, 895 F.2d 1469 (3d Cir. 1990) *1:* 31

Antoine-Tubbs v. Local 513, Transport Workers Union, 50 F. Supp. 2d 601 (N.D. Tex. 1998) *15:* 85

Anzalone v. Allstate, Ins. Co., 5 AD Cases 455 (E.D. La. 1995) *16:* 432

Aquinas v. Federal Express Corp., 940 F. Supp. 73, 6 AD Cases 485 (S.D.N.Y. 1996) *16:* 418

Aramark Corp., Inc.; EEOC v., 208 F.3d 266, 10 AD Cases 798 (D.C. Cir. 2000) *16:* 529

Arenson v. Sullivan, 946 F.2d 90, 2 AD Cases 31 (8th Cir. 1991) *16:* 490

Armstrong v. Turner Indus., Ltd., 950 F. Supp. 162, 7 AD Cases 875 (M.D. La. 1996), *aff'd,* 141 F.3d 554, 8 AD Cases 118 (5th Cir. 1998) *16:* 531, 532

Arnold v. City of Seminole, 614 F. Supp. 853, 40 FEP Cases 1539 (E.D. Okla. 1985) *1:* 25

Atchison, Topeka & Santa Fe Ry. v. Buell, 480 U.S. 557 (1987) *1:* 47

B

Bailey v. Runyon, 220 F.3d 879, 82 FEP Cases 892 (8th Cir. 2000) *1:* 129

Barfield v. BellSouth Telecomms., Inc., 886 F. Supp. 1321, 4 AD Cases 1159 (S.D. Miss. 1995) *16:* 418

Barnes
—v. Cochran, 944 F. Supp. 897, 5 AD Cases 1685 (S.D. Fla. 1996) *16:* 555
—v. Costle. *See* Barnes v. Train
—v. Train, 13 FEP Cases 123 (D.D.C. 1974), *rev'd sub nom.* Barnes v. Costle, 561 F.2d 983, 15 FEP Cases 345 (D.C. Cir. 1977) *14:* 5, 6, 10

Barnett v. U.S. Air, Inc., 228 F.3d 1105, 10 AD Cases 1761 (9th Cir. 2000) *16:* 384, 441

Barnsville Exempted Village Sch. Dist. Bd. of Educ., 209 F.3d 931, 10 AD Cases 787 (6th Cir. 2000) *16:* 524

Barrett v. Applied Radiant Energy Corp., 240 F.3d 262, 85 FEP Cases 252 (4th Cir. 2001) *1:* 44, 45

Barta v. City & County of Honolulu, 169 F.R.D. 132 (D. Haw. 1996) *8:* 114, 115, 139–41, 172, 173

Barth v. Gelb, 2 F.3d 1180, 2 AD Cases 1180 (D.C. Cir. 1993) *16:* 344

Bartlett v. New York State Bd. L. Exam'rs, 225 F.3d 69, 10 AD Cases 1687 (2d Cir. 2001) *16:* 90

Baty v. Willamette Indus., Inc., 985 F. Supp. 987 (D. Kan. 1997), *aff'd,* 172 F.3d 1232, 79 FEP Cases 1451 (10th Cir. 1999) *Preface:* 15

Baulos v. Roadway Express, Inc., 139 F.3d 1147, 7 AD Cases 1753 (7th Cir. 1998) *16:* 137

Baustian v. Louisiana, 910 F. Supp. 274, 4 AD Cases 1692 (E.D. La 1995) *16:* 504

Beagle v. Vasold, 65 Cal. 2d 166, 53 Cal. Rptr. 129 (1966) *1:* 136, 140, 141

Beard v. Flying J, Inc., 116 F. Supp. 2d 1077 (S.D. Iowa 2000) *8:* 138

Beaver v. Delta Air Lines, Inc., 43 F. Supp. 2d 685 (N.D. Tex. 1999) *16:* 477

Beck v. University of Wis. Bd. of Regents, 75 F.3d 1130, 5 AD Cases 304 (7th Cir. 1996) *16:* 351, 385–90

Bekker v. Humana Health Plan, 229 F.3d 662, 10 AD Cases 1776 (7th Cir. 2000) *16:* 654

Benson v. Northwest Airlines, Inc., 62 F.3d 1108, 4 AD Cases 1234 (8th Cir. 1995) *16:* 262, 343, 440, 657

Berg v. Norand Corp., 169 F.3d 1140, 9 AD Cases 207 (8th Cir. 1999) *16:* 195

Berger v. Iron Workers Reinforced Rodment Local 201, 170 F.3d 1111, 79 FEP Cases 1018 (D.C. Cir. 1999) *1:* 238–40

Bergsrud v. Columbia-Lee Reg'l Med. Ctr., 2000 WL 33287447 (D.N.M. June 24, 2000) *16:* 37, 145, 151

Berry
—v. Crown Equip. Corp., 108 F. Supp. 2d 743 (E.D. Mich. 2000) *15:* 63

—v. Detroit, City of, 25 F.3d 1342 (6th Cir. 1994) *15:* 60
Bethel v. Dixie Homecrafters, Inc., 192 F.R.D. 320, 82 FEP Cases 345 (N.D. Ga. 2000) *9:* 38, 79, 104, 113, 138, 139
Bicknell v. Thomas Tile & Carpet, Inc., 45 F. Supp. 2d 538, 9 AD Cases 481 (S.D. W.Va. 1999) *16:* 215, 221
Biggs v. Nicewonger Co., 897 F. Supp. 483, 68 FEP Cases 1771 (D. Or. 1995) *8:* 185, 186
Bilodeau v. Mega Indus., 50 F. Supp. 2d 27, 9 AD Cases 850 (D. Me. 1999) *16:* 160, 161, 183, 184
Blakey v. Continental Airlines, 992 F. Supp. 731, 76 FEP Cases 280 (D.N.J. 1998) *1:* 147–50, 217, 218; *12:* 12
Blankenship v. Parke Care Ctrs., Inc., 913 F. Supp. 1045 (S.D. Ohio 1995), *aff'd,* 123 F.3d 868, 75 FEP Cases 1351 (6th Cir. 1997), *cert. denied,* 118 S. Ct. 1039, 77 FEP Cases 64 (1998) *8:* 227, 229–31
Blanton v. AT&T Communications, 1 AD Cases 1552 (D. Mass. 1990) *16:* 202
Boeing Co.; Doe v., 846 P.2d 531, 2 AD Cases 548 (Wash. 1996) *16:* 199
Boldini v. Postmaster Gen., 928 F. Supp. 125, 5 AD Cases 11 (D.N.H. 1995) *16:* 20, 317
Bolstein v. Reich, 1995 WL 686236 (D.D.C. Oct. 4, 1995) *16:* 327
Booker v. City of Boston, 1999 WL 734644 (D. Mass. Sept. 10, 1999) *8:* 52
Borawick v. Shay, 68 F.3d 597 (2d Cir. 1995) *15:* 115
Borgialli v. Thunder Basin Coal Co., 235 F.3d 1284, 11 AD Cases 484 (10th Cir. 2000) *16:* 646, 673, 674
Borkowski v. Valley Cent. Sch. Dist., 63 F.3d 131, 4 AD Cases 1264 (2d Cir. 1995) *16:* 339, 343
Borquez v. Ozer, 923 P.2d 166, 69 FEP Cases 1415, 11 IER Cases 496 (Colo. App. 1995), *aff'd in part and rev'd in part,* 940 P.2d 371, 12 IER Cases 1665 (Colo. 1997) *9:* 54, 55
Bottomly v. Leucadia Nat'l, 163 F.R.D. 617 (D. Utah 1995) *8:* 58–61, 63
Bowen v. Income Producing Management of Okla., 202 F.3d 1282, 10 AD Cases 296 (10th Cir. 2000) *16:* 149
Bowers v. Multimedia Cablevision, Inc., 1998 WL 856 074 (D. Kan. Nov. 3, 1998) *16:* 39
Bowersox v. P.H. Glatfelter Co., 677 F. Supp. 307, 45 FEP Cases 1443 (M.D. Pa. 1988) *1:* 98, 102
Boyd v. James S. Hayes Living Health Care Agency, 671 F. Supp. 1155, 44 FEP Cases 332 (W.D. Tenn. 1987) *1:* 65
Bragdon v. Abbott, 524 U.S. 624, 8 AD Cases 239 (1998) *16:* 45, 79, 96–98, 121, 122, 127–30, 663
Branch
—v. Homefed Bank, 6 Cal. App. 4th 793, 8 Cal. Rptr. 2d 182 (1992) *1:* 88, 92, 106, 107
—v. New Orleans, 1995 WL 295320 (E.D. La. May 5, 1995) *16:* 65
Breda v. Wolf Camera, Inc., 78 FEP Cases 433 (S.D. Ga. 1998) *9:* 104, 166, 167
Breiland v. Advance Circuits, Inc., 976 F. Supp. 858, 7 AD Cases 619 (D. Minn. 1997) *16:* 104
Bremiller v. Cleveland Psychiatric Inst., 898 F. Supp. 572, 66 FEP Cases 1738 (N.D. Ohio 1995) *1:* 235
Brennan v. National Tel. Directory Corp., 850 F. Supp. 331, 4 AD Cases 76 (E.D. Pa. 1994) *16:* 195
Bridges v. Eastman Kodak Co., 850 F. Supp. 216, 64 FEP Cases 1100 (S.D.N.Y. 1994) *8:* 13, 56, 82–84; *9:* 18, 38, 56
Brookins v. Indianapolis Power & Light Co., 90 F. Supp. 2d 993 (S.D. Ind. 2000) *16:* 468
Brooms v. Regal Tube Co., 881 F.2d 412, 50 FEP Cases 1499 (7th Cir. 1989) *1:* 111
Brown
—v. Northern Trust Bank, 7 AD Cases 548, 1997 WL 543098 (N.D. Ill. Sept. 2, 1997) *12:* 11, 22; *16:* 39
—v. Youth Servs. Int'l of Baltimore, 904 F. Supp. 469, 69 FEP Cases 991 (D. Md. 1995) *1:* 99, 100
Brumley v. Pena, 62 F.3d 277, 4 AD Cases 1239 (8th Cir. 1995) *16:* 549
Brundage v. Hahn, 66 Cal. Rptr. 2d 830,

Brundage v. Hahn (*cont.*)
7 AD Cases 286 (Ct. App. 1997) *16:* 283
Bryant v. Better Bus. Bureau of Greater Md., 923 F. Supp. 720, 5 AD Cases 625 (D. Md. 1996) *16:* 338, 436
Buchanan v. San Antonio, 85 F.3d 196, 5 AD Cases 987 (5th Cir. 1996) *16:* 565
Buckley v. Consolidated Edison Co. of N.Y., Inc., 127 F.3d 270, 7 AD Cases 794 (2d Cir. 1997) *16:* 500
Bultemeyer v. Fort Wayne Community Sch., 100 F.3d 1281, 6 AD Cases 67 (7th Cir. 1996) *16:* 287, 288, 364–66, 384
Bundy v. Jackson, 641 F.2d 934, 24 FEP Cases 1155 (D.C. Cir. 1981) *14:* 12
Burch v. Coca-Cola Co., 119 F.3d 305, 7 AD Cases 241 (5th Cir. 1997) *16:* 38, 58, 206, 223, 424, 445
Burger v. Litton Indus., Inc.
—1995 WL 363741, 68 FEP Cases 737 (S.D.N.Y. June 19, 1995) *9:* 114, 149, 160–62
—1995 WL 476712 (S.D.N.Y. Aug. 10, 1995) *8:* 189
Burlington Indus., Inc. v. Ellerth, 524 U.S. 742, 77 FEP Cases 1 (1998) *14:* 26
Burns v. McGregor Elec. Indus., Inc., 989 F.2d 959, 61 FEP Cases 592 (8th Cir. 1993) *8:* 130
Burrell v. Crown Cent. Petroleum, Inc.
—177 F.R.D. 376 (E.D. Tex. 1997) *8:* 53
—197 F.R.D. 284 (E.D. Tex. 2000) *1:* 232
Buskirk v. Apollo Metals, 116 F. Supp. 2d 591, 11 AD Cases 178 (E.D. Pa. 2000) *16:* 125
Byrd v. Richardson-Greenshields Sec., 552 So. 2d 1099 (Fla. 1989) *1:* 108, 112, 113
Byrne v. Board of Educ., 979 F.2d 560, 2 AD Cases 284 (7th Cir. 1992) *16:* 206

C

Cannice v. Norwest Bank Iowa N.A., 189 F.3d 723, 9 AD Cases 1103 (8th Cir. 1999) *16:* 350, 382

Carey v. Piphus, 435 U.S. 247 (1978) *1:* 16, 114, 127
Carlson v. Inacom Corp., 885 F. Supp. 1314, 4 AD Cases 600 (D. Neb. 1995) *16:* 282
Carmichael
—v. Samyang Tire, Inc., 131 F.3d 1433 (11th Cir. 1997) *15:* 40
—State v., 727 P.2d 918 (Kan. 1986) *8:* 107
Carr
—v. Reno, 23 F.3d 525, 3 AD Cases 434 (D.C. Cir. 1994) *16:* 415, 418, 421, 431
—v. U.S. W. Direct Co., 98 Or. App. 30, 779 P.2d 154 (1989) *1:* 108
Carrier Corp. v. New York Div. of Human Rights, 224 A.D.2d 936, 637 N.Y.S.2d 877 (1996) *9:* 13
Carter v. Casa Central, 849 F.2d 1048, 1 AD Cases 1332 (7th Cir. 1988) *16:* 660
Cehrs v. Northeast Ohio Alzheimer's Research Ctr., 155 F.3d 775, 8 AD Cases 825 (6th Cir. 1998) *16:* 61, 278, 283, 396, 402
Chamberlain v. McNeil Consumer Prods. Co., 1998 WL 42271 (N.D. Ill. Jan. 29, 1998) *16:* 223
Chamberlin v. 101 Realty, 915 F.2d 777, 54 FEP Cases 101 (1st Cir. 1990) *1:* 56
Champagne v. Servister Corp., 138 F.3d 7, 7 AD Cases 1685 (1st Cir. 1998) *16:* 181
Chandler v. City of Dallas, 2 F.3d 1385, 2 AD Cases 1326 (5th Cir. 1993) *16:* 241
Chaparro v. IBP, Inc., 1994 WL 714369 (D. Kan. Dec. 7, 1994) *9:* 48, 52, 53, 66, 67, 82, 113, 158, 165
Chicago; Doe v., 883 F. Supp. 1126 (N.D. 1994) *16:* 565
Chiperas v. Rubin, 1998 WL 765126 (D.D.C. Nov. 3, 1998) *9:* 155, 156
Christian v. St. Anthony Med. Ctr., 117 F.3d 1051, 6 AD Cases 1665 (7th Cir. 1997) *16:* 49
Christopher v. Adam's Mark Hotels, 137 F.3d 1069, 7 AD Cases 1537 (8th Cir. 1998) *16:* 250
Circuit City Stores, Inc. v. Adams, 532

U.S. 105, 85 FEP Cases 266 (2001) *14:* 31

City of. *See name of city*

Clemens v. Gerber Scientific, 1989 U.S. Dist. LEXIS 376 (E.D. Pa. 1989) *1:* 58

Clemente v. Executive Airlines, Inc., 215 F.3d 25, 10 AD Cases 996 (1st Cir. 2000) *16:* 57

Cleveland v. International Paper Co., 74 FEP Cases 1661 (N.D.N.Y. 1997) *8:* 12, 13

Cline v. Wal-Mart Stores, Inc., 144 F.3d 294, 8 AD Cases 154 (4th Cir. 1998) *16:* 219, 222

CNA Ins. Cos.; EEOC v., 96 F.3d 1039, 5 AD Cases 1769 (7th Cir. 1996) *16:* 528

Codrington v. Virgin Islands Port Auth., 911 F. Supp. 907, 70 FEP Cases 213 (D.V.I. 1995) *1:* 34, 35

Cody
—v. Cigna Healthcare of St. Louis, 139 F.3d 595, 7 AD Cases 1716 (8th Cir. 1998) *16:* 39, 153, 226, 235, 237, 244, 245
—v. Marriott Corp., 103 F.R.D. 421, 44 FEP Cases 1228 (D. Mass. 1984) *9:* 15, 16, 21, 47

Colautti; Doe v., 592 F.2d 704 (3d Cir. 1979) *16:* 526

Coleman v. Keeble Co., 997 F. Supp. 1102 (N.D. Ill. 1998) *16:* 215

Collins v. Longview Fibre Co., 63 F.3d 828, 4 AD Cases 1278 (9th Cir. 1995) *16:* 503

Colwell v. Suffolk County Police Dep't, 158 F.3d 635, 8 AD Cases 1232 (2d Cir. 1998) *16:* 46, 137, 185, 206, 238, 239

Cook
—v. Cub Foods, Inc., 99 F. Supp. 2d 945, 83 FEP Cases 536 (N.D. Ill. 2000) *16:* 181, 189
—v. Rhode Island Dep't of Mental Health, 10 F.3d 17, 2 AD Cases 1476 (1st Cir. 1993) *16:* 131

Corbett v. National Prods. Co., 4 AD Cases 987 (E.D. Pa. 1995) *16:* 523

Corne v. Bausch & Lomb, Inc., 390 F. Supp. 161, 10 FEP Cases 289 (D. Ariz. 1975), vacated, 562 F.2d 55 (9th Cir. 1977) *14:* 7, 8

Courder v. Lucent Techs., Inc., 162 F.3d 924, 8 AD Cases 1611 (7th Cir. 1998) *16:* 401

Covell v. CNG Transmission Corp., 863 F. Supp. 202, 70 FEP Cases 914 (M.D. Pa. 1994) *8:* 47, 49

Cox v. Indian Head Indus., Inc., 187 F.R.D. 531 (W.D.N.C. 1999) *1:* 229, 244, 245

Cravens v. Blue Cross & Blue Shield of Kans., 214 F.3d 1011, 10 AD Cases 1057 (8th Cir. 2000) *16:* 384

Criado v. International Bus. Machs. Corp., 145 F.3d 437, 8 AD Cases 336 (1st Cir. 1998) *16:* 64, 103, 182, 283, 402

Crisci v. Security Ins. Co., 66 Cal. 2d 425, 58 Cal. Rptr. 13, 426 P.2d 173 (1967) *1:* 104

Cummings v. Walsh Constr. Co., 561 F. Supp. 872, 31 FEP Cases 930 (S.D. Ga. 1983) *1:* 80, 81, 94

Curtis v. Express, Inc., 868 F. Supp. 467, 66 FEP Cases 449 (N.D.N.Y. 1994) *9:* 38, 56

Cutler v. Jewel Food Stores, Inc., 1998 WL 895453 (N.D. Ill. Dec. 14, 1998) *16:* 52

D

Daddazio v. Kathrine Gibbs Sch. Inc., 9 AD Cases 585 (D.S.D. 1999) *16:* 279

Dahdal v. Thorn Americas, Inc., 76 FEP Cases 88 (D. Kan. 1998) *9:* 35, 36

Daley v. Koch, 892 F.2d 212, 1 AD Cases 1549 (2d Cir. 1989) *16:* 27, 231

Dalton v. Subaru-Isuzu Auto., Inc., 141 F.3d 667, 7 AD Cases 1872 (7th Cir. 1998) *16:* 373, 437, 439

Danka Indus., Inc.; EEOC v., 990 F. Supp. 1138, 75 FEP Cases 685 (E.D. Mo. 1997) *8:* 36, 37, 79

Daubert v. Merrill Dow Pharm., Inc.
—509 U.S. 579 (1993) **Preface:** 10, 12; *1:* 157; *2:* 5; *3:* 6; *9:* 168; *10:* 1; *15:* 3, 9–13, 16, 25–31, 100; 80
—43 F.3d 1311 (9th Cir. 1995) *15:* 17–24, 32, 33, 93

Daugherty v. El Paso, 56 F.3d 695, 4 AD Cases 993 (5th Cir. 1995) *16:* 646

David v. Trugreen Ltd. P'ship, 1999 WL 288686 (N.D. Tex. May 5, 1999) *1:* 249

Davidson v. Midelfort Clinic, Ltd., 133 F.3d 499, 8 AD Cases 77 (7th Cir. 1998) *16:* 99, 211

Davis
—v. Florida Power & Light Co., 205 F.3d 1301, 10 AD Cases 492 (11th Cir. 2000) *16:* 304
—v. Guardian Life Ins. Co. of Am., 11 AD Cases 550 (E.D. Pa. 2000) *16:* 383
—v. Monroe County Bd. of Educ., 526 U.S. 629 (1999) *14:* 20, 22–24
—v. United States Steel Corp., 539 F. Supp. 839, 54 FEP Cases 203 (E.D. Pa. 1982) *Preface:* 24; *1:* 195
—v. University of N.C., 263 F.3d 95, 12 AD Cases 243 (4th Cir. 2001) *16:* 104, 178
—v. York Int'l., Inc., 2 AD Cases 1810 (D. Md. 1993) *16:* 338

Davis-Durnil v. Village of Carpentersville, 128 F. Supp. 2d 575 (N.D. Ill. 2001) *16:* 634, 635

Davoll v. Webb, 194 F.3d 1116, 9 AD Cases 1533 (10th Cir. 1999) *16:* 174, 346, 439

Deane v. Pocono Med. Ctr., 142 F.3d 138, 7 AD Cases 1809 (3d Cir. 1998) *16:* 272

Deas v. River West, 152 F.3d 471, 8 AD Cases 989 (5th Cir. 1998) *16:* 143

Delaney v. City of Hampton, 999 F. Supp. 794 (E.D. Va.), *aff'd,* 135 F.3d 769 (4th Cir. 1998) *8:* 195

Delli Santi v. CNA Ins. Co., 88 F.3d 192, 71 FEP Cases 143 (3d Cir. 1996) *1:* 146

Den Hartog v. Wasatch Academy, 129 F.3d 1076, 7 AD Cases 764 (10th Cir. 1997) *16:* 449–53

Depaoli v. Abbott Labs., 140 F.3d 668, 7 AD Cases 1828 (7th Cir. 1998) *16:* 266

Despears v. Milwaukee County, 63 F.3d 635, 4 AD Cases 1313 (7th Cir. 1995) *16:* 524

Devine; Doe v., 545 F. Supp. 576 (D.D.C. 1982), *aff'd,* 703 F.2d 1319 (D.C. Cir. 1983) *16:* 526

DeWitt v. Carsten, 941 F. Supp. 1232, 6 AD Cases 1255 (N.D. Ga. 1996) *16:* 19, 438

Diamond (In re Doe); United States v., 964 F.2d 1325 (2d Cir. 1992) *8:* 48

Dias v. Sky Chefs, 919 F.2d 1370, 54 FEP Cases 852 (9th Cir. 1990) *1:* 28, 29, 56

Dillon v. Legg, 68 Cal. 2d 728, 69 Cal. Rptr. 72, 441 P.2d 912 (1968) *1:* 105

Dipol v. New York Transit Auth., 999 F. Supp. 309 (S.D. N.Y. 1999) *16:* 215

District of Columbia; Does v., 962 F. Supp.2d 202, 10 NDLR ¶14 (D.D.C. 1997) *16:* 234, 556

District of Columbia; Doe v., 796 F. Supp. 559, 2 AD Cases 197 (D.D.C. 1992) *16:* 579

Dockter v. Rudolf Wolff Futures, 684 F. Supp. 532, 46 FEP Cases 1129 (N.D. Ill. 1988), *aff'd,* 913 F.2d 456, 53 FEP Cases 1642 (7th Cir. 1990) *1:* 62

Doe, In re, 964 F.2d 1325 (2d Cir. 1992) *8:* 48

Doe v. *See name of other party*

Donahue v. Consolidated Rail Corp., 224 F.3d 226, 10 AD Cases 1505 (3d Cir. 2000) *16:* 669, 674

Doolittle v. Ruffo, 1997 WL 151799 (N.D.N.Y. Mar. 31, 1997) *8:* 33

Doren v. Battle Creek Health Sys., 187 F.3d 595, 9 AD Cases 1115 (6th Cir. 1999) *16:* 195

Douris v. County of Bucks, 2000 WL 1358481 (E.D. Pa. Sept. 21, 2000) *9:* 1, 86

Downs v. Massachusetts Bay Transp. Auth., 13 F. Supp. 2d 130, 8 AD Cases 447 (D. Mass. 1998) *16:* 565

Doyal v. Oklahoma Heart, Inc., 213 F.3d 492, 10 AD Cases 991 (10th Cir. 2000) *16:* 46, 142, 145, 148

Doyle v. Superior Ct., 50 Cal. App. 4th 1878, 58 Cal. Rptr. 2d 476 (1996) *8:* 211; *9:* 57, 60

Drinkwalter v. Shipton, 225 Mont. 380, 732 P.2d 1335, 50 FEP Cases 616 (1987) *1:* 57

Duckett v. Dunlop Tire Corp., 120 F.3d 1222, 7 AD Cases 572 (11th Cir. 1997) *16:* 401

Duda v. Board of Educ., 133 F.3d 1054,

8 AD Cases 99 (7th Cir. 1998) *16:* 22, 23, 253, 612–14
Dufresne v. J.D. Fields & Co., 85 FEP Cases 25 (E.D. La. 2001) *8:* 135
Duncan v. State of Wisconsin Dep't of Health & Family Servs., 166 F.3d 930, 8 AD Cases 1800 (7th Cir. 1999) *16:* 231
Dunegan v. City of Council Grove
—77 F. Supp. 2d 1192 (D. Kan. 1999) *16:* 189
—189 F.R.D. 649 (D. Kan. 1999) *8:* 162, 163
Dupre v. Harris County Hosp., 8 F. Supp. 2d 908 (S.D. Tex. 1998) *16:* 43
Durley v. APAC, Inc., 236 F.3d 651, 84 FEP Cases 1177 (11th Cir. 2000) *1:* 39
Durning v. Duffens Optical, Inc., 1996 WL 67640 (E.D. La. Feb. 14, 1996) *16:* 318
Dutton v. Johnson County Bd. of Comm'rs, 859 F. Supp. 498, 3 AD Cases 808 (D. Kan. 1994) *16:* 338, 418

E

Earl v. Mervyns, Inc., 207 F.3d 1361, 10 AD Cases 673 (11th Cir. 2000) *16:* 297, 298, 382, 419, 420
Eber v. Harris County Hosp. Dist., 130 F. Supp. 2d 847 (S.D. Tex. 2001) *1:* 249
Echazabel v. Chevron USA, Inc., 226 F.3d 1063 (9th Cir. 2000) *16:* 272, 644, 645
Edmond v. Fujitsu-ICL Sys., Inc., 1997 WL 118406 (N.D. Tex. Mar. 5, 1997) *16:* 60, 61
Edwards v. Superior Ct., 16 Cal. 3d 905, 130 Cal. Rptr. 14 (1976) *9:* 95–98
EEOC v. *See name of other party*
Eide v. Kelsey-Hayes Co., 427 N.W.2d 488, 47 FEP Cases 1050 (Mich. 1988) *1:* 98, 101
Ellison v. Brady, 924 F.2d 872, 54 FEP Cases 1346 (9th Cir. 1991) *1:* 176; *8:* 220, 221; *11:* 10; *14:* 16, 119, 120
Elshirbiny v. Hewlett Packard Co., 2001 WL 590034 (N.D. Cal. May 24, 2001) *1:* 249
Emberger v. Deluxe Check Printers, 1997 WL 677149 (E.D. Pa. Oct. 30, 1997) *16:* 246–48
Enriquez v. West Jersey Health, 11 AD Cases 1810 (N.J. Super. Ct. 2001) *16:* 199
Erebia v. Chrysler Plastic Prods. Corp., 772 F.2d 1250, 37 FEP Cases 1820 (6th Cir. 1985) *1:* 129
Erjavac v. Holy Family Health Plus, 13 F. Supp. 2d 737 (N.D. Ill. 1998) *16:* 39
Evans v. Federal Express Corp., 133 F.3d 137, 8 AD Cases 151 (1st Cir. 1998) *16:* 338, 523
Everly v. United Parcel Serv., Inc., 1991 WL 18429 (N.D. Ill. Feb. 5, 1991) *9:* 38, 77, 78
Excel Corp. V. Bosley, 165 F.3d 635, 78 FEP Cases 1844 (8th Cir. 1999) *8:* 142
Exxon Corp.; EEOC v., 203 F.3d 871, 10 AD Cases 225 (5th Cir. 2000) *16:* 656, 669

F

Faragher v. City of Boca Raton, 524 U.S. 775, 77 FEP Cases 14 (1998) *14:* 27
Farpella-Crosby v. Horizon Health Care, 97 F.3d 803, 72 FEP Cases 254 (5th Cir. 1996) *1:* 151
Favors v. Alco Mfg. Co., 186 Ga. App. 480, 367 S.E.2d 328 (1988) *1:* 96
Fedio v. Circuit City Stores, Inc., 1998 WL 966000 (E.D. Pa. Nov. 4, 1998) *8:* 126–28, 138, 198
Fehr v. McLean Packaging Co., 3 AD Cases 798 (E.D. Pa. 1994) *16:* 49
Fenton v. Pritchard Corp., 926 F. Supp. 1437, 7 AD Cases 1109 (D. Kan. 1996) *16:* 223, 227
Ferrell
—v. Glen-Gery Brick, 678 F. Supp. 111, 46 FEP Cases 502 (E.D. Pa. 1987) *8:* 11
—v. Shell Oil Co., 1995 WL 688795 (E.D. La. Nov. 20, 1995) *9:* 73, 74, 82, 104, 140
Fields v. Cummings Employees Fed. Credit Union, 540 N.E.2d 631, 53 FEP Cases 1613 (Ind. Ct. App. 1989) *1:* 62, 111

Finical v. Collections Unlimited, Inc., 65 F. Supp. 2d 1032, 9 AD Cases 1162 (D. Ariz. 1999) *16:* 132

Finley v. Johnson Oil Co., 199 F.R.D. 301, 85 FEP Cases 117 (S.D. Ind. 2001) *8:* 8

Fisher v. San Pedro Peninsula Hosp., 214 Cal. App. 3d 590, 262 Cal. Rptr. 842, 54 FEP Cases 584 (1989) *1:* 30, 31

Fitzgerald v. Mountain States Tel. & Tel. Co., 68 F.3d 1257, 69 FEP Cases 163 (10th Cir. 1995) *1:* 129, 144

Fitzpatrick v. QVC, Inc., 1999 WL 1215577 (E.D. Pa. Dec. 7, 1999) *8:* 182, 183

Fjellestad v. Pizza Hut, 188 F.3d 944, 9 AD Cases 1153 (8th Cir. 1999) *16:* 196, 343, 376, 382

Flavel v. Svedala Indus., Inc., 1994 WL 761447 (E.D. Wis. Oct. 25, 1994) *15:* 71

Fliss v. Movado Group, Inc., 10 AD Cases 1524 (N.D. Ill. 2000) *16:* 350

Flynn v. Raytheon Co., 868 F. Supp. 383, 3 AD Cases 1495 (D. Mass. 1994), *aff'd,* 94 F.3d 640 (1st Cir. 1996) *16:* 445, 517

Foley v. Polaroid Corp., 508 N.E.2d 72, 2 IER Cases 328 (Mass. 1987) *1:* 72

Ford
—v. Contra Costa County, 179 F.R.D. 579, 76 FEP Cases 1849 (N.D. Cal. 1998) *9:* 14
—v. Schering-Plough Corp., 145 F.3d 601, 8 AD Cases 190 (3d Cir. 1998) *16:* 529

Foreman v. Babcock & Wilcox Co.
—113 F.3d 1402, 6 AD Cases 1523 (5th Cir. 1997) *16:* 439
—117 F.3d 800, 7 AD Cases 331 (5th Cir. 1997) *16:* 441

Formosa v. Miami Dade Community College, 990 F. Supp. 1433, 7 AD Cases 1768 (S.D. Fla. 1997) *16:* 39, 279

Forshee v. Waterloo Indus., Inc., 178 F.3d 527 (8th Cir. 1999) *1:* 130, 131

Fox v. Gates Corp., 179 F.R.D. 303 (D. Colo. 1998) *8:* 65; *9:* 25, 26

Francis v. Chemical Banking Corp., 62 F. Supp. 2d 948 (E.D.N.Y. 1999) *16:* 125

Franklin
—v. Consolidated Edison Co. of N.Y., Inc., 1999 WL 796170 (S.D.N.Y. Sept. 30, 1999) *16:* 142
—v. United States Postal Serv., 687 F. Supp. 1214, 1 AD Cases 1312 (S.D. Ohio 1988) *16:* 467, 470

Frazier v. Topeka Metal Specialties, Inc., 2001 WL 138893 (D. Kan. Feb. 15, 2001) *1:* 210, 211

Fredenburg v. Contra Costa County Dep't of Health Serv., 172 F.3d 1176, 9 AD Cases 385 (9th Cir. 1999) *16:* 582

Freeman v. Chicago Park Dist., 189 F.3d 613, 80 FEP Cases 1678 (7th Cir. 1999) *Preface:* 6

Fritsch v. City of Chula Vista
—11 AD Cases 273 (S.D. Cal. 2000) *16:* 590
—196 F.R.D. 562 (S.D. Cal. 1999) *8:* 21, 25

Fritz v. Mascotech Auto. Sys. Group, Inc., 914 F. Supp. 1481, 6 AD Cases 1103 (E.D. Mich. 1996) *16:* 282, 418

Fromm-Vane v. Longwood Med. Ctr., Inc., 995 F. Supp. 1471 (S.D. Fla. 1997) *16:* 23

Frye v. United States, 293 F. 1013 (D.C. Cir. 1923) *15:* 6, 7, 8

Fuller v. Frank, 916 F.2d 558, 1 AD Cases 1701 (9th Cir. 1990) *16:* 464

G

Gaines v. Runyon, 107 F.3d 1171, 6 AD Cases 688 (6th Cir. 1997) *16:* 380

Galieti v. State Mut. Auto. Ins. Co., 154 F.R.D. 262 (D. Colo. 1994) *9:* 107

Gallagher Co.; EEOC v., 181 F.3d 645, 9 AD Cases 917 (5th Cir. 1999) *16:* 206

Galloway; United States v., 937 F.2d 542 (10th Cir. 1991) *8:* 105

Gantt v. Wilson Sporting Goods, 143 F.3d 1042, 8 AD Cases 308 (6th Cir. 1998) *16:* 346, 408

Garcia-Ayala v. Lederle Parenterals, Inc., 212 F.3d 638, 10 AD Cases 865 (1st Cir. 2000) *16:* 283, 401, 408

Gardner v. Morris, 752 F.2d 1271, 1 AD Cases 673 (8th Cir. 1985) *16:* 481

Garvey v. Jefferson Smurfit Corp., 11 AD

Cases 154 (E.D. Pa. 2000) *16:* 113, 115, 116, 264, 310
Garza v. Abbott Labs., 940 F. Supp. 1227, 6 AD Cases 1507 (N.D. Ill. 1996) *16:* 495
Gaston v. Bellingrath Gardens & Home, Inc., 167 F.3d 1361, 8 AD Cases 1862 (11th Cir. 1999) *16:* 256, 346
Gatewood v. Stone Container Corp., 170 F.R.D. 455, 78 FEP Cases 1251 (S.D. Iowa 1996) *8:* 19, 20
Gaul v. AT&T, Inc., 955 F. Supp. 346, 6 AD Cases 705 (D.N.J. 1997), *aff'd sub nom.* Gaul v. Lucent Tech. Inc., 134 F.3d 576, 7 AD Cases 1223 (3d Cir. 1998) *16:* 185, 189, 438
Gavenda v. Orleans County, 174 F.R.D. 272 (W.D.N.Y. 1996) *9:* 107, 111, 119
Gazaway v. Makita USA, Inc., 11 F. Supp. 2d 1281 (S.D.N.Y. 1998) *16:* 43, 181
Gebser v. Lago Vista Ind. Sch. Dist., 524 U.S. 274 (1998) *14:* 21
General Elec. Co. v. Joiner, 522 U.S. 136 (1997) *15:* 14, 54
Gier v. Educational Serv. Unit No. 16, 845 F. Supp. 1342 (D. Neb. 1994), *aff'd,* 66 F.3d 940 (8th Cir. 1995) *15:* 98–100, 117
Giladi v. Strauch, 2001 WL 388052 (S.D.N.Y. Apr. 16, 2001) *9:* 91
Gilardi v. Schroeder, 672 F. Supp. 1043, 45 FEP Cases 283 (N.D. Ill. 1986), *aff'd,* 833 F.2d 1226, 45 FEP Cases 346 (7th Cir. 1987) *1:* 27, 69
Gilday v. Mecosta County, 124 F.3d 760, 7 AD Cases 1268 (6th Cir. 1997) *16:* 120
Gile v. United Airlines, Inc.
—95 F.3d 492, 5 AD Cases 1466 (7th Cir. 1996) *16:* 303, 309, 440
—213 F.3d 365, 10 AD Cases 968 (7th Cir. 2000) *16:* 371
Giron v. Corrections Corp. of Am., 981 F. Supp. 1406 (D.N.M. 1997) *8:* 174, 175, 190, 198, 210
Glowacki v. Buffalo Gen. Hosp., 2 F. Supp. 2d 346 (W.D.N.Y. 1998) *16:* 43, 52
Godby v. Electrolux Corp., 65 FEP Cases 211 (N.D. Ga. 1994) *1:* 100
Goebel v. Denver & Rio Grande W. R.R. Co., 215 F.3d 1083 (10th Cir. 2000) *15:* 53
Goins v. West Group, 619 N.W. 424 (Minn. Ct. App. 2000) *16:* 199
Gonzagowski v. Widnall, 115 F.3d 744, 6 AD Cases 1559 (10th Cir. 1997) *16:* 437, 490
Gonzales
—v. Garner Food Servs., 89 F.3d 1523, 5 AD Cases 1202 (11th Cir. 1996) *16:* 528
—v. National Bd. Med. Exam'rs, 225 F.3d 620, 10 AD Cases 1575 (6th Cir. 2000) *16:* 46, 90
—v. Sandoval County, 2 F. Supp. 2d 1442, 8 AD Cases 1337 (D.N.M. 1998) *16:* 591
Goodwin-Haulmark v. Menninger Clinic, Inc., 76 F. Supp. 2d 1235, 5 WH Cases 2d 1548 (D. Kan. 1999) *16:* 58
Gordon v. E.L. Hamm & Assocs., Inc., 100 F.3d 907, 6 AD Cases 282 (11th Cir. 1996) *16:* 220
Gray v. Sears, Roebuck & Co., 131 F. Supp. 2d 895 (N.D. Tex. 2001) *1:* 40, 41
Green v. George L. Smith II World Cong. Ctr. Auth., 987 F. Supp. 1481, 7 AD Cases 1419 (N.D. Ga. 1997) *16:* 445
Greenberg
—v. New York State, 919 F. Supp. 637, 5 AD Cases 1851 (E.D.N.Y. 1996) *16:* 233
—v. New York State Dep't of Correctional Servs., 919 F. Supp. 637, 5 AD Cases 1851 (E.D.N.Y. 1996) *16:* 27
Greer v. Emerson Elec. Co., 185 F.3d 917, 9 AD Cases 1100 (8th Cir. 1999) *16:* 279
Grenier v. Cyanamid Plastics, Inc., 70 F.3d 667, 5 AD Cases 75 (1st Cir. 1995) *16:* 312, 541–44, 555
Griffin v. Steeltek, Inc., 160 F.3d 591, 8 AD Cases 1249 (10th Cir. 1999) *16:* 532
Grinstead v. Pool Co. of Texas, 3 AD Cases 9 (E.D. La. 1994), *aff'd,* 26 F.3d 1118, 4 AD Cases 160 (5th Cir. 1994) *16:* 207
Gruenberg v. Aetna Ins. Co., 9 Cal. 3d 566, 108 Cal. Rptr. 480, 510 P.2d 1032 (1973) *1:* 104

GTE Southwest v. Bruce, 998 S.W.2d 605 (Tex. 1999) *1:* 40
Guice-Mills v. Derwinski
—967 F. 2d 794, 2 AD Cases 187 (2d Cir. 1992) *16:* 295, 299
—772 F. Supp. 188, 1 AD Cases 1886 (S.D.N.Y. 1991) *16:* 418, 421
Gunby v. Pennsylvania Elec. Co., 840 F.2d 1108, 45 FEP Cases 1818 (3d Cir. 1995) *1:* 129
Gutridge v. Clure, 153 F.3d 898, 8 AD Cases 705 (8th Cir. 1998) *16:* 206

H

Hadley v. VAMPTS, 44 F.3d 372, 67 FEP Cases 186 (5th Cir. 1995) *1:* 32, 33
Haensel v. Chrysler Corp., 1997 WL 537995 (E.D. La. Aug. 25, 1997) *9:* 104, 107
Haiman v. Village of Fox Lake, 79 F. Supp. 2d 949, 10 AD Cases 57 (N.D. Ill. 2000) *16:* 215
Hallquist v. Mak Fish Plumbing & Heating Co., 46 FEP Cases 1855 (D. Mass. 1987), *aff'd*, 843 F.2d 18, 47 FEP Cases 323 (1st Cir. 1988) *1:* 61
Hamilton v. Southwestern Bell Tel. Co., 136 F.3d 1047, 8 AD Cases 1219 (5th Cir. 1998) *16:* 43, 52, 180, 458
Hamlin v. Township of Flint, 165 F.3d 426, 8 AD Cases 1688 (6th Cir. 1999) *16:* 268, 667
Hamm v. Runyon, 51 F.3d 721, 4 AD Cases 357 (7th Cir. 1995) *16:* 235
Hammon v. DHL Airways, Inc., 980 F. Supp. 919, 7 AD Cases 900 (S.D. Ohio 1997), *aff'd,* 165 F.3d 441, 8 AD Cases 1707 (6th Cir. 1999) *16:* 347, 350, 357
Handley v. Phillips, 715 F. Supp. 657, 52 FEP Cases 195 (M.D. Pa. 1989) *1:* 56, 98
Hankins v. Gap, Inc., 84 F.3d 797, 5 AD Cases 924 (6th Cir. 1996) *16:* 379
Hanna v. Santa Rosa Mem'l Hosp., 1997 WL 446231 (N.D. Cal. July 29, 1997) *16:* 221
Hardy
—v. ESSROC Materials, Inc., 1998 WL 103306 (E.D. Pa. Feb. 18, 1998) *9:* 22

—v. Sears, Roebuck & Co., 1996 WL 735565 (N.D. Ga. Aug. 28, 1996) *16:* 470
Harris
—v. Forklift Sys., Inc., 510 U.S. 17, 114 S. Ct. 367, 63 FEP Cases 225 (1993) *1:* 5, 242, 243; *8:* 218, 219, 228; *14:* 18
—v. Harris & Hart, Inc., 206 F.3d 838, 10 AD Cases 481 (9th Cir. 2000) *16:* 545–47
Harrison v. Edison Bros. Apparel Stores, 724 F. Supp. 1185 (M.D.N.C. 1989) *1:* 59, 108
Hart v. National Mortgage & Land Co., 189 Cal. App. 3d 1420, 235 Cal. Rptr. 68 (1987) *1:* 108
Hartman v. City of Petaluma, 841 F. Supp. 946, 2 AD Cases 1860 (N.D. Cal. 1994) *16:* 500
Haschmann v. Time Warner Entertainment Co., 151 F.3d 591, 8 AD Cases 692 (7th Cir. 1998) *16:* 283, 400
Hatfield v. Quantum Chem. Corp., 920 F. Supp. 108, 5 AD Cases 765 (S.D. Tex. 1996) *16:* 181, 189
Hawkins v. Trustees of Ind. Univ., 83 F. Supp. 2d 987, 10 AD Cases 819 (S.D. Ind. 1999) *16:* 142, 181
Haw-Len v. F.W. Woolworth Co., 737 F. Supp. 1104, 1106-08 (D. Haw. 1990) *1:* 59
Hearn v. General Elec. Co., 927 F. Supp. 1486, 71 FEP Cases 435 (M.D. Ala. 1996) *1:* 152
Hein
—v. All American Plywood, 232 F.3d 482, 11 AD Cases 308 (6th Cir. 2000) *16:* 132
—v. Merck & Co., 868 F. Supp. 230 (M.D. Tenn. 1994) *1:* 160, 173
Heise v. Genuine Parts Co., 900 F. Supp. 1137, 4 AD Cases 1551 (D. Minn. 1995) *16:* 418
Hendricks-Robinson v. Excel Corp., 154 F.3d 685, 8 AD Cases 875 (7th Cir. 1998) *16:* 350
Hendry v. GTE, North, Inc., 896 F. Supp. 816, 6 AD Cases 451 (N.D. Ind. 1995) *16:* 418
Hennenfant v. Mid Dakota Clinic, 164 F.3d 419, 8 AD Cases 1537 (8th Cir. 1998) *16:* 383

Henson v. City of Dundee, 682 F.2d 897, 29 FEP Cases 787 (11th Cir. 1982) *8:* 93, 117, 234; *14:* 123

Herchenroeder v. Johns Hopkins Univ., 171 F.R.D. 179 (D. Md. 1997) *8:* 131–33, 173

Hernandez v. Prudential Ins. Co., 977 F. Supp. 1160 (M.D. Fla. 1997) *16:* 135

Herring; People v., 20 Cal. App. 4th 1066, 25 Cal. Rptr. 2d 213 (1993) *8:* 211

Hertenstein v. Kimberly Home Health Care, Inc., 80 FEP Cases 355 (D. Kan. 1999) *9:* 110, 143, 144

Hertz Corp.; EEOC v., 7 AD Cases 1097 (E.D. Mich. 1998) *16:* 471

Hetzel v. County of Prince William, 89 F.3d 169, 71 FEP Cases 520 (4th Cir. 1996) *1:* 143

Heyman v. Queens Village Comm. for Mental Health, 198 F.3d 68, 110 AD Cases 27 (2d Cir. 1999) *16:* 174

Hill
—v. Florida Dep't of Pub. Health, 2 AD Cases 177 (M.D. Fla. 1992) *16:* 475
—v. Kansas City Area Transp. Auth., 181 F.3d 891, 9 AD Cases 833 (8th Cir. 1999) *16:* 445
—v. Metropolitan Rapid Transit Auth., 77 F. Supp. 2d 1291 (N.D. Ga. 1998) *16:* 39
—v. Spiegel, Inc., 708 F.2d 233, 31 FEP Cases 1532 (6th Cir. 1983) *1:* 18

Hiller v. Runyon, 95 F. Supp. 2d 1016 (S.D. Iowa 2000) *16:* 135

Hilt v. SFC Inc., 170 F.R.D. 182 (D. Kan. 1997) *8:* 90, 91

Hinnershitz v. Ortep of Pa., Inc., 1998 WL 962096 (E.D. Pa. 1998) *16:* 621–29

Hirschheimer v. Associated Minerals & Minerals Corp., 1995 WL 736901 (S.D.N.Y. Dec. 12, 1995) *9:* 38, 65, 80, 81, 104, 109, 114, 160, 163, 164, 172, 173

Hlinko v. Virgin Atlantic Airways, 1997 WL 68560 (S.D.N.Y. Feb. 19, 1997) *9:* 107

Hoeller v. Eaton Corp., 149 F.3d 621, 8 AD Cases 537 (7th Cir. 1998) *16:* 37

Hogan
—v. Bangor & Aroostook R. Co., 61 F.3d 1034, 4 AD Cases 1251 (1st Cir. 1995) *1:* 8

—v. Forsyth Country Club Co., 79 N.C. App. 483, 340 S.E.2d 116, *review denied,* 317 N.C. 334, 346 S.E.2d 141 (1986) *1:* 113

Hogarth v. Thornburgh, 833 F. Supp. 1077, 2 AD Cases 1777 (S.D.N.Y. 1993) *16:* 325, 482

Holiday v. Chattanooga, 206 F.3d 637, 10 AD Cases 501 (6th Cir. 2000) *16:* 254, 277, 577–79, 682

Holien v. Sears, Roebuck & Co., 298 Or. 76, 689 P.2d 1292, 36 FEP Cases 137 (1984) *1:* 56

Holihan v. Lucky Stores, Inc., 87 F.3d 362, 5 AD Cases 1068 (9th Cir. 1996) *16:* 224

Holt
—v. Northeast Pa. Training P'ship Consortium, Inc., 694 A.2d 1134 (Pa. Commw. Ct. 1997) *16:* 199
—v. Welch Allyn, Inc.
——3 WH Cases 2d 1622 (N.D.N.Y. 1997) *8:* 150, 151, 167–69
——2000 WL 98118 (N.D.N.Y. Jan. 11, 2000) *8:* 130

Horwitz v. L. & J.G. Stickley, Inc., 122 F. Supp. 2d 350 (N.D.N.Y. 2000) *16:* 104

Hoskins v. Oakland County Sheriff's Dep't, 44 F. Supp. 2d 882 (E.D. Mich. 1999) *16:* 125

Howard v. Historic Tours of Am., 177 F.R.D. 48 (D.D.C. 1997) *8:* 148, 149

Howard Univ. v. Best, 484 A.2d 958, 36 FEP Cases 482 (D.C. App. 1984) *1:* 28

Hrabak v. Marquip, Inc., 58 FEP Cases 908 (W.D. Wis. 1992) *1:* 132

Huber v. Howard County, 849 F. Supp. 407, 3 AD Cases 262 (D. Md. 1994) *16:* 669

Hucko v. City of Oak Forest, 185 F.R.D. 526 (N.D. Ill. 1999) *8:* 70

Hudson v. MCI Telecommunications Corp., 87 F.3d 1167, 5 AD Cases 1099 (10th Cir. 1996) *16:* 398

Huff v. UARCO, Inc., 122 F.3d 374, 74 FEP Cases 879 (7th Cir. 1997) *16:* 237

Humiston-Keeling Inc.; EEOC v., 227 F.3d 1024, 10 AD Cases 1665 (7th Cir. 2000) *16:* 441

Humphrey v. Memorial Hosp. Ass'n, 239 F.3d 1128, 11 AD Cases 765 (9th Cir. 2001)   *5:* 8; *16:* 150, 163, 164, 293, 300, 433, 459–61
Hunt-Golliday v. Metropolitan Water Reclamation Dist., 104 F.3d 1004, 6 AD Cases 725 (7th Cir. 1997)   *16:* 351
Hurley v. Atlantic City Police Dep't, 933 F. Supp. 396, 72 FEP Cases 1828 (D.N.J. 1996)   *1:* 189, 190; *8:* 190; *9:* 63
Hypes v. First Commerce Corp., 134 F.3d 721, 7 AD Cases 1546 (5th Cir. 1998)   *16:* 279, 432

I

In re. *See name of party*
Isely v. Capuchin Province, 877 F. Supp. 1055 (E.D. Mich. 1995)   *10:* 2; *15:* 61–63, 77, 99, 116

J

Jackan v. New York State Dep't of Labor, 205 F.3d 562, 10 AD Cases 497 (2d Cir. 2000)   *16:* 439
Jackson
—v. Bayou Indus., 1995 WL 143538 (E.D. La. Mar. 29, 1995)   *15:* 66, 67
—v. Chubb Corp., 193 F.R.D. 216 (D.N.J. 2000)   *8:* 43–46, 70
—v. Entergy Operations, Inc., 76 FEP Cases 85 (E.D. La. 1998)   *9:* 152, 153
Jacobsen v. Tillmann, 17 F. Supp. 2d 1018, 8 AD Cases 913 (D. Minn. 1998)   *16:* 329
Jacques v. Clean-Up Group, Inc., 96 F.3d 506, 5 AD Cases 1594 (1st Cir. 1996)   *16:* 382, 415, 418
Jaffee v. Redmond, 518 U.S. 1 (1996)   ***Preface:*** 21, 22; *8:* 4–6, 9
James v. James River Paper Co., 1995 WL 938383 (D. Or. Apr. 6, 1995), *aff'd,* 101 F.3d 705 (9th Cir. 1996)   *16:* 458
Janopoulos v. Harvey L. Walner & Assocs., 1995 WL 107170 (N.D. Ill. Mar. 7, 1995)   *8:* 112
Jansen v. Packaging Corp. of Am., 158 F.R.D. 409, 66 FEP Cases 556 (N.D. Ill. 1994)   *9:* 14, 65, 76, 80
Jaqua v. Furr's/Bishop's Cafeterias, L.P., 175 F.R.D. 688, 75 FEP Cases 737 (D. Kan. 1997)   *9:* 154
Jarchow v. Transamerica Title Ins. Co., 48 Cal. App. 3d 917, 122 Cal. Rptr. 470 (1975)   *1:* 104
Jefferson v. Ingersoll Int'l Inc., 195 F.3d 894, 81 FEP Cases 170 (7th Cir. 1999)   *1:* 236
Jeffrys v. LRP Publications, Inc., 1999 WL 79058 (E.D. Pa. Feb. 16, 1999)   *9:* 1
Jenson v. Eveleth Taconite Co., 130 F.3d 1287, 75 FEP Cases 852 (8th Cir. 1997)   *1:* 122–24, 183–85, 237; *8:* 179; *9:* 62, 63
Jensvold v. Shalala, 925 F. Supp. 1109, 70 FEP Cases 788 (D. Md. 1996)   *1:* 215, 216
Jerina v. Richardson Auto., 960 F. Supp. 106 (N.D. Tex. 1997)   *16:* 41
Johnson
—v. Boardman Petroleum, Inc., 923 F. Supp. 1563, 5 AD Cases 983 (S.D. Ga. 1996)   *16:* 16, 228, 229
—v. Foulds, Inc., 5 AD Cases 1635 (N.D. Ill. 1996)   *16:* 396
—v. Georgia Highway Express, Inc., 417 F.2d 1122 (5th Cir. 1969)   *1:* 220
—v. Morrison, Inc., 849 F. Supp. 777, 3 AD Cases 259 (N.D. Ala. 1994)   *16:* 323
—v. New York Med. College, 1997 WL 580708 (S.D.N.Y. Sept. 18, 1997)   *16:* 39, 126
—v. Railway Express Agency, Inc., 421 U.S. 454, 10 FEP Cases 817 (1975)   *1:* 15
Johnston v. Long, 30 Cal. 2d 54, 181 P.2d 645 (1947)   *1:* 139
Jones
—v. American Postal Workers Union Nat'l, 192 F.3d 417, 9 AD Cases 1249 (4th Cir. 1999)   *16:* 458
—v. Men's Wearhouse, 1999 WL 134210 (N.D. Tex. Mar. 10, 1999)   *16:* 237
Jovanovic v. In-Sink-Erator, 201 F.3d 894, 10 AD Cases 193 (7th Cir. 2000)   *16:* 279

Judd v. Rodman, 105 F.3d 1339 (11th Cir. 1997) *8:* 109, 110, 111

Judice v. Hospital Serv. Dist. No. 1, 919 F. Supp. 978, 7 AD Cases 825 (E.D. La. 1996) *16:* 603–5, 619

K

Karcher v. Emerson Elec. Co., 94 F.3d 502, 71 FEP Cases 1651 (8th Cir. 1996) *1:* 134; *9:* 63

Karibian v. Columbia Univ., 930 F. Supp. 134, 71 FEP Cases 325 (S.D.N.Y. 1996) *15:* 70, 72

Karlin v. Foust, 975 F. Supp. 1177 (W.D. Wis. 1997) *15:* 67

Katz v. City Metal Co., 87 F.3d 26, 5 AD Cases 1120 (1st Cir. 1996) *16:* 330

Kees v. Wallerstein, 161 F.3d 1196, 8 AD Cases 1629 (9th Cir. 1998) *16:* 276

Kellogg v. Union Pac. R.R. Co., 2000 WL 766281 (D. Neb. Jan. 28, 2000) *16:* 195

Kelly v. Drexel Univ., 94 F.3d 102, 5 AD Cases 1353 (3d Cir. 1996) *16:* 235

Kelly-Zurian v. Wohl Shoe Co., 22 Cal. App. 4th 397, 27 Cal. Rptr. 2d 457, 64 FEP Cases 603 (1994) *1:* 151

Kemer v. Johnson, 900 F. Supp. 677, 4 AD Cases 1832 (S.D.N.Y. 1995), *aff'd,* 101 F.3d 683, 5 AD Cases 1536 (2d Cir. 1996) *16:* 250

Kennedy
—v. Applause, Inc., 3 AD Cases 1734 (C.D. Cal. 1994), *aff'd,* 90 F.3d 1477, 5 AD Cases 1249 (9th Cir. 1996) *16:* 418
—v. Dresser Rand Co., 193 F.3d 120, 9 AD Cases 1335 (2d Cir. 1999) *16:* 339, 438

Kent v. Derwinski, 790 F. Supp. 1032, 2 AD Cases 947 (E.D. Wash. 1991) *16:* 491–93

Kersul v. Skulls Angels, 130 Misc. 2d 345, 495 N.Y.S.2d 886, 42 FEP Cases 987 (Sup. Ct. 1985) *1:* 85

Keys v. U.S. Welding, Fabrication & Mfg., Inc., 59 FEP Cases 1537 (N.D. Ohio 1992) *1:* 152

Kidder, Peabody & Co.; EEOC v., 62 FEP Cases 899 (S.D.N.Y. 1993) *8:* 11

Kimzey v. Wal-Mart Stores, Inc., 107 F.3d 568, 73 FEP Cases 87 (8th Cir. 1997) *1:* 10

King v. Board of Regents, 898 F.2d 533, 52 FEP Cases 809 (7th Cir. 1990) *1:* 16

Kinney Shoe Corp.; EEOC v., 917 F. Supp. 419, 5 AD Cases 506 (W.D. Va. 1996), *aff'd sub nom.* Martinson v. Kinney Shoe Corp., 104 F.3d 683, 6 AD Cases 434 (4th Cir. 1997) *16:* 264, 667

Kiphart v. Saturn Corp., 74 F. Supp. 2d 769, 9 AD Cases 1650 (M.D. Tenn. 1999), *rev'd,* 251 F.3d 573, 11 AD Cases 1473 (6th Cir. 2001) *16:* 104, 142

Kirchner v. Mitsui & Co., 184 F.R.D. 124 (M.D. Tenn. 1998) *8:* 35

Klein v. Florida Dep't of Family Affairs & Child Servs., 34 F. Supp. 2d 1367 (S.D. Fla. 1998) *16:* 37

Knapp v. Northwestern Univ., 101 F.3d 473 (7th Cir. 1996) *16:* 684

Knoettgen v. Superior Ct., 224 Cal. App. 3d 11, 273 Cal. Rptr. 636 (1990) *8:* 196; *9:* 120

Kohn Nast & Graf C.C.; Doe v., 866 F. Supp. 190, 3 AD Cases 1322 (E.D. Pa. 1994) *16:* 592

Kolpas v. G.D. Searle & Co., 959 F. Supp. 525, 8 AD Cases 1285 (N.D. Ill. 1997) *16:* 195, 303

Kotlowski v. Eastman Kodak Co., 922 F. Supp. 790, 6 AD Cases 609 (W.D.N.Y. 1996) *16:* 280, 281, 295

Kralik v. Durbin, 130 F.3d 76, 7 AD Cases 1040 (3d Cir. 1997) *16:* 166

Kravel v. Iowa Methodist Med. Ctr., 95 F.3d 674, 5 AD Cases 1503 (8th Cir. 1996) *16:* 154

Kresko v. Rulli, 432 N.W.2d 764 (Minn. Ct. App. 1988) *1:* 108; *9:* 47, 82

Krocka
—v. Bransfield, 969 F. Supp. 1073, 8 AD Cases 707 (N.D. Ill. 1997), *aff'd,* 203 F.3d 507, 10 AD Cases 289 (7th Cir. 2000) *16:* 113, 582
—v. Chicago, 203 F.3d 507, 10 AD Cases 289 (7th Cir. 2000) *16:* 77, 223, 244, 245

Kumho Tire Co. v. Carmichael, 526 U.S. 137 (1999) *Preface:* 13; *15:* 4, 31, 38, 39, 41–43
Kurncz v. Honda N. Am., Inc., 166 F.R.D. 386 (W.D. Mich. 1996) *1:* 154, 159
Kvintus v. R.L. Polk & Co., 3 F. Supp. 2d 788 (E.D. Mich. 1998) *16:* 140, 237
Kvorjak v. State of Maine, 259 F.3d 48, 12 AD Cases 160 (1st Cir. 2001) *16:* 432

L

Lachance v. Duffy's Draft House, Inc., 146 F.3d 832, 8 AD Cases 652 (11th Cir 1998) *16:* 657
Lahr v. Fulbright & Jaworski, L.L.P., 164 F.R.D. 204 (N.D. Tex. 1996) *9:* 15, 20, 27, 28, 38–42, 77, 78, 107, 157
Lanci v. Arthur Andersen, 10 AD Cases 1004 (S.D.N.Y. 2000) *16:* 44, 61
Lang v. Kohl's Food Stores, Inc., 217 F.3d 919 (7th Cir. 2000) *15:* 45–47
Langford v. County of Cook, 965 F. Supp. 1091 (N.D. Ill. 1997) *16:* 189
Langon v. Department of Health & Human Servs., 959 F.2d 1053, 2 AD Cases 152 (D.C. Cir. 1992) *16:* 431, 432
Lanni v. New Jersey, 177 F.R.D. 295 (D.N.J. 1998) *1:* 204, 205
Lanning v. Southeastern Pa. Transp. Auth., 1997 WL 597905 (E.D. Pa. Sept. 17, 1997) *8:* 14–16
Large v. Our Lady of Mercy Med. Ctr., 76 FEP Cases 1054 (S.D.N.Y. 1998) *9:* 14
Larkins v. CIBA Vision Corp., 858 F. Supp. 1572, 3 AD Cases 715 (N.D. Ga. 1994) *16:* 324, 476
Lassiter v. Reno, 885 F. Supp. 869, 4 AD Cases 609 (E.D. Va. 1995), *aff'd,* 86 F.3d 1151, 5 AD Cases 1343 (4th Cir. 1996) *16:* 250, 325, 648
Laurin v. Providence Hosp., 150 F.3d 52, 8 AD Cases 768 (1st Cir. 1998) *16:* 306, 307, 414, 418, 440
Law v. Garden State Tanning, 2001 WL 322550 (E.D. Pa. Feb. 12, 2001) *16:* 590
Lawson v. CSX Transp., Inc., 245 F.3d 916, 10 AD Cases 832 (7th Cir. 2001) *16:* 86
Layser v. Morrison, 935 F. Supp. 562, 6 AD Cases 1295 (E.D. Pa. 1995) *16:* 675, 676
Leatherwood v. Houston Post Co., 59 F.3d 533, 4 AD Cases 1091 (5th Cir. 1995) *16:* 279
LeFave v. Symbios, Inc., 2000 WL 1644154 (D. Colo. Apr. 14, 2000) *8:* 75, 76; *9:* 37
Legrand v. New York City Transit Auth., 83 FEP Cases 1817 (E.D.N.Y. 1999) *1:* 230, 231
Leisen v. Shelbyville, 968 F. Supp. 409 (S.D. Ind. 1997), *aff'd,* 153 F.3d 805, 8 AD Cases 892 (7th Cir. 1998) *16:* 26, 149
Lemire v. Silva, 104 F. Supp. 2d 80, 11 AD Cases 141 (D. Mass. 2000) *16:* 77, 113, 117–19, 152, 167–69, 184
Lenkar v. Methodist Hosp., 210 F.3d 792, 10 AD Cases 782 (7th Cir. 2000) *16:* 276
Lent v. Goldman Sachs & Co., 1998 WL 915906 (S.D.N.Y. Dec. 30, 1998) *16:* 592
Lewis
—v. Alfa Laval Separation, Inc., 714 N.E.2d 426 (Ohio App. 1999) *1:* 164
—v. K-Mart, 180 F.3d 166, 9 AD Cases 791 (4th Cir. 1999) *16:* 529
—v. Zilog. Inc., 908 F. Supp. 931, 4 AD Cases 1787 (N.D. Ga. 1995) *16:* 338
Lifschutz, In re, 2 Cal. 3d 415, 85 Cal. Rptr. 829 (1970) *8:* 24
Lightfoot v. Union Carbide Corp., 901 F. Supp. 166, 71 FEP Cases 269 (S.D.N.Y. 1995) *1:* 146
Lippman v. Sholom Home, Inc., 945 F. Supp. 188, 6 AD Cases 1389 (D. Minn. 1996) *16:* 223
Lipsett v. University of Puerto Rico, 740 F. Supp. 921 (D.P.R. 1990) *15:* 73, 74
Little v. Edgington, 53 FEP Cases 1061 (D. Or. 1990) *9:* 47, 89
Livitsanos v. Superior Ct., 2 Cal. 4th 744, 7 Cal. Rptr. 2d 808, 7 IER Cases 745 (1992) *1:* 50
Loulseqed v. Akzo Nobel, Inc., 178 F.3d 731, 9 AD Cases 783 (5th Cir. 1999) *16:* 382
Lowe v. Philadelphia Newspapers, Inc.
—594 F. Supp. 123, 54 FEP Cases 167

(E.D. Pa. 1984) *Preface:* 23, 24; *1:* 194, 195; *12:* 7, 8
—101 F.R.D. 296, 44 FEP Cases 1224 (E.D. Pa. 1983) *8:* 16, 91; *9:* 68, 82, 104, 108, 114
Lucas v. Brown & Root, Inc., 736 F.2d 1202, 35 FEP Cases 1855 (8th Cir. 1984) *1:* 28, 58
Luciano v. Olsten Corp., 912 F. Supp. 663, 73 FEP Cases 221 (E.D.N.Y. 1996) *1:* 152
Lusk v. Christ Hosp. & Med. Ctr., 2000 WL 263975 (N.D. Ill. Mar. 6, 2000) *16:* 181
Lussier v. Runyon, 1994 WL 129776, 3 AD Cases 223 (D. Me. 1994) *1:* 152

M

Mackie v. Runyon, 804 F. Supp. 1508, 2 AD Cases 260 (M.D. Fla. 1992) *16:* 178, 194, 259
Macsenti v. Becker, 237 F.3d 1223 (10th Cir. 2001) *15:* 51–53
Maddox v. University of Tenn., 62 F.3d 843, 4 AD Cases 1253 (6th Cir. 1995) *16:* 524
Magee v. Paul Revere Life Ins. Co., 178 F.R.D. 33 (E.D.N.Y. 1998) *7:* 4
Malik v. Carrier Corp., 202 F.3d 97, 81 FEP Cases 1275 (2d Cir. 2000) *1:* 51–53
Mancini v. General Elec. Co., 820 F. Supp. 141, 2 AD Cases 764 (D. Vt. 1993) *16:* 313, 314
Mancuso v. Consolidated Edison Co. of N.Y., 967 F. Supp. 1437 (S.D.N.Y. 1997) *15:* 89, 92, 115
Mantolete v. Bolger, 767 F.2d 1416, 1 AD Cases 811 (9th Cir. 1985) *16:* 645
Marcum v. Consolidated Freightways, 48 F. Supp. 2d 721, 9 AD Cases 1494 (N.D. Ohio 1999) *16:* 142
Margeson v. Springfield Terminal Ry. Co., 2 AD Cases 1240 (D. Mass. 1993) *16:* 242, 243
Marschand v. Norfolk & W. Ry. Co., 876 F. Supp. 1528, 4 AD Cases 1099 (N.D. Ind. 1995), *aff'd,* 81 F.3d 714, 5 AD Cases 1184 (7th Cir. 1996) *16:* 187, 221
Martin v.
—Barnesville Exempted Village, 35 F. Supp. 2d 1038, 9 AD Cases 46 (S.D. Ohio 1999) *16:* 38
—General Mills, Inc., 1996 WL 648721 (N.D. Ill. Nov. 5, 1996) *16:* 181, 185
Martinez v. Bally's La., Inc., 244 F.3d 474, 85 FEP Cases 537 (5th Cir. 2001) *8:* 88
Martinson v. Kinney Shoe Corp. *See* EEOC v.; Kinney Shoe Corp.
Mastio v. Wausau Serv. Corp., 948 F. Supp. 1396 (E.D. Mo. 1996) *16:* 43, 210
Matzo v. Postmaster General, 685 F. Supp. 260, 1 AD Cases 1137 (D.D.C. 1987), *aff'd,* 861 F.2d 1290, 1 AD Cases 1399 (D.C. Cir. 1988) *16:* 279
Maurio v. Borgess Med. Ctr., 886 F. Supp. 1349, 4 AD Cases 737 (W.D. Mich. 1995) *16:* 264
Maynard v. Pneumatic Prods., 233 F.3d 1344, 11 AD Cases 295 (11th Cir. 2000), *vacated,* 256 F.3d 1259, 11 AD Cases 1790 (11th Cir. 2001) *16:* 46, 48
Mazzarolla v. United States Postal Serv., 849 F. Supp. 89 (D. Mass. 1994) *16:* 648
McAlindin v. County of San Diego, 192 F.3d 1226, 9 AD Cases 1217, 10 AD Cases 252 (9th Cir. 1999) *11:* 13; *16:* 77, 108–12, 123, 124, 137
McClam v. Norfolk Police Dep't, 877 F. Supp. 277, 71 FEP Cases 757 (E.D. Va. 1995) *1:* 153
McCleland v. Montgomery Ward & Co., 1995 WL 571324 (N.D. Ill. Sept. 25, 1995) *8:* 191–94
McDaniel
—v. Allied Signal, Inc., 896 F. Supp. 1482, 4 AD Cases 1471 (W.D. Mo. 1995) *16:* 252, 325
—v. Mississippi Baptist Med. Ctr., 877 F. Supp. 321, 4 AD Cases 241 (S.D. Miss. 1998), *aff'd,* 74 F.3d 1238, 6 AD Cases 800 (6th Cir. 1995) *16:* 504, 509, 510
McGinnis v. Wonder Chem. Co., 5 AD Cases 219 (E.D. Pa. 1995) *16:* 350
McGuire v. Santa Fe, 954 F. Supp. 230 (D.N.M. 1996) *1:* 168–72; *15:* 118, 119

McInnis v. Alamo Community College Dist., 207 F.3d 276, 10 AD Cases 597 (5th Cir. 2000) *16:* 215, 235

McIntosh v. Irving Trust Co., 887 F. Supp. 662, 74 FEP Cases 99 (S.D.N.Y. 1995) *1:* 146

McKay v. Toyota Motor Mfg. USA, 110 F.3d 369, 6 AD Cases 933 (6th Cir. 1997) *16:* 180

McKenna v. Cruz, 1998 WL 809533 (S.D.N.Y. Nov. 19, 1998) *8:* 77, 78

McKenzie v. Davala, 242 F.3d 967, 11 AD Cases 936 (10th Cir. 2001) *16:* 217

McKey v. Occidental Chem. Corp., 956 F. Supp. 1313, 6 AD Cases 883 (S.D. Tex. 1997) *16:* 465, 466

McKinnon v. Kwong Wah Restaurant, 83 F.3d 498, 70 FEP Cases 1037 (1st Cir. 1996) *1:* 151, 186–88; *8:* 190

McNeil
—In re Marriage of, 160 Cal. App. 3d 548, 206 Cal. Rptr. 641 (1984) *1:* 89
—v. Time Ins. Co., 205 F.3d 179, 10 AD Cases 415 (5th Cir. 2000) *16:* 529

McNight v. Circuit City Stores, Inc., 73 FEP Cases 841 (E.D. Va. 1997) *1:* 153

Mears v. Gulfstream Aerospace Corp., 905 F. Supp. 1075, 5 AD Cases 1295 (S.D. Ga. 1995) *16:* 279, 438

Mendez v. Gearon, 956 F. Supp. 1520, 8 AD Cases 1181 (N.D. Cal. 1997) *16:* 660

Mercado v. Ahmed, 974 F.2d 863 (7th Cir. 1992) *1:* 161

Meritor Sav. Bank v. Vinson, 477 U.S. 57, 40 FEP Cases 1822 (1986) *1:* 5; *8:* 93, 99, 116, 118, 120, 233; *11:* 11; *14:* 14, 122

Midland, City of v. O'Bryant, 18 S.W.3d 209 (Tex. 2000) *1:* 41

Miller
—v. Aluminum Co. of Am., 679 F. Supp. 495, 45 FEP Cases 1775 (W.D. Pa. 1988), *aff'd,* 856 F.2d 184, 52 FEP Cases 1472 (3d Cir. 1988) *1:* 24, 48
—v. Champaign Community Unit Sch. Dist. No. 4, 983 F. Supp. 1201, 8 AD Cases 1142 (C.D. Ill. 1997) *16:* 595, 606
—v. Illinois Dep't of Corrections, 107 F.3d 483, 6 AD Cases 678 (7th Cir. 1997) *16:* 368, 369
—v. National Cas. Co., 61 F.3d 627, 4 AD Cases 1089 (8th Cir. 1995) *16:* 19, 358–61
—v. Springfield, City of, 146 F.3d 612, 8 AD Cases 321 (8th Cir. 1998) *16:* 221, 241, 574–76

Milton v. Scrivner, 53 F.3d 1118, 4 AD Cases 432 (0th Cir. 1995) *16:* 257

Miners v. Cargill Communications, Inc., 113 F.3d 820, 6 AD Cases 1229 (5th Cir. 1997) *16:* 225, 517

Miranda
—v. Mount Sinai Sch. of Med., 68 FEP Cases 546 (S.D.N.Y. 1995) *8:* 17, 18
—v. Wisconsin Power & Light Co., 91 F.3d 1011, 5 AD Cases 1856 (7th Cir. 1996) *16:* 586

Mister v. Illinois Cent. Gulf R.R., 790 F. Supp. 1411, 61 FEP Cases 1391 (S.D. Ill. 1992) *1:* 166, 167

Mistrella v. Volusia County Dep't of Corrs., 61 F. Supp. 2d 1255 (M.D. Fla. 1999) *16:* 41

Mitchell v. Washington Cent. Sch. Dist., 190 F.3d 1, 9 AD Cases 1123 (2d Cir. 1999) *16:* 396

Molien v. Kaiser Found. Hosps., 27 Cal. 3d 916, 167 Cal. Rptr. 831, 616 P.2d 813 (1980) *1:* 103

Monette v. Electronic Data Sys. Corp., 90 F.3d 1173, 5 AD Cases 1326 (6th Cir. 1996) *16:* 339, 344, 396

Moore v. Ashland Chem., Inc.
—126 F.3d 679 (5th Cir. 1997) *15:* 94, 95
—151 F.3d 269 (5th Cir. 1998) *15:* 96, 97

Morgan v. Hilti, Inc., 108 F.3d. 1319, 4 WH Cases 2d 1226 (10th Cir. 1997) *16:* 279

Morisky v. Broward County, 80 F.3d 445, 5 AD Cases 737 (11th Cir. 1996) *16:* 351

Morton v. Haskell Co., 1995 WL 819182, 5 AD Cases 272 (M.D. Fla. Sept. 12, 1995) *9:* 15, 20, 43, 44, 61, 82, 108, 117, 118, 141, 142

Moses v. American Nonwovens, Inc., 97 F.3d 446, 5 AD Cases 1651 (11th Cir. 1996) *16:* 382, 646, 657

Muller
—v. Automobile Club of S. Cal., 897 F. Supp. 1289, 5 AD Cases 1997 (S.D. Cal. 1995) *16:* 52, 181
—v. Costello, 5 AD Cases 779 (N.D.N.Y. 1996) *16:* 495
—v. Hotsy Corp., 917 F. Supp. 1389, 6 AD Cases 35 (N.D. Iowa 1996) *16:* 273
Mullins v. Crowell, 228 F.3d 1305, 11 AD Cases 38 (11th Cir. 2000) *16:* 174
Munday v. Waste Management of N. Am., 858 F. Supp. 1364, 72 FEP Cases 471 (D. Md. 1994), *rev'd in part,* 126 F.3d 239, 74 FEP Cases 1478 (4th Cir. 1997) *1:* 212–14
Mundo v. Sanus Health Plan of Greater N.Y., 966 F. Supp. 171, 8 AD Cases 937 (E.D.N.Y. 1997) *16:* 19, 185, 222, 236
Murphy
—v. Allstate Ins. Co., 83 Cal. App. 3d 38, 147 Cal. Rptr. 565 (1978) *1:* 91
—v. United Parcel Serv. Inc., 527 U.S. 516, 9 AD Cases 691 (1999) *16:* 36, 69
—v. Village of Hoffman Estates, 1999 WL 160305 (N.D. Ill. Mar. 17, 1999) *16:* 524
Mustafa v. Clark County Sch. Dist., 157 F.3d 1169, 8 AD Cases 1119 (9th Cir. 1998) *16:* 338
Muthler v. Ann Arbor Mach. Inc., 18 F. Supp. 2d 722, 9 AD Cases 365 (E.D. Mich. 1998) *16:* 195
Myers v. Hose, 50 F.3d 278, 4 AD Cases 391 (4th Cir. 1995) *16:* 397

N

Naton v. Bank of California, 649 F.2d 691, 27 FEP Cases 510 (9th Cir. 1981) *1:* 18
Nave v. Woolridge Const. of Pa., Inc., 8 AD Cases 1351 (E.D. Pa. 1997) *16:* 237
Neal v. Siegel-Robert, Inc., 171 F.R.D. 264, 73 FEP Cases 637 (E.D. Mo. 1996) *9:* 15, 19, 22, 55
Nesser v. Trans World Airlines, 160 F.3d 442, 8 AD Cases 1348 (8th Cir. 1998) *16:* 279
Newberry v. East Tex. State Univ., 161 F.3d 276, 8 AD Cases 1595 (5th Cir. 1998) *1:* 206, 207; *16:* 330
Newland v. Dalton, 81 F.3d 904, 5 AD Cases 735 (9th Cir. 1996) *16:* 524
Newman v. Chevron U.S.A., 979 F. Supp. 1085, 7 AD Cases 1821 (S.D. Tex. 1993) *16:* 650
Newsome v. Cooper-Wiss, Inc., 179 Ga. App. 670, 347 S.E.2d 619 (1986) *1:* 68
Nielson v. Moroni Feed Co., 162 F.3d 604, 8 AD Cases 1553 (10th Cir. 1998) *16:* 502
Norman-Bloodshaw v. Lawrence Berkeley Lab., 135 F.3d 1260, 7 AD Cases 1395 (9th Cir. 1998) *16:* 568
Norris v. Sysco Corp., 191 F.3d 1043, 9 AD Cases 1262 (9th Cir. 1994) *16:* 597
Nowak v. St. Rita High Sch., 142 F.3d 999, 8 AD Cases 106 (7th Cir. 1998) *16:* 396, 401
Nunes v. Wal Mart Stores, Inc., 164 F.3d 1243, 8 AD 1813 (9th Cir. 1999) *16:* 658
Nweke v. Prudential Ins. Co., 25 F. Supp. 2d 203, 82 FEP Cases 1621 (S.D.N.Y. 1999) *16:* 39

O

O'Conner v. Commonwealth Edison Co., 13 F.3d 1090 (7th Cir. 1994) *15:* 78–80
Odima v. Westin Tucson Hotel, 53 F.3d 1484, 67 FEP Cases 1222 (9th Cir. 1995) *1:* 153
Old Western Furniture Corp.; EEOC v., 173 F.R.D. 444 (W.D. Tex. 1996) *9:* 28
Oleszko v. State Comp. Ins. Fund, 243 F.3d 1154, 85 FEP Cases 483 (9th Cir. 2001) *8:* 7
Olson
—v. Connerly, 156 Wis. 2d 488, 457 N.W.2d 479 (1990) *1:* 48
—v. Dubuque Community Sch. Dist., 137

F.3d 609, 7 AD Cases 1598 (8th Cir. 1998) *16:* 113, 235
—v. General Elec. Astrospace, 101 F.3d 947, 6 AD Cases 270 (3d Cir. 1996) *16:* 209, 216, 235
Oncale v. Sundowner Offshore Servs., Inc., 523 U.S. 75, 76 FEP Cases 221 (1998) *14:* 25
O'Neal v. Spillane, 45 Cal. App. 3d 147, 119 Cal. Rptr. 245 (1975) *1:* 89
One Feather; United States v., 702 F.2d 736 (8th Cir. 1983) *8:* 106
O'Neill v. Atlanta Gen. & Light Co., 968 F. Supp. 721 (S.D. Ga. 1997) *16:* 8
Onishea v. Hopper, 171 F.3d 1289 (11th Cir. 1999) *16:* 669
O'Quinn v. New York Univ. Med. Ctr., 163 F.R.D. 226, 68 FEP Cases 1798 (S.D.N.Y. 1995) *9:* 21, 56
O'Reilly v. Executone of Albany, 121 A.D.2d 772, 503 N.Y.S.2d 185 (1986) *1:* 62
Osika v. Board of Educ. for Bremen Community High Schs., 1999 WL 1044838 (N.D. Ill. Nov. 16, 1999) *16:* 189
Oswald v. LaRoche Chems., Inc., 894 F. Supp. 988, 5 AD Cases 401 (E.D. La. 1995) *16:* 264
Ouzts v. USAir, Inc., 1996 WL 578514 (W.D. Pa. July 26, 1996) *16:* 158, 159
Overton
—v. Reilly, 977 F.2d 1190, 2 AD Cases 254 (7th Cir. 1992) *16:* 265, 271, 319
—v. Tar Heel Farm Credit, 942 F. Supp. 1066, 9 AD Cases 547 (E.D.N.C. 1996) *16:* 195

P

Pack v. K-Mart Corp., 166 F.3d 1300, 8 AD Cases 1880 (10th Cir. 1999) *16:* 137, 141, 151
Paegle v. Department of Interior, 813 F. Supp. 61, 2 AD Cases 482 (D.D.C. 1993) *16:* 58
Paleologos v. Rehb Consultants, Inc., 990 F. Supp. 1460 (N.D. Ga. 1998) *16:* 24
Palmer v. Circuit Ct. of Cook County, 117 F.3d 351, 6 AD Cases 1569 (7th Cir. 1997) *16:* 192, 193, 315–17, 455
Paoli R.R. Yard PCB Litig., In re, 35 F.3d 717 (3d Cir. 1994) *15:* 111–14
Parker v. Columbia Pictures Indus., Inc., 204 F.3d 326, 10 AD Cases 396 (2d Cir. 2000) *16:* 396, 423
Pascouau v. Martin Marietta Corp., 994 F. Supp. 1276, 76 FEP Cases 651 (D. Colo. 1998), *aff'd in part,* 185 F.3d 874 (10th Cir. 1999) (table) **Preface:** 26–28; *1:* 199–203; *14:* 118
Passantino v. Johnson & Johnson Consumer Prods., Inc., 212 F.3d 493 (9th Cir. 2000) *1:* 11
Pasternak v. Texaco Inc., 1997 WL 621267 (S.D.N.Y. Oct. 7, 1997) *8:* 18
Patterson
—v. Chicago Ass'n for Retarded Citizens, 150 F.3d 719, 8 AD Cases 983 (7th Cir. 1998) *16:* 43, 181
—v. P.H.P. Healthcare Corp., 90 F.3d 927, 72 FEP Cases 613 (5th Cir. 1996) *1:* 126, 128, 129, 225
Pease v. Alford Photo Indus., 667 F. Supp. 1188, 49 FEP Cases 497 (W.D. Tenn. 1987) *1:* 27, 62
People v. *See name of other party*
Perkins v. Spivey, 911 F.2d 22, 53 FEP Cases 973 (8th Cir. 1990) *1:* 109, 110
Perrell v. FinanceAmerica Corp., 726 F.2d 654, 33 FEP Cases 1728 (10th Cir. 1984) *1:* 18
Pesterfield v. Tennessee Valley Auth., 941 F.2d 437, 1 AD Cases 1858 (6th Cir. 1991) *16:* 312, 488
Petermann v. Teamsters Local 396, 174 Cal. App. 2d 184, 344 P.2d 25 (1959) *1:* 54
Pettus v. Cole, 49 Cal. App. 4th 402, 12 IER Cases 74 (Ct. App. 1996) *16:* 473
Pfeifer v. State Farm, 1997 WL 276085 (E.D. La. May 22, 1997) *8:* 87
Phillips v. Smalley Maintenance Serv., 435 So. 2d 705 (Ala. 1983) *1:* 76
Pikora v. Blue Cross/Blue Shield of Mich., 970 F. Supp. 591 (E.D. Mich. 1997) *16:* 477
Pilman v. New York City Housing Auth., 2000 WL 236322 (S.D.N.Y. Feb. 25, 2000) *16:* 240
Polderman v. Northwest Airlines, Inc., 40 F. Supp. 2d 456 (N.D. Ohio 1999) *16:* 39
Pollard v. E.I. duPont de Nemours & Co., __ U.S. __, 121 S. Ct. 1946, 85 FEP Cases 1217 (2001) *1:* 9

Poole v. Copland, Inc., 481 S.E.2d 88, 12 IER Cases 833 (N.C. App. 1997) *1:* 178, 179

Popko v. Pennsylvania State Univ., 84 F. Supp. 2d 589, 10 AD Cases 1404 (M.D. Pa. 2000) *16:* 87, 142

Porter
—v. U.S. Alumoweld Co., 125 F. 3d 243, 7 AD Cases 537 (4th Cir. 1997) *16:* 598
—v. Whitehall Labs., Inc., 9 F.3d 607 (7th Cir. 1993) *15:* 81, 82

Potter v. Xerox Corp., 88 F. Supp. 2d 109, 82 FEP Cases 1116 (W.D.N.Y. 2000) *16:* 488

Pouncy v. Vulcan Materials Co., 920 F. Supp. 1566, 7 AD Cases 1621 (N.D. Ala. 1996) *16:* 223

Powers v. Polygram Holding, Inc., 40 F. Supp. 2d 195, 9 AD Cases 1370 (S.D.N.Y. 1999) *16:* 400, 402

Presta v. Southeastern Pa. Transp. Auth., 1998 WL 310735 (E.D. Pa. 1998) *16:* 188

Prevo's Family Mkt., Inc.; EEOC v., 135 F.3d 1089, 8 AD Cases 401 (6th Cir. 1998) *16:* 606, 633

Price v. City of Charlotte, 93 F.3d 1241, 71 FEP Cases 1289 (4th Cir. 1996) *1:* 125

Priest v. Rotary, 634 F. Supp. 571, 40 FEP Cases 208 (N.D. Cal. 1986) *1:* 26, 27, 76

Pritchard v. Southern Co., 92 F.3d 1130, 5 AD Cases 1480 (11th Cir.), *amended in part on reh'g by* 102 F.3d 1118, 6 AD Cases 206 (11th Cir. 1996) *16:* 137, 212, 213

Prunty v. Arkansas Freightways, Inc., 16 F.3d 649, 9 IER Cases 911 (5th Cir. 1994) *1:* 36, 37

Pryor
—v. Trane Co., 138 F.3d 1024, 8 AD Cases 271 (5th Cir. 1998) *16:* 210
—v. U.S. Gypsum, 585 F. Supp. 311, 47 FEP Cases 159 (W.D. Mo. 1985) *1:* 101

Q

Qualls v. Lack's Stores, Inc., 1999 WL 731758 (N.D. Tex. Mar. 31, 1999) *16:* 125, 135

Quigley v. Austeel Lemont Co., 79 F. Supp. 2d 941, 10 AD Cases 351 (N.D. Ill. 2000) *16:* 504, 515

Quitmeyer v. Southeastern Pa. Trans. Auth., 740 F. Supp. 363 (E.D. Pa. 1990) *1:* 100

R

Ragge v. MCA/Universal Studios, 165 F.R.D. 605 (C.D. Cal. 1995) *9:* 38, 65, 77, 79, 80, 107, 113, 158, 171; *10:* 6

Rakestraw v. Carpenter Co., 898 F. Supp. 386, 5 AD Cases 622 (N.D. Miss. 1995) *16:* 58

Ralph v. Lucent Techs., Inc., 135 F.3d 166, 7 AD Cases 1345 (1st Cir. 1998) *16:* 336, 401, 409, 422

Ramirez
—v. Kelly, 1997 WL 223053 (N.D. Ill. May 1, 1997) *1:* 193
—v. Nabil's, Inc., 1995 WL 609415 (D. Kan. Oct. 5, 1995) *8:* 170, 171
—v. New York City Off-Track Betting Corp., 112 F.3d 38, 73 FEP Cases 573 (2d Cir. 1997) *1:* 146

Rand v. Miller, 408 S.E.2d 655 (W. Va. 1991) *13:* 110

Rascon v. U.S. West Communications, Inc., 143 F.3d 1324, 8 AD Cases 541 (10th Cir. 1998) *16:* 283, 402

Ratts v. Board of County Commissioners, 189 F.R.D. 448 (D. Kan. 1999) *8:* 145

Reed v. LePage Bakeries, Inc., 244 F.3d 254, 11 AD Cases 1150 (1st Cir. 2001) *16:* 342, 344

Reese v. American Food Serv., 2000 WL 1470212 (E.D. Pa. Sept. 29, 2000) *16:* 125

Reeves v. Johnson Controls World Servs., Inc., 140 F.3d 144, 7 AD Cases 1675 (2d Cir. 1998) *16:* 40, 165, 166

Region 13 Mental Health-Mental Retardation Comm'n; Doe v., 704 F.2d 1402, 1 AD Cases 447 (5th Cir. 1983) *16:* 678

Rehling v. Chicago, 207 F.3d 1009, 10 AD Cases 589 (7th Cir. 2000) *16:* 382, 384

Reid v. Lockheed Martin Aeronautics Co., 199 F.R.D. 379 (N.D. Ga. 2001) *1:* 234

Reigel v. Kaiser Found. Health Plan, 859 F. Supp. 963, 3 AD Cases 577 (E.D.N.C. 1994) **16:** 607–9

Renaud v. Wyoming Dep't of Family Servs., 203 F.3d 723, 5 WH Cases 2d 1505 (10th Cir. 2000) **16:** 524

Rentos v. OCE Office Sys., 72 FEP Cases 1717 (S.D.N.Y. 1996) **16:** 199

Reyes v. City of New York, 2000 WL 1528239 (S.D.N.Y. Oct. 16, 2000) **9:** 99, 101

Reynolds v. Octel Communications Corp., 924 F. Supp. 743, 69 FEP Cases 1178 (N.D. Tex. 1995) **1:** 124

Rice v. United Ins. Co., 465 So. 2d 1100, 36 FEP Cases 1641 (Ala. 1984) **1:** 28

Ricks v. Abbott Labs., 198 F.R.D. 647 (D. Md. 2001) **9:** 29–31

Riechman v. Cutler-Hammer, Inc., 95 F. Supp. 2d 1171 (D. Kan. 2000) **16:** 588

Riel v. Electronic Data Sys., 99 F.3d 678, 6 AD Cases 26 (5th Cir. 1996) **16:** 344

Riemer v. Illinois Dep't of Transp., 148 F.3d 800, 8 AD Cases 440 (7th Cir. 1998) **16:** 215

Rizzo v. Children's World Learning Ctrs., Inc., 213 F.3d 209, 10 AD Cases 976 (5th Cir. 2000) **16:** 650, 655

R.J. Gallagher; EEOC v., 181 F.3d 645, 9 AD Cases 917 (5th Cir. 1999) **16:** 175–77

Roads v. Bob Florence Contractor, Inc., 890 F. Supp. 960, 4 AD Cases 1201 (D. Kan. 1995) **16:** 425

Robb v. Horizon Credit Union, 66 F. Supp. 2d 913, 9 AD Cases 1365 (D.C. Ill. 1999) **16:** 77

Roberts
—v. Fairfax, City of, 937 F. Supp. 541, 8 AD Cases 919 (E.D. Va. 1996) **16:** 463
—v. Unidynamics Corp., 126 F.3d 1088, 7 AD Cases 1867 (8th Cir. 1997) **16:** 235

Robertson v. Neuromedical Ctr., 161 F.3d 292 (5th Cir. 1998) **16:** 261, 468, 483, 484, 653

Robin v. Espo Eng'g., 200 F.3d 1081, 81 FEP Cases 1332 (7th Cir. 2000) **16:** 346

Robinson
—v. Canon U.S.A., 82 FEP Cases 1129 (W.D. Mo. 2000) **8:** 178–80
—v. Jacksonville Shipyards, Inc.
——760 F. Supp. 1486, 57 FEP Cases 971 (M.D. Fla. 1991) **14:** 17
——118 F.R.D. 525, 54 FEP Cases 83 (M.D. Fla. 1988) **9:** 15, 17
—v. Metro-North Commuter R.R., 197 F.R.D. 85, 84 FEP Cases 151 (S.D.N.Y. 2000) **1:** 233

Rodriguez-Hernandez v. Miranda-Veletz, 132 F.3d 848, 75 FEP Cases 1228 (1st Cir. 1998) **8:** 134

Roe v. Cheyenne Mountain Conference Resort, Inc., 124 F.3d 1221, 7 AD Cases 779 (10th Cir. 1997) **16:** 592, 615

Rogers
—v. EEOC, 454 F.2d 234, 4 FEP Cases 92 (5th Cir. 1971) **14:** 13
—v. International Marine Terminals, Inc., 87 F.3d 755, 5 AD Cases 1115 (5th Cir. 1996) **16:** 401
—v. Loew's L'Enfant Plaza Hotel, 526 F. Supp. 523, 29 FEP Cases 828 (D.D.C. 1981) **1:** 48, 75

Rojo v. Kliger, 52 Cal. 3d 65, 276 Cal. Rptr. 130, 54 FEP Cases 1146 (1990) **1:** 57, 61

Romero v. Mason & Hanger-Silas Mason Co., 739 F. Supp. 1472 (D.N.M. 1990) **1:** 93

Ross v. Douglas County, 234 F.3d 391, 84 FEP Cases 791 (8th Cir. 2000) **1:** 152

Rouse; United States v., 111 F.3d 561 (8th Cir. 1997) **15:** 72

Roush v. Weastec, Inc., 96 F.3d 840, 5 AD Cases 1713 (6th Cir. 1996) **16:** 59

Rudd v. General Motors Corp., 127 F. Supp. 2d 1330 (M.D. Ala. 2001) **15:** 48

Ruhlmann v. Ulster County Dep't of Soc. Servs., 194 F.R.D. 445 (N.D.N.Y. 2000) **8:** 72–74

Rush v. Scott Specialty Gases, Inc., 930 F. Supp. 194, 73 FEP Cases 1429 (E.D. Pa. 1996), rev'd, 113 F.3d 476, 74 FEP Cases 1745 (3d Cir. 1997) **1:** 145

Ruth v. Fletcher, 377 S.E.2d 412 (Va. 1989) **1:** 45

Ryan v. Grae & Rybicki P.C., 135 F.3d 867, 7 AD Cases 1387 (1st Cir. 1998) **16:** 162

Ryzlak v. McNeil Pharm. Co., 38 Fed. R. Serv. 2d 443 (E.D. Pa. 1982) **9:** 14, 65, 82, 114

S

Sabine Pilot Serv. v. Hauck, 687 S.W.2d 733, 119 LRRM 2187 (Tex. 1985) *1:* 55

Sabree v. Carpenters Local No. 33, 126 F.R.D. 422 (D. Mass. 1989) *9:* 24

Saia v. Sears Roebuck & Co., 47 F. Supp. 2d 141 (D. Mass. 1999) *1:* 156, 158, 160, 162

St. Andre v. Henderson, 2000 WL 1677967 (N.D. Cal. Nov. 6, 2000) *1:* 249

St. Michael Hosp.; EEOC v., 74 FEP Cases 993 (E.D. Wis. 1997) *8:* 11

Salley v. Circuit City Stores, Inc., 160 F.3d 977, 8 AD Cases 1407 (3d Cir. 1997) *16:* 504, 511

Salmon v. Dade County Sch. Bd., 4 F. Supp. 2d 1157 (S.D. Fla. 1998) *16:* 414

Sanchez
—v. U.S. Airways, 2001 WL 311271 (E.D. Pa. Mar. 29, 2001) *8:* 38–42
—v. Zabihi, 166 F.R.D. 500, 71 FEP Cases 835 (D.N.M. 1996) *8:* 146, 147, 173

Sanders
—v. Arneson Prods., Inc., 91 F.3d 1351, 5 AD Cases 1292 (9th Cir. 1996) *16:* 39, 52, 63
—v. Chicago, 2000 WL 198901 (N.D. Ill. Feb. 15, 2000) *16:* 215

Sandford v. Stearn, 2 AD Cases 491 (N.D. Ohio 1992) *16:* 178

Sanfelice v. Dominick's Finer Foods, Inc., 1995 WL 608602 (N.D. Ill. Oct. 13, 1995) *15:* 68, 69, 115

Santelli v. Electro-Motive, 188 F.R.D. 306 (N.D. Ill. 1999) *8:* 66, 67, 70

Sara Lee Corp.; EEOC v., 237 F.3d 349, 11 AD Cases 595 (4th Cir. 2001) *16:* 156, 157

Sarko v. Penn-Del Dir. Co.
—170 F.R.D. 127, 7 AD Cases 195 (E.D. Pa. 1997) *8:* 10; *9:* 37, 38, 47, 48, 56, 65, 73, 80, 145–47; *16:* 39
—968 F. Supp 1026, 7 AD Cases 1201 (E.D. Pa. 1997) *16:* 39

Schlagenhauf v. Holder, 379 U.S. 104 (1964) *9:* 6–9, 75

Schmidt
—v. Bell, 1 AD Cases 491 (E.D. Pa. 1983) *16:* 489

—v. Safeway, Inc., 864 F. Supp. 991, 3 AD Cases 1141 (D. Or. 1994) *16:* 347, 518, 521–23

Schneiker v. Fortis Ins. Co., 200 F.3d 1055, 10 AD Cases 75 (7th Cir. 2000) *16:* 185, 189

Schoffstall v. Henderson, 223 F.3d 818, 84 FEP Cases 1411 (8th Cir. 2000) *8:* 50

School Bd. of Nassau County v. Arline, 480 U.S. 273, 1 AD Cases 1026 (1987) *16:* 206, 636

Schroeder v. Auto Driveaway Co., 11 Cal. 3d 908, 114 Cal. Rptr. 622, 528 P.2d 662 (1974) *1:* 91

Schwartz v. Comex, 8 AD Cases 1223 (S.D.N.Y. 1997) *16:* 42

Scott v. American Airlines, Inc., 1997 WL 278129 (N.D. Tex. May 15, 1997) *16:* 403

Seaman v. C.S.P.H., Inc., 179 F. 3d 297, 5 WH Cases 2d 673 (5th Cir. 1999) *16:* 362, 363

Seamon v. C.S.P. Eight, Inc., 1997 WL 538751 (N.D. Tex. Aug. 25, 1997) *16:* 43

Seffert v. Los Angeles Transit Lines, 56 Cal. 2d 498, 15 Cal. Rptr. 161 (1961) *1:* 138

Shafer v. Preston Mem'l Hosp. Corp., 107 F.3d 274, 6 AD Cases 682 (4th Cir. 1997) *16:* 505–8, 515

Shannon v. Philadelphia, 1999 WL 1065210 (E.D. Pa. Nov. 23, 1999) *16:* 61, 402

Shea v. Icelandair, 925 F. Supp. 1014, 70 FEP Cases 1544 (S.D.N.Y. 1996) *1:* 133, 181, 182

Sheffield v. Hilltop Sand & Gravel Co., 895 F. Supp. 105, 68 FEP Cases 930 (E.D. Va. 1995) *8:* 136–38

Shepherd v. American Broad. Cos., 151 F.R.D. 194 (D.D.C. 1993), *rev'd in part and vacated in part,* 62 F.3d 1469 (D.C. Cir. 1995) *9:* 47, 49, 68, 72, 82, 115, 116

Sherback v. Wright Auto. Group, 987 F. Supp. 433 (W.D. Pa. 1997) *16:* 113

Sherman v. New York Life Ins. Co., 1997 WL 452024 (S.D.N.Y. Aug. 7, 1997) *16:* 185

Sherrod v. Berry, 827 F.2d 195 (7th Cir. 1987) *1:* 155

Shirsat v. Mutual Pharm. Co., 169 F.R.D. 68 (E.D. Pa. 1996) *9:* 73, 74, 90, 107, 109, 160

Shrout v. Black Clawson Co., 689 F. Supp. 774, 46 FEP Cases 1339 (S.D. Ohio 1988) *1:* 27

Shumaker v. West, 196 F.R.D. 454 (S.D. W.Va. 2000) *9:* 87, 92, 93

Sidor v. Reno, 8 AD Cases 18 (S.D.N.Y. 1998) *8:* 34, 35

Siefken v. Village of Arlington Heights, 65 F.3d 664, 4 AD Cases 1441 (7th Cir. 1995) *16:* 445, 470, 648

Siemon v. AT&T Corp., 113 F.3d 1175, 6 AD Cases 1249 (10th Cir. 1997) *16:* 39, 189, 438

Sierra Nat'l Bank v. Brown, 18 Cal. App. 3d 98, 95 Cal. Rptr. 742 (1971) *1:* 89

Silver v. Engelman Secs., Inc., 1995 WL 413456 (N.D. Ill. July 11, 1995) *16:* 186

Simeon v. AT&T Corp., 117 F.3d 1173 (10th Cir. 1997) *16:* 181

Simmerman v. Hardee's Food Sys., Inc., 7 AD Cases 887 (E.D. Pa. 1996), *aff'd,* 118 F.3d 1578, 8 AD Cases 480 (3d Cir. 1997) *16:* 270, 301

Sinkler v. Midwest Property Mgmt. Ltd., 209 F.3d 678, 11 AD Cases 677 (7th Cir. 2000) *16:* 166

Skorup v. Modern Door Corp., 153 F.3d 512, 8 AD Cases 808 (7th Cir. 1998) *16:* 180

Skousen v. Nidy, 90 Ariz. 215, 367 P.2d 248 (1961) *1:* 62

Smartt v. Charlotte Housing Auth., 1998 WL 760866 (W.D.N.C. Apr. 7, 1998) *16:* 403

Smedley v. Capps, Staples, Ward, Hastings & Dodson, 820 F. Supp. 1227, 61 FEP Cases 1360 (N.D. Cal. 1993) *9:* 5, 12, 76

Smith
—v. AmeriTech, 129 F.3d 857, 7 AD Cases 917 (6th Cir. 1997) *16:* 432
—v. Blue Cross & Blue Shield of Kan., Inc.
———102 F.3d 1075, 6 AD Cases 367 (10th Cir. 1996) *16:* 396
———894 F. Supp. 1463, 4 AD Cases 1378 (D. Kan. 1995) *16:* 322
—v. Ford Motor Co., 215 F.3d 713 (7th Cir. 2000) *15:* 50

—v. Ingersoll-Rand Co., 214 F.3d 1235 (10th Cir. 2000) *1:* 163
—v. Midland Brake, Inc., 180 F.3d 1154, 9 AD Cases 738 (10th Cir. Dec. 22, 1999) *16:* 346, 382, 441

Smolinsky v. State Farm Ins. Co., 1999 WL 1285824 (E.D. Pa. Dec. 22, 1999) *9:* 1

Socks-Brunot v. Hirschvogel, Inc., 184 F.R.D. 113 (S.D. Ohio 1999) *8:* 123

Soileau v. Guilford of Maine, Inc., 105 F.3d 12, 6 AD Cases 437 (1st Cir. 1997) *16:* 39, 46, 52, 102, 103

Sommers v. Iowa Civil Rights Comm'n, 337 N.W.2d 470 (Iowa 1993) *16:* 199

Soto-Ocasio v. Federal Express Corp., 150 F.3d 14, 8 AD Cases 1067 (1st Cir. 1998) *16:* 418, 421, 424

Spades v. City of Walnut Ridge, 186 F.3d 897, 9 AD Cases 1015 (8th Cir. 1999) *16:* 39, 52, 77, 679, 680

Spath v. Hayes Wheels Int'l—Ind., Inc., 211 F.3d 392, 10 AD Cases 878 (7th Cir. 2000) *16:* 456, 457

Spearman Indus. v. St. Paul Fire & Marine Ins. Co., 128 F. Supp. 2d 1148 (N.D. Ill. 2001) *15:* 49, 50

Spencer v. General Elec. Co., 697 F. Supp. 204, 51 FEP Cases 1696 (E.D. Va. 1988), *aff'd,* 894 F.2d 651, 51 FEP Cases 1725 (4th Cir. 1990) *1:* 196; *13:* 102

Spoon v. American Agriculturalists, 120 A.D.2d 857, 502 N.Y.S.2d 296 (1986) *1:* 98

Spradley v. Custom Campers, 68 F. Supp. 2d 1225 (D. Kan. 1999) *16:* 132

Sprague v. Frank J. Sanders Lincoln Mercury, Inc., 120 Cal. App. 3d 412, 174 Cal. Rptr. 608 (1981) *1:* 90, 91

Stafford v. Noramco of Delaware, Inc., 2000 WL 1868179 (D. Del. Dec. 15, 2000) *1:* 208, 209

Stalnaker v. K-Mart Corp., 71 FEP Cases 705 (D. Kan. 1996) *8:* 187, 188

Stanley v. Lester M. Pronje, Inc., 25 F. Supp. 2d 581, 8 AD Cases 1157 (E.D. Pa. 1998) *16:* 432

Starzecpysel; United States v., 880 F. Supp. 1027 (S.D.N.Y. 1995) *15:* 34

State v. *See name of other party*

State Personnel Bd. v. Fair Employment & Hous. Comm'n, 39 Cal. 3d 422 (1985) *1:* 20

Stauffer v. Bayer Corp., 1997 WL 588890 (N.D. Ind. July 21, 1997) *16:* 56, 114, 142, 185, 189

Steele v. Offshore Shipbuilding, 867 F.2d 1311, 49 FEP Cases 522 (11th Cir. 1989) *1:* 79

Steffes v. Stepan Co., 144 F.3d 1070, 8 AD Cases 352 (7th Cir. 1998) *16:* 383

Stevenson v. Stanley Bostitch, Inc., 2001 WL 812310, 201 F.R.D. 551 (N.D. Ga. Mar. 21, 2001) *8:* 69–71, 92

Stewart
—v. Brown, County of, 86 F.3d 107, 5 AD Cases 1018 (7th Cir. 1996) *16:* 232
—v. Happy Herman's Cheshire Bridge, Inc., 117 F.3d 1278, 6 AD Cases 1834 (11th Cir. 1997) *16:* 383
—v. Thomas, 538 F. Supp. 891, 30 FEP Cases 1609 (D.D.C. 1982) *1:* 28

Stola v. Joint Indus. Bd., 889 F. Supp. 133, 4 AD Cases 1018 (S.D.N.Y. 1995) *16:* 351

Stoll v. Runyon, 165 F.3d 1238, 78 FEP Cases 1312 (9th Cir. 1998) *1:* 246, 247

Stradlay v. LaFourche Communications, Inc., 869 F. Supp. 442, 3 AD Cases 1507 (E.D. La. 1994) *16:* 218

Sublette v. Glidden Co., 1998 WL 964189 (E.D. Pa. Oct. 1, 1998) *8:* 124, 125, 158

Sudtelgte v. Reno, 63 FEP Cases 1257 (W.D. Mo. 1994) *1:* 175, 177, 197, 198; *8:* 232; *14:* 121

Sullivan v. River Valley Sch. Dist., 197 F.3d 804, 9 AD Cases 1711 (6th Cir. 1999) *16:* 244, 245, 458, 586, 593–95

Sutton
—v. Lader, 185 F.3d 1203, 9 AD Cases 1182 (11th Cir. 1999) *16:* 220
—v. United Airlines, Inc., 527 U.S. 471, 9 AD Cases 673 (1999) *16:* 36, 68, 70, 72–76, 171–73, 221

Swann v. Walters, 620 F. Supp. 741, 35 FEP Cases 1246 (D.D.C. 1984) *16:* 325

T

Tameny v. Atlantic Richfield Co., 27 Cal. 3d 167, 610 P.2d 1330, 164 Cal. Rptr. 839 (1980) *1:* 55

Tangires v. Johns Hopkins Hosp., 79 F. Supp. 587, 10 AD Cases 215 (D. Md. 2000) *16:* 132

Tardie v. Rehabilitation Hosp. of R.I., 168 F.3d 538, 9 AD Cases 155 (1st Cir. 1999) *16:* 195, 302

Tauriac v. Polaroid Corp., 716 F. Supp. 672, 48 FEP Cases 1256 (D. Mass. 1989) *1:* 100

Taylor
—v. Dover Elevator Sys., 917 F. Supp. 455, 5 AD Cases 616 (N.D. Miss. 1996) *16:* 214, 458
—v. Food World, Inc., 133 F.3d 1419 (11th Cir. 1998) *16:* 320, 321
—v. Nimock's Oil Co., 214 F.3d 957, 10 AD Cases 1069 (8th Cir. 2000) *16:* 125, 195
—v. Pathmark Store, Inc., 177 F.3d 180, 9 AD Cases 497 (3d Cir. 1999) *16:* 330
—v. Pepsi-Cola Co., 196 F.3d 1106, 9 AD Cases 1731 (10th Cir. 1999) *16:* 396, 401
—v. Phoenixville Sch. Dist., 184 F.3d 296, 9 AD Cases 1187 (3d Cir. 1999) *16:* 66, 67, 77, 144–47, 347, 350, 376, 382, 384
—v. Principal Fin. Group., Inc., 93 F.3d 155, 5 AD Cases 1653 (5th Cir. 1996) *16:* 352–57

Templeton v. Neodata Servs., 162 F.3d 617, 8 AD Cases 1615 (10th Cir. 1998) *16:* 383

Tenbrink v. Federal Home Loan Bank, 920 F. Supp. 1156, 15 AD Cases 1283 (D. Kan. 1996) *16:* 426

Terrell v. USAir, 132 F.3d 621, 8 AD Cases 529 (11th Cir. 1998) *16:* 424

Testerman v. Chrysler Corp., 1997 WL 820934 (D. Del. Dec. 30, 1997) *16:* 235

Texas Bus Lines; EEOC v., 923 F. Supp. 965, 5 AD Cases 878 (S.D. Tex. 1996) *16:* 579, 682

Thiessen v. General Elec. Capital Corp., 178 F.R.D. 568 (D. Kan. 1998) *9:* 32–34

Thing v. La Chusa, 48 Cal. 3d 644, 257 Cal. Rptr. 865, 771 P.2d 814 (1989) *1:* 105

Thomas
—v. Borg-Warner Protective Servs., 1996

Thomas (*cont.*)
  WL 162990 (N.D. Cal. Mar. 11, 1996) *16:* 557
—v. Mississippi State Dep't of Health, 934 F. Supp. 768 (S.D. Miss. 1996) *16:* 550
Tice v. Centre Area Transp. Auth., 247 F.3d 506, 11 AD Cases 1185 (3d Cir. 2001) *16:* 45, 245
Timbol v. Commercial Bank of Kuwait, 2000 WL 282886 (S.D.N.Y. Mar. 15, 2000) *16:* 267
Tirado v. Erosa, 158 F.R.D. 294 (S.D.N.Y. 1994) *9:* 96, 103
Todd v. Academy Corp., 57 F. Supp. 2d 448, 9 AD Cases 1306 (S.D. Tex. 1999) *16:* 77
Tokar v. Chicago, 2000 WL 1230489 (N.D. Ill. Aug. 25, 2000) *16:* 685–87
Treanor v. MCI Telecomm. Corp., 200 F.3d 570, 10 AD Cases 80 (8th Cir. 2000) *16:* 424
Trombetta v. Detroit, Toledo & Ironton R.R., 81 Mich. App. 489, 265 N.W.2d 385 (1978) *1:* 55
Truong v. Smith, 183 F.R.D. 273 (D. Colo. 1998) *8:* 143, 144, 176, 177
Tsai v. Rockefeller Univ., 137 F. Supp. 2d 276, 85 FEP Cases 358 (S.D. N.Y. 2001) *1:* 248
Tumbler v. American Trading & Prod. Corp., 6 AD Cases 1439 (E.D. Pa. 1997) *16:* 279
Turco v. Hoechst Celanese Chem. Corp., 101 F.3d 1090, 6 AD Cases 278 (5th Cir. 1996) *16:* 308, 328, 430, 439
Turner v. Imperial Stores, 161 F.R.D. 89 (S.D. Cal. 1995) *9:* 15, 19, 21, 23, 37, 38, 47, 48, 71–73
Tylo v. Superior Ct., 55 Cal. App. 4th 1379, 64 Cal. Rptr. 2d 731 (1997) *8:* 27
Tyndall v. National Educ. Ctrs., Inc., 31 F.3d 209, 3 AD Cases 868 (4th Cir. 1994) *16:* 404, 414, 418
Tyus v. Urban Search Management, 102 F.3d 256 (7th Cir. 1996) *15:* 31, 95

U

Ubelacker v. Cincom Sys., Inc., 48 Ohio App. 3d 268, 3 IER Cases 1853 (1988) *1:* 71

United States v. *See name of other party*
University of Md. Med. Sys. Corp.; Doe v., 50 F.3d 1261, 4 AD Cases 379 (4th Cir. 1995) *16:* 650
Usher v. Lakewood Usher Eng'g & Mfg. Co., 158 F.R.D. 411, 66 FEP Cases 558 (N.D. Ill. 1994) *Preface:* 14; *9:* 169

V

Valdez v. Church's Fried Chicken, 683 F. Supp. 596, 47 FEP Cases 1155 (W.D. Tex. 1988) *1:* 62, 69
Vance v. Southern Bell Tel. & Tel. Co., 863 F.2d 1503, 50 FEP Cases 742 (11th Cir. 1989) *1:* 129
Vanderbilt v. Town of Chilmark, 174 F.R.D. 225, 74 FEP Cases 685 (D. Mass. 1997) *8:* 51, 52
Vande Zande v. Wisconsin Dep't of Admin., 851 F. Supp. 353, 2 AD Cases 1846 (W.D. Wis. 1994), *aff'd,* 44 F.3d 538, 3 AD Cases 1636 (7th Cir. 1995) *16:* 62, 339, 344, 431, 434, 435, 472
Vann v. Lone Star Steakhouse, 967 F. Supp. 346, 75 FEP Cases 1131 (C.D. Ill. 1997) *8:* 31
Van Stan v. Family Colours & Co., 125 F.3d 563, 7 AD Cases 426 (7th Cir. 1997) *16:* 132
Vasconcellos v. Cybex Int'l, Inc., 962 F. Supp. 701, 4 WH Cases 2d 1446 (D. Md. 1997) *8:* 54–57
Vazquez v. Bedsole, 888 F. Supp. 727, 4 AD Cases 970 (E.D.N.C. 1995) *16:* 436
Vedernikov v. West Virginia Univ., 55 F. Supp. 2d 518 (D. W.Va. 1999) *16:* 504
Vera v. Williams Hospitality Group, Inc., 73 F. Supp. 2d 161, 9 AD Cases 1626 (D.P.R. 1999) *16:* 284–86
Vinson v. Superior Ct., 43 Cal. 3d 833, 239 Cal. Rptr. 292, 44 FEP Cases 1174 (Cal. 1987) *8:* 1–3; *9:* 3, 4, 58, 59, 80, 85, 104, 111
Violette v. International Bus. Machs. Corp., 962 F. Supp. 446, 7 AD Cases 395 (D. Conn. 1996), *aff'd,* 116 F.3d 466, 7 AD Cases 544 (2d Cir. 1997) *16:* 304
Vollmart v. Wisconsin Dep't of Transp.,

197 F.3d 293, 9 AD Cases 1704 (7th Cir. 1999) *16:* 436
Vorhies v. Pioneer Mfg., Co., 906 F. Supp. 578, 6 AD Cases 572 (D. Colo. 1995) *16:* 418
Vreeland v. Ethan Allen, Inc., 151 F.R.D. 551 (S.D.N.Y. 1993) *9:* 105

W

Waggoner v. Olin Corp., 169 F.3d 481, 9 AD Cases 88 (7th Cir. 1999) *16:* 283, 403, 432
Walker v. Thompson, 214 F.3d 615, 83 FEP Cases 243 (5th Cir. 2000) *1:* 38, 39
Wallace v. Veterans Admin., 683 F. Supp. 758, 1 AD Cases 1263 (D. Kan. 1988) *16:* 664, 665
Wallin v. Minnesota Dep't of Corrs., 153 F.3d 681, 8 AD Cases 1012 (8th Cir. 1998) *16:* 38
Walsh v. United Parcel Serv., Inc., 201 F.3d 718, 10 AD Cases 161 (6th Cir. 2000) *16:* 339, 340, 344, 396
Walsted v. Woodbury County, 113 F. Supp. 2d 1318, 11 AD Cases 20 (N.D. Iowa 2000) *16:* 367
Waltman v. International Paper Co., 47 FEP Cases 671 (W.D. La. 1988), *rev'd*, 875 F.2d 468, 50 FEP Cases 179 (5th Cir. 1989) *1:* 62
Walton v. Mental Health Ass'n of Southeastern Pa., 168 F.3d 661, 9 AD Cases 34 (3d Cir. 1999) *16:* 339, 343, 399
Ward v. Massachusetts Health Research Inst., 209 F.3d 29, 10 AD Cases 776 (1st Cir. 2000) *16:* 292, 293, 296, 413, 416–18
Watkins v. Telsmith, Inc., 121 F.3d 984 (5th Cir. 1997) *15:* 37, 95
Watson v. City of Miami Beach, 177 F.3d 932, 9 AD Cases 760 (11th Cir. 1999) *16:* 27, 601, 602
Webb
—v. Choate Mental Health & Dev. Ctr., 230 F.3d 991, 11 AD Cases 97 (7th Cir. 2000) *16:* 178
—v. Garelick Mfg. Co., 94 F.3d 484, 6 AD Cases 127 (8th Cir. 1996) *16:* 179
—v. Hyman, 861 F. Supp. 1094 (D.D.C. 1994) *9:* 63

—v. Mercy Hosp., 102 F.3d 958, 6 AD Cases 333 (8th Cir. 1996) *16:* 3, 223, 231
—United States v., 115 F.3d 711 (9th Cir. 1997) *15:* 36, 37
Weber v. Strippit, Inc., 186 F.3d 907, 9 AD Cases 961 (8th Cir. 1999) *16:* 87, 330
Webster v. Methodist Occupational Health Ctrs., Inc., 141 F.3d 1236, 8 AD Cases 33 (7th Cir. 1998) *16:* 327
Weiler v. Household Fin. Corp., 101 F.3d 519, 6 AD Cases 106 (7th Cir. 1996) *16:* 181, 190, 191, 438
Weissman v. Dawn Joy Fashions, Inc., 7 AD Cases 365 (S.D.N.Y. 1997) *16:* 215
Weyer v. Twentieth Century Fox Film Corp., 198 F.3d 1104, 10 AD Cases 65 (9th Cir. 2000) *16:* 528, 529
Wheat v. Biesecker, 125 F.R.D. 479 (N.D. Ind. 1989) *9:* 104
Wheaton v. Ogden Newspapers, Inc., 9 AD Cases 1456 (N.D. Iowa 1999) *16:* 206
Wheelock v. Philip Morris, USA, 1997 WL 45292 (E.D. La. Feb. 5, 1997) *16:* 39
Whillock v. Delta Airlines, 926 F. Supp. 1555, 5 AD Cases 1027 (N.D. Ga. 1995) *16:* 432
White v. York Int'l Corp., 45 F.3d 357, 3 AD Cases 1746 (10th Cir. 1995) *16:* 343
Whitney v. Greenberg, Rosenblatt, Kull & Bitsoli, 258 F.3d 30, 12 AD Cases 18 (1st Cir. 2001) *16:* 63
Whitted; United States v., 11 F.3d 782 (8th Cir. 1993) *15:* 75
Williams
—v. Anheuser-Busch, Inc., 957 F. Supp. 1246, 6 AD Cases 905 (M.D. Fla. 1997) *16:* 250, 524
—v. Bell. *See* Williams v. Saxbe
—v. Board of County Commissioners of Wyandotte County, 192 F.R.D. 698 (D. Kan. 2000) *8:* 181
—v. Healthreach Network, 2000 WL 760742 (E.D. Mo. Feb. 22, 2000) *16:* 39
—v. Houston Lighting & Power Co., 980 F. Supp. 879 (S.D. Tex. 1997) *16:* 630–32

Williams (*cont.*)
—v. Pharmacia, Inc., 956 F. Supp. 1457, 73 FEP Cases 294 (N.D. Ind. 1996) *1:* 146
—v. Saxbe, 413 F. Supp. 654, 12 FEP Cases 1093 (D.D.C. 1976), *rev'd sub nom.* Williams v. Bell, 587 F. 2d 1240, 17 FEP Cases 1662 (D.C. Cir. 1978) *14:* 9
—v. Trader Publ'g Co., 218 F.3d 481, 83 FEP Cases 668 (5th Cir. 2000) *1:* 115
—v. Trans World Airlines, 660 F.2d 1267, 27 FEP Cases 487 (8th Cir. 1981) *1:* 2
Williamson v. Handy Button Mach. Co., 817 F.2d 1290, 43 FEP Cases 1465 (7th Cir. 1987) *1:* 180
Willis
—v. Conopco, Inc., 108 F.3d 282, 6 AD Cases 806 (11th Cir. 1997) *16:* 344, 371, 382, 393, 573
—State v., 256 Kan. 837, 888 P.2d 839 (1995) *15:* 67
Winston v. Maine Tech. College, 631 A.2d 70, 2 AD Cases 1228 (Me. 1993) *16:* 203
Wintz v. Northrop Corp., 110 F.3d 508 (7th Cir. 1997) *15:* 83–85
Wisiewski v. Ameritech, 1996 WL 501737 (N.D. Ill. Sept. 3, 1996) *16:* 39
Witter v. Delta Air Lines, Inc., 138 F.3d 1366, 8 AD Cases 747 (11th Cir. 1998) *16:* 37, 221
Wojciechowski v. Emergency Technical Servs. Corp., 6 AD Cases 1290 (N.D. Ill. 1997) *16:* 418, 432
Wolak v. Spucci, 217 F.3d 157, 83 FEP Cases 253 (2d Cir. 2000) *8:* 101, 159–61
Wolk v. Saks Fifth Ave., 728 F.2d 221, 34 FEP Cases 193 (3d Cir. 1984) *1:* 60
Woodard v. Metro I.P.T.C., 2000 WL 684101 (S.D. Ind. Mar. 16, 2000) *8:* 129
Woodman v. Runyon, 132 F.3d 1330, 7 AD Cases 1189 (10th Cir. 1997) *16:* 339, 371
Workman
—v. Carolina Freight Carriers Corp., 65 FEP Cases 1209 (M.D. Ala. 1994) *8:* 29, 30; *9:* 165
—v. Frito-Lay, Inc., 165 F.3d 460, 8 AD Cases 1761 (6th Cir. 1999) *16:* 330
Wormley v. Arkla, Inc., 871 F. Supp. 1079, 3 AD Cases 1703 (E.D. Ark. 1998) *16:* 515
Wright v. Illinois Dep't of Corrections, 204 F.3d 727, 10 AD Cases 408 (9th Cir. 2000) *16:* 244
Wynne v. Loyola Univ. of Chicago, 1999 WL 759401 (N.D. Ill. Sept. 3, 1999) *8:* 32

Y

Yelverton v. Graebel/Houston Movers, Inc., 121 F. Supp. 2d 604 (E.D. Tex. 2000) *1:* 46
Yin v. California, 95 F.3d 864, 5 AD Cases 1487 (9th Cir. 1996) *16:* 589, 590, 633
Yuntis; Doe v., 2000 WL 33162199 (Mass. Super. Ct. Oct. 11, 2000) *16:* 199

Z

Zabkowicz v. West Bend Co.
—585 F. Supp. 635, 35 FEP Cases 209 (E.D. Wis. 1984) *9:* 14, 76, 105, 108, 111
—589 F. Supp. 780 (E.D. Wis. 1984) *8:* 222
Zenor v. El Paso Healthcare Sys., Ltd., 176 F.3d 847, 9 AD Cases 609 (5th Cir. 1999) *16:* 499, 504, 512–14
Ziemann v. Burlington County Bridge Comm'n, 155 F.R.D. 497 (D.N.J. 1994) *9:* 45, 46, 48, 50, 51, 88, 150, 151
Zihala v. Illinois Dep't of Health, 1999 WL 116221 (N.D. Ill. Feb. 26, 1999) *16:* 445
Zirpel v. Toshiba American Info. Sys., Inc., 111 F.3d 80, 6 AD Cases 929 (8th Cir. 1997) *16:* 41

Index

A

Abuse, sexual. *See* Sexual abuse
Accommodation of disability. *See* Americans with Disabilities Act (ADA), *subheading:* reasonable accommodation
ADA. *See* Americans with Disabilities Act
ADEA (Age Discrimination in Employment Act)
  damages, 4
ADHD. *See* Attention Deficit/Hyperactivity Disorder
Adjustment disorders, 206–10
  ADA coverage, 669–72
  diagnostic criteria, 209
  DSM-IV-TR, 136–39
  subtypes, 209
Adolescence
  disorders first diagnosed in, 131
Affective disorders. *See* Mood disorders
Age Discrimination in Employment Act (ADEA)
  damages, 4
Agoraphobia and Panic Disorder, 188–92
Alcoholism. *See* Substance abuse
Alternative dispute resolution
  sexual harassment claims, 581–83
Americans with Disabilities Act (ADA), 659–776
  alcoholism, 749–50
  benefit plans for employees, 750–51
  coverage, 661–703
    exclusions, 693
    major life activities, 675–93
    mental impairments, 661–67
    record of disability, 693–95
    regarded as disabled, 695–703
    substantial limitation, 667–75
  definition of mental disability, 660–703
  direct threat, 767–76
    accommodations, 739
    burden of proof, 768–70
    conflicting medical information, 774–76
    fitness for duty examinations, 762–63
    significant risk, 770–73
    suicide threats, 773–74
  drug use, 746–49
    safe harbor provision, 748
  employee benefit plans, 750–51
  essential job functions, 703–16
  major life activities, 675–93
    caring for oneself, 685–87
    cognitive functions, 683–85
    concentration, 685
    interacting with others, 676–79
    malingering, impact of, 430–31
    memory, 685
    reproduction, 681–82
    sexual relations, engaging in, 679–80
    sleeping, 682–83
    traveling, 687
    working, 687–93
      overtime, 692
      personality conflicts with supervisors or coworkers, 691–92
      shift work, 692
      stress, inability to tolerate, 690–91
  medical evaluations and inquiries, 751–67

Americans with Disabilities Act (*cont.*)
  fitness for duty examinations, 760–67
    direct threat, 762–63
    medication requirements or monitoring, 764–66
    prescription medication use disclosures, 763–64
    refusal by employee, 766–67
    treatment requirements or monitoring, 764–66
  performance-related concerns, 760–67
  postemployment inquires, 758–60
  post-offer preemployment inquiries, 756–58
  preemployment inquires, 752–56
    drug testing, 755
    psychological testing, 754
  mental disabilities, 660–703
    exclusions, 693
    major life activities. *See this heading:* major life activities
    record of disability, 693–95
    regarded as disabled, 695–703
    substantially limiting mental impairments. *See this heading:* substantially limiting mental impairments
  mental expert, distortion by, 422–23
  qualified individual with disability, 703–16
    ability to get along with coworkers and supervisors, 713
    attendance, 707–10
    concentration, 715
    independent work, 715
    interacting with customers or general public, 714
    licensure, 715
    punctuality, 710–11
    security clearances, 715
    shifts and hours worked, 712–13
  reasonable accommodation, 716–46
    burden of proof, 717–18
    common forms, 727–43
    conduct standards, 737–41
    definition of, 717
    discipline, 737–41
    interactive process, 723–26
      liability for failure to engage in process, 724–26
    medication monitoring, 742
    misconduct, 737–41
    modified work schedule, 730–33
    not required, 743–45
    part-time work, 733
    performance standards, 737–41
    regarded as disabled, 701
    return to work agreement, 741
    shift changes, 734
    transfer, 735–37
    treatment requirements, 741–43
    triggers, 718–23
    undue hardship, 745–46
    unpaid leave, 727–30
    work at home, 734–35
    work schedules, 730–34
  regarded as disabled
    accommodation, offer of, 701
    concern, expressions of, 699
    counseling referral, 698–99
    employee assistance program referral, 698–99
    knowledge of symptoms, 700
    medical evaluation, request for, 702–3
    perception of personality traits, 699–700
    referrals to counseling or employee assistance program, 698–99
    safety concerns, 702
  return to work agreements
    medications, monitoring of, 764–66
    reasonable accommodation, 741
  substantially limiting mental impairments, 661–93
    adverse effects of medication, 663
    definitions, 667–75
      major life activity, 675–93
    diagnosable mental disorders, 661–63
    mental conditions, other, 663–65
    mental disorders listed in DSM-IV-TR, 661–63
    mitigating measures, 672–75
    pathological personality traits, 665–67
    personality disorders, 665–67
    substantial limitation, 667–75
    temporary nonchronic impairments, 669–72
    V codes, 663
Amnestic disorder, 132
Analgesic agents, 480–82
Anorexia, 136
Anti-convulsant agents, 474–75

Anti-panic agents, 482–83
Antisocial Personality Disorder
  clinical evaluations, preexisting disorders, 95
  diagnostic criteria, 230
Anxiety disorders, 187–200
  clinical evaluations
    physical disorders with psychological symptoms, 99–108
    preexisting and comorbid disorders, 89–90
  diagnostic criteria
    Generalized Anxiety Disorder, 195–96
    panic attack, 189–90
    panic disorder
      with Agoraphobia, 190–91
      without Agoraphobia, 191
  DSM-IV-TR, 134
  medications
    anti-anxiety agents, 472–73
    anti-panic agents, 482–83
  personality disorders, 239–49
Arbitration
  sexual harassment claims, 581–83
Assault and battery, 12–13
Assessments
  clinical. *See* Clinical evaluations and case formulations
  DSM-IV-TR. *See* Diagnostic and Statistical Manual of Mental Disorders
  mental examinations. *See* Mental examinations
  multiaxial assessments. *See* Multiaxial assessments
  psychological tests, 368–86. *See also* Psychological tests
Attendance as essential job function, 707–10
Attention Deficit/Hyperactivity Disorder (ADHD)
  clinical evaluations and case formulations, 85
  medications, anti-ADHD agents, 477–78
Attorneys
  case preparation for mental health experts, 268–83. *See also* Case preparation for expert
At-will employment and wrongful discharge, 10–12

Avoidant Personality Disorder, 240–42
  diagnostic criteria, 241–42
  preexisting disorders, 96
Axis I disorders, 130–37, 164–210. *See also* Mental disorders
Axis II disorders, 137–39. *See also* Personality disorders
Axis III, 139. *See also* Medical conditions, general
Axis IV, psychosocial and environmental problems, 139–40
Axis V, Global Assessment of Functioning, 140–43

B

Battery, 12–13
Beck Anxiety Inventory, 387
Beck Depression Inventory, 387
Beck Hopelessness Survey, 388
Benefit plans, disability discrimination, 750–51
Billing practices of mental health professionals, 62, 70
Bipolar disorders
  Bipolar Affective Disorder, 181–84
    diagnostic criteria
      manic episode, 182–83
      mixed episode, 183–84
  Bipolar I Disorder, 184–87
    diagnostic criteria, 185–86
  Bipolar II Disorder, 184–87
    diagnostic criteria, 186
  medications, anti-convulsant agents, 474–75
Borderline Personality Disorder, 231–35
  diagnostic criteria, 234–35
  preexisting disorders, 95
  Posttraumatic Stress Disorder distinguished, 551–56
  repetition compulsion, 555–56
  revictimization, 553–56
  "sitting duck" syndrome, 553–54
  trauma, 553
Brain injuries
  factors affecting mental health, 162
  preexisting and comorbid disorders, 93

Burden of proof
  Americans with Disabilities Act (ADA)
    direct threat, 768–70
    reasonable accommodation, 717–18

C

Caring for oneself as major life activity, 685–87
Case formulations by expert. *See* Clinical evaluations and case formulations
Case preparation for expert, 262–83
  attorney's responsibilities, 268–83
    expert's background, 269
    experts from outside jurisdiction, 269–70
    financial arrangements, 270
    issues outside expertise, 270
    litigation process orientation, 269
    orientations
      experts to litigation process, 269
      less experience lawyers, 268
    preliminary matters, 269–70
    retention of mental health expert, 58–63
    timing of expert selection, 269
  checklist, 283
  deposition of plaintiff, information needed for expert, 279–82
  discovery, 271–82
    child custody proceedings, 277
    court cases, prior, 278
    divorce proceedings, 277
    educational records, 276–77
    legal documents, 271
    medical records, 272–76
    medications, 273
    personnel records, 276
    psychotherapy and other treatment records, 271–72
    treatment records, 271–72
    workers' compensation files, 278
  experts, role in, 262–68
    objective forensic opinion formulation, 262–64
    theory formulation, 264–68
  medical examination setup, 282
Categories of mental disorders. *See* Diagnostic and Statistical Manual of Mental Disorders; Mental disorders
Certification of class actions, 43
Children
  child custody proceedings, discovery of, 277
  disorders first diagnosed in childhood, 131
Civil Rights Act of 1866, 4
Civil Rights Act of 1871, 4
Civil Rights Act of 1991, 3–4, 29
Class actions, 41–48
  certification, 43
  damages, 43–47
  emotional distress claims, 46–47
  Federal Rules of Civil Procedure, Rule 23, 42–43
  hybrid class actions, 43
  liability issues, 47
Classification of medications. *See* Medications
Classification of mental disorders. *See* Diagnostic and Statistical Manual of Mental Disorders; Mental disorders
Clinical evaluation and case formulation, 72–117
  case conceptualization, 114–16
  comorbid psychiatric disorders. *See* this heading: preexisting and comorbid psychiatric disorders
  context of claim, 75–78
    qualifications of treaters and experts, 77–78
    referrals, 76
    severity of injury alleged, 75–76
    treatment provided, 76–77
  diagnosis, 78–85
    iatrogenic effects, 84–85
    litigation, effects of, 83
    malingering, 83–84
    multiaxial diagnoses, 79–80
    premorbid functioning, 82–83
    record review, 82–83
    reliability, 80–82
    symptom exaggeration, 83–84
  discovery issues, 111–14
  Factitious Disorder, 115
  general issues and overview, 72–75
  mental disorders, 210–11
  personality disorders, 254–61

preexisting and comorbid disorders, 94–98
physical disorders with psychological symptoms, 99–108
preexisting and comorbid psychiatric disorders, 85–99
  anxiety disorders, 89–90
  developmental disorders, 85–88
    Attention Deficit/Hyperactivity Disorder (ADHD), 85
    intellectual disorders, 86–87
    learning disorders, 87
  mood disorders, 90–93
  organic disorders, 93
  personality disorders, 94–98
  substance abuse, 88–89
  thought disorders, 98–99
psychosocial stressors, 108–10
record review
  diagnosis, 82–83
  discovery, 111–14
testing, role of, 110–11

Clinical psychologists. *See* Mental health professionals

Cognitive disorders, 132, 161

Cognitive functions as major life activity, 683–85

Comorbid disorders
clinical evaluations, 85–99. *See also* Clinical evaluations and case formulations, *subheading:* preexisting and comorbid psychiatric disorders
Posttraumatic Stress Disorder, 520–22
  forensic assessment, 543–47

Compensation. *See* Damages

Concentration as major life activity, 685
qualified individual with disability, 715

Conduct disorder, 227–31

Consultants
clinical evaluations and case formulations. *See* Clinical evaluations and case formulations
discovery and record review, 111–14
experts. *See* Expert testimony
mental health professionals, 71. *See also* Mental health professionals

Contingency fees
mental health professionals, 70

Convulsions
anti-convulsant agents, 474–75

Court records. *See* Record reviews

D

Damages
Age Discrimination in Employment Act (ADEA), 4
assault and battery, 12–13
calculation of, 23–27
Civil Rights Act of 1991, 3
class actions, 43–47
common law bases for recovery, 5–19
defamation, 15
"eggshell plaintiff" rule, 32–34
Equal Employment Opportunity Commission (EEOC) policy guide, 4
false imprisonment, 13
fraud and misrepresentation, 15–16
hedonic damages, 27–32
intentional infliction of emotional distress, 5–9
  extreme or outrageous conduct, 6–9
  severe emotional distress, 9
invasion of privacy, 13–15
  false-light publicity, 14
  intrusion on seclusion, 14
  public disclosure of private facts, 14–15
jury discretion in award amount, 23–26
loss of consortium, 16–17
negligence, 17–19
negligent infliction of emotional distress, 9–10
per diem argument, 24
personality disorders, role in, 219–20
Posttraumatic Stress Disorder, 561–65
preexisting conditions, 32–34
proof of, 19–23
public policy violations, wrongful discharge, 10–12
recovery available, 2–19
Sections 1981 and 1983, 4
sexual harassment, 623–25
state statutes, 4–5
statutory bases for recovery, 3–5

Damages (*cont.*)
  stress of litigation, 41
  theory formulation, 264–68
  tortious interference with contract, 16
  wrongful discharge, 10–12
Daubert **decision,** 66–67, 632–37. *See also* Expert testimony
  clinical evaluations, 83
  diagnoses, reliability of, 81
  hedonic damages, effect on, 28–2
Deception. *See* Distortion and deception issues
Decision trees and differential diagnosis process, 145–46
Defamation, 15
Definitions
  emotional distress, 1
  mental disability, 660–703
  mental disorder, 143, 158
  reasonable accommodation, 717
  sexual harassment, 575–79
  substantially limiting mental impairments, 667–75
    major life activity, 675–93
Delirium, 132
Delusional Disorder, 170–73
  diagnostic criteria, 171
  medications, anti-psychotic agents, 483–85
  subtypes, 172
Dementia, 132
Depositions
  background information on plaintiff needed by expert, 279–82
  medications, 498–99
  privacy, waiver of privileges, 298–99
Depressants, 469
Depression
  bipolar disorders. *See* Bipolar disorders
  clinical evaluations
    physical disorders with psychological symptoms, 99–108
    preexisting disorders, 90–93
  Dysthymic Disorder, 178–80
  Major Depressive Disorder, 173–78
    diagnostic criteria, 175–76
      recurrent, 177
      single episode, 176–77
    medications, anti-depressant agents, 475–77
Depression scale of MMPI-2, 375

Detection of distortion and deception, 437–46. *See also* Distortion and deception issues
Developmental disorders
  medications, anti-ADHD agents, 477–78
  preexisting and comorbid psychiatric disorders, 85–88
    Attention Deficit/Hyperactivity Disorder, 85
    intellectual disorders, 86–87
    learning disorders, 87
Diagnosis
  clinical evaluations and case formulations. *See* Clinical evaluation and case formulation
  DSM-IV-TR. *See* Diagnostic and Statistical Manual of Mental Disorders
  mental disorders. *See* Mental disorders
  personality disorders. *See* Personality disorders
Diagnostic and Statistical Manual of Mental Disorders, 117–57
  ADA coverage
    mental disorders, 661–63
    personality disorders, 665–67
    V codes, 663
  adjustment disorders, 136–37
  admissibility of expert testimony, 66–67
  adolescence, disorders first diagnosed in, 131
  amnestic disorder, 132
  anxiety disorders, 133
  categories, 126–28
  childhood disorders, 131
  clinical judgment, importance of, 149–50
  clinically significant impairment or distress, 144
  cognitive disorders, 132
  common life problems, 137
  commonly used terms, 143–49
  decision trees, 145–46
  deferred diagnosis, 147–49
  delirium, 132
  dementia, 132
  diagnostic uncertainty, 147–49
  differential diagnosis decision trees, 145–46
  dimensions, 126–28
  dissociative disorders, 135

eating disorders, 136
exclusion criteria, 146–47
Factitious Disorder, 134
future directions, 153
  DSM-V, 126
gender identity disorders, 135
general medical conditions, 132, 139
historical background, 118–26
  classification prior to DSM-III, 118–20
  DSM-III and DSM-III-R, 120–22
  DSM-IV, 122–25
  DSM-IV-TR, 125
  DSM-V, 126
impulse-control disorders, 136
inclusion criteria, 146–47
infancy, disorders first diagnosed in, 131
legal standard, use as, 150–52
mental disorder, definition of, 143
mood disorders, 133
multiaxial evaluations, 128–43
  adverse life events, 139–40
  appendixes, 143
  Axis I, 130–37
  Axis II, 137–39
  Axis III, 139
  Axis IV, 139–40
  Axis V, 140–43
  clinical disorders, 130–37. *See also* Mental disorders
  environmental problems, 139–40
  general medical condition, 132, 139
  global assessment of functioning scale, 140–43
  optional axes, 143
  personality disorders, 137–39. *See also* Personality disorders
  psychosocial problems, 139–40
  retardation, mental, 137–39
not otherwise specified (NOS) diagnosis, 147–49
numerical codes, 144
other conditions that merit clinical attention, 137
present status, 152–57
principal diagnosis, 145
prototypes, 126–28
provisional diagnosis, 147–49
psychotic disorders, 133
reason for visit, 145
Schizophrenia, 133

sexual identity disorders, 135
sleep disorders, 136
somatoform disorders, 134
substance-related disorders, 133
subtypes and specifiers, 144
symptom clusters of common mental disorders, 159
unspecified diagnosis, 147–49
V codes, 137

Diagnostic criteria
adjustment disorders, 209
Antisocial Personality Disorder, 230
Avoidant Personality Disorder, 241–42
Bipolar Affective Disorder
  hypomanic episode, 185
  manic episode, 182–83
  mixed episode, 183–84
Bipolar I Disorder, 185–86
Bipolar II Disorder, 186
Borderline Personality Disorder, 234–35
  Posttraumatic Stress Disorder distinguished, 551–56
Conduct Disorder, 230–31
Conversion Disorder, 204
Delusional Disorder, 171
Dependent Personality Disorder, 244
Dysthymic Disorder, 179–80
Generalized Anxiety Disorder, 195–96
Histrionic Personality Disorder, 237
Major Depressive Disorder, 175–76
  recurrent, 177
  single episode, 176–77
Narcissistic Personality Disorder, 239
Obsessive-Compulsive Disorder, 193–94
  Obsessive-Compulsive Personality Disorder, 247
Pain Disorder, 205–6
panic attack, 189–90
Panic Disorder with Agoraphobia, 190–91
Panic Disorder without Agoraphobia, 191
Paranoid Personality Disorder, 223
Personality Disorder, not otherwise specified, 248
personality disorders, 214–15
Posttraumatic Stress Disorder, 198, 504–13
Schizoid Personality Disorder, 224–25
Schizophrenia, 166

Schizotypal Personality Disorder, 225–26
Somatization Disorder, 201–2
Dietary supplements, 468
Differential diagnosis decision trees, 145–46
Direct threat. *See* Americans with Disabilities Act (ADA)
Disability. *See* Americans with Disabilities Act (ADA)
Discovery
  case preparation for expert, 271–82
    child custody proceedings, 277
    court cases, prior, 278
    divorce proceedings, 277
    educational records, 276–77
    legal documents, 271
    medical records, 272–76
    medications, 273
    personnel records, 276
    psychotherapy and other treatment records, 271–72
    treatment records, 271–72
    workers' compensation files, 278
  clinical evaluations and case formulations by expert, 111–14
  distortion and deception issues, 447
  privacy issues, 284–327
    scope, 285–300
    sexual history. *See this heading:* sexual history
    waiver of privileges, 285–300
      depositions, 298–99
      Federal Rules of Civil Procedure, Rule 35, 295–97
      garden variety test, 296
      interrogatories, 299–300
      medical records, 285–97
      other records, 297–98
      psychotherapy records, 285–97
  sexual history, 300–327
    credibility affected by prior sexual abuse, 321–23
    borderline rage, 322
    dissociation, 322–23
    Federal Rules of Evidence, Rule 412, 301–3
      application to, 313–17
      emotional damages, 310–13
      nonparty witnesses, 317–18
      sexual abuse, 318–27
      summary judgment motions, 313
      volitional conduct, 303–10
    prior sexual abuse and welcomeness defense, 325–27
    sexual abuse, 318–27
      alternative causation of damages, 320–21
      credibility, 321–23
      reasonable victim/woman/person standard, 323–25
      repetition compulsion, 325–27
    volitional conduct, 303–10
      behavior types covered, 304–5
      welcomeness issue, 305–10
Dissociative disorders, 135
Distortion and deception issues, 409–52
  classifications of distortion, 410–15
    conscious distortion, 410–12
      deception, 411–12
      evasion, 410–11
    subconscious distortion, 413–15
      Axis I conditions, due to, 413–14
      Axis II conditions, due to, 414
      life events, due to, 414–15
  detection, 437–46
    collateral sources of information, 438–39
    forensic interview, 441–47
    normal response to traumatic events, 440–41
    problems in detecting, 447–52
    psychological testing, 439–40
    records review, 438–39
  dissimulation, 436
  experts, distortion by, 421–25
    ADA mental disability, 422–23
    alternative causes, importance downplayed, 423–24
    defense experts, 425
    diagnosis, exaggeration of, 421
    plaintiff's expert, 421–25
    Posttraumatic Stress Disorder, overdiagnosis of, 421
    prognosis, exaggeration of, 424
    treating clinician, 424–25
    treatment duration, exaggeration of, 424
  forensic interview, 441–47
    alternative motives, 446–47
    attitude toward emotional distress, 446
    background history, 442

collateral data, knowledge of, 441
detailed questions, 442
inconsistencies, 445
leading questions, 442
litigation stress impact, 445–46
nonverbal cues of vagueness and evasiveness, 444
open-ended questions, 442
problems in detecting. *See this heading:* problems in detecting
symptom evaluation in detail, 443
verbal cues of vagueness and evasiveness, 444
malingering, 425–36
plaintiffs, distortion by, 415–20
alternative causes of symptoms, downplaying, 415–16
avoidance of responsibility, 420
normal behaviors, misconstrued as sexual and/or harassing, 417–20
work environment, 416–17
Posttraumatic Stress Disorder, 567–73
overdiagnosis of, 421
problems in detecting, 447–52
ability to work, failure to evaluate, 451–52
discovery, inadequate or blocked, 447
evaluation parameters inadequate, 448–49
major life events, 449
malingering over- or underdiagnoses, 450–51
outdated knowledge, 452
personality traits, failure to evaluate for, 449–50
plaintiff evaluation inadequate, 448–50
therapeutic bias, failure to recognize, 448

Divorce records
discovery of, 277
Drugs. *See* Medications; Substance abuse
DSM. *See* Diagnostic and Statistical Manual of Mental Disorders

E

Eating disorders, 136
Educational records
discovery of, 276–77

EEOC. *See* Equal Employment Opportunity Commission
Eggshell plaintiff rule, 32–34
Emotional distress
case preparation. *See* Case preparation for expert
class actions, 46–47
clinical evaluation and case formulation. *See* Clinical evaluation and case formulation
damage recovery, 2–19
statutory bases, 3–5
definition, 1
Employee benefit plans and disability discrimination, 750–51
Employment at will and wrongful discharge, 10–12
Enjoyment of life valuation. *See* Hedonic damages
Equal Employment Opportunity Commission (EEOC)
ADA guidance. *See* Americans with Disabilities Act
damage recovery policy guide, 4
proof of damages, 20
Equitable tolling, 48–49
Essential job functions, qualified individual with disability, 703–16. *See also* Americans with Disabilities Act (ADA)
Ethics of expert witnesses
professional guidelines, 71
treating therapists, use of as forensic evaluator, 58–60
Evaluations. *See* Clinical evaluations and case formulations
DSM-IV-TR. *See* Diagnostic and Statistical Manual of Mental Disorders
mental examinations. *See* Mental examinations
multiaxial assessments. *See* Multiaxial assessments
psychological testing. *See* Psychological tests
Evidence
admissibility of expert testimony. *See* Expert testimony, *subheading:* admissibility
damages, proof of, 20–23
discovery. *See* Discovery
junk science, 631–58

Evidence (*cont.*)
  Posttraumatic Stress Disorder, 565–67
  sexual history, 301–3
    application to, 313–17
    emotional damages, 310–13
    nonparty witnesses, 317–18
    sexual abuse, 318–27
    summary judgment motions, 313
    volitional conduct, 303–10
      behavior types covered, 304–5
      welcomeness issue, 305–10
Examinations, mental. *See* Clinical evaluation and case formulation; Mental examinations
  DSM-IV-TR. *See* Diagnostic and Statistical Manual of Mental Disorders
  multiaxial assessments. *See* Multiaxial assessments
Expert testimony
  admissibility
    clinical experience, 645–47
    diagnostic technique, 647–54
      differential diagnosis, failure to conduct, 652–54
      DSM-IV-TR, failure to use, 66–67, 648–52
    education and training, 642–45
    legal developments, 632–41
      Daubert, 632–37
      Federal Rule of Evidence 702, revision, 639–41
      Kumho Tire, 637–39
    psychological testing, misuse of, 654–58
      administration improper, 656–57
      interpretation improper, 657–58
      qualifications, 654–55
      scientific basis of test lacking, 655–56
      scoring improper, 657
  case preparation for expert, 262–83. *See also* Case preparation for expert
  medical experts, 23
  mental health professionals, 50–71. *See also* Mental health professionals
  sexual harassment, 601–5
    forensic evaluations and clinical issues, 594–99
      process, 613–15

F

Factitious disorders, 134
  case conceptualization, 115
False imprisonment, 13
Family and Medical Leave Act (FMLA)
  reasonable accommodation under ADA, compared, 709–10
Family therapists. *See* Mental health professionals
Federal Rules of Civil Procedure
  Rule 23, class actions, 42–43
  Rule 35
    discovery of psychotherapy records, 295–97
    mental examinations, 328–63
Federal Rules of Evidence. *See also* Evidence
  Rule 412, discovery of sexual history, 301–3
  Rule 702 revision, expert testimony admissibility, 639–41
Fitness for duty examinations under ADA, 760–67
  return to work agreements, 741
FMLA (Family and Medical Leave Act)
  reasonable accommodation under ADA, compared, 709–10
Forensic evaluations. *See* Clinical evaluation and case formulation
  distortion and deception issues. *See* Distortion and deception issues
  DSM-IV-TR. *See* Diagnostic and Statistical Manual of Mental Disorders
  Posttraumatic Stress Disorder. *See* Posttraumatic Stress Disorder (PTSD)
  sexual harassment. *See* Sexual harassment
Forensic mental health evaluators. *See* Mental health professionals
Fraud and misrepresentation, 15–16

G

GAF. *See* Global Assessment of Functioning scale
Gender identity disorders, 135
General medical conditions. *See* Medical conditions, general

Georgetown Guidelines, 533
Global Assessment of Functioning (GAF) scale
  multiaxial evaluations, 140–43
  Posttraumatic Stress Disorder, 512
Good cause requirement for mental examinations, 341–44

H

Hallucinogens, 469
Hamilton Anxiety Rating Scale, 389
Hamilton Depression Inventory, 391
Hamilton Depression Rating Scale, 390
Harassment. *See* Sexual harassment
Health care plans for employees
  disability discrimination, 750–51
Hedonic damages, 27–32
  Civil Rights Act of 1991, 29
  Daubert decision, 28–29
  willingness-to-pay model, 27
Herbal medicines, 468
Histrionic Personality Disorder, 235–37
  clinical evaluations, preexisting disorders, 96
  diagnostic criteria, 237
Homosexuality
  same-sex harassment, 580–81
Human figure drawing test, 391
Hypochondriasis scale of MMPI-2, 375
Hypomania, 184–87
  MMPI-2 scale, 377
Hysteria scale of MMPI-2, 375

I

Illicit drugs, 464–65. *See also* Substance abuse
Impact of event scale, 392–94
Impulse-control disorders, 136
In controversy requirement for mental examinations, 331–41. *See also* Mental examinations
Infancy, disorders first diagnosed in, 131

Injury claims
  clinical evaluation and case formulation. *See* Clinical evaluation and case formulation
  damages. *See* Damages
Inkblot test, Rorschach, 396–98
Intentional infliction of emotional distress, 5–9
Interviews, forensic. *See* Clinical evaluation and case formulation
  distortion and deception issues. *See* Distortion and deception issues
  DSM-IV-TR. *See* Diagnostic and Statistical Manual of Mental Disorders
Invasion of privacy, 13–15
  discovery issues. *See* Discovery

J

Junk science. *See* Expert testimony, *subheading:* admissibility
Jury discretion in damage calculation, 23–26

K

Kumho Tire, 637–39. *See also* Expert testimony

L

Learning disorders. *See* Developmental disorders
Legal documents. *See* Record reviews
Legal drugs. *See* Medications
Liability
  class actions, 47
  damages. *See* Damages
  "eggshell plaintiff" rule, 32
  personality disorders, 34–40
    righteous rage, validity of claims, 251–53
  role in litigation, 219–20
  theory formulation by expert, 264–68
  torts. *See* Torts
Libel, 15
Licensure as essential job function, 715
Licit drugs. *See* Medications
Liens for services of mental health professionals, 70

Litigation stress. *See* Stress of litigation
Loss of consortium, 16–17

M

Major life activities. *See* Americans with Disabilities Act (ADA)
Malingering, 425–36. *See also* Distortion and deception issues
  claim fabrication, 427–30
  disability benefits, 426–27
  major life activities impacts, ADA protections, 430–31
  misattribution of cause to workplace, 434–36
    cause and effect reversal, 435–36
  overdiagnoses, 450–51
  Posttraumatic Stress Disorder, 567–73
  symptom exaggeration, 431–34
    duration, 432–33
    long-term impact, 433–34
    nature of impairment, 431–32
    permanent or long-term impact, 433–34
    severity of impairment, 431–32
  underdiagnoses, 450–51
  work avoidance, 426–27
Mania
  bipolar disorders. *See* Bipolar disorders
  clinical evaluations, preexisting disorders, 92
  diagnostic criteria, 182–83
  substance abuse. *See* Substance abuse
Marriage and family therapists. *See* Mental health professionals
Masculinity-femininity scale of MMPI-2, 376
Mediation of sexual harassment claims, 581–83
Medical conditions, general
  clinical evaluations, 99–108
  multiaxial evaluations
    Axis I, clinical disorders, compared, 132
    Axis III, 139
  physiologic effects, 132

Medical examinations
  ADA, 751–67. *See also* Americans with Disabilities Act, *subheading:* medical evaluations and inquiries
  attorney arrangements, 282
Medical records
  discovery of, 272–76. *See also* Discovery
Medications, 454–501
  Americans with Disabilities Act (ADA)
    accommodation, monitoring of, 742
    disabilities corrected by, 673
    disclosures of use, 763–64
    fitness for duty examinations, 764–66
    monitoring of
      accommodation, 742
      last chance agreement, 764–66
  classifications, 461–501
    analgesic agents, 480–82
    anti-addiction agents, 470–72
    anti-ADHD agents, 477–78
    anti-anxiety agents, 472–73
    anti-appetite agents, 473–74
    anti-cholinergic medications, 467
    anti-convulsant agents, 474–75
    anti-dementia agents, 475
    anti-depressant agents, 475–77
    anti-insomnia agents, 478–79
    anti-manic agents, 479–80
    anti-obsessive agents, 480
    anti-pain agents, 480–82
    anti-panic agents, 482–83
    anti-parkinsonian medications, 466
    anti-psychotic agents, 483–85
    anti-sex agents, 485–86
    clinical purpose, 465
    depressants, 469
    effects, 465
    hallucinogens, 469
    herbal medicines, vitamins, dietary supplements, 468
    lawfulness of use, 464–65
    over-the-counter (OTC) medications, 467
    stimulants, 468
  depositions, 498–99
  discovery, 273
  dose-response relationships, 458–59
  effects, desired versus undesired, 459–60
  illicit psychotropic agents, 464–65

interactions, 460
licit psychotropic agents, 464–65
nonpsychotropic agents, 486–88
pharmacology
    classification, 461–68
    fundamentals, 458
    interactions, 460
    nonpsychotropic medications, 461–64
    psychotropic medications, 464–501
physical disorders with psychological symptoms, clinical evaluations, 99–108
Posttraumatic Stress Disorder, 528–30
psychopharmacology
    basic principles, 456–68
    diagnosis fundamentals, 457
    fundamentals, 458
side effects, 459–60, 486–90
toxicology, fundamentals of, 458

Memory as major life activity, 685

Mental disorders, 158–211
adjustment disorders, 206–10
anxiety disorders, 187–200
    Agoraphobia and Panic Disorder, 188–92
    Generalized Anxiety Disorder, 195–97
    Obsessive-Compulsive Disorder, 192–95
    Panic Disorder and Agoraphobia, 188–92
    Posttraumatic Stress Disorder, 197–200
Axis I disorders, overview, 164–210
diagnosis, multiaxial, 163
disabilities. *See* Americans with Disabilities Act (ADA)
dual diagnosis, 187–200
factors affecting mental health, 162–63
    functional pathology, 162
    nature, 162
    nurture, 162
    organic pathology, 162
    physical insult to brain, 162
    stressors, 162
forensic evaluations, effective work-ups, 210–11
mood disorders, 173–87
    Bipolar Affective Disorder, 181–84
    Bipolar I Disorder, 184–87
    Bipolar II Disorder, 184–87
    double depression, 180–81
    Dysthymic Disorder, 178–80
    hypomania, 184–87
    Major Depressive Disorder, 173–78
origins, history, and definitions, 143, 158
overview, 164–210
physical illnesses and mental disorders, 159
psychiatric symptoms, 159–62
    affective symptoms, 160–61
    anxiety symptoms, 161
    cognitive symptoms, 161
    conversion symptoms, 161
    psychotic symptoms, 160
    unreasonable attitudes and expectations, 161–62
psychiatry, 158–59
psychology, 158–59
record reviews, 210–11
somatoform disorders, 200–206
    conversion disorder, 203–5
    pain disorder, 205–6
    somatization disorder, 200–203
symptom clusters, 159
thought disorders, 164–73
    Delusional Disorder, 170–73
    Schizophrenia, 165–70

Mental examinations, 328–63
areas of inquiry, 350–52
availability, 330–44
    in controversy requirement, 331–41
    good cause requirement, 341–44
clinical interview, 356–63
    examiner's approach, 357–58
    record review, 356–57
clinical opinion, 362–63
components, 63–65, 358–62
    current functioning assessment, 361–62
    current symptoms, 358–59
    mental status examination, 358–59
    past history, 359–60
    psychological testing, 362
    workplace events, 360–61
in controversy requirement, 331–41
    factors leading to finding of, 335–41
        continuing emotional injury allegations, 338–40
        intentional infliction of emotional distress as separate tort claim, 335–36

Mental examinations (*cont.*)
  mental health expert, plaintiff use of, 337–38
  plaintiff concession, 341
  severe emotional injury allegations, 340–41
  specific psychiatric disorder allegations, 336–37
  garden variety emotional damages claims, 333–35
DSM-IV-TR. *See* Diagnostic and Statistical Manual of Mental Disorders
duration, 349
forensic evaluations. *See* Clinical evaluation and case formulation
observers, 345–48
psychological testing as part of, 353–56
  identity of tests, obligation to disclose, 356
  limitations on tests used, 354–56
recording examinations, 348
scope, 349–53
timing of examination, 344–45

Mental health professionals
clinical psychologists, 53
clinicians with master's degrees, 54
evaluations, approach to conducting, 63–65
  forensic interview, 63–64
  personal interview, 63–64
  personality tests or inventories, 65
  psychological testing, 65
  record review, 63
as expert witnesses, qualifications, 52–55
  forensic or legal training, 54–55
  testimony, nature and scope of, 65–66
  types of professionals, 52–54
litigation consultants, 71
marriage and family therapists, 54
psychiatric social workers, 53–54
psychiatrists, 52
retaining experts, 58–63
  billing, 62
  budgets, 62
  payment, 62
  practical considerations, 61–62
  scheduling, 62
  timing issues, 61
  treating therapists, use of, 58–60
role in legal proceedings, 50–71
selection factors, 55–58
  clinical expertise, 55–56
  forensic expertise, 56–57
  interpersonal issues and problems, 57–58
sexual harassment claims, role as experts, 594–99, 601
testimony, nature and scope of, 65–68
  admissibility, 66–67. *See also* Expert testimony
  opinion of expert, 67–68
    alternative explanations for plaintiff's condition, 68
    diagnosis, 68
    preexisting conditions/psychopathology, 68
    prognosis and possible treatment, 68
  qualifications, 65–66
vulnerabilities in court, 68–71
  contingency fees, 70
  ethical guidelines, 71
  financial bias, 70
  lien for services, 70
  limited evaluation, problems with, 69–70
  malingering or possible exaggeration of symptoms, 69

Millon Clinical Multiaxial Inventory-III (MCMI-III), 381–84

Minnesota Multiphasic Personality Inventory-2 (MMPI-2), 368–81
clinical scales, 374–78
  depression scale, 375
  hypochondriasis scale, 375
  hypomania scale, 377
  hysteria scale, 375
  masculinity-femininity scale, 376
  paranoia scale, 376
  psychasthenia scale, 377
  psychopathic deviate scale, 376
  schizophrenia scale, 377
  social introversion scale, 377
code types, 380–81
content scales, 378
interpretation, 379–80
mental examination, test as part of, 355
preemployment testing and the ADA, 755
supplementary scales, 378–79
validity scales, 369–74

Misrepresentation and fraud, 15–16. *See also* Distortion and deception issues
malingering. *See* Malingering
Mood disorders, 173–87
 bipolar disorders. *See* Bipolar disorders
 clinical evaluations, preexisting disorders, 90–93
 depression. *See* Depression
 DSM-IV-TR, 133
Mood states, profile of, 395–96
Multiaxial assessments
 case formulations, 79–80
 diagnosis, formal report, 163
 Diagnostic and Statistical Manual of Mental Disorders, 128–43. *See also* Diagnostic and Statistical Manual of Mental Disorders
 general medical conditions
  Axis I, clinical disorders, compared, 132
  Axis III, 139
 Global Assessment of Functioning (GAF) scale, 140–43
 posttraumatic stress disorder, 532–33

N

Narcissistic Personality Disorder
 clinical evaluations, preexisting disorders, 96
 diagnostic criteria, 239
Nature as factor in development
 mental disorders, 162
 personality disorders, 215
  arousal theories, 218
  genetic theories, 217
  temperament theories, 218
Negligent infliction of emotional distress, 9–10
Negligent retention and supervision claims, 17–19
Normal behavior misconstrued as sexual harassment, 417–20
Not otherwise specified
 mental disorders, 147–49
 personality disorders, 247–48
  diagnostic criteria, 248
Numerical codes, use in diagnosis, 144
Nurture as factor in development
 mental disorders, 162

 personality disorders, 215
  bonding theories, 216
  efficacy and interaction theories, 216–17
  trauma theories, 217

O

Obsessive-Compulsive Disorder
 clinical evaluations, preexisting disorders, 97
 diagnostic criteria, 193–94
 medications, anti-obsessive agents, 480
Obsessive-Compulsive Personality Disorder, 245–47
 diagnostic criteria, 247
Organic disorders
 factors affecting mental health, 162
 preexisting and comorbid disorders, 93
Over-the-counter (OTC) medications, 467
Overtime, 692

P

Pain disorder
 diagnostic criteria, 205–6
 medications, 480–82
Panic attack, 189–90
 anti-panic agents, 482–83
Panic Disorder
 with Agoraphobia, 190–91
 without Agoraphobia, 191
Paranoia scale of MMPI-2, 376
Paranoid Personality Disorder, 221–23
 clinical evaluations, preexisting disorders, 94
 diagnostic criteria, 223
 medications, anti-psychotic agents, 483–85
Part-time work as reasonable accommodation, 733
Per diem argument of damage calculation, 24
Personality disorders, 212–61
 ADA coverage, 665–67
 characteristics, 215
 clinical evaluations, preexisting disorders, 94–98

Personality disorders (*cont.*)
  cluster groups, 220–48
    cluster A disorders, 221–26
      Paranoid Personality Disorder, 221–23
      Schizoid and Schizotypal Personality Disorder, 223–26
    cluster B disorders, 226–39
      Antisocial Personality Disorder, 227–31
      Borderline Personality Disorder, 231–35
      Histrionic Personality Disorder, 235–37
      Narcissistic Personality Disorder, 237–39
    cluster C disorders, 239–49
      Avoidant Personality Disorder, 240–42
      Dependent Personality Disorder, 242–45
      Obsessive-Compulsive Personality Disorder, 245–47
    not otherwise specified, 247–48
  damages, role in litigation, 219–20
  diagnostic criteria, 214–15
  DSM-IV-TR, Axis II diagnostic entities, 137–39
  factors affecting personality development, 215–19
    etiologic conclusions, 219
    nature, 215
      arousal theories, 218
      genetic theories, 217
      temperament theories, 218
    nurture, 215
      bonding theories, 216
      efficacy and interaction theories, 216–17
      interaction and efficacy theories, 216–17
      trauma theories, 217
  forensic evaluations, effective work-ups, 254–61
    record review, 255–57
  historical background, 212
  liability issues, 34–40
  manifestations, 215
  Posttraumatic Stress Disorder and, 547–61
    interplay, 558–61
  preexisting disorders, 94–98
  qualities of personality, 213–15
  righteous rage, 251–53
  role in employment litigation, 219–20
  sexual harassment, assessment issues, 618–19
  subconscious distortion, 414
  treatment, 253–54
    acute intervention, 253–54
    crisis management, 253–54
    long-term treatment and restructuring, 254
  workplace violence, 248–51
Personality traits, 213–15
  Americans with Disabilities Act (ADA)
    regarded as disabled, 699–700
    substantially limiting mental impairments, 665–67
  failure to evaluate for, 449–50
Personnel records
  discovery of, 276
Pharmacology, 454–501. *See also* Medications
Physical injuries
  clinical evaluations and case formulations
    preexisting and comorbid disorders, 93
    psychological symptoms, 99–108
  factors affecting mental health, 162
  general medical conditions. *See* Medical conditions, general
Plaintiffs
  alternative explanations for condition, 68
  in controversy requirement
    concession, 341
    mental health expert, use of, 337–38
  deposition, information needed for expert, 279–82
  distortion by, 415–20
  eggshell plaintiff rule, 32–34
  sexual harassment, 620–23
    normal behaviors misconstrued, 417–20
Posttraumatic Stress Disorder (PTSD), 502–73
  clinical context, 504–31
  comorbidity, 520–22
    forensic assessment, special issues, 543–47
  course and prognosis, 522–26

Acute Stress Disorder, 522
chronic PTSD, 522–25
diagnostic criteria, 198, 504–13
  duration of symptoms, 511–13
  functional impairment, 511–13
  symptoms, 509–11
  traumatic stressor, 505–9
DSM-IV-TR, 134, 197–200
  forensic evaluations, 532–33
epidemiology, 514–19
  predictive factors, 514–18
  subthreshold PTSD, 518–19
forensic evaluations, 531–43
  bias, 539–43
  Borderline Personality Disorder, clinical presentation, 551–56
    repetition compulsion, 555–56
    revictimization, 553–56
    "sitting duck" syndrome, 553–54
    trauma, 553
  comorbid disorders, 543–47
  damage assessment, 561–65
  Diagnostic and Statistical Manual of Mental Disorders, 532–33
  evidence, use as, 565–67
  functional impairment, 561–65
  Georgetown Guidelines, 533
  guidelines, 532–33
  malingering, 567–73
  misdiagnosis, 539–43
  personality disorders and, 547–61
    Borderline Personality Disorders, 551–56
    interplay, 558–61
  proximate cause, 543–47
  record review, 533–35
  special issues, 543–73
  testing of diagnosis, 535–39
    physiological testing, 535–36
    psychological testing, 536–39
  trauma history, 543–47
Global Assessment of Functioning (GAF) scale, 512
medications, 528–30
predictive factors, 514–18
  magnitude of stressors, 515–16
  postevent recovery factors, 517–18
  preparedness for event, 516
  pretrauma vulnerabilities, 515
  responses, immediate and short-term, 516–17
prognosis, 525–27

risk factors, 514–18
Social and Occupational Functioning Assessment Scale (SOFAS), 512
symptoms, 509–11
  avoidance, 510
  duration, 511–13
  hyperarousal, 511
  reexperiencing, 509–10
treatment, 527–31
Preemployment testing and inquiries, 752–58
drug testing, 755
psychological testing, 754
Preexisting mental disorders
clinical evaluations, 85–99. *See also* Clinical evaluations and case formulations, *subheading:* preexisting and comorbid psychiatric disorders
damages, 32–34
liability issues, 34–40
Prescription medications. *See* Medications
Privacy
damage recovery, public disclosure of private facts, 13–15
discovery, 284–327. *See also* Discovery
Profile of mood states, 395–96
Psychasthenia scale of MMPI-2, 377
Psychiatric social workers. *See* Mental health professionals
Psychiatric symptoms
diagnostic criteria. *See* Diagnostic criteria
DSM-IV-TR. *See* Diagnostic and Statistical Manual of Mental Disorders
exaggeration of, 431–34
malingering. *See* Malingering
mental disorders. *See* Mental disorders
personality disorders. *See* Personality disorders
Psychiatrists. *See* Mental health professionals
Psychological tests, 368–86
approach to conducting by expert, 65
Beck Anxiety Inventory (BAI), 387
Beck Depression Inventory (BDI), 387
Beck Hopelessness Survey (BHS), 388
detection of distortion and deception, 439–40
disclosure of identity of tests, 356
Hamilton Anxiety Rating Scale, 389

Psychological tests (*cont.*)
  Hamilton Depression Inventory, 391
  Hamilton Depression Rating Scale, 390
  human figure drawing test, 391
  impact of event scale, 392–94
  mental examinations, part of, 353–56, 362
  Millon Clinical Multiaxial Inventory-III, 381–84
  Minnesota Multiphasic Personality Inventory-2 (MMPI-2), 368–81
    clinical scales, 374–78
    code types, 380–81
    content scales, 378
    interpretation, 379–80
    supplementary scales, 378–79
    validity scales, 369–74
  misuse of testing, 402–8
    administration of test, 404
    coaching, 407
    examiner qualifications, 403
    expert testimony admissibility, 654–58
    interpretation, 405–6
    scoring, 404
    validity, 406–7
  mood states, profile of, 395–96
  posttraumatic stress diagnostic scale, 394–95
  Posttraumatic Stress Disorder, 536–39
  preemployment testing and inquiries, 754
  profile of mood states, 395–96
  Rorschach inkblot test, 396–98
  sentence completion test, 398
  sexual harassment, 609–13
  Shipley Institute of Living scale, 398–99
  State-Trait Anxiety Inventory, 399
  Symptom Checklist 90-R, 399–401
  terminology, 366–68
  Thematic Apperception Test, 401–02
  use and misuse, 364–408
  Wechsler Adult Intelligence Scale-III, 384
Psychologists. *See* Mental health professionals
Psychopathic deviate scale of MMPI-2, 376
Psychopharmacology, 454–501. *See also* Medications
Psychosocial stressors
  clinical evaluations, 108–10
  multiaxial evaluations, 139–40
Psychotherapy records. *See* Record reviews
Psychotic disorders, 133
  schizophrenia. *See* Schizophrenia
PTSD. *See* Posttraumatic Stress Disorder
Public policy violations
  wrongful discharge, 10–12
Punctuality as essential job function, 710–11

Q

Qualifications of expert witnesses. *See* Expert testimony; Mental health professionals
Qualified individual with disability, 703–16. *See also* Americans with Disabilities Act (ADA)

R

Reasonable accommodation of disability. *See* Americans with Disabilities Act (ADA)
Reasonable victim/woman/person standard
  assessment issues, 619–20
  discovery, sexual history, 323–25
  social science perspective and studies, 592–93
Record reviews
  diagnosis evaluations, premorbid functioning, 82–83
  discovery, 111–14, 271–82
    child custody proceedings, 277
    court cases, prior, 278
    divorce proceedings, 277
    educational records, 276–77
    legal documents, 271
    medical records, 272–76
    medications, 273
    personnel records, 276
    privacy, waiver of privileges
      medical records, 285–97
      other records, 297–98
      psychotherapy records, 285–97
    psychotherapy and other treatment records, 271–72

treatment records, 271–72
workers' compensation files, 278
distortion and deception issues, 438–39
forensic workups
   mental (Axis I) disorders, 210–11
   personality (Axis II) disorders, 255–57
personality disorders, 557
Posttraumatic Stress Disorder, 533–35
Reproduction as major life activity, 681–82
Retaining experts. *See* Case preparation for expert; Mental health professionals
Return to work agreements under ADA
fitness for duty examinations, 760–67
medications, monitoring of, 764–66
reasonable accommodation, 741
Righteous rage, 251–53
Rorschach inkblot test, 396–98

S

Same-sex harassment, 580–81
Schizoid Personality Disorder
clinical evaluations, preexisting disorders, 94
diagnostic criteria, 224–25
Schizophrenia
diagnostic criteria, 166
DSM-IV-TR, 133
medications, anti-psychotic agents, 483–85
mental disorders, 165–70
MMPI-2 scale, 377
personality disorders, 223–26
subtypes, 167–68
Schizotypal Personality Disorder
clinical evaluations, preexisting disorders, 94
diagnostic criteria, 225–26
Security clearances as essential job function, 715
Selection of expert witnesses. *See* Expert testimony; Mental health professionals
Sentence completion test, 398
Sexual abuse
discovery, 318–27

alternative causation of damages, 320–21
credibility due to prior abuse, 321–23
   borderline rage, 322
   dissociation, 322–23
Federal Rules of Evidence, Rule 412, 318–27
reasonable victim/woman/person standard, 323–25
repetition compulsion, 325–27
welcomeness defense, 325–27
sexual harassment assessment issues, 616–18
Sexual harassment, 574–630
alternative dispute resolutions, 581–83
arbitration, 581–83
assessment issues, 615–25
   hypersensitivity issue, 619–20
   personality disorders, 618–19
   plaintiff response, 620–23
   reasonable victim/woman/person exceptions, 619–20
   severity of emotional damages, 623–25
   sexual abuse, 616–18
   welcomeness, 620–23
complaint procedures, internal, 581–83
definitions, 575–79
discovery of sexual history, 300–327. *See also* Discovery
distortion, plaintiff misconstrues normal behaviors, 417–20
employer precautions and employee responsibility, 581
forensic evaluation process, 605–15
   interview, 605–9
   testimony, 613–15
     inference, 614
     objectivity, 613
     tier of fact, usurping role of, 614–15
   testing, 609–13
     credibility, 609–12
     personality assessment, 613
     validity, 609–12
forensic evaluations and clinical issues, 594–601
evaluation process, 605–15
expert, role in cases, 594–99
scope, focus, and assessment practices, 599–601

Sexual harassment (cont.)
  forensic experts, 601–5
    areas of expertise, 602–3
    bias, 603–5
    examiner role, 603
    ground rules, 601–2
    history of examiner, 604–5
    ideological beliefs, 604
    objectivity, 603–5
    political beliefs, 604
    role, 594–99, 601
    testimony, 613–15
    therapist role, 603
  history and background, 574–84
  intellectual history and controversies, 583–84
  investigations, negligent infliction of emotional distress claims, 10
  loss of consortium claims, 16–17
  malingering, 427–30
  mediation, 581–83
  negligent infliction of emotional distress claims, 10
  negligent retention and supervision claims, 17–19
  psychological treatment, 625–30
    confidentiality issues, 626–27
    decision to litigate, 625–26
    therapist and evaluator distinction, 627–28
    treatment approaches, 628–30
  same-sex harassment, 580–81
  school settings, 579–80
  social science perspective and studies, 584–94
    effects on individual, 590–92
    effects on organizations, 592
    gender differences in perception, 588
    individual responses and effects, 590–92
    legal practice, impacts on, 593–94
    legal standards, 592–93
    offender characteristics, 589–90
    organizational characteristics, 589–90
    perception, gender differences, 588
    prevalence, 586–88
    reasonable victim/woman/person, 592–93
    types, 585
    victim characteristics and patterns, 589

Sexual identity disorders, 135
Sexual relations as major life activity, 679–80
Shift work
  major life activities, 692
  qualified individual with disability, 712–13
  reasonable accommodation, 734
Shipley Institute of Living scale, 398–99
Side effects of medications, 459–60, 486–90
Slander, 15
Sleep disorders, 136
Sleeping as major life activity, 682–83
Social and Occupational Functioning Assessment Scale (SOFAS), 512
Social introversion scale of MMPI-2, 377
Social workers, psychiatric. See Mental health professionals
Somatization Disorder, 200–203
  diagnostic criteria, 201–2
Somatoform disorders, 200–206
  Conversion Disorder, 203–5
  Pain Disorder, 205–6
  Somatization Disorder, 200–203
State statutes
  at-will employment, 10–12
  discrimination
    damage recovery, 4–5
    intentional infliction of emotional distress, 6
State-Trait Anxiety Inventory, 399
Statutes of limitations, 48–49
Stimulants, 468
Stress, inability to tolerate, 690–91
Stress of litigation
  damage availability, 41
  forensic interview to assess impact, 445–46
  sexual harassment, 625–26
Substance abuse
  Americans with Disabilities Act (ADA)
  alcoholism, 749–50
  drug use, 746–49
    safe harbor, 748
  preemployment drug testing, 755
  clinical evaluations, preexisting disorders, 88–89

medications, anti-addiction agents, 470
Substance-related disorders, 133. *See also* Substance abuse
Suicide threats, 773–74
Symptom Checklist 90-R, 399–401
Symptoms
 diagnostic criteria. *See* Diagnostic criteria
 DSM-IV-TR. *See* Diagnostic and Statistical Manual of Mental Disorders
 exaggeration of, 431–34
 malingering. *See* Malingering
 mental disorders. *See* Mental disorders
 personality disorders. *See* Personality disorders

T

Testimony. *See also generally* Evidence
 experts. *See* Expert testimony
 proof of damages, 20–23
 sexual abuse, nonparty witnesses, 317–18
Testing
 drug testing, preemployment, 755
 MMPI-2, 368–81. *See also* Minnesota Multiphasic Personality Inventory-2 (MMPI-2)
 psychological, 368–86. *See also* Psychological tests
 Rorschach inkblot test, 396–98
Thematic Appercepton Test, 401–2
Therapeutic bias
 expert witness, use as, 58–60, 424–25
 failure to recognize, 448
Thought disorders, 164–73
 Delusional Disorder, 170–73
 preexisting and comorbid psychiatric disorders, 98–99
 Schizophrenia. *See* Schizophrenia
Torts
 assault and battery, 12–13
 damage recovery for emotional distress, 5–19
 defamation, 15
 false imprisonment, 13
 fraud and misrepresentation, 15–16
 invasion of privacy, 13–15
 negligence, 17–19
 wrongful discharge, 10

Toxicology, 458
Trauma. *See* Posttraumatic Stress Disorder (PTSD)
Traveling as major life activity, 687
Treatment
 ADA
  fitness for duty examinations, 764–66
  reasonable accommodation, 741–43
 context of claim, 76–77
 discovery, 271–72
 distortion by expert
  duration, exaggeration of, 424
 personality disorders, 253–54
  acute intervention, 253–54
  crisis management, 253–54
  long-term treatment and restructuring, 254
 Posttraumatic Stress Disorder, 527–31
 prognosis, opinion of expert, 68
 records. *See* Record reviews
 sexual harassment, 625–30
  confidentiality issues, 626–27
  decision to litigate, 625–26
  therapist and evaluator distinction, 627–28
  treatment approaches, 628–30

V

V codes
 major life activity impairment, 663
 multiaxial diagnosis, 137
Violence
 assault and battery, 12–13
 Posttraumatic Stress Disorder. *See* Posttraumatic Stress Disorder (PTSD)
 suicide threats, 773–74
 workplace violence, 248–51
Vitamins, 468

W

Wechsler Adult Intelligence Scale-III, 384–86
 performance tests, 385
 scoring, 385–86
 verbal tests, 384–85

Welcomeness issues in sexual harassment claims
  assessment issues, 620–23
  discovery
    prior sexual abuse, 325–27
    volitional conduct, 305–10
Witnesses. *See* Expert testimony
  sexual abuse, nonparty witnesses, 317–18
Workers' compensation
  discovery of files, 278
  preemption of negligence claims, 10
  negligent retention and supervision claims, 17–19
Working as major life activity, 687–93
  qualified individual with disability, 712–13
  reasonable accommodation, 730–34
Workplace violence, 248–51
Wrongful discharge, 10–12